Mathematics

with Applications in
Management and Economics

The Irwin Series in Quantitative Analysis for Business

Consulting Editor   **Robert B. Fetter**   Yale University

Mathematics
with Applications in Management and Economics

EARL K. BOWEN

Babson College

GORDON D. PRICHETT

Babson College

JOHN C. SABER

Babson College

Sixth Edition

1987

IRWIN

Homewood, Illinois   60430

Cover photo by COMSTOCK, Inc.

ISBN 0-256-03140-1

Library of Congress Catalog Card No. 86–81793

Printed in the United States of America

3 4 5 6 7 8 9 0 V 4 3 2 1 0 9 8 7

TO:

Steven and Pamela

Jill, Reid, Trevor, and Glenn

Carol, John, Stephen, and Nicholas

Preface

This text was written intending to explain the value of mathematics as a tool in solving actual problems. Earl Bowen's objectives in the First Edition were to present mathematics at a level appropriate to student preparation and directed specifically toward applications in management and economics. This Sixth Edition is motivated by those same objectives.

The systematic presentation in each chapter—explanation, example, answered exercise—which students and teachers have enthusiastically approved through five previous editions is maintained and amplified in this edition. This approach provides a text easily adapted to self-study.

Many of the algebraic details omitted in most texts at this level have been included within the text to help students learn or recall the arithmetic and algebra needed to solve problems. In addition, to limit the prerequisite for study of the text to no more than one year of secondary school algebra, we have included appendixes on the elements of mathematics for study or reference.

Our main concern in preparing this revision has been: *Can students read and understand the text?* The following features have been added or retained primarily with this objective in mind.

Examples. Several hundred worked examples are included in this text to demonstrate applications and techniques in problem solving.

Exercises. Each section contains answered exercises to allow students to reconfirm their understanding of the material while reading the text.

Applications. A greater number and selection of applications in management and economics than is customary is included in each chapter. Many chapters contain special application sections which are optional.

Calculator applications. Calculator applications are presented where appropriate. Examples and exercises using both standard features and preprogrammed functions are explained in detail.

Computer applications. Computer programs in both BASIC and PASCAL and the use of computer packages such as LINDO and Minitab are included where appropriate. Computer exercises have also been added. A disc with all the programs used in the text is available for the Apple IIe and the IBM PC.

Theorems and definitions. All theorems and definitions are boxed and highlighted to emphasize their importance. Care has been taken to state theorems and definitions simply but accurately.

Problems. The text contains over 1,500 numbered problems, with answers, and over 750 additional review problems that can serve as a basis for examination and lecture purposes. Solutions to the review problems, worked out in detail, are included in the Instructor's Manual. In addition, there is a supplemental Student's Manual which contains worked-out solutions to selected problems.

Overhead transparencies. Transparency masters for the text material are available for the instructor. These allow the careful planning and preparation of each class session.

Chapter 1 begins with a review of distance, slope, and straight lines with applications in cost-output analysis, break-even analysis, and linear demand. Chapter 2 starts with solutions of 2 by 2 linear systems by the Elimination Procedure together with applications in supply and demand. This is generalized to 3 by 3 systems before discussing linear inequalities. Chapter 3 is an introduction to linear programming with special attention paid to graphical analysis for 2-variable problems and formulation of general problems. Chapter 4 discusses vectors, matrices, and the summation operation. Here, the Gauss-Jordan Method for solution of an m by n system of linear equations is developed simply as a generalization of the Elimination Procedure with the aid of matrix techniques. Chapter 5 presents the Simplex Method solution for linear programming problems with $\leq$ constraints. Here, the concepts of sensitivity analysis and shadow prices are also introduced. Chapter 6 demonstrates the computer solution of linear programming problems and a complete summary of the entire Simplex Method in an eye-catching flowchart. Chapter 7 is a short treatment of exponential and logarithmic functions, followed by a fairly detailed presentation of the Mathematics of Finance in Chapter 8. At this point, we introduce elementary Probability and Statistics in Chapter 9 and illustrate the use of computer packages. The next four chapters give a detailed presentation of differential and integral calculus. Differential calculus is thoroughly developed in Chapters 10 through 12 with special emphasis on optimization problems and curve sketching for both one- and two-independent variables. Chapter 13 presents integral calculus including area applications, numerical integration, and differential equations. Chapter 14 introduces probability in the continuous case and discusses means, expected values, variance and standard deviation, and the normal probability distribution. Finally, there are three appendixes to help students review the fundamentals of sets, algebra, and graphing that provide the background material for the text.

If the entire text including the appendixes is to be completed, there is sufficient material for a three-semester sequence of courses. However, the book is structured so that it is adaptable to a variety of courses, from one quarter to three semesters in duration by making parts of chapters, whole chapters, and groups independent. This structure permits omissions to be made without loss of continuity or prerequisite topics. A few possible plans are included in the following table:

Course Title	Time Required	Material to Be Covered
Finite Mathematics	3–4 semester hours	Chapters 1–8 (9 optional)
Calculus with Applications	3–4 semester hours	Chapters 1, 7, 8, 10–13
Basic Mathematics for Business Students	9–12 semester hours	Entire book
Introduction to Linear Programming	2–3 semester hours	Chapters 1–6

Many reviewers have been a tremendous help in critiquing this revision. Especially notable is the careful review written by Jerry Rubin of Marshall University. Other reviewers to whom we are indebted are Sufi Nazem and James Conway of the University of Nebraska at Omaha; Tom Obremski of the University of Denver; Roseanne Hofmann of Montgomery County Community College; Frank Jewett of Humboldt State University; Richard Levin of Western Washington University; Elton Lacey of Texas A&M University; Woo Bong Lee of Bloomsburg University; John Shannon of Suffolk University; William Marchal of the University of Toledo; David Ashley of the University of Missouri at Kansas City; Jean Clark of Virginia Commonwealth University; and John Spellman of Southwest Texas State University. Previous editions have benefited as well by suggestions over the years. Of special note are the comments by Christopher J. Toy of New Hampshire College. Others who have contributed to the text over its life include: R. Andres, P. Applebaum, W. Beatty, F. Benn, T. Billesbach, G. Bloom, R. Borman, A. Brunson, R. Carlson, W. Cassidy, D. Chesnut, T. Church, D. Cleaver, C. Crell, R. Davis, W. Davis, E. Dawson, B. Dilworth, R. Dingle, D. Dixon, W. Etterbeek, J. Freigo, R. Fetter, J. Flaherty, J. Foster, R. Fox, Jr., R. Friesen, H. Frisinger, H. Fullerton, W. Furman, E. Goldstein, L. Goldstein, M. Greenberg, V. Heeren, J. Hindle, A. Ho, A. Hoffman, G. Horcutt, J. Hudson, and D. Isaacson.

Also: R. Jaffa, C. I. Jones, R. J. Jones, H. King, R. Kizior, P. Latimer, R. Leezer, R. Leidig, J. Liff, S. Logan, G. Long, T. Lougheed, J. Lovell, T. Lupton, M. Malchow, E. Marrinan, Jr., P. McKeon, A. McLaury, E. Merrick, P. Merry, R. Moreland, J. Moreno, C. Murphy, D. Nichols, J. Papenfuss,

R. Ralls, P. Randolph, G. Reeves, J. ReVelle, R. Salmon, F. Schwab, H. Sendek, P. Sgalla, R. Sheffield, L. Shumway, P. Siegel, B. Smith, J. Smith, W. Soule, Jr., M. Spinelli, H. Stein, D. Stoller, M. Tarrab, T. Taylor, O. Thomas, R. Tibrewalla, T. Tsukahara, E. Tyler, E. Underwood, B. Van Cor, T. Vasper, G. Waldron, B. Walker, and M. Williamson.

Additionally, we wish to acknowledge the encouragement and contributions of our colleagues at Babson: W. Carpenter, I. Dambolena, D. Kopsco, H. Kriebel, J. McKenzie, W. Montgomery, M. Riskalla, A. Shah, and M. Weinblatt; in addition, Samuel C. Hanna of Boston University, who helped develop the authors' approach to linear programming and mathematics of finance.

Finally, special recognition should go to our wives and children who gave up so many long winter nights and summer days with us so that this book could become a reality.

Earl K. Bowen
Gordon D. Prichett
John C. Saber

Contents

1 Linear Equations and Functions, 1

1.1   Introduction,   1
1.2   Vertical and Horizontal Distances,   5
1.3   Problem Set 1–1,   7
1.4   The Distance Formula,   8
1.5   Problem Set 1–2,   11
1.6   Slope,   12
1.7   Problem Set 1–3,   16
1.8   Equation of a Line: Slope-Intercept Form,   18
1.9   Straight-Line Equation Given a Point and Slope,   22
1.10 Straight-Line Equation from Two Points,   24
1.11 Horizontal and Vertical Lines,   25
1.12 Parallel and Perpendicular Lines,   27
1.13 Lines through the Origin,   29
1.14 Problem Set 1–4,   29
1.15 Interpretive Exercise: Cost–Output,   33
1.16 Problem Set 1–5,   35
1.17 Comment on Models,   36
1.18 Break-Even Interpretation: 1,   39
1.19 Break-Even Interpretation: 2,   41
1.20 Linear Demand Functions,   45
1.21 Problem Set 1–6,   48
1.22 Review Problems,   51

2 Systems of Linear Equations and Inequalities, 55

2.1   Introduction,   55
2.2   Number of Solutions Possible,   56
2.3   Intersections of Straight Lines,   56
2.4   Operations on Linear Systems,   58
2.5   Elimination Procedure,   60

2.6   Applications—1,   61

2.7   Problem Set 2–1,   62

2.8   Applications—2: Supply and Demand Analysis,   63

2.9   Problem Set 2–2,   65

2.10   Elimination Procedure: Nonunique Solutions,   66

2.11   Problem Set 2–3,   67

2.12   Definition, m by n System,   68

2.13   3 by 3 System,   68

2.14   Problem Set 2–4,   73

2.15   Applications—3: Introduction to Optimization,   73

2.16   Applications—4: Two-Product Supply and Demand Analysis,   77

2.17   Problem Set 2–5,   78

2.18   Systems of Two Linear Inequalities,   79

2.19   Nonnegativity Constraints,   82

2.20   Applications,   85

2.21   Problem Set 2–6,   88

2.22   Review Problems,   89

3   Introduction to Linear Programming,   92

3.1   Introduction,   92

3.2   Maximization Examples: Product Mix,   93

3.3   Minimization Examples: Ingredient Mix,   100

3.4   Isolines: Three-Step Graphical Procedure,   104

3.5   Problem Set 3–1,   107

3.6   Mix of Constraints,   109

3.7   Problem Set 3–2,   115

3.8   More than Two Variables,   116

3.9   Problem Set 3–3,   121

3.10   More on Formulation,   122

3.11   Problem Set 3–4,   126

3.12   Review Problems,   130

4   Compact Notation: Vectors, Matrices, and Summation,   133

4.1   Introduction,   133

4.2   Matrices and Vectors,   133

4.3   Product of a Number and a Matrix,   135

4.4   Addition and Subtraction of Matrices,   136

4.5   Multiplication of Matrices,   138

4.6   Identity Matrix,   141

4.7   Problem Set 4–1,   142

4.8   Matrix Symbols,   143

4.9   Linear Equations in Matrix Form,   144

4.10   Problem Set 4–2,   146
4.11   Applications—1: Markov Chains,   147
4.12   Problem Set 4–3,   150
4.13   Row Operations,   151
4.14   The Inverse of a Matrix,   152
4.15   Problem Set 4–4,   160
4.16   Applications—2: Matrix Solution of n by n Linear Systems,   161
4.17   Problem Set 4–5,   169
4.18   Applications—3: Matrix Solution of m by n Linear Systems,   171
4.19   Problem Set 4–6,   176
4.20   Summation Symbol,   177
4.21   Problem Set 4–7,   178
4.22   Summation on Indices: Linear Equations,   179
4.23   Problem Set 4–8,   180
4.24   Summation Form for Systems,   180
4.25   Linear Programming Problems in Summation Notation,   182
4.26   Problem Set 4–9,   183
4.27   Properties of the Summation Operation,   184
4.28   Problem Set 4–10,   186
4.29   Review Problems,   186

5   Linear Programming: The Simplex Method,   192

5.1   Introduction,   192
5.2   Fundamental Procedures and Terminology,   193
5.3   Tableaus: Changing Basic Variables,   200
5.4   Problem Set 5–1,   205
5.5   The Simplex Procedure,   206
5.6   Problem Set 5–2,   215
5.7   A Minimizing Problem with "≤" Constraints,   217
5.8   Problem Set 5–3,   221
5.9   Tie for the Entering or Leaving Variable,   222
5.10   Alternative Optimal Solutions,   230
5.11   Problem Set 5–4,   232
5.12   Unbounded Solutions,   233
5.13   Negative Decision Variables,   235
5.14   Two Penalty/Premium Examples with "≤" Constraints,   239
5.15   Problem Set 5–5,   244
5.16   Minimization by Maximizing the Dual,   245
5.17   Problem Set 5–6,   253
5.18   Sensitivity Analysis: Shadow Prices and Right-Hand-Side Ranges,   255
5.19   Problem Set 5–7,   267
5.20   Review Problems,   269

6   The Simplex Method *(continued)***: Computer Solutions,   274**

6.1   Introduction,   274
6.2   Computer Solutions,   274
6.3   Problem Set 6–1,   279
6.4   Preliminaries to Phase I–Phase II: The Big-M Method,   281
6.5   The Phase I–Phase II Method,   286
6.6   Problem Set 6–2,   296
6.7   No Feasible Solutions,   298
6.8   An Example with "=" Constraints; Phase I–Phase II Method,   302
6.9   Grand Summary of the Simplex Method,   312
6.10   Problem Set 6–3,   315
6.11   Sensitivity Analysis on "≥" and "=" Constraints,   316
6.12   Sensitivity Analysis on the Objective Function and New Product Analysis,   322
6.13   Problem Set 6–4,   326
6.14   Review Problems,   336

7   Exponential and Logarithmic Functions,   348

7.1   Introduction,   348
7.2   Exponential Functions,   348
7.3   Problem Set 7–1,   353
7.4   The Need for Logarithms,   353
7.5   Natural (Base e) Logarithms,   357
7.6   Problem Set 7–2,   359
7.7   Definition of Logarithms,   359
7.8   Rules of Logarithms,   360
7.9   Application of Inverse Natural Logarithms,   363
7.10   Graph of $y = \ln x$,   367
7.11   Computing e and Natural Logarithms (Optional),   369
7.12   Problem Set 7–3,   373
7.13   Review Problems,   375

8   Mathematics of Finance,   377

8.1   Introduction,   377
8.2   Simple Interest and the Future Value,   378
8.3   Simple Discount: Present Value,   383
8.4   Bank Discount,   385
8.5   Effective Rate: Simple Interest,   386
8.6   Problem Set 8–1,   389
8.7   Compound Interest and the Future Value,   390
8.8   The Conversion Period,   393

8.9   Finding the Time,   395

8.10   Finding the Interest Rate,   397

8.11   Problem Set 8–2,   398

8.12   Compound Discount: Present Value,   399

8.13   Problem Set 8–3,   402

8.14   Effective Rate: Compound Interest,   402

8.15   Problem Set 8–4,   404

8.16   Continuous (Instantaneous) Compounding,   405

8.17   Effective Rate: Continuous Compounding,   409

8.18   Problem Set 8–5,   411

8.19   Ordinary Annuities: Future Value,   412

8.20   Ordinary Annuities: Sinking Fund,   415

8.21   Problem Set 8–6,   417

8.22   Ordinary Annuities: Present Value,   419

8.23   Ordinary Annuities: Amortization,   421

8.24   Problem Set 8–7,   426

8.25   Summary of Financial Rules,   427

8.26   Multistep Problems,   430

8.27   Problem Set 8–8,   434

8.28   Finding the Interest Rate and Time: Ordinary Annuities,   435

8.29   Ordinary Annuities: Continuous Compounding,   437

8.30   Problem Set 8–9,   438

8.31   Review Problems,   439

9   Elementary Probability and Statistics,   443

9.1   Introduction,   443

9.2   Probability and Odds,   443

9.3   Statistical Inference,   444

9.4   Sources of Probabilities,   445

9.5   Probability Symbols and Definitions,   447

9.6   Problem Set 9–1,   455

9.7   Probability Rules,   456

9.8   Practice with Probability Rules,   461

9.9   Problem Set 9–2,   467

9.10   Bayes' Rule,   469

9.11   Problem Set 9–3,   473

9.12   Experiment, Event, Sample Space,   475

9.13   Problem Set 9–4,   477

9.14   Discrete Random Variables,   478

9.15   Problem Set 9–5,   484

9.16   The Binomial Probability Distribution,   485

9.17   Cumulative Binomial Probabilities,   490

9.18   Problem Set 9–6,   493
9.19   Expected Monetary Value (EMV),   495
9.20   Problem Set 9–7,   499
9.21   Review Problems,   500

10   Introduction to Differential Calculus,   506

10.1   Introduction,   506
10.2   Why Study Calculus?   506
10.3   Functional Notation,   510
10.4   Delta Notation,   513
10.5   Problem Set 10–1,   515
10.6   Limits,   516
10.7   Problem Set 10–2,   526
10.8   Continuity,   527
10.9   Problem Set 10–3,   530
10.10   The Difference Quotient,   531
10.11   Definition of the Derivative,   534
10.12   Problem Set 10–4,   540
10.13   The Simple Power Rule,   541
10.14 d/dx Notation and Rules of Operations,   545
10.15   Problem Set 10–5,   548
10.16   The Derivative of $[f(x)]^n$,   549
10.17   Problem Set 10–6,   553
10.18   Product and Quotient Rules,   553
10.19   Problem Set 10–7,   558
10.20   Review Problems,   559

11   Applications of Differential Calculus,   562

11.1   Introduction,   562
11.2   Maxima and Minima of Functions,   562
11.3   Problem Set 11–1,   572
11.4   The Second Derivative Test,   573
11.5   Problem Set 11–2,   580
11.6   Maxima and Minima: Applications,   581
11.7   Problem Set 11–3,   590
11.8   More Applications,   594
11.9   Problem Set 11–4,   601
11.10   An Inventory Model,   602
11.11   Problem Set 11–5,   606
11.12   Sketching Graphs of Polynomials,   606
11.13   Problem Set 11–6,   611
11.14   Sketching Rational Functions,   612

11.15 Problem Set 11–7, 618
11.16 Review Problems, 618

12 Further Topics in Differential Calculus, 622

12.1 Introduction, 622
12.2 Derivatives of Exponential Functions, 623
12.3 Response Functions, 632
12.4 Problem Set 12–1, 634
12.5 Derivatives of Logarithmic Functions, 635
12.6 Problem Set 12–2, 637
12.7 Relative Rate of Change, 638
12.8 Problem Set 12–3, 643
12.9 The Chain Rule and Implicit Differentiation, 645
12.10 Marginal Propensity to Consume and the Multiplier, 651
12.11 Problem Set 12–4, 655
12.12 Calculus of Two Independent Variables, 656
12.13 Problem Set 12–5, 659
12.14 Maxima and Minima: Two Independent Variables, 661
12.15 Problem Set 12–6, 671
12.16 Least-Squares Curve Fitting, 672
12.17 Problem Set 12–7, 680
12.18 Review Problems, 681

13 Integral Calculus, 685

13.1 Introduction, 685
13.2 Antiderivatives: The Indefinite Integral, 686
13.3 Problem Set 13–1, 694
13.4 Area and the Definite Integral, 694
13.5 Problem Set 13–2, 706
13.6 The Area between Two Curves, 709
13.7 Problem Set 13–3, 714
13.8 Interpretive Applications of Area, 715
13.9 Interpreting the Area Bounded by Two Functions, 720
13.10 Consumers' and Producers' Surplus, 722
13.11 Problem Set 13–4, 727
13.12 The Integral of $(mx + b)^{-1}$, 729
13.13 Problem Set 13–5, 731
13.14 Integrals of Exponential Functions, 732
13.15 Problem Set 13–6, 736
13.16 Tables of Integrals, 737
13.17 Problem Set 13–7, 740
13.18 Asymptotic Areas: Improper Integrals, 740

13.19   Problem Set 13–8,   744
13.20   Numerical Integration,   745
13.21   Problem Set 13–9,   753
13.22   Integration by Parts,   754
13.23   Problem Set 13–10,   757
13.24   Differential Equations,   757
13.25   Separable Differential Equations,   760
13.26   Forms of the Constant,   760
13.27   Problem Set 13–11,   764
13.28   Applications of Differential Equations,   764
13.29   Problem Set 13–12,   770
13.30   Review Problems,   771

14   Probability in the Continuous Case,   777

14.1   Introduction,   777
14.2   The Uniform Probability Density Function,   777
14.3   Converting $f(x)$ to a Density Function over an Interval,   779
14.4   Problem Set 14–1,   781
14.5   Expected Value,   781
14.6   Variance and Standard Deviation,   784
14.7   Problem Set 14–2,   786
14.8   The Exponential Distribution,   787
14.9   Problem Set 14–3,   793
14.10   The Normal Density Function,   794
14.11   Normal Probability Table,   795
14.12   Using the Normal Probability Table,   798
14.13   Problem Set 14–4,   801
14.14   Estimating the Mean and the Standard Deviation,   801
14.15   Problem Set 14–5,   804
14.16 $N(\mu,\sigma)$ in Actual Use,   804
14.17   Problem Set 14–6,   809
14.18   Review Problems,   810

Appendix One   Sets,   813

A1.1   Introduction,   813
A1.2   Set Terminology,   813
A1.3   Set Specification,   815
A1.4   Solution Sets for Equations,   816
A1.5   Relations and Functions,   816
A1.6   Problem Set A1–1,   819
A1.7   Subsets, Unions, and Intersections,   820

A1.8   Problem Set A1–2, 822
A1.9   Review Problems, 823

Appendix Two   Elements of Algebra, 825

A2.1   Introduction, 825
A2.2   The Real Numbers, 825
A2.3   Rules of Sign, 826
A2.4   Addition and Subtraction of Signed Numbers, 826
A2.5   Multiplication and Division of Signed Numbers, 829
A2.6   Problem Set A2–1, 830
A2.7   Representing Numbers by Letters, 831
A2.8   Importance of Fundamental Properties, 832
A2.9   Problem Set A2–2, 834
A2.10   Removing Grouping Symbols, 835
A2.11   Definitions: Expression, Term, Factor, 836
A2.12   Elementary Factoring, 837
A2.13   Problem Set A2–3, 840
A2.14   Properties of the Numbers Zero and One, 842
A2.15   Product of Fractions, 845
A2.16   Addition and Subtraction of Fractions, 849
A2.17   Division of Fractions, 851
A2.18   Problem Set A2–4, 852
A2.19   Exponents, 854
A2.20   Zero Exponent, 855
A2.21   Negative Exponents, 856
A2.22   Power to a Power, 857
A2.23   Fractional Exponents, 858
A2.24   Summary of Exponent Rules, 860
A2.25   Practice Problem Set, 862
A2.26   Problem Set A2–5, 863
A2.27   Review Problems, 865

Appendix Three   Formulas, Equations, Inequalities, and Graphs, 867

A3.1   Introduction, 867
A3.2   Some Axioms, 868
A3.3   Solutions by Addition and Multiplication, with Inverses, 869
A3.4   Problem Set A3–1, 874
A3.5   Transposition, 875
A3.6   Formulas, 875
A3.7   Exact Evaluations, 877

A3.8   Problem Set A3–2,   878
A3.9   Coordinate Axes,   880
A3.10   Plotting Observational Data,   881
A3.11   Plotting Equations in Two Variables: Straight Lines,   883
A3.12   Vertical Parabolas,   884
A3.13   Quadratic Equations,   888
A3.14   Problem Set A3–3,   890
A3.15   Definitions and Fundamental Properties of Inequalities,   891
A3.16   Fundamental Operations on Inequalities,   892
A3.17   Solving Single Inequalities,   893
A3.18   Problem Set A3–4,   898
A3.19   Review Problems,   899

Answers to Problem Sets,   903

Tables,   965

Index,   989

Short exercises have been woven into textual discussions to help you pick up pertinent points as they occur. For example, on page 3 you will see the following:

Exercise. Taxicab fare from an airport to a nearby town is $0.80 per mile driven, plus $2 for tolls. Let y represent fare and x the miles driven on one trip. Write the equation for y in terms of x. Answer: $y = 0.80x + 2$.

To make the best use of these exercises, you should determine the answer to the question without reference to the given answer (it would help to cover up the given answer) and then compare your answer with the given answer.

ONE

Linear Equations and Functions

Mathematicians, economists, statisticians, and others have applied their skills to management problems in some degree for many years, but the first concerted effort in this area occurred during World War II, when these specialists were formed into Operations Analysis Groups to assist in the planning of military operations. The analysts used mathematics and statistics extensively in their studies, and the resulting recommendations were an important contribution to the war effort. Following the war, some analysts, soon joined by others, turned their attention to problems of management operations and accomplished major improvements in inventory control, quality control, warehouse location, oil industry operations, agriculture, purchasing decisions, scheduling of complex tasks such as building a shopping center, and a variety of other areas. Mathematics, old and *newly created*, coupled with innovative applications of the rapidly evolving electronic computer and directed toward management problems, resulted in a new field of study called Quantitative Methods (or Management Science or Operations Research), which has become part of the curriculum of colleges of business. The importance of quantitative approaches to management problems is now widely accepted, and a course in mathematics, with management applications, is included in the core of subjects studied by almost all management students. This text, which has been used in many hundreds of classrooms, develops mathematics in the applied context required for an understanding of the quantitative approach to management problems.

Linear relationships are the subject matter of the first six chapters of the book. Three comments can be made about this material. First, the

1

mathematics has direct management applications; indeed, at this moment computers are manipulating linear relationships and printing out information to aid in making lowest-cost or highest-profit decisions. Second, Chapters 3, 5, and 6 introduce the widely used mathematical technique known as linear programming. Third, most readers will be happy to learn that the mathematics of linear relationships, as we shall develop it, is quite easy. Only a minimal background, such as that provided in the appendixes, is required to get started and to make progress.[1] Every reader should scan these appendixes. Those who feel the need should work through them systematically and refer to them as often as necessary while studying the book.

In this chapter, we will consider in some detail the algebra and geometry of linear equations and functions in two variables, that is, equations and functions whose graphs in a coordinate plane are straight lines. Linear equations are equations whose *terms* (the parts separated by plus, minus, and equal signs) are a constant, or a constant times *one* variable to the first power. Thus,

$$2x - 3y = 7$$

is a linear equation because it consists of the constant 7, the term $2x$, which is the constant 2 times x to the first power, and $-3y$, which is also a term consisting of a constant times one variable to the first power. Similarly,

$$y = \frac{1}{2}x + 3 \quad \text{and} \quad \frac{x}{3} + \frac{y}{2} = 1$$

are linear equations. On the other hand,

$$2x + 3xy = 7$$

is not linear because $3xy$ is a constant times the product of two variables, and

$$x^2 + y + 3x = 16$$

is not linear because of the presence of the second-power term, x^2. Linear equations arise in numerous applied situations.

Example. Taxicab fare from an airport to a nearby city is $1.25 per mile driven, plus $0.75 for a bridge toll. Let y represent the fare and x the number of miles driven on one trip, and write the equation for y in terms of x.

Here the total fare will be

$$\text{Fare} = (1.25)(\text{number of miles driven}) + 0.75$$

---

[1] For a review of the minimal background, read Appendix 2. In Appendix 3 read sections A3.1–3.5, A3.15–3.17, and the parts of A3.6–3.11 that deal with linear equations.

or, using the specified symbols,

$$y = 1.25x + 0.75,$$

which is a linear equation.

Exercise. Taxicab fare from an airport to a nearby town is \$0.80 per mile driven, plus \$2 for tolls. Let y represent fare and x the miles driven on one trip. Write the equation for y in terms of x. Answer: $y = 0.80x + 2$.

The equations of the last example and exercise,

$$y = 1.25x + 0.75 \quad \text{and} \quad y = 0.80x + 2,$$

are linear equations in the two *variables* x and y. Such equations have graphs that are straight lines. To graph a straight line, you will recall that we need only to have the coordinates of two of its points (since there is precisely one line that can be drawn between two given points). It does not matter which two points are chosen, so we may arbitrarily select two values for x and obtain the corresponding values for y. For example, in

$$y = 1.25x + 0.75,$$

if we choose $x = 1$, then

$$y = 1.25(1) + 0.75 = 1.25 + 0.75 = \$2,$$

and we have the point $x = 1$, $y = 2$, which is designated in the conventional form (x, y) as $(1, 2)$. Again, choosing, say, $x = 5$, we find

$$y = 1.25(5) + 0.75 = 6.25 + 0.75 = \$7,$$

and we have the point $x = 5$, $y = 7$, or $(5, 7)$. Plotting $(1, 2)$ and $(5, 7)$ as points, then drawing a line through them, leads to Figure 1–1. The accompanying Figure 1–2 shows the graph of $y = 0.80x + 2$.

Exercise. Verify the points shown in Figure 1–2. Answer: In $y = 0.80x + 2$, if we choose $x = 0$, then $y = 2$, and if we choose $x = 5$, then $y = 6$.

Linear functions. The relationship between y and x expressed by

$$y = 1.25x + 0.75$$

is called a functional relationship because for each value of x, there is one, and only one, corresponding value for y. Notice that the expression

---

FIGURE 1–1   **FIGURE 1–2**

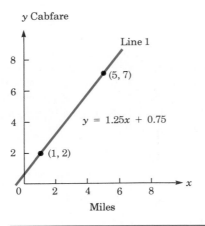

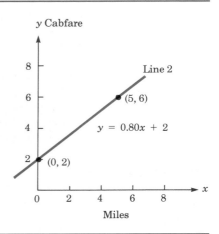

---

states what y is (that is, $y =$) in terms of x, and we connote this by saying *y is a function of x;* of course, this is a linear function. If we write

$$y = \text{an expression involving } x \text{ and constants,}$$

x is called the *independent* variable and is plotted on the horizontal axis. The value of y depends upon what value we assign to x, and so y is called the *dependent* variable, which is plotted on the vertical axis. Thus, when we plot points, the values of x can be chosen independently, but the corresponding values of y depend on the values chosen for x. Later in the text we will encounter situations where an expression has several letters, and we will want to be able to specify which is the independent variable. This is done by writing the independent variable in parentheses next to the dependent variable. Thus, in our example, $y = 1.25x + 0.75$, we would write $y = f(x)$, read "y equals f of x," where

$$f(x) = 1.25x + 0.75.$$

The need for identification of the independent variable can be seen if we write

$$y = kp + n$$

and state that this is a linear function because it is not clear which of the letters on the right is the independent variable. However, writing

$$y = f(p) = kp + n$$

specifies that p is the independent variable and, therefore, k and n are to be considered as being *constants*. In this chapter, the identity of the independent variable will be clear from the context, so we shall not use the parenthetical specification. However, *independent variable, dependent variable*, and *linear function* are phrases that should be a part of our vocabulary.

Returning to Figures 1–1 and 1–2, observe that both lines slant upward to the right, but that line 1, on the left, rises more rapidly (is steeper) than line 2. This means that for a *given* horizontal change, the vertical change on line 1 is greater than the vertical change on line 2. We shall see that the ratio of vertical to horizontal change has numerous applied interpretations. Inasmuch as these changes are horizontal and vertical distances, we turn first to a consideration of such distances.

1.2 VERTICAL AND HORIZONTAL DISTANCES

The distance between two points is the length of the straight-line segment that joins the points. In beginning (plane) geometry and in applied mathematical work, we use a ruler or some other measuring device to determine lengths of segments. In *analytic* geometry, also called coordinate geometry, end points of line segments are specified by their x- and y-coordinates, and algebraic procedures are applied to the coordinates to find the distance between the points.

Distances on horizontal and vertical line segments play an important role in the mathematics of straight lines. Distance on a vertical segment is found by computing the positive difference of the y-coordinates of the end points of the segment. Distance on a horizontal segment is found by computing the positive difference of the x-coordinates of the end points of the segment. Consider, for example, a city that has avenues running east and west and streets running north and south, dividing the city into square blocks. To get from (4th St., 3rd Ave.) to (10th St., 3rd Ave.), we would walk on Third Avenue a distance of $10 - 4 = 6$ blocks.

Exercise. How many blocks would we walk going from (10th St., 6th Ave.) to (10th St., 13th Ave.)? Answer: Seven blocks.

The way we have defined *distance*, it must be a positive number. Hence, if the subtraction of coordinates yields a negative number, the minus sign will be disregarded. Consider Figure 1–3. The segment CD is horizontal. The distance CD is found by subtraction, thus:

CD = horizontal distance = difference of x-coordinates = $9 - 3 = 6$.

If the calculation had been made as $3 - 9 = -6$, the minus sign would have been disregarded.

The segment HG is vertical. The distance HG is found by subtraction:

HG = vertical distance = difference of y-coordinates = $2 - (-4) = 6$.

FIGURE 1–3

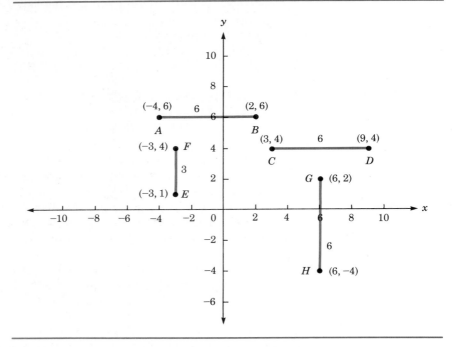

If the x-coordinates of the points at the end of a segment are equal, as in the case of *HG* in Figure 1–3, the segment is vertical, and if the y-coordinates of the two points are equal, as in the case for *AB*, the segment is horizontal. Thus, letting $P(a, b)$ mean the point P whose coordinates are (a, b), and letting $Q(a, c)$ mean the point Q, whose coordinates are (a, c), it follows that the segment

$$P(a, b) \ Q(a, c)$$

is vertical. Similarly, the segment

$$R(a, b) \ S(c, b)$$

is horizontal.

Exercise.   Given $A(-2, -5)$; $B(2, 6)$; $C(3, 10)$; $D(2, -5)$. If each pair of points was connected by a straight-line segment, which segment would be horizontal and which segment would be vertical? Answer: AD and BD, respectively.

Subscript notation. The symbol

$$(x_1, y_1)$$

is read as "x sub-one, y sub-one" or, more briefly, "x-one, y-one," and is used to designate a *particular* point. Similarly, (x_2, y_2) denotes a different particular point. This notation is a handy way to preserve (x, y) to refer to the coordinates of any point, in general, with variations in the subscript serving to designate coordinates of different points. In this notation, a vertical segment would have (x_1, y_1) and (x_1, y_2) as end points. The distance between the points would be

Vertical distance $= |y_2 - y_1|$.

The vertical lines, $|\ |$, are the *absolute value* symbol, which means that the difference is to be taken as positive. For example,

$$|5 - 2| = |+3| = 3$$
$$|2 - 6| = |-4| = 4$$

and, of course,

$$|-3 + 3| = |0| = 0.$$

The coordinates of the end points of a horizontal segment would be written in subscript notation as (x_1, y_1) and (x_2, y_1). The distance between the points would be

Horizontal distance $= |x_2 - x_1|$.

1.3 PROBLEM SET 1–1

1. Given the points $A(3, 6)$, $B(-3, 6)$, $C(3, 9)$, $D(-3, 2)$, plot the points, then figure the following distances from the graph: AB, AC, DB.

2. Given the points $A(-5, -9)$, $B(-3, -9)$, $C(-5, 15)$, $D(12, -9)$, find the distances AB, AC, AD, BD.

1.3 PROBLEM SET 1–1 (*concluded*)

3. Consider the segments AB and CD, where the coordinates are A(p, q), B(p, r), C(n, q), and D(m, q). If the two segments are extended, they will intersect in a right angle. Why?

4. Given $P_1(x_1, y_1)$, $P_2(x_2, y_2)$, $P_3(x_3, y_3)$, what relationships must exist among the coordinates if P_1P_2 is to be horizontal and P_1P_3 is to be perpendicular to P_1P_2?

5. Given P_1, P_2, P_3, P_4 with their respective coordinates in subscript form, what relationships must exist among the coordinates if $P_1 P_2$ is to be horizontal and P_3P_4 is to be parallel to P_1P_2?

6. If cities A, B, and C lie on an east-west line and are collinear (lie on the same straight line), how far would it be between B and C if:
   a) B is 60 miles east of A and C is 100 miles east of A?

   b) B is 30 miles west of A and C is 40 miles east of A?

7. If x represents sales and y represents selling expense, then (30, 22) would mean $30 in sales were accompanied by $22 of selling expense. Suppose last month's figures were (14, 10) and this month's are (30, 22).
   a) How much did sales increase?
   b) How much did selling expense increase?
   c) Make a graph showing the points and labeling the increases.

8. What is the advantage of subscript notation for coordinates of points?

9. A section of a city is divided into square blocks by streets and avenues. How many blocks would we walk on sidewalks going from (6th St., 12th Ave.) to (1st St., 5th Ave.)?

1.4 THE DISTANCE FORMULA

We have been working thus far with horizontal and vertical distances and now wish to develop a formula for the distance between any two points on a line segment. Recall that the Pythagorean theorem states that the sum of the squares of the sides of a right triangle equals the square of the slant side (the hypotenuse). For example, the right triangle in Figure 1–4A has sides 3 and 4, which are a vertical and a horizontal distance, and

$$3^2 + 4^2 = 5^2.$$

That is,

$$9 + 16 = 25.$$

FIGURE 1–4A

$3^2 + 4^2 = 5^2$

FIGURE 1–4B

$a^2 + b^2 = c^2$

More generally, if the sides of the right triangle are a and b as in Figure 1–4B, we may write

$$a^2 + b^2 = c^2.$$

We want the slant distance, which is c, so we write

$$c^2 = a^2 + b^2$$

and take the square root of both sides to obtain

$$c = \sqrt{a^2 + b^2},$$

where, of course, the symbol $\sqrt{}$ means that we take the nonnegative square root so that the distance will be nonnegative.

> **Exercise.** Find the length of the hypotenuse of the right triangle whose sides are 5 and 12 units long. Answer: $c = \sqrt{169} = 13$.

Turning next to an example, Figure 1–5 shows a building whose dimensions are 80 by 90 feet. A sidewalk is to be constructed from a building exit to a point that is 200 feet on the horizontal from the lower left corner of the building. We wish to determine the length of the dotted line which represents the sidewalk. We see that the sidewalk is the hypotenuse of a right triangle whose altitude is 90 feet and whose base is a horizontal line segment of length $(200 - 80) = 120$ feet. According to

FIGURE 1–5

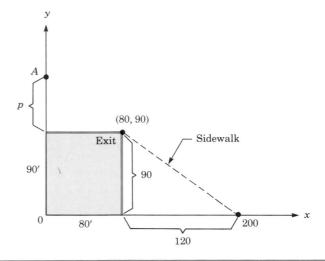

the Pythagorean theorem, the length of the hypotenuse is the square root of the sum of the squares of the sides. Hence, the desired length, L, is

$$L = \sqrt{(120)^2 + (90)^2} = \sqrt{22,500} = 150 \text{ feet.}$$

Exercise. If the sidewalk is continued to meet the vertical at point A, a) find the distance p from the properties of similar triangles; b) find the length of the extension. <u>Answer:</u> a) p is to 80 as 90 is to 120, so p is 60. b) $\sqrt{(60)^2 + (80)^2} = \sqrt{10,000} = 100$ feet.

Now let us develop a formula for finding the distance between any two points that are on a line segment by reference to the segment AB in Figure 1–6. Dashed lines have been drawn to make a right angle at C, so that the distance AB is the length of the hypotenuse of a right triangle. Inasmuch as AC is horizontal, C must have the same y-coordinate as A (namely, 2). Moreover, CB is vertical, so that C must have the same x-coordinate as B (namely, 4). The horizontal distance AC is $|4 - 1| = 3$ and the vertical distance CB is $|6 - 2| = 4$. Employing the Pythagorean

---

FIGURE 1–6

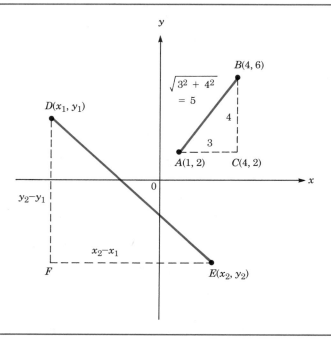

theorem, we find that the hypotenuse, AB, is

$$\sqrt{(AC)^2 + (CB)^2} = \sqrt{3^2 + 4^2} = \sqrt{25} = 5.$$

Applying the same methodology to the segment DE in Figure 1–6, we derive the general formula

Distance between two points $= \sqrt{(x_2 - x_1)^2 + (y_2 - y_1)^2}.$

For example, the distance between $(4, 3)$ and $(7, 2)$ is

$$\sqrt{(7 - 2)^2 + (2 - 3)^2} = \sqrt{9 + 1} = \sqrt{10} = 3.162.$$

1.5 PROBLEM SET 1–2

1. In each case, the given point pairs are the end points of the diagonal of a rectangle whose base is parallel to the x-axis. What are the coordinates of the other corners of the rectangle, and what is the length of the diagonal?
   a) (3, 5), (7, 8).
   b) (−1, −2), (5, 6).
   c) (−1, −2), (−10, −14).

2. Find the distance between the points.
   a) (5, 10), (11, 18).
   b) (0, 0), (9, 12).
   c) (−2, −5), (3, −4).
   d) (−2, 3), (6, 9).
   e) (3, −5), (6, −5).
   f) (4, 7), (4, 9).

3. The coordinates of three cities are shown, in miles, in Figure A. What will be the total distance traveled if one goes from A to B, then B to C, then back to A? Note that ABC is not a right triangle.

4. With reference to an origin, City A is located at (3, 5), City B at (9, 13), and City C at (21, 4), all numbers being miles.
   a) Make a graph showing the positions of the cities.
   b) Compute the total distance covered traveling from A to B, then from B to C.

5. A machine shop occupies a 100-foot by 50-foot rectangular area. The electrical outlets that supply the machines are located

FIGURE A

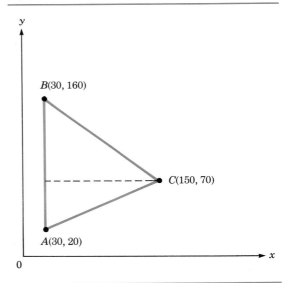

by reference to a grid with origin at one corner of the area and the horizontal axis in the long direction of the area.
   a) What would be the coordinates of the outlet in the center of the shop?
   b) How long a line would it take to reach from the origin to the center of the shop?
   c) How long a line would it take to connect a machine at (10 feet, 5 feet) to a plug at (40 feet, 45 feet)?

1.5 PROBLEM SET 1–2 (*concluded*)

6. Prove that if $P_1(x_1, y_1)$ and $P_2(x_2, y_2)$ are two points on a line parallel to the x-axis, then

$$\sqrt{(x_2 - x_1)^2 + (y_2 - y_1)^2} = |x_2 - x_1|.$$

7. Consider the BASIC program shown in Program 1–1.
   a) Describe what the program is doing line-by-line.

b) Run the program for each pair of points in Problem 2.

8. a) Modify Program 1–1 so that the printout will show the coordinates of the two points inputted.
   b) Run the program in (a) for each pair of points in Problem 2.

Program 1–1

```
10   REM DISTANCE FORMULA/P1(X1,Y1), P2(X2,Y2)
20   INPUT "Enter the coordinates of P1(X1,Y1), then
     P2(X2,Y2)";X1,Y1,X2,Y2
30   D=SQR((X2-X1)^2+(Y2-Y1)^2)
40   PRINT "The distance between P1 and P2 is ";D
50   END
```

1.6 SLOPE

The steepness of a ski slope, the pitch of a roof, and the steepness of the glide path of a descending airplane all are associated with the mathematical concept of the *slope* of a straight line or line segment. Numerically, the slope of a straight line is the ratio of the *rise (or fall)* to the *run* between two points on the line, where the rise or fall is the vertical separation and the run is the horizontal separation of the two points. In Figure 1–7, the slope of the segment *AB* is the ratio

$$\text{Slope} = \frac{\text{Rise}}{\text{Run}} = \frac{6}{2} = 3.$$

Clearly, the rise is a vertical segment and the run is a horizontal segment. Hence the slope (generally called m) of a straight line or line segment joining the points (x_1, y_1) and (x_2, y_2) is

$$\textbf{Slope} = \textbf{m} = \frac{\text{Difference of } y\text{'s}}{\text{Difference of } x\text{'s}} = \frac{y_2 - y_1}{x_2 - x_1}.$$

Consider the segment *CD* in Figure 1–7:

$$m = \frac{\text{Rise}}{\text{Run}} = \frac{-3 - (-7)}{7.5 - 2.5} = \frac{4}{5} = 0.8.$$

It is important to distinguish between segments that rise to the right, such as *AB* in Figure 1–7, and those that fall to the right, such as *KL*. This is done by requiring that lines that slant upward to the right have

FIGURE 1–7

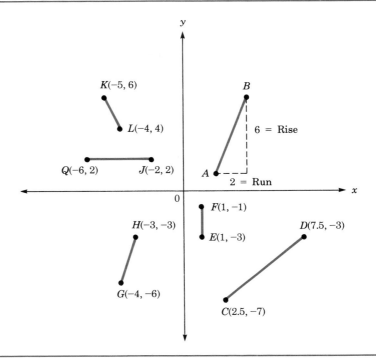

positive slope numbers and those slanting downward to the right have negative slope numbers. This requirement will be met if we *use the same point as the starting point* when computing the rise or fall and the run. For example, the slope of $C(2.5, -7)$, $D(7.5, -3)$ computed above to be 0.8 by starting with point D for both rise and run, is also 0.8 if point C is the starting point for both rise and run. Thus,

$$m = \frac{-7 - (-3)}{2.5 - 7.5} = \frac{-4}{-5} = 0.8.$$

Exercise. See Figure 1–7. Verify that the slopes of KL and GH are, respectively, -2 and 3.

Returning to Figure 1–7, observe the horizontal segment QJ. If we substitute its coordinates into the slope formula we find

$$m = \frac{2 - 2}{-2 - (-6)} = \frac{0}{4} = 0,$$

so the slope is zero. All horizontal segments have a slope of zero, for, as we know, the y-coordinates of two points on a horizontal segment are equal; that is, (x_1, y_1) and (x_2, y_1), with $x_1 \neq x_2$, would represent two points on a horizontal segment because both have the same y-coordinate. The slope of any such segment is

$$m = \frac{y_1 - y_1}{x_2 - x_1} = \frac{0}{x_2 - x_1} = 0.$$

The denominator, $x_2 - x_1$, is not zero here since $x_1 \neq x_2$. Consequently, the quotient is zero because zero divided by any nonzero number is zero.

Next, consider the vertical segment EF in Figure 1–7. From the slope formula we have:

$$m = \frac{-1 - (-3)}{1 - 1} = \frac{2}{0}.$$

The expression 2/0 is undefined since division by 0 is not permitted.[2] Thus, this vertical segment has no well-defined slope number. Saying a line has no slope number may not bring the image of a vertical line to mind. Some find it more descriptive to say a vertical line has infinite slope because a straight up-and-down line is the steepest one we can imagine. However, in using the term infinity, which is symbolized as ∞, it must be remembered that ∞ is not a number, so saying a line has infinite slope means its slope is undefined.

In general, (x_1, y_1) and (x_1, y_2) represent two different points on a vertical segment because they have the same x-coordinate and the slope will be

$$m = \frac{y_2 - y_1}{x_1 - x_1} = \frac{y_2 - y_1}{0}$$

which is undefined. Thus, in general, vertical segments have undefined or infinite slope.

Exercise. Which of the following segments is horizontal and which is vertical? a) The segment joining $(4, -6)$ and $(10, -6)$. b) The segment joining $(4, -6)$ and $(4, 10)$. Answer: a) is horizontal and b) is vertical.

Exercise. Draw three segments through the point $(4, 7)$, one with infinite slope, one with $m = 0$, and one with $m = \frac{2}{3}$. (A slope of $\frac{2}{3}$ is a rise of 2 for a run of 3.)

---

[2] See A2.14.

In applications, the slope of a line segment often is interpreted as the amount of change in the vertical for a unit change (that is, a change of one) in the horizontal, and a number of such slopes have been given names.

Example. This example uses the terms *disposable income, personal consumption expenditures*, and *savings*. It will be sufficient for our purposes here to think of disposable income as the amount of income left after taxes have been paid. The part of disposable income that is placed in a bank or otherwise invested is savings, and the remainder, personal consumption expenditure, is spent on food, clothing, housing, and so on.

A line segment fitted to points whose coordinates are in the order

(Disposable income, Consumption expenditures)

for the United States in recent years passes through

$$(312, 295) \quad \text{and} \quad (575, 537)$$

where the numbers are in billions of dollars. The slope of the segment shown in Figure 1–8 is

$$\frac{\text{Change in consumption expenditures}}{\text{Change in disposable income}} = \frac{537 - 295}{575 - 312} = \frac{242}{263} = 0.92.$$

FIGURE 1–8

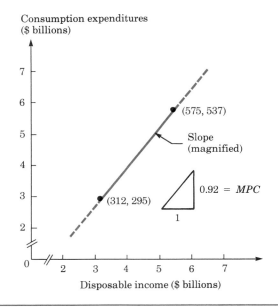

Thus, an increase of $242 billion in consumption expenditures accompanied an increase of $263 billion in disposable income. On a proportionate basis,

$$\frac{\$242}{\$263} = \frac{\$0.92}{\$1} = 0.92,$$

so the slope of the segment, 0.92, when written with a denominator of 1, represents the change in consumption expenditures per *one* dollar of additional income. In economics, this change is called the *marginal propensity to consume*, or MPC for short, as shown in Figure 1–8. The word *marginal*, just used, means *extra*, and MPC is the extra consumption that accompanies a $1 increase in income. Income not used for consumption expenditures is *saved*. We see from the preceding that $0.08 of each extra dollar of disposable income is saved, and 0.08 is called the *marginal propensity to save*, MPS. Clearly,

$$\text{MPS} = 1 - \text{MPC}.$$

The important bearing these two marginals have on the economic well-being of the nation can be understood by noting that savings are the source of investment in the factories and other economic activities that produce the income that becomes available to consumers. It is interesting to note that while many believe saving is a virtue, economics teaches us that when the nation has idle productive capacity, a high propensity to save (with the consequent low propensity to consume) is not necessarily a virtue for the national economy. What may be needed in such times is a high propensity to consume, for this could lead to the increased demand that will bring idle capacity back into use and increase national income.

1.7 PROBLEM SET 1–3

1. If (x_1, y_1) and (x_2, y_2) are the coordinates of two points on a line,
   a) How is the rise computed?
   b) How is the run computed?

2. a) What is the nature of the steepest line that can be drawn through a point?
   b) Why does such a line not have a slope number?

3. If a set of stairs rises 8 inches for every horizontal run of 12 inches, what slope number (assumed positive) describes the steepness of the stairs?

4. If x is the ground path of an airplane and y is its altitude, and at one point in time the plane is at (500, 1000) and soon after it is at (500, 0), what was the path of the airplane during the time interval?

5. A ski slope whose fall line makes a 45° angle with the horizontal is said to have a 100 percent grade. What slope number represents a 100 percent grade?

6. If the total manufacturing cost, y dollars, of producing x units of a product is $500 at 50 units output and $900 at 100 units output, and the cost-output relation is linear,
   a) What is the slope of the cost-output line?
   b) How much does the production of one unit add to total cost?

1.7 PROBLEM SET 1–3 (*concluded*)

7. A line segment fitted to points whose coordinates are in the order (disposable income, personal consumption expenditures) for a nation passes through the points (32, 30), (57, 54), the numbers being in billions of dollars. What are the values, names, and interpretations of the slope and (1 − slope) of this line?

Compute the slope of the segment joining each pair of points:

8. (0, 0), (2, 2).

9. (−3, 5), (4, −2).

10. (6, −1), (−2, 0).

11. (−3, −2), (−3, −4).

12. (2, 3), (6, 3).

13. (1/2, −1/4), (2, −1/4).

14. (−4, 7), (−4, 2).

15. (1, 1), (3, 3).

16. (2/7, −1/3), (−2/9, −2/3).

17. (0, 3), (3, 0).

18. (12, −5), (3, 6).

19. (3, −7), (3, −15).

20. (−1, −2), (−3, −4).

21. (1.6, 3.8), (−3.6, 4.2).

22. Write the formula for the slope of a line segment; then discuss the formula by means of a numerical illustration.

23. Write the expression for the slope of the segment from $P(a, −2)$ to $Q(3, −b)$ in two equivalent forms.

24. Make and label sketches showing segments having positive slope, negative slope, zero slope, and no slope number.

25. Why is division by zero excluded from arithmetic calculations? (See Appendix 2.)

Mark (T) for true or (F) for false:

26. ( ) A line that rises to the right and is almost vertical does not have a slope number.

27. ( ) The slope of the x-axis is zero.

28. ( ) The segment $P(a, b)$ $Q(a, c)$ is vertical.

29. ( ) A line segment of negative slope rises to the left.

30. ( ) The slope of the y-axis is not a number.

31. ( ) A line segment that is very, very close to the vertical has a slope number that has a large absolute value.

32. ( ) No matter how large a number we may write down, there is a line segment whose slope exceeds this number.

33. ( ) A line segment contained entirely in the second quadrant necessarily has a negative slope.

34. ( ) The quadrant in which a line segment lies has no necessary relation to the sign of the slope number of the segment.

35. Consider the BASIC program shown in Program 1–2.
a) Describe what the program is doing line-by-line.
b) Run the program for each pair of points in Problems 8 through 21.

36. a) Modify Program 1–2 so that the printout will show the actual coordinates of the two points inputted.
b) Run the program in (a) for each pair of points in Problems 8 through 21.

Program 1–2

```
10  REM SLOPE FORMULA/P1(X1,Y1), P2(X2,Y2)
20  INPUT "Enter the coordinates of P1(X1,Y1), then P2(X2,Y2)";
    X1,Y1,X2,Y2
30  IF X1<>X2 THEN M=(Y2-Y1)/(X2-X1)
40  PRINT "The slope between P1 and P2 is ";
50  IF X1=X2 THEN PRINT "infinite" ELSE PRINT M
60  END
```

1.8 EQUATION OF A LINE: SLOPE-INTERCEPT FORM

We have been considering line segments and their slopes and now turn to the infinite extension of a segment, which is a straight line. The first linear equation we wrote in the introduction to the chapter,

$$y = 1.25x + 0.75,$$

expressed the fare paid for a taxicab ride, y, in terms of x, the number of miles driven, and the constant 0.75, which was a fixed charge for a bridge toll. For example, the fares for a one-mile ride and a five-mile ride are, respectively,

$$y = 1.25(1) + 0.75 = 2$$
$$y = 1.25(5) + 0.75 = 7,$$

giving rise to the two (x, y) points

$$(1, 2) \quad \text{and} \quad (5, 7).$$

If we now find the slope of the line between these points as

$$\frac{y_2 - y_1}{x_2 - x_1} = \frac{7 - 2}{5 - 1} = \frac{5}{4} = 1.25,$$

we find that the slope is the coefficient of x in

$$y = 1.25x + 0.75.$$

Exercise. If $y = 0.8x + 2$, a) Write the coordinates of the points where $x = 0$ and $x = 5$. b) Compute the slope from the points found in (a). Answer: a) (0, 2) and (5, 6). b) Slope is 0.8, the coefficient of x in $y = 0.8x + 2$.

The last example and exercise suggest that if we write the equation of a line in the form y equals a constant times x, plus another constant, then the coefficient of x is the slope; that is, in

$$y = mx + b, \tag{1}$$

m is the slope. To prove this is so, suppose we take any pair of points on the line (1), (x_1, y_1) and (x_2, y_2). Then we must prove that

$$m = \frac{y_2 - y_1}{x_2 - x_1}.$$

We start by noting that because the points are on the line (1), their co-ordinates must satisfy equation (1). That is, at (x_1, y_1),

$$y_1 = mx_1 + b \tag{2}$$

and at (x_2, y_2),

$$y_2 = mx_2 + b. \tag{3}$$

We can rewrite (2) and (3) as

$$y_1 - mx_1 = b \qquad\qquad (4)$$
$$y_2 - mx_2 = b. \qquad\qquad (5)$$

The left sides of (4) and (5) both equal b, so they are themselves equal, and we have

$$y_1 - mx_1 = y_2 - mx_2$$

and, by transposing terms,

$$mx_2 - mx_1 = y_2 - y_1.$$

Factoring on the left yields

$$m(x_2 - x_1) = y_2 - y_1;$$

then, dividing both sides by $(x_2 - x_1)$, we have

$$\frac{m\cancel{(x_2 - x_1)}}{\cancel{(x_2 - x_1)}} = \frac{y_2 - y_1}{x_2 - x_1}$$

$$m = \frac{y_2 - y_1}{x_2 - x_1},$$

which is what we set out to prove. Thus, if the equation of a line is written in the form

$$y = mx + b,$$

m is the slope. Moreover, if $x = 0$, then

$$y = m(0) + b = b,$$

and $(0, b)$ is the point where the line cuts the y-axis. This point (where $x = 0$), is called the *y-intercept*. Thus, we have

---

Slope-Intercept Form

If the equation of a line is written in the form

$$y = mx + b,$$

then m is the slope and b is the y-intercept.

Example. Write $2y + 3x = 18$ in slope-intercept form and state the value of the slope and the y-intercept.

We proceed to isolate y with a coefficient of 1 on the left-hand side of the equation. First we transpose the term $3x$ to the right-hand side:

$$2y = -3x + 18.$$

Then, dividing both sides by 2, we have

$$\frac{2y}{2} = \frac{-3x + 18}{2}$$

$$y = -\frac{3}{2}x + 9$$

as the desired $y = mx + b$ form. The slope is $-\frac{3}{2}$ and the y-intercept is 9. The line is shown in Figure 1–9. The point (4, 3) shown on the line was obtained by choosing x to be 4, arbitrarily, and computing

$$y = -\frac{3}{2}(4) + 9 = -3(2) + 9 = 3.$$

Plotting by intercepts. When a linear equation is not in slope-intercept form, the simplest points to find and use for plotting the line are its intercepts. To find the x-intercept, set $y = 0$ and solve for x; to find the y-intercept, set $x = 0$ and solve for y. For example, in the equation

$$2y + 3x = 18$$
x-intercept: $2(0) + 3x = 18$; $x = 6$.   Point is $(6, 0)$.
y-intercept: $2y + 3(0) = 18$; $y = 9$.   Point is $(0, 9)$.

This line and its intercepts are shown in Figure 1–9.

The slope-intercept form expresses y as a linear function of x and so from now on in this chapter we will write the final expression for all our linear equations in this form.

FIGURE 1–9

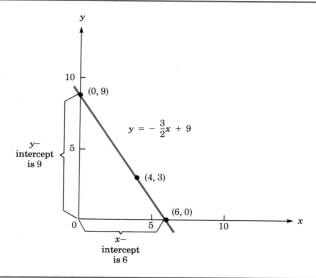

> **Exercise.** a) Write $3y - 2x = 24$ in slope-intercept form. b) What is the slope of the line? c) What is the y-intercept? d) What is the x-intercept? e) Write the coordinates of the points found in (c) and (d). Answer: a) $y = (\tfrac{2}{3})x + 8$. b) $\tfrac{2}{3}$. c) 8. d) -12. e) (0, 8) and $(-12, 0)$.

The next example illustrates one of the many interpretive applications that arise when a line is in slope-intercept form.

Example. It costs \$2,500 to set up the presses and machinery needed to print and bind a paperback book. After setup, it costs \$2 per book printed and bound. Let x represent the number of books made and y the total cost of making this number of books. a) Write the equation for y in terms of x. b) State the slope of the line and interpret this number. c) State the y-intercept of the line, and interpret this number.

a) Here the total cost is y, where

$$y = 2x + 2500,$$

a linear equation in slope-intercept form.

b) The slope, 2, means that every *additional* book printed, starting with the first copy, adds \$2 to total cost. Note that it would *not* be proper to say books cost \$2 per copy. That is, for example, if $x = 100$ books are made, then total cost is

$$y = 2(100) + 2500 = \$2,700$$

and \$2,700 for 100 books is

$$\frac{2700}{100} = \$27 \text{ per copy},$$

not \$2 per copy. It is because of this distinction—between cost per copy and the slope of the line—that economists would call the slope the *marginal* cost, which is the extra cost when an *additional* copy is made.

c) The y-intercept, \$2,500, is total cost when $x = 0$ books are made. That is, at $x = 0$

$$y = 2(0) + 2500 = \$2,500.$$

This means if the machines were made ready and then it was decided not to print the book, this cost would still be incurred. It is an example of a *fixed* cost. Other examples of fixed cost are the cost of insurance on machinery whether or not it is used, and continuing rent on a building used only part time.

Linear equations in a form such as $ax + cy = d$, with a, c, and d constant, arise naturally in many applications. For example, suppose we

> **Exercise.** An agency rents cars for one day and charges $22 plus 20 cents per mile the car is driven. a) Write the equation for one day's rental, y, in terms of x, the number of miles driven. b) Interpret the slope and the y-intercept. c) What is the renter's cost per mile if a car is driven 100 miles? 200 miles? Answer: a) $y = 0.20x + 22$. b) The slope, 0.20, means that each additional mile driven adds 20 cents to total cost. The intercept, 22, is the fixed charge, which would be incurred even if the renter used the car only for a secret meeting with a friend and did not drive it out of the parking lot. c) $0.42 per mile and $0.31 per mile.

have $31.50 to spend on pork and chicken. If we buy p pounds of pork at $2.25 per pound and c pounds of chicken at $1.80 per pound, our expenditures would be $2.25p + 1.80c$ dollars, and this must equal $31.50. Thus,

$$2.25p + 1.80c = 31.50.$$

In slope-intercept form, solving for p, this becomes

$$p = -\frac{1.80}{2.25}c + \frac{31.50}{2.25}, \quad \text{or} \quad p = -0.8c + 14.$$

The intercept tells us that we can buy 14 pounds of pork if we buy no chicken. The slope, -0.8, means that if we increase our purchase of chicken by one pound, we must decrease purchases of pork by 0.8 pounds. Thus, the *substitution rate* is 0.8 pounds of pork per pound of chicken.

> **Exercise.** Solve the above equation for c in terms of p in slope-intercept form, then interpret the intercept and the slope. Answer: $c = -1.25p + 17.5$. We can buy 17.5 pounds of chicken if we buy no pork. The substitution rate is 1.25 pounds of chicken per pound of pork.

1.9 STRAIGHT-LINE EQUATION GIVEN A POINT AND SLOPE

We have seen that the straight-line equation can be written directly if the slope m and a *particular* point, the y-intercept b, are given. The equation then is

$$y = mx + b.$$

If the given point is not the y-intercept, we can easily determine this intercept from the above slope-intercept form.

Example. Find the equation of the line with slope 0.75 that passes through the point (8, 10).

We write first the partially complete equation

$$y = 0.75x + b, \tag{1}$$

and now we must find the value of b. Because the line passes through (8, 10), these coordinates must satisfy (1), so, substituting,

$$10 = 0.75(8) + b$$
$$10 = 6 + b$$
$$4 = b,$$

and the y-intercept is found to be $b = 4$. Hence (1) becomes the desired equation,

$$y = 0.75x + 4.$$

Exercise. Find the equation of the line that has a slope of -0.50 and passes through the point (4, 3). Answer: $y = -0.5x + 5$.

An alternative approach is to let m represent the given slope and (x_1, y_1) represent the given point. The formula we want is the equation that is true not only for the point (x_1, y_1) but also for all other points (x, y) on the line. Thus, we have

$$(x_1, y_1) \text{ and } (x, y) \text{ with slope } m.$$

The slope of the line is

$$\frac{y - y_1}{x - x_1},$$

and this must equal m for all pairs of points on the line. Thus, we have

---

Point-Slope Form

$$\frac{y - y_1}{x - x_1} = m, \quad \text{or} \quad y - y_1 = m(x - x_1).$$

Returning to the last example, where $m = 0.75$ and the given point (x_1, y_1) is (8, 10), substitution into the point-slope form yields

$$\frac{y - 10}{x - 8} = 0.75$$
$$y - 10 = 0.75(x - 8)$$
$$y - 10 = 0.75x - 6$$
$$y = 0.75x + 4,$$

as before. For more practice, redo the last exercise using the point-slope form.

1.10 STRAIGHT-LINE EQUATION FROM TWO POINTS

Two points completely determine a straight line and, of course, they determine the slope of the line. Hence, we can first compute the slope, then use this value of m together with either point in the point-slope form

$$y - y_1 = m(x - x_1)$$

to generate the equation of the line.

Example. The total cost, y, of producing x units is a linear function. Records show that on one occasion 100 units were made at a total cost of $200, and on another occasion, 150 units were made at a total cost of $275. Write the linear equation for total cost in terms of the number of units produced.

The information given consists of two points whose coordinates (x, y) are in the order (units made, total cost). These are:

$$(100, 200) \quad \text{and} \quad (150, 275).$$

The slope of the line is then

$$m = \frac{275 - 200}{150 - 100} = \frac{75}{50} = 1.5.$$

Now picking one of the points, say $(100, 200)$, we substitute in the point-slope form to get

$$y - 200 = 1.5(x - 100).$$

Solving this for y, we have the desired equation

$$y - 200 = 1.5x - 150$$
$$y = 1.5x + 50.$$

Exercise. A publisher asks a printer for quotations on the cost of printing 1,000 and 2,000 copies of a book. The printer quotes $4,500 for 1,000 copies and $7,500 for 2,000 copies. Assume that cost, y, is linearly related to x, the number of books printed. a) Write the coordinates of the given points. b) Write the equation of the line. Answer: a) (1000, 4500); (2000, 7500). b) $y = 3x + 1500$.

To obtain a special two-point form for a straight-line equation, we designate the given points as (x_1, y_1) and (x_2, y_2). Then we let (x, y) represent any other point on the line we seek. Thus we have

$$(x_1, y_1), \quad (x_2, y_2), \quad (x, y).$$

The slope of the line must be the same for any pair of its points. Thus, for (x_1, y_1) and (x, y), the slope is

$$\frac{y - y_1}{x - x_1},$$

and for the given point pair, (x_1, y_1) and (x_2, y_2), the slope is

$$\frac{y_2 - y_1}{x_2 - x_1}.$$

Setting the last two expressions for the same slope equal yields

---

Two-Point Form for a Straight Line

$$\frac{y - y_1}{x - x_1} = \frac{y_2 - y_1}{x_2 - x_1}.$$

To practice with this form, recall that in the last example we found the equation of the line through (100, 200) and (150, 275) was $y = 1.5x + 50$. With the two-point form we write,

$$\frac{y - 200}{x - 100} = \frac{275 - 200}{150 - 100} = \frac{75}{50}$$

$$\frac{y - 200}{x - 100} = 1.5$$

$$y - 200 = 1.5(x - 100)$$

$$y - 200 = 1.5x - 150$$

$$y = 1.5x + 50,$$

as before. For more practice, redo the last exercise using the two-point form.

1.11 HORIZONTAL AND VERTICAL LINES

When the equation of a line is to be determined from two given points, it is a good idea to compare corresponding coordinates because, as we learned earlier in the chapter, if the y values are the same the line is horizontal, and if the x values are the same the line is vertical. For example, given the points

$$(3, 6) \quad \text{and} \quad (8, 6)$$

we see that the line through them is horizontal because both y-coordinates are 6. This line is shown in Figure 1–10. It is clear that y is 6 at every point on this line irrespective of the value assigned to the x-coordinate, and because

$$y = 6$$

describes this line, and this line only, we say $y = 6$ is the equation for the line.

FIGURE 1–10   **FIGURE 1–11**

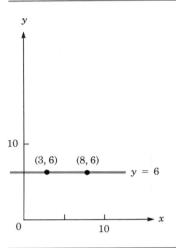

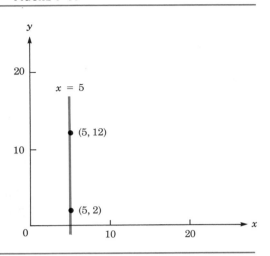

If we had not noticed the equality of the y-coordinates of $(3, 6)$ and $(8, 6)$ and had proceeded with the slope-intercept determination of the equation by first finding

$$m = \frac{6 - 6}{8 - 3} = \frac{0}{5} = 0,$$

then using the point-slope form to get

$$y - 6 = 0(x - 3)$$
$$y - 6 = 0,$$

we would have obtained

$$y = 6$$

as the equation of the line. However, there is no need to proceed beyond the first step because *if the slope, m, turns out to be zero, the line is horizontal and has an equation of the form*

$$y = \text{constant},$$

where the constant is the given y-coordinate.

If the x-coordinates of the two different points are equal, as in

$$(5, 2) \quad \text{and} \quad (5, 12),$$

the line through them is vertical, as shown in Figure 1–11, and its equation is

$$x = 5.$$

If we had proceeded to apply the point-slope procedure, we would obtain

$$m = \frac{12 - 2}{5 - 5} = \frac{10}{0}$$

which is undefined. We need not proceed further because *if the slope is undefined, the line is vertical and has an equation of the form*

$$x = \text{constant},$$

where the constant is the given x-coordinate.

We have become accustomed to seeing both x and y in linear equations but, as we have just learned, the coefficient of x or the coefficient of y (but not both) can be zero, in which case we have a horizontal or a vertical line.

In summary:

> The line through (x_1, y_1); (x_2, y_1) is $y = y_1$.
> The line through (x_1, y_1); (x_1, y_2) is $x = x_1$.

Exercise. What is the equation of the line through a) $(-4, 7)$ and $(-4, -3)$? b) $(3, 6)$ and $(2, 6)$? Answer: a) $x = -4$. b) $y = 6$.

1.12 PARALLEL AND PERPENDICULAR LINES

Lines that have the same slope are parallel. Thus,

$$y = \frac{1}{2}x + 5$$

$$y = \frac{1}{2}x + 2$$

are parallel lines, as shown in Figure 1–12. We shall have occasion to be concerned about parallel lines in coming chapters where the equation of each line expresses a condition that must be satisfied, and we wish both conditions to be satisfied. This means that we will be seeking a point that is on *both* lines; that is, the point of intersection of the lines. Clearly, it is impossible to satisfy both conditions if the two lines are parallel because they do not intersect. The pair of equations associated with parallel lines is called inconsistent.

Exercise. Which of the following pairs of lines are parallel? a) $y = \frac{3}{2}x + 4$; $y = 1.5x + 5$; b) $y = -2x + 2$; $y = -1.5x + 5$. Answer: The pair in (a).

Perpendicular lines. If two slant lines are perpendicular, the slope of one is the negative reciprocal of the slope of the other. Thus,

FIGURE 1–12

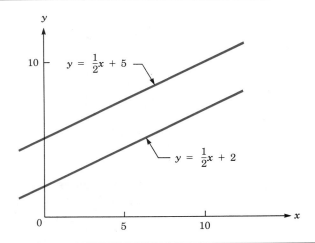

$$y = \frac{2}{3}x + 5 \quad \text{and} \quad y = -\frac{3}{2}x + 10$$

are perpendicular because the negative reciprocal of the slope of the first line is

$$-\frac{1}{\left(\dfrac{2}{3}\right)} = -1\left(\frac{3}{2}\right) = -\frac{3}{2},$$

and $-3/2$ is the slope of the second line. We could as easily say that the product of the slopes of two slant lines that are perpendicular is -1. Thus, for the last pair of lines

$$m_1 m_2 = \frac{2}{3}\left(-\frac{3}{2}\right) = -1.$$

We shall have only occasional use for this relationship, so its proof is left as an exercise in the next set of problems, which also contains an application of the relationship. We should note that

$$y = 6 \quad \text{and} \quad x = 5$$

are perpendicular lines because the first is horizontal and the second is vertical. However, $x = 5$ has an undefined slope, so the $m_1 m_2 = -1$ relationship does not apply if the lines are not both slant lines.

Exercise.   Given line 1 is $y = 2x - 3.5$ and line 2 is $y = -0.5x + 2$, to which of these is $y = 2x + 4$ a) parallel b) perpendicular? Answer: a) 1. b) 2.

1.13 LINES THROUGH THE ORIGIN

Any equation in the variables x and y that has no constant term other than zero will have a graph that passes through the origin. For example, in the case of the straight line

$$y = \frac{2}{3}x,$$

it is obvious that $(0, 0)$, the coordinates of the origin, satisfy the equation. From an applied point of view, such lines are of interest because they are the mathematical expression of a *proportion*. That is, if we write the equation in the form

$$\frac{y}{x} = \frac{2}{3},$$

we may read the statement as "y is to x as 2 is to 3." An assumption that, say, output per man-hour is 3 units would translate to $y/x = 3$, where y is number of units of output and x is number of man-hours worked. Graphical expression of the assumption would be the straight line $y = 3x$, passing through the origin.

When considering revenue obtained from sale of a product, revenue, R, is 0 when the number of units sold, x, is 0. The revenue obtained by selling x units at a constant price of $5 per unit would be

$$R = 5x,$$

a line through the origin.

Exercise. If it costs C dollars to maintain a factory and produce x units of product, would it be reasonable to assume the cost curve goes through the origin? Answer: It would not be reasonable because at $x = 0$ (no output) costs of insurance, security, interest payments and other elements of fixed cost, which do not depend upon output, would still be incurred.

1.14 PROBLEM SET 1–4

Find the equation (in slope-intercept form, if possible) of the line passing through the given point and having the given slope:

1. $(3, 4)$, slope 3.
2. $(-5, 6)$, slope -1.
3. $(-2, 6)$, slope $-2/3$.
4. $(1, -4)$, slope $1/2$.
5. $(-3, -8)$, slope 0.
6. $(2, 7)$, slope $-1/6$.

7. $(-5, -8)$, slope 13.
8. $(0, 0)$, slope 0.
9. $(5, 2)$, vertical.
10. $(0, 0)$, vertical.
11. $(3, 4)$, slope 0.
12. $(4, -3)$, slope 5.

1.14 PROBLEM SET 1–4 (*continued*)

Find the equation (in slope-intercept form, if possible) of the line passing through each of the given pairs of points:

13. (4, 6), (−3, 7).
14. (−5, 3), (2, 9).
15. (1, 1), (3, 3).
16. (−2, −4), (−1, 5).
17. (0, 0), (2, 3).
18. (2, 4), (−3, 4).

19. (1/3, −1/2), (2, −3).
20. (−7, 2), (−7, −8).
21. (3, 5), (1, 4).
22. (3, 5), (−4, 5).
23. (6, 0), (10, 0).
24. (−3, −2), (4, −7).

25. Write the equation of the x-axis.
26. Write the equation of the y-axis.
27. On the line passing through (2, 3) and (−5, 6), what is the y-coordinate of the point where x = 17?
28. On the line of slope −2 passing through (3, 7), what is the x-coordinate of the point where y = 17?
29. What is the equation of the vertical line that passes through (−6, 3)?
30. a) What is the equation of the horizontal line that passes through (−6, 3)?
    b) A curve showing profit (vertical) and number of units produced and sold (horizontal) rises smoothly to a peak and then declines as we move to the right. The peak is at (100, 500). What is the equation of the tangent line at the peak? What is the significance of this equation? Hint: Make a sketch labeling the axes, showing a curve that has a rounded peak.
31. a) What is the equation of the line parallel to, and 5 units above, the x-axis?
    b) What is the equation of the line parallel to, and 10 units to the left of, the y-axis?
32. As sales (x) change from $100 to $400, selling expense (y) changes from $75 to $150.

Assume that the given data establish the relationship between sales and selling expense as the two change, and assume that the relationship is linear. Find the equation of the relationship.

33. As the number of units manufactured increases from 100 to 200, manufacturing cost (total) increases from $350 to $650. Assume that the given data establish the relationship between cost (y) and number of units made (x), and assume that the relationship is linear. Find the equation of the relationship.
34. If the relationship between total cost and number of units made is linear, and if cost increases by $3 for each additional unit made, and if the total cost of 10 units is $40, find the equation of the relationship between total cost (y) and number of units made (x).
35. a) If taxi fare (y) is 50 cents plus 20 cents per quarter mile, write the equation relating fare to number of miles traveled, m.
    b) The weekly earnings of a salesman are $50 plus 10% of the retail value of the goods he sells. Write the equation for earnings, E, in terms of sales volume, V. What is the slope of this line called?

Mark (T) for true or (F) for false:

36. (   ) The horizontal line through (5, 6) has the equation x = 5.

37. (   ) The equation of the x-axis is y = 0.

38. (   ) The slope of the line through (4, 6) and (5, 9) is greater than the slope of the line through (0, 0) and (1, 2).

39. (   ) The equation of the x-axis is x = 0.

1.14 PROBLEM SET 1–4 (*continued*)

40. ( ) The lines $x = 5$ and $x = 10$ are parallel to each other.

41. ( ) The lines $x = 5$ and $y = 10$ are perpendicular to each other.

Graph the following lines, using intercepts:

42. $y = -x + 6$.

43. $y = 1.5x - 6$.

44. $y = 0.4x + 1.2$.

45. $y = x - 4$.

46. $y = (-7/6)x + 1/2$.

What is the slope of each of the following lines?

47. $3x - 2y = 7$.

48. $x + y = 2$.

49. $2x - 6y = 5$.

50. $x - y = 0$.

51. a) A pound of food A contains 8 ounces of a nutrient, and a pound of B contains 12 ounces of the nutrient. Write the expression that must be satisfied if x pounds of A and y pounds of B are to provide 96 ounces of nutrient.
b) What is the substitution rate of A per pound of B?
c) What is the substitution rate of B per pound of A?

52. What is the equation of the line that has a slope of 2 and a y-intercept of -6?

53. If a straight-line equation is in the form

$$ax + by + c = 0$$

then the slope is $-a/b$; that is, the negative of the ratio of the coefficient of x to the coefficient of y. Why is this statement true?

54. If total cost is y and number of units is x, what expression represents a constant cost per unit? What equation would replace the statement that cost per unit is $3? What is the slope and what are the intercepts of the line whose equation was just written?

55. a) Find the equation of the line through $(2, 7)$ parallel to the line $y = 1.5x - 3.5$.
b) Find the equation of the line through $(-2, -6)$ perpendicular to the line $y = (1/3)x + 4/3$.

56. A printer quotes the price of $1,400 for printing 100 copies of a report and $3,000 for printing 500 copies. Assuming a linear relationship, what would be the price for printing 300 copies?

57. What is the equation of the line on which the y-coordinate of any point is twice the x-coordinate?

58. Find the equation of the line through the origin parallel to $y = 0.8x - 2$.

59. a) Figure A shows two perpendicular lines, L_1 and L_2. Clearly, the slope of one is positive and the other negative. Prove that angle 1 = angle 2. Then, using similar-triangle relationships, prove that the slopes of the lines are negative reciprocals.

FIGURE A

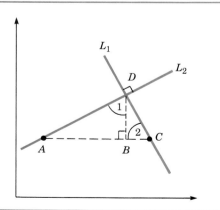

1.14 PROBLEM SET 1-4 (*continued*)

b) In what situation would slopes of perpendicular lines not be negative reciprocals?

60. See Figure B, which shows an existing pipeline passing through two points. Plant *A* is in existence at the point (5, 6) and a new plant, *B*, is to be located on the *x*-axis at a point such that the dotted pipeline that will be constructed to connect *A* and *B* to the existing line will be perpendicular to the existing line.
a) Where should *B* be located?
b) What is the advantage of having the new line meet the existing line at a right angle?

61. Prove that every line whose equation is of the form $ax + by = 0$, where *a* and *b* are any numbers (not both zero), passes through the origin.

FIGURE B

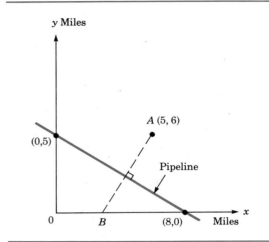

Mark (T) for true or (F) for false:

62. (   ) The *x*-intercept of $3x - 2y = 12$ is -6.

63. (   ) The slope of $2x + 3y = 6$ is $-2/3$.

64. (   ) If the graph of the equation $ax + by + c = 0$ is to pass through the origin, *c* must be 0.

65. (   ) If the ratio of *y* to *x* is constant for an equation, the graph of the equation must pass through the origin.

66. (   ) $x + y = 6$ and $2x + 2y = 8$ are parallel but not identical lines.

67. (   ) $x + y = 6$ and $2x + 2y = 12$ are identical lines.

68. (   ) If the relationship between *x* and *y* can be expressed as $ax + dy = 0$, then *x* and *y* are in proportion.

69. (   ) $x = 10$ has no *y*-intercept.

70. (   ) Any line parallel to $x - 2y = 7$ must have a slope of 1/2.

71. (   ) If *y* is units of output and *x* is man-hours worked, and if $y = 3x$, then output per man-hour is constant.

72. Consider the BASIC program shown in Program 1-3.
a) Describe what the program is doing line-by-line.
b) Run the program for each pair of points in Problems 13 through 24.

73. a) Modify Program 1-3 to print the slope, *y*-intercept, and equation of a line passing through the two points $P_1(x_1, y_1)$ and $P_2(x_2, y_2)$.
b) Run the program in (a) for each pair of points in Problems 13 through 24.

74. a) Modify Program 1-3 to print the equation of a line passing through a given point $P_1(x_1, y_1)$ and having a given slope *m*.

Program 1-3

```
10  REM EQUATION OF LINE/P1(X1,Y1), P2(X2,Y2)
20  INPUT "Enter the coordinates of P1(X1,Y1), then
    P2(X2,Y2)";X1,Y1,X2,Y2
```

1.14 PROBLEM SET 1–4 (concluded)

```
30  IF X1<>X2 THEN M=(Y2-Y1)/(X2-X1)
40  IF X1<>X2 THEN B=Y1-M*X1
50  PRINT "The equation of the line between P1 and P2 is ";
60  IF X1=X2 THEN PRINT "x = ";X1
70  IF X1<>X2 THEN PRINT "y = ";
80  IF X1<>X2 THEN IF Y1=Y2 THEN PRINT Y1 ELSE PRINT M;"x ";
90  IF X1<>X2 AND Y1<>Y2 THEN IF B>0 THEN PRINT "+";B ELSE PRINT
    "-";ABS(B)
100 END
```

1.15 INTERPRETIVE EXERCISE: COST–OUTPUT

The purpose of this exercise is to relate the mathematical terminology of linear equations to a real-world situation. To this end, we shall assume that C is the total factory (manufacturing) cost of production of a product when Q (for quantity) units of the product are made. We assume that the relationship between C and Q is linear,[3] as shown by the line segment LM in Figure 1–13.

FIGURE 1–13

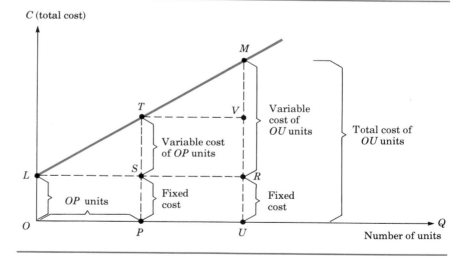

When making interpretations from Figure 1–13, keep in mind that a vertical distance represents a cost and a horizontal distance represents a quantity (number of units). Thus, the segment PT represents the total

---

[3] When the output interval is wide, the cost–output relationship may well be curved rather than straight. We shall consider the case of a curve in later chapters.

cost of producing *OP* units of product, and *UM* is the total cost of producing *OU* units of product.

The distance *OL*, the vertical intercept, corresponds to the cost of operation when zero units are produced, the reasoning here being that some costs (such as insurance on the plant) exist even when no product is being made. Borrowing an accounting term, we interpret *OL* as *fixed cost*, that is, the component of cost that does not vary with the number of units made. In Figure 1–13, fixed cost is

$$OL = PS = UR.$$

If we make *OP* units of product, the total cost is *PT*. *PT*, in turn, is the sum of *PS* and *ST*. *PS* is fixed cost; *ST* we shall call the *variable cost* when *OP* units are made. The term variable cost refers to the component of cost that changes as the number of units produced changes. Thus, *ST* is variable cost when *OP* units are made; *RM* is the (larger) variable cost when *OU* units are made. At each level of output, total cost is the sum of fixed and variable cost.

Consider the ratio *RM/LR*. *RM* is the variable cost when *LR* (or *OU*) units are made. The ratio

$$\frac{\text{Variable cost}}{\text{Number of units made}}$$

is the variable cost *per unit* of product made. By definition, *RM/LR* is the slope of *LM*, and the slope of a straight-line segment is constant. Consequently, variable cost per unit is constant when cost and output are linearly related.[4]

Economic terminology leads us to another description of the slope of *LM* in Figure 1–13. Economists speak of the *extra* cost (the change in total cost) when one more unit is made as the *marginal cost* of that unit. This is the vertical change for a horizontal change of one. It is the slope of the line. We may say that when total cost is linearly related to output, marginal cost is constant. (Marginal cost, of course, will not be constant if the total cost function is not linear.)

For further practice, observe that *UM* is *VM* greater than *PT*, which means that it costs *VM* more dollars to produce *OU* units than to produce *OP* units. *TV*, on the other hand, represents how many more units can be produced for *UM* dollars than for *PT* dollars.

We have said that when total cost is linearly related to output, then variable cost per unit is constant. Average cost per unit, defined as total cost over number of units produced, is not constant. Rather than argue this statement from Figure 1–13, suppose that we interpret the equation

$$y = 3x + 2,$$

---

[4] If, on a cost *curve*, variable cost is divided by number of units produced, the ratio is called *average* variable cost per unit and is *not* constant.

letting y be total cost of producing x units. The fixed cost is $2, and the variable cost per unit (the slope) is $3. However, by substitution, we find that total cost rises from $17 to $32 if x changes from 5 to 10 units. The average cost per unit declines from 17/5 to 32/10, that is, from $3.40 to $3.20. This reduction sometimes is referred to as being a consequence of spreading fixed cost over a larger number of units.

1.16 PROBLEM SET 1–5

Mark (T) for true or (F) for false. (Assume that cost means factory cost.) Given that total cost, y, of making x units is $y = 5x + 10$:

1. ( ) The total cost of making 20 units is $110.

2. ( ) Average cost per unit is $6 if 10 units are made.

3. ( ) The marginal cost of the 11th unit is greater than $5.

4. ( ) The marginal cost of the 20th unit is $5.

5. ( ) The variable cost per unit decreases as the number of units made increases.

6. ( ) The variable cost incurred when making 10 items is $50.

7. ( ) Average cost per unit decreases as the number of units made increases.

8. ( ) Variable cost increases as the number of units made increases.

9. ( ) The marginal cost of every unit is the same.

10. ( ) The slope of the line is the variable cost per unit.

11. If the total factory cost, y, of making x units of a product is given by $y = 3x + 20$, and if 50 units are made:
a) What is the variable cost?
b) What is the total cost?
c) What is the variable cost per unit?
d) What is the average cost per unit?
e) What is the marginal cost of the 50th unit?

12. If total factory cost, y, of making x units of a product is $y = 10x + 500$ and if 1,000 units are made:
a) What is the variable cost?
b) What is the total cost?
c) What is the variable cost per unit?
d) What is the marginal cost of the last unit made?

13. A printer quotes a price of $7,500 for printing 1,000 copies of a book and $15,000 for printing 2,500 copies. Assuming a linear relationship and that 2,000 books are printed:
a) Find the equation relating the total cost, y, to x, the number of books printed.
b) What is the variable cost?

c) What is the fixed cost?
d) What is the variable cost per book?
e) What is the average cost per book?
f) What is the marginal cost of the last book printed?

14. If total factory cost, y, of making x units of a product is given by $y = 2x + 25$:
a) Graph the cost-units equation.
b) Draw a line representing fixed cost on the graph for (a).
c) Erect a vertical line at $x = 10$, intersecting the x-axis at R, the fixed cost line at S, and the given equation at T.
d) What are the numerical values and the interpretations of RS, ST, and RT?

15. In Figure A, the slant line represents the relation between total factory cost, C, of producing a number of units, and the number of units, Q, produced. What line segment(s), or ratios thereof, represent:
a) Fixed cost?
b) Total cost if OA units are made?
c) Variable cost if OA units are made?
d) Variable cost per unit made?

1.16 PROBLEM SET 1–5 (*concluded*)

e) Average cost per unit if *OA* units are made?

f) Fixed cost per unit if *OA* units are made?

g) How many more units can be made for *AD* dollars than for *AF* dollars?

h) Marginal cost?

16. Prior to making a number of units of a certain part, a machine must be made ready, the cost incurred being called the setup cost. The total machine shop cost, *C*, of making *Q* units of the part is shown in Figure B as the segment *RS*. What interpretation would be given to:

   a) *OR*?   c) *PN/OM*?

   b) *PN*?   d) *MN/OM*?

FIGURE A

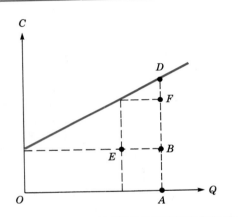

FIGURE B

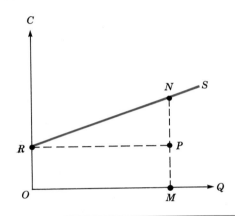

1.17 COMMENT ON MODELS

We call attention here to the distinction between the mathematics of the last discussion and the actual cost-output situation to which the mathematics was related. Nothing was said about whether costs *are* or whether costs *should be* linearly related to output. The theme of the discussion was that *if* the relationship was linear, then certain interpretations suggested themselves. In particular, mathematical analysis of the linear equation showed that the ratio of *y* to *x* decreased as *x* increased, and we interpreted this as being a consequence of spreading fixed cost over an increasing output.

The linear equation under discussion is an example of a mathematical model. In broad context, a *model* is a simplified representation of reality. Thus, for example, engineers will design an airplane by first simulating many possible alternatives on a computer. This technique is currently referred to as CAD (computer-assisted design). The engineer will then make various models of airplane wings to test in a wind tunnel before deciding upon a final design. Architects make several small-scale models of different building designs, often formulated on a computer, to help a client form a mental picture of real buildings before selecting a particular design. A mathematical model is a mathematical expression, or set of expressions, that seeks to capture the essential features of a real-world situation. If this objective can be achieved, then the full force of mathematical analysis can be applied to the model, and the outcome of the analysis may have important interpretations. The key idea here is that mathematical analysis is a highly developed and powerful tool, but before it can be brought to bear on an actual problem, it is necessary to construct an adequate mathematical representation (model) of the situation. We do not expect a model to be an exact replica of the real world. We hope that the model will be adequate. In any event, we must be careful not to exceed the bounds of good sense when interpreting the outcome of mathematical analysis of a model. Thus, it probably would not be realistic to assume a linear relationship between cost and output no matter how large output became, and it certainly would make no sense to extend the linear model to negative outputs.

Physical scientists have had a high degree of success in formulating mathematical models. Witness, for example, the contributions of mathematical analysis of gravitational forces to man's achievements in space. Much effort now is being directed toward model building by workers in the social sciences. The linear programming model we shall encounter a few chapters ahead is a good example of a model widely used in many parts of the world of business and economics.

A model should *fit* actual data reasonably well. To understand what is involved here, recall an earlier example in which a straight line was fitted to points whose coordinates were in the order (disposable income, personal consumption expenditures); the line passed through (312, 295) and (575, 537). The actual data used in determining these points are shown in Figure 1–14, which also shows the plotted points (solid) and a line drawn freehand (with the aid of a stretched thread). Clearly, no line passes through all of the points, but the freehand line comes very close to the points, and the fit is very good—much better than is the case in other situations. Essentially the same line would be obtained if we had used points for all years from 1950 to 1970 and had applied the objective techniques of fitting developed in the study of statistics.

If we let C be personal consumption expenditures and D be disposable income, then use the two-point formula with (312, 295) and (575, 537), we obtain the linear model

$$C = 0.92D + 7.96.$$

The slope, 0.92, is called the marginal propensity to consume, as we learned earlier. What about the intercept, or constant, 7.96? Mechanically, this is consumption when disposable income is zero, but we should not infer anything about consumption when D is zero because we have no

FIGURE 1–14
Linear model fitted to consumption expenditures and disposable
income in the United States. Selected years, 1950–1970.

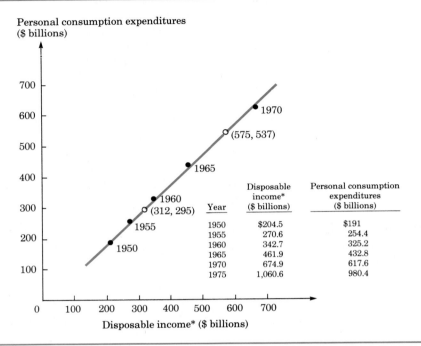

Year	Disposable income* ($ billions)	Personal consumption expenditures ($ billions)
1950	$204.5	$191
1955	270.6	254.4
1960	342.7	325.2
1965	461.9	432.8
1970	674.9	617.6
1975	1,060.6	980.4

* Less interest paid by consumers.
Source: Economic Report of the President, 1973, 1978.

data near zero and, in fact, D will never be zero. Moreover, in this changing economy we should be careful about extrapolating (going beyond the region of experience) very far. An appropriate interpretation of the constant 7.96 is that consumption expenditures are in major part determined by income, but that at any level of income, a part ($7.96 billion) is *independent* of income. This fixed part is called *autonomous* consumption. Thus, a common model of consumption in economics takes the form

$$C = A + MD$$

where the variables C and D are as defined earlier, the constant A is autonomous consumption, and the constant M is the marginal propensity to consume (about 0.92 in recent years).

Having warned about extrapolating beyond the region of experience, we must now admit that a major reason for developing a model is to make projections. Projections answer such questions as, What would consumption be if disposable income were $1,061 billion, assuming the model $C = 0.92D + 7.96$ applies? Mechanical substitution leads to the projection $C = \$984$ billion. As a matter of record, disposable income did reach $1,061 billion in 1975, and in that year consumption expenditures were $980 billion, so the projection was very close to the actual figure. We see that extrapolation can lead to quite accurate results, but we have no assurance of accuracy, and our confidence lessens, the further we depart from the region of experience.

As a final comment, we should point out that many of the equations used in textbooks are simplistic ones, with nice whole numbers as coefficients. Students ask, quite rightly, where they come from. The answer, of course, is that they were designed by the writer of the text to facilitate learning of mathematical techniques, for such is the objective of the text. One of the purposes of the preceding discussion of models was to indicate where equations come from, and to assure the student that simplified equations used for text illustration do have counterparts in actual applications.

1.18 BREAK–EVEN INTERPRETATION: 1

In this section we shall consider a manufacturer who produces q units of a product and sells the product at a price of $\$p$ per unit. The symbols to be used are

C = total cost of producing and selling q units.
q = number of units produced and sold.
v = variable cost *per unit* made, assumed to be constant.
F = fixed cost, a constant.
p = selling price per unit.
R = total revenue received, which is the same as the dollar volume of sales.

The cost function then is given by

$$C = vq + F \tag{1}$$

and

$$\text{Revenue} = (\text{price per unit})(\text{number of units sold})$$
$$R = pq. \tag{2}$$

If the manufacturer is just to break even on operations, neither incurring a loss nor earning a profit, revenue (2) must equal cost (1). That is, at break-even,

$$pq = vq + F. \tag{3}$$

We now may solve (3) for the production volume, q:

$$pq - vq = F$$
$$q(p - v) = F$$

Break-Even Quantity

$$q_e = \frac{F}{p - v} \cdot \tag{4}$$

Example. A manufacturer of records has a fixed cost of $10,000 and variable cost per record made is $5. Selling price per unit is $10. a) Write the revenue and cost equations. b) At what number of units will break-even occur? c) At what sales volume (revenue) will break-even occur?

a) The equations are:

$$\text{Revenue:} \quad R = 10q$$
$$\text{Cost:} \quad C = 5q + 10{,}000.$$

b) We can find the break-even quantity, q, by noting that

$$F = 10{,}000; \quad p = 10; \quad v = 5$$

and substituting these into (4) to obtain

$$q_e = \frac{10{,}000}{10 - 5} = \frac{10{,}000}{5} = 2{,}000 \text{ units.}$$

Alternatively, we can equate the revenue and cost equations in the answer to part (a), obtaining

$$10q = 5q + 10{,}000$$
$$5q = 10{,}000$$
$$q_e = \frac{10{,}000}{5} = 2{,}000 \text{ units.}$$

c) At break-even, 2,000 units would be produced and sold at $10 each, so the break-even sales volume would be

$$R = (10)(2000) = \$20{,}000.$$

Exercise. A manufacturer of cassette tapes has a fixed cost of $60,000 and variable cost is $4 per cassette produced. Selling price is $7 per cassette. a) Write the revenue and cost equations. b) At what number of units will break-even occur? c) At what sales (revenue) volume will break-even occur?
Answer: a) $R = 7q$; $C = 4q + 60{,}000$. b) 20,000 units. c) $140,000.

Break-even charts. Returning to the equations of the last example,

$$R = 10q \quad \text{and} \quad C = 5q + 10{,}000$$

FIGURE 1–15

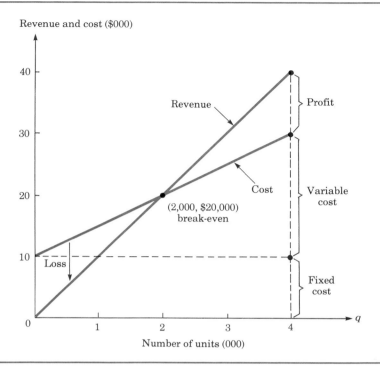

and plotting these in the usual manner, we obtain Figure 1–15. Observe that the revenue line goes through the origin and that the cost line has a y-intercept of $10,000. The dotted horizontal line shows that this fixed cost is constant at all levels of operation. The *total* variable cost, which is the $5q$ in

$$C = 5q + 10{,}000,$$

(not the $5 variable cost per *unit*, which is constant) is the vertical distance from the fixed cost line to the total cost line, which, of course, increases as more units are produced. To the left of the break-even point (2000, $20,000), the cost line is above the revenue line and the vertical separation at any point represents loss, while to the right of break-even the vertical separation represents a profit. Break-even charts are a helpful graphic aid frequently used in planning business operations.

1.19 BREAK–EVEN INTERPRETATION: 2

Production managers and other operations executives tend to think of break-even analysis in the way it was presented in the last section. Comptrollers and other financial managers are more likely to think in accounting terms. To illustrate this latter way of viewing break-even, we shall consider a company that purchases products and sells them at a price that is, presumably, above the cost. Suppose, for example, that an item that cost \$130 is priced to sell at \$200. The *markup* is, therefore, \$70. That is,

$$\text{Cost} = \$130$$
$$\text{Retail price} = \$200$$
$$\text{Markup} = \text{Retail price} - \text{Cost} = 200 - 130 = \$70.$$

From a manager's viewpoint, the dollar amounts of markup on numerous individual items, which will vary widely, are not very useful in planning and controlling operations. What is useful is the overall markup *percentage* on all items. For comparability in different items, markup is viewed in one of two ways: a function of the cost or a function of the retail price. In the current example, the markup as a function of cost is

$$\frac{\text{Markup}}{\text{Cost}} = \frac{70}{130} = 0.54 \text{ or } 54\%.$$

On the other hand, in financial statements, accountants use the concept of *margin*, which is the *markup percentage on retail price*. In our example, this is

$$\text{Margin} = \frac{\text{Markup}}{\text{Retail price}} = \frac{70}{200} = 0.35 \text{ or } 35\%.$$

This means that 35 percent of the retail price of \$200 is margin, and the other 65 percent of \$200, which is

$$0.65(200) = \$130,$$

is the cost.

We now suppose that the company in our illustration uses a margin of 35 percent on *all* items it purchases, so that if the firm sells \$$x$ worth of merchandise, 35 percent of this amount is margin and 65 percent is cost. Thus,

$$\text{Cost of goods sold} = 0.65x. \tag{1}$$

Next, the company incurs selling expenses, which it budgets at 10 percent of the volume of sales. Hence,

$$\text{Selling expense} = 0.10x. \tag{2}$$

Finally, the company budgets fixed expense at \$12,000, so that

$$\text{Fixed expense} = F = \$12,000. \tag{3}$$

If we now let y be total cost, the sum of (1) through (3), we have

$$y = 0.65x + 0.10x + 12,000$$
$$y = 0.75x + 12,000. \tag{4}$$

Thus, at a sales volume of $60,000, cost will be

$$y = 0.75(60{,}000) + 12{,}000 = \$57{,}000$$

and profit before taxes will be

$$60{,}000 - 57{,}000 = \$3{,}000.$$

Exercise. Compute profit if sales are $40,000. Answer: Cost would be $42,000, so a loss of $2,000 would occur.

From the above example of sales levels leading to profit and loss we are led to inquire what the *break-even* level of sales would be; that is, the level of sales that will equal cost. Here, $x of sales must equal the expression for y in (4). That is,

$$x = 0.75x + 12{,}000$$
$$x - 0.75x = 12{,}000$$
$$0.25x = 12{,}000$$
$$x = \frac{12{,}000}{0.25}$$
$$x_e = \$48{,}000,$$

where x_e is the break-even sales level.

Exercise. If cost, y, is related to sales, x, by $y = 0.6x + 100$, show that the break-even point is $250.

If the relationship between cost and sales is written in the general slope-intercept form

$$y = mx + b$$

then the interpretations are that b represents fixed cost, mx represents variable cost, and m itself represents variable cost per dollar of sales. At break-even,

$$y = x = x_e$$

so that, by substitution,

$$x_e = mx_e + b$$
$$x_e(1 - m) = b$$
$$x_e = \frac{b}{1 - m}.$$

Hence, the break-even level occurs when sales are equal to

$$\frac{\text{Fixed cost}}{1 - \text{Variable cost per dollar of sales}}.$$

Suppose that in making a budget for next year's operations, top management has set a sales goal of $200,000. Margin is to be 45 percent of retail (so cost is 55 percent of retail), and other variable cost is estimated at $0.05 per dollar of sales, so that variable cost is $0.55 + 0.05 = 0.60$ per dollar of sales. Fixed cost is projected at $56,000. Then the linear cost-sales model will be

$$y = 0.6x + 56,000.$$

The break-even level of sales will be

$$x_e = \frac{56,000}{1 - 0.6} = 140,000.$$

The calculations show the company will make a profit if its sales exceed $140,000. For example, if sales should turn out to be $190,000, net profit would be

$$190,000 - \text{Cost} = 190,000 - [0.6(190,000) + 56,000] = 20,000.$$

It is useful to keep in mind that a budget establishes *estimates* for coming operations, and that *actual* operations are not expected to be exactly equal to the estimates. However, assuming that the linear model applies, the estimates provide the information needed to predict results (say profit) if sales vary from the estimated value.

Exercise.   Margin is to be 33 percent of retail, and other variable cost is estimated at $0.13 per dollar of sales. Fixed cost is estimated at $4,000. a) What is the break-even point? b) Estimate profit if sales are $50,000. Answer: a) The equation is $y = 0.8x + 4000$ and the break-even point is $4000/(1 - 0.8) = \$20,000$. b) $6,000.

A *break-even chart* can be constructed by plotting

$$y = mx + b$$

and the line where cost equals sales, $y = x$. The point of intersection of these two lines establishes the break-even level of sales. Figure 1–16 shows the break-even chart for the preceding example. The break-even point is seen to be $140,000. The separation of the lines to the right of break-even indicates profit; to the left, loss.

FIGURE 1–16

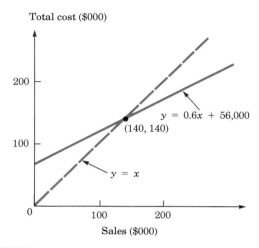

In passing, we should note that the break-even interpretations just discussed rest upon the assumption that total cost can be separated into two components, one fixed and the other varying directly in proportion to sales. These assumptions often are reasonably valid for a restricted range of sales. It is not realistic, however, to assume fixed cost as constant over all ranges of sales. If sales are proving to be considerably below expected levels, management may reduce salaries or take other actions to reduce "fixed" cost. It is not our purpose here to explore managerial action, but rather again to call for exercise of judgment when interpreting mathematical models.

1.20 LINEAR DEMAND FUNCTIONS

In this section we introduce the economic concept of the demand functions for products. Usually these functions are curves rather than straight lines, but lines provide good illustrations of demand characteristics. The demand for a product is the amount, q, of the product consumers are willing and able to buy at a given price per unit, p. Price per unit and demand are related and it is conventional in economics to plot price on the vertical and demand on the horizontal. For example, suppose the demand function for a product at one point in time is

$$DD: \quad p = -0.2q + 20 \tag{1}$$

where q is in millions of pounds and p is in dollars per pound. The line is shown in Figure 1–17, together with the intercepts that were used to plot it, and is labeled in the conventional economic manner as DD.

FIGURE 1–17

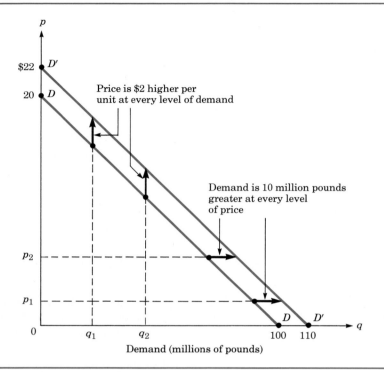

From (1), we compute that at demand $q = 25$ million pounds, $p = -0.2(25) + 20 = \$15$ per pound. Similarly, at $q = 50$, $p = \$10$ per pound. Observe that

At $p = \$15$ per pound, demand $= 25$ million pounds.
At $p = \$10$ per pound, demand $= 50$ million pounds.

Thus, higher prices are associated with lower demand, as we would expect, and this aspect of demand functions is present in (1) because the line has a negative slope and, therefore, slants downward to the right, as shown in Figure 1–17.

Our purpose in this section is to discuss the idea of a parallel *shift* in the demand function DD. The basic idea involved is that as time goes on, various factors such as the prices of competing products, changes in population or family income, or changes in individual tastes, cause the demand function to shift position. Suppose, for example, that an increase in the price of a competing product causes the demand function to shift. And suppose the new demand function, denoted by $D'D'$, is

$$D'D': \quad p = -0.2q + 22,$$

which is also plotted in Figure 1–17. Inasmuch as $D'D'$ is parallel to DD, the vertical separation of the lines is the same wherever it is measured. This separation is the difference in the intercepts on the vertical axis:

$$D'D' \text{ intercept } - DD \text{ intercept } = 22 - 20 = \$2.$$

We describe this *upward* shift by saying that *price per unit is $2 higher at every level of demand.* We can equally well describe the shift in terms of the constant horizontal separation of the lines, which is the difference of the intercepts on the horizontal axis:

$$D'D' \text{ intercept } - DD \text{ intercept } = 110 - 100 = 10 \text{ million pounds.}$$

This shift to the *right* is described by saying that after the shift, *demand is 10 million pounds greater at every level of price.*

Exercise. Suppose that the demand functions just considered were interchanged, so that

$$DD: \quad p = -0.2q + 22, \quad D'D': \quad p = -0.2q + 20,$$

where $D'D'$ arose because of an increase in available supply. In the manner of the foregoing italicized statements, describe: a) The vertical shift. b) The horizontal shift. Answer: a) Price per unit is $2 lower at every level of demand. b) Demand is 10 million pounds less at every price level.

Notice that in the last example and exercise, the shifts were occasioned by changes in available supply, and this leads us to the idea that suppliers have to provide the products consumers demand. The amount suppliers are willing to provide also is a function of price per unit, so there is a supply function that interacts with the demand function. We will return to this matter in the next chapter in our discussion of systems of linear equations.

Horizontal and vertical demand functions. The quantity of water demanded by consumers in a residential area probably remains nearly constant when the price of water varies over a limited range. This gives rise to the notion of a vertical demand function, such as

$$DD: \quad q = 10 \text{ billion cubic feet}$$

shown in Figure 1–18A, and we describe this by saying demand is constant at 10 billion cubic feet at different price levels. On the other hand, consider the small potato farmer who, because of the large competitive market, has no control over the demand price which is fixed at

$$p = \$5 \text{ per bushel}$$

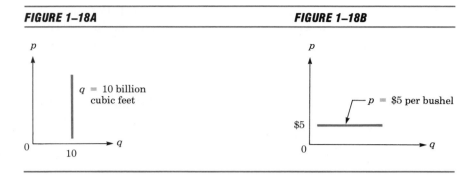

FIGURE 1–18A   **FIGURE 1–18B**

no matter how many potatoes he has to sell. This gives rise to the horizontal demand line in Figure 1–18B. These cases are discussed in economics texts under the headings *perfectly inelastic* demand, Figure 1–18A, and *perfectly elastic* demand, Figure 1–18B.

> **Exercise.**   A college charges $75 per credit hour. If q is the number of credit hours supplied to students, write and interpret the equation of the supply line. Answer: $p = 75$, which means that the price per credit hour is $75 no matter how many credit hours are supplied to students.

1.21 PROBLEM SET 1–6

Given that total cost incurred in producing and selling q units of a product is $C = 6q + 10,000$, and the q units are sold at a price of $46 per unit, mark (T) for true or (F) for false:

1. ( ) Total cost for 1,000 units is $16,000.

2. ( ) Average cost per unit is $6 no matter how many units are made and sold.

3. ( ) Average price is $46 per unit no matter how many units are made and sold.

4. ( ) Every additional unit made and sold increases total cost by $6.

5. ( ) Variable cost is the same at different values of q.

6. ( ) When 1,000 units are made and sold, variable cost will be $6,000.

7. ( ) Marginal cost is the same at all values of q.

8. ( ) Marginal cost is the same as average cost per unit.

9. ( ) A loss will be incurred if 200 units are made and sold.

10. ( ) A profit will be made if 250 units are made and sold.

11. ( ) Total cost is zero if no units are produced.

12. ( ) 250 units must be made and sold in order to break even.

1.21 PROBLEM SET 1–6 (*continued*)

13. A manufacturer has a fixed cost of $60,000 and a variable cost of $2 per unit made and sold. Selling price is $5 per unit.
   a) Write the revenue and cost equations, using C for cost and q for number of units.
   b) Compute profit if 25,000 units are made and sold.
   c) Compute profit if 10,000 units are made and sold.
   d) Find the break-even quantity.
   e) Find the break-even dollar volume of sales (revenue).
   f) Construct the break-even chart. Label the cost and revenue lines, the fixed cost line, and the break-even point.

14. A manufacturer has a fixed cost of $120,000 and a variable cost of $20 per unit made and sold. Selling price is $50 per unit.
   a) Write the revenue and cost equations, using C for cost and q for number of units.
   b) Compute profit if 10,000 units are made and sold.
   c) Compute profit if 1,000 units are made and sold.
   d) Find the break-even quantity.
   e) Find the break-even dollar volume of sales (revenue).
   f) Construct the break-even chart. Label the cost and revenue lines, the fixed cost line, and the break-even point.

15. A company's cost function for the next three months is

$$C = 200,000 + 100q.$$

Find the break-even quantity if the selling price is $180 per unit.

16. A company's cost function for the next three months is

$$C = 500,000 + 5q.$$

Find the break-even *dollar volume of sales* if the selling price is $5.50 per unit.

17. (See Problem 15.)
   a) What would be the company's cost if it decided to shut down operations for the next three months?
   b) If, because of a strike, the most the company can produce is 1,000 units, should it shut down? Why or why not?

18. (See Problem 16.)
   a) What would be the company's cost if it decided to shut down operations for the next three months?
   b) If, because of a strike, the most the company can produce is 100,000 units, should it shut down? Why or why not?

Given that total cost, y, is related to sales volume, x, by the equation $y = 1000 + 0.2x$, mark (T) for true or (F) for false:

19. (   ) Variable cost will be $200 on sales of $1,000.

20. (   ) Variable cost per dollar of sales is $0.20.

21. (   ) Fixed cost is $1,000.

22. (   ) A loss would occur if sales were $1,000.

23. (   ) Sales of $2,000 would lead to a profit of $600.

24. (   ) The cost-sales line rises $2 for each increase of $10 in sales volume.

25. (   ) Average cost per dollar of sales is the same at various sales levels.

26. (   ) The slope of the line is interpreted as variable cost.

27. (   ) Variable cost is a constant.

28. (   ) Variable cost per dollar of sales is constant.

1.21 PROBLEM SET 1–6 (*concluded*)

29. A company expects fixed cost of $22,800. Margin is to be 55 percent of retail. Variable cost in addition to costs of goods is estimated at $0.17 per dollar of sales.
    a) Find the break-even point.
    b) Write the equation relating cost and sales.
    c) What will net profit before taxes be on sales of $75,000?
    d) Make the break-even chart.

30. A company expects fixed cost of $36,000. Margin is to be 52 percent of retail, and variable cost in addition to cost of goods is estimated at $0.07 per dollar of sales.
    a) Find the break-even point.
    b) Write the equation relating sales and cost.
    c) What will net profit before taxes be on sales of $75,000?
    d) Make the break-even chart.

31. If total cost, y, is related to sales volume, x, by the equation $y = 0.47x + 29,786$, find:
    a) Variable cost per dollar of sales.
    b) Fixed cost.
    d) Total cost on sales of $72,000.
    d) The break-even point.
    e) Net profit before taxes on sales of $80,000.

32. If total cost, y, is related to sales volume, x, by the equation $y = 0.32x + 23,800$, find:
    a) Variable cost on sales of $40,000.
    b) Fixed cost.
    c) The break-even point.
    d) Net profit before taxes on sales of $30,000.

33. If variable cost per dollar of sales remains at last year's level, $0.40, but fixed cost this year is $3,600 compared to $3,000 last year,

how much greater will this year's break-even point be than last year's?

34. Make the break-even chart for the equation in
    a) Problem 31.   b) Problem 32.

35. The demand function for a product shifts from

    $$DD: \quad p = -0.10q + 40$$

    to

    $$D'D': \quad p = -0.10q + 35.$$

    Compute the horizontal and vertical shifts and write interpretive descriptions of these numbers.

36. The demand function for a product shifts from

    $$DD: \quad p = -0.05q + 40$$

    to

    $$D'D': \quad p = -0.05q + 50.$$

    Compute the horizontal and vertical shifts and write interpretive descriptions of the numbers.

37. Write a descriptive interpretation of a demand function that is
    a) Vertical.   b) Horizontal.

38. The price of a particular raw material varies markedly from week to week. To be sure that it will be able to obtain this raw material, a company promises a supplier that it will buy 100 tons per week at whatever the going price is. Write the demand function implied by this promise.

39. An electric power company charges residential customers a fixed amount per kilowatt-hour of electricity used. What would be the graphical nature of the demand function in this case?

1.22 REVIEW PROBLEMS

1. Given the points $A(3, -4)$, $B(5, -2)$, $C(3, -2)$, find the distances
   a) AC.
   b) BC.
   c) AB.

2. In Problem 1, which segment is vertical and which is horizontal?

3. In each case, the given points are the end points of the diagonal of a rectangle whose sides are parallel to the axes. What are the coordinates of the other corners of the rectangle, and what is the length of the diagonal?
   a) $(0, 0)$, $(3, 4)$.
   b) $(-1, 2)$, $(8, 14)$.
   c) $(1, 2)$, $(3, 4)$.

4. Find the perimeter of the triangle whose vertices are $(1, 2)$, $(7, 2)$, and $(7, 10)$.

5. a) If City B is 5 miles east and 12 miles north of City A, how far is it from A to B?
   b) A section of a city has square blocks with streets perpendicular to avenues. How far would we walk (in blocks) going by sidewalk from (2nd St., 7th Ave.) to (7th St., 19th Ave.)?
   c) See (b). A subway is to be built under a straight line connecting the corners. If a block is 400 feet long, how long will the subway line be in feet?

6. If y and x represent, respectively, expenses and sales in thousands of dollars, and last week's operations are characterized as $(10, 12)$, compared to this week's $(13, 16)$, by how much did expenses and sales change from last week to this?

7. If sales increased from $12 thousand to $15 thousand, the *percent* increase was (100 percent) $(15 - 12)/12 = 25$ percent.
   a) Write the expression for percent change if sales go from S_1 to S_2.
   b) What would it mean if the answer to a calculation such as that in (a) was negative?

8. Find the slope of the segment joining the following pairs of points:

   a) $(-4, 7)$, $(-1, 3)$.
   b) $(1, 2)$, $(5, 6)$.
   c) $(0, 0)$, $(0, 5)$.
   d) $(5, -1)$, $(10, -1)$.
   e) $(5, 0)$, $(5, 3)$.
   f) $(-2, -1)$, $(2, -4)$.
   g) $(1, -3)$, $(4, -1)$.
   h) $(-2, 5)$, $(3, 5)$.
   i) If personal consumption expenditures increased from $254 billion to $618 billion when disposable income (less consumer interest on loans) increased from $270 billion to $675 billion, compute the marginal propensities to consume and to save.

9. Find the equation of the line passing through each of the pairs of points in Problems 8(a) through 8(h). State answers in slope-intercept form where possible.

10. Find the equation of the line passing through the given point and having the stated slope. State answers in slope-intercept form where possible.
   a) $(1, 3)$, slope 1/5.
   b) $(0, 0)$, slope 0.
   c) $(1, 1)$, slope 1.
   d) $(1, 3)$, slope -2.
   e) $(-2, -4)$, vertical.
   f) $(-3, -4)$, slope 0.

11. What is the equation of the line parallel to and five units below the x-axis?

12. As sales, x, change from $300 to $600, selling expense changes from $250 to $400. Assume that the given data establish a linear relationship between sales and selling expense. Find the equation of the relationship in slope-intercept form.

13. If selling expense is $100 when sales are $150, and if expense increases $1 for each increase of $3 in sales, write the straight-line relationship between expense and sales in slope-intercept form.

14. If a man's weekly pay is computed at $50 (whether or not he works) plus $5 per hour

1.22 REVIEW PROBLEMS (*continued*)

worked, what equation relates weekly pay, y, to hours worked, x?

15. Explain why the lines $y = -6$ and $x = 15$ are perpendicular.

16. What is the slope and y-intercept of the line in Problem 14?

17. Graph the following lines using the intercepts:
a) $y = (3/4)x - 6$.
b) $y = -2x + 10$.
c) $y = 15$.

18. Using the coefficients of x and y, determine the slope of:
a) $y = x - 4$.
b) $y = (1/2)x - 2/3$.
c) $y = (-3/4)x + 7/4$.
d) An ounce of bourbon contains ½ of an ounce of alcohol and an ounce of vermouth contains ⅛ of an ounce of alcohol. Write the relation that exists if b ounces of bourbon and v ounces of vermouth are to be mixed to make a drink containing two ounces of alcohol. What is the substitution rate of bourbon per ounce of vermouth?

19. What is the equation of the line that has a slope of $-\frac{2}{3}$ and a y-intercept of -4?

20. Find the equation of the line through (3, 4) that is parallel to the line $y = (1/2)x - 2$.

21. a) Find the equation of the line through $(-1, 15)$ that is perpendicular to the line $y = (1/2)x - 2$.
b) If an existing pipeline is described by $y = x$ and a plant at (14, 26) wishes to connect to the pipeline on a perpendicular, what is the equation of the perpendicular and how far will it be from the plant to the connecting point? Note: In the equation of the perpendicular, let $y = x$ to find the connecting point.

22. If y and x are in proportion so that y is to x as 2 is to 5, then:
a) Write the equation relating y and x.
b) Graph the equation in (a).

23. If a company sells x units of a product at $4 per unit, write the expression for R, the total revenue received for the x units. Interpret the intercepts of this line.

24. If the first of two lines has the form $ax + by + c = 0$, and the second the form $dx + ey + f = 0$, and if the first line is to pass through the origin and the second is to be parallel to the first, what relationships must exist among a, b, c, d, e, and f?

25. The *productivity* (as contrasted to *production*) of a factory is often measured by the ratio *output per labor-hour*. If a factory has a constant productivity of five units per labor-hour, what is the equation relating units of output, y, to number of labor-hours worked, x?

26. a) If y is a person's weekly pay in dollars and x is the number of hours the person worked, and if $y = 3.5x + 25$, interpret the numbers 3.5 and 25.
b) A machine purchased now ($t = 0$) for $10,000 depreciates in value by a constant amount per year for 20 years to a scrap value of $1,000. Write the equation for D, the depreciated value of the machine at time t years. Interpret the slope and intercept of this line.

27. If total factory cost, y, of making x units of a product is given by $y = 2x + 40$, and if 100 units are made:
a) What is the variable cost?
b) What is total cost?
c) What is the variable cost per unit?
d) What is average cost per unit?
e) What is the marginal cost of the 100th unit?
f) What is the marginal cost of the 1st unit?

28. In Figure A, the slant line represents the total factory cost, C, of producing a number of units, Q. Write an interpretation of each of the following:
a) *OT.*   d) *PL.*
b) *PL/WP.*   e) *SW.*
c) *RW/OR.*

1.22 REVIEW PROBLEMS (*continued*)

FIGURE A

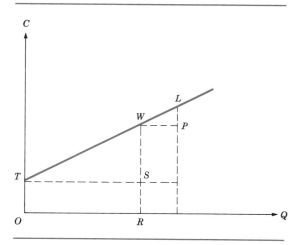

c) Compute profit if 80,000 units are made and sold.
d) Find the break-even quantity.
e) Find the break-even dollar volume of sales (revenue).
f) Construct the break-even chart. Label the cost, revenue, and fixed cost lines, and the break-even point.

31. A company's cost function for the next three months is

$$C = 80,000 + 12q.$$

a) Find the break-even quantity if the company's product sells for $13.25 per unit.
b) What will "profit" be if the company shuts down operations?
c) If, because of a strike, the company will be able to produce only 10,000 units, should it shut down for the next three months? Why or why not?

29. A manufacturer has a fixed cost of $75,000 and a variable cost of $7 per unit made and sold. Selling price is $10 per unit.
a) Using C for cost and q for number of units made and sold, write the revenue and cost equations.
b) Compute profit if 40,000 units are made and sold.
c) Compute profit if 20,000 units are made and sold.
d) Find the break-even quantity.
e) Compute the break-even dollar volume of sales (revenue).
f) Construct the break-even chart. Label the cost, revenue, and fixed cost lines, and the break-even point.

30. A manufacturer has a fixed cost of $40,000 and a variable cost of $1.60 per unit made and sold. Selling price is $2 per unit.
a) Using C for cost and q for number of units made and sold, write the revenue and cost equations.
b) Compute profit if 150,000 units are made and sold.

32. A company expects fixed cost of $25,000. It plans to work on a margin of 46 percent of retail, and to incur other variable costs of $0.06 per dollar of sales.
a) Find the equation relating total cost to sales.
b) Find the break-even point.
c) Make the break-even chart.
d) What will net profit before taxes be if sales are $100,000?

33. If the total cost of operations, y, is related to sales, x, by the equation $y = 10,500 + 0.58x$, find:
a) Fixed cost.
b) Total cost on sales of $60,000.
c) The break-even point.
d) Net profit before taxes on sales of $65,000.

34. If fixed cost is $10,000 and cost increases by $2 for each $3 increase in sales, find:
a) The break-even point.
b) The equation relating cost and sales.

1.22 REVIEW PROBLEMS (*concluded*)

35. A demand function shifts from

$$DD:\ p = -0.2q + 50$$

to

$$D'D':\ p = -0.2q + 60.$$

Compute the horizontal and vertical shifts and write an interpretive description of these numbers.

36. If p, price per unit, is vertical and q, number of units demanded, is horizontal, what is the nature and interpretation of the demand functions $p = 2$ and $q = 100$?

TWO

Systems of Linear Equations and Inequalities

The variables encountered in a problem may have to fulfill more than one condition. In a production problem, for example, the numbers of units of various products made will be restricted by conditions such as time available for production and money available for the purchase of raw materials. When each of the conditions can be expressed in the form of a linear equation, the mathematical description of the problem is a *system* of linear equations. The procedures for finding the values of the variables that satisfy all equations of the system *simultaneously* are the subject matter of this chapter.

Example. The break-even discussion of Chapter 1 introduced a system of two linear equations in two variables. There we saw that if sales, x, and cost, y, were related by the linear condition

$$y = 1200 + 0.4x,$$

we could solve this equation simultaneously with the condition $y = x$ to find where sales revenue just equals cost. If we express the 2 by 2 system as

$$y = 1200 + 0.4x$$
$$y = x,$$

y may be *eliminated* by subtracting the second equation from the first, yielding

$$0 = 1200 - 0.6x,$$

from which the break-even point is at $x = 2000$. Graphically, the simultaneous solution of the system, which is $x = y = 2000$ in this case, is the point of intersection of the graphs of the two equations.

The number of relevant variables in a system, and the number of equations representing conditions to be fulfilled, vary widely. The requirement that *all* conditions expressed by the system be satisfied sometimes cannot be met. In other cases, only one set, or many sets, of values for the variables will satisfy all conditions. In this chapter, we shall learn systematic procedures for solving systems with varying numbers of equations and variables, how to determine if no solution is possible, and how to express the solution if the system is satisfied by more than one set of values. We shall consider the effect of the requirement that values in the solution set not be negative, and also show how the best set can be chosen when the system has more than one solution set. Two of the five sections on applications are concerned with supply and demand analysis.

On the other hand, a mathematical statement of the conditions imposed by a problem often requires the use of inequalities rather than equalities. For instance, if we let x represent the number of hours a plant operates per day, x does not necessarily equal 24, but x must be less than or equal to 24. Moreover, a plant cannot operate a negative number of hours, so x must be greater than or equal to zero. Other examples of conditions leading to inequalities come easily to mind. The volume of fluid stored in a tank must be greater than or equal to zero, but less than or equal to the volume of the tank; the amount of product made is restricted by plant capacity and raw material availability. In this chapter, we shall also offer geometrical interpretations of systems involving one or two variables.

We turn first to a consideration of the relation between solutions and points of intersection.

2.2 NUMBER OF SOLUTIONS POSSIBLE

A specific solution of a system of linear equations is a set of values, one for each variable, that simultaneously satisfy all equations of the system. Geometrically, a set of values for the variables is represented by a point, and a set satisfying all the equations is represented by a point that lies on the graphs of all the equations; that is, a solution is a point of intersection of all the graphs. We shall appeal to the geometry of intersections of lines and planes to illustrate that *the number of solutions of a linear system is either zero, one, or unlimited.*

2.3 INTERSECTIONS OF STRAIGHT LINES

The graphs of linear equations in two-space are straight lines. The parts of Figure 2–1 show the intersection possibilities for such lines. If a system has two equations in two variables, either the corresponding lines intersect in a single point, or they are parallel and have no intersection point, as shown in Figures 2–1A and 2–1B. The three lines representing a system of three equations in two variables may intersect in a single point,

FIGURE 2–1A   **FIGURE 2–1B**

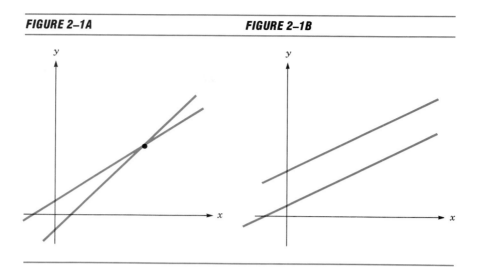

as in Figure 2–1C, or there may be no point that lies on all three lines, as in Figures 2–1D and 2–1E. The same intersection possibilities exist if more than three lines are plotted, and we conclude that two or more different lines have one point in common or no points in common. As a special case, however, we note that if the system has two equations, and the terms of one equation are a constant multiple of the corresponding terms of the other, then both equations have the same graph. All of the (unlimited) points on one line also lie on the "other" line, so that in this special sense the system has an unlimited number of solutions.

FIGURE 2–1C   **FIGURE 2–1D**

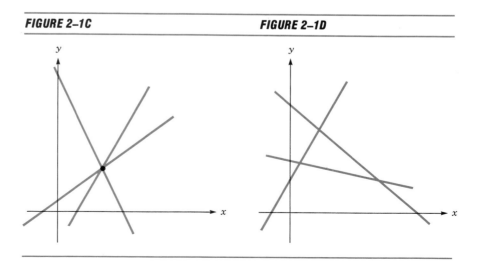

FIGURE 2–1E

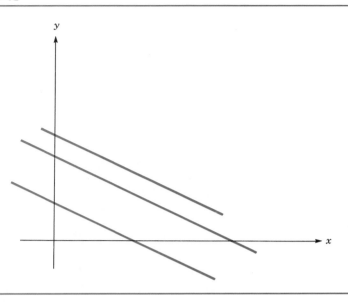

2.4 OPERATIONS ON LINEAR SYSTEMS

When a system of linear equations has a single solution, the solution is a point whose coordinates satisfy all the equations of the system. We start with a system of two equations, the first of which is the line that passes through the points (2, 5) and (8, 3). The equation of this line, determined by the methods of the last chapter, is

$$e_1: \quad x + 3y = 17.$$

The second line passes through the points (2, 5) and (4, 2) and has the equation

$$e_2: \quad 3x + 2y = 16,$$

Notice that the point (2, 5) was used in constructing both e_1 and e_2. Hence (2, 5) satisfies both equations and is the solution of the two-equation system. We purposefully chose (2, 5) to be the solution in order to demonstrate the operations that can be performed on the equations of a system without changing the solution. We will number these operations as we proceed.

Row Operations

1. *The solution is not altered if both sides of one of the equations are multiplied by a constant.*

This is so, of course, because equals times equals are still equal. For example, multiplying both sides of e_1 by 5 gives

$$5e_1: \quad 5(x + 3y = 17) \quad \text{or} \quad 5x + 15y = 85$$

and the solution $(2, 5)$ satisfies this equation, as well as the unchanged e_2, because

$$5(2) + 15(5) = 10 + 75 = 85.$$

> 2. *The solution of a system is not changed if one of its equations is replaced by a linear combination of this and another equation in the system,* where linear combination will mean a nonzero constant times the given equation plus a nonzero constant times another equation.

The reason for this is that equals added to (or subtracted from) equals are still equal. For example, starting with the given

$$\begin{aligned} e_1: & \quad x + 3y = 17 \\ e_2: & \quad 3x + 2y = 16, \end{aligned} \tag{1}$$

let us replace e_1 by $3e_1 - 2e_2$:

$$\begin{aligned} 3e_1: & \quad 3(x + 3y = 17) \quad \text{or} \quad 3x + 9y = 51 \\ 2e_2: & \quad 2(3x + 2y = 16) \quad \text{or} \quad \underline{6x + 4y = 32} \\ e_3 = 3e_1 - 2e_2: & \qquad\qquad\qquad\qquad\qquad\qquad -3x + 5y = 19. \end{aligned}$$

Now observe that e_3 is also satisfied by the solution $(2, 5)$ because

$$-3(2) + 5(5) = -6 + 25 = 19.$$

Hence, the system

$$\begin{aligned} e_3: & \quad -3x + 5y = 19 \\ e_2: & \quad 3x + 2y = 16 \end{aligned} \tag{2}$$

has the same solution as the original system.

> 3. *The solution of a system is not changed if any pair of its equations are interchanged.*

We need not illustrate the obvious fact that interchanging e_1 and e_2 in the system (1) will have no effect on the solution.

Inasmuch as the equations of a system are written horizontally, we often think of them as being *rows*, and refer to the above operations as *row* operations. The manner in which row operations are used to find an unknown solution is presented next.

2.5 ELIMINATION PROCEDURE

The discussion in the last section suggests a method of attack when seeking solutions of a linear system; namely, form linear combinations of pairs of equations in a manner such that a variable is *eliminated.* For example, given the system

$$e_1: \quad 2x + 3y = 2$$
$$e_2: \quad 5x + 4y = 12,$$

we see that multiplication of the first equation by 5 and the second by 2, followed by subtraction, will result in the elimination of x. Thus

$$
\begin{array}{rl}
5e_1: & 10x + 15y = 10 \\
2e_2: & 10x + 8y = 24 \\
\hline
5e_1 - 2e_2: & 7y = -14,
\end{array}
$$

so that

$$y = -2.$$

Rather than forming a linear combination eliminating y in order to obtain the required value for x, we may substitute -2 for y in either of the original equations and find that x is 4. The solution of the system is $(4, -2)$.

We shall use the elimination-substitution method to solve linear systems in most of this chapter. The symbolism illustrated above will be helpful to keep track of the operations performed.

Example. Solve the system

$$e_1: \quad 3x - 2y = 4$$
$$e_2: \quad 2x - 4y = 1.$$

Here we see that elimination of y will occur if we multiply e_1 by minus 2 and add to e_2. We obtain

$$
\begin{array}{rl}
-2e_1: & -6x + 4y = -8 \\
e_2: & 2x - 4y = 1 \\
\hline
-2e_1 + e_2: & -4x = -7,
\end{array}
$$

so that

$$x = \frac{7}{4}.$$

Substitution of this value into e_1 or e_2 yields $y = \frac{5}{8}$, so the solution of the system is $(\frac{7}{4}, \frac{5}{8})$. The geometric nature of the system is shown in Figure 2–2, in which the solution is seen to be the point of intersection of the two lines.

FIGURE 2–2

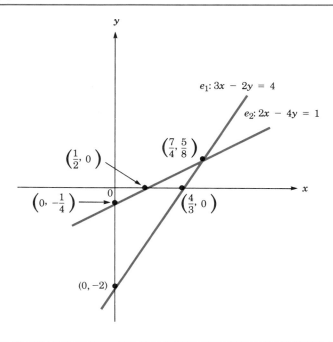

$e_1: 3x - 2y = 4$

$e_2: 2x - 4y = 1$

$\left(\frac{7}{4}, \frac{5}{8} \right)$

$\left(\frac{1}{2}, 0 \right)$

$\left(0, -\frac{1}{4} \right)$

$\left(\frac{4}{3}, 0 \right)$

$(0, -2)$

Exercise. Find the solution of the following system of two equations in two unknowns, then plot the graph of the lines and label the coordinates of the point of intersection.

$$4x - 3y = -3$$
$$5x - y = 10.$$

Answer: $(3, 5)$.

**2.6
APPLICATIONS—1**

Consider a buyer who wants to combine x liters of regular unleaded gasoline, which costs $0.50 per liter, with y liters of super unleaded gasoline, at $0.60 per liter, to obtain 2,000 liters of mixture worth $0.53 per liter. We find two equations by noting that the total amount is $x + y$, which must equal 2000, and by noting that the value of x liters at $0.50 plus y liters at $0.60, which is $0.5x + 0.6y$, must equal the total value of 2,000 liters at $0.53, which is $1,060. Hence,

$$e_1: \quad x + \quad y = 2000$$
$$e_2: \quad 0.5x + 0.6y = 1060.$$

Eliminating x, we obtain

$$
\begin{array}{rrl}
-0.5e_1: & -0.5x - 0.5y = & -1000 \\
e_2: & 0.5x + 0.6y = & 1060 \\
\hline
-0.5e_1 + e_2: & 0.1y = & 60,
\end{array}
$$

so that

$$y = 600 \text{ liters,}$$

and from e_1

$$x = 2000 - y = 1{,}400 \text{ liters.}$$

The buyer should mix 1,400 liters of regular unleaded gasoline with 600 liters of super unleaded gasoline.

Exercise. We plan to invest x dollars in the bonds of Acme Company, which pay 7 percent interest, and y dollars in Star Company bonds, which pay 10 percent interest. We will invest $10,000 and require that we receive $820 interest. How much should be invested in each security? Answer: The equations are $0.07x + 0.1y = 820$ and $x + y = 10{,}000$. The solution is $x = \$6{,}000$ and $y = \$4{,}000$.

2.7 PROBLEM SET 2–1

Solve the following systems:

1. $x + y = 5$
  $2x + y = 7.$

2. $2x + 3y = 10$
  $3x + y = 1.$

3. $5x - 2y = 3$
  $2x + y = 3.$

4. $2x + 3y = 9$
  $4x - 2y = 2.$

5. $4x + 3y = 4$
  $2x + 6y = 5.$

6. $3x + 5y = 9$
  $4x + 2y = 5.$

---

7. If x liters of regular gasoline, which costs $0.50 per liter, are to be mixed with y liters of regular unleaded gasoline, at $0.66 per liter, to obtain 1,000 liters of mixture worth $0.60 per liter, how much of each gasoline should be used?

8. We plan to invest x dollars in Acme Company bonds, which pay 6.5 percent interest, and y dollars in Star Company bonds, which pay 9 percent interest. If $50,000 is to be invested and we require that $4,000 interest be received, how much should be invested in each bond?

9. It takes 20 minutes and costs $2 to make one double-edged razor blade, whereas it takes 30 minutes and costs $1 to make one single-edged razor blade. If 600 minutes and $40 are available, how many of each blade can be made?

10. It takes 10 minutes to make, and 20 minutes to paint, one captain's chair, whereas it takes 5 minutes to make, and 8 minutes to paint, one regular chair. If 300 minutes are available for making these products and 500 minutes are available for painting, how many of each chair can be made?

2.7 PROBLEM SET 2–1 (*concluded*)

11. Consider the general system of two linear equations in two unknowns written in the form

$$a_1x + b_1y = c_1$$
$$a_2x + b_2y = c_2.$$

Show by the elimination procedure that the solution to this system is

$$x = \frac{b_2c_1 - b_1c_2}{b_2a_1 - b_1a_2}, \quad y = \frac{a_1c_2 - a_2c_1}{b_2a_1 - b_1a_2},$$

provided, of course, that $b_2a_1 - b_1a_2 \neq 0$.

12. Using the results of Problem 11, solve each of the systems in Problems 1 through 6.

13. Consider the BASIC program shown in Program 2–1.
   a) Describe what the program is doing line-by-line.
   b) Run the program for each of the systems in Problems 1 through 6.

14. a) Modify Program 2–1 to print "No unique solution" if $D = 0$.
   b) Run the program in (a) for the system

$$2x + 5y = 15$$
$$3.2x + 8y = 24.$$

Program 2–1

```
10  REM TWO LINEAR EQUATIONS IN TWO UNKNOWNS/UNIQUE SOLUTION
20  INPUT "Enter the coefficients and constant of equation 1
    (A1,B1,C1)";A1,B1,C1
30  INPUT "Enter the coefficients and constant of equation 2
    (A2,B2,C2)";A2,B2,C2
40  D=B2*A1-B1*A2
50  PRINT "Solution is x = ";(B2*C1-B1*C2)/D;" and y = ";
    (A1*C2-A2*C1)/D
60  END
```

2.8 APPLICATIONS—2: SUPPLY AND DEMAND ANALYSIS

In the last chapter (Section 1.20), we introduced demand functions, which relate the quantity of product consumers are willing and able to buy to the unit price of the product. Linear demand functions have negative slopes because demand decreases when price increases. A supply function, on the other hand, relates the quantity producers are willing and able to supply to the unit selling price of the product, and linear supply functions have positive slopes because producers increase the supply when the selling price increases. Consider Figure 2–3, which shows supply and demand functions as the straight lines labeled *SS* and *DD* respectively. The equations are

$$e_1: \quad DD: p = -0.1q + 40 \quad \text{(negative slope, demand)}$$
$$e_2: \quad SS: p = 0.2q + 10 \quad \text{(positive slope, supply).}$$

Point *E*, the intersection of *DD* and *SS* in Figure 2–3, is found by

$$
\begin{array}{rl}
e_1: & p + 0.1q = 40 \\
e_2: & p - 0.2q = 10 \\
\hline
e_1 - e_2: & 0.3q = 30
\end{array}
$$

FIGURE 2–3

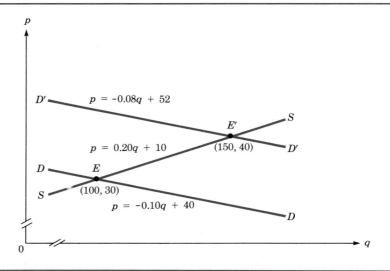

so that

$$q = 100 \text{ units.}$$

From e_1,

$$p = -0.1(100) + 40 = \$30 \text{ per unit}$$

so we have $E(100, 30)$, the *equilibrium* point, which shows the market price that will equate the quantity consumers are willing and able to buy with the quantity producers are willing and able to supply.

What we wish to show in this section is the effect of a change in the demand (but not the supply) function, and the effect of a change in the supply (but not the demand) function. This can be done by finding the new equilibrium point, E', after a change has occurred. For example, suppose demand changes to the function $D'D'$ shown in Figure 2–3, with supply remaining at SS. The two functions now are

$$e_1:\quad D'D': p = -0.08q + 52$$
$$e_2:\qquad SS: p = \quad 0.2q + 10.$$

We now find

$$
\begin{aligned}
e_1:\quad & p + 0.08q = 52 \\
e_2:\quad & p - \;\;0.2q = 10 \\
\hline
e_1 - e_2:\quad & \qquad\;\; 0.28q = 42
\end{aligned}
$$

so that

$$q = 150$$

and, from e_1,

$$p = -0.08(150) + 52 = 40;$$

the new equilibrium point is $E'(150, 40)$, as shown in Figure 2–3. Comparing the equilibrium points whose coordinates are in the order (quantity, price),

$$E(100, 30) \quad \text{and} \quad E'(150, 40),$$

we see that the change in the demand function is an *increase* in demand, which results in a *higher* quantity and *higher* price at the new equilibrium. In economic terminology, the demand function shifted to the right so that a larger quantity is demanded at each price level.

The above discussion shows that to determine the effect of a change in a demand or supply function, we need only to compare the two equilibrium points and interpret the changes in q and p. Thus, if there is a change in a supply function, with the demand function unchanged, and the equilibrium points are

$$E(500, 15) \quad \text{and} \quad E'(400, 20)$$

the *decrease* in supply results in a lower quantity, but a *higher* price at equilibrium. Notice that in Figure 2–3, an *increase* in demand was accompanied by an *increase* in both quantity and price, so a demand change in one direction is accompanied by quantity and price changes in the *same* direction. The effect of a supply change, however, is *inverse* in the sense just illustrated. A decrease in supply lowers the quantity but increases the price, and an increase in supply will increase quantity but lower price.

> **Exercise.** Interpret the results of the change in a supply function if the equilibrium points are $E(400, 50)$, $E'(500, 15)$. Answer: Supply has increased, and at the new equilibrium point, quantity has increased and price has decreased.

2.9 PROBLEM SET 2–2

1. a) Graph the supply and demand functions

$$SS: p = 0.1q + 8$$
$$DD: p = -0.5q + 50.$$

b) Find the equilibrium point, E, for (a).
c) Plot the new demand function $D'D'$:
$p = -0.6q + 36$ on the graph for (a).
d) Find the new equilibrium point, E', and

place its coordinates on the graph.
e) Describe the change in the equilibrium points.

2. a) Graph the supply and demand functions

$$SS: p = 0.20q + 10$$
$$DD: p = -0.40q + 70.$$

2.9 PROBLEM SET 2–2 (concluded)

b) Find the equilibrium point, E, for (a).
c) Plot the new supply function $S'S'$: $p = 0.25q + 18$ on the graph for (a).
d) Find the new equilibrium point, E', and place its coordinates on the graph.
e) Describe the change in equilibrium points.

3. (See Problem 2.) The equilibrium point for the functions in (a) is $E(100, 30)$. Find the new equilibrium point if the demand function changes to $D'D'$: $p = -0.44q + 90$ and describe the change in the equilibrium points.

4. (See Problem 1.) The equilibrium point for the functions in (a) is $E(70, 15)$. Find the new equilibrium point if the supply function changes to $S'S'$: $p = 0.06q + 5.2$ and describe the change in the equilibrium points.

Interpret the following supply and demand changes:

5. $E(100, 10)$ to $E'(125, 14)$ after a change in demand.

6. $E(200, 20)$ to $E'(150, 25)$ after a change in supply.

7. $E(150, 25)$ to $E'(200, 21)$ after a change in supply.

8. $E(200, 40)$ to $E'(180, 35)$ after a change in demand.

9. If either the supply or demand function (but not both) changed and the result was $E(500, 15)$ to $E'(600, 10)$, which function changed? Explain why.

10. If either the supply or demand function (but not both) changed and the result was $E(500, 15)$ to $E'(400, 10)$, which function changed? Explain why.

2.10 ELIMINATION PROCEDURE: NONUNIQUE SOLUTIONS

So far each system of equations we have considered has given rise to a unique solution. It is possible for linear systems to have zero or an unlimited number of solutions. Our next example illustrates how the elimination procedure solves a system which has no solutions.

Example. Solve the system

$$e_1: \quad 2x + 5y = 15$$
$$e_2: \quad 3.2x + 8y = 20.$$

Here we eliminate y by

$$
\begin{array}{rrcr}
8e_1: & 16x + 40y = & & 120 \\
-5e_2: & -16x - 40y = & & -100 \\
\hline
8e_1 - 5e_2: & 0 & = & 20.
\end{array}
$$

This last line is certainly a contradiction! Zero cannot equal 20. We therefore conclude that the system has no solution. The reason for this is that a solution of the system must satisfy any linear combination of the original system. If a linear combination leads to a false statement, then the system must have a built-in contradiction and can have no solution. In this case, we say that the equations in the system are *inconsistent*. On the other hand, when there exists a unique solution or an unlimited number of solutions, the equations in the system are called *consistent*.

Exercise. Prove that the following system is inconsistent.

$$2x + 3y = 17$$
$$9x + 13.5y = 25.$$

The elimination procedure will also tell us when a system of equations has an unlimited (or infinite) number of solutions.

Example. Solve the system

$$e_1: \quad 2x + 5y = 15$$
$$e_2: \quad 3.2x + 8y = 24.$$

If we eliminate y, we get

$$
\begin{array}{rl}
8e_1: & 16x + 40y = 120 \\
-5e_2: & -16x - 40y = -120 \\
\hline
8e_1 - 5e_2: & 0 = 0.
\end{array}
$$

Now this last line is not a contradiction, since zero does indeed equal zero. However, we are unable to solve the system for a unique value of x and y. The reason for this is that e_1 is a precise multiple of e_2; that is,

$$e_2 = 1.6e_1,$$

so that we can actually reduce the system to a single equation. Thus if we were to graph this system we would have two coincident lines (two lines on top of each other so they look like the same line), whereas in our previous example the graph would be two parallel lines.

Exercise. Prove that the following system has an unlimited number of solutions:

$$2x + 3y = 17$$
$$9x + 13.5y = 76.5.$$

2.11 PROBLEM SET 2–3

Solve the following systems:

1. $2x - 3y = 5$
$6x - 9y = 8.$

2. $3x - 6y = 8$
$-5x + 10y = 12.$

3. $2x + 3y = -15$
$-(8/3)x - 4y = 25.$

4. $7x + 2y = 9$
$17.5x + 5y = 14.$

2.11 PROBLEM SET 2–3 (*concluded*)

5. $3x + 12y = -9$
       $-2x - 8y = 6.$

6. $5x + 3y = 15$
       $2x + 1.2y = 6.$

7. $2x + 3y = 15$
       $(8/3)x + 4y = 20.$

8. $6x - 15y = -3$
       $-10x + 25y = 5.$

9. a) Modify the BASIC Program 2–1 (Section 2.7) to handle the cases in which there are zero or unlimited solutions.

b) Run the program in (a) for Problems 1 through 8.

2.12 DEFINITION, *m* BY *n* SYSTEM

The designation m by n means that the number of equations in a system is m and the number of variables is n. The number of variables in a system is the total number appearing in the equations of the system. It is not required that all variables appear in each of the equations. As an example, the system

$$2x + y - z = 4$$
$$x \quad\quad + 2z = 7$$

has two equations and three variables. It is a 2 by 3 system.

We know that linear systems will have either zero, one, or an unlimited number of solutions, and we have discussed the elimination procedure as a method of finding solutions in a 2 by 2 system. This technique of solution can be extended to the general m by n system. In Chapter 4, we will develop a variation of this technique that is easier to use when either m or n is 3 or larger. For now, though, we will illustrate how to use the elimination procedure to solve a 3 by 3 system that has a unique solution.

2.13 3 BY 3 SYSTEM

The procedure for solving a 3 by 3 system is to reduce it to a 2 by 2 system, which is then solved in the usual way to obtain values for two of the three variables. The third variable is then evaluated by substituting these two values into any of the three original equations. To accomplish the reduction, we combine two pairs of equations, eliminating the *same* variable each time and using every equation at least once.

> **Exercise.**   If we label the three equations e_1, e_2, and e_3, what are the possible combinations of two pairs of equations? Answer: e_1e_2 and e_1e_3; e_1e_2 and e_2e_3; e_1e_3 and e_2e_3.

Example. Solve the following system of linear equations.

$$e_1: \quad 2x + y - z = 2$$
$$e_2: \quad x + 2y + z = 1$$
$$e_3: \quad 3x - y + 2z = 9.$$

We reduce this 3 by 3 system to a 2 by 2 system by eliminating x from e_1 and e_2, and also from e_2 and e_3. So we have

$$-2e_2 + e_1 = e_4: \quad -3y - 3z = 0$$
$$-3e_2 + e_3 = e_5: \quad -7y - z = 6.$$

Now we proceed as usual to eliminate, say z, from e_4 and e_5 to get

$$-3e_5 + e_4 = e_6: \quad 18y = -18.$$

The last statement says that y must be -1. We now use backward substitution to find x and z: Setting y equal to -1 in e_5 (or e_4) yields $z = 1$. Finally, putting $y = -1$ and $z = 1$ into e_2 (or e_1 or e_3) leads to $x = 2$.

The solution of the system is the point $(2, -1, 1)$. Check this solution by showing that the number triplet satisfies every one of the original three equations.

Exercise. Find the solution of the following system by use of the elimination procedure.

$$\begin{aligned} x + y + z &= 4 \\ 2x - y + z &= 3 \\ x - 2y + 3z &= 5. \end{aligned}$$

Answer: $(1, 1, 2)$.

Example. Solve the following system of linear equations.

$$\begin{aligned} e_1: \quad x + y + z &= 4 \\ e_2: \quad 5x - y + 7z &= 25 \\ e_3: \quad 2x - y + 3z &= 8. \end{aligned}$$

Eliminating y from e_1 and e_2, and also from e_1 and e_3 leads to

$$e_1 + e_2 = e_4: \quad 6x + 8z = 29$$
$$e_1 + e_3 = e_5: \quad 3x + 4z = 12.$$

Next eliminating x or z from e_4 and e_5 leads to

$$-2e_5 + e_4 = e_6: \quad 0 + 0 = 5.$$

The last line is a contradiction. Zero cannot equal 5. We conclude that the system has no solution and the equations in the system are inconsistent.

Exercise. Prove that the following system has no solution:

$$\begin{aligned} 2x - y + 3z &= 5 \\ x + 2y - z &= 6 \\ 3x + y + 2z &= 8. \end{aligned}$$

The first example of the section had a single solution, the second no solution. Let us turn next to a system that has an unlimited number of solutions and learn how to write the general solution in arbitrary-variable terminology.

Example. Solve the following system of linear equations.

$$
\begin{aligned}
e_1: & \quad x + y + z = 4 \\
e_2: & \quad 5x - y + 7z = 20 \\
e_3: & \quad 2x - y + 3z = 8.
\end{aligned}
$$

Proceeding in the usual manner, we find:

$$
\begin{aligned}
e_1 + e_2 = e_4: & \quad 6x + 8z = 24 \\
e_1 + e_3 = e_5: & \quad 3x + 4z = 12.
\end{aligned}
$$

Eliminating x or z from the last equations yields

$$
-2e_5 + e_4 = e_6: \quad 0 + 0 = 0.
$$

The appearance of the true statement, zero equals zero, means simply, as we saw in the 2 by 2 case, that this linear combination arose from two equivalent equations. Looking back at

$$
\begin{aligned}
e_4: & \quad 6x + 8z = 24 \\
e_5: & \quad 3x + 4z = 12
\end{aligned}
$$

we see that e_4 could be divided by 2 and then would be identical to e_5. Any number pair satisfying one of these equations will satisfy the other. Moreover, any solution of the original system must satisfy these last equations. Solving (either) one, say e_5, for z yields

$$
e_7: \quad z = \frac{12 - 3x}{4}.
$$

To repeat, any solution of the original system requires that z be related to x according to the last equation.

Returning to e_1, or any of the three original equations, and replacing z by

$$
\frac{12 - 3x}{4}
$$

we obtain

$$
e_8: \quad x + y + \frac{12 - 3x}{4} = 4
$$

by substituting e_7 into e_1. Solving the last equation for y leads to

$$
e_9: \quad y = \frac{4 - x}{4}.
$$

Both z and y have now been expressed in terms of x, and we state the *general* solution of the system as follows:

$$x \text{ arbitrary}$$
$$y = \frac{4 - x}{4}$$
$$z = \frac{12 - 3x}{4}.$$

The general solution just written shows that the number of solutions is without limits because x may be assigned any arbitrary value whatsoever. The general solution provides convenient formulas for finding specific solutions. To illustrate the matter of convenience, suppose that we are asked to find the specific solutions for values of x equal to 0, 1, 2, 3, 4, 5, 6, 7, 8, and 9. We could substitute $x = 0$ in the three *original* equations, then solve to get the corresponding y, then substitute to get the corresponding z. Next, we could substitute $x = 1$ in the original equations and repeat the procedure to obtain the corresponding values for y and z. The 10 specific solutions found in this manner would require 10 separate (duplicate) manipulations of the original equations. If, on the other hand, we substitute in the formulas of the general solution, we see immediately that if $x = 0$, then $y = 1$, and $z = 3$. If $x = 1$, then $y = \frac{3}{4}$, and $z = \frac{9}{4}$, and so on.

The general solution also can be of use in actual problems to determine what conditions must be satisfied if the variables in solutions are not permitted to take on negative values. In the above general solution, for example, it is clear that if x, y, and z are all to be nonnegative, then x must not exceed 4; that is, x must be in the interval whose limits are 0 and 4, inclusively.

The tactics of the last example are worth reviewing. First, observation of the identity, zero equals zero, directed attention to the equations from which the statement arose. One of these equations was solved for z in terms of x. This automatically relegated x to the role of arbitrary variable, and we sought to express y also in terms of the same arbitrary variable. To do so, we returned to one of the original equations and replaced z by its x equivalent, leaving an expression that was solved for y in terms of x.

Exercise. Start by eliminating z, then make y arbitrary and prove that the general solution of the system can be expressed as y arbitrary; $x = 2y + 3$; $z = y + 1$.

$$e_1: \quad x - 3y + z = 4$$
$$e_2: \quad x - y - z = 2$$
$$e_3: \quad 2x - 5y + z = 7.$$

Exercise. The general solution just obtained can be checked by substitution into the original equations. For example, substitution into e_1 yields

$$(2y + 3) - 3y + (y + 1) = 4.$$

Removing parentheses, we find the statement is the identity

$$4 = 4.$$

Show that substitution into e_2 and e_3 also leads to identities.

Changing arbitrary variables. The arbitrary variable(s) in one general solution may be changed without solving the entire system again. For example, it may be verified that the general solution of

$$\begin{aligned} e_1: &\quad x + y + z = 6 \\ e_2: &\quad 4x - 2y + z = -9 \\ e_3: &\quad 3x - y + z = -4 \end{aligned}$$

can be written as

$$\begin{aligned} &x \text{ arbitrary} \\ e_4: &\quad y = x + 5 \\ e_5: &\quad z = 1 - 2x. \end{aligned}$$

If we wish to make y, rather than x, arbitrary, then from e_4 we write

$$e_6: \quad x = y - 5$$

and then obtain z by substituting e_6 into e_5:

$$\begin{aligned} z &= 1 - 2x \\ &= 1 - 2(y - 5) \\ &= 1 - 2y + 10 \\ z &= -2y + 11. \end{aligned}$$

The general solution now is

$$\begin{aligned} &y \text{ arbitrary} \\ &x = y - 5 \\ &z = -2y + 11. \end{aligned}$$

Exercise. Write the general solution of the above system with z arbitrary. Answer: z arbitrary; $x = (1 - z)/2$; $y = (11 - z)/2$.

2.14 PROBLEM SET 2–4

1. Define:
   a) An m by n system of equations.
   b) An n by n system of equations.
   c) A 3 by 2 system of equations.
   d) The number of variables in a system of equations.
   e) A linear combination of two equations.

2. Write a general solution of
   a) $3x + 4y = 3$.
   b) $x + 2y - 4z = 15$.

3. What developments in the solution of a system indicate
   a) No solutions?
   b) An unlimited number of solutions?

4. State the situations that may arise in the solution of a 2 by 2 system, and discuss the geometrical interpretation of each.

5. Find the solution of each of the following. Plot the graph of each equation, and label the point of intersection of the lines.
   a) $x - y = 5$
      $x + y = 1$.
   b) $x - 2y = 7$
      $2x + y = 4$.
   c) $2x + 7y = 5$
      $3x + 2y = 6$.

6. Give a geometrical interpretation to the outcome of your attempt to solve
   a) $3x + 2y = 4$
      $6x + 4y = 6$.
   b) $x - y = 4$
      $-2x + 2y = -8$.

Solve each of the following systems:

7. $2x + y + 2z = 5$
   $x + y - z = 0$
   $3x - 2y + z = 1$.

8. $x + z = 5$
   $y + z = 3$
   $x - y = 2$.

9. $5x + y + z = 8$
   $x + 2y - z = 1$
   $2x + y = 3$.

10. $x - 2y + z = 7$
    $x - y + z = 4$
    $2x + y - 3z = -4$.

11. $x + y + z = 10$
    $3x - y + 2z = 14$
    $2x - 2y + z = 8$.

12. $x = 4$
    $x - y - z = 7$
    $x + y + z = 2$.

13. $2x - y + z = 5$
    $x + 4y - 3z = 2$
    $3x + 3y - 2z = 7$.

14. $2x + z = 5$
    $x + y = 3$
    $-y + z = 1$.

15. $2x + y - 3z = 12$
    $x + 3y - 4z = 6$
    $x - 2y + z = 4$.

16. $2x - 5y + z = 7$
    $-3x + y - 2z = -7$
    $x + 2y + 3z = 14$.

When a system has many solutions, some solution or solutions may be better than others because they optimize an objective such as achieving a minimum cost. Two examples follow:

Example 1. A gasoline company wants to provide a customer with 2,000 liters of 85 octane gasoline with a vapor pressure index of 25. To do this, the supplier must mix three kinds of gasoline to form an appropriate mixture at a minimum cost. Regular unleaded gasoline costs $0.40 per liter and has an octane rating of 80 with a vapor pressure index of 30. Premium unleaded gasoline costs $0.50 per liter with an octane rating of 90 and a vapor pressure index of 20. Super unleaded gasoline costs $0.65 per liter and has an octane rating of 100 with a vapor pressure index of 10. What amount of each gasoline should be mixed?

Letting x, y, and z represent, respectively, the number of liters of regular, premium, and super, the cost function, C, is

$$C = 0.4x + 0.5y + 0.65z. \tag{1}$$

The first condition to be satisfied is that the mixture contain precisely 2,000 liters, so

$$e_1: \quad x + y + z = 2000.$$

The second condition to be satisfied is that the octane rating be 85, so we get

$$80x + 90y + 100z = 85(2000)$$

or, dividing by 10,

$$e_2: \quad 8x + 9y + 10z = 17{,}000.$$

The last condition to be satisfied is that the vapor pressure index be 25, so we have

$$30x + 20y + 10z = 25(2000)$$

or, again dividing by 10,

$$e_3: \quad 3x + 2y + z = 5000.$$

Eliminating z from e_1, e_2, and e_3, we find

$$10e_1 - e_2 = e_4: \quad 2x + y = \quad 3000$$
$$e_1 - e_3 = e_5: \quad -2x - y = -3000.$$

Now adding e_4 and e_5 we get

$$e_4 + e_5 = e_6: \quad 0 + 0 = 0$$

so that the system has an unlimited number of solutions. Letting x be arbitrary, we have from e_4

$$e_7: \quad y = 3000 - 2x$$

and then substituting e_7 into e_1

$$e_8: \quad z = x - 1000$$
$$x \text{ arbitrary}$$

Now clearly we cannot permit any of our variables to have a negative value. Inspecting e_7 and e_8, we see that x can take on values from a low of 1000 to prevent z from being negative to a high of 1500 to prevent y from being negative.

Our solution, then, becomes

$$x \text{ arbitrary in the interval}$$
$$1000 \text{ to } 1500, \text{ inclusive}$$
$$y = 3000 - 2x \tag{2}$$
$$z = x - 1000. \tag{3}$$

Now we can express the cost function in terms of the arbitrary variable x by substituting (2) and (3) into (1). This yields

$$C = 0.40x + 0.50(3000 - 2x) + 0.65(x - 1000)$$
$$= 0.40x + 1500 - x + 0.65x - 650$$
$$= 0.05x + 850. \tag{4}$$

From (4) it is clear that cost increases when x increases, so to minimize cost we should use the lowest possible value of x. Because x is arbitrary in the range 1000 to 1500, we choose $x = 1000$, and compute the corresponding values of y and z. We have

$$x = 1{,}000 \text{ liters of regular unleaded}$$
$$y = 1{,}000 \text{ liters of premium unleaded}$$
$$z = 0 \text{ liters of super unleaded}$$

$$\text{Minimum cost} = 0.05(1000) + 850 = \$900.$$

Exercise. a) Convert (2) and (3) of the above example into a solution with z arbitrary. b) What is the permissible interval for z? c) Write the cost function in terms of z. d) What value of z will minimize cost? e) What is the minimum cost? Answer: a) z arbitrary; $x = z + 1000$; $y = 1000 - 2z$. b) 0 to 500. c) Cost $= 0.05z + 900$. d) $z = 0$. e) \$900.

In the next example, we set up the system of equations and leave optimization as an exercise for the reader.

Example 2. A mixture containing x pounds of macadamia nuts, y pounds of almonds, and z pounds of pecans is to be made. The mixture is to weigh five pounds and contain 1,500 units of vitamin and 2,500 calories. The vitamin and caloric content of the three nuts is shown in Table 2–1. The problem is to determine how many pounds of each nut should be in the five-pound mixture.

TABLE 2–1

Nut	Number of Pounds	Units of Vitamin per Pound	Calories per Pound
Macadamia	x	500	300
Almonds	y	200	600
Pecans	z	100	700

The conditions of the problem require that

$$e_1: \quad x + y + z = 5$$
$$e_2: \quad 500x + 200y + 100z = 1500$$
$$e_3: \quad 300x + 600y + 700z = 2500.$$

Proceeding, we find:

$$500e_1 - e_2 = e_4: \quad 300y + 400z = 1000$$
$$300e_1 - e_3 = e_5: \quad -300y - 400z = -1000$$
$$\overline{e_4 + e_5 = e_6: \quad\quad 0 + 0 = 0.}$$

The system does not have a unique solution. Letting z be arbitrary, we get from e_5

$$e_7: \quad y = \frac{10 - 4z}{3}$$

and substituting e_7 into e_1

$$e_8: \quad x = \frac{5 + z}{3}.$$

Applying the nonnegativity condition to

$$e_7: \quad y = \frac{10 - 4z}{3},$$

we see that y will be negative if $4z$ is larger than 10, that is, if z is larger than $10/4$, which is 2.5. If z is restricted to the interval 0 to 2.5, inclusive, none of the variables will be negative. Our final solution is

$$z \text{ arbitrary in the interval}$$
$$0 \text{ to } 2.5, \text{ inclusive}$$
$$y = \frac{10 - 4z}{3}$$
$$x = \frac{5 + z}{3}.$$

Exercise.   (See Example 2.) If the costs of nuts per pound of macadamia, almonds, and pecans are, respectively, $2, $3, and $1, what is the composition and cost of the minimum-cost mixture? Answer: Mix 2.5 pounds of macadamia nuts with 2.5 pounds of pecans. Use no almonds. Minimum cost will be $7.50.

**2.16
APPLICATIONS—4:
TWO-PRODUCT
SUPPLY AND
DEMAND ANALYSIS**

Those planning to work through this section may wish to review the one-product discussion of Section 2.8. Here we consider the case of two products whose supply and demand expressions are interrelated. As an example consider the following expressions in which p_1 and q_1 are the price of product #1 and the quantity demanded of product #1, respectively, and similarly for the price and quantity demanded for product #2.

Product	Demand	Supply
#1	$p_1 = 2000 - 3q_1 - 2q_2$	$p_1 = 100 + 2q_1 + q_2$
#2	$p_2 = 2800 - q_1 - 4q_2$	$p_2 = 200 + 3q_1 + 2q_2.$

To achieve equilibrium, the two price expressions for each product must be equal. Hence,

for product #1: $2000 - 3q_1 - 2q_2 = 100 + 2q_1 + q_2$
for product #2: $2800 - q_1 - 4q_2 = 200 + 3q_1 + 2q_2.$

Rearranging the last two expressions, we have

$$e_1:\ 5q_1 + 3q_2 = 1900$$
$$e_2:\ 4q_1 + 6q_2 = 2600.$$

We obtain the equilibrium quantities supplied and demanded by solving the last pair of equations in the usual manner:

$$5e_2 - 4e_1 = e_3:\ \ 18q_2 = 5400.$$

Hence, $q_2 = 5400/18 = 300$. Then from e_2 we find $q_1 = 200$. Using these quantities in the original supply (or demand) expressions, we find $p_1 = \$800$ and $p_2 = \$1,400$. The equilibrium prices and quantities are

$$E:\quad \begin{array}{ll} p_1 = \$800 & p_2 = \$1,400 \\ q_1 = 200\ \text{units} & q_2 = 300\ \text{units.} \end{array}$$

Now suppose the supply functions remain the same but a change occurs in the demand for product #1 and, since the two products are interrelated, there is a corresponding change in the demand for #2. Then suppose the outcomes are the new demand functions:

Product	Demand
#1	$p_1 = 2270 - 3q_1 - 2q_2$
#2	$p_2 = 2890 - q_1 - 4q_2.$

Equating these new demand expressions with the corresponding original supply expressions leads to

$$5q_1 + 3q_2 = 2170$$
$$4q_1 + 6q_2 = 2690.$$

Solving the last pair, we find $q_1 = 275$ and $q_2 = 265$, and using these values in the new demand or the old supply expressions yields $p_1 = \$915$, $p_2 = \$1,555$. The new equilibrium is

$$E':\quad \begin{array}{ll} p_1 = \$915 & p_2 = \$1,555 \\ q_1 = 275\ \text{units} & q_2 = 265\ \text{units.} \end{array}$$

> **Exercise.** Solve the above pair of equations, then carry out the substitution necessary to verify the values at E'.

Comparing E' and E, we describe what occurred in the following manner. The demand for #1 increased (from 200 to 275) and the price of this product rose (from $800 to $915). At the same time, there was a decrease in demand for #2 (from 300 to 265) but an increase in its price (from $1,400 to $1,555). To gain an understanding of these changes, let us think of product #1 as the standard model of an appliance and #2 as the deluxe model. Then we can see that consumer response to rising prices of appliances (both prices up) might well be to increase their demand for the standard model and decrease demand for the deluxe model, as was the outcome in this example. The outcome of supply and demand shifts depends on the nature of the products involved and relates directly to the constants in the mathematical expressions for supply and demand. Readers interested in pursuing this matter should refer to discussions of *complementary, competing* (or *substitute*), and *independent* products in economics textbooks.

2.17 PROBLEM SET 2–5

1. A mixture of pellets is to be made containing x regular pellets, y large pellets, and z extra large pellets. Cost, weight, and volume data for each type of pellet are shown in the table.

   Is it possible to make a mixture of 45 pellets at a cost of 85 cents if the mixture is to have 120 weight units and 130 volume units? If so, how many of each type of pellet should be in the mixture?

Pellet Type	Number of Pellets	Cost per Pellet in Cents	Weight Units per Pellet	Volume Units per Pellet
Regular	x	2	1	4
Large	y	3	2	2
Extra large	z	1	4	3

2. Replace the volume data in the table for Problem 1 with the numbers 1.6, 2.8, and 3.6 for regular, large, and extra large pellets, respectively. Leaving the other data and the conditions of the problem unchanged, set up and solve the resultant system of equations.

3. Computer chips F, G, and H are each made using three different kinds of transistors, A, B, and C. The number of chips to be made along with their transistor requirements are shown in the table. How many of each kind could be made using all available transistors?

Chip	Number of Chips	Number of Transistors Required per Chip, by Type A	B	C
F	x	1	2	2
G	y	2	7	1
H	z	1	3	1
Total available		(12)	(34)	(14)

4. Solve Problem 3 if the requirement for transistor B in chip G is reduced from 7 to 6.

2.17 PROBLEM SET 2–5 (concluded)

5. Solve Problem 3 if the requirement for transistor C in chip F is increased from 2 to 3.

6. a) The table shows the numbers of hours required in each of three departments to make a unit of various products named A, B, and C. For example, product B requires 1 hour of time in Department I and 3 hours in Department II.

| Department | Hours Required per Unit of Product | | |
	A	B	C
I	1	1	9
II	1	3	7
III	2	7	13

   Find the numbers of units of A, B, and C that could be made if Department I has 75 hours available, Department II has 65 hours available and Department III has 125 hours available.

   b) If profits per unit of A, B, and C are, respectively, $20, $30, and $40, what is the maximum profit and the composition of the maximum-profit combination of outputs?

7. Solve Problem 6(a) and (b) if Departments I and II have 40 hours available, and Department III has 80 hours available.

8. The demand and supply expressions for products #1 and #2 are:

   Demand *Supply*
   $p_1 = 1000 - 5q_1 - 4q_2$ $p_1 = 90 + 2q_1 + 3q_2$
   $p_2 = 900 - 2q_1 - 5q_2$ $p_2 = 120 + q_1 + 4q_2.$

   a) Find the prices and quantities at equilibrium.
   b) If demands change to those below, with the same supply functions, find the new equilibrium point.

Product	Demand
#1	$p_1 = 1210 - 5q_1 - 4q_2$
#2	$p_2 = 984 - 2q_1 - 5q_2.$

9. The demand and supply expressions for products #1 and #2 are:

   Demand *Supply*
   $p_1 = 1500 - 4q_1 - 3q_2$ $p_1 = 400 + 3q_1 + q_2$
   $p_2 = 700 - q_1 - 2q_2$ $p_2 = 200 + q_1 + q_2.$

   a) Find the prices and quantities at equilibrium.
   b) If demands change to those below, with the same supply functions, find the new equilibrium point.

Product	Demand
#1	$p_1 = 1400 - 3q_1 - 3q_2$
#2	$p_2 = 640 - q_1 - q_2.$

2.18 SYSTEMS OF TWO LINEAR INEQUALITIES[1]

The system of inequalities

$$x > 4$$
$$x \leq 9$$

requires that x be greater than 4 but less than or equal to 9. Hence, x is in an interval with the smaller number, 4, at the left and the larger number, 9, at the right. This may be written as

$$4 < x \leq 9.$$

Again, the statement

$$0 \leq x \leq 10$$

says that x is greater than or equal to 0 but less than or equal to 10.

---
[1] For a review of single linear inequalities, see A3.15–A3.17.

> **Exercise.** Write the statement that specifies that y is less than 0 but greater than or equal to -3. Answer: $-3 \le y < 0$.

Two inequalities are said to be *inconsistent* if both cannot be true at the same time, and one of a pair is *redundant* if it is true automatically when the other is true. Thus, if company policy states that workers may not work more than 10 hours a day ($x \le 10$) and the union contract specifies that workers must not work more than 8 hours a day ($x \le 8$), company policy is redundant.

> **Exercise.** How would the system $x < 5$ and $x > 8$ be described? Why? Answer: The inequalities are inconsistent because if x is less than 5, it cannot be greater than 8.

Two linear inequalities are used in describing the space between two lines. For example, the inequalities

$$i_1: \quad y \ge 2x - 1$$
$$i_2: \quad y \le \ x + 2$$

are satisfied by points in the shaded space shown in Figure 2–4. The lines are labeled e_1 and e_2 because they are the graphs of the *equality* parts of the statements. Recall from Appendix 3 that to graph an inequality we first graph the corresponding equality. Then we determine which half space represents the inequality by checking a point, usually the origin $(0, 0)$, to see if it satisfies the inequality. We indicate the resultant solution space by the direction of the arrows on the line.

Now the lines are found in the usual manner to intersect at $(3, 5)$. Hence, for any point in the solution space, the x-coordinate must be less than or equal to 3.

> **Exercise.** Suppose that we let x have the permissible value 0. What y values are permissible if $x = 0$? (See Figure 2–4.) Answer: $-1 \le y \le 2$.

The exercise and Figure 2–4 show that for a given permissible value of x, the permissible values of y are those which are greater than or equal to $2x - 1$ but less than or equal to $x + 2$. That is, the solution space is completely described by

$$x \le 3; \quad 2x - 1 \le y \le x + 2.$$

FIGURE 2–4

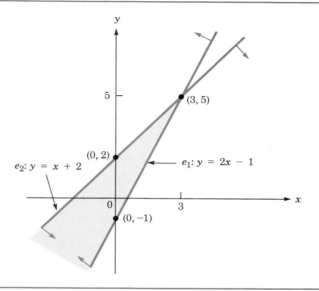

This last result says, for example, that if $x = -1$, then both i_1 and i_2 will be true for any y value in the closed interval

$$-3 \le y \le 1.$$

Exercise. On scratch paper, sketch the lines shown in Figure 2–4 and place arrows on them indicating the solution space for

$$y \le 2x - 1; \quad y \ge x + 2.$$

Describe the solution space algebraically.
Answer: $x \ge 3; \quad x + 2 \le y \le 2x - 1.$

The solution space specified by

$$i_1: \quad y \le 2x - 1$$
$$i_2: \quad y \le \ x + 2$$

is the space *below* both lines in Figure 2–4. This is the space in the lower obtuse angle formed at $(3, 5)$. To the left of $(3, 5)$, that is, for $x < 3$, this means that points must be on or below e_1 (that is, $y \le 2x - 1$), and to the right of $(3, 5)$ points must be on or below e_2 (that is, $y \le x + 2$). Hence, we have

$$x \le 3; \quad y \le 2x - 1$$
$$x \ge 3; \quad y \le \ x + 2.$$

Note in the description just given that to the right of $(3, 5)$

$$i_1: \quad y \le 2x - 1$$

is *redundant* because it holds automatically if

$$i_2: \quad y \le x + 2$$

is true.

Exercise. a) Describe the solution space in the upper obtuse angle formed at $(3, 5)$ in Figure 2–4. b) Which inequality is redundant to the right of $(3, 5)$?
Answer: a) $(x \le 3, y \ge x + 2)$; $(x \ge 3, y \ge 2x - 1)$. b) $y \ge x + 2$.

**2.19
NONNEGATIVITY
CONSTRAINTS**

In the work to come, we shall deal often with quantities and prices of goods, and other variables that cannot take on negative values. In the case of two variables, x and y, this restriction is expressed by writing

$$x \ge 0$$
$$y \ge 0$$

along with the other inequalities at hand. Nonnegativity means that only points in the first quadrant, including the axes, are under consideration.
 The system

$$x \ge 0$$
$$y \ge 0$$
$$x \le 4$$
$$y \le 2$$

has as its solution the points on the boundary and inside the rectangle shown in Figure 2–5.

FIGURE 2–5

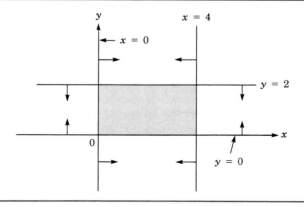

The algebraic solution of 2 by 2 systems of inequalities with nonnegativity constraints is facilitated by graphing the solution space and determining from the graph what algebraic manipulations of the inequalities will lead to the correct general solution. Consider the system

$$
\begin{array}{lrcl}
i_1: & x & \geq & 0 \\
i_2: & y & \geq & 0 \\
i_3: & x + 2y & \leq & 8 \\
i_4: & 7x + 4y & \geq & 28.
\end{array}
$$

The solution space is shown in Figure 2–6 and can be described algebraically by saying that if y is in the interval from 0 to 2.8, inclusive, x must be in the interval from e_4 to e_3. Thus the general solution is

$$
0 \leq y \leq 2.8
$$
$$
\frac{28 - 4y}{7} \leq x \leq 8 - 2y.
$$

Consider the next system

$$
\begin{array}{lrcl}
i_1: & x & \geq & 0 \\
i_2: & y & \geq & 0 \\
i_3: & x + 2y & \leq & 8 \\
i_4: & 7x + 4y & \leq & 28.
\end{array}
$$

FIGURE 2–6

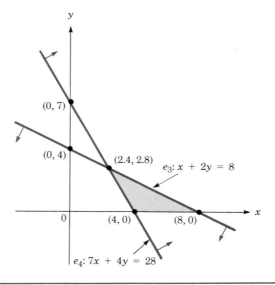

The solution space for this system is shown in Figure 2–7. We see that for x in the interval 0 to 2.4, inclusive, y must be in the interval from 0 to line e_3, inclusive. However, if x is from 2.4 up to and including 4, the interval for y is from 0 to line e_4, inclusive. Hence, the general solution may be written:

$$\text{If } 0 \le x \le 2.4, \text{ then } 0 \le y \le \frac{8-x}{2}.$$

$$\text{If } 2.4 \le x \le 4, \text{ then } 0 \le y \le \frac{28-7x}{4}.$$

Exercise. If the solution space in Figure 2–6 is described by letting x run over the values 2.4 to 8, two statements will be required. The first is

$$2.4 \le x \le 4$$
$$\frac{28-7x}{4} \le y \le \frac{8-x}{2}.$$

The second will be of the form

$$a \le x \le b$$
$$c \le y \le d.$$

Determine from Figure 2–6 the quantities that should appear in the places indicated as a, b, c, and d in the form just written.

Answer: a is 4, b is 8, c is 0, d is $\dfrac{8-x}{2}$.

Exercise. What quantities should appear in the places designated as a, b, c, d, e, and f if the following inequalities are to describe the solution space in Figure 2–7?

$$\text{If } 0 \le y \le 2.8, \text{ then } a \le x \le b.$$
$$\text{If } c \le y \le d, \text{ then } e \le x \le f.$$

Answer: a is 0, b is $\dfrac{28-4y}{7}$, c is 2.8, d is 4, e is 0, f is $8-2y$.

In the next chapter we will frequently encounter solution spaces similar to that in Figure 2–7. Another common type is shown in Figure 2–8, which is the solution space for

$$\begin{array}{llll} i_1 : & x \ge 0 & i_3 : & x + 2y \ge 8 \\ i_2 : & y \ge 0 & i_4 : & 7x + 4y \ge 28. \end{array}$$

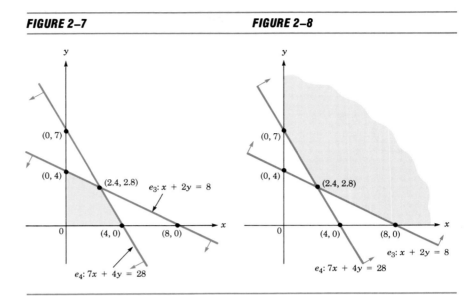

FIGURE 2–7   **FIGURE 2–8**

Exercise.   Write the algebraic expressions for the solution space in Figure 2–8 starting with if $0 \leq x \leq 2.4$. Answer: If $0 \leq x \leq 2.4$, then $y \geq (28 - 7x)/4$. If $2.4 \leq x \leq 8$, then $y \geq (8 - x)/2$. If $x > 8$, then $y > 0$.

2.20 APPLICATIONS

Example 1. The United Parcel Service in Massachusetts accepts a parcel for delivery only if its length plus girth (distance around) does not exceed 108 inches.

a) We want to ship fishing poles in cylindrical containers of radius r. What is the restriction on the length of the poles in terms of the radius of the cylindrical container, and what restrictions apply to the radius?

Here, the girth, g, is $2\pi r$, the circumference of a circle, and using L for the length, we have

$$L + 2\pi r \leq 108$$
$$L \leq 108 - 2\pi r$$

and $r > 0$. Also, $L \geq 0$, so $108 - 2\pi r \geq 0$ and $r \leq 108/2\pi$, which is 17.188 plus a bit more; that is,

$$0 < r \leq 17.188$$

having rounded the right-hand limit *down* to three decimals to insure that the statement is true.

b) From (a), what lengths of poles can be shipped in containers having a one-half inch radius?

Substitution shows that

$$L \le 108 - 2(3.1416)(1/2)$$

or

$$L \le 104.8.$$

Exercise.   Cubical boxes are to be shipped. What is the restriction on x, the dimension of the side of the cube? Answer: $0 < x \le 21.6$ inches.

Example 2. We plan to invest x dollars at 7 percent and y dollars at i percent, and we require that the combined investment yield at least 9 percent. Express the restriction on i in terms of x and y and state the restrictions on x and y.

We have that 7 percent of x plus i percent of y must be equal to or greater than 9 percent of $(x + y)$. Hence, using the decimal equivalents of percents,

$$0.07x + 0.01iy \ge 0.09(x + y)$$
$$0.07x + 0.01iy \ge 0.09x + 0.09y$$
$$0.01iy \ge 0.02x + 0.09y$$
$$iy \ge \frac{0.02x + 0.09y}{0.01}$$
$$iy \ge 2x + 9y$$
$$i \ge \frac{2x + 9y}{y}.$$

Both x and y must be nonnegative. Additionally, x can be zero, but y cannot be zero. Hence,

$$x \ge 0$$
$$y > 0.$$

Exercise.   If $x = \$5,000$ and $y = \$4,000$, what is the minimum interest rate required on the $4,000? Answer: 11.5 percent.

Example 3. A mixture is to be made containing x units of wheat and y units of rye. The weight and amount of nutrient per unit of each component are shown in Table 2–2. If the mixture is to contain not less than 13 ounces of nutrient, and it is to weigh not more than 50 ounces, what combinations (numbers of units) of the foods are permissible?

TABLE 2-2

Component	Number of Units in Mixture	Ounces of Nutrient per Unit	Ounces of Weight per Unit
Wheat	x	0.4	2
Rye	y	0.9	3

To obtain the necessary inequalities, we find the number of ounces of nutrient in a mixture containing x units of wheat and y units of rye, which is $0.4x + 0.9y$. According to the stated requirement, this sum must be 13 or more. Hence, we write

$$0.4x + 0.9y \geq 13.$$

Similarly, the weight constraint is found to be

$$2x + 3y \leq 50.$$

Taking the last two inequalities together with the nonnegativity constraints, we have the system

$$i_1: \qquad\qquad x \geq 0$$
$$i_2: \qquad\qquad y \geq 0$$
$$i_3: \quad 0.4x + 0.9y \geq 13$$
$$i_4: \quad 2.0x + 3.0y \leq 50.$$

The solution space for the system is shown in Figure 2–9. We see that x may take on values from 0 to 10, inclusive. For any x in this interval the

FIGURE 2-9

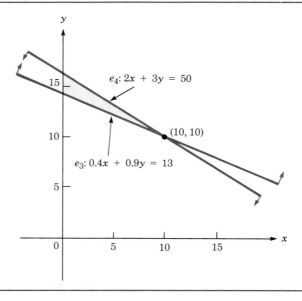

value of y must be selected in the interval from line e_3 to line e_4, inclusive. Hence, the general algebraic solution is

$$0 \leq x \leq 10$$

$$\frac{13 - 0.4x}{0.9} \leq y \leq \frac{50 - 2.0x}{3.0}.$$

2.21 PROBLEM SET 2–6

Make a graph showing the solution space, assuming $x \geq 0$ and $y \geq 0$:

1. $y \geq -1$
   $x \leq 4.$

2. $x \leq 3$
   $x \leq y.$

3. $2x + y \geq 6$
   $x + 4y \leq 8.$

4. $x \leq 3$
   $y \leq 1$
   $x + 3y \geq 3.$

5. $7x + 4y \leq 28$
   $x + 2y \leq 8.$

Find solutions, if any exist, assuming $x \geq 0$ and $y \geq 0$:

6. $2x + 3y \leq 12$
   $x - 2y \geq 2.$

7. $4x + y \leq 12$
   $x + 5y \geq 8.$

8. $4x + y \geq 12$
   $x + 5y \leq 8.$

9. $4x + y \geq 12$
   $x + 5y \geq 8.$

10. A parcel service requires that length plus girth of parcels not exceed 108 inches. Containers with rectangular cross section (girth) of width w, height h, and length L are to be shipped.
   a) If the width is to be 16 inches, state the restriction on the height in terms of the length, and state the restrictions on the length.
   b) If the rectangular cross section is a square of side x, state the restriction on x in terms of L and state the restriction on L.

11. A mixture is to be made containing x units of wheat and y units of rye. Wheat weighs 3 ounces per unit and rye weighs 5 ounces per unit. Wheat contains 0.5 ounces of nutrient per unit and rye 1 ounce of nutrient per unit. The mixture is to have at least 8 ounces of nutrient, and the total weight is not to exceed 45 ounces. Find the general solution, showing all permissible combinations of the two components.

12. Solve Problem 11 if the mixture is not to exceed 40 ounces in total weight.

13. Pencils and pens both require the same amount of storage space per unit. Pencils cost $3 per unit and pens cost $8 per unit. Sufficient storage space is available for 500 units (total), and $2,400 is available to spend on the items. Write the general solution, showing permissible combinations of items that may be purchased and stored without exceeding total space and money restrictions.

14. The table shows, for example, that it takes one hour in Department I and two hours in Department II to make one premium tire. Department I has up to five hours available and Department II has up to seven hours available for making tires. Letting x be the number of premium tires and y the number of regular tires made:
   a) Write the general solution showing permissible combinations of numbers of

2.21 PROBLEM SET 2–6 (*concluded*)

each tire that can be made in the time available.

b) What specific combinations are possible if only complete units of product are allowed?

Department	Hours Required to Make One Tire	
	Premium	Regular
I	1	1
II	2	1

15. It takes two hours to make a single-edged razor blade and three hours to make a double-edged razor blade. The number of double-edged blades must not be more than twice the number of single-edged blades. If up to 36 hours are available for making the products, find the permissible combinations of numbers of each blade.

16. Cashew nuts cost $2 per pound and walnuts cost $5 per pound. If we mix x pounds of cashews with y pounds of walnuts, the mixture contains $x + y$ pounds. The *proportion* of cashews in the mixture then is $x/(x + y)$. Mixtures are to be made at a total cost not exceeding $286, and in these mixtures the proportion of cashews must be not less than 0.2 (20 percent) and not greater than 0.8 (80 percent). Write the general so-

lution showing permissible combinations of the two nuts.

17. The table shows, for example, that Department III has 190 hours available and that one unit of A requires six hours of Department III time. Write the general solution showing the combinations of A and B that can be made in the time available.

Department	Available Hours	Hours Required to Make One Unit of:	
		A	B
I	120	4	3
II	40	1	2
III	190	6	7

18. (This problem is a new interpretation of the numbers in Problem 17.) Each unit of A made contributes $6 to overhead and profit and each unit of B contributes $7. Write the general solution showing permissible combinations that can be made in the available time if total contribution to overhead and profit is to be at least $190.

Department	Available Hours	Hours Required to Make One Unit of:	
		A	B
I	120	4	3
II	40	1	2

2.22 REVIEW PROBLEMS

Solve each of the following systems by the elimination method:

1. $x + 10y = 25$
$3x - 7y = 1.$

2. $6x + 8y = 15$
$9x + 12y = 25.$

3. $x + 2y - 3z = 11$
$3x + 2y + z = 1$
$2x + y - 5z = 11.$

4. $3x + y + z = 4$
$x - 2y - 3z = 0$
$2x + 3y + 4z = 6.$

5. $2x + z = 4$
$3y + 2z = 6$
$4x - 3y = 2.$

6. $x - y = 1$
$2x + y - 3z = 2$
$x + y - 2z = 1.$

2.22 REVIEW PROBLEMS (*continued*)

7. The table shows, for example, that a pound of cashews contains two ounces of nutrient P, three ounces of Q, and one ounce of R. Similar relations are shown for walnuts and almonds. If a mixture of x pounds of cashews, y pounds of walnuts, and z pounds of almonds is to contain exactly 9 ounces of P, 13 ounces of Q, and 4 ounces of R, find the permissible values for x, y, and z.

	Ounces per Pound of Nuts		
Nut	**Nutrient P**	**Nutrient Q**	**Nutrient R**
Cashews	2	3	1
Walnuts	1	2	1
Almonds	1	1	0

Write the solution in arbitrary-variable form, and state the permissible ranges of values for the variables.

8. See Problem 7. If the per-pound costs are 20, 10, and 5 cents for cashews, walnuts, and almonds, respectively, find the cost and composition of the minimum-cost mixture.

9. We wish to mix x liters of regular unleaded gasoline with y liters of premium unleaded and z liters of super premium unleaded to obtain 1,000 liters of 90 octane gasoline with a vapor pressure index of 27.5. Costs per liter are $0.50, $0.55, and $0.65, respectively, octane ratings are 84, 92, and 100, respectively, and vapor pressure indices are 20, 30, and 40, respectively.
a) Write the solution in arbitrary-variable form.
b) What is the composition and cost of the minimum-cost mixture?

10. The table shows the number of hours required to make one unit of various products (A, B, and C) in each of three departments (I, II, and III). For example, it takes one hour of Department I time, three hours of Department II time, and four hours of Department III time to make one unit of product C.

	Hours to Make One Unit of:		
Department	**Product A**	**Product B**	**Product C**
I	1	1	1
II	2	1	3
III	3	2	4

a) Find the numbers of units, x, y, and z of products A, B, and C that can be made if exactly 8 hours of Department I time, 14 hours of Department II time, and 22 hours of Department III time are to be utilized.
b) If the maximum possible number of units of C are made, how many hours of each department's time will be spent on making C?
c) Is it possible to utilize the hours exactly if no units of B are made? Explain.

11. The demand and supply expressions for products #1 and #2 are

Demand	Supply
$p_1 = 1700 - 3q_1 - q_2$	$p_1 = 100 + 2q_1 + q_2$
$p_2 = 1650 - q_1 - 2q_2$	$p_2 = 50 + q_1 + 2q_2$

a) What will be the prices and quantities at equilibrium?
b) If the demand functions change to those below and the supply functions are unchanged, find the new equilibrium point.

Product	Demand
#1	$p_1 = 1730 - 3q_1 - q_2$
#2	$p_2 = 1710 - q_1 - 2q_2$

12. The demand and supply expressions for products #1 and #2 are

Demand	Supply
$p_1 = 2300 - 30q_1 - 10q_2$	$p_1 = 180 + 5q_1 + 2q_2$
$p_2 = 2000 - 10q_1 - 20q_2$	$p_2 = 120 + q_1 + 4q_2$

a) What will be the prices and quantities at equilibrium?
b) If the demand functions change to those below and the supply functions remain the same, find the new equilibrium point.

Product	Demand
#1	$p_1 = 4424 - 30q_1 - 10q_2$
#2	$p_2 = 2708 - 10q_1 - 20q_2$

2.22 REVIEW PROBLEMS (*concluded*)

Make a graph showing the solution space for each of the following, assuming in each system that the nonnegativity constraints $x \geq 0$ and $y \geq 0$ prevail, and write the algebraic statement of the solution space:

13. $x - 2y \leq 0$
$\quad x + y \leq 2.$

14. $x + y \geq 2$
$\quad x + 2y \leq 4.$

15. $x - 2y \leq 0$
$\quad x + 2y \leq 4.$

16. $x - 2y \geq 0$
$\quad x + 2y \geq 4$
$\quad x \geq 3.$

17. $x + y \geq 2$
$\quad x - 2y \leq 0$
$\quad x + 2y \leq 4.$

18. $x + y \geq 2$
$\quad x - 2y \geq 0$
$\quad x \leq 3$
$\quad x + 2y \leq 4.$

---

19. a) We plan to invest x dollars at 6 percent and y dollars at i percent and require that the combined investment yield at least 8 percent. Express the restriction on i in terms of x and y, and state the restrictions on x and y.
  b) If $x = \$2,000$ and $y = \$1,000$, what is the minimum interest rate that must be obtained on the $1,000?

20. A mixture of nuts is to weigh not more than five pounds and contain at least 24 ounces of nutrient. Spanish nuts contain 6 ounces of nutrient per pound and beer nuts contain 4 ounces of nutrient per pound. Write the general solution showing the permissible mixtures of the two nuts.

21. See Problem 20. If, in addition to the stated constraints, the mixture must contain at least three pounds of spanish nuts, write the general solution showing the permissible nut mixtures.

22. See Problem 20. If, in addition to the stated constraints in Problem 20, it is required that the mixture must not cost more than 21 cents, and if spanish nuts cost 6 cents a pound and beer nuts cost 2 cents a pound, write the general solution showing the permissible nut mixtures.

23. A high-quality batch of a substance contains 3 ounces of butter and 4 ounces of margarine. A low-quality batch contains 1 ounce of butter and 3 ounces of margarine. If 70 ounces of butter and 110 ounces of margarine are available, write the general solution showing permissible combinations of numbers of high- and low-quality batches.

24. See Problem 23. Write the solution if a high-quality batch contributes $1 to profit and a low-quality batch contributes $2 to profit, and total profit is to be at least $65.

25. If, in addition to the conditions and facts stated in Problems 23 and 24, it is required that at least 5 percent of total output be high-quality batches, write the solution showing permissible combinations of the numbers of batches of each quality.

26. The table shows, for example, that it takes two hours in Department I, one hour in II, and one hour in III to make a premium tire. If hours available in I, II, and III are, respectively, 12, 7, and 15, write the solution showing the permissible combinations of the two products.

	Hours Required to Make One Tire	
Department	Premium	Regular
I	2	1
II	1	1
III	1	3

THREE

Introduction to Linear Programming

In our everyday lives, we are often confronted with a number of ways of accomplishing a certain objective, some ways being better in a certain sense than others. For example, there are many different combinations of foods that will provide a satisfactory diet, but some combinations are more costly than others, and we may be interested in finding the *minimum* cost of providing dietary requirements. Again, there are many combinations of products a plant can manufacture, and we may be interested in finding the combination that leads to *maximum* profit.

The variables in real-life situations are subject to restrictions that we shall call *constraints.* In the first place, it is required in most instances that the variables not take on negative values. Furthermore, certain combinations of the variables are not permissible. For example, a product mix that requires a plant to operate more than 24 hours a day obviously is not permissible, nor is it permissible to schedule output at levels exceeding capacity.

Let us suppose that the relevant variables in a certain situation are x and y, and that the constraints can be expressed as a system of inequalities in these variables. Then suppose we have an expression called the *objective function*, which states how profit (or cost) is computed for specific values of x and y. The problem is to find the set of values for x and y that satisfies the constraints *and* maximizes profit (or minimizes cost). If the constraints and the objective function are linear, we have a problem in *linear programming*.

To be more specific, suppose that a textile mill buys unfinished cloth and uses 10 processes to convert it into 12 styles of finished material.

The styles require varying amounts of time in each of the processes, and there is a capacity limitation on the time available for each process, making 10 capacity constraints. Further, a certain quantity (at least) of each style must be produced to satisfy customer demand, making 12 demand constraints, so we have a total of 10 + 12 = 22 linear inequality constraints, not counting nonnegativity constraints.

By deducting raw material and processing cost from selling price, the profit contribution per yard produced for each of the 12 styles can be computed, and these profit contributions may be combined to form a linear objective function containing as its variables the unknown number of yards of each of the 12 styles to be produced. The problem is to determine the set of *nonnegative* values for these variables that will maximize total profit, and not violate any of the 22 constraints. This set of values can then be used to establish the production schedule, which is a *program* of operations.

The situation just described involved 22 constraints on 12 variables (a 22 by 12 system), but it is by no means a large system compared to many encountered in practice. We need not be concerned about problem size, however, because large systems can be solved in a matter of seconds by entering the coefficients of the variables into one of the many computers equipped to solve such problems. In this chapter we present the fundamentals of linear programming by use of small systems, and in the next two chapters we shall develop a procedure for solving larger problems.

3.2 MAXIMIZATION EXAMPLES: PRODUCT MIX

Table 3–1 shows that lounge chairs and swivel chairs are made using the equipment of two departments, I and II. It requires one hour in each department to make a lounge chair, but making a swivel chair takes one hour in Department I and two hours in Department II. Department I has four hours of time available, and II has six hours available. Each lounge chair made and sold contributes $1 to profit, and each swivel chair contributes $0.50 to profit.

The problem is to determine the maximum profit that can be achieved, keeping in mind the four- and six-hour time limitations in the departments. The profit achieved from x lounge chairs and y swivel chairs is

(Profit per lounge chair)(Number of lounge chairs)
+ (Profit per swivel chair)(Number of swivel chairs),

TABLE 3–1

Chair	Number of Units Made	Profit per Unit	Department I (4 hours available)	Department II (6 hours available)
			Hours Required per Unit in:	
Lounge	x	$1.00	1	1
Swivel	y	0.50	1	2

which is

$$\$1x + \$0.5y.$$

The last expression is the *objective function*, which we shall name θ (theta) for simplicity[1]

$$\text{Profit} = \theta = x + 0.5y.$$

From Table 3–1, we see that to make x lounge chairs and y swivel chairs will require $x + y$ hours in Department I and $x + 2y$ hours in Department II. The time limitations, 4 hours available in I and 6 hours available in II, therefore are

$$x + \ \ y \le 4$$
$$x + 2y \le 6.$$

The above conditions, taken together with nonnegativity constraints on x and y,

$$x \ge 0$$
$$y \ge 0,$$

lead to the following statement of the problem:

Maximize the objective function

$$\theta = x + 0.5y$$

subject to the constraint inequalities labeled i_1 through i_4:

Department I $\quad i_1: \ x + \ \ y \le 4$
Department II $\quad i_2: \ x + 2y \le 6$
Nonnegativity $i_3, i_4: \quad x, y \ge 0$

where the last expression combines the two nonnegativity constraints in a simplified form. Clearly, we can find nonnegative values of x and y (that is, values satisfying i_3 and i_4) that also satisfy i_1 and i_2. The obvious values are $x = 0$ and $y = 0$. However, if we substitute $(0, 0)$ into the objective function, we find that the profit is 0. We must make some product to achieve a profit. If we make one lounge chair and one swivel chair ($x = 1$ and $y = 1$), we find $\theta = 1.5$ and all inequalities are satisfied.

> **Exercise.** Is it possible to make two units of each product? If so, what profit will be achieved? Answer: Yes; $x = 2$, $y = 2$ satisfy all constraints in the problem. The profit will be $3.

---

[1] Z is another common name given to the objective function. We choose θ to avoid ambiguity later when z is used as a variable.

Our goal is not simply to list all the various profits that might be achieved but, rather, to find the *maximum* profit that can be achieved. Consider Figure 3–1.

The solution space for the inequalities i_1 through i_4 is shown in Figure 3–1 as the space bounded by lines whose intersections (which we shall call *corners*) are at O, A, B, and C. The coordinates of $A(0, 3)$ and $C(4, 0)$, of course, are found as a result of graphing the equalities e_1 and e_2. $O(0, 0)$ is precisely the origin, while $B(2, 2)$ is found by solving the equalities e_1 and e_2 by the elimination procedure. Now each point in the shaded solution space has a pair of coordinates (x, y) that, when substituted into the objective function, yield the value of θ associated with that point. For example, the point $P(1, 2)$ is in the solution space. At P, we find

$$\theta = 1 + 0.5(2) = 2.$$

Again, point $A(0, 3)$ is in the solution space. At A,

$$\theta = 0 + 0.5(3) = 1.5.$$

Clearly, the value of θ varies from point to point in the solution space.

FIGURE 3–1

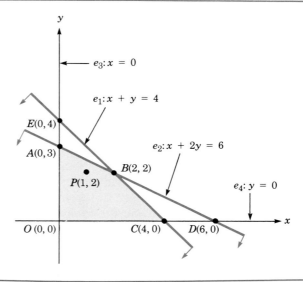

But observe that for a given x, we obtain the largest value of θ, for this given x, by making y as large as possible, that is, by going all the way to the boundary of the solution space. We see, therefore, that any point that will maximize θ must lie on the boundary of the solution space.

Consider the boundary segment from $A(0, 3)$ to $B(2, 2)$:

$$\text{at } A, \quad \theta = 1.5$$
$$\text{at } B, \quad \theta = 3.$$

This means that as we go from A toward B on the boundary AB, θ is increasing. Clearly, therefore, in seeking the maximum θ, we should go as far as possible in this direction, that is, to corner B.

Consider next the boundary segment from $B(2, 2)$ to $C(4, 0)$:

$$\text{at } B, \quad \theta = 3$$
$$\text{at } C, \quad \theta = 4.$$

Following the above reasoning, we move along the boundary to corner C, and then consider the segment from C to O. Obviously, θ decreases along this boundary. Whichever direction we move from C, toward O or toward B, we find θ decreases. Hence the maximum value occurs at $C(4, 0)$ and is

$$\theta_{max} = 4.$$

The solution of our problem is to make four lounge chairs and no swivel chairs. This schedule will provide a profit of \$4, the maximum possible with the stated constraints.

Exercise. Suppose that the profit function related to Figure 3–1 is

$$\theta = 2x + 3y.$$

a) Which values of x and y will now maximize profit? b) What is the maximum profit? Answer: a) $x = 2$, $y = 2$. b) $\theta_{max} = \$10$.

At this point, we would like to discuss the technique of formulation, whereby a word problem is transformed into a mathematical model that can subsequently be solved by some algorithm such as we have just seen.

Example. Ace Rubber Company manufactures two types of tires: Model P, the premium, and Model R, the regular. Model P sells for \$95 per tire and costs \$85 per tire to make, whereas Model R sells for \$50 per tire and costs \$42 per tire to make. To make one Model P tire, it requires two hours on Machine A and four hours on Machine B. On the other hand, to make one Model R tire, it takes nine hours on Machine A and three hours on Machine B. Production scheduling indicates that during the coming week Machine A will be available for at most 36 hours and Machine B for at most 42 hours. How many of each tire should the company make in the coming week in order to maximize its profit? What is this maximum profit?

The first step in the formulation of a linear programming problem is to determine what our specific objective is. In our example above, we can see that we are being asked to find the respective number of Model P and Model R tires to be made in the coming week that will maximize the company's profit, keeping in mind, of course, the limited resources available on Machines A and B.

The second step is to assign variables to each of the unknown quantities for which we wish to solve. Thus, in our example, we let

$$x = \text{Number of Model P tires to be made in the coming week}$$

and

$$y = \text{Number of Model R tires to be made in the coming week.}$$

(Note that x and y are the customary variable names, although any other letters would do just as well.)

The third step is to find a mathematical expression or function that represents our objective in terms of the unknowns just chosen. Since in our example we wish to maximize the profit made by the company, we now examine the profit data given in the statement of the example for each of the two types of tires. First since each Model P tire sells for $95 and costs $85 to make, the company clearly makes a profit of $95 − $85 = $10 per tire. Similarly since each Model R tire sells for $50 and costs $42 to make, the company makes a profit of $50 − $42 = $8 per tire. These facts are summarized, for convenience, as shown in Table 3–2. From this table (or equivalently, our analysis above), we can see that the profit on each Model P tire which is *manufactured and sold* is $10, while the profit on each Model R tire which is *manufactured and sold* is $8. Since the company realizes a profit on each tire *manufactured and sold*, it obviously would like to *manufacture and sell* as many tires as possible. We now make the simplifying assumption that the company can sell all the tires it manufactures. (We will adopt the convention of assuming that a company can sell all that it produces. In actuality, of course, it is the responsibility of the marketing division of a company to set production levels and any associated restrictions.) Thus, the profit from the

TABLE 3–2

	Tire Model	
	P	R
Selling price	$95/tire	$50/tire
Cost	$85/tire	$42/tire
Profit	$10/tire	$8/tire

Model P line is

$$(\$10/\text{tire}) \cdot (x \text{ tires}) = \$10x$$

and the profit from the Model R line is

$$(\$8/\text{tire}) \cdot (y \text{ tires}) = \$8y,$$

so that the total profit for the company is

$$\$10x + \$8y.$$

Therefore, the company would like to choose x and y in such a way as to maximize the objective or profit function

$$\theta = 10x + 8y.$$

Exercise.   Suppose each Model P tire sells for $120 and costs $88 to make, and each Model R tire sells for $67 and costs $49 to make. What is the objective function?   Answer: $\theta = 32x + 18y$.

The fourth step in the formulation of a linear programming problem is to find mathematical expressions that represent any limited resources or constraints in terms of our unknowns. In our example, we see that the company is not free to select just any value of x (i.e., the number of Model P's) and any value of y (i.e., the number of Model R's) since each tire must be processed on the two Machines A and B, both of which have limited availability. These time limitations, then, constrain the choices of x and y. In particular, the resource data can be summarized, for convenience, as shown in Table 3–3. From this table, we can see that since each Model P tire (x) requires 2 hours on Machine A, each Model R tire (y) requires 9 hours on Machine A, and since there are at most 36 hours available on Machine A, we must have

$$(2 \text{ hours/tire}) \cdot (x \text{ tires}) + (9 \text{ hours/tire}) \cdot (y \text{ tires}) \leq 36 \text{ hours}.$$

Similarly since each Model P tire takes 4 hours on Machine B, each Model R tire takes 3 hours on Machine B, and since there are at most 42 hours available on Machine B, we must also have

$$(4 \text{ hours/tire}) \cdot (x \text{ tires}) + (3 \text{ hours/tire}) \cdot (y \text{ tires}) \leq 42 \text{ hours}.$$

TABLE 3–3

Resources	Tire Model		Total
	P	**R**	**Total**
Machine A	2 hours/tire	9 hours/tire	at most 36 hours
Machine B	4 hours/tire	3 hours/tire	at most 42 hours

Thus, the constraints on x and y resulting from the limited resources of Machines A and B, respectively, are

$$\text{Machine A:} \quad 2x + 9y \leq 36$$
$$\text{Machine B:} \quad 4x + 3y \leq 42.$$

Exercise. What would the constraints be if the availabilities on Machine A and B were 41 and 38, respectively? Answer: $2x + 9y \leq 41$ and $4x + 3y \leq 38$.

The fifth and last step is to include any additional constraints on our unknowns that are not explicitly stated in the problem but are implicit from the context of the problem. In our case, we have the obvious requirements that x and y must both be nonnegative since we cannot make a negative number of tires

$$x, y \geq 0.$$

It is important to realize that, in practice, we would also have to require that x and y both be integers since we cannot make a fractional number of tires. Doing this, though, would lead us to the concept of integer programming, which is beyond the scope of our text, and hence, the integer constraints are omitted. However, for the sake of accuracy, all the problems in our text have been designed so that the integer constraints can be omitted without affecting the final solution.

In summary, then, the linear programming problem the company has is:

Maximize the profit function

$$\theta = 10x + 8y$$

subject to the constraints

$$\text{Machine A:} \quad 2x + 9y \leq 36$$
$$\text{Machine B:} \quad 4x + 3y \leq 42$$
$$\text{Nonnegativity:} \quad x, y \geq 0.$$

At this point, we summarize our five-step procedure for formulating a linear programming problem as we have just seen in our example above as follows:

1. Determine what the specific objective is.
2. Assign variables to each of the unknown quantities for which we are solving.
3. Express the desired objective in terms of the chosen variables as an objective function and state how it is to be optimized (maxi-

mized or minimized). If helpful, use a table to summarize the appropriate data.

4. Express the limited resources or constraints in terms of the chosen variables. Again, if helpful, use a table to summarize the appropriate data.

5. Add any additional constraints that are implicit in the nature of the problem.

Lastly we wish to point out that the constraints in Steps 4 and 5 above take on one of three forms: a mathematical expression involving the variables can be "at most" ($\leq$) some number, must be "at least" ($\geq$) some number, or is precisely "equal to" ($=$) some number. We saw the first two kinds of constraints in our example above, and we will see the third kind of constraint in a later section of this chapter.

3.3 MINIMIZATION EXAMPLES: INGREDIENT MIX

Suppose we want to minimize the cost function

$$\theta = 1.25x + y$$

subject to the constraints

$$
\begin{aligned}
i_1: \quad & 2x + y \geq 10 \\
i_2: \quad & x + 2y \geq 8 \\
i_3, i_4: \quad & x, y \geq 0.
\end{aligned}
$$

If we write the equality parts of the first two constraints,

$$
\begin{aligned}
e_1: \quad & 2x + y = 10 \\
e_2: \quad & x + 2y = 8
\end{aligned}
$$

and plot these from their intercepts, the slant lines shown in Figure 3–2 are obtained. Substituting the coordinates of the origin, $(0, 0)$, into i_1 and i_2 leads to

$$
\begin{aligned}
2(0) + \quad 0 &= 0 \not\geq 10 \\
0 + 2(0) &= 0 \not\geq 8,
\end{aligned}
$$

so that neither of these is a true statement. The origin and other points *below* the lines are not in the solution space. Hence, the solution space lies above the slant lines as shown in Figure 3–2. Notice that this space is not enclosed but extends indefinitely above the lines in the first quadrant. This means simply that cost increases without limit as more and more units are produced. Clearly, the smaller the number of units made, the lower will be cost, and minimum cost will occur at a point along the inner boundary of the solution space. Computing total cost, θ, at the corners A, B, and C, we find

FIGURE 3–2

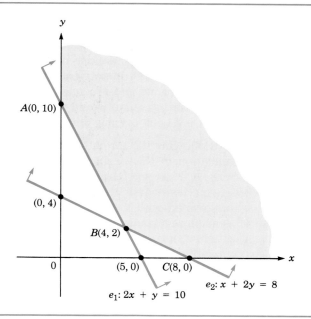

$$
\begin{array}{lll}
\text{at } A(0, 10): & \theta = 1.25(0) + 10 = & 10 \\
\text{at } B(4, 2): & \theta = 1.25(4) + 2 = & 7^* \\
\text{at } C(8, 0): & \theta = 1.25(8) + 0 = & 10.
\end{array}
$$

The asterisk on 7* shows

$$
\theta_{\min} = 7 \text{ at } x = 4, y = 2.
$$

Exercise. Find minimum cost for the last example if

$$
\theta = 2x + 3y.
$$

Answer: $\theta_{\min} = 14$ at $x = 4$, $y = 2$.

Our next example continues the discussion of the formulation of linear programming problems.

Example. Pure Gasoline Company operates two refineries with different production capacities. Refinery A can produce 4,000 gallons per day of super unleaded gasoline, 2,000 gallons per day of regular unleaded gasoline, and 1,000 gallons per day of leaded gasoline. On the other hand, Refinery B can produce 1,000 gallons per day of super unleaded, 3,000 gallons per day of regular unleaded, and 4,000 gallons per day of leaded. The company has made a contract with an automobile manufacturer to provide 24,000 gallons of super unleaded, 42,000 gallons of regular unleaded, and 36,000 gallons of leaded. Determine the number of days the company should operate each refinery in order to meet the terms of the above contract most economically, the minimum cost, and also what grade(s) of gasoline would be overproduced if the cost of running Refinery A is $1,500 per day and Refinery B is $2,400 per day.

Following the format of the previous section, our first step in the formulation of this problem is to determine our specific objective. In this case, we can see that we want to find the respective number of days that Refineries A and B are to be operated to minimize the company's cost associated with producing the required number of gallons of super unleaded, regular unleaded, and leaded gasoline.

Now our second step is to assign variables to each of the unknown quantities. In our example, an obvious choice is to let

$$x = \text{Number of days Refinery A is operated}$$

and

$$y = \text{Number of days Refinery B is operated.}$$

Then our third step is to determine the objective function to be optimized. Since in our example we want to minimize the cost incurred by the company, we now examine the cost data for each refinery. In particular, since Refinery A costs $1,500 per day to operate and since it is operated x days, the cost for Refinery A is

$$\$1,500x;$$

and since Refinery B costs $2,400 per day to operate and since it is operated y days, the cost for Refinery B is

$$\$2,400y.$$

Thus, since the company's objective is to minimize the total cost of operation, we want to minimize the objective or cost function

$$\theta = 1500x + 2400y.$$

(Note that we did not use a table to summarize the cost figures because the data were straightforward.)

Next our fourth step is to determine the constraints on the variables. This time we do not have limited resources to be concerned about, but rather contractual obligations that we must meet. For convenience, we summarize this data as shown in Table 3–4. From this table, we can see that since Refinery A can produce 4,000 gallons per day of super un-

TABLE 3-4

Grade	Refinery A	Refinery B	Total
Super unleaded	4,000 gallons/day	1,000 gallons/day	At least 24,000 gallons
Regular unleaded	2,000 gallons/day	3,000 gallons/day	At least 42,000 gallons
Leaded	1,000 gallons/day	4,000 gallons/day	At least 36,000 gallons

leaded for each of the x days that it is operated, Refinery B can produce 1,000 gallons of super unleaded for each of the y days that it is operated, and since at least 24,000 gallons of super unleaded are needed, we must have

$$(4{,}000 \text{ gallons/day}) \cdot (x \text{ days}) + (1{,}000 \text{ gallons/day}) \cdot (y \text{ days})$$
$$\geq 24{,}000 \text{ gallons.}$$

Similarly since Refinery A can produce 2,000 gallons per day of regular unleaded, Refinery B can produce 3,000 gallons per day of regular unleaded, and since at least 42,000 gallons of regular unleaded are required, we must also have

$$(2{,}000 \text{ gallons/day}) \cdot (x \text{ days}) + (3{,}000 \text{ gallons/day}) \cdot (y \text{ days})$$
$$\geq 42{,}000 \text{ gallons.}$$

In the same way, the requirement on the leaded gasoline becomes

$$(1{,}000 \text{ gallons/day}) \cdot (x \text{ days}) + (4{,}000 \text{ gallons/day}) \cdot (y \text{ days})$$
$$\geq 36{,}000 \text{ gallons.}$$

Thus, our constraints on x and y due to the contractual obligations are

$$\text{Super unleaded:} \quad 4{,}000x + 1{,}000y \geq 24{,}000$$
$$\text{Regular unleaded:} \quad 2{,}000x + 3{,}000y \geq 42{,}000$$
$$\text{Leaded:} \quad 1{,}000x + 4{,}000y \geq 36{,}000.$$

Lastly, simplifying the above constraints and introducing the non-negativity or real constraints, we have that the linear programming problem is:

Minimize the cost function

$$\theta = 1500x + 2400y$$

subject to the constraints

$$\text{Super unleaded:} \quad 4x + y \geq 24$$
$$\text{Regular unleaded:} \quad 2x + 3y \geq 42$$
$$\text{Leaded:} \quad x + 4y \geq 36$$
$$\text{Nonnegativity:} \quad x, y \geq 0,$$

where, of course, there are two nonnegativity constraints specified by the last expression.

> **Exercise.** a) What would the objective function become if the cost of running Refinery A is \$1,600 per day and Refinery B is \$2,400 per day? b) What additional constraints are needed if the automobile manufacturer wants delivery in no more than 14 days? Answer: a) $\theta_{\min} = 1600x + 2400y$; b) $x \leq 14$ and $y \leq 14$.

3.4 ISOLINES: THREE–STEP GRAPHICAL PROCEDURE

The term isobar may be familiar since it is used often in weather forecasts. An isobar is drawn on a weather map by connecting points that have the *same barometric pressure*. We shall also use *iso* to mean *same* when we talk of *isocost* and *isoprofit* lines. Thus, in the first example of the last section, for which cost was

$$\theta = 1.25x + y \quad \text{or} \quad y = -1.25x + \theta,$$

if we wish to speak of all points (x, y) where cost is, say, $\theta_1 = \$5$, then

$$\theta_1: \quad 1.25x + y = 5 \quad \text{or} \quad y = -1.25x + 5$$

is an isocost line. This line, plotted in the usual manner, is shown in Figure 3–3 along with the inner boundary of the solution space of Figure 3–2. At any point on $\theta_1 = 5$, cost is the same, \$5. Similarly isocost lines for costs of \$7, \$9, and \$13, which are

$$\begin{aligned}
\theta_2: & \quad 1.25x + y = 7 \quad \text{or} \quad y = -1.25x + 7 \\
\theta_3: & \quad 1.25x + y = 9 \quad \text{or} \quad y = -1.25x + 9 \\
\theta_4: & \quad 1.25x + y = 13 \quad \text{or} \quad y = -1.25x + 13,
\end{aligned}$$

are shown in Figure 3–3. The four isocost lines have the same slope, -1.25, so they are a family of parallel lines, and all of the isocost lines for this cost function will be parallel. More generally, the isocost for any linear cost function is a family of parallel lines. All of the first quadrant points of $\theta_4 = \$13$ are in the solution space. If we now think of laying a ruler along $\theta_4 = \$13$, then sliding toward the origin while holding it parallel to θ_4, cost is decreasing. Thus we can reduce cost to $\theta_3 = \$9$ by choosing any point on the first quadrant section of θ_3 that lies in the solution space. Sliding inward to $\theta_2 = \$7$, we see that there is just one point $(4, 2)$ on this isocost line that is in the solution space, and sliding further inward, no points on the isocost lines will be in the solution space. Consequently, the minimum cost occurs at $(4, 2)$ and is $\theta_2 = \$7$.

The isocost demonstration just given shows a situation where the minimum occurs at a corner of the solution space. Now suppose that we have a different cost function

$$\theta = x + 2y \quad \text{or} \quad x + 2y = \theta$$

FIGURE 3–3

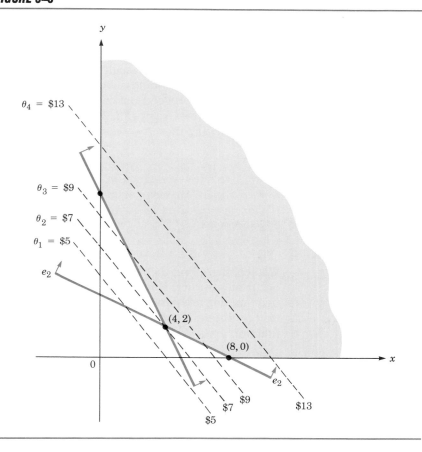

and solve it for y to obtain

$$y = -\frac{1}{2}x + \frac{\theta}{2}.$$

We see that all isocost lines have a slope of $-\frac{1}{2}$. Observe that the con-straining line

$$e_2: \quad x + 2y = 8 \quad \text{or} \quad y = -\frac{1}{2}x + 4$$

also has a slope of $-\frac{1}{2}$, so the isocost lines are parallel to e_2 and the innermost isocost line that contains points in the solution space is the line e_2 itself. Consequently not only will the corners $(4, 2)$ and $(8, 0)$ lead to minimum cost but any point on the segment joining these two points will also lead to the same minimum cost.

If we had analyzed the first maximization problem of Section 3.2 whose solution space is shown in Figure 3–1, we would have used *iso-profit* lines for the profit objective function

$$\theta = x + 0.5y$$

and would be led to a result like that obtained for Figure 3–3. In that case, though, we would investigate increasing values of θ which, of course, would proceed out into the first quadrant until we reached the maximum at the corner $B(2, 2)$.

Summarizing these two results, we can now observe that

> *An optimum (maximum or minimum) value of the objective function in the two-variable case occurs at one corner of the solution space, or at points along a line segment joining two corner points.*

We see, therefore, that a solution of a linear programming problem does occur at a corner. However, in the case where the isolines of the objective function are parallel to a constraint line, different algebraic steps can lead to different corner points that have the same value for the objective function.

> **Exercise.** Suppose the objective function in the Ace Rubber Company example of Section 3.2 were changed to $\theta_{max} = 4x + 18y$, subject to the same four constraints $2x + 9y \leq 36$, $4x + 3y \leq 42$, $x \geq 0$, $y \geq 0$. a) Find all the corners. b) Evaluate θ_{max} at each corner. c) What is the optimum? Answer: a) $(0, 0)$, $(0, 4)$, $(2\frac{1}{2}, 0)$, $(9, 2)$. b) $\theta(0, 0) = 0$, $\theta(0, 4) = 72$, $\theta(2\frac{1}{2}, 0) = 42$, $\theta(9, 2) = 72$. c) $\theta_{max} = 72$ at any point on the line segment joining $(0, 4)$ and $(9, 2)$.

As a consequence of the above discussion, we can in principle solve a two-variable linear programming problem by changing all the constraints to equalities, finding the intersection point of each pair of inequalities to obtain all the corners, checking the corners and substituting the permissible ones into the objective function, then choosing a corner that optimizes the objective function. However, even in the simple two-variable case, this procedure involves unnecessary work because there is no reason for finding corners that are not in the solution space. For example, the axes and the constraint lines in Figure 3–2 contain the intersections $(0, 0)$, $(0, 4)$, and $(5, 0)$, which are not corners of the solution space and therefore need not be calculated. An efficient method of proceeding in the two-variable case is to sketch the constraining lines, identify the solution space, and calculate only intersections that are on the boundary of the solution space.

Three-step graphical procedure. We now summarize the three-step graphical procedure which we have illustrated to this point:

> 1. Graph the constraints in the plane.
> 2. Use the graph as a visual aid to identify the corners and then determine the coordinates of these corners either from the graphing procedure or by the elimination procedure.
> 3. Evaluate the objective function at each corner. The largest value is the maximum (if a maximum exists) and the smallest value is the minimum (if a minimum exists). If two corners have the same optimal value, then the optimum occurs at every point on the line segment joining the respective corners.

Be alert, since a maximum and/or minimum need not exist. For example, in Figure 3–3 we saw that the minimum is $\theta(4, 2) = 7$ but there is no maximum. Of course, in Figure 3–1 the maximum is $\theta(4, 0) = 4$ and the minimum would be $\theta(0, 0) = 0$. The distinction between the two configurations is that Figure 3–1 is bounded in both optimizing directions, whereas Figure 3–3 is bounded in the minimizing direction *but not the maximizing direction.*

3.5 PROBLEM SET 3–1

Use the three-step graphical procedure to find the optimum, as required, assuming $x \geq 0$ and $y \geq 0$:

1. Subject to
$$4x + 3y \leq 24$$
$$x + 2y \leq 11,$$
find θ_{max} if:
a) $\theta = x + y$.
b) $\theta = x + 3y$.
c) $\theta = 3x + y$.
d) $\theta = 2x + 1.5y$.

2. Subject to
$$3x + 7y \leq 42$$
$$x + 5y \leq 22,$$
find θ_{max} if:
a) $\theta = 4x + 10y$.
b) $\theta = 2x - 3y$.
c) $\theta = -3x + 10y$.
d) $\theta = 1.5x + 3.5y$.

3. Subject to
$$2x + 3y \geq 12$$
$$5x + y \geq 17,$$
find θ_{min} if:
a) $\theta = x + 2y$.
b) $\theta = 5x + 7y$.
c) $\theta = 8x + y$.
d) $\theta = 5x + y$.

4. Subject to
$$4x + 5y \geq 30$$
$$3x + 2y \geq 19,$$
find θ_{min} if:
a) $\theta = 2x + 8y$.
b) $\theta = 4x + 2y$.
c) $\theta = 2x + 2y$.
d) $\theta = 8x + 10y$.

3.5 PROBLEM SET 3–1 (*continued*)

5. Subject to
$$3x + y \leq 9$$
$$x + y \leq 5$$
$$x \quad \leq 4$$
$$y \leq 4,$$
find θ_{max} if:
a) $\theta = 0.3x + 0.5y$.
b) $\theta = 2x + y$.
c) $\theta = 5x + y$.
d) $\theta = 3x + 3y$.

6. Subject to
$$x + y \leq 13$$
$$x + 2y \leq 22$$
$$2x + y \leq 20$$
$$x \quad \leq 4,$$
find θ_{max} if:
a) $\theta = 5x + 8y$.
b) $\theta = 4x - y$.
c) $\theta = -2x + 7y$.
d) $\theta = 5x + 10y$.

7. Subject to
$$4x + y \geq 16$$
$$3x + 2y \geq 24$$
$$-x + y \geq 0,$$
find θ_{min} if:
a) $\theta = 2x + y$.
b) $\theta = x + 2y$.
c) $\theta = 8x + 2y$.
d) $\theta = 6x + 4y$.

8. Subject to
$$x + 3y \geq 24$$
$$2x + y \geq 18$$
$$3x + 4y \geq 52,$$
find θ_{min} if:
a) $\theta = x + y$.
b) $\theta = 4x + 3y$.
c) $\theta = 6x + 2y$.
d) $\theta = 6x + 8y$.

---

9. Solve the Ace Rubber Company example of Section 3.2:

$$\theta_{max} = 10x + 8y$$

subject to

Machine A: $2x + 9y \leq 36$
Machine B: $4x + 3y \leq 42$
Nonnegativity: $x, y \geq 0$.

10. Solve the Pure Gasoline Company example of Section 3.3:

$$\theta_{min} = 1500x + 2400y$$

subject to

Super unleaded: $4x + y \geq 24$
Regular unleaded: $2x + 3y \geq 42$
Leaded: $x + 4y \geq 36$
Nonnegativity: $x, y \geq 0$.

11. Star Insulating Company manufactures two types of storm windows: Model H, the heavy duty, and Model R, the regular. Model H sells for $45 per window and costs $36 per window to make, whereas Model R sells for $35 per window and costs $27 per window to make. To make one Model H window, it requires 4 hours on Machine A and 3 hours on Machine B. On the other hand, to make one Model R window, it takes 5 hours on Machine A and 2 hours on Machine B. Production scheduling indicates that during the coming week Machine A will be available for at most 30 hours and Machine B for at most 19 hours. How many of each window should the company make in the coming week in order to maximize its profit? What is this maximum profit?

12. Safety Lock Company makes two kinds of locks: Model SS, the super safe, and Model S, the safe. Each Model SS lock sells for $24 and costs $19 to make, while each Model S lock sells for $18 and costs $15 to make. Each of the locks must be processed on two machines: Model SS requires 3 hours on Machine A and 2 hours on Machine B, whereas Model S requires 7 hours on A and 1 hour on B. During the coming week Machine A will be free for no more than 42 hours and Machine B for no more than 17 hours. Determine the number of each kind

3.5 PROBLEM SET 3–1 (*concluded*)

of lock to be made in the coming week in order for the company to maximize its profit. What is this maximum profit?

13. XYZ Steel Company manufactures two kinds of wrought-iron rails: Model E, the elegant, and Model D, the distinctive. Model E rails sell for $59 and cost $50 to make, whereas Model D rails sell for $48 and cost $41 to make. To make one Model E rail requires 2 hours on Machine A, 1 hour on Machine B, and 4 hours on Machine C. On the other hand, to make one Model D rail requires 1 hour on A, 2 hours on B, and 5 hours on C. Production scheduling indicates that during the coming week Machine A will be available for at most 30 hours, Machine B for at most 24 hours, and Machine C for at most 72 hours. Find the number of each kind of rail to be made in the coming week in order for the company to maximize its profit. What is this maximum profit? At the maximum, which machines, if any, are not fully utilized?

14. A special food for athletes is to be developed from two foods: Food X and Food Y. The new food is to be designed so that it contains at least 16 milligrams of vitamin A, at least 20 milligrams of vitamin B, and at least 12 milligrams of vitamin C. Each pound of Food X costs $1.50 and contains 1 milligram of vitamin A, 5 milligrams of vita-

min B, and 1 milligram of vitamin C. On the other hand, each pound of Food Y costs $2.50 and contains 2 milligrams of A, 1 milligram of B, and 1 milligram of C. How many pounds of each food should be used in the mixture in order to meet the above requirements at a minimum cost? What is this minimum cost?

15. Repeat Problem 14 if, in addition, the amount of Food Y in the mixture must be no more than one-half the amount of Food X.

16. Strong Steel Company operates two steel mills with different production capacities. Mill I can produce 1,000 tons per day of AAA steel, 3,000 tons per day of AA steel, and 5,000 tons per day of A steel. Mill F can produce 2,000 tons per day of each grade of steel. The company has made a contract with the construction firm to provide 24,000 tons of AAA steel, 32,000 tons of AA steel, and 40,000 tons of A steel. For each of the following costs, determine the number of days the company should operate each mill in order to meet the terms of the above contract most economically, the minimum cost, and also what grade(s) of steel would be overproduced:
a) The cost of running Mill I is $1,400 per day and Mill F is $1,000 per day.
b) The cost of running Mill I is $1,500 per day and Mill F is $3,000 per day.

3.6 MIX OF CONSTRAINTS

Up to this point, all our examples have had either all "≤" constraints (ignoring the nonnegativity constraints) or all "≥" constraints. In practice, problems are not restricted to these forms and, in addition, it is possible to have "=" constraints. Our first example will illustrate a problem which has a mix of "≤" and "≥" constraints.

Recall the Pure Gasoline Company example and exercise of Section 3.3 where, subject to the constraints

$$
\begin{array}{lrl}
\text{Super unleaded:} & 4x + y & \geq 24 \\
\text{Regular unleaded:} & 2x + 3y & \geq 42 \\
\text{Leaded:} & x + 4y & \geq 36 \\
\text{Refinery A:} & x & \leq 14
\end{array}
$$

$$\text{Refinery B:} \qquad y \le 14$$
$$\text{Nonnegativity:} \qquad x, y \ge 0,$$

we wanted to minimize two objective functions

a) $\theta = 1500x + 2400y$
b) $\theta = 1600x + 2400y.$

We shall solve the two parts of the problem together by using the three-step graphical procedure. Figure 3–4 shows the solution space for the system of constraints.

The boundary lines are plotted in the usual manner, using intercepts. Of course, the lines obtained by plotting equations e_4 and e_5 are parallel to the y-axis and x-axis, respectively.

Using the symbol 1#2 to designate the corner where lines e_1 and e_2 intersect, and similarly for the other corners, we see from Figure 3–4 that the only corners A, B, C, D, and E that are part of the solution space are 1#5, 4#5, 3#4, 2#3, and 1#2. The coordinates of these corners are found in the usual manner by elimination and substitution. Thus, for 1#5,

---

FIGURE 3–4

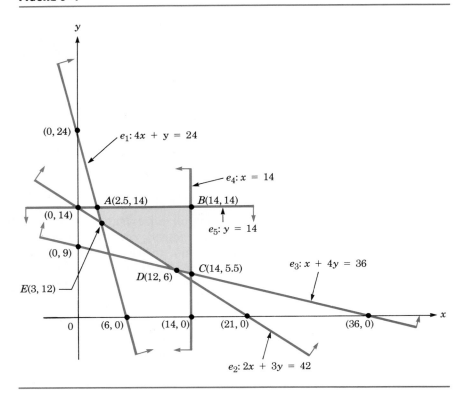

$$e_1: \quad 4x + y = 24$$
$$e_5: \qquad\quad y = 14.$$

Substituting e_5 into e_1, we see that the corner 1#5 is the point $(2.5, 14)$.

Exercise. Find the coordinates of the corners 4#5 and 3#4.
Answer: $(14, 14)$ and $(14, 5.5)$.

The corners, their coordinates, and values of the two objective functions are shown in Table 3–5. Notice that for (a), $\theta_{min} = \$32{,}400$ when Refinery A is operated 12 days and Refinery B is operated 6 days. On the other hand for (b), $\theta_{min} = \$33{,}600$ at any point on the line segment from $(12, 6)$ to $(3, 12)$.

For all practical purposes, there are not an infinite number of solutions in the last example. That is, even though the minimum occurs along an entire line segment, it is impractical for a refinery to operate only part of a working day. Thus, the choice is limited to those solution points with integral coordinates on the line segment from $(12, 6)$ to $(3, 12)$. One such point is $(9, 8)$.

Exercise. Are there any other points with integral coordinates on the line segment? Answer: Yes, the point $(6, 10)$.

One last point before we leave this example. What about the question of any overproduction of gasoline? To answer this in (a), for example, we simply substitute the optimum point $(12, 6)$ back into the constraints and check for any overage. Thus for super unleaded,

$$4(12) + 1(6) = 54,$$

which is larger than our requirement of 24,000 gallons by $54 - 24 = 30{,}000$ gallons. Note that in practice any overproduction should be taken into consideration in the final decision-making process. For example, if

TABLE 3–5

Corner	Coordinates	Objective Function, θ	
		1500x + 2400y	1600x + 2400y
A: 1#5	(2.5, 14)	37,350	37,600
B: 4#5	(14, 14)	54,600	56,000
C: 3#4	(14, 5.5)	34,200	35,600
D: 2#3	(12, 6)	32,400*	33,600*
E: 1#2	(3, 12)	33,300	33,600*

*Indicates the minimum.

the excess can be utilized, then this fact should be used to *reduce* the cost function appropriately. On the other hand, if the excess cannot be utilized, then the cost of storage should be *added* to the cost function.

Exercise.   Are either regular unleaded or leaded gasoline overproduced?   Answer: No, since $2(12) + 3(6) = 42$ and $1(12) + 4(6) = 36$.

The above results concerning overproduction can be observed directly from Figure 3–4 by noting that the corner $(12, 6)$ lies *precisely on* e_2 and e_3, so that regular unleaded and leaded are not overproduced. Of course, $(12, 6)$ lies *above* e_1 so that super unleaded is overproduced.

Exercise.   What grades of gasoline are overproduced for part (b) of the example? Answer: At $(12, 6)$, super unleaded is overproduced. At $(3, 12)$, leaded is overproduced. At any other point on the line segment from $(12, 6)$ to $(3, 12)$ both super unleaded and leaded are overproduced.

Our next example illustrates a problem that has an " $=$ " constraint.

Example. Klean Soap Company wishes to make a new detergent from two of its current soaps: Soap A and Soap B. The company wants the new detergent to contain at least 20 ounces of cleaning ingredient D. Each pound of Soap A costs $0.20 and contains five ounces of D, whereas each pound of Soap B costs $0.25 and contains one ounce of D. Furthermore, for ecological reasons, the amount of Soap A must be no more than that of Soap B. Finally, the new mixture must weigh exactly 12 pounds. How many pounds of each soap should be used in the mixture in order to meet the above requirements at a minimum cost? What is this minimum cost?

In this example, we wish to determine the respective number of pounds of Soaps A and B to be mixed together to minimize the company's cost associated with making a new mixture that not only satisfies the cleaning ingredient and ecological constraints, but also weighs precisely 12 pounds. Thus we assign our variables as follows: We let

$$x = \text{Number of pounds of Soap A in the mixture}$$

and

$$y = \text{Number of pounds of Soap B in the mixture.}$$

Next since Soap A costs $0.20 per pound and Soap B costs $0.25 per pound, the cost of the new mixture will be

$$\$0.20x + \$0.25y;$$

so that the company wants to minimize the objective or cost function

$$\theta = 0.2x + 0.25y.$$

Turning now to our constraints, we first see that the new detergent is to contain at least 20 ounces of cleaning ingredient D. Since each pound of Soap A (x) contains 5 ounces of D while each pound of Soap B (y) contains 1 ounce of D, we must have

$$(5 \text{ ounces/lb of A}) \cdot (x \text{ lbs of A}) + (1 \text{ ounce/lb of B}) \cdot (y \text{ lbs of B})$$
$$\geq 20 \text{ ounces}$$

or simply

$$5x + y \geq 20.$$

Also, since the amount of Soap A must be no more than that of Soap B, we get

$$x \leq y$$

or

$$x - y \leq 0.$$

For reasons that will become clear later, we always write our constraints with all the variables on the left-hand side and with the constant on the right-hand side. Furthermore, we require that the constant on the right-hand side be nonnegative (i.e., ≥ 0). Of course, when the constant is negative, we can transform it into a nonnegative number simply by multiplying the constraint through by -1 (recall that in doing this, we must change the direction of the inequality).

Lastly, since the mixture is to weigh exactly 12 pounds, we have

$$x + y = 12.$$

Adding the nonnegativity constraints, then, the linear programming problem is:

Minimize the cost function

$$\theta = 0.2x + 0.25y$$

subject to the constraints

Ingredient D:	$5x + y$	≥ 20
Ecology:	$x - y$	≤ 0
Weight:	$x + y$	$= 12$
Nonnegativity:	x, y	$\geq 0.$

Figure 3–5 shows the solution space for the system of constraints.

FIGURE 3–5

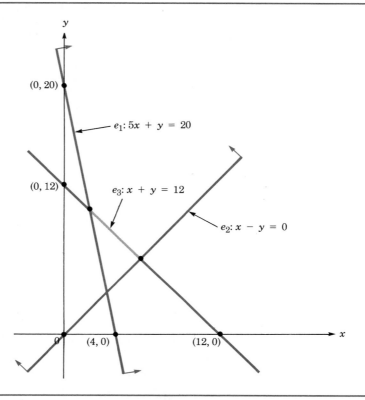

Note that our third constraint is an *equality* so that our solution space is limited to points on this line itself. From Figure 3–5, we see that there are two corners, 1#3 and 2#3. Thus we get the results shown in Table 3–6, from which we see that the minimum cost is $2.70 when six pounds of each soap are mixed together to form the new product.

TABLE 3–6

Corner	Coordinates	$\theta = 0.2x + 0.25y$
1#3	(2, 10)	2.9
2#3	(6, 6)	2.7*

*Indicates the minimum.

> **Exercise.** Would there be any change in the corner points if the weight constraint were changed so that it were "no more than 12 pounds?" Would there be a new minimum? Answer: Yes, there would be an additional corner at (10/3, 10/3), which would represent a new minimum cost of $2.17.

3.7 PROBLEM SET 3–2

Use the three-step graphical procedure to find the optimum, as required, assuming $x \geq 0$ and $y \geq 0$:

1. Subject to
$$2x + y \geq 8$$
$$6x + 10y \leq 60,$$
find θ_{min} if:
a) $\theta = 3x + 2y$.
b) $\theta = 10x + y$.

2. Subject to
$$0.15x + 0.10y \geq 15$$
$$x + y \leq 120$$
$$0.4x \leq 32,$$
find θ_{min} if:
$$\theta = 0.20x + 0.15y.$$

3. Subject to
$$2x + 4y \geq 36$$
$$x + y \leq 12,$$
find θ_{max} and θ_{min} if:
a) $\theta = 3x + 5y$.
b) $\theta = 6x + 2y$.
c) $\theta = 3x + 3y$.

4. Subject to
$$2x + 4y \geq 36$$
$$x + y \leq 12$$
$$-2x + y \geq 0,$$
find θ_{max} and θ_{min} if:
a) $\theta = 3x + 5y$.
b) $\theta = 6x + 2y$.
c) $\theta = 3x + 3y$.

5. Subject to
$$2x + 4y \geq 36$$
$$x + y \leq 12$$
$$x - 2y \leq 0,$$
find θ_{max} and θ_{min} if:

a) $\theta = 3x + 5y$.
b) $\theta = 6x + 2y$.
c) $\theta = 3x + 3y$.

6. Subject to
$$2x + 4y \geq 36$$
$$x + y \leq 12$$
$$x - 2y \geq 0,$$
find θ_{max} and θ_{min} if:
a) $\theta = 3x + 5y$.
b) $\theta = 6x + 2y$.
c) $\theta = 3x + 3y$.

7. Subject to
$$x + 3y \leq 24$$
$$x + y \geq 10$$
$$2x + y = 18,$$
find θ_{max} and θ_{min} if:
a) $\theta = 5x + 2y$.
b) $\theta = x + 7y$.
c) $\theta = 4x + 2y$.

8. Subject to
$$x + 3y \leq 24$$
$$x + y \geq 10$$
$$2x + y = 18$$
$$4x - 3y = 16,$$
find θ_{max} and θ_{min} if:
a) $\theta = 5x + 2y$.
b) $\theta = x + 7y$.
c) $\theta = 4x + 2y$.

9. Subject to
$$x + 3y \leq 24$$
$$x + y \geq 10$$
$$2x + y = 18$$

3.7 PROBLEM SET 3–2 (concluded)

$5x + y = 20$,
find θ_{max} and θ_{min} if:
a) $\theta = 5x + 2y$.
b) $\theta = x + 7y$.
c) $\theta = 4x + 2y$.

10. Subject to
    $2x + 3y \leq 24$

$2x - y \leq 8$
$-2x + 3y \leq 12$,
find θ_{max} and θ_{min} if:
a) $\theta = 6x + y - 7$.
b) $\theta = -3x + 7y + 10$.
c) $\theta = -x - 3y + 25$.
d) $\theta = 8x - 4y + 18$.

11. Strong Steel Company operates two steel mills with different production capacities. Mill I can produce 1,000 tons per day of AAA steel, 3,000 tons per day of AA steel, and 5,000 tons per day of A steel. Mill F can produce 2,000 tons per day of each grade of steel. The company has made a contract with the construction firm to provide 24,000 tons of AAA steel, 32,000 tons of AA steel, and 40,000 tons of A steel in no more than 10 days. For each of the following costs, determine the number of days the company should operate each mill in order to meet the terms of the above contract most economically, the minimum cost, and also what grade(s) of steel would be overproduced:
    a) The cost of running Mill I is $1,400 per day and Mill F is $1,000 per day.
    b) The cost of running Mill I is $1,500 per day and Mill F is $3,000 per day.

12. ABC Dairy Company wishes to make a new cheese from two of its current cheeses: Cheese X and Cheese Y. The mixture is to weigh no more than four pounds and is to contain at least six ounces of the sharpness ingredient S. Each pound of X costs $4 and contains three ounces of S, whereas each pound of Y costs $1 and contains one ounce of S. How many pounds of each cheese should be used in the mixture in order to meet the above requirements at a minimum cost? What is this minimum cost?

13. Repeat Problem 12 if, in addition, the amount of Cheese Y cannot exceed the amount of Cheese X by more than one pound.

14. Slim Soda Company wishes to make a new drink from two of its current sodas: Soda A and Soda B. The new drink is to contain at least six ounces of the taste ingredient T. Each quart of A costs $0.20 and contains one ounce of T, whereas each quart of B costs $0.30 and contains three ounces of T. Furthermore, for dietary reasons, the amount of B must not exceed the amount of A. Finally, the volume of the new drink must be exactly four quarts. How many quarts of each soda should be used in the mixture in order to meet the above requirements at a minimum cost? What is this minimum cost?

15. Repeat Problem 14 if, instead of requiring that the volume of the new drink be exactly four quarts, we require that it be no more than six quarts.

3.8 MORE THAN TWO VARIABLES

In principle, a system in three variables can be represented graphically because linear equations in three variables are planes. However, sketching planes that are in three-dimensional space on a flat (two-dimensional) piece of paper and trying to identify the solution space is too complex to be a practical method of eliminating intersections that are not in the solution space. Of course, it is impossible even to graph systems in more than three variables. In Chapter 5, we shall present a systematic procedure that provides a permissible corner to start with and rules that show how to go to another permissible corner that *improves* the objective function. When no permissible corner improving the solution exists, the current corner provides the optimum value. Those who plan to study Chapter 5 need only scan the remainder of this chapter to see first the need for a procedure that eliminates the extensive computation of non-permissible corners and, second, to fix in mind the key principle that if a system has m constraints on n variables ($m < n$) in addition to the non-negativity constraints on the variables, then at every corner *at least* $(n - m)$ of the variables have the value zero.

First, consider our chair factory example of Section 3.2, which was

Maximize the objective function

$$\theta = x + 0.5y$$

subject to the constraints

Department I $\quad i_1$: $\quad x + \ y \leq 4$
Department II $\quad i_2$: $\quad x + 2y \leq 6$
Nonnegativity i_3, i_4: $\qquad x, y \geq 0.$

We can see from Figure 3–1 that there are six corners O, A, B, C, D, and E, of which two (D and E) are not in the solution space. If we did not have the graph available as a visual aid, we could determine these facts as follows: Each corner is the solution of a two-by-two system of equations. Since there are four equations in all (e_1, e_2, e_3, and e_4), the number of corners can be found using the formula for counting the number of combinations of four equations taken two at a time. This is

$$\text{Number of corners} = \frac{4!}{2!2!},$$

where the factorial symbol, !, means, for example,

$$4! = 4(3)(2)(1)$$
$$2! = 2(1)$$

so

$$\text{Number of corners} = \frac{24}{(2)(2)} = 6.$$

In general, if there are c constraints (including nonnegativity) and n variables, then

$$\text{Number of corners} = \frac{c!}{n!(n - c)!}.$$

Exercise. How many corners would there be if the problem had 5 constraints and 2 variables? Answer: 10.

TABLE 3–7

Corner	Coordinates	Check	$\theta = x + 0.5y$
1#2	$B(2, 2)$	Yes	3
1#3	$E(0, 4)$	No	
1#4	$C(4, 0)$	Yes	4*
2#3	$A(0, 3)$	Yes	1.5
2#4	$D(6, 0)$	No	
3#4	$O(0, 0)$	Yes	0

*Indicates the maximum.

The results of calculating and checking the six corners in our example are shown in Table 3–7. Note that each pair of equations is solved and then the resultant solution is checked against the remaining constraints. For example, at 1#4 we check $C(4, 0)$ in i_2 and i_3:

$$i_2: \quad x + 2y = 4 + 2(0) = 4 \leq 6$$
$$i_3: \qquad\qquad x = 4 \geq 0,$$

so that C is a permissible corner. However, at 1#3 we see that for $E(0, 4)$

$$i_2: \quad x + 2y = 0 + 2(4) = 8 \not\leq 6,$$

so that E is not a permissible corner.

Exercise. Which constraint does $D(6, 0)$ not satisfy? Answer: i_1.

Our next example illustrates the situation where the number of constraints (not counting nonnegativity) is less than the number of variables.

Example. Solve the following three-variable linear programming problem:

Minimize

$$\theta = x + 4y + 3z$$

subject to:

$$i_1: \quad 0.5x + y + 0.2z \geq 600$$
$$i_2: \quad 2x + 3y + z \leq 2000$$
$$i_3, i_4, i_5: \qquad x, y, z \geq 0.$$

The problem has three variables, so each corner is the solution of a three-by-three system of equations. For example, writing the equality part of i_1, i_2, and i_3, we have

Corner 1#2#3
$$e_1: \quad 0.5x + y + 0.2z = 600$$

$$e_2: \quad 2x + 3y + \quad z = 2000$$
$$e_3: \quad x \qquad\qquad = \quad 0.$$

Substituting $e_3(x = 0)$ into e_1 and e_2, we have

$$y + 0.2z = \quad 600$$
$$3y + \quad z = 2000,$$

which we can solve for z to get

$$z = 500.$$

Substituting $z = 500$, we find $y = 500$, so the desired corner is $(0, 500, 500)$. These coordinates satisfy all inequalities, i_1 through i_5.
  On the other hand,

$$\text{Corner } 1\#3\#4$$
$$e_1: \quad 0.5x + y + 0.2z = 600$$
$$e_2: \qquad x \qquad\qquad = \quad 0$$
$$e_3: \qquad\qquad y \qquad = \quad 0.$$

Substitution of $x = y = 0$ into e_1 yields $z = 3000$. However, $(0, 0, 3000)$ does not satisfy i_2 and so is not a permissible corner at which to evaluate the objective function.

Exercise. Find and check the corner $1\#2\#4$. Answer: $x = 2000$, $y = 0$, $z = -2000$ does not check because z is negative, contrary to constraint i_5.

For the system at hand we have

$$c = 5 \text{ constraints}$$
$$n = 3 \text{ variables}$$
$$c - n = 5 - 3 = 2,$$

so that

$$\text{Number of corners} = \frac{5!}{3!2!} = \frac{5(4)(3)(2)(1)}{(3)(2)(1)(2)(1)} = 10.$$

The results of calculating and checking these ten corners are shown in Table 3–8. The desired minimum is seen to be 2000 and occurs at $x = 400$, $y = 400$, and $z = 0$.

  In Table 3–8, each corner is the solution of a three-by-three system of equations because there are $n = 3$ variables, and each set of coordinates has *at least one zero value*. The reason for this is that, of the total number of constraints, $c = 5$, three of them are nonnegativity constraints that become

$$x = 0, \quad y = 0, \quad z = 0$$

TABLE 3–8

Corner	Coordinates	Check	$\theta = x + 4y + 3z$
1#2#3	(0, 500, 500)	Yes	3500
1#2#4	(2000, 0, −2000)	No	
1#2#5	(400, 400, 0)	Yes	2000*
1#3#4	(0, 0, 3000)	No	
1#3#5	(0, 600, 0)	Yes	2400
1#4#5	(1200, 0, 0)	No	
2#3#4	(0, 0, 2000)	No	
2#3#5	(0, 2000/3, 0)	Yes	8000/3
2#4#5	(1000, 0, 0)	No	
3#4#5	(0, 0, 0)	No	

*Indicates the minimum.

when written as equalities. The number of remaining constraints is $n = 2$, and written as equalities these are

$$0.5x + y + 0.2z = 600$$
$$2x + 3y + z = 2000.$$

Clearly, any three-by-three system formed from the five equalities has to include at least one of the first three, $x = 0$, $y = 0$, $z = 0$, and this accounts for the presence of at least one zero in the coordinates of every corner shown in Table 3–8. In linear programming, nonnegativity constraints are always assumed to be present. Consequently, when we say that the problem has $m = 2$ constraints on $n = 3$ variables, it is to be understood that there are three nonnegativity constraints and $m = 2$ means two constraints in addition to nonnegativity. In our example,

$$n = 3, \quad m = 2, \quad n - m = 3 - 2 = 1$$

tells us that every corner will have *at least* one zero coordinate. Similarly, every corner for a problem that has $m = 4$ constraints on $n = 7$ variables will have zero values for at least three variables because

$$n - m = 7 - 4 = 3.$$

The fact just illustrated is a key principle in the procedure to be developed in Chapter 5, so we highlight it here.

> *If a linear programming problem has* m *constraints[2] (not counting nonnegativity constraints) on* n *variables, where* n ≥ m, *then the coordinates of every corner of the solution space will contain at least* n − m *zeros.*

---

[2] This assumes the constraints are linearly independent, that is, that no constraint is a linear combination of other constraints. If, for example, one constraint is a linear combination of two others (in the simplest case, one is a constant times another), this constraint is not counted in specifying m.

> **Exercise.** A linear programming problem has a *total* number of 16 constraints on $n = 10$ variables. a) How many nonnegativity constraints are there? b) What is m? c) How many zeros will every corner have? Answer: a) 10. b) $m = 6$. c) At least 4.

3.9 PROBLEM SET 3–3

1. Find θ_{max}, and write the coordinates of the point at which the maximum occurs if
$\theta = 0.5x + y + 0.2z$
$x + 4y + 3z \leq 1800$
$2x + 3y + z \leq 2000$
$x, y, z \geq 0.$

2. Find θ_{min} if: $\theta = 0.4x + 1.2y + 0.5z$
$x + 2y + 3z \geq 1200$
$2x + y + z \geq 600$
$x, y, z \geq 0.$

3. Find θ_{max} if: $\theta = 1.5x + 2.5y + 2z$
$x + 1.5y \leq 4$
$y + 2.5z \leq 5$
$1.5x + 5y + z \leq 7.5$
$x, y, z \geq 0.$

4. Find θ_{min} if: $\theta = 4x + 2y + 3z$
$x + 2y + 4z \geq 29$
$3x + 2y + z \geq 23$
$10x + 4y + 3z \geq 62$
$x, y, z \geq 0.$

5. A wholesaler has 9,600 feet of space available, and $5,000 he can spend to buy merchandise of types A, B, and C. Type A costs $4 per unit and requires 4 feet of storage space in the warehouse. B costs $10 per unit and requires 8 feet of space. C costs $5 per unit and requires 6 feet of space. Only 500 units of type A are available to the wholesaler. Assuming that the wholesaler expects to make a profit of $1 on each unit of A he buys and stocks, $3 per unit on B, and $2 per unit on C, how many units of each should he buy and stock in order to maximize his profit?

6. A diet is to contain at least 10 ounces of nutrient P, 12 ounces of R, and 20 ounces of S. These nutrients are to be obtained from foods A, B, and C. Each pound of A costs 3 cents and contains 4 ounces of P, 2 ounces of R, and 1 ounce of S. Each pound of B costs 6 cents and contains 1 ounce of P, 3 ounces of R, and 3 ounces of S. Each pound of C costs 9 cents and contains 1 ounce of P, 1 ounce of R, and 5 ounces of S. How many pounds of each food should be purchased if the stated dietary requirements are to be met at minimum cost?

7. Products A, B, and C are sold door-to-door. A costs $3 per unit, takes 10 minutes to sell (on the average), and costs $0.50 to deliver to a customer. B costs $5, takes 15 minutes to sell, and is left with the customer at the time of sale. C costs $4, takes 12 minutes to sell, and costs $1 to deliver. During any week, a salesman is allowed to draw up to $500 worth of A, B, and C (at cost) and he is allowed delivery expenses not to exceed $75. If a salesman's selling time is not expected to exceed 30 hours (1,800 minutes) in a week, and if the salesman's profit (net after all expenses) is $1 each on a unit of A or B and $2 on a unit of C, what combination of sales of A, B, and C will lead to maximum profit, and what is this maximum profit?

8. AAA Electrical Company makes three kinds of automobile batteries: Model S, the super, Model N, the normal, and Model E, the economy. Each battery must be processed on three machines: Machine I, Machine II, and Machine III. To make one Model S battery requires 2 hours on I, 1 hour on II, and 3 hours on III; whereas to make one Model N battery requires 2 hours on I, 4 hours on

3.9 PROBLEM SET 3–3 (*concluded*)

II, and 1 hour on III; while to make one Model E battery requires 5 hours on I, 2 hours on II, and 3 hours on III. Production scheduling indicates that during the coming week Machine I will be available for at most 40 hours, Machine II for at most 26 hours, and Machine III for at most 27 hours. If the company makes an $8 profit on each Model S battery, a $6 profit on each Model N battery, and a $12 profit on each Model E battery, how many of each kind should be made in the coming week in order to maximize profit? What is this maximum profit?

9. A special food for athletes is to be developed from three foods: Food X, Food Y, and Food Z. The new food is to contain at least 66 milligrams of vitamin A, at least 48 milligrams of vitamin B, at least 40 milligrams of vitamin C, and at least 58 milligrams of vitamin D. Each pound of Food X costs $1.50 and contains 2 milligrams of vitamin A, 4 milligrams of vitamin B, 1 milligram of vitamin C, and 6 milligrams of vitamin D. On the other hand, each pound of Food Y costs $2.50 and contains 9 milligrams of A, 3 milligrams of B, 4 milligrams of C, and 2 milligrams of D; whereas each pound of Food Z costs $2.00 and contains 7 milligrams of A, 2 milligrams of B, 8 milligrams of C, and 1 milligram of D. How many pounds of each food should be used in the mixture in order to meet the above requirements at a minimum cost? What is this minimum cost?

10. Safety Lock Company makes three kinds of locks: Model SS, the super safe, Model S,

the safe, and Model O, the economy. Each Model SS lock sells for $16 and costs $11 to make, whereas each Model S lock sells for $9 and costs $6 to make, and each Model O lock sells for $7 and costs $3 to make. Each of the locks must be processed on five machines: Model SS requires 3 hours on Machine A, 1 hour on Machine B, 2 hours on Machine C, 4 hours on Machine D, and 3 hours on Machine E. On the other hand, Model S requires 2 hours on A, 3 hours on B, 1 hour on C, 5 hours on D, and 4 hours on E; while Model O requires 1 hour on A, 2 hours on B, 2 hours on C, 3 hours on D, and 4 hours on E. During the coming week Machine A will be free for no more than 23 hours, Machine B for no more than 26 hours, Machine C for no more than 19 hours, Machine D for no more than 49 hours, and Machine E for no more than 45 hours. Determine the number of each kind of lock to be made in the coming week in order for the company to maximize its profit. What is this maximum profit?

11. a) Write a computer program that will locate all the permissible corners of the solution space of a linear programming problem with two variables, evaluate each of these corners at any given objective function, and then print the associated optimum.
    b) Run the program in (a) for Problems 1 through 10 of Problem Set 3–1.
    c) Run the program in (a) for Problems 1 through 10 of Problem Set 3–2.

3.10 MORE ON FORMULATION

As we have already seen, one of the most important phases in the solution of a linear programming problem is the formulation, which translates the verbiage into an objective function together with a set of constraints. The more complicated the problem, of course, the more involved the formulation itself. Our next example will help to illustrate this fact.

Example. A certain professor likes to give weekly quizzes composed of multiple-choice questions divided into two groups, A and B. By closely observing the format of the first few quizzes, one rather clever student has determined that although there are always 30 questions of each type, the student is allowed to answer at most 40 total questions. In addition, the student is prohibited from answering more than 25 A questions but is required to answer at least as many B questions as A questions. Furthermore, while each A question counts two points, each B question counts three points. Lastly, the student is always restricted by having the number of B questions answered not exceed the number of A questions answered by more than 8; and, indeed, is penalized ½ point each for the number of B questions answered over the number of A questions answered. After some deliberation, the student has worked out a scheme for the number of each kind of question that should be answered to attain the best possible grade and finds that there are five alternative combinations. What is the scheme and what will be the grade?

In this example, we clearly want to maximize the student's grade. Thus, we first let

$$x = \text{Number of A questions that the student answers}$$

and

$$y = \text{Number of B questions that the student answers.}$$

Now since each A question counts two points while each B question counts three points, the student's grade is given by

$$2x + 3y.$$

However, the student is penalized ½ point each for the number of B questions answered over the number of A questions answered. In other words, we must deduct ½ point for the difference between y and x. This penalty, of course, is meaningful only if $y \geq x$, which we will see later on is actually one of the constraints. Thus the goal is to maximize the objective or grade function

$$2x + 3y - \left(\frac{1}{2}\right)(y - x)$$

or simply

$$\theta = 2.5x + 2.5y.$$

Exercise. What would the objective function be if the student were awarded one point for the number of B questions answered in excess of the number of A questions answered?
Answer: $\theta_{\max} = x + 4y$.

Turning now to our constraints, we first see that there are always 30 questions of each type and that the student is allowed to answer at most 40 questions. These conditions give rise to the three constraints

$$x \quad\ \leq 30, \tag{1}$$
$$y \leq 30, \tag{2}$$
$$x + y \leq 40. \tag{3}$$

Next we see that the student is prohibited from answering more than 25 A questions but is required to answer at least as many B questions as A questions. Thus we have the two additional constraints

$$x \leq 25 \tag{4}$$
$$y \geq x.$$

As stated in Section 3.6, we rewrite the latter constraint with all the variables on the left-hand side to get

$$-x + y \geq 0. \tag{5}$$

(Alternatively, of course, this constraint could have been written as $x - y \leq 0$ simply by multiplying through by -1.)

Lastly we see that the student is always restricted by having the number of B questions that he answers not exceed the number of A questions by more than 8. This gives rise to the constraint

$$y \leq x + 8,$$

which, again, we rewrite as

$$-x + y \leq 8. \tag{6}$$

Exercise. Can we rewrite the last constraint in the form $x - y \geq -8$? Why? Answer: No, since we want the constant on the right-hand side to be nonnegative.

Adding the nonnegativity constraints, then, the linear programming problem becomes

Maximize the grade function

$$\theta = 2.5x + 2.5y$$

subject to the constraints

$$x \quad\ \leq 30 \tag{1}$$
$$y \leq 30 \tag{2}$$
$$x + y \leq 40 \tag{3}$$
$$x \quad\ \leq 25 \tag{4}$$

$$-x + y \geq 0 \qquad\qquad (5)$$
$$-x + y \leq 8 \qquad\qquad (6)$$
$$x, y \geq 0. \qquad\qquad (7), (8)$$

Although we could stop with the formulation at this point, an inspection of the constraints will show that some are *redundant* or unnecessary. It would clearly simplify the solution process if these redundancies were removed.

Examining the constraints, then, we first see that constraint (1), $x \leq 30$, is clearly unnecessary because of constraint (4), $x \leq 25$.

Secondly constraint (4), $x \leq 25$, is itself unnecessary because of constraint (3), $x + y \leq 40$, together with constraint (5), $-x + y \geq 0$ (or $y \geq x$). In other words, if the two variables x and y can sum to no more than 40 and if y must be at least as large as x, then x must in fact be no larger than 20.

Thirdly, constraint (2), $y \leq 30$, is unnecessary because of constraint (6), $-x + y \leq 8$ (or $y \leq x + 8$), together with constraint (3), $x + y \leq 40$. This last redundancy is not so evident, but becomes clear upon some reflection of the numbers involved or alternatively upon adding the two constraints; i.e.,

$$
\begin{aligned}
y &\leq & x &+ 8 \\
y &\leq & -x &+ 40 \\
\hline
2y &\leq & & 48
\end{aligned}
$$

which means, of course, that

$$y \leq 24.$$

Thus, in summary, the linear programming problem is:

Maximize the grade function

$$\theta = 2.5x + 2.5y$$

subject to the constraints

$$x + y \leq 40$$
$$-x + y \geq 0$$
$$-x + y \leq 8$$
$$x, y \geq 0.$$

Exercise. Solve the latter problem by the graphical procedure. How many practical solutions are there? Why? Answer: The maximum is 100 at any point on the line segment from (16, 24) to (20, 20). Only (16, 24), (17, 23), (18, 22), (19, 21), and (20, 20) are practical since the student cannot answer a fractional number of questions.

3.11 PROBLEM SET 3–4

1. To introduce its new economy automobile to the public, the marketing department of Guarantee Motors, Inc., has decided to sponsor a 90-minute television special featuring the world-famous comedian I. M. Hilarious. From past experience, it is known that to reach a maximum number of viewers, a delicate balance must be maintained between the number of minutes devoted to commercials and the number of minutes that the comedian is on the air. In fact, although Hilarious' popularity is such that he attracts 15,000 viewers for every minute that he is on the air, any television program tends to lose about 150 viewers for each minute devoted to commercials. Furthermore, the time devoted to commercials should be no more than 25 percent of the time Hilarious is on the air. On the other hand, the president of Guarantee insists that the commercial time be at least 20 percent of the comedian's time. Under all of these conditions, what is the optimum strategy for allotting the 90 minutes between commercials and Hilarious? What is the maximum number of viewers that Guarantee will reach?

2. Lifetime Siding Company sells both aluminum and vinyl siding for homes with a 30-year guarantee on all materials and labor. The company has to order its stock at least six months in advance, but must pay the manufacturer within fifteen days of delivery. Since business in the current economic times is slow, management wants to place its next order very carefully so as to minimize its cost. Aluminum siding costs the company $75 per square (10-foot by 10-foot section), while vinyl siding costs the company $100 per square. The company has to carry the inventory in stock until sold and has determined that the carrying cost is $5 per square (aluminum or vinyl) for the average number of squares in the inventory (the average being typically one-half of the number originally acquired). On the basis of past experience, the sales department of the company has projected that its needs for the period to be covered by the order will call for at most 4,000 but at least 2,000 total squares. Furthermore, no more than 3,000 but at least 1,000 squares of aluminum will be needed; and, in addition, the number of vinyl squares should be at least 20 percent of the total.
    a) What order should the company place and what will be its cost?
    b) If the company had, by mistake, maximized its cost, what would the results be?

3. In the last days before the election, the political prospects of I. M. Hopeful look rather dim unless he can reach a very large part of his constituency immediately. His campaign manager has hit upon an idea of staging a rally highlighted by performances by the leading male and female singers in the area. Unfortunately, there are a few complications. First of all, the two singers dislike each other intensely and so will not do a song together but only sing solos. In addition, the female singer insists on having at least equal time, while the male singer will not perform for less than 30 minutes. Also, the rally is to last two hours with at least 20 minutes devoted to political speeches. Finally, the personalities of the two singers are such that they not only attract large audiences, but also tend to drive some people away. In fact, for every minute the male singer is on the stage alone he ordinarily draws 300 people, while for every minute the female singer is on stage alone she ordinarily draws 200 people. However, the male singer's presence in the program drives away 10 percent of the people who would have come to see the female singer perform solo, whereas the female singer's presence in the program drives away 5 percent of the people who would have come to see the male singer perform solo.
    a) How should the two hours be divided

3.11 PROBLEM SET 3–4 (continued)

up to maximize the number of people drawn to the rally? What is this maximum number?

b) If the male singer charges $100 per minute and the female singer charges $90 per minute, what is the cost of the results of (a)?

c) If the campaign manager decided to minimize the total cost rather than maximize the size of the audience, how would the time be divided up and what would the cost be?

4. Premium Brewing Company has to decide the optimal mix of two blending processes for making rye whiskey and bourbon. Each unit of Process A uses 25 pounds of malted grain and 50 pounds of unmalted grain to make 100 gallons of rye whiskey and 1,500 gallons of bourbon. On the other hand, each unit of Process B needs 40 pounds of malted grain and 20 pounds of unmalted grain to make 120 gallons of rye whiskey and 400 gallons of bourbon. The company has only 500 pounds of malted grain and only 400 pounds of unmalted grain on hand. Furthermore, the sales department has projected that they will need a minimum of 1,200 gallons of rye whiskey and a minimum of 7,500 gallons of bourbon. If the company makes a profit of $1,500 per unit of Process A and $2,000 per unit of Process B, find the blending mix that maximizes the total profit. What is this maximum profit?

In Problems 5 through 7, formulate the problem and then determine the number of corners in the feasible solution space.

5. The brothers of XYZ fraternity have kept a record of a certain logic professor's final examinations and have determined the following interesting facts: The examination is always divided into three categories of questions: T/F, the true-false, M/C, the multiple-choice, and S/E, the short-essay. Now the student is given a choice of 50 T/F questions each counting one point, 50 M/C questions each counting two points, and 10 S/E questions each counting four points. However, the student must select at least 40 questions but no more than 60 questions, and must answer at least 5 S/E questions. In addition, the student must answer more M/C questions than T/F questions, but the student's score is penalized one point each for the number of M/C questions answered over the number of T/F questions answered. Finally, the number of T/F questions answered must be smaller by at least 10 than the difference between the number of M/C questions answered and twice the number of S/E questions answered. The president of the fraternity, now enrolled in the logic professor's course, has decided that one phase of the initiation of the new pledges will be to find all possible combinations of the number of each kind of question that should be answered to attain the best possible grade on the upcoming final examination. Determine the maximum score and all alternative combinations.

6. Superior Paint Company sells three kinds of exterior finishes: oil-base paint, water-base paint, and stain. In order to keep all its distributors properly supplied, the company must manufacture and store at least three months' sales in advance. Oil-base paint costs the company $5.50 per gallon to make, whereas water-base paint costs $4.50 per gallon, and stain costs $3.50 per gallon. The company has determined that the carrying cost for all three finishes is $0.50 per gallon for the average number of gallons in the inventory (the average being typically one half of the number originally manufactured). On the basis of past experience, the sales department of the company has projected that its needs for the next three months will be at most 10,000 but at least 6,000 total gallons. Furthermore, no

3.11 PROBLEM SET 3–4 (*continued*)

more than 2,000 gallons of stain but at least 1,000 gallons of each finish will be needed. In addition, the number of gallons of paint should be at least 75 percent of the total. How many gallons of each finish should the company make and what will be the cost?

7. Pure Tobacco Company makes three kinds of cigarettes: filter regulars, filter kings, and filter super kings. Management has to decide the optimal production mix of three blending processes for making each cigarette: Process X, Process Y, and Process Z. Each unit of Process X uses 4 pounds of tobacco, 1 ream of paper, and 3 ounces of charcoal to make 800 filter regulars, 700 filter kings, and 600 filter super kings. On the other hand, each unit of Process Y uses 5 pounds of tobacco, 2 reams of paper, and 4 ounces of charcoal to make 1,000 filter regulars, 800 filter kings, and 600 filter super kings; whereas each unit of Process Z uses 3 pounds of tobacco, 1 ream of paper, and 3 ounces of charcoal to make 900 filter regulars, 400 filter kings, and 700 filter super kings. The company has only 425 pounds of tobacco, 140 reams of paper, and 350 ounces of charcoal on hand. Furthermore, the sales department has projected that they will need a minimum of 50,000 filter regulars, 40,000 filter kings, and 30,000 filter super kings. If the company makes a profit of $18 per unit of Process X, $23 per unit of Process Y, and $15 per unit of Process Z, find the production mix that maximizes the total profit. What is this maximum profit?

In Problems 8 through 12, formulate the problem only.

8. Growth Investment Company is planning a pension fund of $10,000,000 for one of its valued clients. Federal and state regulations require that, for the workers' protection, the fund must be made up of stocks, bonds, and a reserve in the form of bank notes or savings accounts. After much investigation, the company has decided upon the following combination: Three stocks, S_1, S_2, and S_3; two bond issues, B_1 and B_2; and a particular bank note, N. Their study shows that the expected yield from S_1 will be 8 percent, S_2 will be 9 percent, S_3 will be 7 percent, B_1 will be 10 percent, B_2 will be 11 percent, and N will be 6 percent. There are, however, some very stringent limitations on the investment possibilities written in the above-mentioned regulations on pension funds. First, the amount invested in stocks must be no more than 40 percent of that invested in bonds. Second, a minimum of 25 percent of the total fund must be held in reserve. Third, no more than 35 percent of the total fund can be invested in stocks. Finally, no single investment other than a bank note or savings account can constitute more than 30 percent of the total fund. What portfolio will the company recommend for the pension fund and what will be its expected yield?

9. True Sound Radio Company makes four kinds of radios for automobiles: AM, AM/FM, AM/FM stereo, and AM/FM stereo tape. Each radio can be manufactured by either one of two methods: Method I, which involves two processes, P_1 and P_2, and Method II, which involves three processes, P_3, P_4, and P_5. Revenue and cost data on the radios are as shown in Table A, while manufacturing data are as shown in Table B. What is the optimal number of each kind of radio for the company to make and what

TABLE A

		Radio		
	AM	AM/FM	AM/FM Stereo	AM/FM Stereo Tape
Unit selling price ($)	100	150	250	300
Unit cost, Method I	70	90	150	225
Unit cost, Method II	95	70	185	190
Maximum quantity that can be sold	5000	3000	2000	1000

3.11 PROBLEM SET 3–4 (continued)

TABLE B

| | Manufacturing Time (hours) | | | | |
	AM	AM/FM	AM/FM Stereo	AM/FM Stereo Tape	Maximum Hours Available
Method I					
Process P_1	4	4	3	0	2,100
Process P_2	8	10	6	7	14,000
Method II					
Process P_3	1	0	5	5	1,500
Process P_4	3	8	0	6	2,400
Process P_5	1	1	11	20	2,500

is the associated profit? (Hint: Let x_{1A}, x_{1F}, x_{1S}, x_{1T} be the number of AM, AM/FM, AM/FM stereo, and AM/FM stereo tape radios made by Method I, and similarly x_{2A}, x_{2F}, x_{2S}, x_{2T} for Method II.)

10. Precision Instruments, Inc., has a contract to supply Electronic Calculator Company 600 minicircuits in July and 500 minicircuits in August. Precision makes and tests the minicircuits on an assembly line, using people on both a regular- and second-shift basis. In July, because of other commitments, only 650 minicircuits can be produced during regular time and only 200 during the second shift. On the other hand, only 450 minicircuits can be produced during regular time in August and only 150 in the second shift. The problem is that production costs differ not only for each shift, but also for each of the two months. Specifically, in the month of July the regular-shift cost is $250 per minicircuit, while the second-shift cost is $350 per minicircuit. The respective costs for August are $300 and $375. Of course, Precision can make more than the 600 minicircuits required by Electronic in July; but, in this case, Precision must store the difference over from July to August at a unit inventory cost of $25. What should Precision's production schedule be and what is the associated cost?

a) Formulate the problem with the following variables: x_{JR} and x_{JS} are the number of minicircuits produced in July during reg-

ular and second shift, respectively; x_{AR} and x_{AS} in August; and x_I the inventory from July to August. (Hint: Be careful to remember that, for consistency, the inventory must be the excess over the 600.)

b) Formulate the problem with the following variables: x_{JRJ} and x_{JRA} are the numbers of minicircuits produced in July, regular shift, for use in July and August, respectively; x_{JSJ} and x_{JSA} the numbers of minicircuits produced in July, second shift; x_{AR} and x_{AS} as in (a) above.

11. The intensive care unit of City Hospital has to schedule the shifts for its nursing staff on a round-the-clock basis so as to ensure that a certain minimum number of nurses are on duty at various times. The supervisor of nurses has broken the day into six slots of four hours each and has determined that in order to maintain efficiency at least 12 nurses must be on duty from 8 AM to 12 noon, at least 14 from 12 noon to 4 PM, at least 16 from 4 PM to 8 PM, at least 10 from 8 PM to 12 midnight, at least 6 from 12 midnight to 4 AM, and at least 9 from 4 AM to 8 AM. Of course, the nurses work eight-hour shifts, but they are scheduled to arrive (and depart) every four hours starting at 8 AM; i.e., Shift 1 works from 8 AM to 4 PM, Shift 2 from 12 noon to 8 PM, Shift 3 from 4 PM to 12 midnight, etc. Find the optimal schedule that meets the above requirements and, at the same time, employs the smallest total number of nurses. What is this total? (Hint: Let x_i be the number of nurses who are scheduled to work Shift i where $i = 1, 2, 3, 4, 5, 6$).

12. Fine Paper Mill produces paper in reels having a standard width of 60 inches and a fixed length. The mill receives orders from its customers for reels of the same fixed length but smaller widths. One customer's order calls for 50 reels of width 10, 75 reels of width 16, and 85 reels of width 23; all of which the mill cuts from the standard size reel. The mill wants to meet the customer's

3.11 PROBLEM SET 3–4 (concluded)

needs in such a way as to minimize the total trim waste. This trim waste occurs, of course, when the standard reel is cut into smaller reels; i.e., if one 60-inch reel is cut into one 10-inch reel and two 23-inch reels, then there is a trim waste of $60 - [10(1) + 23(2)] = 4$ inches.

a) Find every possible combination of cutting the standard 60-inch reel into combinations of 10-inch, 16-inch, and 23-inch reels, and calculate the trim waste

for each such combination. (Hint: There are eight such combinations.)

b) Formulate the problem minimizing the total trim waste, assuming that the mill ignores the extra 10-inch, 16-inch, and 23-inch reels made. What is this total waste?

c) Formulate the problem minimizing the total trim waste assuming that the extra reels are also waste. What is this total waste?

3.12 REVIEW PROBLEMS

Solve each of the following two-variable linear programming problems, assuming $x \geq 0$ and $y \geq 0$:

1. $x + 2y \leq 40$
$3x + y \leq 45$
a) Find θ_{max} if $\theta = 2x + 3y$.
b) Find θ_{max} if $\theta = 6x + 2y$.

2. $x + 2y \geq 40$
$3x + y \geq 45$
a) Find θ_{min} if $\theta = 4x + y$.
b) Find θ_{min} if $\theta = 2x + 4y$.

3. $x - y \geq -1$
$3x + 2y \leq 17$
$x + 4y \geq 9$
Find θ_{max} if $\theta = 2x + y$.

4. $x - y \geq -1$
$3x + 2y \geq 17$
$x + 4y \geq 9$
Find θ_{min} if $\theta = 2x + y$.

5. $x \geq 2$
$x + y \geq 7$
$3x + 4y \geq 24$
Find θ_{min} if $\theta = 3x + 2y$.

6. $x + y \leq 13$
$x + 2y \leq 22$
$2x + y \leq 20$
Find θ_{max} if $\theta = 10x + 10y$.

7. $x - y \leq 7$
$-x + y \geq 2$
$-5x + y = 0$
Find θ_{min} if $\theta = 3x + 4y$.

8. $x + y \leq 10$
$3x + y = 18$
Find θ_{max} if $\theta = 2x + y$.

9. One pound of Food A costs $1 and contains 2 ounces of Nutrient I and 4 ounces of Nutrient II. One pound of B costs $2 and contains 3 ounces of I and 1 ounce of II. A mixture is to contain at least 90 ounces of I and 80 ounces of II. Find the minimum-cost mixture.

10. (See Problem 9.) Suppose the mixture must weigh not more than 40 pounds. What will be the minimum-cost mixture now?

11. (See Problem 9). What will be the minimum-cost mixture if at least 80 percent of the mixture must be food B?

12. To make one unit of product A requires three minutes each in Departments I and II. A unit of B requires two minutes in I and four minutes in II. A unit of either product contributes $1 to profit. If Departments I and II have 900 and 1,200 minutes available, respectively, for making A and B, find the

3.12 REVIEW PROBLEMS (*continued*)

numbers of each that should be made to maximize profit, and find what the maximum profit is.

13. (See Problem 12.) Solve the problem if the number of units of A must be at least as great as the number of units of B.

Solve each of the following three-variable linear programming problems, assuming $x \geq 0$, $y \geq 0$, and $z \geq 0$:

14. $x + 3y + 4z \leq 30$
$x + 4y + 2z \leq 40$
Find θ_{max} if $\theta = x + 4y + 3z$.

15. $4x + 8y + z \leq 52$
$8x + 28y + 3z \leq 168$
Find θ_{max} if $\theta = 3x + 9y + z$.

16. $x + 3y + 3z \leq 50$
$x + 4y + 2z \leq 60$
$z \leq 10$
Find θ_{max} if $\theta = x + 4y + 2z$.

17. $x + 2y + 7z \leq 21$
$5x + 17y + 28z \leq 140$
$x + 9y + 10z \leq 66$
Find θ_{max} if $\theta = x + 3y + 7z$.

18. $x + 2y + z \leq 14$
$0.5x + 2y + 0.5z \leq 10$
$x + 5y + 4z \leq 26$
Find θ_{max} if $\theta = x + 3y + 3z$.

19. $x + 2y + 3z \leq 25$
$x + 3y + 2z \leq 30$
Find θ_{max} if $\theta = x + 3y + 2z$.

---

20. A man sells and installs products A, B, and C. The table shows, for example, that it takes three hours to sell a unit of B, four hours to install it, and net profit per unit is $40.

Product	Number of Units	Selling Hours per Unit	Installation Hours per Unit	Profit per Unit
A	x	1	1	$10
B	y	3	4	40
C	z	2	1	10

During a 38-hour week, the man allots no more than 18 hours to selling and no more than 20 hours to installation. Find the combination of numbers of units of A, B, and C that would yield maximum profit.

21. The table shows, for example, that two labor-hours are needed to sell a unit of B, three labor-hours to deliver it, and three

Product	Number of Units	Selling Hours per Unit	Delivery Hours per Unit	Installation Hours per Unit	Profit per Unit
A	x	1	1	2	$20
B	y	2	3	3	60
C	z	3	2	5	40

labor-hours to install it. Profit per unit of B is $60.

If 220 labor-hours are available, of which not more than 50 are to be used for selling, not more than 60 for delivery, and not more than 110 for installation, find the combination of A, B, and C that yields maximum profit and state what this maximum is.

22. The table shows, for example, that in making a unit of B, 3 minutes are required for stamping, 13 minutes for forming, and 5 minutes for painting, and each unit of B contributes $4 to profit.

Product	Number of Units	Minutes per Unit for			Profit per Unit
		Stamping	Forming	Painting	
A	x	1	3	1	$1
B	y	3	13	5	4
C	z	2	2	5	2

Minutes available for stamping, forming, and painting are 40, 144, and 70, respectively. Find the combination of numbers of units of A, B, and C that leads to maximum profit. (Note: Assume that fractional units are permissible and that a fractional unit contributes its fraction to profit.)

3.12 REVIEW PROBLEMS (concluded)

In Problems 23 through 25, formulate the problem and then determine the number of corners in the feasible solution space.

23. Strong Steel Company operates three steel mills with different production capacities: Mill I can produce 4,000 tons per day of AAAA steel, 1,000 tons per day of AAA steel, 3,000 tons per day of AA steel, and 10,000 tons per day of A steel. Mill F can produce 3,000 tons per day of AAAA steel, 2,000 tons per day of AAA steel, 2,000 tons per day of AA steel, and 4,000 tons per day of A steel. Mill S can produce 2,000, 4,000, 1,000, and 3,000 tons per day, respectively. The company has made a contract with a construction firm to provide 35,000 tons of AAAA steel, 29,000 tons of AAA steel, 23,000 tons of AA steel, and 62,000 tons of A steel. If it costs $1,400 per day to run Mill I, $1,000 per day to run Mill F, and $1,200 per day to run Mill S, determine the number of days the company should operate each mill in order to meet the terms of the above contract most economically. What is this minimum cost?

24. Ace Rubber Company manufactures three types of tires: Model P, the premium, Model S, the second line, and Model E, the economy. Model P sells for $95 per tire and costs $60 per tire to make, whereas Model S sells for $75 per tire and costs $45 to make, while Model E sells for $55 per tire and costs $30 to make. To make one Model P tire, it requires 1 hour on Machine A, 1 hour on Machine B, 2 hours on Machine C, and 3 hours on Machine D. On the other hand, to make one Model S tire, it takes 1 hour on A, 2 hours on B, 1 hour on C, and 4 hours on D. Model E requires 4 hours on A, 3 hours on B, 2 hours on C, and 1 hour on D. Production scheduling indicates that during the coming week Machine A will be available for at most 42 hours, Machine B for at most 40 hours, Machine C for at most 30 hours, and Machine D for at most 44 hours. How many of each tire should the company make in

the coming week in order to maximize its profit? What is this maximum profit?

25. The Hickory Desk Company, an office furniture manufacturer, produces two types of desks: executive desks and secretary/stenographer desks. The company has two plants at which desks are made. Plant 1, which is an older plant, operates on a double shift of 80 hours per week. Plant 2 is a newer plant and is not running at full capacity. However, since management plans to operate the second plant on a double-shift basis similar to Plant 1, operators have been employed to work two shifts. Currently each shift at Plant 2 works 25 hours per week. No premium is paid to second-shift workers. The following table shows production time (in hours/unit) and standard costs (in dollars/unit) at each plant.

	Production Time (hours/unit)		Standard Costs (dollars/unit)	
	Plant 1	Plant 2	Plant 1	Plant 2
Executive desks	7.0	6.0	250	260
Sec./steno. desks	4.0	5.0	200	180

The company has been competitive in the past by pricing the executive desks at $350. However, it appears the company will have to drop the price on the secretary/stenographer desks to $275 in order to be competitive. The company has been experiencing cost overruns in the past eight to ten weeks; therefore, the management has set a weekly budget restraint on production costs. The weekly budget for the total production of executive desks is $2,000, while the budget for the secretary/stenographer desks is $2,200. Management would like to determine the number of each type of desk that should be produced at each plant in order to maximize profit.

FOUR

Compact Notation: Vectors, Matrices, and Summation

Brevity in mathematical statements is achieved through the use of symbols. Thus the brief expression $247 \div 793$ takes the place of what would be a very lengthy statement if one chose to write a complete description of the steps involved in the long division. The price paid for brevity, of course, is the effort spent in learning the meaning of the symbol.

In this chapter, we shall learn the symbols for matrices and vectors and apply them in the statement and solution of input-output problems and other problems involving linear systems. Then we shall introduce the summation symbol and show its application in linear systems and in statistics.

4.2 MATRICES AND VECTORS

Numerical data arranged in a form that we shall come to call a matrix are very common in everyday life. For example, suppose that a company has six gasoline stations, three in region #1 and three in region #2. January sales volume, in thousands of gallons, is shown for each station in Table 4–1.

TABLE 4–1
Tiger Oil Company: Sales in thousands of gallons, January

Station	Region #1	Region #2
#1	10	15
#2	12	18
#3	8	12

We note that sales of Station #1 in Region #2 were 15 thousand gallons. The position of the *entry* (also called *element*) 15 is at the intersection of the first row and second column, and we may symbolize the entry as a_{12} (read "a sub one two")[1] where the first subscript refers to the row and the second to the column. To avoid having to specify which of a pair of subscripts specifies the row and which the column, we shall *always* use the row, column order convention.

> **Exercise.** In Table 4–1, a) what are a_{11} and a_{32}? b) Write the symbol for the entry 8.   Answer: a) 10 and 12. b) a_{31}.

If we keep in mind that rows are stations and columns are regions, we can omit the stub and caption of the table and write the *matrix:*

Station by region sales matrix

$$\begin{pmatrix} 10 & 15 \\ 12 & 18 \\ 8 & 12 \end{pmatrix}. \tag{1}$$

> **Definition.** A *matrix* is a rectangular array of numbers. Matrices are enclosed in grouping symbols such as parentheses or brackets.

If a matrix has m rows and n columns, m by n is called the *order* of the matrix or, more descriptively, the *dimension* of the matrix. Thus, a 5 by 4 matrix has the dimensions of a rectangle 5 (rows) down by 4 (columns) across.

Matrices that have precisely one row or precisely one column are given special names.

> **Definition.** A 1 by n matrix is called a *row vector of dimension n,* and an m by 1 matrix is called a *column vector of dimension m.* Entries in row and column vectors often are referred to as the *components* of the vectors.

Thus, the 1 by 3 matrix

$$(4 \quad 7 \quad 6)$$

---

[1] A comma is required to avoid ambiguity if the number of rows or columns exceeds nine. For example, an entry in the 12th row, 3rd column would be $a_{12,3}$.

is a row vector of dimension 3, while the 2 by 1 matrix

$$\begin{pmatrix} 5 \\ 7 \end{pmatrix}$$

is a column vector of dimension 2. The station by region sales matrix (1) may be thought of as consisting of two column vectors, each of dimension 3, or three row vectors, each of dimension 2.

Exercise. Write the first row vector in the matrix (1).
Answer: (10   15).

Next, suppose Tiger Oil Company sells one grade of gasoline but, due to transportation costs, prices vary in the two regions as shown in Table 4–2.

TABLE 4–2
Tiger Oil Company: Regional price variation

Region	Price per Gallon
#1	$1.10
#2	$1.20

We can represent the price matrix either as a 2-dimensional column or row vector. Thus,

Regional price vector

$$\begin{pmatrix} 1.10 \\ 1.20 \end{pmatrix} \quad \text{or} \quad (1.10 \quad 1.20). \tag{2}$$

Finally, an n by n matrix has the same number of rows and columns and is called a square matrix. We may specify a square matrix simply by stating the order n. Thus, a 3 by 3 matrix is a square matrix of order 3.

4.3 PRODUCT OF A NUMBER AND A MATRIX

In matrix algebra, an ordinary number is called a *scalar*. To multiply a matrix by a scalar, we multiply each entry in the matrix by the scalar. For example

$$12 \begin{pmatrix} 1 & 3 \\ 4 & 2 \end{pmatrix} = \begin{pmatrix} 12 & 36 \\ 48 & 24 \end{pmatrix}.$$

To see the origin of the word scalar, think of the entries 1, 3, 4, 2 in the left matrix as being in feet. Scaling these to inches requires that each entry be multiplied by 12. Similarly, Tiger Oil Company may wish to set February sales quotas that are 10 percent higher than actual January sales. The February quota matrix will then be obtained by multiplying the January sales matrix by the scalar 1.1; thus,

$$\begin{pmatrix} Scaling \\ factor \end{pmatrix} \times \begin{pmatrix} January \\ sales \end{pmatrix} = \begin{pmatrix} February \\ quota \end{pmatrix}$$

$$1.1 \qquad \begin{pmatrix} 10 & 15 \\ 12 & 18 \\ 8 & 12 \end{pmatrix} = \begin{pmatrix} 11 & 16.5 \\ 13.2 & 19.8 \\ 8.8 & 13.2 \end{pmatrix}.$$

Exercise. Tiger Oil Company's price vector is (1.10 1.20) in dollars per gallon. What would be the scaling factor and the resultant price vector if prices are to be in dollars per 1,000 gallons? Answer: The scaling factor is 1000. Hence, 1000 (1.10 1.20) = (1100 1200).

4.4 ADDITION AND SUBTRACTION OF MATRICES

Matrices are added or subtracted by adding or subtracting *corresponding* entries. Since entries must correspond, the matrices involved must have the same dimensions. We cannot compute

$$\begin{pmatrix} 3 & 1 & 5 \\ 2 & 4 & 7 \end{pmatrix} + \begin{pmatrix} 5 & 2 \\ -3 & 6 \end{pmatrix}$$

because the first matrix is 2 by 3 and the second is 2 by 2. However,

$$\begin{pmatrix} 3 & 1 \\ 2 & 4 \end{pmatrix} + \begin{pmatrix} 5 & -6 \\ 2 & 0 \end{pmatrix} = \begin{pmatrix} 8 & -5 \\ 4 & 4 \end{pmatrix}$$

and

$$\begin{pmatrix} 5 & 8 \\ -1 & 3 \end{pmatrix} - 2\begin{pmatrix} 1 & 0 \\ 3 & -2 \end{pmatrix} = \begin{pmatrix} 5 & 8 \\ -1 & 3 \end{pmatrix} - \begin{pmatrix} 2 & 0 \\ 6 & -4 \end{pmatrix}$$

$$= \begin{pmatrix} 3 & 8 \\ -7 & 7 \end{pmatrix}.$$

Exercise. Compute

$$3\begin{pmatrix} 4 & -1 \\ 2 & 5 \end{pmatrix} - 2\begin{pmatrix} 1 & 2 \\ -3 & 4 \end{pmatrix}. \quad \text{Answer:} \begin{pmatrix} 10 & -7 \\ 12 & 7 \end{pmatrix}.$$

Returning to the affairs of Tiger Oil Company, recall its February sales quota matrix, (3). This is the middle matrix in the following. The left is the new matrix, (4), of *actual* February sales, and the difference in matrix (5), which shows the deviation of actual February sales from quota.

$$(4) \qquad\qquad (3) \qquad\qquad\qquad (5)$$
$$\textit{February sales} \ - \ \textit{February quota} \ = \ \textit{Deviation from quota}$$

$$\begin{pmatrix} 12 & 15.5 \\ 13 & 20 \\ 8.5 & 12.9 \end{pmatrix} - \begin{pmatrix} 11 & 16.5 \\ 13.2 & 19.8 \\ 8.8 & 13.2 \end{pmatrix} = \begin{pmatrix} 1 & -1 \\ -0.2 & 0.2 \\ -0.3 & -0.3 \end{pmatrix}.$$

From (5) we see, for example, that Station #1, Region #2 sales were 1,000 gallons below quota.

Exercise. In (5), interpret the entry a_{21}. Answer: Station #2, Region #1 sales were 0.2 thousand gallons below quota.

Two important properties of addition are the *commutative* and *associative laws.*

$$A + B = B + A \qquad \text{Commutative law}$$
$$A + (B + C) = (A + B) + C \qquad \text{Associative law}$$

These laws are valid because addition of matrices is accomplished by adding corresponding entries, and the commutative and associative laws hold for ordinary numbers. For example, we saw that

$$\begin{pmatrix} 3 & 1 \\ 2 & 4 \end{pmatrix} + \begin{pmatrix} 5 & -6 \\ 2 & 0 \end{pmatrix} = \begin{pmatrix} 8 & 5 \\ 4 & 4 \end{pmatrix},$$

and if we commute these matrices the result remains the same

$$\begin{pmatrix} 5 & -6 \\ 2 & 0 \end{pmatrix} + \begin{pmatrix} 3 & 1 \\ 2 & 4 \end{pmatrix} = \begin{pmatrix} 8 & 5 \\ 4 & 4 \end{pmatrix}.$$

Just as with ordinary numbers, the associative law allows us to drop the parentheses and simply write $A + B + C$.

Exercise. Compute $A + (B + C)$ and $(A + B) + C$ for

$$A = \begin{pmatrix} 3 & 1 \\ 2 & 4 \end{pmatrix}, B = \begin{pmatrix} 5 & -6 \\ 2 & 0 \end{pmatrix}, \text{ and } C = \begin{pmatrix} 7 & 1 \\ -8 & 9 \end{pmatrix}.$$

$$\text{Answer: } \begin{pmatrix} 15 & -4 \\ -4 & 13 \end{pmatrix}.$$

One special matrix is the *zero matrix*, in which all of the entries are zeros. For example,

$$\begin{pmatrix} 0 & 0 & 0 \\ 0 & 0 & 0 \end{pmatrix}$$

is a 2 by 3 zero matrix. Using O to denote the zero matrix, it is clear that O behaves like the number 0 in ordinary arithmetic. So we have the *identity law* for matrix addition:

$$A + O = A.$$

Of course, we also have the usual properties

$$A - O = A \quad \text{and} \quad O - A = -A,$$

where $-A$ means the matrix $(-1)A$. For example,

$$\begin{pmatrix} 0 & 0 & 0 \\ 0 & 0 & 0 \end{pmatrix} - \begin{pmatrix} 2 & 3 & 4 \\ 5 & 2 & -3 \end{pmatrix} = \begin{pmatrix} -2 & -3 & -4 \\ -5 & -2 & 3 \end{pmatrix}.$$

4.5 MULTIPLICATION OF MATRICES

Matrix multiplication is a specialized form of multiplication devised for very practical reasons. Consider the following:

$$(3 \quad 2)\begin{pmatrix} 5 \\ 4 \end{pmatrix} = 23.$$

We obtain the product, 23, as the sum of $3 \cdot 5 + 2 \cdot 4$. To fix this in mind, we may place our left index finger on the 3 and our right index finger on the 5. Multiply to obtain 15. Then move the left finger *across* to the 2 and the right finger *down* to the 4, multiply to obtain 8, then add this to 15 to get 23. A product obtained in this manner is called the *inner product*. Observe that the inner product of a row vector by a column vector is an ordinary number, a scalar. As another example,

$$(2 \quad -3 \quad 1 \quad 0)\begin{pmatrix} 4 \\ -2 \\ 3 \\ -1 \end{pmatrix} = 2(4) - 3(-2) + 1(3) + 0(-1)$$

$$= 8 + 6 + 3 + 0 = 17.$$

Exercise. Evaluate

$$(3 \quad -1)\begin{pmatrix} 4 \\ 2 \end{pmatrix}. \quad \text{Answer: 10.}$$

It is clear that if the "left finger across, right finger down" technique is to be defined there must be as many numbers across as there are down. That is, the first matrix must have as many columns as the second has rows. In our last example, we had a 1 by 4 matrix multiplied by a 4 by 1 matrix. If we indicate this as (1 by 4) · (4 by 1), observe that the two middle numbers are the same, 4. When the dimensions of two matrices are indicated in this manner and the middle numbers are the same, the two are said to be *conformable for multiplication.* Alternatively, we may say that two matrices are conformable for multiplication if the number of columns in the first is the same as the number of rows in the second. In the next example, we multiply a (2 by 2) and a (2 by 3).

$$\begin{pmatrix} 1 & 2 \\ 3 & 4 \end{pmatrix}\begin{pmatrix} 5 & 6 & 7 \\ 8 & 9 & 10 \end{pmatrix} = \begin{pmatrix} 21 & 24 & 27 \\ 47 & 54 & 61 \end{pmatrix}.$$

The calculations leading to the rightmost matrix are:

First row: $1(5) + 2(8) = 21$
$1(6) + 2(9) = 24$
$1(7) + 2(10) = 27.$

Second row: $3(5) + 4(8) = 47$
$3(6) + 4(9) = 54$
$3(7) + 4(10) = 61.$

Exercise. Compute the following product:

$$\begin{pmatrix} 1 & 2 & 3 \\ 4 & 5 & 6 \end{pmatrix}\begin{pmatrix} 0 & 1 \\ 2 & 3 \\ 4 & 5 \end{pmatrix}. \quad \text{Answer: } \begin{pmatrix} 16 & 22 \\ 34 & 49 \end{pmatrix}.$$

As an example of the applied meaning of matrix multiplication, let us multiply the gallons sold matrix (entries in thousands of gallons) by the price per thousand gallons vector for the Tiger Oil Company.

Station	Region #1	#2		Region	Dollars per thousand gallons
#1	10	15		#1	1100
#2	12	18		#2	1200
#3	8	12			

The product is

Station	Total dollar volume of sales, both regions
#1	$10(1100) + 15(1200) = \$29,000$
#2	$12(1100) + 18(1200) = \$34,800$
#3	$8(1100) + 12(1200) = \$23,200.$

Thus, if Mr. Jones owns both #1 stations, his dollar volume of sales is 10 thousand gallons at $1,100 per thousand in Region #1, plus 15 thousand gallons at $1,200 per thousand in Region #2 for a total of $29,000 in both regions. Similarly, the owner of the #2 stations grosses $34,800 and the owner of the #3 stations grosses $23,200.

We saw that matrix addition has the associative and commutative properties of ordinary algebra. On the other hand, matrix multiplication has the associative property but *the commutative property does not hold in general for matrix multiplication*. Thus it is possible that

$$A \cdot B \neq B \cdot A,$$

but it is always true that

$$A \cdot (B \cdot C) = (A \cdot B) \cdot C = A \cdot B \cdot C.$$

For example,

$$\begin{pmatrix} 1 & 2 \\ 3 & 4 \end{pmatrix} \begin{pmatrix} 5 & 6 \\ 7 & 8 \end{pmatrix} = \begin{pmatrix} 19 & 22 \\ 43 & 50 \end{pmatrix},$$

but if we interchange the matrices on the left we find

$$\begin{pmatrix} 5 & 6 \\ 7 & 8 \end{pmatrix} \begin{pmatrix} 1 & 2 \\ 3 & 4 \end{pmatrix} = \begin{pmatrix} 23 & 34 \\ 31 & 46 \end{pmatrix}.$$

Thus, if we *premultiply* by

$$\begin{pmatrix} 1 & 2 \\ 3 & 4 \end{pmatrix}$$

we get one result, but if we *postmultiply* by the same matrix we get a different result.

Exercise.   What do we obtain if we

a) Premultiply $\begin{pmatrix} 1 \\ 2 \end{pmatrix}$ by $(3 \quad 4)$?

b) Postmultiply $\begin{pmatrix} 1 \\ 2 \end{pmatrix}$ by $(3 \quad 4)$?

Answer: a) 11.   b) $\begin{pmatrix} 3 & 4 \\ 6 & 8 \end{pmatrix}$.

We *can* design matrices that commute with each other in multiplication. For example,

$$\begin{pmatrix} 1 & 0 \\ 0 & 1 \end{pmatrix}\begin{pmatrix} 2 & 3 \\ 4 & 5 \end{pmatrix} = \begin{pmatrix} 2 & 3 \\ 4 & 5 \end{pmatrix}\begin{pmatrix} 1 & 0 \\ 0 & 1 \end{pmatrix} = \begin{pmatrix} 2 & 3 \\ 4 & 5 \end{pmatrix}.$$

However, as we have seen, the commutative property does not hold in general.

On the other hand,

$$\begin{pmatrix} 1 & 2 \\ -2 & -1 \end{pmatrix}\left[\begin{pmatrix} 1 & 2 \\ 3 & 4 \end{pmatrix}\begin{pmatrix} 5 & 6 \\ 7 & 8 \end{pmatrix}\right] = \begin{pmatrix} 1 & 2 \\ -2 & -1 \end{pmatrix}\begin{pmatrix} 19 & 22 \\ 43 & 50 \end{pmatrix}$$
$$= \begin{pmatrix} 105 & 122 \\ -81 & -94 \end{pmatrix}$$

and

$$\left[\begin{pmatrix} 1 & 2 \\ -2 & -1 \end{pmatrix}\begin{pmatrix} 1 & 2 \\ 3 & 4 \end{pmatrix}\right]\begin{pmatrix} 5 & 6 \\ 7 & 8 \end{pmatrix} = \begin{pmatrix} 23 & 34 \\ 31 & 46 \end{pmatrix}\begin{pmatrix} 5 & 6 \\ 7 & 8 \end{pmatrix}$$
$$= \begin{pmatrix} 105 & 122 \\ -81 & -94 \end{pmatrix}.$$

Here both results are the same, and this will always be the case.

We repeat the suggestion that an m by n matrix can be postmultiplied by an n by p matrix (they are conformable), and the result will be an m by p matrix. Thus, we can postmultiply a 5 by 8 matrix by an 8 by 11 matrix, and the product matrix will be 5 by 11.

Exercise. a) What will be the dimensions of the product matrix if a 5 by 7 is postmultiplied by a 7 by 6? b) What happens if we pre-multiply the 5 by 7 by the 7 by 6? Answer: a) 5 by 6. b) The matrices are not conformable for multiplication.

Of course, as the reader would expect, any matrix postmultiplied or premultiplied by the zero matrix results in the zero matrix. Thus

$$\boldsymbol{A} \cdot \boldsymbol{O} = \boldsymbol{O} \cdot \boldsymbol{A} = \boldsymbol{O}.$$

4.6 IDENTITY MATRIX

An *identity* or *unit* matrix is a square matrix with 1 as the element in each position on the main diagonal (upper left to lower right) and 0 as the element in all other positions. Thus,

$$\boldsymbol{I} = \begin{pmatrix} 1 & 0 & 0 \\ 0 & 1 & 0 \\ 0 & 0 & 1 \end{pmatrix}$$

is a 3 by 3 identity matrix or *the* identity matrix of order 3. We can call it *the* identity matrix since there is precisely one unit matrix for each square order.

The identity matrix of order 2 is

$$I = \begin{pmatrix} 1 & 0 \\ 0 & 1 \end{pmatrix}.$$

The most important property of the identity matrix is illustrated by the statements

$$A \cdot I = A \quad \text{and} \quad I \cdot A = A.$$

That is, the product of any given matrix and the identity matrix is the given matrix itself. Thus, the identity matrix behaves in matrix multiplication like the number 1 in ordinary arithmetic, where we say

$$(a)(1) = (1)(a) = a.$$

The reader may verify the unity property of I by carrying out the following multiplication, in which the first written matrix, I, when multiplied by the second matrix, yields the second matrix as the product.

$$\begin{pmatrix} 1 & 0 & 0 \\ 0 & 1 & 0 \\ 0 & 0 & 1 \end{pmatrix} \begin{pmatrix} 2 & 3 & 4 \\ -1 & -2 & 0 \\ 5 & 2 & -3 \end{pmatrix} = \begin{pmatrix} 2 & 3 & 4 \\ -1 & -2 & 0 \\ 5 & 2 & -3 \end{pmatrix}.$$

Exercise. Given

$$A = \begin{pmatrix} 2 & 3 & 4 \\ 5 & 2 & -3 \end{pmatrix}$$

verify that $A \cdot I = A$ and that $I \cdot A = A$. What is the dimension of the I matrices?

Answer: To postmultiply, I is 3 by 3; to premultiply, I is 2 by 2.

4.7 PROBLEM SET 4–1

Perform the following operations:

1. (2 3 4) + (1 −2 3).

2. $\begin{pmatrix} 1 \\ -3 \end{pmatrix} + \begin{pmatrix} -3 \\ 5 \end{pmatrix}.$

3. $\begin{pmatrix} 2 \\ 4 \end{pmatrix} + \begin{pmatrix} 5 \\ 7 \end{pmatrix} + \begin{pmatrix} 3 \\ 2 \end{pmatrix}.$

4. (6 −1 2) − (3 −2 4) + (5 −1 6).

5. $3\begin{pmatrix} 7 \\ 2 \end{pmatrix}.$

6. −2(5 −9 3).

7. $(2 \ 7)\begin{pmatrix} 3 \\ 5 \end{pmatrix}.$

8. $(1 \ -3 \ 6 \ 2)\begin{pmatrix} 2 \\ 1 \\ 2 \\ -3 \end{pmatrix}$.

14. $\begin{pmatrix} 3 & 0 \\ -5 & 4 \end{pmatrix}\begin{pmatrix} 1 & 6 \\ 2 & 0 \end{pmatrix}$.

9. $\begin{pmatrix} 3 & 1 & 2 \\ 1 & 4 & 1 \end{pmatrix} + \begin{pmatrix} 1 & -5 & -2 \\ -3 & 2 & 4 \end{pmatrix}$.

15. $\begin{pmatrix} 2 & 1 & 1 & 0 \\ 1 & 3 & 0 & 2 \\ -1 & -2 & 1 & 4 \end{pmatrix}\begin{pmatrix} 5 & 6 \\ 1 & 1 \\ 2 & 3 \\ 0 & -1 \end{pmatrix}$.

10. $\begin{pmatrix} 4 & 7 \\ 1 & 3 \end{pmatrix} + \begin{pmatrix} 1 & -2 \\ 6 & -3 \end{pmatrix} - \begin{pmatrix} 2 & -4 \\ 5 & 7 \end{pmatrix}$.

16. $\begin{pmatrix} 1 & -1 & 2 \\ 2 & 0 & 3 \end{pmatrix}\begin{pmatrix} 4 & 0 & 1 & 2 \\ -1 & 3 & 0 & 2 \\ 1 & 1 & 2 & 3 \end{pmatrix}$.

11. $4\begin{pmatrix} 1 & -3 & 2 \\ 5 & 1 & -3 \end{pmatrix} - 3\begin{pmatrix} 2 & 5 & -3 \\ 1 & 2 & -1 \end{pmatrix}$.

12. $\begin{pmatrix} 1 & 2 \\ 3 & 5 \end{pmatrix}\begin{pmatrix} 3 & 0 & 5 \\ 1 & -2 & 0 \end{pmatrix}$.

17. $\begin{pmatrix} 1 & 0 & 0 \\ 0 & 1 & 0 \\ 0 & 0 & 1 \end{pmatrix}\begin{pmatrix} 1 & 4 \\ 2 & 5 \\ 3 & 6 \end{pmatrix}$.

13. $(5 \ 6 \ 7)\begin{pmatrix} 1 & 2 \\ 0 & 3 \\ 3 & 1 \end{pmatrix}$.

18. $\begin{pmatrix} 1 & 2 & 3 \\ 3 & 2 & 1 \end{pmatrix}\begin{pmatrix} 1 & 0 & 0 \\ 0 & 1 & 0 \\ 0 & 0 & 1 \end{pmatrix}$.

---

19. Interest at the rates 0.06, 0.07, and 0.08 is earned on respective investments of $3,000, $2,000, and $4,000. a) Express the total amount of interest earned as the product of a row vector by a column vector. b) Compute the total interest by matrix multiplication.

20. Two canned meat spreads, Regular and Superior, are made by grinding beef, pork, and lamb together. The numbers of pounds of each meat in a 15-pound batch of each brand are as follows:

Brand	Pounds of		
	Beef	Pork	Lamb
Superior	8	2	5
Regular	4	8	3

a) Suppose we wish to make 10 batches of Superior and 20 of Regular. Multiply the meat matrix in the table and the batch vector (10 20) and interpret the result.

b) Suppose that the per pound prices of beef, pork, and lamb are $2.50, $2.00, and $3.00, respectively. Multiply the price vector and the meat matrix and interpret the results.

4.8 MATRIX SYMBOLS

We have used a boldface capital letter for a matrix. Thus, A is a matrix. You may use a wavy underscore, $\underset{\sim}{A}$, to designate a matrix. Similarly, boldface small letters, such as b, will be used to designate a vector. Subscripted small letters will be used to symbolize the entries in a matrix. Thus, a_{23} is the entry at the intersection of the 2nd row and 3rd column. The 3 by 4 matrix A will then be denoted by

$$A = \begin{pmatrix} a_{11} & a_{12} & a_{13} & a_{14} \\ a_{21} & a_{22} & a_{23} & a_{24} \\ a_{31} & a_{32} & a_{33} & a_{34} \end{pmatrix}.$$

We shall refer to A as the *compact* form and to the righthand expression as the *expanded matrix form.*

Exercise.   Write the expanded matrix form of the 2 by 3 matrix B.
Answer:

$$B = \begin{pmatrix} b_{11} & b_{12} & b_{13} \\ b_{21} & b_{22} & b_{23} \end{pmatrix}.$$

4.9 LINEAR EQUATIONS IN MATRIX FORM

To secure the advantage of matrix representation of equations, we shall use the same letter with varying subscripts to designate different variables. That is, instead of using x, y, and z as three variables, we shall use x_1, x_2, and x_3. Consider the linear equation

$$3x_1 + 2x_2 = 7$$

and observe that the technique of matrix multiplication makes it possible to express the equation as

$$(3 \quad 2)\begin{pmatrix} x_1 \\ x_2 \end{pmatrix} = 7.$$

Exercise.   Write the linear equation specified by

$$(5 \quad 1 \quad 4)\begin{pmatrix} x_1 \\ x_2 \\ x_3 \end{pmatrix} = 10.$$

Answer: $5x_1 + x_2 + 4x_3 = 10$.

Similarly, the equation

$$a_1 x_1 + a_2 x_2 + a_3 x_3 = b$$

is

$$(a_1 \quad a_2 \quad a_3)\begin{pmatrix} x_1 \\ x_2 \\ x_3 \end{pmatrix} = b$$

and the general linear equation in n variables,

$$a_1 x_1 + a_2 x_2 + a_3 x_3 + \cdots + a_n x_n = b$$

becomes

$$(a_1 \quad a_2 \quad a_3 \cdots a_n) \begin{pmatrix} x_1 \\ x_2 \\ x_3 \\ \vdots \\ x_n \end{pmatrix} = b.$$

We can now see the advantage of compact form. Namely, all the information in the expanded vector expression just written can be summarized by stating simply that the equation is

$$\boldsymbol{ax} = b$$

and that $\boldsymbol{a}$ is 1 by n. *We do not have to state the dimensions of $\boldsymbol{x}$* because conformability requires that this vector be n by 1.

Exercise. If $\boldsymbol{p}$ is 1 by 2 and we have $\boldsymbol{py} = q$, a) what are the dimensions of $\boldsymbol{y}$? b) Write the expanded vector form of the equation. c) Write the usual algebraic form.   Answer: a) $\boldsymbol{y}$ must be 2 by 1.

b) $(p_1 \quad p_2)\begin{pmatrix} y_1 \\ y_2 \end{pmatrix} = q.$ c) $p_1 y_1 + p_2 y_2 = q.$

Exercise. If a customer buys u_1 units of product #1, u_2 units of #2, and so on to u_g units of product #g at unit prices of, respectively, $p_1, p_2, \ldots, p_g$, write the expression for the total cost, t, in usual algebraic form and in compact form. What are the dimensions of $\boldsymbol{p}$ and $\boldsymbol{u}$? Answer: $p_1 u_1 + p_2 u_2 + \cdots + p_g u_g = t$; $\boldsymbol{pu} = t$; $\boldsymbol{p}$ is 1 by g, and $\boldsymbol{u}$ is g by 1.

It is now easy to express any system of linear equalities or inequalities in matrix form. For example,

$$3x_1 + 2x_2 + x_3 = 5$$
$$2x_1 + x_2 - x_3 = 4$$

becomes

$$\begin{pmatrix} 3 & 2 & 1 \\ 2 & 1 & -1 \end{pmatrix} \begin{pmatrix} x_1 \\ x_2 \\ x_3 \end{pmatrix} = \begin{pmatrix} 5 \\ 4 \end{pmatrix}.$$

The general 2 by 3 system (2 equations, 3 variables) is

$$a_{11} x_1 + a_{12} x_2 + a_{13} x_3 = b_1$$
$$a_{21} x_1 + a_{22} x_2 + a_{23} x_3 = b_2,$$

where now we need double subscripts to specify the row and column position of a coefficient. The preceding system can be described in compact form as

$$Ax = b, \quad \text{where } A \text{ is 2 by 3.}$$

Exercise. If $cy \le d$ represents a 3 by 2 system of $\le$ inequalities, write a) the expanded matrix form and b) the usual algebraic form of the system.

Answer: a) $\begin{pmatrix} c_{11} & c_{12} \\ c_{21} & c_{22} \\ c_{31} & c_{32} \end{pmatrix} \begin{pmatrix} y_1 \\ y_2 \end{pmatrix} \le \begin{pmatrix} d_1 \\ d_2 \\ d_3 \end{pmatrix}.$ b) $c_{11} y_1 + c_{12} y_2 \le d_1$
$c_{21} y_1 + c_{22} y_2 \le d_2$
$c_{31} y_1 + c_{32} y_2 \le d_3.$

The general m by n system,

$$a_{11}x_1 + a_{12} x_2 + a_{13} x_3 + \cdots + a_{1n} x_n = b_1$$
$$a_{21}x_1 + a_{22} x_2 + a_{23} x_3 + \cdots + a_{2n} x_n = b_2$$
$$\vdots$$
$$a_{m1}x_1 + a_{m2}x_2 + a_{m3}x_3 + \cdots + a_{mn}x_n = b_m,$$

can be specified simply as

$$Ax = b, \quad \text{where } A \text{ is } m \text{ by } n.$$

Checking the dimensions again, we see that if A is m by n, the vector x is n by 1, and the product vector b is m by 1.

Exercise. In the p by q system $Cy = d$, what are the dimensions of $C, y,$ and d? Answer: C is p by q, y is q by 1, and d is p by 1.

4.10 PROBLEM SET 4–2

Write the following in expanded matrix form:

1. $2x_1 + 3x_2 = 5$
$x_1 + 2x_2 = 3.$

2. $x_1 + 2x_2 + y_1 = 10$
$2x_1 + 3x_2 + y_2 = 12.$

3. $3x_1 + x_3 - x_4 \le 5$
$2x_1 + x_2 - 5x_4 \le 10$
$x_2 + 3x_3 + x_4 \le 8.$

4.10 PROBLEM SET 4–2 (concluded)

Write the following in usual algebraic form:

4. $\begin{pmatrix} 3 & 1 & 2 \\ 1 & 4 & 1 \end{pmatrix} \begin{pmatrix} x_1 \\ x_2 \\ x_3 \end{pmatrix} = \begin{pmatrix} 5 \\ 4 \end{pmatrix}$.

5. $\begin{pmatrix} 2 & 3 \\ 4 & 6 \\ 1 & 7 \end{pmatrix} \begin{pmatrix} x_1 \\ x_2 \end{pmatrix} = \begin{pmatrix} 5 \\ 10 \\ 6 \end{pmatrix}$.

6. $(x_1 \ x_2) \begin{pmatrix} 3 & 5 \\ 1 & 4 \end{pmatrix} = \begin{pmatrix} 2 \\ 6 \end{pmatrix}$.

7. $\begin{pmatrix} p_{11} & p_{12} & p_{13} & p_{14} \\ p_{21} & p_{22} & p_{23} & p_{24} \\ p_{31} & p_{32} & p_{33} & p_{34} \end{pmatrix} x = q$,

if x and q are appropriate vectors.

8. $\begin{pmatrix} 2 & 1 & 5 \\ 4 & 6 & 2 \end{pmatrix} \begin{pmatrix} x_1 \\ x_2 \\ x_3 \end{pmatrix} + \begin{pmatrix} y_1 \\ y_2 \end{pmatrix} = \begin{pmatrix} 10 \\ 5 \end{pmatrix}$.

9. The coefficient matrix of a system of equalities, A, is p by q. The variables y, and the constants, g, are vectors with the proper number of components.

a) What are the proper dimensions for y and for g?

b) Write the system in compact matrix notation.

**4.11
APPLICATIONS—1:
MARKOV CHAINS**

To set the stage for this section, suppose that a restaurant chain notes that 30 percent of the dinners it sells each week are beef dinners, and 70 percent are other dinners. The chain manager has a special arrangement for volume buying of beef at relatively low prices, and would like to raise the proportion of beef dinners sold. He carries out a promotional campaign to increase beef sales and collects the information shown in Table 4–3.

The matrix of proportions is called the *transition matrix*. The number 0.8 means that 80 percent of those buying beef dinners one week buy beef dinners again the next week. Similarly, 20 percent of those buying beef one week buy other dinners the next week.

> **Exercise.** Interpret the second row of Table 4–3. Answer: 60 percent of those buying other dinners one week change to beef dinners the next week, and the remaining 40 percent buy other dinners again the next week.

**TABLE 4–3
Transition proportions, one week to the next week**

	Next Week	
One Week	Beef	Other
Beef	0.8	0.2
Other	0.6	0.4

The state of affairs at the beginning of the section was 30 percent beef and 70 percent other. We shall call the vector (0.3   0.7) the *state* vector. Writing the state vector to the left of the transition matrix, we have

$$\begin{array}{cc} \textit{Beef} & \textit{Other} \\ (0.3 & 0.7) \end{array} \quad \begin{array}{c} \textit{Beef} \\ \textit{Other} \end{array} \begin{array}{cc} \textit{Beef} & \textit{Other} \\ \begin{pmatrix} 0.8 & 0.2 \\ 0.6 & 0.4 \end{pmatrix}. \end{array}$$

If we wish to find what proportion will buy beef after a one-week transition, we note that 80 percent of the 30 percent who bought beef one week will buy it the next and an additional 60 percent of the 70 percent who bought other dinners one week will buy beef the next week. The sum is 0.3(0.8) + 0.7(0.6) = 0.66, and we found this by the usual inner product matrix multiplication procedure. In the same manner 0.3(0.2) + 0.7(0.4) = 0.34 is the proportion buying other dinners next week, and the new state vector is

$$\begin{array}{cc} \textit{Beef} & \textit{Other} \\ (0.66 & 0.34) \end{array}$$

In brief,

$$(0.3 \quad 0.7) \begin{pmatrix} 0.8 & 0.2 \\ 0.6 & 0.4 \end{pmatrix} = (0.66 \quad 0.34).$$

Now suppose the promotion activity is maintained and the transition matrix remains constant from week to week. Then the state vector for week #1, (0.66 0.34) can be used as a premultiplier of the transition matrix to obtain the state vector for week #2.

Exercise.   What proportions will buy beef and other in week #2?

Answer: $(0.66 \quad 0.34) \begin{pmatrix} 0.8 & 0.2 \\ 0.6 & 0.4 \end{pmatrix} = (0.732 \quad 0.268)$,

which is 73.2 percent beef and 26.8 percent other dinners.

If we continue this procedure forming a chain, we may examine the successive state vectors as shown in Table 4–4.

TABLE 4–4
Successive state vectors

Week	Beef	Other
Beginning	(0.30	0.70)
#1	(0.66	0.34)
#2	(0.732	0.268)
#3	(0.7464	0.2536)
#4	(0.74928	0.25072)
#5	(0.749856	0.250144)

Observe that the components of each state vector sum to 1, as must be the case because they are proportions of a whole. Also, for the same reason, the rows of any transition matrix must each sum to 1. Note also that the state vector appears to be approaching $(0.75 \quad 0.25)$. What would happen if we used this state vector as a multiplier of the transition matrix? We would obtain

$$(0.75 \quad 0.25) \begin{pmatrix} 0.8 & 0.2 \\ 0.6 & 0.4 \end{pmatrix} = (0.75 \quad 0.25).$$

We see that the transition of $(0.75 \quad 0.25)$ leads to the same state, $(0.75 \quad 0.25)$, and we call this vector the *steady state*. The actual calculation of successive state vectors will never yield exactly $(0.75 \quad 0.25)$, so it is a matter of importance to learn how to find the steady state by a method other than tabulating successive state vectors and guessing the steady state from the sequence of results. In our problem, let us call the steady state $(v_1 \quad v_2)$. Then it must be true that

$$(v_1 \quad v_2) \begin{pmatrix} 0.8 & 0.2 \\ 0.6 & 0.4 \end{pmatrix} = (v_1 \quad v_2),$$

where, of course, $v_1 + v_2 = 1$. The matrix multiplication yields

$$\begin{array}{ll} e_1: & 0.8v_1 + 0.6v_2 = v_1 \\ e_2: & 0.2v_1 + 0.4v_2 = v_2 \end{array} \quad \text{or} \quad \begin{array}{l} -0.2v_1 + 0.6v_2 = 0 \\ 0.2v_1 - 0.6v_2 = 0. \end{array}$$

Clearly, e_1 and e_2 are the same equation, so we need only one of them. Taking e_1 with $v_1 + v_2 = 1$ we have

$$\begin{array}{ll} e_1: & -0.2v_1 + 0.6v_2 = 0 \\ e_3: & v_1 + v_2 = 1. \end{array}$$

Eliminating v_1, we obtain

$$e_4: \quad 0.8v_2 = 0.2.$$

From the last statement, $v_2 = 0.25$ and from e_3, $v_1 = 0.75$, so we have the steady state vector $(0.75 \; 0.25)$ that we obtained by guessing from the sequence in Table 4–4.

Exercise. Find the steady state for the transition matrix

$$\begin{pmatrix} 0.5 & 0.5 \\ 1 & 0 \end{pmatrix}.$$

Answer: $(2/3 \quad 1/3)$.

Next, let us suppose that once a customer buys beef he is so satisfied that he will buy beef the next time. This results in a 1 in the upper left corner of the transition matrix. Thus,

$$\begin{array}{cc} Beef & Other \\ (0.3 & 0.7) \end{array} \qquad \begin{array}{c} \\ Beef \\ Other \end{array} \begin{array}{cc} Beef & Other \\ \begin{pmatrix} 1.0 & 0.0 \\ 0.6 & 0.4 \end{pmatrix}. \end{array}$$

Inasmuch as 60 percent of those buying other meals change to beef, then continue to buy beef, it is reasonable to expect that ultimately all customers will buy beef and the steady state will be (1 0). In this situation, beef has absorbed all the business, and the chain leading to this steady state is called an *absorbing Markov chain.*

Exercise. Verify that the steady state for the last written beef-other matrix is (1 0).

We have used 2 by 2 transition matrices to illustrate the concept of Markov chains. Clearly, the methodology can be applied to n by n matrices. All that would change is the complexity of the calculations, so we shall not pursue this topic further. We should mention that Markov was a mathematician whose name has been given to processes of the type discussed in this section; namely, processes in which the future state is completely determined by the present state and not at all by the way in which the present state arose. Finally, we should call attention to the fact that the transition matrices in our discussion have been constant as we changed from state to state, and this fact can be made explicit by referring to the processes as *stationary* Markov processes.

4.12 PROBLEM SET 4-3

1. Technics and Soneton Companies each have 50 percent of the market for a product. Because of a promotion campaign, buyers are switching between Technics and Soneton according to the following transition matrix.

$$\begin{array}{c} \\ Technics \\ Soneton \end{array} \begin{array}{cc} Technics & Soneton \\ \begin{pmatrix} 0.6 & 0.4 \\ 0.5 & 0.5 \end{pmatrix}. \end{array}$$

a) What do the numbers 0.6 and 0.4 mean?
b) What will be the market shares after the first and second transitions?
c) What are the steady state market shares?

2. At a point in time, 95 percent of the population were spenders of copper pennies and 5 percent were savers. Because of the increasing value of pennies, only 30 percent of the spenders remain spenders, and 10 percent of the savers become spenders.
a) What will be the (spender saver) state vector after one transition?
b) What is the steady state vector?

3. At a point in time, 1 percent of the population use a drug and 99 percent do not. In a year, $\frac{1}{10}$ of one percent of nonusers become users, but all users remain users.

4.12 PROBLEM SET 4–3 (*concluded*)

a) What will be the percent of users and nonusers after one transition?
b) What is the steady state?

4. A recent survey showed that 20 percent of the population own some kind of microcomputer and 80 percent do not. Market experts predict that in a year 1 percent of the nonowners will become owners, and $\frac{1}{100}$ of one percent of the owners will become nonowners.
    a) What will be the predicted percent of owners and nonowners next year?
    b) What is the predicted steady state?

5. Currently it is known that 85 percent of the population own an automobile and 15 percent do not. Based upon past experience, 1¼ percent of the nonowners will become

owners, and $\frac{1}{1000}$ of one percent of the owners will become nonowners.

6. Carry out the multiplication and interpret the result.

$$
\begin{array}{c}
State \\
\begin{array}{cc} \#1 & \#2 \\ (a & b) \end{array}
\end{array}
\quad
\begin{array}{c}
 \\
\begin{array}{c} \#1 \\ \#2 \end{array}
\begin{pmatrix} 1 & 0 \\ 0 & 1 \end{pmatrix}.
\end{array}
$$

a) What will be the percent of owners and nonowners next year?
b) What is the steady state?

7. The following chain is cyclical, meaning that it returns periodically to the same state. Write the successive state vectors until the initial one, (0.6 0.3 0.1), reappears.

$$(0.6 \quad 0.3 \quad 0.1) \begin{pmatrix} 0 & 0 & 1 \\ 1 & 0 & 0 \\ 0 & 1 & 0 \end{pmatrix}.$$

4.13 ROW OPERATIONS

Row operations on a matrix consist either of multiplying (dividing) a row by a nonzero constant, adding a multiple of one row to another row, or interchanging two rows.[2] For example, given the matrix

$$A = \begin{pmatrix} 1 & 2 \\ 3 & 9 \end{pmatrix},$$

we may multiply the first row by -2 to give another matrix

$$\begin{pmatrix} -2 & -4 \\ 3 & 9 \end{pmatrix}.$$

Or, dividing the second row of A by 3 leads to the matrix

$$\begin{pmatrix} 1 & 2 \\ 1 & 3 \end{pmatrix}.$$

If we multiply the first row of A by -3 and add the result to the second row (leaving the first row unchanged), we have

$$\begin{pmatrix} 1 & 2 \\ 0 & 3 \end{pmatrix}.$$

---

[2] See also Chapter 2, Section 4.

Exercise.   What row operation performed on

$$\begin{pmatrix} 2 & 5 \\ 6 & 13 \end{pmatrix}$$

will lead to another matrix that will have a 0 in place of the 6, and what will the new matrix be? Answer: Multiply the first row of the given matrix by -3 and add to the second row, obtaining

$$\begin{pmatrix} 2 & 5 \\ 0 & -2 \end{pmatrix}.$$

In summary, we have

Matrix Row Operations

1. Multiply or divide a row by a nonzero constant.
2. Add a multiple of one row to a multiple of another row.
3. Interchange two rows.

4.14 THE INVERSE OF A MATRIX

In ordinary algebra, we write

$$a(a^{-1}) = (a^1)(a^{-1}) = a^{1-1} = a^0 = 1.$$

Thus,

$$aa^{-1} = 1,$$

and a^{-1} is called the multiplicative inverse of a because the product of a and a^{-1} is the identity. For example, 3^{-1} is the inverse of 3 because

$$3(3^{-1}) = 3 \cdot \frac{1}{3} = 1.$$

In matrix algebra, we have an analogous operation illustrated by

$$\begin{pmatrix} 1 & 2 \\ 2 & 3 \end{pmatrix}\begin{pmatrix} -3 & 2 \\ 2 & -1 \end{pmatrix} = \begin{pmatrix} 1 & 0 \\ 0 & 1 \end{pmatrix} = \boldsymbol{I}.$$

That is, the product of the matrices at the left is the identity matrix $\boldsymbol{I}$ of order 2. If we call the leftmost matrix $\boldsymbol{A}$, that is,

$$\boldsymbol{A} = \begin{pmatrix} 1 & 2 \\ 2 & 3 \end{pmatrix},$$

we define the second matrix as the *multiplicative inverse*, $\boldsymbol{A}^{-1}$, and write

$$\boldsymbol{A}^{-1} = \begin{pmatrix} -3 & 2 \\ 2 & -1 \end{pmatrix}.$$

Thus,

$$\begin{pmatrix} 1 & 2 \\ 2 & 3 \end{pmatrix} \cdot \begin{pmatrix} -3 & 2 \\ 2 & -1 \end{pmatrix} = I$$

$$A \quad \cdot \quad A^{-1} \quad = I$$

> **Definition.** Two square matrices are inverses of each other if their product is the identity matrix, I.

Observe that the definition says *inverses of each other*. This means that either matrix can be called A and the other is A^{-1} or, more to the point, we may write the product as AA^{-1} or $A^{-1}A$ and still obtain

> $$AA^{-1} = A^{-1}A = I.$$

Hence, any two square matrices that are inverses of one another will satisfy the rule of commutativity of multiplication.

For example, in the above, we have

$$A^{-1}A = \begin{pmatrix} -3 & 2 \\ 2 & -1 \end{pmatrix}\begin{pmatrix} 1 & 2 \\ 2 & 3 \end{pmatrix} = \begin{pmatrix} 1 & 0 \\ 0 & 1 \end{pmatrix} = I.$$

> **Exercise.** Verify that the following matrices are inverses of each other:
>
> $$\begin{pmatrix} 13 & 3 \\ 4 & 1 \end{pmatrix}\begin{pmatrix} 1 & -3 \\ -4 & 13 \end{pmatrix}.$$
>
> Answer: Multiplication of the two matrices leads to the unit matrix
>
> $$\begin{pmatrix} 1 & 0 \\ 0 & 1 \end{pmatrix}.$$

We shall see later that not every square matrix has an inverse. However, if the inverse of A does exist, it is unique: that is, a matrix that has an inverse has exactly one inverse.

Gauss-Jordan inversion. We are now ready to attack the main objective of this section, which is to compute the inverse of a given square matrix, if one exists. After we have learned computational procedures, we shall discover that they are directly applicable to the solution of n by n systems of linear equations. We present first the method attributed to Gauss and Jordan, which is the method we shall use as we continue our work.

Briefly, the Gauss-Jordan method starts by writing the given matrix at the left, and the corresponding identity matrix next to it, at the right. Then select and carry out row operations that will convert the given matrix into the identity matrix, and *apply the same operations to the matrix at the right.* When the left (given) matrix becomes the identity matrix, the matrix on the right will be the desired inverse. To illustrate, let us find the inverse of the matrix

$$\begin{pmatrix} 3 & 2 \\ 1 & 1 \end{pmatrix}.$$

We start by writing the given matrix to the left and the identity matrix to the right; thus,

$$\left(\begin{array}{cc|cc} 3 & 2 & 1 & 0 \\ 1 & 1 & 0 & 1 \end{array}\right).$$

To change the left matrix into the identity matrix will require several steps (row operations which we perform on both matrices). We start by getting a 1 in the upper left corner. This could be accomplished by dividing the first row above by 3. However, to avoid fractions and thus simplify the arithmetic, we simply interchange the first and second rows to obtain

$$\left(\begin{array}{cc|cc} 1 & 1 & 0 & 1 \\ 3 & 2 & 1 & 0 \end{array}\right).$$

Next, get a 0 in the second row, first column of the left matrix by multiplying the first row above by -3 and adding to the second row. We then have

$$\left(\begin{array}{cc|cc} 1 & 1 & 0 & 1 \\ 0 & -1 & 1 & -3 \end{array}\right).$$

Now divide the second row, just above, by -1 to obtain a 1 in the second row, second column of the left matrix. Thus,

$$\left(\begin{array}{cc|cc} 1 & 1 & 0 & 1 \\ 0 & 1 & -1 & 3 \end{array}\right).$$

Finally, multiply the second row, just above, by -1 and add to the first to obtain a 0 in the first row, second column of the left matrix. This gives

$$\left(\begin{array}{cc|cc} 1 & 0 & 1 & -2 \\ 0 & 1 & -1 & 3 \end{array}\right).$$

We now have the identity matrix at the left, so the inverse of

$$\begin{pmatrix} 3 & 2 \\ 1 & 1 \end{pmatrix}$$

is the matrix at the right; namely,

$$\begin{pmatrix} 1 & -2 \\ -1 & 3 \end{pmatrix}.$$

As a check, we have

$$\begin{pmatrix} 3 & 2 \\ 1 & 1 \end{pmatrix} \begin{pmatrix} 1 & -2 \\ -1 & 3 \end{pmatrix} = \begin{pmatrix} 1 & 0 \\ 0 & 1 \end{pmatrix}.$$

Exercise. Apply the procedure of the last example and find the inverse of the matrix

$$A = \begin{pmatrix} 7 & 3 \\ 2 & 1 \end{pmatrix}.$$

Answer: The inverse is the matrix

$$A^{-1} = \begin{pmatrix} 1 & -3 \\ -2 & 7 \end{pmatrix}.$$

Note in the exercise that interchanging of rows to avoid fractions was of no use. Another situation, where interchange *is* useful, occurs when the matrix is in a form that does not lend itself to the inversion process. For example, in

$$\left(\begin{array}{cc|cc} 0 & 1 & 1 & 0 \\ 2 & 3 & 0 & 1 \end{array} \right)$$

we have an unwanted zero as the upper left diagonal element. Interchanging rows, we have

$$\left(\begin{array}{cc|cc} 2 & 3 & 0 & 1 \\ 0 & 1 & 1 & 0 \end{array} \right).$$

We can now proceed to the inverse in the usual manner. Thus, add -3 times row 2 to row 1

$$\left(\begin{array}{cc|cc} 2 & 0 & -3 & 1 \\ 0 & 1 & 1 & 0 \end{array} \right).$$

Then, divide the first row by 2

$$\left(\begin{array}{cc|cc} 1 & 0 & -3/2 & 1/2 \\ 0 & 1 & 1 & 0 \end{array} \right)$$

and we have that

$$\text{if} \quad A = \begin{pmatrix} 0 & 1 \\ 2 & 3 \end{pmatrix}, \quad \text{then} \quad A^{-1} = \begin{pmatrix} -3/2 & 1/2 \\ 1 & 0 \end{pmatrix}.$$

Often, a matrix such as the above is rewritten for convenience by factoring out the common denominator. Thus, we would write

$$A^{-1} = (1/2) \begin{pmatrix} -3 & 1 \\ 2 & 0 \end{pmatrix}.$$

We next illustrate the computation of the inverse of a square matrix of order 3, the left matrix in the following:

$$\begin{pmatrix} 2 & 3 & 1 & | & 1 & 0 & 0 \\ 1 & 4 & 2 & | & 0 & 1 & 0 \\ 5 & 6 & 4 & | & 0 & 0 & 1 \end{pmatrix}.$$

First, we interchange rows 1 and 2 to obtain

$$\begin{pmatrix} 1 & 4 & 2 & | & 0 & 1 & 0 \\ 2 & 3 & 1 & | & 1 & 0 & 0 \\ 5 & 6 & 4 & | & 0 & 0 & 1 \end{pmatrix}.$$

Multiply the first row above by -2 and add to the second row to obtain

$$\begin{pmatrix} 1 & 4 & 2 & | & 0 & 1 & 0 \\ 0 & -5 & -3 & | & 1 & -2 & 0 \\ 5 & 6 & 4 & | & 0 & 0 & 1 \end{pmatrix}.$$

Multiply the first row above by -5 and add to the third row to obtain

$$\begin{pmatrix} 1 & 4 & 2 & | & 0 & 1 & 0 \\ 0 & -5 & -3 & | & 1 & -2 & 0 \\ 0 & -14 & -6 & | & 0 & -5 & 1 \end{pmatrix}.$$

The tactics we have followed are these: first get a 1 in the first column, first row, then use combinations of this row with each of the other rows to get zeros in the first columns of these rows. We now repeat these tactics, starting by getting a 1 in the second column of the second row, then using this row to get zeros in the second columns of the other rows.

Interchanging rows does not avoid fractions, so we divide the second row by -5 to obtain the new second row

$$(0 \quad 1 \quad 3/5 \quad | \quad -1/5 \quad 2/5 \quad 0).$$

If we multiply this new second row by -4 and add to the first row, then multiply the new second row by 14 and add to the third row, we obtain

$$\begin{pmatrix} 1 & 0 & -2/5 & | & 4/5 & -3/5 & 0 \\ 0 & 1 & 3/5 & | & -1/5 & 2/5 & 0 \\ 0 & 0 & 12/5 & | & -14/5 & 3/5 & 1 \end{pmatrix}.$$

Finally, we repeat the tactics by getting a 1 in the third row of the third column and then using this row to get zeros in the third column of the other rows. The new third row, obtained by dividing the previous third row by $12/5$, is

$$(0 \quad 0 \quad 1 \quad | \quad -7/6 \quad 1/4 \quad 5/12).$$

If we multiply this new third row by $2/5$ and add to the first row, then multiply the new third row by $-3/5$ and add to the second row we find

$$\begin{pmatrix} 1 & 0 & 0 & | & 1/3 & -1/2 & 1/6 \\ 0 & 1 & 0 & | & 1/2 & 1/4 & -1/4 \\ 0 & 0 & 1 & | & -7/6 & 1/4 & 5/12 \end{pmatrix},$$

which has the matrix I to the left and the desired inverse to the right.

Exercise. a) Multiply the original matrix of the last illustration by the inverse and verify that the product is I. b) Rewrite the inverse by factoring out the common denominator. Answer:

$$A^{-1} = (1/12)\begin{pmatrix} 4 & -6 & 2 \\ 6 & 3 & -3 \\ -14 & 3 & 5 \end{pmatrix}.$$

Zeros first. The Gauss-Jordan method proceeds to obtain ones on the main diagonal and zeros for the off-diagonal elements. A variation on this procedure is to obtain the off-diagonal zeros first and, following this, obtain ones on the diagonal.[3] This *zeros-first* variation can simplify the work involved in hand calculation by avoiding fractions until the last step.

Example. By the zeros-first method, find the inverse of

$$A = \begin{pmatrix} 2 & 3 \\ 4 & 7 \end{pmatrix}.$$

We start in the usual manner by writing

$$\begin{pmatrix} 2 & 3 & | & 1 & 0 \\ 4 & 7 & | & 0 & 1 \end{pmatrix}.$$

Multiplying the first row by -2 and adding to the second row, we have

$$\begin{pmatrix} 2 & 3 & | & 1 & 0 \\ 0 & 1 & | & -2 & 1 \end{pmatrix}.$$

---

[3] Suggested by Professor Van Cor of New Hampshire College.

We now have a zero as the lower off-diagonal element and proceed to obtain a zero as the upper off-diagonal element. Multiplying the second row by -3 and adding to the first yields

$$\begin{pmatrix} 2 & 0 & \bigm| & 7 & -3 \\ 0 & 1 & \bigm| & -2 & 1 \end{pmatrix}.$$

The off-diagonal elements now are zero, and ones are obtained on the main diagonal by dividing the first row by 2 to give

$$\begin{pmatrix} 1 & 0 & \bigm| & 7/2 & -3/2 \\ 0 & 1 & \bigm| & -2 & 1 \end{pmatrix}.$$

The desired inverse is

$$A^{-1} = \begin{pmatrix} 7/2 & -3/2 \\ -2 & 1 \end{pmatrix}.$$

As we stated earlier, this latter matrix is often rewritten for convenience by factoring out the common denominator to get

$$A^{-1} = (1/2) \begin{pmatrix} 7 & -3 \\ -4 & 2 \end{pmatrix}.$$

Exercise. Use the zeros-first method to find the inverse of

$$A = \begin{pmatrix} 3 & 2 & -1 \\ 1 & -1 & 0 \\ 2 & 0 & -1 \end{pmatrix}.$$

Answer:

$$A^{-1} = (1/3) \begin{pmatrix} 1 & 2 & -1 \\ 1 & -1 & -1 \\ 2 & 4 & -5 \end{pmatrix}.$$

The above example and exercise illustrate how the zeros-first method postpones the introduction of fractions until the final step. This is an advantage for hand calculation, and we recommend its use. Matrix inversion on high-speed computers, on the other hand, is usually carried out by programs following the Gauss-Jordan method. However, the computer program can be adapted to make use of the interchange of rows and/or the zeros-first method. In large-scale problems, these modifications can lead to significant improvements in speed and accuracy.

To see why the Gauss-Jordan method works, consider the true statement

$$A = IA.$$

Suppose that we carry out row operations on the left of the equal sign to change the left matrix to I, and maintain the equality by applying the same operations to the first matrix on the right of the equal sign (which starts out as I). The end result will be I on the left and something times A on the right; thus,

$$I = (?)A.$$

We showed earlier that the inverse of a matrix is unique. Hence, there is only one appropriate entry for (?) in the above. It is A^{-1}. It follows that if we write a given square matrix A with I to its right, then change the left to I by row operations that are applied also to the right, the end result will be A^{-1} on the right.

Symbolically, then, the Gauss-Jordan method for finding the inverse of a square matrix A is to start with the matrix

$$(A \mid I)$$

and use the row operations to transform the latter matrix into

$$(I \mid A^{-1}).$$

Of course, the above process will work only when there exists an inverse. Now clearly not every square matrix has an inverse. For example, the zero matrix O has no inverse since $O \cdot B = O$ for every matrix B. As an example of a nonzero square matrix that has no inverse, consider the matrix

$$\begin{pmatrix} 1 & 1 \\ 2 & 2 \end{pmatrix}.$$

If we set this matrix up with the unit matrix to the right, we have

$$\left(\begin{array}{cc|cc} 1 & 1 & 1 & 0 \\ 2 & 2 & 0 & 1 \end{array} \right).$$

The indicated row operation is to multiply the first row by -2 and add to the second row. We find

$$\left(\begin{array}{cc|cc} 1 & 1 & 1 & 0 \\ 0 & 0 & -2 & 1 \end{array} \right).$$

No row operations for the left matrix can be found that will provide a 1 in the lower right corner and a 0 in the upper right. The given matrix has no inverse and is said to be *singular*. In the matrix context, the word singular does not mean one or single but, rather, connotes that the matrix is special in that it has no inverse.

4.15 PROBLEM SET 4-4

Find the inverse of each of the following, if one exists.

1. $\begin{pmatrix} 7 & 3 \\ 2 & 1 \end{pmatrix}$.

2. $\begin{pmatrix} 9 & 4 \\ 2 & 1 \end{pmatrix}$.

3. $\begin{pmatrix} 2 & 2 \\ 3 & 5 \end{pmatrix}$.

4. $\begin{pmatrix} 1 & -1 \\ -1 & 2 \end{pmatrix}$.

5. $\begin{pmatrix} 2 & 2 \\ 6 & 6 \end{pmatrix}$.

6. $\begin{pmatrix} 3 & 3 \\ 2 & 2 \end{pmatrix}$.

7. $\begin{pmatrix} 1 & 3 \\ 2 & 0 \end{pmatrix}$.

8. $\begin{pmatrix} 2 & 5 \\ 3 & 4 \end{pmatrix}$.

9. $\begin{pmatrix} 0 & 1 \\ 2 & 3 \end{pmatrix}$.

10. $\begin{pmatrix} 0 & 3 \\ 2 & 5 \end{pmatrix}$.

11. $\begin{pmatrix} 2 & 8 & -11 \\ -1 & -5 & 7 \\ 1 & 2 & -3 \end{pmatrix}$.

12. $\begin{pmatrix} 2 & 2 & 3 \\ 0 & 1 & 1 \\ 4 & 0 & 3 \end{pmatrix}$.

13. $\begin{pmatrix} 1 & 1 & 1 \\ 1 & 1 & 1 \\ 2 & 2 & 2 \end{pmatrix}$.

14. $\begin{pmatrix} 0 & -1 & 1 \\ -1 & 1 & 2 \\ 1 & 0 & -2 \end{pmatrix}$.

15. $\begin{pmatrix} 2 & 1 & 4 \\ 3 & 0 & 2 \\ 1 & 2 & 3 \end{pmatrix}$.

16. $\begin{pmatrix} 1 & -1 & 0 \\ 2 & 1 & 3 \\ 3 & 0 & 3 \end{pmatrix}$.

17. Let

$$A = \begin{pmatrix} 2 & -1 & 0 \\ -1 & 1 & 3 \\ 2 & 1 & 4 \end{pmatrix}.$$

Find a matrix that
a) Commutes multiplicatively with **A**.
b) Does not commute multiplicatively with **A**.

18. Consider the BASIC program shown in Program 4–1.
a) Describe what the program is doing line-by-line.
b) Run the program for Problems 1 through 8 and 11 through 16.

19. a) Modify Program 4–1 to allow for the interchange of two rows.
b) Run the program in (a) for Problems 1 through 16.

20. a) Modify Program 4–1 to perform the zeros-first method.
b) Run the program in (a) for Problems 1 through 16.

Program 4-1

```
10  REM INVERSE OF n by n MATRIX, n <= 10
20  INPUT "Enter the dimension n";N
30  FOR I=1 TO N
40  PRINT "Enter the elements one-by-one in row";I
50  FOR J=1 TO N
60  INPUT A(I,J)
```

4.15 PROBLEM SET 4–4 (*concluded*)

```
 70    NEXT J
 80    NEXT I
 90    FOR I=1 TO N
100    FOR J=N+1 TO N+N
110    A(I,J)=0
120    IF J=I+N THEN A(I,J)=1
130    NEXT J
140    NEXT I
150    I=1
160    C=A(I,I)
170    IF C=0 THEN PRINT "No inverse exists"
180    IF C=0 THEN GOTO 390
190    FOR J=1 TO N+N
200    A(I,J)=A(I,J)/C
210    NEXT J
220    IF I=1 THEN P=2 ELSE P=1
230    D=-A(P,I)
240    FOR K=I TO N+N
250    A(P,K)=D*A(I,K)+A(P,K)
260    NEXT K
270    IF P=N THEN I=I+1
280    IF P=N THEN GOTO 160
290    P=P+1
300    IF P<>I THEN GOTO 230 ELSE IF I=N THEN GOTO 320 ELSE P=P+1
310    GOTO 230
320    PRINT "The inverse is"
330    FOR I=1 TO N
340    FOR J=N+1 TO N+N
350    PRINT A(I,J),
360    NEXT J
370    PRINT
380    NEXT I
390    END
```

4.16 APPLICATIONS—2: MATRIX SOLUTION OF *n* BY *n* LINEAR SYSTEMS

In this section, we shall show how the solution of an n by n system of linear equations is accomplished by the Gauss-Jordan method. To set the stage, consider first the manner in which a simple linear equation such as

$$2x = 3$$

is solved for x. To bring out what we have in mind, two procedures using slightly different symbols are presented side by side.

Regular solution symbols	*Inverse solution symbols*
$2x = 3$	$2x = 3$
$\frac{1}{2}(2x) = \frac{1}{2}(3)$	$(2^{-1})(2x) = (2^{-1})(3)$

Regular solution symbols   *Inverse solution symbols*

$$(1)\ x = \frac{1}{2}(3)$$ $$(1)\ x = (2^{-1})(3)$$

$$x = \frac{1}{2}(3).$$ $$x = (2^{-1})(3).$$

Notice on the right that the solution was obtained by multiplying both sides of the original equation by the multiplicative inverse of 2, which is 2^{-1}. More generally, if we start with

$$ax = b$$

then multiply both sides of the equation by the inverse, a^{-1}, to obtain

$$(a^{-1})(a^1x) = (a^{-1})b$$

we have

$$(a^{-1+1})\,x = (a^{-1})b$$
$$a^0x = a^{-1}b$$
$$(1)\,x = a^{-1}b$$
$$x = a^{-1}b.$$

The solution of a linear system proceeds in a manner analogous to that just illustrated for a single equation, except that now we multiply both sides of the matrix form of the system by the inverse of the coefficient matrix. To see how this works out, consider the 2 by 2 system

$$2x_1 + 3x_2 = 17$$
$$x_1 + 2x_2 = 10.$$

The system can be written in expanded matrix form as

$$\begin{pmatrix} 2 & 3 \\ 1 & 2 \end{pmatrix} \begin{pmatrix} x_1 \\ x_2 \end{pmatrix} = \begin{pmatrix} 17 \\ 10 \end{pmatrix},$$

or equivalently in the form

$$\boldsymbol{Ax} = \boldsymbol{b}.$$

In this equation,

$$\boldsymbol{A} = \begin{pmatrix} 2 & 3 \\ 1 & 2 \end{pmatrix}$$

is the matrix of coefficients,

$$\boldsymbol{x} = \begin{pmatrix} x_1 \\ x_2 \end{pmatrix}$$

is the column vector of unknowns, and

$$\boldsymbol{b} = \begin{pmatrix} 17 \\ 10 \end{pmatrix}$$

is the column vector of constants. If both sides of the matrix equation $Ax = b$ are multiplied by the inverse of the coefficient matrix, namely A^{-1}, we have

$$A^{-1} Ax = A^{-1}b,$$

from which it follows that

$$x = A^{-1}b.$$

Now recall that we solved for the inverse matrix A^{-1} by using row operations to transform the matrix

$$(A \mid I)$$

into the matrix

$$(I \mid A^{-1}).$$

If we then start with the matrix

$$(A \mid b),$$

we can rewrite this in the form

$$(A \mid I \cdot b).$$

Using the row operations, we would be transforming the latter matrix into

$$(I \mid A^{-1} \cdot b),$$

thereby giving us the solution to the system of equations.

For example, consider the system given earlier,

$$2x_1 + 3x_2 = 17$$
$$x_1 + 2x_2 = 10.$$

If we set this up in the form $(A \mid b)$, we have

$$\begin{pmatrix} 2 & 3 & \vline & 17 \\ 1 & 2 & \vline & 10 \end{pmatrix}.$$

Proceeding in the usual manner with the Gauss-Jordan method, we interchange rows to obtain

$$\begin{pmatrix} 1 & 2 & \vline & 10 \\ 2 & 3 & \vline & 17 \end{pmatrix}.$$

Then, we add -2 times row 1 to row 2:

$$\begin{pmatrix} 1 & 2 & \vline & 10 \\ 0 & -1 & \vline & -3 \end{pmatrix}.$$

Next, we divide row 2 by -1:

$$\begin{pmatrix} 1 & 2 & \vline & 10 \\ 0 & 1 & \vline & 3 \end{pmatrix}$$

and add -2 times row 2 to row 1:

$$\begin{pmatrix} 1 & 0 & \bigm| & 4 \\ 0 & 1 & \bigm| & 3 \end{pmatrix}.$$

From the last matrix, we see that the solution is

$$\begin{pmatrix} x_1 \\ x_2 \end{pmatrix} = \begin{pmatrix} 4 \\ 3 \end{pmatrix}$$

so that $x_1 = 4$ and $x_2 = 3$.

Exercise. If the system

$$\begin{aligned} 7x_1 + 3x_2 &= 5 \\ 2x_1 + x_2 &= 7 \end{aligned}$$

is expressed in matrix form as $Ax = b$, what are A, x, and b; what is the solution? Answer: A is the coefficient matrix

$$\begin{pmatrix} 7 & 3 \\ 2 & 1 \end{pmatrix},$$

x is the solution vector

$$\begin{pmatrix} x_1 \\ x_2 \end{pmatrix},$$

b is the vector of constants

$$\begin{pmatrix} 5 \\ 7 \end{pmatrix},$$

and the solution is

$$x_1 = -16 \quad \text{and} \quad x_2 = 39.$$

Now consider the 3 by 3 system

$$\begin{aligned} 2x_1 + 2x_2 + 3x_3 &= 3 \\ x_2 + x_3 &= 2 \\ x_1 + x_2 + x_3 &= 4. \end{aligned}$$

This time, we start with the matrix

$$\begin{pmatrix} 2 & 2 & 3 & \bigm| & 3 \\ 0 & 1 & 1 & \bigm| & 2 \\ 1 & 1 & 1 & \bigm| & 4 \end{pmatrix}.$$

We then interchange rows 1 and 3

$$\begin{pmatrix} 1 & 1 & 1 & \bigm| & 4 \\ 0 & 1 & 1 & \bigm| & 2 \\ 2 & 2 & 3 & \bigm| & 3 \end{pmatrix}.$$

and add -2 times row 1 to row 3:

$$\left(\begin{array}{ccc|c} 1 & 1 & 1 & 4 \\ 0 & 1 & 1 & 2 \\ 0 & 0 & 1 & -5 \end{array}\right).$$

At this point, we add -1 times row 2 to row 1:

$$\left(\begin{array}{ccc|c} 1 & 0 & 0 & 2 \\ 0 & 1 & 1 & 2 \\ 0 & 0 & 1 & -5 \end{array}\right).$$

Lastly, we add -1 times row 3 to row 2:

$$\left(\begin{array}{ccc|c} 1 & 0 & 0 & 2 \\ 0 & 1 & 0 & 7 \\ 0 & 0 & 1 & -5 \end{array}\right)$$

so that the solution is given by

$$x_1 = 2, \quad x_2 = 7, \quad \text{and} \quad x_3 = -5.$$

An alternative approach to solving the system $Ax = b$ would be to use the Gauss-Jordan method to determine A^{-1} and then find the solution by multiplication of $A^{-1} \cdot b$. This method is no shorter than the one we developed above since the row operations would be the same; i.e., instead of transforming

$$(A \mid b) \rightarrow (I \mid s)$$

where s is the solution vector, we would have transformed

$$(A \mid I) \rightarrow (I \mid A^{-1}).$$

In addition, matrix inversion is defined *only for square matrices* (n by n systems), whereas, as we will see in Section 4.20, the Gauss-Jordan method of transforming $(A \mid b) \rightarrow (I \mid s)$ works for any m by n system regardless of whether $m = n$ or $m \neq n$.

One advantage, though, of using the inverse appears when we are trying to solve a system of equations whose coefficient matrix is A, for a variety of different constant vectors. As an example of this, suppose a company makes liquid products Primeoil, Midoil, and Lastoil, which contain different amounts of additives A_1, A_2, and A_3 per gallon, as shown in Table 4–5.

TABLE 4–5

Liquid	Gallons Made	Pounds of Additive per Gallon		
		A_1	A_2	A_3
Primeoil	x_1	1	1	1
Midoil	x_2	1	2	1
Lastoil	x_3	2	0	1

The additives deteriorate if not used within a week, so each Saturday the company schedules production of $(x_1 \quad x_2 \quad x_3)$ gallons of Primeoil, Midoil, and Lastoil to use up the additives on hand. These amounts vary from week to week and are represented by the vector $(a_1 \quad a_2 \quad a_3)$. If we schedule $(x_1 \quad x_2 \quad x_3)$ gallons of the liquids, the pounds of additive A_1 used will be $x_1(1) + x_2(1) + x_3(2)$, and this should equal a_1, the amount available. Hence, $x_1 + x_2 + 2x_3 = a_1$. Combining this condition with the conditions on additives A_2 and A_3 leads us to the system

$$\begin{aligned}
x_1 + x_2 + 2x_3 &= a_1 \\
x_1 + 2x_2 &= a_2 \\
x_1 + x_2 + x_3 &= a_3.
\end{aligned}$$

The coefficient matrix is

$$A = \begin{pmatrix} 1 & 1 & 2 \\ 1 & 2 & 0 \\ 1 & 1 & 1 \end{pmatrix}$$

and it may be verified that the inverse is

$$A^{-1} = \begin{pmatrix} -2 & -1 & 4 \\ 1 & 1 & -2 \\ 1 & 0 & -1 \end{pmatrix}.$$

Hence, the solution vector is

$$\begin{pmatrix} x_1 \\ x_2 \\ x_3 \end{pmatrix} = \begin{pmatrix} -2 & -1 & 4 \\ 1 & 1 & -2 \\ 1 & 0 & -1 \end{pmatrix} \begin{pmatrix} a_1 \\ a_2 \\ a_3 \end{pmatrix}.$$

Suppose that on a given Saturday the amounts of additives available are $a_1 = 20$ pounds of A_1, $a_2 = 30$ pounds of A_2, and $a_3 = 20$ pounds of A_3. To use up these additives, the production schedule should be

$$\begin{pmatrix} x_1 \\ x_2 \\ x_3 \end{pmatrix} = \begin{pmatrix} -2 & -1 & 4 \\ 1 & 1 & -2 \\ 1 & 0 & -1 \end{pmatrix} \begin{pmatrix} 20 \\ 30 \\ 20 \end{pmatrix} = \begin{pmatrix} 10 \\ 10 \\ 0 \end{pmatrix},$$

which is 10 gallons of Primeoil, 10 gallons of Midoil, and no Lastoil.

Exercise. If the additives available at a week's end are $(a_1 \ a_2 \ a_3) = (80 \ 100 \ 70)$, what should the production schedule be?
Answer: $(x_1 \quad x_2 \quad x_3) = (20 \quad 40 \quad 10)$.

Of course, it may not be possible to schedule production to use all the additives available on a given Saturday. For example, if $(a_1 \quad a_2 \quad a_3) = (40 \quad 60 \quad 50)$, the solution vector is $(x_1 \quad x_2 \quad x_3) = (60 \quad 0 \quad -10)$, and the value $x_3 = -10$ is not possible. In such a case we might choose to maximize either the total amount of liquid made or the total amount of additive used, depending upon cost considerations, and we would apply the linear programming techniques begun in Chapter 3 and continued in Chapters 5 and 6 to determine the optimum production schedule.

Finally, the Gauss-Jordan method can be used to solve systems of equations that have no solution or an unlimited number of solutions. For example, consider the system

$$2x_1 + 5x_2 = 15$$
$$3.2x_1 + 8x_2 = 20,$$

which was shown in Section 2.10 to have no solutions. Starting with the matrix

$$\begin{pmatrix} 2 & 5 & | & 15 \\ 3.2 & 8 & | & 20 \end{pmatrix},$$

we first divide row 1 by 2 to obtain

$$\begin{pmatrix} 1 & 2.5 & | & 7.5 \\ 3.2 & 8 & | & 20 \end{pmatrix}$$

and add -3.2 times row 1 to row 2

$$\begin{pmatrix} 1 & 2.5 & | & 7.5 \\ 0 & 0 & | & -4 \end{pmatrix}.$$

At this point, we can proceed no further! Why? To see exactly what has happened, we retranslate the latter matrix back into equations, so we have

$$x_1 + 2.5x_2 = 7.5$$
$$0 + 0 = -4.$$

The last equation is an absurd contradiction since $0 \neq -4$; so that, as in Section 2.10, there can be no solution.

Exercise. Show that the following system has no solutions:

$$2x_1 + 3x_2 = 17$$
$$9x_1 + 13.5x_2 = 25.$$

Now consider the system

$$2x_1 + 5x_2 = 15$$
$$3.2x_1 + 8x_2 = 24,$$

which we showed in Section 2.10 to have an unlimited number of solutions. This time, we start with the matrix

$$\begin{pmatrix} 2 & 5 & | & 15 \\ 3.2 & 8 & | & 24 \end{pmatrix}$$

and obtain

$$\begin{pmatrix} 1 & 2.5 & | & 7.5 \\ 3.2 & 8 & | & 24 \end{pmatrix}$$

and then

$$\begin{pmatrix} 1 & 2.5 & | & 7.5 \\ 0 & 0 & | & 0 \end{pmatrix}.$$

The latter matrix represents the system

$$\begin{aligned} x_1 + 2.5x_2 &= 7.5 \\ 0 + 0 &= 0, \end{aligned}$$

which means we really have a single equation,

$$x_1 + 2.5x_2 = 7.5.$$

On a graph, the original two lines would be coincident, and hence the system has an unlimited number of solutions.

Exercise. Show that the following system has an unlimited number of solutions.

$$\begin{aligned} 2x_1 + 3x_2 &= 17 \\ 9x_1 + 13.5x_2 &= 76.5. \end{aligned}$$

Summarizing our results for solving an n by n system, we start with the matrix

$$(A \mid b)$$

and attempt to transform it into the matrix

$$(I \mid s).$$

One of three things will result:

    1. An n by n matrix together with the unique solution; e.g.,

$$\begin{pmatrix} 1 & 0 & 0 & | & 5 \\ 0 & 1 & 0 & | & -2 \\ 0 & 0 & 1 & | & 6 \end{pmatrix}.$$

2. A row that is all zeros *except in the constant column*, indicating that there are no solutions; e.g.,

$$\left(\begin{array}{ccc|c} 1 & 0 & 2 & -4 \\ 0 & 1 & 3 & 8 \\ 0 & 0 & 0 & 2 \end{array}\right).$$

3. A matrix in a form different from (1) and (2), indicating that there are an unlimited number of solutions. Note that for an n by n system, this case occurs when there is a row with all zeros, including the constant column; e.g.,

$$\left(\begin{array}{ccc|c} 1 & 0 & 2 & -4 \\ 0 & 1 & 3 & 8 \\ 0 & 0 & 0 & 0 \end{array}\right).$$

4.17 PROBLEM SET 4–5

1. Consider the system

$$8x_1 + 5x_2 = 2$$
$$3x_1 + 2x_2 = 1.$$

a) Relating the system to $Ax = b$, what is A?, x?, b?
b) Solve the system using the Gauss-Jordan method.
c) Compute A^{-1}.
d) Write $x = A^{-1}b$ in expanded matrix form.
e) Compute the solution from part (d).
f) What would be the solution vector if the elements in the vector of constants, 2 and 1, were changed to each of the following:
(1) 1, 0.   (2) 0, 1.   (3) 1, 1.
(4) 3, 4.   (5) −3, 1.

2. Answer parts (a) through (e) of Problem 1 for the system

$$4x_1 + 3x_2 = 2$$
$$9x_1 + 7x_2 = 3.$$

f) What would be the solution vector if the elements in the vector of constants, 2 and 3, were changed to each of the following:
(1) 1, 0.   (2) 0, 1.   (3) 1, 1.
(4) 2, 1.   (5) −1, 2.

3. Answer parts (a) through (e) of Problem 1 for the system

$$6x_1 + 8x_2 = 3$$
$$2x_1 + 3x_2 = 1.$$

f) What would be the solution vector if the elements in the vector of constants, 3 and 1, were changed to each of the following:
(1) 1, 1.   (2) 0, 1.   (3) 1, 0.
(4) 2, 3.   (5) −1, 1.

4. Given the system

$$8x_1 - 7x_2 = b_1$$
$$-5x_1 + 5x_2 = b_2$$

find the missing elements to complete the following equation:

$$\begin{pmatrix} x_1 \\ x_2 \end{pmatrix} = \begin{pmatrix} \end{pmatrix} \begin{pmatrix} b_1 \\ b_2 \end{pmatrix}.$$

5. Answer parts (a) through (e) of Problem 1 for the system

$$3x_1 + 5x_3 = 3$$
$$2x_1 + 2x_2 + 5x_3 = 7$$
$$ x_2 + x_3 = 2.$$

f) What would be the solution vector if the elements in the vector of constants, 3, 7,

4.17 PROBLEM SET 4–5 (continued)

and 2, were changed to each of the following:

(1) 1, 2, 1. (2) 2, 3, 4. (3) 1, 0, − 1.
(4) 1, 6, 2. (5) 2, 10, 1.

6. Answer parts (a) through (e) of Problem 1 for the system

$$7x_1 + 3x_2 \qquad = 1$$
$$3x_2 + 5x_3 = 2$$
$$x_1 + \quad x_2 + \quad x_3 = 3.$$

f) What would be the solution vector if the elements in the vector of constants were changed from 1, 2, and 3 to each of the following:

(1) 1, − 1, 1. (2) 2, 3, 0. (3) − 1, 2, − 2. (4) 10, − 1, 1. (5) 0, − 1, 0.

7. Given the system

$$2x_1 + 2x_2 + 3x_3 = b_1$$
$$x_2 + \quad x_3 = b_2$$
$$4x_1 \qquad + 3x_3 = b_3$$

find the missing elements to complete the following equation:

$$\begin{pmatrix} x_1 \\ x_2 \\ x_3 \end{pmatrix} = \begin{pmatrix} \end{pmatrix} \begin{pmatrix} b_1 \\ b_2 \\ b_3 \end{pmatrix}.$$

8. Given the system

$$x_1 + 2x_2 + \quad x_3 = b_1$$
$$2x_1 + \quad x_2 + \quad x_3 = b_2$$
$$3x_1 \qquad + 2x_3 = b_3$$

a) Verify by multiplication that the inverse of the coefficient matrix is

$$\mathbf{A}^{-1} = \begin{pmatrix} -2/3 & 4/3 & -1/3 \\ 1/3 & 1/3 & -1/3 \\ 1 & -2 & 1 \end{pmatrix}.$$

b) Compute the solution vector if the b's are, respectively,

(1) 3, 0, 3. (2) 6, 3, 0.

9. Given the system

$$x_1 + \quad x_2 + \quad x_3 + \quad x_4 = b_1$$
$$x_1 + 2x_2 + 2x_3 + 2x_4 = b_2$$
$$x_1 + 2x_2 + 3x_3 + 3x_4 = b_3$$
$$x_1 + 2x_2 + 3x_3 + 4x_4 = b_4$$

a) Verify by multiplication that the inverse of the coefficient matrix is

$$\begin{pmatrix} 2 & -1 & 0 & 0 \\ -1 & 2 & -1 & 0 \\ 0 & -1 & 2 & -1 \\ 0 & 0 & -1 & 1 \end{pmatrix}.$$

b) What is the solution vector if the b's are, respectively,

(1) 1, 1, 1, 1. (2) 1, 0, 1, 0.

10. The table shows that we plan to make x_1 Primers. Making each Primer requires one hour on machine M_1 and one hour on M_3. Other entries in the table have corresponding interpretations. H_1, H_2, and H_3 are the total numbers of hours available on M_1, M_2, and M_3, respectively.

a) Set up the system of equations that must be solved if all available machine hours are to be used in making $(x_1 \quad x_2 \quad x_3)$ units of the products.

Product	Units Made	Machine Hours per Unit on Machine		
		M_1	M_2	M_3
Primer	x_1	1	0	1
Middler	x_2	0	1	2
Laster	x_3	2	3	0

b) Set up the coefficient matrix and find its inverse.

What number of units can be made if the numbers of available hours, $(H_1 \quad H_2 \quad H_3)$, are:

c) (160 80 200)?   d) (400 400 400)?
e) (320 192 256)?

Solve the following systems:

11. $2x_1 − 3x_2 = 5$
$6x_1 − 9x_2 = 8.$

12. $3x_1 − 6x_2 = 8$
$−5x_1 + 10x_2 = 12.$

4.17 PROBLEM SET 4–5 (concluded)

13.
$$2x_1 + 3x_2 = -15$$
$$-(8/3)x_1 - 4x_2 = 25.$$

14.
$$7x_1 + 2x_2 = 9$$
$$17.5x_1 + 5x_2 = 14.$$

15.
$$3x_1 + 12x_2 = -9$$
$$-2x_1 - 8x_2 = 6.$$

16.
$$5x_1 + 3x_2 = 15$$
$$2x_1 + 1.2x_2 = 6.$$

17.
$$2x_1 + 3x_2 = 15$$
$$(8/3)x_1 + 4x_2 = 20.$$

18.
$$6x_1 - 15x_2 = -3$$
$$-10x_1 + 25x_2 = 5.$$

---

19. a) Modify the BASIC program in Program 4–1 (Section 4.15) to compute and print the solution of an n by n system of equations using the Gauss-Jordan method.
b) Run the program in (a) for Problems 1 through 6 and Problems 11 through 18.

20. a) Modify the computer program in Problem 19(a) to allow for the interchange of two rows. (Hint: Refer to Problem 19 of Problem Set 4–4 in Section 4.15.)

b) Run the program in (a) for Problems 1 through 6 and Problems 11 through 18.

21. a) Modify the computer program in Problem 19(a) to perform the zeros-first method. (Hint: Refer to Problem 20 of Problem Set 4–4.)
b) Run the program in (a) for Problems 1 through 6 and Problems 11 through 18.

4.18 APPLICATIONS—3: MATRIX SOLUTION OF m BY n LINEAR SYSTEMS

In this section, we will show how to use the Gauss-Jordan method to solve m by n linear systems of equations where $m \neq n$. For ease in understanding, we first present the case where the number of rows m is greater than the number of columns n; i.e., $m > n$.

Consider the 3 by 2 system

$$4x_1 + 5x_2 = 30$$
$$3x_1 + 2x_2 = 19$$
$$2x_1 + 5x_2 = 20.$$

Proceeding in the usual manner, we start with the matrix

$$\begin{pmatrix} 4 & 5 & | & 30 \\ 3 & 2 & | & 19 \\ 2 & 5 & | & 20 \end{pmatrix}.$$

Then, we divide row 1 by 4:

$$\begin{pmatrix} 1 & 5/4 & | & 15/2 \\ 3 & 2 & | & 19 \\ 2 & 5 & | & 20 \end{pmatrix}.$$

Next, we add -3 times row 1 to row 2 and -2 times row 1 to row 3:

$$\begin{pmatrix} 1 & 5/4 & | & 15/2 \\ 0 & -7/4 & | & -7/2 \\ 0 & 5/2 & | & 5 \end{pmatrix}.$$

Now we divide row 2 by $-\frac{7}{4}$:

$$\begin{pmatrix} 1 & 5/4 & \Big| & 15/2 \\ 0 & 1 & \Big| & 2 \\ 0 & 5/2 & \Big| & 5 \end{pmatrix},$$

then add $-\frac{5}{4}$ times row 2 to row 1 and $-\frac{5}{2}$ times row 2 to row 3:

$$\begin{pmatrix} 1 & 0 & \Big| & 5 \\ 0 & 1 & \Big| & 2 \\ 0 & 0 & \Big| & 0 \end{pmatrix}.$$

At this point, the method terminates since there is no entry in the third row and third column on the left-hand side of the matrix. What does this last matrix mean? The first row tells us

$$x_1 = 5,$$

the second row,

$$x_2 = 2,$$

and the third row,

$$0 = 0.$$

Thus, our solution is given by

$$x_1 = 5 \quad \text{and} \quad x_2 = 2.$$

Exercise. Solve the system

$$\begin{aligned} 2x_1 + 3x_2 &= 17 \\ x_1 + 2x_2 &= 10 \\ 4x_1 + x_2 &= 19. \end{aligned}$$

Answer: $x_1 = 4$ and $x_2 = 3$.

Now consider the 3 by 2 system

$$\begin{aligned} 4x_1 + 5x_2 &= 30 \\ 3x_1 + 2x_2 &= 19 \\ 2x_1 + 5x_2 &= 30. \end{aligned}$$

Here we start with

$$\begin{pmatrix} 4 & 5 & \Big| & 30 \\ 3 & 2 & \Big| & 19 \\ 2 & 5 & \Big| & 30 \end{pmatrix},$$

then obtain

$$\begin{pmatrix} 1 & 5/4 & \bigm| & 15/2 \\ 3 & 2 & \bigm| & 19 \\ 2 & 5 & \bigm| & 30 \end{pmatrix}$$

and

$$\begin{pmatrix} 1 & 5/4 & \bigm| & 15/2 \\ 0 & -7/4 & \bigm| & -7/2 \\ 0 & 5/2 & \bigm| & 15 \end{pmatrix}.$$

Next we have

$$\begin{pmatrix} 1 & 5/4 & \bigm| & 15/2 \\ 0 & 1 & \bigm| & 2 \\ 0 & 5/2 & \bigm| & 15 \end{pmatrix},$$

and finally,

$$\begin{pmatrix} 1 & 0 & \bigm| & 5 \\ 0 & 1 & \bigm| & 2 \\ 0 & 0 & \bigm| & 10 \end{pmatrix}.$$

Again the method terminates, but this time the final matrix gives

$$x_1 = 5$$
$$x_2 = 2$$
$$0 = 10.$$

Of course, the statement $0 = 10$ is absurd, so that the system has no solution. By the way, the result above still tells us something about the system. Indeed, $x_1 = 5$ and $x_2 = 2$ is a solution to the first two equations of the system but not the third. How much is the third equation off by? If you guessed precisely the 10 in the last absurd statement, $0 = 10$, you were correct.

Lastly, it is possible but rare that a 3 by 2 system (in general, m by n with $m > n$) will have an unlimited number of solutions. The Gauss-Jordan method will identify this situation, as indicated by the following summary of all three possibilities.

To solve an m by n system of equations with $m > n$, we start with the matrix

$$(A \mid b)$$

and attempt to transform it into the matrix

$$(I \mid s).$$

One of three things will result:

1. An n by n identity matrix above $m - n$ bottom rows that are all zeros, giving the unique solution; e.g.,

$$\begin{pmatrix} 1 & 0 & 0 & \bigm| & 5 \\ 0 & 1 & 0 & \bigm| & -2 \\ 0 & 0 & 1 & \bigm| & 6 \\ 0 & 0 & 0 & \bigm| & 0 \\ 0 & 0 & 0 & \bigm| & 0 \end{pmatrix}.$$

2. A row that is all zeros *except in the constant column*, indicating that there are no solutions; e.g.,

$$\begin{pmatrix} 1 & 0 & 0 & \bigm| & 5 \\ 0 & 1 & 0 & \bigm| & -2 \\ 0 & 0 & 1 & \bigm| & 6 \\ 0 & 0 & 0 & \bigm| & 2 \\ 0 & 0 & 0 & \bigm| & 0 \end{pmatrix}.$$

3. A matrix in a form different from (1) and (2), indicating that there are an unlimited number of solutions; e.g.,

$$\begin{pmatrix} 1 & 0 & 2 & \bigm| & -4 \\ 0 & 1 & 3 & \bigm| & 8 \\ 0 & 0 & 0 & \bigm| & 0 \\ 0 & 0 & 0 & \bigm| & 0 \\ 0 & 0 & 0 & \bigm| & 0 \end{pmatrix}.$$

Note the similarity between this summary and that for n by n systems at the end of Section 4.16.

Now let us consider the case where the number of rows m is less than the number of columns n; i.e., $m < n$. This time, the system has either no solutions or else an unlimited number of solutions. There cannot be just one common solution! Why? Picture the situation where $m = 2$ and $n = 3$ so that we have two planes in three-dimensional space. What can happen? The planes are parallel, intersect in a line, or are coincident. They can never intersect in a single point. Can you guess, then, how the Gauss-Jordan method will identify the two possibilities?

Our attempt to transform $(A \mid b)$ into $(I \mid s)$ in the case where $m < n$ will result in:

1. A row which is all zeros except in the constant column, indicating that there are no solutions; or
2. A matrix in a form different from (1), indicating that there are an unlimited number of solutions.

Typically, the latter situation occurs. Don't two planes in three-dimensional space intersect in a line more often than not? Let us look at an example of this; namely the 2 by 3 system

$$2x_1 + 2x_2 + x_3 = 36$$
$$x_1 + 3x_2 + 2x_3 = 30.$$

Starting with the matrix

$$\left(\begin{array}{ccc|c} 2 & 2 & 1 & 36 \\ 1 & 3 & 2 & 30 \end{array} \right),$$

we interchange rows 1 and 2, obtaining

$$\left(\begin{array}{ccc|c} 1 & 3 & 2 & 30 \\ 2 & 2 & 1 & 36 \end{array} \right),$$

and then add -2 times row 1 to row 2:

$$\left(\begin{array}{ccc|c} 1 & 3 & 2 & 30 \\ 0 & -4 & -3 & -24 \end{array} \right).$$

Next, we divide row 2 by -4:

$$\left(\begin{array}{ccc|c} 1 & 3 & 2 & 30 \\ 0 & 1 & 3/4 & 6 \end{array} \right)$$

and add -3 times row 2 to row 1:

$$\left(\begin{array}{ccc|c} 1 & 0 & -1/4 & 12 \\ 0 & 1 & 3/4 & 6 \end{array} \right).$$

At this point, the method terminates. Why? There is no entry in the third row and third column. In fact, there is no third row at all. Thus, we have an unlimited number of solutions given by

$$x_1 + 0 - \frac{1}{4}x_3 = 12$$
$$0 + x_2 + \frac{3}{4}x_3 = 6,$$

or solving both equations in terms of x_3,

$$x_1 = \frac{1}{4}x_3 + 12$$
$$x_2 = -\frac{3}{4}x_3 + 6.$$

In this solution, we say x_3 is "free" and can take on any real number as a value. Once a value is chosen for x_3, the corresponding values for x_1 and x_2 can be found from the above equations.

Exercise. Solve the system

$$x_1 + 3x_2 + x_3 = 6$$
$$-x_1 + x_2 + x_3 = 2.$$

Answer: $x_1 = (\frac{1}{2})x_3$ and $x_2 = (-\frac{1}{2})x_3 + 2$.

4.19 PROBLEM SET 4–6

Solve each of the following systems of equations:

1. $2x_1 - 3x_2 = 6$
$x_1 + 5x_2 = 29$
$3x_1 - 4x_2 = 11.$

2. $-3x_1 + 4x_2 = -11$
$4x_1 - 5x_2 = 13$
$x_1 + 2x_2 = -13.$

3. $2x_1 + x_2 = 30$
$x_1 + 2x_2 = 24$
$4x_1 + 5x_2 = 72.$

4. $6x_1 + 5x_2 = 20$
$9x_1 + (15/2)x_2 = 30$
$(36/5)x_1 + 6x_2 = 24.$

5. $3x_1 + 2x_2 + x_3 = 23$
$x_1 + 3x_2 + 2x_3 = 26$
$2x_1 + x_2 + 2x_3 = 19$
$4x_1 + 5x_2 + 3x_3 = 49.$

6. $2x_1 - 5x_2 + x_3 = 7$
$-3x_1 + x_2 - 2x_3 = -7$
$x_1 + 2x_2 + 3x_3 = 14$
$-x_1 + 3x_2 - 4x_3 = -25.$

7. $3x_1 + 4x_2 - 6x_3 = 10$
$12x_1 + 16x_2 - 24x_3 = 7$
$x_1 + 2x_2 + 3x_3 = 8$
$5x_1 + 3x_2 + 2x_3 = 12.$

8. $3x_1 + 2x_2 + x_3 = 6$
$2x_1 + (4/3)x_2 + (2/3)x_3 = 4$
$(9/2)x_1 + 3x_2 + (3/2)x_3 = 9$
$(15/2)x_1 + 5x_2 + (5/2)x_3 = 15.$

9. $-2x_1 + x_2 - 3x_3 = 0$
$x_1 + 3x_2 - 4x_3 = 34$

10. $-3x_1 + 4x_2 + 2x_3 = 16$
$2x_1 + 2x_2 - 5x_3 = 24$
$x_1 + 3x_2 + 6x_3 = 47$
$-x_1 + x_2 - 3x_3 = -5$
$4x_1 - 2x_2 + x_3 = 16.$

11. $-3x_1 + x_2 - 2x_3 = 9$
$-5x_1 + (5/3)x_2 - (10/3)x_3 = 15$
$-2x_1 + (2/3)x_2 - (4/3)x_3 = 18$
$-7x_1 + (7/3)x_2 - (14/3)x_3 = 21$
$4x_1 - (4/3)x_2 + (8/3)x_3 = -12.$

12. $-3x_1 + x_2 - 2x_3 = 9$
$-5x_1 + (5/3)x_2 - (10/3)x_3 = 15$
$-2x_1 + (2/3)x_2 - (4/3)x_3 = 6$
$7x_1 - (7/3)x_2 + (14/3)x_3 = -21$
$6x_1 - 2x_2 + 4x_3 = -18.$

13. $4x_1 + 6x_2 - 3x_3 = 12$
$6x_1 + 9x_2 - (9/2)x_3 = 20.$

14. $3x_1 - 2x_2 + 4x_3 = 15$
$4x_1 - (8/3)x_2 + (16/3)x_3 = 20.$

15. $2x_1 + 4x_2 + 3x_3 - 2x_4 = 12$
$3x_1 + 6x_2 + (9/2)x_3 - 3x_4 = 18$
$5x_1 + 10x_2 + (15/2)x_3 - 5x_4 = 25.$

16. $3x_1 + 5x_2 - 6x_3 + 4x_4 = 36$
$2x_1 + (10/3)x_2 - 4x_3 + (8/3)x_4 = 24$
$5x_1 + (25/3)x_2 - 10x_3 + (20/3)x_4 = 60.$

17. Stay Trim Bakery makes two kinds of diet candy: Luscious and Delicious. To make one dozen of Luscious Candy requires 1 gallon of milk, 2 pounds of butter, and 1 pint of cream. To make one dozen of Delicious Candy requires 3 gallons of milk, 1 pound of

4.19 PROBLEM SET 4–6 (concluded)

butter, and 1 pint of cream. Find the number of dozens of each candy to be made in the coming week if exactly 24 gallons of milk, exactly 13 pounds of butter, and exactly 10 pints of cream are to be consumed.

18. A special food for athletes is to be developed from two foods: Food X and Food Y. The new food is to be designed so that it contains exactly 16 ounces of vitamin A, exactly 44 ounces of vitamin B, and exactly 12 ounces of vitamin C. Each pound of Food X contains 1 ounce of vitamin A, 5 ounces of vitamin B, and 1 ounce of vitamin C. On the other hand, each pound of Food Y contains 2 ounces of A, 1 ounce of B, and 1 ounce of C. Find the number of pounds of each food to be used in the mixture in order to meet the above requirements.

19. A candy manufacturer regularly makes three kinds of candy, each of which requires milk and butter as follows: Candy 1 requires 3 gallons of milk and 1 pound of butter per dozen, Candy 2 requires 2 gallons of milk and 3 pounds of butter per dozen, and Candy 3 requires 1 gallon of milk and 2 pounds of butter per dozen. The purchasing department buys a variable amount of milk and butter each week, depending upon the market prices; the production department must then determine each week the

amounts of each candy to be made in order to consume the quantities of milk and butter bought. If in the current week 23 gallons of milk and 26 pounds of butter are purchased, find the number of dozens of each candy to be made.

20. Safety Tire Company makes four kinds of tires: Model SS, the super sport, Model P, the premium, Model S, the second line, and Model E, the economy. Each tire must be processed on three machines as follows: Each Model SS tire requires two hours on Machine I, one hour on Machine II, and three hours on Machine III. Each Model P tire requires three hours on I, two hours on II, and one hour on III. Each Model S tire requires four, three, and one hour, respectively; whereas each Model E tire requires one, two, and three hours, respectively. Find the number of each tire to be made in the coming week if exactly 37 hours on Machine I, exactly 24 hours on Machine II, and exactly 33 hours on Machine III are to be utilized.

21. a) Modify the BASIC computer program in Problems 19(a), 20(a), and 21(a) of Problem Set 4–5 in Section 4.17 to solve m by n systems of equations in which $m \neq n$.
b) Run the program in (a) for Problems 1 through 16.

4.20 SUMMATION SYMBOL

The Greek capital letter Σ (sigma) is the mathematical symbol for summation. If $f(j)$ denotes some quantity whose value depends on the value of j, the expression

$$\sum_{j=1}^{3} j$$

is read as "sigma j, j going from 1 to 3" and means to insert 1 for j, then 2 for j, then 3 for j, and *sum* the results. Thus,

$$\sum_{j=1}^{3} j = 1 + 2 + 3 = 6.$$

In this example, the j under the sigma symbol is called the *index* of the summation. Similarly,

$$\sum_{j=2}^{5} j = 2 + 3 + 4 + 5 = 14$$

$$\sum_{j=1}^{4} 2j = 2(1) + 2(2) + 2(3) + 2(4) = 20$$

$$\sum_{j=1}^{3} (j - 1) = (1 - 1) + (2 - 1) + (3 - 1) = 3$$

$$\sum_{j=2}^{3} j^3 = 2^3 + 3^3 = 8 + 27 = 35.$$

We shall have frequent occasion for indicating the sum of n terms, without specifying a particular value for n. Consider, for example, the sum of the first n integers. In expanded form, we would indicate this sum by

$$1 + 2 + 3 + \cdots + n$$

where the three dots are read "and so on" and mean that the unwritten terms of the series are formed according to the same rule that applies to the first written terms; that is, in the present case, each number is formed by adding one to the preceding number. In compact summation notation the sum of the first n integers is

$$\sum_{j=1}^{n} j$$

because, by definition, this symbol expands to

$$\sum_{j=1}^{n} j = 1 + 2 + 3 + \cdots + n.$$

4.21 PROBLEM SET 4–7

Find the numerical values of

1. $\displaystyle\sum_{p=4}^{7} p$.

2. $\displaystyle\sum_{q=1}^{n} q$, if n is 5.

3. $\displaystyle\sum_{u=6}^{9} u^2$.

4. $\displaystyle\sum_{j=1}^{5} 3j$.

5. $\displaystyle\sum_{p=1}^{3} p^3$.

Express in summation notation:

6. The sum of the first q integers.

7. The sum of the squares of the first n integers.

8. $1 + 8 + 27 + 64$.

9. $(1 + 2) + (2 + 2) + (3 + 2) + (4 + 2)$.

10. $3(1) + 3(2) + 3(3) + 3(4) + 3(5)$.

As a first step toward expressing equations in compact summation form, we choose one letter and tag it with different subscripts to indicate different variables, or choose one letter and tag it with subscripts to indicate different constants. For example, x_1, x_2, x_3 can be used to represent three different variables, and c_1, c_2, c_3 to represent three different constants.

Now, consider the expression

$$\sum_{j=1}^{3} x_j,$$

which, as before, means to replace j first by 1, then by 2, then by 3, and sum the results. We see that

$$\sum_{j=1}^{3} x_j = x_1 + x_2 + x_3.$$

Similarly,

$$\sum_{j=1}^{5} a_j = a_1 + a_2 + a_3 + a_4 + a_5$$

$$\sum_{j=1}^{n} x_j = x_1 + x_2 + x_3 + \cdots + x_n.$$

It is clear that

$$\sum_{j=1}^{3} a_j x_j = a_1 x_1 + a_2 x_2 + a_3 x_3,$$

and

$$\sum_{j=1}^{n} a_j x_j = a_1 x_1 + a_2 x_2 + \cdots + a_n x_n.$$

Next, consider the expression

$$\sum_{j=1}^{2} a_j x_j = b,$$

where the a_j and b are constants. In expanded form, the expression becomes

$$a_1 x_1 + a_2 x_2 = b,$$

which is a linear equation in the two variables, x_1 and x_2. It is clear that any linear equation can be written in compact summation notation as

$$\sum_{j=1}^{n} a_j x_j = b,$$

because any linear equation is of the form to which the last expression expands; namely,

$$a_1x_1 + a_2x_2 + \cdots + a_nx_n = b.$$

For example, the linear equation

$$5x_1 + 2x_2 + 4x_3 = 6$$

is of the stated form, with

$$n = 3$$
$$a_1 = 5$$
$$a_2 = 2$$
$$a_3 = a_n = 4$$
$$b = 6.$$

4.23 PROBLEM SET 4–8

Write the expanded form of:

1. $\sum_{j=1}^{5} y_j.$ **2.** $\sum_{j=1}^{3} c_j x_j.$ **3.** $\sum_{j=1}^{n} b_j y_j.$ **4.** $\sum_{j=1}^{5} p_j x_j = 10.$ **5.** $\sum_{j=1}^{n} a_j x_j = c.$

Express in compact summation form:

6. $x_1 + x_2 + x_3 + x_4.$

7. $a_1x_1 + a_2x_2 + a_3x_3 + a_4x_4 + a_5x_5 + a_6x_6 = b.$

8. $c_1x_1 + c_2x_2 + \cdots + c_9x_9.$

9. $a_1x_1 + a_2x_2 + \cdots + a_qx_q.$

10. Identify n, b, and each of the a's in

$$\sum_{j=1}^{n} a_j x_j = b$$

with a number in the equation

$$x_1 + 2x_3 + 5x_4 = 7.$$

4.24 SUMMATION FORM FOR SYSTEMS

We have seen how to express a single linear equation in terms of the summation symbol by tagging variables with a subscript. To extend the notation to systems of equations, another subscript is required to identify the different equations of the system. Consider the following expression:

$$\sum_{j=1}^{3} a_{ij}x_j = b_i \qquad i = 1, 2.$$

Here we are to insert $i = 1$ first, obtaining

$$\sum_{j=1}^{3} a_{1j}x_j = b_1.$$

Then insert $i = 2$ in the original summation, obtaining

$$\sum_{j=1}^{3} a_{2j}x_j = b_2.$$

The expression with $i = 1$ expands to

$$\sum_{j=1}^{3} a_{1j}x_j = a_{11}x_1 + a_{12}x_2 + a_{13}x_3 = b_1.$$

The expression with $i = 2$ expands in the same manner. Thus the original expression

$$\sum_{j=1}^{3} a_{ij}x_j = b_i \qquad i = 1, 2$$

means the following system of two linear equations in three variables:

$$a_{11}x_1 + a_{12}x_2 + a_{13}x_3 = b_1$$
$$a_{21}x_1 + a_{22}x_2 + a_{23}x_3 = b_2.$$

The first number in each double subscript names the equation; the second names the variable. Thus, a_{21} is in the second equation, and it is the coefficient of variable number one, that is, x_1. Similarly, a_{49} would be in the fourth equation, and would be the coefficient of x_9 in that equation.

Exercise. Write the system of equations specified by

$$\sum_{j=1}^{2} c_{ij}x_j = b_i \qquad i = 1, 2, 3.$$

Answer: The system has three equations, each of the form $c_{i1}x_1 + c_{i2}x_2 = b_i$. The three equations can be generated by letting i equal 1, then 2, then 3.

Consider the linear system

$$a_{11}x_1 + a_{12}x_2 + a_{13}x_3 + a_{14}x_4 = b_1$$
$$a_{21}x_1 + a_{22}x_2 + a_{23}x_3 + a_{24}x_4 = b_2$$
$$a_{31}x_1 + a_{32}x_2 + a_{33}x_3 + a_{34}x_4 = b_3.$$

Note that the beginning subscript on all a's in an equation and the subscript on b are the same as the equation number. For example, the first equation has ones in the positions just described. If we let i represent the equation number, it follows in the present case that i must take on the values 1, 2, and 3 to generate the three equations. Next, letting j be the number indicating the variable, it follows that each equation is a summation with j going from 1 to 4, inclusive. The above system of equations, therefore, is represented by

$$\sum_{j=1}^{4} a_{ij}x_j = b_i \qquad i = 1, 2, 3.$$

The first equation of the system is generated from the last expression by letting i be 1, and then constructing the sum for j going from 1 through 4. The other two equations are generated in the same manner after letting i be 2, then 3.

> **Exercise.**   How would a system of three equations in five variables be symbolized in sigma notation? Answer: The symbols would be the same as those written in the immediately foregoing expression, except the upper limit on j would be 5 rather than 4.

We are now ready to symbolize any system of linear equations. Suppose that we have m linear equations in n variables, an m by n system. To indicate this system in expanded form, we would write

$$\begin{aligned}
a_{11}x_1 + a_{12}x_2 + \cdots + a_{1n}x_n &= b_1 \\
a_{21}x_1 + a_{22}x_2 + \cdots + a_{2n}x_n &= b_2 \\
\vdots \qquad \vdots \qquad\qquad \vdots \quad\ \ &\ \ \vdots \\
a_{m1}x_1 + a_{m2}x_2 + \cdots + a_{mn}x_n &= b_m.
\end{aligned}$$

In compact summation form the system is simply

$$\sum_{j=1}^{n} a_{ij}x_j = b_i \qquad i = 1, 2, \ldots, m.$$

4.25 LINEAR PROGRAMMING PROBLEMS IN SUMMATION NOTATION

The linear programming problems of the last chapter consisted of a system of linear inequalities with nonnegativity constraints and an objective function that was to be maximized. The nonnegativity constraints can be expressed as

$$x_j \geq 0 \qquad \text{for all } j.$$

The objective function is of the form

$$\theta = c_1x_1 + c_2x_2 + \cdots + c_nx_n$$

where the letter c is adopted to represent the constants in this function.

In symbols,

$$\theta = \sum_{j=1}^{n} c_j x_j.$$

The system of linear inequalities can be expressed in the same manner as a system of equalities. Hence the compact summation form of the linear programming problems of the last chapter is

Maximize

$$\theta = \sum_{j=1}^{n} c_j x_j$$

subject to

$$\sum_{j=1}^{n} a_{ij} x_j \leq b_i \qquad i = 1, 2, \ldots, m$$

$$x_j \geq 0 \qquad \text{for all } j.$$

4.26 PROBLEM SET 4–9

1. Write in expanded form:

$$\sum_{j=1}^{4} a_{ij} x_j = b_i \qquad i = 1, 2.$$

2. Write in expanded form:
Maximize

$$\sum_{j=1}^{3} c_j x_j$$

subject to:

$$\sum_{j=1}^{3} a_{ij} x_j \leq b_i \qquad i = 1, 2, \ldots, 4$$

$$x_j \geq 0 \qquad \text{for all } j.$$

3. A system has p linear equations in q variables.
a) Write the system in expanded form, using . . . where necessary.
b) Write the system in compact summation form.

4. A linear programming maximization problem has p "less than or equal" constraints on q variables.
a) Write the statement of the problem in expanded form, using . . . where necessary.
b) Write the problem in compact summation form.

5. Express the following in compact summation notation:

$$a_{11} x_1 + a_{12} x_2 + \cdots + a_{18} x_8 = b_1$$
$$a_{21} x_1 + a_{22} x_2 + \cdots + a_{28} x_8 = b_2$$
$$\vdots \qquad \vdots \qquad \qquad \vdots \qquad \vdots$$
$$a_{61} x_1 + a_{62} x_2 + \cdots + a_{68} x_8 = b_6.$$

6. In the system

$$2x_1 + 3x_2 + 4x_4 = 20$$
$$x_1 + 9x_3 + 8x_4 = 50$$
$$5x_1 + 7x_3 + 6x_4 = 100,$$

a) What is m? What is n?
b) What symbol would represent the follow-

4.26 PROBLEM SET 4–9 (concluded)

ing constants, which appear in the system: 2, 3, 8, 9, 7, 6?

c) What constants in the system correspond to a_{13}, b_1, a_{31}, a_{22}, a_{32}?

7. We buy x_1 units of item number one at d_1 dollars per unit, x_2 units of item two at d_2

dollars per unit, and so on. Write the expression for the total cost of 10 different items:

a) In expanded form.

b) In compact summation notation.

8. Repeat parts (a) and (b) of Problem 7 if we buy p different items.

4.27 PROPERTIES OF THE SUMMATION OPERATION

An elementary, but important, property of summation is illustrated by

$$\sum_{i=1}^{3} 5 = 5 + 5 + 5 = 15.$$

We see here that the quantity being summed is the *constant*, 5, when $i = 1$, $i = 2$, and $i = 3$. We could write more concisely

$$\sum_{i=1}^{3} 5 = 3(5) = 15.$$

Exercise.   Compute the value of $\sum\limits_{i=1}^{8} 2$.   Answer: $8(2) = 16$.

In general, if c is any *constant*, then

$$\sum_{i=1}^{n} c = nc.$$

The word *constant* here means that the quantity has the same value for all values of the index of summation.

Exercise.   What is $\sum\limits_{j=1}^{m} p$?   Answer: mp.

The point of the last exercise is that the quantity p is constant with respect to the index of summation.

A second property of the summation operation is that it may be applied term by term to an expression.

To illustrate,

$$\sum_{i=1}^{3}(x_i + y_i) = x_1 + y_1 + x_2 + y_2 + x_3 + y_3$$

$$= x_1 + x_2 + x_3 + y_1 + y_2 + y_3$$

$$\sum_{i=1}^{3}(x_i + y_i) = \sum_{i=1}^{3}x_i + \sum_{i=1}^{3}y_i.$$

The property obviously applies whatever the value of n; that is,

$$\sum_{i=1}^{n}(x_i + y_i - z_i) = \sum_{i=1}^{n}x_i + \sum_{i=1}^{n}y_i - \sum_{i=1}^{n}z_i.$$

Finally, a constant factor of the quantity being summed can be taken outside the summation symbol. Thus,

$$\Sigma 3x_i = 3\,\Sigma x_i \quad \text{and, in general,} \quad \Sigma cx_i = c\,\Sigma x_i,$$

where c is a constant with respect to the index of summation.

Summarizing the properties just discussed, we have

1. $\displaystyle\sum_{i=1}^{n}cx_i = c\sum_{i=1}^{n}x_i$ or $\Sigma\,cx_i = c\,\Sigma x_i.$

2. $\displaystyle\sum_{i=1}^{n}c = nc$ or $\Sigma c = nc$, assuming c is constant with respect to the index, which goes from 1 to n.

3. $\displaystyle\sum_{i=1}^{n}(x_i + y_i - z_i) = \sum_{i=1}^{n}x_i + \sum_{i=1}^{n}y_i - \sum_{i=1}^{n}z_i$
   or
   $\Sigma(x_i + y_i - z_i) = \Sigma x_i + \Sigma y_i - \Sigma z_i.$

For practice with these properties, let us compute

$$\Sigma(4x + 2)$$

for the following data: $x = 1, 3,$ and 5. We may write

$$\Sigma(4x + 2) = \Sigma 4x + \Sigma 2 = 4\,\Sigma x + 3(2)$$

where, in the last term, the factor 3 is the number of terms being summed. Now, Σx is $1 + 3 + 5 = 9$, so

$$4\,\Sigma x + 3(2) = 4(9) + 6 = 42.$$

Alternatively, we could have performed the calculation as shown in Table 4–6, which shows that $\Sigma(4x + 2) = 42$.

TABLE 4–6

x	4x + 2
1	6
3	14
5	22
	42

Exercise. Given the data y: 4, 7, 2, 9, compute $\Sigma(2y - 1)$ by the two procedures just illustrated. Answer: 40.

4.28 PROBLEM SET 4–10

Simplify and evaluate each of the following summations:

1. $\displaystyle\sum_{i=1}^{4} 3$.

2. $\displaystyle\sum_{i=1}^{3} 7$.

3. $\displaystyle\sum_{i=1}^{5} (x_i - a)$.

4. $\displaystyle\sum_{i=1}^{4} (x_i - a)^2$.

Given the data below, evaluate each of the following summations:

i	1	2	3	4	5	6	7	8	9	10
x_i	2	11	−4	5	8	3	−5	−2	6	−9

5. $\displaystyle\sum_{i=1}^{10} (3x_i + 4)$.

8. $\displaystyle\sum_{i=1}^{10} (x_i^2 + 3x_i + 2)$.

6. $\displaystyle\sum_{i=1}^{10} (2x_i - 3)$.

9. $\displaystyle\sum_{i=1}^{10} x_i^2 - (1/10)\left(\sum_{i=1}^{10} x_i\right)^2$.

7. $\displaystyle\sum_{i=1}^{10} (x_i^2 - 2x_i + 1)$.

10. $\displaystyle\sum_{i=1}^{10} \left(x_i - (1/10)\sum_{i=1}^{10} x_i\right)^2$.

4.29 REVIEW PROBLEMS

Perform the following operations:

1. $(1\ \ 4\ \ 6) + (3\ \ -1\ \ 0) - 5(3\ \ 5\ \ -4)$.

2. $\begin{pmatrix} 8 \\ 2 \end{pmatrix} - 3\begin{pmatrix} 4 \\ 6 \end{pmatrix} + 2\begin{pmatrix} 1 \\ 5 \end{pmatrix}$.

3. If p and q are two-component column vectors, express the compact vector statement

$$px + qy = o$$

a) In expanded vector form.

b) In usual algebraic form.

4.29 REVIEW PROBLEMS (*continued*)

4. If **x, y,** and **r** are three-component row vectors, express the compact vector statement
   x + **y** = **r**
   a) In expanded vector form.
   b) In usual algebraic form.

5. If **x** and **o** are four-component column vectors, express the compact vector statement
   $x \geq o$
   a) In expanded vector form.
   b) In usual algebraic form.

6. $\begin{pmatrix} 3 & 2 & 0 \\ 1 & 5 & 4 \end{pmatrix} + \begin{pmatrix} 1 & -3 & 6 \\ 2 & 4 & 5 \end{pmatrix} - 2\begin{pmatrix} 1 & 1 & 3 \\ 4 & 0 & -1 \end{pmatrix}.$

7. $\begin{pmatrix} 3 & -2 \\ 1 & 7 \end{pmatrix} - \begin{pmatrix} -3 & 4 \\ 6 & 0 \end{pmatrix} - 3\begin{pmatrix} 1 & 2 \\ 1 & 3 \end{pmatrix}$
   $+ 5\begin{pmatrix} 1 & -1 \\ -2 & 2 \end{pmatrix}.$

8. $(1 \ 0 \ 2)\begin{pmatrix} 2 & -1 & 3 & 5 \\ 0 & 2 & -2 & 1 \\ 1 & 4 & 2 & 3 \end{pmatrix}.$

9. $\begin{pmatrix} 1 & 3 & 2 \\ 2 & 0 & 1 \\ 0 & 1 & 2 \end{pmatrix}\begin{pmatrix} 2 & 3 & 4 \\ -1 & 2 & 0 \\ 3 & -1 & 5 \end{pmatrix}.$

10. $\begin{pmatrix} 2 & 3 \\ 1 & -1 \end{pmatrix}\begin{pmatrix} 1 & 3 & 5 \\ 2 & 4 & 6 \end{pmatrix}.$

11. $\begin{pmatrix} 4 & 1 & -1 \\ 2 & 0 & 3 \\ 0 & -2 & 4 \end{pmatrix}\begin{pmatrix} 0 & 1 & -1 \\ 1 & -1 & 0 \\ -1 & 0 & 1 \end{pmatrix}.$

---

12. The number of trees, bushes, and shrubs used in landscaping small, medium, and large lots are shown as the requirements matrix in the table. Costs per unit are shown at the left.

    a) A contractor orders plantings for 6 small, 10 medium, and 5 large lots. Multiply the planting vector and the requirements matrix and interpret the results.
    b) Multiply the cost vector and the requirements matrix and interpret the results.

Unit Cost	Item	Requirements Matrix Number Needed to Landscape a		
		Small Lot	Medium Lot	Large Lot
$30	Red maple	0	1	2
20	Hard maple	1	1	1
20	Yew	2	4	5
40	Arbovitae	0	2	2
50	Spruce	0	2	3
20	Rhododendron	2	3	6
10	Laurel	2	2	4
20	Azalea	2	5	8

Write the following in expanded matrix form:

13. $\begin{aligned} x_1 + 2x_2 \quad\quad + x_4 &= 12 \\ 3x_2 - x_3 + 2x_4 &= 6 \\ 5x_1 - x_2 + x_3 - x_4 &= 7. \end{aligned}$

14. $\begin{aligned} x_1 + 2x_2 &\leq 18 \\ 2x_1 + 3x_2 &\leq 24 \\ -x_1 &\leq 0 \\ -x_2 &\leq 0. \end{aligned}$

15. $\begin{aligned} x_1 + 2x_2 + s_1 &= 10 \\ x_1 + 3x_2 + s_2 &= 15. \end{aligned}$

Write the following in usual algebraic form:

16. $\begin{pmatrix} 1 & 2 \\ 3 & 4 \\ 5 & 5 \end{pmatrix}\begin{pmatrix} x_1 \\ x_2 \end{pmatrix} = \begin{pmatrix} 7 \\ 8 \\ 9 \end{pmatrix}.$

17. $\begin{pmatrix} 3 & 0 & 1 \\ 0 & 2 & 4 \\ 2 & 3 & 0 \end{pmatrix}\begin{pmatrix} x_1 \\ x_2 \\ x_3 \end{pmatrix} \leq \begin{pmatrix} 14 \\ 10 \\ 12 \end{pmatrix}.$

18. $\begin{pmatrix} 3 & 1 \\ 2 & 2 \\ 1 & 4 \end{pmatrix}\begin{pmatrix} x_1 \\ x_2 \end{pmatrix} + \begin{pmatrix} s_1 \\ s_2 \\ s_3 \end{pmatrix} = \begin{pmatrix} 20 \\ 30 \\ 40 \end{pmatrix}.$

4.29 REVIEW PROBLEMS (*continued*)

19. In a section of the country, 35 percent live in urban areas and 65 percent in rural areas at a point in time. Urban-rural movement each year is described by the transition matrix

$$\begin{array}{cc} & \begin{array}{cc} \textit{Urban} & \textit{Rural} \end{array} \\ \begin{array}{c} \textit{Urban} \\ \textit{Rural} \end{array} & \begin{pmatrix} 0.8 & 0.2 \\ 0.4 & 0.6 \end{pmatrix}. \end{array}$$

What will be the proportions in urban and rural areas after
a) One year?
b) Two years?
c) Three years?
d) What is the steady state?

20. Brand X has 25 percent of the market and other brands share the rest of the market. Because of a promotional effort, 50 percent of those buying other brands shift to Brand X each month, while 70 percent of those buying Brand X continue to buy this brand.
a) What percent of the market will Brand X have after one month?
b) What is the steady state?

Find the inverse of each of the following matrices (if an inverse exists):

21. $\begin{pmatrix} 0 & 1 \\ 1 & 0 \end{pmatrix}.$

22. $\begin{pmatrix} 3 & 1 \\ 0 & 2 \end{pmatrix}.$

23. $\begin{pmatrix} 1 & 2 \\ 3 & 3 \end{pmatrix}.$

24. $\begin{pmatrix} 1 & 1 \\ 2 & 1 \end{pmatrix}.$

25. $\begin{pmatrix} 5 & 3 \\ 2 & 2 \end{pmatrix}.$

26. $\begin{pmatrix} 1 & 2 \\ 3 & 4 \end{pmatrix}.$

27. $\begin{pmatrix} 1 & 0 & 1 \\ 0 & 1 & 2 \\ 2 & 3 & 0 \end{pmatrix}.$

28. $\begin{pmatrix} 1 & 2 & -1 \\ 1 & 0 & 1 \\ 0 & 5 & -5 \end{pmatrix}.$

29. $\begin{pmatrix} 1 & 0 & 2 \\ 0 & 1 & 3 \\ 1 & 2 & 0 \end{pmatrix}.$

30. $\begin{pmatrix} 0 & 0 & 1 \\ 0 & 1 & 0 \\ 1 & 0 & 0 \end{pmatrix}.$

31. $\begin{pmatrix} 60 & 30 & 20 \\ 30 & 20 & 15 \\ 20 & 15 & 12 \end{pmatrix}.$

32. $\begin{pmatrix} 1 & 1 & 1 \\ 2 & 1 & 1 \\ 1 & 2 & 2 \end{pmatrix}.$

33. $\begin{pmatrix} 1 & 2 & 1 \\ 2 & 1 & 1 \\ 1 & 2 & 2 \end{pmatrix}.$

34. $\begin{pmatrix} 2 & 4 & 1 \\ 3 & 1 & 2 \\ 0 & 5 & 6 \end{pmatrix}.$

35. $\begin{pmatrix} 2 & 0 & 1 \\ 3 & 1 & 3 \\ 0 & 1 & 4 \end{pmatrix}.$

---

36. Consider the system

$$7x_1 + 11x_2 = 3$$
$$5x_1 + 8x_2 = 5.$$

a) Relating the system to $Ax = b$, what is A? x? b?
b) Solve the system using the Gauss-Jordan method.
c) Compute A^{-1}.
d) Write $x = A^{-1}b$ in expanded matrix form.
e) Compute the solution from part (d).
f) What would be the solution vector if the elements in the vector of constants, 3 and 5, were changed to
(1) 1, 1.   (2) 0, 1.   (3) 1, 0.
(4) 2, −3.

4.29 REVIEW PROBLEMS (*continued*)

37. Answer parts (a) through (e) of Problem 36 for the system

$$2x_1 + 4x_2 = 4$$
$$5x_1 + 6x_2 = 8.$$

f) What would be the solution vector if the elements in the vector of constants, 4 and 8, were changed to
(1) 4, 12. (2) 12, 16. (3) 20, 40.
(4) 0, 4.

38. Answer parts (a) through (e) of Problem 36 for the system

$$3x_1 \quad\quad + 2x_3 = 1$$
$$5x_1 + 2x_2 + 5x_3 = 2$$
$$x_2 + \quad x_3 = 3.$$

f) What would be the solution vector if the elements in the vector of constants, 1, 2, and 3, were changed to
(1) 1, 1, 1. (2) 1, 0, 1. (3) 1, 1, 0.

39. Answer parts (a) through (e) of Problem 36 for the system

$$2x_1 + 3x_2 - 15x_3 = 3$$
$$-5x_1 - 7x_2 + 35x_3 = 2$$
$$3x_1 + 4x_2 - 21x_3 = 1.$$

f) What would be the solution vector if the elements in the vector of constants, 3, 2, and 1, were changed to
(1) 1, 1, 1. (2) 0, 1, 1. (3) 1, 1, 0.

40. The table shows that x_1 units of product X_1 are to be made and that a unit of X_1 requires one hour of time on machine M_1, three hours on M_2, and two hours on M_3. For $i = 1, 2, 3$, machine M_i has H_i hours of time available. Similar interpretations apply to other entries.

Product	Units to Be Made	Hours of Machine Time per Unit of Product on		
		M_1	M_2	M_3
X_1	x_1	1	3	2
X_2	x_2	2	1	3
X_3	x_3	3	2	1

Find the number of units that can be made if the machine time availability vector

$(H_1 \quad H_2 \quad H_3)$ is
a) (180 540 360).
b) (180 180 180).
c) (270 360 360).

41. Given the system

$$3x_1 + 2x_2 = b_1$$
$$4x_1 + 3x_2 = b_2$$

find the missing elements to complete the following equation:

$$\begin{pmatrix} x_1 \\ x_2 \end{pmatrix} = \begin{pmatrix} & \\ & \end{pmatrix} \begin{pmatrix} b_1 \\ b_2 \end{pmatrix}.$$

42. Given the system

$$2x_1 + \quad x_2 + x_3 = b_1$$
$$x_1 + \quad x_2 + x_3 = b_2$$
$$x_1 + 2x_2 + x_3 = b_3$$

find the missing elements to complete the following equation:

$$\begin{pmatrix} x_1 \\ x_2 \\ x_3 \end{pmatrix} = \begin{pmatrix} & \\ & \\ & \end{pmatrix} \begin{pmatrix} b_1 \\ b_2 \\ b_3 \end{pmatrix}.$$

43. Consider the system

$$x_1 + \quad x_2 + \quad x_3 = 3$$
$$2x_1 + 3x_2 + 2x_3 = 5$$
$$x_1 + 2x_2 + \quad x_3 = 2.$$

a) Show that the matrix of coefficients does not have an inverse.
b) Find the solution of the system by the methods of Chapter 2.
c) Change the constant in the first equation from 3 to 4.
 (1) Does the change in the constant have an effect upon the matrix of coefficients?
 (2) Does the change have an effect upon the solution in part (b)?
 (3) Our example illustrates what it means if the matrix of coefficients in an n by n system has no inverse. What does it mean if the coefficient matrix has no inverse?

4.29 REVIEW PROBLEMS (*continued*)

Find the numerical values of:

44. $\displaystyle\sum_{n=3}^{6} (n^2 - n)$.

45. $\displaystyle\sum_{i=1}^{5} 2i^2$.

46. $\displaystyle\sum_{p=3}^{7} (2p + 1)$.

Express in summation notation:

47. The sum of the first 100 positive integers.

48. The sum of the fifth power of the first 10 positive integers.

49. The sum of the first 50 positive even integers.

50. The sum of the first 50 positive odd integers.

Write in expanded form:

51. $\displaystyle\sum_{j=10}^{15} c_j y_j$.

52. $\displaystyle\sum_{j=10}^{10+n} c_j x_j$.

53. $\displaystyle\sum_{i=m}^{m+n} a_i x_i$.

54. $\displaystyle\sum_{i=1}^{4} x_i = 25$.

55. $\displaystyle\sum_{j=1}^{3} 2x_j = 7$.

56. $\displaystyle\sum_{j=1}^{6} c_j x_j = 15$.

Express in compact summation form:

57. $a_1 x_1 + a_2 x_2 + a_3 x_3$.

58. $a_1 x_1 + a_2 x_2 + \ldots + a_9 x_9$.

59. $a_1 x_1 + a_2 x_2 + \ldots + a_n x_n$.

60. $a_1 x_1 + a_2 x_2 + \ldots + a_n x_n + a_{n+1} x_{n+1} + a_{n+2} x_{n+2} + \ldots + a_{n+m} x_{n+m}$.

---

61. Identify m, c, and each of the b's in
$$\sum_{j=1}^{m} b_j y_j = c$$
with a number in the equation
$$5y_1 + 3y_2 - y_3 + 4y_6 = 12.$$

62. Write the following system in expanded form
$$\sum_{j=1}^{3} a_{ij} x_j = b_i \qquad i = 1, 2, 3, 4.$$

63. Write in expanded form
Maximize
$$\sum_{j=1}^{2} c_j x_j$$
subject to
$$\sum_{j=1}^{2} a_{ij} x_j \le b_i \qquad i = 1, 2$$
$$x_j \ge 0 \qquad \text{for all } j.$$

64. A linear system has p equations in p variables.
a) Write the system in expanded form, using . . . where necessary.
b) Write the system in compact summation form.

65. A linear programming minimization problem has 15 "greater than or equal" constraints on 25 variables.
a) Write the problem in expanded form using . . . to shorten the expressions.
b) Write the problem in compact summation form.

4.29 REVIEW PROBLEMS (*concluded*)

66. Consider the following system and its compact representation

$$3x_1 + 2x_2 + 5x_3 = 6$$
$$x_1 + 7x_2 - x_3 = 10$$
$$4x_2 - 8x_3 = 2$$
$$6x_1 + 9x_2 = 11.$$

$$\sum_{j=1}^{n} a_{ij}x_j = b_i \qquad i = 1, 2, \ldots, m.$$

a) What is m? What is n?

b) What symbol would represent the following constants, which appear in the system: 3, 7, 10, 9, 11?

c) What constants in the system correspond to a_{23}, a_{31}, b_4, a_{33}, a_{12}?

FIVE

Linear Programming: The Simplex Method

The graphic solution of two-variable linear programming problems in Chapter 3 introduced the fundamental concept of optimizing a linear objective function subject to linear constraints. However, applied problems contain numerous constraints involving many variables and cannot be solved by graphic procedures. Solution by determination of all corners as carried out for the simple three-variable example at the end of Chapter 3, while conceptually possible, would require a tremendous amount of computation, most of which would serve only to eliminate corners that are not in the solution space. The efficient way to solve an applied problem is to start with a corner that is in the solution space, then move to another corner in the solution space that *improves* the objective function, continuing the process of moving to another corner until no corner can be found that will further improve the objective function. This process works only with corners of the solution space and stops at the optimum corner, where no further improvement can be made in the objective function. The process just described is called the *simplex method* of solving linear programming problems.

This chapter starts with an example showing the general idea of the simplex procedure, then provides practice in carrying out each of the simplex steps. Following this practice, the full simplex procedure is again demonstrated as it applies to problems with ≤ constraints. Next we discuss several special cases that can occur when using the simplex method. Then we show how to change a minimization problem with ≥ constraints into a maximization problem with ≤ constraints by applying the dual theorem, so that at this point the simplex method can be used to solve both maximization and minimization problems. The last part of the chapter involves analyses that can be made after the optimal simplex solution has been reached. These analyses provide information (shadow prices, for example) that can be more important than the optimal solution itself.

5.2 FUNDAMENTAL PROCEDURES AND TERMINOLOGY

The introductory illustration of Chapter 3 will serve as our starting point; we shall repeat it here.

Example. Table 5–1 shows lounge chairs and swivel chairs are made using the equipment of Departments I and II. It requires one hour in each department to make a lounge chair, but making a swivel chair takes one hour in Department I and two hours in Department II. Department I has four hours of available time, and Department II has six hours of available time. Each lounge chair made contributes $1 to profit and each swivel chair contributes $0.50 to profit. Determine how many lounge and swivel chairs should be made to maximize profit, and compute the maximum profit.

TABLE 5–1

Chair	Number of Units Made	Profit per Unit	Hours Required per Unit in: Department I (4 hours available)	Department II (6 hours available)
Lounge	x_1	$1.00	1	1
Swivel	x_2	$0.50	1	2

Recall that we formulated the linear programming problem as follows:

Maximize

$$\theta = 1 \cdot x_1 + 0.5 \cdot x_2$$

subject to:

$$\begin{array}{llll} \text{Department I} & i_1 & : & x_1 + x_2 \leq 4 \\ \text{Department II} & i_2 & : & x_1 + 2x_2 \leq 6 \\ \text{Nonnegativity} & i_3, i_4: & & x_1, x_2 \geq 0, \end{array} \quad (1)$$

where we now have changed x and y to x_1 and x_2, respectively.

Step 1. Conversion of the constraints and objective function. The first step in our procedure converts the inequalities in the problem statement to equalities. To do this, we need to introduce one new variable for each constraint. Thus,

$$x_1 + x_2 \leq 4$$

requires that a *nonnegative* quantity be added to the left side to increase its value to 4. Let us call this quantity s_1 and write

$$x_1 + x_2 + s_1 = 4.$$

For example, if we do not make any lounge or swivel chairs, then

$$x_1 = x_2 = 0$$

so that

$$s_1 = 4.$$

Remembering that the inequality at hand is the Department I constraint, the last equation says that if we do not make any lounge or swivel chairs, the four hours of available time in I are not used. This unused time is called *slack*.

In a similar manner, we convert

$$x_1 + 2x_2 \leq 6$$

to

$$x_1 + 2x_2 + s_2 = 6$$

by adding the nonnegative slack variable s_2.

Exercise. What does s_2 represent? Answer: Unused time in Department II.

Inasmuch as slack time does not produce any product, the slack variables ordinarily contribute nothing to profit, so our objective function is now

$$\theta = x_1 + 0.5x_2 + 0s_1 + 0s_2.$$

At the moment, we shall not bother to write the slack variables in the objective function, θ. We will see later on in Section 5.14 how to handle problems where the slack variables do actually contribute something to the objective function. Thus the formulation of the problem is as follows:

$$
\begin{aligned}
e_1&: & x_1 + \ \ x_2 + s_1 &= 4 \\
e_2&: & x_1 + 2x_2 + s_2 &= 6 \\
e_3&: & \theta = \ \ x_1 + 0.5x_2 & \\
& & x_1, x_2, s_1, s_2 &\geq 0.
\end{aligned}
\tag{2}
$$

The original problem, (1), had *two* constraints (i_1 and i_2) which have been converted to the equalities e_1 and e_2. However, in the conversion we introduced two more variables, s_1 and s_2, so that we now have $m = 2$ constraints on $n = 4$ variables ($x_1, x_2, s_1,$ and s_2) and hence, four nonnegativity constraints. According to the principle illustrated and stated in Chapter 3, Section 3.8, in any solution of the system at least $n - m$ of the variables must have the value zero. Here,

$$n - m = 4 - 2 = 2,$$

so at least two of the variables must be zero in a solution of system (2). The critical question, now, is which two are zero in the optimal solution.

Step 2. Finding an initial solution. We start our search by making sure that we have a permissible solution, which we now refer to as a *feasible* solution. The easiest starting point when all constraints are $\leq$ is the origin, where $x_1 = x_2 = 0$. To be clear on this point, refer to Figure 5–1. Any point on the boundary of the shaded space, or within it, is a *feasible* solution, and the corner $(0, 0)$, which is a *vertex* of the solution space, is indeed feasible.

Our next step is to write the system (2) with the zero-valued variables (x_1 and x_2) as independent variables. Thus,

$$x_1 + x_2 + s_1 = 4$$

becomes

$$s_1 = 4 - x_1 - x_2.$$

Similarly,

$$x_1 + 2x_2 + s_2 = 6$$

FIGURE 5–1

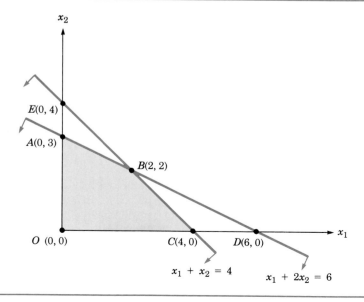

becomes

$$s_2 = 6 - x_1 - 2x_2.$$

The variable θ is already expressed in terms of x_1 and x_2. We have

$$
\begin{aligned}
e_4: \quad & s_1 = 4 - x_1 - x_2 \\
e_5: \quad & s_2 = 6 - x_1 - 2x_2 \\
e_6: \quad & \theta = x_1 + 0.5x_2.
\end{aligned}
\tag{3}
$$

Remembering that the variables x_1 and x_2 on the *right* side take on the value zero at the origin, we have the feasible solution

$$x_1 = x_2 = 0; \quad s_1 = 4; \quad s_2 = 6; \quad \theta = 0. \tag{4}$$

Now for more terminology. The variables that are *in* the solution, the ones on the *left* side of (3), s_1 and s_2, are called *basic* variables. The basic variables, all of them, form the *basis*. Thus, currently, s_1 is in the basis and s_2 is in the basis. Together, s_1 and s_2 are the basis. The variables that are *out of* the solution, the ones on the right side of (3) that have the value zero, are called nonbasic variables, that is, x_1 and x_2 are nonbasic variables at the present time. The solution, (4), which is *on the boundary of* the feasible solution space exhibited in Figure 5–1 (it is the vertex at the origin) is called a *basic feasible* solution to distinguish it from feasible solutions that are not on the boundary. Our interest centers on the vertices of the feasible solution space, so we will confine our attention to the basic feasible solutions at the vertices.

The basic feasible solution (4), in which $x_1 = x_2 = 0$, means, of course, that no lounge or swivel chairs are produced, so Department I has $s_1 = 4$ hours of unused time (slack time) and Department II has $s_2 = 6$ hours of slack. No product is made, so the profit $\theta = 0$. *This vertex serves the important purpose of providing an initial basic feasible solution.* It is, however, merely a starting point.

Step 3. Choosing the entering variable. We now wish to choose an improved vertex of the feasible solution space; i.e., a vertex with a larger profit. To do this, we need to replace a basic variable with another variable. What we plan to do at this point is decide which vertex we should move to next. Examining

$$\theta = 1x_1 + 0.5x_2,$$

which currently is zero, we note that if we *increase* x_1 from its zero value, then every increase of 1 in x_1 (every lounge chair made) will add $1 to profit, but another swivel chair (increasing x_2 by 1) will add only $0.50 to profit. We now plan to bring only *one* new variable into the basis (and subsequently take *one* out). Because a lounge chair provides more profit than a swivel chair, it is reasonable to choose to bring in all the lounge chairs we can, leaving the number of swivel chairs at zero. Thus, we want to increase x_1 *as much as possible.*

Step 4. Choosing the leaving variable. If we look at (3), we see

$$e_4: \quad s_1 = 4 - x_1 - x_2$$
$$e_5: \quad s_2 = 6 - x_1 - 2x_2.$$

Covering up the x_2 terms (which remain at zero), we see from e_4 that

$$s_1 = 4 - x_1$$

and x_1 must not be increased to more than 4, because if it is, s_1 will become negative. Similarly, from e_5 with $x_2 = 0$, we see that

$$s_2 = 6 - x_1$$

and x_1 cannot be increased to more than 6. The controlling condition, therefore, is that x_1 not be increased by more than 4 (which in turn guarantees that it will not be increased by more than 6). Thus, we have found that x_1 should be brought *into* the basis and that it should be brought in at e_4, so that s_1 must go out of the basis.

Step 5. Determining the new solution. To accomplish the necessary change in basis, we solve e_4 for x_1 to obtain

$$e_7: \quad x_1 = 4 - x_2 - s_1.$$

Thus x_1 is now a basic variable and s_1 is now nonbasic along with x_2. We must next change e_5 and e_6 in (3) so that s_1 and x_2 become the nonbasic variables. We start with

$$e_5: \quad s_2 = 6 - x_1 - 2x_2.$$

We have, by substituting e_7 into e_5,

$$s_2 = 6 - (4 - x_2 - s_1) - 2x_2$$
$$= 6 - 4 + x_2 + s_1 - 2x_2$$

or

$$e_8: \quad s_2 = 2 - x_2 + s_1.$$

Finally, to convert θ, we start with

$$e_6: \quad \theta = x_1 + 0.5x_2$$

and substitute from e_7 to obtain

$$\theta = (4 - x_2 - s_1) + 0.5x_2$$

or

$$e_9: \quad \theta = 4 - 0.5x_2 - s_1.$$

Our new system is

$$
\begin{aligned}
e_7: \quad & x_1 = 4 - && x_2 - s_1 \\
e_8: \quad & s_2 = 2 - && x_2 + s_1 \\
e_9: \quad & \theta \ = 4 - 0.5x_2 - s_1,
\end{aligned}
\tag{5}
$$

in which x_1 and s_2 are the basic variables. The variables x_2 and s_1 are nonbasic and have the value zero. The solution at this juncture (setting the nonbasic variables x_2 and s_1 equal to 0) is

$$
x_1 = 4, \quad s_2 = 2; \quad x_2 = s_1 = 0; \quad \theta = 4.
\tag{6}
$$

This is a basic feasible solution and appears as the vertex $C(4, 0)$ in Figure 5–1. Thus, our procedure started with the obvious basic feasible solution, the origin, and moved to another basic feasible solution that increased the objective function.

Returning to Step 3. We look again at the objective function, which is now

$$
e_9: \quad \theta = 4 - 0.5x_2 - s_1
$$

and note that both nonbasic variables (x_2 and s_1 on the right) have *negative* coefficients. We should not increase them from their current values of zero because to do so will *decrease* the value of the objective function. There is no way to increase θ so the current solution is optimal and the maximum value of θ is

$$
\theta_{\max} = \$4 \quad \text{at} \quad x_1 = 4 \quad \text{and} \quad x_2 = 0.
$$

Hence, as in Section 3.2, four lounge chairs and no swivel chairs should be made. From Table 5–1 we see that if four lounge chairs are made (and no swivel chairs) the lounge chairs will use up all four available hours in Department I, so there is no slack in I, and $s_1 = 0$, as the solution (6) states. However, only four of the six hours in II will be used, so the unused time is two hours, which is the value $s_2 = 2$ in the solution.

The procedure illustrated above is summarized in Figure 5–2 and what follows, using the word constraint to refer to constraints other than non-negativity constraints.

1. Introduce a nonnegative slack variable to convert each $\leq$ constraint to an equality.
2. Write the first system with the slacks as the basic variables (on the left).
3. a) If θ can be increased by bringing in a new basic variable and taking one out, determine which variable is to be brought in. Go to Step 4.
   b) If at any juncture θ cannot be increased (all coefficients negative), the present solution is optimal. Stop.

4. Determine which variable is to come out.
5. Adjust the equations to bring in the new variable, taking one out (see Step 4). Write the new system. Return to Step 3.

Step 5 turns out to be the most laborious when the number of variables and constraints increases, so we shall first develop a mechanical procedure for adjusting solutions to bring one variable in and take one out. Then we shall proceed step-by-step to develop and practice the rules used to perform Steps 1 through 5 in the above. We present no problem

FIGURE 5–2
An outline of the simplex method

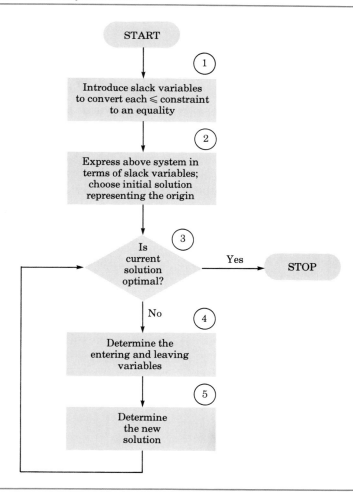

set here because the purpose of this section has been only to introduce fundamental procedures and definitions.

5.3 TABLEAUS: CHANGING BASIC VARIABLES

An efficient way to perform the steps of the preceding section is to use the matrix techniques developed in Chapter 4. To this end, we return to our starting equations (2) of Section 5.2,

$$e_1: \quad x_1 + \quad x_2 + s_1 = 4$$
$$e_2: \quad x_1 + 2x_2 + s_2 = 6$$
$$e_3: \quad \theta = x_1 + 0.5x_2,$$

and rewrite e_3 as

$$e_4: \quad \theta - x_1 - 0.5x_2 = 0$$

by moving all the variables to the left-hand side. Now we view e_1, e_2, and e_4 as a system of three equations in the five unknowns x_1, x_2, s_1, s_2, and θ in the form

$$0 + x_1 + \quad x_2 + s_1 + \quad 0 = 4$$
$$0 + x_1 + \quad 2x_2 + 0 + s_2 = 6 \qquad (1)$$
$$\theta - x_1 - 0.5x_2 + \quad 0 + \quad 0 = 0.$$

Here we have filled out the equations with zeros in the appropriate places. At this point, we summarize system (1) as shown in the tableau of Table 5–2. In this Preliminary tableau, the starting basic variables s_1 and s_2 are contained in the left-most column. The fact that we are maximizing the variable θ, representing the objective function, is entered at the bottom of this column. The rest of the tableau is precisely the matrix representation of system (1) with the last column containing the current values of our basis and θ; namely,

$$s_1 = 4, s_2 = 6, \text{ and } \theta = 0.$$

Recall that the nonbasic variables x_1 and x_2 were assigned the value zero, so that

$$x_1 = x_2 = 0.$$

TABLE 5–2
Preliminary tableau

Basic Variables	θ	Coefficient of				Current Values
		x_1	x_2	s_1	s_2	
s_1	0	1	1	1	0	4
s_2	0	1	2	0	1	6
(max) θ	1	−1	−0.5	0	0	0

Now in the last section we saw that we should bring x_1 into the basis with s_1 going out of the basis. We indicate this by the arrows $\uparrow$ and $\rightarrow$, respectively, as shown in Table 5–3. We call this table the Initial tableau since it contains the initial solution together with the optimality analysis on that solution.

TABLE 5–3
Initial tableau

Basic Variables	θ	Coefficient of				Current Values
		x_1	x_2	s_1	s_2	
s_1	0	1	1	1	0	4
s_2	0	1	2	0	1	6
(max) θ	1	-1	-0.5	0	0	0

(arrow $\rightarrow$ at s_1 row, arrow $\uparrow$ under x_1 column)

To perform the change of basis indicated in Table 5–3, we use the techniques of Chapter 4 to first get a 1 in the asterisked pivotal entry, where the entering-variable column (x_1-column) intersects with the leaving-variable row (s_1-row). By chance, this is already the case:

$$\left(\begin{array}{c|cc|cc|c} 0 & 1^* & 1 & 1 & 0 & 4 \\ 0 & 1 & 2 & 0 & 1 & 6 \\ 1 & -1 & -0.5 & 0 & 0 & 0 \end{array}\right) \rightarrow .$$

This 1^* in the pivotal row and pivotal column is called the pivot element. To find the new solution, we must now change all other values in the pivotal column to 0. To do this, we add -1 times row 1 to row 2 and $+1$ times row 1 to row 3 to obtain

$$\left(\begin{array}{c|cc|cc|c} 0 & 1 & 1 & 1 & 0 & 4 \\ 0 & 0 & 1 & -1 & 1 & 2 \\ 1 & 0 & 0.5 & 1 & 0 & 4 \end{array}\right),$$

TABLE 5–4
Second tableau

Basic Variables	θ	Coefficient of				Current Values
		x_1	x_2	s_1	s_2	
x_1	0	1	1	1	0	4
s_2	0	0	1	-1	1	2
(max) θ	1	0	0.5	1	0	4

which becomes the Second tableau, shown in Table 5–4. Note that x_1 has replaced s_1 in the basic variable (left-most) column, thus indicating the new basis of x_1 and s_2 together with the objective function variable θ. If we write out the system summarized in Table 5–4, we have

$$0 + x_1 + \quad x_2 + s_1 + 0 = 4$$
$$0 + \ 0 + \quad x_2 - s_1 + s_2 = 2$$
$$\theta + \ 0 + 0.5x_2 + s_1 + 0 = 4,$$

or solving for our basic variables x_1 and s_2 together with θ,

$$x_1 = 4 - \quad x_2 - s_1$$
$$s_2 = 2 - \quad x_2 + s_1$$
$$\theta = 4 - 0.5x_2 - s_1.$$

This is precisely system (5) of the previous section.

Exercise. Starting from the Preliminary tableau of Table 5–2, what would the Second tableau have been if we had made x_2 basic in place of s_2? What is the corresponding system of equations?
Answer:

Basic Variables	θ	Coefficient of				Current Values
		x_1	x_2	s_1	s_2	
s_1	0	1/2	0	1	− 1/2	1
x_2	0	1/2	1	0	1/2	3
(max) θ	1	− 3/4	0	0	1/4	3/2

$$s_1 = \ 1 - (1/2)x_1 + (1/2)s_2$$
$$x_2 = \ 3 - (1/2)x_1 - (1/2)s_2$$
$$\theta = 3/2 + (3/4)x_1 - (1/4)s_2.$$

Now consider the linear programming problem:

Maximize

$$\theta = 8x_1 + 5x_2$$

subject to

$$x_1 + \ x_2 \le 13$$
$$x_1 + 2x_2 \le 18$$
$$2x_1 + \ x_2 \le 20$$
$$x_1, x_2 \ge \ 0.$$

This time, we need three slack variables, s_1, s_2, and s_3. Why? Our system then becomes

$$0 + x_1 + x_2 + s_1 + 0 + 0 = 13$$
$$0 + x_1 + 2x_2 + 0 + s_2 + 0 = 18$$
$$0 + 2x_1 + x_2 + 0 + 0 + s_3 = 20$$
$$\theta - 8x_1 - 5x_2 + 0 + 0 + 0 = 0.$$

The Preliminary tableau is shown in Table 5–5. Suppose we wanted to make x_1 basic instead of s_3, as shown in Table 5–6. Then we could change the 2 to a 1 in the x_1-column of the s_3-row by dividing everything in this row by 2; i.e.,

$$\begin{pmatrix} 0 & 1 & 1 & 1 & 0 & 0 & 13 \\ 0 & 1 & 2 & 0 & 1 & 0 & 18 \\ 0 & 1 & 1/2 & 0 & 0 & 1/2 & 10 \\ 1 & -8 & -5 & 0 & 0 & 0 & 0 \end{pmatrix}.$$

TABLE 5–5
Preliminary tableau

Basic Variables	θ	Coefficient of					Current Values
		x_1	x_2	s_1	s_2	s_3	
s_1	0	1	1	1	0	0	13
s_2	0	1	2	0	1	0	18
s_3	0	2	1	0	0	1	20
(max) θ	1	−8	−5	0	0	0	0

TABLE 5–6
Initial tableau

Basic Variables	θ	Coefficient of					Current Values
		x_1	x_2	s_1	s_2	s_3	
s_1	0	1	1	1	0	0	13
s_2	0	1	2	0	1	0	18
s_3	0	2*	1	0	0	1	20
(max) θ	1	−8	−5	0	0	0	0

To convert all other values in the pivotal column to 0, we need to add -1 times row 3 to row 1, -1 times row 3 to row 2, and $+8$ times row 3 to row 4 to get the Second tableau shown in Table 5–7 on the next page. The system corresponding to this tableau is

$$0 + 0 \ + (1/2)x_2 + s_1 + 0 \ - (1/2)s_3 = \ 3$$

$$0 + 0 \ + (3/2)x_2 + 0 \ + s_2 - (1/2)s_3 = \ 8$$

$$0 + x_1 + (1/2)x_2 + 0 \ + 0 \ + (1/2)s_3 = 10$$

$$\theta + 0 \ - \qquad x_2 + 0 \ + 0 \ + \qquad 4s_3 = 80,$$

or in terms of our basis, s_1, s_2, and x_1 together with θ,

$$s_1 = \ 3 - (1/2)x_2 + (1/2)s_3$$

$$s_2 = \ 8 - (3/2)x_2 + (1/2)s_3$$

$$x_1 = 10 - (1/2)x_2 - (1/2)s_3$$

$$\theta = 80 + \qquad x_2 - \qquad 4s_3.$$

Exercise.   Starting from the Preliminary tableau of Table 5–5, what would the Second tableau have been if we had made x_2 basic in place of s_2? What is the corresponding system of equations? Answer:

Basic Variables	θ	Coefficient of					Current Values
		x_1	x_2	s_1	s_2	s_3	
s_1	0	1/2	0	1	$-1/2$	0	4
x_2	0	1/2	1	0	1/2	0	9
s_3	0	3/2	0	0	$-1/2$	1	11
(max) θ	1	$-11/2$	0	0	5/2	0	45

$$s_1 = \ 4 - (1/2)x_1 + (1/2)s_2$$

$$x_2 = \ 9 - (1/2)x_1 - (1/2)s_2$$

$$s_3 = 11 - (3/2)x_1 + (1/2)s_2$$

$$\theta = 45 + (11/2)x_1 - (5/2)s_2$$

TABLE 5-7
Second tableau

Basic Variables	θ	Coefficient of					Current Values
		x_1	x_2	s_1	s_2	s_3	
s_1	0	0	1/2	1	0	$-1/2$	3
s_2	0	0	3/2	0	1	$-1/2$	8
x_1	0	1	1/2	0	0	1/2	10
(max) θ	1	0	-1	0	0	4	80

5.4 PROBLEM SET 5-1

For each of the following linear programming problems, assume all variables are non-negative and construct (a) the Preliminary tableau, (b) the Second tableau corresponding to the change of basis indicated, and (c) the equations corresponding to the Second tableau:

1. Maximize

$$\theta = 3x_1 + x_2$$

subject to

$$4x_1 + 3x_2 \leq 24$$
$$x_1 + 2x_2 \leq 11.$$

Make x_1 basic in place of s_1.

2. Maximize

$$\theta = 4x_1 + 10x_2$$

subject to

$$3x_1 + 7x_2 \leq 42$$
$$x_1 + 5x_2 \leq 22.$$

Make x_2 basic in place of s_2.

3. Maximize

$$\theta = 0.3x_1 + 0.5x_2$$

subject to

$$3x_1 + x_2 \leq 9$$
$$x_1 + x_2 \leq 5$$
$$x_1 \qquad \leq 4$$
$$x_2 \leq 4.$$

Make x_2 basic in place of s_4.

4. Maximize

$$\theta = 4x_1 - x_2$$

subject to

$$x_1 + x_2 \leq 13$$
$$x_1 + 2x_2 \leq 22$$
$$2x_1 + x_2 \leq 20$$
$$x_1 \qquad \leq 4.$$

Make x_1 basic in place of s_4.

5. Maximize

$$\theta = 0.5x_1 + x_2 + 0.2x_3$$

subject to

$$x_1 + 4x_2 + 3x_3 \leq 1800$$
$$2x_1 + 3x_2 + x_3 \leq 2000.$$

Make x_2 basic in place of s_1.

6. Maximize

$$\theta = 1.5x_1 + 2.5x_2 + 2.0x_3$$

subject to

$$x_1 + 5x_2 \qquad \leq 4$$
$$x_2 + 2.5x_3 \leq 5$$
$$1.5x_1 + x_2 + x_3 \leq 7.5.$$

Make x_2 basic in place of s_1.

5.4 PROBLEM SET 5–1 (*concluded*)

7. Maximize

$$\theta = 8x_1 + 6x_2 + 12x_3$$

subject to

$$2x_1 + 2x_2 + 5x_3 \leq 40$$
$$x_1 + 4x_2 + 2x_3 \leq 26$$
$$3x_1 + x_2 + 3x_3 \leq 27.$$

Make x_3 basic in place of s_1.

8. Maximize

$$\theta = 5x_1 + 3x_2 + 4x_3$$

subject to

$$3x_1 + 2x_2 + x_3 \leq 23$$
$$x_1 + 3x_2 + 2x_3 \leq 26$$
$$2x_1 + x_2 + 2x_3 \leq 19$$
$$4x_1 + 5x_2 + 3x_3 \leq 49$$
$$3x_1 + 4x_2 + 4x_3 \leq 45.$$

Make x_1 basic in place of s_1.

5.5 THE SIMPLEX PROCEDURE

Linear programming problems can be solved by a procedure called the *simplex* method. The word simplex is a mathematical term used in *n*-space geometry and is not a synonym for *simple*. The important attribute of the simplex method is that it provides a step-by-step solution of linear programming problems in which each step brings us closer to the optimal value of the objective function. The steps in the simplex procedure have already been broadly outlined in Sections 5.2 and 5.3. In this section we shall describe them in detail. At any step, we can read the current solution (not necessarily optimal) from the tableau. We can determine also whether the solution is optimal; if it is not, we select the proper pivot and construct the next tableau, continuing in this manner until the optimum is reached.

The example of Section 5.2 was to maximize

$$\theta = x_1 + 0.5x_2$$

subject to

$$x_1 + x_2 \leq 4$$
$$x_1 + 2x_2 \leq 6$$
$$x_1, x_2 \geq 0.$$

We already performed Steps 1 and 2 of the simplex procedure in Sections 5.2 and 5.3, but we repeat them here for ease of understanding and completeness.

Step 1. Conversion of the constraints and objective function. To convert our inequalities into equalities, we introduced the slack variables s_1 and s_2, transforming our problem into the system

$$x_1 + x_2 + s_1 = 4$$
$$x_1 + 2x_2 + s_2 = 6 \tag{1}$$
$$\theta = x_1 + 0.5x_2.$$

Step 2. Finding an initial solution. We selected the origin $(0, 0)$ as our initial solution so that x_1 and x_2 were our initial nonbasic variables, while s_1 and s_2 were our initial basic variables. Thus, we have

$$x_1 = x_2 = 0$$

with

$$s_1 = 4, \quad s_2 = 6, \quad \text{and} \quad \theta = 0.$$

This solution caused us to rewrite system (1) as

$$
\begin{aligned}
0 + x_1 + x_2 + s_1 + 0 &= 4 \\
0 + x_1 + 2x_2 + 0 + s_2 &= 6 \\
\theta - x_1 - 0.5x_2 + 0 + 0 &= 0,
\end{aligned}
\tag{2}
$$

which was summarized in the Preliminary tableau shown in Table 5–8. Note that the current solution can be read from this tableau by letting all nonbasic variables be zero, and assigning the basic variables the numbers in the current values column.

TABLE 5–8
Preliminary tableau

Basic Variables	θ	Coefficient of x_1	x_2	s_1	s_2	Current Values
s_1	0	1	1	1	0	4
s_2	0	1	2	0	1	6
(max) θ	1	-1	-0.5	0	0	0

Exercise. Verify that the solution represented in Table 5–8 is indeed the initial solution.

Step 3. Choosing the entering variable. We saw that we should bring x_1 into the solution since every increase of 1 in x_1 would add \$1 to $\theta = x_1 + 0.5x_2$, whereas every increase of 1 in x_2 would add only \$0.50. Note in the Preliminary tableau of Table 5–8 that these coefficients of 1 and 0.5 have become -1 and -0.5, respectively, in the θ row. Why? How did we get from system (1) in Step 1 to system (2) in Step 2? What happened is that when we transposed x_1 and x_2 to the left-hand side of the θ-equation, their coefficients became negative. *Thus, the entering-variable column or pivot column for a maximizing problem is always the one that has the most negative value in the θ-row.* So our tableau becomes that

TABLE 5–9

Basic Variables	θ	Coefficient of				Current Values
		x_1	x_2	s_1	s_2	
s_1	0	1	1	1	0	4
s_2	0	1	2	0	1	6
(max) θ	1	−1	−0.5	0	0	0

$\uparrow$

shown in Table 5–9, where, as usual, the " $\uparrow$ " indicates the entering variable. By the way, if there are no negative values in the θ-row, we would stop the procedure, since we would be at the maximum.

Step 4. Choosing the leaving variable. To select the leaving variable, we solved system (1) for our current basic variables s_1 and s_2:

$$s_1 = 4 - x_1 - x_2$$
$$s_2 = 6 - x_1 - 2x_2.$$

Covering up the x_2 terms since x_2 is to remain at zero, we saw that the first equation restricted the increase of x_1 to no more than 4, while the second equation restricted the increase of x_1 to no more than 6. Why? Remember all our variables are constrained to be nonnegative! The controlling condition, then, was that x_1 could not be increased by more than 4, so that s_1 should leave the basis when x_1 enters. Now notice from Table 5–9 that if we divide the coefficients in the pivot column for x_1 into the corresponding current values in the last column, we have

$$s_1\text{-row:}\quad 4/1 = 4$$
$$s_2\text{-row:}\quad 6/1 = 6.$$

These ratios, then, represent the upper limits on the number of units of x_1 we can introduce, and we obviously must select the controlling one. *Thus, the leaving-variable row or pivot row is the one which corresponds to the smallest nonnegative ratio of the current values to the corresponding pivot column values.* This procedure for selection is shown in the Initial tableau of Table 5–10. Here we have boxed in the entries that are used to compute the ratios, shown the ratios to the right of the tableau, and indicated the leaving variable with the usual arrow.

Exercise. What would the ratios be if x_2 were the entering variable? What would the leaving variable be?
Answer: $4/1 = 4$ and $6/2 = 3$; s_2.

TABLE 5–10
Initial tableau

Basic Variables	θ	x_1	x_2	s_1	s_2	Current Values	
s_1	0	1	1	1	0	4	$4/1 = 4 \rightarrow$
s_2	0	1	2	0	1	6	$6/1 = 6$
(max) θ	1	-1	-0.5	0	0	0	

$\uparrow$

At this point, it suffices to say that we ignore negative ratios since a negative ratio indicates no limiting value. An example of such an occurrence, with a more detailed explanation, will be seen in Section 5.7. Since the current values are always nonnegative, a negative ratio can occur only when an entry in the pivotal column is negative. Thus, we need not even compute the ratio if the pivotal column entry is negative. What if the pivotal column entry were 0? In this case, the ratio is not finite and again produces no limiting value. Obviously, then, the ratios need be computed only for positive entries in the pivotal column.

Step 5. Determining the new solution. We saw the procedure for changing the basis in Section 5.3. There we simply used the row operations associated with matrices to transform the entry in the pivot column and pivot row to a 1 and transform all other entries in the pivot column to 0. This process is summarized in tableau form as shown in Table 5–11, where, for ease of understanding, we have included the steps necessary to perform the change of basis in a Working tableau and boxed in the first column and pivot row operations. As we did in Section 5.3, we first get a 1 in the asterisked pivotal entry of the pivot column. Then we add -1 times the new pivot row to the old s_2-row and $+1$ times the new pivot row to the old θ-row. The purpose of the Working tableau is to indicate the values used to change from the Initial tableau to the Second tableau. The resultant Second tableau is shown in Table 5–11.

> **Exercise.** What is the current solution? Answer: $x_1 = 4$, $s_2 = 2$, $x_2 = s_1 = 0$, and $\theta = 4$.

TABLE 5–11
Initial tableau

Basic Variables	θ	Coefficient of				Current Values	
		x_1	x_2	s_1	s_2		
s_1	0	1*	1	1	0	4	$4/1 = 4 \rightarrow$
s_2	0	1	2	0	1	6	$6/1 = 6$
(max) θ	1	-1	-0.5	0	0	0	

↑

Working tableau

Order	Operation	θ	Coefficient of				Current Values	Use
			x_1	x_2	s_1	s_2		
(1)	pivot row = (old s_1-row) ÷ 1	0	1	1	1	0	4	replaces old s_1-row
(2)	$(-1) \cdot$ (pivot row)	0	-1	-1	-1	0	-4	is added to old s_2-row
(3)	$(+1) \cdot$ (pivot row)	0	1	1	1	0	4	is added to old θ-row

Second tableau

Basic Variables	θ	Coefficient of				Current Values
		x_1	x_2	s_1	s_2	
x_1	0	1	1	1	0	4
s_2	0	0	1	-1	1	2
(max) θ	1	0	0.5	1	0	4

Returning to Step 3. Look again at the objective function in the θ-row for improvement. Since there are no negative values in the θ-row of the Second tableau of Table 5–11, we have reached the maximum. Since x_2 and s_1 are nonbasic, we have

$$x_2 = s_1 = 0.$$

From the Second tableau, we see that the current values of the basic variables are

$$x_1 = 4 \quad \text{and} \quad s_2 = 2$$

with, of course,

$$\theta = 4.$$

This is precisely the same result as found in Section 5.2.

As another example of the simplex procedure, let us recall the Ace Rubber Company example of Section 3.2:

Maximize

$$\theta = 10x_1 + 8x_2$$

subject to

Machine A: $2x_1 + 9x_2 \le 36$
Machine B: $4x_1 + 3x_2 \le 42$
Nonnegativity: $x_1, x_2 \ge 0.$

Again we have changed x and y to x_1 and x_2, respectively. Our first step is to introduce two slack variables, s_1 and s_2, one for each machine. Thus we have

Machine A: $2x_1 + 9x_2 + s_1 = 36$
Machine B: $4x_1 + 3x_2 + s_2 = 42.$

Since there is no specified contribution to profit from the slack times, θ remains unchanged

$$\theta = 10x_1 + 8x_2.$$

The Preliminary tableau, then, is as shown in Table 5–12.

TABLE 5–12
Preliminary tableau

Basic Variables	θ	Coefficient of				Current Values
		x_1	x_2	s_1	s_2	
s_1	0	2	9	1	0	36
s_2	0	4	3	0	1	42
(max) θ	1	-10	-8	0	0	0

Exercise. What is the current solution? Answer: $x_1 = x_2 = 0$, $s_1 = 36$, $s_2 = 42$, and $\theta = 0$.

Examining the θ-row of Table 5–12, we see that the maximum has not been reached. Why? We see also that x_1 should now enter the solution. Why? To determine the leaving variable, we perform the ratio analysis on the x_1 (pivot) column, as shown in Table 5–13.

TABLE 5–13
Initial tableau

Basic Variables	θ	x_1	x_2	s_1	s_2	Current Values	
s_1	0	2	9	1	0	36	36/2 = 18
s_2	0	4	3	0	1	42	42/4 = 21/2 →
(max) θ	1	−10	−8	0	0	0	

From this Initial tableau, we see that the smallest nonnegative ratio is the $21\!/\!2$ for s_2, so that s_2 should now leave the solution.

We next perform the change of basis specified in Table 5–13, bringing x_1 into the solution (making x_1 basic) and taking s_2 out of the solution (making s_2 nonbasic), as shown in Table 5–14.

TABLE 5–14
Preliminary second tableau

Basic Variables	θ	x_1	x_2	s_1	s_2	Current Values
s_1	0	0	15/2	1	−1/2	15
x_1	0	1	3/4	0	1/4	21/2
(max) θ	1	0	−1/2	0	5/2	105

Exercise. What is the current solution? Answer: $s_1 = 15$, $x_1 = 21\!/\!2$, $x_2 = s_2 = 0$, and $\theta = 105$.

Exercise. Why is the tableau in Table 5–14 labeled "Preliminary second tableau?" Answer: Because it represents the second solution without any optimality analysis.

Inspecting the tableau in Table 5–14, we see that we still have not reached the maximum. Why? So, as usual, we perform the entering and leaving variable analysis to get the Second tableau, shown in Table 5–15.

TABLE 5–15
Second tableau

Basic Variables	θ	Coefficient of				Current Values	
		x_1	x_2	s_1	s_2		
s_1	0	0	15/2	1	$-1/2$	15	$15/(15/2) = 2 \rightarrow$
x_1	0	1	3/4	0	1/4	21/2	$(21/2)/(3/4) = 14$
(max) θ	1	0	$-1/2$	0	5/2	105	

$\uparrow$

Exercise. Why do we select x_2 as the entering variable? Why do we select s_1 as the leaving variable? Answer: The most (in fact, only) negative value in the θ-row is $-\frac{1}{2}$, while 2 is the smallest nonnegative ratio.

Performing the change of basis specified in Table 5–15, we obtain the result shown in the Third tableau of Table 5–16. From this tableau, we see that we have reached the maximum. Why? The optimal solution, as seen from this tableau, is

$$x_1 = 9, \quad x_2 = 2, \quad s_1 = s_2 = 0, \quad \text{and} \quad \theta = 106,$$

so that the maximum profit is $\theta = \$106$, which is attained when $x_1 = 9$ Model P tires and $x_2 = 2$ Model R tires are made. Furthermore, both Machines A and B are fully utilized, since $s_1 = s_2 = 0$.

TABLE 5–16
Third tableau

Basic Variables	θ	Coefficient of				Current Values
		x_1	x_2	s_1	s_2	
x_2	0	0	1	2/15	$-1/15$	2
x_1	0	1	0	$-1/10$	3/10	9
(max) θ	1	0	0	1/15	37/15	106

Now before we go on, take a look at the θ-column in Tables 5–11 through 5–16. You should notice that the θ-column never changes from its original form of

$$\begin{pmatrix} 0 \\ 0 \\ 1 \end{pmatrix}.$$

Why? The reason is that the entry in the pivot row of the θ-column is always a zero. So, no matter what number we multiply the pivot row by, the entry in the θ-column will always be 0 (zero times any number is still zero). For this reason, we no longer include the θ-column in our tableaus.

Lastly, it should be clear that the simplex procedure will handle minimizing problems with all $\le$ constraints (except for nonnegativity constraints) in the same way as a maximizing problem, but with one change. Can you guess what that is? Since we are trying to improve our objective function by *reducing* it rather than increasing it, we will look for *positive* values rather than negative values in the θ-row. Another way to look at this is to note that *minimizing* θ is equivalent to *maximizing* $(-\theta)$ so we look for the opposite sign in the θ-row. With this in mind, we present the following summary of the simplex method for $\le$ constraints.

Summary of the Simplex Method for "$\le$" Constraints

Step 1. Convert each "$\le$" constraint into an equality by introducing one slack variable for each such constraint, and also convert the objective function into a θ-equation containing these slack variables.

Step 2. For the system derived in Step 1, set up the associated tableau which represents the initial solution at the origin together with the corresponding θ value by choosing the slack variables as the initial basic variables.

Step 3. Determine whether the current solution is the maximum (minimum) by examining the θ-row for negative (positive) entries. If there are no negative (positive) entries in the θ-row, then the maximum (minimum) has been obtained. Otherwise, choose as the entering variable in a maximizing (minimizing) problem the one corresponding to the most negative (positive) entry in the θ-row.

Step 4. Determine the leaving variable (in both maximizing and minimizing problems) by examining the ratios of the current values to the respective coefficients of the entering variable and choosing as the leaving variable the one corresponding to the smallest nonnegative ratio.

Step 5. Use the row operations to transform the pivotal entry in the column of the entering variable and row of the leaving variable to a 1 and transform all other entries in the pivot column to 0. Then, return to Step 3.

It is possible to have a tie for the entering or leaving variable, or both, in Steps 3 and 4. We will discuss both of these cases in detail in Section 5.9, where we will see that, for all practical purposes, we can arbitrarily choose either one of the tied variables. In addition, it is possible to have negative ratios in Step 4 of the solution of a problem. As stated earlier, the reason that negative ratios are ignored will be explained in detail in Section 5.7, where we will see how such a ratio occurs.

Finally, we want to reemphasize the following two properties of the simplex method:

1. The current values of all nonbasic variables are zero *by choice*.
2. The coefficients of the basic variables in the θ-row are zero *by design*.

5.6 PROBLEM SET 5–2

In each of the following, find the maximum value of θ by the simplex method, and state the values of the variables which make θ maximum. It is to be assumed that all variables must be nonnegative.

1. $\theta = x_1 + 2x_2$
subject to
$$x_1 + x_2 \leq 5$$
$$2x_1 + 3x_2 \leq 12.$$

2. $\theta = 2x_1 - 3x_2$
subject to
$$3x_1 + 7x_2 \leq 42$$
$$x_1 + 5x_2 \leq 22.$$

3. $\theta = 5x_1 + 8x_2$
subject to
$$x_1 + x_2 \leq 13$$
$$x_1 + 2x_2 \leq 22$$
$$2x_1 + x_2 \leq 20.$$

4. $\theta = 5x_1 + 8x_2$
subject to
$$x_1 + x_2 \leq 13$$
$$x_1 + 2x_2 \leq 22$$
$$2x_1 + x_2 \leq 20$$
$$x_1 \leq 4.$$

5. $\theta = x_1 + 2x_2 + 4x_3$
subject to
$$x_1 + 2x_2 + 3x_3 \leq 50$$
$$x_1 + 3x_2 + 5x_3 \leq 60.$$

6. $\theta = 2x_1 + 4x_2 + 3x_3$
subject to
$$x_1 + 3x_2 + 4x_3 \leq 30$$
$$x_1 + 5x_2 + 2x_3 \leq 40.$$

7. $\theta = x_1 + 4x_2 + 6x_3$
subject to
$$x_1 + 3x_2 + 6x_3 \leq 48$$
$$x_1 + 6x_2 + 3x_3 \leq 90$$
$$x_1 + 9x_2 + 10x_3 \leq 137.$$

8. $\theta = 0.5x_1 + 6x_2 + x_3$
subject to
$$x_1 + 5x_2 + 2x_3 \leq 30$$
$$x_1 + 7x_2 \leq 40$$
$$2x_1 + x_2 + 3x_3 \leq 70.$$

9. $\theta = 3x_1 + 7x_2 + 6x_3$
subject to
$$x_1 + x_2 + x_3 \leq 4.$$
$$x_1 + x_2 \leq 3.$$

10. $\theta = 1.5x_1 + 2.5x_2 + 2x_3$
subject to
$$1.5x_1 + x_2 + x_3 \leq 7.5$$
$$x_1 + x_2 + x_3 \leq 4$$
$$x_2 + 2.5x_3 \leq 5.$$

11. $\theta = 3x_1 + 5x_2 + 3x_3$
subject to
$$2x_1 + 3x_2 + 6x_3 \leq 50$$
$$3x_1 + 4x_2 + x_3 \leq 40$$
$$3x_1 + 5x_2 + 2x_3 \leq 20.$$

5.6 PROBLEM SET 5–2 (*concluded*)

12. $\theta = 2x_1 + 3x_2 + x_3$
subject to
$$2x_1 + x_2 + 3x_3 \le 10$$
$$x_1 + 3x_2 + 2x_3 \le 20.$$

13. $\theta = x_1 + 2x_2 + x_3$
subject to
$$2x_1 + x_2 + 3x_3 \le 12$$

$$x_1 + 2x_2 \qquad \le 6$$
$$2x_1 \qquad + x_3 \le 4.$$

14. $\theta = x_1 + x_2 + x_3$
subject to
$$x_1 + 2x_2 + x_3 \le 12$$
$$2x_1 + x_2 + x_3 \le 20$$
$$x_1 + x_2 + 3x_3 \le 15.$$

---

15. Star Insulating Company manufactures two types of storm windows: Model H, the heavy duty, and Model R, the regular. Model H sells for $35 per window and costs $26 per window to make, whereas Model R sells for $28 per window and costs $20 per window to make. To make one Model H window, it requires four hours on Machine A and three hours on Machine B. On the other hand, to make one Model R window, it takes five hours on Machine A and two hours on Machine B. Production scheduling indicates that during the coming week Machine A will be available for at most 30 hours and Machine B for at most 19 hours. How many of each window should the company make in the coming week in order to maximize its profit? What is this maximum profit?

16. Ace Rubber Company manufactures two types of tires: Model P, the premium, and Model S, the second line. Each tire must be processed on three machines: A, B, and C. To make one Model P tire requires 0.5 hours on Machine A, 1 hour on Machine B, and 2 hours on Machine C. To make one Model S tire requires 0.5 hours on A, 2 hours on B, and 1 hour on C. Production scheduling indicates that during the coming week Machine A will be free for at most 6.5 hours, B for at most 22 hours, and C for at most 20 hours. In addition, no more than eight Model S tires may be made. If the company makes a $5 profit on each Model P tire and an $8 profit on each Model S tire, determine the number of each model to be made in the coming week in order for the company to

maximize its profit. What is this maximum profit? At the maximum, which machines, if any, are not fully utilized?

17. A wholesaler has 9,600 feet of space available, and $5,000 he can spend to buy merchandise of types A, B, and C. Type A costs $4 per unit and requires four feet of storage space in the warehouse. B costs $10 per unit and requires eight feet of space. C costs $5 per unit and requires six feet of space. Only 500 units of type A are available to the wholesaler. Assuming that the wholesaler expects to make a profit of $1 on each unit of A he buys and stocks, $3 per unit on B, and $2 per unit on C, how many units of each should he buy and stock in order to maximize his profit, and what is this maximum profit?

18. Products A, B, and C are sold door to door. A costs $3 per unit, takes 10 minutes to sell (on the average), and costs $0.50 to deliver to a customer. B costs $5, takes 15 minutes to sell, and is left with the customer at the time of sale. C costs $4, takes 12 minutes to sell, and costs $1 to deliver. During any week, a salesman is allowed to draw up to $500 worth of A, B, and C (at cost) and he is allowed delivery expenses not to exceed $75. If a salesman's selling time is not expected to exceed 30 hours (1,800 minutes) in a week, and if the salesman's profit (net after all expenses) is $1 each on a unit of A or B and $2 on a unit of C, what combination of sales of A, B, and C will lead to maximum profit, and what is this maximum profit?

5.7 A MINIMIZING PROBLEM WITH "$\leq$" CONSTRAINTS

We now reinforce the simplex method by presenting the solution of the following minimizing linear programming problem, all of whose constraints other than the nonnegativity constraints are "$\leq$":

Example. Clear Film company has won a much-desired contract with the CIA to supply standard microfilm dots for their agents. The contract, in addition, requires the company to provide a second specially designed kind of microfilm dot whose cost, because of its unusual requirements, is actually subsidized by the government. In fact, whereas the standard microfilm dot costs the company \$1 apiece to make, the company is given \$2 apiece above its cost for the special microfilm dot. Each dot is processed for one hour on a single Machine A, which has no more than seven hours available during the coming week. Furthermore, the fixed or setup cost for the processing is \$8 per week. Finally the CIA has specified that the number of special dots cannot exceed the number of standard dots by more than one and that the number of standard dots must be limited to no more than five per week. Find the number of each kind of dot the company should make in the coming week in order to minimize its cost. What is this minimum cost?

If we let x_1 and x_2 be the number of standard and special microfilm dots, respectively, to be made in the coming week, then the total cost function to be minimized is simply

$$\theta = x_1 - 2x_2 + 8.$$

Note that the negative coefficient, -2, of x_2 is due to the fact that the cost of the special microfilm dots is subsidized at the rate of \$2 apiece. Note also that the constant term, 8, is the fixed or setup cost.

The constraints for this problem are

$$\text{Machine A:}\quad x_1 + x_2 \leq 7,$$

together with

$$\text{Relative quantities:}\quad x_2 \leq x_1 + 1$$

which, as usual, we rewrite in the form

$$-x_1 + x_2 \leq 1,$$

and

$$\text{Production limit:}\quad x_1 \leq 5.$$

Thus, our problem is to minimize the objective function

$$\theta = x_1 - 2x_2 + 8$$

subject to the five constraints

$$\text{Machine A:}\quad x_1 + x_2 \leq 7 \qquad\qquad (1)$$
$$\text{Relative quantities:}\quad -x_1 + x_2 \leq 1 \qquad\qquad (2)$$

Production limit: x_1 ≤ 5 (3)
Nonnegativity: $x_1, x_2 \ge 0.$ (4), (5)

The graph of these constraints gives rise to the feasible solution set shown in Figure 5–3.

Proceeding in the usual manner, we first add a slack variable to each of the three $\le$ constraints (1), (2), and (3) to get

$$x_1 + x_2 + s_1 + 0 + 0 = 7$$
$$-x_1 + x_2 + 0 + s_2 + 0 = 1$$
$$x_1 + 0 + 0 + 0 + s_3 = 5,$$

where, of course, s_1 is the slack on Machine A, s_2 is the slack on the relative quantities, and s_3 is the slack on the production limit of standard microfilm dots. Next, we assign the coefficient zero to each slack variable (since no penalty or premium was specified for any of them) to get the θ-equation

$$\theta = x_1 - 2x_2 + 0s_1 + 0s_2 + 0s_3 + 8$$

or

$$\theta - x_1 + 2x_2 + 0 + 0 + 0 = 8.$$

At this point, then, we can generate our initial tableau, as shown in Table 5–17.

FIGURE 5–3

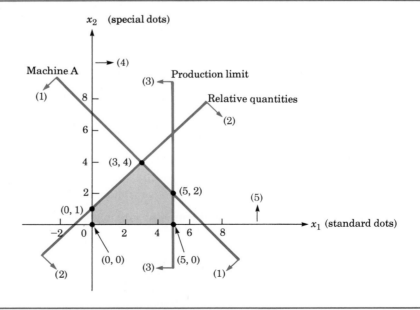

TABLE 5–17
Initial tableau

Basic Variables	Coefficient of					Current Values	
	x_1	x_2	s_1	s_2	s_3		
s_1	1	1	1	0	0	7	7
s_2	−1	1	0	1	0	1	1 →
s_3	1	0	0	0	1	5	∞
(*min*) θ	−1	2	0	0	0	8	
	↑						

Second tableau

Basic Variables	Coefficient of					Current Values	
	x_1	x_2	s_1	s_2	s_3		
s_1	2	0	1	−1	0	6	3 →
x_2	−1	1	0	1	0	1	−1
s_3	1	0	0	0	1	5	5
(*min*) θ	1	0	0	−2	0	6	
				↑			

Third tableau

Basic Variables	Coefficient of					Current Values
	x_1	x_2	s_1	s_2	s_3	
x_1	1	0	1/2	−1/2	0	3
x_2	0	1	1/2	1/2	0	4
s_3	0	0	−1/2	1/2	1	2
(*min*) θ	0	0	−1/2	−3/2	0	3

Exercise. What point in Figure 5–3 is represented by the Initial tableau? Answer: The origin $(0, 0)$, where $x_1 = 0$, $x_2 = 0$, $s_1 = 7$, $s_2 = 1$, $s_3 = 5$, and $\theta = 8$.

Now from the Initial tableau of Table 5–17, we see that x_2 enters first. Why? Since we are *minimizing* θ, the entering variable corresponds to the *most positive* entry in the θ-row and the coefficient 2 of x_2 is the most (in fact, only) positive entry in the θ-row.

> **Exercise.** What variable would have entered if we had been maximizing θ? Answer: x_1.

Now the ratio analysis in the Initial tableau of Table 5–17 shows that s_2 is to leave the solution since the ratio 1 for s_2 is the smallest nonnegative ratio. Note that, for simplicity, we are no longer computing the ratios on the right of the tableau, but simply stating the results. Note also that the ratio for s_3 is $5/0 = \infty$ or unbounded and hence, is ignored. Performing the change of basis in the usual manner, then, we find the result shown in the Second tableau of Table 5–17, which corresponds to the solution:

$$x_1 = 0, \quad x_2 = 1, \quad s_1 = 6, \quad s_2 = 0, \quad s_3 = 5, \quad \text{and} \quad \theta = 6.$$

> **Exercise.** What point in Figure 5–3 is represented by the second tableau? How did we get there from the origin? Answer: (0, 1). We moved from (0, 0) along the x_2-axis to (0, 1).

From the Second tableau of Table 5–17, we see that we should now bring x_1 into the solution and remove s_1. Note here that the negative ratio $1/(-1) = -1$ for x_2 comes from its negative exchange coefficient and indicates that increasing x_1 by 1 unit actually results in an *increase* in x_2 of 1 unit; hence, x_2 *would never decrease to 0*. Specifically, we see from the x_2-row of this tableau that the constraint equation is

$$-x_1 + x_2 + 0 + s_2 + 0 = 1$$

so that if we increase x_1 by 1 unit from 0 to 1 while keeping $s_2 = 0$, we get

$$-(+1) + x_2 + 0 + (0) + 0 = 1$$

or simply

$$x_2 = 2;$$

which, of course, is an *increase* of 1 from the current value of $x_2 = 1$. This fact can be confirmed graphically in Figure 5–3, where we see that as we move along boundary line (2), $-x_1 + x_2 = 1$, increasing x_1 by 1 unit from (0, 1) takes us to the point (1, 2); *this is precisely the reason why the simplex method ignores negative ratios.* Changing the basis, then, as indicated in the Second tableau of Table 5–17, we get the result shown in the Third tableau of that table, which corresponds to the solution

$$x_1 = 3, \quad x_2 = 4, \quad s_1 = 0, \quad s_2 = 0, \quad s_3 = 2, \quad \text{and} \quad \theta = 3.$$

Exercise. What point in Figure 5–3 is represented by the third tableau? How did we get there from $(0, 1)$? Answer: $(3, 4)$. We moved out from $(0, 1)$ along line (2) to $(3, 4)$.

Lastly, we can see from the Third tableau of Table 5–17 that the optimal solution is to make three standard and four special microfilm dots for a total cost of \$3 ($x_1 = 3$, $x_2 = 4$, and $\theta = 3$). Doing this would fully utilize Machine A ($s_1 = 0$), would result in one more special dot than standard ($s_2 = 0$), and would be two less than the production limit of standard dots ($s_3 = 2$).

5.8 PROBLEM SET 5–3

In each of the following, find the minimum value of θ by the simplex method, and state the values of the variables that make θ minimum. It is to be assumed that all variables must be nonnegative.

1. $\theta = 2x_1 - 3x_2 + 14$
subject to
$$3x_1 + 7x_2 \leq 42$$
$$x_1 + 5x_2 \leq 22.$$

2. $\theta = 2x_1 - 3x_2 + 14$
subject to
$$3x_1 + 7x_2 \leq 42$$
$$x_1 + 5x_2 \leq 22$$
$$x_2 \leq 3.$$

3. $\theta = 8x_1 - 12x_2 + 150$
subject to
$$-x_1 + x_2 \leq 10$$
$$x_1 + x_2 \leq 20.$$

4. $\theta = 8x_1 - 12x_2 + 150$
subject to
$$-x_1 + x_2 \leq 10$$
$$x_1 + x_2 \leq 20$$
$$x_2 \leq 8.$$

5. $\theta = 4x_1 - 3x_2 + 50$
subject to
$$x_1 + x_2 \leq 13$$

$$x_1 + 2x_2 \leq 22$$
$$2x_1 + x_2 \leq 20.$$

6. $\theta = 4x_1 - 3x_2 + 50$
subject to
$$x_1 + x_2 \leq 13$$
$$x_1 + 2x_2 \leq 22$$
$$2x_1 + x_2 \leq 20$$
$$x_1 \leq 8$$
$$x_2 \leq 8.$$

7. $\theta = 3x_1 - 5x_2 + 24$
subject to
$$2x_1 + 3x_2 \leq 24$$
$$2x_1 - x_2 \leq 8$$
$$-2x_1 + 3x_2 \leq 12.$$

8. $\theta = 3x_1 - 5x_2 + 24$
subject to
$$2x_1 + 3x_2 \leq 24$$
$$2x_1 - x_2 \leq 8$$
$$-2x_1 + 3x_2 \leq 12$$
$$x_1 \leq 5$$
$$x_2 \leq 5.$$

5.8 PROBLEM SET 5–3 (concluded)

9. Pure Powder Company, one of several subsidiaries of Sure Fire Munitions, Inc., supplies the parent company with most of its gunpowder. The management of Sure Fire requires all of its subsidiaries to make dynamite, the production of which is subsidized by the parent company. Specifically, each company is given $5 per dozen sticks above its cost of manufacturing dynamite. The management of Pure Powder has determined that its cost for making gunpowder is $3 per pound and that its fixed production costs for all manufacturing in any given week are $24. The gunpowder and dynamite are both processed on a single Machine A, which has at most 24 hours available during the coming week. The production of the gunpowder requires two hours per pound on A while the dynamite requires three hours per dozen sticks on A. Sure Fire has further stipulated that twice the number of pounds of gunpowder must not exceed the number of dozens of sticks of dynamite by more than eight. On the other hand, Sure Fire insists that three times the number of dozens of sticks of dynamite must not exceed twice the number of pounds of gunpowder by more than 12. How many pounds of gunpowder and dozens of sticks of dynamite should the company make in the coming week in order to minimize its total cost? What is this minimum cost?

10. Fine Motor Company, a truck manufacturer, has been ardently pursuing a long-term exclusive contract with Near East Oil Company, located in Asia, to supply tractors and tractor bodies. The oil company has asked the truck manufacturer to produce a sample of such tractors and tractor bodies. The tractors themselves are fairly standard items and cost $8,000 each to manufacture. The tractor bodies, on the other hand, are very specialized items, since they have to meet stringent temperature, humidity, and corrosion requirements due to the climate; and, indeed, the oil company has agreed to subsidize these units by giving the truck manufacturer $12,000 per tractor body above its actual cost. The truck manufacturer, in addition, has estimated that the cost of negotiations to date, together with the subsequent tractor body design specifications, amount to $150,000. There are certain restrictions accompanying the oil company's request. First, the oil company wants to see no more than eight tractors. Second, the oil company does not want the number of tractor bodies to exceed the number of tractors by more than 10. Third and last, the oil company wants the total number of pieces of equipment (tractors together with tractor bodies) not to exceed 20. Determine the number of tractors and tractor bodies the truck manufacturer should make in order to minimize its total cost. What is this minimum cost?

5.9 TIE FOR THE ENTERING OR LEAVING VARIABLE

In the summary of the simplex method in Section 5.5, we pointed out that it was possible to have a tie for the entering and/or leaving variable in one of the tableaus. The following example shows that when there is a tie for the entering variable, we can choose either one of the tied variables without affecting the optimal solution.

Example. Let us return to the Ace Rubber Company example, but change the objective function to

$$\theta = 10x_1 + 10x_2,$$

so that we are to maximize this objective function subject to

$$2x_1 + 9x_2 \leq 36$$
$$4x_1 + 3x_2 \leq 42$$
$$x_1, x_2 \geq 0.$$

TABLE 5–18A
Preliminary tableau

Basic Variables	Coefficient of				Current Values
	x_1	x_2	s_1	s_2	
s_1	2	9	1	0	36
s_2	4	3	0	1	42
(max) θ	-10	-10	0	0	0

The Preliminary tableau, then, is as shown in Table 5–18A. In this table, the entry in the θ-row for both x_1 and x_2 is -10, so that we have a tie for the entering variable; i.e., the unit gain in introducing either x_1 or x_2 is the same, and hence, we can choose either one. The resultant tableaus for entering x_1 are shown in Table 5–18B, whereas those for entering x_2 are shown in Table 5–18C. Note that, although the Second tableaus are different, the Third tableaus are identical, with the maximum value of θ occurring at

$$x_1 = 9, \quad x_2 = 2, \quad s_1 = \frac{1}{3}, \quad s_2 = \frac{7}{3}.$$

It is interesting to note in the example above that, although the *unit gains* in moving from the origin along the x_1-axis and the x_2-axis are the same, the *total gains* are different. The total gain, of course, is the unit gain *times the maximum number of units which can be introduced.* Thus, as can be seen from the Initial tableau of Table 5–18B, the total

TABLE 5–18B
Initial tableau

Basic Variables	Coefficient of				Current Values	
	x_1	x_2	s_1	s_2		
s_1	2	9	1	0	36	18
s_2	4	3	0	1	42	21/2 →
(max) θ	-10	-10	0	0	0	

↑

TABLE 5–18B (concluded)
Second tableau

Basic Variables	Coefficient of				Current Values	
	x_1	x_2	s_1	s_2		
s_1	0	15/2	1	−1/2	15	2 →
x_1	1	3/4	0	1/4	21/2	14
(max) θ	0	−5/2	0	5/2	105	

↑

Third tableau

Basic Variables	Coefficient of				Current Values
	x_1	x_2	s_1	s_2	
x_2	0	1	2/15	−1/15	2
x_1	1	0	−1/10	3/10	9
(max) θ	0	0	1/3	7/3	110

TABLE 5–18C
Initial tableau

Basic Variables	Coefficient of				Current Values	
	x_1	x_2	s_1	s_2		
s_1	2	9	1	0	36	4 →
s_2	4	3	0	1	42	14
(max) θ	−10	−10	0	0	0	

↑

Second tableau

Basic Variables	Coefficient of				Current Values	
	x_1	x_2	s_1	s_2		
x_2	2/9	1	1/9	0	4	18
s_2	10/3	0	−1/3	1	30	9 →
(max) θ	−70/9	0	10/9	0	40	

↑

TABLE 5–18C (concluded)
Third tableau

Basic Variables	Coefficient of				Current Values
	x_1	x_2	s_1	s_2	
x_2	0	1	2/15	– 1/15	2
x_1	1	0	– 1/10	3/10	9
(max) θ	0	0	1/3	7/3	110

gain in moving along the x_1-axis is

$$(\$10/\text{unit of } x_1)(21/2 \text{ units of } x_1) = \$105;$$

whereas, as can be seen from the Initial tableau of Table 5–18C, the total gain in moving along the x_2-axis is

$$(\$10/\text{unit of } x_2)(4 \text{ units of } x_2) = \$40.$$

Exercise. Compare the unit and total gains for the Second tableaus. Answer: In Table 5–18B, the unit gain for x_2 is $2.50 and the total gain is $5. In Table 5–18C, the unit gain for x_1 is $7.78 and the total gain is $70.

Since, as we saw above, any tied variable may be selected without affecting the final solution, we henceforth adopt the *convention* of choosing the left-most entering variable.

Now suppose that there is a tie for the leaving variable in one of the tableaus. This tie indicates that the associated basic variables are decreasing to zero *simultaneously*. Thus, after one of these basic variables is chosen to leave the basis to become zero as a nonbasic variable, the other(s) will remain basic but, nevertheless, have its (their) current value(s) decreased to zero. Moreover, such an occurrence of a basic variable with a current value of zero in a tableau is called "degeneracy" and arises, as we will see below, in two dimensions when three or more constraints intersect in a single point, in three dimensions when four or more constraints intersect in a single point, and so on.

When a tie for the leaving variable does occur in a tableau, one way to handle the tie is simply to choose any one of the tied basic variables. However, as will be seen in the problems, in so doing, there is a slight chance that the simplex method may not converge or lead to an answer; i.e., the solution of the problem may begin to cycle by returning to a previously generated tableau. One *sure* way to avoid cycling is by applying the following simple rule (developed by Charnes, Cooper, and

Henderson[1]): *Divide each coefficient in the tied rows by the respective coefficient of the entering variable. Compare the resultant ratios from left to right, ignoring negative ratios, until they are not equal. At that point, select the variable corresponding to the smallest nonnegative ratio as the leaving variable.* The following example illustrates this rule.

Example. Resolve the Ace Rubber Company example, but with the additional constraint that

$$2x_1 + x_2 \leq 21,$$

so that we are to maximize the objective function

$$\theta = 10x_1 + 8x_2$$

subject to

$$2x_1 + 9x_2 \leq 36 \tag{1}$$
$$4x_1 + 3x_2 \leq 42 \tag{2}$$
$$2x_1 + x_2 \leq 21 \tag{3}$$
$$x_1, x_2 \geq 0. \tag{4)(5}$$

The feasible solution set for this set of constraints is shown in Figure 5–4. Note that constraints (2), (3), and (5) all intersect in the single point $(2\frac{1}{2}, 0)$, so that, as stated above, we have a case of degeneracy. Note also that the third constraint (3) that we added is, in fact, redundant since it does not affect the feasible solution set resulting from the other constraints. Thus the solution of this problem will be the same as before except, of course, that here we will have another row and column in each of the tableaus to reflect the additional constraint (3).

Specifically, the Preliminary tableau is as shown in Table 5–19A, where we have introduced the slack variable s_3 to handle the additional third constraint (3). Note in this tableau that x_1 is the entering variable and that there is a tie between s_2 and s_3 for the leaving variable. Using the above rule, then, we now divide each coefficient in the s_2-row by 4 and each coefficient in the s_3-row by 2 to get

s_2-row ÷ 4:

1	3/4	0	1/4	0	21/2

and

s_3-row ÷ 2:

1	1/2	0	0	1/2	21/2

.

Next, comparing the corresponding entries from left to right, we see that

---

FIGURE 5–4

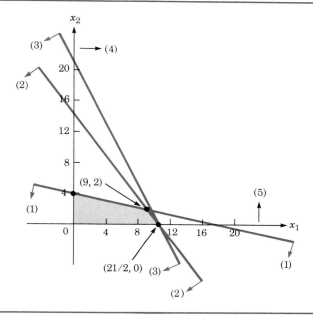

the tie is broken in the second column, where the entry $\frac{1}{2}$ for s_3 is smaller than the entry $\frac{3}{4}$ for s_2. Thus, as shown in the Initial tableau of Table 5–19B, we now select s_3 as the leaving variable.

In the usual manner, then, we get the remaining three tableaus in Table 5–19B. Note in the Second tableau that, consistent with our earlier discussion, the current value of the basic variable s_2 (which was tied with the leaving variable s_3 in the Initial tableau) now equals zero; of course, the nonbasic variables x_2 and s_3 also equal zero.

Next in the Third tableau, we see that the same three variables s_2, x_2,

TABLE 5–19A
Preliminary tableau

Basic Variables	Coefficient of					Current Values	
	x_1	x_2	s_1	s_2	s_3		
s_1	2	9	1	0	0	36	18
s_2	4	3	0	1	0	42	21/2
s_3	2	1	0	0	1	21	21/2
(max) θ	− 10	− 8	0	0	0	0	

TABLE 5–19B
Initial tableau

Basic Variables	Coefficient of					Current Values	
	x_1	x_2	s_1	s_2	s_3		
s_1	2	9	1	0	0	36	18
s_2	4	3	0	1	0	42	21/2
s_3	2	1	0	0	1	21	21/2 →
(max) θ	− 10	− 8	0	0	0	0	

↑

Second tableau

Basic Variables	Coefficient of					Current Values	
	x_1	x_2	s_1	s_2	s_3		
s_1	0	8	1	0	− 1	15	15/8
s_2	0	1	0	1	− 2	0	0 →
x_1	1	1/2	0	0	1/2	21/2	21
(max) θ	0	− 3	0	0	5	105	

↑

Third tableau

Basic Variables	Coefficient of					Current Values	
	x_1	x_2	s_1	s_2	s_3		
s_1	0	0	1	− 8	15	15	1 →
x_2	0	1	0	1	− 2	0	− 0*
x_1	1	0	0	− 1/2	3/2	21/2	7
(max) θ	0	0	0	3	− 1	105	

↑

TABLE 5–19B (concluded)
Fourth tableau

Basic Variables	Coefficient of					Current Values
	x_1	x_2	s_1	s_2	s_3	
s_3	0	0	1/15	−8/15	1	1
x_2	0	1	2/15	−1/15	0	2
x_1	1	0	−1/10	3/10	0	9
(max) θ	0	0	1/15	37/15	0	106

and s_3 are still zero, but s_2 is now nonbasic whereas x_2 is now basic. Furthermore, the values of s_1, x_1, and θ are the same as those in the Second tableau, since we are still at the *same* point of intersection of Figure 5–4; namely, the point ($2\frac{1}{2}$, 0). Lastly, note in the Third tableau that we have asterisked the ratio $0/(-2) = -0$ to indicate that, although it is 0, it should be interpreted as negative (since the exchange rate, -2, is negative) and hence, is to be ignored.

Finally, we see that the Fourth tableau of Table 5–19B corresponds to the solution

$$x_1 = 9, \quad x_2 = 2, \quad s_1 = s_2 = 0, \quad s_3 = 1, \quad \text{and} \quad \theta = 106.$$

This solution is exactly the same as that obtained earlier, except, of course, that we now have the additional result that $s_3 = 1$, reflecting the consequences of the additional constraint (3).

At this point, we wish to emphasize that although in the example above we had both a degeneracy and a redundancy, these two concepts are independent of one another.

Exercise. Graph each of the following sets of constraints and determine whether there is a degeneracy and/or a redundancy.

a) $x_1 + x_2 \le 3$
    $x_2 \le 4$
    $x_1, x_2 \ge 0.$

b) $x_1 + x_2 \le 3$
    $x_1 + x_2 \ge 3$
    $x_1, x_2 \ge 0.$

c) $x_1 + x_2 = 3$
    $x_1, x_2 \ge 0.$

d) What is the relationship between the constraint sets in (b) and (c)? Answer: a) Redundancy, but no degeneracy. b) Degeneracy, but no redundancy. c) No degeneracy and no redundancy. d) They are equivalent.

We saw in Section 3.4 that alternative optimal solutions can result when the objective function is parallel to one of the constraints. In such a case, there will be a zero in the θ-row for *one or more of the nonbasic variables* in the last simplex tableau. (Recall from Section 5.5 that the coefficients of the *basic variables* in the θ-row are always zero.) The next example shows that the way to find an alternative optimum (maximum or minimum) is simply to introduce into the solution the nonbasic variable that has the zero coefficient in the θ-row.

Example. Resolve the Ace Rubber Company example, but change the objective function to

$$\theta = 4x_1 + 18x_2,$$

as we did in Section 3.4, so that we are to maximize this objective function subject to

$$2x_1 + 9x_2 \leq 36$$
$$4x_1 + 3x_2 \leq 42$$
$$x_1, x_2 \geq 0.$$

This time, the simplex tableaus are as shown in Table 5–20A. Note that the Second tableau corresponds to the solution

$$x_1 = 0, \quad x_2 = 4, \quad s_1 = 0, \quad s_2 = 30, \quad \text{and} \quad \theta = 72,$$

which is optimal since there are no negative entries in the θ-row.

TABLE 5–20A
Initial tableau

Basic Variables	Coefficient of				Current Values	
	x_1	x_2	s_1	s_2		
s_1	2	9	1	0	36	$4 \rightarrow$
s_2	4	3	0	1	42	14
(max) θ	-4	-18	0	0	0	

$\uparrow$

Second tableau

Basic Variables	Coefficient of				Current Values
	x_1	x_2	s_1	s_2	
x_2	2/9	1	1/9	0	4
s_2	10/3	0	$-1/3$	1	30
(max) θ	0	0	2	0	72

At this point, we can see from the Second tableau of Table 5–20A that the θ-entry for the nonbasic variable x_1 is 0. The zero value here means that we can bring x_1 into the solution without any gain or loss; i.e., without changing the value of $\theta = 72$. Doing this in the usual manner, we get the Third tableau shown in Table 5–20B. Note that, as expected, the θ-row of this tableau is precisely the same as that of the Second tableau. Note also that this tableau corresponds to the solution

$$x_1 = 9, \quad x_2 = 2, \quad s_1 = s_2 = 0, \quad \text{and} \quad \theta = 72.$$

Combining this with our previous solution, we see that the maximum of 72 occurs at any point on the line segment between $(0, 4)$ and $(9, 2)$, which, of course, agrees with our result in Section 3.4.

TABLE 5–20B
Second tableau

Basic Variables	Coefficient of				Current Values	
	x_1	x_2	s_1	s_2		
x_2	2/9	1	1/9	0	4	18
s_2	10/3	0	− 1/3	1	30	9 →
(max) θ	0	0	2	0	72	

Third tableau

Basic Variables	Coefficient of				Current Values
	x_1	x_2	s_1	s_2	
x_2	0	1	2/15	− 1/15	2
x_1	1	0	− 1/10	3/10	9
(max) θ	0	0	2	0	72

It is important to realize in the example above that the simplex method only determined the two alternative optimal solution *points* $(0, 4)$ and $(9, 2)$. The reason that we were able to state that the maximum occurred at every point on the line segment between these two points was that we had previously solved this problem in Section 3.4. Of course, whenever there are alternative optimal solutions in two dimensions, they must occur on a line segment; and hence, we can always use the simplex method as we did in the example above to determine the two endpoints. In more than two dimensions, however, alternative optimal solutions do not necessarily occur only on a line segment. There are techniques for determining the set of all possible alternative solutions in these cases, but they are rather complicated and hence, are omitted. In any case, though, we can always determine the alternative optimal solution *points* by bringing into the solution any nonbasic variables that have a coefficient of zero in the θ-row.

Exercise. Resolve the example above if the objective function is changed to $\theta = 8x_1 + 6x_2$. Answer: 84 at any point on the line segment between $(2\frac{1}{2}, 0)$ and $(9, 2)$.

5.11 PROBLEM SET 5-4

In each of the following, assume that all variables must be nonnegative:

1. Maximize

$$\theta = 2x_1 + 2x_2$$

subject to

$$3x_1 + 7x_2 \leq 42$$
$$x_1 + 5x_2 \leq 22.$$

2. Minimize

$$\theta = -3x_1 - 3x_2 + 45$$

subject to

$$x_1 + x_2 \leq 13$$
$$x_1 + 2x_2 \leq 22$$
$$2x_1 + x_2 \leq 20.$$

3. Maximize

$$\theta = 6x_1 + 6x_2 - 4$$

subject to

$$x_1 + 2x_2 \leq 8$$
$$-x_1 + x_2 \leq 1$$
$$x_1 \leq 6.$$

4. Minimize

$$\theta = -3x_1 - 4x_2 + 25$$

subject to

$$x_1 - 2x_2 \leq 4$$
$$2x_1 + 3x_2 \leq 15$$
$$x_2 \leq 5.$$

5. Maximize

$$\theta = x_1 + 2x_2$$

subject to

$$-x_1 + x_2 \leq 0$$
$$x_1 + x_2 \leq 18$$
$$x_1 \leq 12.$$

6. Maximize

$$\theta = 5x_1 + 6x_2 + 10x_3$$

subject to

$$x_1 + 2x_2 + 3x_3 \leq 24$$
$$2x_1 + x_2 + x_3 \leq 18$$
$$x_1 + 2x_2 + 4x_3 \leq 32.$$

7. This problem illustrates that cycling can occur if an arbitrary rule is used to break ties for the leaving variable; namely, choose the variable in the uppermost row:
Maximize

$$\theta = (3/4)x_1 - 150x_2 + (1/50)x_3 - 6x_4$$

subject to

$$(1/4)x_1 - 60x_2 - (1/25)x_3 + 9x_4 \leq 0$$
$$(1/2)x_1 - 90x_2 - (1/50)x_3 + 3x_4 \leq 0$$
$$x_3 \leq 1.$$

5.11 PROBLEM SET 5–4 (*concluded*)

8. Maximize

$$\theta = 4x_1 + 6x_2$$

subject to

$$x_1 + x_2 \leq 5$$
$$2x_1 + 3x_2 \leq 12.$$

9. Maximize

$$\theta = 1.5x_1 + 3.5x_2$$

subject to

$$3x_1 + 7x_2 \leq 42$$
$$x_1 + 5x_2 \leq 22.$$

10. Maximize

$$\theta = x_1 + x_2$$

subject to

$$x_1 + x_2 \leq 7$$
$$-x_1 + x_2 \leq 1$$
$$x_1 \qquad \leq 5.$$

11. Maximize

$$\theta = x_1 - x_2$$

subject to

$$x_1 - x_2 \leq 4$$
$$x_1 \qquad \leq 5.$$

12. Maximize

$$\theta = 3x_1 + 3x_2 + 12x_3$$

subject to

$$x_1 + x_2 + 4x_3 \leq 36$$
$$2x_1 + 2x_2 + 3x_3 \leq 42.$$

5.12 UNBOUNDED SOLUTIONS

Another special case that can occur with linear programming problems is to have an unbounded feasible solution set in the "optimizing direction." This case gives rise to a tableau in which the ratios of the current values of the basic variables to the respective coefficients of the entering variable will all be either negative or undefined, so that no leaving variable can be selected. Recall from Section 5.7 that a negative ratio corresponds to increasing the associated current basic variable away from zero rather than decreasing it towards zero. Thus, if all the ratios are negative or undefined, then we can bring in an unlimited amount of the proposed entering variable without any of the current basic variables ever decreasing to zero, indicating, therefore, that the solution set is unbounded in the direction of that proposed entering variable.

The following example illustrates an unbounded solution set.

Example. Maximize the objective function

$$\theta = x_1 + x_2$$

subject to

$$-x_1 + x_2 \leq 1 \qquad\qquad (1)$$
$$x_2 \leq 3 \qquad\qquad (2)$$
$$x_1, x_2 \geq 0. \qquad\qquad (3), (4)$$

The feasible solution set for this set of constraints is shown in Figure 5–5. Note that this feasible solution set is unbounded in the x_1-direction.

FIGURE 5–5

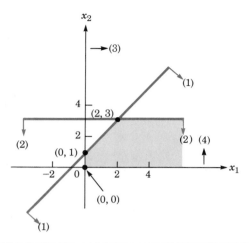

The Initial tableau is as shown in Table 5–21. Note in this tableau that we have a tie for the entering variable between x_1 and x_2; as is our convention, stated in Section 5.9, we have chosen x_1 (the left-most variable). At this point, then, no leaving variable can be chosen since the ratio for s_1 is negative (i.e., -1) while that for s_2 is undefined (i.e., ∞). Thus, the solution is unbounded in the x_1-direction; i.e., as we saw in Figure 5–5, if we proceed out from the origin $(0, 0)$ along the x_1-axis, then the feasible solution set is unbounded in this direction.

TABLE 5–21
Initial tableau

Basic Variables	Coefficient of				Current Values	
	x_1	x_2	s_1	s_2		
s_1	$\boxed{-1}$	1	1	0	$\boxed{1}$	-1
s_2	$\boxed{0}$	1	0	1	$\boxed{3}$	∞
(max) θ	-1	-1	0	0	0	

$\uparrow$

Exercise. Choose x_2 as the entering variable in Table 5–21. In which tableau is it impossible to find a leaving variable? What is the entering variable? Answer: Third. s_1.

Now it is interesting to note in the Initial tableau of Table 5–21 that we need not have computed the actual ratios, since all the coefficients of the entering variable were negative or zero. Thus the ratios themselves would have to be negative or undefined, since the current values of the basic variables are always nonnegative. This fact will hold in general; i.e., the only way for all the ratios to be negative or undefined, so that there is an unbounded solution, is for all the coefficients of the entering variable to be nonpositive.

Finally, we wish to emphasize that if we were to encounter an unbounded solution in a real-world problem, then we should carefully reexamine the formulation of the problem to determine whether or not it is an accurate model.

5.13 NEGATIVE DECISION VARIABLES

It is possible to have a linear programming problem where one or more of the decision variables may be *negative*. Such negativity can arise, for example, when one of the variables represents an inventory level; of course, negative inventory indicates a shortage. Although it is possible to have negative decision variables in the formulation of a linear programming problem, we saw in Section 5.5 that the simplex method requires that all variables be nonnegative. One way to handle problems with variables that may be negative is to replace each such variable by the difference of two variables *both of which are nonnegative*.

The following example illustrates how to handle negative decision variables.

Example. Maximize the objective function

$$\theta = 8x_1 + 10x_2$$

subject to

$$-x_1 + x_2 \leq 4 \tag{1}$$
$$x_1 + x_2 \leq 6 \tag{2}$$
$$x_1 \geq 0 \tag{3}$$
$$x_2 \text{ unrestricted in sign.} \tag{4}$$

First we note that constraint (4) is really a "pseudo-constraint" that allows x_2 to be nonnegative or negative. As stated above, negative variables are not permissible in the simplex method but are acceptable as constraints of a linear programming problem.

The graph of the feasible solution set for the above set of constraints is as shown in Figure 5–6. Note that this graph is unbounded in the negative x_2-direction and, as a consequence, there are only two extreme points; namely, (0, 4) and (1, 5).

At this point, we must overcome the difficulty of the possible negativ-

FIGURE 5–6

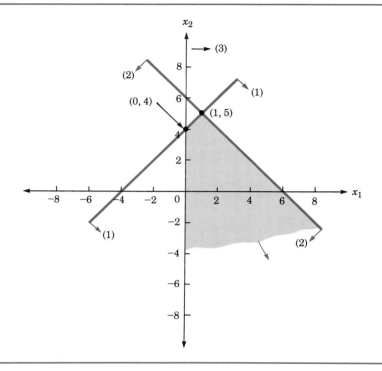

ity of the x_2-variable insofar as the simplex method is concerned. We do this simply by making the substitution

$$x_2 = x_{2p} - x_{2n}$$

in the objective function and in all the constraints where, now, x_{2p} and x_{2n} are both nonnegative variables; i.e.,

$$x_{2p}, x_{2n} \geq 0.$$

The purpose of the above substitution is to break the value of x_2 up into its *positive* portion, represented by x_{2p}, and its *negative* portion, represented by x_{2n}; e.g., if $x_2 = 4$, then $x_{2p} = 4$ and $x_{2n} = 0$, whereas if $x_2 = -4$, then $x_{2p} = 0$ and $x_{2n} = 4$. In general, as will be seen below, one of the two variables x_{2p} and x_{2n} will be zero and the other will be nonnegative.

Making the above substitution, then, our modified problem is to maximize

$$\theta = 8x_1 + 10x_{2p} - 10x_{2n}$$

subject to

$$-x_1 + x_{2p} - x_{2n} \leq 4$$
$$x_1 + x_{2p} - x_{2n} \leq 6$$
$$x_1, x_{2p}, x_{2n} \geq 0.$$

The simplex tableaus for this modified problem are as shown in Table 5–22. From the last tableau, we see that the maximum is 58, which occurs when

$$x_{2n} = s_1 = s_2 = 0,$$

(nonbasic variables) while

$$x_1 = 1 \quad \text{and} \quad x_{2p} = 5$$

(basic variables). Now since

$$x_2 = x_{2p} - x_{2n},$$

we have

$$x_2 = 5 - 0 = 5,$$

so that, in terms of our original variables, the optimal solution is

$$x_1 = 1, \quad x_2 = 5, \quad s_1 = s_2 = 0, \quad \text{and} \quad \theta = 58.$$

TABLE 5–22
Initial tableau

Basic Variables	Coefficient of					Current Values	
	x_1	x_{2p}	x_{2n}	s_1	s_2		
s_1	-1	$\boxed{1}$	-1	1	0	$\boxed{4}$	$4 \rightarrow$
s_2	1	$\boxed{1}$	-1	0	1	$\boxed{6}$	6
$(max)\ \theta$	-8	-10	10	0	0	0	

$\uparrow$

Second tableau

Basic Variables	Coefficient of					Current Values	
	x_1	x_{2p}	x_{2n}	s_1	s_2		
x_{2p}	$\boxed{-1}$	1	-1	1	0	$\boxed{4}$	-4
s_2	$\boxed{2}$	0	0	-1	1	$\boxed{2}$	$1 \rightarrow$
$(max)\ \theta$	-18	0	0	10	0	40	

$\uparrow$

TABLE 5–22 (concluded)
Third tableau

Basic Variables	Coefficient of					Current Values
	x_1	x_{2p}	x_{2n}	s_1	s_2	
x_{2p}	0	1	-1	1/2	1/2	5
x_1	1	0	0	$-1/2$	1/2	1
(max) θ	0	0	0	1	9	58

It is interesting to see how the simplex method forced one of the two variables x_{2p} and x_{2n} to be equal to zero. First we note that, by reason of the substitution $x_2 = x_{2p} - x_{2n}$, the x_{2p}- and x_{2n}-columns start off in the Initial tableau of Table 5–22 as negatives of each other. Then, by reason of the diagonalization process, these two columns remain negatives of each other in the subsequent tableaus of Table 5–22. Thus when both are nonbasic, as in the Initial tableau, both are equal to zero. When one becomes basic, however, as does x_{2p} in the Second tableau, the other (nonbasic) variable x_{2n} will always have a single -1 and then zeros in its column. This, in turn, prevents the variable from subsequently entering the basis as long as the former variable is in the basis since, in computing the appropriate ratios, the exchange rates of -1 and zero will always result in negative and undefined ratios. Therefore, the two variables cannot be basic at the same time; hence, at least one must be nonbasic; i.e., at least one must be equal to zero.

As a consequence of the above analysis, when either variable has a θ-coefficient of zero, then they both must. This can be seen in the Second and also the Third tableaus of Table 5–22. However, if in either of these two tableaus we tried to introduce the nonbasic variable x_{2n} (e.g., for an alternative optimal solution in the Third tableau), then, as stated above, we would find only negative or undefined ratios. This means, as we saw

Exercise. Reformulate the example above if x_1 were unrestricted in sign and $x_2 \geq 0$. Answer:

Maximize

$$\theta = 8x_{1p} - 8x_{1n} + 10x_2$$

subject to

$$-x_{1p} + x_{1n} + x_2 \leq 4$$
$$x_{1p} - x_{1n} + x_2 \leq 6$$
$$x_{1p}, x_{1n}, x_2 \geq 0.$$

in the previous section, that the feasible solution set is unbounded in the x_{2n}-direction. This latter fact is consistent, of course, with the fact that the original variable x_2 was unrestricted in sign and that x_{2n} represented the *negative* portion of x_2; this was previously noted in Figure 5–6, where we saw that the feasible solution set was unbounded in the *negative* x_2 direction.

5.14 TWO PENALTY/ PREMIUM EXAMPLES WITH "≤" CONSTRAINTS

In Section 5.2, we stated that there were situations where the slack variables may contribute (positively or negatively) to the objective function. Obviously then, the coefficient of such a variable in the θ-equation will not be zero. The following two examples will illustrate linear programming problems in which penalties and/or premiums are assigned to the slack variables.

Example 1. Star Insulating Company manufactures three types of storm windows: Model H, the heavy duty, Model R, the regular, and Model E, the economy. Model H sells for $25 per window and costs $16 per window to make, Model R sells for $22 per window and costs $10 per window to make, and Model E sells for $17 per window and costs $7 per window to make. To make one Model H window, it requires two hours on Machine A and one hour on Machine B. To make one Model R window, it takes two hours on Machine A and three hours on Machine B; to make one Model E window requires one hour on A and two hours on B. Production scheduling indicates that during the coming week Machine A will be available for at most 36 hours and Machine B for at most 30 hours. *However, any unused time on Machine A creates an expense (penalty) of $2 per hour allocated for idle time for an operator, but any unused time on Machine B can be rented to another firm at a rate (premium) of $2 per hour.* How many of each window should the company make in the coming week in order to maximize its profit? What is this maximum profit?

The constraints for this problem are

$$
\begin{aligned}
\text{Machine A:} \quad & 2x_1 + 2x_2 + \ x_3 \le 36 \\
\text{Machine B:} \quad & x_1 + 3x_2 + 2x_3 \le 30 \\
\text{Nonnegativity:} \quad & x_1, x_2, x_3 \ge \ 0,
\end{aligned}
$$

where x_1, x_2, and x_3 represent the respective numbers of Model H, Model R, and Model E windows to be made in the coming week. Ignoring the unused time for the moment, the objective function is

$$ \theta = 9x_1 + 12x_2 + 10x_3. $$

If we now let s_1 and s_2 be the slack times on Machines A and B, respectively, we can modify θ for the unused times. Since any unused time s_1 on Machine A has an associated expense (penalty) of $2 per hour, while any unused time s_2 on Machine B has an associated rental (premium) of $2 per hour, the new θ-equation is

$$\theta = 9x_1 + 12x_2 + 10x_3 - 2s_1 + 2s_2.$$

Thus the Preliminary tableau is as shown in Table 5–23A.

TABLE 5–23A
Preliminary tableau

Basic Variables	Coefficient of					Current Values
	x_1	x_2	x_3	s_1	s_2	
s_1	2	2	1	1	0	36
s_2	1	3	2	0	1	30
(max) θ	-9	-12	-10	2	-2	0

Do you notice anything peculiar about this tableau? Look at the coefficients of the basic variables s_1 and s_2 in the θ-row. They should both be zero. In addition, if we start out at the origin with $x_1 = x_2 = x_3 = 0$, $s_1 = 36$, and $s_2 = 30$, then we should have

$$\theta = 9(0) + 12(0) + 10(0) - 2(36) + 2(30)$$
$$= -12.$$

But what is the value of θ in Table 5–23A? The tableau indicates $\theta = 0$. So we do not have a proper starting tableau.

To transform the θ-row coefficients of s_1 and s_2, we use the usual row operations as shown in Table 5–23B. We add -2 times the s_1-row and 2 times the s_2-row to get the new θ-row. Note that we now do have a correct value of $\theta = -12$.

> **Exercise.**   Why is $\theta = -12$? Answer: We pay a penalty of $2 per hour on Machine A for $s_1 = 36$ hours, gain a value of $2 per hour on Machine B for $s_2 = 30$ hours, and $(-2)(36) + (2)(30) = -\$12$.

We now continue in Table 5–23B to generate the simplex tableaus in the usual manner. From the Third tableau, we see that the optimal solution is

$$x_1 = 14, \quad x_2 = 0, \quad x_3 = 8, \quad s_1 = s_2 = 0, \quad \text{and} \quad \theta = 206$$

for a profit of $206 when 14 Model H and 8 Model E windows are made. Since $s_1 = s_2 = 0$, there are no unused hours on either machine and so no penalty or value occurs in the optimal solution.

TABLE 5–23B
Preliminary tableau

Basic Variables	Coefficient of					Current Values
	x_1	x_2	x_3	s_1	s_2	
s_1	2	2	1	1	0	36
s_2	1	3	2	0	1	30
(max) θ	−9	−12	−10	2	−2	0

Working rows for θ

	x_1	x_2	x_3	s_1	s_2	
$(-2) \cdot (s_1\text{-row})$	−4	−4	−2	−2	0	−72
$(2) \cdot (s_2\text{-row})$	2	6	4	0	2	60

Initial tableau

Basic Variables	Coefficient of					Current Values	
	x_1	x_2	x_3	s_1	s_2		
s_1	2	2	1	1	0	36	18 →
s_2	1	3	2	0	1	30	30
(max) θ	−11	−10	−8	0	0	−12	

↑

Second tableau

Basic Variables	Coefficient of					Current Values	
	x_1	x_2	x_3	s_1	s_2		
x_1	1	1	1/2	1/2	0	18	36
s_2	0	2	3/2	−1/2	1	12	8 →
(max) θ	0	1	−5/2	11/2	0	186	

↑

Third tableau

Basic Variables	Coefficient of					Current Values
	x_1	x_2	x_3	s_1	s_2	
x_1	1	1/3	0	2/3	−1/3	14
x_3	0	4/3	1	−1/3	2/3	8
(max) θ	0	13/3	0	14/3	5/3	206

Our second example illustrates a minimizing linear programming problem with penalties or premiums; it is simply a modification of the previous example.

Example 2. Suppose in the previous example that instead of *maximizing the profit* the supervisor of the machine shop of the company wished to *minimize the cost of operation.* Suppose also that the cost of operating Machine A is $15 per hour and Machine B is $10 per hour. Suppose finally that the supervisor places an "opportunity cost" (i.e., cost due to lost opportunities) on the slack time for each machine because of the special nature of the respective machines and the skill of the corresponding operators. In particular, the supervisor feels that each slack hour on Machine A gives rise to an opportunity cost of $12 while each slack hour on Machine B creates an opportunity cost of $14 (the latter machine being an uncommon and rather expensive device that, in addition, requires a skilled operator). Now find how many of each window the supervisor recommends be made in the coming week in order to minimize the cost of operation. What is this minimum cost?

The constraints for this problem are clearly the same as those for the previous problem; namely,

$$\text{Machine A:} \quad 2x_1 + 2x_2 + x_3 \le 36 \qquad (1)$$
$$\text{Machine B:} \quad x_1 + 3x_2 + 2x_3 \le 30 \qquad (2)$$
$$\text{Nonnegativity:} \quad x_1, x_2, x_3 \ge 0 \qquad (3),(4),(5)$$

so that we still need the two slack variables s_1 and s_2. The objective function, this time, is given by

$$\theta = 15(2x_1 + 2x_2 + x_3) + 10(x_1 + 3x_2 + 2x_3) + 12s_1 + 14s_2.$$

In this equation, the coefficients 15 and 10 are the respective costs per hour on Machines A and B, the parenthetical expressions are the respective hours required on each machine, as can be seen from constraints (1) and (2), and the coefficients 12 and 14 are the respective opportunity costs per slack hour on each machine. Simplifying the above expression, we have

$$\theta = 40x_1 + 60x_2 + 35x_3 + 12s_1 + 14s_2.$$

This time the simplex tableaus are as shown in Table 5–24. From the Third tableau in this table, we see that the optimal solution is

$$x_1 = x_2 = 0, x_3 = 15, s_1 = 21, s_2 = 0, \text{ and } \theta = 777$$

for a profit of $777 when 15 Model E windows are made. Note that since $s_1 = 21$, there is an opportunity cost of $(12) \cdot (21) = \$252$ associated with the optimal solution.

TABLE 5–24
Preliminary tableau

Basic Variables	Coefficient of					Current Values
	x_1	x_2	x_3	s_1	s_2	
s_1	2	2	1	1	0	36
s_2	1	3	2	0	1	30
$(min)\ \theta$	-40	-60	-35	-12	-14	0

Initial tableau

Basic Variables	Coefficient of					Current Values	
	x_1	x_2	x_3	s_1	s_2		
s_1	2	2	1	1	0	36	18
s_2	1	3	2	0	1	30	10 →
$(min)\ \theta$	-2	6	5	0	0	852	

↑

Second tableau

Basic Variables	Coefficient of					Current Values	
	x_1	x_2	x_3	s_1	s_2		
s_1	4/3	0	$-1/3$	1	2/3	16	-48
x_2	1/3	1	2/3	0	1/3	10	15 →
$(min)\ \theta$	-4	0	1	0	-2	792	

↑

Third tableau

Basic Variables	Coefficient of					Current Values
	x_1	x_2	x_3	s_1	s_2	
s_1	3/2	1/2	0	1	$-1/2$	21
x_3	1/2	3/2	1	0	1/2	15
$(min)\ \theta$	$-9/2$	$-3/2$	0	0	$-5/2$	777

Exercise. What is the value of θ in the initial tableau? Why? Answer: $\theta = 852$. This represents a cost of ($12/hour of A) · ($s_1 = 36$ hours) + ($14/hour of B) · ($s_2 = 30$ hours) = $852.

5.15 PROBLEM SET 5–5

In each of the following, assume that all variables must be nonnegative unless otherwise indicated:

1. Maximize

$$\theta = 2x_1 + 3x_2$$

subject to

$$-2x_1 + x_2 \leq 2$$
$$x_2 \leq 6.$$

2. Maximize

$$\theta = x_1 + x_2$$

subject to

$$x_1 - x_2 \leq 4$$
$$x_1 \qquad \leq 5.$$

3. Maximize

$$\theta = -5x_1 + x_2$$

subject to

$$x_1 - 4x_2 \leq 8$$
$$-7x_1 + x_2 \leq 7.$$

4. Maximize

$$\theta = 20x_1 + 12x_3$$

subject to

$$5x_1 - x_2 + x_3 \leq 1/5$$
$$x_1 + x_2 + x_3 \leq 1/4$$
$$x_3 \text{ unrestricted in sign.}$$

5. Maximize

$$\theta = -24x_1 + 10x_2 + 18x_3$$

subject to

$$-x_1 + x_2 + 2x_3 \leq 1$$
$$-3x_1 + x_2 + x_3 \leq 7$$
$$x_3 \text{ unrestricted in sign.}$$

6. Maximize

$$\theta = 6x_1 + 4x_3$$

subject to

$$x_1 + x_2 + x_3 \leq 1/5$$
$$3x_1 - x_2 + x_3 \leq 3/10$$
$$x_3 \text{ unrestricted in sign.}$$

---

7. a) Suppose in Example 1 of Section 5.14 that the storm windows had to be processed on a third Machine C as follows: Each Model H window and each Model R window require one hour on C; each Model E window requires two hours on C. Suppose also that during the coming week Machine C will be available for at most 24 hours. Now find the number of each window the company should make in the coming week in order to maximize its profit, assuming no penalties or premiums for any unused time. What is this maximum profit?

b) Resolve (a) if, this time, any unused time on Machine A creates an expense of $1 per hour allocated for idle time for an operator, while any unused time on Machines B and C can be rented to other firms at a rate of $1 per hour.

c) Resolve (a) if, this time, the company wished to minimize its cost of operation where the cost of operating Machine A is $15 per hour, Machine B is $10 per hour, and Machine C is $9 per hour; while each slack hour on A creates an opportunity cost of $16, each slack hour on B creates an opportunity cost of $11, and each slack hour on C creates an opportunity cost of $8.

8. Ace Rubber Company makes two types of tires: Model P, the premium, and Model S, the second line. Each tire must be processed on three machines: A, B, and C. To make one Model P tire requires one hour on Machines A and B and two hours on Machine C. To make one Model S tire requires one hour on Machines A and C and two hours on Machine B. Production scheduling indicates that during the coming week Ma-

5.15 PROBLEM SET 5–5 (concluded)

chine A will be free for at most 13 hours, Machine B for at most 22 hours, and Machine C for at most 20 hours. In addition, no more than eight Model S tires may be made.

a) If the company makes a $25 profit on each Model P tire and a $30 profit on each Model S tire, find the number of each kind of tire to be made in the coming week in order to maximize the profit. What is this maximum profit?

b) Resolve (a) if, this time, any unused time on Machine A creates an expense of $1 per hour allocated for idle time for an op-

erator, while any unused time on Machines B and C can be rented to another firm at a rate of $3 per hour.

c) Resolve (a) if, this time, the company wished to minimize its cost of operation where the cost of operating Machine A is $8 per hour, Machine B is $6 per hour, and Machine C is $9 per hour; while each slack hour on A creates an opportunity cost of $6, each slack hour on Machine B creates an opportunity cost of $10, and each slack hour on Machine C creates an opportunity cost of $7.

5.16 MINIMIZATION BY MAXIMIZING THE DUAL

Our discussion to this point has involved only problems with $\leq$ constraints. In this section we shall learn how to change a minimization problem with $\geq$ constraints into a maximization problem with $\leq$ constraints, so that the solution method already developed can be applied to either type of problem. Thus, we shall solve a "less than or equal to max or min" by the methods already shown, but change a "greater than or equal to min" to a "less than or equal to max" and then solve by the method already shown.

In the next chapter, we will develop a method to solve problems with mixes of $\leq$ and $\geq$ constraints and/or equality constraints.

The original "greater than or equal to min" will be called the *primal* problem. The "less than or equal to max" to which we change will be called the *dual* problem. We first illustrate how the primal is converted to the dual, then give the necessary rules for reading the solution of the primal from the solution of the dual.

Example. Write the dual of the following problem:
Minimize

$$\theta = 2x_1 + 3x_2$$

subject to

$$i_1: \quad 3x_1 + 2x_2 \geq 12$$
$$i_2: \quad 7x_1 + 2x_2 \geq 20$$
$$i_3, i_4: \qquad x_1, x_2 \geq 0.$$

First, observe that in i_1, if $3x_1 + 2x_2$ is, say, 15, the inequality is satisfied because 15 is 3 *more* than 12; that is, there is a *surplus* of 3. Hence, to convert i_1 and i_2 to equalities, *positive* variables would be *subtracted*, and these are called *surplus* variables rather than slack variables. We denote the surplus variables here by p_1 and p_2, and indicate them next to their respective constraints. We also rewrite the primal for ease of manipulation with the nonnegativity constraints first and the objective function last, as follows:

$$Primal$$
$$x_1, x_2 \geq 0$$
$$p_1: \quad 3x_1 + 2x_2 \geq 12$$
$$p_2: \quad 7x_1 + 2x_2 \geq 20$$
$$\text{Minimize:} \quad 2x_1 + 3x_2 = \theta.$$

To form the *dual* problem, which is a maximization problem with $\leq$ constraints, we look at the x_1-column in the primal, make 3 the coefficient of the new variable p_1 and 7 the coefficient of the new variable p_2 and obtain

$$3p_1 + 7p_2.$$

Next, change $\geq$ to $\leq$, use the coefficient of x_1 in θ as the right-hand constant, and write

$$3p_1 + 7p_2 \leq 2.$$

Now repeat the process with the x_2-column to obtain

$$2p_1 + 2p_2 \leq 3.$$

Finally, the new objective function is formed in a similar manner from the right-hand column of constants. It is

$$12p_1 + 20p_2 = \theta.$$

The dual problem is
    Maximize

$$\theta = 12p_1 + 20p_2$$

    subject to

$$x_1: \quad 3p_1 + 7p_2 \leq 2$$
$$x_2: \quad 2p_1 + 2p_2 \leq 3$$
$$p_1, p_2 \geq 0.$$

Notice that the dual is a "less than or equal to max" problem and has x_1 and x_2 as *slack* variables, as indicated at the left of the first two inequalities. We offer another illustration for practice.

Example. Write the dual of the following problem:

    Minimize

$$\theta = 5x_1 + 8x_2 + 6x_3$$

subject to

$$2x_1 + \quad x_2 + 4x_3 \geq 4$$
$$2x_1 + 3x_2 + \quad x_3 \geq 2$$
$$4x_1 + 10x_2 + 3x_3 \geq 6$$
$$x_1, x_2, x_3 \geq 0.$$

We rewrite the primal for clarity, as follows:

Primal

$$x_1, x_2, x_3 \geq 0$$

p_1: $\quad 2x_1 + \quad x_2 + 4x_3 \geq 4$

p_2: $\quad 2x_1 + 3x_2 + \quad x_3 \geq 2$

p_3: $\quad 4x_1 + 10x_2 + 3x_3 \geq 6$

Minimize: $5x_1 + \quad 8x_2 + 6x_3 = \theta,$

where p_1, p_2, and p_3 are surplus variables. Attaching the column of x_1 coefficients to p_1, p_2, and p_3, and using the θ-coefficient in the x_1-column as the constant, leads to the dual $\leq$ constraint

$$2p_1 + 2p_2 + 4p_3 \leq 5.$$

In a similar manner, the second and third columns of the primal lead to the corresponding constraints in the dual. The new objective function is formed from the column of constants on the right. We have:

Dual

$$p_1, p_2, p_3 \geq 0$$

x_1: $\quad 2p_1 + 2p_2 + \quad 4p_3 \leq 5$

x_2: $\quad p_1 + 3p_2 + 10p_3 \leq 8$

x_3: $\quad 4p_1 + \quad p_2 + \quad 3p_3 \leq 6$

Maximize: $4p_1 + 2p_2 + \quad 6p_3 = \theta.$

In the dual, x_1, x_2, and x_3 become the slack variables.

Exercise. a) Construct the dual of the following, using p_1 and p_2 as surplus variables: Minimize $\theta = 4x_1 + 3x_2$ subject to $2x_1 + x_2 \geq 10$; $x_1 + 5x_2 \geq 20$; $x_1, x_2 \geq 0$. b) What are the slack variables in the dual? Answer: a) Maximize $\theta = 10p_1 + 20p_2$ subject to $2p_1 + p_2 \leq 4$; $p_1 + 5p_2 \leq 3$; $p_1, p_2 \geq 0$. b) x_1 and x_2.

We have formed the dual of a primal "greater than or equal to min" problem because the dual is a "less than or equal to max" problem that can be solved by the simplex procedure developed earlier in the chapter. We should mention, however, that a "greater than or equal to max" can be considered the primal, in which case the dual is a "less than or equal to min," and it is clear that whichever problem is the primal, the dual of its dual is the original primal problem. In any event, the dual theorem proves that all of the information contained in the solution of the primal (dual) is present in the solution of the dual (primal). The development of the dual theorem is outside the scope of this text, so we shall state without proof the part of the theorem that we want to use.

> *If a minimization problem with $\geq$ constraints has an optimum (minimum) value, this value equals the maximum of the dual problem.*

Thus, to solve a primal "greater than or equal to min" we shall set up the dual and find its maximum in the usual manner. The dual theorem then assures us that this maximum of the dual is the minimum of the primal.

Example. Solve the following:

Minimize

$$\theta = (5/4)x_1 + x_2$$

subject to

$$
\begin{array}{ll}
i_1: & 2x_1 + x_2 \geq 10 \\
i_2: & x_1 + 2x_2 \geq 8 \\
i_3, i_4: & x_1, x_2 \geq 0.
\end{array}
$$

This is precisely the first two-variable problem of Section 3.3, which we solved by the graphical procedure to obtain

$$\theta_{\min} = 7 \quad \text{at} \quad x_1 = 4 \quad \text{and} \quad x_2 = 2.$$

To solve by maximizing the dual, we first set up the dual as follows:

Maximize

$$\theta = 10p_1 + 8p_2$$

subject to

$$
\begin{array}{l}
2p_1 + p_2 \leq 5/4 \\
p_1 + 2p_2 \leq 1 \\
p_1, p_2 \geq 0.
\end{array}
$$

As stated earlier, x_1 and x_2 now become the slacks in the first two constraints, so we have the modified constraints and θ-equation

$$2p_1 + p_2 + x_1 + 0 = 5/4$$
$$p_1 + 2p_2 + 0 + x_2 = 1$$
$$\theta - 10p_1 - 8p_2 + 0 + 0 = 0.$$

Proceeding in the usual manner, then, we get the results shown in Table 5–25. From the Third tableau of this table, we have for the *dual*,

$$\theta_{max} = 7.$$

The dual theorem states that the minimum of the primal must equal the maximum of the dual. Hence, for the *primal*,

$$\theta_{min} = 7.$$

At the start of the example we found by graphical means that

$$\theta_{min} = 7 \quad at \quad x_1 = 4 \quad and \quad x_2 = 2.$$

The values for x_1 and x_2 at the minimum can also be obtained from the solution of the dual by the following rules.

To obtain the values of the variables in the solution of the primal, set the basic variables of the optimal dual tableau equal to zero and set the values of the nonbasic variables equal to the number under their respective columns in the θ-row. The nonbasic variables in the dual are the basic variables in the primal.

TABLE 5–25
Initial tableau

Basic Variables	Coefficient of				Current Values	
	p_1	p_2	x_1	x_2		
x_1	2	1	1	0	5/4	5/8 →
x_2	1	2	0	1	1	1
(max) θ	− 10	− 8	0	0	0	

↑

Second tableau

Basic Variables	Coefficient of				Current Values	
	p_1	p_2	x_1	x_2		
p_1	1	1/2	1/2	0	5/8	5/4
x_2	0	3/2	− 1/2	1	3/8	1/4 →
(max) θ	0	− 3	5	0	25/4	

↑

TABLE 5–25 (concluded)
Third tableau

Basic Variables	Coefficient of				Current Values
	p_1	p_2	x_1	x_2	
p_1	1	0	2/3	− 1/3	1/2
p_2	0	1	− 1/3	2/3	1/4
(max) θ	0	0	4	2	7

Applying the rules, we have $\theta_{min} = 7$ and

$$\begin{aligned} p_1 &= 0 \\ p_2 &= 0 \\ x_1 &= 4 \\ x_2 &= 2. \end{aligned} \qquad (1)$$

To see the full significance of the complete solution (1), recall the original primal problem, which contained

$$\begin{aligned} i_1: \quad 2x_1 + \quad x_2 &\geq 10 \qquad \text{(surplus variable is } p_1) \\ i_2: \quad x_1 + 2x_2 &\geq \ \ 8 \qquad \text{(surplus variable is } p_2). \end{aligned}$$

The solution (1) has $x_1 = 4$, $x_2 = 2$. Placing these in i_1 yields

$$\begin{aligned} 2(4) + \ \ 2 &\geq 10 \\ 10 &\geq 10, \end{aligned}$$

so i_1 is satisfied precisely and has *no surplus*. This zero surplus is the value $p_1 = 0$ in the solution (1). Similarly, placing $x_1 = 4$, $x_2 = 2$ into i_2 yields

$$\begin{aligned} 4 + 2(2) &\geq 8 \\ 8 \ &\geq 8, \end{aligned}$$

and again there is no surplus, which is the meaning of $p_2 = 0$ in the solution (1).

In Section 3.8, we stated a minimization problem in three variables and proceeded to solve it by the laborious method of finding all 10 intersections, eliminating 6 vertices as infeasible, then determining the optimum from the remaining four basic feasible solutions. We shall now illustrate how to solve such a problem by maximizing the dual.

Example. Three variables. A diet is to contain at least 10 ounces of nutrient R, 12 ounces of nutrient S, and 20 ounces of nutrient T. These nutrients are to be obtained by some combination of foods A, B, and C. Each pound of A costs 4 cents and has 4 ounces of R, 3 of S, and no T. Each pound of B costs 7 cents and has 1 ounce of R, 2 of S, and 4 of T.

Each pound of C costs 5 cents and has no R, 1 ounce of S, and 5 of T. How many pounds of A, B, and C should be combined to provide the required amount of nutrient at minimum cost?

Letting x_1, x_2, and x_3 represent, respectively, the number of pounds of A, B, and C, the data of the problem lead to the following:

Minimize

$$\theta = 4x_1 + 7x_2 + 5x_3$$

subject to

p_1:	$4x_1 + \ x_2 \qquad\qquad \geq 10$	(Nutrient R constraint)
p_2:	$3x_1 + 2x_2 + \ x_3 \ \geq 12$	(Nutrient S constraint)
p_3:	$4x_2 + 5x_3 \ \geq 20$	(Nutrient T constraint),

$$x_1, x_2, x_3 \geq 0$$

where p_1, p_2, and p_3 are surplus variables in the primal, and x_1, x_2, and x_3 will become slack variables in the dual.

We first write the dual as follows

Maximize

$$\theta = 10p_1 + 12p_2 + 20p_3$$

subject to

x_1:	$4p_1 + 3p_2 \qquad\qquad \leq 4$
x_2:	$p_1 + 2p_2 + 4p_3 \leq 7$
x_3:	$p_2 + 5p_3 \leq 5$

$$p_1, p_2, p_3 \geq 0.$$

Introducing x_1, x_2, and x_3 as slacks, we change the constraints and the θ-equation to

$$4p_1 + \ 3p_2 + \ 0 \ + x_1 + 0 \ + 0 \ = 4$$
$$p_1 + \ 2p_2 + \ 4p_3 + 0 \ + x_2 + 0 \ = 7$$
$$0 + \ p_2 + \ 5p_3 + 0 \ + 0 \ + x_3 = 5$$
$$\theta - 10p_1 - 12p_2 - 20p_3 + 0 \ + 0 \ + 0 \ = 0.$$

Using the simplex method, we get the results shown in Table 5–26.

Following the rules for writing the minimum of the primal from the last tableau (which provides the maximum of the dual), we have for the minimum cost of the mixture,

$$\theta_{min} = {}^{92}\!/\!3 \text{ cents;}$$

and for the contents of the minimum-cost mixture,

$$x_1 = {}^{8}\!/\!3 \text{ pounds of food A}$$
$$x_2 = 0 \text{ pounds of food B}$$
$$x_3 = 4 \text{ pounds of food C.}$$

TABLE 5–26
Initial tableau

Basic Variables	Coefficient of						Current Values	
	p_1	p_2	p_3	x_1	x_2	x_3		
x_1	4	3	0	1	0	0	4	∞
x_2	1	2	4	0	1	0	7	7/4
x_3	0	1	5	0	0	1	5	1 $\rightarrow$
(max) θ	-10	-12	-20	0	0	0	0	

↑

Second tableau

Basic Variables	Coefficient of						Current Values	
	p_1	p_2	p_3	x_1	x_2	x_3		
x_1	4	3	0	1	0	0	4	1 $\rightarrow$
x_2	1	6/5	0	0	1	$-4/5$	3	3
p_3	0	1/5	1	0	0	1/5	1	∞
(max) θ	-10	-8	0	0	0	4	20	

↑

Third tableau

Basic Variables	Coefficient of						Current Values	
	p_1	p_2	p_3	x_1	x_2	x_3		
p_1	1	3/4	0	1/4	0	0	1	4/3 $\rightarrow$
x_2	0	9/20	0	$-1/4$	1	$-4/5$	2	40/9
p_3	0	1/5	1	0	0	1/5	1	5
(max) θ	0	$-1/2$	0	5/2	0	4	30	

↑

TABLE 5–26 (concluded)
Fourth tableau

Basic Variables	Coefficient of						Current Values
	p_1	p_2	p_3	x_1	x_2	x_3	
p_2	4/3	1	0	1/3	0	0	4/3
x_2	−3/5	0	0	−2/5	1	−4/5	7/5
p_3	−4/15	0	1	−1/15	0	1/5	11/15
(max) θ	2/3	0	0	8/3	0	4	92/3

Exercise. What are the values of p_1, p_2, and p_3 in the optimal solution? What do these values mean? Answer: $p_1 = \frac{2}{3}$, $p_2 = p_3 = 0$. There is a surplus of $\frac{2}{3}$ ounce of nutrient R, but no surplus of either nutrient S or nutrient T.

From this example, we can see the superiority of the simplex method to that of Section 3.8. Indeed, the method of Section 3.8 is an unthinkable procedure to apply to problems with numerous variables and constraints. The simplex method is a general procedure that can solve any linear programming problem efficiently. It is true, of course, that an extensive amount of arithmetic has to be done in applying the simplex method to large problems, but the fact that the method applies the *same* steps to go from one tableau to another means that these steps can be carried out by an electronic computer. We will see an example of a computer program that does this in the next chapter after we have had more experience with the simplex method.

5.17 PROBLEM SET 5–6

Convert each of the primal problems into its dual and write the *first* tableau for the dual. It is not necessary to carry out iterations and all variables are assumed to be nonnegative.

1. Given $\theta = 5x_1 + 3x_2$, find θ_{min} subject to

$$4x_1 + 2x_2 \geq 20$$
$$6x_1 + x_2 \geq 10.$$

2. Given $\theta = 4x_1 + 2x_2$, find θ_{min} subject to

$$3x_1 + 2x_2 \geq 10$$
$$x_1 + 2x_2 \geq 20.$$

3. Given $\theta = x_1 + x_2 + x_3$, find θ_{min} subject to

$$3x_1 + 3x_2 + x_3 \geq 2$$
$$2x_1 + x_2 \qquad \geq 4$$
$$4x_1 + 2x_2 + 2x_3 \geq 6.$$

4. Given $\theta = 2x_1 + 3x_2 + x_3$, find θ_{min} subject to

$$x_1 + x_2 + x_3 \geq 10$$
$$2x_1 + 3x_2 + x_3 \geq 15$$
$$3x_1 + x_2 + 2x_3 \geq 20.$$

5.17 PROBLEM SET 5–6 (concluded)

Find the minimum value of θ by maximizing the dual.

5. $\theta = 3x_1 + 2x_2$
subject to
$$4x_1 + 3x_2 \geq 24$$
$$x_1 + 2x_2 \geq 11.$$

6. $\theta = 5x_1 + 4x_2$
subject to
$$3x_1 + 2x_2 \geq 24$$
$$x_1 + x_2 \geq 9.$$

7. $\theta = x_1 + x_2 + 3x_3$
subject to
$$x_1 + 2x_2 + 3x_3 \geq 1200$$
$$2x_1 + x_2 + x_3 \geq 600.$$

8. $\theta = 18x_1 + 30x_2 + 4x_3$
subject to
$$x_1 + 2x_2 - x_3 \geq 2$$
$$2x_1 + 3x_2 + 8x_3 \geq 6.$$

---

9. A special food for athletes is to be developed from two foods, food R and food S. The new food is to be designed so that it contains at least 16 milligrams of vitamin A, at least 20 milligrams of vitamin B, and at least 12 milligrams of vitamin C. Each pound of food R costs $1.50 and contains 1 milligram of vitamin A, 5 milligrams of vitamin B, and 1 milligram of vitamin C. Each pound of food S costs $2.50 and contains 2 milligrams of A, 1 milligram of B, and 1 milligram of C. How many pounds of each food should be used in the mixture in order to meet the above requirements at a minimum cost? What is this minimum cost?

10. Strong Steel Company operates two steel mills with different production capacities. Mill I can produce 1,000 tons per day of AAA steel, 3,000 tons per day of AA steel, and 5,000 tons per day of A steel. Mill F can produce 2,000 tons per day of each grade of steel. The company has made a contract with a construction firm to provide 24,000 tons of AAA steel, 32,000 tons of AA steel, and 40,000 tons of A steel. Determine the number of days the company should operate each mill in order to meet the terms of the above contract most economically, the minimum cost, and also what grade(s) of steel would be overproduced, if the cost of running Mill I is $1,400 per day and Mill F is $1,000 per day.

11. A special food for athletes is to be developed from three foods: food R, food S, and food T. The new food is to contain at least 66 milligrams of vitamin A, at least 48 milligrams of vitamin B, and at least 40 milligrams of vitamin C. Each pound of food R costs $1.50 and contains 2 milligrams of vitamin A, 4 milligrams of vitamin B, and 1 milligram of vitamin C. Each pound of food S costs $2.50 and contains 9 milligrams of vitamin A, 3 milligrams of vitamin B, and 4 milligrams of vitamin C. Each pound of food T costs $2.00 and contains 7 milligrams of A, 2 milligrams of B, and 8 milligrams of C. How many pounds of each food should be used in the mixture in order to meet the above requirements at a minimum cost? What is this minimum cost?

12. Strong Steel Company operates three steel mills with different production capacities. Mill I can produce 1,000 tons per day of AAA steel, 3,000 tons per day of AA steel, and 10,000 tons per day of A steel. Mill F can produce 2,000 tons per day of AAA steel, 2,000 tons per day of AA steel, and 4,000 tons per day of A steel. Mill S can produce 4,000, 1,000, and 3,000 tons per day, respectively. The company has made a contract with a construction firm to provide 29,000 tons of AAA steel, 23,000 tons of AA steel, and 62,000 tons of A steel. If it costs $1,400 per day to run Mill I, $1,000 per day to run Mill F, and $1,200 per day to run Mill S, determine the number of days the company should operate each mill in order to meet the terms of the above contract most economically. What is this minimum cost?

5.18 SENSITIVITY ANALYSIS: SHADOW PRICES AND RIGHT-HAND-SIDE RANGES

In practice, the constants and coefficients of the constraints and/or the objective function in a linear programming problem cannot be determined precisely. In other words, statements such as "Machine A will be available for at most 36 hours" are actually educated guesses and management must have the flexibility to vary the numerical values slightly *one way or the other.* The purpose of "postoptimality analysis" or "sensitivity analysis" is to determine the effects of such changes on the solution to the linear programming problem. Of course, we could reformulate the problem and resolve it in its entirety. As we will see, this procedure is not only inefficient but also unnecessary. Rather, we can start from the optimal solution to the original linear programming problem, determine the effects of the proposed modifications, and then, if necessary, proceed from there to the optimal solution of the modified problem. In this way, we can save all of the work done in solving the original problem.

The following illustration will give us a better understanding of sensitivity analysis and the associated concept of shadow prices. Recall the Ace Rubber Company example of Section 5.5 (and Section 3.2):

Maximize

$$\theta = 10x_1 + 8x_2$$

subject to

$$\text{Machine A:} \quad 2x_1 + 9x_2 \leq 36$$
$$\text{Machine B:} \quad 4x_1 + 3x_2 \leq 42$$
$$\text{Nonnegativity:} \quad x_1, x_2 \geq 0.$$

We saw in Section 5.5 that the optimal solution was

$$x_1 = 9, \quad x_2 = 2, \quad s_1 = s_2 = 0, \quad \text{and} \quad \theta = 106,$$

where s_1 and s_2 represented the slack time on Machines A and B, respectively. We shall say that when a slack variable is zero in an optimal solution, the associated constraint is *binding.* The binding constraints in the present case mean simply that no more Model P or R tires can be manufactured because all of the available resources (Machine A and B time) have been used. Consequently, the only way to increase output, all other things remaining unchanged, is to increase the amount of available time on the machines. By way of contrast, a slack that turns out to be greater than zero in the optimal solution is associated with a nonbinding constraint because the corresponding available resource is not fully utilized.

The management of Ace Rubber Company, noting that the binding constraints on resources limit the number of tires that can be made and consequently limit profit, wishes to know the effect of freeing up machine time. What if, for example, Machine A could be available for 66 hours instead of 36? The only change to the original problem would be to raise the right-hand side of the Machine A constraint to a new limit of 66:

$$\text{Machine A:} \quad 2x_1 + 9x_2 \le 66;$$

the effect of this new Machine A constraint is shown in Figure 5–7.

Exercise.   What would be the change in the original problem if Machine B could be available for 76 hours? Draw the graph showing both the old and new constraints. Answer: The right-hand side of the Machine B constraint would change from 42 to 76:

$$\text{Machine B:} \quad 4x_1 + 3x_2 \le 76.$$

Using the simplex method with the new Machine A constraint, we get the results shown in Table 5–27. From the last tableau in this table, we see that the new optimal solution is

$$x_1 = x_2 = 6, s_1 = s_2 = 0, \theta = 108,$$

or a profit of \$108 when six of each model tire are made.

Now compare Table 5–27 with Tables 5–13, 5–15, and 5–16 for the original problem. What do you notice? In both Initial tableaus, x_1 entered the basis and s_2 left. In both Second tableaus, x_2 entered the basis and s_1 left. Thus, exactly the same row operations were performed in both so-

---

FIGURE 5–7

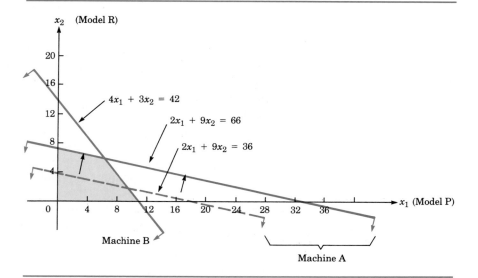

TABLE 5–27
Initial tableau

Basic Variables	Coefficient of				Current Values	
	x_1	x_2	s_1	s_2		
s_1	2	9	1	0	66	33
s_2	4	3	0	1	42	21/2 →
(max) θ	−10	−8	0	0	0	

↑

Second tableau

Basic Variables	Coefficient of				Current Values	
	x_1	x_2	s_1	s_2		
s_1	0	15/2	1	−1/2	45	6 →
x_1	1	3/4	0	1/4	21/2	14
(max) θ	0	−1/2	0	5/2	105	

↑

Third tableau

Basic Variables	Coefficient of				Current Values
	x_1	x_2	s_1	s_2	
x_2	0	1	2/15	−1/15	6
x_1	1	0	−1/10	3/10	6
(max) θ	0	0	1/15	37/15	108

lutions. The fact that we changed the right-hand side of the Machine A constraint from 36 to 66 shows up only in the current values column. Naturally, such a simple matchup will not always occur since the entering and/or leaving variable can be affected by a change in the right-hand side.

Exercise. What would be the entering and leaving variable in the initial tableau if the original problem were changed so that Machine B became available for 76 hours? Answer: x_1 would enter and s_1 would leave.

However, the matchup of Tables 5–13, 5–15, and 5–16 with Table 5–27 suggests an alternative way of solving a modified problem. Why not go directly to the last tableau and compute the effect of the change? Maybe, as in the present situation, the tableau will still be optimal, so we will be done. Even if the tableau is not optimal, we can continue on without repeating all the calculations done to that point. How, then, can we determine the new tableau directly? One way is to look at the tableaus in terms of their column vectors. For example, in the Initial tableau of Table 5–27 the x_1 column vector, $\boldsymbol{x}_1$, is

$$\boldsymbol{x}_1 = \begin{pmatrix} 2 \\ 4 \\ -10 \end{pmatrix}.$$

Exercise.   What is the x_2 column vector in this tableau?

Answer: $\boldsymbol{x}_2 = \begin{pmatrix} 9 \\ 3 \\ -8 \end{pmatrix}$.

Now notice that the column vectors for our initial basic variables s_1 and s_2 are

$$\boldsymbol{s}_1 = \begin{pmatrix} 1 \\ 0 \\ 0 \end{pmatrix} \quad \text{and} \quad \boldsymbol{s}_2 = \begin{pmatrix} 0 \\ 1 \\ 0 \end{pmatrix},$$

respectively. Recall also that in the solution of the original problem in Tables 5–13, 5–15, and 5–16 there was a never-changing θ column of

$$\boldsymbol{\theta} = \begin{pmatrix} 0 \\ 0 \\ 1 \end{pmatrix},$$

which we subsequently dropped from the solution. Now then we can express $\boldsymbol{x}_1$ in terms of $\boldsymbol{s}_1$, $\boldsymbol{s}_2$, and $\boldsymbol{\theta}$ as

$$\boldsymbol{x}_1 = \begin{pmatrix} 2 \\ 4 \\ -10 \end{pmatrix} = 2 \cdot \begin{pmatrix} 1 \\ 0 \\ 0 \end{pmatrix} + 4 \cdot \begin{pmatrix} 0 \\ 1 \\ 0 \end{pmatrix} - 10 \cdot \begin{pmatrix} 0 \\ 0 \\ 1 \end{pmatrix}$$

or

$$\boldsymbol{x}_1 = 2 \cdot \boldsymbol{s}_1 + 4 \cdot \boldsymbol{s}_2 - 10 \cdot \boldsymbol{\theta}.$$

Exercise.   Express $\boldsymbol{x}_2$ in terms of $\boldsymbol{s}_1$, $\boldsymbol{s}_2$, and $\boldsymbol{\theta}$.
Answer: $\boldsymbol{x}_2 = 9 \cdot \boldsymbol{s}_1 + 3 \cdot \boldsymbol{s}_2 - 8 \cdot \boldsymbol{\theta}$.

For the current values (or CV) column of the Initial tableau, we have a column vector that we symbolize by

$$CV = \begin{pmatrix} 66 \\ 42 \\ \hline 0 \end{pmatrix}$$

or

$$CV = 66 \cdot \boldsymbol{s}_1 + 42 \cdot \boldsymbol{s}_2 + 0 \cdot \boldsymbol{\theta}. \qquad (1)$$

Now look at the CV-column in the last tableau of Table 5–27:

$$CV = \begin{pmatrix} 6 \\ 6 \\ \hline 108 \end{pmatrix}.$$

Does the vector relationship (1) above still hold?

$$66 \cdot \boldsymbol{s}_1 + 42 \cdot \boldsymbol{s}_2 + 0 \cdot \boldsymbol{\theta} = 66 \cdot \begin{pmatrix} 2/15 \\ -1/10 \\ \hline 1/15 \end{pmatrix} + 42 \cdot \begin{pmatrix} -1/15 \\ 3/10 \\ \hline 37/15 \end{pmatrix} + 0 \cdot \begin{pmatrix} 0 \\ 0 \\ \hline 1 \end{pmatrix}$$

$$= \begin{pmatrix} 6 \\ 6 \\ \hline 108 \end{pmatrix}.$$

It does; indeed this will always be the case.

> *Every column vector of the Initial tableau can be expressed in terms of the initial basic variable column vectors together with the θ-column vector. Furthermore, the same vector relationship holds throughout all the tableaus.*

> **Exercise.** Verify that $x_1 = 2 \cdot \boldsymbol{s}_1 + 4 \cdot \boldsymbol{s}_2 - 10 \cdot \boldsymbol{\theta}$ and $x_2 = 9 \cdot \boldsymbol{s}_1 + 3 \cdot \boldsymbol{s}_2 - 8 \cdot \boldsymbol{\theta}$ in all the tableaus of Table 5–27.

Now we return to the original problem and consider a different modification. What if the hours available on Machine A must remain at 36, but Machine B can be made available for 72 hours instead of 42? This time, the only change to the original problem will affect the right-hand side of the Machine B constraint; the new limit will be 72:

$$\text{Machine B:} \quad 4x_1 + 3x_2 \le 72.$$

Once again, the Initial tableau of Table 5–13 would be affected only in the CV-column, which would become

$$CV = \begin{pmatrix} 36 \\ 72 \\ 0 \end{pmatrix}.$$

Expressing this column vector in terms of the initial basic vectors s_1 and s_2 together with θ, we have

$$CV = 36 \cdot s_1 + 72 \cdot s_2 + 0 \cdot \theta.$$

Thus, the only change in the Third tableau of Table 5–16 would be a new CV-column

$$CV = \begin{pmatrix} x_2 \\ x_1 \\ \hline \theta \end{pmatrix} = 36 \cdot s_1 + 72 \cdot s_2 + 0 \cdot \theta$$

$$= 36 \cdot \begin{pmatrix} 2/15 \\ -1/10 \\ 1/15 \end{pmatrix} + 72 \cdot \begin{pmatrix} -1/15 \\ 3/10 \\ 37/15 \end{pmatrix} + 0 \cdot \begin{pmatrix} 0 \\ 0 \\ 1 \end{pmatrix}$$

$$= \begin{pmatrix} 0 \\ 18 \\ \hline 180 \end{pmatrix},$$

so that the tableau would be as shown in Table 5–28.

TABLE 5–28
Third tableau

Basic Variables	Coefficient of				Current Values
	x_1	x_2	s_1	s_2	
x_2	0	1	2/15	-1/15	0
x_1	1	0	-1/10	3/10	18
(max) θ	0	0	1/15	37/15	180

From the table, we see that the new optimal solution is

$$x_1 = 18, \quad x_2 = s_1 = s_2 = 0, \quad \text{and} \quad \theta = 180,$$

or a profit of \$180 when 18 Model R tires are made.

Exercise. Suppose the management of Ace Rubber Company is forced to reduce the availability on both machines from their original levels to 15 hours each. a) What would be the change to the original problem? b) What is the new CV-column for the Initial tableau?

c) What is the CV-column for the Third tableau? d) What is the new optimal solution? Answer: a) The original constraints on Machine A and B become

$$\text{Machine A: } 2x_1 + 9x_2 \leq 15$$
$$\text{Machine B: } 4x_1 + 3x_2 \leq 15.$$

b) $CV = \begin{pmatrix} 15 \\ 15 \\ \hline 0 \end{pmatrix}$. c) $CV = \begin{pmatrix} 1 \\ 3 \\ \hline 36 \end{pmatrix}$. d) \$36 profit when three Model P tires and one Model R tire are made.

Now let us generalize the previous discussion by returning to the original problem and assuming that the availability of Machine A is changed by an amount of c hours from its original value of 36. This time, the constraint on Machine A becomes

$$\text{Machine A: } 2x_1 + 9x_2 \leq 36 + c \tag{2}$$

so that the CV-column of the Initial tableau would be

$$CV = \begin{pmatrix} 36 + c \\ 42 \\ \hline 0 \end{pmatrix}.$$

Thus in our Third tableau, we would have

$$CV = (36 + c) \cdot s_1 + 42 \cdot s_2 + 0 \cdot \theta$$

$$= (36 + c) \cdot \begin{pmatrix} 2/15 \\ -1/10 \\ \hline 1/15 \end{pmatrix} + 42 \cdot \begin{pmatrix} -1/15 \\ 3/10 \\ \hline 37/15 \end{pmatrix} + 0 \cdot \begin{pmatrix} 0 \\ 0 \\ \hline 1 \end{pmatrix} \tag{3}$$

$$= \begin{pmatrix} 2 + 2c/15 \\ 9 - c/10 \\ \hline 106 + c/15 \end{pmatrix}$$

so that the tableau would be as shown in Table 5–29.

TABLE 5–29
Third tableau

Basic Variables	Coefficient of				Current Values
	x_1	x_2	s_1	s_2	
x_2	0	1	2/15	-1/15	2 + 2c/15
x_1	1	0	-1/10	3/10	9 - c/10
(max) θ	0	0	1/15	37/15	106 + c/15

The new solution is

$$x_1 = 9 - c/10, \quad x_2 = 2 + 2c/15, \quad s_1 = s_2 = 0,$$
$$\text{and} \quad \theta = 106 + c/15, \tag{4}$$

where c is the change in the number of hours available on Machine A. Recall our first modification in this section was to increase the availability from 36 to 66 hours. In this case, then, the change is

$$c = 66 - 36 = 30$$

so our solution would be

$$x_1 = 9 - \frac{30}{10} = 6$$

$$x_2 = 2 + \frac{2(30)}{15} = 6$$

$$s_1 = s_2 = 0$$

$$\theta = 106 + \frac{30}{15} = 108,$$

which is precisely the same answer as before.

Shadow Price

On the other hand, what if there had been an increase from the original 36 to 37 hours? The new profit would be

$$\theta = 106 + \frac{c}{15}$$

$$= 106 + \frac{1}{15},$$

or an increase of $1/15 \approx \$0.07$. This particular value is called the *shadow price* of an hour of Machine A time. It is also called the *marginal value* of an hour of Machine A time, because it is the additional profit when the available amount of the resource is increased by *one* unit. Finally, it may be referred to as the *imputed price* of an hour of Machine A time, because the original problem statement did not provide a dollar value for Machine A time, and the $0.07 per hour was imputed from the analysis.

By the way, where did the $1/15$ come from in the new value of $\theta = 106 + 1/15$? Looking back at (3), we see that it came from multiplying c times the θ-row entry $1/15$ for s_1. This $1/15$, of course, is precisely the θ-row entry of the s_1-column in the Third tableau of Table 5–29 (or the original Table

---

Exercise. a) What is the shadow price of an hour of Machine B time? b) Which entry in Table 5–29 gives us this value? c) Why? Answer: a) $37/15$ or $\$2.47$. b) The $37/15$ in the θ-row of the s_2-column. c) s_2 is the slack variable for Machine B.

5–16 of Section 5.5). Recall that s_1 is the slack variable for Machine A.

Right-Hand-Side Ranges

The solutions we considered above were still optimal because the change c did not change the basis. Clearly, if a change of c caused x_1 or x_2 to be negative in (4), the simplex procedure would not have produced (3), because adherence to the simplex rules insures that basic variables will not be negative. Thus, it follows that in (4), the values of x_1 and x_2 must be greater than or equal to zero

$$x_1 = 9 - \frac{c}{10} \geq 0 \quad \text{and} \quad x_2 = 2 + \frac{2c}{15} \geq 0.$$

Working first with x_1, we find

$$9 - \frac{c}{10} \geq 0$$
$$-\frac{c}{10} \geq -9$$
$$\frac{c}{10} \leq 9$$
$$c \leq 90. \tag{5}$$

Working next with x_2, we have

$$2 + \frac{2c}{15} \geq 0$$
$$\frac{2c}{15} \geq -2$$
$$2c \geq -30$$
$$c \geq -15. \tag{6}$$

Taking (5) and (6) together gives

$$-15 \leq c \leq 90. \tag{7}$$

Recalling our time constraint (2) on Machine A

$$\text{Machine A:} \quad 2x_1 + 9x_2 \leq 36 + c,$$

the result (7) means that we can decrease the right-hand side by as much as 15 to $36 - 15 = 21$; i.e.,

$$2x_1 + 9x_2 \leq 21$$

or increase it by as much as 90 to $36 + 90 = 126$; i.e.,

$$2x_1 + 9x_2 \leq 126$$

without changing the variables that are in the basis. In summary, then, the shadow price of an hour of Machine A time is $0.07 for available Machine A times in the range 21 to 126 hours.

TABLE 5–30

Basic Variables	Coefficient of				Current Values	
	x_1	x_2	s_1	s_2		
x_2	0	1	2/15	−1/15	2	15
x_1	1	0	−1/10	3/10	9	−90
(max) θ	0	0	1/15	37/15	106	

↑

The price we have found in the shadows, \$0.07 per hour of Machine A time, is an important value because it shows that profit can be increased by \$0.07 for each hour of increased Machine A time made available. It follows that it would be profitable to increase Machine A time availability if the cost per additional hour is less than \$0.07.

An alternative way to determine the right-hand-side range is to compute the ratios in the last tableau of the original problem. For example, the last tableau in our present example from Table 5–16 of Section 5.5 is repeated for convenience in Table 5–30. If we were to try to change the availability of Machine A time by bringing s_1, the slack variable for Machine A, into this optimal solution, we see the ratios are 15 and −90, respectively. Recall that the original constraint *equation* for Machine A is

$$\text{Machine A:} \quad 2x_1 + 9x_2 + s_1 = 36$$

or

$$2x_1 + 9x_2 = 36 - s_1.$$

So, *subtracting* the two limiting ratios for s_1 of 15 and −90, we have

$$36 - 15 = 21$$

and

$$36 - (-90) = 126,$$

which is precisely the same result as before. Note that if there were more than one positive (negative) ratio, we would select the one with the smallest magnitude.

Exercise. Using Table 5–30, determine a) the ratios for Machine B and b) the associated right-hand-side range.
Answer: a) −30 and 30. b) 42 − 30 = 12 and 42 − (−30) = 72, so the constraint ranges between $4x_1 + 3x_2 \leq 12$ and $4x_1 + 3x_2 \leq 72$.

At this point, we present an example illustrating how the vector relationship approach can be used to perform sensitivity analysis on the coefficients of the constraints.

Example. Suppose that the management of Ace Rubber Company is forced to change the Machine A time requirement for Model R tires from the original nine hours per tire to three hours per tire. What is the optimal solution of the modified problem?

The only change to the original problem is to the coefficient of x_1 in the Machine A constraint so we want to

Maximize

$$\theta = 10x_1 + 8x_2$$

subject to

$$
\begin{aligned}
\text{Machine A:} \quad & 2x_1 + 3x_2 \leq 36 \\
\text{Machine B:} \quad & 4x_1 + 3x_2 \leq 42 \\
\text{Nonnegativity:} \quad & x_1, x_2 \geq 0.
\end{aligned}
$$

Thus the only change to the Initial tableau would be a new x_2-column.

$$
x_2 = \begin{pmatrix} 3 \\ 3 \\ -8 \end{pmatrix}
$$

$$
= 3 \cdot s_1 + 3 \cdot s_2 - 8 \cdot \theta.
$$

Hence in our Third tableau we would have

$$
x_2 = 3 \cdot s_1 + 3 \cdot s_2 - 8 \cdot \theta
$$

$$
= 3 \cdot \begin{pmatrix} 2/15 \\ -1/10 \\ 1/15 \end{pmatrix} + 3 \cdot \begin{pmatrix} -1/15 \\ 3/10 \\ 37/15 \end{pmatrix} - 8 \cdot \begin{pmatrix} 0 \\ 0 \\ 1 \end{pmatrix}
$$

or

$$
x_2 = \begin{pmatrix} 1/5 \\ 3/5 \\ -2/5 \end{pmatrix}.
$$

so that the Third tableau would be as shown in Table 5–31.

Is this tableau optimal? Certainly not, because of the negative entry $-2/5$ in the θ-row for x_2. But something else is wrong with this tableau. It does not have the proper form for a simplex tableau. Why not? Look at the x_2-column. x_2 is part of the basis, so the column should be

$$
\begin{pmatrix} 1 \\ 0 \\ 0 \end{pmatrix}.
$$

TABLE 5–31
Third tableau

Basic Variables	Coefficient of				Current Values
	x_1	x_2	s_1	s_2	
x_2	0	1/5	2/15	−1/15	2
x_1	1	3/5	−1/10	3/10	9
(max) θ	0	−2/5	1/15	37/15	106

Thus we cannot even begin to consider the question of optimality until the tableau is transformed into its proper form. We do this in the usual way, as shown in Table 5–32. From the New third tableau, we see that we have the optimal solution

$$x_1 = 3, \quad x_2 = 10, \quad s_1 = s_2 = 0, \quad \theta = 110,$$

or a profit of $110 when 3 Model P and 10 Model R tires are made.

It should be clear, at this point, that the vector relationship approach can be used to perform sensitivity analysis on any combination of coefficients and/or constants of the ≤ constraints. We will see in the next chapter that this same approach also works for ≥ and = constraints. What we will do is use the vector relationship(s) to modify the last tab-

TABLE 5–32
Third tableau

Basic Variables	Coefficient of				Current Values
	x_1	x_2	s_1	s_2	
x_2	0	1/5	2/15	−1/15	2
x_1	1	3/5	−1/10	3/10	9
(max) θ	0	−2/5	1/15	37/15	106

New third tableau

Basic Variables	Coefficient of				Current Values
	x_1	x_2	s_1	s_2	
x_2	0	1	2/3	−1/3	10
x_1	1	0	−1/2	1/2	3
(max) θ	0	0	1/3	7/3	110

leau of the original problem. Then we examine the new tableau as follows:

Step 1. Check that all the basic variable columns are in the proper form. If not, transform them as we did in the last example.

Step 2. Check that the current values column is feasible, that is, has no negative entries. If not, then a special technique that is beyond the scope of our work, known as the dual simplex method,[2] must be used.

Step 3. Check that the θ-row is optimal. If not, proceed in the usual manner, starting from the new tableau.

5.19 PROBLEM SET 5–7

1. If we were to maximize

$$\theta = 5x_1 + 8x_2$$

subject to

$$x_1 + x_2 \leq 13$$
$$x_1 + 2x_2 \leq 22$$
$$2x_1 + x_2 \leq 20$$
$$x_1, x_2 \geq 0,$$

the Final tableau would be

Basic Variables	Coefficient of					Current Values
	x_1	x_2	s_1	s_2	s_3	
x_1	1	0	2	-1	0	4
x_2	0	1	-1	1	0	9
s_3	0	0	-3	1	1	3
(max) θ	0	0	2	3	0	92

Find the new optimal solution if
a) Only the right-hand side of the first constraint is changed from 13 to 14.

b) Only the right-hand side of the second constraint is changed from 22 to 20.
c) Only the right-hand side of the third constraint is changed from 20 to 18.

2. Find the right-hand-side ranges of each of the first three constraints in Problem 1.

3. Consider the original Problem 1.
a) Find the new optimal solution if the right-hand sides of the first three constraints were simultaneously changed to 14, 20, and 24, respectively.
b) Find the Preliminary final tableau if the right-hand sides of the first three constraints were simultaneously changed to 14, 20, and 18, respectively. Explain why this tableau does not represent the optimal solution.

4. If we were to maximize

$$\theta = 3x_1 + 2x_2$$

subject to

$$x_1 + 3x_2 \leq 24$$
$$2x_1 + x_2 \leq 18$$
$$x_1 + x_2 \leq 10$$
$$x_1, x_2 \geq 0,$$

---

[2] See any textbook in management science or operations research for a discussion of the dual simplex method; for example, H. M. Wagner, *Principles of Management Science* (Englewood Cliffs, N.J.: Prentice-Hall, 1975) or F. S. Hillier and G. J. Lieberman, *Introduction to Operations Research* (San Francisco: Holden-Day, 1986).

5.19 PROBLEM SET 5-7 (continued)

the Final tableau would be

Basic Variables	Coefficient of					Current Values
	x_1	x_2	s_1	s_2	s_3	
s_1	0	0	1	2	-5	10
x_1	1	0	0	1	-1	8
x_2	0	1	0	-1	2	2
(max) θ	0	0	0	1	1	28

a) Find the right-hand-side ranges of each of the first three constraints.
b) Find the new optimal solution if the right-hand side of the first constraint was decreased to 21, simultaneously the second was increased to 22, and also the third was increased to 11.

5. If we were to maximize

$$\theta = 5x_1 + 6x_2 + 10x_3$$

subject to

$$x_1 + 2x_2 + 3x_3 \le 24$$
$$2x_1 + x_2 + x_3 \le 18$$
$$x_1, x_2, x_3 \ge 0,$$

then the Final tableau would be

Basic Variables	Coefficient of					Current Values
	x_1	x_2	x_3	s_1	s_2	
x_3	0	3/5	1	2/5	$-1/5$	6
x_1	1	1/5	0	$-1/5$	3/5	6
(max) θ	0	1	0	3	1	90

a) Find the right-hand-side ranges of each of the first two constraints.
b) Find the new optimal solution if the right-hand sides of the first two constraints were simultaneously changed to 30 and 20, respectively.

6. Find the new optimal solution to the Ace Rubber Company example if the requirement on Machine A for Model R tires were again changed to three hours per tire and simultaneously the requirement on Machine B for Model R tires were changed to one hour per tire.

7. Find the new optimal solution to Problem 4 if the original problem were changed so that each unit of x_1 were to require two units of the first resource and simultaneously each unit of x_2 were to require four units of the first resource.

8. Find the new optimal solution to Problem 4 if the original problem were changed so that each unit of x_1 were to require two units of the first resource, simultaneously each unit of x_2 were to require four units of the first resource, and also the number of available units of the first resource were increased to 36.

9. A glass manufacturer makes x_1 4-ounce, x_2 8-ounce, and x_3 12-ounce glasses, each glass made contributing to profit. Resources available are 80 man-hours of moulding time (slack is s_1), 40 manhours of grinding time (slack is s_2), and 24 manhours of polishing time (slack is s_3). Suppose the optimal profit-maximizing tableau is that given below, where θ is dollars of profit.

Basic Variables	Coefficient of						Current Values
	x_1	x_2	x_3	s_1	s_2	s_3	
x_1	1	-2	0	0	20	25	100
s_1	0	3	0	1	-1	5	5
x_3	0	-5	1	0	40	-20	80
(max) θ	0	3	0	0	30	50	1500

a) How many of each type of glass should be made to maximize profit? What is the maximum profit?

5.19 PROBLEM SET 5–7 (*concluded*)

b) Find the shadow price of any resource for which the constraint is binding and state the meaning of this price.

c) Find the right-hand-side ranges for the constraints in (b).

10. A contractor plans to build x_1 Superdeluxe, x_2 Deluxe, and x_3 Standard houses, each of which contributes to θ, the profit function. Resources available are the amounts of money a bank will loan for land purchase, building, and landscaping. Maximum amounts that will be loaned are $100,000 for land (slack is s_1), $500,000 for building (slack is s_2), and $40,000 for landscaping (slack is s_3). Suppose the optimal tableau is as follows:

Basic Variables	Coefficient of						Current Values
	x_1	x_2	x_3	s_1	s_2	s_3	
x_1	1	0	2/3	−1	0	2	4
x_2	0	1	−1/4	−3	0	1/3	9
s_2	0	0	0	1	1	−1/2	5
(*max*) θ	0	0	2	1/5	0	1/20	125

a) How many of each type of house should

be built to maximize profit? What is the maximum profit?

b) Find the shadow price of any resource for which the constraint is binding and state the meaning of this price.

c) Find the right-hand-side ranges for the constraints in (b).

11. The table shows, for example, that making one unit of Product A requires one minute for stamping, three minutes for forming, and one minute for painting and contributes $1 to profit.

Product	Number of Units	Minutes per Unit for			Profit per Unit
		Stamping	Forming	Painting	
A	x_1	1	3	1	$1
B	x_2	3	10	5	$4
C	x_3	2	5	5	$2

Minutes available for stamping, forming, and painting are, respectively, 48, 150, and 70.

a) How many units of each product should be made to maximize profit? What is the maximum profit?

b) Find the shadow price of any resource for which the constraint is binding and state the meaning of this price.

c) Find the right-hand-side range for constraints in (b).

5.20 REVIEW PROBLEMS

Solve by the simplex procedure.

1. Given $\theta = x_1 + 6x_2 + 10x_3$, find θ_{max} subject to $x_1, x_2, x_3 \geq 0$ and

$$x_1 + 5x_2 + 10x_3 \leq 150$$
$$3x_1 + 20x_2 + 25x_3 \leq 500$$
$$x_1 + 15x_2 + 15x_3 \leq 300.$$

2. Given $\theta = x_1 + 6x_2 + 3x_3$, find θ_{max} subject to $x_1, x_2, x_3 \geq 0$ and

$$x_1 + 5x_2 + 4x_3 \leq 39$$
$$2x_1 + 13x_2 + 5x_3 \leq 90$$
$$x_1 + 2x_2 + 3x_3 \leq 40.$$

3. Given $\theta = 2x_1 + 3x_2 + x_3$, find θ_{max} subject to $x_1, x_2, x_3 \geq 0$ and

$$3x_1 + 2x_2 + x_3 \leq 8$$
$$2x_1 + 3x_2 + x_3 \leq 10$$
$$5x_1 + 3x_2 + 2x_3 \leq 17.$$

5.20 REVIEW PROBLEMS (*continued*)

4. Given $\theta = x_1 + 4x_2 + 7x_3$, find θ_{max} subject to $x_1, x_2, x_3 \geq 0$ and

$$x_1 + 3x_2 + 7x_3 \leq 70$$
$$x_1 + 5x_2 + 5x_3 \leq 100$$
$$x_1 + 10x_2 + 8x_3 \leq 190.$$

5. Given $\theta = 3x_1 + 2x_2 + x_3$, find θ_{max} subject to $x_1, x_2, x_3 \geq 0$ and

$$3x_1 + x_2 + x_3 \leq 35$$
$$2x_1 + 10x_2 + 3x_3 \leq 140$$
$$4x_1 + 4x_2 + x_3 \leq 50.$$

6. Given $\theta = x_1 + 10x_2 + 3x_3$, find θ_{max} subject to $x_1, x_2, x_3 \geq 0$ and

$$x_1 + 9x_2 + 3x_3 \leq 240$$
$$3x_1 + 35x_2 + x_3 \leq 800$$
$$x_1 + 12x_2 + 5x_3 \leq 300.$$

7. Given $\theta = 2x_1 + x_2 + 2x_3$, find θ_{max} subject to $x_1, x_2, x_3 \geq 0$ and

$$x_1 + x_2 + 2x_3 \leq 8$$
$$2x_1 + x_2 + x_3 \leq 10$$
$$3x_1 + x_2 + 3x_3 \leq 15.$$

8. Given $\theta = 3x_1 + x_2 + 7x_3$, find θ_{max} subject to $x_1, x_2, x_3 \geq 0$ and

$$2x_1 + x_2 + 7x_3 \leq 21$$
$$17x_1 + 5x_2 + 28x_3 \leq 140$$
$$9x_1 + x_2 + 10x_3 \leq 66.$$

9. XYZ Steel Company manufactures two kinds of wrought-iron rails: Model E, the elegant, and Model D, the distinctive. Model E rails sell for $99 and cost $90 to make, whereas Model D rails sell for $88 and cost $81 to make. To make one Model E rail requires two hours on Machine A, one hour on Machine B, and four hours on Machine C. To make one Model D rail requires one hour on A, two hours on B, and five hours on C. Production scheduling indicates that during the coming week Machine A will be available for at most 30 hours, Machine B for at most 24 hours, and Machine C for at most 72 hours. Find the number of each kind of rail to be made in the coming week in order for the company to maximize its profit. What is this maximum profit? At the maximum, which machines, if any, are not fully utilized?

10. Ace Rubber Company manufactures three types of tires: Model P, the premium, Model S, the second line, and Model E, the economy. Model P sells for $95 per tire and costs $85 per tire to make, Model S sells for $78 per tire and costs $72 per tire to make, while Model E sells for $75 per tire and costs $63 per tire to make. To make one Model P tire, it requires one hour on Machine A and one hour on Machine B. To make one Model S tire, it takes one hour on Machine A and two hours on Machine B; to make one Model E tire requires four hours on A and three hours on B. Production scheduling indicates that during the coming week Machine A will be available for at most 42 hours and Machine B for at most 40 hours. How many of each tire should the company make in the coming week in order to maximize its profit? What is this maximum profit?

11. AAA Electrical Company makes three kinds of automobile batteries: Model S, the super, Model N, the normal, and Model E, the economy. Each battery must be processed on three machines: Machine I, Machine II, and Machine III. To make one Model S battery requires two hours on I, one hour on II, and three hours on III; to make one Model N battery requires two hours on I, four hours on II, and one hour on III; to make one Model E battery requires five hours on I, two hours on II, and three hours on III. Production scheduling indicates that during the coming week Machine I will be available for at most 40 hours, Machine II for at most 26 hours, and Machine III for at most 27 hours. If the company makes an $8 profit on each Model S battery, a $6 profit on each model N battery, and a $12 profit on each Model E battery, how many of each kind of battery should be made in the coming week in order to maximize profit? What is this maximum profit?

5.20 REVIEW PROBLEMS (*continued*)

12. Maximize

$$\theta = 3x_1 + 3x_2 + 2x_3$$

subject to

$$2x_1 + 2x_2 + x_3 \leq 36$$
$$x_1 + 3x_2 + 2x_3 \leq 30$$
$$x_1, x_2, x_3 \geq 0.$$

13. Safety Lock Company makes three kinds of locks: Model SS, the super safe, Model S, the safe, and Model O, the economy. Each Model SS lock sells for $16 and costs $11 to make, each Model S lock sells for $9 and costs $6 to make, and each Model O lock sells for $7 and costs $3 to make. Each of the locks must be processed on five machines: Model SS requires three hours on Machine A, one hour on Machine B, two hours on Machine C, four hours on Machine D, and three hours on Machine E. Model S requires two hours on A, three hours on B, one hour on C, five hours on D, and four hours on E; Model O requires one hour on A, two hours on B, two hours on C, three hours on D, and four hours on E. During the coming week Machine A will be free for no more than 23 hours, Machine B for no more than 26 hours, Machine C for no more than 19 hours, Machine D for no more than 49 hours, and Machine E for no more than 45 hours. Determine the number of each kind of lock to be made in the coming week in order for the company to maximize its profit. What is this maximum profit?

14. Subject to

$$x_1 + x_2 + 4x_3 \leq 36$$
$$2x_1 + 2x_2 + 3x_3 \leq 42$$
$$x_1, x_2, x_3 \geq 0,$$

maximize

a) $\theta = 3x_1 + 3x_2 + 12x_3$.
b) $\theta = 6x_1 + 6x_2 + 7x_3$.

15. A certain professor likes to give weekly quizzes composed of multiple-choice questions divided into two groups, A and B. By closely observing the format of the first few quizzes, one rather clever student has de-

termined that although there are always 30 questions of each type, the student is allowed to answer at most 40 total questions. In addition, the student is prohibited from answering more than 25 A questions but is required to answer at least as many B questions as A questions. Furthermore, while each A question counts two points, each B question counts three points. Lastly, the student is always restricted by having the number of B questions answered not exceed the number of A questions by more than 8; and, indeed, is penalized ½ point each for the number of B questions answered over the number of A questions answered. After some deliberation, the student has worked out a scheme for the number of each kind of question that should be answered to attain the best possible grade and finds five alternative combinations. What is his scheme and what will be his score?

16. Subject to

$$-x_1 + x_2 \leq 4$$
$$x_1 + x_2 \leq 6$$
$$x_1 \geq 0$$
$$x_2 \text{ unrestricted in sign,}$$

a) Maximize $\theta = 10x_1 + 10x_2$.
b) Maximize $\theta = 10x_1 + 8x_2$.
c) Minimize $\theta = 8x_1 + 10x_2$.

17. XYZ Steel Company manufactures two kinds of wrought-iron rails: Model E, the elegant, and Model D, the distinctive. Model E rails sell for $84 and cost $75 to make; Model D rails sell for $73 and cost $66 to make. To make one Model E rail requires two hours on Machine A, one hour on Machine B, and four hours on Machine C. On the other hand, to make one Model D rail requires one hour on A, two hours on B, and five hours on C. Production scheduling indicates that during the coming week Machine A will be available for at most 30 hours, Machine B for at most 24 hours, and Machine C for at most 72 hours. In addition, each unused hour on Machine A is worth $2, on Machine B costs $2, and on Machine C is worth $1.

5.20 REVIEW PROBLEMS (*continued*)

Find the number of each kind of rail to be made in the coming week in order for the company to maximize its profit.

18. Ace Rubber Company makes two types of tires: Model P, the premium, and Model S, the second line. Each tire must be processed on three machines: A, B, and C. To make one Model P tire requires one hour on Machines A and B, and two hours on Machine C. To make one Model S tire requires one hour on Machines A and C, and two hours on Machine B. Production scheduling indicates that during the coming week Ma-

chine A will be free for at most 13 hours, Machine B for at most 22 hours, and Machine C for at most 20 hours. In addition, no more than eight Model S tires may be made. The cost of operating Machine A is $10 per hour, Machine B is $4 per hour, and Machine C is $8 per hour; while each slack hour on A creates an opportunity cost of $8, each slack hour on B creates an opportunity cost of $9, and each slack hour on C creates an opportunity cost of $6. Find the number of each type of tire to be made in the coming week for the company to minimize its cost of operation.

Solve Problems 19–24 by the dual procedure.

19. Given $\theta = 6x_1 + 24x_2 + 12x_3$, find θ_{min} subject to $x_1, x_2, x_3 \geq 0$ and

$$x_1 + 2x_2 + x_3 \geq 1$$
$$x_1 + x_2 + 3x_3 \geq 2$$
$$x_1 + 3x_2 + x_3 \geq 3.$$

20. Given $\theta = 2x_1 + x_2 + x_3$, find θ_{min} subject to $x_1, x_2, x_3 \geq 0$ and

$$2x_1 + 3x_2 + 2x_3 \geq 10$$
$$x_1 + 4x_2 + 3x_3 \geq 20.$$

21. Given $\theta = 12x_1 + 6x_2 + 4x_3$, find θ_{min} subject to $x_1, x_2, x_3 \geq 0$ and

$$2x_1 + x_2 + 2x_3 \geq 1$$
$$x_1 + 2x_2 \geq 2$$
$$3x_1 + x_3 \geq 1.$$

22. Given $\theta = 8x_1 + 10x_2 + 15x_3$, find θ_{min} subject to $x_1, x_2, x_3 \geq 0$ and

$$x_1 + 2x_2 + 3x_3 \geq 2$$
$$x_1 + x_2 + x_3 \geq 1$$
$$2x_1 + x_2 + 3x_3 \geq 2.$$

23. Given $\theta = 2x_1 + 3x_2 + x_3$, find the *minimum* value of θ subject to $x_1, x_2, x_3 \geq 0$ and

$$x_1 + x_2 + x_3 \geq 10$$
$$2x_1 + 3x_2 + x_3 \geq 15$$
$$3x_1 + x_2 + 2x_3 \geq 20.$$

24. Given $\theta = 5x_1 + 7x_2 + 6x_3$, find θ_{min} subject to $x_1, x_2, x_3 \geq 0$ and

$$x_1 + x_3 \geq 3$$
$$x_1 + x_2 \geq 2$$
$$x_2 + x_3 \geq 1.$$

25. If we were to maximize

$$\theta = 2x_1 + x_2$$

subject to

$$x_1 + x_2 \leq 7$$
$$-x_1 + x_2 \leq 1$$
$$x_1 \leq 5$$
$$x_1, x_2 \geq 0,$$

the final tableau would be

Basic Variables	Coefficient of					Current Values
	x_1	x_2	s_1	s_2	s_3	
x_2	0	1	1	0	-1	2
s_2	0	0	-1	1	2	4
x_1	1	0	0	0	1	5
(*max*) θ	0	0	1	0	1	12

5.20 REVIEW PROBLEMS (*concluded*)

a) Find the right-hand-side ranges for each of the first three constraints.

b) Find the new optimal solution to the original problem if the right-hand sides of the first three constraints were simultaneously changed to 8, 6, and 4, respectively.

26. Find the new optimal solution to Problem 25 if only the first constraint were changed to $2x_1 + x_2 \leq 10$.

27. A doll manufacturer makes x_1 dresses, x_2 hats, and x_3 gloves a day, each of which contributes to the profit function θ. Resources available are 100 hours of cutting time (slack is s_1), 40 hours of assembly time (slack time is s_2), and 50 hours of stitching time (slack is s_3). Suppose the optimal profit-maximizing tableau is that given opposite.

a) How many of each item should be made to maximize profit? What is the maximum profit?

b) Find the shadow price of any resource for which the constraint is binding and state the meaning of this price.

c) Find the right-hand-side ranges for the constraints in (b).

Basic Variables	Coefficient of						Current Values
	x_1	x_2	x_3	s_1	s_2	s_3	
s_1	1	0	2	50	−40	0	200
x_3	0	0	−1	−1	−1	1	10
s_2	0	1	−3	20	50	0	300
(*max*) θ	0	0	5	60	30	0	800

The Simplex Method *(continued)*: Computer Solutions

6.1 INTRODUCTION

The simplex method for solving linear programming problems in Chapter 5 was a systematic technique that moved from one corner of the solution space to another, always improving the objective function. The computations involved, however, can become tedious and time-consuming to do by hand. It seems natural, then, to use the computer as a tool to aid us in the step-by-step solution process. We will present here two such computer solutions. One will correspond identically to the step-by-step hand technique developed in Chapter 5. The other will be a commercially available package that currently runs on most mainframes, minicomputers, and microcomputers and uses more advanced techniques to speed up the solution and to reduce the amount of time required to solve large-scale problems.

This chapter starts by illustrating the computer solutions for problems with all $\leq$ constraints other than nonnegativity. Following this, the general technique used by the simplex method to handle $\geq$ and $=$ constraints will be explained and illustrated. Next, a special case will be discussed, followed by a detailed summary of the simplex method. The last part of this chapter will deal with sensitivity analysis on $\geq$ and $=$ constraints as well as the objective function and new product analysis.

6.2 COMPUTER SOLUTIONS

We use the Ace Rubber Company example of Sections 3.2 and 5.5 to illustrate computer solutions. Recall that our problem was

Maximize

$$\theta = 10x_1 + 8x_2$$

subject to

$$\text{Machine A:} \quad 2x_1 + 9x_2 \le 36$$
$$\text{Machine B:} \quad 4x_1 + 3x_2 \le 42$$
$$\text{Nonnegativity:} \quad x_1, x_2 \ge 0.$$

The first computer solution we will discuss is called "P1P2," an abbreviation for the "Phase I–Phase II Method," which will be introduced in Section 6.5. This is shown in Table 6–1 as it was run on a VAX™ 11/780[1], where the information entered by the user has been underlined for ease of understanding. In this table, the user signs on to the computer and then accesses the P1P2 program. The computer responds with a query, asking the user if all the tableaus are to be printed. We responded with a "Y" for yes. Next, the computer asks for the type of optimum. We responded with a "1." Why? Then, the user is asked to supply the number of constraints and the number of variables. The response is "2,2." What about the nonnegativity constraints? The computer will automatically assume them. Now, the computer requests the number of each kind of constraint. We entered "2,0,0." At this point, the user is asked to enter each constraint, followed by the objective function coefficients. The responses were "2,9,36" followed by "4,3,42" for the constraints, and then "10,8" for the objective function.

Table 6–1 then shows each of the tableaus together with the optimal solution. Compare these tableaus to those in Tables 5–13, 5–15, and 5–16 of Section 5.5. What do you see? They are indeed identical, as is the optimum of

$$x_1 = 9, \quad x_2 = 2, \quad s_1 = s_2 = 0, \quad \text{and} \quad \theta = 106.$$

The dual variables in the answer, by the way, are precisely the θ-row coefficients of s_1 and s_2 (slack variables 3 and 4) in the last tableau of computer printout.

Exercise. What are the dual variables called? Answer: Shadow prices.

The second computer solution was generated by the commercial package LINDO, which stands for Linear Interactive and Discrete Optimizer; it was developed by Linus Schrage at the Graduate School of Business, University of Chicago.[2] This solution is shown in Table 6–2, again as it was run on a VAX. As before, the user signs on to the computer and then accesses the LINDO program.

---

[1] VAX is a trademark of Digital Equipment Corporation.
[2] For a detailed explanation of LINDO, see L. Schrage, *Linear, Integer, and Quadratic Programming with LINDO* (Palo Alto, Cal.: Scientific Press, 1984).

TABLE 6–1

Username: SABER
Password:
        Welcome to VAX/VMS version V4.3 on node VAX2

$ RUN LIB:P1P2

PHASE I – PHASE II ALGORITHM

Do you want all the tableaus printed (Y/N) ? Y

Enter '1' for MAX, '-1' for MIN ? 1

Enter number of constraints, number of variables ? 2,2
Enter number of <=, number of >=, number of =? 2,0,0

Enter coefficients and constants of <= constraints
Constraint 1   ? 2,9,36

Constraint 2   ? 4,3,42

Enter the objective function coefficients
? 10,8

****
        Decision Variables   1   through   2
          Slack Variables   3   through   4

Simplex Tableau Number   1

      2.00   9.00   1.00   0.00   36.00

      4.00   3.00   0.00   1.00   42.00

    -10.00   -8.00   0.00   0.00   0.00

Basic   Current
Variables   Value
3   36
4   42
****
Simplex Tableau Number   2

      0.00   7.50   1.00   -0.50   15.00

      1.00   0.75   0.00   0.25   10.50

      0.00   -0.50   0.00   2.50   105.00

Basic   Current
Variables   Value
3   15
1   10.5
****
Simplex Tableau Number   3

      0.00   1.00   0.13   -0.07   2.00

      1.00   0.00   -0.10   0.30   9.00

      0.00   0.00   0.07   2.47   106.00

TABLE 6–1 (concluded)

```
Basic           Current
Variables       Value
2               2
1               9

************************************************************
Answers:

Basic           Current
Variables       Value
2               2
1               9

Dual
Variables       Value
3               .666667E-01
4               2.46667

Optimum Objective Function Value =   106
in 3 Tableaus

************************************************************
DO YOU WISH TO RUN THIS PROGRAM AGAIN? N
$ LO
```

The format used in LINDO is first to input the type of optimization together with the objective function in response to the ":" prompt. Next we respond to the first query ("?") with "ST", meaning subject to, to indicate that the constraints are forthcoming. At the next set of queries, we input the specific constraints, again excluding nonnegativity. The final response of "END" signifies that we have finished the constraint set and the command "GO" at the next ":" prompt instructs LINDO to proceed with the optimization process. The optimal solution is

$$x_1 = 9, \quad x_2 = 2, \quad s_1 = s_2 = 0, \quad \text{and} \quad \theta = 106,$$

with the same dual or shadow prices as before. LINDO then allows the option of doing sensitivity analysis. The subsequent results give us a range on the objective function coefficients, which we will fully discuss in Section 6.12 together with the right-hand-side ranges. These ranges are precisely the same as in Section 5.18, so that the right-hand side 36 of the Machine A constraint can be increased by 90 to 126, and decreased by 14.999999 or 15 to 21. Similarly, the right-hand side 42 of the Machine B constraint can be increased by 29.999998 or 30 to 72, and decreased by 29.999998 or 30 to 12.

Lastly, it is important to note that computer solutions will handle the special cases discussed in Chapter 5, with two exceptions. First, an alternative optimal solution is not usually identified, so the user must inspect the last tableau for a zero in the θ-row, corresponding to a nonbasic

TABLE 6–2

```
Username: SABER
Password:
        Welcome to VAX/VMS version V4.3 on node VAX2

$ RUN LIB:LINDO
  LINDO (UC 1 APRIL 82)
:MAX 10X1 + 8X2
?ST
?2X1 + 9X2 <= 36
?4X1 + 3X2 <= 42
?END

:GO
    LP OPTIMUM FOUND  AT STEP      2
           OBJECTIVE FUNCTION VALUE

  1)        106.000000

VARIABLE          VALUE        REDUCED COST
       X1        9.000000        0.000000
       X2        2.000000        0.000000

ROW         SLACK OR SURPLUS    DUAL PRICES
   2)         0.000000          0.066667
   3)         0.000000          2.466667

NO. ITERATIONS=         2

 DO RANGE(SENSITIVITY) ANALYSIS?
?YES

   RANGES IN WHICH THE BASIS IS UNCHANGED

                         OBJ COEFFICIENT RANGES
VARIABLE         CURRENT       ALLOWABLE        ALLOWABLE
                  COEF         INCREASE         DECREASE
       X1       10.000000       0.666667        8.222222
       X2        8.000000      37.000000        0.500000

                       RIGHTHAND SIDE RANGES
   ROW           CURRENT       ALLOWABLE        ALLOWABLE
                  RHS          INCREASE         DECREASE
    2           36.000000      90.000000       14.999999
    3           42.000000      29.999998       29.999998
:QUIT
FORTRAN STOP
$ LO
```

Exercise. What would be the format to run P1P2 and LINDO for the example of Section 5.2, which was to

Maximize

$$\theta = x_1 + 0.5x_2$$

subject to

$$x_1 + x_2 \leq 4$$
$$x_1 + 2x_2 \leq 6$$
$$x_1, x_2 \geq 0.$$

Answer: For P1P2,

```
Y
1
2,2
2,0,0
1,1,4
1,2,6
1,0.5.
```

For LINDO,

```
MAX X1+ 0.5X2
ST
X1 + X2 <= 4
X1 + 2X2 <= 6
END
GO
```

variable (see Section 5.10). Second, all variables are assumed to be non-negative, so a negative decision variable must be transformed, as we did in Section 5.13, *before* inputting the information into the computer. In addition, a constant appearing in the objective function is not entered into the computer, but simply added to (subtracted from) the final answer.

6.3 PROBLEM SET 6–1

Use a computer program such as P1P2 or LINDO to solve each of the following, assuming all variables to be nonnegative.

1. Maximize

$$\theta = 5x_1 + 7x_2$$

subject to

$$x_1 + x_2 \leq 5$$
$$2x_1 + 3x_2 \leq 12.$$

2. Maximize

$$\theta = 4x_1 + 10x_2$$

subject to

$$3x_1 + 7x_2 \leq 42$$
$$x_1 + 5x_2 \leq 22.$$

6.3 PROBLEM SET 6–1 (*continued*)

3. Maximize

$$\theta = 4x_1 - x_2$$

subject to

$$x_1 + x_2 \le 13$$
$$x_1 + 2x_2 \le 22$$
$$2x_1 + x_2 \le 20.$$

4. Repeat Problem 1 with the additional constraint that $x_1 \le 4$.

5. Repeat Problem 2 with the additional constraint that $x_2 \le 3$.

6. Repeat Problem 3 with the additional constraints that $x_1 \le 8$ and $x_2 \le 8$.

7. Maximize

$$\theta = 6x_1 + x_2 - 7$$

subject to

$$2x_1 + 3x_2 \le 24$$
$$2x_1 - x_2 \le 8.$$
$$-2x_1 + 3x_2 \le 12.$$

8. Repeat Problem 7 but, this time, minimize the objective function.

9. Maximize

$$\theta = 5x_1 + 6x_2 + 10x_3$$

subject to

$$x_1 + 2x_2 + 3x_3 \le 24$$
$$2x_1 + x_2 + x_3 \le 18.$$

10. Maximize

$$\theta = -2x_1 + 5x_2 + 9x_3$$

subject to

$$x_1 + x_2 + 4x_3 \le 36$$
$$2x_1 + 2x_2 + 3x_3 \le 42.$$

11. Maximize

$$\theta = 2x_1 + 5x_2 + 8x_3 - 10$$

subject to

$$x_1 + x_2 + 4x_3 \le 36$$
$$x_1 + 2x_2 + 3x_3 \le 42.$$

12. Maximize

$$\theta = 3x_1 + 5x_2 + 12x_3$$

subject to

$$x_1 + 2x_2 + 3x_3 \le 36$$
$$x_2 + 2x_3 \le 12.$$

13. Repeat Problem 9 with the additional constraint that $x_2 \le 5$.

14. Repeat Problem 9 with the additional constraint that $x_3 \le 5$.

15. Repeat Problem 10 with the additional constraint that $x_1 \le 4$.

16. Maximize

$$\theta = 3x_1 + 4x_2 + 10x_3$$

subject to

$$x_1 + x_2 + 4x_3 \le 42$$
$$x_1 + 2x_2 + 3x_3 \le 40$$
$$2x_1 + x_2 + 2x_3 \le 30.$$

17. Maximize

$$\theta = 10x_1 + 8x_2 + 14x_3$$

subject to

$$2x_1 + 2x_2 + 5x_3 \le 40$$
$$3x_1 + x_2 + 3x_3 \le 27$$
$$x_1 + 4x_2 + 2x_3 \le 26.$$

18. Ace Rubber Company manufactures three types of tires: Model P, the premium, Model S, the second line, and Model E, the economy. Model P sells for $96 per tire and costs $86 per tire to make; Model S sells for $79 per tire and costs $73 per tire to make; Model E sells for $76 per tire and costs $64 per tire to make. To make one Model P tire, it requires one hour on Machine A, one hour on Machine B, and two hours on Machine C. To make one Model S tire, it takes one hour on Machine A, two hours on Machine B, and one hour on Machine C; to make one Model E tire requires four hours on A, three hours on B, and two hours on C. Production scheduling indicates that during the coming

6.3 PROBLEM SET 6–1 (*concluded*)

week Machine A will be available for at most 42 hours, Machine B for at most 40 hours, and Machine C for at most 30 hours. How many of each tire should the company make in the coming week in order to maximize its profit? What is this maximum profit?

19. True Sound Radio Company makes four kinds of radios for automobiles: AM, AM/FM, AM/FM stereo, and AM/FM stereo tape. Each radio can be manufactured by either one of two methods: Method I, which involves two processes, P_1 and P_2, and Method II, which involves three processes, P_3, P_4, and P_5. Revenue and cost data on the radios are as shown in Table A, while manufacturing data are as shown in Table B. What is the optimal number of each kind of radio for the company to make and what is the associated profit? (Hint: Let x_{1A}, x_{1F}, x_{1S}, x_{1T} be the number of AM, AM/FM, AM/FM stereo, and AM/FM stereo tape radios made by Method I, and similarly x_{2A}, x_{2F}, x_{2S}, x_{2T} for Method II.)

TABLE A

	Radio			
	AM	AM/FM	AM/FM Stereo	AM/FM Stereo Tape
Unit selling price ($)	100	150	250	300
Unit cost, Method I	70	90	150	225
Unit cost, Method II	95	70	185	190
Maximum quantity that can be sold	5,000	3,000	2,000	1,000

TABLE B

Manufacturing Time (Hours)					
	AM	AM/FM	AM/FM Stereo	AM/FM Stereo Tape	Maximum Hours Available
Method I					
Process P_1	4	4	3	0	2,100
Process P_2	8	10	6	7	14,000
Method II					
Process P_3	1	0	5	5	1,500
Process P_4	3	8	0	6	2,400
Process P_5	1	1	11	20	2,500

6.4 PRELIMINARIES TO PHASE I–PHASE II: THE BIG-M METHOD

In Section 5.16 we saw how to solve a minimization problem with all $\geq$ constraints by transforming the problem into its dual, a maximization problem with all $\leq$ constraints (other than nonnegativity). This technique, as we noted, will not work if the problem has a mix of $\leq$ and $\geq$ constraints and/or equality constraints. In this and the next section, we will develop the general technique used to handle $\geq$ and $=$ constraints.

The Pure Gasoline Company example of Section 3.3 will serve as our starting point, and we shall repeat it here.

Example. Pure Gasoline Company operates two refineries with different production capacities. Refinery A can produce 4,000 gallons per day of super unleaded gasoline, 2,000 gallons per day of regular unleaded gasoline, and 1,000 gallons per day of leaded gasoline. Refinery B can produce 1,000 gallons per day of super unleaded, 3,000 gallons per day of regular unleaded, and 4,000 gallons per day of leaded. The company has made a contract with an automobile manufacturer to provide 24,000 gallons of super unleaded, 42,000 gallons of regular unleaded, and 36,000 gallons of leaded. Determine the number of days the company should operate each refinery in order to meet the terms of the above contract most economically, the minimum cost, and also what grade(s) of gasoline would be overproduced if the cost of running Refinery A is $1,500 per day and Refinery B is $2,400 per day.

Recall that we formulated this linear programming problem as follows:

Minimize

$$\theta = 1500x_1 + 2400x_2$$

subject to

Super unleaded:	$4x_1 + x_2 \geq 24$	(1)
Regular unleaded:	$2x_1 + 3x_2 \geq 42$	(2)
Leaded:	$x_1 + 4x_2 \geq 36$	(3)
Nonnegativity:	$x_1, x_2, \geq 0,$	(4), (5)

so that all the constraints are $\geq$. (Note that once again we have changed the unknowns from x and y to x_1 and x_2, respectively.) Recall that x_1 and x_2 represent the respective number of days Refineries A and B are operated, the coefficients in the objective function represent the costs in dollars per day, and the coefficients in the constraints represent the number of gallons (in thousands) of gasoline produced at each respective refinery. Now the above constraints give rise to the feasible solution set shown in Figure 6–1. As can be seen from this figure, the feasible solution set consists of the four extreme points (0, 24) from boundary lines (1) and (4), (3, 12) from boundary lines (1) and (2), (12, 6) from boundary lines (2) and (3), and (36, 0) from boundary lines (3) and (5).

Exercise. Determine the minimum by evaluating θ at each extreme point. Answer: $32,400 at (12, 6).

We will see in Section 6.5 that the simplex method will start at the point of intersection at the origin (0, 0), will then proceed along the x_2-axis to the point of intersection at (0, 9) of Figure 6–1, next along boundary line (3) to the point of intersection at (4, 8), after this along boundary line (1) to the point of intersection (extreme point) at (3, 12), and finally along boundary line (2) to the point of intersection (extreme point) at (12, 6). We wish to point out that the simplex method does not proceed directly from the point of intersection at (4, 8) along boundary line (3) to the final solution at (12, 6), as we might expect. The reason for this is that the simplex method selects the best *unit* gain at each step and so it does not always take the shortest possible path to the optimum. In solving this problem, then, the simplex method will examine five points of intersection before finding the optimum; and furthermore, the first three solution points are nonfeasible, whereas the last two are feasible (extreme).

FIGURE 6–1

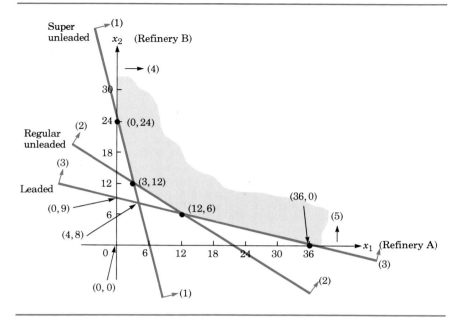

Exercise. In Figure 6–1, how many points of intersection (feasible and nonfeasible) are there? Answer: 10.

As in Section 5.16, we convert the constraints, other than nonnegativity, into equalities by introducing a surplus variable to take up the surplus or excess gallons of each grade of gasoline:

p_S = surplus variable (excess in 1,000 gallons) of super unleaded,
p_R = surplus variable (excess in 1,000 gallons) of regular unleaded,
p_L = surplus variable (excess in 1,000 gallons) of leaded.

Thus, constraints (1), (2), and (3) become

$$4x_1 + x_2 - p_S + 0 + 0 = 24 \qquad (1')$$
$$2x_1 + 3x_2 + 0 - p_R + 0 = 42 \qquad (2')$$
$$x_1 + 4x_2 + 0 + 0 - p_L = 36. \qquad (3')$$

Now, to choose an initial solution from equations $(1')$, $(2')$, and $(3')$ corresponding to the origin, we have to choose $x_1 = x_2 = 0$ so that

$$p_S = -24, \quad p_R = -42, \quad \text{and} \quad p_L = -36.$$

These three values are obviously impossible since negative values are not allowed for the variables used in the simplex method. Therefore, for each surplus variable we now *add* an associated "artificial" variable that will allow us to circumvent the problem of negative values. In particular, we respectively add the artificial variables a_S, a_R, and a_L to equations (1'), (2'), and (3') to get

$$
\begin{array}{llllllllll}
4x_1 & + & x_2 & - & p_S & + & 0 & + & 0 & + & a_S & + & 0 & + & 0 & = 24 & \quad (1'') \\
2x_1 & + & 3x_2 & + & 0 & - & p_R & + & 0 & + & 0 & + & a_R & + & 0 & = 42 & \quad (2'') \\
x_1 & + & 4x_2 & + & 0 & + & 0 & - & p_L & + & 0 & + & 0 & + & a_L & = 36, & \quad (3'')
\end{array}
$$

so that we now have a system of three equations in eight unknowns.

To see how the artificial variables allow us to circumvent the negative surpluses, let us reconsider the origin where $x_1 = x_2 = 0$. At this point, we operate both Refineries A and B zero days, so that no gasoline is produced and hence, we have no surpluses; i.e.,

$$p_S = p_R = p_L = 0.$$

This, in turn, means from equations (1''), (2''), and (3'') that

$$a_S = 24, \quad a_R = 42, \quad \text{and} \quad a_L = 36;$$

i.e., we have (positive) "shortages" (in terms of meeting the contract) of 24,000 gallons of super unleaded, 42,000 gallons of regular unleaded, and 36,000 gallons of leaded.

Exercise.   Using Figure 6–1, verify the following three facts for constraining lines (1), (2), and (3):

1. Below each constraining line, the corresponding surplus variable is zero while the artificial variable is greater than zero; i.e., there is no surplus, but there is a shortage.
2. On each constraining line, both the corresponding surplus variable and artificial variable are zero; i.e., there is no surplus and no shortage.
3. Above each constraining line, the corresponding surplus variable is greater than zero but the artificial variable is zero; i.e., there is a surplus so that there is, of course, no shortage.

Now that we have introduced the surplus and artificial variables, we must redefine our objective function,

$$\theta = 1500x_1 + 2400x_2,$$

in terms of all eight variables x_1, x_2, p_S, p_R, p_L, a_S, a_R, and a_L rather than in terms of simply x_1 and x_2. The surplus variables p_S, p_R, and p_L represent the numbers of excess gallons of super unleaded, regular unleaded, and leaded gasolines, respectively. Thus, they clearly do not contribute anything directly to the cost function being minimized. Therefore, as with slack variables in Chapter 5, we assign a coefficient of zero to p_S, p_R, and p_L in the objective function. Of course, just as with slack variables, there are cases where there is a penalty or premium associated with surplus variables. In these situations, as will be seen in the problems, the coefficients would not be zero. On the other hand, the artificial variables a_S, a_R, and a_L represent the shortages of each respective gasoline. Since we cannot have any shortages in our final solution, we assign each artificial variable a large cost coefficient, which will literally *drive it out of the solution;* i.e., all artificial variables will be driven to zero, since the cost of leaving any amount, however small, of an artificial variable in any solution will be prohibitive. In particular, we assign each artificial variable a coefficient of M (called "big M") where M is some very large positive number or penalty (e.g., we can think of M as being a cost of $1 million per thousand gallons). Thus our objective function becomes

$$\theta = 1500x_1 + 2400x_2 + 0p_S + 0p_R + 0p_L + Ma_S + Ma_R + Ma_L. \quad (4)$$

We now select the initial solution to the system of equations (1″), (2″), (3″), and (4) that represents the origin (0, 0). At the origin, we clearly have $x_1 = x_2 = 0$ and, in addition, $p_S = p_R = p_L = 0$ (i.e., we have no surpluses since neither refinery is being operated). Substituting these five values into equations (1″), (2″), (3″), and (4), we get

$$a_S = 24, \quad a_R = 42, \quad a_L = 36$$

and

$$\theta = 102M.$$

Exercise. What do these initial values mean? Answer: The artificial variables represent the shortages (in thousands of gallons) for each grade of gasoline. $\theta = 102M$ means there is a cost or penalty of $102M$ created by these shortages.

The Preliminary tableau for our initial solution, then, is as shown in Table 6–3. Now this tableau is not in the proper form in the θ-row. Why?

Exercise. How would the θ-row be transformed into the proper form? What would the current value of θ then be? Answer: Add $M \cdot (a_S\text{-row})$ plus $M \cdot (a_R\text{-row})$ plus $M \cdot (a_L\text{-row})$ to the θ-row. $24M + 42M + 36M = 102M$.

TABLE 6–3
Preliminary tableau

Basic Variables	Coefficient of								Current Values
	x_1	x_2	p_S	p_R	p_L	a_S	a_R	a_L	
a_S	4	1	-1	0	0	1	0	0	24
a_R	2	3	0	-1	0	0	1	0	42
a_L	1	4	0	0	-1	0	0	1	36
(min) θ	-1500	-2400	0	0	0	$-M$	$-M$	$-M$	0

We could now proceed to apply the simplex method to solve this example, but the computations become cumbersome when using the big-M method. The next section presents an easier way to complete the solution.

6.5 THE PHASE I–PHASE II METHOD

The Phase I–Phase II method is equivalent to the big-M method but is computationally easier since it avoids the complexity of carrying M throughout the calculations. To illustrate this, we will use the Pure Gasoline Company example of Section 6.4 (and 3.3). We first rewrite the objective function equation (4) of Section 6.4

$$\theta = 1500x_1 + 2400x_2 + 0p_S + 0p_R + 0p_L + Ma_S + Ma_R + Ma_L$$

in the form

$$\theta = 1500x_1 + 2400x_2 + 0p_S + 0p_R + 0p_L + M \cdot W$$

where, of course,

$$W = a_S + a_R + a_L.$$

Thus, W is precisely the sum of the artificial variables (note W is an upside-down M) and hence, represents the infeasibility portion or part arising from the need for artificial variables to generate an initial solution. Now to minimize θ, it is obvious that we must minimize W *all the way down to zero* (because of the positive M coefficient together with the fact that the artificial variables a_S, a_R, and a_L must be nonnegative). This can be true, of course, only if $a_S = a_R = a_L = 0$; i.e., we must drive out all the artificial variables.

Using this analysis, then, we can break our minimizing problem into two phases as follows: In the first phase, Phase I, we minimize W to zero where, as we saw above,

$$W = a_S + a_R + a_L.$$

In the second phase, Phase II, we complete the solution by minimizing θ

where we now modify θ to

$$\theta = 1500x_1 + 2400x_2 + 0p_S + 0p_R + 0p_L$$

since W is now zero; i.e., at this point, θ simply represents the "nonartificial" variables. Of course, if we cannot complete Phase I then we terminate the procedure since, as we will see in Section 6.7, there will be no solution to the problem.

This two-phase procedure is represented as shown in the Preliminary tableau of Table 6–4A. Compare this tableau with Table 6–3 of Section

TABLE 6–4A
Preliminary tableau

Basic Variables	Coefficient of								Current Values
	x_1	x_2	p_S	p_R	p_L	a_S	a_R	a_L	
a_S	4	1	−1	0	0	1	0	0	24
a_R	2	3	0	−1	0	0	1	0	42
a_L	1	4	0	0	−1	0	0	1	36
(*min*) θ	−1500	−2400	0	0	0	0	0	0	0
(*min*) W	0	0	0	0	0	−1	−1	−1	0

6.4. You will notice that the θ-row of Table 6–3 has been split in Table 6–4A into a θ-row containing all the nonartificial-variable coefficients and a W-row containing all the artificial-variable coefficients.

Now Phase I consists of minimizing the W-row while *including the θ-row in all the calculations.* After Phase I is completed, Phase II consists of subsequently omitting the W-row and also the artificial variable columns from the tableaus, and then proceeding to minimize the θ-row *as it appears at that stage.* We wish to point out, as will be seen below, that since the θ-row itself is included in all the calculations of Phase I and since it is in the proper form for the initial basis, then it will necessarily be expressed in terms of the proper basis for the start of Phase II.

To start Phase I of the solution, then, we first examine the W-row of Table 6-4A. We can see immediately that this tableau is *not* in the proper form for W. Why?

> **Exercise.** How would the W-row be transformed into the proper form? Answer: Add $1 \cdot (a_S\text{-row})$ plus $1 \cdot (a_R\text{-row})$ plus $1 \cdot (a_L\text{-row})$ to the W-row.

TABLE 6–4B
Preliminary tableau

Basic Variables	Coefficient of								Current Values
	x_1	x_2	p_S	p_R	p_L	a_S	a_R	a_L	
a_S	4	1	-1	0	0	1	0	0	24
a_R	2	3	0	-1	0	0	1	0	42
a_L	1	4	0	0	-1	0	0	1	36
(min) θ	-1500	-2400	0	0	0	0	0	0	0
(min) W	0	0	0	0	0	-1	-1	-1	0

Working rows for W

$1 \cdot (a_S$-row)	4	1	-1	0	0	1	0	0	24
$1 \cdot (a_R$-row)	2	3	0	-1	0	0	1	0	42
$1 \cdot (a_L$-row)	1	4	0	0	-1	0	0	1	36

New W-row

(min) W	7	8	-1	-1	-1	0	0	0	102

The transformation of the W-row into proper form is shown in Table 6–4B. Note that, for ease in understanding, we have included the working rows for W in an intermediate tableau.

At this point, we minimize W in the usual manner. Therefore, we now examine the new W-row of Table 6–4B for positive entries. The coefficient 8 for x_2 is the most positive entry in the new W-row; and hence, as shown in the Initial tableau of Table 6–5, x_2 enters the basis first. Next computing the ratios, we see that the smallest nonnegative ratio is the 9 for a_L, so that a_L now leaves the basis. Performing the change of basis in the usual way, we get the Second tableau shown in Table 6–5. Note that, once more for ease in understanding, we have included the working tableau. Note also that the θ-row is included in the process.

Continuing with Phase I, we then see from the Second tableau of Table 6–5 that x_1 enters next while a_S leaves. The result of this change of basis is as shown in the Third tableau of Table 6–5.

Again continuing with Phase I, we see from the Third tableau of Table 6–5 that we should introduce p_L into the basis, while a_R should leave. Performing this change of basis in the usual manner, we get the Fourth tableau shown in Table 6–5.

Once more continuing with Phase I, we see from the W-row of the Fourth tableau of Table 6–5 that we are done with Phase I since there are no positive entries. Note that, as mentioned earlier, the minimum

TABLE 6–5
Initial tableau

Basic Variables	Coefficient of								Current Values	
	x_1	x_2	p_S	p_R	p_L	a_S	a_R	a_L		
a_S	4	1	−1	0	0	1	0	0	24	24
a_R	2	3	0	−1	0	0	1	0	42	14
a_L	1	4	0	0	−1	0	0	1	36	9 →
(*min*) θ	−1500	−2400	0	0	0	0	0	0	0	
(*min*) W	7	8	−1	−1	−1	0	0	0	102	

↑

Working tableau

(−1) · (pivotal row)	−1/4	−1	0	0	1/4	0	0	−1/4	−9	
(−3) · (pivotal row)	−3/4	−3	0	0	3/4	0	0	−3/4	−27	
pivotal row = (a_L-row) ÷ 4	1/4	1	0	0	−1/4	0	0	1/4	9	
2400 · (pivotal row)	600	2400	0	0	−600	0	0	600	21,600	
(−8) · (pivotal row)	−2	−8	0	0	2	0	0	−2	−72	

Second tableau

Basic Variables	Coefficient of								Current Values	
	x_1	x_2	p_S	p_R	p_L	a_S	a_R	a_L		
a_S	15/4	0	−1	0	1/4	1	0	−1/4	15	4 →
a_R	5/4	0	0	−1	3/4	0	1	−3/4	15	12
x_2	1/4	1	0	0	−1/4	0	0	1/4	9	36
(*min*) θ	−900	0	0	0	−600	0	0	600	21,600	
(*min*) W	5	0	−1	−1	1	0	0	−2	30	

↑

TABLE 6–5 (continued)
Third tableau

Basic Variables	x_1	x_2	p_S	p_R	p_L	a_S	a_R	a_L	Current Values	
						Coefficient of			**Current Values**	
x_1	1	0	−4/15	0	1/15	4/15	0	−1/15	4	60
a_R	0	0	1/3	−1	2/3	−1/3	1	−2/3	10	15 →
x_2	0	1	1/15	0	−4/15	−1/15	0	4/15	8	−30
(min) θ	0	0	−240	0	−540	240	0	540	25,200	
(min) W	0	0	1/3	−1	2/3	−4/3	0	−5/3	10	

↑

Fourth tableau

Basic Variables	x_1	x_2	p_S	p_R	p_L	a_S	a_R	a_L	Current Values
				Coefficient of					**Current Values**
x_1	1	0	−3/10	1/10	0	3/10	−1/10	0	3
p_L	0	0	1/2	−3/2	1	−1/2	3/2	−1	15
x_2	0	1	1/5	−2/5	0	−1/5	2/5	0	12
(min) θ	0	0	30	−810	0	−30	810	0	33,300
(min) W	0	0	0	0	0	−1	−1	−1	0

Abbreviated fourth tableau

Basic Variables	x_1	x_2	p_S	p_R	p_L	Current Values	
			Coefficient of			**Current Values**	
x_1	1	0	−3/10	1/10	0	3	−10
p_L	0	0	1/2	−3/2	1	15	30 →
x_2	0	1	1/5	−2/5	0	12	60
(min) θ	0	0	30	−810	0	33,300	

↑

TABLE 6–5 (concluded)
Fifth tableau

Basic Variables	Coefficient of					Current Values
	x_1	x_2	p_S	p_R	p_L	
x_1	1	0	0	− 4/5	3/5	12
p_S	0	0	1	− 3	2	30
x_2	0	1	0	1/5	− 2/5	6
(*min*) θ	0	0	0	− 720	− 60	32,400

value of W is indeed zero and the artificial variables a_S, a_R, and a_L have been removed from the basis.

Now we start Phase II, as we stated earlier, by omitting the W-row and the a_S, a_R, and a_L columns from the Fourth tableau of Table 6–5 to get the Abbreviated fourth tableau shown in Table 6–5. Note, also as we stated earlier, that the θ-row of this tableau is in the proper form. Proceeding to minimize θ, then, we can see from the Abbreviated fourth tableau that p_S enters next and p_L leaves. The result of this change of basis is as shown in the Fifth tableau of Table 6–5.

Continuing with Phase II, now, we see that there are no positive entries in the θ-row of the Fifth tableau of Table 6–5. Thus, we are done with Phase II and, consequently, with the solution of the entire problem. The minimum from this tableau is

$$x_1 = 12, \quad x_2 = 6, \quad p_S = 30, \quad p_R = p_L = 0, \quad \text{and} \quad \theta = 32,400.$$

This is precisely the extreme point (12, 6) of Figure 6–1 of Section 6.4, and the minimum cost is $32,400 when Refinery A is operated 12 days and Refinery B is operated 6 days. Furthermore, since $p_S = 30$ the company has a surplus of 30,000 gallons of super unleaded gasoline.

Exercise. Substitute the optimum solution of (12, 6) into the original constraint set (1), (2), (3) of Section 6.4 and verify that only super unleaded is overproduced.

The computer solutions in P1P2 and LINDO for our current example are shown in Tables 6–6A and 6–6B, respectively. Compare the P1P2 output in Table 6–6A with the results in Table 6–5. What do you see? They are indeed identical, step by step. Of course, the computer printout maintains all the columns throughout and does not use the abbreviated format for Phase II. In Section 6.11, we will see the value of having all the col-

TABLE 6–6A

```
Username: SABER
Password:
        Welcome to VAX/VMS version V4.3 on node VAX2

$ RUN LIB:P1P2
PHASE I  -  PHASE II ALGORITHM

Do you want all the tableaus printed (Y/N) ? Y

Enter '1' for MAX, '-1' for MIN ? -1

Enter number of constraints, number of variables ? 3,2
Enter number of <=, number of >=, number of =? 0,3,0

Enter coefficients and constants of >= constraints
Constraint  1    ? 4,1,24

Constraint  2    ? 2,3,42

Constraint  3    ? 1,4,36

Enter the objective function coefficients
? 1500,2400
*******************************************************************************
         Decision Variables   1    through   2
         Surplus Variables    3    through   5
         Artificial Variables 6    through   8

Simplex Tableau Number   1
        4.00       1.00      -1.00       0.00       0.00       1.00       0.00
        0.00      24.00

        2.00       3.00       0.00      -1.00       0.00       0.00       1.00
        0.00      42.00

        1.00       4.00       0.00       0.00      -1.00       0.00       0.00
        1.00      36.00

   -1,500.00  -2,400.00       0.00       0.00       0.00       0.00       0.00
        0.00       0.00

        7.00       8.00      -1.00      -1.00      -1.00       0.00       0.00
        0.00     102.00

    Basic         Current
    Variables     Value
    6             24
    7             42
    8             36

*******************************************************************************
```

TABLE 6–6A (continued)

Simplex Tableau Number 2

3.75	0.00	−1.00	0.00	0.25	1.00	0.00
−0.25	15.00					
1.25	0.00	0.00	−1.00	0.75	0.00	1.00
−0.75	15.00					
0.25	1.00	0.00	0.00	−0.25	0.00	0.00
0.25	9.00					
−900.00	0.00	0.00	0.00	−600.00	0.00	0.00
600.00	21,600.00					
5.00	0.00	−1.00	−1.00	1.00	0.00	0.00
−2.00	30.00					

Basic Variables	Current Value
6	15
7	15
2	9

****

Simplex Tableau Number 3

1.00	0.00	−0.27	0.00	0.07	0.27	0.00
−0.07	4.00					
0.00	0.00	0.33	−1.00	0.67	−0.33	1.00
−0.67	10.00					
0.00	1.00	0.07	0.00	−0.27	−0.07	0.00
0.27	8.00					
0.00	0.00	−240.00	0.00	−540.00	240.00	0.00
540.00	25,200.00					
0.00	0.00	0.33	−1.00	0.67	−1.33	0.00
−1.67	10.00					

Basic Variables	Current Value
1	4
7	10
2	8

****

TABLE 6–6A (continued)

```
Simplex Tableau Number  4
     1.00      0.00     -0.30      0.10      0.00      0.30     -0.10
       0.00      3.00

     0.00      0.00      0.50     -1.50      1.00     -0.50      1.50
      -1.00     15.00

     0.00      1.00      0.20     -0.40      0.00     -0.20      0.40
       0.00     12.00

     0.00      0.00     30.00   -810.00      0.00    -30.00    810.00
       0.00 33,300.00

     0.00      0.00      0.00      0.00      0.00     -1.00     -1.00
      -1.00      0.00
```

Basic Variables	Current Value
1	3
5	15
2	12

```
*************************************************************************
PHASE I COMPLETED WITH TABLEAU NUMBER  4
*************************************************************************
Simplex Tableau Number  5
     1.00      0.00      0.00     -0.80      0.60      0.00      0.80
      -0.60     12.00

     0.00      0.00      1.00     -3.00      2.00     -1.00      3.00
      -2.00     30.00

     0.00      1.00      0.00      0.20     -0.40      0.00     -0.20
       0.40      6.00

     0.00      0.00      0.00   -720.00    -60.00      0.00    720.00
      60.00 32,400.00
```

Basic Variables	Current Value
1	12
3	30
2	6

```
*************************************************************************
```

Answers:

Basic Variables	Current Value
1	12
3	30
2	6

TABLE 6–6A (concluded)

```
Dual
Variables      Value
   3             0
   4            720
   5             60

Optimum Objective Function Value = 32400
in 5 Tableaus

**************************************************************************
DO YOU WISH TO RUN THIS PROGRAM AGAIN? N
$ LO
```

TABLE 6–6B

```
Username: SABER
Password:
        Welcome to VAX/VMS version V4.3 on node VAX2

$ RUN LIB:LINDO
 LINDO (UC 1 APRIL 82)
:MIN 1500X1 + 2400X2
?ST
?4X1 + X2 >= 24
?2X1 + 3X2 >=42
?X1 + 4X2 >= 36
?END

:GO
   LP OPTIMUM FOUND  AT STEP      3
         OBJECTIVE FUNCTION VALUE

 1)        32400.0000

VARIABLE         VALUE          REDUCED COST
      X1      12.000000           0.000000
      X2       6.000000           0.000000

ROW          SLACK OR SURPLUS     DUAL PRICES
   2)           30.000000           0.000000
   3)            0.000000        -720.000000
   4)            0.000000         -60.000000

NO. ITERATIONS=         3

 DO RANGE(SENSITIVITY) ANALYSIS?
?NO
:QUIT
FORTRAN STOP
$ LO
```

---

umns when doing sensitivity analysis. What else do you notice about the tableaus in Tables 6–5 and 6–6A? Look at the p- and a-columns. Except for the W-rows, the a-columns are precisely the negatives of the corresponding p-columns (compare the a_S- and p_S-columns, the a_R- and p_R-columns, and the a_L- and p_L-columns). Why? If you look back in Section 6.4, you will see that we effectively replaced $-p_S$ in (1′) by $a_S - p_S$ in (1″), $-p_R$ in (2′) by $a_R - p_R$ in (2″), and $-p_L$ in (3′) by $a_L - p_L$ in (3″). So this relationship will *always* hold. One further point before we go to the LINDO solution. Look back in Section 5.13, where we saw how to handle negative decision variables. This same type of substitution was made there.

Now compare the LINDO solution in Table 6–6B with the P1P2 solution in Table 6–6A. You will notice that the LINDO solution uses only three steps or four tableaus rather than the five tableaus used in P1P2. The reason for this, as stated in Section 6.1, is that LINDO uses advanced solution techniques.

6.6 PROBLEM SET 6–2

Use the Phase I–Phase II method or a computer program to solve each of the following, assuming that all variables are nonnegative.

1. Minimize
$$\theta = 5x_1 + 7x_2$$
subject to
$$2x_1 + 3x_2 \geq 12$$
$$5x_1 + x_2 \geq 17.$$

2. Minimize
$$\theta = 2x_1 + 8x_2$$
subject to
$$4x_1 + 5x_2 \geq 30$$
$$3x_1 + 2x_2 \geq 19.$$

3. Minimize
$$\theta = 6x_1 + 2x_2$$
subject to
$$x_1 + 3x_2 \geq 24$$
$$2x_1 + x_2 \geq 18$$
$$3x_1 + 4x_2 \geq 52.$$

4. Minimize
$$\theta = 3x_1 + 5x_2 + 4x_3$$
subject to
$$2x_1 + x_2 + 2x_3 \geq 30$$
$$x_1 + x_2 + 2x_3 \geq 20.$$

5. Minimize
$$\theta = 5x_1 + 2x_2 + 6x_3 + 8$$
subject to
$$2x_1 + 2x_2 + 5x_3 \geq 30$$
$$3x_1 + x_2 + 3x_3 \geq 27.$$

6. Minimize
$$\theta = 2x_1 + 5x_2 + 8x_3 - 15$$
subject to
$$x_1 + x_2 + 4x_3 \geq 36$$
$$3x_1 + 2x_2 + 2x_3 \geq 48.$$

6.6 PROBLEM SET 6–2 (*continued*)

7. Minimize

$$\theta = 4x_1 + 2x_2 + 5x_3 - 20$$

subject to

$$x_1 + 2x_2 + 3x_3 \geq 36$$
$$x_1 \qquad + 2x_3 \geq 16.$$

8. Minimize

$$\theta = 5x_1 + 2x_2 + 3x_3 - 24$$

subject to

$$2x_1 + x_2 + 3x_3 \geq 36$$
$$x_2 \qquad \geq 18.$$

9. Strong Steel Company operates three steel mills with different production capacities. Mill I can produce 1,000 tons per day of AAA steel, 3,000 tons per day of AA steel, and 10,000 tons per day of A steel. Mill F can produce 2,000 tons per day of AAA steel, 2,000 tons per day of AA steel, and 4,000 tons per day of A steel. Mill S can produce 4,000, 1,000, and 3,000 tons per day, respectively. The company has made a contract with a construction firm to provide 29,000 tons of AAA steel, 23,000 tons of AA steel, and 62,000 tons of A steel. If it costs $1,400 per day to run Mill I, $1,000 per day to run Mill F, and $1,200 per day to run Mill S, determine the number of days the company should operate each mill in order to meet the terms of the above contract most economically. What is this minimum cost?

10. A special food for athletes is to be developed from three foods: food X, food Y, and food Z. The new food is to contain at least 66 milligrams of vitamin A, at least 48 milligrams of vitamin B, and at least 40 milligrams of vitamin C. Each pound of food X costs $1.50 and contains 2 milligrams of vitamin A, 4 milligrams of vitamin B, and 1 milligram of vitamin C. Each pound of food Y costs $2.50 and contains 9 milligrams of vitamin A, 3 milligrams of vitamin B, and 4 milligrams of vitamin C; each pound of food Z costs $2.00 and contains 7 milligrams of A, 2 milligrams of B, and 8 milligrams of C. How many pounds of each food should be used in the mixture in order to meet the above requirements at a minimum cost? What is this minimum cost?

11. The intensive care unit of City Hospital has to schedule the shifts for its nursing staff on

a round-the-clock basis so as to ensure that a certain minimum number of nurses are on duty at various times. The supervisor of nurses has broken the day into six slots of four hours each and has determined that in order to maintain efficiency, at least 12 nurses must be on duty from 8 AM to 12 noon, at least 14 from 12 noon to 4 PM, at least 16 from 4 PM to 8 PM, at least 10 from 8 PM to 12 midnight, at least 6 from 12 midnight to 4 AM, and at least 9 from 4 AM to 8 AM. The nurses work eight-hour shifts, but they are scheduled to arrive (and depart) every four hours starting at 8 AM; i.e., Shift 1 works from 8 AM to 4 PM, Shift 2 from 12 noon to 8 PM, Shift 3 from 4 PM to 12 midnight, etc. Find the optimal schedule that meets the above requirements and, at the same time, employs the fewest total nurses. What is this total? (Hint: Let x_i be the number of nurses who are scheduled to work shift i where $i = 1, 2, 3, 4, 5, 6$.)

12. Fine Paper Mill produces paper in reels having a standard width of 60 inches and a fixed length. The mill receives orders from its customers for reels of the same fixed length but smaller widths. One customer's order calls for 50 reels of width 10 inches, 75 reels of width 16, and 85 reels of width 23, all of which the mill cuts from the standard size reel. The mill wants to meet the customer's needs in such a way as to minimize the total trim waste. This trim waste occurs when the standard reel is cut into narrower reels; i.e., if one 60-inch reel is cut into one 10-inch reel and two 23-inch reels, then there is a trim waste of $60 - [10(1) + 23(2)] = 4$ inches.
a) Find every possible combination of cut-

6.6 PROBLEM SET 6–2 (concluded)

ting the standard 60-inch reel into combinations of 10-inch, 16-inch, and 23-inch reels, and calculate the trim waste for each such combination. (Hint: There are eight such combinations.)

b) Formulate the problem of minimizing the total trim waste, assuming that the mill

ignores the extra 10-inch, 16-inch, and 23-inch reels made. What is this total waste?

c) Formulate the problem of minimizing the total trim waste, assuming that the extra reels are also waste. What is this total waste?

6.7 NO FEASIBLE SOLUTIONS

There is one last special case that can occur in linear programming problems—the empty feasible solution set. This occurs when no point satisfies all the constraints simultaneously, so that the constraints contradict themselves. If this happens the associated objective function can have no optimum (maximum or minimum). When we try to solve such a problem by the simplex method, we will find that we are unable to complete Phase I; i.e., we will not be able to get $W = 0$ and hence, an artificial variable will be left in the basis. Recall from Section 6.4 that when an artificial variable is not zero (so that it is still in the basis), then the constraint corresponding to that artificial variable is not satisfied; i.e., we have a shortage.

The following modification of the Ace Rubber Company example will serve to illustrate a linear programming problem with no feasible solutions.

Example. Maximize

$$\theta = 10x_1 + 8x_2$$

subject to

Machine A:	$2x_1 + 9x_2 \le 36$		(1)
Machine B:	$x_1 + x_2 \ge 20$		(2)
	$x_1, x_2 \ge 0.$		(3),(4)

The graph of the constraint set is shown in Figure 6–2. Note that the feasible solution set is indeed empty.

We begin the simplex method solution, as usual, by converting the constraints (1) and (2) into equalities. Thus, we introduce the *slack* variable s_A into the $\le$ constraint (1), while we introduce the *surplus* variable p_B together with the *artificial* variable a_B into the $\ge$ constraint (2). Doing this, we get

$$2x_1 + 9x_2 + s_A + 0 + 0 = 36 \qquad (1')$$
$$x_1 + x_2 + 0 - p_B + a_B = 20. \qquad (2')$$

Next we convert the objective function into the θ-equation for the non-

FIGURE 6–2

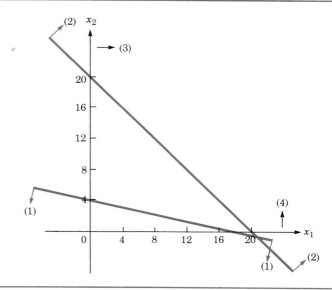

artificial variables x_1, x_2, s_A, and p_B, together with the W-equation for the artificial variable a_B. The θ-equation becomes

$$\theta = 10x_1 + 8x_2 + 0s_A + 0p_B \tag{5}$$

(since there are no penalties and/or premiums for the slack or surplus variables), whereas the W-equation becomes

$$W = a_B \tag{6}$$

so that, as always, W is simply the sum of the artificial variables.

The initial solution to the system of equations $(1')$, $(2')$, (5), and (6) representing the origin is

$$x_1 = x_2 = p_B = 0$$

so that

$$s_A = 36 \quad \text{and} \quad a_B = 20$$

and hence,

$$\theta = 0 \quad \text{and} \quad W = 20.$$

Thus the *slack* variable s_A and the *artificial* variable a_B are our initial basic variables, and our Preliminary tableau is as shown in Table 6–7. This tableau, however, is not in the proper diagonalized form for W because of the -1 coefficient in the W-row for the basic variable a_B. Therefore we add 1 times the a_B-row to the W-row, as shown in the Working

TABLE 6–7
Preliminary tableau

Basic Variables	Coefficient of					Current Values
	x_1	x_2	s_A	p_B	a_B	
s_A	2	9	1	0	0	36
a_B	1	1	0	−1	1	20
(max) θ	−10	−8	0	0	0	0
(min) W	0	0	0	0	−1	0

Working row for W

$1 \cdot (a_B$-row)	1	1	0	−1	1	20

New W-row

(min) W	1	1	0	−1	0	20

Initial tableau

Basic Variables	Coefficient of					Current Values	
	x_1	x_2	s_A	p_B	a_B		
s_A	2	9	1	0	0	36	18 →
a_B	1	1	0	−1	1	20	20
(max) θ	−10	−8	0	0	0	0	
(min) W	1	1	0	−1	0	20	

↑

Second tableau

Basic Variables	Coefficient of					Current Values
	x_1	x_2	s_A	p_B	a_B	
x_1	1	9/2	1/2	0	0	18
a_B	0	−7/2	−1/2	−1	1	2
(max) θ	0	37	5	0	0	180
(min) W	0	−7/2	−1/2	−1	0	2

row for W, to get the new W-row also shown in Table 6–7. Note that we did not use the row corresponding to the basic variable s_A since the coefficient of s_A is already (and will always be) zero in the W-row of the Preliminary tableau. Note also that the Preliminary tableau with its new W-row corresponds to the point of intersection $(0, 0)$ on boundary lines (3) and (4) of Figure 6–2.

Now, as usual, we perform the initial optimality analysis to get the Initial tableau of Table 6–7. From this tableau, we see that we have a tie for the entering variable between x_1 and x_2. As we saw in Section 5.9, we can choose either one and the end-result will be identical. However, as we agreed for conformity, we bring the left-most entering variable, x_1, into the basis so that s_A leaves. Performing this change of basis, then, we

---

TABLE 6–8

```
Username: SABER
Password:
        Welcome to VAX/VMS version V4.3 on node VAX2

$ RUN LIB:LINDO
 LINDO (UC 1 APRIL 82)
:MAX 10X1 + 8X2
?ST
?2X1 + 9X2 <= 36
?X1 + X2 >= 20
?END

:GO

    NO FEASIBLE SOLUTION AT STEP     1
      SUM OF INFEASIBILITIES=  2.00000
VIOLATED ROWS HAVE NEGATIVE SLACK,
OR(EQUALITY ROWS) NONZERO SLACKS.
ROWS CONTRIBUTING TO INFEASIBILITY HAVE
NONZERO DUAL PRICE.
            OBJECTIVE FUNCTION VALUE
  1)        180.000000

VARIABLE          VALUE         REDUCED COST
       X1      18.000000          0.000000
       X2       0.000000          3.500000

ROW         SLACK OR SURPLUS     DUAL PRICES
   2)             0.000000          0.500000
   3)            -2.000000         -1.000000

NO. ITERATIONS=         1
:QUIT
FORTRAN STOP
$ LO
```

get the result shown in the Second tableau of Table 6–7, which corresponds to the point of intersection (18, 0) on boundary lines (1) and (4) of Figure 6–2.

From the Second tableau of Table 6–7, we see that there are no positive entries left in the W-row, indicating that W has been minimized. However, at this "minimum," $W = 2$ and, furthermore, $a_B = 2$ is still in the basis. Therefore, Phase I cannot be completed; and hence, as stated earlier in our graphical analysis of Figure 6–2, the feasible solution set is empty.

> **Exercise.** Which constraint is violated by the last solution point (18, 0)? Why? Verify this fact by substitution into the constraint itself. Answer: 2. a_B corresponds to constraint (2). $x_1 + x_2 = 18 + 0 = 18$, which is not greater than or equal to 20.

The LINDO solution of this example is shown in Table 6–8. Note in this table the line

$$\text{SUM OF INFEASIBILITIES} = 2.000000,$$

which corresponds precisely to our result in Table 6–7.

Lastly, we wish to emphasize that a linear programming problem with *all* $\leq$ constraints (and nonnegative right-hand-side constants) other than the nonnegativity constraints would always have a nonempty feasible solution set. Algebraically, this makes sense since we would not need to introduce any artificial variables and hence, the Phase I portion of the Phase I–Phase II method is not even necessary.

6.8 AN EXAMPLE WITH "=" CONSTRAINTS; PHASE I–PHASE II METHOD

We now complete the discussion of the simplex method by illustrating the solution of a linear programming problem that has = constraints. The Klean Soap example of Section 3.6 will serve as our example and we repeat it here.

Example. Klean Soap Company wishes to make a new detergent from two of its current soaps: soap A and soap B. The company wants the new detergent to contain at least 20 ounces of cleaning ingredient D. Each pound of soap A costs $0.20 and contains 5 ounces of D, whereas each pound of soap B costs $0.25 and contains 1 ounce of D. Furthermore, for ecological reasons, the amount of soap A must be no more than that of soap B. Finally, the new mixture must weigh exactly 12 pounds. How many pounds of each soap should be used in the mixture in order to meet the above requirements at a minimum cost? What is this minimum cost?

We saw in Section 3.6 that the linear programming problem is to minimize

$$\theta = 0.2x_1 + 0.25x_2$$

subject to

Ingredient D:	$5x_1 + x_2 \geq 20$	(1)
Ecology:	$x_1 - x_2 \leq 0$	(2)
Weight:	$x_1 + x_2 = 12$	(3)
Nonnegativity:	$x_1, x_2 \geq 0.$	(4),(5)

(Once again, we have changed the unknowns from x and y to x_1 and x_2, respectively.) Recall that these constraints gave rise to the feasible solution set shown in Figure 6–3, which is nothing more than Figure 3–5 of Section 3.6 repeated here for convenience. From this figure, we see that there are two extreme points; namely, (2, 10) from boundary lines (1) and (3), and (6, 6) from boundary lines (2) and (3). Recall also that the minimum value was $2.70 at (6, 6).

We begin the simplex method solution, as usual, by converting the constraints (1), (2), and (3) into equalities. To conform with the P1P2 input format, we reorder the constraints with the $\leq$ constraints first, then the $\geq$ constraints, and lastly the $=$ constraints; i.e.,

---

FIGURE 6–3

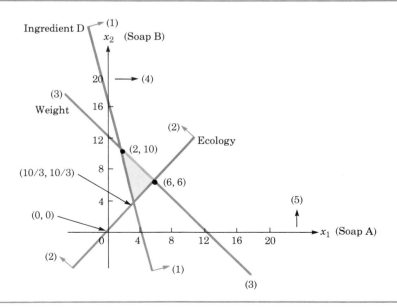

$$\text{Ecology:} \quad x_1 - x_2 \leq 0 \qquad (6)$$
$$\text{Ingredient D:} \quad 5x_1 + x_2 \geq 20 \qquad (7)$$
$$\text{Weight:} \quad x_1 + x_2 = 12. \qquad (8)$$

Now, as usual, we introduce the *slack* variable s_E into the $\leq$ constraint (6), and next the *surplus* variable p_D together with the *artificial* variable a_D into the $\geq$ constraint (7). At this point, we note that although constraint (8) is already an equality, we cannot at one and the same time satisfy this constraint and select an initial solution representing the origin; i.e., substituting $x_1 = x_2 = 0$ in equation (8) gives $0 = 12$, *which is impossible.* Thus we now introduce an *artificial* variable a_W into constraint (8) so that our constraints become

$$x_1 - x_2 + s_E + 0 \quad + 0 \quad + 0 \ = \ 0 \qquad (6')$$
$$5x_1 + x_2 + 0 \ - p_D + a_D + 0 \ = 20 \qquad (7')$$
$$x_1 + x_2 + 0 \ + 0 \quad + 0 \quad + a_W = 12. \qquad (8')$$

Next we convert the objective function

$$\theta = 0.2x_1 + 0.25x_2$$

into a θ-equation and a W-equation in the usual manner to get

$$\theta = 0.2x_1 + 0.25x_2 + 0s_E + 0p_D \qquad (9)$$

and

$$W = a_D + a_W. \qquad (10)$$

The initial solution to the system of equations (6'), (7'), (8'), (9), and (10) representing the origin (0, 0) is

$$x_1 = x_2 = p_D = 0$$

so that

$$s_E = 0, \quad a_D = 20, \quad a_W = 12$$

and hence

$$\theta = 0 \quad \text{and} \quad W = 32.$$

Note that we have a basic variable, s_E, which *equals* zero. Do you remember what this means? In Section 5.9, we saw that this meant that the problem had a degeneracy. Recall that this presented no difficulty in the simplex method solution.

Exercise. Refer to Figure 6–3 and identify the degeneracy. Answer: Ecology constraint (2) passes through the origin (0, 0), where two other constraints (4), $x_1 = 0$, and (5), $x_2 = 0$, intersect.

The Preliminary tableau, then, is as shown in Table 6–9, where, for ease in computation, we have converted the decimals in the θ-equation to their fractional equivalents. As usual, this tableau must be properly converted to begin the simplex method. Doing this by means of the working rows for W as shown in Table 6–9 (again using only the rows corresponding to the artificial variables), we get the new W-row also shown in Table 6–9. The Preliminary tableau, then, with its new W-row corresponds to the point of intersection $(0, 0)$ on boundary lines (2), (4), and (5) of Figure 6–3.

TABLE 6–9
Preliminary tableau

Basic Variables	Coefficient of						Current Values
	x_1	x_2	s_E	p_D	a_D	a_W	
s_E	1	-1	1	0	0	0	0
a_D	5	1	0	-1	1	0	20
a_W	1	1	0	0	0	1	12
(*min*) θ	$-1/5$	$-1/4$	0	0	0	0	0
(*min*) W	0	0	0	0	-1	-1	0

Working rows for W

$1 \cdot (a_D\text{-row})$	5	1	0	-1	1	0	20
$1 \cdot (a_W\text{-row})$	1	1	0	0	0	1	12

New W-row

(*min*) W	6	2	0	-1	0	0	32

Initial tableau

Basic Variables	Coefficient of						Current Values	
	x_1	x_2	s_E	p_D	a_D	a_W		
s_E	1	-1	1	0	0	0	0	$0 \rightarrow$
a_D	5	1	0	-1	1	0	20	4
a_W	1	1	0	0	0	1	12	12
(*min*) θ	$-1/5$	$-1/4$	0	0	0	0	0	
(*min*) W	6	2	0	-1	0	0	32	

$\uparrow$

TABLE 6–9 (continued)
Second tableau

Basic Variables	Coefficient of						Current Values	
	x_1	x_2	s_E	p_D	a_D	a_W		
x_1	1	$\boxed{-1}$	1	0	0	0	$\boxed{0}$	-0^*
a_D	0	$\boxed{6}$	-5	-1	1	0	$\boxed{20}$	$10/3 \rightarrow$
a_W	0	$\boxed{2}$	-1	0	0	1	$\boxed{12}$	6
(min) θ	0	$-9/20$	1/5	0	0	0	0	
(min) W	0	8	-6	-1	0	0	32	

$\uparrow$

Third tableau

Basic Variables	Coefficient of						Current Values	
	x_1	x_2	s_E	p_D	a_D	a_W		
x_1	1	0	$\boxed{1/6}$	$-1/6$	1/6	0	$\boxed{10/3}$	20
x_2	0	1	$\boxed{-5/6}$	$-1/6$	1/6	0	$\boxed{10/3}$	-4
a_W	0	0	$\boxed{2/3}$	1/3	$-1/3$	1	$\boxed{16/3}$	$8 \rightarrow$
(min) θ	0	0	$-7/40$	$-3/40$	3/40	0	3/2	
(min) W	0	0	2/3	1/3	$-4/3$	0	16/3	

$\uparrow$

Fourth tableau

Basic Variables	Coefficient of						Current Values
	x_1	x_2	s_E	p_D	a_D	a_W	
x_1	1	0	0	$-1/4$	1/4	$-1/4$	2
x_2	0	1	0	1/4	$-1/4$	5/4	10
s_E	0	0	1	1/2	$-1/2$	3/2	8
(min) θ	0	0	0	1/80	$-1/80$	21/80	29/10
(max) W	0	0	0	0	-1	-1	0

TABLE 6–9 (concluded)
Abbreviated fourth tableau

Basic Variables	Coefficient of				Current Values	
	x_1	x_2	s_E	p_D		
x_1	1	0	0	-1/4	2	-8
x_2	0	1	0	1/4	10	40
s_E	0	0	1	1/2	8	16 →
(*min*) θ	0	0	0	1/80	29/10	

↑

Fifth tableau

Basic Variables	Coefficient of				Current Values
	x_1	x_2	s_E	p_D	
x_1	1	0	1/2	0	6
x_2	0	1	-1/2	0	6
p_D	0	0	2	1	16
(*min*) θ	0	0	-1/40	0	27/10

Our initial optimality analysis, now, leads us to the Initial tableau shown in Table 6–9. From this tableau, we see that x_1 enters the basis first, while s_E leaves. This change of basis gives the Second tableau shown in Table 6–9. Note that s_E and x_1 are both still zero, but s_E is now nonbasic whereas x_1 is now basic. Note also that the values of a_D, a_W, θ, and W, as well as x_2, are the same as in the Initial tableau since we are still at the *same* point of intersection (0, 0) of Figure 6–3.

Next, as shown in the Second tableau of Table 6–9, x_2 is brought into the basis and a_D is removed. Note that, as usual, we have asterisked (*) the ratio $0/(-1) = -0$ to indicate that, although it is zero, it should be interpreted as negative and hence, is to be ignored. Performing the change of basis indicated in the Second tableau, then, we get the result shown in the Third tableau of Table 6–9. This solution corresponds to the point of intersection (10/3, 10/3) on boundary lines (1) and (2) of Figure 6–3. *Thus, this time, we did not move from the origin out along either the* x_1- *or* x_2-*axis, but rather we did move up along the ecology constraint* (2).

Now from the Third tableau of Table 6–9, we see that s_E enters next, while a_W leaves. This change of basis gives us the Fourth tableau of Table 6–9, which corresponds to the extreme point (2, 10) on boundary lines (1) and (3) of Figure 6–3.

At this point, then, we find in the Fourth tableau of Table 6–9 that Phase I is done; and hence, as always, we begin Phase II by omitting the W-row and the a_D- and a_W-columns to get the Abbreviated fourth tableau shown in Table 6–9. Continuing with Phase II, now, we see from the latter tableau that p_D enters next and s_E leaves. Doing this, we get the result shown in the Fifth tableau of Table 6–9, which corresponds to the extreme point (6, 6) on boundary lines (2) and (3) of Figure 6–3.

From the Fifth tableau of Table 6–9, we see that Phase II is now completed so that the minimum is (6, 6) = $^{27}/_{10}$ (or 2.7) with $p_D = 16$, which is precisely the same result as in Section 3.6. Specifically, the minimum cost is \$2.70, which arises from a mixture of six pounds each of soaps A and B with a surplus of 16 ounces of cleaning ingredient D.

> **Exercise.** Substitute the optimum solution of (6, 6) into the original constraint set (1), (2), (3) and verify the surplus of 16 ounces of D.

The P1P2 and LINDO solutions of this example are shown in Tables 6–10A and 6–10B, respectively. Note that both tables give precisely the same result as obtained in our example above.

TABLE 6–10A

```
Username: SABER
Password:
        Welcome to VAX/VMS version V4.3 on node VAX2

$ RUN LIB:P1P2

PHASE I  -  PHASE II ALGORITHM

Do you want all the tableaus printed (Y/N) ? Y

Enter '1' for MAX, '-1' for MIN ? -1

Enter number of constraints, number of variables ? 3,2
Enter number of <=, number of >=, number of =? 1,1,1

Enter coefficients and constants of <= constraints
Constraint 1   ? 1,-1,0

Enter coefficients and constants of >= constraints
Constraint 2   ? 5,1,20
```

TABLE 6–10A (continued)

```
Enter coefficients and constants of = constraints
Constraint 3   ? 1,1,12

Enter the objective function coefficients
? .2,.25
```

****

```
          Decision Variables  1   through  2
             Slack Variables  3   through  3
           Surplus Variables  4   through  4
        Artificial Variables  5   through  6
```

Simplex Tableau Number 1

1.00	-1.00	1.00	0.00	0.00	0.00	0.00
5.00	1.00	0.00	-1.00	1.00	0.00	20.00
1.00	1.00	0.00	0.00	0.00	1.00	12.00
-0.20	-0.25	0.00	0.00	0.00	0.00	0.00
6.00	2.00	0.00	-1.00	0.00	0.00	32.00

Basic Variables	Current Value
3	0
5	20
6	12

****

Simplex Tableau Number 2

1.00	-1.00	1.00	0.00	0.00	0.00	0.00
0.00	6.00	-5.00	-1.00	1.00	0.00	20.00
0.00	2.00	-1.00	0.00	0.00	1.00	12.00
0.00	-0.45	0.20	0.00	0.00	0.00	0.00
0.00	8.00	-6.00	-1.00	0.00	0.00	32.00

Basic Variables	Current Value
1	0
5	20
6	12

****

Simplex Tableau Number 3

1.00	0.00	0.17	-0.17	0.17	0.00	3.33
0.00	1.00	-0.83	-0.17	0.17	0.00	3.33
0.00	0.00	0.67	0.33	-0.33	1.00	5.33
0.00	0.00	-0.17	-0.08	0.08	0.00	1.50
0.00	0.00	0.67	0.33	-1.33	0.00	5.33

TABLE 6–10A *(continued)*

Basic Variables	Current Value
1	3.33333
2	3.33333
6	5.33333

****

Simplex Tableau Number 4

1.00	0.00	0.00	-0.25	0.25	-0.25	2.00
0.00	1.00	0.00	0.25	-0.25	1.25	10.00
0.00	0.00	1.00	0.50	-0.50	1.50	8.00
0.00	0.00	0.00	0.01	-0.01	0.26	2.90
0.00	0.00	0.00	0.00	-1.00	-1.00	0.00

Basic Variables	Current Value
1	2
2	10
3	8

****

PHASE I COMPLETED WITH TABLEAU NUMBER   4

****

Simplex Tableau Number 5

1.00	0.00	0.50	0.00	0.00	0.50	6.00
0.00	1.00	-0.50	0.00	0.00	0.50	6.00
0.00	0.00	2.00	1.00	-1.00	3.00	16.00
0.00	0.00	-0.03	0.00	0.00	0.23	2.70

Basic Variables	Current Value
1	6
2	6
4	16

****

Answers:

Basic Variables	Current Value
1	6
2	6
4	16

Dual Variables	Value
3	.025
4	0
6	.225

TABLE 6–10A (concluded)

```
Optimum Objective Function Value = 2.7
in 5 Tableaus

***********************************************************************

DO YOU WISH TO RUN THIS PROGRAM AGAIN? N
$ LO
```

TABLE 6–10B

```
Username: SABER
Password:
        Welcome to VAX/VMS version V4.3 on node VAX2
$ RUN LIB:LINDO
 LINDO (UC 1 APRIL 82)
:MIN .2X1 + .25X2
?ST
?X1 - X2 <= 0
?5X1 + X2 >= 20
?X1 + X2 = 12
?END

:GO

    LP OPTIMUM FOUND  AT STEP    4

          OBJECTIVE FUNCTION VALUE

 1)        2.70000005

VARIABLE         VALUE          REDUCED COST
      X1         6.000000          0.000000
      X2         6.000000          0.000000

ROW         SLACK OR SURPLUS     DUAL PRICES
   2)            0.000000           0.025000
   3)           16.000000           0.000000
   4)            0.000000          -0.225000

NO. ITERATIONS=        4

 DO RANGE(SENSITIVITY) ANALYSIS?
?N
:QUIT
FORTRAN STOP
$ LO
```

6.9 GRAND SUMMARY OF THE SIMPLEX METHOD

At this point, it is helpful to collect all our techniques of this chapter and the previous chapter into a grand summary of the simplex method. Before doing so, however, we wish to reemphasize three important points associated with using the method. The first point concerns the constraints of the linear programming problem being solved, the second concerns the objective function (specifically, the θ-equation and the W-equation), while the third concerns the Phase I–Phase II Method; namely,

---

1. We always convert the constraints into equalities where
   a) We add a slack variable to each $\leq$ constraint.
   b) We subtract a surplus variable and simultaneously add an artificial variable to each $\geq$ constraint (other than the non-negativity constraints).
   c) We add an artificial variable to each $=$ constraint.
2. The objective function is always separated into a θ-equation and a W-equation where
   a) The θ-equation contains all the original decision variables together with all the slack and surplus variables (slack and surplus variables are given a coefficient of zero unless there is an associated penalty or premium).
   b) The W-equation is simply the sum of all the artificial variables.
3. a) Phase I always consists of *minimizing the W-row*, the initial basic variables being the slack variables (if any) together with the artificial variables.
   b) Phase II consists of *optimizing (maximizing or minimizing) the θ-row* depending upon the original objective of the problem.

Of course, as we have seen in this chapter, the W-row must be transformed into the proper form before beginning Phase I. Also, as we saw in the previous chapter, if there is a penalty and/or premium for the slack variables, then the θ-row too will have to be put into the proper form before starting Phase I. (We need not be concerned about surplus variables since they are never in the initial basis.) Furthermore, Phase I is completed when there are no positive entries left in the W-row and $W = 0$; but if Phase I cannot be completed, then, as we saw in Section 6.7, the feasible solution set is empty. Lastly, we wish to point out that if initially there are no artificial variables, then obviously Phase I is not needed and only Phase II must be performed. This was the case, of course, in the previous chapter where we treated problems with all $\leq$ constraints (other than the nonnegativity constraints); i.e., *the method used in the previous chapter was precisely Phase II.*

The grand summary of the simplex method can be viewed as shown in the self-explanatory flowchart of Figure 6–4. Note that this flowchart is broken into four separate sections; namely, Preliminaries, Phase I, Phase II, and Improving the Solution.

FIGURE 6–4
Grand summary of the simplex method

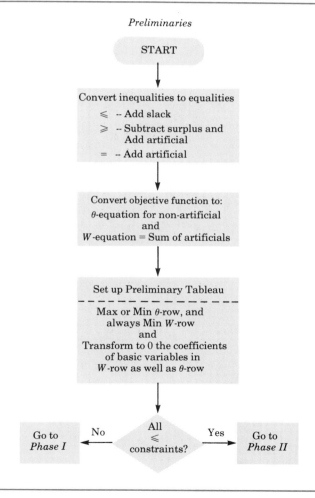

FIGURE 6–4 (concluded)

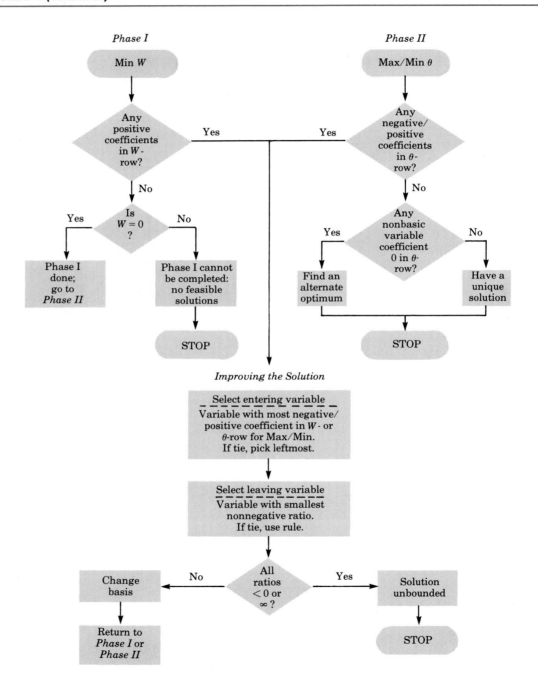

6.10 PROBLEM SET 6–3

Use the Phase I–Phase II method or a computer program to solve each of the following, assuming that all variables are nonnegative.

1. Maximize
$$\theta = 3x_1 + 5x_2$$
subject to
$$x_1 + x_2 \le 12$$
$$2x_1 + 4x_2 \ge 36$$
$$x_1 - 2x_2 \ge 0.$$

2. Maximize
$$\theta = 5x_1 + 2x_2$$
subject to
$$x_1 + 3x_2 \le 24$$
$$x_1 + x_2 \ge 10$$
$$2x_1 + x_2 = 18$$
$$5x_1 + x_2 = 20.$$

3. Minimize
$$\theta = 2x_1 + 3x_2$$
subject to
$$x_1 + x_2 \le 10$$
$$2x_1 + x_2 \ge 12$$
$$x_2 \ge 10.$$

4. Minimize
$$\theta = 5x_1 + 6x_2$$
subject to
$$x_1 + x_2 \le 15$$
$$-x_1 + x_2 \ge 3$$
$$x_1 \ge 9.$$

5. Minimize
$$\theta = 6x_1 + 2x_2$$
subject to
$$x_1 + x_2 \le 10$$
$$3x_1 + x_2 = 18$$
$$x_2 = 9.$$

6. Maximize
$$\theta = 4x_1 + 2x_2$$
subject to

$$x_1 + 3x_2 \le 24$$
$$x_1 + x_2 \ge 10$$
$$2x_1 + x_2 = 18$$
$$x_2 = 8.$$

7. Minimize
$$\theta = 3x_1 + 3x_2$$
subject to
$$x_2 \le 6$$
$$-x_1 + 3x_2 \ge 0$$
$$x_1 + x_2 = 12$$
$$x_1 = 10.$$

8. Minimize
$$\theta = 5x_1 + 2x_2$$
subject to
$$x_1 \le 5$$
$$2x_1 + 3x_2 \ge 12$$
$$5x_1 + x_2 \ge 17.$$

9. Minimize
$$\theta = 8x_1 + 10x_2$$
subject to
$$x_2 \le 8$$
$$4x_1 + 5x_2 \ge 30$$
$$3x_1 + 2x_2 \ge 19.$$

10. Maximize and minimize
$$\theta = 3x_1 + 5x_2$$
subject to
$$x_1 + x_2 \le 12$$
$$2x_1 + 4x_2 \ge 36.$$

11. Repeat Problem 10 with the additional constraint that $-2x_1 + x_2 \ge 0$.

12. Repeat Problem 10 with the additional constraint that $x_1 - 2x_2 \le 0$.

13. Maximize and minimize
$$\theta = x_1 + 5x_2$$

6.10 PROBLEM SET 6–3 (*concluded*)

subject to

$$x_1 \leq 8$$
$$x_1 + x_2 \geq 12$$
$$-x_1 + x_2 \geq 0.$$

14. Maximize and minimize

$$\theta = 2x_1 + 3x_2$$

subject to

$$x_1 + x_2 \leq 10$$
$$2x_1 + x_2 \geq 12$$
$$x_2 \geq 4.$$

15. Maximize and minimize

$$\theta = 5x_1 + 6x_2$$

subject to

$$x_1 + x_2 \leq 15$$
$$-x_1 + x_2 \geq 3$$
$$x_1 \geq 4.$$

16. Maximize and minimize

$$\theta = 2x_1 + x_2$$

subject to

$$x_1 + x_2 \leq 10$$
$$3x_1 + x_2 = 18.$$

17. Maximize and minimize

$$\theta = 5x_1 + 2x_2$$

subject to

$$x_1 + 3x_2 \leq 24$$

$$x_1 + x_2 \geq 10$$
$$2x_1 + x_2 = 18.$$

18. Maximize and minimize

$$\theta = 6x_1 + 3x_2$$

subject to

$$x_2 \leq 6$$
$$-x_1 + 3x_2 \geq 0$$
$$x_1 + x_2 = 12.$$

19. Subject to

$$3x_1 + x_2 \leq 18$$
$$x_1 + x_2 \geq 12,$$

maximize

$$\theta = 5x_1 + 2x_2,$$

where there is both a premium of $3 per unit of slack associated with the first constraint and a penalty of $2 per unit of surplus associated with the second constraint.

20. Subject to

$$4x_1 + 3x_2 + x_3 \leq 36$$
$$2x_1 + 3x_2 + 2x_3 \geq 24,$$

minimize

$$\theta = 8x_1 + 6x_2 + 2x_3,$$

where we treat θ as a cost function and, furthermore, there is both a premium of $3 per unit of slack associated with the first constraint and a penalty of $2 per unit of surplus associated with the second constraint.

6.11 SENSITIVITY ANALYSIS ON "≥" AND "=" CONSTRAINTS

In Section 5.18, we developed a vector relationship approach to performing sensitivity analysis on $\leq$ constraints. This same approach can be used to perform sensitivity analysis on $\geq$ and $=$ constraints. Before illustrating how to do this, though, we will show how to interpret the associated LINDO output for $\geq$ and $=$ constraints, as we did in Section 6.2 for $\leq$ constraints.

The Pure Gasoline Company example of Section 6.4 will serve as a starting point, and the LINDO solution from Table 6–6B is repeated here in Table 6–11 with its associated sensitivity analysis. Examining the right-hand-side ranges in this table, we see that the right-hand-side 24 of the

TABLE 6–11

```
Username: SABER
Password:
        Welcome to VAX/VMS version V4.3 on node VAX2

$ RUN LIB:LINDO
 LINDO (UC 1 APRIL 82)
:MIN 1500X1 + 2400X2
?ST
?4X1 + X2 >= 24
?2X1 + 3X2 >= 42
?X1 + 4X2 >= 36
?END

:GO
    LP OPTIMUM FOUND  AT STEP      3

          OBJECTIVE FUNCTION VALUE

  1)        32400.0000

VARIABLE          VALUE          REDUCED COST
       X1       12.000000          0.000000
       X2        6.000000          0.000000

ROW          SLACK OR SURPLUS      DUAL PRICES
   2)            30.000000           0.000000
   3)             0.000000        -720.000000
   4)             0.000000         -60.000000

NO. ITERATIONS=          3

 DO RANGE(SENSITIVITY) ANALYSIS?
?YES

   RANGES IN WHICH THE BASIS IS UNCHANGED

                      OBJ COEFFICIENT RANGES
VARIABLE          CURRENT        ALLOWABLE         ALLOWABLE
                   COEF          INCREASE          DECREASE
       X1       1500.000000      99.999992        900.000000
       X2       2400.000000    3600.000000        150.000000

                      RIGHTHAND SIDE RANGES
  ROW             CURRENT        ALLOWABLE         ALLOWABLE
                   RHS           INCREASE          DECREASE
    2            24.000000      30.000000          INFINITY
    3            42.000000      30.000000         10.000000
    4            36.000000      15.000000         15.000000
:QUIT
FORTRAN STOP
$ LO
```

super unleaded constraint can be increased by 30 to 54, and decreased by ∞, indicating that there is no lower limit. Why is there no lower limit? Recall that the surplus variable p_S associated with super unleaded was basic in the optimal solution at a value of $p_S = 30$, indicating that the lower limit of 24 is not really a restricting value. Similarly, the right-hand-side 42 of the regular unleaded constraint can be increased by 30 to 72, and decreased by 10 to 32.

> **Exercise.**   What is the right-hand-side range for leaded gasoline. Answer: 21 to 51.

In Section 5.18, we saw that the initial basic variable column vectors and the θ-column vector were all that were needed to develop the vector relationship approach. We also saw that the right-hand-side ranges could easily be computed by the usual ratio analysis on these initial basic variables in the optimal tableau. In our current example, the artificial variables a_S, a_R, and a_L form our initial basis. If we examine the optimal tableau in Table 6–5, repeated here as Table 6–12, we see that there are no a-columns. But remember from Section 6.5 the relationship between the a- and p-columns. They are simply negatives of each other, as can be verified by the P1P2 output for this example in Table 6–6A. So using the negatives of the p-columns in Table 6–12, the ratios for super unleaded from the p_S-column are

$$\frac{12}{0} = \infty$$

$$\frac{30}{-1} = -30$$

$$\frac{6}{0} = \infty.$$

TABLE 6–12
Fifth tableau

Basic Variables	Coefficient of					Current Values
	x_1	x_2	p_S	p_R	p_L	
x_1	1	0	0	$-4/5$	3/5	12
p_S	0	0	1	-3	2	30
x_2	0	1	0	1/5	$-2/5$	6
(*min*) θ	0	0	0	-720	-60	32,400

Remember that $-0 = 0$. Thus our limiting ratios are ∞ and -30, meaning that the original right-hand-side 24 can range from

$$24 - \infty = -\infty,$$

or no lower limit, to

$$24 - (-30) = 54.$$

This is precisely the same result as we had with LINDO.

In the same way, the ratios for regular unleaded from the negatives of the p_R-column of Table 6–12 are

$$\frac{12}{-(-4/5)} = 15$$
$$\frac{30}{-(-3)} = 10$$
$$\frac{6}{-1/5} = -30.$$

Here, our limiting ratios are 10 and -30, meaning that the original right-hand side of 42 can range from

$$42 - 10 = 32$$

to

$$42 - (-30) = 72.$$

Again, this result coincides precisely with our previous LINDO analysis.

Exercise. What are the ratios for leaded gasoline? What is the right-hand-side range? Answer: -20, -15, 15. 21 to 51.

Now what about = constraints? For example, the LINDO solution of the Klean Soap Company example of Section 6.8 was given in Table 6–10B and is repeated here in Table 6–13 with its associated sensitivity analysis. Examining the right-hand-side range for the = constraint of weight, we see that the right-hand-side 12 can be increased by ∞, indicating that there is no upper limit, and decreased by 5.333333 or 16/3 to 20/3.

Exercise. Using Table 6–13, determine the right-hand-side ranges for ecology and ingredient D. Answer: -8 to 12, and 36 with no lower limit.

TABLE 6–13

```
Username: SABER
Password:
         Welcome to VAX/VMS version V4.3 on node VAX2

$ RUN LIB:LINDO
 LINDO (UC 1 APRIL 82)
:MIN .2X1 + .25X2
?ST
?X1 - X2 <= 0
?5X1 + X2 >= 20
?X1 + X2 = 12
?END

:GO
    LP OPTIMUM FOUND  AT STEP     4

         OBJECTIVE FUNCTION VALUE

  1)        2.70000005

VARIABLE          VALUE          REDUCED COST
       X1       6.000000           0.000000
       X2       6.000000           0.000000


ROW          SLACK OR SURPLUS      DUAL PRICES
   2)             0.000000           0.025000
   3)            16.000000           0.000000
   4)             0.000000          -0.225000

NO. ITERATIONS=        4

 DO RANGE(SENSITIVITY) ANALYSIS?
?YES


   RANGES IN WHICH THE BASIS IS UNCHANGED

                        OBJ COEFFICIENT RANGES
VARIABLE          CURRENT          ALLOWABLE         ALLOWABLE
                  COEF             INCREASE          DECREASE
       X1       0.200000           0.050000          INFINITY
       X2       0.250000           INFINITY          0.050000

                      RIGHTHAND SIDE RANGES
   ROW            CURRENT          ALLOWABLE         ALLOWABLE
                  RHS              INCREASE          DECREASE
    2           0.000000          12.000000          8.000000
    3          20.000000          16.000000          INFINITY
    4          12.000000          INFINITY           5.333333
:QUIT
FORTRAN STOP
$ LO
```

TABLE 6–14
Fifth tableau

Basic Variables	Coefficient of				Current Values
	x_1	x_2	s_E	p_D	
x_1	1	0	1/2	0	6
x_2	0	1	− 1/2	0	6
p_D	0	0	2	1	16
(*min*) θ	0	0	− 1/40	0	27/10

Now the initial basic variable for the = constraint in this example was the artificial variable a_W. Examining the optimal tableau in Table 6–9, repeated here as Table 6–14, we see that again there is no column for the artificial variable a_W. This time, though, there is no p_W-column either, since there was no p_W variable. The P1P2 computer printout in Table 6–10A shows that if we had carried the a_W-column throughout, then it would have been

$$\begin{pmatrix} 0.50 \\ 0.50 \\ 3.00 \\ \hline 0.23 \end{pmatrix}.$$

Thus the ratios for weight are

$$\frac{6}{0.5} = 12$$
$$\frac{6}{0.5} = 12$$
$$\frac{16}{3} = \frac{16}{3},$$

so the only limiting ratio is 16/3. This means that the original right-hand-side 12 can range from

$$12 - \frac{16}{3} = \frac{20}{3}$$

with no upper limit, since there are no negative ratios. Again, this is precisely the same result that we had with LINDO.

Exercise. Using ratios from Table 6–14, determine the right-hand-side ranges for ecology and ingredient D. Answer: −8 to 12, and 36 with no lower limit.

6.12 SENSITIVITY ANALYSIS ON THE OBJECTIVE FUNCTION AND NEW PRODUCT ANALYSIS

Now let's return to the Ace Rubber Company example of Section 6.2 and discuss sensitivity analysis on the objective function coefficients. Management might like to know how much the profit coefficients 10 for Model P tires and 8 for Model R tires can be changed *without affecting the optimal solution point of* (9, 2). This range is contained in the LINDO solution of Table 6–2. Under the columns headed

OBJ COEFFICIENT RANGES

we see that the coefficient 10 for Model P tires can be increased by 0.666667 to $10.67, and decreased by 8.222222 to $1.78. Similarly, the coefficient 8 for Model R tires can be increased by 37 to $45, and decreased by 0.5 to $7.50.

> **Exercise.** Verify the ranges by running a computer program for the Ace Rubber Company example with the objective function coefficients of 5 and 8, next 10 and 40, and then 5 and 10. What are the new optimal solutions? What happened in the last case? Answer: $61 at (9, 2). $170 at (9, 2). $160 at (0, 4). We moved away from the original optimal solution point of (9, 2), since the range analysis applies only when changing precisely one coefficient at a time.

> **Exercise.** Using the LINDO solution of the Pure Gasoline Company example in Table 6–11, determine the ranges for the objective function coefficients of Refinery A and Refinery B. Answer: $600 to $1,600. $2,250 to $6,000.

The vector relationship analogy carries over to this type of sensitivity analysis also. However, the mechanics are somewhat cumbersome and hence, are omitted.[3]

As another example, suppose we were to maximize

$$\theta = 9x_1 + 12x_2 + 10x_3$$

subject to

$$\text{Resource 1:}\quad 2x_1 + 2x_2 + x_3 \le 36$$
$$\text{Resource 2:}\quad x_1 + 3x_2 + 2x_3 \le 30$$
$$x_1, x_2, x_3 \ge 0.$$

---

[3] For a full treatment showing that the vector relationship approach can be used to do any type of sensitivity analysis, see *Linear Programming and Matrix Algebra* by S. Hanna and J. Saber, (Babson Park, Mass.: Babson College Press, 1978.)

The LINDO solution of this example, together with the associated sensitivity analysis, is shown in Table 6–15. Here, we can see that the original objective function coefficient 9 of x_1 can be increased by 11 to \$20, and decreased by 4 to \$5. Similarly, the objective function coefficient 12 of x_2 can be increased by 4.333333 to \$16.33 with no lower limit.

Exercise. What is the range for the objective function coefficient 10 of x_3 in this example?   Answer: \$6.75 to \$18.

Now let's take a closer look at this example. Note that x_2 is nonbasic in the optimal solution. Why? Note also that the reduced cost of 4.333333 is the same as the allowable increase. This will always be true.

In a maximizing (minimizing) linear programming problem, the θ-row coefficients of the *final nonbasic variables* represent the largest increase (decrease) of the original objective function coefficients that will leave the optimal solution unaffected. Any decrease (increase) in these coefficients has no effect on the optimal solution.

Exercise. In Table 6–15, what other variables are nonbasic? What were the original objective function coefficients of these variables? What are their respective ranges? Answer: The slack variables s_1 and s_2. Both were zero. The variable s_1 can be increased to \$2.67, s_2 can be increased to \$3.67.

One final type of sensitivity analysis that can be performed is the introduction of a new product. In this case, management is interested in the level at which it makes sense to introduce such an item. For example, let's go back to our previous maximization example, where

$$\theta = 9x_1 + 12x_2 + 10x_3$$

subject to

$$\text{Resource 1: } 2x_1 + 2x_2 + x_3 \leq 36$$
$$\text{Resource 2: } x_1 + 3x_2 + 2x_3 \leq 30.$$

Now suppose that a new product is proposed that would contribute \$P to θ while using R_1 units of the first resource and R_2 units of the second resource. This modification would simply result in one additional initial

---

TABLE 6–15

```
Username: SABER
Password:
        Welcome to VAX/VMS version V4.3 on node VAX2

$ RUN LIB:LINDO
 LINDO (UC 1 APRIL 82)
:MAX 9X1 + 12X2 + 10X3
?ST
?2X1 + 2X2 + X3 <= 36
?X1 + 3X2 + 2X3 <= 30
?END

:GO
    LP OPTIMUM FOUND  AT STEP      3

        OBJECTIVE FUNCTION VALUE

  1)       206.000000

VARIABLE          VALUE           REDUCED COST
        X1      14.000000           0.000000
        X2       0.000000           4.333333
        X3       8.000000           0.000000

ROW        SLACK OR SURPLUS     DUAL PRICES
    2)          0.000000          2.666667
    3)          0.000000          3.666667

NO. ITERATIONS=          3

 DO RANGE(SENSITIVITY) ANALYSIS?
?YES

    RANGES IN WHICH THE BASIS IS UNCHANGED
                          OBJ COEFFICIENT RANGES
VARIABLE          CURRENT        ALLOWABLE        ALLOWABLE
                  COEF           INCREASE         DECREASE
        X1        9.000000       11.000000         4.000000
        X2       12.000000        4.333333        INFINITY
        X3       10.000000        8.000000         3.250000
                        RIGHTHAND SIDE RANGES
    ROW           CURRENT        ALLOWABLE        ALLOWABLE
                  RHS            INCREASE         DECREASE
        2        36.000000       24.000000        21.000000
        3        30.000000       42.000000        12.000000
:QUIT
FORTRAN STOP
$ LO
```

column,

$$\begin{pmatrix} R_1 \\ R_2 \\ \hline P \end{pmatrix}.$$

Why? In terms of our vector relationship, this column is

$$R_1 \cdot \boldsymbol{s}_1 + R_2 \cdot \boldsymbol{s}_2 - P \cdot \boldsymbol{\theta}$$

and would remain so throughout all the tableaus. The θ-row entries in the last tableau are simply the DUAL PRICES in LINDO, so from Table 6–15, we would get

$$R_1 \cdot (2.666667) + R_2 \cdot (3.666667) - P \cdot 1. \tag{1}$$

Why is the θ-row coefficient a 1 for θ itself? Simplifying (1), we get a θ-row coefficient of

$$R_1 \cdot \left(\frac{8}{3}\right) + R_2 \cdot \left(\frac{11}{3}\right) - P. \tag{2}$$

Since we have a maximizing problem, we would bring this new product into the solution *only if its θ-row coefficient were less than zero*. From (2), then, we would want

$$R_1 \cdot \left(\frac{8}{3}\right) + R_2 \cdot \left(\frac{11}{3}\right) - P < 0$$

or

$$8R_1 + 11R_2 - 3P < 0$$
$$8R_1 + 11R_2 < 3P. \tag{3}$$

Suppose, then, that the new product required one unit of R_1 and three units of R_2. From (3), we have

$$8(1) + 11(3) < 3P$$
$$41 < 3P$$
$$\frac{41}{3} < P,$$

so that the product would have to contribute at least $41\frac{1}{3}$ or $13.67 to θ before it would be introduced into the solution.

As another example, suppose that the new product contributed $13 to θ and used three units of resource 2. Then from (3), we have

$$8R_1 + 11(3) < 3(13)$$
$$8R_1 + 33 < 39$$
$$8R_1 < 6$$
$$R_1 < \frac{3}{4}.$$

Thus the new product can use no more than ¾ units of resource 1.

Exercise. Suppose that the new product contributed $15 to θ and used two units of resource 1. How many units of resource 2 can the product use if it is to be introduced into the solution? Answer: No more than $^{29}/_{11}$.

6.13 PROBLEM SET 6–4

Solve each of the following problems, using the accompanying LINDO printout and/or P1P2 optimal tableau:

1.
```
$ RUN LIB:LINDO
  LINDO (UC 1 APRIL 82)
:MIN 6X1 + 2X2
?ST
?X1  + 3X2 >= 24
?2X1 +  X2 >= 18
?3X1 + 4X2 >= 52
?END

:GO
    LP OPTIMUM FOUND  AT STEP     3
          OBJECTIVE FUNCTION VALUE

  1)         36.0000000

VARIABLE         VALUE         REDUCED COST
      X1       0.000000          2.000000
      X2      18.000000          0.000000

ROW         SLACK OR SURPLUS    DUAL PRICES
   2)         30.000000          0.000000
   3)          0.000000         -2.000000
   4)         20.000000          0.000000

NO. ITERATIONS=        3

 DO RANGE(SENSITIVITY) ANALYSIS?
?YES

    RANGES IN WHICH THE BASIS IS UNCHANGED
                      OBJ COEFFICIENT RANGES
VARIABLE        CURRENT       ALLOWABLE        ALLOWABLE
                 COEF         INCREASE         DECREASE
      X1       6.000000       INFINITY         2.000000
      X2       2.000000       1.000000         2.000000
```

6.13 PROBLEM SET 6–4 (*continued*)

```
                        RIGHTHAND SIDE RANGES
     ROW         CURRENT       ALLOWABLE      ALLOWABLE
                 RHS           INCREASE       DECREASE
      2        24.000000      30.000000       INFINITY
      3        18.000000       INFINITY       5.000000
      4        52.000000      20.000000       INFINITY
Simplex Tableau Number   5

    2.00       1.00       0.00      -1.00       0.00       0.00       1.00
    0.00      18.00

    5.00       0.00       0.00      -4.00       1.00       0.00       4.00
   -1.00      20.00

    5.00       0.00       1.00      -3.00       0.00      -1.00       3.00
    0.00      30.00

   -2.00       0.00       0.00      -2.00       0.00       0.00       2.00
    0.00      36.00
```

a) Find the right-hand-side ranges of each of the first three constraints.
b) Find the new optimal solution if the right-hand sides of the first three constraints were simultaneously changed to 18, 20, and 48, respectively.
c) Find the new optimal solution to the orig-

inal problem if only the third constraint were changed to $3x_1 + 3x_2 \geq 48$.
d) Find the Preliminary final tableau if in the original problem only the third constraint were changed to $3x_1 + 2x_2 \geq 48$. Explain why this tableau does not represent the optimal solution.

---

2. RUN LIB:LINDO

```
   LINDO (UC 1 APRIL 82)
  :MIN X1 + 5X2
  ?ST
  ?X1 <= 8
  ?X1 + X2 >= 12
  ?-X1 + X2 >=   0
  ?END

  :GO
     LP OPTIMUM FOUND   AT STEP      2

            OBJECTIVE FUNCTION VALUE

   1)        36.0000000

  VARIABLE         VALUE          REDUCED COST
         X1       6.000000          0.000000
         X2       6.000000          0.000000

  ROW          SLACK OR SURPLUS     DUAL PRICES
     2)          2.000000            0.000000
     3)          0.000000           -3.000000
     4)          0.000000           -2.000000
```

6.13 PROBLEM SET 6–4 (*continued*)

```
NO. ITERATIONS=        2

 DO RANGE(SENSITIVITY) ANALYSIS?
?YES

    RANGES IN WHICH THE BASIS IS UNCHANGED
                       OBJ COEFFICIENT RANGES
VARIABLE        CURRENT       ALLOWABLE      ALLOWABLE
                COEF          INCREASE       DECREASE
     X1         1.000000      4.000000       6.000000
     X2         5.000000      INFINITY       4.000000
                       RIGHTHAND SIDE RANGES
    ROW         CURRENT       ALLOWABLE      ALLOWABLE
                RHS           INCREASE       DECREASE
     2          8.000000      INFINITY       2.000000
     3         12.000000      4.000000      12.000000
     4          0.000000     12.000000       4.000000
Simplex Tableau Number   3

    0.00      0.00      1.00      0.50     -0.50     -0.50      0.50
    2.00

    1.00      0.00      0.00     -0.50      0.50      0.50     -0.50
    6.00

    0.00      1.00      0.00     -0.50     -0.50      0.50      0.50
    6.00

    0.00      0.00      0.00     -3.00     -2.00      3.00      2.00
   36.00
```

a) Find the right-hand-side ranges of each of the first three constraints.
b) Find the new optimal solution if the right-hand sides of the first three constraints were simultaneously changed to 12, 16, and 2, respectively.
c) Find the new optimal solution to the orig-inal problem if only the first constraint were changed to $x_1 + 2x_2 \leq 32$.
d) Find the Preliminary final tableau if in the original problem only the first constraint were changed to $x_1 + 8x_2 \leq 32$. Explain why this tableau does not represent the optimal solution.

3.
```
$ RUN LIB:LINDO
 LINDO (UC 1 APRIL 82)
:MAX 2X1 + 3X2
?ST
?X1 + X2 <= 10
?2X1 + X2 >= 12
?X1 >= 2
?END

:GO
    LP OPTIMUM FOUND   AT STEP      3
```

6.13 PROBLEM SET 6—4 (*continued*)

```
              OBJECTIVE FUNCTION VALUE

   1)          28.000000

VARIABLE          VALUE            REDUCED COST
        X1         2.000000            0.000000
        X2         8.000000            0.000000


ROW          SLACK OR SURPLUS      DUAL PRICES
    2)            0.000000          3.000000
    3)            0.000000          0.000000
    4)            0.000000         -1.000000

NO. ITERATIONS=          3

 DO RANGE(SENSITIVITY) ANALYSIS?
?YES

   RANGES IN WHICH THE BASIS IS UNCHANGED
                         OBJ COEFFICIENT RANGES
VARIABLE          CURRENT          ALLOWABLE          ALLOWABLE
                  COEF             INCREASE           DECREASE
        X1         2.000000         1.000000          INFINITY
        X2         3.000000         INFINITY           1.000000
                         RIGHTHAND SIDE RANGES
    ROW           CURRENT          ALLOWABLE          ALLOWABLE
                  RHS              INCREASE           DECREASE
     2            10.000000        INFINITY           0.000000
     3            12.000000         0.000000          INFINITY
     4             2.000000         8.000000          0.000000

Simplex Tableau Number  5
      0.00        0.00        1.00        1.00       -1.00       -1.00        1.00
      0.00

      0.00        1.00        1.00        0.00        1.00        0.00       -1.00
      8.00

      1.00        0.00        0.00        0.00       -1.00        0.00        1.00
      2.00

      0.00        0.00        3.00        0.00        1.00        0.00       -1.00
     28.00
```

a) Find the right-hand-side ranges of each of the first three constraints.

b) Find the new optimal solution if the right-hand sides of the first three constraints were simultaneously changed to 6, 1, and 2, respectively.

c) Find the new optimal solution to the original problem if only the first constraint were changed to $x_1 + 2x_2 \leq 16$.

d) Find the new optimal solution to the original problem if only the first constraint were changed to $3x_1 + x_2 \geq 18$ and the objective function were to be minimized.

6.13 PROBLEM SET 6–4 (*continued*)

4.
```
$ RUN LIB:LINDO
  LINDO (UC 1 APRIL 82)
:MIN 5X1 + 2X2
?ST
?X1 + 3X2 <= 24
?X1 + X2 >= 10
?2X1 + X2 = 18
?END

:GO
    LP OPTIMUM FOUND  AT STEP    4

        OBJECTIVE FUNCTION VALUE

  1)      42.0000000

VARIABLE        VALUE        REDUCED COST
      X1      6.000000        0.000000
      X2      6.000000        0.000000

ROW        SLACK OR SURPLUS   DUAL PRICES
   2)          0.000000        0.200000
   3)          2.000000        0.000000
   4)          0.000000       -2.600000

NO. ITERATIONS=       4

DO RANGE(SENSITIVITY) ANALYSIS?
?YES

    RANGES IN WHICH THE BASIS IS UNCHANGED

                    OBJ COEFFICIENT RANGES
VARIABLE        CURRENT      ALLOWABLE     ALLOWABLE
                COEF         INCREASE      DECREASE
      X1      5.000000      INFINITY       1.000000
      X2      2.000000      0.500000      INFINITY

                    RIGHTHAND SIDE RANGES
ROW             CURRENT      ALLOWABLE     ALLOWABLE
                RHS          INCREASE      DECREASE
   2          24.000000     30.000000     10.000000
   3          10.000000      2.000000     INFINITY
   4          18.000000     30.000000      5.000000

Simplex Tableau Number   4
     0.00     0.00     0.20     1.00    -1.00     0.40     2.00
     0.00     1.00     0.40     0.00     0.00    -0.20     6.00
     1.00     0.00    -0.20     0.00     0.00     0.60     6.00
     0.00     0.00    -0.20     0.00     0.00     2.60    42.00
```

6.13 PROBLEM SET 6–4 (*continued*)

a) Find the right-hand-side ranges of each of the first three constraints.

b) Find the new optimal solution if the right-hand sides of the first three constraints were simultaneously changed to 30, 12, and 20, respectively.

c) Find the new optimal solution to the original problem if only the first constraint were changed to $x_1 + 2x_2 \leq 30$.

d) Find the maximum corresponding to the changes in (c).

5.
```
$ RUN LIB:LINDO
  LINDO (UC 1 APRIL 82)
:MIN 6X1 + 3X2
?ST
?X2 <= 6
?-X1 + 3X2 >= 0
?X1 + X2 = 12
?END

:GO
    LP OPTIMUM FOUND  AT STEP    2

          OBJECTIVE FUNCTION VALUE

  1)         54.0000000

VARIABLE        VALUE          REDUCED COST
      X1       6.000000          0.000000
      X2       6.000000          0.000000


ROW          SLACK OR SURPLUS    DUAL PRICES
    2)            0.000000         3.000000
    3)           12.000000         0.000000
    4)            0.000000        -6.000000

NO. ITERATIONS=        2

 DO RANGE(SENSITIVITY) ANALYSIS?
?YES

    RANGES IN WHICH THE BASIS IS UNCHANGED
                        OBJ COEFFICIENT RANGES
VARIABLE        CURRENT        ALLOWABLE        ALLOWABLE
                COEF           INCREASE         DECREASE
      X1       6.000000        INFINITY         3.000000
      X2       3.000000        3.000000         INFINITY
                        RIGHTHAND SIDE RANGES
    ROW         CURRENT        ALLOWABLE        ALLOWABLE
                RHS            INCREASE         DECREASE
     2         6.000000        6.000000         3.000000
     3         0.000000       12.000000         INFINITY
     4        12.000000       12.000000         6.000000
```

6.13 PROBLEM SET 6–4 (*continued*)

```
Simplex Tableau Number   4
    0.00      0.00      4.00      1.00     -1.00     -1.00     12.00
    0.00      1.00      1.00      0.00      0.00      0.00      6.00
    1.00      0.00     -1.00      0.00      0.00      1.00      6.00
    0.00      0.00     -3.00      0.00      0.00      6.00     54.00
```

a) Find the right-hand-side ranges of each of the first three constraints.
b) Find the new optimal solution if the right-hand sides of the first three constraints were simultaneously changed to 8, 4, and 16, respectively.
c) Find the new optimal solution to the original problem if only the first constraint were changed to $(\frac{1}{2})x_1 + x_2 \leq 9$.
d) Repeat (c), but, this time, with the constraint changed to the equivalent restraint $x_1 + 2x_2 \leq 18$. Compare the slack variable column in the Final tableau of this problem with that in (c) and explain the difference.

6. ```
$ RUN LIB:LINDO
  LINDO (UC 1 APRIL 82)
:MAX 3X1 + 2X2
?ST
?X1 + 3X2 <= 24
?2X1 + X2 <= 18
?X1 + X2 <= 10
?END

:GO
    LP OPTIMUM FOUND AT STEP   2
          OBJECTIVE FUNCTION VALUE

  1)   28.0000000

VARIABLE   VALUE   REDUCED COST
      X1   8.000000   0.000000
      X2   2.000000   0.000000

ROW   SLACK OR SURPLUS   DUAL PRICES
   2)   10.000000   0.000000
   3)   0.000000   1.000000
   4)   0.000000   1.000000

NO. ITERATIONS=   2

  DO RANGE(SENSITIVITY) ANALYSIS?
?YES

    RANGES IN WHICH THE BASIS IS UNCHANGED
                      OBJ COEFFICIENT RANGES
VARIABLE   CURRENT   ALLOWABLE   ALLOWABLE
                 COEF   INCREASE   DECREASE
      X1   3.000000   1.000000   1.000000
      X2   2.000000   1.000000   0.500000
```
```

6.13 PROBLEM SET 6–4 (*continued*)

```
                      RIGHTHAND SIDE RANGES
    ROW          CURRENT          ALLOWABLE         ALLOWABLE
                   RHS            INCREASE          DECREASE
      2         24.000000         INFINITY          10.000000
      3         18.000000         2.000000          5.000000
      4         10.000000         2.000000          1.000000
```

Simplex Tableau Number   3

0.00	0.00	1.00	2.00	-5.00	10.00
1.00	0.00	0.00	1.00	-1.00	8.00
0.00	1.00	0.00	-1.00	2.00	2.00
0.00	0.00	0.00	1.00	1.00	28.00

a) What is the range for the objective function coefficient 3 of x_1?

b) What is the range for the objective function coefficient 2 of x_2?

c) What is the range for the objective function coefficient 0 of s_2?

d) What is the range for the objective function coefficient 0 of s_3?

---

7. The following are the computer printouts for Example 1 of Section 5.14, where $\theta_{max} = 9x_1 + 12x_2 + 10x_3 - 2s_1 + 2s_2$ was transformed into $\theta_{max} = 11x_1 + 10x_2 + 8x_3 - 12$.

```
$ RUN LIB:LINDO
 LINDO (UC 1 APRIL 82)
:MAX 11X1 + 10X2 + 8X3
?ST
?2X1 + 2X2 + X3 <= 36
?X1 + 3X2 + 2X3 <= 30
?END

:GO
    LP OPTIMUM FOUND   AT STEP     2

          OBJECTIVE FUNCTION VALUE

 1)          218.000000

VARIABLE          VALUE          REDUCED COST
      X1        14.000000          0.000000
      X2         0.000000          4.333333
      X3         8.000000          0.000000

ROW         SLACK OR SURPLUS     DUAL PRICES
   2)          0.000000            4.666667
   3)          0.000000            1.666667

NO. ITERATIONS=       2

 DO RANGE(SENSITIVITY) ANALYSIS?
?YES

    RANGES IN WHICH THE BASIS IS UNCHANGED
```

6.13 PROBLEM SET 6–4 (*continued*)

```
                        OBJ COEFFICIENT RANGES
    VARIABLE        CURRENT        ALLOWABLE        ALLOWABLE
                    COEF           INCREASE         DECREASE
        X1          11.000000       5.000000         7.000000
        X2          10.000000       4.333333         INFINITY
        X3           8.000000      13.999999         2.500000
                        RIGHTHAND SIDE RANGES
      ROW           CURRENT        ALLOWABLE        ALLOWABLE
                    RHS            INCREASE         DECREASE
        2           36.000000      24.000000        21.000000
        3           30.000000      42.000000        12.000000
    Simplex Tableau Number   3
        1.00       0.33       0.00       0.67      -0.33       14.00
        0.00       1.33       1.00      -0.33       0.67        8.00
        0.00       4.33       0.00       4.67       1.67      218.00
```

a) What is the optimal solution?
b) What is the range for the objective function coefficient 9 of x_1?
c) What is the range for the objective function coefficient 12 of x_2?

d) What is the range for the objective function coefficient 10 of x_3?
e) What is the range for the objective function coefficient -2 of s_1?
f) What is the range for the objective function coefficient 2 of s_2?

---

8. In Problem 1,
a) What is the range for the objective function coefficient 6 of x_1?

b) What is the range for the objective function coefficient 2 of x_2?
c) What is the range for the objective function coefficient 0 of p_2?

---

9. The following are the computer printouts for Example 2 of Section 5.14, where
$\theta_{min} = 40x_1 + 60x_2 + 35x_3 + 12s_1 + 14s_2$ was transformed into
$\theta_{min} = 2x_1 - 6x_2 - 5x_3 + 852$.

```
$ RUN LIB:LINDO
 LINDO (UC 1 APRIL 82)
:MIN 2X1 - 6X2 - 5X3
?ST
?2X1 + 2X2 + X3 <= 36
?X1 + 3X2 + 2X3 <= 30
?END

:GO
    LP OPTIMUM FOUND  AT STEP     2
        OBJECTIVE FUNCTION VALUE
  1)        -75.0000000

VARIABLE           VALUE          REDUCED COST
        X1         0.000000         4.500000
        X2         0.000000         1.500000
        X3        15.000000         0.000000
```

6.13 PROBLEM SET 6–4 (*continued*)

```
ROW              SLACK OR SURPLUS     DUAL PRICES
   2)                21.000000          0.000000
   3)                 0.000000          2.500000

NO. ITERATIONS=         2

 DO RANGE(SENSITIVITY) ANALYSIS?
?YES

    RANGES IN WHICH THE BASIS IS UNCHANGED
                        OBJ COEFFICIENT RANGES
VARIABLE            CURRENT          ALLOWABLE         ALLOWABLE
                     COEF            INCREASE          DECREASE
        X1          2.000000         INFINITY          4.500000
        X2         -6.000000         INFINITY          1.500000
        X3         -5.000000         1.000000          INFINITY
                        RIGHTHAND SIDE RANGES
    ROW             CURRENT          ALLOWABLE         ALLOWABLE
                     RHS             INCREASE          DECREASE
     2             36.000000         INFINITY          21.000000
     3             30.000000         42.000000         30.000000
Simplex Tableau Number   3
     1.50          0.50          0.00          1.00         -0.50          21.00
     0.50          1.50          1.00          0.00          0.50          15.00
    -4.50         -1.50          0.00          0.00         -2.50         -75.00
```

a) What is the optimal solution?

b) What is the range for the objective function coefficient 40 of x_1?

c) What is the range for the objective function coefficient 60 of x_2?

d) What is the range for the objective function coefficient 35 of x_3?

e) What is the range for the objective function coefficient 14 of s_2?

---

10. In Problem 6,

a) Find the inequality relating the profit P associated with the introduction of a new product and its corresponding resource requirements R_1, R_2, and R_3.

b) Suppose the new product utilized 2 units of resource 1, 3 units of resource 2, and 1 unit of resource 3. How much would it have to contribute to the profit for it to be introduced into the solution?

c) Suppose the new product utilized 3 units of resource 1, 1 unit of resource 2, and contributed $5 to the profit. How many units of resource 3 can the product use if it is to be introduced into the solution?

d) What is the restriction on the number of units the new product can use of resource 1 if it is to be introduced into the solution?

11. In Problem 1,

a) Find the inequality relating the cost C associated with the introduction of a new product and its corresponding resource requirements R_1, R_2, and R_3.

b) Suppose the new product utilized 4 units of resource 1, 3 units of resource 2, and 5 units of resource 3. How much could it add to the cost for it to be introduced into the solution?

c) Suppose the new product added $14 to the cost? How many units of resource 2

6.13 PROBLEM SET 6–4 (concluded)

can the product use if it is to be introduced into the solution? Resource 1? Resource 3?

12. In Problem 7,
a) Find the inequality relating the profit P
associated with the introduction of a new
product and its corresponding resource
requirements R_1 and R_2.
b) Suppose the new product utilized 2 units
of resource 1 and 1 unit of resource 2.
How much would it have to contribute to
the profit for it to be introduced into the
solution?
c) Suppose the new product utilized 3 units
of resource 1 and contributed $19 to the
profit. How many units of resource 2 can
the product use if it is to be introduced
into the solution?
d) Suppose the new product utilized 4 units
of resource 2 and contributed $20 to the
profit. How many units of resource 1 can

the product use if it is to be introduced
into the solution?

13. In Problem 9,
a) Find the inequality relating the cost C associated with the introduction of a new
product and its corresponding resource
requirements R_1 and R_2.
b) Suppose the new product utilized 2 units
of resource 1 and 2 units of resource 2.
How much could it add to the cost for it
to be introduced into the solution?
c) Suppose the new product utilized $\frac{1}{8}$ unit
of resource 1 and added $36 to the cost.
How many units of resource 2 can the
product use if it is to be introduced into
the solution?
d) Suppose the product utilized 2 units of
resource 2 and added $35 to the cost.
How many units of resource 1 can the
product use if it is to be introduced into
the solution?

6.14 REVIEW PROBLEMS

Use a computer program such as P1P2 or LINDO to solve Problems 1 through 22,
assuming all variables to be nonnegative.

1. Maximize

$$\theta = 2x_1 + x_2$$

subject to

$$x_1 + x_2 \le 5$$
$$2x_1 + 3x_2 \le 12.$$

2. Maximize

$$\theta = -3x_1 + 10x_2$$

subject to

$$3x_1 + 7x_2 \le 42$$
$$x_1 + 5x_2 \le 22.$$

3. Maximize

$$\theta = -2x_1 + 7x_2$$

subject to

$$x_1 + x_2 \le 13$$
$$x_1 + 2x_2 \le 22$$
$$2x_1 + x_2 \le 20.$$

4. Repeat Problem 1 with the additional constraint that $x_1 \le 4$.

5. Repeat Problem 2 with the additional constraint that $x_2 \le 3$.

6. Repeat Problem 3 with the additional constraints that $x_1 \le 8$ and $x_2 \le 8$.

7. Maximize and minimize

$$\theta = -3x_1 + 7x_2 + 10$$

subject to

6.14 REVIEW PROBLEMS (*continued*)

$$2x_1 + 3x_2 \leq 24$$
$$2x_1 - x_2 \leq 8$$
$$-2x_1 + 3x_2 \leq 12.$$

8. Maximize

$$\theta = 3x_1 + 5x_2 - 4x_3$$

subject to

$$x_1 + 2x_2 + 3x_3 \leq 24$$
$$2x_1 + 2x_2 + x_3 \leq 18.$$

9. Maximize

$$\theta = 4x_1 + 3x_2 + 7x_3$$

subject to

$$x_1 + x_2 + 4x_3 \leq 36$$
$$2x_1 + x_2 + 3x_3 \leq 42.$$

10. Maximize

$$\theta = 4x_1 + 3x_2 + 2x_3 - 10$$

subject to

$$x_1 + x_2 + 4x_3 \leq 36$$
$$x_1 + 2x_2 + 3x_3 \leq 42.$$

11. Maximize

$$\theta = 3x_1 + 5x_2 + 8x_3$$

subject to

$$x_1 + 2x_2 + 3x_3 \leq 36$$
$$x_1 + 3x_2 \leq 18.$$

12. Repeat Problem 8 with the additional constraint that $x_2 \leq 5$.

13. Repeat Problem 8 with the additional constraint that $x_3 \leq 3$.

14. Repeat Problem 9 with the additional constraint that $x_1 \leq 4$.

15. Minimize

$$\theta = 2x_1 + 5x_2 + 6x_3$$

subject to

$$4x_1 + 3x_2 + 2x_3 \geq 48$$
$$x_1 + 4x_2 + 8x_3 \geq 40$$
$$2x_1 + 9x_2 + 7x_3 \geq 66.$$

16. Ace Rubber Company manufactures three types of tires: Model P, the premium, Model S, the second line, and Model E, the economy. Model P sells for $95 per tire and costs $85 per tire to make; Model S sells for $78 per tire and costs $72 per tire to make; Model E sells for $75 per tire and costs $63 per tire to make. To make one Model P tire, it requires one hour on Machine A and one hour on Machine B. To make one Model S tire, it takes one hour on Machine A and two hours on Machine B; to make one Model E tire requires four hours on A and three hours on B. Production scheduling indicates that during the coming week Machine A will be available for at most 42 hours and Machine B for at most 40 hours. How many of each tire should the company make in the coming week in order to maximize its profit? What is this maximum profit?

17. Suppose in Problem 16 that each tire must be processed on two additional machines C and D as follows: Model P requires two hours on C and three hours on D, Model S requires one hour on C and four hours on D, and Model E requires two hours on C and one hour on D. Suppose also that during the coming week Machine C will be available for at most 30 hours and Machine D for at most 44 hours. Find the number of each tire the company should make in the coming week in order to maximize its profit. What is this maximum profit?

18. The brothers of XYZ fraternity have kept a record of a certain logic professor's final examinations and have determined the following interesting facts: The examination is always divided into three categories of questions: T/F, the true-false, M/C, the multiple-choice, and S/E, the short-essay. Now the student is given a choice of 50 T/F questions, each counting one point, 50 M/C questions, each counting two points, and 10 S/E questions, each counting four points. However, the student must select at least 40 questions but no more than 60 questions, and must answer at least five S/E questions.

6.14 REVIEW PROBLEMS (*continued*)

In addition, the student must answer more M/C questions than T/F questions, but the student's score is penalized one point each for the number of M/C questions answered over the number of T/F questions answered. Finally, the number of T/F questions answered must be smaller by at least 10 than the difference between the number of M/C questions answered and twice the number of S/E questions answered. The president of the fraternity, now enrolled in the logic professor's course, has decided that one phase of the initiation of the new pledges will be to find all possible combinations of the number of each kind of question that should be answered to attain the best possible grade on the upcoming final examination. Determine the maximum score and all alternative combinations.

19. Superior Paint Company sells three kinds of exterior finishes: oil-base paint, water-base paint, and stain. In order to keep all its distributors properly supplied, the company must manufacture and store at least three months' sales in advance. Since the color preferences of the consumer tend to change rapidly and since warehousing costs are high, management wishes to carefully select its next manufacturing choices. Oil-base paint costs the company $5.50 per gallon to make, water-base paint costs $4.50 per gallon, and stain costs $3.50 per gallon. The company has determined that the carrying cost for all three finishes is $0.50 per gallon for the average number of gallons in the inventory (the average being typically one-half of the number originally manufactured). Based on past experience, the sales department of the company has projected that its needs for the next three months will be at most 10,000 but at least 6,000 total gallons. Furthermore, no more than 2,000 gallons of stain but at least 1,000 gallons of each finish will be needed. In addition, the number of gallons of paint should be at least 75 percent of the total. How many gallons of each finish should the company make and what will be the cost?

20. Pure Tobacco Company makes three kinds of cigarettes: filter regulars, filter kings, and filter super kings. Management has to decide the optimal production mix of three blending processes for making each cigarette: Process X, Process Y, and Process Z. Each unit of Process X uses 4 pounds of tobacco, 1 ream of paper, and 3 ounces of charcoal to make 800 filter regulars, 700 filter kings, and 600 filter super kings. Each unit of Process Y uses 5 pounds of tobacco, 2 reams of paper, and 4 ounces of charcoal to make 1,000 filter regulars, 800 filter kings, and 600 filter super kings; each unit of Process Z uses 3 pounds of tobacco, 1 ream of paper, and 3 ounces of charcoal to make 900 filter regulars, 400 filter kings, and 700 filter super kings. The company has only 425 pounds of tobacco, 140 reams of paper, and 350 ounces of charcoal on hand. Furthermore, the sales department has projected that they will need a minimum of 50,000 filter regulars, 40,000 filter kings, and 30,000 filter super kings. If the company makes a profit of $18 per unit of Process X, $23 per unit of Process Y, and $15 per unit of Process Z, find the production mix that maximizes the total profit. What is this maximum profit?

21. Growth Investment Company is planning a pension fund of $1 million for one of its valued clients. Federal and state regulations require that, for the workers' protection, the fund must be made up of stocks, bonds, and a reserve in the form of bank notes or savings accounts. After much investigation, the company has decided upon the following combination: Three stocks, S_1, S_2, and S_3; two bond issues, B_1 and B_2; and a particular bank note, N. Their study shows that the expected yield from S_1 will be 8 percent, S_2 will be 9 percent, S_3 will be 7 percent, B_1 will be 10 percent, B_2 will be 11 percent, and N will be 6 percent. There are, however, some very stringent limitations on the investment possibilities written in the above-mentioned regulations on pension funds. First, the amount invested in stocks must be

6.14 REVIEW PROBLEMS (*continued*)

no more than 40 percent of that invested in bonds. Second, a minimum of 25 percent of the total fund must be held in reserve. Third, no more than 35 percent of the total fund can be invested in stocks. Finally, no single investment other than a bank note or savings account can constitute more than 30 percent of the total fund. What portfolio will the company recommend for the pension fund and what will be its expected yield?

22. Precision Instruments, Inc. has a contract to supply Electronic Calculator Company 600 minicircuits in July and 500 minicircuits in August. Precision makes and tests the minicircuits on an assembly line, using people on both a regular- and second-shift basis. In July, because of other commitments, only 650 minicircuits can be produced during regular time and only 200 during the second shift. On the other hand, only 450 minicircuits can be produced during regular time in August and only 150 in the second shift. The problem is that production costs differ not only for each shift, but also for each of the two months. Specifically, in the month of July the regular-shift cost is $250

per minicircuit, while the second-shift cost is $350 per minicircuit. The respective costs for August are $300 and $375. Of course, Precision can make more than the 600 minicircuits required by Electronic in July; but, in this case, Precision must store the excess from July to August at a unit inventory cost of $25. What should Precision's production schedule be and what is the associated cost?

a) Formulate the problem with the following variables: x_{JR} and x_{JS} are the number of minicircuits produced in July during regular and second shift, respectively: x_{AR} and x_{AS} in August; and x_i the inventory from July to August. (Hint: Be careful to remember that, for consistency, the inventory must be the excess over the 600.)

b) Formulate the problem with the following variables: x_{JRJ} and x_{JRA} are the number of minicircuits produced in July, regular shift, for use in July and August, respectively; x_{JSJ} and x_{JSA}, the number of minicircuits produced in July, second shift; x_{AR} and x_{AS} as in (a).

Use the Phase I–Phase II Method or a computer program to solve Problems 23 through 51, assuming all variables to be nonnegative.

23. Minimize

$$\theta = 5x_1 + x_2$$

subject to

$$2x_1 + 3x_2 \geq 12$$
$$5x_1 + x_2 \geq 17.$$

24. Minimize

$$\theta = 8x_1 + 10x_2$$

subject to

$$4x_1 + 5x_2 \geq 30$$
$$3x_1 + 2x_2 \geq 19.$$

25. Minimize

$$\theta = 6x_1 + 8x_2$$

subject to

$$x_1 + 3x_2 \geq 24$$
$$2x_1 + x_2 \geq 18$$
$$3x_1 + 4x_2 \geq 52.$$

26. Minimize

$$\theta = 2x_1 + x_2 + 3x_3$$

subject to

$$2x_1 + 2x_2 + 5x_3 \geq 30$$
$$3x_1 + x_2 + 3x_3 \geq 27.$$

27. Minimize

$$\theta = 3x_1 + 4x_2 + 6x_3 + 10$$

subject to

6.14 REVIEW PROBLEMS (*continued*)

$$x_1 + x_2 + 4x_3 \geq 36$$
$$3x_1 + 2x_2 + 2x_3 \geq 48.$$

28. Minimize

$$\theta = 3x_1 + x_2 + 4x_3 - 5$$

subject to

$$x_1 + 2x_2 + 3x_3 \geq 36$$
$$x_1 \qquad + 2x_3 \geq 16.$$

29. Maximize and minimize

$$\theta = 4x_1 + 6x_2 + 5x_3$$

subject to

$$x_1 + 2x_2 + 3x_3 \leq 18$$
$$x_1 + x_2 + x_3 \geq 12.$$

30. Maximize and minimize

$$\theta = 8x_1 + 6x_2 + 2x_3$$

subject to

$$x_1 + 3x_2 + x_3 \leq 36$$
$$2x_1 + x_2 + 2x_3 \geq 24.$$

31. Strong Steel Company operates three steel mills with different production capacities: Mill I can produce 4,000 tons per day of AAAA steel, 1,000 tons per day of AAA steel, 3,000 tons per day of AA steel, and 10,000 tons per day of A steel. Mill F can produce 3,000 tons per day of AAAA steel, 2,000 tons per day of AAA steel, 2,000 tons per day of AA steel, and 4,000 tons per day of A steel. Mill S can produce 2,000, 4,000, 1,000, and 3,000 tons per day, respectively. The company has made a contract with a construction firm to provide 35,000 tons of AAAA steel, 29,000 tons of AAA steel, 23,000 tons of AA steel, and 62,000 tons of A steel. If it costs $1,400 per day to run Mill I, $1,000 per day to run Mill F, and $1,200 per day to run Mill S, determine the number of days the company should operate each mill in order to meet the terms of the above contract most economically. What is this minimum cost?

32. Maximize

$$\theta = 6x_1 + 2x_2$$

subject to

$$x_1 + x_2 \leq 12$$
$$2x_1 + 4x_2 \geq 36$$
$$x_1 - 2x_2 \geq 0.$$

33. Maximize

$$\theta = x_1 + 7x_2$$

subject to

$$x_1 + 3x_2 \leq 24$$
$$x_1 + x_2 \geq 10$$
$$2x_1 + x_2 = 18$$
$$5x_1 + x_2 = 20.$$

34. Minimize

$$\theta = 3x_1 + 2x_2$$

subject to

$$x_1 + x_2 \leq 10$$
$$2x_1 + x_2 \geq 12$$
$$x_2 \geq 9.$$

35. Minimize

$$\theta = 4x_1 + 5x_2$$

subject to

$$x_1 + x_2 \leq 15$$
$$-x_1 + x_2 \geq 3$$
$$x_1 \geq 8.$$

36. Minimize

$$\theta = 2x_1 + x_2$$

subject to

$$x_1 + x_2 \leq 10$$
$$3x_1 + x_2 = 18$$
$$x_2 = 7.$$

37. Maximize

$$\theta = 5x_1 + 2x_2$$

subject to

6.14 REVIEW PROBLEMS (*continued*)

$$x_1 + 3x_2 \leq 24$$
$$x_1 + x_2 \geq 10$$
$$2x_1 + x_2 = 18$$
$$x_2 = 6.$$

38. Minimize

$$\theta = 5x_1 + 7x_2$$

subject to

$$x_1 \leq 5$$
$$2x_1 + 3x_2 \geq 12$$
$$5x_1 + x_2 \geq 17.$$

39. Minimize

$$\theta = 2x_1 + 8x_2$$

subject to

$$x_2 \leq 8$$
$$4x_1 + 5x_2 \geq 30$$
$$3x_1 + 2x_2 \geq 19.$$

40. Minimize

$$\theta = 3x_1 + 5x_2 + 4x_3$$

subject to

$$x_1 + 2x_2 + x_3 \leq 24$$
$$2x_1 + x_2 + 2x_3 \geq 30$$
$$x_1 + x_2 + 2x_3 \geq 20.$$

41. Maximize and minimize

$$\theta = 6x_1 + 2x_2$$

subject to

$$x_1 + x_2 \leq 12$$
$$2x_1 + 4x_2 \geq 36.$$

42. Repeat Problem 41 with the additional constraint that $-2x_1 + x_2 \geq 0$.

43. Repeat Problem 41 with the additional constraint that $x_1 - 2x_2 \leq 0$.

44. Maximize and minimize

$$\theta = 2x_1 + 3x_2$$

subject to

$$x_1 \leq 8$$

$$x_1 + x_2 \geq 12$$
$$-x_1 + x_2 \geq 0.$$

45. Maximize and minimize

$$\theta = 3x_1 + 4x_2$$

subject to

$$x_1 + x_2 \leq 10$$
$$2x_1 + x_2 \geq 12$$
$$x_2 \geq 4.$$

46. Maximize and minimize

$$\theta = 4x_1 + 5x_2$$

subject to

$$x_1 + x_2 \leq 15$$
$$-x_1 + x_2 \geq 3$$
$$x_1 \geq 4.$$

47. Maximize and minimize

$$\theta = x_1 + 2x_2$$

subject to

$$x_1 + x_2 \leq 10$$
$$3x_1 + x_2 = 18.$$

48. Maximize and minimize

$$\theta = 6x_1 + 5x_2$$

subject to

$$x_1 + 3x_2 \leq 24$$
$$x_1 + x_2 \geq 10$$
$$2x_1 + x_2 = 18.$$

49. Maximize and minimize

$$\theta = 5x_1 + x_2$$

subject to

$$x_2 \leq 6$$
$$-x_1 + 3x_2 \geq 0$$
$$x_1 + x_2 = 12.$$

50. Subject to

$$3x_1 + x_2 \leq 18$$
$$x_1 + x_2 \geq 12,$$

6.14 REVIEW PROBLEMS (*continued*)

minimize

$$\theta = 5x_1 + 2x_2$$

where there is both a premium of $3 per unit of slack associated with the first constraint and a penalty of $2 per unit of surplus associated with the second constraint.

51. Subject to

$$x_1 + 2x_2 + 3x_3 \le 18$$
$$x_1 + x_2 + x_3 \ge 12,$$

maximize the objective function

$$\theta = 4x_1 + 6x_2 + 5x_3$$

where there is both a premium of $3 per unit of slack associated with the first constraint and a penalty of $2 per unit of surplus associated with the second constraint.

Solve Problems 52 through 58, using the accompanying LINDO printout and/or P1P2 optimal tableau.

52.
```
$ RUN LIB:LINDO
  LINDO (UC 1 APRIL 82)
:MIN 1500X1 + 2400X2
?ST
?4X1 + X2 >= 24
?2X1 + 3X2 >= 42
?X1 + 4X2 >= 36
?END

:GO
    LP OPTIMUM FOUND   AT STEP      3
            OBJECTIVE FUNCTION VALUE

  1)          32400.0000

VARIABLE          VALUE          REDUCED COST
      X1        12.000000           0.000000
      X2         6.000000           0.000000

ROW          SLACK OR SURPLUS      DUAL PRICES
   2)            30.000000           0.000000
   3)             0.000000        -720.000000
   4)             0.000000         -60.000000

NO. ITERATIONS=        3

 DO RANGE(SENSITIVITY) ANALYSIS?
?YES

    RANGES IN WHICH THE BASIS IS UNCHANGED
                        OBJ COEFFICIENT RANGES
VARIABLE          CURRENT        ALLOWABLE        ALLOWABLE
                   COEF          INCREASE         DECREASE
      X1        1500.000000      99.999992       900.000000
      X2        2400.000000    3600.000000       150.000000
```

6.14 REVIEW PROBLEMS (*continued*)

```
                         RIGHTHAND SIDE RANGES
       ROW          CURRENT         ALLOWABLE        ALLOWABLE
                      RHS           INCREASE         DECREASE
        2          24.000000       30.000000        INFINITY
        3          42.000000       30.000000        10.000000
        4          36.000000       15.000000        15.000000

   Simplex Tableau Number   5

      1.00          0.00         0.00        -0.80       0.60        0.00        0.80
     -0.60         12.00

      0.00          0.00         1.00        -3.00       2.00       -1.00        3.00
     -2.00         30.00

      0.00          1.00         0.00         0.20      -0.40        0.00       -0.20
      0.40          6.00

      0.00          0.00         0.00      -720.00     -60.00        0.00      720.00
     60.00      32,400.00
```

a) Find the right-hand-side ranges of each of the first three constraints.

b) Find the new optimal solution if the right-hand sides of the first three constraints were simultaneously changed to 10, 20, and 15, respectively.

c) Find the new optimal solution to the orig-

inal problem if only the first constraint were changed to $3x_1 + x_2 \geq 24$.

d) Find the Preliminary final tableau if in the original problem only the third constraint were changed to $3x_1 + 4x_2 \geq 36$. Explain why this tableau does not represent the optimal solution.

53.
```
$ RUN LIB:LINDO
 LINDO (UC 1 APRIL 82)
:MAX 3X1 + 5X2 - 4X3
?ST
?X1 + 2X2 + 3X3 <= 24
?2X1 + X2 + X3 <= 18
?X3 >= 3
?END

:GO
   LP OPTIMUM FOUND  AT STEP      3

          OBJECTIVE FUNCTION VALUE

  1)        28.0000000

VARIABLE          VALUE         REDUCED COST
      X1         5.000000         0.000000
      X2         5.000000         0.000000
      X3         3.000000         0.000000

ROW        SLACK OR SURPLUS     DUAL PRICES
   2)         0.000000           2.333333
   3)         0.000000           0.333333
   4)         0.000000         -11.333333

NO. ITERATIONS=       3
```

6.14 REVIEW PROBLEMS (*continued*)

```
DO RANGE(SENSITIVITY) ANALYSIS?
?YES

    RANGES IN WHICH THE BASIS IS UNCHANGED
                        OBJ COEFFICIENT RANGES
VARIABLE          CURRENT        ALLOWABLE        ALLOWABLE
                  COEF           INCREASE         DECREASE
      X1          3.000000       7.000000         0.500000
      X2          5.000000       1.000000         3.500000
      X3         -4.000000      11.333333         INFINITY
                       RIGHTHAND SIDE RANGES
  ROW             CURRENT        ALLOWABLE        ALLOWABLE
                  RHS            INCREASE         DECREASE
      2          24.000000      15.000000         7.500000
      3          18.000000      15.000000         7.500000
      4           3.000000       3.000000         3.000000

Simplex Tableau Number   4

    0.00      1.00      0.00      0.67     -0.33      1.67     -1.67
    5.00

    1.00      0.00      0.00     -0.33      0.67     -0.33      0.33
    5.00

    0.00      0.00      1.00      0.00      0.00     -1.00      1.00
    3.00

    0.00      0.00      0.00      2.33      0.33     11.33    -11.33
   28.00
```

a) Find the right-hand-side ranges of each of the first three constraints.

b) Find the new optimal solution if the right-hand sides of the first three constraints were simultaneously changed to 27, 15, and 6, respectively.

c) Find the new optimal solution to the orig-inal problem if only the first constraint were changed to $x_1 + 2x_2 + 4x_3 \leq 24$.

d) Find the Preliminary final tableau if in the original problem only the third constraint were changed to $x_2 + x_3 \geq 3$. Explain why this tableau does not represent the optimal solution.

54.
```
$ RUN LIB:LINDO
 LINDO (UC 1 APRIL 82)
:MAX -2X1 + 5X2 + 9X3
?ST
?X1 + X2 + 4X3 <= 36
?2X1 + 2X2 + 3X3 <= 42
?X1 = 4
?END

:GO
    LP OPTIMUM FOUND   AT STEP      3

          OBJECTIVE FUNCTION VALUE

  1)          86.0000000
```

6.14 REVIEW PROBLEMS (*continued*)

```
VARIABLE         VALUE          REDUCED COST
       X1         4.000000          0.000000
       X2         8.000000          0.000000
       X3         6.000000          0.000000


ROW          SLACK OR SURPLUS      DUAL PRICES
    2)            0.000000           0.600000
    3)            0.000000           2.200000
    4)            0.000000          -7.000000

NO. ITERATIONS=          3

 DO RANGE(SENSITIVITY) ANALYSIS?
?YES


    RANGES IN WHICH THE BASIS IS UNCHANGED

                        OBJ COEFFICIENT RANGES
VARIABLE          CURRENT        ALLOWABLE       ALLOWABLE
                  COEF           INCREASE        DECREASE
       X1        -2.000000       INFINITY        INFINITY
       X2         5.000000       1.000000        2.750000
       X3         9.000000      11.000000        1.500000

                        RIGHTHAND SIDE RANGES
    ROW           CURRENT        ALLOWABLE       ALLOWABLE
                  RHS            INCREASE        DECREASE
     2           36.000000      13.333333       15.000000
     3           42.000000      30.000000       10.000000
     4            4.000000       8.000000        4.000000

Simplex Tableau Number   4
     0.00      0.00      1.00      0.40     -0.20      0.00      6.00

     0.00      1.00      0.00     -0.60      0.80     -1.00      8.00

     1.00      0.00      0.00      0.00      0.00      1.00      4.00

     0.00      0.00      0.00      0.60      2.20     -7.00     86.00
```

a) Find the right-hand-side ranges of each of the first three constraints.

b) Find the new optimal solution if the right-hand sides of the first three constraints were simultaneously changed to 35, 40, and 5, respectively.

c) Find the new optimal solution to the orig-inal problem if only the first constraint were changed to $x_1 + 3x_2 + 4x_3 \leq 36$.

d) Find the Preliminary final tableau if in the original problem only the third constraint were changed to $x_1 + 2x_2 = 4$. Explain why this tableau does not represent the optimal solution.

6.14 REVIEW PROBLEMS (*continued*)

55.
```
$ RUN LIB:LINDO
  LINDO (UC 1 APRIL 82)
:MAX 5X1 + 6X2 + 10X3
?ST
?X1 + 2X2 + 3X3 <= 24
?2X1 + X2 + X3 <= 18
?END

:GO
    LP OPTIMUM FOUND  AT STEP    2
            OBJECTIVE FUNCTION VALUE

  1)        90.0000000

VARIABLE        VALUE          REDUCED COST
       X1       6.000000          0.000000
       X2       0.000000          1.000000
       X3       6.000000          0.000000


ROW         SLACK OR SURPLUS     DUAL PRICES
   2)          0.000000          3.000000
   3)          0.000000          1.000000

NO. ITERATIONS=        2

 DO RANGE(SENSITIVITY) ANALYSIS?
?YES

    RANGES IN WHICH THE BASIS IS UNCHANGED
                        OBJ COEFFICIENT RANGES
VARIABLE        CURRENT       ALLOWABLE       ALLOWABLE
                COEF          INCREASE        DECREASE
       X1       5.000000      15.000000        1.666667
       X2       6.000000       1.000000       INFINITY
       X3      10.000000       5.000000        1.666667
                        RIGHTHAND SIDE RANGES
ROW             CURRENT       ALLOWABLE       ALLOWABLE
                RHS           INCREASE        DECREASE
    2          24.000000      30.000000       15.000000
    3          18.000000      30.000000       10.000000
Simplex Tableau Number  3
     0.00       0.60       1.00       0.40      -0.20       6.00

     1.00       0.20       0.00      -0.20       0.60       6.00

     0.00       1.00       0.00       3.00       1.00      90.00
```

a) What is the range for the objective function coefficient 5 of x_1?

b) What is the range for the objective function coefficient 6 of x_2?

c) What is the range for the objective function coefficient 10 of x_3?

d) What is the range for the objective function coefficient 0 of s_1?

e) What is the range for the objective function coefficient 0 of s_2?

6.14 REVIEW PROBLEMS (*concluded*)

56. In Problem 52,
  a) What is the range for the objective function coefficient 1,500 of x_1?
  b) What is the range for the objective function coefficient 2,400 of x_2?
  c) What is the range for the objective function coefficient 0 of p_2?

57. In Problem 55,
  a) Find the inequality relating the profit P associated with the introduction of a new product and its corresponding resource requirements R_1 and R_2.
  b) Suppose the new product utilized 2 units of resource 1 and 3 units of resource 2. How much would it have to contribute to the profit for it to be introduced into the solution?
  c) Suppose the new product utilized 4 units of resource 1 and contributed $18 to profit. How many units of resource 2 can the product use if it is to be introduced into the solution?
  d) Suppose the new product utilized 5 units of resource 2 and contributed $14 to profit. How many units of resource 1 can the product use if it is to be introduced into the solution?

58. In Problem 52,
  a) Find the inequality relating the cost C associated with the introduction of a new product and its corresponding resource requirements R_1, R_2, and R_3.
  b) Suppose the new product utilized 5 units of resource 1, 2 units of resource 2, and 3 units of resource 3. How much could it add to the cost for it to be introduced into the solution?
  c) Suppose the new product used 10 units of resource 1, 1 unit of resource 2, and added $1,800 to the cost. How many units of resource 3 can the product use if it is to be introduced into the solution?
  d) Suppose the new product added $2,100 to the cost. How many units of resource 1 can the product use if it is to be introduced into the solution?

SEVEN

Exponential and Logarithmic Functions

7.1 INTRODUCTION

The object of this chapter is to review the nature and properties of exponents, exponential functions, logarithms, and logarithmic functions. We will look at some of the many applications of these very important functions, and in Chapter 8 we will see useful applications of both exponential and logarithmic functions to the mathematics of finance. Until twenty years ago, students labored with extensive tables of logarithms and exponential values, but today we are fortunate to have these numerical values at our fingertips via the calculator and computer. We shall include in our discussion important techniques in the use of the calculator.

7.2 EXPONENTIAL FUNCTIONS

We are all familiar with the functions

$$s(x) = x^2, \qquad t(x) = \sqrt{x} \qquad \text{and} \qquad u(x) = x^{-1}.$$

Each of these is of the same form as the function

$$f(x) = x^n,$$

where we have chosen a particular value of the exponent n and allowed the base x to vary over all appropriate real values. What if we were to choose a particular value for the base and allow the exponent to vary over all real values? We then obtain functions such as

$$w(x) = 2^x \qquad \text{or} \qquad z(x) = \left(\frac{1}{2}\right)^x.$$

The general form of these functions is

$$f(x) = a^x \quad (a > 0),$$

where the value of the base, a, is fixed and the exponent, x, varies over all real numbers. Such a function is called an exponential function since the variable now appears as an exponent.

It is helpful to review the important properties of exponents before we continue our discussion of exponential functions.[1] The following seven properties are the most important.

Properties of Exponents (a, $b > 0$)

1. $a^0 = 1$ 4. $(a^x)^y = a^{xy}$
2. $a^x \cdot a^y = a^{x+y}$ 5. $(ab)^x = a^x b^x$
3. $a^x/a^y = a^{x-y}$ 6. $(a/b)^x = a^x/b^x$
                 7. $a^{-x} = 1/a^x$

---

1. Any number to the power 0 is 1; $a^0 = 1$.
2. Always add exponents when multiplying two powers of the same base; $a^x \cdot a^y = a^{x+y}$.
3. When dividing a^x by a^y, subtract exponents; $a^x/a^y = a^{x-y}$.
4. The quantity a^x to the power y is equal to a^{xy}; $(a^x)^y = a^{xy}$.
5. The base ab to the power x is equal to a^x times b^x; $(ab)^x = a^x \cdot b^x$.
6. The base a/b to the power x is equal to a^x over b^x; $(a/b)^x = a^x/b^x$.
7. A base to the power $-x$ is equivalent to one over that base to the power x; $a^{-x} = 1/a^x$.

The graph of an exponential function is easy to sketch. Consider the function

$$f(x) = 2^x.$$

Since $2^0 = 1$, the point $(x, f(x)) = (0, 1)$ is on the graph. Looking at the values

x	-4	-3	-2	-1	0	1	2	3	4
2^x	$\frac{1}{16}$	$\frac{1}{8}$	$\frac{1}{4}$	$\frac{1}{2}$	1	2	4	8	16

---

[1] A more detailed review of exponents is given in Appendix 2.

FIGURE 7–1

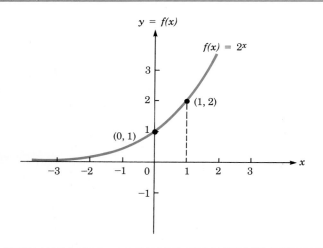

---

we see that as x becomes large positively, 2^x increases rapidly; and as x takes on values more and more negative, 2^x seems to decrease to zero. This is indeed the case, as shown in Figure 7–1.

Some more graphs of exponential functions are given in Figure 7–2. Notice how these graphs all look like the one in Figure 7–1. When the base a is between 0 and 1, however, the graphs look like those shown in Figure 7–3. Why?

From these sketches we can see that exponential functions come in

Exercise.   Sketch a graph of $f(x) = 5^x$ and $f(x) = (\frac{1}{5})^x$.
Answer:

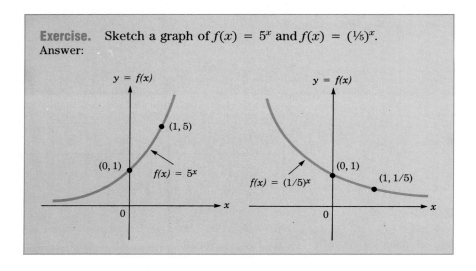

FIGURE 7–2

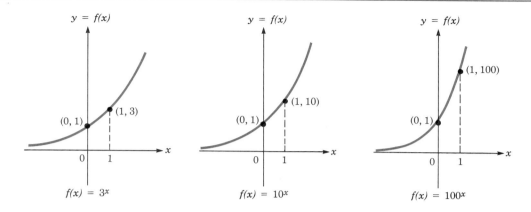

two forms; those with $a > 1$ increase to the right and those with $0 < a < 1$ decrease to the right. All exponential functions of the form a^x

1. pass through $(0, 1)$;
2. are positive for all values of x; and
3. tend to infinity in one direction and zero in the other.

Now that we have recalled the general properties of exponential functions and exponents, we wish to look at a particularly important exponential function for a specific base a. It turns out that in many

FIGURE 7–3

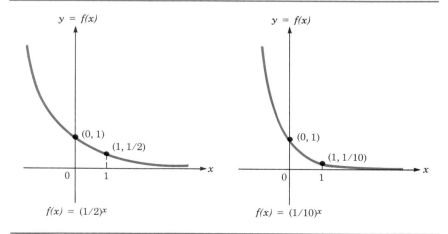

FIGURE 7–4

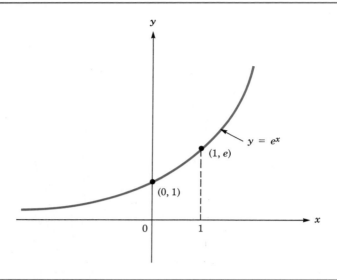

applications the most natural (and hence, convenient) choice for a base is the irrational number e, approximated by decimals as

$$e \approx 2.7182818 \ldots .$$

This number appears to be anything but convenient, and in fact we cannot express e in a simple form since it is an irrational number. In Chapter

Exercise. Graph $y = e^{-x}$. Answer:

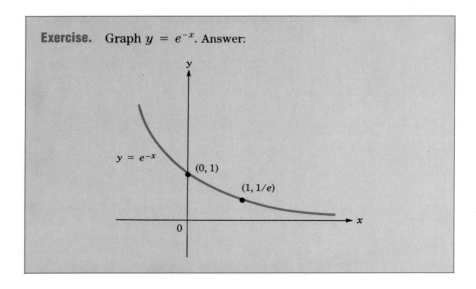

8, we will see how this base evolves naturally out of the formulas for compound interest. Notice that the graph $y = e^x$ in Figure 7–4 displays the fundamental properties of all exponential functions described above.

7.3 PROBLEM SET 7–1

Evaluate each of the expressions in Problems 1 through 10:

1. $4(4^3)$.

2. $64^{1/2}$.

3. $27^{2/3}$.

4. $(8^{1/2})(2^{1/2})$.

5. $(1/5)^{-2}$.

6. $[(9^{1/2})(9^2)]^{1/5}$.

7. $[(3^{-1})(3^{2/3})]^3$.

8. $(e^2)(e^4)$.

9. $(e^3)^{-2}$.

10. $(1/e)^{-4}$.

Sketch a graph of the exponential functions in Problems 11 through 20:

11. $f(x) = 3^x$.

12. $f(x) = 12^x$.

13. $f(x) = 4^{-x}$.

14. $f(x) = (1/5)^x$.

15. $f(x) = (1/4)^{-x}$.

16. $f(x) = 2^{-x}$.

17. $f(x) = 3^{-x}$.

18. $f(x) = 2^x + 1$.

19. $f(x) = 2^{-x} + 3$.

20. $f(x) = 2^x/2$.

7.4 THE NEED FOR LOGARITHMS

In the early part of this century, and for centuries before, logarithms were extensively used to ease calculational difficulties arising in a variety of fields including finance, navigation, and engineering. At the present time such calculations are made accurately and rapidly by computers. However, computers have not outmoded logarithms. For one thing, computers routinely find logarithms and use them in calculations. For example, calculations like

$$1000(1.005)^{60}$$

are performed millions of times a day by banks' data-processing computers, and the computers routinely apply logarithms in carrying out such calculations.

A second reason that logarithms have not been outmoded is that they are *necessary* in the solution of certain types of equations. Third, as we shall see, the *rules* of logarithms continue to play an important role in mathematical analysis and data analysis.

Logarithms are necessary in the solution of the exponential equation

$$10^x = 5,$$

TABLE 7–1

Number N	Logarithm to the Base 10 $\log_{10} N$ (Common Logs)
1	0.000 000
1.02	0.008 600
1.04	0.017 033
1.06	0.025 306
1.08	0.033 424
2	0.301 030
3	0.477 121
4	0.602 060
5	0.698 970
6	0.778 151
7	0.845 098
8	0.903 090
9	0.954 243
10	1.000 000
16	1.204 120

which requires that we find the power of 10 that equals 5. We know that

$$10^0 = 1$$
$$10^1 = 10,$$

so x is between 0 and 1, but this is not a sufficiently accurate answer. The answer can be found easily by referring to a table of logarithms that have the 10 in 10^x as their "base" number. Such a table consists of numbers together with the power of 10 that equals each of the numbers. This power of 10 for a number, N, is called the *logarithm of N to the base 10*. Base 10 logarithms are also called *common* logarithms. In symbols, the common logarithm of a number N is written

$$\log_{10} N.$$

Table 7–1 provides a few logarithms, correct to six decimal places, for our use here.

These values can easily be found on your calculator if you have a $\log x$ or a $\log_{10} x$ key. Look carefully because many calculators have a key labeled 2nd to enable each key to perform two functions, one written on the key and a second written above the key. After you have located the $\log x$ or $\log_{10} x$ key, verify some of the entries in Table 7–1. Returning to

$$10^x = 5$$

we see from Table 7–1 that the power of 10 that equals 5, that is, $\log_{10} 5$, is

$$x = \log_{10} 5 = 0.698\,970.$$

Exercise.   Solve for x: $10^x = 8$.   Answer: 0.903 090.

Next, in Table 7–1, observe that

$$\log_{10} 4 = 0.602\,060$$
$$\log_{10} 16 = 1.204\,120,$$

and we see that the logarithm of 16 is two times the logarithm of 4; that is,

$$\log_{10} 16 = 2(0.602060) = 2\log_{10} 4 = 1.204120.$$

This result occurs because 16 is 4 to the second power, and a *rule of logarithms*, which we will prove later, states that *the logarithm of a number to a power equals the power times the logarithm of the number.* That is,

$$\log_{10} 16 = \log_{10} 4^2 = 2\log_{10} 4.$$

In general terms, we have

$$\log_{10} a^b = b(\log_{10} a)$$

so that

$$\log_{10} 5^4 = 4\log_{10} 5$$
$$\log_{10} 7^3 = 3\log_{10} 7,$$

and so on.

Exercise. From Table 7–1: a) Compute 3 times $\log_{10} 2$. b) The result in (a) is the logarithm of what number? Answer: a) 0.903090. b) 8, which is 2^3.

We introduced the above rule to illustrate the point that logarithms are needed in the solution of practical problems. To pursue this point, suppose that Jan has $1,000 to invest and finds that interest can be earned at the rate of 6 percent, compounded annually. Jan wants to know how many years, n, it will take at this interest rate for $1,000 to grow to $2,000. A friend who knows some formulas from finance (which we study in the next chapter) says the answer is the solution of the equation

$$1000(1.06)^n = 2000.$$

Here the unknown is an exponent, and logarithms are needed to determine the value of the exponent. First, dividing both sides by 1000, we have

$$(1.06)^n = 2.$$

Next, take the logarithms of both sides of the equation. Thus:

$$\log_{10} (1.06)^n = \log_{10} 2.$$

Now apply the rule of logarithms stated a little earlier to obtain

$$n \log_{10} (1.06) = \log_{10} 2.$$

$$n = \frac{\log_{10} 2}{\log_{10} 1.06}.$$

We find the required logarithms using Table 7–1 or a calculator and have

$$n = \frac{0.301\ 030}{0.025\ 306}$$
$$= 11.9,$$

so it will take 11.9 years, or about 12 years, for Jan's investment of $1,000 to grow to $2,000.

Note that from this point onward we shall simplify writing $\log_{10} N$ in our discussion by agreeing that log without any base shall always mean $\log_{10}$.

Definition. $\log N$ means $\log_{10} N$.

Example. Solve for x: $3^x = 8$.

As before, we first take the logarithm of both sides to obtain

$$\log 3^x = \log 8.$$

Next we apply the rule for the power giving

$$x \log 3 = \log 8$$
$$x = \frac{\log 8}{\log 3}.$$

Lastly, inserting logarithms from Table 7–1, we find

$$x = \frac{0.903090}{0.477121}$$
$$= 1.893.$$

If you solve this using your calculator, you can find the answer using the sequence of key strokes shown in Table 7–2.[2] That is,

$$x = 1.893,$$

when rounded to three places.

Whenever you use a calculator you want to keep all values in the

---

[2] If your calculator does not have a $\log_{10} x$ or log key but does have a ln x key, then use this key as a substitute for the log key. The result should be the same. The function ln x is discussed in Section 7.5.

TABLE 7–2

Keystroke	Calculator Display
8	8
$\log_{10} x$ (or log x)	0.90309
$\div$	0.90309
3	3
$\log_{10} x$ (or log x)	0.47712
=	1.89279

calculator to avoid round-off error. *Don't* write down values from the display and reenter them at a later point in the computation. With a little practice you will be able to choose the right starting point and perform almost all calculations with a single continuous sequence of keystrokes.

Exercise. Solve for x: $9^x = 2$. Answer: 0.31546.

7.5 NATURAL (BASE e) LOGARITHMS

Just as the exponential function

$$y = e^x$$

is important in many applications, the logarithm to the base e is equally useful in many situations. These logarithms are called natural logarithms and are designated by the symbol $\ln x$ (pronounced as the name Lynn x) in practice and on your calculator.

Definition. $\ln N = \log_e N$

To find the value of $\ln 2$, just press the sequence on your calculator shown in Table 7–3.

Now use a calculator to verify the following:

$$\begin{aligned} \ln 6.7 &= 1.90211; \\ \ln 0.1 &= -2.30259; \\ \ln 6.14 &= 1.81482; \\ \ln 603 &= 6.40192. \end{aligned}$$

The problems we solved earlier with common (base 10) logarithms can be solved in the same manner with natural (base e) logarithms.

Example. Solve for n by natural logarithms:

$$(1.06)^n = 2.$$

TABLE 7–3

Keystroke	Calculator Display
2	2
ln *x*	0.693147

Taking the natural logarithm of both sides and solving for n, we have

$$\ln(1.06)^n = \ln 2$$
$$n \ln(1.06) = \ln 2$$
$$n = \frac{\ln 2}{\ln 1.06}$$
$$n = \frac{0.69315}{0.05827}$$
$$n = 11.9.$$

Exercise.   Solve $9^x = 2$ for x by natural logarithms. Answer: 0.31547.

When working with logarithms, it makes no difference (until we get into calculus) whether we work with the common or natural system. If, for some reason, we have a logarithm to one base and want to find the corresponding logarithm to the other base, the conversion is simple. It is

Ln to Log Conversion

$$\ln N = (\ln 10) \log N = 2.30259 \log N.$$
$$\log N = (\log e) \ln N = 0.434294 \ln N.$$

Exercise.   Table 7–1 shows log 5 = 0.698970 and Table II (at the back of the book) shows ln 5 = 1.60944. a) How can ln 5 be computed from log 5? b) How can log 5 be computed from ln 5? Answer: a) ln 5 = (2.30259) log 5 = 2.30259(0.698970) = 1.60944. b) log 5 = (0.434294) ln 5 = (0.434294)(1.60944) = 0.698970.

To avoid confusion, we will use ln x whenever possible.

7.6 PROBLEM SET 7–2

Solve the following for x by reference to Table 7–1 or by use of a calculator:

1. $2^x = 3$.

2. $3^x = 2$.

3. $10^x = 5$.

4. $10^x = 6$.

5. $2^x = 1.08$.

6. $5^x = 1.02$.

7. $(1.06)^x = 3$.

8. $(1.08)^x = 2$.

9. $10^x = 7$.

10. $10^x = 3$.

Apply the power rule and Table 7–1 or a calculator to find the following:

11. $\log 125$.

12. $\log 27$.

13. $\log 81$.

14. $\log 625$.

Solve the following for x by use of a calculator:

15. $20^x = 100$.

16. $4^x = 500$.

17. $(0.5)^x = 8$.

18. $(0.25)^x = 10$.

19. $(1.08)^x = 3$.

20. $(1.03)^x = 5$.

7.7 DEFINITION OF LOGARITHMS

The need for logarithms in certain calculations was demonstrated in the previous sections of this chapter. Logarithms also play an important role, independent of their calculational use, in applied mathematical analysis. To understand this role, it is necessary to be thoroughly familiar with the definition of a logarithm and the rules that apply to operations with logarithms. We start by recalling that the logarithm of a given number is the exponent of the power to which another number, the base, must be raised to equal the given number. If we write

$$2^3 = 8,$$

then 3 is the power to which 2, the base, must be raised to equal 8 and we say the logarithm of 8 to the base 2 equals 3. Thus,

$$2^3 = 8 \quad \text{means} \quad \log_2 8 = 3,$$

and conversely. The two statements are called *inverse* forms. Similarly

$$\log_5 125 = 3 \quad \text{means} \quad 5^3 = 125$$
$$\log_2 \left(\frac{1}{2}\right) = -1 \quad \text{means} \quad 2^{-1} = \frac{1}{2}$$
$$\log_b M = x \quad \text{means} \quad b^x = M.$$

Example. Write $2^5 = 32$ and $\log_{10} N = x$ in inverse form.

For the first part,

$$2^5 = 32,$$

we identify the base as 2. The exponent, 5, equals the logarithm, which is the logarithm of 32. Hence,

$$\log_2 32 = 5.$$

The arrows below show a system for remembering how to do the second part, starting with the base.

$$\log_{10} N = x \quad \text{means} \quad 10^x = N.$$

Exercise. Write the following in inverse form. a) $\log_{10} 100 = 2$. b) $\log_a N = x$. c) $(0.5)^2 = 0.25$. d) $x^2 = 10$. e) $a^z = M$. Answer: a) $10^2 = 100$. b) $a^x = N$. c) $\log_{0.5} (0.25) = 2$. d) $\log_x 10 = 2$. e) $\log_a M = z$.

7.8 RULES OF LOGARITHMS

Logarithms, as we stated, are exponents and therefore must obey rules corresponding to exponent rules. Three of the exponent rules we reviewed in Section 7.2 are

$$x^a \cdot x^b = x^{a+b}$$
$$\frac{x^a}{x^b} = x^{a-b}$$
$$(x^a)^b = x^{ab}.$$

Briefly, the above say that when the bases are the same, exponents of the powers are added in multiplication, subtracted in division, and multiplied when a power is raised to a power. The corresponding rules for logarithms are

---

Logarithm Rules

Product: $\log ab = \log a + \log b.$

Quotient: $\log \left(\dfrac{a}{b} \right) = \log a - \log b.$

Power: $\log a^b = b(\log a).$

Warning. Logarithms of sums and differences *cannot* be taken term by term. That is, $\log (a + b)$ *cannot* be written as $\log a + \log b$, and similarly for $\log (a - b)$.

Thus, the logarithm of a product is the sum of the logarithms of the factors, the logarithm of a quotient is the logarithm of the numerator minus the logarithm of the denominator, and the logarithm of a number to a power is the power times the logarithm of the number. These rules apply whatever the base of the logarithms is.

Let us prove the product rule. To do this, we assume the base is some number c, and let

$$\log_c a = x \quad \text{so that} \quad c^x = a$$
$$\log_c b = y \quad \text{so that} \quad c^y = b.$$

If we multiply a by b, at the right, the result is the same as multiplying the equivalent values, c^x and c^y. Hence,

$$(c^x)(c^y) = ab.$$
$$c^{x+y} = ab.$$

Writing the inverse of the last statement gives

$$\log_c ab = x + y.$$

Now, remembering that $x = \log_c a$ and $y = \log_c b$, we have

$$\log_c ab = \log_c a + \log_c b$$

which proves the product rule. Similar proofs can be written for the quotient and power rules, but we shall leave these for the next problem set.

Example. Assume that for some base, $\log a = 0.3000$, $\log b = 2.8642$, and $\log c = 1.7642$. Find

$$\log \left(\frac{a^3 b^{1/2}}{c} \right).$$

The purpose of this example is to fix the rules of logarithms in mind. If we apply the product and quotient rules, then the power rule, we have

$$\log \left(\frac{a^3 b^{1/2}}{c} \right) = \log a^3 + \log b^{1/2} - \log c$$

$$= 3 \log a + \frac{1}{2} \log b - \log c$$

$$= 3(0.3000) + \frac{1}{2}(2.8642) - 1.7642$$

$$= 0.9000 + 1.4321 - 1.7642$$

$$= 0.5679.$$

Exercise. Assume that, for some base, $\log x = 0.5$, $\log y = 1.5$, and $\log z = 3$. Compute the value of $\log (xy/z^{1/3})$. Answer: 1.

Example. Rewrite the following using the log symbol only once:

$$\log a \; - \; 2 \log b \; + \; \frac{1}{2} \log c.$$

We proceed to use the power rule first, then apply the product and quotient rules. Doing this, we obtain

$$\log a \; - \; 2 \log b \; + \; \frac{1}{2} \log c = \log a \; - \; \log b^2 \; + \; \log c^{\frac{1}{2}}$$

$$= \log \left(\frac{ac^{\frac{1}{2}}}{b^2} \right).$$

Exercise. Rewrite $2 \log x - \log y - 0.5 \log z$ using the log symbol only once. Answer: $\log (x^2/yz^{0.5})$.

Points to remember. The base, b, of a system of logarithms can be any positive number except 1. For such a number

$$\log_b b = 1; \quad \text{that is,} \quad b^1 = b$$
$$\log_b 1 = 0; \quad \text{that is,} \quad b^0 = 1.$$

Thus, for example, remembering that $\log N$ means $\log_{10} N$ and $\ln N = \log_e N$,

$$\log 10 = 1; \quad \ln e = 1; \quad \log 1 = 0; \quad \ln 1 = 0.$$

These points are worthy of special note because they arise often in applications.

Example. If $y = x(x - \ln x)$, compute y when $x = 1$.

Substituting $x = 1$, we find

$$\begin{aligned} y &= 1(1 - \ln 1) \\ &= 1(1 - 0) \\ &= 1. \end{aligned}$$

Example. Solve for x:

$$e^{-0.1x} = 0.2.$$

Inasmuch as the base of this exponential is e, taking the natural logarithm of both sides of the equation is the simplest way to proceed. Thus,

$$\ln (e^{-0.1x}) = \ln 0.2$$
$$(-0.1x) \ln e = \ln 0.2,$$

and $\ln e = 1$, so

$$-0.1x = -1.60944$$
$$x = \frac{-1.60944}{-0.1}$$
$$= 16.0944.$$

Exercise. a) Evaluate $\ln (x^2 - 3)$ when $x = 2$.
b) Solve $0.5x \log 10 = 2$ for x. Answer: a) 0. b) $x = 4$.

Log$_b$ N requires that N be positive. There are no logarithms for 0 or for negative numbers, and an attempt to obtain logarithms for such numbers on a calculator will lead to an error signal. This is because the base of a logarithm system, which must be positive, when raised to any power, is always positive. For example, for base 10,

$$\log_{10} N = x \quad \text{means} \quad 10^x = N.$$

If we examine various values of 10^x, we can see that these values are always positive. Thus,

$$10^2 = 100$$
$$10^0 = 1$$
$$10^{-1} = 0.1$$
$$10^{-5} = 0.00001,$$

and, in general,

$$10^x > 0$$
$$10^{-x} = \frac{1}{10^x} > 0.$$

Hence, for every value of x in

$$\log_{10} N = x,$$

N must be strictly positive; that is, N cannot be zero or negative.

7.9 APPLICATION OF INVERSE NATURAL LOGARITHMS

By definition of a natural logarithm,

$$\ln N = \log_e N = x \quad \text{means} \quad N = e^x.$$

That is, for example, if

$$\ln N = 2$$

then

$$N = e^2 = (2.718282)^2$$
$$= 7.38906$$

to five decimal places. Again, if

$$\ln N = -2$$

then

$$N = e^{-2} = \frac{1}{e^2}$$
$$= \frac{1}{(2.718282)^2}$$
$$= 0.13534.$$

Positive and negative powers of e can be obtained from a calculator having an e^x key by simply entering the value of x and depressing the e^x key. Some calculators do not have a separate e^x key but have a ln x key and an INV key designating inverse. Since e^x and ln x are inverse functions the sequence shown in Table 7–4 will produce the value e^2 on these calculators. Remember to push the key marked 2nd when the operation you desire is shown above the key.

TABLE 7–4

Keystroke	Calculator Display
2	2
INV	2
ln x	7.389056

Exercise.   Using a calculator, find: a) e^3. b) e^{-3}. c) $e^{0.05}$. d) $e^{-0.1}$. Answer: (Accurate to 5 decimal places.) a) 20.08554. b) 0.04979. c) 1.05127. d) 0.90484.

Occasionally it is helpful to use the symbol antiln x instead of e^x.

Definition. antiln $x = e^x$.

The operations ln and antiln are inverse operations in the sense that one annuls the effect of, or undoes, the other. For example, if we find

$$\ln 2 = 0.69315$$

and take the antiln, we obtain

$$\text{antiln (ln 2)} = \text{antiln (0.69315)}$$
$$= e^{0.69315}$$
$$\text{antiln (ln 2)} = 2.$$

Rule

$$\text{antiln (ln } x) = x \quad \text{or} \quad e^{ln\,x} = x.$$

Example. One dollar has been deposited in a bank account. At time n years later, the expression relating F, the amount in the account, to the time n is

$$\ln F = 0.08n.$$

Find the amount in the account at time $n = 20$ years.

Substituting $n = 20$, we have

$$\ln F = 0.08(20) = 1.6.$$

Hence,

$$\text{antiln (ln } F) = \text{antiln (1.6)}$$
$$F = e^{1.6} = \$4.95.$$

Example. A \$1,000 deposit in a bank account grows to \$2,000 in 10 years at an interest rate of i, where i must be computed from

$$1000(1 + i)^{10} = 2000.$$

Find i.

We first divide by 1000, giving

$$(1 + i)^{10} = 2.$$

An easy way to proceed is to isolate $(1 + i)$ by raising both sides of the equation to the 0.1 power; that is, by taking the tenth root. Thus,

$$[(1 + i)^{10}]^{0.1} = 2^{0.1}$$
$$(1 + i)^1 = 2^{0.1}$$

because, on the left, we multiply exponents when a power is raised to a power. Consequently,

$$1 + i = 2^{0.1}$$
$$i = 2^{0.1} - 1.$$

With a calculator we find 2 to the 0.1 power is 1.07177. Hence,

$$i = 1.07177 - 1 = 0.07177.$$

An alternate way of solving

$$(1 + i)^{10} = 2$$

is to take the logarithms of both sides of the equation. Thus,

$$\ln (1 + i)^{10} = \ln 2$$
$$10 \ln (1 + i) = 0.69315$$
$$\ln (1 + i) = 0.069315.$$

The last, in inverse form, says

$$1 + i = e^{0.069315}$$

and by calculator e to the 0.069315 power is 1.07177, so

$$1 + i = 1.07177$$
$$i = 1.07177 - 1 = 0.07177,$$

as before.

The precise steps to use when solving this example on a calculator are shown in Table 7–5. Note in this table that, for simplicity, the process of finding ln 2 has been simplified from two steps to the single step "2, *then* ln x" (two keystrokes). What two steps are combined in the single step "2nd, *then* e^x"?

The last example illustrates a commonly occurring problem in finance, that of determining an unknown interest rate. The answer 0.07177, or 7.177 percent, means that \$1,000 at this interest rate, applied in the compounding procedure described in the next chapter, will grow to \$2,000 in 10 years.

TABLE 7–5

Keystroke	Calculator Display
2, *then* ln x	0.69315
÷	0.69315
10	10
=	0.06931
2nd, *then* e^x	1.07177
−	1.07177
1	1
=	0.07177

Exercise.   a) If $\ln F = 3 + 0.1n$, find F when $n = 5$. b) Find i if $10,000(1 + i)^{10} = 30,000$.   Answer: a) 33.11545. b) 0.11612.

7.10 GRAPH OF
$y = \ln x$

To sketch the graph of

$$y = \ln x,$$

we start at $x = 1$, where $y = \ln 1 = 0$, and move to the right (x increasing) to

$$x = 2 \quad \text{and} \quad y = \ln 2 = 0.69,$$

then to

$$x = 3, \quad y = \ln 3 = 1.10,$$

and so on. We see that as we move to the right, $\ln x$ increases, and the curve of $y = \ln x$ rises. If we move to the left of $x = 1$ to

$$x = 0.5, \quad y = \ln 0.5 = -0.69$$

then to

$$x = 0.1, \quad y = \ln 0.1 = -2.30,$$

and so on, the curve of $y = \ln x$ falls even further below the x-axis. Figure 7–5 illustrates the behavior of $y = \ln x$. The curve rises slowly, but always rises, to the right of $x = 1$. Recalling that x cannot be zero or negative, we conclude that to the left of $x = 1$ the curve falls indefinitely as x gets closer to zero, but never touches the y-axis (where $x = 0$). It is not important to graph $y = \ln x$ carefully, but it is useful to know its characteristics, including the intercept point, $(1, 0)$.

FIGURE 7–5 (not to scale)

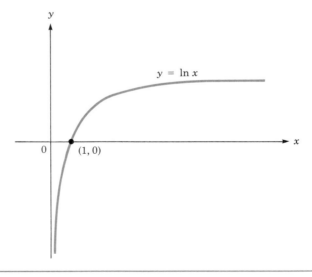

FIGURE 7–6   **FIGURE 7–7**

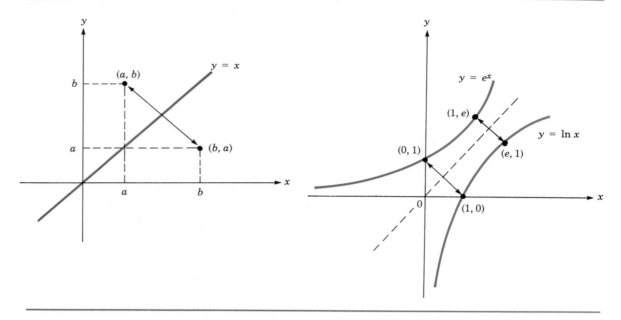

FIGURE 7–8

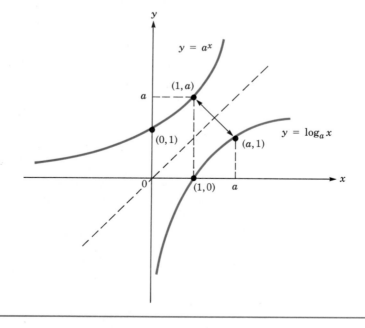

There is an easy way to remember the graph of $y = \ln x$; we only need to remember that e^x and $\ln x$ are inverse functions. This method is based on the geometric fact that the point (b, a) is the reflection across the line $y = x$ of the point (a, b) as shown in Figure 7–6. Since $y = \ln x$ is inverse to $y = e^x$, the graph of $y = \ln x$ is the reflection across the line $y = x$ of $y = e^x$, as shown in Figure 7–7. Notice that $(0, 1)$ is on the graph of $y = e^x$ since $e^0 = 1$, and $(1, 0)$ is on the graph of $y = \ln x$ since $\ln 1 = 0$. Hence if you can sketch the graph of $y = e^x$, then you can sketch the graph of $y = \ln x$.

This technique will work for the sketch of the graph of any pair of functions that are inverses of each other. For example, consider

$$y = \log_a x.$$

Since $y = \log_a x$ and $y = a^x$ are inverse functions, we can sketch both graphs as shown in Figure 7–8.

7.11 COMPUTING e AND NATURAL LOGARITHMS (OPTIONAL)

A calculator is a black box that determines logarithms by some process known to only a relatively small number of people, and logarithms found in a table are computed by methods known to only a few. This is understandable because one person cannot know all fields. However, it is not difficult to learn one process for computing logarithms. We are going to illustrate the computation of natural logarithms, so let us first learn how their base, e, can be calculated to any desired degree of accuracy.

The mathematical definition of e, developed in a later chapter, says that e can be approximated to any degree of accuracy from the expression

$$\left(\frac{n + 1}{n}\right)^n$$

by using a sufficiently large value of n. Unfortunately, sufficiently large is very large indeed if high accuracy is required. For example, Table 7–6 shows a BASIC and PASCAL program to compute $[(n + 1)/n]^n$ for values up to $n = 10{,}000$ in steps of $1{,}000$. Look closely at the two outputs in Table 7–6. You see the values seem to be jumping back and forth around the true six-place value,

$$e = 2.718282.$$

Now compare the previous results with the output from a calculator as shown in Table 7–7. Notice that there is no jumping back and forth. There are two reasons for this. The first comes from the way the computer performs exponentiation. As can be seen from Table 7–6, the BASIC and PASCAL compilers perform exponentiation differently and hence the outputs are different. The second reason is that the computer operates in binary arithmetic, which can cause significant round-off errors. *This is an excellent example of why computer output is not always*

TABLE 7–6

BASIC	PASCAL

```
10 REM e-APPROXIMATION
20 PRINT "n","((n+1)/n)^n"
30 PRINT
40 FOR n=1000 TO 10000 STEP 1000
50 PRINT n,((n+1)/n)^n
60 NEXT n
70 END
```

```
program eapprox (input, output);

var
   i,n:integer;

begin
   writeln('n':3,'((n+1)/n)^n':15);
   writeln;
   for i:=1 to 10 do
   begin
      n:=1000*i;
      writeln(n:5,exp(n*ln((n+1)/n)):10:5);
   end(*loop*);
end.
```

n	((n+1)/n)^n	n	((n+1)/n)^n
1000	2.717042	1000	2.71705
2000	2.717365	2000	2.71741
3000	2.717758	3000	2.71763
4000	2.717365	4000	2.71775
5000	2.718023	5000	2.71846
6000	2.717758	6000	2.71786
7000	2.717313	7000	2.71724
8000	2.718637	8000	2.71921
9000	2.717605	9000	2.71793
10000	2.718023	10000	2.71860

TABLE 7–7

n	$[(n + 1)/n]^n$
1000	2.716924
2000	2.717603
3000	2.717829
4000	2.717942
5000	2.718010
6000	2.718056
7000	2.718087
8000	2.718112
9000	2.718131
10000	2.718146

precise and should never be considered infallible. The calculator, however, does not operate in binary arithmetic and has a much more precise method of exponentiation.

To obtain an alternate and more precise method of approximating *e*,

$$\left(\frac{n + 1}{n}\right)^n$$

can be expanded by the binomial theorem, and mathematicians have proved from this expansion that

$$e = 1 + \frac{1}{1!} + \frac{1}{2!} + \frac{1}{3!} + \frac{1}{4!} + \frac{1}{5!} + \frac{1}{6!} + \frac{1}{7!} + \frac{1}{8!} + \cdots$$

where the three dots $\cdots$ mean to continue indefinitely. That is, the more terms included in the sum, the closer the sum is to e. The meaning of the factorial symbol, !, is illustrated by

$$4! = 4 \text{ factorial} = 4 \cdot 3 \cdot 2 \cdot 1 = 24$$
$$3! = 3 \text{ factorial} = 3 \cdot 2 \cdot 1 \quad = \quad 6.$$

The endless sum just presented is the infinite-series definition of e. Computing the factorials, we have

$$e = 1 + \frac{1}{1} + \frac{1}{2} + \frac{1}{6} + \frac{1}{24} + \frac{1}{120} + \frac{1}{720} + \frac{1}{5040} + \frac{1}{40320} + \cdots$$
$$= 2.7182788 + \cdots.$$

Rounded to five decimal places, the last is 2.71828 and is the value of e correct to five decimal places. Including three more terms yields 2.718281828, which is e correct to nine decimal places. Lest the reader be led to think the last set of digits is a repeating decimal (note the 1828, 1828 sequence) we point out that this is not so, and correct to 12 decimal places, e is 2.7182 8182 8459. In any event, the series approximation leads quickly to a value of e as accurate as we need in any application. Check this value on your calculator.

Mathematicians have also derived a set of series approximation formulas for computing natural logarithms of numbers. One of them is

$$\ln(1 + x) = x - \frac{x^2}{2} + \frac{x^3}{3} - \frac{x^4}{4} + \frac{x^5}{5} - \frac{x^6}{6} \cdots; \quad 0 < x \le 1,$$

where the signs of the terms alternate. This series will settle in (converge) on a value for a logarithm only if x is positive and not greater than 1, but other formulas and the rules of logarithms can be applied to obtain logarithms for all nonnegative numbers. To illustrate a logarithm calculation, we compute

$$\ln 1.2 = \ln(1 + 0.2).$$

This is

$$\ln(1 + x)$$

with $x = 0.2$. Hence,

$$\ln 1.2 = 0.2 - \frac{(0.2)^2}{2} + \frac{(0.2)^3}{3} - \frac{(0.2)^4}{4} + \frac{(0.2)^5}{5} - \frac{(0.2)^6}{6} + \cdots$$
$$\approx 0.18232,$$

where, as usual, $\approx$ means equals approximately. Verify by calculator or from Table II that the value calculated is ln 1.2 correct to five decimal places.

Exercise. a) Approximate ln 1.01 using only the first two terms of the above series. b) By how much does the result in (a) differ from the value 0.00995 for ln 1.01 in Table II? Answer: a) 0.00995. b) No difference.

After the logarithm of one number, N, has been computed by the series approximation, logarithms of all powers of N can be computed by simple multiplication because

$$\ln N^x = x \ln N.$$

Similarly, after the logarithms of two numbers have been computed, logarithms of their product and quotient can be found by simple addition and subtraction. That is,

$$\ln MN = \ln M + \ln N$$
$$\ln \frac{M}{N} = \ln M - \ln N.$$

Example. Two logarithms, correct to eight decimal places, have been computed. They are

$$\ln 4 = 1.3862\ 9436$$
$$\ln 10 = 2.3025\ 8509.$$

Compute the following, correct to five decimals, from the values of ln 4 and ln 10: a) ln 64. b) ln 40. c) ln 0.04.

We have a) $64 = 4^3$; $\ln 64 = 3 \ln 4$
$$= 3(1.3862\ 9436)$$
$$= 4.1588\ 8308$$
$$= 4.15888.$$

b) $40 = 4(10)$; $\ln 40 = \ln 4 + \ln 10$
$$= 1.3862\ 9436 + 2.3025\ 8509$$
$$= 3.6888\ 7945$$
$$= 3.68888.$$

c) $0.04 = \dfrac{4}{100} = \dfrac{4}{10^2}$;

$$\ln(0.04) = \ln\left(\frac{4}{10^2}\right) = \ln 4 - 2 \ln 10$$
$$= 1.3862\ 9436 - 2(2.3025\ 8509)$$
$$= -3.2188\ 7582$$
$$= -3.21888.$$

> **Exercise.** Given $\ln 4 = 1.3862\,9436$ and $\ln 10 = 2.3025\,8509$, show how the following can be computed, and carry out the computation correct to five decimal places. a) $\ln 1000$. b) $\ln 0.01$. c) $\ln 25$. Answer: a) $\ln 1000 = 3 \ln 10 = 6.90776$. b) $\ln (0.01) = \ln 1 - 2 \ln 10 = -4.60517$. c) $\ln 25 = 2 \ln 10 - \ln 4 = 3.21888$.

It is clear from the preceding that only a selected group of logarithms has to be calculated by the series approximation. With these and the rules of logarithms, a table can be constructed.

7.12 PROBLEM SET 7–3

Note: Remember that $\log x = \log_{10} x$ and $\ln x = \log_e x$. Write the following in inverse form.

1. $3^2 = 9$.

2. $2^5 = 32$.

3. $\log_3 N = x$.

4. $\log_2 N = y$.

5. $(1/2)^3 = 0.125$.

6. $(0.2)^2 = 0.04$.

7. $\log_{16} 4 = 1/2$.

8. $\log_{27} 3 = 1/3$.

9. $2^{-3} = 0.125$.

10. $3^{-2} = 1/9$.

11. $\log_5 0.04 = -2$.

12. $\log_2 0.0625 = -4$.

13. $\log 100 = 2$.

14. $\ln 20 = 2.9957$.

15. $\ln 10 = 2.3026$.

16. $\log 10 = 1$.

17. $\log 0.5 = -0.3010$.

18. $\ln 0.5 = -0.6931$.

What is the value of x in Problems 19 through 26?

19. $\ln e = x$.

20. $\log 10 = x$.

21. $\log_2 4 = x$.

22. $\log_3 27 = x$.

23. $\log_7 7 = x$.

24. $\log_{0.5} (0.5) = x$.

25. $\log_4 2 = x$.

26. $\log_{64} 4 = x$.

27. By taking natural logarithms and antilogarithms of both sides, prove that $x = 2$ if

$$e^{\ln x} = 2.$$

28. By taking common logarithms and antilogarithms of both sides, prove that $x = 3$ if

$$10^{\log x} = 3.$$

29. What value must x have if

$$10^{\log 5} = x?$$

30. What value must x have if

$$e^{\ln 4} = x?$$

31. Find the value of x:

$$7^{\log_7 6} = x.$$

7.12 PROBLEM SET 7–3 (concluded)

32. Find the value of x:
$$4^{\log_4 5} = x.$$

33. Rewrite the following, using the ln symbol only once.
$$\frac{\ln x}{0.5} - 2 \ln y + 3 \ln z.$$

34. Rewrite the following, using the log symbol only once.
$$\frac{\log x}{0.2} + (1/2)\log y - 2 \log z.$$

Given that $\log_a x = 4.2$, $\log_a y = 1.4$, $\log_a z = -1.2$, compute the value of each of the following:

35. $\log_a (xyz)$.

36. $\log_a \sqrt{z}$.

37. $\log_a (x/z)$.

38. $\log_a (xy/z)$.

39. $\log_a (z^{3/2})$.

40. $\log_a z^2$.

41. $\log_a \sqrt{xy}$.

42. $\log_a (xz)^{1/3}$.

43. $\log_a x/\log_a z$.

44. $\log_a (xy)/\log_a z$.

Using the rules of logarithms, write the following in a different, but equivalent form:

45. $2 \ln x + 3 \ln y$.

46. $3 \ln x - 2 \ln y$.

47. $0.2 \ln x^5$.

48. $(1/2) \ln x^4$.

49. $(\ln y)/x$.

50. $(1/y) \ln x$.

Solve for x:

51. $\ln x = 0.42$.

52. $\ln x = 1.2$.

53. $\ln x = -1.1$.

54. $\ln x = -0.01$.

55. $\ln (1 + x) = 0.3$.

56. $\ln (2 + x) = 1$.

57. $\ln (0.5x - 2) = -0.5$.

58. $\ln (1 - 0.1x) = -0.65$.

Use the compound interest formula, $F = P(1 + i)^n$, to solve the following:

59. Compute n if $F = 5000$, $P = 2000$, and $i = 0.085$.

60. Compute n if $F = 10,000$, $P = 5000$, and $i = 0.12$.

61. Compute i if $F = 4000$, $P = 1000$ and $n = 10$.

62. Compute i if $F = 2500$, $P = 1000$, and $n = 5$.

(Optional) Compute the following by summing five terms of the series approximation,
$$\ln (1 + x) = x - \frac{x_2}{2} + \frac{x^3}{3} - \frac{x^4}{4} + \frac{x^5}{5} \cdots \quad 0 < x \le 1.$$

63. $\ln 1.1$

64. $\ln (1.3)$.

65. Write a computer program to estimate e, using 5, 6, 7, 8, 9, and 10 terms of an infinite series.

7.13 REVIEW PROBLEMS

1. What is the value of e accurate to six decimal places?

2. State the definition of the natural logarithm of a number N.

Find the following:

3. ln 8.46.

4. ln 33.

5. ln 0.08.

6. ln 0.1.

7. ln 2.27.

8. ln 3.36.

9. ln 58.

10. ln 8.18.

11. ln 425.

12. ln 786.

13. ln e.

14. ln 1.

15. In $\log_b N$, why must N be positive?

16. Sketch a graph showing the characteristics of $y = \ln x$.

Find the following:

17. $e^{0.25}$.

18. $e^{0.01}$.

19. $e^{-0.25}$.

20. $e^{-0.01}$.

21. $e^{1.6}$.

22. $e^{2.3}$.

23. e^{-2}.

24. e^{-3}.

Find the following:

25. antiln 0.17.

26. antiln 0.08.

27. antiln (-1.3).

28. antiln (-2.1).

29. antiln (-0.01).

30. antiln 1.

Write the following in inverse form:

31. $5^2 = 25$.

32. $2^3 = 8$.

33. $\log_7 49 = 2$.

34. $\log_5 125 = 3$.

35. $27^{1/3} = 3$.

36. $64^{1/2} = 8$.

37. $\log_8 2 = 1/3$.

38. $\log_{81} 3 = 1/4$.

39. ln $e = 1$.

40. log 1 = 0.

41. $7^0 = 1$.

42. $5^1 = 5$.

What is the value of x in each of the following?

43. $\log_2 32 = x$.

44. $\log_3 81 = x$.

45. $\log_{0.2} (0.04) = x$.

46. $\log_{0.2} 5 = x$.

7.13 REVIEW PROBLEMS (*concluded*)

47. $\log_3 x = 3$.

48. $\log_2 x = 4$.

49. $\ln x = 1$.

50. $\log x = 0$.

51. $e^{\ln e} = x$.

52. $10^{\log 10} = x$.

53. $3^{\log_3 5} = x$.

54. $5^{\log_5 4} = x$.

55. If, for base a, $\log_a x = 0.6$, $\log_a y = 1.8$, $\log_a z = 1.2$, compute the value of

$$\log_a \left[\frac{x^2}{(yz)^{1/3}} \right].$$

56. Using the logarithms of Problem 55, compute the value of

$$\log_a \left[\frac{z^{1/4}}{x^{1/3} y^{1/6}} \right].$$

57. Rewrite the following, using the ln symbol only once.

$$2 \ln x - (1/2) \ln y^2 + \ln z.$$

58. Rewrite the following, using the ln symbol only once.

$$3 \ln x^{1/3} - (1/2) \ln y - 2 \ln z.$$

Solve the following for x:

59. $\ln x = 0.84$.

60. $\ln x = 2.4$.

61. $\ln x = -2.3$.

62. $\ln x = -0.08$.

63. $\ln (1 + x) = 1.2$.

64. $\ln (1 + x) = -0.5$.

65. $(6.75)^x = 4$.

66. $(25)^x = 127$.

67. $(0.23)^x = 0.15$.

68. $(0.55)^x = 1.8$.

69. $3^{-x} = 2$.

70. $4^{-x} = 8$.

71. $(0.2)^{-x} = 0.7$.

72. $(0.8)^{-x} = 0.5$.

73. $(4/x)^{-5} = 0.26$.

74. $(x/5)^{2.1} = 8$.

75. $e^x = 25$.

76. $10^x = 80$.

77. $x^{10} - 1 = 0$.

78. $x^{10} - 2 = 0$.

79. $(1 + x)^{15} = 2.5$.

80. $(1 + x)^{-10} = 0.5$.

81. $(1 + x) = \text{antiln } 0.14$.

82. $(1 + x) = \text{antiln } 0.1239$.

83. $x[1 + (1.01)^{50}] = 5$.

84. $2500[1 + (1.02)^{-x}] = 3000$.

EIGHT

Mathematics of Finance

Just about everyone becomes involved in transactions where interest rates affect the amount of money to be paid or received. For many, the largest such transaction is the purchase of a home. As we shall learn, a person who borrows $80,000 for such a purchase and cancels the debt by making monthly payments over a period of 30 years, will pay back about $296,240 if the interest rate is 12 percent per year, compounded monthly. Not very many years ago, when the interest rate was about 9 percent, the corresponding payback would have been about $231,731. The size of these paybacks serves to show both the effect of compound interest and the effect of changes in interest rates. In this chapter, we first look at simple interest calculation, then turn to the major objective of the chapter, which is to develop and apply formulas for financial transactions that involve compound interest calculations. In so doing, we shall ask and answer questions such as the following, for various interest rates and frequencies of compounding:

1. If $5,000 is deposited in a bank account now, what will be the amount in the account 10 years from now?
2. How much must be deposited in a bank account now if the amount in the account 5 years from now is to be $10,000?
3. If $1,000 is added to an account every year, to what amount will the account grow in 15 years?
4. How much must be deposited in an account each year if the amount in the account at the end of 10 years is to be $15,000?

5. What sum deposited now will provide an income of $10,000 per year each year for the next 20 years?
6. If $30,000 is borrowed now to pay for a home, how much must be paid back each month if the debt is to be cancelled in 20 years?

We shall also answer questions like the preceding if interest is compounded instantaneously (continuously) rather than at discrete points in time such as the end of each day, month, four months, six months, or one year.

Extensive tabulations are available to aid in carrying out the calculations involved in financial tabulations. However, we shall show how these calculations are easily carried out on a calculator and/or computer. We prefer this approach because even the most extensive tabulations provide a limited cross-section of interest rates and time periods. It is important, however, to understand that the chapter has been designed so that it is possible to learn the subject matter and do practice calculations using either approach. Also, we should point out that compound interest calculations involve exponents and, as a consequence, logarithms play a role in some of these calculations.

8.2 SIMPLE INTEREST AND THE FUTURE VALUE

Interest rates are generally quoted in percentage form and, for use in calculations, must be converted to the equivalent decimal value by dividing the percentage by 100; that is, by moving the decimal point in the percentage two places to the left. For example,

$$i = 8\tfrac{1}{4}\% = 8.25\% = 0.0825.$$

Unless otherwise stated, *a quoted rate is a rate per year.* Thus, $1 at 8 percent means that interest of $0.08 will be earned in a year, and $100 at this rate provides

$$100(0.08) = \$8$$

of interest in one year. Interest on $100 at 8 percent for 9 months is interest for $\tfrac{9}{12}$ year; that is,

$$\text{Interest} = \underset{\uparrow}{100} \quad \underset{\uparrow}{(0.08)} \quad \underset{\uparrow}{\left(\frac{9}{12}\right)} \quad = \$6.00.$$

$$\text{Interest} = (\text{Principal})(\text{Rate})(\text{Time in years})$$

The last line introduces the following definitions, which apply in simple interest calculations:

Definitions

I = Interest, in dollars.
P = Principal, the sum of money on which interest is being earned.

> i = Rate of interest per period (assumed to be one year).
> n = Number of years, or fraction of one year.
>
> Simple interest formula: $I = Pin$.

Thus, interest on $600 at 7½ percent for 10 months is computed using $P = 600$, $i = 0.075$, and $n = {}^{10}\!/_{12}$ year. This is

$$I = 600(0.075)\left(\frac{10}{12}\right) = \$37.50.$$

> **Exercise.** Compute the interest on $480 at 6¼ percent for 9 months. Answer: $22.50.

The simple interest formula can be solved easily for any of its variables.

Example. Find the interest rate if $1,000 earns $45 interest in 6 months.

Here, $I = 45$, $P = 1000$, $n = {}^{6}\!/_{12} = 0.5$. Hence,

$$I = Pin$$
$$45 = 1000(i)(0.5)$$
$$45 = 500i$$
$$\frac{45}{500} = i$$
$$0.09 = i.$$

To obtain the percent rate, the decimal rate, $i = 0.09$, is multiplied by 100. Thus,

$$i = 0.09 = 100(0.09)\% = 9\%.$$

The *yield* on the common stock of a company is a percent obtained by dividing the amount (called the *dividend*) that a shareholder receives per share of stock held by the price of a share of the stock. Thus, yield is like an interest rate with the dividend analogous to the interest for n = 1 year and the price per share analogous to the principal. A stock market report showing

GenEl   2.50   77½

means that at the time of the quotation, a share of General Electric stock sold for $77.50 and the annual dividend was estimated to be $2.50 per share.

Exercise. Compute the yield for General Electric from the market report in the above. Answer: 3.23 percent.

When time is given in days, there are two ways of computing the interest: the exact method and the ordinary method (often called the Banker's Rule). If the exact method is used, then the time is

$$n = \frac{\text{Number of days}}{365};$$

but if the ordinary method is used, then

$$n = \frac{\text{Number of days}}{360}.$$

Banks, for convenience, often count a year as twelve 30-day months, 360 days for a year.

Example. Find the interest on $1,460 for 72 days at 10 percent interest using (a) the exact method and (b) the ordinary method.

In both methods, $P = 1460$ and $i = 0.1$. For (a),

$$I = Pin$$
$$= (1460)(0.1)\left(\frac{72}{365}\right)$$
$$= \$28.80.$$

On the other hand, for (b)

$$I = Pin$$
$$= (1460)(0.1)\left(\frac{72}{360}\right)$$
$$= \$29.20.$$

As you can see from this example, the ordinary interest is more than the exact interest. This will always be the case. Why? In fact,

$$\frac{\text{Ordinary interest}}{\text{Exact interest}} = \frac{Pi(\text{Number of days}/360)}{Pi(\text{Number of days}/365)}$$
$$= \frac{365}{360}$$
$$= \frac{73}{72}.$$

So

$$\text{Ordinary interest} = \left(\frac{73}{72}\right)(\text{Exact interest}).$$

We will adopt the common practice of using ordinary interest unless otherwise specified.

Exercise. Find the exact and ordinary interest on $2,190 for 75 days at 12 percent interest. Answer: $54.00, $54.75.

The future value. If interest on $1,000 at 9 percent for 8 months is computed as

$$I = Pin = 1000(0.09)\left(\frac{8}{12}\right) = \$60$$

and the interest is added to the principal, the sum is called the *future value*, F. Thus,

$$F = 1000 + 1000(0.09)\left(\frac{8}{12}\right)$$
$$= 1000 + 60$$
$$= \$1,060.$$

Definition. Future value: $F = P + Pin = P(1 + in)$.

Example. Find the future value if $20,000 is borrowed at 6 percent for 3 months.

Here, 3 months is $3/12 = 1/4$ of a year, so $n = 1/4$. Hence,

$$F = 20,000\left[1 + 0.06\left(\frac{1}{4}\right)\right]$$
$$= 20,000(1 + 0.015)$$
$$= \$20,300.$$

It is often helpful to visualize money transactions in a "time diagram." In our current example, such a diagram is shown in Figure 8–1. Here, we have started at the present with $P = \$20,000$, drawn a line pointing out to the unknown F in the future three months hence, and indicated the 6 percent interest rate over the line.

Exercise. Find the future value of $5,000 at 10 percent for 9 months. Answer: $5,375.00.

Table 8–1 shows a BASIC and PASCAL program to compute the future

FIGURE 8–1

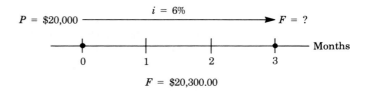

$$P = \$20,000 \xrightarrow{\quad i = 6\% \quad} F = ?$$

Months

0   1   2   3

$$F = \$20,300.00$$

value, along with the results of running the program for the example above.

The future value formula can be solved easily for any one of its variables.

Example. Jan received $50 for a diamond at a pawn shop and a month later paid $53.50 to get the diamond back. Find the percent interest rate.

Here,

$$P = \$50, \quad F = \$53.50, \quad n = \frac{1}{12} \text{ year}$$

and the associated time diagram is shown in Figure 8–2.

TABLE 8–1

BASIC	PASCAL

10 REM FUTURE VALUE/SIMPLE INTEREST
20 INPUT "Enter P, i, and n";P,I,N
30 F=P*(1+I*N)
40 PRINT "Future Value F = ";
50 PRINT USING "$###,###.##",F
60 END
	program fut_val_simp_int(input,
	  output);
	
	  var
	    p,f,i,n:real;
	  (* p=principal,f=future val,i=int.
	  rate,n=# yrs. *)
	
	begin
	
	  writeln('Enter principal,interest
	    rate,# years');
	  readln(p,i,n);
	  f:=p*(1+i*n);
	  writeln('Future Value F = $',f:8:2)
	end. (*program*)

RUN	
	$ run
Enter P, i, and n? 20000,.06,.25 Future Value F = $ 20,300.00	Enter principal,interest rate,# years 20000 .06 .25 Future Value F = $20300.00

FIGURE 8–2

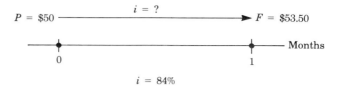

Therefore,

$$53.50 = 50\left[1 + i\left(\frac{1}{12}\right)\right].$$

Dividing both sides by 50 yields

$$\frac{53.50}{50} = 1 + \frac{i}{12}.$$

Multiplying both sides by 12, we find

$$12\left(\frac{53.50}{50}\right) = 12 + i$$
$$12.84 = 12 + i$$
$$0.84 = i$$

The last is the *decimal* rate. The percent rate is 100 times the decimal rate

$$0.84 = 100(0.84)\% = 84\%.$$

Exercise.   Fran has placed $500 in an employees' savings account that pays 8 percent simple interest. How long will it be, in months, until the investment amounts to $530? Answer: ¾ of a year = 9 months.

8.3 SIMPLE DISCOUNT: PRESENT VALUE

In the last exercise, $500 now amounts to $530 nine months from now if the interest rate is 8 percent. In reverse, we say that the *present value* of $530 receivable in nine months is $500 now if the interest rate is 8 percent. This present value is analogous to a principal, so we shall denote it by P. Inasmuch as

$$F = P(1 + in)$$

we obtain the simple present value formula by dividing both sides by

$(1 + in)$. Thus,

$$\frac{F}{1 + in} = P.$$

> **Definition.** Present value: $P = \dfrac{F}{1 + in}$.

Thus, the present value of $530 receivable 9 months from now if the interest rate is 8 percent is

$$P = \frac{530}{1 + 0.08(9/12)}$$
$$= \frac{530}{1.06}$$
$$= \$500.$$

The time diagram for this example is shown in Figure 8–3.

FIGURE 8–3

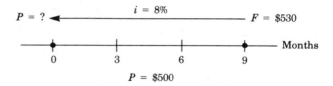

> **Exercise.** How much will Fran have to invest now in the employees' 8 percent savings account in order to have $600 a year from now? Answer: $600/1.08 = \$555.56$.

It is important in this chapter to keep in mind that a future amount of money, F, is worth less than F now. The sense of this is that certainly, in a business transaction, a person who promises to pay back $1,000 to a lender at some time in the future cannot expect to receive as much as $1,000 now.

> **Exercise.** Find the present value of $1,000 at 9 percent due 8 months from now. Answer: $943.40.

TABLE 8–2

BASIC	PASCAL
| ```
10 REM PRESENT VALUE/SIMPLE INTEREST
20 INPUT "Enter F, i, and n";F,I,N
30 P=F/(1+I*N)
40 PRINT "Present Value P = ";
50 PRINT USING "$###,###.##",P
60 END



RUN



Enter F, i, and n? 530,.08,.75
Present Value P = $     500.00
``` | ```
program pres_val_simp_int(input,
  output);

  var
     p,f,i,n:real;
(* f=future val,i=int. rate,n=#
  yrs. *)

begin

  writeln('Enter future value,
    interest rate,# years');
  readln(f,i,n);
  p:=f/(1+i*n);
  writeln('Present Value p =
    $',p:8:2)
end. (*program*)
$ run




Enter future value, interest rate,
  # years
530 .08 .75
Present Value P = $   500.00
``` |

Table 8–2 shows a BASIC and PASCAL program to compute the present value, along with the results of running the program for our example above.

8.4 BANK DISCOUNT

In many loans, the interest charge is computed not on the amount the borrower receives, but on the amount that is repaid later. A charge for a loan computed in this manner is called the *bank discount*, and the amount the borrower receives is called the *proceeds* of a loan. Proceeds begins with P and it is an amount received now. The future amount to be paid back is F, now called the *maturity value* of the loan. If $1,000 is borrowed at 12 percent for 6 months, the borrower receives the proceeds, P, and pays back $F = \$1,000$. The proceeds will be $1,000 minus the interest on $1,000. This will be

$$P = 1000 - 1000\,(0.12)\left(\frac{6}{12}\right)$$

$$P = \overset{\uparrow}{F} - \overset{\uparrow}{F}\ \overset{\uparrow}{(d)}\ \overset{\uparrow}{(n)}$$

$$= 1000 - 60$$

$$= \$940.$$

In the preceding, the interest rate was designated as d and is called the *bank discount rate*. This method is also called *interest deducted-in-advance* because the interest amount is deducted from the maturity value F before the proceeds P are given to the borrower.

> **Definition.** Proceeds: $P = F(1 - dn)$.

The example just completed shows that the borrower receives $940 but pays interest on the maturity value $1,000. If the borrower wants to receive proceeds of $P = \$1,000$, then

$$1000 = F\left[1 - 0.12\left(\frac{6}{12}\right)\right]$$
$$1000 = F(1 - 0.06)$$
$$1000 = 0.94F$$
$$\frac{1000}{0.94} = F$$
$$\$1,063.83 = F.$$

Thus, the borrower who wants $1,000 now will pay back $1,063.83 six months from now.

> **Exercise.** a) A borrower signs a note promising to pay a bank $5,000 ten months from now. How much will the borrower receive if the discount rate is 8.4 percent? b) How much would the borrower have to repay in order to receive $5,000 now? Answer: a) $4,650. b) $5,376.34.

Proceeds are an amount received now for repayment in the future, so they are analogous to present value, which was discussed in the last section. However, proceeds are not equal to present value because the proceeds from a future obligation to pay are always *less than* the present value of that obligation if, of course, the same rate of interest is used in both calculations. In general, proceeds should be computed when the interest rate is stated as a *discount rate* or a *bank discount* or *interest deducted-in-advance*, and present value should be computed where the interest rate is given without the qualifier, discount.

8.5 EFFECTIVE RATE: SIMPLE INTEREST

We have just seen the difference between the bank discount (proceeds) and the simple discount (present value). These two methods can be compared from an "effective" or "true" interest rate point of view. By the effective interest rate we mean the actual true simple interest rate for one year

> ### Effective Interest Rate
>
> $$i_e = \frac{\text{Interest amount for one year}}{\text{Amount borrower receives}}.$$

In the simple discount (present value) example of Section 8.3, we had $F = \$530$, $i = 8\%$, $n = 9/12$, and computed $P = \$500$. So the interest amount for one year is

$$(530 - 500)\frac{12}{9} = (30)\frac{4}{3}$$
$$= \$40.00,$$

and

$$i_e = \frac{40}{500} = 0.08,$$

or 8 percent. It will always be the case with the simple discount that $i_e = i$. Why? Because the interest amount is charged against the actual amount (present value)

$$i_e = \frac{(P)(i)(1 \text{ year})}{P}$$
$$= \frac{Pi}{P}$$
$$= i.$$

Thus, *the effective interest rate for a simple discount (present value) transaction is precisely the quoted rate.*

On the other hand, for the bank discount (proceeds) example of Section 8.4, we had $F = \$1{,}000$, $d = 12\%$, $n = 6/12$, and computed $P = \$940$. Here the interest for one year is

$$(1000 - 940)\frac{12}{6} = (60)(2)$$
$$= \$120.00,$$

and

$$i_e = \frac{120}{940} = 0.1277,$$

or 12.77 percent. This is more than the quoted rate of 12 percent, and this will always be the case. Why? Because here the interest amount is charged against the amount to be paid back (maturity value), not the actual amount received (proceeds). Writing i_e as a function of F, d, and n, we have

$$i_e = \frac{(F)(d)(1 \text{ year})}{F(1 - dn)}$$

$$i_e = \frac{Fd}{F(1 - dn)}$$

$$i_e = \frac{d}{1 - dn}. \tag{1}$$

Exercise.   a) Find the present value and effective rate of $1,000 due in 4 months at 12 percent interest. b) Find the proceeds and effective rate of $1,000 due in 4 months at 12 percent interest. Answer: a) $961.54, 12%. b) $960.00, 12.5%.

An interesting application of (1) occurs when a lender wishes to determine the discount rate d that should be quoted in order to receive a desired effective rate i_e. Solving (1) for d, we have

$$i_e = \frac{d}{1 - dn}$$

$$i_e(1 - dn) = d$$

$$i_e - i_e dn = d$$

$$i_e = d + i_e dn$$

$$i_e = d(1 + i_e n)$$

$$d = \frac{i_e}{1 + i_e n}. \tag{2}$$

Returning to our example where $F = \$1,000$ and $n = \frac{6}{12}$, if the lender only wants to earn 12 percent true interest, then from (2) the discount rate should be

$$d = \frac{0.12}{1 + (0.12)(6/12)}$$

$$= 0.1132,$$

or 11.32 percent.

Exercise.   Suppose a lender wishes to earn 15 percent true interest on a 4-month transaction using interest deducted-in-advance. What discount rate should be quoted?   Answer: 14.29 percent.

8.6 PROBLEM SET 8–1

In Problems 1 through 10, find a) the interest and b) the amount for each of the principals for the stated simple interest rate and time period:

1. $500; 7 percent; 1 year.
2. $1,000; 8 percent; 1 year.
3. $1,000; 9 percent; 6 months.
4. $2,000; 6 percent; 6 months.
5. $100; 36 percent; 4 months.

6. $500; 24 percent; 3 months.
7. $200; 12 percent; 18 months.
8. $500; 18 percent; 16 months.
9. $5,000; 24 percent; 3 years.
10. $4,000; 30 percent; 2 years.

11. How many months will it take until the interest on $900 at 12 percent will be $135?

12. A credit card holder has owed the credit card company $200 for a month and receives a bill containing an interest charge of $3. Find the interest rate.

13. Compute the yield of New England Electric Company stock from the following stock market report.

    NEngE   1.92   24

14. How much must be deposited in an account paying 7 percent if interest of $100 is to be earned in 24 months?

In solving Problems 15 through 26, draw the associated time diagram.

15. How many months will it take at 8 percent interest for $2,000 to grow to an amount of $2,400?

16. Fran deposits $1,000 in an employees' savings account at 6 percent. How many months will it be until the amount in the account is $1,100?

17. Dan buys a TV set priced at $500 and is to pay this amount, plus interest, 3 months later. The total bill was $520. Compute the interest rate.

18. At what rate of interest will an investment of $1,000 for 2 years grow to the amount of $1,100?

19. Find the present value of $460 receivable 18 months from now if the interest rate is 10 percent.

20. Find the present value of $1,000 receivable 2 years from now if the interest rate is 8.5 percent.

21. How much will Sam have to invest now in an employees' savings account at 7 percent in order to have $1,000 in the account 18 months from now?

22. (See Problem 21.) How much would Sam have to invest if the interest rate was 10 percent?

23. Find the proceeds of a $2,000, 18-month loan from a bank if the discount rate is 12 percent.

24. Find the proceeds of a $500, 9-month loan from a bank if the discount rate is 9 percent.

25. Dan wants $2,000 now from a bank, to be repaid 18 months from now. How much will the repayment be if the discount rate is 15 percent?

26. Fran signs a note promising to pay a bank $1,000 ten months from now and receives $900. Find the discount rate.

27. Find the effective interest rate in Problem 23.

28. Find the effective interest rate in Problem 24.

8.6 PROBLEM SET 8–1 (concluded)

29. Find the effective interest rate in Problem 25.

30. What discount rate should a lender quote to earn 9 percent true interest on a 90-day transaction?

31. What discount rate should a lender quote to earn 11 percent true interest on a 6-month transaction?

32. What discount rate should a lender quote to earn 15 percent true interest on a 9-month transaction?

33. Run the computer program in Section 8.2 for Problems 1 through 10.

34. Run the computer program in Section 8.3 for Problems 19 through 22.

35. a) Modify the computer programs in Sections 8.2 and 8.3 into a single program that will compute any one of the four parameters F, P, i, and n, given the other three. Include a modification that will allow n to be entered directly in terms of days, months, or years.
    b) Run the program in (a) for Problems 1 through 10 and 15 through 22.

36. a) Modify the computer program in Problem 35(a) for the bank discount.
    b) Run the program in (a) for Problems 23 through 26.

37. a) Write a computer program to determine the effective interest rate for a quoted discount rate.
    b) Run the program in (a) for Problems 27 through 29.

38. a) Write a computer program to determine the quoted discount rate for a given effective rate.
    b) Run the program in (a) for Problems 30 through 32.

8.7 COMPOUND INTEREST AND THE FUTURE VALUE

To see how compound interest works and develop a formula for computing the future value, suppose $5,000 is invested at 10 percent interest compounded each year. The amount at the end of the first year would be

$$F_1 = 5000 + 5000(0.10)(1)$$
$$= 5000 + 500$$
$$= \$5,500.$$

This $5,500 becomes the principal at the beginning of the second year, and the amount at the end of the second year is

$$F_2 = 5500 + 5500(0.10)(1)$$
$$= 5500 + 550$$
$$= \$6,050.$$

Thus, in the second year, interest is earned on not only the $5,000 invested, but also on the $500 of interest earned in the first year. This common practice of computing interest on interest is called *compounding* interest.

To obtain a formula for computing the future value, we will again use *i as the interest rate per period*. It will suffice for the moment to think of the period as being a year, and we will adjust our formula accordingly later when the period is something other than a year.

> Definition. i = Interest rate per period.

Assuming, then, that the period is 1 year, a principal of $\$P$ will amount to

$$F_1 = P(1 + i)^1$$

at the end of the first year. At the beginning of the second year, $P(1 + i)$ becomes the new beginning principal, which is multiplied by $(1 + i)$ to find the future value at the end of the second year. Thus,

$$F_2 = P(1 + i)(1 + i) = P(1 + i)^2$$

after two years. At the beginning of the third year, the new principal is $P(1 + i)^2$, and to obtain the future value at the end of the third year, this must be multiplied by $(1 + i)$. Thus,

$$F_3 = P(1 + i)^2(1 + i) = P(1 + i)^3$$

after three years. Similarly, the future value at the end of 10 years would be

$$F_{10} = P(1 + i)^{10}$$

and, in general, at the end of n years, the future value will be

$$F_n = P(1 + i)^n.$$

Conventionally, the subscript n on F_n is not written.

> Definition. Future value: $F = P(1 + i)^n.$

This last expression is the *future value of $\$P$ for n periods at an interest rate of i per period.*

Example. Find the future value of $\$1,000$ at 7 percent per year for 10 years.

We have

$$\begin{aligned}
F &= 1000(1 + 0.07)^{10} \\
&= 1000(1.07)^{10} \\
&= 1000(1.96715) \\
&= \$1,967.15.
\end{aligned}$$

The time diagram for this example is shown in Figure 8–4.

There are two ways to compute the answer to this example on a calculator. One way is to calculate $(1.07)^{10}$ and then multiply this by 1000, as shown in Table 8–3.

FIGURE 8–4

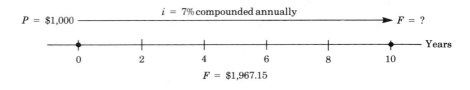

On the other hand, some calculators are preprogrammed with the financial functions, and then this example is solved as shown in Table 8–4.

For those who do not have a calculator with either option, values such as $(1.07)^{10}$ can be obtained from Table III at the back of the book. The title of this table is the *Compound Amount of $1*. The reader should verify that the entry for 7 percent, 10 periods, is 1.96715. This is the future value of $1, so the future value of $1,000 is 1000 times 1.96715.

> **Exercise.** If $500 is invested at 6 percent compounded annually, what will be the future value 30 years later? Answer: $2,871.75.

TABLE 8–3

Keystroke	Calculator Display
1.07	1.07
2nd, *then* y^x (or just y^x)	1.07
10	10
=	1.96715
×	1.96715
1000	1000
=	1967.15

TABLE 8–4

Keystroke	Calculator Display
1000, *then* PV	1000
7, *then* % i	7
10, *then* n	10
CPT, *then* FV	1967.15

TABLE 8–5

BASIC	PASCAL
| ```
10 REM FUTURE VALUE/COMPOUND INTEREST
20 INPUT "Enter P, i, and n";P,I,N
30 F=P*(1+I)^N
40 PRINT "Future Value F = ";
50 PRINT USING "$###,###.##";F
60 END

RUN

Enter P, i, and n? 1000,.07,10
Future Value F = $  1,967.15
``` | ```
program fut_val_comp_int(input,
  output);

  var
    p,f,i,n:real;
(* p=principal,f=future val,i=int.
   rate,n=# yrs. *)

begin

  writeln('Enter principal,interest
     rate,# years');
  readln(p,i,n);
  f:=p*exp(n*ln(1+i));
  writeln('Future Value F =$',f:8:2)
end.   (*program*)
$ run
Enter principal,interest rate,# years
1000 .07 10
Future Value F =$ 1967.15
``` |

Table 8–5 shows a BASIC and PASCAL program to compute the future value, along with the results of running the program for our example above.

8.8 THE CONVERSION PERIOD

Quoted interest rates are rates *per year* if not accompanied by a qualifying statement such as 1½ percent per month. In the absence of a qualifier, the quoted annual rate is called the *nominal* rate and it is symbolized by j.

> **Definition.** Nominal rate = Rate per year = j.

Although the quoted nominal rate is per year, it is common practice to compound interest more frequently than once a year. Many banks compound interest on savings accounts on a daily basis, or 365 times a year. In other transactions, interest is compounded monthly, quarterly, or semiannually as shown in Table 8–6.

TABLE 8–6

Conversion	Number of Conversions per Year, m
Daily	365
Monthly	12
Quarterly	4
Semiannually	2

> **Definition.** Number of conversions per year $= m$.

Example. Find the future value of $500 at 8 percent compounded quarterly for 10 years.

There are four quarters in one year and

$$4(10) = 40$$

quarters in 10 years. Thus we multiply the number of years by the number of conversions per year. We shall now use this number of periods (40 quarters) as n in the future value formula.

Next, inasmuch as the quoted 8 percent is a nominal or per-year rate, we divide 8 percent by the number of conversions per year to obtain

$$i = \frac{8\%}{4} = 2\% \text{ per period.}$$

Using a calculator or Table III, we then have

$$F = 500\left(1 + \frac{0.08}{4}\right)^{10(4)}$$
$$= 500(1.02)^{40}$$
$$= 500(2.208040)$$
$$= \$1,104.02.$$

On a calculator with preprogrammed financial functions, we would proceed as shown in Table 8–7.

TABLE 8–7

Keystroke	Calculator Display
500, *then* PV	500
8	8
÷	8
4	4
=, *then* % i	2
10	10
×	10
4	4
=, *then* n	40
CPT, *then* FV	1104.02

In summary, *when interest is compounded more often than once a year,* n is the total number of conversion periods, so that

$$n = \text{(Number of years)(Number of conversions per year)}$$

and

$$i = \frac{\text{Nominal rate per year}}{\text{Number of conversions per year}} = \frac{j}{m}.$$

Exercise. If $800 is invested at 6 percent compounded semi-annually, what will be the amount in 5 years? Answer: $1,075.13.

Example. Compute the future value of $5,000 at 9 percent compounded monthly for 10 years.

Here we have

$$n = \text{(10 years)(12 months per year)} = 120$$

and

$$i = \frac{0.09}{12}.$$

Hence,

$$F = 5000\left(1 + \frac{0.09}{12}\right)^{120}$$
$$= \$12,256.79.$$

Exercise. A bank pays 7.25 percent compounded daily on 90-day notice accounts. If $500 is deposited in such an account, what will be the amount in 90 days? (Use 365 days per year.) Answer: $509.02.

8.9 FINDING THE TIME

In the formula

$$F = P(1 + i)^n,$$

we can determine n if F, P, and i are given; that is, we can find how many periods it will take for P dollars deposited now at i percent to grow to an amount of F dollars.

Example. At 8 percent compounded annually, how many years will it take for $2,000 to grow to $3,000?

We have

$$3000 = 2000(1 + 0.08)^n$$
$$\frac{3000}{2000} = (1.08)^n$$
$$1.5 = (1.08)^n.$$

Taking the natural logarithm of both sides,

$$\ln 1.5 = \ln (1.08)^n = n(\ln 1.08).$$

Thus

$$\frac{\ln 1.5}{\ln 1.08} = n,$$
$$5.27 = n.$$

so n is a bit more than $5\frac{1}{4}$ years.

To solve the above example on a calculator, we would proceed as shown in Table 8–8. If the calculator has preprogrammed financial functions, then we would proceed as shown in Table 8–9.

TABLE 8–8

Keystroke	Calculator Display
1.5, *then* ln x	0.40547
÷	0.40547
1.08, *then* ln x	0.07696
=	5.26845

TABLE 8–9

Keystroke	Calculator Display
8, *then* %i	8
2000, *then* PV	2000
3000, *then* FV	3000
CPT, *then* n	5.26845

Exercise. Find how many years it will take at 9 percent compounded annually for $1,000 to grow to $2,000. Answer: About 8.04 years.

$$2000 = 1000(1.09)^N$$
$$2 = (1.09)^N$$

The next example illustrates how to determine an unknown interest rate.

Example. At what interest rate compounded annually will a sum of money double in 10 years?

Here, double means $100 grows to $200, $25 grows to $50, $1 grows to $2, and so on, and the time required is the same in any doubling. We shall use

$$P = \$1, \qquad F = \$2.$$

Hence, in

$$F = P(1 + i)^n$$

or

$$P(1 + i)^n = F$$

we have

$$(1)(1 + i)^{10} = 2$$
$$(1 + i)^{10} = 2.$$

Then, taking the natural logarithm of both sides,

$$\ln (1 + i)^{10} = \ln 2$$
$$10 \ln (1 + i) = \ln 2$$
$$\ln (1 + i) = \frac{\ln 2}{10}.$$

To obtain $(1 + i)$, we must take the antilogarithm of both sides. Thus,

$$1 + i = e^{(\ln 2)/10}$$
$$i = e^{(\ln 2)/10} - 1$$
$$= 1.0718 - 1$$
$$= 0.0718$$
$$i = 7.18\%.$$

To solve the above example on a calculator, we would proceed as shown in Table 8–10, which is precisely Table 7–5 of Section 7.9, repeated here for convenience. If the calculator has preprogrammed financial functions, then we would proceed as shown in Table 8–11.

Exercise. Find the rate of interest that, compounded annually, will result in tripling a sum of money in 10 years. Answer: 11.61 percent.

TABLE 8–10

Keystroke	Calculator Display
2, *then* ln x	0.69315
÷	0.69315
10	10
=	0.06931
2nd, *then* e^x	1.07177
−	1.07177
1	1
=	0.07177

TABLE 8–11

Keystroke	Calculator Display
1, *then* PV	*1*
2, *then* FV	*2*
10, *then* n	*10*
CPT, *then* % i	*7.177*

8.11 PROBLEM SET 8–2

In Problems 1 through 4, find the future value at the stated nominal interest rate compounded annually (once a year): (Compute by calculator or Table III.)

1. $200; 20 years; 5 percent.

2. $300; 10 years; 6 percent.

3. $400; 40 years; 8 percent.

4. $500; 15 years; 7 percent.

In Problems 5 through 8, find the future value using the appropriate interest rate and number of periods:

5. $150; 8 years; 8 percent compounded quarterly.

6. $250; 3 years; 12 percent compounded monthly.

7. $600; 20 years; 8 percent compounded semiannually.

8. $1,000; 10 years; 16 percent compounded quarterly.

9. How many years will it take at 7 percent compounded annually for $5,000 to amount to $20,000?

10. How many years will it take for a sum of money to double at 10 percent compounded annually?

11. Find the rate of interest compounded annually at which a sum of money will double in 20 years.

12. Find the rate of interest compounded semiannually at which $5,000 will grow to $12,000 in 8 years.

8.11 PROBLEM SET 8–2 (concluded)

Solve Problems 13 through 16 using a calculator:

13. A bank pays 5.25 percent compounded daily on certificate accounts running for 6 years. Using 365 days per year, compute the future value of a deposit of $5,000 for 6 years.

14. A bank pays 5.25 percent compounded daily on certain accounts. Find the future value of a deposit of $2,000 for 45 days.

15. How many years will it take at 9 percent compounded annually for $5,000 to grow to $10,000?

16. At what rate of interest compounded annually will $1,000 grow to $5,000 in 10 years?

17. Run the computer program in Section 8.7 for Problems 1 through 4.

18. a) Modify the computer program in Section 8.7 so that it will compute any one of the three parameters F, i, and n, given P and the other two parameters.

b) Run the program in (a) for Problems 5 through 16.
c) Modify the program in (a) so that you can enter j and m into the program instead of i and n.
d) Run the program in (c) for Problems 5 through 16.

8.12 COMPOUND DISCOUNT: PRESENT VALUE

Dividing both sides of the future value formula

$$F = P(1 + i)^n$$

by $(1 + i)^n$ leads to

$$\frac{F}{(1 + i)^n} = P \quad \text{or} \quad P = \frac{F}{(1 + i)^n}$$

By the definition of a negative exponent,

$$P = \frac{F}{(1 + i)^n} = F(1 + i)^{-n}.$$

> **Definition.** Present value: $P = F(1 + i)^{-n}$
> Compound discount factor $= (1 + i)^{-n}$.

Values of the compound discount factor are available in Table IV, which has the title *Present Value of $1*. In this, as in all the financial tables, the tabular entry is multiplied by the number of dollars specified in the problem at hand. On a calculator, of course, it is as easy to divide by $(1 + i)^n$ as it is to multiply by $(1 + i)^{-n}$, but multiplication is easier for handwork without a calculator.

Example. What is the present value of $2,500 payable four years from now at 8 percent compounded quarterly?

Here, the amount four years hence is $F = \$2,500$. With quarterly compounding,

$$n = (4 \text{ periods per year})(4 \text{ years}) = 16 \text{ periods.}$$

$$i = \frac{0.08}{4} = 0.02.$$

Therefore,

$$P = 2500(1 + 0.02)^{-16}$$
$$= 2500(0.728446),$$

where 0.728446 is the compound discount factor taken from Table IV. Multiplication gives

$$P = \$1,821.115.$$

There is no generally applied rule for rounding a monetary number to the last cent, and we shall follow the practice of rounding a digit up when the next digit is 5 or more. Thus,

$$P = \$1,821.12.$$

A calculator shows the last result is, more accurately, $\$1,821.1145$, which would round to $\$1,821.11$.

On a calculator with preprogrammed financial functions, we would proceed as shown in Table 8–12.

Exercise.   What is the present value of $4,000 payable in 20 years at 8 percent compounded semiannually?   Answer: $833.16.

Example. How much must be deposited now in an account paying 7.3 percent compounded daily in order to have just enough in the account 3 years from now to make $10,000 available for investment in a business enterprise?

With one day as a period,

$$n = (365 \text{ days per year})(3 \text{ years}) = 1,095 \text{ periods}$$

and

$$i = \frac{0.073 \text{ per year}}{365 \text{ conversions per year}}.$$

Hence,

$$P = 10,000\left(1 + \frac{0.073}{365}\right)^{-1095}$$
$$= \$8,033.39.$$

TABLE 8–12

Keystroke	Calculator Display
2500, *then* FV	2500
4	4
×	4
4	4
=, *then n*	16
8	8
÷	8
4	4
=, *then* % *i*	2
CPT, *then* PV	1821.11

Exercise. How much must be deposited now in an account paying 8 percent compounded monthly in order to have just enough in the account 5 years from now to make a $10,000 down payment on a home? Answer: $6,712.10.

Table 8–13 shows a BASIC and PASCAL program to compute the present value, along with the results of running the program for our first example of this section. Notice that the BASIC computer result is not as

TABLE 8–13

BASIC	PASCAL
| ```
10 REM PRESENT VALUE/COMPOUND INTEREST
20 INPUT "Enter F, i, and n";F,I,N
30 P=F*(1+I)^(-N)
40 PRINT "Present Value P = ";
50 PRINT USING "$###,###.##";P
60 END

RUN

Enter F, i, and n? 2500,.02,16
Present Value P = $  1,821.12
``` | ```
program pres_val_comp_int(input,
  output);

  var
     p,f,i,n:real;
(* f=future val,i=int. rate,n=#
  yrs. *)

begin

  writeln('Enter future value,
     interest rate,# years');
  readln(f,i,n);
  p:=f*exp((-n)*ln(1+i));
  writeln('Present Value P =$',p:8:2)
end. (*program*)
$ run
Enter future value,interest rate,
  # years
2500 .02 16
Present Value P =$ 1821.11
``` |

accurate as the PASCAL computer result, or as accurate as the calculator result in Table 8–12. Why? Recall from Section 7.11 our earlier explanation of the difference in accuracy between a calculator and a computer.

8.13 PROBLEM SET 8–3

In Problems 1 through 8, compute the present value using a calculator or Table IV.

1. $1,000 at 8 percent compounded annually, due in 20 years.

2. $2,000 at 7 percent compounded annually, due in 10 years.

3. $5,000 at 10 percent compounded semi-annually, due in 5 years.

4. $4,000 at 12 percent compounded monthly, due in 3 years.

5. What sum of money deposited now at 8 percent compounded quarterly will provide just enough money to pay a $1,000 debt due 7 years from now?

6. What sum of money invested now at 12 percent compounded monthly will provide just enough to pay a debt of $2,500 due in 3 years?

7. If output per manhour increases by 5 percent compounded annually and is currently 100 units per manhour, what was output per manhour 5 years ago?

8. An account bearing interest at 6 percent compounded semiannually was established 10 years ago. The account balance now is $9,030.55. What was the initial amount when the account was established?

Solve Problems 9 and 10 using a calculator.

9. Find the present value of $1,000 due in 2 years at 8 percent compounded daily. (365 days in a year.)

10. Find the present value of $2,000 due in 10 years at 9 percent compounded monthly.

11. Run the computer program in Section 8.12 for Problems 1 and 2.

12. a) Modify the computer program in Problem 18 of Problem Set 8–2 (Section 8.11) so

that it will compute any one of the four parameters F, P, i, and n, given the other three.

b) Run the program in (a) for Problems 3 through 10.

8.14 EFFECTIVE RATE: COMPOUND INTEREST

Because of lack of comparability, it is hard to judge whether interest quoted at 8 percent compounded semiannually results in more or less interest than would be the case if the rate was 7.9 percent compounded monthly. To make the comparison possible, we change both to their equivalent annual rates; these equivalents are called *effective* rates as in Section 8.5. For example, $1 at 8 percent compounded quarterly for *one* year would amount to

$$F = 1\left(1 + \frac{0.08}{4}\right)^4$$

$$= (1.02)^4$$
$$= 1.08243,$$

which is the same as the amount of $1 at a rate of 0.08243, or 8.243 percent for one year. Similarly, by calculator, $1 at 7.9 percent compounded monthly for *one* year would amount to

$$F = 1\left(1 + \frac{0.079}{12}\right)^{12}$$
$$= 1.08192,$$

which is equivalent to the amount of $1 at a rate of 8.192 percent for one year.

In general, at nominal (annual) rate j compounded m times a year, $1 grows to

$$F = (1)(1 + i)^m, \quad i = \frac{j}{m},$$

in one year. At the *effective* rate, r_e, $1 grows to

$$F = 1 + r_e$$

in a year. Hence,

$$1 + r_e = (1 + i)^m$$
$$r_e = (1 + i)^m - 1.$$

Effective Rate of i Compounded m Times a Year

$$r_e = (1 + i)^m - 1; \quad i = \frac{j}{m}.$$

Example. Find the effective rate of 24 percent compounded monthly.

Here, as usual,

$$i = \frac{24\%}{12} = 2\%$$
$$m = 12 \text{ months in a year.}$$

Consequently,

$$r_e = (1 + 0.02)^{12} - 1$$
$$= 1.26824 - 1$$
$$= 0.26824$$
$$= 26.824\%.$$

Table III provides

$$(1 + i)^m$$

for some values of i and, of course, this power can be found easily on a calculator for any i and m in common use.

> **Exercise.** Find the effective rate of 16 percent compounded quarterly.   Answer: 16.99%.

Example. Find the effective rate of 12 percent compounded annually, semiannually, quarterly, monthly, semimonthly, weekly, and daily.

In this case,

$$i = \frac{12\%}{m},$$

where $m = 1, 2, 4, 12, 24, 52,$ and 365. The results for

$$r_e = (1 + i)^m - 1$$

are shown in Table 8–14. Note that r_e increases as m increases, but the amount of increase in r_e is gradually diminishing, especially after $m = 12$. What do you think will happen if we compounded by the hour, minute, or second? More will be said about this in Section 8.16.

TABLE 8–14

m	1	2	4	12	24	52	365
r_e	12%	12.36%	12.551%	12.683%	12.716%	12.734%	12.747%

> **Exercise.** Find the effective rate of 15 percent compounded annually, semiannually, quarterly, monthly, semimonthly, weekly, and daily.   Answer: 15%, 15.563%, 15.865%, 16.075%, 16.129%, 16.158%, 16.180%.

8.15 PROBLEM SET 8–4

In Problems 1 through 10, find the effective interest rate using a table or a calculator.

1. 8 percent, compounded quarterly.

2. 10 percent, compounded semiannually.

3. 12 percent, compounded monthly.

4. 16 percent, compounded quarterly.

5. 10 percent, compounded monthly.

6. 7 percent, compounded quarterly.

7. 18 percent, compounded monthly.

8. 9 percent, compounded quarterly.

8.15 PROBLEM SET 8–4 (*concluded*)

9. 9 percent, compounded monthly.

10. 9 percent, compounded daily (365 days).

Solve Problems 11 and 12 using a calculator.

11. Find the effective rate of 11 percent compounded annually, semiannually, quarterly, monthly, semimonthly, weekly, and daily.

12. Find the effective rate of 14 percent compounded annually, semiannually, quarterly, monthly, semimonthly, weekly, and daily.

13. a) Write a computer program that will compute the effective rate of interest.

b) Run the program in (a) for Problems 1 through 12.

8.16 CONTINUOUS (INSTANTANEOUS) COMPOUNDING

Before the appearance of modern high-speed data processing computers, calculation and recording of interest for even a few thousand bank accounts was too costly in time to be done at frequent intervals. Consequently, the common practice was to compound quarterly—once every three months—and depositors who withdrew money from their accounts between interest dates did not receive interest for the time between the last interest calculation and the date of withdrawal. Now, with high-speed computers, it is possible to calculate and add interest whenever any account transaction takes place. A common practice currently is to compute interest from the day of deposit to the day of withdrawal, with interest compounded daily. The number of compoundings in a year would then be 365, or 366 for a leap year. However, as stated in Section 8.2, banks may, for convenience, count a year as twelve 30-day months, 360 days for a year.

We start on our way toward continuous, or instantaneous, compounding by recalling the number e, which is the base of the system of natural logarithms (Chapter 7). This constant, like the constant π, has an unending sequence of digits and therefore cannot be expressed exactly by any finite sequence of digits. However, e can be expressed as accurately as needed for any applied problem. To twelve decimal places,

$$e = 2.7182\ 8182\ 8459^{+}.$$

The value of e can be computed to any desired degree of accuracy by calculating

$$\left(1 + \frac{1}{m}\right)^{m}$$

using a *sufficiently large* value of m. For example, with $m = 200{,}000$

$$\left(1 + \frac{1}{200{,}000}\right)^{200{,}000} = 2.7182\ 8182\ 8,$$

which is e correct to eight decimal places. The important point to note is that the expression

$$\left(1 + \frac{1}{m}\right)^m$$

can be interpreted as the future value, F, of \$1 at 100 percent interest ($i = 1.00$) for one year, compounded m times a year. Thus, for example, \$1 at 100 percent compounded monthly for a year would yield

$$F = 1\left(1 + \frac{1}{12}\right)^{12} = \$2.61.$$

This is illustrated in Figure 8–5, which shows 12 discrete points (that is, separated points) representing the 12 compoundings that make \$1 at 100 percent grow to \$2.61 in a year.

If we compound \$1 at 100 percent for a year with daily compoundings, $m = 365$ and

$$F = 1\left(1 + \frac{1}{m}\right)^m = 1\left(1 + \frac{1}{365}\right)^{365} = \$2.71,$$

as shown in Figure 8–6, which has a discrete set of 365 points representing the daily compoundings. Note that in the result, \$2.71, we have the first two decimal digits of e. Note also that the discrete set of 365 points is beginning to look like a *continuous* line; that is a line drawn without lifting the pencil from the paper. Now, going one step further, suppose we compound every hour for a year so that

$$m = (365 \text{ days})(24 \text{ hours per day}) = 8760.$$

Then

$$F = \left(1 + \frac{1}{m}\right)^m = \left(1 + \frac{1}{8760}\right)^{8760} = 2.7181,$$

a result that has the first four decimal digits of e. It might be possible with the aid of a magnifying glass and a very sharp point to make a figure like Figure 8–6 showing these 8,760 compoundings, but if the magnifying glass were removed, the result would appear to be a continuous line without gaps, but the set of points is discrete, and the gaps are there.

To approach the core concept of instantaneous compounding, we now contemplate compounding every minute ($m = 525,600$ compoundings per year), every second ($m = 31,536,000$ compoundings a year), and so on, with the duration of the compounding period getting smaller and the number of compounding points increasing. There is no limit to the number of compounding periods but, as it grows, the duration of a period approaches *zero*, and this leads us to the concept of a *point* in time of zero duration, which is connoted by the word *instant*. The nature of time in the real world forces us to attach meaning to a point in time—an instant—because, for example, the time from 9 A.M. to 11 A.M. goes

FIGURE 8–5

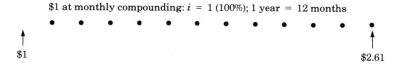

$1 at monthly compounding: $i = 1$ (100%); 1 year = 12 months

$1 $2.61

FIGURE 8–6

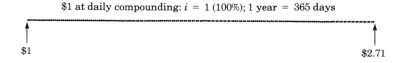

$1 at daily compounding: $i = 1$ (100%); 1 year = 365 days

$1 $2.71

FIGURE 8–7

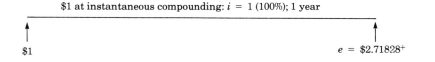

$1 at instantaneous compounding: $i = 1$ (100%); 1 year

$1 $e = \$2.71828^{+}$

through all times in the interval, and at some point the time must be precisely 10 o'clock. We cannot, of course, mark a clock dial in instants. However, real time does not progress in discrete jumps—it is *continuous*. A real time line, then, is not a discrete set of points, but a continuous line with no gaps. It is a line we represent on paper by drawing a pencil along a straight edge without removing the pencil from the paper, as shown on Figure 8–7, which represents instantaneous compounding. As this figure shows, instantaneous compounding of $1 at 100 percent for one year yields a compound amount of $e. For present purposes, we state that *the sequence of digits generated by calculating*

$$\left(1 + \frac{1}{m}\right)^{m}$$

using larger and larger values of m becomes closer and closer to the sequence of digits representing e. Of course, the letter m is arbitrary, and we can say equally well that e is generated by

$$\left(1 + \frac{1}{x}\right)^{x} \qquad \text{or} \qquad \left(1 + \frac{1}{p}\right)^{p}$$

as x, on the left, or p, on the right, becomes larger and larger.

We have demonstrated that $1 at 100 percent for one year, compounded continuously (instantaneously), yields e. If we have $1 at nominal rate j per year for t years, the future value is

$$F = 1e^{jt}.$$

as shown in the footnote.[1] If $P rather than $1 is the principal, we have:

Future Value with Continuous Compounding

$$F = Pe^{jt}$$

Note: We shall use the symbol t to denote a number of years. This number can be a fraction or a decimal. We do this to distinguish t from n because n has been defined to be a *whole* number of periods.

Example. Find the future value of $500 at 8 percent compounded continuously for 9 years and 3 months.

Remembering that t is the number of years, we find

$$t = 9 + \frac{3}{12} = 9.25 \text{ years.}$$

Hence,

$$\begin{aligned} F &= 500e^{0.08(9.25)} \\ &= 500e^{0.74} \\ &= \$1,047.97. \end{aligned}$$

Exercise. Find the amount of $200 at 6 percent compounded continuously for 30 months. Answer: $232.37.

---

[1] The compound amount of $1 at rate j compounded m times a year for t years is

$$\left(1 + \frac{j}{m}\right)^{mt}. \tag{1}$$

Now let $p = m/j$ so that $j/m = 1/p$ and $m = pj$, and substitute these into (1), giving

$$\left(1 + \frac{1}{p}\right)^{pjt} = \left[\left(1 + \frac{1}{p}\right)^{p}\right]^{jt} \tag{2}$$

Now as m becomes larger and larger, p, which is m/j, becomes larger and larger, the bracketed expression in (2) generates e, and we obtain e^{jt}.

If both sides of the formula

$$F = Pe^{jt}$$

are divided by the exponential term, we have

$$\frac{F}{e^{jt}} = P,$$

or, using the negative exponent,

$$Fe^{-jt} = P.$$

This is the present value, P, of a future amount, F.

Present Value with Continuous Compounding

$$P = Fe^{-jt}$$

Exercise. How much must be deposited now in an account earning 7.5 percent compounded continuously if the amount in the account 8 years from now is to be $10,000? Answer: $5,488.12.

8.17 EFFECTIVE RATE: CONTINUOUS COMPOUNDING

At a nominal rate $j = 0.08$, $1 compounded continuously for one year amounts to

$$F = e^{0.08} = 1.0833,$$

so the interest earned is

$$1.0833 - 1 = 0.0833 \text{ or } 8.33\%.$$

In general,

Effective Rate of Nominal Rate j

$$r_e = e^j - 1.$$

Exercise. Find the effective rate of 10 percent compounded continuously. Answer: 10.52 percent.

Current banking practice. There are legal limits on the interest rates banks can offer for various types of accounts. In the last decade, these limits have not compared favorably with interest rates that can be obtained from non-bank investments and, in an effort to attract more deposits, some banks have adopted not only the ultimate in compounding, continuous compounding, but also the *modified* year. Although banks customarily use a 360-day year, they sometimes give the investor the advantage of the full 365-day year by using the multiplier,

$$\frac{365}{360}$$

which is greater than one. For example, we might read a newspaper advertisement that states that the effective rate on 8 percent is 8.45 percent. To obtain this result, we replace the exponent in

$$e^{0.08} - 1$$

by

$$\frac{365}{360}(0.08) \quad \text{or} \quad 0.08111$$

to obtain

$$r_e = e^{0.08111} - 1$$
$$= 1.08449 - 1$$
$$= 0.08449.$$

The last number, rounded, is 0.0845, or 8.45 percent.

Exercise.   Using the modified year, what is the effective rate of 6 percent compounded continuously?   Answer: 6.27 percent.

In passing, we note that going from daily to continuous compounding contributes very little to interest earned, but the modified year makes a significant contribution when large sums of money are involved. *We shall use one year as t = 1 unless specifically instructed to use the modified year.*

We return now to the nominal rate j compounded continuously, for which the effective rate is

$$r_e = e^j - 1.$$

If we solve this for j we have the nominal rate, which, compounded continuously, yields a *given* effective rate, r_e. Rearranging the terms of the last equation, we have

$$e^j = 1 + r_e.$$

Taking the natural logarithm of both sides,

$$\ln e^j = \ln (1 + r_e).$$

By the power rule of logarithms,

$$j\ln e = \ln (1 + r_e),$$

where $\ln e = 1$. Hence,

Continuous j Equivalent of r_e Effective

$$j = \ln (1 + r_e).$$

Example. A bank states that the effective interest on savings accounts that earn continuous interest is 7 percent. Find the nominal rate.

Here,

$$r_e = 0.07,$$

so

$$j = \ln (1 + r_e)$$
$$= \ln (1.07)$$
$$= 0.06766$$

or 6.766%.

Exercise. What nominal rate compounded continuously gives an effective rate of 8 percent? Answer: 7.696 percent.

8.18 PROBLEM SET 8–5

Note: Problems 1 through 20 can be solved by table or calculator.
In Problems 1 through 4, find the future value if interest is compounded continuously:

1. $1,000; 6 percent; 5 years.
2. $500; 8 percent; 10 years.
3. $5,000; 8 percent; 4 years and 6 months.
4. $4,000; 6 percent; 5 years and 8 months.

In Problems 5 through 8, find the present value if interest is compounded continuously:

5. $800; 8.5 percent; due in 10 years.
6. $2,500; 9.5 percent; due in 12 years.
7. $1,000; 12 percent; due in 9 months.
8. $3,000; 10 percent; due in 18 months.

8.18 PROBLEM SET 8–5 (*concluded*)

The rates in Problem 9 through 12 are nominal rates. Find the effective rate if interest is compounded continuously:

9. $j = 0.05$.   **11.** $j = 0.07$.

10. $j = 0.06$.   **12.** $j = 0.08$.

What nominal rate compounded continuously will yield the effective rates in Problems 13 through 16?

13. $r_e = 0.12$.   **15.** $r_e = 0.05$.

14. $r_e = 0.09$.   **16.** $r_e = 0.10$.

In Problems 17 through 25, use continuous compounding:

17. How much will a deposit of $5,000 grow to in 20 years at 6.8 percent interest compounded continuously?

18. How much should be deposited now at 8.4 percent compounded continuously if the amount in the account 10 years from now is to be $10,000?

19. Sam invests $10,000 in a bank account paying 7.6 percent compounded continuously for 15 years. How much will the account amount to at the end of this time?

20. How much must be deposited now in an account paying 7.5 percent interest compounded continuously if the amount in the account 6 years from now is to be $7,500?

Solve Problems 21 through 25 using a calculator.

21. History tells us that Peter Minuit purchased Manhattan Island in New York from the Indians for $24 about 360 years ago. If the $24 had been invested at 5 percent compounded continuously, what would be its amount after 360 years?

22. How much should be deposited now in an account paying 7.6 percent compounded continuously if the account is to grow to $10,000 in 8 years?

23. What is the effective rate of 7.9 percent compounded continuously?

24. What nominal rate compounded continuously will yield an effective rate of 8.22 percent?

25. A bank offers 7.6 percent compounded continuously and uses the modified year. Find the effective rate.

8.19 ORDINARY ANNUITIES: FUTURE VALUE

An *ordinary* annuity is a series of equal periodic payments in which each payment is made at the *end* of the period. In our work we shall use the following symbols:

n = Number of periods
i = Interest rate per period
R = Payment per period
F = Future value of the annuity.

FIGURE 8–8

Figure 8–8 illustrates the ordinary annuity. Here we see that the first payment of $R accumulates interest for $n - 1$ periods, the second payment R for $n - 2$ periods, etc. The next-to-last payment R accumulates one period of interest, and the last payment R accumulates no interest. So using the future value formula for compound interest from Section 8.7, we set the future value of the annuity:

$$F = R(1 + i)^{n-1} + R(1 + i)^{n-2} + \cdots + R(1 + i)^1 + R. \qquad (1)$$

To simplify (1), we multiply both sides by $(1 + i)$ to get

$$F(1 + i) = R(1 + i)^n + R(1 + i)^{n-1} + \cdots + R(1 + i)^2 + R(1 + i). \qquad (2)$$

Next we subtract (1) from (2),

$$
\begin{aligned}
F(1 + i) - F &= [R(1 + i)^n + R(1 + i)^{n-1} + \cdots + R(1 + i)] \\
&\quad - [R(1 + i)^{n-1} + \cdots + R(1 + i) + R] \\
&= R(1 + i)^n - R.
\end{aligned}
$$

This last operation becomes

$$F + Fi - F = R(1 + i)^n - R$$

or

$$Fi = R(1 + i)^n - R,$$

which gives us

Future Value of Ordinary Annuity

$$F = R\left[\frac{(1 + i)^n - 1}{i}\right]. \qquad (3)$$

Formula (3) is often abbreviated to

$$F = Rs_{\overline{n}|i}$$

by defining $s_{\overline{n}|i}$ as the bracketed quantity. Table V at the back of the book entitled *Amount of $1 per Period* provides values of $s_{\overline{n}|i}$. To apply the table when the payment is R per period, we multiply the appropriate entry by R. Of course, these values can also be computed on a calculator or by means of preprogrammed financial functions on a calculator.

Example. If $100 is deposited in an account at the end of every quarter for the next 5 years, how much will be in the account at the time of the final deposit if interest is 8 percent compounded quarterly?

We have

$$n = (5 \text{ years})(4 \text{ quarters per year}) = 20 \text{ periods},$$
which means 20 quarterly payments.

$$i = \frac{8\%}{4} = 2\%$$

$$R = \$100.$$

From Table V, with $i = 2\%$, $n = 20$, we find that $1 per period would amount to $24.29737. Hence, with $R = \$100$ per period

$$F = 100(24.29737) = \$2,429.74.$$

Observe that 20 payments of $100 each amount to $2,000. The $2,429.74 amount in this $2,000 plus interest for varying lengths of time on all payments except the last one.

On a calculator with preprogrammed financial functions, we would proceed as shown in Table 8–15.

TABLE 8–15

Keystroke	Calculator Display
100, *then* PMT	100
8	8
÷	8
4	4
= , *then* %i	2
5	5
×	5
4	4
= , *then* n	20
CPT, *then* FV	2429.74

Exercise. Sums of $500 are deposited in an account at the end of each 6-month period for 8 years. Find the amount in the account after the last deposit has been made if interest is earned at the rate of 10 percent compounded semiannually. Answer: $11,828.75.

Example. If $100 is deposited in an account each month for 10 years and the account earns 7 percent compounded monthly, how much will be in the account after the last deposit is made?

We have

$$n = 10 \text{ years } (12 \text{ months per year}) = 120 \text{ periods}$$
$$r = \frac{0.07}{12}$$
$$R = \$100.$$

Hence,

$$F = 100\left[\frac{(1 + 0.07/12)^{120} - 1}{0.07/12}\right]$$
$$= \$17{,}308.48.$$

Exercise. Sums of $500 are deposited in an account at the end of each 6-month period for 25 years. Find the amount in the account after the last deposit is made if interest is computed at 6 percent compounded semiannually. Answer: $56,398.43.

8.20 ORDINARY ANNUITIES: SINKING FUND

A sinking fund is a fund into which periodic payments are made in order to accumulate a specified amount at some point in the future. For example, a corporation that obtains money needed to expand by selling $1 million worth of bonds payable in 10 years must pay interest to bond holders (usually semiannually) while the bonds mature and, at maturity 10 years later, pay $1 million to redeem the bonds. To be sure that the $1 million is available 10 years hence, the corporation may set up a sinking fund to accumulate this amount. The problem is to determine R, the required periodic payment into the sinking fund. The n payments constitute an ordinary annuity of R per period, and the known future value of this annuity is

$$F = Rs_{\overline{n}|i}.$$

Solving this for the unknown periodic payment R, we have

$$R = \frac{F}{s_{\overline{n}|i}} = F\left(\frac{1}{s_{\overline{n}|i}}\right)$$
$$= F\left[\frac{1}{\dfrac{(1 + i)^n - 1}{i}}\right].$$

Inverting the simple fraction in the denominator, and multiplying this by the numerator, 1, we have

> **Sinking Fund Payment**
>
> $$R = F\left(\frac{1}{s_{\overline{n}|i}}\right) = F\left[\frac{i}{(1 + i)^n - 1}\right].$$

Table VIII at the back of the book, entitled *Per-Period Equivalent of $1 Future Value*, provides values for $1/s_{\overline{n}|i}$.

Example. How much should be deposited in a sinking fund at the end of each quarter for 5 years to accumulate $10,000 if the fund earns 8 percent compounded quarterly?

Table VIII, for

$$i = \frac{8\%}{4} = 2\%$$

$$n = (5 \text{ years})(4 \text{ quarters per year}) = 20 \text{ periods}$$

shows

$$\frac{1}{s_{\overline{n}|i}} = 0.0411567.$$

Hence,

$$R = 10,000(0.0411567) = \$411.567.$$

Thus, the quarterly payment is, rounded, $411.57. Over the life of the sinking fund, the sum of the deposits will be

$$20(411.567) = \$8,231.34.$$

This sum, plus interest earned, will provide the desired $10,000.

On a calculator with preprogrammed financial functions, we would proceed as shown in Table 8–16.

TABLE 8–16

Keystroke	Calculator Display
10000, *then* FV	10000
8	8
÷	8
4	4
=, *then* %i	2
5	5
×	5
4	4
=, *then* n	20
CPT, *then* PMT	411.57

Exercise. Instead of creating a sinking fund at a bank, a company has its controller create a reserve fund in the company's accounts to which a contribution is made each quarter. By so doing, the company can realize a return of 12 percent compounded quarterly. What should be the amount transferred quarterly to the reserve fund to accumulate $10,000 in 5 years?   Answer: $372.16.

Example. A company wants to accumulate $100,000 to purchase replacement machinery eight years from now. To accomplish this, equal semiannual payments are made to a fund that earns 7 percent compounded semiannually. Find the amount of each payment.

We have

$$F = 100{,}000$$
$$i = \frac{0.07}{2} = 0.035$$
$$n = 8(2) = 16.$$

From

$$R = F\left[\frac{i}{(1 + i)^n - 1}\right]$$

we have

$$R = 100{,}000\left[\frac{0.035}{(1.035)^{16} - 1}\right]$$
$$= \$4{,}768.48.$$

Exercise. A company issues $1 million of bonds and sets up a sinking fund at 8 percent compounded quarterly to accumulate $1 million 15 years hence to redeem the bonds. Find the quarterly payment to the sinking fund.   Answer: $8,767.97.

8.21 PROBLEM SET 8–6

Find the future value of the ordinary annuities in Problems 1 through 4:

1. $500 per month for 3 years at 12 percent compounded monthly.

2. $1,000 every 3 months for 10 years at 8 percent compounded quarterly.

3. $2,000 per year for 20 years at 7 percent compounded annually.

4. $2,500 a year for 34 years at 8 percent compounded annually.

8.21 PROBLEM SET 8–6 (concluded)

5. When Kathy was born, her parents decided to deposit $500 every 6 months thereafter for 15 years in an account earning 6 percent compounded semiannually. How much will be in the account after the last deposit is made?

6. Greg has $100 deducted from his salary at the end of each month and invested in an employees' fund that, because of company contributions, pays 12 percent interest compounded monthly. How much will Greg's account amount to when he retires 3 years from now after receiving his last salary check?

7. What amount should be deposited at the end of each quarter in a sinking fund earning 8 percent compounded quarterly if the amount in the fund after 4 years is to be $90,000?

8. What amount should be deposited at the end of each six-month period in a sinking fund earning 6 percent compounded semiannually if the amount in the fund after 15 years is to be $75,000?

9. New Venture Corporation has decided to transfer a sum of money to a reserve account at the end of each year to accumulate $100,000 to be used to replace machinery 10 years from now. How much should be transferred each year if interest at 8 percent compounded annually is credited to the reserve?

10. The Joneses are going to deposit a sum of money at the end of each six-month period in an account earning 8 percent compounded semiannually in order to accumulate $15,000 for a down payment on a home 8 years from now. What should be the amount of each deposit?

Solve Problems 11 and 12 using a calculator:

11. Find the future value of an ordinary annuity of $1,000 per quarter for 25 years at 8 percent compounded quarterly.

12. Septech Corporation has issued $10 million worth of bonds to obtain money now for expanding its corporate activities. To redeem the bonds, which fall due in 30 years, Septech will transfer an amount to a reserve fund at the end of each six-month period. How much should be transferred if the account earns 7 percent compounded semiannually?

---

13. a) Write a computer program that will compute the future value F of an ordinary annuity given R, i, and n. (Hint: Refer to the program in Section 8.7.)
    b) Run the program in (a) for Problems 1 through 6, and 11.

14. a) Modify the program in Problem 13(a) to print out the period-by-period amounts under the headings Period, Current Balance, Interest, Payment, New Balance.

15. a) Write a computer program that will compute the sinking fund payment R of an ordinary annuity given F, i, and n. (Hint: Refer to Problem 13a.)
    b) Run the program in (a) for Problems 7 through 10, and 12.

16. a) Modify the program in Problem 15(a) to print out the period-by-period amounts under the headings Period, Present Fund, Interest, Payment, Accumulated Fund, Sinking Fund.

8.22 ORDINARY ANNUITIES: PRESENT VALUE

We have learned earlier that the present value of any amount due n periods from now is found by multiplying the amount by the compound discount factor,

$$(1 + i)^{-n}.$$

If we multiply the future amount of an annuity of $1 per period, $s_{\overline{n}|i}$, by the compound discount factor we have the present value of an annuity of $1 per period, which is symbolized by $a_{\overline{n}|i}$. Hence,

$$a_{\overline{n}|i} = s_{\overline{n}|i}(1 + i)^{-n}$$

$$= \left[\frac{(1 + i)^n - 1}{i} \right](1 + i)^{-n}$$

$$= \left[\frac{(1 + i)^n(1 + i)^{-n} - 1(1 + i)^{-n}}{i} \right]$$

$$= \left[\frac{(1 + i)^0 - (1 + i)^{-n}}{i} \right]$$

$$= \left[\frac{1 - (1 + i)^{-n}}{i} \right].$$

Values for $a_{\overline{n}|i}$ are given in Table VI, entitled *Present Value of $1 per Period*, at the back of the book. The present value P of an ordinary annuity of R per period is R times the tabular entry.

Present Value of Ordinary Annuity

$$P = R\left[\frac{1 - (1 + i)^{-n}}{i} \right].$$

Present value annuity calculations arise when we wish to determine what lump sum must be deposited in an account now if this sum and the interest it earns are to provide equal payments for a stated number of periods, with the last payment making the account balance zero.

Example. What sum deposited now in an account earning 8 percent interest compounded quarterly will provide quarterly payments of $1,000 for 10 years, the first payment to be made 3 months from now?

Here we have

$$n = (10 \text{ years})(4 \text{ quarters per year}) = 40$$

$$i = \frac{8\%}{4} = 2\%$$

$$a_{\overline{40}|2} = 27.35548 \text{ (from Table VI)}.$$

Hence,

$$P = 1000(27.35548) = \$27,355.48.$$

On a calculator with preprogrammed financial functions, we would proceed as shown in Table 8–17.

TABLE 8–17

Keystroke	Calculator Display
1000, *then* PMT	1000
8	8
÷	8
4	4
=, *then* %*i*	2
10	10
×	10
4	4
=, *then* n	40
CPT, *then* PV	27355.48

Exercise. a) A sum of money invested now at 10 percent compounded semiannually is to provide payments of $1,500 every 6 months for 8 years, the first payment due 6 months from now. How much should be invested? b) How much interest will the investment earn?   Answer: a) $16,256.65 b) $7,743.35.

Example. a) The directors of a company have voted to establish a fund that will pay a retiring accountant, or his estate, $1,000 per month for the next 10 years, the first payment to be made a month from now. How much should be placed in the fund if it earns interest at 7 percent compounded monthly? b) How much interest will the fund earn during its existence?

Here, for part (a)

$$n = (10 \text{ years})(12 \text{ months per year}) = 120$$
$$i = \frac{0.07}{12}$$
$$R = 1000.$$

Hence,

$$P = 1000 \left[\frac{1 - (1 + 0.07/12)^{-120}}{0.07/12} \right]$$

$$= \$86,126.35.$$

For part (b) we have

$$(120 \text{ payments})(\$1,000 \text{ per payment}) = \$120,000.$$
$$\text{Interest earned} = \$120,000 - \$86,126.35 = \$33,873.65.$$

Exercise. Answer (a) and (b) of the last example if the interest rate is 8 percent compounded monthly. Answer: a) $82,421.48. b) $37,578.52.

8.23 ORDINARY ANNUITIES: AMORTIZATION

In many financial transactions, a current obligation is discharged by making a series of payments in the future. After the last payment, the obligation ceases to exist—it is dead—and it is said to have been *amortized* by the payments. Prominent examples of amortization are loans taken to buy a home or a car and amortized over a period of 20 to 30 years in the case of a home mortgage and over 2, 3, or 4 years in the case of a car purchase loan. Given the amount of the loan (the current principal, P), the number of periods (n), and the interest rate (i), the quantity to be calculated is R, the amount of the periodic payment. The n payments of R dollars each constitute an ordinary annuity whose present value is P, and we have learned that P is R times the present value of an annuity of $1, which is $a_{\overline{n}|i}$. Therefore,

$$P = Ra_{\overline{n}|i}.$$

Solving this for the unknown R, we have

$$R = \frac{P}{a_{\overline{n}|i}} = P\left(\frac{1}{a_{\overline{n}|i}}\right).$$

Therefore, to find the periodic payment needed to amortize a debt of P, we need only to divide P by $a_{\overline{n}|i}$, or multiply by $1/a_{\overline{n}|i}$, the reciprocal of $a_{\overline{n}|i}$. The complete formula for the amortization payment is

$$R = \frac{P}{a_{\overline{n}|i}} = \frac{P}{\left[\dfrac{1 - (1 + i)^{-n}}{i} \right]}.$$

The denominator on the right is a simple fraction, so we may invert it and multiply by the numerator to obtain

Amortization Payment

$$R = P\left[\frac{i}{1 - (1 + i)^{-n}}\right] = P\left(\frac{1}{a_{\overline{n}|i}}\right).$$

Values of $1/a_{\overline{n}|i}$ are provided in Table VII, entitled *Per-Period Equivalent of \$1 Present Value*, at the back of the book.

Example. Sam borrowed \$5,000 to buy a car. He will amortize the loan by monthly payments of \$R each over a period of 3 years. a) Find the monthly payment if interest is 12 percent compounded monthly. b) Find the total amount Sam will pay.

For part (a) we have

$$P = 5000$$
$$n = (3 \text{ years})(12 \text{ months per year}) = 36$$
$$i = \frac{12\%}{12} = 1\% \text{ per month.}$$

From Table VII with $i = 1\%$, $n = 36$, we find $1/a_{\overline{n}|i}$ is 0.033214. Hence,

$$R = 5000(0.033214) = \$166.07.$$

b) Sam pays \$166.07 a month for 36 months. The total paid will be

$$36(166.07) = \$5,978.52,$$

of which \$978.52 is interest.

On a calculator with preprogrammed financial functions, we would proceed as shown in Table 8–18.

TABLE 8–18

Keystroke	Calculator Display
5000, *then* PV	5000
12	12
÷	12
12	12
=, *then* %i	1
3	3
×	3
12	12
=, *then* n	36
CPT, *then* PMT	166.07

> **Exercise.** (See the preceding example.) Sam paid for his car, but more than once was late in making payments because of financial reverses, one being an accident that badly damaged the car. He now wishes to buy another car and receives a 3-year loan for $5,000, but the interest charge is 24 percent compounded monthly. a) What will Sam's monthly payment be for the new car? b) How much interest will he pay on this loan? Answer: a) $196.17 from Table VII; by calculator, $196.16. b) $2,062.12; by calculator, $2,061.91.

Example. A company has borrowed $50,000 at 10 percent compounded quarterly. The debt is to be amortized by equal payments each quarter over 15 years. a) Find the quarterly payment. b) How much interest will be paid?

a) We have $P = 50,000$, $i = 0.10/4$, and $n = 15(4) = 60$. Hence,

$$R = 50,000 \left[\frac{0.10/4}{1 - (1 + 0.10/4)^{-60}} \right]$$

$$= \$1,617.67 \text{ per quarter.}$$

b) Payments for 60 quarters will be

$$60(1617.6698) = \$97,060.19.$$

Interest paid will be

$$\$97,060.19 - \$50,000 = \$47,060.19.$$

> **Exercise.** A real estate developer borrows $100,000 at 12 percent compounded monthly. The debt is to be discharged by monthly payments for the next 6 years. a) Find the monthly payment. b) How much interest will be paid? Answer: a) $1,955.02. b) $40,761.44.

Mortgage payments. In a typical home purchase transaction, the homebuyer pays part of the cost in cash and borrows the remainder needed, usually from a bank or a savings and loan institution. As security for the loan, the lending agency ordinarily obtains conditional title to the property, a *mortgage*. The buyer amortizes the indebtedness by periodic payments over a period of time. Typically, payments are monthly and the time period is long—30 years is not unusual. A mortgage loan at 11.5 percent monthly for 30 years means

$$n = (12)(30) = 360 \text{ periods,}$$

$$i = \frac{11.5\%}{12} = \frac{0.115}{12} = 0.009\,583\,333\,333.$$

Because large sums of money are involved, amortization calculations require carrying 10 or more digits. Consequently, tables for $1/a_{\overline{n}|i}$ for varying interest rates and mortgage durations are too lengthy to include in this book. We have, however, provided entries for selected rates and durations in Table IX at the back of the book.

Example. A $70,000 home is to be purchased by paying $10,000 in cash and a $60,000 mortgage for 30 years at 9.75 percent compounded monthly. a) Find the monthly payment on the mortgage. b) What will be the total amount of interest paid?

In Table IX, all entries have been computed for monthly compounding, so it is not necessary to calculate the rate per period. We simply enter the table at the nominal rate $j = 9.75$ percent,

$$n = 30 \text{ years}(12 \text{ months per year}) = 360 \text{ months}$$

and find

$$0.008\,591\,5441.$$

a) For a principal amount of $60,000, the monthly payment is

$$R = 60{,}000(0.008\,591\,5441) = \$515.49265,$$

or, rounded, $515.49 per month. A calculator will give the same result.
b) The total amount paid in 360 months will be

$$360(515.49265) = \$185{,}577.35.$$

Interest paid will be

$$\$185{,}577.55 - \$60{,}000 = \$125{,}577.35.$$

The amount of interest just calculated is very large, but it must be remembered that the buyer has a home to live in for 30 years and, moreover, real estate values have risen, and are predicted to continue to rise as time goes on. If the experience of the past 30 years is repeated, the value of the home when the mortgage has been paid off could easily be three times its purchase cost.

Exercise. A manufacturer has a 15-year, 8.5 percent, mortgage for $100,000 on a building. Payments are made monthly. a) Find the monthly payment. b) How much interest will be paid? Answer: a) $984.74. b) $77,253.12.

Amortization schedules. When a debt is amortized, part of each payment is interest on the balance outstanding, and the remainder is used to reduce the balance outstanding. The largest interest charge occurs at the first payment because then interest is due on the entire principal and, of course, the smallest reduction of principal occurs at the time of the first payment. To see how this works, recall the $60,000, 9.75 percent, 30-year mortgage of the last example. The monthly payment is $515.49. At the time the first payment is due, one month has passed and the interest on the $60,000 is

$$I = 60,000(0.0975)\left(\frac{1}{12}\right) = \$487.50.$$

The amount applied to reduce the balance outstanding is

$$\$515.49 - \$487.50 = \$27.99,$$

so the new balance is

$$\$60,000 - \$27.99 = \$59,972.01.$$

It is clear that the first payment is almost entirely absorbed by the interest charge, with little left to reduce the balance still owed. Each month, of course, the interest charge decreases and the reduction of the amount owed increases. However, in financial jargon, early payments do not increase the homeowner's equity very much.

Continuing to the second payment, the beginning balance is now $59,972.01, and we proceed as follows:

Beginning balance owed		$59,972.01
Payment	$515.49	
Interest charge $(59,972.01)(.0975)\left(\frac{1}{12}\right)$:	487.27	
Reduction of balance owed	28.22	28.22
Ending balance owed		$59,943.79

When the process just described is repeated for the entire period of the loan (360 months for the example) and the results tabulated, the table is called an *amortization schedule*. The process is simple, but it must be repeated many times, and the chore is best left to a computer that can be programmed to do the process once and then instructed to repeat it over and over again, printing out a line of entries in an amortization schedule at the end of each repetition.

> **Exercise.** For the $100,000, 15-year, 8.5 percent mortgage of the last exercise, the monthly payment is $984.74. For the first and second payments, find the a) Interest charge. b) Reduction in balance owed. c) Ending balance owed. Answer: First month: a) $708.33. b) $276.41. c) $99,729.59. Second month: a) $706.42. b) $278.32. c) $99,451.27.

8.24 PROBLEM SET 8–7

Find the present value of the ordinary annuities in Problems 1 through 4:

1. $400 every three months for five years at 8 percent compounded quarterly.

2. $1,000 per month for three years at 12 percent compounded monthly.

3. $2,000 every six months for 18 years at 8 percent compounded semiannually.

4. $1,000 every year for 40 years at 6 percent compounded annually.

5. A company offers its salespeople a bonus of $500 per quarter for 3 years. To win a bonus, a salesperson must have sold at least $1 million worth of the company's products in the period January 1 through December 31, and the first bonus payment is made at the end of the first quarter following. The company funds each bonus on December 31 by a lump-sum deposit in a bank account that pays 8 percent compounded quarterly, and the bank sends out the bonus checks. a) What total sum is received by each bonus winner? b) How much does it cost the company to fund each bonus?

6. A college alumni club has decided to establish a scholarship fund that will provide grants of $5,000 a year for 25 years, the first grants to be made a year from now. a) What should be the sum placed in the fund if interest on it is earned at the rate of 8 percent compounded annually? b) What is the total amount of scholarship aid the fund will provide over its life?

7. What payment at the end of each month for two years will discharge a current debt of $1,000 if the interest charge on the debt balance at any time is 12 percent compounded monthly?

8. What payment at the end of each six-month period for 10 years will discharge a current debt of $2,500 if the interest charge on the debt balance is 10 percent compounded semiannually?

9. A company borrows $100,000 at 12 percent compounded semiannually. The debt is amortized by making equal payments at the end of each 6 months for 7 years.
   a) Find the amount of each payment.
   b) How much of the first payment is for interest, and by how much does it reduce the balance owed?
   c) How much of the second payment is for interest, and by how much does it reduce the balance owed?

10. Fran borrowed $6,000 at 24 percent compounded monthly to buy a car. The debt is to be discharged by equal payments at the end of each month for 3 years.
    a) Find the amount of each payment.
    b) How much of the first payment is for interest, and by how much does it reduce the balance owed?
    c) How much of the second payment is for interest, and by how much does it reduce the balance owed?

8.24 PROBLEM SET 8-7 (concluded)

11. First Realty Development Corporation has taken out a $1,500,000, 25-year mortgage on its new office building, with interest at 9 percent compounded monthly.
   a) Find the monthly payment.
   b) How much of the first payment is for interest, and by how much does it reduce the balance owed?

12. The Smiths have taken out a $35,000, 30-year mortgage on their home, with interest at 8.75 percent compounded monthly.
   a) Find the monthly payment.
   b) How much of the first payment is for interest, and by how much does it reduce the balance owed?

Solve Problems 13 and 14 using a calculator:

13. Find the present value of an ordinary annuity of $1,000 per month for 10 years at 7 percent compounded monthly.

14. New Venture Corporation has borrowed

$5,000,000 at 7 percent compounded semi-annually. The debt is discharged by equal payments at the end of each six-month period for 30 years. Find the amount of each payment.

15. a) Write a computer program that will compute the present value P of an ordinary annuity given R, i, and n. (Hint: Refer to the program in Section 8.12.)
   b) Run the program in (a) for Problems 1 through 6, and 13.

16. a) Write a computer program that will compute the amortization payment R of an ordinary annuity given P, i, and n. (Hint: Refer to Problem 15a.)

   b) Run the program in (a) for Problems 7 through 12, and 14.

17. a) Modify the program in Problem 16(a) to print out the period-by-period amounts under the headings Period, Current Balance, Interest, Payment, Principal, New Balance.
   b) Run the program in (a) for Problems 7 through 12, and 14.

8.25 SUMMARY OF FINANCIAL RULES

The purpose of this section and the subsequent problem set is to provide guidance in identifying the type of problem at hand and the proper rule or rules to be selected to solve the problem. We shall use time diagrams to analyze problems, and you are encouraged to do the same.

Example. How much money should be deposited now in an account earning 8 percent compounded quarterly if the amount in the account 10 years from now is to be $10,000?

The time diagram, Figure 8-9, demonstrates that the $10,000 is a *future value*, and the unknown amount, P, is the present value of the future amount. A calculator or Table IV gives

$$P = 10{,}000\left[1 + \frac{0.08}{4}\right]^{-40} = \$4{,}528.90.$$

FIGURE 8–9

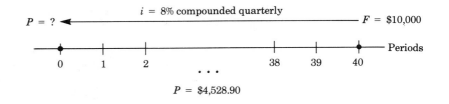

$i = 8\%$ compounded quarterly

$P = \,?$ $F = \$10,000$

Periods

0   1   2   . . .   38   39   40

$P = \$4,528.90$

Example. How much will be accumulated at the end of 10 years by depositing $1,000 at the end of each six-month period in an account paying 6 percent compounded semiannually?

Figure 8–10 shows the given $1,000 deposits at the end of each six-month period, with the unknown future value, F, at the end of 10 years. Thus, using a calculator or Table V,

$$F = 1000\left[\frac{(1 + 0.06/2)^{20} - 1}{0.06/2}\right] = \$26,870.37.$$

FIGURE 8–10

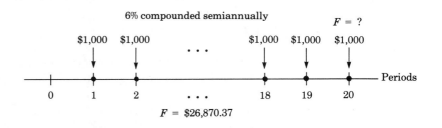

6% compounded semiannually

$F = \,?$

$1,000 $1,000   . . . $1,000 $1,000 $1,000

Periods

0   1   2   . . .   18   19   20

$F = \$26,870.37$

Example. Ms. Smith borrows $5,000 from a bank at 12 percent compounded monthly and promises to discharge the debt by equal payments at the end of each month for 3 years. Find the amount of each payment.

Figure 8–11 shows the present debt is $5,000, and the R payments are the per-period equivalent of the $5,000 plus interest. So, a calculator or Table VII gives

$$R = 5000\left[\frac{0.12/12}{1 - (1 + 0.12/12)^{-36}}\right] = \$166.07.$$

FIGURE 8–11

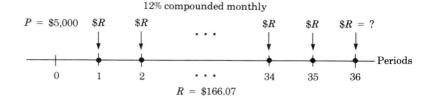

Example. Sue will start college six months from now, and her parents have decided to establish a bank account now to provide $2,500 every six months for tuition payments. If eight tuition payments are to be made and the account earns 6 percent compounded semiannually, how much should be deposited?

Figure 8–12 shows the unknown deposit, P, to be made now, is the present value of $2,500 per period. Thus, a calculator or Table VI results in

$$P = 2500\left[\frac{1 - (1 + 0.06/2)^{-8}}{0.06/2}\right] = \$17,\!549.23.$$

FIGURE 8–12

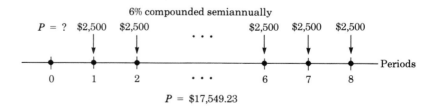

Example. If the gross national product now is $1,683.5 billion and is growing at the compound annual rate of 6 percent, what will the GNP be 20 years from now?

Figure 8–13 shows that we want the future value of the single value, $1,683.5 billion. We have, from a calculator or Table III,

$$F = 1683.5(1 + 0.06)^{20} = \$5,\!399.2 \text{ billion.}$$

FIGURE 8–13

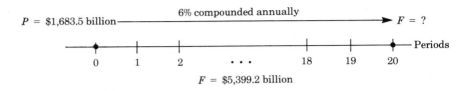

P = \$1,683.5 billion ——— 6% compounded annually ———→ F = ?

0   1   2 $\cdots$ 18   19   20 — Periods

F = \$5,399.2 billion

Example. Sam plans to buy a new car 2 years from now and decides to accumulate \$3,000 to help pay for it by having a deduction made from his monthly salary at the end of each month and deposited in an employees' savings account that, because of employer contributions, earns 12 percent interest compounded monthly. How much will be deducted each month?

Figure 8–14 shows the amount Sam desires as a future value. The periodic payment, $R, needed to accumulate this amount is the per-period equivalent of \$3,000 future value. A calculator or Table VIII gives

$$R = 3000 \left[\frac{0.12/12}{(1 + 0.12/12)^{24} - 1} \right] = \$111.22.$$

FIGURE 8–14

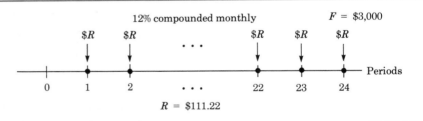

12% compounded monthly F = \$3,000

$R $R $\cdots$ $R $R $R

0   1   2 $\cdots$ 22   23   24 — Periods

R = \$111.22

8.26 MULTISTEP PROBLEMS

The solution of a problem may require more than one step and involve more than one interest rate, as illustrated by the following examples.

Example. Sam wants to determine how much he should deposit in a retirement account now at 8 percent compounded quarterly so that the amount in the account 10 years from now will provide an income of \$5,000 every 6 months for 12 years, with the first \$5,000 to be received in 10½ years. Sam estimates that 10 years from now he should be able to earn 6 percent compounded semiannually on the account when it is used to provide his semiannual income of $5,000. How much should Sam deposit now?

Figure 8–15 shows the structure of the problem. Sam's goal is to have $\$P_1$ in his account at the point shown, where P_1 must be the then present value of $5,000 per period. Applying a calculator or Table VI, we find

$$P_1 = 5000\left[\frac{1 - (1 + 0.06/2)^{-24}}{0.06/2}\right] = \$84,677.71,$$

as shown in the lower portion of Figure 8–15. The current deposit now, at time zero, is the present value of $\$P_1$. Hence, from a calculator or Table IV,

$$P = 84,677.71(1 + 0.08/4)^{-40} = \$38,349.72,$$

as shown in the upper portion of Figure 8–15.

FIGURE 8–15

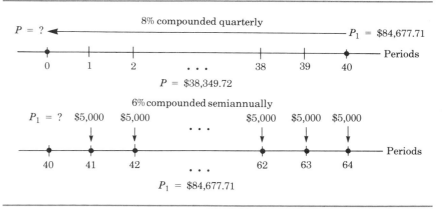

The previous example was an illustration of a *deferred annuity;* that is, an annuity purchased now with the annuity payments being deferred so that they start at a time later than would be the case for an ordinary annuity.

Example. Fran borrows $2,000 from Silverbank and signs a note promising to discharge the debt with interest at 12 percent compounded monthly at a maturity date two years from now. Six months later, Silverbank needed more cash and sold Fran's note to Goldbank. Goldbank computed the maturity amount of Fran's note, and gave Silverbank the present value of this amount, computed at 8 percent compounded quarterly. How much did Silverbank receive?

Figure 8–16 shows the structure of the problem. The maturity value of

---

FIGURE 8–16

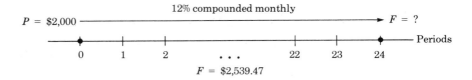

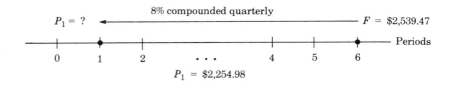

the note, F, is the future value of $2,000, which, using a calculator or Table III, is

$$F = 2000\left(1 + \frac{0.12}{12}\right)^{24} = \$2,539.47.$$

When Goldbank buys the note, it still has 1½ years or 6 quarters until maturity. Thus the amount Silverbank receives, P_1, is the present value of $F = \$2,539.47$, which, using a calculator or Table IV, is

$$P_1 = 2539.47\left(1 + \frac{0.08}{4}\right)^{-6} = \$2,254.98.$$

The previous example illustrated the *compound discounting of a note.* Simple interest calculations are frequently used to discount notes, but we shall not use simple interest in this section.

Example. Sam wishes to provide himself, or his estate, with an income of $5,000 every 6 months, starting 15½ years from now and continuing for 20 years. He deposits $25,000 in the account now, and he has a guaranteed inheritance of $10,000, which he will receive 10 years from now and add to the account. He knows these sums will not provide the income he wants, so he plans to make periodic deposits to the account at the end of every 6 months for 15 years to make up the difference. How much should the periodic deposits be if all interest is computed at 6 percent compounded semiannually?

Figure 8–17 brings all amounts back to time zero. There, from diagram (a), Sam has available $P_1 = \$25,000$ plus the present value, P_2, of the $10,000 inheritance, which is

$$P_2 = 10,000\left(1 + \frac{0.06}{2}\right)^{-20} = \$5,536.76.$$

FIGURE 8–17

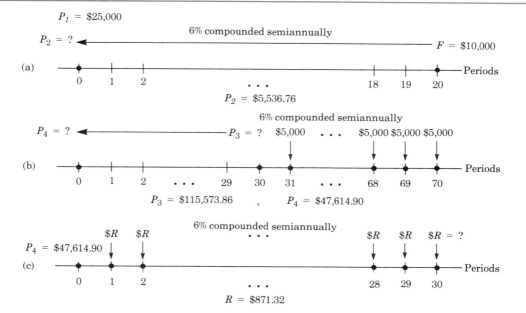

Thus the total amount available so far is $P_1 + P_2 = \$30{,}536.76$. Now from diagram (b), the deferred annuity Sam wants to establish has a principal of $\$P_3$, and it is an annuity of \$5,000 for 20 years at 6 percent compounded semiannually. Hence,

$$P_3 = 5000\left[\frac{1 - (1 + 0.06/2)^{-40}}{0.06/2}\right] = \$115{,}573.86.$$

The present value P_4, then, of $\$P_3$ is the amount Sam needs. This is

$$P_4 = 115{,}573.86\left(1 + \frac{0.06}{2}\right)^{-30} = \$47{,}614.90,$$

as shown in diagram (b). The annuity Sam must provide by his additional payments to the account must make up the difference between the amount needed and the amount available, which is

$$\$47{,}614.90 - \$30{,}536.76 = \$17{,}078.14.$$

Consequently, as shown in diagram (c), Sam needs to know the per-period equivalent of \$17,078.14 present value for 15 years at 6 percent compounded semiannually

$$R = 17{,}078.14\left[\frac{0.06/2}{1 - (1 + 0.06/2)^{-30}}\right] = \$871.32.$$

Hence, Sam should deposit \$871.32 to the account every 6 months for the next 15 years.

8.27 PROBLEM SET 8–8

Solve the following by use of a calculator or the appropriate tables at the back of the book. All periodic payments are in the form of ordinary annuities:

1. If $100 is deposited at the end of every 6 months for 5 years at 6 percent compounded semiannually, what will be the amount in the account after the last deposit?

2. Sue borrowed $7,000 at 12 percent compounded monthly for 3 years to buy a car. How much will she have to pay at the end of each month to discharge the debt?

3. At 8 percent compounded quarterly, what will be the amount of a current deposit of $5,000 in 10 years?

4. How much should be deposited at the end of each year to an account earning 8 percent compounded annually in order to accumulate $10,000 at the time of the last deposit 9 years from now?

5. What sum of money deposited now at 8 percent compounded annually will grow to $10,000 in 20 years?

6. How much should be deposited now at 7 percent compounded annually to provide an income of $20,000 at the end of each year for the next 22 years?

7. The population of a town now is 52,000. Population five years ago is unknown, but it is estimated that population has increased at the rate of 6 percent compounded annually. Estimate the population 5 years ago.

8. Sam borrowed $4,000 at 24 percent compounded monthly to pay for construction of a garage. The debt is to be discharged by payments at the end of each month for 30 months. Find the amount of the monthly payment.

9. Jill has $250 taken from her salary at the end of each quarter and deposited in an employees' fund that earns 8 percent compounded quarterly. What will be the amount in the account after the last deposit is made 5 years from now?

10. The board of directors of a company has voted to establish a fund that will provide a retiring executive with an income of $5,000 at the end of each quarter for 10 years. The fund will be invested in the company, which earns 12 percent compounded quarterly. Find the amount that should be invested.

11. The real estate tax on a piece of property now is $2,000 per year. If taxes increase at the rate of 5 percent compounded annually, what will the tax on this property be 10 years from now?

12. Sam wants to accumulate $10,000 for a down payment on a home 8 years from now. He will do this by making a deposit at the end of each quarter in an account earning 8 percent compounded quarterly. How much should he deposit each quarter?

13. A note for $3,000 with interest at 12 percent compounded monthly is payable 40 months from now. Find the (then present) value of the note 19 months from now if this value is computed at 8 percent compounded quarterly.

14. Sue has purchased $20,000 worth of securities earning 10 percent compounded semiannually. Ten years from now, she plans to use the securities and interest to establish an account earning 7 percent compounded annually, and to exhaust this account by equal withdrawals at the end of each year for 5 years. How much will each withdrawal be?

15. How much should be deposited now at 8 percent compounded semiannually to make possible equal withdrawals of $5,000 at the end of each year for 5 years, the first withdrawal to be made 10 years from now. Interest during the withdrawal period is to be 7 percent compounded annually.

8.27 PROBLEM SET 8–8 (concluded)

16. Nine years from now, Sam wants to have an amount available to deposit to an account that earns 6 percent compounded annually. This account is to provide Sam with an income of $10,000 at the end of each year for 10 years. To accomplish this, Sam invests in an 8-year bank certificate that pays 8 percent compounded semiannually, and he will use this certificate, plus its interest, to establish his income account. What should the principal value of the certificate be?

17. Fran will make 20 equal semiannual deposits to an account earning 8 percent compounded semiannually then, after the last deposit, she will use the amount in the account to establish an ordinary annuity earning 6 percent compounded annually which will provide her with $10,000 at the end of each year for 5 years. How much should Fran's semiannual deposit be?

18. During a three-year period when his business was prospering, Jack was able to deposit $1,000 at the end of each month in an account earning 12 percent compounded monthly. The business slackened, and Jack could not continue the deposits. Moreover, the interest rate on his accumulated deposits fell to 8 percent compounded quarterly and remained at this level for 10 years, at which time Jack decided to exhaust the account by withdrawing equal amounts at the end of every 6 months for 5 years. The interest rate remained at 8 percent compounded semiannually over the time of the withdrawals. How much did Jack withdraw every 6 months?

19. (All interest rates are 7 percent compounded annually.) Jill wishes to provide herself, or her estate, an income of $10,000 at the end of each year for 10 years. She will make a lump sum deposit when the account is established and add $3,000 at the end of each year for 12 years. The income is to start at the end of the year following the year in which the last deposit was made. Compute the lump sum deposit.

8.28 FINDING THE INTEREST RATE AND TIME: ORDINARY ANNUITIES

An unknown interest rate i can be approximated by interpolation in the periodic payment tables, or by calculator. However, the annuity formulas cannot be solved for i, and so a precise value is not easily attainable. The annuity formulas also cannot be solved for an unknown time n, and in this case, interpolation is not even useful. We prefer not to burden the reader with the interpolation approach. Rather, we will show how a calculator with preprogrammed financial functions can be used to determine an unknown interest rate or an unknown time.

Example. Sam purchased a piece of property by making a down payment and signing an agreement to pay the remaining amount, $5,000, by making equal year-end payments of $700 for 10 years. Find the rate of annually compounded interest that Sam is paying.

In this example, we know that $700 is the per-period equivalent of the $5,000 plus interest at an unknown interest rate i. So we proceed as shown in Table 8–19. From this table, we see that the desired interest rate is $i = 6.64\%$.

TABLE 8–19

Keystroke	Calculator Display
5000, *then* PV	5000
700, *then* PMT	700
10, *then* n	10
CPT, *then* %i	6.637

Exercise.   At what interest rate, compounded semiannually, will an ordinary annuity of $100 per year amount to $2,500 in 8 years? Answer: 11.35%.

The next example illustrates how to compute an unknown time.

Example. Mary bought a new sports car for $26,000. She was able to put 10 percent down and wanted to finance the rest with payments of $500 per month. If she is charged 12 percent interest, how many payments must she make?

Mary is putting down 10 percent of $26,000,

$$(0.10)(26,000) = \$2,600,$$

and so her balance will be

$$\$26,000 - \$2,600 = \$23,400.$$

So she has to make a series of $500 payments every month at 12 percent interest (1 percent per month) until the $23,400 is amortized. From Table 8–20, we see that the desired number of payments n turns out to be 63.426 periods or months. What does this mean? One interpretation is 63 payments of $500 each, and then a final or 64th payment equal to 0.426 times $500 for a total of

$$(63)(500) + (0.426)(500) = 31,500 + 213$$
$$= \$31,713.$$

TABLE 8–20

Keystroke	Calculator Display
23400, *then* PV	23400
500, *then* PMT	500
1, *then* %i	1
CPT, *then* n	63.426

> **Exercise.** George buys a chalet in the mountains for $250,000. He puts 20 percent down and finances the balance with payments of $3,000 per month at 15 percent interest. How many payments does he make? What is the total amount paid to the nearest dollar? Answer: 145. $432,704.

8.29 ORDINARY ANNUITIES: CONTINUOUS COMPOUNDING

In this section we shall present without development the continuous compounding counterparts of the formulas developed earlier in the chapter for periodic compounding. Table 8–21 contains the formulas for periodic payments of $R each, where payment is made at the end of the period, and between payments the amount in the account is compounded continuously.

TABLE 8–21
Continuous compounding formulas
(t = number of years; j = nominal rate; m = number of periods per year)

Quantity	Formula
1. Amount of $R per period	$F = R\left[\dfrac{e^{jt} - 1}{e^{j/m} - 1}\right]$
2. Per-period equivalent of $F future value	$R = F\left[\dfrac{e^{j/m} - 1}{e^{jt} - 1}\right]$
3. Present value of $R per period	$P = R\left[\dfrac{1 - e^{-jt}}{e^{j/m} - 1}\right]$
4. Per-period equivalent of $P present value	$R = P\left[\dfrac{e^{j/m} - 1}{1 - e^{-jt}}\right]$

Example. How much must be deposited at the end of each quarter for 5 years at 8 percent compounded continuously to accumulate $10,000 at the time of the last deposit?

Here we have to find the per-period equivalent of $10,000 future value, so Formula 2 of Table 8–21 applies with $t = 5$, $j = 0.08$, $m = 4$, and $F = 10,000$.

$$\frac{j}{m} = \frac{0.08}{4} = 0.02; \quad jt = 0.08(5) = 0.4.$$

Substituting into Formula 2 yields

$$R = 10,000\left[\frac{e^{0.02} - 1}{e^{0.4} - 1}\right]$$
$$= \$410.74.$$

> **Exercise.** How much should be deposited now at 6 percent compounded continuously to provide payments of $2,000 at the end of each 6 months for 8 years? Answer: (Formula 3 of Table 8–21). $25,035.13.

8.30 PROBLEM SET 8–9

Solve Problems 1 through 16 using a table or a calculator.

1. At what rate of interest compounded annually will payments of $2,000 at the end of each year for 8 years amount to $20,000?

2. At what rate of interest compounded annually will $50,000 be accumulated by payments of $2,000 at the end of each year for 15 years?

3. At what rate of interest will a principal of $20,000 provide payments of $2,000 at the end of each year for 20 years?

4. At what rate of interest compounded annually will $5,000 payments at the end of each year for 11 years be provided by a principal investment now of $40,000?

5. Joan deposits $500 in her savings account at the end of every 6 months until she has $5,800. If she is getting 12 percent interest compounded semiannually, how many deposits will she make? What will be the amount of her last deposit?

6. Chris wants to accumulate $10,000 and is able to put $300 into his credit union monthly. If he is getting 15 percent interest compounded monthly, how long will it take him? What is his last contribution?

7. Nick has a chance to buy a new power boat for $14,000. His uncle, who owns the boat, has agreed to allow Nick to pay $600 per month and will charge him 10 percent interest compounded monthly. How many payments will Nick make? What is the total amount paid to the nearest dollar?

8. Rita wants to buy a vacation condominium for $75,000. She is able to put 10 percent down and wants to pay $800 per month to amortize the balance. If she is charged 11 percent interest compounded monthly, how many payments will she make? What is the total amount paid to the nearest dollar?

In Problems 9 through 20, use continuous compounding:

9. Sam deposits $500 at the end of each six months for 10 years in an account earning 6 percent. How much will be in the account after the last payment?

10. Bill wants to accumulate $5,000 to buy a boat 5 years from now by making deposits at the end of each quarter to an account earning 8 percent. How much should Bill deposit each quarter?

11. George has $100 deducted from his salary at the end of each month and invested in an employees' fund that earns 12 percent interest. How much will he have after the last payment 10 years from now?

12. A company wants to accumulate $15,000 to replace a machine 5 years from now. To do this, equal payments are to be made at the end of each six-month period to an account earning 10 percent interest. Find the periodic payment.

13. Fran has an opportunity to lend a growing company a sum of money and earn 10 percent interest. The company will discharge its debt to Fran by sending her equal amounts every 6 months for 5 years. How much should Fran lend if she wants to receive $2,000 every 6 months?

8.30 PROBLEM SET 8–9 (*concluded*)

14. How much invested now at 8 percent will provide an income of $1,000 per quarter for the next 7 years?

15. Jan has lent a new company $10,000 at 12 percent. The company will discharge its debt by sending Jan checks of equal

amounts, one each month, for 6 years. How much will Jan receive each month?

16. Bill has borrowed $5,000 at 24 percent to purchase a car. He will discharge the debt by equal end-of-the-month payments for 3 years. Find the payment.

Solve Problems 17 through 20 using a calculator.

17. Fran deposits $150 at the end of each month for 6 years in an account earning 7.2 percent compounded continuously. What will be the amount in the account after the last deposit?

18. How much should be deposited at the end of each month for 10 years to accumulate $20,000 if the account earns 8 percent compounded continuously?

19. What sum of money deposited at 7.5 percent compounded continuously will yield an income of $1,500 at the end of each month for 6 years?

20. Bill borrowed $6,000 at 18 percent compounded continuously to buy a car. He will discharge the debt by equal end-of-the-month payments for 3 years. Find the amount of the payment.

8.31 REVIEW PROBLEMS

1. Compute the simple interest at 9 percent on $500 for 15 months.

2. Compute the future value of $1,500 at 8 percent simple interest for 10 months.

3. How many months will it take for the simple interest on $2,000 at 7 percent to be $175?

4. A credit card holder has owed the card company $400 for one month and receives a bill for $405. Find the simple rate of interest.

5. Compute the yield of the stock of Detroit Edison Company from the following stock market report.

DetE   1.52   15½

6. How much must be deposited in an account paying 8.5 percent simple interest if $210 interest is to be earned in 30 months?

7. At what rate of simple interest will $500 grow to $560 in 9 months?

8. How many months will it take at 8.4 percent simple interest for $2,000 to grow to $2,280?

9. Find the present value of $1,500 due two years from now with simple interest at 10 percent.

10. How much will Fran have to deposit now in an employees' savings account earning 10 percent simple interest in order to have $2,500 in the account 2½ years from now?

11. Find the proceeds of a $1,000, two-year loan from a bank if the simple bank discount rate is 18 percent.

12. Bill receives $2,000 from a bank now, to be repaid in 30 months. If the bank discount rate is 12 percent, how much will Bill have to pay back?

13. Sam signs a note promising to pay a bank $3,000 in two years. If Sam receives $2,400 when he signs the note, what is the bank's discount rate?

8.31 REVIEW PROBLEMS (*continued*)

14. Find the future value of $10,000 at 12 percent compounded monthly for 3 years and 4 months.

15. Find the future value of $4,000 at 8 percent compounded quarterly for 7 years.

16. Find the future value of $5,000 at 7 percent compounded annually for 20 years.

17. An employees' Credit Union Fund pays interest at 12 percent compounded monthly. How much will an employee who invests $2,500 now have 3 years from now?

18. How many years will it take at 8 percent compounded annually for $2,000 to grow to $10,000?

19. How many years will it take for a sum of money to double at 9 percent compounded annually?

20. Find the rate of interest compounded annually at which $1,000 will grow to $2,500 in 10 years.

21. A company sold 125,000 machines five years ago and this year sold 350,000 machines. Find the annually compounded percentage rate of increase in sales over the 5-year period.

22. Find the present value of $5,000 payable 10 years from now with interest at 10 percent compounded semiannually.

23. The population of a town now is about 500,000. If population has increased at the rate of 7 percent compounded semi-annually, estimate the population 20 years ago.

24. What sum invested now at 8 percent compounded quarterly will grow to $10,000 in 9 years?

25. Find the future value of an ordinary annuity of $500 per quarter for 10 years at 8 percent compounded quarterly.

26. Sam deposits $250 at the end of every three months for 10 years to an account earning 8 percent compounded quarterly. How much will he have in the account after the last deposit?

27. Sue plans to accumulate $8,000 for a trip around the world 5 years from now. Find how much she should deposit to the trip fund at the end of each quarter if the fund earns 8 percent compounded quarterly.

28. How much should be deposited now in an account earning 6 percent compounded semiannually to provide an income of $5,000 at the end of each 6-month period for 17½ years?

29. Sam has borrowed $12,000 at 12 percent, compounded monthly, from a bank. He will discharge the debt by end-of-the-month payments for the next 30 months. Find the monthly payment.

30. a) New Venture Corporation has taken out a $5 million, 30-year, 10 percent mortgage on its new manufacturing facility. How much will New Venture pay each month to discharge this mortgage?
 b) How much of the first payment is for interest, and by how much does it reduce the balance owed?
 c) How much of the second payment is for interest, and by how much does it reduce the balance owed?

31. a) The Browns have taken out a $50,000, 20-year, 8 percent mortgage on their home. How much will they pay each month to discharge this mortgage?
 b) How much of the first payment is for interest, and by how much does it reduce the balance owed?
 c) How much of the second payment is for interest, and by how much does it reduce the balance owed?

32. A note for $3,000 with interest at 12 percent compounded monthly is payable 30 months from now. Find the (then present) value of the note 12 months from now if this value is computed at 8 percent compounded quarterly.

33. Bill promises to pay off a current debt of $10,000 at 7 percent compounded annually by making equal end-of-the-year payments for the next 10 years. Compute the payment.

8.31 REVIEW PROBLEMS (*continued*)

34. How much should be deposited now at 7 percent compounded annually to make possible withdrawals of $7,500 at the end of each year for 10 years, the first withdrawal to be made 15 years from now? Interest during the withdrawal period is 6 percent compounded annually.

35. If fuel is now consumed by a plant at the rate of 25,000 barrels a year, and the rate increases by 7 percent compounded annually, what will yearly fuel consumption be 15 years from now?

36. Septech Corporation is setting up a reserve account earning 10 percent compounded semiannually. At the end of each six-month period, equal sums are transferred to this account. The purpose of the account is to provide $20,000 after the last transfer 8 years from now to be used to replace equipment. Compute the semiannual transfer to the account.

37. (All interest at 7 percent compounded annually.) A business man has an obligation to pay $8,000 four years from now, and another obligation to pay $12,000 nine years from now. The money needed is to be provided by setting up an account into which equal deposits are made at the end of each year for 9 years. Find the annual deposit.

38. Sam wants to buy a boat for $10,000 nine years from now. How much should he deposit now at 8 percent compounded quarterly in order to have the desired amount available?

39. A company will need 1,500 barrels of fuel at the end of this month, and its needs will increase at the rate of 1 percent per month (12 percent compounded monthly). The company plans to take advantage of a currently favorable price situation and purchase a 3-year supply of fuel. How many barrels should be purchased?

40. How much should be deposited now in an account at 7 percent compounded annually to provide an income of $10,000 at the end of each year for 22 years?

41. (All interest compounded annually.) Sue has an investment that will pay her $20,000 plus interest at 5 percent in 10 years. She can obtain the present value of this investment, computed at 6 percent, and deposit this amount in an account paying 8 percent. If she does so, what will be the amount of the account in 10 years?

42. At what rate of interest compounded annually will payments of $1,000 per year for 15 years discharge a current debt of $10,000?

43. At what rate of interest compounded annually will a series of end-of-the-year deposits of $2,500 amount to $41,000 in 12 years?

44. At what rate of interest compounded annually will a series of end-of-the-year deposits of $1,000 amount to $25,000 in 15 years?

45. How many monthly payments will it take to amortize a debt of $150,000 with payments of $1,800 per month at an interest rate of 14 percent compounded monthly? What is the total amount paid to the nearest dollar?

46. How many monthly payments will it take to amortize a debt of $125,000 with payments of $1,500 per month at an interest rate of 13 percent compounded monthly? What is the total amount paid to the nearest dollar?

47. Find the effective interest rate of 12 percent compounded quarterly.

48. Find the effective interest rate of 24 percent compounded monthly.

49. Find the effective interest rate for 6 percent compounded daily, using 365 days per year.

50. Find the amount of $5,000 for nine years at 7 percent compounded continuously.

51. How much should be deposited now at 8 percent compounded continuously to have $10,000 seven years from now?

52. What is the effective rate of 12 percent compounded continuously?

53. What nominal rate of interest compounded

8.31 REVIEW PROBLEMS (*concluded*)

continuously will yield an effective rate of 12 percent?

54. Fran wants to have $4,000 available 3 years from now. She makes equal deposits at the end of each quarter in an employees' fund earning 12 percent compounded continuously. Compute the amount of the deposit.

55. Bill has lent a company $20,000 at 14 percent compounded continuously. The company will discharge the debt by sending Bill a check at the end of each six-month period for 10 years. Compute the amount of the check.

56. How much should be deposited now in an account earning 6.6 percent compounded continuously in order to have $12,000 fifteen years from now?

57. Sam has an opportunity to invest in an income account at 12 percent compounded continuously. The amount invested, plus interest, comes back to Sam in the form of a check at the end of each month for 8 years. How much should Sam invest if he wants the monthly income check to be $1,000?

58. How much will a deposit of $2,500 amount to in 10 years at 8.3 percent compounded continuously?

59. Sue deposits $400 at the end of each six-month period for 12 years in an account earning 8 percent compounded continuously. What will the amount in the account be after the last payment?

NINE

Elementary Probability and Statistics

9.1 INTRODUCTION

Almost all students of management and economics study statistics at some point during their undergraduate years. Typically, statistics courses devote only a small amount of time to probability, even though probability forms the foundation upon which statistical inference rests. Consequently, one objective of this chapter is to lay the foundation for the study of statistical inference. A second objective is to encourage thinking in the probabilistic mode that is characteristic of decision-making problems. Finally, we should add, probability has its own interesting and useful applications and is worthy of study in its own right.

9.2 PROBABILITY AND ODDS

A weather forecaster may state in his radio broadcast that the probability of rain tomorrow is 60 percent and later, while playing poker, tell friends that the odds on rain tomorrow are 3 to 2. Other methods exist for expressing the degree of certainty, or uncertainty. In mathematics, we always express probabilities as numbers on a scale from zero to one, inclusive. Thus, letting $P(R)$ represent the probability of rain, we convert 60 percent to its decimal equivalent and write

$$P(R) = 0.60.$$

The odds statement 3 to 2 is viewed as meaning there are $3 + 2 = 5$ "chances" on tomorrow's weather, of which 3 are for rain, so

$$P(R) = \frac{3}{3 + 2} = \frac{3}{5} = 0.60$$

as before.

443

> **Exercise.**   If the odds are 13 to 7 that the stock market will rise tomorrow, what is the decimal value of the probability of a rise? Answer: 0.65.

Odds are in common use, but suffer lack of comparability because they do not have a fixed base. Thus, if the odds for a stock price rise are 11 to 7 while those for a rise in bond yields are 3 to 2, a conversion is needed to express the likelihood of rises in comparable form, and probabilities in decimal form are an appropriate conversion.

> **Exercise.**   Convert the last two odds statements into decimal probabilities.   Answer: 0.611 and 0.600.

9.3 STATISTICAL INFERENCE

One of the most important areas in which comparability is fundamental is that of statistical inference. Many times in making important business decisions we need to know the profile of a certain population. This could be a population of consumers, a population of inventory items, or a population of numerical values.

> **Definition.** A *population* is the entire set or collection of elements associated with a particular study.

Since many populations are too large to yield to a total census, we frequently scrutinize a sample from the population.

> **Definition.** A *sample* is any subset of a population.

Using the characteristics of a sample we make inferences about the characteristics of the entire population. For example, statisticians regularly predict the outcome of pending elections by polling a sample of voters out of the population of all voters. A statistical inference could be a decision, an estimate, or a prediction about a population that is based on information contained in a sample. Any statistical inference should be accompanied by a measure of reliability, which defines the confidence we have in the correctness of the inference. These measures of reliability depend heavily upon the theory of probability.

9.4 SOURCES OF PROBABILITIES

If we plan to draw a card from a well-shuffled standard deck of 52 cards, we would find it natural to assess the probability that the card will be a spade as

$$P(S) = \frac{13 \text{ spades}}{52 \text{ cards}} = \frac{13}{52} = \frac{1}{4} = 0.25.$$

What this implies is that if we repeat the experiment of drawing a card from a well-shuffled deck of 52 cards many times, we would expect the proportion or *relative* frequency of drawing a spade to approach 0.25 as a limit as the number of drawings increases. *Relative frequency over the long run* under constant conditions (*e.g.*, drawing from a well-shuffled deck) is one source of probability measures. Most people feel confident in such probability assignments and refer to them as *objective* probabilities that can be verified by experiment. A novice in a poker game may feel that a pair of kings and a pair of aces should beat three deuces, but such is not the case. In poker, the more unusual (less probable) hand wins, and three of a kind is more unusual than two pairs—not because of intuition or any subjective factor, but because of mathematical computations that can be verified by experiment.

In general, if we perform an experiment with all outcomes equally likely to occur, then we assign the probability $P(E)$ to an event E following the rule:

$$P(E) = \frac{\text{Number of all favorable outcomes}}{\text{Number of all possible outcomes}}.$$

For example, if we were to toss two coins A and B, then there are four possible outcomes we could obtain

Coin A	Coin B
H	H
H	T
T	H
T	T

What is the probability of obtaining two tails?

$$P(2 \text{ tails}) = \frac{\text{Number of outcomes yielding 2 tails}}{\text{Number of all possible outcomes}} = \frac{1}{4}.$$

You should verify that

$$P(1 \text{ tail}) = \frac{2}{4} = \frac{1}{2}.$$

Exercise. If we toss three coins, a) How many possible outcomes are there? b) What is the probability of obtaining exactly 2 heads? Answer: a) 8. b) ⅜.

We should point out at once that objective probabilities, which arise as relative frequencies over the long run under constant conditions, are not as prevalent in management decision-making as they are in games of chance. To see why, consider a firm that is deciding on whether or not to bid on a $5 million project, at a point in time, and in the competitive environment of that time. The firm knows it will cost about $100,000 to prepare the bid so, naturally, it will not prepare a bid unless the probability of winning the contract is sufficiently high to justify the cost. How does the firm assess the probability of winning? Past experience will be of some help, but it is unlikely that the circumstances surrounding this particular situation have occurred very often, if at all, in the past, so that a relative-frequency objective probability is not at hand. Nevertheless, a decision based upon a probability assessment must be made. We may assume that the appropriate officials of the firm, drawing upon both quantified and nonquantified experience and projection, will make the assessment. We refer to the results as a *subjective* probability.

In practice, probability assessments range from highly objective to highly subjective. In this chapter, we shall not distinguish between the two because probability theory is not concerned with the source of the probabilities we assign. The theory requires only that we consider *all* of the *different* events that may occur in a given situation and assign to each event a *nonnegative* number between zero and one in a manner such that the sum of all the probabilities is one. For example, in drawing a card from a deck, the events red card, spade and club are one way to specify *all* the *different* events that can occur, and we may assign probabilities 0.5, 0.25, and 0.25, respectively, to these events.

Certain and impossible events. We assign a probability of one to an event that is certain to occur, such as the event of getting a red or a black card when drawing from a deck. The probability zero is assigned to an impossible event, such as drawing a red spade from the deck. Again, a weatherman may assign a probability of zero for rain tomorrow if he believes rain is impossible, or one if he believes rain is certain. In summary, if $P(E)$ is the probability of event E,

$$0 \leq P(E) \leq 1$$
$$P(\text{impossible event}) = 0$$
$$P(\text{certain event}) = 1.$$

9.5 PROBABILITY SYMBOLS AND DEFINITIONS

We shall introduce probability terminology by reference to the data in Table 9–1. These data show the results of a poll of *all* 500 employees in a firm on the question of whether to change the work week from five 8-hour days to four 10-hour days.

The right margin shows there are 100 men in the group of 500 workers. If we were to draw an individual at random[1] from the 500, it would be natural to assign the probability of selecting a man, $P(M)$, as

$$P(M) = \frac{100}{500} = 0.20.$$

Similarly, the probability that the individual disfavors, $P(D)$, is

$$P(D) = \frac{160}{500} = 0.32.$$

TABLE 9–1

	Favor (*F*)	Disfavor (*D*)	Neutral (*N*)	Totals
Men *(M)*	70	10	20	100
Women *(W)*	170	150	80	400
Totals	240	160	100	500

Exercise. From Table 9–1 find: a) $P(W)$. b) $P(F)$. Answer: a) 0.80. b) 0.48.

Joint events: Intersection. In Table 9–1, draw a horizontal line across the *M* row and a vertical line down the *F* column. At the *intersection* of the two lines there are 70 people who are both men *and* in favor. In set terminology, the symbol ∩ represents intersection, so the event at hand is *M* intersection *F*, or

$$M \cap F.^{2}$$

An alternative description refers to the intersection as the *joint* event, *M* and *F*. Clearly,

$$P(M \cap F) = \frac{70}{500} = 0.14.$$

---

[1] The concept of random selection underlies all probability rules. In the case of card playing, randomness is sought by shuffling the cards before dealing a hand. In the case of Table 9–1, we could shuffle the 500 employee time cards or use other methods to insure random selection.

[2] Later in the chapter we will, for brevity, omit ∩ and express the intersection as *MF*. See also Appendix 1, Section A1.7.

Similarly,

$$P(W \cap N) = \frac{80}{500} = 0.16,$$

and is the probability that the selected individual is a woman *and* is neutral. Remember always that the intersection means *both* occur and is characterized by the word *and*.

Exercise.   Write the symbols for the probability that a man who disfavors is selected, and compute this probability. Answer: $P(M \cap D) = \frac{10}{500} = 0.02$.

Mutually exclusive (disjoint) events. In Table 9–1 the intersection

$$F \cap D$$

is empty (has no elements) because an individual cannot both favor and disfavor the proposal. In set terminology,

$$F \cap D = \phi,$$

where ϕ is the *empty* or *null* set. We shall say F and D are disjoint or, more commonly, that they are *mutually exclusive*. Clearly,

$$P(F \cap D) = 0$$

and, in general,

A and B are mutually exclusive if $A \cap B = \phi$ so that $$P(A \cap B) = 0.$$

Exercise.   If a card is drawn from a deck, what is the probability that it will be red and be a spade? Why? Answer: $P(R \cap S) = 0$ because red and spade are mutually exclusive.

Conditional probability. Suppose next that an individual has been selected from the population of employees. We are told that the individual is a man, but not told his attitude toward the proposal. What now is the probability that this individual is in favor? Here it is *given* that we have a man, so in Table 9–1 we consider only the 100 men and the 70 of these who are in favor. We find that

$$P(\text{in favor, given man}) = P(F \mid M) = \frac{70}{100} = 0.70,$$

where the vertical line segment in $P(F \mid M)$ is read as *given,* and the whole symbol as the probability of F, given M.

Similarly, if we are told the person selected disfavors the proposal and are asked to find the probability that the person is a man, we compute

$$P(M \mid D) = \frac{10}{160} = 0.0625.$$

Exercise. If the person selected is in favor, write the symbols for, and compute the probability that, the person is a woman. **Answer:** $P(W \mid F) = {}^{170}\!/_{240} = 0.708.$

Dependent and independent events. Table 9–1 shows

$$P(M) = \frac{100}{500} = 0.200 \quad \text{but} \quad P(M \mid F) = \frac{70}{240} = 0.292.$$

We note that

$$P(M \mid F) \neq P(M)$$

and say that M and F are *dependent* in the probability sense. The idea is that the probability that the selected person is a male is related to, or depends on, whether the person is in favor. In this case, the *unconditional* probability that the selected person is a man is 0.200, but it is more likely (0.292) that the person is a man if we are given that the person is in favor.

On the other hand, we note that

$$P(M) = \frac{100}{500} = 0.20 \quad \text{and} \quad P(M \mid N) = \frac{20}{100} = 0.20$$

so that

$$P(M \mid N) = P(M)$$

which we translate by saying that the probability that the selected person is a male does not depend on (is independent of) whether the person is neutral. In general, we state that *in the probability sense,*

If $P(A \mid B) = P(A)$, *A and B are independent.*

If $P(A \mid B) \neq P(A)$, *A and B are dependent.*

Exercise. See Table 9–1. Are the following independent or dependent? Why? a) W and D. b) W and N. Answer: a) $P(W \mid D) = {}^{150}/_{160}$ which does not equal $P(W) = 0.8$, so W and D are dependent. b) $P(W \mid N) = 0.80 = P(W)$, so W and N are independent.

In the preceding definition of independence, we emphasized that independence as a mathematical concept is independence *in the probability sense*. We should note that events that we think or feel (intuitively) are independent or dependent may or may not prove to be so in the probability sense. Thus, in the poll of workers under discussion, we might feel intuitively that women would tend not to be in favor of changing from an 8-hour to a 10-hour day because the longer workday would interfere with the home responsibilities of some women. That is, intuitively we might feel that women would be more likely not to favor a longer day than workers in general and, therefore, that Disfavor and Women are dependent. The test in the probability sense may or may not bear out this intuitive feeling, and the test is:

$$\text{If } P(D \mid W) = P(D) \qquad D \text{ and } W \text{ are independent.}$$

$$\text{If } P(D \mid W) \neq P(D) \qquad D \text{ and } W \text{ are dependent.}$$

From Table 9–1 we find

$$P(D \mid W) = \frac{150}{400} = 0.375.$$

$$P(D) = \frac{160}{500} = 0.32$$

so D and W are dependent. Moreover, the last two numbers confirm the intuitive feeling that women are more likely to disfavor a longer workday than workers in general. By way of contrast, we might feel intuitively that men would be less likely to be neutral on the question than workers in general because men would prefer to work longer days in order to have a three-day weekend. Here intuition is again suggesting dependence. However, if we compute from Table 9–1

$$P(N \mid M) = \frac{20}{100} = 0.2$$

$$P(N) = \frac{100}{500} = 0.2,$$

we see that N and M are independent *in the probability sense*, and the data do not support intuition in this case.

Another matter worthy of special attention is the distinction between mutual exclusiveness and independence. The first point to note is that *if each of two events, A and B, has a nonzero probability and the events are mutually exclusive they are necessarily dependent;* that is, they cannot be independent. To see why this is so, suppose that

$$P(A) = 0.3 \qquad P(B) = 0.7.$$

Now, if A occurs, B *cannot* occur because A and B are mutually exclusive. Hence,

$$P(B \mid A) = 0,$$

but

$$P(B) = 0.7,$$

so

$$P(B \mid A) \neq P(B),$$

and the events are dependent. The question of independence for mutually exclusive events thus always has the answer that the events are dependent in the probability sense. On the other hand, *if A and B are not mutually exclusive, they may be independent or they may be dependent.* The last statement will be made clear in the next example.

Example. An urn (jar) contains 200 small glass balls. Each ball has a left and a right half of different colors. The left half may be R, W, or B (for Red, White, or Blue) and the right side may be G or Y (for Green or Yellow). A ball with red and yellow can be said to have some red (or some yellow). There are 80 balls with some red; 70 with white and green; 30 with white and yellow; 20 with blue and green; 140 with some green. Answer the following:

1. Are blue and green mutually exclusive? Why?
2. Are blue and green independent? Why?
3. Are white and yellow mutually exclusive? Why?
4. Are white and yellow independent? Why?
5. Are blue and yellow mutually exclusive? Why?
6. Are blue and yellow independent? Why?

The numbers given in this problem are summarized in the left table, and the table at the right provides the remaining numbers by using the given data and the requirements of row and column sums; that is, for example, the row sum for white must be 100, and to make the column sum for green be 140, the red and green element must be 50.

Given Data

	Green	Yellow	Totals
Red			80
White	70	30	
Blue	20	____	____
Totals	140		200

Completed Table

	Green	Yellow	Totals
Red	50	30	80
White	70	30	100
Blue	20	0	20
Totals	140	60	200

We turn now to questions 1–6 of the example statement, using the completed table at the right.

1. There are 20 balls that are both blue and green, so blue and green are not mutually exclusive; that is, $P(B \cap G) \neq 0$.
2. If we compute

$$P(B \mid G) = \frac{20}{140} = \frac{1}{7}; \quad P(B) = \frac{20}{200} = \frac{1}{10}$$

we see that $P(B \mid G) \neq P(G)$, so blue and green are dependent, not independent. Or, we could have computed

$$P(G \mid B) = \frac{20}{20} = 1; \quad P(G) = \frac{140}{200} = \frac{7}{10}$$

and $P(G \mid B) \neq P(G)$, showing again that blue and green are not independent.
3. There are 30 balls that are white and yellow, so white and yellow are not mutually exclusive; that is, $P(W \cap Y) \neq 0$.
4. If we compute

$$P(W \mid Y) = \frac{30}{60} = 0.5; \quad P(W) = \frac{100}{200} = 0.5,$$

we note that $P(W \mid Y) = P(W)$, so white and yellow are independent. Or, we could have computed

$$P(Y \mid W) = \frac{30}{100} = 0.3; \quad P(Y) = \frac{60}{200} = 0.3$$

and $P(Y \mid W) = P(Y)$ showing again that yellow and white are independent.

Note: Observe in the answers to 1–4 that if two events are not mutually exclusive, they may be either dependent (as in 1 and 2) or independent (as in 3 and 4).

5. There is no ball with blue and yellow, so blue and yellow are mutually exclusive; that is, $P(B \cap Y) = 0$.
6. Mutually exclusive events with nonzero probabilities automatically are dependent, so blue and yellow are dependent. Numerically, the dependence is exhibited by showing that $P(B \mid Y) \neq P(B)$. These probabilities are

$$P(B \mid Y) = \frac{0}{60} = 0; \quad P(B) = \frac{20}{200} = 0.1.$$

Summarizing the last example, we observe in the answer to 1 that if a ball has blue, it also can have green, so blue and green are not mutually exclusive; moreover, the two demonstrations of the answer to 2 show that *if we know* one color is green (blue), this knowledge does affect the probability that the ball also has blue (green) because green and blue are dependent. Then, in 3, we determine yellow and white also are not mutually exclusive, but 4 shows that *if we know* one color is yellow (white) this knowledge does not affect the probability that the other color is white (yellow) because yellow and white are independent. Finally, 5 shows blue and yellow are mutually exclusive, so of necessity they are dependent; that is, as 6 shows, *if we know* one color is blue (yellow) this does affect the probability that the other color is yellow (blue); that is, this latter probability must be zero.

Exercise.   If we draw two cards from a deck and let A_1 and A_2 represent the event that the first card is an ace and the event that the second card is an ace, respectively, are A_1 and A_2 mutually exclusive? Independent? Explain. Answer: The events A_1 and A_2 (e.g., first card ace of spades, second card ace of clubs) both can occur, so $P(A_1 \cap A_2) \neq 0$ and the events are not mutually exclusive. However, the probability that the second card is an ace *does* depend upon whether the first card was an ace. That is, because there are four aces in the deck of 52 cards, the probability that the first card is an ace is $4/52$. If we know the first card drawn was an ace, 3 aces remain in a deck of 51 cards and the probability of the second card being an ace, *given* that the first card is an ace, is $3/51$.

Union of events. Refer to Table 9–1. The expression

$$M \cup F,$$

where $\cup$ is read as *union* and $M \cup F$ as *M union F*, means the set of individuals who are either men *or* in favor *or* both. The table shows there are 100 men in total and an additional uncounted 170 women in favor, for a grand total of 270 that are either men or in favor or both, so

$$P(M \cup F) = \frac{270}{500} = 0.54.$$

Another counting method we shall soon find useful is to add the number of men to the number of people in favor, then subtract the number of men in favor because they were counted *twice*. This yields $100 + 200 - 70$, so

$$P(M \cup F) = \frac{100 + 240 - 70}{500} = \frac{270}{500} = 0.54,$$

as before.

On the other hand, F and D are mutually exclusive (the intersection is empty), so

$$P(F \cup D) = \frac{240 + 160 - 0}{500} = 0.8.$$

Exercise. From Table 9–1, find: a) $P(M \cup W)$. b) $P(F \cup N)$. c) $P(W \cup D)$. d) $P(W \cup F)$.   Answer: a) 1. b) 0.68. c) 0.82. d) 0.94.

Complementary events. Two events are said to be complementary if the sum of their probabilities is one. That is, letting E' (E prime) be the complement of E, then

$$P(E) + P(E') = 1$$
$$P(E') = 1 - P(E).$$

E' may be read as "not E." Similarly, if R means "rain," R' means "not rain" and if $P(R) = 0.40$, then

$$P(R') = 1 - P(R) = 1 - 0.40 = 0.60.$$

Again, if W means woman, W' is not woman (therefore man). In Table 9–1

$$P(W') = 1 - P(W) = 1 - \frac{400}{500} = 0.2.$$

Exercise. From Table 9–1, a) What would constitute F'? b) What is $P(F')$? Answer: a) F' (not Favor) would include Disfavor and Neutral. b) $P(F') = 1 - P(F) = 1 - {}^{240}\!/_{500} = 0.52.$

For further practice with complements, note that $F \cup D$ includes all joint events containing an F or a D (or both). The only remaining event is not F and not D; that is, $F' \cap D'$, so $F' \cap D'$ is the complement of $F \cup D$ and we may write

$$P(F \cup D) = 1 - P(F' \cap D') \quad \text{or} \quad P(F' \cap D') = 1 - P(F \cup D).$$

Similarly,

$$P(M \cup F) = 1 - P(M' \cap F') \quad \text{or} \quad P(M' \cap F') = 1 - P(M \cup F).$$

Further practice with these symbols is provided in the following set of problems.

9.6 PROBLEM SET 9–1

1. The table shows, for example, that area A has 30 large stores and area C has 150 small stores.

Geographic Area	Store Size ($ Volume)		
	Large L	Medium M	Small S
A	30	45	75
B	150	125	275
C	20	130	150

Find the following probabilities:

a) $P(M)$.
b) $P(B)$.
c) $P(M \cap S)$.
d) $P(B \cap M)$.
e) $P(A \cap C)$.
f) $P(A \cap L)$.
g) $P(L \cap A)$.
h) $P(A \mid L)$.
i) $P(L \mid A)$.
j) $P(A \mid M)$.
k) $P(S \mid B)$.
l) $P(L \cup M)$.
m) $P(B \cup S)$.
n) $P(M \cup C)$.
o) $P(B \cup C)$.
p) $P(A')$.
q) $P(M')$.
r) $P(L' \cap M')$.

What event, joint event, or union of events is the complement of

s) $M' \cap S'$?
t) $B' \cap C'$?
u) $A \cup C$?
v) $A \cup M$?
w) $B' \cap M'$?
x) $L' \cap C'$?

2. See the table of Problem 1.
   a) Does $P(M \mid A) = P(M)$?
   b) What does the answer to (a) mean?
   c) Are A and L independent? Explain.
   d) Are B and L independent? Explain.
   e) What is $P(A \cap B)$? What does this mean?

3. a) Voters in an area are classified as Democrat, Independent, or Republican. If 48 percent are Democrats and 10 percent are Independents, what is the probability that a voter selected at random is a Republican?
   b) If the probability of rain tomorrow is 0.4, what is the probability that it will not rain?

4. An urn contains 600 glass balls. Each ball has a left half and a right half of different colors. The left may be G or Y (for green or yellow) and the right half may be R, W, or B (for red, white, or blue). The numbers of balls of various colors are shown in the table.

	R	W	B
G	30	42	138
Y	270	78	42

a) Are white and blue mutually exclusive? Why?
b) Are white and blue independent? Why?
c) Are yellow and white mutually exclusive? Why?
d) Are yellow and white independent? Why?
e) Are yellow and red mutually exclusive? Why?
f) Are yellow and red independent? Why?

5. An urn contains 400 small glass balls. Each ball has a left half and a right half of different colors. The left half may be R, W, or B (for red, white, or blue), and the right half may be Y, G, or T (for yellow, green, or tan). Each ball has R, W, or B on one side and Y, G, or T on the other, except that none of the balls has red on one side and green on the other. A ball that has, say, red and yellow, can be said to have some red (or some yellow). There are 200 balls having some red; 40 are red and yellow; 10 are white and yellow; 50 are blue and yellow; 50 have some green and 20 are white and green; 120 have some blue. Construct a tabular form having three rows labeled R, W, and B and three columns headed Y, G, and T. Place the given numbers in their proper position in the table, then fill in the remaining elements and totals.

   A ball is selected at random. What is the probability that it has the following colors on it?
   a) Some red.
   b) Some green.

9.6 PROBLEM SET 9–1 (concluded)

c) White or green.
d) Red and blue.
e) Red and green.
f) Both sides red.
g) Some yellow.
h) Red or green.
i) Blue and tan.

A ball (which we cannot see) has been selected. Answer the following according to the information provided:

j) If the ball drawn has some blue, what is the probability that the other color is green?
k) If the ball drawn has some yellow, what is the probability that the other color is red?
l) If the ball drawn is green, what is the probability that the other color is red?

Answer the following:

m) Are white and yellow mutually exclusive? Why?
n) Are white and yellow independent? Why?
o) Are white and tan mutually exclusive? Why?
p) Are white and tan independent? Why?

q) Are red and green mutually exclusive? Why?
r) Are red and green independent? Why?

6. In the table, *H, M, L* stand for "high absenteeism," "medium absenteeism," and "low absenteeism," respectively. *S* stands for "salaried" and *P* for "hourly paid." The table shows, for example, that there were 40 salaried workers who had high absentee records. Assigning probabilities as relative frequencies, show that method of pay and absenteeism (for these data) are independent in the probability sense.

	H	M	L
S	40	60	100
P	60	90	150

7. A plant has 300 workers, 200 of whom are females. Classified by *H, M, L* absenteeism, there are 30 workers in the *H* class and 30 workers in the *L* class. Assuming independence of sex and absenteeism, how many workers should there be in each of the six possible classes?

9.7 PROBABILITY RULES

Table 9–1 showed the numbers of people in each category, the marginal totals, and the grand total, 500. We now divide each number in Table 9–1 by 500 to yield the *probabilities* shown in Table 9–2.

Intersections, such as $M \cap F$, are very often of interest, and for brevity we shall henceforth omit the intersection symbol and express a joint event such as $M \cap F$ as simply *MF*. We shall refer to *MF* as *M and F*, keeping in mind that the word *and* means *both M* and *F*. The union symbol, as in $M \cup F$, shall be retained, and we shall refer to $M \cup F$ as *M or F*, keeping in mind that this includes *M*, or *F*, or *MF*.

From Table 9–1 we computed

$$P(M \cup F) = \frac{100 + 240 - 70}{500}$$

$$= \frac{100}{500} + \frac{240}{500} - \frac{70}{500}$$

$$= 0.20 + 0.48 - 0.14 = 0.54.$$

TABLE 9–2

	Favor (F)	Disfavor (D)	Neutral (N)	Totals
Men (M)	0.14	0.02	0.04	0.20
Women (W)	0.34	0.30	0.16	0.80
Totals	0.48	0.32	0.20	1.00

The corresponding calculation can be made directly from Table 9–2 as

$$P(M \cup F) = P(M) + P(F) - P(MF)$$
$$= 0.20 + 0.48 - 0.14 = 0.54.$$

On the other hand, from Table 9–2,

$$P(F \cup D) = P(F) + P(D) - P(FD)$$
$$= 0.48 + 0.32 - 0$$
$$= 0.80$$

where, here, $P(FD) = 0$ because F and D are mutually exclusive. We have the following rule:

Addition Rule

The probability that A or B occurs is the probability of A plus the probability of B, minus the probability of A *and* B. Thus,

$$P(A \cup B) = P(A) + P(B) - P(AB).$$

If A and B are mutually exclusive, then

$$P(A \cup B) = P(A) + P(B).$$

Exercise.   From Table 9–2 find: a) $P(M \cup N)$. b) $P(M \cup W)$. c) $P(D \cup N)$. Answer: a) $0.20 + 0.20 - 0.04 = 0.36$. b) $0.20 + 0.80 - 0 = 1$. c) $0.32 + 0.20 - 0 = 0.52$

As another example, suppose a political candidate runs for two offices, A and B. She assesses her probabilities of winning at 0.30 and 0.20 for A and B, respectively, and thinks she has an outside chance, probability 0.05, of winning both offices. The probability of winning A or B would then be

$$P(A \cup B) = P(A) + P(B) - P(AB)$$
$$= 0.30 + 0.20 - 0.05$$
$$= 0.45.$$

> **Exercise.** An investor thinks the probability that stock P will rise tomorrow is 0.70, and that Q will rise is 0.80. He thinks there is a 50–50 chance that both will rise. What is his probability that P or Q will rise? Answer: $0.70 + 0.80 - 0.50 = 1.00$.

It is worth noting in the last exercise that the investor's subjective probability assignments lead logically to the conclusion that he is certain (probability 1) that P or Q will rise. Note also that if the investor had assessed the probability that both will rise at 0.4 (rather than 0.5), then $0.7 + 0.8 - 0.4 = 1.1$. This would lead the investor to reassess probabilities because the probability of an event cannot exceed 1. The last sentence illustrates a fundamental reason for understanding probability rules; namely, to monitor probability assessments and insure the internal logical consistency of such assessments.

Returning to Table 9–1, recall that

$$P(F \mid M) = \frac{70}{100} = 0.70.$$

If we express the latter in the equivalent manner,

$$P(F \mid M) = \frac{70/500}{100/500} = \frac{0.14}{0.20} = 0.70$$

and relate the 0.14 and 0.20 to Table 9–2, we observe that

$$P(MF) = 0.14 \quad \text{and} \quad P(M) = 0.20.$$

It follows that

$$P(F \mid M) = \frac{P(FM)}{P(M)}.$$

Thus, the probability of F given M is the probability of the joint event, FM, divided by the probability of M. Correspondingly,

$$P(M \mid F) = \frac{P(MF)}{P(F)}$$

which, from Table 9–2, is

$$P(M \mid F) = \frac{0.14}{0.48} = 0.292.$$

> **Exercise.** Complete the following: a) $P(N \mid W) =$ _____ b) $P(W \mid N) =$ _____ . Compute a) and b) from Table 9–2. Answer: a) $P(N \mid W) = P(NW)/P(W)$. b) $P(W \mid N) = P(WN)/P(N)$. The probabilities are a) 0.20 and b) 0.80.

Conditional Probability Rule

The probability that B will occur, given that A has occurred, is the probability of AB divided by the probability of A. Thus,

$$P(B \mid A) = \frac{P(AB)}{P(A)}.$$

The rule just stated can be solved for $P(AB)$ after multiplying both sides by $P(A)$. The result is:

Joint Probability Rule

The probability of AB is the probability of A times the probability of B, given A. Thus,

$$P(AB) = P(A)P(B \mid A).$$

As an example, suppose a box contains two defective and three good items, $DDGG$. Two items are to be selected and we seek the probability, $P(GD)$, that the first is good and the second defective.

$$P(GD) = P(G)P(D \mid G).$$

The probability, $P(G)$, that the first is good is ⅗. We reason that if the first selected is G, the four remaining are $DDGG$, so the probability, $P(D \mid G)$, that the second is defective, given the first is good, is ²⁄₄. Hence,

$$P(GD) = \frac{3}{5} \cdot \frac{2}{4} = 0.30.$$

Observe that *order* is significant in the context of the last example. Thus, GD means *first* good, *second* defective. Similarly, GGD means first good, second good, third defective. Using a continuation of the joint probability rule,

$$P(GGD) = P(G)P(G \mid G)P(D \mid GG),$$

which means that $P(GGD)$ is the probability that the first is good times the probability that the second is good, given that the first is good, times the probability that the third is defective, given that the first two are good. Arithmetically,

$$P(GGD) = \frac{3}{5} \cdot \frac{2}{4} \cdot \frac{2}{3} = 0.20.$$

Exercise.   For the preceding example, compute: a) $P(DD)$.
b) $P(DDG)$. c) $P(DDD)$.   Answer: a) 0.1. b) 0.1. c) 0.

Recalling that independence means

$$P(B \mid A) = P(B),$$

we may substitute $P(B)$ for $P(B \mid A)$ in the joint probability rule and obtain $P(AB) = P(A)P(B)$.

Joint Probability Rule, Independent Events

If A and B are independent in the probability sense, then the probability of the joint event AB is the probability of A times the probability of B. Thus,

$$P(AB) = P(A)P(B).$$

We may use this rule as a test for independence. For example, in Table 9–2, we note that

$$P(M) = 0.2, \quad P(N) = 0.2, \quad \text{and} \quad P(MN) = 0.04.$$

Hence,

$$P(M)P(N) = (0.2)(0.2) = 0.04 = P(MN),$$

so M and N are independent.

Exercise.   Refer to Table 9–2. Are W and D independent? Explain. Answer: $P(W) = 0.80$, $P(D) = 0.32$, whereas $P(WD) = 0.30$. $P(WD) \neq P(W)P(D)$, so W and D are not independent.

The *assumption* of independence underlies a number of probability applications. For example, suppose that, by test, a fire alarm functions successfully, S, in the presence of fire 90 percent of the time and fails, F, 10 percent of the time. For added protection, a store installs two alarms that operate independently. If there is a fire, what is the probability that both will fail? Here $P(F) = 0.1$ and because of independence,

$$P(FF) = P(F)P(F) = (0.1)(0.1) = 0.01.$$

> **Exercise.** For the above example, find the probability that: a) Both will function successfully. b) The first will function and the second fail. Answer: a) $P(SS) = (0.9)(0.9) = 0.81$. b) $P(SF) = (0.9)(0.1) = 0.09$.

9.8 PRACTICE WITH PROBABILITY RULES

In this section we present a series of examples to provide further practice with probability rules.

Example 1. A job applicant assigns probabilities as follows: The probability, $P(A)$, of being offered a job at company A is 0.6; the probability, $P(B)$, of being offered a job at company B is 0.5; the probability of being offered a job at both companies is 0.4. What is the probability of being offered a job with at least one of the two companies?

Here we shall apply a tabular approach to the problem. The given probabilities are entered in the table at the left, and the entries in the table at the right follow as logical consequences.

Given

	B	B'	Totals
A	0.4		0.6
A'	—	—	—
Totals	0.5		

Completed Table

	B	B'	Totals
A	0.4	0.2	0.6
A'	0.1	0.3	0.4
Totals	0.5	0.5	1.0

The event in question consists of the mutually exclusive events AB', $A'B$, and AB. By the addition rule, then, we have

$$P(AB' \cup A'B \cup AB) = P(AB') + P(A'B) + P(AB)$$
$$= 0.2 + 0.1 + 0.4$$
$$= 0.7.$$

The complement of the event in question is $A'B'$, so that the desired probability could alternatively have been found as

$$P[(A'B')'] = 1 - P(A'B')$$
$$= 1 - 0.3$$
$$= 0.7.$$

When only two events are at hand, problems often can be solved quite easily by construction of a two-by-two table as in Example 1.

> **Exercise.** The probability of good weather, G, is 0.6 and the probability of accident, A, is 0.014. The probability of the joint event, accident and good weather, is 0.006. Find the probability of accident if the weather is not good. (Hint: Make a two-by-two table.) Answer: 0.02.

The completion of a two-by-two table may require application of the probability rule for joint events, as shown next.

Example 2. Ten percent of the workers in an area are accountants; 60 percent of accountants read the area paper *Goodnews*, and 30 percent of those who are not accountants read *Goodnews*. If a worker is selected at random, what is the probability that the worker reads *Goodnews*?

If we make a tabular format with *A* meaning accountant and *G* meaning a reader of *Goodnews*, the only direct entry that can be made from the given information is $P(A) = 0.10$, which follows from the fact that 10 percent are accountants. From the latter, we find $P(A') = 1 - 0.10 = 0.90$ and start the table as shown next.

	G	G'	Totals
A			0.10
A'	—	—	0.90
Totals			1.00

In order to complete the table we need joint probabilities. *The key matter to think about is the meaning of a statement such as* "60 percent of the accountants read *Goodnews*." The proper interpretation starts by observing that the statement is limited to accountants; that is, *accountant is given,* and the 60 percent is the probability of reading *Goodnews* given accountant,

$$P(G \mid A) = 0.60.$$

By similar reasoning, the meaning of "30 percent of those who are not accountants read *Goodnews*" is

$$P(G \mid A') = 0.30.$$

We can now determine the probabilities for the joint events *AG* and *A'G*. These are

$$P(AG) = P(A)P(G \mid A) \quad = (0.10)(0.6) \quad = 0.06$$
$$P(A'G) = P(A')P(G \mid A') = (0.90)(0.30) = 0.27.$$

Completing the table, we have

	G	G'	Totals
A	0.06	0.04	0.10
A'	0.27	0.63	0.90
Totals	0.33	0.67	1.00

and the answer to the question is the probability of G, which is

$$P(G) = 0.33.$$

Tree diagrams. A tree diagram such as that used in the next example often is helpful in solving probability problems, especially when more than two events are involved.

Example 3. Solve the problem of Example 2 by a tree diagram.

We start by showing an initial *fork* (the oblong at the left of Figure 9–1A) and drawing two *branches* from the fork. One is A, for "accountant," and the other A', for "not accountant." The respective probabilities for A and A' (0.1 and 0.9) are shown at the right ends of the two branches that end at the righthand forks. Next, Figure 9–1B shows two branches from each of the righthand forks of Figure 9–1A. Each of the new pair of branches contains G and G', for those who are and are not readers of *Goodnews.* The new branch probabilities, indicated in parentheses, are *conditional* probabilities. Thus, $G(0.6)$ on the top right branch of Figure 9–1B is the probability of G *given* A, as stated in Example 2. Inasmuch as

$$P(G \mid A) + P(G' \mid A) = 1$$

we have the conditional probability

$$P(G' \mid A) = 1 - P(G \mid A) = 1 - 0.6 = 0.4,$$

which is shown as $G'(0.4)$ on Figure 9–1B. Similarly, from Example 2, $P(G \mid A') = 0.3$, so

$$P(G' \mid A') = 1 - 0.3 = 0.7,$$

as shown by $G(0.3)$ and $G'(0.7)$ on the bottom pair of branches of Figure 9–1B. Finally, the probability at the end of a branch is the probability at the beginning fork times the (conditional) branch probability. We complete the tree by filling in the conditional branch probabilities, then

---

FIGURE 9–1A

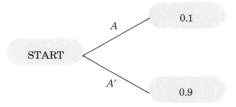

FIGURE 9–1B

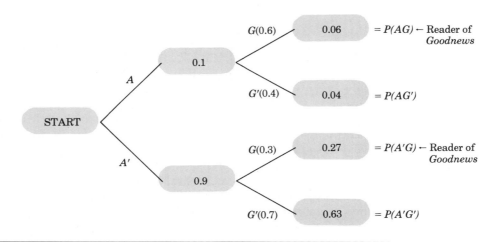

multiplying these by beginning fork probabilities to obtain the end probabilities, as shown in Figure 9–1B. The first and third joint events, AG and $A'G$, represent readers of *Goodnews*, so

$$P(G) = 0.06 + 0.27 = 0.33,$$

as before.

Defining a *fork* as a point from which *branches* emerge, we may state the following rules each of which should be verified using the preceding example:

Rules for Trees

1. The sum of the probabilities on all branches from a fork is one.
2. The probability at the end of a branch is the probability at the beginning fork multiplied by the (conditional) branch probability.
3. The sum of the probabilities at the ends of the branches from a fork equals the probability at the fork.
4. The probability at a fork is the joint probability of all events leading to that fork.
5. The probability of an event X is the sum of the probabilities of all joint events in which X appears.

Example 4. To advertise the opening of a new store, management plans to hold one large outdoor display of fireworks on Thursday, Friday, or Saturday of the opening week if it does not rain. A meteorologist states that the probability of rain on Thursday is 0.6, but if it rains on Thursday, the probability of rain on Friday is 0.7, and if it rains on both Thursday and Friday, the probability of rain on Saturday is 0.10. What is the probability that the fireworks display will occur?

The tree in Figure 9–2 contains the given information, using R for rain and R' for not rain. We want only events containing R' (not rain) and, furthermore, if R' appears on a branch the fireworks display is held on the corresponding day and that part of the tree ceases at the end of that branch. Figure 9–2 presents the relevant branches of the tree and the given probabilities.

Exercise. Verify the probabilities in Figure 9–2. What is the probability that the fireworks display will be held?
Answer: $0.378 + 0.18 + 0.4 = 0.958$.

Now that we have done the problem the "hard" way, we can see that the only joint event that would result in the fireworks display *not* being

FIGURE 9–2

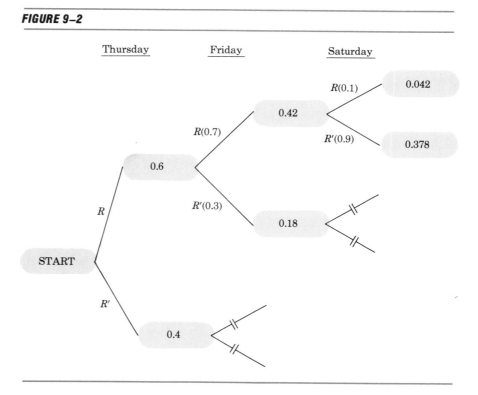

held is rain on all three days. Hence, the top path, *RRR*, with probability 0.042, is the *complement* of the desired event, so the answer to our problem is

$$1 - 0.042 = 0.958,$$

as shown in the exercise.

Situations often arise where events are, or are assumed to be, independent, and the complementary approach is the best way to solve the problem.

Example 5. In a lottery, a person buys a ticket containing four digits, and each digit is selected by a random procedure from the digits 0, 1, 2, · · · , 8, 9. The ticket holder wins a prize if the ticket held contains the same digit at least twice. What is the probability of having a winning ticket?

There are numerous ways of having a number occur at least twice. We have, as examples, 3537, 3339, 3333. The *only* way for a digit not to appear at least twice is for every digit to be different. Thus, *all digits different* is the complement of the event whose probability is sought. To compute the probability of this complement, we start with the observation that the first digit may be any digit, but the second digit must be different from the first. Hence, whatever digit is drawn first in the lottery, there remain 9 different digits in the 10 that can appear when the second is drawn. Therefore,

$$P(\text{Second different from first}) = \frac{9}{10}.$$

There are now eight digits different from the first and second remaining when the third digit is drawn. Hence,

$$P(\text{Third different from first and second}) = \frac{8}{10}.$$

Similarly,

$$P(\text{Fourth different from first, second, and third}) = \frac{7}{10}.$$

Because the outcome of the drawing of a digit does not depend on what happened in previous drawings, we have independent events, and the probability that all three occur is the product of the three probabilities.

$$P(\text{All digits different}) = \frac{9}{10} \cdot \frac{8}{10} \cdot \frac{7}{10} = \frac{504}{1000} = 0.504.$$

Finally,

$$P(\text{At least two digits same}) = 1 - P(\text{All digits different})$$
$$= 1 - 0.504 = 0.496.$$

9.9 PROBLEM SET 9–2

1. Convert the following to a probability table.

Geographic Area	Store Size ($ Volume)		
	Large L	Medium M	Small S
A	30	45	75
B	150	125	275
C	20	130	150

2. a) Complete the following probability table. (Note C' and F' are complements of C and F, respectively.)

	F	F'	Totals
C	0.24		0.60
C'			
Totals	0.40	——	——

Find the following probabilities:
b) $P(CF')$.
c) $P(C \cup F)$.
d) $P(C \cap C')$.
e) $P(F \mid C)$.
f) $P(C \mid F)$.
g) $P(F \mid F')$.
h) Are C and F independent? Why?
i) Why is $P(F \cup F') = 1$?

3. A political candidate runs for two offices, A and B. She assesses her probabilities of winning at 0.6 and 0.2, respectively, and thinks she has only a probability of 0.01 of winning both.
a) What is the probability that she wins one office *or* the other?
b) If the candidate sets $P(A) = 0.7$, $P(B) = 0.4$, and $P(AB) = 0.01$, what advice should she be given? Why?

4. A weatherman states that if it is colder tomorrow, the probability of snow is 0.7. He also states the probability that it will be colder is 0.5. What is the probability it will be colder *and* snow tomorrow? Why?

5. The probability that a student will graduate with honors and get a good job is 0.09, whereas the probability that a student will graduate with honors is 0.1. What is the probability that a student will get a good job if he graduates with honors?

6. A salesman has two prospective customers, A and B, to call on one day. He assigns the probability of making a sale to A at 0.4, of making a sale to B at 0.3, and the probability of making a sale to both at 0.1. What is the probability of making a sale to at least one of the customers?

7. In order to insure that weather will not prevent making an air trip, an executive makes plane reservations for two successive days and assesses the probability of being able to fly either day at 0.95. What is the probability that the executive will be able to make the trip? (Assume independence.)

8. If $P(X \mid Y) = 0.7$, what is $P(X' \mid Y)$?

9. Given $P(X) = 0.6$, $P(Y) = 0.4$, and $P(XY) = 0.1$. Find: $P(X \mid Y)$ and $P(Y \mid X)$.

10. If $P(Y \mid X) = 0.4$, $P(X \mid Y) = 0.5$, and $P(XY) = 0.2$, find $P(X)$ and $P(Y)$.

11. If $P(Y \mid X) = 0.72$, $P(XY) = 0.18$, and $P(Y') = 0.4$, find $P(X \cup Y)$.

12. A candidate runs for two political offices, A and B. He assigns 0.4 as the probability of being elected to both, 0.7 as the probability of being elected to A if he is elected to B, and 0.8 as the probability of being elected to B if he is elected to A.
a) What is the probability of being elected to A?
b) What is the probability of being elected to B?
c) What is the joint probability of being elected to neither?
d) What is the probability of being elected to at least one of the offices?

13. The probability of snow is 0.4, of colder 0.5; and the conditional probability of snow if colder is 0.7. Find the probability of:
a) Colder and snow.
b) No snow.
c) Either colder or snow.
d) Neither colder nor snow.

9.9 PROBLEM SET 9–2 (*continued*)

14. Job candidates are screened by means of a preliminary interview. The probability is 0.6 that a screened candidate will be a good worker. Screened candidates are given a test. If the candidate is one who will prove to be a good worker, the probability of his passing the test is 0.8. If the candidate is one who will prove to be a poor worker, the probability of his passing the test is 0.4.
 a) What is the probability that a screened candidate will be a good worker and pass the test?
 b) What is the probability that a screened candidate will not be a good worker and will pass the test?

15. Fran plans to offer a new product for sale and, in assessing the chances that the product will be successful, Fran has to take her competitor, Judy, into account because Judy may offer a competing new product for sale. Fran thinks that the chance of Judy competing is 0.4. Fran assesses the probability that she will be successful to be 0.85 if Judy does not compete, but only 0.25 if Judy does compete. Compute Fran's chance of being successful.

16. The first time an insurance salesman calls on a new client, he has a probability of 0.1 of selling a policy. *If* he does not sell the policy on the first call, he makes a second call and has a probability of 0.3 of making the sale. *If* he does not make the sale on either of the first two calls, he makes one final call and has a probability of 0.05 of making the sale. What is the probability that the insurance man will sell the policy to a client?

17. A company assesses the probability that its product will fail during the first month after sale as 0.01. The probability it will fail during the next 11 months if it did not fail during the first month is 0.001. The company guarantees the product for the first year. What is the probability that the product will fail in the first year?

18. See Problem 17. Suppose the probability of failure during the first month is 0.05, the probability of failure during the next five months (if the product did not fail in the first month) is 0.02, and the probability of failure for the remainder of the year if failure did not occur during the first noted time intervals is 0.01. What is the probability of failure during the first year?

19. If snow, colder are the events with $P(S) = 0.8$, $P(C) = 0.6$, and $P(S'C) = 0.1$:
 a) Show that the events are not independent in the probability sense.
 b) What probability would $S'C$ have if the events were to be independent in the probability sense?

20. The probability that machine A will break down on a particular day is

$$P(A) = 1/50.$$

Similarly, for Machine B:

$$P(B) = 1/80.$$

Assuming independence, on a particular day:
 a) What is the probability that both will break down?
 b) What is the probability that neither will break down?
 c) What is the probability that one or the other will break down?
 d) What is the probability that exactly one machine will break down?

21. A pair of dice is rolled, and a coin is tossed. Assuming independence, what is the probability of
 a) Heads on the coin and a seven on the dice?
 b) Heads on the coin or a seven on the dice?
 c) Heads on the coin and an even number on the dice?
 d) Heads on the coin and a number greater than eight on the dice?

9.9 PROBLEM SET 9–2 (*concluded*)

22. Five parts go into the assembly of item X. The assembly is defective if any one of the parts is defective, and each part has a probability of 0.03 of being defective. Assuming independence, what is the probability that an assembly is defective?

23. Suppose an arena has two events, hockey and basketball, scheduled on Thursday and another two, hockey and track, on Friday. If two are selected to be played and two cancelled, calculate by probability rules the probability that there will be a hockey game on Thursday or on Friday.

24. Company A plans to bid on a contract. It does not know whether or not a competitor, Company B, will bid, but assesses the probability that it will bid at 0.6. A judges that it has a probability of 0.8 of winning if B does not bid, but only a probability of 0.4 if B does bid. What is the probability that A wins?

25. An arena has scheduled two events on Thursday and three on Friday of a particular week. To obtain time to carry out repairs, two of the events, selected at random, are to be postponed. Find the probability that there will be an event on Thursday and an event on Friday.

26. Five people at a party were born in the month of December. What is the probability that at least two of the five have the same birthday?

27. (For those with calculators.) A mathematics class has 30 students. What is the probability that at least two have the same birthday? (The same day of the same month.) Assume independence and assume a year has 365 days.

9.10 BAYES' RULE

As a result of past hiring procedure, a company finds that 60 percent of its employees are good workers, G, and 40 percent are poor workers, which we shall designate by the complement, G'. The woman in charge of hiring believes that the proportion of good workers can be increased by designing a test to be administered to job applicants, and hiring only those who pass, P, the test. A consulting firm supplies the test and offers to administer it for a fee to applicants. Because of the cost, it is decided to determine first how well the test discriminates between good and poor workers by trying it on current employees. It is found that 80 percent of the good workers and 40 percent of the poor workers pass the test. It is important to understand that these last two numbers are *conditional* probabilities because the first applies only to good workers and the second applies to poor workers. That is, *if* a worker is a good worker, the probability of passing is 0.80, so

$$P(P \mid G) = 0.80.$$

Similarly,

$$P(P \mid G') = 0.40.$$

Note carefully that in general

$$P(P \mid G) \neq 1 - P(P \mid G')$$

because there is no *necessary* relationship between a good worker's passing the test and a poor worker's passing the test.[3]

At first glance it may appear that the test functions well because it is twice as likely (0.80 versus 0.40) that an employee will pass if he is a good worker as it is that he will pass if he is a poor worker. The important point to note, however, is that the real question at hand is whether the test should be used in selecting employees from job applicants. Thus, the issue is not whether an employee will pass if he is a good worker, $P(P \mid G)$, but rather $P(G \mid P)$, which is the probability that an employee will be a good worker if he passes the test. Thus, we know $P(P \mid G)$ and we seek the *inverse* probability, $P(G \mid P)$. We have given:

$$P(G) = 0.60 \qquad P(G') = 1 - P(G) = 0.40.$$
$$P(P \mid G) = 0.80 \qquad P(P \mid G') = 0.40.$$

From the above, we can compute:

$$P(PG) = P(G)P(P \mid G) = (0.60)(0.80) = 0.48.$$
$$P(PG') = P(G')P(P \mid G') = (0.40)(0.40) = 0.16.$$

We now have

	P	P'	Totals
G	0.48		0.6
G'	0.16		
Totals	0.64	—	—

It follows from the table that

$$P(G \mid P) = \frac{0.48}{0.64} = 0.75.$$

To see the significance of the last result, recall that 60 percent of current employees are good workers. This means that past or prior employment procedures, without the test, had a probability of $P(G) = 0.60$, which we shall call the *prior* probability, of selecting a good worker. If, now, we change the selection procedure and employ only those who pass the test, we *revise* the probability of hiring a good worker to $P(G \mid P) = 0.75$, and this revised probability is called the *posterior* probability. Management must decide whether the additional information provided by a test, which results in an increase in the probability of hiring good workers from 0.60 to 0.75, is worth the cost of administering the test.

---

[3] Similarly, the probability that it will snow tomorrow if it is colder, $P(S \mid C)$, tells us nothing about $P(S \mid C')$, the probability that it will snow if it does not get colder. However, if the *given* is the *same* as in $P(S \mid C)$ and $P(S' \mid C)$, then $P(S' \mid C) = 1 - P(S \mid C)$, which means simply that if it is colder it *must* snow or not snow, so $P(S \mid C) + P(S \mid C') = 1$.

To develop the symbolic procedure (Bayes' Rule) for determining $P(G|P)$ from $P(P|G)$, refer to the preceding calculation of $P(G|P) = 0.75$,

$$P(G|P) = 0.75 = \frac{0.48}{0.64}.$$

From the above table, we see that the numerator 0.48 on the right is

$$P(PG) = 0.48$$

and the denominator 0.64 is

$$P(PG) + P(PG') = 0.48 + 0.16.$$

Hence,

$$P(G|P) = 0.75 = \frac{0.48}{0.48 + 0.16}$$

$$P(G|P) = \frac{P(PG)}{P(PG) + P(PG')}. \tag{1}$$

In the denominator of (1), we have probabilities for the joint events PG and PG'. The rule for joint probabilities allows us to write

$$P(PG) = P(P|G)P(G)$$
$$P(PG') = P(P|G')P(G').$$

Substituting this into (1) yields

Bayes' Rule

$$P(G|P) = \frac{P(P|G)P(G)}{P(P|G)P(G) + P(P|G')P(G')}.$$

Bayes' Rule can be remembered easily if we note that in the numerator on the right we start with $P(P|G)$ which is simply the left side, $P(G|P)$, reversed. The numerator is completed in the manner of any joint probability by multiplying by $P(G)$ to give $P(P|G)P(G)$. The first term in the denominator repeats the numerator, and the second term follows by replacing the G in the first term by G'. As another example,

$$P(B|A) = \frac{P(A|B)P(B)}{P(A|B)P(B) + P(A|B')P(B')}.$$

Exercise. Write Bayes' Rule for $P(X|Y)$. Answer: $P(X|Y) = [P(Y|X)P(X)]/[P(Y|X)P(X) + P(Y|X')P(X')]$.

To help fix in mind the inverse probability concept expressed by Bayes' Rule, we shall review the last example by constructing tree diagrams. Recall that the given information was

$$P(G) \ = 0.60 \quad \text{so} \qquad P(G') = 0.40.$$
$$P(P\,|\,G) = 0.80 \quad \text{and} \quad P(P\,|\,G') = 0.40.$$

From these probabilities, we compute

$$P(GP) \ = P(G)P(P\,|\,G) \ \ = (0.6)(0.8) = 0.48.$$
$$P(G'P) = P(G')P(P\,|\,G') = (0.4)(0.4) = 0.16.$$

Figure 9–3A shows the probabilities now at hand. Note that this figure has *good* as given and shows the branch probability of passing the test, if good, is 0.8. Figure 9–3B is what we want because it shows *pass* as given, and the branch (conditional) probability $P(G\,|\,P)$ is the desired probability of good, given pass. To determine this, we first observe that the probabilities for the joint events GP and $G'P$ on Figure 9–3A are the same as the probabilities for PG and PG', respectively, on Figure 9–3B, as shown. Moreover, the sum of these branch probabilities is the fork probability, 0.64, shown in Figure 9–3B, and, finally, following a tree rule,

$$(0.64)P(G\,|\,P) = 0.48.$$

From this, we have

$$P(G\,|\,P) = \frac{0.48}{0.64} = 0.75,$$

as before.

The tree presentation just given serves well to show the inverse probability concept inherent in Bayes' Rule. For problem solving, one may use the symbolic formula, a table, or the tree approach.

We now offer a second application of Bayes' Rule.

Example. Suppose the probability that a person has disease X is

$$P(X) = 0.09.$$

The probability that medical examination will indicate the disease if a person has it is

$$P(I\,|\,X) = 0.6.$$

The probability that medical examination will indicate the disease if a person does not have it is

$$P(I\,|\,X') = 0.05.$$

What is the probability that a person has the disease if medical examination so indicates?

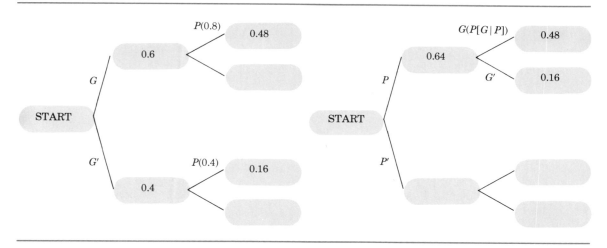

FIGURE 9–3A

FIGURE 9–3B

By Bayes' Rule:

$$P(X \mid I) = \frac{P(I \mid X)P(X)}{P(I \mid X)P(X) + P(I \mid X')P(X')}$$

$$= \frac{(0.6)(0.09)}{(0.6)(0.09) + (0.05)(0.91)}$$

$$= \frac{0.054}{0.0995} = 0.543.$$

The same result could be obtained by applying the tabular analysis used earlier in this section. We see that the prior probability of the person having the disease, 0.09, has been revised to the posterior probability 0.543 as a consequence of the additional information that medical examination indicated the disease.

9.11 PROBLEM SET 9–3

1. Supervisors rate 87.5 percent of the workers as good workers. On a work-aptitude test, 64 percent of the good workers and 24 percent of the other (not good) workers obtained passing grades. If a worker passes the test, what is the probability that this is a good worker?

2. The probability that a person has disease X is 0.05. The probability that a medical test will indicate the disease is present is 0.80 if the person has the disease and 0.02 if the person does not have the disease. What is the probability that a person has the disease if the medical test so indicates?

3. A fellow notes that his girl friend is happy on 60 percent of his visits to her home and that 40 percent of the times when she is happy she makes a drink for him. She makes drinks on 10 percent of the visits when she is not happy. If the fellow arrives on a visit

9.11 PROBLEM SET 9–3 (concluded)

and finds his friend making drinks, what is the probability that she is happy?

4. The probability that a customer will be a bad debt is 0.01. The probability that he will make a large down payment if he is a bad debt is 0.20, and the probability that he will make a large down payment if he is not a bad debt is 0.60.
   a) Suppose that a customer makes a large down payment. Find the posterior probability that he will be a bad debt.
   b) What is the probability that a customer who does not make a large down payment will be a bad debt?

5. The probability that a machine is running properly is 0.95. From time to time, samples of output are selected and measured, and the sample average is computed. If the machine is running properly, the probability that the sample average will be in a certain range is 0.9. If the machine is not running properly, the probability that the sample average will be in this range is 0.04.
   a) A sample is selected, and its average is in the range. What is the probability that the machine is running correctly?
   b) What is the probability that the machine is running correctly if the sample average is not in the range?

6. Two economic theories, T_1 and T_2, are proposed by two leading economists to predict the behavior of the GNP in the coming year. In the past, the two economists have been equally reliable, so we assign an equal prior probability of 0.50 to each theory. Let I be the event that the GNP increases, D the event that the GNP decreases, and S the event that the GNP is about the same as the previous year. Suppose that we have the following probabilities

Theory	$P(T_i)$	$P(I \mid T_i)$	$P(D \mid T_i)$	$P(S \mid T_i)$
T_1	0.50	0.25	0.50	0.25
T_2	0.50	0.125	0.75	0.125

a) Applying Bayes' Rule, find the probabilities that we would now assign to T_1 and T_2 if the GNP is actually the same or about the same as the previous year.
b) Find the probabilities that we would now assign to T_1 and T_2 if the GNP has decreased from the previous year.

7. In Problem 6, assume that the two economists are not equally reliable from past experience, so that we assign $P(T_1) = 0.40$ and $P(T_2) = 0.60$. Find the probabilities that we would now assign to T_1 and T_2 if the GNP has increased over the previous year.

8. The following table is developed by a manufacturing firm indicating production by three machines, A, B, and C.

Machine	A	B	C
Percent of total number of items produced	40%	25%	35%
Probability of a defective item	0.02	0.005	0.15

If one item selected at random from the production line is defective, find the probability that the item was produced by
a) Machine A.
b) Machine B.
c) Machine C.

9. The Business People Computer Company loses a shipment of its goods because of a mistake by one of its partners. The firm has three partners (John, Anne, and Sally) who could have made the mistake and it cannot tell with certainty which one was responsible. On the basis of past performance, it is known that the probability that John would make such a mistake is 0.001 (if he is responsible for the shipment), the probability for Anne is 0.002, and for Sally is 0.001. If John is responsible for 50 percent of the shipments, and Anne and Sally share the rest of the responsibilities equally, what is the probability that each partner was responsible for the lost shipment?

9.12 EXPERIMENT, EVENT, SAMPLE SPACE

The word *experiment* usually is associated with the natural sciences. However, it is also used in a very broad sense in probability to specify what we plan to do. For example, one experiment may be to select 10 items from a continuous production line, examine them, and record the number of defectives. Another experiment may be to select a sample of 100 families and record the date at which they last purchased an automobile.

A formal definition of an experiment would be

> **Definition.** An *experiment* is the process of making an observation or taking a measurement.

An outcome of an experiment is called an *event*.

> **Definition.** A *simple event* is an event that cannot be decomposed into two or more events. The collection of all simple events of our experiment is called a *sample space*.

For example, consider the experiment of testing two fire alarms by subjecting them to fire and recording whether they worked or failed. *One* way to construct the sample space is to use ordered pairs such as *SF*, which means the first was successful and the second failed. We have

Events, Sample Space 1

SS
SF
FS
FF

Observe that the occurrence of one of the events (say *SS*) excludes the possibility of occurrence of any of the others, so the events are mutually exclusive. Moreover, every possible event is listed, so this is a proper sample space.

Often, more than one sample space can be constructed for an experiment. In the case at hand, we could describe all possible events by listing the three mutually exclusive events 0 fail, 1 fails, 2 fail. Thus,

Events, Sample Space 2

Number Failing
0
1
2

Returning to Sample Space 1 and recalling the assumption of independence with $P(S) = 0.9$ and $P(F) = 0.1$, we can compute $P(SS) = (0.9)(0.9) = 0.81$, and so on leading to the following listing of the sample space and probabilities.

Sample Space 1, with Probabilities

Event	Probability
SS	0.81
SF	0.09
FS	0.09
FF	0.01
	1.00

The sum of the probabilities of the simple events in a sample space must be one, as indicated above.

Turning now to probabilities for Sample Space 2, the event *zero fail* is the event *SS*, so $P(0) = 0.81$. Similarly, the event *two fail* is the event *FF*, so $P(2) = 0.01$. However, the event *one fails* occurs if *FS* or *SF* occurs. Keeping in mind that the latter two are mutually exclusive, we have

$$P(FS \cup SF) = P(FS) + P(SF) = 0.09 + 0.09 = 0.18.$$

We thus have

Sample Space 2, with Probabilities

Number Failing	Probability
0	0.81
1	0.18
2	0.01
	1.00

A special way of constructing a sample space is to place each event in one or the other of two categories. In the last table, for example, we could say E is the event *zero fail* and E' is the event *one or more fail.* We have

$$P(E) = 0.81$$
$$P(E') = 0.19$$
$$P(E) + P(E') = 1.00.$$

According to our earlier definition, E' is the complement of E. Clearly, complementary events constitute a sample space because they are mutually exclusive and the sum of their probabilities is one. The rule for complementary events,

$$P(E') = 1 - P(E),$$

finds frequent application. Returning to the fire alarm example, the most important consideration is the probability that at least one of the two alarms functions in case of fire. This could be computed as

$$P(SS) + P(SF) + P(FS),$$

but the computation is simplified if we note that the event FF is the complement of the three just mentioned. Hence, the desired probability is

$$1 - P(FF) = 1 - 0.01 = 0.99.$$

Exercise. If the store had three independent alarms with $P(S) = 0.9$ and $P(F) = 0.1$, what is the probability that at least one functions successfully? Answer: $1 - P(0) = 1 - P(FFF) = 1 - (0.1)(0.1)(0.1) = 0.999$.

Note on terminology. Readers are sometimes puzzled by the term *at least*, and similar terms. Some equivalences are shown in the following to help make clear the meaning of terms that appear quite frequently. In reading the equivalences, assume x can be zero or any positive whole number; that is, 0, 1, 2, 3, $\cdots$ and so on.

Equivalences

x is at least 5;	x is 5 or more;	$x \geq 5$;	$x > 4$.
x is at most 4;	x is 4 or less;	$x \leq 4$;	$x < 5$.
x is exactly 3;	x is 3;	$x = 3$.	
x is less than 5;	x is 4 or less;	$x < 5$;	$x \leq 4$.
x is greater than 6;	x exceeds 6;	$x > 6$;	$x \geq 7$.

9.13 PROBLEM SET 9–4

1. A box contains seven good and three defective items. If a sample of two items is selected, what is the probability that:
   a) Both will be good?
   b) Both will be defective?
   c) Exactly one will be defective. (Note: Two events are involved.)
   d) If a sample of three items is selected, what is the probability that at least one will be defective? (Hint: What is the complement of at least one defective?)

2. In the manufacture of an expensive product, each item is inspected independently by two women. The probability that either

woman will correctly classify an item as defective is 0.95. If a defective item is inspected, what is the probability that:
   a) Both will correctly classify the item?
   b) Neither will correctly classify the item?
   c) At least one will correctly classify the item?
   d) Exactly one will correctly classify the item? (Two events.)
   e) The second will correctly classify the item if the first did not? Why?

3. Three coins are to be tossed.
   a) Write the sample space in terms of *HHT*, and so on, where *HHT* means first coin

9.13 PROBLEM SET 9–4 (concluded)

heads, second heads, and third tails. (There are eight events.)
b) Write the sample space in terms of the number of heads.
c) Construct a probability table for (a).
d) Construct a probability table for (b).

What is the probability of:
e) At least one head?
f) At least two heads?
g) Exactly one head?
h) Exactly two heads?

4. An election results in a tie among two women (W_1 and W_2) and one man (M). It is decided to select two people at random from the three and appoint the first selected as president and the second selected as vice president.
a) Construct a sample space using, for example, W_1M to mean woman one is president, and the man is vice president. Assign probabilities to each event in the sample space.

Using the results of (a), what is the probability that:
b) The man will be president?
c) The man will be either president or vice president?

d) What is the probability women will occupy both offices?

5. See Problem 4, but do not refer to the sample space.
a) Using W to represent either woman, write the symbol for the joint event that specifies the man is vice president.
b) Compute the probability for the event in (a) using the conditional probability rule.
c) Write the symbols for the event that a man is selected for neither office.
d) Compute the probability for the event in (c) using the conditional probability rule.

6. A sample space consists of the five simple events E_1, E_2, E_3, E_4, and E_5. The events E_1, E_2, E_3, and E_4 are equally likely, but $P(E_5) = 2P(E_2)$. Find
a) $P(E_1)$.
b) $P(E_2 \cup E_5)$.
c) $P(E_3 \cup (E_1 \cap E_5))$.

7. Describe the associated sample space and state how many simple events are in it if the experiment is to:
a) Draw a poker hand of five cards from a standard deck of 52 cards.
b) Toss a coin n times, and the result, heads or tails, is recorded.

9.14 DISCRETE RANDOM VARIABLES

In many situations, we are not interested in each simple event, but in some numerical value associated with each event. For example, if we toss two dice we are more interested in the sum of the values showing on the dice than the individual value on each die. In sampling 100 households for an election poll, we are more interested in the number of positive responses than in which households had a particular response. In each of these examples, we are considering a rule that assigns a numerical value to each simple event in an experiment. Such a rule or function is called a random variable and is usually denoted by the capital letter X.

Definition. A *random variable* is a rule that assigns one (and only one) numerical value to each simple event of an experiment.

Consider the experiment of tossing two coins. Let X be the random variable that assigns the number of heads in each toss as a numerical value. From Table 9–3, we can see for example that there are two simple events, E_2 and E_3, which produce a random variable value of 1.

TABLE 9–3

Simple Event	Number of Heads, x	P(X = x)
E_1: HH	2	$\frac{1}{4}$
E_2: HT	1	$\frac{1}{4}$
E_3: TH	1	$\frac{1}{4}$
E_4: TT	0	$\frac{1}{4}$

We are really interested in the probability $P(X = x)$, abbreviated $p(x)$, of occurrence of each of the values x that X will take on. In the current example, we have $p(0) = \frac{1}{4}$ from E_4, $p(1) = \frac{1}{2}$ from E_2 and E_3, and $p(2) = \frac{1}{4}$ from E_1. Such a function $p(x)$ is called a probability density function or probability distribution of the random variable X. We exhibit these probabilities for the current example of Table 9–3 in Table 9–4.

We can also present this same probability distribution on a graph called a histogram, as shown in Figure 9–4. A table and a histogram are the two customary ways of presenting a probability distribution of the random variable X.

There are two properties that a random variable must satisfy. The first property is the obvious one that the probability of each outcome must be between zero and one. The second is that the sum of the probabilities of all possible outcomes must be one. Why? Because every time an experiment is performed, some event (i.e., some value of the random variable) must occur and the total probability must be distributed throughout these events so that their probabilities will sum to one.

TABLE 9–4

Number of Heads, x	Probability of X = x, p(x)
0	$\frac{1}{4}$
1	$\frac{1}{2}$
2	$\frac{1}{4}$

FIGURE 9–4

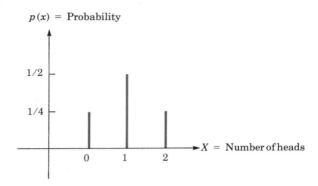

We can formalize these two properties as follows:

If we have any random variable X that has possible values $x_1, x_2, \ldots,$ x_n, then

$$\text{a)} \quad 0 \le p(x_i) \le 1, \quad i = 1, 2, \ldots, n$$

and

$$\text{b)} \quad p(x_1) + p(x_2) + \cdots + p(x_n) = 1.$$

In our coin-tossing example, it is easy to verify property (a). As for property (b), note from Table 9–4 that

$$p(0) + p(1) + p(2) = \frac{1}{4} + \frac{1}{2} + \frac{1}{4} = 1.$$

Example. Consider the tossing of two dice. What is the probability distribution of the random variable representing the sum of the faces of the two dice?

Let the random variable X be the sum of the two faces. We first need to list the possible outcomes x for X, then compute the probability of each outcome.

Sum, x	2	3	4	5	6	7	8	9	10	11	12
Probability $p(x)$	$\frac{1}{36}$	$\frac{2}{36}$	$\frac{3}{36}$	$\frac{4}{36}$	$\frac{5}{36}$	$\frac{6}{36}$	$\frac{5}{36}$	$\frac{4}{36}$	$\frac{3}{36}$	$\frac{2}{36}$	$\frac{1}{36}$

What do you suppose the average value of the sum of the dice is? We expect to toss two 1's for a sum of $x = 2$ one out of every 36 times. Also we would expect to toss a sum of 3 two out of every 36 times, a sum of 4 three out of every 36 times, and so on. Verify these values by listing all possible ways of throwing a sum of 2, 3, and 4 out of the 36 possible rolls. Thus in the long run, the expected value of X, which we write as $E(X)$, is

$$E(X) = 2\left(\frac{1}{36}\right) + 3\left(\frac{2}{36}\right) + 4\left(\frac{3}{36}\right) + \cdots + 12\left(\frac{1}{36}\right) = \frac{252}{36} = 7.$$

Does this mean that we can expect with certainty to toss a 7 eventually? Absolutely not! It is very important to realize that the expected value of a random variable is the average value of the outcomes over a large number of experiments. It is not a guaranteed outcome and indeed may not even be an actual outcome itself.

Exercise.   Consider the experiment of tossing one die and let $X =$ the number of dots on the upper face. Compute $E(X)$.   Answer: 3.5.

Definition. If we have a random variable X with values $x_1, x_2, \ldots, x_n$ and corresponding probabilities $p_1, p_2, \ldots, p_n$, then $E(X) = p_1 x_1 + p_2 x_2 + \cdots + p_n x_n = \sum_{i=1}^{n} p_i x_i$. $E(X)$ is called the *expected value* or *mean value of X.*

In some sense, the mean value of X is the central balance point around which the actual X values occur. For this reason, the expected value or mean value of a random variable X is called a measure of central tendency of X and is frequently denoted by μ to denote mean.

We will now look at a second important measure for X. To do this, let us assume we toss a single die 20 times and get two 1's, three 2's, four 3's, five 4's, four 5's, and two 6's; i.e.;

$$1, 1, 2, 2, 2, 3, 3, 3, 3, 4, 4, 4, 4, 4, 5, 5, 5, 5, 6, 6.$$

The probability distribution for this experiment is shown in Table 9–5, and the histogram is shown in Figure 9–5. What do you think about this die? Would you not have expected each face of the die to have come up about an equal number of times if the die were "fair"? This certainly

---

TABLE 9–5

x	1	2	3	4	5	6
p(x)	0.10	0.15	0.20	0.25	0.20	0.10

FIGURE 9–5

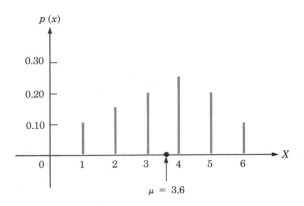

should be the case in the long run, but we have only $n = 20$ outcomes in the current experiment. If such a probability distribution were to hold up in the long run, then the die would be called "unfair" or "loaded."

> **Exercise.** Find $\mu = E(X)$ for a loaded die with the same probability distribution as that given in Table 9–5. Answer: 3.6, as shown in Figure 9–5.

In addition to the central balance point μ of the distribution, it would be useful to see how scattered the distribution is. For this purpose, we obtain a measure of the dispersion or a measure of the amount of spread in the distribution of probabilities about the central point μ. The two most common measures of dispersion are the variance and the standard deviation of the random variable X.

> **Definition.** For a random variable X with values $x_1, x_2, \ldots, x_n$ and corresponding probabilities $p_1, p_2, \ldots, p_n$, the *variance* is defined as
>
> $$\sigma^2(X) = (x_1 - \mu)^2 p_1 + (x_2 - \mu)^2 p_2 + \cdots + (x_n - \mu)^2 p_n$$
>
> where
>
> $$\mu = E(X) = x_1 p_1 + x_2 p_2 + \cdots + x_n p_n$$
>
> is the mean of the distribution.

The *standard deviation* of X is the positive square root of the variance, so

$$\sigma(X) = \sqrt{\sigma^2(X)}.$$

The standard deviation is the most frequently referred to measure of dispersion since it has the same units as the values of X.

As an example of how to compute the variance and standard deviation, let us reconsider the loaded die. We first compute

$$\sigma^2(X) = (x_1 - \mu)^2 p_1 + (x_2 - \mu)^2 p_2 + (x_3 - \mu)^2 p_3$$
$$+ (x_4 - \mu)^2 p_4 + (x_5 - \mu)^2 p_5 + (x_6 - \mu)^2 p_6$$

$$= (1 - 3.6)^2(0.10) + (2 - 3.6)^2(0.15) + (3 - 3.6)^2(0.20)$$
$$+ (4 - 3.6)^2(0.25) + (5 - 3.6)^2(0.20) + (6 - 3.6)^2(0.10)$$

$$= 2.14.$$

Thus, the standard deviation is

$$\sigma(X) = \sqrt{2.14} = 1.46.$$

Exercise. Compute the variance and standard deviation for the random variable $X =$ the number of dots on the face of a fair die. Answer: $\sigma^2(X) = 2.92$, $\sigma(X) = 1.71$.

The computations involving the mean, variance, and standard deviation of a set of data from an experiment can become very complex and tedious. However, computer packages such as Minitab, SAS, and SPSS have been developed to help us compute the important descriptive statistical values. As an example, the computer output in Table 9–6 uses Minitab on a VAX 11/780 to draw a histogram and find a set of measures including the mean and standard deviation of the 20 rolls of our loaded die. Notice that the standard deviation, STDEV, in this table is 1.501, whereas we earlier computed $\sigma(X)$ to be 1.46. The reason for the difference is that the computer package treats the data as a sample of a larger population, whereas we treated the data as an entire population.

In addition to computer packages, some calculators have special function keys to simplify the computation of the mean, variance, and standard deviation of a set of data. If you have such a calculator, compute the mean and standard deviation of the 20 rolls of our loaded die.

TABLE 9-6

```
Username: SABER
Password:
         Welcome to VAX/VMS version V4.3 on node VAX2
$ MINITAB
MTB > SET C1
DATA> 1,1,2,2,2,3,3,3,3,4,4,4,4,4,5,5,5,5,6,6
DATA> END
MTB > HIST C1

Histogram of C1    N = 20

Midpoint              Count
       1                2    **
       2                3    ***
       3                4    ****
       4                5    *****
       5                4    ****
       6                2    **

MTB > DESC C1

                   N      MEAN    MEDIAN    TRMEAN     STDEV    SEMEAN
C1                20     3.600     4.000     3.611     1.501     0.336

                 MIN       MAX        Q1        Q3
C1             1.000     6.000     2.250     5.000
MTB > STOP
$LO
```

9.15 PROBLEM SET 9–5

In Problems 1–6, draw a histogram of the probability distribution and find the expected value and standard deviation of the random variable X.

1.

x	1	2	3	4	5	6
$p(x)$	0.1	0.2	0.2	0.2	0.2	0.1

2.

x	1	2	3	4	5	6
$p(x)$	0.1	0.2	0.2	0.3	0.1	0.1

3.

x	1	2	3	4	5	6
$p(x)$	0.4	0.3	0.1	0.1	0.05	0.05

4.

x	−1	0	1	2	3
$p(x)$	0.3	0.1	0.1	0.1	0.4

5.

x	−2	−1	0	1	2
$p(x)$	0.1	0.1	0.3	0.4	0.1

6.

x	−3	−2	−1	0	1
$p(x)$	0.3	0.4	0.1	0.1	0.1

9.15 PROBLEM SET 9–5 (*concluded*)

7. Explain why each of the following is or is not a valid probability distribution for a random variable X.

a)

x	p(x)
0	0.3
1	0.6
2	0.2

b)

x	p(x)
−1	0.25
0	0.30
1	0.20
2	0.25

c)

x	p(x)
3	−0.25
8	0.50
11	0.75

8. Given the following probability distribution for the random variable X:

x	10	20	30	40	50	60
p(x)	0.10	0.15	0.25	0.25	0.15	0.10

a) Find μ, σ^2 and σ.
b) Graph p(x).
c) Locate μ and the interval $\mu \pm 2\sigma$ on your graph. What is the probability that X will fall within the interval $\mu \pm 2\sigma$, $\mu \pm \sigma$?

9. Given the following probability distribution for the random variable X:

x	1	2	3	4	5
p(x)	0.05	0.15	0.30	0.25	0.25

a) Find μ, σ^2 and σ.
b) Graph p(x).
c) Locate μ and the interval $\mu \pm 3\sigma$ on your graph. What is the probability that x will fall within the interval $\mu \pm 3\sigma$, $\mu \pm \sigma$?

10. A local weekly newspaper receives orders for one-, two-, and three-year subscriptions, with probabilities ¼, ½, and ¼, respectively. For each subscription year, it receives $2. What is the expected return for each order received?

11. Use a calculator or computer package to solve Problems 1 through 6, 8, and 9.

9.16 THE BINOMIAL PROBABILITY DISTRIBUTION

We now look at a special discrete probability distribution called the binomial probability distribution. Let us assume that a basketball player is successful (hits) on 40 percent of his free-throw trials. Letting H represent *hit* and M represent *miss*, we assign

$$P(\text{Hit}) = P(H) = p = 0.40$$
$$P(\text{Miss}) = P(M) = q = 1 - p = 0.60.$$

We assume further that the outcome of one trial is *independent* of the outcomes of other trials and that p and q are the same on every trial.[4] If we consider the probability of the five hits in a row, we find

$$P(5) = P(HHHHH) = (0.4)(0.4)(0.4)(0.4)(0.4) = (0.4)^5$$
$$= 0.01024.$$

Next, consider $P(4)$, the probability of four hits in the next five trials. One way this can be done is *HHHHM;* that is, hit on the first four trials

---

[4] This assumption, which is *required* in the development of the binomial distribution, may be subject to question in this case because players do have their ups and downs.

and miss on the fifth. Another way is *HHHMH*. Writing all the events which constitute four hits and a miss, together with their probabilities, we find:

Components of Event Four Hits	Probability
HHHHM	$(0.4)(0.4)(0.4)(0.4)(0.6) = (0.4)^4(0.6)^1$
HHHMH	$(0.4)(0.4)(0.4)(0.6)(0.4) = (0.4)^4(0.6)^1$
HHMHH	$(0.4)(0.4)(0.6)(0.4)(0.4) = (0.4)^4(0.6)^1$
HMHHH	$(0.4)(0.6)(0.4)(0.4)(0.4) = (0.4)^4(0.6)^1$
MHHHH	$(0.6)(0.4)(0.4)(0.4)(0.4) = (0.4)^4(0.6)^1$

The five events just written are mutually exclusive, so the total probability, $P(4)$, is the sum of the five probabilities. Moreover, the five probabilities are equal, so that

$$P(4) = 5(0.4)^4(0.6)^1 = 5(0.01536) = 0.0768.$$

In the last statement, note that

$$P(4) = \text{(Number of ways of getting four hits and a miss)} \ p^4q^1.$$

If we next ask for the probability of three hits in the next five trials, we would have

$$P(3) = \text{(Number of ways of getting three hits and two misses)} \ p^3q^2.$$

One way to get three hits is *HHHMM*, another way is *HHMHM*, and if we persist we will find there are 10 different sequences in the event (three hits, two misses) in five trials. Fortunately, we can compute this number by the formula

$$C_3^5 = \frac{5!}{3!(5-3)!} = \frac{5!}{3!(2!)} = \frac{5(4)3!}{3!(2)(1)} = \frac{20}{2} = 10.$$

The symbol at the left in the above is read as *the number of combinations of five things taken three at a time*. In the present application, it is the number of different ways of arranging five things of which three are of one kind and the remaining $5 - 3 = 2$ are of another kind.

We now have

$$P(3) = C_3^5 p^3q^2$$
$$= 10(0.4)^3(0.6)^2 = 10(0.02304) = 0.2304.$$

Exercise. Find the probability of two hits and three misses in the next five trials. Answer: $C_2^5 \ p^2q^3 = 10(0.4)^2(0.6)^3 = 10(0.03456) = 0.3456.$

We may now generalize our demonstrations and state that if n independent trials are made, where p is the probability of outcome A and $q = 1 - p$ is the probability of the complementary outcome A' on any trial, then the probability that A will occur x times in the n trials is:

Binomial Probability Rule

$$P(x) = C_x^n p^x q^{n-x}.$$

As an example, let us compute the probability that the basketball player hits exactly three times in his next 10 tries. We have

$$n = 10, \quad p = 0.4, \quad q = 0.6, \quad x = 3,$$

and

$$P(3) = C_3^{10} p^3 q^{10-3} = \frac{10!}{3!7!}(0.4)^3(0.6)^7$$

$$= \frac{10(9)(8)}{3!}(0.4)^3(0.6)^7$$

$$= 120(0.064)(0.0279936)$$

$$= 0.215.$$

Exercise. Compute the probability that the player will hit exactly twice in his next six trials. Answer: $15(0.16)(0.1296) = 0.31104$.

If we seek the probability that $x = 0$ in $n = 7$ trials, it is clear that there is only *one* way, *MMMMMMM*, that this can occur. The binomial rule states

$$P(0) = C_0^7(0.4)^0(0.6)^7$$

$$= \frac{7!}{0!7!}(0.4)^0(0.6)^7.$$

The count,

$$\frac{7!}{0!7!},$$

must be *one* so, for consistency, we state

Definition. $0! = 1$.

Then,

$$P(0) = \frac{7!}{0!7!}(0.4)^0(0.6)^7 = 1(1)(0.6)^7$$
$$= 0.0280.$$

One can compute the mean, variance, and standard deviation of the binomial probability distribution as we did in the last section. It turns out that some very nice formulas can be found for these values

> Mean: $\mu = np$
>
> Variance: $\sigma^2 = npq$
>
> Standard deviation: $\sigma = \sqrt{npq}.$

So, the expected value for our basketball player in five free throws is

$$\mu = 5(0.4) = 2.0$$

hits; i.e., in the long run he can expect to average two out of every five free throws.

> **Exercise.**   Compute the mean, variance, and standard deviation of the binomial random variable for $n = 7, p = 0.4$.
> Answer: $\mu = 2.8, \sigma^2 = 1.68, \sigma = 1.30$.

Binomial situations arise in many applications. For example, we may record an inspected item as good or defective, check male or female on a questionnaire, classify accounts receivable as active or bad debts, and so on. In some situations we apply the binomial rule even though the requisite constancy of probability from trial to trial is only approximately correct. For example, if we draw items from a batch of 100,000 items, of which 100 are defective, we would have

$$P(\text{First is defective}) = P(D_1) = \frac{100}{100,000} = 0.001.$$

The probability that the second is also defective, correctly computed, is not 0.001 but is

$$P(D_2 \mid D_1) = \frac{99}{99,999} = 0.00099.$$

The difference noted between 0.001 and 0.00099 would be lessened if we were drawing from a batch larger than 100,000. To call attention to this approximate use of the binomial, we shall indicate that selection is made from a (very) *large* group and *not* state the number in the group. For example, suppose that 35 percent of the people in a *large* area are independent voters. We select 10 people and compute the probability that exactly six are independents as, approximately,

$$P(6) = C_6^{10}(0.35)^6(0.65)^4$$
$$= \frac{10(9)(8)(7)}{(4)(3)(2)(1)}(0.35)^6(0.65)^4$$
$$= 210(0.001838)(0.1785) = 0.0689.$$

Exercise. In a large batch of items, 10 percent are defective. If a sample of five is selected, what is the probability that exactly three will be defective? Answer: $C_3^5 (0.1)^3(0.9)^2 = 10(0.001)(0.81) = 0.0081$.

At least one occurrence. Some applications require the computation of the probability of at least one occurrence. For example, suppose the assembly of a machine requires five independent operations, and the probability that any operation will result in a defect is 0.01. Further, the assembly is defective if one or more operations is defective; that is, if the number of defective operations is 1, 2, 3, 4, or 5. Hence, we seek the probability of at least one defective operation, which is the complement of zero defective.

$$P(\text{At least one defective}) = 1 - P(0 \text{ defective})$$
$$= 1 - C_0^5(0.01)^0(0.99)^5$$
$$= 1 - 1(1)(0.99)^5$$
$$= 1 - 0.951$$
$$= 0.049.$$

Exercise. A town has three ambulances for emergency transportation to the hospital. The probability that any one of the ambulances will be available at a point in time is 0.90. If a person calls for an ambulance, what is the probability that at least one will be available? Answer: $1 - (0.1)^3 = 0.999$.

As a variation on the last example and exercise, consider a car salesman who makes telephone calls during the day to obtain prospective car buyers. He assesses the probability of obtaining a prospect on a given call as 0.10. How many calls should he make if his goal is to have a probability of 0.90 of obtaining at least one prospect? Here we have:

$$P(\text{At least one prospect}) = 1 - P(\text{No prospects}) = 0.90,$$

or

$$1 - C_0^n(0.10)^0(0.90)^n = 0.90$$
$$1 - (0.90)^n = 0.90$$
$$-(0.90)^n = -0.10$$
$$(0.90)^n = 0.10.$$

We solve for n by taking natural logarithms of both sides,

$$n \ln (0.90) = \ln (0.10)$$
$$n = \frac{\ln (0.10)}{\ln (0.90)}$$
$$= \frac{-2.30259}{-0.10536} = 21.9,$$

or about 22 calls.

Exercise.   A complicated computer program has a flaw or "bug" in it, and will not execute properly. The program is to be sent to n experts, each of whom has a probability of 0.4 of finding the bug. What should n be if the probability that at least one expert will find the flaw is to be 0.99?   Answer: 9.

9.17 CUMULATIVE BINOMIAL PROBABILITIES

The binomial rule as applied in the preceding section computes the probability of *exactly* x occurrences in n trials. Thus, in examples where we drew, say, five items from a large lot and recorded the number of defectives, the binomial rule calculates $P(2)$, the probability of exactly two defectives, or $P(1)$, and so on. In actual application, the purpose of drawing the sample is to make a decision on whether or not to *accept the whole lot* on the basis of the sample evidence. Thus, the quality control department may have a *sampling plan* that specifies that five items are to be drawn and inspected, and the *whole lot* is to be accepted if no more than one defective is found in the sample. That is, the lot is accepted if the sample contains zero or one defective; otherwise, the lot is rejected. Hence, if the *lot* is 10 percent defective

$$P(\text{Acceptance}) = P(\text{None defective}) + P(\text{One defective})$$
$$= P(0) + P(1)$$
$$= C_0^5(0.1)^0(0.9)^5 + C_1^5(0.1)^1(0.9)^4$$
$$= (0.9)^5 + 5(0.1)(0.9)^4$$
$$= 0.59049 + 0.32805$$
$$= 0.91854.$$

The probability of acceptance is about 0.92, so if lots 10 percent defective are submitted to this sampling plan, 92 percent will be accepted and only 8 percent rejected.

> **Exercise.** If, in the preceding, lots submitted are 1 percent defective, what is the probability of acceptance and rejection? Answer: $(0.99)^5 + 5(0.01)(0.99)^4 = 0.951 + 0.048 = 0.999$ as the probability of acceptance and 0.001 as the probability of rejection.

If we consider 10 percent defective as poor quality and 1 percent defective as good quality, then the sampling plan at hand, with a sample of $n = 5$, has a high probability (0.999) of accepting good quality, but also an undesirably high probability (0.92) of accepting poor quality. We can easily see that the probability of accepting poor quality would be reduced by selecting a larger sample, say 20, and accepting the lot only if *none* of the 20 is defective. Now, if lots are 10 percent defective,

$$P(\text{Acceptance}) = P(\text{None defective}) = C_0^{20}(0.1)^0(0.9)^{20} = 0.12.$$

This plan offers better protection against the acceptance of poor lots. On the other hand, a good lot (say, 1 percent defective) now has

$$P(\text{Acceptance}) = P(\text{None defective}) = C_0^{20}(0.01)^0(0.99)^{20} = 0.82,$$

so in reducing the probability of accepting poor lots (from 0.92 to 0.12) we also lower the probability of accepting good lots (from 0.999 to 0.82). Clearly, the choice of sampling plan (number in the sample to be inspected and the number of defectives permitted in the sample) can be adjusted to achieve a balance between the chances of accepting good and poor lots. For example, we may select 25, and accept the lot if it has no more than three defectives. If p is the proportion defective in a lot, then

$$
\begin{aligned}
P(\text{Acceptance}) &= P(0, 1, 2, \text{ or } 3 \text{ defectives}) \\
&= P(0) + P(1) + P(2) + P(3) \\
&= C_0^{25}\,p^0 q^{25} + C_1^{25}\,p^1 q^{24} + C_2^{25}\,p^2 q^{23} + C_3^{25}\,p^3 q^{22} \\
&= \sum_{x=0}^{3} C_x^{25}\,p^x q^{25-x}.
\end{aligned}
$$

We refer to the last expression as a *cumulative* binomial probability, and hasten to add that tables are available for these cumulative probabilities. Tables X–A ($n = 10$) and X–B ($n = 25$) at the end of the book will be used in our examples and exercises. For the problem at hand, we find from Table X–B that for $p = 0.01$

$$\sum_{x=0}^{3} C_x^{25}\,(0.01)^x(0.99)^{25-x} = 1.000.$$

The tabular entries have been rounded to three decimals and the last-written number, 1.000, does not mean exactly one, but a number less than 1 that rounds to 1.000. We interpret this result by saying that if $n = 25$

items are selected from a lot which is one percent defective and three defectives are allowed in the sample, it is almost certain that the lot will be accepted.

> **Exercise.** For the preceding find the probability of acceptance if the lot is 10 percent defective. Answer: 0.764.

To demonstrate an understanding of cumulative probabilities, we should be able to write summation expressions similar to the one we wrote in the above. Thus, if we toss a coin 50 times and seek the probability of getting *at most* 10 heads, we have $n = 50$, $p = 0.5$. The probability of $0, 1, 2, \ldots, 10$ heads would be expressed as

$$\sum_{x=0}^{10} C_x^{50} (0.5)^x (0.5)^{50-x}.$$

> **Exercise.** If a salesperson's probability of making a sale on any contact is 0.08, express in summation symbols the probability of making at most 15 sales in 100 contacts.
>
> Answer: $\sum_{x=0}^{15} C_x^{100} (0.08)^x (0.92)^{100-x}.$

Now, for brevity, we shall express the cumulative probability for, say, 0, 1, 2, 3, 4, 5, as

$$\sum_0^5 .$$

Thus, from Table X–B, with $n = 25$, $p = 0.4$,

$$\sum_0^5 = 0.029$$

is the probability of *at most* five occurrences. If we seek the probability of *at least* five occurrences, which would be $5, 6, 7, \ldots, 25$, it would be found as the complementary probability

$$1 - \sum_0^4 = 1 - 0.009 = 0.991.$$

Again, the probability of 6 to 10 occurrences, inclusive, would be

$$\sum_0^{10} - \sum_0^5 = 0.586 - 0.029 = 0.557.$$

Finally, if we want the probability of *exactly* five occurrences, we compute

$$\sum_0^5 - \sum_0^4 = 0.029 - 0.009 = 0.020.$$

Exercise. For $n = 25, p = 0.3$, find the probability of: a) Less than 8 occurrences. b) At most 5 occurrences. c) At least 10 occurrences. d) From 5 to 11 occurrences, inclusive. e) Exactly 8 occurrences. Answer: a) 0.512. b) 0.193. c) 0.189. d) 0.866. e) 0.165.

As an application of Table X–B, suppose a student takes a 25-question true-false test and determines the answer to each by flipping a coin, so that the probability of getting the correct answer is $p = 0.5$ for each question. If 60 percent or more correct is passing, what is the probability of passing? We note that 60 percent or more is $25(0.6) = 15$ or more correct. Hence,

$$P(\text{Pass}) = \sum_{15}^{25} = 1 - \sum_0^{14} = 1 - 0.788 = 0.212.$$

The student's probability of not passing is 0.788, or about 0.8. In other terminology, the odds are about 4 to 1 against passing.

Exercise. If a student takes a 25-question four-choice multiple choice examination and judges that his probability of getting any question correct is about 0.6, what is the probability that he will get 80 percent or more correct? Answer: 0.029.

9.18 PROBLEM SET 9–6
Compute the answers to Problems 1–8 using the binomial rule.

1. A basketball player has a probability of 0.3 of hitting on any shot from the foul line. What is the probability of:
   a) Exactly one hit in three trials?
   b) At least one hit in three trials?
   c) Exactly two hits in five trials?
   d) More than two hits in four trials?

2. The probability that an inspector will properly classify an item is 0.8. If each item is inspected independently by three inspectors, what is the probability that at least one will properly classify the item?

3. A company has bid on five projects, assessing the probability of winning a contract at 0.6. To have a successful year, it must win at least two of the contracts. What is the probability for a successful year?

9.18 PROBLEM SET 9–6 (concluded)

4. A sample of six items is selected from a large lot. The *lot* is accepted if the *sample* contains no more than one defective item. Find the probabilities of accepting and rejecting a lot if the proportion defective in the lot is a) 0.1. b) 0.2.

5. A department store employs four people who take orders over the telephone. Each person is busy taking an order 70 percent of the time. What is the probability that an operator will be free to take an order at the time of a call:
   a) If one customer calls at a point in time?
   b) If three customers call at the same time?

6. See Problem 5. How many telephone operators should the store have if the probability that an operator will be free when a customer calls is to be 0.83?

7. A true-false examination has five questions, and a student guesses the answer for each question, assigning probability of 0.5 of being correct. Assuming independence, what is the probability that he gets
   a) All five correct?
   b) At least four correct?
   c) Exactly three correct?
   d) At least three correct?
   e) At least four incorrect?

8. A test has five four-choice questions, and a student guesses the answer to each question. Assuming independence, what is the probability of
   a) All five correct?
   b) At least four correct?
   c) Exactly three correct?
   d) At least three correct?

9. The probability that an item in a large group is defective is 0.05. Express the following by use of the summation symbol, but do not try to calculate the answer.

   a) The probability that at most 15 of 100 items purchased are defective.
   b) The probability that more than 10 of 200 items purchased are defective.

Use Tables X–A and X–B to answer Problems 10–15.

10. A sample of 25 items is selected from a large lot and the lot is rejected if the sample contains more than four defectives. Find the probability of acceptance if the proportion defective in a lot is: a) 0.05. b) 0.20.

11. Repeat Problem 10 assuming the lot is rejected if more than one defective is found in the sample.

12. A test has 25 five-choice questions. A student gives answers at random. What is the probability that he gets:
    a) Less than 40 percent correct?
    b) More than 40 percent correct?
    c) At least 20 percent correct?
    d) Exactly eight correct?
    e) Six to 10, inclusive, correct?
    f) At most five correct?

13. Repeat Problem 12 if the student assesses his probability of getting a correct answer at 0.5.

14. Ten percent of the (very large) supply of tires offered for sale around the country have faulty valves. If a person buys 10 of these tires (assumed to be a random selection), what is the probability that the buyer will get
    a) No faulty tires?
    b) Exactly one faulty tire?
    c) At least one faulty tire?
    d) Two or three faulty tires?

15. A company has 10 employees who, on the average, are absent from work on 5 percent of the working days. What is the probability that on a given day
    a) Exactly two are absent?
    b) Exactly nine are present?
    c) More than two are absent?
    d) One or two are absent?

9.19 EXPECTED MONETARY VALUE (EMV)

If we bet $1 that heads will appear on the toss of a coin for which we have assigned

$$P(H) = P(T) = \frac{1}{2},$$

we win $1 if heads appears, and win $-$1 (lose $1) if tails appears. We compute the *expected monetary value of the act* of tossing the coin as

$$\text{EMV} = (\text{payoff if } event\ H \text{ occurs})\ P(H)$$
$$+ (\text{payoff if } event\ T \text{ occurs})\ P(T)$$
$$= \$1\left(\frac{1}{2}\right) + (-\$1)\left(\frac{1}{2}\right) = 0.$$

More generally, the expected monetary value of an *act* is the sum of the products formed by multiplying the dollar payoff of each *event* by the probability of the event. It is assumed that the events constitute a sample space. For example, if we consider act A as having three events, E_1, E_2, and E_3, with probabilities 0.4, 0.5, and 0.1, respectively, and payoffs, $10, $-$8, and $2, then

$$\text{EMV of act } A = (0.4)(10) + (0.5)(-8) + (0.1)(2) = \$0.20.$$

Example. An urn contains five red, one white, and four green balls, and we assign probabilities

$$P(R) = 0.5$$
$$P(W) = 0.1$$
$$P(G) = 0.4.$$

A ball is to be drawn, and the payoffs are red ball, lose $1; white ball, win $3; green ball, win nothing. Compute the EMV of the act of drawing a ball.

First we build the payoff table:

P	Event	Payoff
0.5	*R*	-1
0.1	*W*	3
0.4	*G*	0

From the table, we have

$$\text{EMV} = (0.5)(-1) + (0.1)(3) + (0.4)(0)$$
$$= -\$0.20.$$

> **Exercise.** What is the expected monetary value of the act of tossing two coins if the payoffs are $0 for zero heads, $1 for one head, and $-\$1$ (loss of $1) for two heads? Answer: $(0)(\frac{1}{4}) + (\$1)(\frac{1}{2}) + (-\$1)(\frac{1}{4}) = \$0.25$.

Expected monetary value has been advanced as one criterion to aid decision making. The notion is that we list the various events that might arise in a certain situation and assign a probability to each event. In addition, we consider the payoffs that would occur for each event for each decision we might make, the decisions being the choice of act 1, act 2, and so on. Suppose that we use EMV to choose between act 1 and act 2 in Table 9–7. According to the EMV criterion, the decision maker would choose act 1 rather than act 2 because act 1 has the higher expected monetary value.

TABLE 9–7
Payoff Table

		Act	
P	Events	*A₁*	*A₂*
0.3	E_1	$2.00	$2.00
0.4	E_2	1.00	3.00
0.3	E_3	8.00	3.00
1.0			

$$\text{EMV, act 1} = (0.3)(2) + (0.4)(1) + (0.3)(8) = 3.4.$$
$$\text{EMV, act 2} = (0.3)(2) + (0.4)(3) + (0.3)(3) = 2.7.$$

Example. Items are manufactured for sale. Each unit made and sold yields a profit of $3; each unit made but not sold yields a loss of $1. It is believed that zero, one, two, or three units might be demanded by customers, but the event *four or more* units demanded is considered impossible and assigned probability zero. Other probabilities are assigned by experience and judgment (Table 9–8). Use the expected monetary value to decide whether to make zero units (act 1), one unit (act 2), two units (act 3) or three units (act 4).

The payoff table can be filled in from the given information. For example, if two units are made and one unit is demanded, one of the two would yield a profit of $3 and the other a loss of $1, for a payoff of $2 net. Again, if one unit is made and two are demanded, the payoff is $3 on the single unit made. These and the remaining payoffs are shown in Table 9–9.

TABLE 9–8

Events (Number of Units Demanded)	Probability of Number of Units Being Demanded
0	0.2
1	0.4
2	0.3
3	0.1
4 or more	0.0
	1.0

TABLE 9–9
Payoff Table

		Acts			
P	Events (Units Demanded)	A_1 (Make 0)	A_2 (Make 1)	A_3 (Make 2)	A_4 (Make 3)
0.2	0	0	−1	−2	−3
0.4	1	0	3	2	1
0.3	2	0	3	6	5
0.1	3	0	3	6	9
0.0	4 or more .	0	3	6	9
1.0					

$$\text{EMV of } A_1 = 0.0$$
$$\text{EMV of } A_2 = 2.2$$
$$\text{EMV of } A_3 = 2.8$$
$$\text{EMV of } A_4 = 2.2$$

The decision would be to choose A_3, the act with the highest EMV, and so make two units.

EMV can be useful criterion in some decisions. However, it is easy to illustrate that this criterion does not have general applicability. For example, the EMV of A_1 in the following table is \$2,500, compared to an EMV of \$200 for A_2, and yet some persons would prefer A_2 to A_1.

P	Event	A_1	A_2
0.5	E_1	\$10,000	\$400
0.5	E_2	−5,000	0

$$\text{EMV of } A_1 = \$2,500$$
$$\text{EMV of } A_2 = \$\ 200$$

The point here is that even though the EMV of A_1 is much larger than that of A_2, some people would not feel they could afford a loss of \$5,000, which would arise if they chose A_1 and event E_2 occurred. Others would prefer A_2 on the ground that they cannot lose if they choose A_2, and have a 0.5 probability of gaining \$400. Of course, a person possessing a large amount of money might well choose A_1 because he can afford to lose \$5,000 and thinks a 50–50 gamble of winning \$10,000 or losing \$5,000 is sensible.

The last illustration shows that the act chosen depends upon the person making the decision and the amounts involved. EMV may or may not be a proper guide for action. A criterion applicable when EMV is not appropriate is *expected utility value* (EUV), which allows a person to inject his or her own circumstances and inclinations into the analysis. Exploration of the EUV criterion would carry us beyond our immediate goals.[5]

One-time decisions. The probability of heads when a coin is tossed, 0.5, means that as the number of tosses increases (approaches infinity in the limit sense), the proportion or relative frequency of heads approaches 0.5 as a limit. However, if we toss a coin only once, heads or tails will appear and the 0.5 probability does not tell us which will occur. Similarly, the EMV of an act is computed from probabilities and means the average payoff we would expect to arise if the act was performed an increasingly large number of times under constant conditions, but this EMV does not tell us what will occur if the act is performed only once. Consequently, some people contend that it is not correct to apply the EMV criterion to a one-time decision. Other people, while agreeing with the long-run interpretation of EMV, contend that EMV may be applied to one-time decisions, arguing that if a person would choose act A over and over again in a repeated series of decisions, it would not be unreasonable to choose A if the decision circumstances occur only once. The latter group would also point out that management-administrative decisions typically are of the one-time variety because the circumstances under which actual decisions are made are not "constant over the long run." The controversy between those who would and those who would not use probability considerations in one-time decisions really centers upon the question of what information a decision maker would choose to consider in making a one-time decision where the outcome is uncertain. Thus, whether or not probabilities would be considered in chancy one-time decisions is a choice left to the decision maker. An informed manager or administrator should consider probabilities when making decisions where the outcome is uncertain, even if a one-time decision is at hand.

---

[5] The reader is encouraged to investigate Robert Schlaifer, *Introduction to Statistics for Business Decisions* (New York: McGraw-Hill Book Co., 1961) as the next step toward achieving a fuller understanding of the role of probability in business decisions.

9.20 PROBLEM SET 9–7

1. A pair of dice is to be rolled. If the number appearing is even, you win that even number of dollars; if the number appearing is odd, you lose that odd number of dollars. Compute the EMV of the act "rolling the pair of dice."

2. An act is accompanied by three possible events with probabilities 0.2, 0.3, and 0.5, and payoffs $2, $3, and − $1, respectively. Compute the expected monetary value of the act.

3. Urn number one contains four red, nine white, and seven green balls with payoffs $2, − $4, and $2, respectively. Urn number two contains four red and six black balls with payoffs $3 and − $1.80, respectively. If act 1 is selecting a ball from urn number one and act 2 is selecting a ball from urn number two, which act should be chosen according to the criterion of expected monetary value?

4. Which act should be chosen according to EMV?

Payoff Table

P	Event	A_1	A_2	A_3	A_4
0.2	E_1	$2	$1	$0	$0
0.1	E_2	2	2	− 1	− 3
0.4	E_3	2	3	3	3
0.3	E_4	2	2	4	5

5. If you make a unit of product and it is sold (demanded), you gain $5; if you make a unit that is not sold, you lose $2. You assign probabilities as follows:

Number of Units Demanded	Probability of Number of Units Demanded
0	0.10
1	0.20
2	0.25
3	0.40
4	0.05
5 or more	0.00

According to the EMV criterion, how many units should you make?

6. In setting premiums to charge for protection against various hazards, insurance companies must start with a base figure (exclusive of overhead and profit), which represents their expected loss. A building is to be insured in the amount of $60,000 for fire damage. The probabilities of total, 75 percent, 50 percent, and 25 percent losses in a year are, respectively, 0.0001, 0.00015, 0.0005, and 0.001. Assuming these are the only losses to be considered,
   a) What base figure should be used in computing the annual premium?
   b) Why do the probabilities given not add up to 1?

7. Think seriously about your present circumstances, and then decide in each case whether you would choose act 1 or act 2. For example, in part (a), would you prefer a 0.6 probability of gaining $3, 0.4 of losing $1, to a gamble which has a 0.6 probability of gaining $1? (There are no correct answers to this question.)

a)

P	A_1	A_2
0.6	$3	$1
0.4	− 1	0.

b)

P	A_1	A_2
0.6	$30	$10
0.4	− 10	0.

c)

P	A_1	A_2
0.5	$3,000	$500
0.5	− 1,000	0.

9.21 REVIEW PROBLEMS

1. The table shows, for example, that 40 cars of make Y had gear train malfunctions.

Make of Car	Malfunction		
	Electrical (E)	Gear Train (G)	Carburetor (C)
X	17	60	23
Y	20	40	60
Z	15	48	117

Find the following probabilities:
a) $P(Y)$.
b) $P(E)$.
c) $P(C)$.
d) $P(X \cap G)$.
e) $P(G \cap X)$.
f) $P(E \cap G)$.
g) $P(Z \cap X)$.
h) $P(Y \cap C)$.
i) $P(X \mid C)$.
j) $P(C \mid X)$.
k) $P(E \mid Z)$.
l) $P(Z \mid G)$.
m) $P(X \cup Y)$.
n) $P(X \cup C)$.
o) $P(G \cup C)$.
p) $P(Y \cup G)$.

2. See the table of Problem 1.
a) Are Z and C independent? Explain.
b) Are Y and C independent? Explain.
c) What is $P(X \cap Y)$? What does this mean?

3. a) In some areas, one may often predict tomorrow's weather correctly by stating it will be the same as today's weather. In such areas, is tomorrow's weather independent of today's weather? Explain.
b) A card is to be drawn from a deck. Let B represent black card and D represent diamond. Are B and D mutually exclusive? Independent? Explain.
c) Consider the physical traits of brown eyes, B, and dark hair, D. Are B and D mutually exclusive? Do *you* think B and D are independent?

4. a) Complete the following table if all event pairs such as AX are independent.

	X	Y	Z	Totals
A				0.40
B				0.60
Totals	0.30	0.20	0.50	

Find the following probabilities from the completed table.
b) $P(A \mid X)$.
c) $P(X \mid A)$.
d) $P(X)$.
e) $P(A)$.
f) $P(A \cup X)$.
g) $P(X \cup Y)$.

5. a) Complete the following probability table. (Note: A' and B' are complements of A and B, respectively.)

	B	B'	Total
A			0.70
A'		0.12	
Total		0.34	

b) Are A and B independent? Explain.

Compute:
c) $P(B' \mid A')$.
d) $P(A \cup B')$.

6. An investor assesses the probability that the Dow-Jones stock market average will rise tomorrow as 0.65, and the probability that the price of stock X will rise if the Dow-Jones rises as 0.90. What is the probability that the Dow-Jones will rise and X will rise? Why?

7. A candidate runs for offices A and B, assessing the probability of winning both at 0.10, and the probability of winning B at 0.25. What is the probability of winning A if he wins B? Why?

8. An investor has funds in banks A and B. He assesses the probability that A will fail at 0.0001, and assigns the same failure probability to B. Further, he thinks the probability that both banks will fail is 0.00001.
a) What is the probability that A or B will fail?

9.21 REVIEW PROBLEMS (*continued*)

b) Are the events *A* fails, *B* fails independent? Why?

c) What is the probability that *B* fails if *A* fails?

9. A box of eight items contains six good and two defective items. If a sample of two items is selected, what is the probability that:
   a) Both will be good?
   b) Both will be defective?
   c) Exactly one will be defective? (Note: Two events are involved.)
   d) If three items are drawn, what is the probability that at least one will be defective?

10. A box contains four items, of which two are good and two defective. A sample of two items is selected.
    a) Letting *G* and *D* stand for good and defective, write a sample space for the experiment using four events and enter the probabilities for each event.
    b) Write a sample space using as events the count of the number of defectives in the sample, and enter the probabilities for each event.
    c) Write a sample space using equally likely events. (Hint: Let G_1D_2 mean good number one and defective number two.)

11. Graduation exercises are to be held outdoors on Friday if it does not rain. If it rains on Friday, the exercises will be postponed until Saturday and held outdoors if it does not rain, and indoors if it rains. The probability that it will rain on Friday is 0.3, and the probability it will not rain on Saturday if it rains on Friday is 0.4. Find the probability that the exercises will be held outdoors.

12. Two women and three men are equally qualified for two positions in a firm. The firm decides to select two of the five at random.
    a) Write a sample space for the experiment using equally likely events.
    b) From (a) determine the probability that a man and a woman are selected.
    c) Calculate the answer to (b) by probability rules.

13. A job applicant assigns probabilities as follows: The probability, $P(A)$, of being offered a job at company A is 0.4, the probability of being offered a job at B is $P(B) = 0.3$, and the probability of being offered jobs at both companies is 0.12. What is the probability of being offered a job at at least one of the two companies? At exactly one of the two companies?

14. Probability of colder is assigned at 0.7, probability of snow at 0.4, and probability of neither colder nor snow at 0.2. What is the probability
    a) That it will get colder and snow?
    b) That it will get colder but not snow?
    c) That it will snow but not get colder?

15. A test has two questions. A student assigns probability 0.6 of getting the first correct, 0.3 of getting the second correct, and 0.25 of getting both wrong.
    a) Show that with this assignment of probabilities, the outcome of the second question is not independent of the outcome of the first in the probability sense.
    b) What would the probability of getting both wrong be if the outcomes are to be independent in the probability sense?

16. The claim is made that whether or not an employee's attendance record is good depends upon the sex of the employee. On the basis of the table, using probability terminology, refute the claim.

	Number of Employees with	
Sex	Good Attendance Records	Poor Attendance Records
Male	40	10
Female	80	20

17. The probability that machine A will break down on a particular day is $P(A) = 1/100$; similarly, for machine B, $P(B) = 1/200$. Assuming independence, on a particular day,
    a) What is the probability that both will break down?

9.21 REVIEW PROBLEMS (*continued*)

b) What is the probability that neither will break down?

c) What is the probability that one or the other will break down?

d) What is the probability that exactly one will break down?

18. Five parts go into the assembly of item X. The assembly is defective if any one of the parts is defective, and each part has probability of 0.01 of being defective. Assuming independence, what is the probability that an assembly is defective?

19. There are five intersections between two cities where a driver can bear left or bear right. If, and only if, the proper turn is made at each intersection will a driver starting from one city arrive at the second city. Suppose that the driver flips a coin to choose each turn. What is the probability that he will arrive at the second city?

20. Given $P(X) = 0.5$, $P(Y) = 0.7$, and $P(XY) = 0.30$, find $P(X \mid Y)$ and $P(Y \mid X)$.

21. If $P(Y \mid X) = 0.80$, $P(X \mid Y) = 0.75$, and $P(XY) = 0.60$, find $P(X)$ and $P(Y)$.

22. If $P(Y \mid X) = 0.80$, $P(XY) = 0.20$, $P(Y') = 0.30$, find $P(X \cup Y)$.

23. Job candidates are screened by means of a preliminary interview. The probability is 0.6 that a screened candidate will be a good worker. Screened candidates are given a test. If the candidate is one who will prove to be a good worker, the probability of his passing the test is 0.90. If the candidate is one who will prove to be a poor worker, the probability of his passing the test is 0.40.

a) What is the probability that a screened candidate will be a good worker and pass the test?

b) What is the probability that a screened candidate will not be a good worker and will pass the test?

24. A candidate runs for two political offices, A and B. He assigns 0.27 as the probability of being elected to both, 0.50 as the probability of being elected to A if he is elected to B,

and 0.90 as the probability of being elected to B if he is elected to A.

a) What is the probability of being elected to A?

b) What is the probability of being elected to B?

c) What is the probability of being elected to neither?

d) What is the probability of being elected to at least one of the offices?

25. Mr. M thinks his probability of winning an election is 0.9 if Ms. W does not run, but only 0.3 if Ms. W does run. Mr. M judges the probability that Ms. W will run to be 0.4. What is the probability that Mr. M wins the election?

26. Complete the Bayes' Rule formulation that starts with $P(A' \mid B) =$

27. The probability that a customer will be a bad debt is 0.01. The probability that he will make a large down payment if he is a bad debt is 0.10, and the probability that he will make a large down payment if he is not a bad debt is 0.50. Suppose that a customer makes a large down payment. Find the posterior probability that he will be a bad debt.

28. Complete the tabular analysis for Problem 27, and find the probability that a customer will not be a bad debt if he does not make a large down payment.

29. The probability that a person has disease X is $P(X) = 0.008$. The probability that medical examination will indicate the disease if a person has it is $P(I \mid X) = 0.75$, and the probability that examination will indicate the disease if a person does not have it is $P(I \mid X') = 0.01$. What is the probability that a person has the disease if medical examination so indicates?

30. The probability that a machine is running properly is 0.80. From time to time, samples of output are selected and measured, and the sample average is computed. If the machine is running properly, the probability that the sample average will be in a certain range is 0.95. If the machine is not running

9.21 REVIEW PROBLEMS (*continued*)

properly, the probability that the sample average will be in this range is 0.05. A sample is selected, and its average is outside the range. What is the probability that the machine is running properly?

31. Let X be a random variable with the probability distribution given in the following table.

x	0	1	2	3
p(x)	.55	.35	.05	.05

Find
a) The expected value $E(X)$ of X.
b) The variance $\sigma^2(X)$ of X.
c) The standard deviation $\sigma(X)$ of X.

32. A multiple choice examination consists of four questions, each of which has five possible answers. If a student guesses on all four questions,
a) What is the probability distribution of the random variable X, the number of correct answers?
b) What is the most likely number of correct answers?
c) What is the expected value $E(X)$ of the random variable X?
d) What are the variance $\sigma^2(X)$ and standard deviation $\sigma(X)$ of the random variable X?

33. During a 20-week tourist season, the number of vacancies after 6 PM on weekdays at the Roadside Motel was as follows.

Number of vacancies	0	1	2	3	4	5
Number of days	25	15	20	18	12	10

a) Graph the probability distribution of vacancies.
b) If two parties arrived after 6 PM on a weekday, what is the probability that they are accommodated?
c) How many parties could arrive after 6 PM before the probability exceeded 0.75 that they could not all be accommodated?
d) Find the expected number of vacancies on a weekday.
e) Find the mean and variance of the probability distribution.

34. To save time and money, but still provide safeguards on the quality of incoming goods, buyers often inspect a portion of a shipment and judge the quality of the entire shipment on the basis of the quality of the inspected sample. Suppose a buyer has received a shipment of 10 microcomputer disk drives, 2 of which are defective. Three disk drives are selected at random from the shipment and tested. If d is the number of defective disk drives observed, then d = 0, 1, or 2. Find the probability distribution for d and present the results graphically.

35. Simulate the experiment in Problem 34, using a computer simulation or a deck of cards with eight black cards (representing satisfactory disk drives) and two red cards (representing defective disk drives). Repeat this simulation 100 times so that 100 observations have been made of the value of d. Construct a relative frequency histogram for this sample and compare it to the graph of the probability distribution constructed in Problem 34.

Do Problems 36–46 using the binomial rule.

36. A baseball player assesses his probability of getting on base each time at bat at 0.20. What is the probability that he will get on base:
a) Exactly once in his next three times at bat?
b) At least once in his next three trips?
c) At least twice in his next three trips?
d) Exactly twice in six trips?

37. The four engines of an airplane operate independently, and on an overseas flight the probability that an engine will fail is 0.001. On such a flight, what is the probability that:
a) Exactly one will fail?
b) More than one will fail?

38. A true-false examination has five questions, and a student assigns probability of 0.7 of

9.21 REVIEW PROBLEMS (*continued*)

being correct on each of the questions. Assuming independence, what is the probability that he gets:
a) All five correct?
b) At least four correct?
c) Exactly three correct?
d) At least three correct?
e) At least four incorrect?

39. A test has five five-choice questions and a student guesses the answer to each question. Assuming independence, what is the probability of:
a) All five correct?
b) At least four correct?
c) Exactly three correct?
d) At least three correct?

40. A test has five four-choice questions and a student assigns probability 0.8 of getting each one correct. What is the probability of getting:
a) All five correct?
b) At least three correct?
c) At least one correct?

41. The probability of success on a single trial of an event is 0.3. In 100 independent trials, write, but do not evaluate, the expression for the probability of:
a) At least one success.
b) At most one success.
c) Exactly five successes.
d) At most three successes.

42. A test has 50 five-choice questions and a student guesses the answer to each question. Write, but do not evaluate, the expression for each of the following probabilities:
a) Ninety percent or more correct.
b) At least one correct.

43. The probability that any particular item is defective is 0.10. Using binomial probabilities, find:
a) The probability of at most one defective in 10 items.
b) How many items would have to be selected to have a probability of 0.99 that the group would contain at least one good item.

44. A binomial experiment consists of m trials. Write the summation expression using m, p, q, r, and x for:
a) The probability of at most r occurrences in the m trials.
b) The probability of more than r occurrences in the m trials.

45. A department store employs three people who take orders over the telephone. Each person is busy taking an order 80 percent of the time. What is the probability that an operator will be free to take an order at the time of the call:
a) If one customer calls at a point in time?
b) If two customers call at a point in time?

46. See Problem 45. How many telephone operators should the store have if the probability that an operator will be free when a customer calls is to be approximately 0.6?

Do Problems 47–49, using Table X–B.

47. A sample of 25 items is selected from a large lot, and the lot is rejected if the sample contains any defective items. Find the probability of acceptance if the proportion defective in the lot is:
a) 0.01
b) 0.10.
c) 0.20.

48. Repeat Problem 47, assuming the lot is rejected if more than two defectives are found in the sample.

49. From past experience, a market research firm knows that 60 percent of the people contacted by telephone will agree to a telephone interview. If the firm calls 25 people, what is the probability of completing:

a) At most 10 interviews?
b) At least 10 interviews?
c) More than 15 interviews?
d) From 15 to 20 interviews, inclusive?
e) Exactly 10 interviews?

9.21 REVIEW PROBLEMS (*concluded*)

50. The act is to draw a card. If the card is a face card you win $20; if it is not a face card, you lose $20. Compute the expected monetary value of the act. (Face cards are jack, queen, king, and ace.)

51. The act is rolling a pair of dice. If the dice come up 2, 7, or 11, you win $100; otherwise you lose $16. Compute the expected monetary value of the act.

52. Which act should be chosen according to the EMV criterion?

Probability	Event	Payoffs		
		A_1	A_2	A_3
0.5	E_1	$5	$4	$4
0.3	E_2	5	7	7
0.2	E_3	5	3	5

53. If you make a unit of a product and it is sold (demanded), you gain $10; if you make a unit and it is not sold, you lose $5. You assign probabilities as follows:

Number of Units Demanded	Probability of Number of Units Demanded
0	0.1
1	0.2
2	0.4
3	0.3
4 or more	0.0

According to the EMV criterion, how many units should you make?

54. One million tickets are sold at $1 each for a lottery. There is a first prize of $100,000, 2 second prizes of $50,000, 10 third prizes of $1,000, and 20 fourth prizes of $500. What is the (expected) value of a ticket?

55. A company offers insurance covering damage of 20 percent, 40 percent, 60 percent, 80 percent, or 100 percent. The owner of a particular property wishes to insure it for $200,000. The company assesses yearly damage probabilities (for the various respective damage percentages) at 0.0010, 0.0008, 0.0006, 0.0004, and 0.0002. What base figure (before overhead and profit) should the company use in establishing the annual premium to charge for insuring the property?

TEN

Introduction to Differential Calculus

10.1 INTRODUCTION

In this and the next two chapters, we provide a discussion of elementary differential calculus and its applications. One of our major objectives is to present these concepts with a minimum of prerequisite study. Only algebra and a study of straight lines and slopes (Chapter 1) are needed for Chapters 10 and 11. In Chapter 12, we introduce and apply exponential and logarithmic functions that have the material in the first part of Chapter 7 (the modern treatment of logarithms) as an additional prerequisite.

The present chapter is an introduction to the basic concepts of differential calculus including the definition of the derivative, limits, continuity, and the fundamental rules of taking derivatives. Chapter 11 shows how to use the derivative to solve optimization problems; that is, for example, to determine how to maximize profit or minimize cost. We also present a simple technique to help in sketching graphs of polynomials and rational functions. Chapter 12 includes the chain rule, implicit differentiation, and an introduction to the calculus of two independent variables.

10.2 WHY STUDY CALCULUS?

The answer to the question posed in the title of this section has several parts, but we select the part we consider most significant; namely, that the tools of calculus can be used to solve applied problems. The purpose of this section is to document the last statement by first posing a simple applied problem and showing how it can be solved approximately by 'brute force' without calculus. Then we shall explain what tools are needed to obtain an *exact* solution in a *simple* manner. The tools, of course, are the procedures of calculus.

FIGURE 10–1

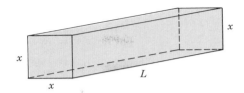

Example. The United Parcel Service operates a fleet of trucks that pick up and deliver packages. UPS will not handle packages whose length plus girth[1] exceeds 108 inches. Seafare Fruit Company ships a fresh product that requires as much ventilation as possible, and its boxes are made of a perforated material. To obtain maximum ventilation, Seafare Fruit wants the boxes to have as large a surface area as possible. The problem then is to find what box dimensions will utilize the entire 108 inches allowed *and* provide maximum surface area. The box is to be rectangular, with square ends, as shown in Figure 10–1. The length of the box is L, and its girth is $4x$. Thus,

$$\text{Length plus girth} = L + 4x.$$

When all 108 inches are utilized,

$$L + 4x = 108$$

so that

$$L = 108 - 4x. \tag{1}$$

To find the expression for the surface area, which is to be maximized, we note first that the area of each square end is x^2, and there are two such ends. Hence,

$$\text{Area of the two ends} = 2x^2.$$

The area of the rectangle forming one side is $x \cdot L$, and there are four such sides, so that

$$\text{Side area} = 4xL.$$

Thus,

$$\text{Total area} = A = 2x^2 + 4xL.$$

---

[1] For example, the length of this book is the vertical (longer) dimension of the cover, and the girth is the distance around the book in the horizontal direction.

Substituting the expression (1) for L into the last expression, we can write A in terms of the single variable x as

$$A(x) = 2x^2 + 4x(108-4x)$$
$$= 2x^2 + 432x - 16x^2$$
$$= 432x - 14x^2. \tag{2}$$

Our objective, then, is to find the value of x that makes $A(x)$ as large as possible. This value can then be substituted back into (1) to get the required value of L. In the 'brute force' approach to the solution, we let $x = 1$, then $x = 2, 3, 4$, and so on. For each value of x, the area is computed using (2) and tabulated. For example,

$$x = 1: \quad A(1) = 432(1) - 14(1)^2 = 418 \text{ square inches.}$$
$$x = 2: \quad A(2) = 432(2) - 14(2)^2 = 808 \text{ square inches.}$$

We see that $x = 2$ provides a larger area than $x = 1$, so we try $x = 3$.

$$x = 3: \quad A(3) = 432(3) - 14(3)^2 = 1{,}170 \text{ square inches.}$$

Continuing in this manner, we obtain the results shown in Table 10–1. Observe that as x increases, the area increases until the point marked with * at the bottom of the fourth column. When x went from 15 to 16, the area decreased from 3330 to 3328. We conclude that the maximum area occurs near $x = 15$. In the right section of Table 10–1, we find that $x = 15.1$ gives a larger area than $x = 15$, so we continue by steps of 0.1 until 15.5 where the area once again decreases. Now we change to steps of 0.01 until we encounter a decrease at 15.44. Clearly, we could proceed to steps of 0.001 and so on to get a more exact value for x. However, we have demonstrated that this time-consuming procedure, even if we use a computer, is a 'brute force' attack on the problem.

We leave the preceding work with the conclusion that the area is maximized when x is approximately 15.4 inches. Of course, we have no absolute assurance, without looking at the graph, that $A(x)$ does not take on a larger value at some value of x quite a bit larger than 16. We can only assume that once $A(x)$ begins to decrease at $x = 16$ it continues to do so.

TABLE 10–1

x	Area	x	Area	x	Area
1	418	9	2754	15.1	3331.06
2	808	10	2920	15.2	3331.84
3	1170	11	3058	15.3	3332.34
4	1504	12	3168	15.4	3332.56
5	1810	13	3250	15.5	3332.5*
6	2088	14	3304	15.41	3332.5666
7	2338	15	3330	15.42	3332.5704
8	2560	16	3328*	15.43	3332.5714
				15.44	3332.5696*

* Marks a point in a sequence where area decreases.

The calculus method of solving this problem can be understood by reference to the graph of

$$A(x) = 432x - 14x^2$$

shown in Figure 10–2. Observe that the graph is mound-shaped and the largest area possible is the vertical height of the peak of the mound. Note also that the line tangent to the curve at the peak of the mound is horizontal, so this tangent has a slope of zero. In this chapter, we shall learn that the tangent to

$$A(x) = 432x - 14x^2$$

is horizontal when

$$28x = 432$$
$$x = \frac{432}{28}$$
$$= \frac{108}{7},$$

exactly, or 15.43 inches, correct to two decimal places. Note that since this is the *only* value of x, there can be no other candidate for a maximum value. The corresponding value for L, computed from $L = 108 - 4x$ is $324/7$ inches exactly, or 46.29 inches, correct to two decimals. The question, of course, is how we obtained $28x = 432$, and that is the question we shall answer in this chapter. In the course of developing the tools needed to answer the question, and in the application of these tools, functional notation will be used extensively, so we shall review functions before proceeding.

FIGURE 10–2

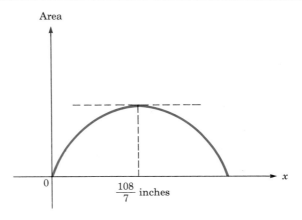

10.3 FUNCTIONAL NOTATION

In Chapter 1, the expression

$$y = mx + b$$

was called the slope-intercept form of the equation of a straight line. The quantities m (the slope) and b (the y-intercept) for any *specific* line are constants, as in

$$y = 2x + 5,$$

whereas x and y are variables. Thus, even though

$$y = mx + b$$

contains four letters (y, m, x, b), we know from the context that x and y are to be considered as the variables, while m and b are called "parameters" since they represent constant rather than variable values. The first advantage of functional notation is to ensure that the variable in any expression is stated specifically. To do this for $y = mx + b$, we write, as we saw in Chapter 1,

$$f(x) = mx + b,$$

and read $f(x)$ as "the function f of x" or, more briefly, "f of x." In the symbol $f(x)$, recall x is called the *independent* variable. Similarly, in

$$C(L) = \frac{NF}{L} + \frac{iL}{2},$$

L is the independent variable and, this being the case, N, F, and i are parameters as are m and b in

$$f(x) = mx + b.$$

If we write

$$g(x) = 3x^3 - 2x + 10,$$

g is the name of the function, x is the independent variable, and $g(x)$ represents values of the function. To find the value of the function when $x = 2$, written as $g(2)$, we evaluate

$$g(x) = 3x^3 - 2x + 10$$

at $x = 2$ to find

$$g(2) = 3(2^3) - 2(2) + 10$$
$$= 30.$$

Exercise.   Given $h(q) = 2q - 10/q$, find: a) $h(1)$. b) $h(5)$. c) $h(100)$.
Answer: a) -8. b) 8. c) 199.9.

The preceding exercise shows a second advantage of functional notation; namely, brevity of statement. That is, the instruction "Find $h(1)$" replaces the longer instruction "Find the value of the expression when the independent variable q equals 1." For emphasis, we note that if

$$f(k) = k^2 - 2kg$$

then

$$f(5) = 25 - 10g,$$

but if, for the same expression, g is the independent variable as in

$$h(g) = k^2 - 2kg,$$

then

$$h(5) = k^2 - 10k.$$

Exercise. If $p(q) = q^2 - r^2 + 5$ and $h(r) = q^2 - r^2 + 5$, what is:
a) $p(2)$? b) $h(2)$? Answer: a) $9 - r^2$. b) $q^2 + 1$.

It is helpful to think of a function as a rule that specifies how to find the value of the function for a stated value of the independent variable. For example, given

$$f(x) = x^2 - 6,$$

the rule, $x^2 - 6$, tells us to square the value of the independent variable and then subtract 6. Thus, $f(5)$ is obtained by squaring 5, then subtracting 6, and the resulting function value is 19. Similarly,

$$f(x + a)$$

will be obtained by squaring $(x + a)$ and subtracting 6, so

$$f(x + a) = (x + a)^2 - 6$$
$$= x^2 + 2ax + a^2 - 6.$$

Example. Find $g(a) - g(x - a)$ if $g(x) = x^2 + 10$.

We find

$$g(a) = a^2 + 10$$
$$g(x - a) = (x - a)^2 + 10.$$

Hence,

$$g(a) - g(x - a) = (a^2 + 10) - [(x - a)^2 + 10]$$
$$= a^2 + 10 - (x - a)^2 - 10$$
$$= a^2 - (x^2 - 2ax + a^2)$$
$$= a^2 - x^2 + 2ax - a^2$$
$$= 2ax - x^2.$$

> **Exercise.**   Find $f(x + a) - f(x)$ if $f(x) = x^2 - 3$.
> Answer: $2ax + a^2$.

A function must be single-valued. To avoid ambiguity in the meaning of *the* value of a function, we require that a function shall have one, and only one, value for each permissible value of the independent variable. In particular, in

$$f(x) = x^{1/2} = \sqrt{x}$$

we define $f(x)$ to be the *nonnegative* square root of x. That is,

$$f(4) = 4^{1/2} = 2.$$

This does not mean that

$$y^2 = 4$$

has only $y = 2$ as a solution, because $y^2 = 4$ is a *conditional equality*, not a function, and both $y = 2$ and $y = -2$ satisfy the conditional equality.

What has been said for

$$f(x) = x^{1/2}$$

applies also to any other fractional power that has an even denominator, such as

$$g(x) = x^{3/4}, \quad h(x) = x^{-5/6}.$$

That is, the function value for such even roots is the nonnegative value. Note also that for even roots, x must not be negative, so only positive numbers (or zero if the exponent is positive) are permissible values for x. An odd root, such as

$$p(x) = x^{2/3}$$

raises no question of ambiguity because such roots are single-valued. Thus,

$$p(8) = 8^{2/3}$$
$$= (8^{1/3})^2$$
$$= (2)^2$$
$$= 4$$

and

$$p(-8) = (-8)^{2/3}$$
$$= (-8^{1/3})^2$$
$$= (-2)^2$$
$$= 4.$$

We note in passing that while odd roots of negative numbers are permissible, we shall not use them in our work.

Exercise. For

$$g(x) = \frac{x^{3/2}}{32} - 16x^{-1/2} + 2x^{1/3},$$

find: a) $g(64)$. b) $g(-1)$. Answer: a) 22. b) $x = -1$ is not permissible.

10.4 DELTA NOTATION

Calculus has been described as the mathematics of change because it was invented to solve problems involving rates of change. In this section we show how to find the general expression for the change in the value of a function when its independent variable changes value. Conventionally, the symbol Δ, delta, is taken to mean *the change in*. Thus, Δx, read as "delta x," is the change in x; that is, the change in the value of the independent variable. In summary:

$$\Delta \text{ means the change in}$$
$$\Delta x \text{ means the change in } x.$$

Example. Find the expression for $g(z + \Delta z) - g(z)$ if

$$g(z) = z^2 + 3z.$$

Here, z is the independent variable, so we seek the change in $g(z)$ when z changes by Δz. We can picture the change in z as

$$\Delta z$$

$$z \qquad z + \Delta z$$

so that z changes to $z + \Delta z$. The change in $g(z)$ is therefore

$$
\begin{aligned}
g(z + \Delta z) - g(z) &= [(z + \Delta z)^2 + 3(z + \Delta z)] - (z^2 + 3z) \\
&= [z^2 + 2z(\Delta z) + (\Delta z)^2 + 3z + 3(\Delta z)] - z^2 - 3z \\
&= 2z(\Delta z) + (\Delta z)^2 + 3(\Delta z) \\
&= \Delta z[2z + \Delta z + 3].
\end{aligned}
$$

The last expression says, for example, that if z changes from, say, 5 to 5.5, so that

$$\Delta z = 5.5 - 5 = 0.5,$$

then $g(z)$ will change by

$$
\begin{aligned}
g(5 + 0.5) - g(5) &= 0.5[2(5) + 0.5 + 3] \\
&= 0.5(13.5) \\
&= 6.75.
\end{aligned}
$$

This may be verified as follows:

$$g(z) = z^2 + 3z$$
$$g(5.5) = (5.5)^2 + 3(5.5) = 46.75$$
$$g(5) = 5^2 + 3(5) \qquad\quad = 40$$
$$g(5.5) - g(5) = 46.75 - 40 \quad = 6.75.$$

Attention should be called to the fact that in the little figure at the beginning of the example, $z + \Delta z$ was shown at the right of z. This will be the case if Δz is positive, but $z + \Delta z$ would be to the left of z for negative values of Δz. However, the expression we derived for $g(z + \Delta z) - g(z)$ is correct for both positive and negative values of Δz.

Exercise.   a) Find the algebraic expression for $g(y + \Delta y) - g(y)$ if $g(y) = 2y^2 - 5$. b) Find $g(y + \Delta y) - g(y)$ if y goes from 2 to 3 by substitution into the answer for (a). c) Compute $g(y + \Delta y) - g(y)$ as $g(3) - g(2)$. Answer: a) $2(\Delta y)[2y + \Delta y]$. b) 10. c) 10.

As an application to help fix the preceding in mind, recall that in Chapter 1 the marginal cost of a unit of production was defined as the change in total cost when that unit is produced. Thus, if the total cost of making g gallons of olive oil is $C(g)$, then the marginal cost of the 10th gallon is

$$C(10) - C(9),$$

which is the total cost of 10 gallons minus the total cost of 9 gallons. In general, the marginal cost of the gth gallon is

$$C(g) - C(g - 1).$$

Now suppose we have the cost function

$$C(g) = 1000 + 5g + 0.01g^2,$$

and we want the expression for the marginal cost of the gth gallon;

$$
\begin{aligned}
C(g) &- C(g - 1) \\
&= [1000 + 5g + 0.01g^2] - [1000 + 5(g - 1) + 0.01(g - 1)^2] \\
&= 1000 + 5g + 0.01g^2 - [1000 + 5g - 5 + 0.01(g^2 - 2g + 1)] \\
&= 1000 + 5g + 0.01g^2 - 1000 - 5g + 5 - 0.01g^2 + 0.02g - 0.01 \\
&= 5 + 0.02g - 0.01 \\
&= 4.99 + 0.02g.
\end{aligned}
$$

Thus,

$$\text{Marginal cost of the } g\text{th gallon} = 4.99 + 0.02g.$$

> **Exercise.** For the cost function of the last example, find the marginal cost of the a) 10th gallon. b) 50th gallon. Answer: a) $5.19. b) $5.99.

In the answer to the last exercise, note that the marginal cost of the 50th gallon is greater than that of the 10th gallon. In Chapter 1, where *linear* cost functions were considered, marginal cost was the *constant* slope of a straight line. The cost function of the exercise has a second-degree term ($0.01g^2$) and is a curve. After we have discussed slope as it applies to a curve, we will see the reason for the increase in marginal cost observed in the answer to the last exercise.

10.5 PROBLEM SET 10–1

1. If $f(x) = 3x - 2$, find the value of, or the algebraic expression for:
a) $f(3)$.
b) $f(-2)$.
c) $f(a)$.
d) $[f(a)]^2$.
e) $f(ab)$.
f) $f(3y + 4)$.
g) $f(x + 1)$.
h) $f(x + 1) - f(x)$.

2. If $h(x) = x^2 + 3x$, find the value of, or the algebraic expression for:
a) $h(2)$.
b) $h(-3)$.
c) $h(1/2)$.
d) $h(2/a)$.
e) $h(x + 0.5)$.
f) $h(a + 1)$.
g) $h(a - 1)$.
h) $h(x) - h(x - 1)$.

3. a) If $g(x) = x^2y - y^2$, write the expression for $g(a)$.
b) If $f(y) = x^2y - y^2$, write the expression for $f(a)$.

4. a) If $h(y) = 2x + 5y$, write the expression for $h(3)$.
b) If $p(x) = 2x + 5y$, write the expression for $p(3)$.

5. If $p(x) = 2x^{-1} - 3x^{-2}$, write the value of, or the algebraic expression for:
a) $p(2)$.   b) $p(3)$.   c) $p(a)$.   d) $p(x + 1)$.

6. If $f(x) = 2x^{1/3} + 3x^{-2/3}$, find the value of:
a) $f(1)$.   b) $f(64)$.   c) $f(1/8)$.

7. What is the meaning of:
a) Δx?
b) $f(x + \Delta x)$?
c) $f(x + \Delta x) - f(x)$?

8. Given $f(x) = x^2 - 3x + 5$, find $f(x + \Delta x) - f(x)$ if x changes from 2 by the amount $\Delta x = 0.5$.

9. Given $f(x) = 2x^2 - 10x + 8$, find $f(x + \Delta x) - f(x)$ if x changes from 0 by the amount $\Delta x = 0.1$.

10. Find the expression for $f(x + \Delta x) - f(x)$ if $f(x) = 10 - 3x$.

11. Find the expression for $g(x + \Delta x) - g(x)$ if $g(x) = mx + b$.

12. Find the expression for:
a) $f(x + \Delta x) - f(x)$ if $f(x) = x^2$.
b) $g(x + \Delta x) - g(x)$ if $g(x) = 2x^2 - 3x + 5$.

13. Find the expression for:
a) $f(x + \Delta x) - f(x)$ if $f(x) = 2x^2$.
b) $g(x + \Delta x) - g(x)$ if $g(x) = x^2 + 2x - 10$.

14. If the total cost of making g gallons of olive oil is $C(g)$ dollars and
$$C(g) = 100 + 3g + 0.01g^2,$$

10.5 PROBLEM SET 10–1 (concluded)

a) Find the expression for the marginal cost of the gth gallon, which is $C(g) - C(g - 1)$.

b) Find the marginal cost of the 10th gallon.

c) Find the marginal cost of the 50th gallon.

15. If the total cost of making g gallons of corn oil is $C(g)$ dollars and

$$C(g) = 50 + g + 0.1g^2$$

a) Find the expression for the marginal cost of the gth gallon, which is $C(g) - C(g - 1)$.

b) Find the marginal cost of the 10th gallon.

c) Find the marginal cost of the 50th gallon.

10.6 LIMITS

Limits are the core concept in the development of calculus. We shall not pursue the theory of limits in detail in this text, but in this section you will become familiar enough with the limit concept to use it when needed as we proceed. We start by observing that the function

$$g(x) = \frac{x^2}{x}$$

does not have a value at $x = 0$, because at $x = 0$ the ratio is the meaningless expression 0/0, and we shall say $g(x)$ is *not defined* at $x = 0$. Those who think this ratio has the value 1 should look up the Index reference to discussion of *zero*. There it is shown why we cannot divide any number, including zero, by zero. To emphasize this exception, we can write

$$g(x) = \frac{x^2}{x}; \quad x \neq 0.$$

It is true, though, that

$$g(x) = \frac{x^2}{x} = x; \quad x \neq 0.$$

That is, $g(x) = x$ for any value of x except zero. Because this is true, it is correct to state that $g(x)$ is close to zero if x is close to zero or that $g(x)$ approaches zero if x approaches zero. We describe this behavior of $g(x)$ by saying that $g(x)$ approaches zero as a limiting value as x approaches zero and that as x goes to zero, the limit of $g(x)$ is zero. This is expressed symbolically as

$$\lim_{x \to 0} g(x) = 0,$$

where the symbol "$x \to 0$" means x approaches zero or gets closer and closer to zero without ever equalling zero. Thus, in the case of $g(x)$ we are able to state that a limit exists. It is especially important to note that

$\lim\limits_{x \to 0} g(x)$ is not always related to the value of $g(x)$ at $x = 0$. In this particular example, $g(0)$ does not exist but $\lim\limits_{x \to 0} g(x) = 0$.

By way of contrast, consider

$$f(x) = \frac{x}{x^2}; \quad x \neq 0.$$

Like the earlier $g(x)$, $f(x)$ at $x = 0$ becomes the meaningless expression $0/0$ and $f(x)$ is not defined at $x = 0$. It is true, of course, that

$$f(x) = \frac{x}{x^2} = \frac{1}{x}; \quad x \neq 0.$$

that is, $f(x) = 1/x$ for any value except $x = 0$. But $f(x)$, unlike $g(x)$, does not have a limit as x approaches zero. For example, if x takes on the sequence of values

$$1, 0.1, 0.01, 0.001,$$

and so on, approaching zero, then

$$f(1) \quad = \frac{1}{1} \quad = 1$$

$$f(0.1) \quad = \frac{1}{0.1} \quad = 10$$

$$f(0.01) \quad = \frac{1}{0.01} = 100$$

$$f(0.001) = \frac{1}{0.001} = 1000,$$

and so on, and this last sequence of values becomes larger and larger and approaches ∞ as x gets closer and closer to zero. Similarly, if we took $x = -1, -0.1, -0.01, -0.001$, and so on, as a sequence approaching zero, then

$$f(-1) = \frac{1}{-1} \quad = -1$$

$$f(-0.1) = \frac{1}{-0.1} \quad = -10$$

$$f(-0.01) = \frac{1}{-0.01} \quad = -100$$

$$f(-0.001) = \frac{1}{-0.001} = -1000$$

and so on. Again, the sequence $-1, -10, -100, -1000$ continues indefinitely and approaches $-\infty$. Hence,

$$\lim\limits_{x \to 0} \frac{x}{x^2} \quad \text{does not exist (abbreviated as d.n.e.).}$$

Comparing

$$g(x) = \frac{x^2}{x}; \quad x \neq 0$$

and

$$f(x) = \frac{x}{x^2}; \quad x \neq 0,$$

we see that they are alike at $x = 0$ in that both become the meaningless ratio, 0/0. However, they have the important difference that $g(x)$ has a limit as x approaches zero and $f(x)$ does not. The distinction is important because, as we shall see, the central definition of the differential calculus always leads to 0/0, but we can attach a meaningful interpretation to the expression that leads to 0/0 when this expression has a limit.

The limits we shall use in the major part of the chapter are easily found. We start by stressing the real meaning of the limit concept, and then we will show an easy way to find the limits without formally applying the concept. The real meaning of the concept is embodied in the proper interpretation of $x \rightarrow a$. This is that x gets closer and closer to, *but never reaches (and thus never equals), a.*

Sometimes a picture is worth a thousand words. Study Figure 10–3. Do you see any source of confusion when we say that x approaches a? Let us take a closer look at the behavior of x as it approaches a. The value of x could remain larger than a (to the right of a on the x-axis) or smaller than a (to the left of a on the x-axis), or it could jump back and forth, taking values alternately larger and smaller than a as it approaches

FIGURE 10–3

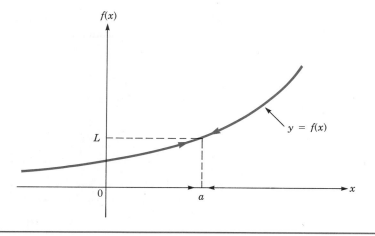

a. Think first of x as approaching a from the right side only, always remaining greater than a. We designate this process by

$$x \to a^+,$$

read "x approaches a from above." Similarly, as x approaches a from the left side only, we write

$$x \to a^-$$

and say "x approaches a from below." In each of these expressions, a is called a one-sided limit.

What happens to $f(x)$ in Figure 10–3 while this is going on? As x approaches a from above, $f(x)$ approaches L from above, and as x approaches a from below, $f(x)$ approaches L from below. Clearly, if

$$\lim_{x \to a} f(x) = L,$$

then as x approaches a in any fashion the height of the function curve $f(x)$ must approach the height L. With this discussion in mind we are ready for a definition.

Definition. The limit of $f(x)$ as x approaches a is L,

$$\lim_{x \to a} f(x) = L,$$

if and only if $f(x)$ approaches L as x approaches a along any sequence of values.

Example. Find

$$\lim_{x \to 2} (x + 3).$$

Keeping in mind that $x \to 2$ means x must not equal 2, we set up any sequence of x values approaching 2, and compute the corresponding values of the function $x + 3$. For example,

x	1.9	1.99	1.999	1.9999	$\to$	2
$f(x) = x + 3$	4.9	4.99	4.999	4.9999	$\to$	?

or

x	1.5	2.25	1.875	2.0625	$\to$	2
$f(x) = x + 3$	4.5	5.25	4.875	5.0625	$\to$	?

All indications seem to be that the "?" at the right of the sequence for $f(x) = x + 3$ is 5, so that we can conclude

$$\lim_{x \to 2} (x + 3) = 5.$$

There are many more (in fact, an infinite number) of such sequences. For every one of these sequences $x + 3$ approaches 5 as x approaches 2.

Exercise. Use a calculator or write a computer program to generate some of these sequences and to reconfirm this fact.

Example. Not all functions are as easy to handle as the last example. Let's try another one. Let

$$f(x) = \begin{cases} 1 \text{ if } x \geq 2 \\ -1 \text{ if } x < 2. \end{cases}$$

What is $\lim\limits_{x \to 2} f(x)$?

When working with functions, it is often helpful to draw a graph, as shown in Figure 10–4.

Now, observe the following sequences:

x	3	2.5	2.25	2.125	→	2
f(x)	1	1	1	1	→	1

and

x	1	1.5	1.75	1.875	→	2
f(x)	−1	−1	−1	−1	→	−1

In the first instance,

$$\lim_{x \to 2^+} f(x) = 1$$

FIGURE 10–4

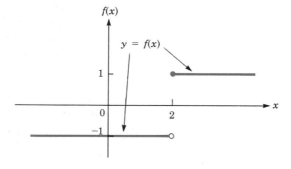

as x approaches 2 from above. But in the second instance,

$$\lim_{x \to 2^-} f(x) = -1$$

as x approaches 2 from below. For

$$\lim_{x \to 2} f(x)$$

to exist, we must have

$$\lim_{x \to 2^+} f(x) = \lim_{x \to 2^-} f(x) = \lim_{x \to 2} f(x).$$

The only logical conclusion to be drawn in this case is that

$$\lim_{x \to 2} f(x)$$

does not exist (d.n.e.).

This technique of examining the limits of the function as the variable approaches its limit from the left and from the right is especially useful in showing that limits do not exist.

Exercise. If

$$f(x) = \begin{cases} x \text{ if } x > 0 \\ -1 \text{ if } x \le 0, \end{cases}$$

find

$$\lim_{x \to 0} f(x).$$

Answer: The limit does not exist since

$$\lim_{x \to 0^-} f(x) = -1 \text{ and } \lim_{x \to 0^+} f(x) = 0.$$

Example. Find, if it exists,

$$\lim_{x \to 2} \frac{x}{x - 2}.$$

The graph of $x/(x - 2)$ is shown in Figure 10–5. Utilizing the new-found significance of left-hand-side and right-hand-side limits, let us check

$$\lim_{x \to 2} \frac{x}{x - 2}$$

as x approaches 2 from above and from below. To check the right-hand

FIGURE 10–5

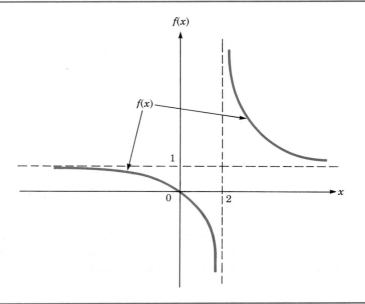

limit, we can use the sequence in the following table:

x	3	2.5	2.25	2.125	2.0625	$\rightarrow$	2
$x - 2$	3	5	9	17	33	$\rightarrow$	$+\infty$

We conclude that

$$\lim_{x \to 2^+} \frac{x}{x - 2} = +\infty.$$

Exercise. Choose a sequence to show that

$$\lim_{x \to 2^-} \frac{x}{x - 2} = -\infty.$$

Using either of the sequences, we conclude that

$$\lim_{x \to 2} \frac{x}{x - 2}$$

does not exist.

A few more examples will help us fully understand the limits we need in this text.

Example. Find, if it exists,

$$\lim_{x \to 2} \frac{x^2 - 4}{x - 2}.$$

A graph of the function is again useful. First we see that the function is not defined for $x = 2$ since the denominator would be zero. Next we see that if $x \neq 2$, then $x - 2$ is not zero, so we can cancel $x - 2$ with a factor of $x^2 - 4$; i.e.,

$$\lim_{x \to 2} \frac{x^2 - 4}{x - 2} = \lim_{x \to 2} \frac{(x + 2)(x - 2)}{x - 2} = \lim_{x \to 2} (x + 2).$$

We emphasize the fact that we can perform the above cancellation because the value of x is never equal to 2 when we let x approach 2, hence $x - 2$ is never zero in the above limit. Thus, the graph of $(x^2 - 4)/(x - 2)$ must look just like the graph of $x + 2$ everywhere except at $x = 2$, as shown in Figure 10–6.

Now it is easy to see that

$$\lim_{x \to 2} \frac{x^2 - 4}{x - 2} = \lim_{x \to 2} (x + 2) = 4.$$

This technique of cancellation occurs frequently in limit problems, so be alert. Think before you jump to the limit.

FIGURE 10–6

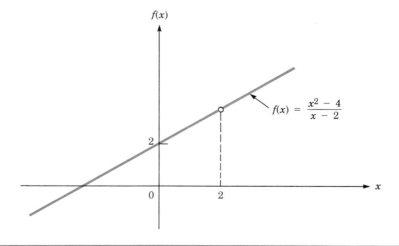

Exercise. Find, if it exists, a) $\lim\limits_{x\to 5}\dfrac{x^2-25}{x-5}.$ b) $\lim\limits_{x\to 1}\dfrac{x+1}{x^2-1}.$

Answer: a) 10. b) Limit does not exist.

Example. Find, if it exists,

$$\lim_{a\to b}(3a+2b).$$

We note that for any sequence of values of a, approaching b, $3a$ will approach $3b$ and $3a+2b$ will approach $3b+2b$. Hence,

$$\lim_{a\to b}(3a+2b)=3b+2b=5b.$$

Example. Find, if it exists,

$$\lim_{b\to a}\frac{a^2-b^2}{a-b}.$$

Factoring leads to

$$\lim_{b\to a}\frac{a^2-b^2}{a-b}=\lim_{b\to a}\frac{(a+b)(a-b)}{a-b}$$
$$=\lim_{b\to a}(a+b)$$
$$=2a.$$

Note that in this example b approaches a, whereas in the previous example a approaches b.

Exercise. Find, if it exists, a) $\lim\limits_{y\to x}(2x+y).$ b) $\lim\limits_{x\to y}\dfrac{x^2-y^2}{x-y}.$

Answer: a) $3x$. b) $2y$.

Limit theorems. We now state and illustrate limit theorems we shall refer to from time to time as our work progresses. These theorems are intuitively reasonable, but their proof requires attention to details that are not appropriate for this text. The following are true if all of the indicated limits exist.

1. If k is any constant, $\lim\limits_{x\to a}k=k.$

Here note that $x \to a$ specifies that x is changing and approaching a. The constant k does not change (it does not involve x). Thus, the limit of a constant is the constant.

$$\text{\textit{Examples.}} \quad \lim_{x \to 5} 10 = 10. \quad \lim_{a \to b} c = c.$$

2. $\lim_{x \to a} k\, f(x) = k \lim_{x \to a} f(x).$

That is, a constant factor, here k, may be placed inside or outside the limit symbol.

$$\text{\textit{Example.}} \quad \lim_{x \to a} 3x^2 = 3(\lim_{x \to a} x^2) = 3(a^2) = 3a^2.$$

3. $\lim_{x \to a} [f(x) \pm g(x)] = \lim_{x \to a} f(x) \pm \lim_{x \to a} g(x).$

That is, the limit of a sum or difference is the sum or difference of the limits. Or, we can say that the limit of an expression can be taken term by term.

$$\text{\textit{Example.}} \quad \lim_{x \to a} (x^2 - 2x + 3) = \lim_{x \to a} x^2 - 2\lim_{x \to a} x + \lim_{x \to a} 3$$
$$= a^2 - 2a + 3.$$

4. $\lim_{x \to a} [f(x)g(x)] = [\lim_{x \to a} f(x)][\lim_{x \to a} g(x)].$

That is, the limit of a product is the product of the limits.

$$\text{\textit{Example.}} \quad \lim_{x \to 2} (x + 3)(x - 2) = [\lim_{x \to 2} (x + 3)][\lim_{x \to 2} (x - 2)]$$
$$= [5][0]$$
$$= 0.$$

5. $\lim_{x \to a} [f(x)]^n = [\lim_{x \to a} f(x)]^n.$

That is, the limit of a power of $f(x)$ is the power of the limit of $f(x)$.

$$\text{\textit{Example.}} \quad \lim_{x \to 3} (x - 1)^5 = [\lim_{x \to 3} (x - 1)]^5 = 2^5 = 32.$$

6. If $\lim_{x \to a} f(x) = L$ and $\lim_{x \to a} g(x) = M$, then

(a) if $M \neq 0$, then $\lim_{x \to a} [f(x)/g(x)] = L/M$;

(b) if $M = 0$ and $L \neq 0$, then $\lim_{x \to a} [f(x)/g(x)]$ does not exist (d.n.e.);

(c) if $M = 0$ and $L = 0$, then $f(x)$ and $g(x)$ have a common factor and the limit can be evaluated after employing the process of cancellation.

10.7 PROBLEM SET 10–2

Find each of the following, if it exists:

1. $\lim\limits_{x \to 1} (x^2 + 2x - 2)$.

2. $\lim\limits_{x \to 2} (x^3 - 5x^2 - 1)$.

3. $\lim\limits_{x \to b} ax^2$.

4. $\lim\limits_{b \to a} a^2 b^2$.

5. $\lim\limits_{x \to 1} \dfrac{x^2 - 1}{x + 1}$.

6. $\lim\limits_{x \to 1} \dfrac{x^2 + 1}{x + 1}$.

7. $\lim\limits_{x \to 2} \dfrac{x + 5}{x - 2}$.

8. $\lim\limits_{x \to 1} \dfrac{x^2 + 1}{x - 1}$.

9. $\lim\limits_{x \to a} (x - 1)^{1/3}$.

10. $\lim\limits_{x \to 24} (x + 1)^{1/2}$.

11. $\lim\limits_{b \to a} (3a + 5b)$.

12. $\lim\limits_{a \to b} (5a - b)$.

13. $\lim\limits_{x \to 3/2} \dfrac{4x^2 - 9}{2x - 3}$.

14. $\lim\limits_{x \to 5/3} \dfrac{9x^2 - 25}{3x - 5}$.

15. $\lim\limits_{x \to 0} \dfrac{x^4}{x^3}$.

16. $\lim\limits_{x \to 0} \dfrac{x^3}{x^4}$.

17. $\lim\limits_{x \to 1/2} \dfrac{2x + 1}{2x - 1}$.

18. $\lim\limits_{x \to 1/3} \dfrac{3x - 1}{3x + 1}$.

19. $\lim\limits_{\Delta x \to 0} \dfrac{(\Delta x)(2x + 3\Delta x)}{\Delta x}$.

20. $\lim\limits_{\Delta x \to 0} \dfrac{(\Delta x)[3x^2 + 2x(\Delta x)]}{\Delta x}$.

21. $\lim\limits_{a \to 0} \dfrac{\dfrac{1}{2 + a} - \dfrac{1}{2}}{a}$.

22. $\lim\limits_{a \to 0} \dfrac{\dfrac{1}{5 + a} - \dfrac{1}{5}}{a}$.

23. $\lim\limits_{x \to 1} \dfrac{x^3 - 1}{x - 1}$.

24. $\lim\limits_{x \to 2} \dfrac{x^3 - 2}{x - 2}$.

25. $\lim\limits_{x \to 2} \left(\dfrac{x}{x - 2} - \dfrac{2}{x - 2} \right)$.

26. $\lim\limits_{x \to 1} \left(\dfrac{x^2}{x - 1} - \dfrac{1}{x - 1} \right)$.

27. $\lim\limits_{x \to 3} \left(\dfrac{x^3}{x - 3} + \dfrac{27}{x - 3} \right)$.

28. $\lim\limits_{x \to 2} \left(\dfrac{x^2}{x - 2} + \dfrac{4}{x - 2} \right)$.

29. $\lim\limits_{x \to 2} \dfrac{x^2 + x - 6}{x^2 - 4}$.

30. $\lim\limits_{x \to -1} \dfrac{x^3 + 1}{x + 1}$.

31. $\lim\limits_{x \to -2} \dfrac{x - 3}{x^2 + x - 2}$.

---

32. The BASIC program shown in Program 10–1 generates the values of

$$f(x) = \frac{x^3 - 2}{x}$$

corresponding to the x values in the sequence

$$x: \quad 1, \tfrac{1}{2}, \tfrac{1}{2}^2, \tfrac{1}{2}^3, \ldots, \tfrac{1}{2}^{10}.$$

Program 10–1

```
10 REM LIMIT
20 PRINT TAB(7);"X",TAB(27);"F(X)"
30 FOR N = 0 TO 10
40 X=1/2^N
50 PRINT X,TAB(25);(X^3-2)/X
60 NEXT N
70 END
```

10.7 PROBLEM SET 10–2 (*concluded*)

a) Describe what the program is doing line-by-line.

b) Run the program.

c) What is $\lim\limits_{x \to 0+} f(x)$?

33. a) Modify Program 10–1 for

$$f(x) = \frac{x^2 - 4\sqrt{x} + 2}{x - 1}.$$

b) Run the program in (a).

c) What is $\lim\limits_{x \to 0+} f(x)$?

34. a) Modify Program 10–1 for

$$f(x) = \begin{cases} 1/x, & x < 0 \\ x, & x \ge 0. \end{cases}$$

b) Run the program in (a).

c) What is $\lim\limits_{x \to 0+} f(x)$?

10.8 CONTINUITY

It is often useful to consider sets of functions with a common property. Continuity is such a property. In simple terms, continuous functions are functions with graphs that are unbroken. Let us sketch a graph of

$$f(x) = \begin{cases} x + 1, & x \ge 0 \\ x - 1, & x < 0 \end{cases}$$

as shown in Figure 10–7. This graph is fragmented in that we cannot draw the graph in one continuous stroke without having to lift our pencil from the paper. Roughly speaking, a function is called continuous if its graph can be drawn without lifting the pencil from the paper. In what

---

FIGURE 10–7

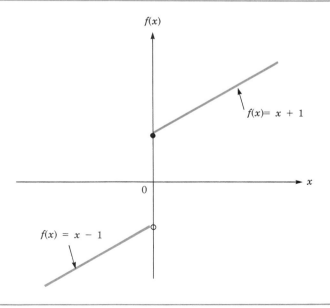

$f(x)$

$f(x) = x + 1$

0

x

$f(x) = x - 1$

circumstances do we have to lift the pencil from the paper while drawing? As we see in Figures 10–7 and 10–8, if there is a jump in the graph, or, as in Figure 10–9, a gap or hole in the graph, at $x = a$, we then must lift the pencil. In the first instance, the jump in Figure 10–8, we notice that $\lim_{x \to a} f(x)$ does not exist at the jump point a since the right-hand limit does not equal the left-hand limit. Think about this a moment and it will become clear that to avoid a jump at a point a, $\lim_{x \to a} f(x)$ must exist.

In the second instance, the gap in Figure 10–9, the function $f(x)$ does not have a value at $x = a$. Clearly $f(x)$ must have a value $f(a)$ if we are to draw the graph in one continuous motion. Are these two conditions enough? Before you answer let us look at one more special case in Figure 10–10. In this picture, $\lim_{x \to a} f(x)$ exists and $f(a)$ is defined, but $\lim_{x \to a} f(x) \neq f(a)$.

FIGURE 10–8

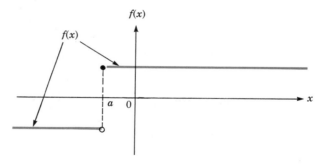

FIGURE 10–9

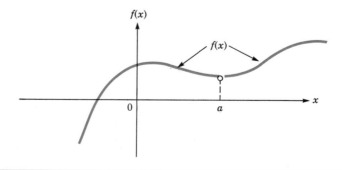

FIGURE 10–10

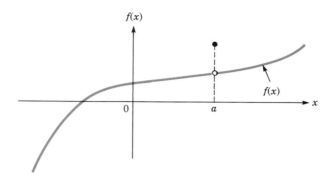

Now, with all this in mind, we are ready for a formal definition of continuity.

> **Definition.** A function $f(x)$ is said to be continuous at a point a if the following three conditions are met:
>
> 1. $f(a)$ is defined.
> 2. $\lim_{x \to a} f(x)$ exists.
> 3. $\lim_{x \to a} f(x) = f(a)$.
>
> If a function is not continuous at a point a we say it is discontinuous at a or has a discontinuity at a.

Example. Discuss the continuity of

$$f(x) = \frac{x + 2}{x^2 - 3x + 2}.$$

First, we factor the denominator

$$f(x) = \frac{x + 2}{(x - 1)(x - 2)}.$$

Now we can go through the three conditions of our definition to check for points of discontinuity. Once we have found these points of discontinuity, if any, then the function will clearly be continuous at all other points.

Condition 1: $f(x)$ is defined for all x except $x = 1$ and $x = 2$.

Condition 2: By limit theorem 6 of Section 10.6, $\lim\limits_{x \to a} f(x)$ exists for all x except $x = 1$ and $x = 2$.

Condition 3: Again by limit theorem 6, we see that $\lim\limits_{x \to a} f(x) = f(a)$ for all x except $x = 1$ and $x = 2$.

Hence, $f(x)$ is continuous at all x except $x = 1$ and $x = 2$, where it has discontinuities.

The concepts of continuity and discontinuity can be simplified by recognizing that certain classes of functions are always continuous. For our purposes, the following list, presented without justification, will be very helpful in determining the continuity of functions.

1. All polynomial functions are continuous. A polynomial function is one of the form

$$a_n x^n + a_{n-1} x^{n-1} + \cdots + a_1 x + a_0.$$

So, $f(x) = 3$ (or $f(x) = k$ for any constant) and $f(x) = x^2$ (or $f(x) = x^n$ for any integer n) are always continuous. We will talk more about polynomials later.

2. If $f(x)$ is continuous and $g(x)$ is continuous, then
   a) $f(x) \pm g(x)$ is continuous.
   b) $f(x) \cdot g(x)$ is continuous.
   c) $f(x)/g(x)$ is continuous when $g(x) \neq 0$.

10.9 PROBLEM SET 10–3

In Problems 1 through 10, find the discontinuities, if any, for each function:

1. $f(x) = x^3 + 2x - 4$.

2. $f(x) = \dfrac{1}{x - 1}$.

3. $f(x) = \dfrac{x}{x^2 + 1}$.

4. $f(x) = \dfrac{x - 2}{x^2 - 4}$.

5. $f(x) = \dfrac{x^2 - 4}{x - 2}$.

6. $f(x) = \dfrac{x + 2}{x^2 - 5x + 6}$.

7. $f(x) = \begin{cases} x + 1, & x > 1 \\ x, & x \le 1 \end{cases}$.

8. $f(x) = \begin{cases} x + 1, & x \ge 1 \\ 2, & x < 1 \end{cases}$.

9. $f(x) = \begin{cases} x^2 + 1, & x \ge 2 \\ x + 3, & x < 2 \end{cases}$.

10. $f(x) = \begin{cases} \dfrac{x}{2} + 1, & x \ge -2 \\ x + 2, & x < -2 \end{cases}$.

10.9 PROBLEM SET 10–3 (concluded)

11. The BASIC program shown in Program 10–2 generates the values of $f(x)$ for Problem 7.

Program 10–2

```
10 REM CONTINUITY
20 PRINT " X","F(X)"
30 FOR X = 0 TO 1.1 STEP 0.1
40 PRINT X,X
50 NEXT X
60 PRINT "*****","*****"
70 FOR X = 2 TO 1 STEP -0.1
80 PRINT X,X+1
90 NEXT X
100 END
```

a) Describe what the program is doing line-by-line.

b) Run the program and verify the answer to Problem 7.

12. a) Modify Program 10–2 for each function in Problems 8 through 10.

b) Run the program in (a) and verify the answers to Problems 8 through 10.

13. A direct-dial long distance call between Boston and New York costs $0.49 for the first three minutes and $0.21 for each additional minute or fraction thereof. Sketch a graph of this function and discuss its continuity.

14. An electric utility company used to make the following charges for usage of electricity: $8.50 flat charge for 0–70 kilowatt hours (kwh) of usage, 10 cents per kwh for the next 380 kwh, and 8 cents per kwh for the excess over 450 kwh. Sketch a graph of this function and discuss its continuity.

10.10 THE DIFFERENCE QUOTIENT

The function

$$f(x) = mx + b$$

is a *linear* function represented graphically by a straight line. Thus,

$$f(x) = 0.8x + 3$$

is a linear function. Conventionally when graphing functions, the function values, $f(x)$, are on the vertical axis, and the independent variable values are on the horizontal axis. The graph of $f(x)$, which has a slope of 0.8 and a vertical intercept of 3, is shown in Figure 10–11. If the independent variable changes from x to $x + \Delta x$, the value of the function changes from $f(x)$ to $f(x + \Delta x)$, so the change in the function, $\Delta f(x)$, is

$$\Delta f(x) = f(x + \Delta x) - f(x),$$

as shown in Figure 10–11. The slope of the line can be determined from any two of its points, such as P and Q. It is the vertical change divided by the horizontal change; that is, the change in the function divided by the change in x, which is

$$\frac{\Delta f(x)}{\Delta x}.$$

FIGURE 10–11

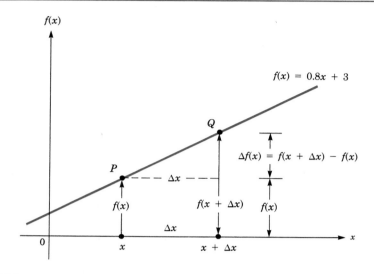

This expression is called the *difference quotient*. Thus, the difference quotient is simply the slope of a straight line. For our function,

$$f(x) = 0.8x + 3,$$

we find

$$\Delta f(x) = f(x + \Delta x) - f(x) = [0.8(x + \Delta x) + 3] - [0.8x + 3]$$
$$= 0.8x + 0.8(\Delta x) + 3 - 0.8x - 3$$
$$= 0.8(\Delta x).$$

Hence, the difference quotient is

$$\frac{\Delta f(x)}{\Delta x} = \frac{0.8(\Delta x)}{\Delta x} = 0.8.$$

The result, a constant, is not surprising, of course, because $f(x)$ is a straight line and we know that a given line has the same slope number for any pair of its points.

Exercise.   If $g(x) = mx + b$, what will the difference quotient be? Answer: m, the slope of the line specified by $g(x)$.

FIGURE 10-12

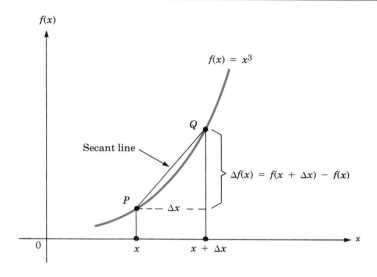

Consider next the function x^3, a section of which is shown in Figure 10-12. A line, called a *secant* line, has been drawn through two points, P and Q, on the curve. The difference quotient for this pair of points we shall call m_s, where m stands for slope and s for secant. We have

$$m_s = \frac{\Delta f(x)}{\Delta x} = \frac{f(x + \Delta x) - f(x)}{\Delta x} = \frac{(x + \Delta x)^3 - x^3}{\Delta x}.$$

First we find $(x + \Delta x)^3$:

$$
\begin{aligned}
(x + \Delta x)^3 &= (x + \Delta x)(x + \Delta x)^2 \\
&= (x + \Delta x)[x^2 + 2x(\Delta x) + (\Delta x)^2] \\
&= x^3 + 2x^2(\Delta x) + x(\Delta x)^2 + x^2(\Delta x) + 2x(\Delta x)^2 + (\Delta x)^3 \\
&= x^3 + 3x^2(\Delta x) + 3x(\Delta x)^2 + (\Delta x)^3.
\end{aligned}
$$

Hence,

$$
\begin{aligned}
m_s &= \frac{(x + \Delta x)^3 - x^3}{\Delta x} \\
&= \frac{x^3 + 3x^2(\Delta x) + 3x(\Delta x)^2 + (\Delta x)^3 - x^3}{\Delta x} \\
&= \frac{3x^2(\Delta x) + 3x(\Delta x)^2 + (\Delta x)^3}{\Delta x} \\
&= \frac{\Delta x[3x^2 + 3x(\Delta x) + (\Delta x)^2]}{\Delta x}
\end{aligned}
$$

$$= 3x^2 + 3x(\Delta x) + (\Delta x)^2$$
$$= 3x^2 + (\Delta x)(3x + \Delta x).$$

Here the difference quotient, m_s, is not constant as it is in the case of a straight line but depends, instead, upon the size of Δx and the particular value of x at hand. We could call m_s the average rate of change of $f(x)$ over the interval $(x, x + \Delta x)$. For example, over the interval $(2, 2.5)$, $x = 2$ and $\Delta x = 0.5$ so $m_s = 3(2)^2 + (0.5)(6 + 0.5) = 15.25$. On the other hand, over the interval $(2, 2.4)$, $m_s = 3(2)^2 + (0.4)(6 + 0.4) = 14.56$.

Exercise.   Find m_s over the interval $(1, 1.7)$. Answer: 5.59.

Example. Compute the average rate of change m_s for $f(x) = x^2$ over the interval $(x, x + \Delta x)$ when $\Delta x = 0.1, 0.01, 0.001$ and $x = 1$.

First we compute

$$m_s = \frac{\Delta f(x)}{\Delta x} = \frac{(x + \Delta x)^2 - x^2}{\Delta x} = \frac{x^2 + 2x(\Delta x) + (\Delta x)^2 - x^2}{\Delta x}$$
$$= \frac{2x(\Delta x) + (\Delta x)^2}{\Delta x} = 2x + \Delta x.$$

So we have

Δx	$(x, x + \Delta x)$	m_s
0.1	(1, 1.1)	2.1
0.01	(1, 1.01)	2.01
0.001	(1, 1.001)	2.001

Do you see a pattern?

Exercise.   Find the expression for the difference quotient for $f(x) = 2x^2 + 1$. Answer: $4x + 2(\Delta x)$.

10.11 DEFINITION OF THE DERIVATIVE

We now have the tools needed to obtain the rules of differential calculus. The problem at hand can be thought of as that of determining the slope of a line tangent to a curve at *a* point on the curve. This is a new problem because until now it has been necessary to have *two* points to compute a slope and here we have only one point. But we also have the function that determines the shape of the graph, and this shape governs the slopes of the tangents.

We start, as shown in Figure 10–13, by taking the stated point on a curve, P, and a nearby point, Q. The secant line through these points has

FIGURE 10–13

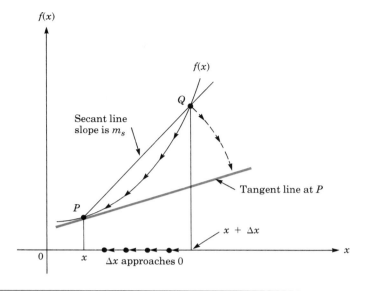

the slope m_s. We will take the slope of the secant line,

$$m_s = \frac{\Delta f(x)}{\Delta x},$$

as an approximation of the slope of the tangent line. Clearly, the closer Q is to P, the more closely will the secant slope approximate the tangent slope. Thus, if we move Q down the curve toward P, as indicated by the arrowheads on the curve, so that Q *approaches* P, secant slopes will change and *approach* the slope of the tangent line at P.[2] Thus, as Q approaches P,

$$\text{Secant line} \rightarrow \text{Tangent line at } P$$
$$\text{Secant slope} \rightarrow \text{Tangent slope at } P$$
$$m_s = \frac{\Delta f(x)}{\Delta x} \rightarrow \text{Tangent slope at } P.$$

The next step is to find a mathematical procedure that can be used to make Q approach P. Returning to Figure 10–13, note the points at the

---

[2] To see this clearly, construct a curve on a full sheet of paper, and use a ruler to sketch a tangent line at a point, P. Then take a piece of thread and stretch it across P and another point Q to represent the secant line in Figure 10–13. Now, holding the thread fixed at point P, rotate the stretched thread so that it cuts the curve at points successively closer to P. Observe that as the thread, which represents the secant line, moves downward, it approaches the tangent line.

arrowheads on the x-axis. The distance from x to one of these points is a value of Δx. We generate these arrowhead points by letting Δx approach zero. The corresponding points vertically above on the curve then move from Q toward P as Δx approaches zero. Hence, as

$$\Delta x \to \text{zero}$$
$$Q \to P$$
$$\frac{\Delta f(x)}{\Delta x} \to \text{Tangent slope at } P.$$

The smaller Δx is, the closer the secant slope is to the tangent slope at P. As a consequence, it is intuitively reasonable to define the tangent slope at P to be the limit of the secant slope as Δx approaches zero.

$$\text{Tangent slope} = \lim_{\Delta x \to 0} \frac{\Delta f(x)}{\Delta x}.$$

The function derived when this limit is obtained is called the *derivative* of $f(x)$ and is symbolized by $f'(x)$.

Definition. $f'(x) = $ the derivative of $f(x)$

$$f'(x) = \lim_{\Delta x \to 0} \frac{\Delta f(x)}{\Delta x} = \lim_{\Delta x \to 0} \frac{f(x + \Delta x) - f(x)}{\Delta x}.$$

The definition just stated is the fundamental definition of differential calculus, and all rules for finding derivatives are developed by starting from this definition. Its statement requires the use of functions, delta procedures, and limits, which we have studied earlier in the chapter. It is worth noting in particular that the need for the limit concept arises because the secant slope in Figure 10–13 is

$$m_s = \frac{\Delta f(x)}{\Delta x} = \frac{f(x + \Delta x) - f(x)}{\Delta x}.$$

If Δx is set equal to zero, m_s becomes

$$m_s = \frac{f(x + 0) - f(x)}{0} = \frac{f(x) - f(x)}{0} = \frac{0}{0},$$

so m_s is not defined at $\Delta x = 0$. What has happened here, of course, is that $\Delta x = 0$ means that on Figure 10–13, points P and Q are the same point and the slope of a line cannot be determined from one of its points. But, if we let $\Delta x \to 0$, rather than set $\Delta x = 0$, and a limit exists, then this limit has an important interpretation; namely, the limit is the slope of a tangent line at a (one) point on the curve. Thus, the problem that is solved by finding $f'(x)$ is that of finding the expression that gives the slope of a tangent line when only one point on such a line is specified. A function that has a derivative at a point P is said to be differentiable at P. If a function $f(x)$ has a derivative at all points for which it is defined, we merely say that $f(x)$ is differentiable.

Before going on to an example, we state the following definition in order to simplify statements:

Definition. The slope of a curve at a point means the slope of the line tangent to the curve at that point.

Example. Find the slope of $f(x) = x^3$ at the point where $x = 0.5$.

First we must find the expression for the derivative, $f'(x)$. This will be done in steps that we shall number so that the reader can refer to them. For convenience and to emphasize the use of the three-step procedure, we repeat the algebra done in Section 10.10.

1. Find $f(x + \Delta x)$. For $f(x) = x^3$,

$$
\begin{aligned}
f(x + \Delta x) &= (x + \Delta x)^3 \\
&= (x + \Delta x)(x + \Delta x)^2 \\
&= (x + \Delta x)[x^2 + 2x(\Delta x) + (\Delta x)^2] \\
&= x^3 + 2x^2(\Delta x) + x(\Delta x)^2 + x^2(\Delta x) + 2x(\Delta x)^2 + (\Delta x)^3 \\
&= x^3 + 3x^2(\Delta x) + 3x(\Delta x)^2 + (\Delta x)^3.
\end{aligned}
$$

2. Set up the difference quotient. This is

$$
\begin{aligned}
\frac{\Delta f(x)}{\Delta x} &= \frac{f(x + \Delta x) - f(x)}{\Delta x} \\
&= \frac{x^3 + 3x^2(\Delta x) + 3x(\Delta x)^2 + (\Delta x)^3 - x^3}{\Delta x} \\
&= \frac{3x^2(\Delta x) + 3x(\Delta x)^2 + (\Delta x)^3}{\Delta x} \\
&= \frac{\Delta x[3x^2 + 3x(\Delta x) + (\Delta x)^2]}{\Delta x} \\
&= 3x^2 + 3x(\Delta x) + (\Delta x)^2.
\end{aligned}
$$

3. Find $f'(x)$, which is the limit of the difference quotient as $\Delta x \to 0$, if a limit exists. Here we have

$$
f'(x) = \lim_{\Delta x \to 0} [3x^2 + 3x(\Delta x) + (\Delta x)^2] = 3x^2.
$$

Observe in the last line that Δx is the changing quantity and the terms with Δx as a factor vanish as Δx approaches zero. However, the first term does not involve Δx, so it will not change, and

$$
f'(x) = 3x^2
$$

This says the slope of

$$f(x) = x^3$$

at any point is computed as three times the square of the x-coordinate of the point. Thus, for the point where $x = 0.5$,

$$f'(0.5) = 3(0.5)^2 = 3(0.25) = 0.75.$$

Figure 10–14 shows $f(x)$ and the tangent line at the point P where

$$x = 0.5; \quad f(x) = f(0.5) = (0.5)^3 = 0.125.$$

Exercise. Given $f(x) = x^2$, follow the preceding three steps and write the results of a) Step 1. b) Step 2. c) Step 3. d) Compute the slope of $f(x)$ at the point where $x = 1$.
Answer: a) $x^2 + 2x(\Delta x) + (\Delta x)^2$. b) $2x + \Delta x$. c) $2x$. d) 2.

We now return to the introductory example in Section 10.2. There the problem was that of finding box dimensions that provided a box of maximum surface area. The problem, illustrated in Figure 10–2, was to find x so that the slope of the tangent to

$$A = A(x) = 432x - 14x^2$$

was zero. This horizontal tangent marked the peak (highest value) of the area function in Figure 10–2. Applying the three-step procedure to find $A'(x)$, we have

1. $A(x + \Delta x) = 432(x + \Delta x) - 14(x + \Delta x)^2$
$$= 432x + 432(\Delta x) - 14[x^2 + 2x(\Delta x) + (\Delta x)^2]$$
$$= 432x + 432(\Delta x) - 14x^2 - 28x(\Delta x) - 14(\Delta x)^2.$$

2. $\dfrac{\Delta A(x)}{\Delta x} = \dfrac{A(x + \Delta x) - A(x)}{\Delta x}$

$$= \frac{[432x + 432(\Delta x) - 14x^2 - 28x(\Delta x) - 14(\Delta x)^2] - [432x - 14x^2]}{\Delta x}$$

$$= \frac{432(\Delta x) - 28x(\Delta x) - 14(\Delta x)^2}{\Delta x}$$

$$= \frac{\Delta x[432 - 28x - 14(\Delta x)]}{\Delta x}$$

$$= 432 - 28x - 14(\Delta x).$$

3. $A'(x) = \lim\limits_{\Delta x \to 0} [432 - 28x - 14(\Delta x)]$
$$= 432 - 28x,$$

where, as before, terms with Δx as a factor vanish when $\Delta x \to 0$. Now

FIGURE 10-14

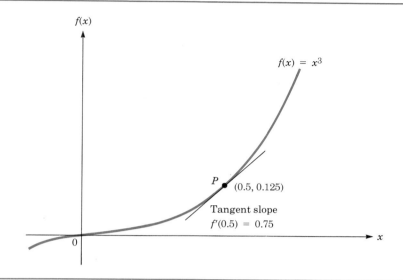

we wish to know where the slope of the curve is zero. This is where $A'(x) = 0$.

$$A'(x) = 0 \quad \text{where} \quad 432 - 28x = 0$$
$$432 = 28x$$
$$\frac{432}{28} = x$$
$$\frac{108}{7} = x,$$

which is the result stated in Section 10.2.

With practice, this three-step procedure will become second nature and problem solutions will appear as in the next example.

Example. Find the slope of $f(x) = x^2 + 1$ at $x = -1, 0,$ and 1.

First we must find the difference quotient

$$\frac{\Delta f(x)}{\Delta x} = \frac{[(x + \Delta x)^2 + 1] - [x^2 + 1]}{\Delta x}$$
$$= \frac{x^2 + 2x(\Delta x) + (\Delta x)^2 + 1 - x^2 - 1}{\Delta x}$$
$$= \frac{2x(\Delta x) + (\Delta x)^2}{\Delta x}$$
$$= 2x + \Delta x.$$

Now to find $f'(x)$ we must evaluate

$$\lim_{\Delta x \to 0} \frac{\Delta f(x)}{\Delta x} = \lim_{\Delta x \to 0} (2x + \Delta x) = 2x.$$

Thus, we have

x	$f'(x)$
-1	-2
0	0
1	2

Figure 10–15 shows the three tangent lines at the three designated values of x.

We shall pause now for a brief problem set that will serve to fix the fundamental definition of the derivative in mind and then return to develop a simple rule that can be applied to take derivatives quickly.

FIGURE 10–15

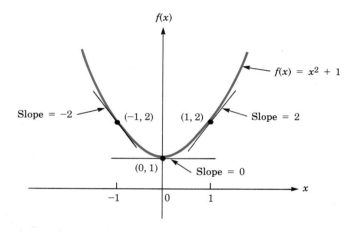

10.12 PROBLEM SET 10–4

Apply the three steps of the delta method to determine $f'(x)$ for each of the following, and find the slope of the curve of $f(x)$ for the stated value of x.

1. $f(x) = 3x + 2$, at $x = 1$.

2. $f(x) = 2 - 0.5x$, at $x = 1$.

3. $f(x) = x^2 - 2x - 1$, at $x = 1$.

4. $f(x) = 3x^2 - 12x + 2$, at $x = 3$.

5. $f(x) = 1/x$, at $x = 2$.

6. $f(x) = 1/x^2$, at $x = -1$.

7. $f(x) = x^3 + 2x$, at $x = 2$.

8. $f(x) = x^3 - 1/2x^2 + x + 1$, at $x = -1$.

9. $f(x) = x^4$, at $x = -1$.

10. $f(x) = \sqrt{x}$, at $x = 1$.

10.12 PROBLEM SET 10–4 (*concluded*)

The definition of the derivative of $f(x) = x^2$ is

$$f'(x) = \lim_{\Delta x \to 0} \frac{(x + \Delta x)^2 - x^2}{\Delta x}.$$

Write the corresponding definition of the derivative of the following. Do not continue beyond writing the definition.

11. $f(x) = x^5 - 2x^4$.

12. $f(x) = 3x^6 + 2x^3$.

13. $f(x) = x^{1/3}$.

14. $f(x) = x^{1/2}$.

---

15. The BASIC program shown in Program 10–3 computes the derivative in Problem 1.

Program 10–3
```
10  REM DERIVATIVE
20  PRINT " X","F(X)"
30  FOR X = 2 TO 1 STEP -0.1
40  PRINT X,((3*X+2)-(3*1+2))/(X-1)
50  NEXT X
60  END
```

a) Describe what the program is doing line-by-line.
b) Run the program and verify the answer to Problem 1.

16. a) Modify Program 10–3 for each function in Problems 2 through 10.
b) Run the program in (a) and verify the answers to Problems 2 through 10.

10.13 THE SIMPLE POWER RULE

There is a simple rule that can be applied to find the derivative of any power of x. To see where the rule comes from, we state some results obtained earlier. Namely,

$$\text{for } f(x) = x^2, \quad \frac{f(x + \Delta x) - f(x)}{\Delta x} = 2x + \Delta x;$$

$$\text{for } f(x) = x^3, \quad \frac{f(x + \Delta x) - f(x)}{\Delta x} = 3x^2 + \Delta x(3x + \Delta x).$$

Omitting the algebra, we state the further results that:

$$\text{for } f(x) = x^4, \quad \frac{f(x + \Delta x) - f(x)}{\Delta x} = 4x^3 + \Delta x(\quad)$$

$$\text{for } f(x) = x^5, \quad \frac{f(x + \Delta x) - f(x)}{\Delta x} = 5x^4 + \Delta x(\quad),$$

where, in the last two lines, $\Delta x(\quad)$ means that all remaining terms have Δx as a factor and hence will vanish in the limit,

$$f'(x) = \lim_{\Delta x \to 0} \frac{f(x + \Delta x) - f(x)}{\Delta x}.$$

Thus, taking the limit of each of the above, we find that:

$$\text{if } f(x) = x^2, \quad f'(x) = 2x;$$

$$\text{if } f(x) = x^3, \quad f'(x) = 3x^2;$$
$$\text{if } f(x) = x^4, \quad f'(x) = 4x^3.$$

We see that in each case,

$$f'(x) = (\text{power})(x \text{ to the power minus one}),$$

and this can be proved to be true for x to any power that is a constant, for all values of x where the derivative is defined. To see the need for the last clause, which implies a restriction on values of x, observe that

$$\text{if } f(x) = x^{1/2},$$

then

$$f'(x) = \frac{1}{2} x^{1/2 - 1}$$
$$= \frac{1}{2} x^{-1/2}$$
$$= \frac{1}{2x^{1/2}}$$

and note that $f'(x)$ is not defined at $x = 0$ because

$$f'(0) = \frac{1}{2(0)^{1/2}} = \frac{1}{0}$$

is not defined. *To avoid endless repetition, we shall follow convention and omit the necessary qualification that a derivative rule holds only for values of the independent variable where the derivative is defined.*

Simple Power Rule

$$\text{If } f(x) = x^n, \quad f'(x) = nx^{n-1}.$$

Example. Find $f'(x)$ if: a) $f(x) = x^{10}$.   b) $f(x) = x^{2/3}$.   c) $f(x) = \dfrac{1}{x^3}$.

We have the following:

a) $n = 10$, so $f'(x) = 10x^{10-1} = 10x^9$.

b) $n = \dfrac{2}{3}$, so $f'(x) = \dfrac{2}{3} x^{2/3 - 1} = \dfrac{2}{3} x^{-1/3} = \dfrac{2}{3x^{1/3}}$.

c) $f(x) = \dfrac{1}{x^3} = x^{-3}$, so $n = -3$.

Hence, $f'(x) = -3x^{-3-1} = -3x^{-4} = -\dfrac{3}{x^4}$.

Exercise. Find $g'(x)$ for each of the following. a) $g(x) = x^7$. b) $g(x) = x^{6.5}$. c) $g(x) = x^{4/3}$. d) $g(x) = x^{1/2}$. e) $g(x) = x$. f) $g(x) = \dfrac{1}{x}$. Answer: a) $7x^6$. b) $6.5x^{5.5}$. c) $\dfrac{4}{3}x^{1/3}$. d) $\dfrac{1}{2x^{1/2}}$ e) 1. f) $-\dfrac{1}{x^2}$.

We have called the rule at hand the *simple* power rule to distinguish it from the *function power rule* we shall develop later in Section 10.16 and apply to cases where the base of the power is a function of x other than simply x itself. Thus, the derivative of

$$f(x) = x^9$$

is found by the simple power rule, but the derivative of

$$g(x) = (3x^2 + 2x - 7)^9$$

will be found later by the function power rule.

Parabolic cost functions: Marginal cost. Suppose the total cost, in dollars, of producing g gallons of Galloil can be represented on the interval $0 \le g \le 150$ by the cost function

$$C(g) = 0.1g^2 + 2g + 30.$$

This function is sketched as the vertical parabola shown in Figure 10–16. In Chapter 1, and earlier in this chapter, we determined the marginal cost of, say, the 51st gallon as

$$C(51) - C(50);$$

that is, the additional cost incurred with the 51st gallon is produced. In Figure 10–16, this will be the slope of the secant line joining the points where $g = 50$ and $g = 51$. However, we should realize that a gallon is an arbitrary unit and we could as easily deal with quarts, in which case the interval from 50 to 51 gallons becomes 200 to 204 quarts. Now we could compute the marginal cost of the 201st, 202nd, 203rd, and 204th quarts. These again would be secant slopes, all of which will be different because our cost function curves, and all of which will be different from the marginal cost of the 51st gallon, $C(51) - C(50)$. Again, quarts are an arbitrary unit, and we could think in terms of pints, in which case each of the 8 pints in the 51st gallon would have a different marginal cost. The way out of the ambiguity caused by the fact that measuring units are arbitrary is to define marginal cost *at a point*; that is, to use the slope of the tangent line, $C'(g)$, as marginal cost.

FIGURE 10–16 (not to scale)

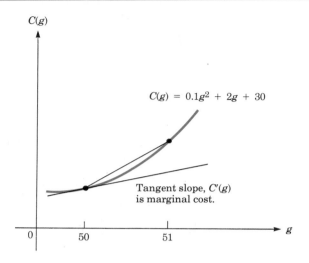

$C(g) = 0.1g^2 + 2g + 30$

Tangent slope, $C'(g)$ is marginal cost.

Definition. If $C(x)$ is the total cost of producing x units of a product, $C'(x)$ is the point marginal cost.

Hereafter in this text, marginal cost will mean point marginal cost.

Example. If $C(g) = 0.1g^2 + 2g + 30$, find the marginal cost at 50 and 51 units of output.

Using the simple power rule, the derivative of g^2 is $2g$, the derivative of g is 1, and the derivative of $30 = 30g^0$ is 0. So

$$\text{Marginal cost} = C'(g) = 0.2g + 2.$$
$$C'(50) = 0.2(50) + 2 = \$12 \text{ per gallon.}$$
$$C'(51) = 0.2(51) + 2 = \$12.20 \text{ per gallon.}$$

Exercise. If the total cost of producing p pounds of Poundum is $C(p) = 0.0015p^3 - 0.9p^2 + 200p + 60,000$, compute the marginal cost at outputs of a) 100 pounds. b) 200 pounds. c) 300 pounds. Answer: a) \$65 per pound. b) \$20 per pound. c) \$65 per pound.

10.14 *d/dx* NOTATION AND RULES OF OPERATIONS

The two-part statement,

$$\text{if } f(x) = x^3, \quad \text{then} \quad f'(x) = 3x^2,$$

is awkward, and it will be convenient to use a symbol that means to take the derivative with respect to an independent variable.

Definition. $\dfrac{d}{dx}$ means take the derivative with respect to x.

$$\frac{df(x)}{dx} \quad \text{means} \quad f'(x).$$

Thus, the symbol d/dx is an instruction and should *never* be read as d over d times x. Instead, say "the derivative with respect to x." The symbol may be written apart from the function, as in

$$\frac{d}{dx}f(x),$$

or it may appear as

$$\frac{df(x)}{dx}.$$

We now can make simple one-part statements such as

$$\frac{d}{dx}x^3 = 3x^2; \quad \frac{d(x^4)}{dx} = 4x^3.$$

Next we state the rules that govern operations with derivatives, and give an example of each. We shall prove the first two rules and leave the third one for the reader to prove in the coming problem set.

1. If k is any constant, $\dfrac{d}{dx}(k) = 0$.

That is, the derivative of any constant is zero. Thus, if we have

$$f(x) = 10, \quad \frac{df(x)}{dx} = \frac{d}{dx}(10) = 0.$$

Graphically, this means simply that $f(x) = 10$, or $f(x) = k$, is a *horizontal* straight line, and the slope of a horizontal line is zero.

Proof: a) If $f(x) = k$, meaning $f(x)$ is the same no matter what the value of x is, then $f(x + \Delta x) = k$.

b) $\dfrac{f(x + \Delta x) - f(x)}{\Delta x} = \dfrac{k - k}{\Delta x} = 0.$

c) $f'(x) = \lim\limits_{\Delta x \to 0} (0) = 0$, because the limit of a constant is the constant.

2. If k is any constant, $\dfrac{d}{dx}[kf(x)] = k\dfrac{df(x)}{dx} = kf'(x).$

That is, a constant factor (multiplier) remains in the derivative or, we may say, a constant factor may be placed inside or outside of the derivative symbol.

Examples

$$\frac{d}{dx}(2x) = 2\frac{d}{dx}(x) = 2(1) = 2.$$

$$\frac{d}{dx}(3x) = 3\frac{d}{dx}(x) = 3.$$

$$\frac{d}{dx}(3x^2) = 3\frac{d}{dx}(x^2) = 3(2x) = 6x.$$

Proof: Let $g(x) = kf(x)$ and apply steps a, b, and c of the preceding to $g(x)$.

a) $g(x + \Delta x) = kf(x + \Delta x).$

b) $\dfrac{g(x + \Delta x) - g(x)}{\Delta x} = \dfrac{kf(x + \Delta x) - kf(x)}{\Delta x}$

$$= \frac{k[f(x + \Delta x) - f(x)]}{\Delta x}.$$

c) $\lim\limits_{\Delta x \to 0} \dfrac{g(x + \Delta x) - g(x)}{\Delta x} = \lim\limits_{\Delta x \to 0} \dfrac{k[f(x + \Delta x) - f(x)]}{\Delta x}$

$$= k \lim\limits_{\Delta x \to 0} \frac{f(x + \Delta x) - f(x)}{\Delta x}$$

$$= kf'(x),$$

which is rule number two. Note in the next to the last step that we applied the limit theorem that states that a constant factor may be placed inside or outside of the limit symbol.

3. $\dfrac{d}{dx}[f(x) \pm g(x)] = \dfrac{df(x)}{dx} \pm \dfrac{dg(x)}{dx}.$

That is, the derivative of an expression may be taken term by term. This follows from the limit theorem which says the limit may be taken term by term. (See the last problem in Section 10.15.)

Example

$$\frac{d}{dx}(5x^4 + 3x^2 + 2x + 7)$$

$$= \frac{d}{dx}(5x^4) + \frac{d}{dx}(3x^2) + \frac{d}{dx}(2x) + \frac{d}{dx}(7)$$
$$= 5(4x^3) + 3(2x) + 2(1) + 0$$
$$= 20x^3 + 6x + 2.$$

Summary of Rules

1. The derivative of a constant is zero.
2. The derivative of a constant times a function equals the constant times the derivative of the function.
3. The derivative of an expression may be taken term by term.

Because the point seems unclear to some students, we call special attention to the fact that

$$f(x) = kx \text{ is } f(x) = kx^1.$$

By the power rule,

$$\frac{df(x)}{dx} = k(1)x^{1-1} = kx^0 = k.$$

That is, for example,

$$\frac{d}{dx}\left(\frac{x}{3}\right) = \frac{1}{3}, \quad \frac{d}{dx}(5x) = 5, \quad \frac{d}{dx}(0.2x) = 0.2, \quad \text{and} \quad \frac{d}{dx}(-2x) = -2.$$

Note also that in

$$\frac{d}{dx}(3x^2 + ax - b),$$

the derivative is *with respect to* x. This means that other letters are treated as constants because x is the independent variable. Thus,

$$\frac{d}{dx}(3x^2 + ax - b) = 6x + a.$$

Again,

$$\frac{d}{dq}(3q^2 - pq + 4r) = 6q - p.$$

Exercise. Find: a) $\dfrac{d}{dx}(2x^{3/2} - 4x^3 + 5x - 10)$.

b) $\dfrac{d}{dp}(2q^3 - 4p^2q^2 + 3p)$.

Answer: a) $3x^{1/2} - 12x^2 + 5$. b) $-8pq^2 + 3$.

10.15 PROBLEM SET 10–5

In Problems 1 through 18, find $f'(x)$. Do not leave negative exponents in answers.

1. $f(x) = 2 + k$.

2. $f(x) = x$.

3. $f(x) = x/2$.

4. $f(x) = 2x + 3$.

5. $f(x) = x/3 + 4$.

6. $f(x) = 2/3 - 3x/2$.

7. $f(x) = 3x^2 + 2x - 5$.

8. $f(x) = x^3/3 - x^2/2 + x + 12$.

9. $f(x) = 0.01x^2 + 2x + 100$.

10. $f(x) = 0.5x^3 - x^2/2 + 7$.

11. $f(x) = mx + b$.

12. $f(x) = ax^2 + bx + c$.

13. $f(x) = 2/x - 1/x^2$.

14. $f(x) = 1/2x + 1/x^3$.

15. $f(x) = 2x^{3/2} - 4x^{1/2} + 3x^{2/3} + 2x - 7$.

16. $f(x) = 2x^{1/3} + x^{4/3} + 5x^{1.2} + x - 1$.

17. $f(x) = 1/3x + 2/x^{1/2}$.

18. $f(x) = 3/x^{1/3} - 12/x^{1/4}$.

Find each of the following:

19. $\dfrac{d}{dx}(3x^2 - 2x + 5)$.

20. $\dfrac{d}{dy}(10y^2 - 4x + 7)$.

21. $\dfrac{d}{dz}(az + b)$.

22. $\dfrac{d}{dx}(3pw^2 - 2p^3)$.

23. $\dfrac{d}{dh}(kh^2 - ah^{1/3} + 5ak)$.

24. $\dfrac{d}{dm}\left(\dfrac{a}{m} - 3m^2 + 5a^3\right)$.

Find the slope of the tangent to each of the following curves at the indicated value of x:

25. $f(x) = 3$; $x = 1$.

26. $f(x) = -5$; $x = 4$.

27. $f(x) = 2x + 6$; $x = -0.5$.

28. $f(x) = 3 - 4x$; $x = -3$.

29. $f(x) = 3x^2 - 2x + 5$; $x = 0.5$.

30. $f(x) = 10x - 2x^2 + 3$; $x = 2.5$.

31. $f(x) = 3x + 12/x$; $x = 2$.

32. $f(x) = 12x^{1/2} - 3x$; $x = 9$.

33. $f(x) = 8x^{1/3} + x$; $x = 8$.

34. $f(x) = 1/x^2 - 1/x + x$; $x = 2$.

In Problems 35–40, find the value of x for which the slope is zero.

35. $f(x) = 10 - 3x^2 + 3x$.

36. $f(x) = 0.2x^2 - 40x + 50$.

37. $f(x) = 3x^{1/3} - 4x$; $x > 0$.

38. $f(x) = 3x^{1/2} - 2x$.

39. $f(x) = x + 9/x$; $x > 0$.

40. $f(x) = 3x + 48/x$; $x > 0$.

10.15 PROBLEM SET 10–5 (*concluded*)

41. If the total cost of producing y yards of Yardall is

$$C(y) = 0.001y^2 + 2y + 500$$

find the marginal cost at outputs of:
a) 1,000 yards.
b) 2,000 yards.

42. If the total cost of producing t tons of Tonal, in dollars, is

$$C(t) = 0.0005t^3 - 0.3t^2 + 100t + 30,000,$$

compute marginal cost at outputs of:
a) 100 tons.
b) 200 tons.
c) 300 tons.

43. Prove from the definition of derivatives and limit theorems that

$$\frac{d}{dx}[f(x) + g(x)] = f'(x) + g'(x).$$

10.16 THE DERIVATIVE OF $[f(x)]^n$

Now that we are familiar with the use of the *simple* power rule,

$$\frac{d}{dx}(x^n) = nx^{n-1},$$

we wish to learn how to expand this rule to take the derivative of expressions such as

$$\frac{d}{dx}(2x - 7)^{10}$$

$$\frac{d}{dx}(3x^2 - 2x + 5)^{3/2},$$

where the base of the power is something other than simply x; that is, we want a rule for finding

$$\frac{d}{dx}[f(x)]^n.$$

The rule is easily learned and applied. We shall state it, give illustrations, and then show its source.

Function Power Rule

$$\frac{d}{dx}[f(x)]^n = n[f(x)]^{n-1}\frac{df(x)}{dx}$$
$$= n[f(x)]^{n-1}f'(x).$$

Thus, the new rule starts out as does the simple rule with the (power) times the (function to the power minus one), then is completed by multiplying by the derivative of the function.

Example. Find the derivative of $g(x) = (2x - 7)^{10}$.

Here we could expand $g(x)$ by raising $(2x - 7)$ to the tenth power and take the derivative of the result term by term using the simple power rule—but this is almost unthinkable. By the function power rule,

$$\frac{d}{dx}(2x - 7)^{10} = 10(2x - 7)^9 \frac{d}{dx}(2x - 7)$$

$$= 10(2x - 7)^9 (2)$$

$$= 20(2x - 7)^9.$$

Exercise.   Find $h'(x)$ if $h(x) = (3x^2 + 5)^{100}$. Answer: $600x(3x^2 + 5)^{99}$.

Example.   Find $f'(x)$ if $f(x) = (3x^2 - 2x + 5)^{3/2}$.

We have

$$\frac{d}{dx}(3x^2 - 2x + 5)^{3/2} = \frac{3}{2}(3x^2 - 2x + 5)^{1/2} \frac{d}{dx}(3x^2 - 2x + 5)$$

$$= \frac{3}{2}(3x^2 - 2x + 5)^{1/2} (6x - 2)$$

$$= \frac{3}{2}(3x^2 - 2x + 5)^{1/2} (2)(3x - 1)$$

$$= 3(3x^2 - 2x + 5)^{1/2} (3x - 1).$$

Exercise.   Find $f'(x)$ if $f(x) = (2x^3 - 3x^2 - 10)^{4/3}$.
Answer: $8(2x^3 - 3x^2 - 10)^{1/3} (x)(x - 1)$.

Example. Find $f'(x)$ if $f(x) = \dfrac{50}{0.2x + 5}$.

To obtain proper form, $[f(x)]^n$, which is not a fractional form, we write

$$f(x) = \frac{50}{0.2x + 5} = 50(0.2x + 5)^{-1}.$$

Then

$$f'(x) = 50\frac{d}{dx}(0.2x + 5)^{-1}$$

$$= 50(-1)(0.2x + 5)^{-2}\frac{d}{dx}(0.2x + 5)$$

$$= -50(0.2x + 5)^{-2}(0.2)$$
$$= -10(0.2x + 5)^{-2}$$
$$= -\frac{10}{(0.2x + 5)^2}.$$

Example. Find $f'(1)$ if $f(x) = 10x - \dfrac{54}{(5x^2 + 4)^{1/2}}$.

Changing to proper form, we have

$$f(x) = 10x - 54(5x^2 + 4)^{-1/2}$$
$$f'(x) = 10 - 54(-1/2)(5x^2 + 4)^{-3/2}\frac{d}{dx}(5x^2 + 4)$$
$$= 10 + 27(5x^2 + 4)^{-3/2}(10x)$$
$$= 10 + \frac{270x}{(5x^2 + 4)^{3/2}}.$$

Then,

$$f'(1) = 10 + \frac{270 \cdot 1}{(5 \cdot 1^2 + 4)^{3/2}} = 10 + \frac{270}{9^{3/2}} = 10 + \frac{270}{(9^{1/2})^3} = 10 + \frac{270}{3^3}$$
$$= 10 + \frac{270}{27} = 20.$$

Source of the function power rule. This, like all derivative rules, starts with the limit definition of a derivative. For a function $g(x)$ this is

$$\frac{d}{dx}g(x) = g'(x) = \lim_{\Delta x \to 0}\frac{\Delta g(x)}{\Delta x} = \lim_{\Delta x \to 0}\frac{g(x + \Delta x) - g(x)}{\Delta x}.$$

Here we shall use

$$[f(x)]^n \quad \text{as} \quad g(x)$$

so

$$\frac{d}{dx}[f(x)]^n = \lim_{\Delta x \to 0}\frac{\Delta[f(x)]^n}{\Delta x}.$$

To show the results more clearly, we shall for the present write f in place of $f(x)$, leave off the limit symbol until the end, and manipulate the difference quotient

$$\frac{[\Delta f(x)]^n}{\Delta x} = \frac{\Delta f^n}{\Delta x}.$$

Next, we apply a device often used by mathematicians to change a form at hand into a different, but equivalent, form that is wanted. The device is to multiply and divide the given form by the *same* quantity, which, in this case, is Δf. Thus,

$$\frac{\Delta f^n}{\Delta x} = \frac{\Delta f^n}{\Delta x} \left(\frac{\Delta f}{\Delta f}\right) = \frac{\Delta f^n}{\Delta f} \left(\frac{\Delta f}{\Delta x}\right),$$

where, at the right, the factors have been rearranged as permitted by the commutative property for multiplication. Then we take the limit as Δx approaches zero to obtain the derivative:

$$\lim_{\Delta x \to 0} \frac{\Delta f^n}{\Delta x} = \lim_{\Delta x \to 0} \frac{\Delta f^n}{\Delta f} \left(\frac{\Delta f}{\Delta x}\right).$$

A limit theorem says the limit of a product is the product of the limits, so

$$\lim_{\Delta x \to 0} \frac{\Delta f^n}{\Delta x} = \left[\lim_{\Delta x \to 0} \frac{\Delta f^n}{\Delta f}\right] \left[\lim_{\Delta x \to 0} \frac{\Delta f}{\Delta x}\right].$$

Now we must remember that as Δx approaches zero, $\Delta f(x)$, which is

$$\Delta f(x) = \Delta f = f(x + \Delta x) - f(x),$$

also approaches zero. Hence, changing $\Delta x \to 0$ to $\Delta f \to 0$ in the first factor on the right of the above limit expression, we have

$$\lim_{\Delta x \to 0} \frac{\Delta f^n}{\Delta x} = \left[\lim_{\Delta f \to 0} \frac{\Delta f^n}{\Delta f}\right] \left[\lim_{\Delta x \to 0} \frac{\Delta f}{\Delta x}\right]. \tag{1}$$

We may now write

$$\lim_{\Delta x \to 0} \frac{\Delta f^n}{\Delta x} = [nf^{n-1}][f'(x)] \tag{2}$$

because, by definition, in (1),

$$\lim_{\Delta f \to 0} \frac{\Delta f^n}{\Delta f} = \frac{d}{df} f^n = nf^{n-1}$$

and

$$\lim_{\Delta x \to 0} \frac{\Delta f}{\Delta x} = f'(x).$$

Finally, recalling that f is $f(x)$, (2) becomes

$$\lim_{\Delta x \to 0} \frac{\Delta [f(x)]^n}{\Delta x} = n[f(x)]^{n-1} f'(x),$$

which is the function power rule.

We pause now for a practice problem set.

10.17 PROBLEM SET 10–6

Find $f'(x)$. Simplify where possible. Leave no negative exponent in answers.

1. $f(x) = (6x - 5)^5.$

2. $f(x) = (2x + 6)^5.$

3. $f(x) = (2x)^3.$

4. $f(x) = (6x)^{1/3}.$

5. $f(x) = (4x)^{1/2}.$

6. $f(x) = (9x)^{4/3}.$

7. $f(x) = (8x - 3)^{3/2}.$

8. $f(x) = (12x - 9)^{5/3}.$

9. $f(x) = (3x^2 - 6x + 2)^{5/2}.$

10. $f(x) = (x^3 - 3x^2 + 6x)^{4/3}.$

11. $f(x) = (2x - 3)^{1/2}.$

12. $f(x) = (3x^2 + 5)^{2/3}.$

13. $f(x) = \dfrac{4}{2x - 3}.$

14. $f(x) = \dfrac{6}{3x - 5}.$

15. $f(x) = (1/x - 2)^2.$

16. $f(x) = (5 - 1/x^2)^3.$

17. $f(x) = \dfrac{9}{(3x - 5)^2}.$

18. $f(x) = \dfrac{12}{(2x + 10)^3}.$

19. $f(x) = 5x + \dfrac{10}{3x + 2}.$

20. $f(x) = 0.1x + \dfrac{5}{5 - 0.2x}.$

21. $f(x) = 3x + \dfrac{1}{(5 + 2x)^{1/2}}.$

22. $f(x) = \dfrac{1}{(3x - 7)^{1/2}} - 2x.$

23. Find $g'(2)$ if $g(x) = 10x + \dfrac{18}{(5 + 2x)^{1/2}}.$

24. Find $h'(3)$ if $h(x) = 7x + \dfrac{4}{(x^2 - 1)^{1/3}}.$

10.18 PRODUCT AND QUOTIENT RULES

We now extend our list of rules to include the derivative of the product of two functions and the quotient of two functions; that is, for example, to find

$$\frac{d}{dx}(x - 1)(x^2 + 2)^{4/3} \quad \text{and} \quad \frac{d}{dx}\left(\frac{2x^2 + 3}{x + 1}\right),$$

or, more generally,

$$\frac{d}{dx}[f(x)g(x)] \quad \text{and} \quad \frac{d}{dx}\left[\frac{f(x)}{g(x)}\right].$$

The product rule. To find the derivative of any function, we start with the definition that the derivative is the limit of the difference quotient as $\Delta x \to 0$. For

$$f(x)g(x)$$

the difference quotient is

$$\frac{f(x + \Delta x)g(x + \Delta x) - f(x)g(x)}{\Delta x}. \tag{1}$$

Now

$$\Delta f(x) = f(x + \Delta x) - f(x)$$

so

$$f(x + \Delta x) = f(x) + \Delta f(x).$$

For clarity, we shall abbreviate the last expression as

$$f(x + \Delta x) = f + \Delta f.$$

Similarly,

$$g(x + \Delta x) = g + \Delta g.$$

The difference quotient, (1), then is

$$\frac{(f + \Delta f)(g + \Delta g) - fg}{\Delta x} = \frac{fg + f(\Delta g) + g(\Delta f) + (\Delta f)(\Delta g) - fg}{\Delta x}$$

$$= \frac{f(\Delta g) + g(\Delta f) + (\Delta f)(\Delta g)}{\Delta x}$$

$$= f\left(\frac{\Delta g}{\Delta x}\right) + g\left(\frac{\Delta f}{\Delta x}\right) + \Delta f\left(\frac{\Delta g}{\Delta x}\right).$$

The derivative is the limit of the last expression as Δx approaches zero, and the limit may be taken term by term. Thus,

$$\frac{d}{dx}[f(x)g(x)] = \frac{d}{dx}[fg]$$

$$= \lim_{\Delta x \to 0} f\left(\frac{\Delta g}{\Delta x}\right) + \lim_{\Delta x \to 0} g\left(\frac{\Delta f}{\Delta x}\right) + \lim_{\Delta x \to 0} \Delta f\left(\frac{\Delta g}{\Delta x}\right). \tag{2}$$

Now f and g are to be thought of as function values (at a *given* point x) that do not vary as we approach the point by letting Δx approach zero, so f and g may be placed outside the limit symbols. And, of course, as Δx approaches zero, so also do Δf and Δg approach zero. Finally, the limit of the product at the right end of (2) is the product of the limits. Hence, (2) may be written as

$$\frac{d}{dx}[fg] = f \lim_{\Delta x \to 0}\left(\frac{\Delta g}{\Delta x}\right) + g \lim_{\Delta x \to 0}\left(\frac{\Delta f}{\Delta x}\right) + [\lim_{\Delta f \to 0} \Delta f]\left[\lim_{\Delta x \to 0}\left(\frac{\Delta g}{\Delta x}\right)\right]. \tag{3}$$

Now, because

$$\lim_{\Delta x \to 0}\left(\frac{\Delta g}{\Delta x}\right) = g' = g'(x),$$

$$\lim_{\Delta x \to 0} \left(\frac{\Delta f}{\Delta x} \right) = f' = f'(x),$$

and

$$[\lim_{\Delta f \to 0} \Delta f] \left[\lim_{\Delta x \to 0} \left(\frac{\Delta g}{\Delta x} \right) \right] = 0(g') = 0,$$

the expression (3) becomes

$$\frac{d}{dx}[fg] = fg' + gf'.$$

Replacing the independent variable, we have

Product Rule

$$\frac{d}{dx}[f(x)g(x)] = f(x)g'(x) + g(x)f'(x).$$

In words, *the derivative of the product of two functions is the first times the derivative of the second, plus the second times the derivative of the first.*

To show that the product rule works, note that

$$\frac{d}{dx}(x^3)(x^5) = \frac{d}{dx}(x^8) = 8x^7$$

by the power rule. If we now think of

$$f(x) = x^3 \quad \text{as the first function,}$$

and

$$g(x) = x^5 \quad \text{as the second function,}$$

then by the product rule

$$\frac{d}{dx}(x^3)(x^5) = x^3 \frac{d}{dx}(x^5) + x^5 \frac{d}{dx}(x^3)$$
$$= x^3(5x^4) + x^5(3x^2)$$
$$= 5x^7 + 3x^7$$
$$= 8x^7,$$

as it should be.

Example. Find

$$\frac{d}{dx}(x - 1)(x^3 + 2)^{4/3}.$$

Here, the first function is $(x - 1)$ and the second is $(x^3 + 2)^{4/3}$.

$$\frac{d}{dx}(x - 1)(x^3 + 2)^{4/3} = (x - 1)\frac{d}{dx}(x^3 + 2)^{4/3} + (x^3 + 2)^{4/3}\frac{d}{dx}(x - 1)$$

$$= (x - 1)(4/3)(x^3 + 2)^{1/3}(3x^2)^* + (x^3 + 2)^{4/3}(1)$$

$$= 4x^2(x - 1)(x^3 + 2)^{1/3} + (x^3 + 2)^{4/3},$$

where * (two lines above) calls attention to application of the function power rule. The expression last written has $(x^3 + 2)^{1/3}$ as a common factor, and to show this we write $(x^3 + 2)^{4/3}$ as $(x^3 + 2)^1 (x^3 + 2)^{1/3}$, giving

$$4x^2(x - 1)(x^3 + 2)^{1/3} + (x^3 + 2)^1 (x^3 + 2)^{1/3}$$

$$= (x^3 + 2)^{1/3} [4x^2 (x - 1) + (x^3 + 2)]$$

$$= (x^3 + 2)^{1/3} (4x^3 - 4x^2 + x^3 + 2)$$

$$= (x^3 + 2)^{1/3} (5x^3 - 4x^2 + 2).$$

Exercise. a) By the simple power rule, find

$$\frac{d}{dx}(2x + 1)(x - 1) = \frac{d}{dx}(2x^2 - x - 1).$$

b) Do (a) by the product rule. c) Find $\frac{d}{dx}(x^2 + 3)(2x + 5)^{3/2}$.

Answer: a) $4x - 1$. b) $(2x + 1)(1) + (x - 1)(2) = 4x - 1$.
c) $3(x^2 + 3)(2x + 5)^{1/2} + 2x(2x + 5)^{3/2}$. Factoring the last yields $(2x + 5)^{1/2} (7x^2 + 10x + 9)$.

The quotient rule. This rule can be derived easily from the product rule if we remember that by the function power rule

$$\frac{d}{dx}\left[\frac{1}{g(x)}\right] = \frac{d}{dx}[g(x)]^{-1} = -1[g(x)]^{-2} g'(x).$$

We start by changing the quotient to a product, then apply the product rule.

$$\frac{d}{dx}\left[\frac{f(x)}{g(x)}\right] = \frac{d}{dx}(f(x)[g(x)]^{-1})$$

$$= f(x)\frac{d}{dx}[g(x)]^{-1} + [g(x)]^{-1}\frac{d}{dx}f(x)$$

$$= f(x)(-1)[g(x)]^{-2} g'(x) + [g(x)]^{-1}f'(x)$$

$$= \frac{-f(x)g'(x)}{[g(x)]^2} + \frac{f'(x)}{g(x)}$$

$$= \frac{-f(x)g'(x)}{[g(x)]^2} + \frac{f'(x)}{g(x)}\left[\frac{g(x)}{g(x)}\right]$$

$$= \frac{-f(x)g'(x) + f'(x)g(x)}{[g(x)]^2},$$

where in the next to the last step we multiplied the rightmost term by $g(x)/g(x)$ to obtain a common denominator. Rearranging the last expression, we have

---

Quotient Rule

$$\frac{d}{dx}\left[\frac{f(x)}{g(x)}\right] = \frac{g(x)f'(x) - f(x)g'(x)}{[g(x)]^2}.$$

In words, *the derivative of a quotient is the denominator times the derivative of the numerator, minus the numerator times the derivative of the denominator, all over the denominator squared.* For example,

$$\frac{d}{dx}\left(\frac{2x + 5}{3x - 7}\right) = \frac{(3x - 7)\dfrac{d}{dx}(2x + 5) - (2x + 5)\dfrac{d}{dx}(3x - 7)}{(3x - 7)^2}$$

$$= \frac{(3x - 7)(2) - (2x + 5)(3)}{(3x - 7)^2}$$

$$= \frac{6x - 14 - (6x + 15)}{(3x - 7)^2}$$

$$= -\frac{29}{(3x - 7)^2}.$$

Exercise. Find $\dfrac{d}{dx}\left(\dfrac{5x}{3 - 4x}\right)$. Answer: $\dfrac{15}{(3 - 4x)^2}$.

Example. Find the derivative of $x^2/(3x + 2)^{1/2}$.

We have

$$\frac{d}{dx}\left[\frac{x^2}{(3x + 2)^{1/2}}\right] = \frac{(3x + 2)^{1/2}(2x) - x^2(1/2)(3x + 2)^{-1/2}(3)}{[(3x - 2)^{1/2}]^2}$$

$$= \frac{(3x + 2)^{1/2}(2x) - \dfrac{3x^2(3x + 2)^{-1/2}}{2}}{3x + 2}.$$

To remove the divisor, 2, and the negative exponent in the numerator, we multiply the numerator and denominator by

$$2(3x + 2)^{1/2}$$

as follows:

$$\left[\dfrac{(3x + 2)^{1/2}(2x) - \dfrac{3x^2(3x + 2)^{-1/2}}{2}}{3x + 2} \right] \left[\dfrac{2(3x + 2)^{1/2}}{2(3x + 2)^{1/2}} \right]$$

$$= \dfrac{(3x + 2)^{1/2}(2x)(2)(3x + 2)^{1/2} - \dfrac{3x^2(3x + 2)^{-1/2}}{2}(2)(3x + 2)^{1/2}}{(3x + 2)(2)(3x + 2)^{1/2}}$$

$$= \dfrac{4x(3x + 2) - 3x^2}{2(3x + 2)^{3/2}} = \dfrac{9x^2 + 8x}{2(3x + 2)^{3/2}} = \dfrac{x(9x + 8)}{2(3x + 2)^{3/2}}.$$

It may help to refer to the preceding examples when working on the next set of problems.

10.19 PROBLEM SET 10–7

Find the first derivative of each of the following. Simplify results and factor where possible. Do not leave negative exponents or complex fractions (fractions containing fractions) in answers.

1. $f(x) = (3x - 2)(2x + 5)$.

2. $f(x) = (7x + 3)(4 - 3x)$.

3. $f(x) = (x^2 + 2)(3x - 5)$.

4. $f(x) = (3 - x^2)(5x + 6)$.

5. $f(x) = x(x - 1)^4$.

6. $f(x) = x^2(x + 5)^3$.

7. $f(x) = x^2(x + 3)^{3/2}$.

8. $f(x) = x^3(6x - 1)^{2/3}$.

9. $f(x) = 2x(3x^2 + 7)^{1/3}$.

10. $f(x) = 3x(2x^3 + 5)^{1/2}$.

11. $f(x) = \dfrac{x}{x - 1}$.

12. $f(x) = \dfrac{x - 2}{x + 1}$.

13. $f(x) = \dfrac{x^2}{2x + 3}$.

14. $f(x) = \dfrac{x^3}{3x + 5}$.

15. $f(x) = \dfrac{x}{3 + 2x^2}$.

16. $f(x) = \dfrac{3x}{1 - 2x^2}$.

17. $f(x) = \dfrac{x}{(3x + 2)^{1/2}}$.

18. $f(x) = \dfrac{2x}{(2x + 3)^{1/2}}$.

19. $f(x) = \dfrac{2x + 1}{(x^2 + 5)^{1/3}}$.

20. $f(x) = \dfrac{3 - 5x}{(x^3 + 2)^{1/3}}$.

10.20 REVIEW PROBLEMS

1. If $f(x) = 3x^2 + 2x + 5$, find the value of, or the algebraic expression for:
   a) $f(0)$.
   b) $f(1)$.
   c) $f(-1)$.
   d) $f(5)$.
   e) $f(2a)$.
   f) $f\left(\dfrac{1}{x+1}\right)$.
   g) $f(x + 1) - f(x)$.
   h) $f(x) - f(x - a)$.

2. a) If $f(x) = 2xy$, write the expression for $[f(a)]^2$.
   b) If $g(y) = 2xy$, write the expression for $g(a - 1)$.

3. If $f(x) = 32x^{-1} - 2x^{-2/3} + 24x^{-1/2}$, find $f(64)$.

4. Find the expression for $\Delta f(x)$ if
   a) $f(x) = 7 - 2x$.   b) $f(x) = x^2 + 3x - 6$.

5. If $f(x) = 3x^2 - 2x + 4$;
   a) Write the expression for $\Delta f(x)$.
   b) Compute $\Delta f(x)$ if x changes from 2 by the amount $\Delta x = 0.1$.

6. The total cost of making p pounds of Poundal is $C(p)$ dollars, where

$$C(p) = 50 + 1.5p + 0.02p^2.$$

   a) Write the expression for the marginal cost of the pth gallon.
   b) Find the marginal cost of the fifth gallon.
   c) Find the marginal cost of the 40th gallon.

Find each of the following, if it exists:

7. $\lim\limits_{x \to 0} (3x^2 - 2x + 5)$.

8. $\lim\limits_{b \to a} (a^3 + 3a^2b + 3ab^2 + b^3)$.

9. $\lim\limits_{x \to 1} \dfrac{x^2 + 1}{x - 1}$.

10. $\lim\limits_{x \to 4} \dfrac{3x}{0.5x - 2}$.

11. $\lim\limits_{x \to 8} 2x^{-2/3}$.

12. $\lim\limits_{x \to 0} \dfrac{x^{3/2}}{x}$.

13. $\lim\limits_{a \to b} (a^2 + 2ab + b^2)$.

14. $\lim\limits_{x \to 1.25} \dfrac{16x^2 - 25}{4x - 5}$.

15. $\lim\limits_{x \to 0} \dfrac{x}{x^{1/3}}$.

16. $\lim\limits_{\Delta x \to 0} \dfrac{\Delta x(x - 1)}{\Delta x}$.

17. $\lim\limits_{x \to 0} \left(8 + \dfrac{x^2}{x}\right)^{1/3}$.

18. $\lim\limits_{a \to 0} \dfrac{\dfrac{1}{(x + a)^2} - \dfrac{1}{x^2}}{a}; x \neq 0$.

19. Write the delta limit definition for the derivative of $f(x)$.

Apply the delta definition of Problem 19 to find the derivatives for Problems 20–25.

20. $f(x) = 2x^2 + 3$.

21. $f(x) = x^2 + 3x - 2$.

22. $f(x) = \dfrac{1}{1 - x}$.

23. $f(x) = \dfrac{2}{3x - 5}$.

24. $f(x) = x^{1/2}$. [Hint: After the difference quotient has been set up, multiply its numerator and denominator by $(x + \Delta x)^{1/2} + x^{1/2}$ and proceed.]

25. $f(x) = x^{3/2}$. [Hint: After the difference quotient has been set up, multiply its numerator and denominator by $(x + \Delta x)^{3/2} + x^{3/2}$ and proceed.]

26. Find the derivative by the delta limit definition, then find the slope of the curve at the point where $x = 2$ if $f(x) = x^2 - 5x$.

27. Find the derivative by the delta limit definition, then find the slope of the curve at the point where $x = 2$ if $f(x) = 12/x$.

10.20 REVIEW PROBLEMS (*continued*)

In Problems 28–39, find $f'(x)$. Do not leave negative exponents in answers.

28. $f(x) = 2x - 3$.

29. $f(x) = 5 - 4x$.

30. $f(x) = 1.5x^2 - 2x^3 - 4x + 5$.

31. $f(x) = 0.25x^4 - 2.5x^2 + x - 6$.

32. $f(x) = ax^3 - bx + 1$.

33. $f(x) = xy - ax^2$.

34. $f(x) = 3/2x^2 - 5/x$.

35. $f(x) = 1/3x^2 - 1/x$.

36. $f(x) = 3x^{1/2} + 2x^{1/3} + 1$.

37. $f(x) = 6x^{4/3} - 3x^{2/3} - 2x + 6$.

38. $f(x) = 12/x^{2/3} - 16/x^{3/4} + x$.

39. $f(x) = x^{-1/2} - x^{-1/3} + 4x - 25$.

Find each of the following:

40. $\dfrac{d}{dx}(ax^3 - bx^2 + cx - d)$.

41. $\dfrac{d}{dy}(xy^2 - 2y + 3x^2y - 2x + 3)$.

Find the slope of the line tangent to each curve at the indicated value of x:

42. $f(x) = 2 - 0.5x$; $x = 2$.

43. $f(x) = x^3/6 - 18/x + 2x - 1$; $x = 2$.

44. $f(x) = 18x^{1/3}$; $x = 8$.

45. $f(x) = x + 12/x^{1/2}$; $x = 4$.

Find the value(s) of x for which the slope is zero:

46. $f(x) = 0.25x^2 - x + 4$.

47. $f(x) = 2x + 72/x$.

48. $f(x) = 4x^3 - 3x^2$.

49. $f(x) = x^3 - 12x$.

50. $f(x) = x - 3x^{1/2}$.

51. $f(x) = 0.1x + 12.8/x^{1/2}$.

In Problems 52–59, find $f'(x)$. Simplify where possible. Leave no negative exponents in answers.

52. $f(x) = (3x - 2)^{15}$.

53. $f(x) = (2x^3 + 3x^2 + 4x - 50)^{3/2}$.

54. $f(x) = (x^3 - 3x^2 + 5)^{1/3}$.

55. $f(x) = (10x)^{1/2}$.

56. $f(x) = \dfrac{1}{4(8x - 6)}$.

57. $f(x) = (5 - 2/x)^3$.

58. $f(x) = \dfrac{2}{27(10 - 3x)^{3/2}}$.

59. $f(x) = x - \dfrac{1}{(5 - 0.3x)^{1/3}}$.

60. Find the slope of the curve at the point where $x = 1$.

$$f(x) = \left(5 + \frac{3}{x}\right)^{1/3}.$$

61. Find the value of x at the points on the curve where the tangent line is horizontal.

$$f(x) = x + \frac{50}{2 + 0.5x}.$$

10.20 REVIEW PROBLEMS (*concluded*)

Find the first derivative for Problems 62–69. Simplify results where possible. Do not leave negative exponents or complex fractions (fractions containing fractions) in answers.

62. $f(x) = x(2x - 1)^6$.

63. $f(x) = 2x(x^3 - 5x)^{1/2}$.

64. $f(x) = 2x^2(3x^2 + 5)^{1/2}$.

65. $f(x) = (2x + 1)(4x - 5)^{1/2}$.

66. $f(x) = \dfrac{3x + 2}{2 - 3x}$.

67. $f(x) = \dfrac{x}{1 - 0.5x^2}$.

68. $f(x) = \dfrac{3x + 2}{(6x^2 + 5)^{1/3}}$.

69. $f(x) = \dfrac{2x - 1}{(2x + 3)^{1/2}}$.

ELEVEN

Applications of Differential Calculus

In this chapter, we will show how to apply the techniques of differential calculus to solve optimization problems and sketch curves. We will begin by illustrating maxima and minima of simple polynomial functions and develop the concept of critical points along with the first derivative test. Next we will use concavity to introduce the second derivative test and illustrate how to use this test in many different applications. Lastly we will give the detailed presentation of curve sketching including both polynomial and rational functions.

11.2 MAXIMA AND MINIMA OF FUNCTIONS

One of the most useful applications of calculus in management and economics is finding the maximum and minimum values for a function. To find these optimum values, we need to develop a keener sense of the behavior of the graph of a function. This section is intended to help us develop that sense.

Consider the graph of the function $f(x)$ shown in Figure 11–1. First we note that $f(x)$ is defined only on the interval $[a, \infty)$. When we use the brackets [and] to enclose an interval we indicate that the endpoint of the interval next to the bracket is included in the interval. The parentheses (and) mean that the interval contains all points except the endpoints next to the parentheses. Certainly no interval can contain ∞, so when ∞ or $-\infty$ appear in place of a finite endpoint we always use a parenthesis.

Where are the maxima and minima of our function $f(x)$? If you look carefully at the graph you will see three optima, one at a (an endpoint maximum), one at b (a local minimum), and one at c (a local and global

FIGURE 11–1

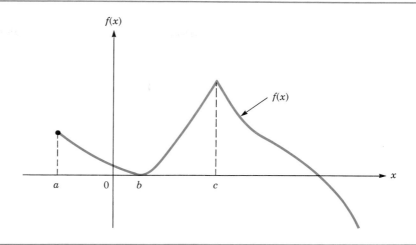

or absolute maximum). You probably already have gleaned that a local maximum or minimum point p is a point where $f(x)$ takes on a maximum or minimum value for all points in the immediate vicinity of p. An absolute (or global) maximum for $f(x)$ would be the largest value of $f(x)$ over all values of $f(x)$. Notice that the function in Figure 11–1 has no absolute minimum. We shall now show how to test whether a point is a maximum or minimum (or neither) for most functions. We lead up to the tests by discussing critical points and increasing and decreasing properties.

Critical points are those points that are *candidates* for maximum and minimum values. There are three kinds of critical points: stationary points, cusps, and endpoints.

Stationary points. The slope of a line tangent to a curve at a point is, by definition, the value of the first derivative at that point. Hence, when the first derivative is zero, the tangent line is horizontal and points where this occurs are called *stationary* points.

Definition. A stationary point on $f(x)$ is a point where $f'(x) = 0$.

Figure 11–2 shows

$$f(x) = x^3 - 6x^2 + 37.$$

To find the stationary points, we write

$$f'(x) = 3x^2 - 12x$$

FIGURE 11–2 (not to scale)

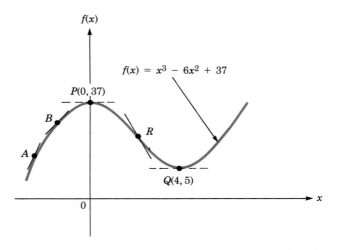

so that

$$f'(x) = 0 \quad \text{when} \quad 3x^2 - 12x = 0$$
$$x(3x - 12) = 0.$$

The values of x are found by setting each factor of the last expression equal to zero. Thus,

$$x = 0; \quad 3x - 12 = 0$$
$$3x = 12$$
$$x = 4.$$

The function values for $x = 0$ and $x = 4$ are

$$f(0) = 0^3 - 6(0)^2 + 37 = 37$$
$$f(4) = 4^3 - 6(4)^2 + 37 = 5,$$

and the stationary points $P(0, 37)$ and $Q(4, 5)$ are shown in Figure 11–2. P is called a *local* maximum because it is the highest point in its neighborhood, but not the highest point on the curve. Similarly, Q is a *local* minimum. By way of contrast, the stationary point on a vertical parabola is the highest or lowest point on the entire curve, so it is called a *global* as well as a local maximum or minimum.

Cusps. A cusp is a point on a curve where a tracing of the curve would exactly reverse its direction of motion. There is no unique tangent line at such a point: at a cusp, the function is defined but the derivative is not defined.

> **Definition.** A cusp on the function $f(x)$ in an interval (a,b) is a point in (a,b) at which $f(x)$ is defined but $f'(x)$ does not exist.

Example. Consider $f(x) = 6x^{5/3} - 15x^{2/3}$, as shown in Figure 11–3.

FIGURE 11–3

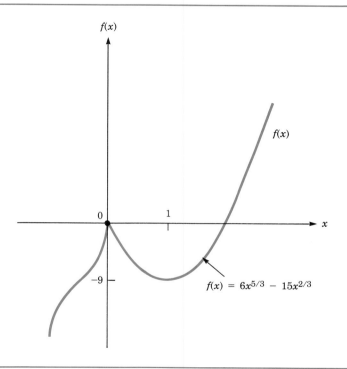

$$f(x) = 6x^{5/3} - 15x^{2/3}$$

Taking the derivative,

$$f'(x) = 10x^{2/3} - 10x^{-1/3}$$
$$= 10x^{-1/3}(x - 1)$$
$$= \frac{10(x - 1)}{x^{1/3}}.$$

Looking closely at this derivative, you see that $f(x)$ has a stationary point at $(1, -9)$. But when $x = 0$, $f'(x)$ does not exist. Since $f(0)$ exists but $f'(0)$ does not exist, we conclude that $f(x)$ has a cusp at $x = 0$. Figure 11–3 does indeed show this cusp.

Endpoints. When a function is defined only for a restricted set of points $[a,b]$, then it will have endpoints at $x = a$ and $x = b$. These endpoints will usually be local maxima or minima.

Example. Consider $f(x) = x^2 + 1$ on $[-1, 2)$ as shown in Figure 11–4. From the figure it is clear that $f(x)$ on $[-1, 2)$ has an endpoint maximum at $f(-1) = 2$. But what is happening at $x = 2$? Since $f(2)$ is not defined (because $x = 2$ is not included in the interval for which the function is defined), we cannot say that $f(x)$ has an endpoint maximum at $x = 2$. Instead, we must conclude that $f(x)$ has a local maximum at $f(-1) = 2$ but *no* absolute maximum since the function is not defined at $x = 2$.

We now summarize the tests for critical points.

1. *Stationary points:* Points where $f'(x) = 0$.
2. *Cusps:* Points where $f(x)$ is defined but $f'(x)$ does not exist.
3. *Endpoints:* Points that bound the admissible values of x for which $f(x)$ is defined.

Once we have identified the critical points of a function $f(x)$, it is very helpful to have some mechanism to determine which of these critical points are maxima, minima, or neither. It is easiest to do this by first understanding the concept of an increasing or decreasing function.

FIGURE 11–4

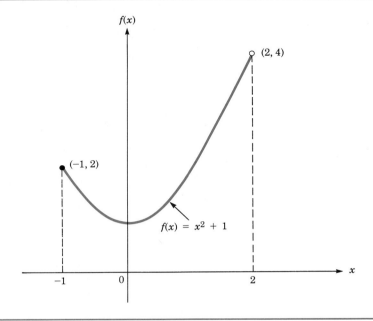

If we choose *any* two values x_1 and x_2 in an interval with $x_1 < x_2$, then we say that $f(x)$ is *increasing* on the interval if $f(x_1) < f(x_2)$. Looking at an increasing function, the function will go up as we move from left to right along the x-axis. Hence, if $f(x)$ is increasing, then $f'(x) > 0$.

Example. Let $f(x) = x^2$, as shown in Figure 11–5.

Clearly $f(x)$ is increasing on the interval $[0, \infty)$. We say $f(x)$ is *decreasing* on $(-\infty, 0]$ since for any $x_1 < x_2$ on this interval $f(x_1) > f(x_2)$. A decreasing function will go down as we move from left to right along the x-axis, so $f'(x) < 0$ when $f(x)$ is decreasing.

Look again at Figure 11–5. The point $(0, 0)$ is a local and absolute minimum of $f(x)$, with $f(x)$ decreasing to the left of $(0, 0)$ and increasing to the right of $(0, 0)$. If you think about it for a moment, you will realize that $f(x)$ must decrease to the left (and increase to the right) of any local minimum not at an endpoint.

Exercise. What must be the case for a local maximum not at an endpoint? Answer: $f(x)$ increases to the left and decreases to the right.

At an endpoint maximum (minimum), of course, the function must be increasing up (decreasing down) to that endpoint itself. So, all we need to do is to find the intervals in which $f(x)$ increases and decreases to determine the nature of the critical points.

FIGURE 11–5

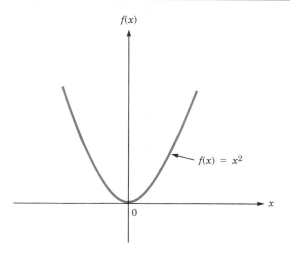

Example. Analyze $f(x) = \dfrac{x^3}{3} + x^2 - 8x + 4$ on $(-\infty, \infty)$.

First, we find $f'(x)$:

$$f'(x) = x^2 + 2x - 8$$
$$= (x + 4)(x - 2).$$

Second, we locate the critical points:

1. *Stationary points:* $f'(x) = 0$ when $x = -4$ and $x = 2$.
2. *Cusps:* None; $f'(x)$ exists for all x in $(-\infty, \infty)$.
3. *Endpoints:* None.

Third, we find whether the function is increasing or decreasing in the intervals defined by the critical points. There are two critical points, $x = -4$ and $x = 2$. Plotting these on a coordinate line, we can see that

there are three intervals to be considered; namely, $(-\infty, -4)$, $(-4, 2)$, and $(2, \infty)$. Consider first the interval $(-\infty, -4)$. The function $f(x)$ must *always increase* or *always decrease* in this interval. Why? Because if $f(x)$ went from up to down (or down to up), then the point of change would be a new critical point. But $x = -4$ and $x = 2$ are the only critical points of $f(x)$. So we need only test one spot in the interval $(-\infty, -4)$ to determine the behavior of $f(x)$ in the entire interval $(-\infty, -4)$. Of course, this same analysis will apply to the other two intervals $(-4, 2)$ and $(2, \infty)$. Thus, we need only test the value of $f'(x)$ at one point in each interval to determine the behavior of the function in the interval.

Interval	Point, x	f'(x)	Behavior of f'(x)
$(-\infty, -4)$	-5	7	Increases
$(-4, 2)$	0	-8	Decreases
$(2, \infty)$	3	7	Increases

We show this graphically on the coordinate line as follows:

From the graph, it is clear that $f(x)$ has a local maximum at $f(-4) = 92\frac{2}{3}$ and a local minimum at $f(2) = -16\frac{1}{3}$.

This method of determining the nature of critical points is frequently called the first derivative test, which we may summarize as follows:

First Derivative Test

If $f(x)$ has a critical point at $x = p$, then

a) If p is an interval point (i.e., not an endpoint) and $f'(x) < 0$ to the left of p and $f'(x) > 0$ to the right of p, then $f(x)$ has a local minimum at $x = p$;

b) If p is an interval point and $f'(x) > 0$ to the left of p and $f'(x) < 0$ to the right of p, then $f(x)$ has a local maximum at $x = p$.

We can also use our knowledge of the increasing-decreasing behavior of a function to determine the nature of endpoint optima.

Endpoint Test

If $f(x)$ has an endpoint value at $x = p$, then

a) If p is a right-hand endpoint and $f'(x) < 0$ $(f'(x) > 0)$ to the left of p so that $f(x)$ is decreasing down (increasing up) to $f(p)$, then $f(x)$ has an endpoint minimum (maximum) at $x = p$;

b) If p is a left-hand endpoint and $f'(x) < 0$ $(f'(x) > 0)$ to the right of p, then $f(x)$ has an endpoint maximum (minimum) at $x = p$.

The graph in Figure 11–6 illustrates both of the above tests.

FIGURE 11–6

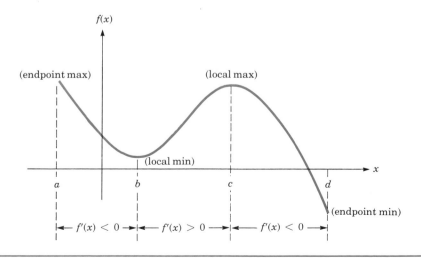

Exercise. Find all local and endpoint maxima and minima for $f(x) = x^2 - 4x + 4$ on $[0, 3]$. Answer: Endpoint maximum at $f(0) = 4$, local minimum at $f(2) = 0$, endpoint maximum at $f(3) = 1$.

In applied problems endpoint tests are needed when there is a restriction on the *range* of permissible values the independent variable may have. Typically, x must not be negative ($x \geq 0$), or x must be strictly positive ($x > 0$). Again, if x is the number of hours a machine is operated during a day, then

$$\text{Range:} \quad 0 \leq x \leq 24.$$

When we find a local optimum point by setting the derivative equal to zero, the x obtained may be outside the range. For example, if

$$f(x) = 0.01x^2 - 1.2x + 100; \quad 0 \leq x \leq 50$$

it may be verified that $x = 60, f(x) = 64$ would be a local minimum, but this is outside the range, and the minimum (global) value of the function occurs at the endpoint, 50, and is $f(50) = 65$.

Secondly, the value of a function at the endpoint of the range may be greater (less) than the value found at a local maximum (minimum) and, finally, a function may have no local optimum points, in which case its global maximum and minimum occur at the endpoints of the range.

It follows that in working with an unfamiliar function it would be wise to keep endpoint considerations in mind. However, in this book, problems have been designed so that we need not be preoccupied with endpoints, and we shall call attention to these considerations on the rare occasion where they are relevant.

A function may have several local maxima and minima, as we saw above. However, a function will never have more than one absolute maximum or minimum. The absolute maximum (minimum) of a function is the largest (smallest) value of the function over all points for which it is defined. In applied problems these are almost always the values we seek, and we find them by enumerating every optimum value and choosing the appropriate absolute optima.

Example. Find local optimum points of the following function, if any exist. State the nature of points found and prove by testing.

$$f(x) = 20x^{1/2} - 2x.$$

First we notice that $x^{1/2}$ is defined only for nonnegative values of x, so that $f(x)$ is defined over the interval $[0, \infty)$. With this in mind, we first find $f'(x)$:

$$f'(x) = 10x^{-1/2} - 2.$$

Next, we locate the critical points.

1. *Stationary points:* We find that $f'(x) = 0$ when

$$10x^{-1/2} - 2 = 0$$

or

$$\frac{10}{x^{1/2}} - 2 = 0.$$

Now multiply both sides by $x^{1/2}$ to obtain

$$\left(\frac{10}{x^{1/2}}\right)x^{1/2} - 2(x^{1/2}) = 0(x^{1/2})$$
$$10 - 2x^{1/2} = 0$$
$$10 = 2x^{1/2}$$
$$5 = x^{1/2}.$$

To obtain x we must *square* both sides.

$$5^2 = (x^{1/2})^2$$
$$25 = x$$
$$x = 25.$$

2. *Cusps:* There are no cusps, since $f'(x)$ is defined for all x in $[0, \infty)$ except at $x = 0$. But $x = 0$ is an endpoint.
3. *Endpoints:* There is one endpoint, at $x = 0$.

Next, we determine the intervals within which the function increases or decreases.

Interval	Point, x	$f'(x)$	Behavior of $f'(x)$
(0, 25)	1	8	Increases
(25, ∞)	36	$-1/3$	Decreases

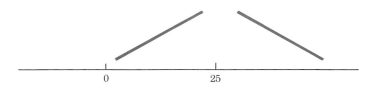

The preceding analysis leads to the conclusions that at $f(25) = 50$, $f(x)$ has a local maximum; at $f(0) = 0$, $f(x)$ has an endpoint minimum.

> **Exercise.** Find the local maxima or minima, if any, and state which has been found. Prove by testing.
>
> $$f(x) = x^3 - 3x^2 + 3x + 5.$$
>
> Answer: No local optimum points exist. There is a critical point where $x = 1, f(1) = 6$.

11.3 PROBLEM SET 11–1

1. When x gallons of antifreeze are produced, the average cost per gallon is $A(x)$ where

   $$A(x) = 100/x + 0.04x + 1.$$

   a) How many gallons should be produced if average cost per gallon is to be minimized?
   b) Compute the minimum average cost per gallon.
   c) Prove (b) is a minimum.

2. If we use 100 linear feet of fence to enclose a rectangular plot of land, we need $2x$ feet for one pair of sides (or x feet for one of these sides), leaving $100 - 2x$ feet for the other pair of sides (or $50 - x$ feet for one of these sides). The rectangle is then x feet by $(50 - x)$ feet and its area, $A(x)$, is

   $$A(x) = x(50 - x) = 50x - x^2.$$

   a) Find the value of x that maximizes the area of the plot.
   b) Prove (a) yields a maximum.
   c) What are the dimensions of the maximum area rectangle?
   d) What is the maximum area?

3. In many sampling surveys, only a small number n of a large population of people are interviewed. Published survey results state what proportion p of the n people interviewed answered yes to a particular question. Inherently, because only a fraction of the population was interviewed, the proportion p is expected to be in error. Statisticians measure this error by $V(p)$, where V stands for *variance,* and

   $$V(p) = \frac{p}{n} - \frac{p^2}{n}.$$

   Thus variance or error is a function of p for a *given n.*
   a) Find the value of p that maximizes $V(p)$; that is, the proportion that leads to the largest expected error.
   b) Prove (a) is a maximum.
   c) Taking $n = 10$, find $V(0.5)$ and $V(0.1)$.

4. The profit realized when y gallons of distilled water are made and sold is

   $$P(y) = 20y - 0.005y^2.$$

   a) Find the number of gallons that should be made to maximize profit.
   b) Prove (a) yields a maximum.
   c) Compute the maximum profit.

For each of the following, find the coordinates of local optimum points, if any exist. In each case, state the type of point that has been found and prove the statement by showing a test.

5. $f(x) = 5x - x^2$.

6. $f(x) = 2x^2 - 12x + 20$.

7. $f(x) = 3 - x^2$.

8. $f(x) = 2x^2 + 20$.

9. $f(x) = 30x - 3x^2 + 10$.

10. $f(x) = x^2 - x + 1$.

11.3 PROBLEM SET 11–1 (*concluded*)

11. $f(x) = x^3 - 12x^2 + 12$.

12. $f(x) = x^3 - 3x^2 + 2$.

13. $f(x) = 3x^3 + 27$.

14. $f(x) = 14 - 2x^3$.

15. $f(x) = 21x^2 - 2x^3 - 60x + 20$.

16. $f(x) = 6x^2 - x^3 - 9x$.

17. $f(x) = x^3 - 9x^2 + 27x$ on $[-1,1]$.

18. $f(x) = x^3 + 15x^2 + 75x$ on $[-2,2]$.

19. $f(x) = x^4 - 32x + 100$ on $[0,3]$.

20. $f(x) = 108x - x^4$ on $[0, 2]$.

21. $f(x) = 4x^3 - 3x^4 + 4$ on $[-1,2)$.

22. $f(x) = x^4 - 4x^3 + 30$ on $[0,3)$.

23. $f(x) = 2x - 8x^{1/2}$.

24. $f(x) = 9x^{2/3} - 2x$.

25. $f(x) = x^{3/2} - 12x^{1/2}$.

26. $f(x) = 10x^{1/3} - x^{2/3}$.

27. $f(x) = 4x + 64/x$.

28. $f(x) = 4x + 250/x^2$.

11.4 THE SECOND DERIVATIVE TEST

In this section we introduce a new test that is simple to use and is very helpful in optimization problems and curve sketching. Consider the point R in Figure 11–7. To the left of R, the curve is shaped like a cup that will spill water, and this section is said to be *concave downward* so that the curve always lies below the tangent line. To the right of R, the shape is like a cup that holds water and is said to be *concave upward* so that the curve always lies above the tangent line. The point R, which separates downward and upward concavity, is called an *inflection point*. We will now develop a technique using the second derivative of the function that will help us to effectively determine when a function is concave up or concave down.

FIGURE 11–7

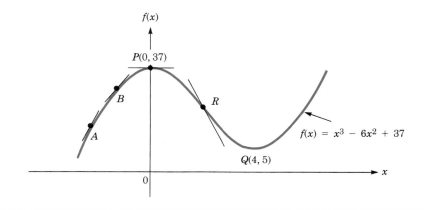

The derivative of a function, $f'(x)$, is itself a function—the slope function. Its derivative is

$$\frac{d}{dx}f'(x) = f''(x),$$

where $f''(x)$ is the *second derivative.*[1] If the derivative of $f'(x)$, which is $f''(x)$, is positive (negative), the slope function is increasing (decreasing). Now look at points A and B in Figure 11–7. The slope at B is less than the slope at A because the curve is concave downward. When the slopes decrease in this way, it means that the slope function is *decreasing,* so its derivative, $f''(x)$, must be *negative.* In general, a curve is concave downward at a point where the second derivative is negative. This will be true, for example, at $x = -1$, $x = 0$, and $x = +1$ for the function plotted in Figure 11–7, that is,

$$f(x) = x^3 - 6x^2 + 37$$
$$f'(x) = 3x^2 - 12x$$
$$f''(x) = 6x - 12$$

and

$$f''(-1) = -18$$
$$f''(0) = -12$$
$$f''(1) = -6.$$

Moreover, we have

$f'(0) = 0;$ stationary point where $x = 0$.
$f''(0) = -12;$ curve concave downward at $x = 0$.
Conclusion: There is a local maximum where $x = 0$.

Turning next to the point $Q(4, 5)$ in Figure 11–7, we find

$f'(4) = 0;$ stationary point where $x = 4$.
$f''(4) = +12;$ curve concave upward where $x = 4$.
Conclusion: There is a local minimum where $x = 4$.

In summary, if x is a value such that $f(x) = 0$ (stationary point), the point is a local maximum (minimum) if $f''(x)$ is negative (positive). We now formulate a procedure for finding possible local optimum points and testing to determine whether they are local maxima or minima.

---

[1] The second derivative may also be symbolized as

$$\frac{d^2f(x)}{dx^2},$$

which is read as "*d* second *f* of *x*, *dx* second."

> ### Second Derivative Test
>
> 1. Find $f'(x)$, set it equal to zero, and solve for candidate values, x.
> 2. Find $f''(x)$ and evaluate $f''(x)$.
>   a) If $f''(x)$ is negative, a local maximum occurs at x.
>   b) If $f''(x)$ is positive, a local minimum occurs at x.
>   c) If $f''(x)$ is zero, the test fails to determine what happens at x.

The reason the test fails when $f''(x) = 0$ can be seen by examining Figures 11–8, 11–9, and 11–10. All of the stationary points in these figures, $S(0, 8)$, $T(0, 5)$, and $V(0, 6)$, have $x = 0$ and the second derivative is also zero at these points.

> **Exercise.** Write the expression for the second derivatives of the functions under consideration and compute the values of these derivatives at $x = 0$. The functions are: a) $g(x) = x^3 + 8$. b) $h(x) = x^4 + 5$. c) $k(x) = 6 - x^4$. Answer: a) $g''(x) = 6x$; $g''(0) = 0$. b) $h''(x) = 12x^2$; $h''(0) = 0$. c) $k''(x) = -12x^2$; $k''(0) = 0$.

Thus, we see that if both first and second derivatives are zero, the point at hand could be a stationary inflection point (Figure 11–8), a minimum (Figure 11–9), or a maximum (Figure 11–10). These three figures show us that the second derivative test gives us no help in determining the type of point at hand if both derivatives are zero at the point. Notice

FIGURE 11–8 (not to scale)   *FIGURE 11–9 (not to scale)*   *FIGURE 11–10 (not to scale)*

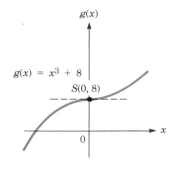

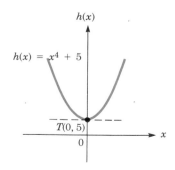

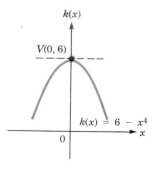

that in this case, we can always rely on the first derivative test. Fortunately, the second derivative test does work in a majority of the problems we will encounter.

Example. Find the local optimum points, if any exist, and state which type of point has been found. Prove by testing.

$$f(x) = 2x^2 - 12x + 50.$$

We start with this problem because we know the answer. The curve is a vertical parabola opening upward, and its optimum point is the vertex, which is a local (and global) minimum. Applying the second derivative test, we obtain

$$f'(x) = 4x - 12$$
$$f''(x) = 4$$

so that

$$f'(x) = 0 \quad \text{when} \quad 4x - 12 = 0 \quad \text{or} \quad x = 3.$$

Now checking the second derivative, we have

$$f''(x) = f''(3) = 4,$$

which is positive. Hence, a local minimum occurs where $x = 3$. The minimum value of the function is

$$f_{\min} = f(3) = 2(3)^2 - 12(3) + 50 = 32.$$

Note that

$$f''(x) = 4$$

is a positive constant not depending on x. This means the curve is concave upward at all points, which, of course, is the case for an upward-opening parabola.

Exercise. Find the local optimum point of the function and prove which type it is by testing. a) $f(x) = 30x - 3x^2 + 25$. b) $g(x) = x - 6x^{1/2} + 20$. Answer: a) $x = 5$, $f(5) = 100$ is a local maximum because $f''(5) = -6$. b) $x = 9$, $g(9) = 11$ is a local minimum because $g''(9) = 3/[2(9)^{3/2}]$ is positive.

A function of a single variable, such as

$$f(x) = 0.1x^3 - 1.8x^2 + 8.1x + 2,$$

in which each term is either a constant or a constant times the variable to a power that is a positive whole number, is called a polynomial. The *degree* of a polynomial is its highest power, so $f(x)$ just written is of degree three. Third-degree polynomials are called *cubics*. Quadratics, which graph as vertical parabolas, are second-degree polynomials; first-degree polynomials are straight lines. A particularly nice property of polynomials is that all polynomials are continuous and differentiable everywhere. This means that whenever we work with a polynomial we know that the tangent line exists at all points.

If a polynomial is set equal to zero and solved for x, it can be proved that the maximum possible number of roots is the degree of the polynomial or less than the degree by a multiple of two. For example, if we write

$$f(x) = 0.1x^3 - 1.8x^2 + 8.1x + 2$$
$$f'(x) = 0.3x^2 - 3.6x + 8.1$$

and set the resultant *second*-degree polynomial $f'(x)$ equal to zero to solve for optimum points, we have

$$0.3x^2 - 3.6x + 8.1 = 0.$$

This last polynomial has either *two* roots or two minus two (that is, zero) roots. Hence, a cubic (whose derivative is second-degree) can have two local optimum points or none. In the case at hand, we factor the last expression to obtain

$$0.3(x^2 - 12x + 27) = 0$$
$$0.3(x - 9)(x - 3) = 0$$
$$x - 9 = 0, \quad \text{so } x = 9$$
$$x - 3 = 0, \quad \text{so } x = 3.$$

The second derivative is

$$f''(x) = 0.6x - 3.6$$
$$f''(9) = 5.4 - 3.6 = \quad 1.8, \quad \text{so a local minimum occurs at } x = 9,$$
$$f''(3) = 1.8 - 3.6 = -1.8, \quad \text{so a local maximum occurs at } x = 3.$$

Evaluating $f(x)$ at these optimum points we find

$$f(9) = 0.1(9^3) - 1.8(9^2) + 8.1(9) + 2 = 2,$$

so $(9, 2)$ is the local minimum, and

$$f(3) = 0.1(3^3) - 1.8(3^2) + 8.1(3) + 2 = 12.8,$$

so $(3, 12.8)$ is the local maximum. A *sketch* showing the important characteristics of $f(x)$ can be made from these two points. See Figure 11–11. We have included the intercept, $x = 0$, $f(0) = 2$, in the figure because it is easily obtained. Note that just to the right of the peak, P, the curve is concave downward, so the second derivative is negative. However, beyond point I, the curve becomes concave up so the second derivative is now positive. This would imply that the second derivative is zero at point $I(6, 7.4)$, and this is indeed the case. Such a point, where the concavity of a function changes, is called an inflection point. All inflection points

FIGURE 11–11 (not to scale)

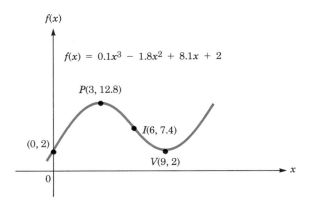

occur at points where the second derivative is zero (or is undefined), but *beware*: Not all points where the second derivative is zero are inflection points.

The next example incorporates the second derivative test for local maxima and local minima, along with the analysis of concavity and inflection points.

Example. Determine all local maxima, local minima, and inflection points, and discuss the concavity of

$$f(x) = 15x^4 + 8x^3 - 18x^2 + 1.$$

We begin by finding the first and second derivatives

$$f'(x) = 60x^3 + 24x^2 - 36x$$
$$f''(x) = 180x^2 + 48x - 36.$$

Be careful! Always double check each of your derivatives because if any one is incorrect, all subsequent ones will be wrong and the rest of the work you do will be useless.

Next we set the first derivative equal to zero and solve

$$60x^3 + 24x^2 - 36x = 0$$
$$12x(5x^2 + 2x - 3) = 0$$
$$x(5x^2 + 2x - 3) = 0$$
$$x(x + 1)(5x - 3) = 0$$

or

$$x = 0, \quad x = -1, \quad \text{and} \quad x = \frac{3}{5}.$$

Then checking the second derivative

$$f''(0) = -36, \quad f''(-1) = 96, \quad f''\left(\frac{3}{5}\right) = \frac{288}{5}$$

so we have a local maximum at $x = 0$ and local minima at $x = -1$ and $x = 3/5$. The corresponding values of $f(x)$ are

$$f(0) = 1, \quad f(-1) = -10, \quad \text{and} \quad f\left(\frac{3}{5}\right) = -\frac{9}{5}.$$

Now to locate the inflection points, if any, we set the second derivative equal to zero and solve

$$180x^2 + 48x - 36 = 0$$
$$12(15x^2 + 4x - 3) = 0$$
$$15x^2 + 4x - 3 = 0$$
$$(5x + 3)(3x - 1) = 0$$

so that

$$x = -\frac{3}{5} \quad \text{and} \quad x = \frac{1}{3}$$

are *possible* points of inflection. To prove that they are actual points of inflection we must show that $f(x)$ changes concavity at these points. We now repeat the use of the coordinate line as a mechanism, this time to determine concavity. Recall that when $f''(x) > 0, f(x)$ is concave up, and when $f''(x) < 0, f(x)$ is concave down. Since $f''(x) = 0$ only at $-3/5$ and $1/3, f''(x)$ must be positive or negative throughout each of the intervals $(-\infty, -3/5), (-3/5, 1/3),$ and $(1/3, \infty)$. We need only choose a representative point in each interval (as we did to determine the increasing-decreasing properties) to determine the concavity properties of $f(x)$. Thus we obtain

Interval	Point, x	f''(x)	Concavity
$(-\infty, -3/5)$	-1	96	Up
$(-3/5, 1/3)$	0	-36	Down
$(1/3, \infty)$	1	192	Up

and designate this information on the number line drawn with the cups shown. Now we can clearly see that $f(x)$ changes concavity at both $x =$

$-3/5$ and $x = 1/3$, so

$$f(-3/5) = -\frac{657}{125} \quad \text{and} \quad f(1/3) = -\frac{14}{27}$$

are each points of inflection. Also $f(x)$ is concave up on the intervals $(-\infty, -3/5)$ and $(1/3, \infty)$, and concave down on the interval $(-3/5, 1/3)$. Figure 11–12 indicates what we have found.

It is important to realize that $f''(x)$ can be zero and yet not produce an inflection point. A quick look back at Figures 11–10 and 11–11 and the accompanying exercise should convince you. More will be said about inflection points in Section 11.12.

FIGURE 11–12 (not to scale)

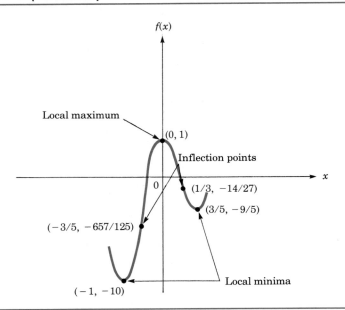

11.5 PROBLEM SET 11–2

In Problems 1–10, find the first and second derivatives of the function.

1. $f(x) = x^5 - 2x^4 + x^3 + 3$.

2. $f(x) = x^3 - x^2 - x - 1$.

3. $f(x) = 8x^3 - 2x^2$.

4. $f(x) = x^6 - x^4 + 3x^2 + 7$.

5. $f(x) = 3x^4 - 5x^3 + 2x^2$.

6. $f(x) = x^2\sqrt{x} - 5x^2 + x$.

7. $f(x) = (x + 5)^3$.

8. $f(x) = (x^2 + 1)^{1/2}$.

9. $f(x) = \dfrac{3x + 4}{x - 3}$.

10. $f(x) = \dfrac{x + 2}{x - 2}$.

11.5 PROBLEM SET 11–2 (*concluded*)

In Problems 11–20, determine all local maxima, local minima, and points of inflection. Also discuss the concavity of the function.

11. $f(x) = x^2 - 4x + 3$.

12. $f(x) = x^2 + 10x - 9$.

13. $f(x) = x^3 - 6x^2 + 9x + 1$.

14. $f(x) = x^3 + 9x$.

15. $f(x) = x^3 - 2x^2 - 4x + 3$.

16. $f(x) = x^3 + 3x^2 - 9x - 3$.

17. $f(x) = -x^3 - 12x^2 - 45x + 2$.

18. $f(x) = x^4 - 8x^3 + 24x^2$.

19. $f(x) = 0.1(x - 10)^4 - 25.6x + 340.8$.

20. $f(x) = x^4 - 8x^3 + 18x^2 - 27$.

11.6 MAXIMA AND MINIMA: APPLICATIONS

In this section we present a series of examples that involve the application of calculus rules and procedures developed in earlier sections. Our examples will concentrate on local maxima and minima so we will be concerned only with stationary points and will use the second derivative test.

Example 1. A rectangular warehouse with a flat roof is to have a floor area of 9,600 square feet. The interior is to be divided into storeroom and office space by an interior wall parallel to one pair of the sides of the building. The roof and floor areas will be 9,600 square feet for any building, but the total wall length will vary for different dimensions. For example, a 96 foot by 100 foot building could have a 96-foot interior wall, two 96-foot and two 100-foot exterior walls for a total length of $3(96) + 2(100) = 488$ feet.

> **Exercise.** If the building dimensions are $40 \times 240 = 9,600$ square feet, what will be the total length of wall if the interior wall is 40 feet long? Answer: $3(40) + 2(240) = 600$ feet.

The problem is to find the dimensions that minimize the total amount of wall. Letting x and y be the dimensions as in Figure 11–13, we see that the total amount of wall, w, is

$$w = 3x + 2y,$$

subject to the constraint that

$$xy = 9600 \quad \text{or} \quad y = \frac{9600}{x}.$$

As first stated, w depends upon *two* variables, x and y, and our calculus to this point deals with only *one* independent variable. However, since

FIGURE 11–13

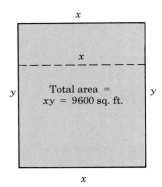

$xy = 9600$, we can replace y by $9600/x$ and write w as a function of the single variable, x. Thus,

$$w(x) = 3x + 2\,\frac{9600}{x}, \quad x > 0.$$

The condition that x be positive holds because x is the length of a wall.
    We next find

$$w'(x) = 3 - \frac{2(9600)}{x^2}$$

and determine stationary points by setting $w'(x) = 0$. Thus we have

$$3 - \frac{2(9600)}{x^2} = 0 \quad \text{so} \quad x^2 = \frac{2(9600)}{3} = 6400.$$

$$x = \pm 80.$$

We discard $x = -80$ because x must be positive in this problem. There are no cusps or endpoints in this problem. To determine the type of stationary point at $x = 80$, we find the second derivative,

$$w''(x) = \frac{4(9600)}{x^3},$$

and note that $w''(80)$ is positive, so we have a local minimum. Recalling that $y = 9600/x = 9600/80 = 120$, we find that the building dimensions should be 80×120, with the interior wall being 80 feet long. The minimum total wall length is

$$w = 3x + 2y = 3(80) + 2(120) = 480 \text{ feet.}$$

Exercise. Suppose the floor area is to be 10,000 square feet, with no interior wall. a) What is the function $w(x)$? b) What dimensions minimize $w(x)$? Answer: a) $w(x) = 2x + 20{,}000/x$. b) A square building, 100 by 100 feet.

Example 2. A rectangular plot of land is to be enclosed by a fence. Fence for the north-south (N–S) sides costs $10 per running foot, while that for the east-west (E–W) sides costs $5 per running foot. What is the maximum area that can be enclosed if $1,500 is available for purchasing the fence?

We shall carry through the solution of this problem by listing questions and answers in a step-by-step sequence in order to provide a reference framework for solving optimization problems. We shall use x and y, respectively, for the N–S and E–W dimensions, and A for the area.

1. What quantity is to be maximized? Answer: The area, A.
2. What is the formula for this quantity? Answer: $A = xy$.
3. How can this quantity be made a function of a single variable? Answer: By expressing y in terms of x, or vice versa, and substituting into (2).
4. What information is available to accomplish (3)? Answer: We know the total amount to be spent is $1,500 and this must equal the cost of the two N–S sides, which will be 2(10x$), plus the cost of the E–W sides, which will be 2(5y$); hence,

$$2(10x) + 2(5y) = 1500 \quad \text{or} \quad 20x + 10y = 1500.$$

Therefore,

$$y = \frac{1500 - 20x}{10} = 150 - 2x.$$

5. Express the quantity to be optimized as a function of a single variable. Answer: $A(x) = x(150 - 2x) = 150x - 2x^2$.
6. Find the first derivative, set it equal to zero, and solve. Answer: $A'(x) = 150 - 4x$ is zero when $x = {}^{150}\!/_4 = 37.5$.
7. Test the result in (6) by the second derivative. Answer: $A''(x) = -4$ is always negative, so we have a local maximum.
8. Evaluate the remaining variable, and find the optimum. Answer: $y = 150 - 2(37.5) = 75$. $A = (37.5)(75) = 2812.5$.
9. Write a concluding statement directly answering the original problem. Answer: The dimensions of the maximum area enclosure are 37.5 feet by 75 feet, and the maximum area is 2,812.5 square feet.

Example 3. *Parameterizing a model.* When we write $y = mx + b$ to represent the equation of a straight line, the arbitrary letters m and b represent constants (slope and y-intercept) that distinguish one line from another. Such *arbitrary constants* (that is, letters standing for constants) are called *parameters*. Now return to Example 2 and let $\$n$ (instead of $10) be the cost per N–S foot, and $\$e$ (instead of $5) be the cost per E–W foot.

Similarly, let $\$C$ (instead of $1500) represent the total cost. We would then have

$$C = 2x(\$n) + 2y(\$e)$$

from which

$$y = \frac{C - 2xn}{2e} \tag{1}$$

and

$$A(x) = x\left(\frac{C - 2xn}{2e}\right). \tag{2}$$

The model for $A(x)$ has now been parameterized, and we seek the optimal solution in terms of the parameters, C, n, and e. We have from (2)

$$A(x) = \frac{xC}{2e} - \frac{x^2 n}{e}.$$

Remembering that the parameters represent constants, we find

$$A'(x) = \frac{C}{2e} - \frac{2xn}{e} \tag{3}$$

and $A'(x) = 0$ when

$$\frac{C}{2e} - \frac{2xn}{e} = 0.$$

Multiplying by $2e$, we have

$$C - 4xn = 0 \quad \text{or} \quad x = \frac{C}{4n}. \tag{4}$$

From (1) we obtain

$$y = \frac{C - 2xn}{2e} = \frac{C - (2C/4n)n}{2e} = \frac{C - C/2}{2e}$$

and, multiplying numerator and denominator of the last by 2, we find

$$y = \frac{2C - C}{4e} = \frac{C}{4e}. \tag{5}$$

The parameterized expression for the area is, from (4) and (5),

$$A = xy = \left(\frac{C}{4n}\right)\left(\frac{C}{4e}\right) = \frac{C^2}{16ne}.$$

To show that we have a local maximum, we start with the first derivative (3), and take the second derivative, which is

$$A''(x) = \frac{-2n}{e}.$$

$A''(x)$ is negative because n and e, which are costs, are positive, so we have a local maximum.

The obvious advantage of using parameters instead of specific numbers in solving a problem of a given type is that the solution of the parameterized model is a *general* solution that covers all specific cases. For the problem type under discussion, we see that if C = $1,500 is to be spent, with n = $10 and e = $5, then from (4) and (5), the optimal dimensions are

$$x = \frac{C}{4n} = \frac{1500}{4(10)} = 37.5 \text{ feet}$$

and

$$y = \frac{C}{4e} = \frac{1500}{4(5)} = 75 \text{ feet.}$$

Exercise. If, in Example 2, the N–S and E–W costs per foot are $2 and $3, and $2,400 is to be spent, what dimensions will maximize the area? Answer: 300 by 200 feet.

Example 4. A rectangular manufacturing plant with a floor area of 16,875 square feet is to be built on a straight road. The front of the plant must be set back 60 feet from the road, and buffer strips (grass and trees) 30 feet on each side and 20 feet at the back must be provided, as shown in Figure 11–14. Because of the high cost of land, builders seek to minimize the total area, plant plus buffers. This area is

$$A = (x + 80)(y + 60).$$

Since the *plant* area is 16,875 square feet, we have

$$xy = 16,875 \quad \text{so} \quad y = \frac{16,875}{x}.$$

FIGURE 11–14

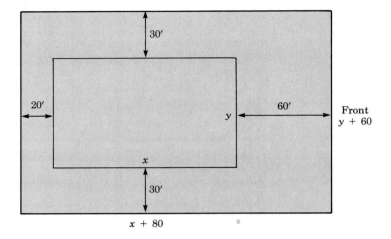

Hence,

$$A(x) = (x + 80)\left(\frac{16{,}875}{x} + 60\right)$$

$$= 16{,}875 + 60x + \frac{80(16{,}875)}{x} + 4800.$$

We find

$$A'(x) = 60 - \frac{80(16{,}875)}{x^2},$$

and $A'(x)$ is zero when

$$60 - \frac{80(16{,}875)}{x^2} = 0$$

$$x^2 = \frac{80(16{,}875)}{60} = 22{,}500,$$

$$x = 150 \text{ feet.}$$

The second derivative test shows this dimension will minimize $A(x)$. It follows that

$$y = \frac{16{,}875}{x} = \frac{16{,}875}{150} = 112.5 \text{ feet.}$$

The plant dimensions should be 112.5 feet at the front by 150 feet deep. The total land dimensions will then be

$$x + 80 = 230 \text{ feet} \quad \text{by} \quad y + 60 = 172.5 \text{ feet.}$$

The minimal total land area is $(230)(172.5) = 39{,}675$ square feet.

Example 5. Figure 11–15 shows a box with square top and bottom and rectangular sides. The total surface area of this box is $2x^2$ for top and bottom, plus $4xy$ for the four sides. Thus,

$$A = 2x^2 + 4xy.$$

The volume of the box is the area of the base times the altitude. Thus,

$$V = x^2y.$$

Suppose that we require a box of volume 2,592 cubic inches, and we seek to minimize the cost of materials for the sides, top, and bottom. Side material costs 6 cents per square inch, and top and bottom material 9 cents per square inch. Total cost, C, will be

$$C = \text{(Top and bottom area) at 9 cents} + \text{(Side areas) at 6 cents}$$
$$C = (2x^2)(9) + (4xy)(6).$$

From

$$V = x^2y$$

or

$$2592 = x^2y$$

we have

$$y = \frac{2592}{x^2}.$$

Substituting for y in the cost equation yields

$$C(x) = 18x^2 + \frac{24(2592)}{x}.$$

The derivative is

$$C'(x) = 36x - \frac{(2592)(24)}{x^2},$$

FIGURE 11–15

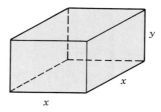

and $C'(x) = 0$ when

$$36x = \frac{(2592)(24)}{x^2}.$$

Multiplying by x^2 we find

$$36x^3 = (2592)(24)$$

or

$$x^3 = 1728.$$

Hence,

$$x = (1728)^{\frac{1}{3}} = 12 \text{ inches.}$$

It follows that

$$y = \frac{2592}{x^2} = \frac{2592}{144} = 18 \text{ inches.}$$

As the following exercise shows, the cost function has a local minimum at $x = 12$ inches and $y = 18$ inches.

Exercise.   For the preceding: a) Find the cost of a 12 by 12 by 18 inch box. b) Prove this cost is a minimum by the second derivative test.   Answer: a) 7,776 cents, or \$77.76. b) $C''(x) = 36 + (48)(2592)/x^3$ is positive when $x = 12$.

Example 6. According to United Parcel Service requirements stated at the opening of the chapter, the length plus girth of a package must not exceed 108 inches. Suppose packages are to be cylinders, as shown in Figure 11–16, and we seek the dimensions (length L and radius r) that will yield maximum volume. The volume of a cylinder is the circular base area, πr^2, times the height L, so

$$V = \pi r^2 L.$$

The girth of the cylinder is the perimeter of the circular cross-section, $2\pi r$, so length plus girth is $L + 2\pi r$ and

$$L + 2\pi r = 108 \quad \text{or} \quad L = 108 - 2\pi r.$$

Hence, substituting

$$V(r) = \pi r^2 (108 - 2\pi r) = 108\pi r^2 - 2\pi^2 r^3.$$

The derivative is

$$V'(r) = 216\pi r - 6\pi^2 r^2.$$

FIGURE 11-16

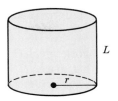

Setting $V'(r) = 0$,

$$6\pi r(36 - \pi r) = 0$$

from which

$$r = 0 \quad \text{and} \quad r = \frac{36}{\pi}.$$

Of course, we discard $r = 0$ since this value would be impractical. The second derivative is

$$V''(r) = 216\pi - 12\pi^2 r$$

and

$$V''\left(\frac{36}{\pi}\right) = 216\pi - 12\pi^2\left(\frac{36}{\pi}\right) = -216\pi,$$

so $r = 36/\pi$ yields a local maximum. Next,

$$L = 108 - 2\pi\left(\frac{36}{\pi}\right) = 36$$

so the optimal dimensions for maximum volume are a radius of $36/\pi$ (about 11.5 inches) and a height of 36 inches. The maximum volume will be

$$V = \pi\left(\frac{36}{\pi}\right)^2 (36) = \frac{(36)^3}{\pi} = \frac{46{,}656}{\pi} = 14{,}851 \text{ cubic inches.}$$

Exercise. In the last example, suppose the limitation on length plus girth is the parameter, M inches. Express the dimensions r and L for maximum volume in terms of M. Answer: $r = M/3\pi$ and $L = M/3$.

Example 7. In normal operations, a plant employs 100 workers working eight hours a day for a total of $100(8) = 800$ labor-hours of work per day. In normal operations, productivity averages 30 units per labor-hour worked. Thus, in a normal day, production is

$$P = \text{(Labor-hours worked)(Output per labor-hour)}$$
$$= (800)(30) = 24{,}000 \text{ units.}$$

If the work level (labor-hours) is raised above 800, management estimates that average output per labor-hour falls off at the rate of 2.5 units for each extra 100 labor-hours, or by 0.025 units for each labor-hour in excess of 800. For example, if 840 labor-hours are worked, the excess would be $840 - 800 = 40$ and average productivity would be $30 - 40(0.025) = 29$ units per labor-hour. Total output would then be

$$P = 840(29) = 24{,}360 \text{ units.}$$

The problem is to find the work level, x labor-hours, that maximizes output. Reviewing the illustrative calculations, we find that for $x = 840$ labor-hours,

$$P(840) = 840[30 - (840 - 800)(0.025)].$$

In general,

$$P(x) = x[30 - (x - 800)(0.025)]$$
$$= 30x - 0.025x^2 + 20x$$
$$= 50x - 0.025x^2.$$

We find

$$P'(x) = 50 - 0.05x$$

and

$$P'(x) = 0 \quad \text{when} \quad x = 1{,}000 \text{ labor-hours.}$$

Also,

$$P''(x) = -0.05$$

so we have a local maximum, which is

$$P(1000) = 50(1000) - 0.025(1000)^2 = 25{,}000 \text{ units.}$$

11.7 PROBLEM SET 11–3

1. A rectangular warehouse is to have 3,300 square feet of floor area and is to be divided into two rectangular rooms by an interior wall. Cost per running foot is $125 for exterior walls and $80 for the interior wall.
   a) What dimensions will minimize total wall cost?
   b) What is the minimum cost?

2. (Similar to Problem 1, but the area is to be found.) If $49,500 has been allocated for walls,
   a) What are the dimensions of the largest warehouse that can be built?
   b) What is the floor area of this warehouse?

3. (Problem 1 in parameterized form.) The floor area is to be A square feet and the cost per

11.7 PROBLEM SET 11–3 (*continued*)

running foot is $e for exterior walls and $i for the interior wall. Let x and y be the warehouse dimensions, with x being the length of the interior wall.
   a) Write the expression for total wall cost $C(x)$.
   b) Find the expression for x that minimizes $C(x)$.

4. (Problem 2 in parameterized form.) If D are allocated for wall construction then, using the parameters in Problem 3,
   a) Write the expression for the enclosed area, $A(x)$.
   b) Find the expression for x that will maximize $A(x)$.

5. Both interior and exterior walls of a 13,500-square-foot rectangular warehouse cost $100 per running foot. The warehouse is to be divided into eight rooms by three interior walls running in the x direction and one running in the y direction.
   a) What dimension will lead to minimal total wall cost?
   b) What is this minimal cost?

6. A rectangular area of 1,050 square feet is to be enclosed by a fence, then divided down the middle by another piece of fence. The fence down the middle costs $0.50 per running foot, and the other fence costs $1.50 per running foot. Find the minimum cost for the required fence.

7. Fence is required on three sides of a rectangular plot. Fence for the two ends costs $1.25 per running foot; fence for the third side costs $2 per running foot. Find the maximum area that can be enclosed with $100 worth of fence.

8. A rectangular cardboard poster is to contain a 96-square-inch rectangular section of printed material, have a 2-inch border top and bottom, and a 3-inch border on each side. Find the dimensions and area of the smallest poster that meets these specifications. (Note: Let x and y be the dimensions of the 96-square-inch area).

9. A rectangular-shaped manufacturing plant with a floor area of 600,000 square feet is to be built in a location where zoning regulations require buffer strips 50 feet wide front and back, and 30 feet wide at either side. (A buffer strip is a grass and tree belt that must not be built upon.) What plot dimensions will lead to minimum total area for plant and buffer strips? What is this minimum total area? (Note: Let x and y be the dimensions of the 600,000-square-foot area.) If the plant dimensions were made 1,500 by 400 feet rather than the dimensions leading to minimum area, by how much would the total plot area exceed the minimum area?

10. In the United Parcel Service example at the beginning of the chapter, the length plus girth of a package was restricted to 108 inches. Suppose a shipper uses rectangular boxes with square ends made of a perforated material to provide ventilation to the box contents. To secure maximum ventilation, the shipper wants the total surface area to be as large as possible. Use x as the side of the square base and L as the length.
   a) Write the expression for the area, A, in terms of L and x.
   b) Express $A(x)$ as a function of x alone.
   c) What value of x maximizes $A(x)$? Prove this is a maximum.
   d) What are the dimensions of the maximum-area box?

11. (See Problem 10.) Suppose the maximum length plus girth is M. Express the optimal x and L in terms of M.

12. A box with a square top and bottom is to be made to contain a volume of 64 cubic inches. What should be the dimensions of the box if its surface area is to be a minimum? What is this minimum surface area?

13. A box with a square bottom and no top is to be made to contain a volume of 500 cubic inches. What should be the dimensions of the box if its surface area is to be a minimum? What is this minimum surface area?

11.7 PROBLEM SET 11–3 (*continued*)

14. A box with a square top and bottom is to be made to contain 250 cubic inches. Material for top and bottom costs $2 per square inch and material for the sides costs $1 per square inch. What should be the dimensions of the box if its cost is to be a minimum? What is the minimum cost?

15. A box with a square bottom and no top is to be made to contain 100 cubic inches. Bottom material costs five cents per square inch and side material costs two cents per square inch. Find the cost of the least expensive box that can be made.

16. A box with a square bottom and no top is to be made from a 6 by 6 inch piece of material by cutting equal-sized squares from the corners, then turning up the sides. What should the dimensions of the squares be if the box is to have maximum volume?

17. A box with a rectangular bottom and no top is to be made from a rectangular piece of material with dimensions 16 by 30 inches by cutting equal-sized squares from the corners, then turning up the sides. What should the dimensions of the squares be if the box is to have maximum volume?

18. A cylindrical storage tank is to contain $V = 16,000\pi$ cubic feet (about 400,000 gallons). The cost of the tank is proportional to its area, so the minimal-cost tank will be the one with minimum area. The volume of a cylinder of radius r and height h is $V = \pi r^2 h$. Its surface area is the area of top and bottom, $2\pi r^2$, plus the side area, $2\pi rh$. Find the dimensions, r and h, of the minimal-area tank.

19. Suppose the tank in Problem 18 is to be built into the ground to catch runoff water, so it needs no top. Suppose, further, that the cost of the base of the tank is $10 per square foot and the sides $8.64 per square foot. What dimensions will lead to the minimal-cost tank?

20. A consulting firm conducts training sessions for employees of various companies. The charge to a company sending employees to a session is $50 per employee, less $0.50 for each employee in excess of 10. That is, for example, if 12 employees are sent, the charge per employee would be $49.00 and the total prorated charge to the company would be 12(49.00) = $588.00. The consulting firm further has a fixed total charge for groups of x or more, where x is the number that maximizes the prorated group charge. What should x be, and what is the maximum total group charge to a company?

21. A household appliance service organization has a parts stockroom and a garage at its central office location. Its trucks and drivers service customers in a roughly circular area of radius r around the central office. The number of customers per square mile is approximately $80/\pi$ (about 25) in any circular area around the office. Therefore the number of calls in a month is found by multiplying the number of customers per square mile by the number of square miles in the service area.
    a) What is the expression for the number of calls in a month?
    b) The company figures travel cost at $2 per mile and computes mileage per call at $r/2$ miles out from the garage plus $r/2$ miles back in, for a total of r miles per call, on the average. The travel charge per call, excluding parts and labor, is fixed at $24. What is the expression for the net travel income per call? ("Net" means after deducting mileage cost.)
    c) What is the expression for the total net monthly travel income?
    d) What service area radius will maximize total net monthly travel income?
    e) What is the maximum net monthly travel income?

22. When State College charges $195 for a continuing education class in the uses of microcomputers, it attracts 125 students. For each $10 decrease in the charge, an additional eight students will attend the class. Find the tuition value State should charge to

11.7 PROBLEM SET 11–3 (*continued*)

maximize revenue, and find this maximum revenue.

23. A company operates a fleet of Beta model trucks. Study shows that gallons of fuel consumed per mile of driving, $F(x)$, is related to the speed at which a truck is driven, x miles per hour, by the function

$$F(x) = \frac{k_1}{x} + k_2x; \; 10 \le x \le 80,$$

where k_1 and k_2 are parameters that vary somewhat from truck to truck.
a) Find and write the expression for the speed, x, that will lead to minimal fuel consumption per mile of driving.
b) What speed will provide minimal fuel consumption per mile of driving for a truck having $k_1 = 4.9$ and $k_2 = 0.004$?

24. (See Problem 23.) Fuel cost is d dollars per gallon and truck drivers are paid p dollars per hour of driving.
a) Write the expression for the value of x that will minimize the combined cost of fuel and driver, per mile driven, in terms of the parameters d, p, k_1 and k_2.
b) With $k_1 = 4.9$ and $k_2 = 0.004$, what speed will minimize the cost in (a) if fuel is $0.52 per gallon and drivers are paid $9 per hour?

25. The United Parcel Service (UPS) will pick up and deliver packages whose length plus girth does not exceed 108 inches. Zeeall Corporation ships a granular grinding abrasive in rectangular boxes with square ends. What is the largest volume of abrasive Zeeall can ship in a box? (Neglect the volume of the materials of which the box is made.)

26. When a Jack truck is driven at a speed of x miles per hour, it travels $m(x)$ miles per gallon of fuel consumed, where

$$m(x) = \frac{x}{5.76 + 0.0036x^2}.$$

At what speed should a truck be driven if $m(x)$ is to be maximized?

27. Answer Problem 26 for a Jill truck for which

$$m(x) = \frac{x}{4.5 + 0.005x^2}.$$

28. Answer Problem 26 in terms of the parameters k_1 and k_2 if

$$m(x) = \frac{x}{k_1 + k_2x^2}.$$

29. If the proportion of defective transistors in a very large stock of transistors is p, then the proportion of good transistors is $1 - p$. For example, if 5 percent (0.05 as a proportion) are defective, then 95 percent (0.95) are good. Now suppose that p is unknown. One transistor is selected at random and inspected; then a second is selected and inspected, and so on until the *first* defective is found, and this is the *10th* one. It is shown in probability that the chance that this will happen if the proportion defective is p, is $C(p)$, where

$$C(p) = p(1 - p)^9.$$

What value of p will maximize $C(p)$, the chance that the first defective will be the 10th one inspected?

30. (See Problem 29.) The chance that the first defective found is the nth transistor inspected is

$$C(p) = p(1 - p)^{n-1},$$

where, of course, n is a parameter. In terms of this parameter, what value of p maximizes $C(p)$?

31. In one run of a process, the number of pounds of Hypop that can be produced is x, where $0 < x \le 300$. The production cost *per pound* is, in dollars,

$$\frac{100}{40 - 0.1x}.$$

Hypop sells for $10 *per pound*.
a) Find the number of pounds that should be made in a run of the process if profit

11.7 PROBLEM SET 11–3 (*continued*)

(revenue from sales, minus cost) is to be maximized.

b) Compute the maximum profit.

32. (See Problem 31.) A new process has been designed to make an improved product, Hypop-II, which sells at $15 *per pound*. In one run of this process, x pounds are produced at a *per-pound* cost of

$$\frac{100}{60 - 0.05x}; \ 0 < x \le 750.$$

a) Find the number of pounds to be made in a run if profit is to be maximized.

b) Compute the maximum profit.

33. Sam, a modern artist, has submitted a sketch of a proposed piece to a client who wants a simple, clean-lined decoration to place in the lobby of a new office building. Sam's sketch shows an eight-foot column whose cross section is a right triangle, so the column has three plane surfaces. The client commissions Sam to do the work, but stipulates that the hypotenuse of the triangle must be 40 inches *and* the triangular cross-sectional area is to be maximized. What dimensions should be used for the two sides of the right triangle if these stipulations are to be met? Recall that the area of a right triangle is one-half the product of the lengths of the sides, and the sum of the squares of the sides equals the square of the hypotenuse. State answer to the nearest one-hundredth of an inch.

11.8 MORE APPLICATIONS

In this section, we present applications, using some more complicated functions.

Example 1. When x gallons of alcohol are produced, the average cost per gallon is $A(x)$ dollars, where

$$A(x) = \frac{200}{0.1x + 5} + 0.05x, \quad x > 0.$$

a) Find the value of x where $A(x)$ is stationary.

b) Prove that this value of x occurs at a local minimum of $A(x)$.

c) Compute the minimum average cost per gallon.

a) We start by rewriting $A(x)$ as

$$A(x) = 200(0.1x + 5)^{-1} + 0.05x.$$

Differentiating $A(x)$, we obtain

$$A'(x) = 200(-1)(0.1x + 5)^{-2}(0.1) + 0.05.$$

Continuing, we set $A'(x)$ equal to zero and solve for x.

$$A'(x) = -20(0.1x + 5)^{-2} + 0.05$$
$$= \frac{-20}{(0.1x + 5)^2} + 0.05$$

and $A'(x) = 0$ when

$$\frac{-20}{(0.1x + 5)^2} + 0.05 = 0$$

$$0.05 = \frac{20}{(0.1x + 5)^2}.$$

Multiplying both sides by the denominator,

$$0.05(0.1x + 5)^2 = 20$$

$$(0.1x + 5)^2 = \frac{20}{0.05} = 400.$$

Taking the square root of both sides (the ½ power)

$$[(0.1x + 5)^2]^{1/2} = (400)^{1/2}$$
$$0.1x + 5 = \pm 20$$

$$\begin{array}{ll} 0.1x + 5 = 20 & \quad 0.1x + 5 = -20 \\ 0.1x = 15 & \quad 0.1x = -25 \\ x = 150. & \quad x = -250. \end{array}$$

We discard $x = -250$ because it is negative and the problem statement requires that x be greater than zero.

b) To show $x = 150$ yields a local minimum, we start with

$$A'(x) = -20(0.1x + 5)^{-2} + 0.05$$

and find the second derivative,

$$A''(x) = -20(-2)(0.1x + 5)^{-3}(0.1)$$
$$= \frac{4}{(0.1x + 5)^3}$$

then

$$A''(150) = \frac{4}{(15 + 5)^3},$$

which is positive, so there is a local minimum where $x = 150$.

c) To find the minimum average cost per gallon of alcohol, we write

$$A(x) = \frac{200}{0.1x + 5} + 0.05x.$$

Then,

$$A(150) = \frac{200}{0.1(150) + 5} + 0.05(150)$$
$$= \frac{200}{20} + 7.5$$
$$= \$17.5 \text{ per gallon.}$$

Example 2. a) Find the slope of the line tangent to the curve representing

$$f(x) = (169 - x^2)^{1/2}$$

at the point where $x = 12$.

b) Find the y-intercept of the tangent line in (a).

A meaningful application of the method of solving this problem appears in the next problem set.

a) We first find the slope function, which is the derivative

$$f'(x) = \frac{1}{2}(169 - x^2)^{-1/2}(-2x)$$

$$f'(x) = \frac{-x}{(169 - x^2)^{1/2}}.$$

Hence the tangent slope where $x = 12$ is

$$f'(12) = \frac{-12}{(169 - 12^2)^{1/2}} = \frac{-12}{(169 - 144)^{1/2}} = \frac{-12}{(25)^{1/2}} = \frac{-12}{5} = -2.4.$$

b) The function value at $x = 12$ is

$$f(12) = (169 - 12^2)^{1/2} = (25)^{1/2} = 5,$$

so the point at hand has coordinates $(12, 5)$. The intercept of the tangent line we seek has coordinates $(0, b)$, as shown in Figure 11–17. If we now

FIGURE 11–17

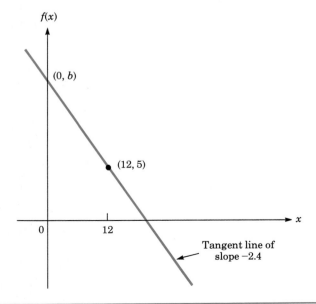

set the slope of the line through (12, 5) and (0, b) equal to -2.4, from (a), we have

$$\frac{b - 5}{0 - 12} = -2.4$$
$$b - 5 = (-12)(-2.4)$$
$$b - 5 = 28.8$$
$$b = 33.8,$$

which is the desired intercept.

Example 3. A bus company uses the function

$$P(x) = (3 + 0.6x)^{1/2} - 0.1x, \quad x > 0$$

to estimate the net weekly profit, in hundreds of dollars, if a particular bus route is x miles long. How long should the route be to maximize the net profit, and what is the maximum net profit?

First, we obtain

$$P'(x) = \frac{1}{2}(3 + 0.6x)^{-1/2}(0.6) - 0.1 = 0.3(3 + 0.6x)^{-1/2} - 0.1.$$

Continuing,

$$P'(x) = \frac{0.3}{(3 + 0.6x)^{1/2}} - 0.1$$

and $P'(x) = 0$ where

$$\frac{0.3}{(3 + 0.6x)^{1/2}} - 0.1 = 0$$
$$\frac{0.3}{(3 + 0.6x)^{1/2}} = 0.1.$$

Multiplying by the denominator leads to

$$0.3 = (0.1)(3 + 0.6x)^{1/2}$$

so

$$3 = (3 + 0.6x)^{1/2}.$$

Then, *squaring* both sides, we have

$$3^2 = [(3 + 0.6x)^{1/2}]^2$$
$$9 = 3 + 0.6x$$
$$6 = 0.6x$$
$$\frac{6}{0.6} = x$$
$$10 = x,$$

so a stationary point exists at $x = 10$ miles.

Exercise. Verify that there are no cusps or endpoints. (Hint: $P(x)$ is defined only for $x > 0$.)

To test this point, we return to

$$P'(x) = 0.3(3 + 0.6x)^{-1/2} - 0.1$$

and find the second derivative,

$$
\begin{aligned}
P''(x) &= (0.3)(-1/2)(3 + 0.6x)^{-3/2}(0.6) \\
&= -0.09(3 + 0.6x)^{-3/2} \\
&= -\frac{0.09}{(3 + 0.6x)^{3/2}}
\end{aligned}
$$

and

$$P''(10) = -\frac{0.09}{(3 + 6)^{3/2}},$$

which is negative, proving there is a maximum at $x = 10$. From

$$P(x) = (3 + 0.6x)^{1/2} - 0.1x,$$

the maximum is

$$
\begin{aligned}
P_{\text{max}} = P(10) &= [3 + 0.6(10)]^{1/2} - (0.1)(10) \\
&= (9)^{1/2} - 1 \\
&= \$200 \text{ per week.}
\end{aligned}
$$

Example 4. Points A and D on Figure 11–18 are to be connected by highways. Construction cost above BD is \$200,000 per mile and cost along BD is \$160,000 per mile. Consequently, it would be more costly to run a highway directly from A to D, the shortest distance, than to run a section from A to a point C, and another section from C to D. The problem is to find where the intersection, C, should be if cost is to be minimized. As shown in Figure 11–18, AB is 6 miles and BD is 20 miles. If we let BC be x miles, then CD is $20 - x$ miles. Also, because ABC is a right triangle,

$$AC = \sqrt{x^2 + 6^2} = (x^2 + 36)^{1/2} \text{ miles.}$$

Total highway cost then will be, in hundreds of thousands of dollars,

$$2(AC) + 1.6(CD)$$

so

$$C(x) = 2(x^2 + 36)^{1/2} + 1.6(20 - x).$$

Proceeding to the derivative, we have

FIGURE 11–18

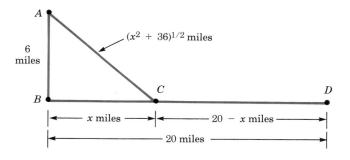

$$C'(x) = 2\left(\frac{1}{2}\right)(x^2 + 36)^{-\frac{1}{2}}(2x) - 1.6$$

$$= \frac{2x}{(x^2 + 36)^{\frac{1}{2}}} - 1.6.$$

Setting $C'(x)$ equal to zero yields

$$\frac{2x}{(x^2 + 36)^{\frac{1}{2}}} - 1.6 = 0$$

$$\frac{2x}{(x^2 + 36)^{\frac{1}{2}}} = 1.6.$$

Now multiply both sides by the denominator, then square both sides to obtain

$$2x = 1.6(x^2 + 36)^{\frac{1}{2}}$$
$$(2x)^2 = (1.6)^2[(x^2 + 36)^{\frac{1}{2}}]^2$$
$$4x^2 = 2.56(x^2 + 36)$$
$$4x^2 = 2.56x^2 + 92.16$$
$$4x^2 - 2.56x^2 = 92.16$$
$$1.44x^2 = 92.16$$
$$x^2 = \frac{92.16}{1.44}$$
$$x^2 = 64$$
$$x = 8, x = -8 \text{ miles.}$$

We discard $x = -8$ because x must be in the interval $0 \le x \le 20$ in this problem. To test $x = 8$ by the second derivative, we have to find the derivative of

$$C'(x) = \frac{2x}{(x^2 + 36)^{\frac{1}{2}}} - 1.6.$$

Using the quotient rule, we find

$$C''(x) = \frac{2(x^2 + 36)^{1/2}(x^2 + 36)^{-1/2} \cdot 2x}{[(x + 36)^{1/2}]^2}$$

$$= \frac{2(x^2 + 36)^{1/2} - \dfrac{2x^2}{(x^2 + 36)^{1/2}}}{(x^2 + 36)}$$

$$= \frac{2(x^2 + 36)^{1/2}(x^2 + 36)^{1/2} - 2x^2}{(x^2 + 36)^{1/2}(x^2 + 36)}$$

$$= \frac{2(x^2 + 36) - 2x^2}{(x^2 + 36)^{3/2}}$$

$$= \frac{2x^2 + 72 - 2x^2}{(x^2 + 36)^{3/2}}$$

$$= \frac{72}{(x^2 + 36)^{3/2}},$$

so

$$C''(8) = \frac{72}{(64 + 32)^{3/2}} > 0,$$

and hence a minimum occurs at the stationary point $x = 8$ miles.
    The cost at $x = 8$ is

$$C(8) = \$39.2 \text{ hundred thousand}$$
$$= \$3{,}920{,}000.$$

We have two endpoint considerations at $x = 0$ and $x = 20$. A direct road from A to D, that is when $x = 20$, in **Figure 11–18** would have a length of

$$[(20)^2 + (6)^2]^{1/2} = (436)^{1/2} = 20.880613$$

and the cost would be

$$\$2(20.880613) = \$41.76123 \text{ hundred thousand}$$
$$= \$4{,}176{,}123.$$

This exceeds the cost at $x = 8$, $\$3{,}920{,}000$, found in the preceding by

$$\$4{,}176{,}123 - \$3{,}920{,}000 = \$256{,}123.$$

Solve the following exercise to prove that

$$C_{\min} = C(8) = \$3{,}920{,}00.$$

Exercise.   a) Compute the cost when $x = 0$. b) By how much does this exceed the cost at $x = 8$?   Answer: a) \$4,400,000. b) \$480,000.

In the solution of this example, the algebra to obtain $C''(x)$ was very complicated. We might have been better off to use the first derivative test to determine the behavior of $C(x)$ at $x = 8$. Let's try it. Recall that $C'(x) = 2x/(x^2 + 36)^{1/2} - 1.6$, so we obtain

Interval	Point, x	C'(x)	Behavior of f(x)
[0, 8)	1	~ −1.3	Decreases
(8, 20]	12	~0.2	Increases

8

Thus we can conclude, with much less work, that (8, 39.2) is a minimum. Through practice, you will learn to recognize the easiest route to the final solution of most problems.

11.9 PROBLEM SET 11–4

1. When y gallons of crude oil are produced, the average cost per barrel is $A(y)$, where

$$A(y) = \frac{2500}{0.04y + 9} + 0.16y, \; y > 0.$$

a) Find the value, y, that minimizes average cost per barrel.
b) Compute the minimum average cost per barrel.

2. When x gallons of olive oil are produced, the average cost per barrel is $A(x)$, where

$$A(x) = \frac{4000}{0.1x + 20} + 0.25x, \; x > 0.$$

a) Find the value, x, which minimizes average cost per barrel.
b) Compute the minimum average cost per barrel.

3. Profit realized when x thousand gallons of antifreeze are produced and sold is $P(x)$ thousand dollars, where

$$P(x) = (100 + 10x)^{1/2} - 0.2x.$$

a) Find the value, x, which leads to maximum profit.
b) Compute the maximum profit.

4. The output of a chemical process that is applied for t hours is $k(t)$ hundreds of pounds, where

$$k(t) = (6 + 0.3t)^{1/2} - 0.05t.$$

a) Find the value, t hours, which leads to maximum output.
b) Compute the maximum output.

5. The section of circular roadway on Figure A is part of the graph of the function

$$f(x) = (10,000 - x^2)^{1/2}.$$

An exit is planned at $P(60, 80)$, and the straight exit path is to be tangent to the circular roadway at point P. Find the vertical intercept, b, of the intersection point, Q.

11.9 PROBLEM SET 11–4 *(concluded)*

FIGURE A

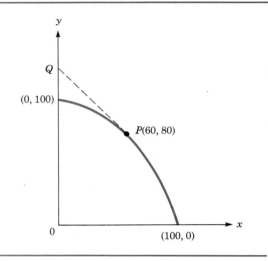

b) Compute the minimum cost.

c) How much more than the minimum would be the cost of a single segment from A to D?

FIGURE B

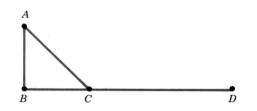

8. Answer (a), (b), and (c) of Problem 7 if A is 8.4 miles above B, BD is 15 miles, cost along BD is $200,000 per mile, and cost above BD is $290,000 per mile.

9. a) Find the expression for x at the stationary point on

$$f(x) = \frac{a}{bx + c} + kx.$$

b) If a, b, c, k, and x are all positive, determine by the second derivative test whether x is at a local maximum or a local minimum.

10. a) Find the expression for x at the stationary point on

$$f(x) = (ax + b)^{1/2} - kx.$$

b) If a, b, and k are all positive, determine by the second derivative test whether x is at a local maximum or a local minimum.

6. (See Problem 5.) Find the vertical intercept if the circular section is

$$f(x) = (225 - x^2)^{1/2}$$

and the point on this section is P(12, 9).

7. In Figure B, points B, C, and D are on a horizontal line and A is three miles above B on a perpendicular to BD. Straight line sections of road are to be constructed from A to C, then from C to D. Construction cost along BD is $200,000 per mile, but the cost above BD is $250,000 per mile. The distance BD is 10 miles.

a) How many miles from B should the intersection C be located if cost is to be minimized?

11.10 AN INVENTORY MODEL

We all have seen advertisements featuring inventory clearance sales. Such sales serve to emphasize that it costs money to carry a stock in inventory. *Carrying* costs include the cost of warehouse space, record keeping, insurance, damage losses, and obsolescence. Additionally, inventory often is acquired with borrowed money, and interest charges on this money can be a significant cost. In this model, we consider the case of a manufacturer who produces a product in batches, or lots, periodically, places the produced lot in inventory, then sells from this inventory until it is exhausted and a new lot is produced. On the production side, the manufacturer can achieve the cost economies of mass production if large lots are produced, but large lots will incur higher inventory carrying costs than small lots. The problem at hand, then, is to determine what lot size, L, should be produced to obtain an estimate of the optimal (minimum-cost) balance between production costs and inventory carrying costs.

To make the problem more specific, suppose that a manufacturer plans to produce 98,000 units of a product during a year. A lot, of size L, to be determined, is to be made periodically, and every time a lot is made it is necessary to set up the appropriate machinery and other production facilities before production starts. The *setup cost* is then a fixed cost incurred for each lot produced. Let us suppose this setup cost is $500. When production commences, the cost of making a unit is constant at $5 per unit. Inventory cost is to be determined on the basis that it costs $0.50 per year to carry one unit in inventory. However, when a lot is made and placed in inventory, there are L units in inventory, but as the product is sold during the interval until production of the next lot, the number of units in inventory decreases to zero. Thus the largest and smallest numbers of units in inventory are, respectively, L and 0, and we shall assume that on the average,

$$\frac{L + 0}{2} = \frac{L}{2}$$

units are carried in inventory during the year. We assign parameters as follows:

Number of units to be made in a year:	$N = 98,000$
Number of units to be made in each lot:	L
Fixed setup cost per lot:	$F = \$500$
Variable cost per unit made:	$v = \$5$
Average annual inventory carrying cost per unit:	$i = \$0.50$
Average inventory during a year:	$\dfrac{L}{2}.$

We now determine the expressions for costs incurred. First we note that if, for example, each lot contains 14,000 units, then to make 98,000 units in a year, the number of lots required would be

$$\text{Lots per year} = \frac{\text{Units per year}}{\text{Units per lot}} = \frac{98,000}{14,000} = 7.$$

Consequently, if the optimal lot size (to be determined) is L, we would have

$$\text{Lots per year} = \frac{98{,}000}{L} = \frac{N}{L}.$$

Each time a lot is made, the setup cost is $F = \$500$, so the total setup cost for a year will be

$$\text{Total setup cost per year} = (\text{Lots per year})(\text{Setup cost per lot})$$

$$= \frac{N}{L}(F) = \frac{98{,}000(500)}{L}. \tag{1}$$

Next we consider total annual inventory cost, which is the number of units carried in inventory during the year, on the average, times the carrying cost per unit.

$$\text{Inventory carrying cost for year} = \left(\frac{L}{2}\right)i = \frac{0.50L}{2}. \tag{2}$$

Finally, no matter what the lot size, 98,000 units will be made after setups during the year, and add a cost of 98,000 units times $v = \$5$ per unit to total cost. Thus:

$$\text{Total variable cost for year} = vN = 5(98{,}000). \tag{3}$$

The sum of the costs (1), (2), and (3) is the total cost for the year, and this, a function of L, is

$$C(L) = \frac{98{,}000(500)}{L} + \frac{0.50L}{2} + 5(98{,}000)$$

or, in parameterized form,

$$C(L) = \frac{NF}{L} + \frac{iL}{2} + vN. \tag{4}$$

Seeking to minimize $C(L)$ in (4), we find

$$C'(L) = -\frac{NF}{L^2} + \frac{i}{2}$$

and $C'(L) = 0$ when

$$-\frac{NF}{L^2} + \frac{i}{2} = 0 \quad \text{so} \quad L = \sqrt{\frac{2NF}{i}}.$$

Inasmuch as

$$C''(L) = \frac{2NF}{L^3}$$

is positive for any applied problem (that is, N, F, and L are positive), we have a local minimum. For the illustrative parameter values,

$$L = \sqrt{\frac{2(98,000)(500)}{0.5}} = \sqrt{196,000,000} = 14,000 \text{ units/lot.}$$

It follows that the firm would make $98,000/14,000 = 7$ lots each year or a lot every $^{365}/_7$ days, that is, a lot every 52 days.

Exercise. The annual requirement for another product made by the above firm is 7,200 units. The setup cost per batch is $100 and the inventory cost is $1 per unit in average inventory. a) What batch size will minimize total annual cost? b) How often should a lot be made? Answer: a) 1,200 per lot. b) Six lots will be made in a year, or a lot every two months.

In the model

$$C(L) = \frac{NF}{L} + \frac{iL}{2} + vN$$

note that vN is constant, so its derivative is zero. Consequently, the parameter v does not appear in the optimal solution. Notice also that when L is small, the setup cost term NF/L is large but the inventory cost $iL/2$ is small, and the reverse holds when L is large. The optimal balance of the cost terms occur when

$$L = \sqrt{\frac{2NF}{i}}.$$

Finally, observe that the optimal L is not proportional to N. That is, if the annual requirement was reduced by 19 percent to 81 percent of its old value, so that the new requirement is $0.81N$, then

$$L = \sqrt{\frac{2(0.81N)F}{i}} = 0.9\sqrt{\frac{2NF}{i}}$$

so the optimal lot size is now 0.9 or 90 percent of (or 10 percent below) its old value.

Exercise. If the annual requirement is cut to one-fourth of its old value, how would this affect the optimal lot size? Answer: The optimal lot size would now be one-half the old value.

11.11 PROBLEM SET 11–5

1. A retail firm orders a product from a supplier Q units at a time. During a year, the firm will order $N = 2,400$ units. The cost per unit ordered is $u = \$4$, and the cost of preparing and handling is figured at $c = \$12$ per order. The annual cost of carrying the average inventory of $Q/2$ units is $p = 0.25$ times (or 25 percent of) the purchase cost of $Q/2$ units. What are the parameterized expressions for:

   a) The number of orders placed in a year?
   b) The total handling cost per year?
   c) The purchase cost of Q units?
   d) Inventory cost per year?
   e) $S(Q)$, the sum of the handling, purchase, and inventory cost per year?
   f) The order quantity, Q, which minimizes $S(Q)$?
   g) What is the optimal order quantity for the parameter values given in the problem statement?

2. A manufacturing process generates $W = 4,096$ cubic feet of waste per year. The waste is accumulated in a cubical container of side x feet (area $= 6x^2$, volume $= x^3$), which lasts one year and is then discarded. The container costs $K = \$2$ per square foot to make. When full, the container is emptied and the interior surface (also assumed to be $6x^2$ square feet) is decontaminated at a cost of $d = \$0.50$ per square foot. What are the parameterized expressions for:

   a) The cost of the container?
   b) The number of decontaminations per year?
   c) The yearly decontamination cost?
   d) The yearly sum, $C(x)$, of the container cost plus the decontamination cost?
   e) The container dimension, x, which minimizes $C(x)$?

   Finally,
   f) What is the optimum container dimension for the parameter values given in the problem statement?

11.12 SKETCHING GRAPHS OF POLYNOMIALS

We saw in Section 11.4 that all candidate inflection points must have their second derivative equal to zero (a special case, which we will not encounter in this book, occurs when the second derivative is undefined). We checked for an actual point of inflection by determining whether the second derivative changed sign (so that the concavity changed) as we passed by the candidate point from left to right. An alternative technique using the third derivative will be shown in the next problem set. At the same time, a higher-order derivative test for local maximum and minimum will be shown.

We next present an example of curve sketching, using the critical point analysis of Section 11.4.

Example. Sketch the graph of

$$f(x) = x^3 - 12x^2 + 50x - 60.$$

First we find $f'(x)$ and $f''(x)$:

$$f'(x) = 3x^2 - 24x + 50$$
$$f''(x) = 6x - 24.$$

Next we determine the critical points.

1. *Stationary points:* We find

$$f'(x) = 3x^2 - 24x + 50$$
$$f'(x) = 0 \quad \text{when} \quad 3x^2 - 24x + 50 = 0.$$

The quadratic last written cannot be factored, so we shall apply the quadratic formula

$$x = \frac{-b \pm \sqrt{b^2 - 4ac}}{2a}$$

with $a = 3$, $b = -24$, $c = 50$ to obtain

$$x = \frac{24 \pm \sqrt{576 - 600}}{6} = \frac{24 \pm \sqrt{-24}}{6}.$$

The square root of a negative number is not a real number, so we conclude that $f(x)$ has no stationary points.

2. *Cusps:* None; $f'(x)$ exists for all x in $(-\infty, \infty)$ since $f'(x)$ is a polynomial and hence everywhere differentiable.

3. *Endpoints:* None.

Now we look at the increasing-decreasing behavior of $f(x)$. There are no critical points, so $f(x)$ is always increasing or always decreasing. We then draw the number line and use the representative point $x = 0$ to show that $f'(x) > 0$ for all x in $(-\infty, \infty)$.

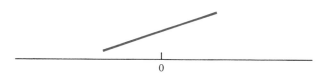

Then we examine $f(x)$ for inflection points and concavity. Turning to the second derivative, $f''(x) = 6x - 24$, we find that it is equal to zero when $x = 4$, which may mean there is an inflection point. If so, concavity must be different to the left and right of $x = 4$. We draw another number line to indicate $x = 4$ as a possible inflection point and test for inflection points to obtain

Interval	Point, x	f"(x)	Concavity
$(-\infty, 4)$	0	-24	Down
$(4, \infty)$	5	6	Up

So there is an inflection point when $x = 4$. The corresponding value of $f(x)$ is

$$f(4) = (4)^3 - 12(4)^2 + 50(4) - 60$$
$$= 64 - 192 + 200 - 60$$
$$= 12$$

so the inflection point is located at $(4, 12)$.

Finally, we use all the information we have collected to sketch a graph of $f(x)$, the function, as shown in Figure 11–19.

If you follow the above procedure in sketching the graphs of functions, you will find that you can draw the graph of almost any well behaved function accurately and quickly. This is an important skill since cubics with no local optimum points play an important role in economic cost analyses. Our next example illustrates curve sketching of a fourth-degree polynomial, a *quartic*, on a restricted set of points.

FIGURE 11–19

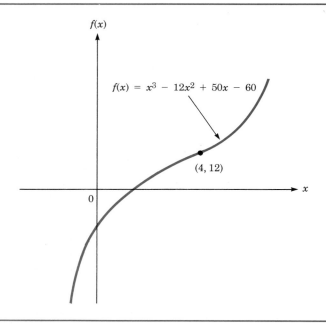

$f(x) = x^3 - 12x^2 + 50x - 60$

$(4, 12)$

Example. Sketch the graph of $f(x) = x^4 - 8x^2 + 26$ on the interval $[-4, 6]$.

Following the procedure from above, we first find

$$f'(x) = 4x^3 - 16x$$

and

$$f''(x) = 12x^2 - 16,$$

then proceed as before with the analysis of critical points.

 1. *Stationary points:* Since $f'(x) = 0$ when

$$4x^3 - 16x = 0$$
$$4x(x^2 - 4) = 0$$
$$4x(x - 2)(x + 2) = 0,$$

the values of x are 0, 2, and -2.
 2. *Cusps:* None.
 3. *Endpoints:* $x = -4$ and 6.

To find out whether the function increases and decreases in the intervals between critical points, we evaluate $f'(x)$ at a point in each interval.

Interval	Point, x	f'(x)	Behavior of f(x)
$(-4, -2)$	-3	-60	Decreases
$(-2, 0)$	-1	12	Increases
$(0, 2)$	1	-12	Decreases
$(2, 6)$	3	60	Increases

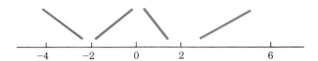

So we have local maxima at $x = -4$, $x = 0$, and $x = 6$, and local minima at $x = -2$ and $x = 2$. Computing the value of $f(x)$ at each of these points, we have

Maxima	Minima
$f(-4) = 154$	$f(-2) = 10$
$f(0) = 26$	$f(2) = 10$
$f(6) = 1034$	

Hence the absolute maximum for $f(x)$ on the interval $[-4, 6]$ is 1034, and the absolute minimum value is 10.

Exercise. Use the second derivative test of Section 11.4 to verify that there is a local maximum at $x = 0$ and local minima at $x = -2$ and $x = 2$.

To investigate inflection points and concavity, we set the second derivative equal to zero:

$$f''(x) = 12x^2 - 16$$
$$12x^2 - 16 = 0$$
$$4(3x^2 - 4) = 0$$
$$x^2 = \frac{4}{3}$$
$$x = \pm \sqrt{\frac{4}{3}}.$$

Checking intervals, we find

Interval	Point, x	f''(x)	Concavity
$(-4, -\sqrt{4/3})$	−2	32	Up
$(-\sqrt{4/3}, \sqrt{4/3})$	0	−16	Down
$(\sqrt{4/3}, 6)$	2	32	Up

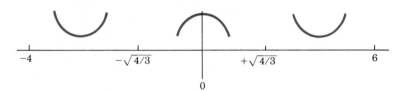

The graph of the function is sketched in Figure 11–20.

FIGURE 11–20

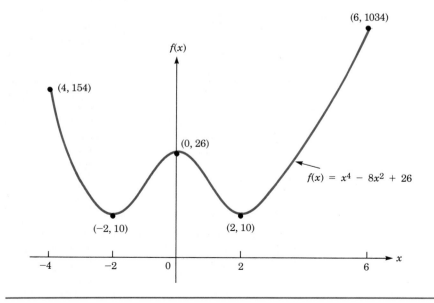

The procedure we have discussed can, in principle, be applied to sketch any polynomial. However, as the degree of the polynomial rises above four, problems arise in solving the equations $f'(x) = 0$ and $f''(x) = 0$, so we shall not discuss higher degree polynomials. Because our discussion has been quite detailed, it is worth noting that the procedures presented involved only finding and interpreting the first and second derivatives.

11.13 PROBLEM SET 11–6

Sketch the graphs of the following polynomials. Find all critical points. Indicate where the function is increasing, decreasing, concave up, and concave down. Place coordinates of optimum points and inflection points on the sketch.

1. $f(x) = x^3 - 18x^2 + 96x - 100$.

2. $f(x) = 9x^2 - x^3 - 15x$.

3. $f(x) = 5 - x^3$.

4. $f(x) = 0.2x^3 + 4$.

5. $f(x) = x^3 - 15x^2 + 80x - 70$.

6. $f(x) = -0.5x^3 + 6x^2 - 25x + 42$.

7. $f(x) = 50x^2 - x^4 - 100$.

8. $f(x) = x^4 - 18x^2 + 90$.

9. $f(x) = (0.001)(x - 10)^4 + 20$.

10. $f(x) = 0.01(6 - x)^4 + 0.32x + 0.56$.

11. $f(x) = x^4 - 8x^3 + 18x^2 - 27$.

12. $f(x) = 10 - 24x^2 - x^4$.

13. Recall the difficulty with the second derivative test if $f''(x) = 0$. There is an alternative. Consider the following tests:

Inflection point test
1. Find $f''(x)$ and determine candidates x where either
   a) $f''(x) = 0$, or
   b) $f''(x)$ is undefined (which could occur if $f(x)$ is not a polynomial).
2. Then there is an inflection point at $(x, f(x))$ if either
   a) $f'''(x) \neq 0$, or
   b) $f''(x)$ changes sign as we pass x from left to right.

Higher-order test for maximum, minimum, stationary inflection point
1. Find $f'(x)$, set it equal to zero, and solve for candidates x (stationary points).
2. a) If $f''(x) < 0$, then there is a local maximum at $(x, f(x))$.
   b) If $f''(x) > 0$, then there is a local minimum at $(x, f(x))$.

c) If $f''(x) = 0$, then find f''', f^{iv}, f^{v}, as needed.
   i) If the lowest derivative that is not zero is of odd order, then there is a stationary inflection point at $(x, f(x))$.
   ii) If the lowest derivative that is not zero is of even order, then there is a local maximum (minimum) at $(x, f(x))$ if this derivative is < 0 (> 0).

Apply these tests to graph the following functions:
a) Problems 1 through 12.
b) $f(x) = x^3 + 8$.
c) $f(x) = x^4 + 5$.
d) $f(x) = 6 - x^4$.
e) $f(x) = x^4 - 3x^3$.
f) $f(x) = x^5 + x^4$.
g) $f(x) = x^7 - x$.

A rational function is a function that is the quotient, or ratio, of two polynomials. Examples are

$$f(x) = \frac{2x^2 - 3}{x + 5}$$

$$f(x) = \frac{x^3 - 3x^2 + 2x - 7}{x^2 + 3x}$$

$$f(x) = \frac{x}{x - 5}.$$

We start with the last function

$$f(x) = \frac{x}{x - 5}$$

and our first concern is the discontinuity at $x = 5$. Here the denominator becomes zero, and $f(5) = \frac{5}{0}$ is undefined. However, if x approaches 5 from the right through a sequence such as 5.1, 5.01, 5.001, and so on, we find

$$f(5.1) = \frac{5.1}{0.1} = 51$$

$$f(5.01) = \frac{5.01}{0.01} = 501$$

$$f(5.001) = \frac{5.001}{0.001} = 5001.$$

The closer x is to 5, the larger is $f(x)$. Thus the curve rises higher and higher as x becomes closer to 5, but x cannot equal 5. Similarly, as x approaches 5 from the left through a sequence such as 4.9, 4.99, 4.999, and so on,

$$f(4.9) = \frac{4.9}{-0.1} = -49$$

$$f(4.99) = \frac{4.99}{-0.01} = -499$$

$$f(4.999) = \frac{4.999}{-0.001} = -4999,$$

so as x approaches 5 from the left, the curve falls further and further downward, but, again, x cannot equal 5. These characteristics are shown in the partial sketch of $f(x)$ in Figure 11–21, where the vertical line is $x = 5$. Coming in from the left of $x = 5$ the curve falls forever, *becoming closer to but never touching* $x = 5$. We describe this by saying $x = 5$ is an *asymptote* of $f(x)$ or that $f(x)$ falls, approaching $x = 5$ *asymptotically* from the left. Similarly, $f(x)$ rises and approaches $x = 5$ asymptotically as the curve comes in from the right.

FIGURE 11–21 (not to scale)

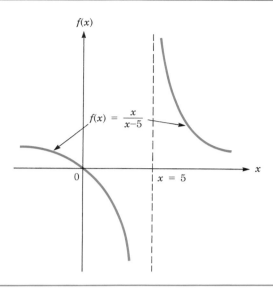

$$f(x) = \frac{x}{x-5}$$

The next questions concern what happens to $f(x)$ as x moves off indefinitely to the left and to the right. We shall use the symbols

$x \to -\infty$ to mean x decreases (moves off to the left) without limit.
$x \to \infty$ to mean x increases (moves off to the right) without limit.

The symbol ∞ (infinity) is not a number, and to investigate $x \to -\infty$, we use a sequence such as $x = -100, -1000, -10,000$ and so on, and similarly for $x \to \infty$. In

$$f(x) = \frac{x}{x - 5}$$

$$f(-1000) = \frac{-1000}{-1000 - 5} = \frac{1000}{1005} = 0.995$$

$$f(-10,000) = \frac{-10,000}{-10,000 - 5} = \frac{10,000}{10,005} = 0.9995$$

and it does not take many such trials before it becomes clear that for very large values of x, the constant -5 in the denominator of

$$f(x) = \frac{x}{x - 5}$$

becomes almost, but not quite, inconsequential, so $f(x)$ becomes almost, but not quite, x/x, which equals 1. A simple way to determine the limiting value of any rational function is to divide the numerator and denominator by the largest power of x that appears in the fraction of polynomials. In this case, we are considering

$$\lim_{x \to \infty} \frac{x}{x - 5} = \lim_{x \to \infty} \frac{x/x}{(x - 5)/x} = \lim_{x \to \infty} \frac{1}{1 - 5/x} = \frac{1}{1} = 1$$

and

$$\lim_{x \to -\infty} \frac{x}{x - 5} = \lim_{x \to -\infty} \frac{1}{1 - 5/x} = \frac{1}{1} = 1.$$

Notice that as $x \to \infty$ or $x \to -\infty$, $5/x \to 0$.

Now, as the above sequence shows, when $x \to -\infty$, $f(x)$ increases, but is always a bit less than 1. Hence $f(x)$ approaches the horizontal line one unit above the x-axis asymptotically as $x \to -\infty$. Figure 11–22 shows the asymptote as the constant function $A(x) = 1$. Verify by using a sequence such as 100, 1000, 10,000, . . . that as $x \to \infty$, $f(x)$ approaches $A(x) = 1$ asymptotically from above, as shown in Figure 11–22. Separately, the two branches are smooth curves, but the function $f(x)$ itself has a discontinuity at $x = 5$. The function has no local optimum points. It is instructive to verify this by the usual first derivative method, and also verify from the derivative that $f'(x)$ is always negative (except at $x = 5$). This is consistent with Figure 11–22, which shows that tangents to the

FIGURE 11–22

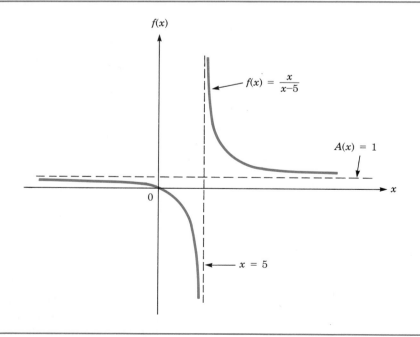

curve always slant downward to the right. The concavity (downward for $x < 5$ and upward for $x > 5$) can be verified by the second derivative, which is negative for $x < 5$ and positive for $x > 5$.

Example. Sketch the graph of

$$f(x) = 15x - \frac{100x}{60 - 0.5x}.$$

In the last example, we went immediately to the new idea of asymptotes. However, as we did when we sketched curves in Section 11.12, it is useful first to examine the function for optimum points. To do so, we apply the quotient rule to find

$$f'(x) = 15 - \frac{(60 - 0.5x)(100) - (100x)(-0.5)}{(60 - 0.5x)^2}$$

$$= 15 - \frac{6000}{(60 - 0.5x)^2}$$

and

$$f''(x) = 0 - (6000) \cdot (-2) (60 - 0.5x)^{-3} \cdot (-0.5)$$

$$= -\frac{6000}{(60 - 0.5x)^3}.$$

1. *Stationary points:* $f'(x) = 0$ where

$$15 - \frac{6000}{(60 - 0.5x)^2} = 0$$

$$15(60 - 0.5x)^2 - 6000 = 0$$

$$(60 - 0.5x)^2 = \frac{6000}{15} = 400.$$

Taking the square root of both sides yields ± 20 for the square root of 400.

$$60 - 0.5x = +20, \qquad x = \frac{40}{0.5} = 80$$

$$60 - 0.5x = -20, \qquad x = \frac{80}{0.5} = 160$$

$$f(80) = 15(80) - \frac{100(80)}{60 - 0.5(80)} = 800$$

$$f(160) = 15(160) - \frac{100(160)}{60 - 0.5(160)} = 3200.$$

Note that in the solution of the conditional equality, we took both the positive and negative values for the square root of 400. We now have $(80, 800)$ and $(160, 3200)$ as candidate optimum points.

2. *Cusps:* Returning to

$$f(x) = 15x - \frac{100x}{60 - 0.5x},$$

we note that a discontinuity occurs where the denominator is zero; that is, where

$$60 - 0.5x = 0$$
$$x = \frac{60}{0.5} = 120.$$

This is not a cusp, but we should be aware of the discontinuity when we sketch the graph.

3. *Endpoints:* None.

Since $f(x)$ is not defined at $x = 120$, this must be treated as a critical point, for $f(x)$ may change its behavior at $x = 120$. Checking increasing-decreasing behavior, we find

Interval	Point, x	f'(x)	Behavior of f(x)
$(-\infty, 80)$	60	25/3	Increases
$(80, 120)$	100	-45	Decreases
$(120, 160)$	140	-45	Decreases
$(160, \infty)$	180	25/3	Increases

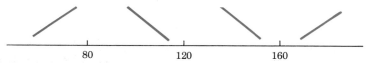

So we have a local maximum at $f(80) = 800$ and a local minimum at $f(160) = 3200$.

Checking inflection points and concavity, we see that

$$f''(x) = -6000/(60 - 0.5x)^3$$

is never zero, so concavity can only change at the discontinuity $x = 120$. In the usual way, we obtain

Interval	Point, x	f''(x)	Concavity
$(-\infty, 120)$	100	-6	Down
$(120, \infty)$	140	6	Up

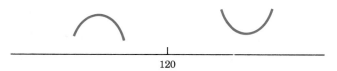

Is there an inflection point at $x = 120$? No, because $f(120)$ is not defined.

FIGURE 11–23 (not to scale)

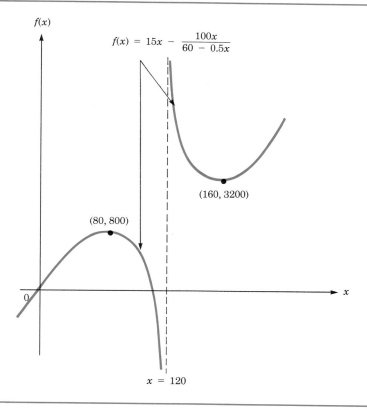

$$f(x) = 15x - \frac{100x}{60 - 0.5x}$$

(160, 3200)

(80, 800)

$x = 120$

As in the previous example, $f(x)$ will approach $x = 120$ asymptotically. We now have sufficient information to sketch the graph of $f(x)$, as shown in Figure 11–23.

Note that the left branch falls forever and the right branch rises forever. Why? Let's examine

$$\lim_{x \to \infty} f(x) = \lim_{x \to \infty} \left(15x - \frac{100x}{60 - 0.5x} \right).$$

To do this, we write the latter limit as

$$\lim_{x \to \infty} \left[15x - \frac{100x/x}{(60 - 0.5x)/x} \right] = \lim_{x \to \infty} \left[15x - \frac{100}{60/x - 0.5} \right].$$

It is now fairly easy to see that this limit is $+\infty$, so the right branch does indeed rise forever.

Exercise. By looking at

$$\lim_{x \to -\infty} \left(15x - \frac{100x}{60 - 0.5x} \right),$$

show that the left branch of **Figure 11–23** does indeed fall forever.

It is now time to practice some more curve sketching. We shall show how to sketch curves of additional functions as they arise in the next chapter.

11.15 PROBLEM SET 11–7

Sketch the graphs of the following functions. Place coordinates of optimum points and inflection points on the sketch. If a curve has an asymptote, put it and its equation on the graph.

1. $f(x) = 1/x$.

2. $f(x) = 100/x^2$.

3. $f(x) = \dfrac{2x}{x - 4}$.

4. $f(x) = \dfrac{x}{0.1x - 1}$.

5. $f(x) = 9x - \dfrac{48x}{3 - x}$.

6. $f(x) = \dfrac{2x}{x - 2} + x$.

7. $f(x) = \dfrac{x - 1}{x + 2}$.

8. $f(x) = x + 1/x$.

11.16 REVIEW PROBLEMS

For Problems 1 and 2, find the maximum or minimum value of $f(x)$, state which has been found, and describe the graph of $f(x)$.

1. $f(x) = 0.5x^2 - 50x + 2500$.

2. $f(x) = 10x - 0.2x^2 - 5$.

3. If the total cost of producing y yards of madras is, in dollars,

$$C(y) = 0.002y^2 + 5y + 100,$$

find the marginal cost at outputs of
a) 2000 yards.   b) 2500 yards.

4. If the total cost of producing t tons of coal is, in dollars,

$$C(t) = 0.001t^3 - 0.15t^2 + 10t + 100,$$

find the marginal cost at outputs of
a) 10 tons.   b) 50 tons.   c) 60 tons.

For Problems 5–14, find the coordinates of local optimum points, if any exist. In each case, state the type of point that has been found, and prove the statement by testing.

5. $f(x) = 0.1x^2 - 4x + 50$.

6. $f(x) = 20x - x^2$.

11.16 REVIEW PROBLEMS (*continued*)

7. $f(x) = 2x^3 - 3x^2 - 12x$.

8. $f(x) = 8x - x^3 - 5x^2 + 50$.

9. $f(x) = x^3 + x^2 + x - 4$.

10. $f(x) = 2x^4 - 216x + 500$.

11. $f(x) = 3x^4 - 16x^3 + 24x^2 + 10$.

12. $f(x) = 2x^3 - 9x^2 + 12x$.

13. $f(x) = 2x + 98/x$.

14. $f(x) = 96x^{1/2} - 6x$.

---

15. Interior and exterior walls of a rectangular 80,000-square-foot warehouse cost $90 per running foot. The warehouse is to be divided into 10 rooms by four interior walls in the x direction and one interior wall in the y direction. What should be the warehouse dimensions if the wall cost is to be minimized?

16. A rectangular area is to be enclosed, then divided into thirds by two fences across the area parallel to one pair of the sides. If the area to be enclosed is 1,250 square feet, what dimensions will lead to the use of a minimum amount of fence?

17. (See Problem 16.) If the fence on the two ends costs $0.64 per running foot and the dividers and the sides cost $1 per running foot, what should be the dimensions if the cost of the fence is to be a minimum, and what is this minimum cost?

18. If a rectangular area is to be fenced in the manner of Problem 16, what is the maximum area that could be enclosed with 1,000 feet of fence?

19. A rectangular manufacturing plant with a floor area of 5,400 square feet is to be built in a location where zoning regulations require buffer strips 30 feet wide front and back, and 20 feet wide at either end. (A buffer strip is a grass and tree belt that must not be built upon.) What plot dimensions will lead to minimum total area for plant and buffer strips? What is this minimum total area?

20. A box with square bottom and no top is to contain 32 cubic inches. Find the dimensions that will lead to a box of minimum area. What is this minimum area?

21. If the bottom material for the box in Problem 20 costs 8 cents per square inch, and the side material costs 1 cent per square inch, what dimensions will lead to minimum cost? What is this minimum cost?

22. A box with no top is to be made from an 8 by 15 inch piece of cardboard by cutting equal sized squares from the corners, then turning up the sides. What should be the dimensions of the squares if the box is to have maximum volume?

23. A parcel delivery service accepts cylindrical packages whose length, L, plus girth, $2\pi r$, does not exceed 120 inches. A shipper who uses cylindrical cartons, perforated, wishes to design a carton with maximum ventilation (area). What should be the length and radius of the carton?

24. An appliance service company is located centrally in a roughly square area x miles on a side. It charges $27 per call, not including parts and labor, and travel cost is figured at $1.50 per mile. The average distance traveled per call is $1.2x$ miles. In a month, the average number of calls per square mile of service area is 30.
   a) What should x be if net travel income (which excludes parts and labor) is to be maximized?
   b) What is this maximum?

25. Following the inventory model of this chapter (Section 11.10), suppose it costs $250 to set up a plant to make a batch (lot) of a product and $2 for each unit made after set-up. Inventory cost is $1.20 per year per unit in average inventory. The annual requirement for the product is 9,600 units.
   a) Write the expression for total annual cost as a function of the lot size, L.
   b) What lot size yields minimum cost?

26. A parcel delivery service picks up and delivers packages whose length plus girth

11.16 REVIEW PROBLEMS (*continued*)

does not exceed M inches. A shipper uses rectangular cartons with square ends. In terms of the parameter M, find the dimensions the carton should have if its volume is to be maximized.

27. Given the function

$$f(x) = 25(x^2 + 9)^{1/2} + 20(10 - x), \quad x \geq 0,$$

a) Find the x-coordinate of the local optimum point.
b) Determine whether the optimum point is a local maximum or minimum.

28. When x tons of magnesium are produced, the average cost per ton is $A(x)$, where

$$A(x) = \frac{4000}{0.1x + 20} + 0.25x, \quad x > 0.$$

a) Find the value of x at the local optimum point of $A(x)$.
b) Prove that (a) is a local minimum.
c) Compute the minimum average cost per ton.

29. Profit per tree grown and sold by a tree grower depends upon the height of a tree at the time of sale. Taking h as tree height in inches, the profit per tree, in dollars, is approximated by

$$p(h) = (10 + 2h)^{1/2} - 0.1h.$$

a) What tree height provides maximum profit per tree?
b) What is the maximum profit per tree?

30. Points B, C, and D are on a horizontal line with C between B and D. Point A is 4.2 miles vertically above B, and BD is 14 miles. Straight road sections are to be constructed from A to C, then from C to D. Along BD, construction cost is $200,000 per mile and above BD, cost is $290,000 per mile.
a) How far from B should the intersection at

C be if construction cost is to be minimized?
b) Compute the minimum construction cost.
c) How much is saved by the two-section construction choice rather than a single road from A to D?

31. This question has the material on summation (see Chapter 4) as a prerequisite. Given any set of n numbers,

$$x_1, x_2, x_3, \ldots, x_n:$$

a) What is the summation expression for the average of the n numbers?
b) Let a be an arbitrary number, subtract a from each x_i, square this, and sum for all x_i to obtain

$$S(a) = \sum_{i=1}^{n} (x_i - a)^2.$$

Find the expression for a that will minimize the sum of squares, $S(a)$.
c) How is this expression related to the set of numbers?

32. (Note: This problem is algebraically difficult, so we shall give the answer, $x = 5/3$ mile.) Point $R(x, 0)$ is on the x-axis. To its left, and above, is point $P(1, 1)$ and to its right, also above, is $Q(3, 2)$. A plant is to be built at R and the sum of its distances from points P and Q is to be minimized. Find the x-coordinate of $R(x, 0)$. Note that x is between 1 and 3, so x must be positive.

33. Given

$$f(x) = h(a^2 + x^2)^{1/2} + g(b - x),$$

where a, b, h, and g are all positive and $h < g$, find the expression for x if it is to mark a point where $f(x)$ has a local optimum point.

Find the value of x at local optimum points for Problems 34–36. State whether each optimum point is a local maximum or minimum.

34. $f(x) = \dfrac{3x}{8 + 0.5x^2}$, $x > 0$.

35. $f(x) = x(1 - x)^{1/2}$, $x \leq 1$.

36. $f(x) = 2x + \dfrac{8x}{0.5x - 1}$.

11.16 REVIEW PROBLEMS (*concluded*)

For Problems 37–46, sketch graphs of the functions. Place coordinates of optimum points and inflection points on the sketch. If a curve has an asymptote, put it and its equation on the graph.

37. $f(x) = 8x - 0.5x^2 - 20$.

38. $f(x) = x^2 - 10x + 35$.

39. $f(x) = x^3 - 6x^2 + 15x - 4$.

40. $f(x) = x^3 - 12x^2 + 21x + 100$.

41. $f(x) = 32x - (x + 7)^4 + 200$.

42. $f(x) = 0.04x^4 - 2x^2 + 30$.

43. $f(x) = x^4 - 16x^3 + 72x^2 - 128$.

44. $f(x) = 2x - \dfrac{50x}{1 - 0.2x} + 15$.

45. $f(x) = \dfrac{2x}{0.5x - 4}$.

46. $f(x) = 36/x$.

TWELVE

Further Topics in Differential Calculus

In Chapters 10 and 11, we learned the basic ideas of differential calculus and applied them to solve numerous problems involving maxima and minima of polynomial functions. Such problems arise in many situations where the appropriate formulation includes functions other than polynomial functions, so in the first part of this chapter, problem-solving ability is expanded by developing derivative rules for exponential and logarithmic functions and applying them to optimization problems. Then we introduce the application of the derivative as a relation between the rate of change of the variable and the rate of change of the function. Next we provide a rule (the chain rule) that makes it possible to find the derivative when a functional form is implied, but not stated explicitly, and apply this rule to develop the formula for the *multiplier*, which is a fundamental determinant of the behavior of the economy. As we shall see, the derivative involved in the multiplier is also a *rate*, and rate interpretations are a new application of the derivative, not necessarily related to maxima or minima. In the last part of the chapter we again expand our set of calculus tools by showing how optimization problems can be solved, and rate interpretations can be made, when a function has *two* independent variables rather than one, as has been the case up to this point. This introduction to multivariate calculus and its applications concludes our work in differential calculus.

The presentation in this chapter assumes that the reader is familiar with the basic ideas presented in Chapters 10 and 11. Additionally, it is assumed that the reader is familiar with natural logarithms and the rules of logarithms presented in the first part of Chapter 7.

If $1,000 is deposited in a bank account that earns interest at the rate of 8 percent compounded annually, the amount in the account after t years is

$$A(t) = 1000(1.08)^t.$$

Observe that the independent variable, t, in the last expression is the exponent of the power of the constant base, 1.08. Functions that have a constant base and a variable exponent are called *exponential functions*. Other examples are

$$f(x) = 2^x, \quad g(x) = e^{-0.1x}, \quad h(x) = 3e^{2x-5},$$

where, in $g(x)$ and $h(x)$,

$$e = 2.718282$$

to six decimal places. This important constant is the base of the system of natural logarithms presented in Chapter 7. Calculus applications involving exponential functions typically are expressed with e as the base because this choice leads to a remarkably simple derivative, which is

$$\frac{d}{dx}(e^x) = e^x.$$

This says that the derivative of the function e^x is the function itself. To show how the last statement comes about, we start as always with the definition of the derivative,

$$\frac{df(x)}{dx} = \lim_{\Delta x \to 0} \frac{f(x + \Delta x) - f(x)}{\Delta x}.$$

Hence,

$$\frac{d(e^x)}{dx} = \lim_{\Delta x \to 0} \frac{e^{x + \Delta x} - e^x}{\Delta x}. \tag{1}$$

Now, by a rule of exponents, we can write

$$e^{x + \Delta x} = e^x e^{\Delta x}$$

and use this to rewrite (1) as

$$\frac{d(e^x)}{dx} = \lim_{\Delta x \to 0} \frac{e^x e^{\Delta x} - e^x}{\Delta x}$$

and, by factoring,

$$\frac{d(e^x)}{dx} = \lim_{\Delta x \to 0} e^x \left[\frac{e^{\Delta x} - 1}{\Delta x} \right]$$

$$= e^x \lim_{\Delta x \to 0} \left[\frac{e^{\Delta x} - 1}{\Delta x} \right] \tag{2}$$

where, in the last line, we have placed e^x outside the limit symbol. This is permitted because x is to be thought of as being a coordinate of a fixed point that does not vary as Δx changes and approaches zero.

We cannot evaluate the limit needed in the above by any elementary procedure so, instead, we state and illustrate what happens to

$$\frac{e^{\Delta x} - 1}{\Delta x}$$

as Δx approaches zero. The important point, which can be proved rigorously, is that as Δx becomes smaller and smaller, approaching zero, $e^{\Delta x}$ gets closer and closer to the value $(1 + \Delta x)$. To illustrate, use a calculator to show that for $\Delta x = 0.02$

$$e^{\Delta x} = e^{0.02} = 1.0202 \text{ compared to } (1 + \Delta x) = 1.02,$$

and with a smaller Δx, $\Delta x = 0.01$,

$$e^{\Delta x} = e^{0.01} = 1.0101 \text{ compared to } (1 + \Delta x) = 1.01.$$

Those having appropriate calculators may verify that with $\Delta x = 0.001$,

$$e^{\Delta x} = e^{0.001} = 1.0010005 \text{ compared to } (1 + \Delta x) = 1.001.$$

Note in the last three arithmetic expressions that as Δx becomes smaller, $e^{\Delta x}$ becomes closer to $(1 + \Delta x)$. Accepting as a fact that

$$e^{\Delta x} \text{ approaches } (1 + \Delta x) \text{ as } \Delta x \text{ approaches } 0,$$

the ratio in (2) approaches 1 as a limit. That is,

$$\frac{e^{\Delta x} - 1}{\Delta x} \text{ approaches } \frac{(1 + \Delta x) - 1}{\Delta x} = \frac{\Delta x}{\Delta x} = 1.$$

Hence, (2) becomes

$$\frac{d(e^x)}{dx} = e^x \lim_{\Delta x \to 0} \left(\frac{e^{\Delta x} - 1}{\Delta x} \right) = e^x(1) = e^x.$$

Simple Exponential Rule, Base e

$$\frac{d(e^x)}{dx} = e^x.$$

The simple function, e^x, is not nearly as common as expressions such as

$$e^{-0.1x}, \qquad e^{-0.5x^2}, \qquad e^{2x-3},$$

or, in general,

$$e^{f(x)},$$

where $f(x)$ is some function other than simply x itself. We have had much practice with the function power rule, which states

$$\frac{d[f(x)]^n}{dx} = n[f(x)]^{n-1}f'(x).$$

The procedure that led to this rule, when applied to

$$\frac{de^{f(x)}}{dx},$$

yields a corresponding result.

Exponential Function Rule, Base e

$$\frac{d}{dx}[e^{f(x)}] = e^{f(x)}f'(x).$$

Example. Find the first and second derivatives of

$$f(x) = e^{-0.5x}.$$

We have

$$\begin{aligned}
f'(x) &= \frac{d}{dx}(e^{-0.5x}) = e^{-0.5x}\frac{d}{dx}(-0.5x) \\
&= e^{-0.5x}(-0.5) \\
&= -0.5e^{-0.5x}
\end{aligned}$$

and so

$$\begin{aligned}
f''(x) &= \frac{d}{dx}[-0.5e^{-0.5x}] \\
&= -0.5\frac{d}{dx}e^{-0.5x} \\
&= -0.5(-0.5e^{-0.5x}) \\
&= 0.25e^{-0.5x}.
\end{aligned}$$

Exercise. Find the first and second derivatives of

$$f(x) = e^{0.1x+2}.$$

Answer: $f'(x) = 0.1e^{0.1x+2}$. $f''(x) = 0.01e^{0.1x+2}$.

The important idea to be kept in mind is that the derivative of an exponential expression with base e consists of two factors. The first is the expression itself, and the second is the derivative of the function in the exponent.

Example.   Find the local optimum point of $f(x)$, and prove it is a local minimum, if

$$f(x) = e^{0.2x} - 3x + 50.$$

We have

$$f'(x) = e^{0.2x}(0.2) - 3$$
$$= 0.2e^{0.2x} - 3$$
$$f'(x) = 0 \quad \text{when} \quad 0.2e^{0.2x} - 3 = 0$$
$$0.2e^{0.2x} = 3$$
$$e^{0.2x} = \frac{3}{0.2}$$
$$e^{0.2x} = 15.$$

We next take the natural logarithm of both sides of the last equation and write

$$\ln (e^{0.2x}) = \ln 15.$$

By a rule of logarithms (see Chapter 7), this may be written as

$$0.2x \ln e = \ln 15$$
$$0.2x(1) = \ln 15$$

because $\ln e = 1$. Hence,

$$x = \frac{\ln 15}{0.2} = \frac{2.70805}{0.2} = 13.54025$$

is a stationary point. There are no endpoints or cusps. To prove we have a local minimum, we return to

$$f'(x) = 0.2e^{0.2x} - 3$$

and find

$$f''(x) = 0.2e^{0.2x}(0.2)$$
$$= 0.04e^{0.2x}$$

so that

$$f''(13.54025) = 0.04e^{0.2(13.54025)}.$$

There is no need to evaluate this because *e to any power is positive*, so $f''(x)$ is positive, proving there is at a local minimum at $x = 13.54025$.
    To evaluate the function

$$f(x) = e^{0.2x} - 3x + 50$$

at $x = 13.54025$, recall that this was the solution to

$$e^{0.2x} = 15.$$

Thus, we have

$$f_{min} = f(13.54025) = 15 - 3(13.54025) + 50$$
$$= 24.37925.$$

Exercise. Given $f(x) = e^{2x} - 7x + 5.88466$: a) Find the local minimum value of $f(x)$. b) Prove (a) is a local minimum. Answer: a) $f_{min} = 5$. b) $f''(x) = 4e^{2x}$, which is always positive.

The derivative of $f(x) = a^x$. The exponential rule we have used requires that the base of the exponential be e. To generalize the rule to cover all bases, a, where $a > 0$ but not equal to 1, we consider the function a^x. By a rule of logarithms,

$$\ln a^x = x \ln a.$$

Exponentiating both sides of the equation, we have

$$e^{\ln a^x} = e^{x \ln a}$$

or simply

$$a^x = e^{x \ln a}. \tag{3}$$

Here we have converted a^x into a form whose derivative we can take by applying the exponential function rule. Thus,

$$\frac{d}{dx}(a^x) = \frac{d}{dx} e^{x \ln a}$$

$$= e^{x \ln a} \frac{d}{dx}(x \ln a)$$

$$\frac{d}{dx}(a^x) = e^{x \ln a}(\ln a). \tag{4}$$

Substituting from (3) into (4) we have

$$\frac{d}{dx}(a^x) = e^{x \ln a}(\ln a) = a^x \ln a.$$

This says that for a base a, the exponential rule contains a conversion factor, $\ln a$. The same factor appears in the exponential function rule. Thus

Exponential Rules, Base *a*

$$\frac{d(a^x)}{dx} = a^x \ln a$$

$$\frac{d}{dx}[a^{f(x)}] = a^{f(x)} \cdot f'(x) \ln a.$$

Example. Find the derivative of a) $f(x) = 2(3)^x$. b) $g(x) = 10^{-0.3\,x}$.

We have

a) $f'(x) = 2\dfrac{d}{dx}(3)^x$

$\qquad = 2(3)^x \ln 3$

$\qquad = 2(3^x)(1.09861)$

$\qquad = (2.19722)(3^x).$

b) $g'(x) = \dfrac{d}{dx}(10^{-0.3\,x})$

$\qquad = 10^{-0.3x}(-0.3) \ln 10$

$\qquad = 10^{-0.3x}(-0.3)(2.30259)$

$\qquad = -(0.69078)(10^{-0.3\,x}).$

Exercise. Find the derivative of: a) $f(x) = 2^x$. b) $g(x) = 5 - (4^{1-2x})$. Answer: a) $f'(x) = (0.69315)(2^x)$. b) $g'(x) = (2.77258)(4^{1-2x})$ or, by calculator, $(2.77259)(4^{1-2x})$.

Graphs of exponential functions. The characteristics of exponential functions are shown in Figures 12–1 and 12–2 by the sketches of

$$f(x) = 2^x \quad \text{and} \quad g(x) = e^{-0.1x}.$$

FIGURE 12–1 (not to scale)

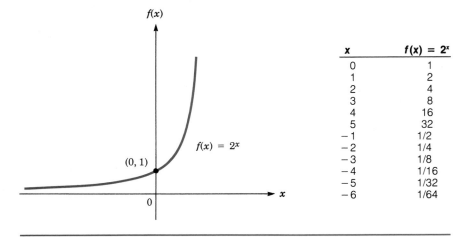

x	f(x) = 2^x
0	1
1	2
2	4
3	8
4	16
5	32
−1	1/2
−2	1/4
−3	1/8
−4	1/16
−5	1/32
−6	1/64

FIGURE 12–2 (not to scale)

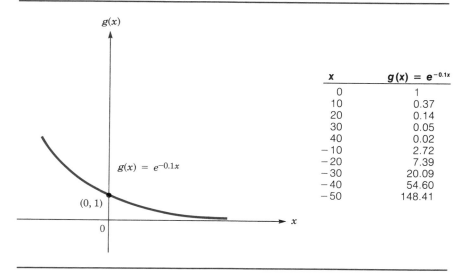

x	$g(x) = e^{-0.1x}$
0	1
10	0.37
20	0.14
30	0.05
40	0.02
−10	2.72
−20	7.39
−30	20.09
−40	54.60
−50	148.41

$g(x) = e^{-0.1x}$

$(0, 1)$

Observe that the value $x = 0$, making the exponent zero, yields the value 1 in the case of both $f(x)$ and $g(x)$. Also, both functions approach the x-axis asymptotically. In the case of $f(x) = 2^x$, we see that

$$\lim_{x \to -\infty} f(x) = 0,$$

so this function approaches zero (the x-axis) as we move to the left. Conversely, $g(x)$ approaches 0 as we move to the *right*, as shown in the table accompanying Figure 12–2. It is important to remember that the base of an exponential function must be positive, but not 1, and such a base to *any* power is *always positive*, never zero or negative.

It follows from the preceding that an exponential can be sketched if we know what its asymptote is, in which direction (to the left or right) it approaches the asymptote, and have one point, the *zero exponent point*, as a starting point. The functions we will want to sketch consist of a constant term C, which may be zero, and an exponential term Kb^p as in

$$h(x) = C + Kb^p.$$

For example, consider

$$h(x) = 10 + 3(2^{1-x}).$$

Here $C = 10$, $K = 3$, $b = 2$, and $p = 1 - x$, so that the constant term is 10 and the exponential term is

$$3(2^{1-x}).$$

Observe that the base of the exponential, 2, is greater than one and that the coefficient of x is negative. If we move to the right on the graph to larger values of x, such as $x = 100$, then

$$3(2^{1-x}) = 3(2^{-99}) = \frac{3}{2^{99}}$$

is a very small number, and becomes ever smaller as x increases. This means the curve approaches its asymptote to the right. Inasmuch as the exponential term approaches zero,

$$h(x) = 10 + 3(2^{1-x})$$

approaches 10, so the asymptote, which we shall symbolize as $A(x)$, is the horizontal line

$$A(x) = 10.$$

To obtain the zero exponent starting point, we note that the exponent $1 - x = 0$ where $x = 1$ and

$$h(1) = 10 + 3(2)^0 = 10 + 3(1) = 13.$$

Hence (1, 13) is the starting point. The curve may now be sketched as shown in Figure 12–3.

If the base of the exponential is greater than one and the coefficient of x in the exponent is positive, as in Figure 12–1, the curve approaches its asymptote to the left. Hence for bases greater than one, the curve approaches its asymptote to the right (left) if the coefficient of x in the

FIGURE 12–3 (not to scale)

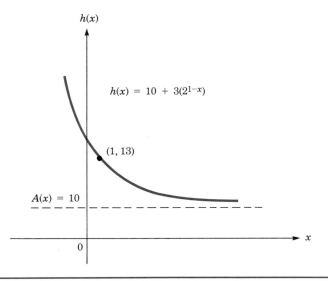

exponent is negative (positive). If the base is between zero and one, its *reciprocal* is greater than one, and we can change to the reciprocal by changing the sign of the exponent. For example,

$$f(x) = (0.4)^x = \left(\frac{1}{0.4}\right)^{-x} = (2.5)^{-x},$$

and, by the right-left principle just stated for bases greater than $1, f(x)$ approaches its asymptote to the right.

Procedure for Sketching Exponentials $f(x) = C + Kb^p$

1. Draw the horizontal asymptote, which is $A(x) = C$ (the constant term).
2. Find the zero exponent point (the point where $p = 0$) to locate on which side of the asymptote the curve will lie.
3. Find the *direction of approach indicator* to see how the curve approaches the asymptote by taking the sign of x in the exponent p for bases greater than 1 and the opposite sign for bases between zero and one. A positive (negative) indicator means the approach is to the left (right).

Example. Describe the characteristics of the graph of

$$f(x) = 20 - 9(2^{0.5x-3}).$$

1. The asymptote is the horizontal line $A(x) = 20$.
2. The zero exponent occurs where

$$0.5x - 3 = 0$$
$$0.5x = 3$$
$$x = \frac{3}{0.5} = 6.$$
$$f(6) = 20 - 9(2^0) = 11.$$

Hence, $(6, 11)$ is a starting point which is located below the asymptote since the y-coordinate, 11, of the point is smaller than the y-coordinate, 20, of the asymptote.

3. The base is greater than 1, so the positive coefficient of x means the curve approaches its asymptote to the left.

As shown in Figure 12–4, the curve rises to the left of $(6, 11)$ toward the asymptote and falls ever more steeply to the right of $(6, 11)$.

Exercise. Describe the graph of $f(x) = 20 + 10e^{3-0.5x}$. Answer: Starting at $(6, 30)$ the curve falls to the right toward its asymptote, $A(x) = 20$. To the left of $(6, 30)$ it rises ever more steeply.

FIGURE 12–4 (not to scale)

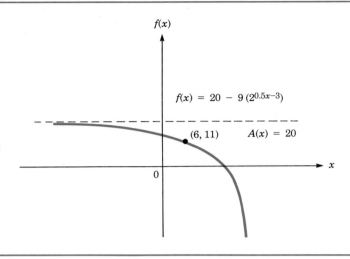

$f(x)$

$f(x) = 20 - 9 (2^{0.5x-3})$

$(6, 11)$ $A(x) = 20$

x

0

12.3 RESPONSE FUNCTIONS

In the planning stages of a promotional effort to sell a new product, the Newprod Company uses the exponential function

$$r(t) = 0.40 - 0.40e^{-0.02\,t}$$

as an indicator of the proportion of all potential customers who will have responded to the promotion in its first t days of operation. Thus, for example, during the first 50 days

$$\begin{aligned}
r(50) &= 0.40 - 0.40e^{-0.02(50)} \\
&= 0.40 - 0.40e^{-1} \\
&= 0.40 - 0.40(0.3679) \\
&= 0.253
\end{aligned}$$

or 25.3 percent of potential customers are expected to respond. It follows from the discussion in the last section that the exponential response function has $A(x) = 0.40$ as its asymptote and that the proportion responding rises as time goes on (t increases), but never reaches 0.40.

Newprod market research personnel estimate the total number of potential customers at 5,000,000 and that, on the average, one response will yield a revenue of $2. The cost of running the promotion consists of a fixed cost of $155,200 plus a variable cost of $24,000 each day the promotion is continued. In summary:

Proportion responding in t days: $r(t) = 0.40 - 0.40e^{-0.02t}$.
Number of potential customers: 5,000,000.

Average revenue per response: $2.

Cost in t days: $C(t) = (155{,}200 + 24{,}000t)$ dollars.

Total revenue in t days, symbolized as $R(t)$, will be $2 times the number of responses, and the number of responses will be $r(t)$, the proportion responding, times 5,000,000. Thus

$$R(t) = \$2(\text{proportion responding})(5{,}000{,}000)$$
$$R(t) = 10{,}000{,}000(0.4 - 0.4e^{-0.02t}).$$

Profit at t days, $P(t)$, will be total revenue minus cost:

$$P(t) = R(t) - C(t)$$
$$= 10{,}000{,}000(0.4 - 0.4e^{-0.02t}) - (155{,}200 + 24{,}000t)$$
$$P(t) = 4{,}000{,}000 - 4{,}000{,}000e^{-0.02t} - 155{,}200 - 24{,}000t.$$

Newprod now wants to know how many days the promotion should be continued to maximize profit. Taking the derivative,

$$P'(t) = -4{,}000{,}000e^{-0.02t}(-0.02) - 24{,}000$$
$$= 80{,}000e^{-0.02t} - 24{,}000.$$

To have an optimum point $P'(t)$ must be zero. Hence,

$$80{,}000e^{-0.02t} - 24{,}000 = 0$$
$$80{,}000e^{-0.02t} = 24{,}000$$
$$e^{-0.02t} = \frac{24{,}000}{80{,}000}$$
$$e^{-0.02t} = 0.3.$$

Taking the natural logarithm of both sides yields

$$\ln(e^{-0.02t}) = \ln 0.3$$
$$-0.02t \ln e = \ln 0.3$$
$$-0.02t = \ln 0.3$$
$$t = \frac{\ln 0.3}{-0.02}$$
$$= \frac{-1.20397}{-0.02}$$
$$t = 60.2 \text{ days.}$$

It may be verified that $P''(t)$ is negative for all values of t, so we have maximum profit if the promotion is continued for about 60 days. To compute the maximum, we find $P(t)$, remembering that $e^{-0.02t} = 0.3$. Thus,

$$P_{\max} = P(60.2) = 4{,}000{,}000 - 4{,}000{,}000(0.3) - 155{,}200 - 24{,}000(60.2)$$
$$= \$1{,}200{,}000.$$

Practice with response functions will be provided in the next set of problems.

12.4 PROBLEM SET 12–1

Find the first and second derivatives of each of the following functions:

1. $f(x) = 2e^x$.

2. $f(x) = 5^x$.

3. $f(x) = 7^x$.

4. $f(x) = 3e^x$.

5. $f(x) = 5e^{-0.2x}$.

6. $f(x) = 2.5e^{-0.4x}$.

7. $f(x) = 20e^{3-0.1x}$.

8. $f(x) = 10e^{0.3x-6}$.

9. $f(x) = e^{x^2}$.

10. $f(x) = e^{-x^2}$.

11. $f(x) = (1/2)^{-3x}$.

12. $f(x) = (0.4)^{-0.3x}$.

13. $f(x) = 1000(1.06)^x$.

14. $f(x) = 500(1.08)^{-x}$.

In Problems 15–22, sketch the curve. Show the starting point coordinates and the asymptote with its equation. The sketches need not be to scale, and the coordinate axes need not be shown.

15. $f(x) = 5^x$.

16. $f(x) = 5^{-x}$.

17. $f(x) = 2^{3-0.5x}$.

18. $f(x) = 3^{0.5x-2}$.

19. $f(x) = (0.5)^x$.

20. $f(x) = (0.25)^{-x}$.

21. $f(x) = 15 - 10e^{3-0.1x}$.

22. $f(x) = 20 + 15e^{2-0.1x}$.

23. Find the slope of the line tangent to the following at the point where $x = 2$.

$$f(x) = e^{-0.1x^2+2x-3}.$$

24. Newprod Company estimates the total potential number of customers for a new product is 1,000,000. It plans to operate a promotional campaign to sell the product and uses the response function

$$r(t) = 0.25 - 0.25e^{-0.01t}$$

as a measure of the proportion of total customer potential responding to the promotion after it has been in operation for t days. On the average, one response generates $5 in revenue. Campaign costs consist of a fixed cost of $15,000 plus a variable cost of $1,000 per day of operation.
a) How long should the campaign continue if profit (revenue minus cost) is to be maximized?
b) Compute the maximum profit.

25. Solve Problem 24 if the response function is

$$r(t) = 0.25 - 0.25e^{-0.02t}$$

and other facts remain as given.

26. An oil deposit contains 1,000,000 barrels of oil, which, after being pumped from the deposit, yields a revenue of $12 per barrel. The proportion of the deposit that will have been pumped out after t years of pumping is

$$0.9 - 0.9e^{-0.16t}.$$

Operating costs are $345,600 per year.
a) How long should pumping be continued to maximize profit?
b) Compute the maximum profit.

27. Answer Problem 26 if revenue per barrel is $15.

28. The revenue from, and cost of, operating an undertaking for t years are, respectively,

$$R(t) = 4e^{0.3t} \quad \text{and} \quad C(t) = 1.5e^{0.4t}$$

millions of dollars. How long should the undertaking be continued if profit is to be maximized?

12.4 PROBLEM SET 12–1 (*concluded*)

In Problems 29–34, find the value of the function at its local optimum point and state whether this is a local maximum or minimum.

29. $f(x) = 25x - e^x$.

30. $f(x) = 0.1x + e^{-0.1x}$.

31. $f(x) = 0.02x + e^{-0.1x}$.

32. $f(x) = e^{x - 0.1 x^2}$.

33. $f(x) = 10x - e^{0.2x}$.

34. $f(x) = 0.05x + e^{-0.1x} + 4$.

12.5 DERIVATIVES OF LOGARITHMIC FUNCTIONS

To obtain the simple logarithmic derivative rule, we start with

$$g(x) = \ln x. \tag{1}$$

Applying the definition of a logarithm, equation (1) means

$$e^{g(x)} = x. \tag{2}$$

Taking the derivative with respect to x by application of the exponential function rule, we have

$$\frac{d}{dx}[e^{g(x)}] = \frac{d}{dx}(x)$$

$$e^{g(x)}g'(x) = 1$$

$$g'(x) = \frac{1}{e^{g(x)}}.$$

But from (2), the right side of the last expression is $1/x$. Hence,

$$g'(x) = \frac{1}{x}.$$

Thus,

$$\frac{d}{dx}[g(x)] = g'(x) = \frac{1}{x},$$

and from (1), $g(x)$ is $\ln x$, so

$$\frac{d}{dx}(\ln x) = \frac{1}{x}.$$

Thus, the simple logarithmic function, $\ln x$, has the reciprocal of x as its derivative. Moreover, as might by now be expected, the logarithm of $f(x)$, $\ln f(x)$, has as its derivative the reciprocal of $f(x)$ multiplied by $f'(x)$.

Logarithmic Rules, Base e

$$\frac{d}{dx}(\ln x) = \frac{1}{x}$$

$$\frac{d}{dx}\ln[f(x)] = \frac{1}{f(x)} \cdot f'(x) = \frac{f'(x)}{f(x)}$$

Because of the simplicity of the derivative rules when the natural logarithm system is used, we shall not use base 10 (common) logarithms in our work with calculus. If we wish to find the derivative of $f(x) = \log_{10} f(x)$, we need only remember

$$\log_{10} f(x) = \frac{\ln f(x)}{\ln 10},$$

so

$$\frac{d}{dx}(\log_{10} f(x)) = \frac{1}{\ln 10} \cdot \frac{1}{f(x)} \cdot f'(x)$$

$$= (0.4343)\frac{f'(x)}{f(x)}.$$

Example. Find $f'(2)$ if

$$f(x) = \ln(2x + 1) + \ln x.$$

We have

$$f'(x) = \frac{1}{2x + 1} \cdot 2 + \frac{1}{x}$$

$$= \frac{2}{2x + 1} + \frac{1}{x}.$$

Thus,

$$f'(2) = \frac{2}{5} + \frac{1}{2} = 0.4 + 0.5 = 0.9.$$

Exercise. Find $h'(1)$ if $h(x) = \ln(x^2 + 3x + 1) + 2\ln x$.
Answer: 3.

Sketching the graph of $g(x) = \ln x$. Inasmuch as $\ln 1 = 0$, the graph of this function passes through $(1, 0)$ as shown in Figure 12–5. The table accompanying the graph shows that to the right of $(1, 0)$ the curve rises, but not very rapidly, because $\ln x$ increases slowly as x increases. To the

FIGURE 12–5 (not to scale)

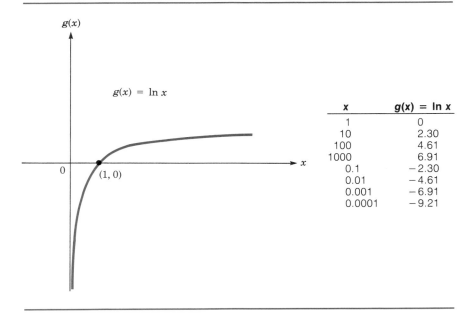

$g(x)$

$g(x) = \ln x$

$(1, 0)$

x	g(x) = ln x
1	0
10	2.30
100	4.61
1000	6.91
0.1	−2.30
0.01	−4.61
0.001	−6.91
0.0001	−9.21

left of $(1, 0)$, where x is less than one, $\ln x$ is negative and the closer x is to zero, the further the curve drops below the x-axis. But note that x cannot be zero or negative because only positive numbers have logarithms. It follows that as x approaches zero, the curve falls and approaches the vertical axis asymptotically.

Exercise.   Prove that $f(x) = \ln x$ is concave downward at all permissible values of x. Answer: This is true because $f''(x) = -1/x^2$, which is negative for all values of x.

12.6 PROBLEM SET 12–2
Find the derivatives of the following functions:

1. $f(x) = \ln x$.

2. $f(x) = 3 \ln(2x)$.

3. $f(x) = \ln(2x + 3)$.

4. $f(x) = \ln(1/x)$.

5. $f(x) = \ln e^x$.

6. $f(x) = \ln(2x + 5)^{1/3}$.

7. $f(x) = \ln(x^2 + 2x)$.

8. $f(x) = \ln(2x^3 - 6x)$.

9. $f(x) = \ln(3x + 2)^{1/2}$.

12.6 PROBLEM SET 12–2 (*concluded*)

In Problems 10–15, find the value of $f(x)$ at its local optimum point and state whether this is a local maximum or minimum.

10. $f(x) = 20x - 10 \ln x$.

11. $f(x) = 100 \ln x - 0.5x^2$.

12. $f(x) = 3x - 12 \ln x$.

13. $f(x) = \ln(x^2 - 10x + 35)$.

14. $f(x) = 100x^2 - 72 \ln x$.

15. $f(x) = 0.5x^2 - 4x - 5 \ln x + 25$.

16. When x ounces of seed costing $2 per ounce are sown on a plot of land, the crop yield is $\ln(2x + 1)$ bushels worth $25 per bushel. How many ounces should be sown if the worth of the crop minus the cost of the seed is to be maximized?

17. Solve Problem 16 if seed cost changes to $2.50 per ounce and the crop is worth $30 per bushel.

12.7 RELATIVE RATE OF CHANGE

The word *rate* has many meanings, so it is important at the outset to review what it means in the calculus context as we first introduced it in Section 10.10. Refer to Figure 12–6, which shows $P(t)$ as the total profit from a venture at time t days. Point Q is at 25 days and $P(25) = \$60,000$ is total profit at 25 days. The derivative at $t = 25$,

$$P'(25) = 3000,$$

is the slope of the tangent line at point Q. As the figure shows, this value is

$$\frac{\$3,000}{1 \text{ day}}.$$

To describe this ratio by saying profit is $3,000 per day does not bring out the full meaning of what is shown in Figure 12–6, and, furthermore, it is easy to misinterpret the statement and assume it means that profit from the venture is $3,000 per day *every* day. The value $3,000 does not mean profit per day every day, nor does it mean average profit per day. It does mean that the *tangent line at point Q* rises at a rate of $3,000 per day, and we describe this by saying that *at* $t = 25$ days profit is increasing at the rate of $3,000 per additional day the venture continues. Thus, in calculus, rates are tangent slopes at points, so we call them *point* rates or, when time is the independent variable, *instantaneous* rates, and whenever we describe a derivative in rate terminology it is to be understood that this means a point rate.

As examples of point rates already introduced, recall that marginal cost *at* output level q units is the change (increase) in total cost per additional unit made, and that marginal propensity to consume *at* income

FIGURE 12–6 (not to scale)

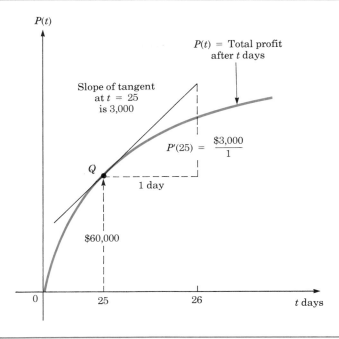

level Y is the change (increase) in total amount spent per additional dollar of income received.

Example. The cost of renting a car for one day consists of a fixed charge of $15, plus $0.20 per mile the car is driven. Letting m be the number of miles driven, one day's cost, $C(m)$, is

$$C(m) = 15 + 0.20m.$$

Interpret $C'(m)$ in rate terminology.

We have

$$C'(m) = 0.20,$$

which is a constant because $C(m)$ is a linear function. The rate interpretation is that the day's cost increases at the rate of $0.20 (or 20 cents) per additional mile driven. Note that it would be incorrect to state that the $0.20 means the cost is 20 cents per mile, because, for example, if the car is driven 100 miles, the cost is $35 and cost per mile is $0.35. This $0.35 is the *average* cost per mile if the car is driven 100 miles.

Exercise. The cost of printing and binding a paperback book is $C(n)$ dollars, where n is the number of copies made. If $C(n) = 1500 + 1.5n$, find $C'(n)$ and interpret it in rate terminology. Answer: $C'(n) = 1.5$ means that total cost increases at the rate of $1.50 per additional book made.

Example. In an attempt to attract renters who drive a car many miles in one day, an enterprising car rental manager decided to offer a one-day rental cost computed from

$$C(m) = 15 + 0.20m - 0.00004m^2.$$

Find $C'(500)$ and $C'(1000)$ and interpret these values in rate terminology.

Observe the negative term in $C(m)$. This represents a reduction in cost that, though modest when the car is driven a small number of miles, becomes significant if the car is driven, say, 1,000 miles. We find

$$C'(m) = 0.20 - 0.00008m$$
$$C'(500) = 0.16$$
$$C'(1000) = 0.12.$$

Here, the cost function is not linear, so $C'(m)$ varies as m changes. $C'(500) = 0.16$ means that at 500 miles, cost is increasing at the rate of 16 cents per additional mile driven, and $C'(1000) = 0.12$ means that at 1,000 miles, cost is increasing at the rate of 12 cents per additional mile driven.

Sometimes it is useful to consider the ratio of the rate of change of a function to the value of the function itself. This ratio is referred to as a *relative* rate of change and may be expressed as a proportion or as a percent. In Figure 12–6, for example, the $3,000 is a change from $P(25) = $60,000$, so the relative rate is

$$\frac{3000}{60,000} = 0.05 \quad \text{or} \quad 5 \text{ percent.}$$

We describe the last result by saying that *at* $t = 25$ days profit is increasing at the rate of 5 percent per additional day. This rate is

$$\frac{P'(25)}{P(25)}$$

and, in general,

Relative rate of change of $f(x)$ **at a point** $= \dfrac{f'(x)}{f(x)}.$

Example. If $1,000 is deposited in a bank savings account that pays 6 percent interest compounded annually, the amount in the account at time t years is $A(t)$ where

$$A(t) = 1000(1.06)^t.$$

Find the relative rate of change at $t = 5$ years and describe this number in rate terminology.

First we find

$$A'(t) = 1000(1.06)^t \ln(1.06).$$

The relative rate expression then is

$$\frac{A'(t)}{A(t)} = \frac{1000(1.06)^t \ln(1.06)}{1000(1.06)^t}$$
$$= \ln 1.06$$
$$= 0.05827$$
$$= 5.827\%.$$

Noting that the rate is independent of t, we state that at any point in time the amount in the account is increasing at the rate of 5.827 percent per additional year. This result may seem to be incorrect because the example states that interest is 6 percent per year, not 5.827 percent. The reason for this is that the procedure we have used translates the rate of 6 percent compounded *once* a year to an equivalent rate of 5.827 percent compounded *continuously* (or instantaneously). A complete discussion of this matter can be found in Chapter 8. The next exercise shows that if interest is compounded continuously, the difference just noted does not occur.

Exercise. If $1,000 is deposited in an account paying 6 percent interest compounded continuously, the amount in the account at time t years is

$$A(t) = 1000e^{0.06t}.$$

Find the percent rate of change at time $t = 5$ years and describe this in rate terminology. Answer: At any time, t years, the amount is increasing at the rate of 6 percent per additional year.

Example. Total sales volume of a new product, in thousands of gallons, is $G(t)$ at time t years, where

$$G(t) = 12t + 4(e^{-0.5t} - 1).$$

Find the percent rate of change at $t = 4$ years and describe this in rate terminology.

First we find

$$G'(t) = 12 + 4e^{-0.5t}(-0.5)$$
$$= 12 - 2e^{-0.5t}.$$

The relative rate is

$$\frac{G'(t)}{G(t)} = \frac{12 - 2e^{-0.5t}}{12t + 4(e^{-0.5t} - 1)}$$

and at $t = 4$

$$\frac{G'(4)}{G(4)} = \frac{12 - 2e^{-2}}{48 + 4(e^{-2} - 1)} = \frac{11.7293}{44.5413} = 0.263,$$

so at $t = 4$ years sales volume is increasing at the rate of 26.3 percent per additional year.

Sensitivity analysis. In Chapter 11 we developed an inventory model to describe the costs associated with acquiring units of a product and carrying some of these units in inventory. The objective was to determine the lot size (the number of units to be acquired periodically during the year) so that cost would be minimized. In parameterized form the solution for L, the lot size, was

$$L = \left(\frac{2NF}{i}\right)^{1/2}$$

where

$N =$ Number of units to be acquired in one year.
$F =$ Fixed cost when a lot is acquired.
$i =$ Average annual inventory cost per unit.

If i is subject to error, or to change, we would like to know what effect a variation in i would have on the optimum lot size, L. If this effect is small, we say the lot size formula is not very sensitive to changes in i. We now consider L to be a function of i and write

$$L(i) = \left(\frac{2NF}{i}\right)^{1/2} = (2NF)^{1/2}i^{-1/2}.$$

Then

$$L'(i) = (2NF)^{1/2}\left(-\frac{1}{2}\right)i^{-3/2}$$

$$= \underbrace{(2NF)^{1/2}(i^{-1/2})}_{L(i)}\left(-\frac{1}{2}\right)i^{-1}$$

$$= L(i)\left(-\frac{1}{2}\right)i^{-1}$$

$$= -\frac{L(i)}{2i}. \tag{1}$$

Now suppose the parameter values used to compute the optimum L were

$$N = 500, \quad F = \$100, \quad i = \$10$$

so

$$L = \left[\frac{2(500)(100)}{10}\right]^{\frac{1}{2}} = 100 \text{ units.}$$

If $L = 100$ and $i = 10$, then (1) is

$$L'(i) = -\frac{L}{2i} = -\frac{100}{2(10)} = -5,$$

which says that the optimum lot size decreases at the rate of five units per additional \$1 of inventory cost per unit. Consequently, if the unit inventory cost changes from \$10 to, say, \$10.20, the optimal lot size would decrease by *approximately* one from 100 to 99; that is, the change from \$10 to \$10.20 is an additional \$0.20 and the decrease at the rate of five units per \$1 is, proportionately, one unit for \$0.20. Note that the word approximately in the last sentence was italicized. This was done to call attention to the fact that the derivative applies precisely only at a point, and only approximately if we move one unit from the point. In effect, the approximation means we are moving along the tangent line rather than along the curve. The exact change would be found by computing $L(10.20)$ − $L(10)$, and this turns out to be a decrease of 0.985 units rather than one unit.

Exercise. The minimal value of a function $g(h)$ occurs at $h = 600/k$, where k is a parameter. a) Write the expression for the rate of change of h with respect to k. b) Evaluate (a) if $k = 4$. c) Using (b), by how much, approximately, would h change if k increased by 0.2? Answer: a) $-600/k^2$. b) -37.5. c) h would decrease by about 7.5.

12.8 PROBLEM SET 12–3

1. If $C(x)$ is the cost in dollars of making (printing and binding) x books, and

$$C(x) = 2000 + 2.50x,$$

find $C'(1,000)$ and interpret the number in rate terminology.

2. If the total cost in dollars of renting a car for one day and driving it x miles is

$$C(x) = 20 + 0.2x - 0.00005x^2,$$

find $C'(500)$ and $C'(1000)$ and interpret them in rate terminology.

12.8 PROBLEM SET 12–3 *(continued)*

3. Two thousand dollars deposited in a bank account paying 8 percent interest compounded annually will grow to the amount

$$A(t) = 2000(1.08)^t$$

in t years. Find $A'(5)$ and $A'(10)$ and interpret the results in rate terminology.

4. Two thousand dollars deposited in an account paying 8 percent interest compounded continuously will grow to the amount

$$A(t) = 2000e^{0.08t}$$

in t years. Find $A'(5)$ and $A'(10)$ and interpret the results in rate terminology.

5. The cost in dollars of renting a car for one day and driving it x miles is

$$C(x) = 16 + 0.20x.$$

a) Write the expression for $a(x)$, the *average* cost per mile if the car is driven x miles.
b) Find $a'(40)$ and interpret it in rate terminology.

6. The total cost in dollars of producing x tons of a product is

$$C(x) = 0.01x^3 - 3x^2 + 300x + 10,000.$$

a) Write the expression for $a(x)$, the average cost per ton if x tons are produced.
b) Find $a'(100)$ and interpret it in rate terminology.
c) Find $a'(500)$ and interpret it in rate terminology.

7. [Note: If a group of 10 miners work a "shift" of 8 hours each, the product (10 laborers) times (8 hours) = 80 is called 80 labor-hours.]

A shift of miners produce $T(m)$ tons of ore when m labor-hours are worked, where

$$T(m) = 1.2m - 0.15m(\ln m).$$

Find $T'(100)$ and interpret it in rate terminology.

8. Total sales of a new product in thousands of dollars when the product has been sold for t years is

$$G(t) = 20t + 18(e^{-0.8t} - 1).$$

Find $G'(2)$ and interpret it in rate terminology.

9. The potential number of customers in a store's trading area t years from the time the store opens is $N(t)$, where

$$N(t) = \frac{200,000}{1 + 50e^{-0.8t}}.$$

Find $N'(5)$ and interpret it in rate terminology.

10. Find the relative rate of change in the function

$$f(x) = x^{1/2}$$

at $x = 5$ and interpret it in percent terminology.

11. The potential number of customers in a store's trading area t years from the time the store opens is

$$N(t) = 50,000e^{0.1t}.$$

Find the relative rate of change at $t = 5$ years and interpret it in percent terminology.

12. Total sales volume of a new product, in thousands of gallons, when the product has been sold for t years is

$$G(t) = 20t + 18(e^{-0.8t} - 1).$$

Find the relative rate of change at $t = 2$ years and interpret it in percent terminology.

13. A deposit of $5,000 in a bank account paying 7 percent interest compounded annually will grow in t years to the amount

$$A(t) = 5000(1.07)^t.$$

Find the relative rate of change at $t = 10$ years and interpret it in percent terminology.

14. A formula for the optimum lot size, L, which minimizes cost, is

$$L = \left(\frac{2NF}{i}\right)^{1/2}$$

where N, F, and i are parameters.

12.8 PROBLEM SET 12–3 (*concluded*)

a) What is the optimal lot size if $N = 500$, $F = 100$, and $i = 10$?

b) How sensitive is the optimum lot size to a change in the parameter F? To answer this, write the expression for the rate at which L changes per unit change in F.

c) Using the expression in (b) and the numbers from (a), estimate how much the optimum lot size would change if F increased from its value of 100 to the value 104.

15. (See Problem 14.)

a) What is the optimal lot size if $N = 1,000$, $F = 200$, and $i = 10$?

b) How sensitive is optimal lot size to changes in the parameter N?

c) Using the expression in (b) and the numbers from (a), estimate how much the optimal lot size would change if N decreased from its value of 1000 to the value 900.

16. A revenue function is maximized if its independent variable takes the value

$$x = \frac{50}{h} + \frac{k}{2},$$

where h and k are parameters.

a) What is the optimal value of x if $h = 10$ and $k = 20$?

b) How sensitive is the optimal value of x to

changes in the parameter h? To answer this, write the expression for the rate at which x changes per unit change in h.

c) Using the expression in (b) and the numbers from (a), estimate how much the optimal value of x would change if h increased from its value of 10 to the value 10.5.

17. a) Find $f'(5)$ and interpret it in rate terminology if

$$f(x) = \ln x.$$

b) Table II at the back of the book shows

$$f(5) = \ln 5 = 1.60944,$$

but the table does not give ln 5.001. Estimate how much $\ln x$ will change if x changes from 5 to 5.001.

c) Determine from (b) the approximate value of $\ln 5.001$.

18. a) Find $f'(4)$ and interpret it in rate terminology if

$$f(x) = \sqrt{x}.$$

b) We know $f(4) = 2$ and wish to estimate $f(4.01) = \sqrt{4.01}$. Estimate how much the square root of x will change if x increases from 4 to 4.01.

c) Determine from (b) the approximate value of $\sqrt{4.01}$.

12.9 THE CHAIN RULE AND IMPLICIT DIFFERENTIATION

The function power rules we have developed and worked with are special cases of a general rule called the chain rule. What if, for example, we wish to find

$$\frac{d}{dx} z^5. \tag{1}$$

We must be careful not to confuse this with

$$\frac{d}{dz} z^5 = 5z^4$$

because (1) asks for the derivative with respect to x not with respect to

z. Thus we need to know exactly how z depends upon x to find the derivative. For example, suppose

$$z = x^3 + x^2.$$

Then

$$\frac{d}{dx} z^5 = \frac{d}{dx}(x^3 + x^2)^5$$

$$= \underbrace{5(x^3 + x^2)^4}_{5z^4} \cdot \underbrace{(3x^2 + 2x)}_{dz/dx}$$

so

$$\frac{d}{dx} z^5 = 5z^4 \cdot \frac{dz}{dx}. \tag{2}$$

If we do not know an explicit expression for z as a function of x, we can still find

$$\frac{d}{dx} z^5$$

using (2).

Now what about a problem like

$$\frac{d}{dx} e^{f(x)} = ?$$

If we think of $f(x)$ as a single variable z, then

$$\frac{d}{dx} e^{f(x)} = \frac{d}{dx} e^z = \frac{d}{dz} e^z \cdot \frac{dz}{dx} = e^z \cdot \frac{dz}{dx}$$

or replacing z by $f(x)$

$$\frac{d}{dx} e^{f(x)} = e^{f(x)} \cdot f'(x).$$

This is precisely the exponential function rule we used in Section 12.2.
The above discussion leads us to the general chain rule.

Chain Rule

$$\frac{d}{dx} g[f(x)] = \frac{d}{df} g[f(x)] \cdot \frac{d}{dx} f(x) \quad \text{(Complete form)}$$

$$\frac{dg(f)}{dx} = \frac{dg(f)}{df} \cdot \frac{df}{dx} \quad \text{(Abbreviated form)}$$

Applied to the problem of finding

$$\frac{d}{dx}z^5,$$

the chain rule says to take the derivative of the function of z, which is z^5, with respect to z (which is what we would expect), then multiply this by the derivative of z with respect to x. Thus,

$$\frac{d}{dx}z^5 = \frac{d}{dz}z^5 \cdot \frac{dz}{dx} = 5z^4 \cdot \frac{dz}{dx}.$$

which is precisely equation (2).

Again, to determine

$$\frac{d}{dw}e^{2y}$$

we must use the chain rule because the derivative is with respect to w, and the expression whose derivative is sought, e^{2y}, is a function not of w, but of y. Hence,

$$\frac{d}{dw}e^{2y} = \frac{d}{dy}e^{2y} \cdot \frac{dy}{dw} \tag{3}$$
$$= e^{2y}(2) \cdot \frac{dy}{dw}.$$

To be sure the chain rule has been applied correctly, refer to (3) and, on the right, cover the denominator of the first factor with one finger and the numerator of the second factor with another finger. What remains in view should be the same as the expression on the left. Note that we avoided saying cancel dy on the right because d/dy does not mean d divided by dy but rather is an instruction meaning to take the derivative with respect to y, and we cannot cancel part of an instruction. Note also that we wrote

$$\frac{dy}{dw}$$

rather than the more formal statement for the derivative of y with respect to w,

$$\frac{d}{dw}y,$$

which is what dy/dw means.

Definition. $\dfrac{dy}{dx}$ means $\dfrac{d}{dx}y.$

Example. Write the expression for the derivative with respect to w for the following.

a) $2y^3$.   b) $e^{x^2} + 5w$.   c) $\ln(3z + 2)$.

We have

a) $\dfrac{d}{dw}(2y^3) = \dfrac{d}{dy}(2y^3) \cdot \dfrac{dy}{dw} = 6y^2 \cdot \dfrac{dy}{dw}$.

b) $\dfrac{d}{dw}(e^{x^2} + 5w) = \dfrac{d}{dw}(e^{x^2}) + \dfrac{d}{dw}(5w) = e^{x^2}(2x) \cdot \dfrac{dx}{dw} + 5$.

Notice that $\dfrac{d}{dx}(e^{x^2}) = e^{x^2} \cdot 2x$ by the chain rule.

c) $\dfrac{d}{dw}\ln(3z + 2) = \dfrac{d}{dz}\ln(3z + 2) \cdot \dfrac{dz}{dw} = \dfrac{3}{3z + 2} \cdot \dfrac{dz}{dw}$.

Notice that $\dfrac{d}{dz}\ln(3z + 2) = \dfrac{3}{3z + 2}$ by the chain rule.

Exercise.   Write the expressions for the derivative with respect to x of: a) $\ln y$. b) $2z^{3/2} + x^2$. c) e^{3w}.

Answer: a) $\left(\dfrac{1}{y}\right) \cdot \dfrac{dy}{dx}$. b) $3z^{1/2} \cdot \dfrac{dz}{dx} + 2x$. c) $3e^{3w} \cdot \dfrac{dw}{dx}$.

Note that the function power rule, exponential function rule, and logarithmic function rule are all special cases of the chain rule. No purpose would be served by applying the chain rule to problems we can solve with the function rules.

One of the important applications of the chain rule arises in problems where a function cannot be stated explicitly. To see what is meant here, recall that prior to this section all expressions were of the form

$$f(x) = \quad \text{or} \quad g(x) =$$

where the expression on the right involved x and constants, but *not* the function. These expressions are said to define the function *explicitly*. By way of contrast, consider

$$2[f(x)]^5 + 7[f(x)] = 3x^2 - 2.$$

Here it is impossible to solve this expression explicitly to obtain $f(x)$ above on the left. For convenience, and in keeping with convention, we shall write y instead of $f(x)$ and say that

$$2y^5 + 7y = 3x^2 - 2$$

implies y is a function of x. The method of finding

$$\frac{d}{dx}f(x) = \frac{dy}{dx}$$

is then called *implicit* differentiation, and the chain rule must be invoked. Thus, taking the derivative with respect to x, we have

$$\frac{d}{dx}(2y^5 + 7y) = \frac{d}{dx}(3x^2 - 2)$$

$$\frac{d}{dx}(2y^5) + \frac{d}{dx}(7y) = 6x$$

$$10y^4 \cdot \frac{dy}{dx} + 7 \cdot \frac{dy}{dx} = 6x.$$

Factoring dy/dx on the left yields

$$\frac{dy}{dx}(10y^4 + 7) = 6x$$

$$\frac{dy}{dx} = \frac{6x}{10y^4 + 7}.$$

Exercise. Find dy/dx if: a) $y^4 = x^3$. b) $y^3 - 3y^2 - 2x^3 + 3x = 0$. c) In (a) and (b), y is an abbreviation of what symbol?

Answer: a) $\dfrac{dy}{dx} = \dfrac{3x^2}{4y^3}$. b) $\dfrac{dy}{dx} = \dfrac{6x^2 - 3}{3y^2 - 6y} = \dfrac{2x^2 - 1}{y^2 - 2y}$. c) $f(x)$.

It is instructive to review part (a) of the exercise because

$$y^4 = x^3 \tag{4}$$

can be written in *explicit* form by taking the fourth root of both sides to give

$$(y^4)^{1/4} = (x^3)^{1/4}$$

$$y = x^{3/4} \tag{5}$$

or

$$f(x) = x^{3/4}.$$

We now can find $f'(x)$ by the simple power rule as,

$$f'(x) = \frac{3}{4}x^{-1/4} = \frac{3}{4x^{1/4}}.$$

Hence, we now have dy/dx, or $f'(x)$ as

$$f'(x) = \frac{dy}{dx} = \frac{3}{4x^{1/4}} \tag{6}$$

and, from the exercise answer,

$$\frac{dy}{dx} = \frac{3x^2}{4y^3}. \tag{7}$$

The two results certainly look different, but they are, in fact, equivalent. To see that this is true, let us replace the y^3 in (7) using (5) to obtain

$$\frac{dy}{dx} = \frac{3x^2}{4y^3} = \frac{3x^2}{4(x^{3/4})^3} = \frac{3x^2}{4x^{9/4}} = \frac{3x^{2-9/4}}{4} = \frac{3x^{-1/4}}{4} = \frac{3}{4x^{1/4}},$$

so (7) is equivalent to (6).

There is no need to invoke the chain rule for an expression that can be stated as an explicit function but, as the last discussion illustrates, we may choose to use the chain rule if we wish and the outcome of implicit differentiation will be equivalent to the derivative of the explicit function, although the expression for the two may appear to be different. Our immediate interest in the chain rule arises in the next section, where we encounter expressions such as

$$f(y) = y - x^2$$

and we want to find the expression for the derivative, dy/dx, of y with respect to x. We start by writing the expression for the derivative with respect to x,

$$\frac{d}{dx}f(y) = \frac{d}{dx}y - \frac{d}{dx}x^2.$$

On the left, see the need for the chain rule because we have to take the derivative of a function of y with respect to x. The chain rule says this is carried out by doing what is natural; that is, take the derivative of $f(y)$ with respect to y, then multiply this by dy/dx. Thus,

$$\frac{df(y)}{dy} \cdot \frac{dy}{dx} = \frac{dy}{dx} - 2x.$$

To solve for the desired dy/dx, we isolate terms containing dy/dx on one side, factor, and proceed as follows:

$$\frac{df(y)}{dy} \cdot \frac{dy}{dx} - \frac{dy}{dx} = -2x$$

$$\frac{dy}{dx}\left[\frac{df(y)}{dy} - 1\right] = -2x$$

$$\frac{dy}{dx} = \frac{-2x}{\dfrac{df(y)}{dy} - 1} = \frac{2x}{1 - \dfrac{df(y)}{dy}}.$$

The significance of what seems to be symbol manipulation in the last example will be seen in the next section when we attach interpretations to the derivatives in the result.

> **Exercise.** Find the expression for dy/dx if $y = C(y) + x$.
> Answer:
> $$\frac{dy}{dx} = \frac{1}{1 - \dfrac{dC(y)}{dy}}.$$

12.10 MARGINAL PROPENSITY TO CONSUME AND THE MULTIPLIER

The major part of the income people have available for their use is spent on food, clothing, shelter, medical care, transportation, recreation, and so on, and the remainder is saved in one form or another. The amount spent is called consumption expenditure or, briefly, consumption. Consumption, of course, is a function of income. If we symbolize income by Y, as is conventional in economics, and consumption as the function $C(Y)$, then $C(Y)$ is called a *consumption function.* Suppose, for example, that

$$C(Y) = 30 + 0.6Y$$

and that Y and $C(Y)$ are in billions of dollars. At income level $Y = \$100$ billion,

$$C(Y) = C(100) = 30 + 0.6(100) = \$90 \text{ billion,}$$

so that people having $100 billion of income available for use (referred to as *disposable* income) spend $90 billion on consumption, and the remaining $10 billion represents savings. While aggregate numbers for consumption and savings are important numbers, the topic of this section is concerned with the *rate at which consumption changes per additional $1 of income received.* This is the derivative of $C(Y)$ with respect to Y and is called the *marginal propensity to consume,* MPC, as introduced in Section 1.6.

> **Definitions**
> $$\text{Marginal Propensity to Consume} = \text{MPC} = \frac{dC(Y)}{dY}.$$
> $$\text{Marginal Propensity to Save} = \text{MPS} = 1 - \text{MPC} = 1 - \frac{dC(Y)}{dY}.$$

The second part of this definition means simply that if *MPC* is the part of an extra $1 of income going to consumption, the remaining part of the $1, 1 − MPC, goes to savings.

For the above consumption function, we have

$$C(Y) = 30 + 0.6Y$$

$$\text{MPC} = \frac{dC(Y)}{dY} = 0.6$$

$$\text{MPS} = 1 - \text{MPC} = 1 - 0.6 = 0.4.$$

Thus, of an additional $1 of income, $0.60 is spent on consumption and $0.40 is saved.

Exercise.   For the consumption function $C(Y) = 20 + 0.75Y$:
a) Find MPC and MPS. b) Interpret the answer to (a). c) What *proportion* (or percentage) of an income of $100 billion would be spent? Answer: a) MPC = 0.75, MPS = 0.25. b) Seventy-five cents of an *additional* $1 of income would be spent and twenty-five cents would be saved. c) 0.95 or 95 percent.

Note in part (c) of the last exercise that

$$C(100) = 20 + 0.75(100) = 95,$$

so $95 billion of the $100 billion, or 95 percent, would be spent. The *proportion spent is not the same as the marginal propensity to consume* because in economics marginals always refer to the rate at which a function changes per increase of 1 in the independent variable. That is, marginals are slopes of lines (derivatives).

The multiplier. At income level Y, $C(Y)$ is spent on consumption, and the difference

$$\text{Income} - \text{Consumption expenditure} = Y - C(Y)$$

is the amount saved. In our elementary analysis, we shall suppose that business investment opportunities exist, and all savings are invested, so savings equal investment. Letting I represent investment, we have

$$I = Y - C(Y).$$

Now, of course, investment by someone generates income for others. For example, a businessman who invests $1,000 to pay the wages for two workers to build an addition on a building, using material the businessman owns, generates a first round of a matching $1,000 of income to the workers. However, this is only the beginning round, and the important point we wish to demonstrate is that the $1,000 investment generates a multiple of $1,000 of income, and the multiplier is greater than one. To see this, we start with the $1,000 investment, which generates $1,000 of income to the workers. However, the workers now spend part of the

$1,000 income (remember MPC) on consumption, and this part becomes income to the suppliers of the consumption items. In turn, these suppliers spend part of their income on consumption, and so on, and on. Just how much income received at one link in this chain is spent on consumption and becomes income at the next link depends, of course, on the marginal propensity to consume, MPC. We now analyze the situation, starting with the algebraic expression

$$I = Y - C(Y).$$

What we want to know is by how much does income, Y, change per additional dollar of investment; that is, we want dY/dI. Taking the derivative of the last *with respect to I*, we have

$$\frac{d}{dI}(I) = \frac{d}{dI}(Y) - \frac{d}{dI}[C(Y)].$$

We must invoke the chain rule for the rightmost term. We have

$$1 = \frac{dY}{dI} - \frac{dC(Y)}{dY} \cdot \frac{dY}{dI}.$$

Remembering that dY/dI is sought, we proceed as follows:

$$1 = \frac{dY}{dI}\left[1 - \frac{dC(Y)}{dY}\right]$$

$$\frac{dY}{dI} = \frac{1}{1 - dC(Y)/dY}.$$

Next, remembering that $dC(Y)/dY$ is the marginal propensity to consume, MPC, we may write

$$\frac{dY}{dI} = \frac{1}{1 - \text{MPC}} = \frac{1}{\text{MPS}}.$$

The rate at which income increases per additional $1 of investment (investment = saving), dY/dI, is called the *multiplier*. Thus,

$$\text{Multiplier} = \frac{dY}{dI} = \frac{1}{1 - \text{MPC}} = \frac{1}{\text{MPS}}.$$

Returning to the consumption function at the beginning of this section,

$$C(Y) = 30 + 0.6Y$$

$$\text{MPC} = \frac{dC(Y)}{dY} = 0.6$$

$$\text{Multiplier} = \frac{1}{1 - \text{MPC}} = \frac{1}{1 - 0.6} = \frac{1}{0.4} = 2.5.$$

The multiplier here means that 2.5 dollars of income is generated by an additional $1 of investment. It is clear that MPC is a critical factor in income generation. When investment opportunities exist, a high MPC generates new income in an amount that is a large multiple of the sum invested.

Exercise. a) Find the multiplier if the consumption function is $C(Y) = 10 + 0.9Y$. b) Interpret the answer to (a). Answer: a) 10. b) One additional dollar of investment generates $10 of additional income.

We must leave more extensive analysis of the topics introduced in this section for courses in economics. However, our introduction serves to demonstrate the important contribution calculus can make to this analysis and also serves our purpose of illustrating a situation where the chain rule arises. We close the section by an example involving a consumption function that is not linear.

Example. a) Suppose Y is family income in tens of thousands of dollars so that, for example, $Y = 2$ means $20,000, and

$$C(Y) = 6 + 0.6Y - e^{-0.4Y}$$

represents the family consumption function. Find MPC for families with $1 and $2 of income.

b) Suppose Y is in trillions of dollars and the $C(Y)$ in part (a) represents the national income of a country. Find the multiplier at an income level of $0.8 trillion.

Here $C(Y)$ is not linear so MPC is a function of income that we shall symbolize as MPC(Y).

a) For

$$C(Y) = 6 + 0.6Y - e^{-0.4Y}$$

$$\text{MPC}(Y) = \frac{dC(Y)}{dY} = 0.6 - (e^{-0.4Y})(-0.4) = 0.6 + 0.4e^{-0.4Y}.$$

$$\text{MPC}(1) = 0.6 + 0.4e^{-0.4(1)} = 0.6 + 0.4e^{-0.4}$$
$$= 0.6 + 0.4(0.6703) = 0.87$$
$$\text{MPC}(2) = 0.6 + 0.4e^{-0.4(2)} = 0.6 + 0.4e^{-0.8}$$
$$= 0.6 + 0.4(0.4493) = 0.78.$$

Part (a) is illustrative of a common observation that the higher the income level of a family, the smaller MPC tends to be. That is, at a higher income, a smaller fraction of an additional dollar is spent on consumption and a larger fraction is saved.

b) Here we have the same MPC function as in (a),

$$MPC(Y) = 0.6 + 0.4e^{-0.4Y}.$$
$$MPC(0.8) = 0.6 + 0.4e^{-0.4(0.8)}$$
$$= 0.6 + 0.4e^{-0.32}$$
$$= 0.6 + 0.4(0.7261)$$
$$= 0.89.$$

Then, from our earlier derivation,

$$\text{Multiplier} = \frac{1}{1 - MPC} = \frac{1}{1 - 0.89} = \frac{1}{0.11} = 9.1.$$

12.11 PROBLEM SET 12–4

Employ the chain rule to carry out each of the following:

1. $\dfrac{d}{dx} f(y)$.

2. $\dfrac{d}{dz} f(x)$.

3. $\dfrac{d}{dh} p(q)$.

4. $\dfrac{d}{dw} g(f)$.

5. $\dfrac{d}{dx} (y^4)$.

6. $\dfrac{d}{dy} (x^3)$.

7. $\dfrac{d}{dz} (e^{2w})$.

8. $\dfrac{d}{dq} (2e^{-0.5p})$.

9. $\dfrac{d}{dx} \ln(2y + 3)$.

10. $\dfrac{d}{dw} \ln(z^3 - 3z)$.

11. $\dfrac{d}{dy} (xy)$.

12. $\dfrac{d}{dx} (x/y)$.

Find $\dfrac{dy}{dx}$ by implicit differentiation:

13. $y^3 - x^2 = 0$.

14. $y^5 - 3x^3 = 0$.

15. $2y^3 - 3y^2 - x^6 - 6x + 10 = 0$.

16. $4y^5 - 2y^2 + y - 2x - 50 = 0$.

17. $x = y + e^{-y}$.

18. $x = 2y - e^{y^2}$.

19. $e^x \ln y = 5$.

20. $e^{-y} \ln x = 1$.

21. $xy^3 = x^2 + 5$.

22. $x^2y^3 = 2x + 10$.

23. Find the expression for $\dfrac{dy}{dx}$ if y is a function of x and

$$x = y - g(y).$$

24. Find the expression for $\dfrac{dw}{dz}$ if w is a function of z and

$$w^2 = z^2 + f(w).$$

25. At income level Y, consumption expenditures are $C(Y)$ billion dollars, where

$$C(Y) = 34 + 0.68Y.$$

a) Find the marginal propensity to consume.

b) Interpret (a).

12.11 PROBLEM SET 12–4 (*continued*)

c) How much income is generated by an additional dollar of investment?

d) At income level 200, what proportion of total income is spent?

26. At income level Y, consumption expenditures are $C(Y)$ billion dollars, where

$$C(Y) = 54 + 0.63Y.$$

a) Find the marginal propensity to consume.
b) Interpret (a).
c) How much income is generated by an additional dollar of investment?

d) At income level 200, what proportion of total income is spent?

27. For the consumption function

$$C(Y) = 9 + 0.7Y - e^{-0.3Y},$$

find the multiplier at income level
a) 3.   b) 10.

28. Find the consumption function

$$C(Y) = 6 + 0.8Y - e^{-0.2Y},$$

find the multiplier at income level
a) 2.   b) 15.

12.12 CALCULUS OF TWO INDEPENDENT VARIABLES

All of our work in differential calculus thus far has involved functions having one independent variable. Thus, for example, if a producer makes only the product antifreeze, the cost of producing x gallons of antifreeze is $C(x)$, a function of the single variable x. However, if the producer makes two products, x gallons of antifreeze and y gallons of windshield cleaner, production cost is a function of both x and y, which we symbolize as

$$C(x, y),$$

and C is now a function of two independent variables. Clearly, the function concept can be extended to more than two independent variables and we refer to calculus of two or more independent variables as *multivariate* calculus. This subject area is too extensive to treat in any detail in this book, but we can learn some of its important aspects and applications by considering the case of two independent variables.

Consider the function

$$f(x, y) = 3x^2 - 2xy - 8y + y^2 + 44.$$

A pair of numbers, one for x and the other for y, yield a value for $f(x, y)$. Thus, at $x = 1$, $y = 2$, we find

$$f(1, 2) = 3(1)^2 - 2(1)(2) - 8(2) + (2)^2 + 44 = 31.$$

Exercise.   Find $f(2, 6)$ for the preceding function. Answer: 20.

If we treat y in $f(x, y)$ as a constant and take the derivative of $f(x, y)$ with respect to x, the procedure is called taking the *partial derivative* with respect to x or, more briefly, the partial with respect to x. Among the symbols used to designate this procedure are

$$f_x; \quad \frac{\partial f(x, y)}{\partial x}; \quad \frac{\partial f}{\partial x}$$

where ∂ is called a "round delta." Actually, the large and small Greek deltas are Δ and δ; ∂ is really not a letter but is a symbol devised to represent taking a partial derivative. For

$$f(x, y) = 3x^2 - 2xy - 8y + y^2 + 44$$
$$f_x = 6x - 2y;$$

that is, if y is treated as a constant then in the second term, $-2xy$, $-2y$ is constant and the derivative of $(-2y)x$ with respect to x is the constant, $-2y$. Similarly, the derivatives with respect to x of $-8y$, y^2, and 44 are all zero. In round delta notation we would write

$$\frac{\partial}{\partial x} f(x, y) = \frac{\partial}{\partial x} (3x^2 - 2xy - 8y + y^2 + 44)$$
$$= 6x - 2y.$$

Next we find f_y, the partial of f with respect to y. This means to take the derivative of $f(x, y)$ treating x as a constant. We find

$$f_y = -2x - 8 + 2y.$$

The *second partial of $f(x, y)$ taken twice with respect to x* is symbolized as

$$f_{xx}; \quad \frac{\partial^2 f(x, y)}{\partial x^2}; \quad \frac{\partial^2 f}{\partial x^2},$$

and it means to take the partial with respect to x, then take the partial of this result again with respect to x. For our example,

$$f_x = 6x - 2y,$$

so

$$f_{xx} = 6.$$

In round delta notation, we would write

$$\frac{\partial^2 f}{\partial x^2} = \frac{\partial}{\partial x}\left(\frac{\partial f}{\partial x}\right) = \frac{\partial}{\partial x}(6x - 2y) = 6.$$

Similarly, we have

$$f_y = -2x - 8 + 2y$$
$$f_{yy} = 2.$$

Finally we may take the partial with respect to x,

$$f_x = 6x - 2y,$$

then take the partial of f_x *with respect to y.* This is symbolized as

$$f_{xy} \quad \text{or} \quad \frac{\partial f}{\partial y \partial x}$$

and is called the second partial of $f(x, y)$, first with respect to x, then with respect to y or simply the mixed partial with respect to x, then y. Thus, with $f_x = 6x - 2y$,

$$f_{xy} = -2.$$

For all functions in this book, we can obtain the same result by finding the mixed partial with respect to y, then x,

$$f_{yx} \quad \text{or} \quad \frac{\partial f}{\partial x \partial y};$$

that is, find the partial of $f(x, y)$ first with respect to y, then take the partial of the result with respect to x. In our example,

$$f_y = -2x - 8 + 2y$$
$$f_{yx} = -2,$$

which is the same as f_{xy}. The equality of f_{xy} and f_{yx} is true wherever these derivatives are continuous, and will be true for all functions we shall deal with.

Exercise. $f(x, y) = 2x + 3y + x^2y + 2xy^3 - 20$. Find: a) f_x. b) f_y. c) f_{xx}. d) f_{yy}. e) f_{xy}. f) f_{yx}.   Answer: a) $2 + 2xy + 2y^3$. b) $3 + x^2 + 6xy^2$. c) $2y$. d) $12xy$. e) $2x + 6y^2$. f) $2x + 6y^2$.

Partial derivatives, like derivatives of a function of one variable, can be interpreted as slopes or rates of change. For example, if the cost in dollars of making x gallons of antifreeze and y gallons of windshield cleaner is

$$C(x, y) = 3x + 2y + 10,$$

then

$$C_x = 3 \quad \text{and} \quad C_y = 2.$$

We can say that if production of windshield cleaner is held constant, cost increases at the rate of $C_x = 3$ dollars for each additional gallon of antifreeze made, whereas if production of antifreeze is held constant, cost increases at the rate of $C_y = 2$ dollars for each additional gallon of windshield cleaner made.

If, unlike the example just given, the partials are not constant, then the rate interpretation is made at a point; that is, a pair of values, (x, y).

Example. Total profit in dollars when x tons of oats and y tons of hay are produced and sold is given by

$$P(x, y) = 100x - x^2 - 2xy + 200y - 3y^2.$$

Find $P(15, 20)$, $P_x(15, 20)$, and $P_y(15, 20)$. Interpret the partials in rate terminology.

First we find

$$P(15, 20) = 100(15) - (15)^2 - 2(15)(20) + 200(20) - 3(20)^2 = \$3,475.$$

Next,

$$P_x(x, y) = 100 - 2x - 2y$$
$$P_x(15, 20) = 100 - 2(15) - 2(20) = 30.$$

Thus, with hay production held constant (at $y = 20$), profit is increasing at the rate of \$30 per additional ton of oats produced and sold. Similarly

$$P_y(x, y) = -2x + 200 - 6y$$
$$P_y(15, 20) = -2(15) + 200 - 6(20) = 50$$

and with production of oats constant (at $x = 15$), profit is increasing at the rate of 50 dollars per additional ton of hay produced and sold.

Note in the preceding example that profit at the point where $x = 15$, $y = 20$, is $P(15, 20) = \$3,475$, and both partials indicate that profit can be increased by making and selling additional amounts of oats and hay. This suggests that production should be increased and raises the question of whether profit increases indefinitely or reaches a local maximum at some combination of outputs of oats and hay. We shall answer this question after the next set of problems.

Exercise. For the profit function of the last example, find:
a) $P(26, 27)$. b) $P_x(26, 27)$. c) $P_y(26, 27)$. d) Interpret the answer to parts (b) and (c). Answer: a) \$3,733. b) $P_x = -6$. c) $P_y = -14$. d) At 26 units of oats and 27 units of hay, profit is *decreasing* at the rate of \$6 per additional unit of oats and 14 dollars per additional unit of hay.

12.13 PROBLEM SET 12–5

For the following find: a) f_x. b) f_{xx}. c) f_y. d) f_{yy}. e) f_{xy}.

1. $f(x, y) = 3x - 2y + 6$.
2. $f(x, y) = 2x + 5y - 10$.
3. $f(x, y) = x^2 + y^2 + 3x - 2y - 9$.

4. $f(x, y) = x^2 - y^2 - 5x + 4y + 7$.
5. $f(x, y) = 3x^2 - 2xy + y^2 + 4$.
6. $f(x, y) = 2x^3 + 3xy + 4y - 6$.

12.13 PROBLEM SET 12–5 *(concluded)*

7. $f(x, y) = x^{1/2}y^{1/2}$.

8. $f(x, y) = x^{2/3}y^{1/3}$.

9. $f(x, y) = 2xy^{1/2} - 3x^{1/3}y$.

10. $f(x, y) = x^{3/2}y^2$.

11. $f(x, y) = xye^x$.

12. $f(x, y) = xy \ln y$.

13. $f(x, y) = \dfrac{x - y}{x + y}$.

14. $f(x, y) = \dfrac{x + y}{x - y}$.

15. $f(x, y) = \ln(3x + 2y)$.

16. $f(x, y) = e^{2x + 3y}$.

Perform the following:

17. $\dfrac{\partial}{\partial z}(3z^2 - 2xz)$.

18. $\dfrac{\partial}{\partial w}(w^2 - 3z^2w)$.

19. $\dfrac{\partial^2}{\partial w^2}(w^3 - 3z^2w)$.

20. $\dfrac{\partial^2}{\partial z^2}(3z^2 - 2xz)$.

21. $\dfrac{\partial^2}{\partial w \partial z}(w^3 - 3zw)$.

22. $\dfrac{\partial^2}{\partial z \partial x}(z^3 + 3xz)$.

---

23. If $f(x, y) = 3x + 2y$, find:
    a) $f(1, 2)$.
    b) $f_x(1, 2)$.
    c) $f_{xx}(1, 2)$.
    d) $f_y(1, 2)$.
    e) $f_{yy}(1, 2)$.
    f) $f_{xy}(1, 2)$.

24. If $f(x, y) = 2x + 3y - 6$, find:
    a) $f(2, 3)$.
    b) $f_x(2, 3)$.
    c) $f_{xx}(2, 3)$.
    d) $f_y(2, 3)$.
    e) $f_{yy}(2, 3)$.
    f) $f_{xy}(2, 3)$.

25. If $f(x, y) = x^2 + xy - 3y^2 + 5$, compute:
    a) $f(2, 1)$.
    b) $f_x(2, 1)$.
    c) $f_{xx}(2, 1)$.
    d) $f_y(2, 1)$.
    e) $f_{yy}(2, 1)$.
    f) $f_{xy}(2, 1)$.

26. If $f(x, y) = 2x^2 - 5xy + y^2 - 6$, compute:
    a) $f(3, 2)$.
    b) $f_x(3, 2)$.
    c) $f_{xx}(3, 2)$.
    d) $f_y(3, 2)$.
    e) $f_{yy}(3, 2)$.
    f) $f_{xy}(3, 2)$.

27. During a period of operation a producer makes and sells x tons of oats and y tons of hay at a cost in dollars of

$$C(x, y) = 3x^2 - 2xy + y^2 - 12x - 4y + 61$$

Find $C_x(3, 5)$ and $C_y(3, 5)$ and interpret these numbers in rate terminology.

28. (See the cost function in Problem 27.) Find $C_x(3, 7)$ and $C_y(3, 7)$ and interpret these numbers in rate terminology.

29. A producer makes and sells x tons of oats and y tons of hay during a period of operation. Profit in dollars is

$$P(x, y) = 50x - 0.05x^2 + 110y - 0.10y^2$$

Compute each of the following and interpret the result in rate terminology.
    a) $P_x(400, 500)$.
    b) $P_y(400, 500)$.
    c) $P_x(600, 500)$.
    d) $P_y(400, 600)$.

30. The total output of an industry, V million dollars, is a function of L (expenditure for labor) and C (dollars of capital invested in the industry). Suppose

$$V(L, C) = 8L^{1/3}C^{2/3}.$$

Compute the following and interpret the result in rate terminology.
    a) $V_L(64, 27)$.
    b) $V_C(64, 27)$.

12.14 MAXIMA AND MINIMA: TWO INDEPENDENT VARIABLES

Reviewing the example of the last section, where $P(x, y)$ was the profit function for a producer who made and sold x tons of oats and y tons of hay,

$$P(x, y) = 100x - x^2 - 2xy + 200y - 3y^2, \qquad (1)$$

we found

$$P_x = 100 - 2x - 2y \quad \text{and} \quad P_y = -2x + 200 - 6y.$$

At $x = 15$, $y = 20$

$$P_x(15, 20) = 30 \quad \text{and} \quad P_y(15, 20) = 50,$$

so profit is increasing per additional unit of oats if production of hay is constant, and profit also is increasing per additional unit of hay if oats production is held constant. However, the opposite (profit rates decreasing) occurs when $x = 26$ and $y = 27$ because

$$P_x(26, 27) = -6 \quad \text{and} \quad P_y(26, 27) = -14$$

are both negative. The change from increasing to decreasing rates suggest that a maximum profit exists. If such is the case at some pair of values (x, y), then for this pair of values profit must be neither increasing nor decreasing, so *both* P_x and P_y must be zero. This is similar to the one-variable case condition that the first derivative must be zero at a local optimum point, except that with two independent variables, both first partial derivatives must be zero.

Condition: Both first partial derivatives must be zero at a local optimum point.

It may at first be hard to visualize what the maximum of a function of two independent variables looks like. Since $P(x, y)$ has two independent variables, x and y, then $z = P(x, y)$ is a third, dependent, variable in (1), which we can now rewrite as

$$z = 100x - x^2 - 2xy + 200y - 3y^2.$$

In this form, it is easy to realize that the graph of $P(x, y)$ must be drawn in three-dimensional space. We will not discuss graphing in three dimensions since it is very technical and sometimes very complex, but a few generic graphs are included in this section to help you see how maxima and minima appear in three dimensions.

For example, a minimum might appear as shown in Figure 12–7, where we see a local minimum at $z = P(0, 0)$. On the other hand, a maximum might appear, as shown in Figure 12–8. Here, there is a local maximum at the point (x_0, y_0, z_0) and the value of this maximum is $P(x_0, y_0) = z_0$.

Now that we can visualize optima in three dimensions, how do we locate these optima? Our condition stated earlier in this section required

FIGURE 12–7

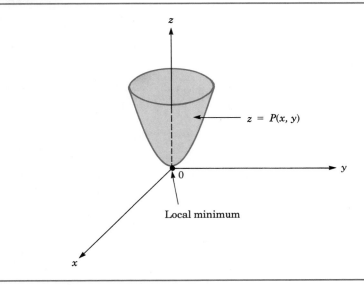

$z = P(x, y)$

0

Local minimum

FIGURE 12–8

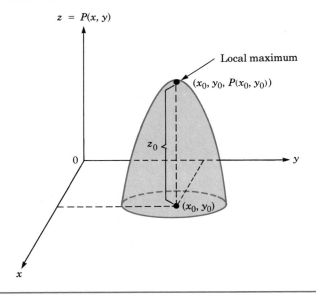

$z = P(x, y)$

Local maximum

$(x_0, y_0, P(x_0, y_0))$

z_0

0

(x_0, y_0)

that both first partial derivatives must be zero at a local optimum point. Consequently, in seeking to maximize the profit function $P(x, y)$ at hand, we set $P_x = 0$ and $P_y = 0$ to give equations e_1 and e_2:

$$e_1: \quad 100 - 2x - 2y = 0$$
$$e_2: \quad 200 - 2x - 6y = 0.$$

These equations are now solved simultaneously. The simplest procedure is to rewrite them and subtract, as follows:

$$
\begin{array}{rl}
e_1: & 2x + 2y = 100 \\
e_2: & 2x + 6y = 200 \\
\hline
e_1 - e_2: & -4y = -100
\end{array}
$$

so that

$$y = 25.$$

Substituting $y = 25$ into e_1, we find

$$
\begin{aligned}
2x + 2(25) &= 100 \\
2x &= 50 \\
x &= 25,
\end{aligned}
$$

and so $x = 25$, $y = 25$ marks a stationary point that may (or may not) be a local optimum point. In any event,

$$
\begin{aligned}
P(25, 25) &= 100(25) - (25)^2 - 2(25)(25) + 200(25) - 3(25)^2 \\
&= \$3,750.
\end{aligned}
$$

To determine whether we have a local optimum point and, if so, whether it is a maximum or minimum, we use a test that, as might be anticipated, involves the second partial derivatives. We shall not develop the source of this test because to do so would carry us too far afield.

Test for Local Optima Points: Two Independent Variables

1. Find f_x and f_y, set both equal to zero, and solve the resultant equations simultaneously to obtain the candidate values x^* and y^*.
2. Compute $f_{xx}(x^*, y^*)$, $f_{yy}(x^*, y^*)$, and $f_{xy}(x^*, y^*)$.
3. Set $A = f_{xx}(x^*, y^*)$

$$
\begin{aligned}
B &= f_{xy}(x^*, y^*) \\
C &= f_{yy}(x^*, y^*)
\end{aligned}
$$

and

$$D = B^2 - AC.$$

D is called the *discriminant* of f.

4. If $D < 0$:
$$\begin{cases} \text{if } A \text{ or } C \text{ is negative, there is a local maximum} \\ \text{at } (x^*, y^*). \\ \text{if } A \text{ or } C \text{ is positive, there is a local minimum} \\ \text{at } (x^*, y^*).^1 \end{cases}$$

If $D > 0$: there is a saddle point (neither a maximum nor a minimum) at (x^*, y^*).

If $D = 0$: The test fails.

In the example at hand, with $x = 25$, $y = 25$,

$$P_x = 100 - 2x - 2y, \quad \text{so} \quad P_{xx} = -2$$
$$P_y = -2 + 200 - 6y, \quad \text{so} \quad P_{yy} = -6$$
$$P_{xy} = -2.$$

Hence, step (3) in the above test provides

$$A = -2, \quad B = -2, \quad C = -6$$
$$D = B^2 - AC = (-2)^2 - (-2)(-6) = -8.$$

So in step (4), we have $D < 0$. Since both A and C are negative, this proves we have a maximum, and

$$\text{Maximum profit} = P_{\max} = P(25, 25) = \$3{,}750,$$

as previously computed. The producer should produce and sell 25 tons of oats and 25 tons of hay to achieve this maximum profit.

Exercise.   a) Find the candidate optimum point for

$$f(x, y) = 3x^2 - 2xy + y^2 - 12x - 4y + 61.$$

b) Evaluate the function at this point. c) Show by test whether (b) is a local maximum or minimum. Answer: a) $x = 4$, $y = 6$. b) $f(4, 6) = 25$. c) $D = -8$, $f_{xx} = 6$, $f_{yy} = 2$. Local minimum.

If D, in the above test for optimum points, is positive we have a point that is the three-dimensional version of an inflection point. Such points are called *saddle points* and are neither maxima nor minima. Figure 12–9 is a clear demonstration of why such points are called saddle points.

---

[1] It can be shown that when D is negative, A and C are either *both negative* or *both positive*, so that we need only test one of the two to determine whether the candidate point is a local maximum or local minimum.

FIGURE 12–9

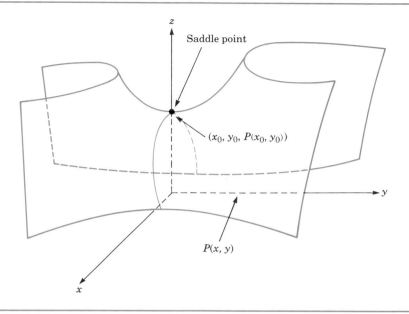

However, if D equals zero, the test fails and the point in question may not be a local optimum point. Situations where D is zero will not occur for the functions we shall deal with, but in passing we note that when D is zero it is possible to determine whether or not an optimum point occurs at (x, y). We do this by moving to nearby points, which we may symbolize as $[(x + h), (y + k)]$, where h and k are arbitrary small numbers. We then determine, either algebraically or by computation, whether the function values at the nearby points are greater than (less than) $f(x, y)$, thus making $f(x, y)$ a local minimum (maximum).

Example. Find the value of the function

$$f(x, y) = x^3 + x^2 + y^2 - xy + 8$$

at its extreme and saddle point(s), if any exist. State whether each point is a local maximum, a local minimum, or a saddle point.

Since $f(x, y) = x^3 + x^2 + y^2 - xy + 8$, we have the partial derivatives

$$f_x = 3x^2 + 2x - y$$
$$f_y = 2y - x$$
$$f_{xx} = 6x + 2$$
$$f_{xy} = -1$$
$$f_{yy} = 2.$$

Setting $f_x = f_y = 0$, we get

$$e_1: \quad 3x^2 + 2x - y = 0$$
$$e_2: \quad 2y - x = 0.$$

To solve this system, we multiply e_1 by 2 and add the result to e_2, so

$$2e_1: \quad 6x^2 + 4x - 2y = 0$$
$$e_2: \qquad \quad - x + 2y = 0$$
$$\overline{2e_1 + e_2: \quad 6x^2 + 3x \qquad \quad = 0.}$$

Hence,

$$x(6x + 3) = 0$$

so that

$$x = 0, -\tfrac{1}{2}.$$

Substituting these values back into e_2, we find

$$y = 0 \quad \text{and} \quad y = -\tfrac{1}{4},$$

respectively. Thus, in this case we have two points that are possible optima:

$$(0, 0) \quad \text{and} \quad (-\tfrac{1}{2}, -\tfrac{1}{4}).$$

Beginning with $(0, 0)$,

$$A = f_{xx}(0, 0) = 2; \quad B = f_{xy}(0, 0) = -1; \quad C = f_{yy}(0, 0) = 2$$

so that

$$D = B^2 - AC = (-1)^2 - (2)(2) = -3 < 0.$$

Since A (and C) > 0, then $f(x, y)$ has a local minimum at $(0, 0)$, and the value of this minimum is

$$f(0, 0) = 8.$$

Now consider the point $(-\tfrac{1}{2}, -\tfrac{1}{4})$. Here

$$A = f_{xx}(-\tfrac{1}{2}, -\tfrac{1}{4}) = 6(-\tfrac{1}{2}) + 2 = -1;$$
$$B = f_{xy}(-\tfrac{1}{2}, -\tfrac{1}{4}) = -1;$$
$$C = f_{yy}(-\tfrac{1}{2}, -\tfrac{1}{4}) = 2;$$

so that

$$D = B^2 - AC = (-1)^2 - (-1)(2) = 3 > 0.$$

We conclude that $f(x, y)$ has a saddle point at $(-\tfrac{1}{2}, -\tfrac{1}{4})$ and the value of $f(x, y)$ at this saddle point is

$$f(-\tfrac{1}{2}, -\tfrac{1}{4}) = (-\tfrac{1}{2})^3 + (-\tfrac{1}{2})^2 + (-\tfrac{1}{4})^2 - (-\tfrac{1}{2})(-\tfrac{1}{4}) + 8$$
$$= 8\tfrac{1}{16}.$$

Example. A rectangular box with a volume of 16 cubic feet is to be manufactured from three different types of cardboard. The cost of the cardboard for the top and bottom is nine cents per square foot, the cost of the cardboard for the front and back is eight cents per square foot, and the cost of the cardboard for the other two sides is six cents per square foot. Find the dimensions of the box for which the cost of the materials is a minimum.

First we need to isolate an objective. In this problem, we see that we wish to minimize cost C for the box shown in Figure 12–10.

The cost function is then

$$\begin{aligned} C &= (2)(6)\, lh \,+\, (2)(8)\, wh \,+\, (2)(9)\, lw \\ &= 12lh \,+\, 16wh \,+\, 18lw. \end{aligned} \qquad (2)$$

We know that the box must have a volume of 16 cubic feet, so

$$16 = lwh.$$

We can solve this equation for any one of the three variables l, w, and h in terms of the other two. Solving for h, we have

$$h = \frac{16}{lw}.$$

Substituting this into (2), we obtain

$$C(l, w) = 12l\left(\frac{16}{lw}\right) + 16w\left(\frac{16}{lw}\right) + 18\, lw$$

FIGURE 12–10

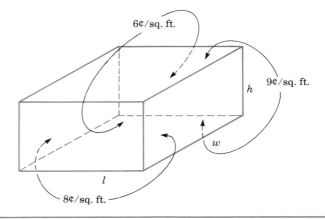

6¢/sq. ft.

9¢/sq. ft.

h

w

l

8¢/sq. ft.

or

$$C(l, w) = \frac{(12)(16)}{w} + \frac{(16)^2}{l} + 18\,lw.$$

We can now test this function for optima as usual by starting with the first partial derivatives,

$$C_l = -\frac{(16)^2}{l^2} + 18w$$

$$C_w = -\frac{(12)(16)}{w^2} + 18l,$$

and setting them equal to zero:

$$C_l = 0 \quad \text{when} \quad \frac{(16)^2}{l^2} = 18w, \quad \text{or } l^2 = \frac{(16)^2}{18w}$$

$$C_w = 0 \quad \text{when} \quad \frac{(12)(16)}{w^2} = 18l, \quad \text{or } l = \frac{(12)(16)}{18w^2}.$$

For both of these to be true, we must have

$$\left(\frac{(12)(16)}{18w^2}\right)^2 = \frac{(16)^2}{18w}$$

or

$$\left(\frac{(12)(16)}{18}\right)^2 \cdot \frac{18}{(16)^2} = w^3$$

or

$$\frac{(12)^2}{18} = w^3$$

$$8 = w^3$$

$$w = 2 \text{ feet.}$$

Substituting back into the equation for $C_w = 0$, we have

$$l = \frac{(12)(16)}{18(2)^2} = \frac{8}{3} \text{ feet}$$

and hence the candidate optimum point

$$(8/3, 2).$$

Computing the second partials, we obtain

$$C_{ll} = \frac{(16)^2 \cdot 2}{l^3}$$

$$C_{lw} = 18$$

$$C_{ww} = \frac{(12)(16)(2)}{w^3},$$

so

$$A = \frac{(16)^2(2)}{(8/3)^3} = 27; \quad B = 18; \quad C = \frac{(12)(16)(2)}{(2)^3} = 48$$

and

$$D = B^2 - AC = (18)^2 - (27)(43) = -972 < 0.$$

Since $D < 0$ and $A > 0$, we have a minimum cost when

$$l = 8/3 \text{ feet}, \quad w = 2 \text{ feet}, \quad \text{and} \quad h = \frac{16}{2 \cdot 8/3} = 3 \text{ feet}.$$

The value of the minimum cost is

$$C(8/3, 2) = \frac{(12)(16)}{2} + \frac{(16)^2}{(8/3)} + 18(2)(8/3) = \$288.$$

Example. To meet customer demand for a product, the producer makes a batch, or *lot*, of L units of the product periodically. The producer's strategy is to establish the period of time between lot productions so that a new lot is not made until some time after current inventory has been exhausted. Thus, there is an out-of-stock or stock-out interval. During this interval, orders received from customers are placed in "back-order" status and are filled immediately when a new lot is made. Thus, the producer makes L units, uses some to fill back-orders, and places the remainder, I units, in inventory. Taking into account various costs, including a cost associated with being out of stock, the producer has developed the following cost-function model.

$$C(L, I) = \frac{1,350,000}{L} + \frac{20I^2}{L} + 15L - 30I.$$

What values of L and I will minimize this cost function?

We proceed by taking the first partial derivatives:

$$C_L = -\frac{1,350,000}{L^2} - 20\frac{I^2}{L^2} + 15$$

$$C_I = \frac{40I}{L} - 30.$$

If there is an optimum point, the first partials must equal zero. Hence,

$$-\frac{1,350,000}{L^2} - 20\frac{I^2}{L^2} + 15 = 0 \tag{3}$$

$$\frac{40I}{L} - 30 = 0. \tag{4}$$

The common solution of the pair of equations can be found by solving

(4) for I in terms of L and substituting this into (3). Thus, from (4)

$$\frac{40I}{L} - 30 = 0$$

$$40I - 30L = 0$$

$$40I = 30L$$

$$I = \frac{30L}{40} = 0.75L. \tag{5}$$

Substituting (5) into (3), we have

$$-\frac{1,350,000}{L^2} - \frac{20(0.75L)^2}{L^2} + 15 = 0$$

$$-\frac{1,350,000}{L^2} - \frac{20(0.75)^2L^2}{L^2} + 15 = 0$$

$$-\frac{1,350,000}{L^2} - 11.25 + 15 = 0$$

$$3.75 = \frac{1,350,000}{L^2}$$

$$3.75L^2 = 1,350,000$$

$$L^2 = \frac{1,350,000}{3.75}$$

$$L^2 = 360,000$$

$$L = 600 \text{ units.}$$

With $L = 600$, we find from (5) that

$$I = 0.75L$$
$$= 0.75(600)$$
$$I = 450 \text{ units.}$$

To prove the values found do minimize cost, $C(L, I)$, we find

$$C_{LL} = \frac{2(1,350,000)}{L^3} + 40\frac{I^2}{L^3}$$

$$C_{LL}(600, 450) = \frac{2(1,350,000)}{(600)^3} + \frac{40(450)^2}{(600)^3} = 0.05.$$

$$C_{II} = \frac{40}{L} \quad \text{and} \quad C_{II}(600, 450) = \frac{40}{600} = 0.06667.$$

$$C_{LI} = -\frac{40I}{L^2} \quad \text{and} \quad C_{LI}(600, 450) = -\frac{40(450)}{(600)^2} = -0.05.$$

Both C_{LL} and C_{II} are positive and

$$D = (C_{LI})^2 - (C_{LL})(C_{II}) = (-0.05)^2 - (0.05)(0.06667) = -0.0008,$$

which is less than zero, so we have a minimum at

$$C(600, 450) = \frac{1{,}350{,}000}{600} + \frac{20(450)^2}{600} + 15(600) - 30(450) = \$4{,}500.$$

Hence, the producer should make $L = 600$ units in each lot and place $I = 450$ units in inventory. This means that the remaining 150 units are used to fill back orders. The advantage the producer achieves by his out-of-stock strategy arises from the cost saving achieved by not having to carry these 150 units in inventory.

The last example serves not only to illustrate a current application of multivariate calculus but also to bring out the point that the set of simultaneous equations encountered when first partials are set equal to zero may be very difficult to solve. The task was relatively easy in our example because we had only two variables and a relatively simple cost function. Typically, when the function is more complicated and there are more than two variables, solutions of the set of simultaneous equations are approximated by specially prepared computer programs that also deal with the situation, earlier mentioned, where $D = 0$. Procedure for approximating solutions are treated in texts on *numerical analysis*.

12.15 PROBLEM SET 12–6

Find the value of the function at its optimum and saddle points, if any exist. State whether each point is a local maximum, a local minimum, or a saddle point.

1. $f(x, y) = 2x^2 + 3y^2 + 10.$

2. $f(x, y) = 4x + 6y - x^2 - y^2 + 10.$

3. $f(x, y) = 10xy - 5x^2 - 6y^2 + 20x.$

4. $f(x, y) = 3x^2 + y^2 - 2xy - 12y + 104.$

5. $f(x, y) = x + y + 9/x + 4/y$ (x and y positive).

6. $f(x, y) = 4xy + 8x + 20y - 4x^2 - 4y^2.$

7. $f(x, y) = xy - x - 2y + 2.$

8. $f(x, y) = 2x^2 - 3y^2.$

9. $f(x, y) = 3xy - 3x^2 - y^2 + 6x + 10y + 3.$

10. $f(x, y) = x^2 + 3y^2 - 4xy + 8x - 6y + 5.$

11. $f(x, y) = 10e^{-x^2} - y^2.$

12. $f(x, y) = 3x^2 - 5e^{-y^2}.$

13. Profit in dollars earned by making and selling x gallons of molasses and y gallons of maple syrup is

$$P(x, y) = 50x - 0.05x^2 + 110y - 0.10y^2$$

a) What number of units of each product will maximize profit?

b) Prove (a) is a maximum.

c) Compute the maximum profit.

14. One unit of product can be made by using Machine A for x hours and Machine B for y hours. The cost in dollars of making one unit is

$$C(x, y) = 3x^2 - 2xy + y^2 - 12x - 4y + 50$$

a) What numbers of hours on each machine

12.15 PROBLEM SET 12–6 (concluded)

will minimize the cost of making one unit?

b) Prove (a) is a minimum.

c) Compute the minimum cost.

15. Assume a store's profit is dependent on the number of salespersons, s, and the amount of inventory, i (in hundreds of dollars). If the profit is given by

$$P(s, i) = 1400 - (12 - s)^2 - (40 - i)^2,$$

then what values of s and i will maximize profit? Find the maximum profit.

16. A sporting goods store sells two kinds of lacrosse sticks, which are similar but are made by different manufacturers. The cost to the store of the first kind is $40, and the cost to the store of the second kind is $50. Experience has shown that if the selling price of the first kind is x dollars and the selling price of the second kind is y dollars, then the number sold monthly of the first kind is

$$3200 - 50x + 25y,$$

and the number sold monthly of the second kind is

$$25x - 30y.$$

What should be the selling price of each kind of lacrosse stick for the greatest gross profit?

17. The inventory cost model discussed in the example near the end of the last section is to be applied to another product, and the

cost function is

$$C(L, I) = \frac{750,000}{L} + \frac{20I^2}{L} + \frac{25L}{2} - 25I,$$

where L is the number of units to be made in each lot and I is the number to be placed in inventory each time a lot is made. The remaining part of the lot is used to fill back orders.

a) Find the values of L and I that minimize $C(L, I)$.

b) Compute the minimum cost.

18. Another company follows the strategy of the company in Problem 17, but uses the cost model

$$C(L, p) = \frac{108,160}{L} + \frac{Lp^2}{2} + 2L(1 - p)^2,$$

where $C(L, p)$ is in thousands of dollars, L is the lot size, and p is the *proportion* of a lot which is to be placed in inventory.

a) Find the values of L and p that minimize $C(L, p)$.

b) Prove (a) is a minimum.

c) Compute the minimum cost.

19. (This problem is somewhat difficult, algebraically.) The cost model in Problem 17 is a special case of the general model

$$C(L, I) = \frac{cd}{L} + \frac{(a + b)I^2}{2L} + \frac{bL}{2} - bI,$$

where a, b, c, and d are parameters. Find the expressions for L and I that minimize cost in terms of these parameters.

12.16 LEAST– SQUARES CURVE FITTING

Suppose that we have selected a sample of $n = 3$ people and found from them that their weekly incomes, in hundreds of dollars, are

$$x_1 = 3, \quad x_2 = 5, \quad x_3 = 10$$

where the subscripts refer, respectively, to the first, second, and third persons. The *average* of this sample of $n = 3$, designated by $\bar{x}$ (read as "x bar"), is

$$\bar{x} = \frac{3 + 5 + 10}{3} = \frac{18}{3} = 6.$$

This is

$$\bar{x} = \frac{x_1 + x_2 + x_3}{3}$$

or, in summation symbols (see Section 4.24),

$$\bar{x} = \frac{\sum\limits_{i=1}^{n} x_i}{n}, \text{ with } n = 3.$$

Next, we show the three numbers in our sample as points on a line segment, Figure 12–11. We have placed an arbitrary point, a, on this line.

FIGURE 12–11

Now we express the distance between each of the sample numbers and a as

$$a - 3, \quad a - 5, \quad \text{and} \quad a - 10.$$

These distances we call the *deviations* of the sample numbers from the point a. We wish to find the value of a that will minimize the sum of the squares of the deviations. This sum is

$$S = (a - 3)^2 + (a - 5)^2 + (a - 10)^2.$$

Taking the derivative with respect to a, we find

$$\frac{dS}{da} = 2(a - 3) + 2(a - 5) + 2(a - 10),$$

and

$$\frac{dS}{da} = 0 \quad \text{when} \quad 2(a - 3) + 2(a - 5) + 2(a - 10) = 0$$

$$a - 3 + a - 5 + a - 10 = 0$$
$$3a = 3 + 5 + 10$$
$$a = \frac{3 + 5 + 10}{3} = 6$$
$$a = \bar{x}.$$

The second derivative is 6 which is positive, so we have a minimum and have proved that a must be the average of the x's. That is, the sum of the squares of the deviations of this group of numbers from their average, $\bar{x}$, is less than the sum of the squares of the deviations from any other number.

We now show that this result is true for any set of n numbers $\{x_i\}$. The expression for the sum of squares of the deviations of the x_i from a number a is

$$S = \sum_{i=1}^{n} (a - x_i)^2.$$

Taking the derivative, we write

$$\frac{dS}{da} = \frac{d}{da} \sum_{i=1}^{n} (a - x_i)^2,$$

but the derivative of a sum is the sum of the derivatives, so we may place d/da inside the Σ symbol, thus:

$$\frac{dS}{da} = \sum_{i=1}^{n} \frac{d}{da} (a - x_i)^2$$

$$= \sum_{i=1}^{n} [2(a - x_i)]$$

$$= \sum_{i=1}^{n} (2a - 2x_i)$$

$$= \sum_{i=1}^{n} 2a - \sum_{i=1}^{n} 2x_i.$$

Now the sum of a constant with respect to i as i goes from 1 to n is n times the constant, and $2a$ is a constant, so

$$\frac{dS}{da} = n(2a) - 2 \sum_{i=1}^{n} x_i$$

$$\frac{dS}{da} = 0 \quad \text{where} \quad n(2a) - 2 \sum_{i=1}^{n} x_i = 0$$

$$n(2a) = 2 \sum_{i=1}^{n} x_i$$

$$a = 2 \frac{\sum_{i=1}^{n} x_i}{2n}$$

$$= \frac{\sum_{i=1}^{n} x_i}{n}$$

$$= \bar{x}.$$

The second derivative is

$$\frac{d}{da} \left[n(2a) - 2 \sum_{i=1}^{n} x_i \right] = 2n,$$

which is positive because n, the count of the numbers in a set, is positive.

Hence, we have a minimum, and we have proved that for any group of numbers, the sum of the squares of their deviations from their average is less than the sum of their squared deviations from any other number.

We now turn to the main objective of this section, which is to develop the procedure most generally used to fit mathematical models to actual observed data. This procedure is called *least-squares curve fitting*. In applications, the user determines by examination of the data, or from knowledge of applicable functions, the type of curve that is to be used. The unknown quantities are the constants or *parameters* that the selected curve function should have if it is to match actual observations as closely as possible. For example, if the choice of curve is a straight line, the functional form is

$$y(x) = mx + b,$$

and the problem is to take actual observed data and apply the least-squares method to them to get values for m and b so that the line with this slope and intercept fits the observed data more closely than any other line.

To see what is involved, suppose the observed data in Table 12–1 are x_i, the number of units made, and y_i, the corresponding cost of making the x_i units.

The (x_i, y_i) points, (1, 4), (2, 3), and so on, are plotted in Figure 12–12. Notice that the points scatter somewhat and do not all fall on one straight line. The figure is called, aptly, a scatter diagram. To begin with, a straight line has been drawn *freehand* to describe the tendency for cost to rise as output increases. We do not yet have an equation for this line and, clearly, freehand drawing by different people would lead to varying lines. To say which of all possible lines is the line that "best" fits the actual observed data, it is necessary to specify the criterion by which a line is to be judged to be the best-fitting line. In descriptive, but imprecise, terms, we want the line that comes *closest* to the points taken as a group. To make this more precise, look at Figure 12–12 and notice that for $x_i = 2$, the actual observed value, which is 3, has been labeled y_i. Now, denoting the as yet unknown value for y on the line when $x_i = 2$ as y_f (where y_f means the fitted value for y), the equation of the line is

$$y_f = mx_i + b,$$

TABLE 12–1

Number of Units Made x_i	Total Cost y_i
1	4
2	3
3	8
4	11
5	10

FIGURE 12–12

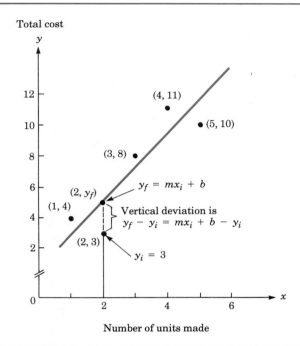

and the *vertical* deviation of the observed point from the line is the difference of the vertical coordinates; that is,

$$\text{Deviation} = y_f - y_i$$
$$= mx_i + b - y_i.$$

Moreover,

$$\text{Squared deviation} = (mx_i + b - y_i)^2.$$

The smaller this squared deviation, the closer is the line to the point, and the smaller the sum of the squared deviations for *all* observed points, the closer the line is to the group of points. Hence,

---

Least-Squares Best-Fitting Line Criterion

The line that best fits a set of observed points is the one whose slope and intercept, m *and* b, *are such that the sum of the squares of the vertical deviations of the points from the line is a minimum.*

If we write the sum of squares as

$$S(m, b) = \sum_{i=1}^{n} (mx_i + b - y_i)^2,$$ (1)

the problem then becomes that of finding the expressions for m and b that will minimize S. Consequently, m and b are independent variables. We must set the first partials with respect to m and to b equal to zero and solve the resultant pair of equations for m and b. We have

$$\frac{\partial S}{\partial m} = \sum_{i=1}^{n} \frac{\partial}{\partial m} (mx_i + b - y_i)^2$$

$$= \sum_{i=1}^{n} 2(mx_i + b - y_i)(x_i)$$

$$= 2 \sum_{i=1}^{n} (mx_i^2 + bx_i - x_iy_i).$$

Now, although m and b are variables in taking the derivative, i is the index (or variable) in the summations, so in these summations, m and b are treated as constants. Hence,

$$\frac{\partial S}{\partial m} = 2 \left[m \sum_{i=1}^{n} x_i^2 + b \sum_{i=1}^{n} x_i - \sum_{i=1}^{n} x_iy_i \right].$$ (2)

Taking the partial of (1) with respect to b yields

$$\frac{\partial S}{\partial b} = \frac{\partial}{\partial b} \sum (mx_i + b - y_i)^2$$

$$= \sum_{i=1}^{n} 2(mx_i + b - y_i)(1)$$

$$= 2 \left[m \sum_{i=1}^{n} x_i + \sum_{i=1}^{n} b - \sum_{i=1}^{n} y_i \right].$$

The middle term in the last expression is the summation of a constant with i going from 1 to n and equals nb. Hence,

$$\frac{\partial S}{\partial b} = 2 \left[m \sum_{i=1}^{n} x_i + nb - \sum_{i=1}^{n} y_i \right].$$ (3)

After setting (2) and (3) equal to zero and dividing both sides of each equation by 2, we have

$$e_1: \quad m \sum_{i=1}^{n} x_i^2 + b \sum_{i=1}^{n} x_i - \sum_{i=1}^{n} x_iy_i = 0$$

$$e_2: \quad m \sum_{i=1}^{n} x_i + nb \quad - \sum_{i=1}^{n} y_i = 0$$

which are to be solved. First we solve e_2 to get b in terms of m. Thus,

$$e_2: \quad m \sum_{i=1}^{n} x_i + nb - \sum_{i=1}^{n} y_i = 0$$

$$nb = \sum_{i=1}^{n} y_i - m \sum_{i=1}^{n} x_i$$

$$b = \frac{\sum_{i=1}^{n} y_i - m \sum_{i=1}^{n} x_i}{n}. \tag{4}$$

We now substitute (4) into e_1 and solve for m.

$$e_1: \quad m \sum_{i=1}^{n} x_i^2 + b \sum_{i=1}^{n} x_i - \sum_{i=1}^{n} x_i y_i = 0$$

$$m \sum_{i=1}^{n} x_i^2 + \left[\frac{\sum_{i=1}^{n} y_i - m \sum_{i=1}^{n} x_i}{n} \right] \sum_{i=1}^{n} x_i - \sum_{i=1}^{n} x_i y_i = 0.$$

Next, expanding the center term and multiplying both sides by n,

$$nm \sum_{i=1}^{n} x_i^2 + \sum_{i=1}^{n} x_i \sum_{i=1}^{n} y_i - m \left(\sum_{i=1}^{n} x_i \right)^2 - n \sum_{i=1}^{n} x_i y_i = 0$$

$$m \left[n \sum_{i=1}^{n} x_i^2 - \left(\sum_{i=1}^{n} x_i \right)^2 \right] + \sum_{i=1}^{n} x_i \sum_{i=1}^{n} y_i - n \sum_{i=1}^{n} x_i y_i = 0.$$

Placing the two terms at the right on the other side of the equation and then dividing both sides by the coefficient of m, we obtain

$$m = \frac{n \sum_{i=1}^{n} x_i y_i - \left(\sum_{i=1}^{n} x_i \right)\left(\sum_{i=1}^{n} y_i \right)}{n \sum_{i=1}^{n} x_i^2 - \left(\sum_{i=1}^{n} x_i \right)^2}. \tag{5}$$

Expression (5) tells us how to compute the slope of the best fitting line from the observed data. Having done this, we can then compute the intercept, b, from expression (4).

To compute m and b according to the formulas at the top of the next page, we need

n = Number of points
Σx_i = Sum of the x observations
Σy_i = Sum of the y observations
$\Sigma x_i y_i$ = Sum of the products: (x observation)(y observation)
$(\Sigma x_i)^2$ = Square of the sum of the x observations.

**Formulas for Slope and Intercept of the Best-Fitting
(Least-Squares) Straight Line**

(Note: The summations are over all n values of x_i and y_i.)

$$m = \frac{n\Sigma\, x_i y_i - (\Sigma x_i)(\Sigma y_i)}{n\Sigma \mathrm{x}_i^2 - (\Sigma x_i)^2}$$

$$b = \frac{\Sigma y_i - m\Sigma \mathrm{x}_i}{n}$$

We carry out the necessary calculation for the data of Table 12–1 in Table 12–2.

TABLE 12–2

x_i	y_i	$x_i y_i$	x_i^2
1	4	4	1
2	3	6	4
3	8	24	9
4	11	44	16
5	10	50	25
15	36	128	55
Σx_i	Σy_i	$\Sigma x_i y_i$	Σx_i^2

For the $n = 5$ points

$$m = \frac{5(128) - (15)(36)}{5(55) - (15)^2} = \frac{100}{50} = 2;$$

$$b = \frac{36 - 2(15)}{5} = \frac{6}{5} = 1.2;$$

$$y_f = 2x + 1.2.$$

Thus, the sum of the squares of the vertical deviations of the five points on Figure 12–12 is at the smallest possible value if the line has the equation

$$y_f = 2x + 1.2.$$

The line can be plotted using its intercept $(0, 1.2)$ and another point, say

$$x = 5, \quad y_f = 2(5) + 1.2 = 11.2.$$

or $(5, 11.2)$. This is, in fact, the line shown on Figure 12–12, so examination of that figure will show how closely the line fits the points.

Exercise.   Given the three observed points (1, 2); (2, 4); (3, 3), find:
a) Σx_i. b) Σy_i. c) $\Sigma x_i y_i$. d) Σx_i^2. e) $(\Sigma x_i)^2$. Now compute: f) m.
g) b. Then, h) Write the equation of the best fitting least-squares
straight line. Answer: a) 6. b) 9. c) 19. d) 14. e) 36. f) 0.5. g) 2. h) $y_f = 0.5x + 2$.

Least-squares methodology is widely used to fit functions of various
types to observed data. It is interesting to note that some relatively in-
expensive calculators have been designed so that the user need only enter the observed data values and press the appropriate keys to obtain the
slope and intercept of the best-fitting least-squares line. We should remark in passing that the methodology can be extended to fit functions
other than straight lines to observed data, and also to fit functions that
have more than one independent variable. These topics are treated in
statistics under the heading of *regression analysis*.

12.17 PROBLEM SET 12–7

For each of the following data sets, find m and b for the best-fitting least-squares line
and write the equation of the line. [Note: It is helpful in each case to plot the given
data and the fitted line to see graphically how well the line fits the data.]

1.

x_i	y_i
3	4
4	3
11	11

2.

x_i	y_i
7	12
2	10
3	11

3.

x_i	y_i
2	7
2	6
1	8
3	5

4.

x_i	y_i
1	8
1	9
4	1
2	7

5. The following data are values of x_i, hours
worked, and y_i, number of units produced.
Find and write the equation of the best-
fitting least-squares line.

x_i: 10 20 14 35 40 25 15 31 50 58 50 62
y_i: 25 40 30 45 50 45 35 47 52 54 55 56.

6. The following are data for 12 new different
model automobiles. (x_i = Automobile engine size in cubic inches, obtained from
stickers on the automobiles; y_i = Miles per
gallon for highway driving as provided by
the Environmental Protection Agency.)

x_i: 85 140 151 200 231 232 250 301 302 305 400 425
y_i: 28 26 26 21 18 20 18 15 16 16 13 11

Find and write the equation of the best-
fitting least-squares straight line.

12.18 REVIEW PROBLEMS

Find the first and second derivatives of each of the following functions:

1. $f(x) = 5e^{0.4x}$.

2. $f(x) = (1.09)^x$.

3. $f(x) = 4e^{0.5x - 5}$.

4. $f(x) = e^{-0.5x^2}$.

5. $f(x) = e^{2x - x^2}$.

6. $f(x) = (1/4)^x$.

Find local optimum values, if any exist, and state which type of value has been found:

7. $f(x) = e^{2x} - 10x + 4$.

8. $f(x) = e^{-0.1x} + 0.9x$.

9. $f(x) = xe^{-0.2x} + 3$.

10. $f(x) = 11 - x^2 - e^{x^2}$.

Sketch graphs of the functions in Problems 11 and 12. Show the starting point coordinates and the asymptote with its equation. Sketches need not be to scale, and the coordinate axes need not be shown.

11. $f(x) = 30 + 20e^{3 + 0.2x}$.

12. $f(x) = 30 - 20(0.5)^{x - 10}$.

13. The revenue from, and the cost of, operating an undertaking for t years are, respectively, in millions of dollars,

$$R(t) = 3e^{0.05t} \quad \text{and} \quad C(t) = 1.5e^{0.08t}.$$

a) How long should operations continue if profit is to be maximized?
b) Compute maximum profit.

14. The total potential audience for a promotional campaign is 10,000 customers. Revenue averages $3 per response to the campaign. Campaign costs are a fixed amount of $500, plus $300 per day the campaign continues. The proportion of the total audience responding by time t days is

$$1 - e^{-0.25t}.$$

a) How long should the campaign continue if profit is to be maximized?
b) Compute maximum profit.

15. The total potential audience for a promotional campaign is 2,000 customers. Revenue averages $5 per response to the campaign. Costs are $105.36 per day, plus a fixed cost of $100. The proportion of potential audience responding by time t days is

$$1 - (0.9)^t.$$

a) How long should the campaign continue if profit is to be maximized?
b) Compute maximum profit.

Find the derivatives of the following functions:

16. $f(x) = 2 \ln 3x$.

17. $f(x) = \ln(5x - 4)$.

18. $f(x) = \ln(1/2x^2)$.

19. $f(x) = \ln(x^3 + x^2 + x - 5)$.

20. $f(x) = \ln(2x + 3)^{1/2}$.

21. $f(x) = \ln(xe^x)$.

Find the value of $f(x)$ at its local optimum point, if any exists, and state whether this value is a local maximum or minimum.

22. $f(x) = 50 \ln x - x^2, x > 0$.

23. $f(x) = x^2 - 4x - 16 \ln x + 30, x > 0$.

12.18 REVIEW PROBLEMS (*continued*)

24. $f(x) = 100(\ln 0.5x)/x$, $x > 0$.

25. $f(x) = 0.5x^2 + 5x + 50 \ln x$, $x > 0$.

26. $f(x) = 3 \ln(2x^2 - 16x + 40)$.

By the chain rule, carry out each of the following:

27. $\dfrac{d}{dh} p(q)$.

28. $\dfrac{d}{dx} (3y^5)$.

29. $\dfrac{d}{dx} \ln(y^2 - 2y)$.

30. $\dfrac{d}{dx} (e^{y^2})$.

31. $\dfrac{d}{dx} (2y^{3/2} - x^2)$.

32. $\dfrac{d}{dy} (x^3 - 3y)$.

Find dy/dx by implicit differentiation.

33. $y^4 - x^2 = 0$.

34. $2y^3 - 3y^2 - x^3 + 2x^2 + 10 = 0$.

35. $e^y \ln x = x^2$.

36. $xy^3 = x^3 + 10$.

37. $y + e^y = x$.

38. $y = h(y) + x^2$.

---

39. At income level Y, consumption expenditures are $C(Y)$ billion dollars, where

$$C(Y) = 25 + 0.875Y.$$

   a) Find the marginal propensity to consume.
   b) Interpret (a).
   c) How much income is generated by an additional dollar of investment?
   d) At income level $500 billion, what proportion of total income is spent?

40. For the consumption function

$$C(Y) = 10 + 0.75Y - e^{-0.25Y}$$

   find the multiplier at income levels
   a) 1.   b) 4.

41. Find the expression for the multiplier if the consumption function is

$$C(Y) = a + bY.$$

42. Find the expression for the multiplier if the consumption function is

$$C(Y) = a + bY + e^{kY}.$$

43. If $P(x)$ is total profit when x gallons of homogenized milk are made and sold and

$$P(x) = 4x - 200,$$

compute $P'(500)$ and interpret the result in rate terminology.

44. A car rental agency rents a car for one day at a cost in dollars figured from

$$C(x) = 15 + 0.10x - 0.00005x^2,$$

where x is the number of miles the car is driven. Compute $C'(500)$ and interpret the result in rate terminology.

45. Five thousand dollars deposited in a bank account paying 7 percent interest compounded annually will grow to the amount

$$A(t) = 5000(1.07)^t$$

in t years. Compute $A'(20)$ and interpret the result in rate terminology.

46. (See Problem 45.) If interest is 7 percent compounded continuously,

$$A(t) = 5000e^{0.07t}.$$

12.18 REVIEW PROBLEMS (*continued*)

Compute $A'(20)$ and interpret the result in rate terminology.

47. The cost in dollars of making (printing and binding) x books is

$$C(x) = 2500 + 2.5x.$$

a) Write the expression for $a(x)$, the average cost per book if x books are made.
b) Compute $a'(100)$ and interpret the result in rate terminology.

48. The cost in dollars of producing x tons of a product is

$$C(x) = 0.0002x^3 - 0.06x^2 + 8x + 500$$

a) Write the expression for $a(x)$, the average cost per ton if x tons are produced.
b) Compute $a'(50)$ and interpret the result in rate terminology.

49. If $1,500 is deposited in a bank account paying 9 percent interest compounded annually, the amount in the account at time t years is

$$A(t) = 1500(1.09)^t.$$

Find the percent rate of change of $A(t)$ at time $t = 10$ years.

50. (See Problem 49.) If the account pays 9 percent compounded continuously, then

$$A(t) = 1500e^{0.09t}.$$

Find the percent rate of change of the amount in the account at $t = 10$ years.

51. The number of potential customers in a store's trading area t years from the time the store opens is

$$N(t) = \frac{200,000}{1 + 50e^{-0.1t}}.$$

Find the percent rate of change in number of potential customers at $t = 5$ years.

52. Find the percent rate of change in $f(t)$ at time $t = 7$ years, if

$$f(t) = 5t + 2te^{-0.4t}.$$

53. A cost function is minimized when its independent variable, y, has the optimal value

$$y = \frac{10}{k} + 2a,$$

where a and k are parameters.
a) What is the optimal value of y if $k = 5$ and $a = 10$?
b) How sensitive is y to changes in the parameter k? To answer this, write the expression for the rate at which y changes per unit change in k.
c) Using the expression in (b) and the numbers from (a), estimate by how much the optimal value of y would change if k changes from 5 to 5.5.

54. a) Find $f'(0)$ and interpret it in rate terminology if

$$f(x) = e^x.$$

b) What is the value of $f(0) = e^0$?
c) Using (a), estimate by how much e^x will change if x increases from 0 to 0.001.
d) From (b) and (c), estimate the value of $e^{0.001}$.

For each of the following find: a) f_x. b) f_{xx}. c) f_y. d) f_{yy}. e) f_{xy}.

55. $f(x, y) = 2x^3 - 3xy + 4y^2 - 6$.

56. $f(x, y) = (x^2 + y^2)^{1/2}$.

57. $f(x, y) = 2y^5 - 6x^2y^3 + 3x - 2y$.

58. $f(x, y) = y \ln x$.

59. $f(x, y) = xe^y$.

60. $f(x,y) = \dfrac{x^2}{2y + 1}$.

12.18 REVIEW PROBLEMS (*concluded*)

Carry out the following:

61. $\dfrac{\partial}{\partial y}(x^2 - 3y^2)$.

62. $\dfrac{\partial^2}{\partial x^2}(x^3y^2)$.

63. $\dfrac{\partial^2}{\partial x \partial y}(x^3y^2)$.

64. $\dfrac{\partial^2}{\partial x^2}(xe^y)$.

---

65. If $f(x, y) = 5x - 4y$, compute
   a) $f_x(1, 2)$.
   b) $f_{xx}(1, 2)$.
   c) $f_y(1, 2)$.
   d) $f_{yy}(1, 2)$.
   e) $f_{xy}(1, 2)$.

66. During a period of operations, a gasoline producer makes and sells x gallons of regular and y gallons of super at a cost, in cents, of

$$C(x, y) = 2x^2 - 4xy + 3y^2 - 6x + 10y.$$

Find $C_x(10, 15)$ and $C_y(10, 15)$ and interpret these numbers in rate terminology.

For the following, find the value of the function at its local optimum and saddle points, if any exist, and state whether a value found is a local maximum, a local minimum, or a saddle point:

67. $f(x, y) = xy - x^2 - y^2 + 15x$.

68. $f(x, y) = x + y + 25/x + 16/y$;
   x and y positive.

69. $f(x, y) = 3x^2 - 3xy + y^2 - 6x + 32$.

70. $f(x, y) = \ln x + \ln y - 0.2x - 0.5y + 5$.

71. $f(x, y) = \dfrac{1,600,000}{x} + 2xy^2 + \dfrac{x(1 - y)^2}{2}$,
   $x > 0$.

72. (This problem is difficult, algebraically.) Given

$$f(x, y) = \frac{ab}{x} + \frac{cxy^2}{2} + \frac{dx(1 - y)^2}{2}$$

where x, y, and all parameters (a, b, c, and d) are positive.
   a) Find the expressions for x and y that minimize $f(x, y)$, in terms of the parameters a, b, c, and d.
   b) Prove (a) yields a minimum.

For the following data sets: a) Find the equation of the best-fitting least-squares straight line. b) Plot the data and the line on a graph.

73. x_i: 2 4 8 10 16
   y_i: 2 5 4 10 9

74. x_i: 5 6 3 2 6 4 6 2 7 4
   y_i: 4 3 2 5 5 3 6 3 5 5

THIRTEEN

Integral Calculus

13.1 INTRODUCTION

We have learned how to find the derivatives of functions and that numerous applications of the derivative stem from its interpretation as the slope of the curve representing the function. It is quite surprising to learn that if we start with a function, $f(x)$, carry out the process that is the inverse of taking the derivative, the result provides an area that has $f(x)$ as part of its boundary. The inverse process is first called taking the *antiderivative of* $f(x)$ then, later, we shall refer to it as *integrating* $f(x)$. Many of the applications of the inverse process stem from interpreting the result as an area that represents quantities such as dollars of profit or pounds of output.

Students generally find elementary integral calculus easy because, having had extensive practice in finding derivatives, the idea of doing the process in reverse, so to speak, is not hard to grasp. However, experience indicates that, at the beginning, students tend to get the two procedures mixed up. The need, therefore, is to concentrate on practicing integration until it is firmly fixed in mind.

In the first part of the chapter, only rational functions to a power are considered, and emphasis is placed on practicing integrating such functions; then attention turns to areas having these functions as part of their boundaries. Next, again using only rational functions to a power, applications involving area interpretations are presented. At this point, we will have learned most of the new ideas covered in the chapter. The middle part of the chapter simply expands the list of integration rules to include exponential and logarithmic forms. The final sections of the chapter introduce differential equations and illustrate some applications of this important branch of mathematics.

13.2 ANTIDERIVATIVES: THE INDEFINITE INTEGRAL

Addition and subtraction are examples of *inverse* operations where one operation annuls the effect of the other. Thus, if we start with the number 50, add 10 to it, then subtract 10, we have the original number 50. Similarly, multiplication and division are inverse operations and, as a last example, cubing a number is annulled by the inverse operation of taking the cube root. Thus, starting with 2,

$$2^3 = 8 \quad \text{and} \quad \sqrt[3]{8} = 2.$$

Now recall the rule for the operation of taking the derivative of x to a power n, that is, multiply the function x^n by the power n and subtract one from the power to obtain a new power, $n - 1$, thus getting

$$\frac{d}{dx}(x^n) = n \cdot x^{n-1}.$$

Keeping this rule in mind, then, the correct inverse procedure would be to add one to the power $n - 1$ to obtain a new power n and subsequently divide the entire expression by this new power to get the original function x^n; i.e.,

$$\frac{n \cdot x^{(n-1)+1}}{(n-1)+1} = \frac{n \cdot x^n}{n} = x^n.$$

So if we take

$$\frac{d}{dx}(x^3) = 3x^2$$

and attempt to reverse the process of differentiation, we obtain

$$\frac{3x^{2+1}}{2+1} = \frac{3x^3}{3} = x^3,$$

as desired. However, the correct procedure just shown is still incomplete, because if we have

$$\frac{d}{dx}(x^3 + 10) = 3x^2,$$

and apply the above procedure to $3x^2$, we cannot recover the constant 10. What we can say is that $3x^2$ is the derivative of x^3 plus an arbitrary constant, C, and write

$$\text{antiderivative } (3x^2) = x^3 + C.$$

The word *antiderivative* denotes the result of the operation that is the inverse of taking the derivative. Thus,

$$\text{antiderivative } (3x^2)$$

means all expressions whose derivative is $3x^2$. Again,

$$\text{antiderivative } (x^3) = \frac{x^{3+1}}{3+1} + C = \frac{x^4}{4} + C$$

and means that $x^4/4$ plus an arbitrary constant constitutes all expressions that have x^3 as their derivative.

Exercise. a) Find antiderivative (x). b) What does the answer to (a) mean? Answer: a) $(x^2/2) + C$. b) $(x^2/2) + C$ constitutes all expressions that have x as their derivative.

For reasons that will become clear when we introduce interpretations of the antiderivative operation, we shall represent this operation by an elongated S; thus,

$$\int$$

is called the *integral symbol* and means the antiderivative of the expression following, as in

$$\int x^2 \, dx = \frac{x^3}{3} + C.$$

In general, we write

$$\int f(x) \, dx = F(x) + C$$

where $F(x)$ is an antiderivative of $f(x)$.

The dx is a *single* symbol and is called the *differential of x*. That is, just as Δx means the change in x and not Δ times x, so dx does not mean d times x. For the moment, we shall think of dx in the same sense as we did when we wrote

$$\frac{d}{dx}$$

to mean the derivative with respect to x. That is, the dx means the independent variable is x and we are to integrate with respect to x. Continuing with terminology, the function to be integrated is called the *integrand*, the outcome of the integration is called the *integral*, and the arbitrary constant is called the *constant of integration*. Thus, in

$$\int x^2 \, dx = \frac{x^3}{3} + C,$$

the integrand is x^2, the constant of integration is C, and

$$\frac{x^3}{3} + C$$

is the *indefinite* integral, where the italicized word is inserted because of the presence of the arbitrary constant, C.

The general rule for the indefinite integral of x to a constant power is

Simple Power Rule

$$\int x^n \, dx = \frac{x^{n+1}}{n+1} + C; \quad \text{if } n \neq -1.$$

Observe that the rule is inapplicable if the power is $n = -1$ for then the divisor, $(n+1)$, in the integral would be zero. We shall see later that if $n = -1$, the integral is the natural logarithm of x.

Example. Integrate the following functions:

a) $f(y) = 1/y^2$.   b) $f(x) = x^{1/2}$.

For part (a), we have

a) $\displaystyle\int \frac{1}{y^2} \, dy = \int y^{-2} \, dy = \frac{y^{-2+1}}{-2+1} + C = \frac{y^{-1}}{-1} + C = -\frac{1}{y} + C.$

For part (b), we obtain

b) $\displaystyle\int x^{1/2} \, dx = \frac{x^{1/2+1}}{1/2+1} + C = \frac{x^{3/2}}{3/2} + C = \frac{2}{3}x^{3/2} + C.$

Exercise. Integrate the following: a) z^5. b) $1/(w^{1/2})$.
Answer: a) $(z^6/6) + C$. b) $2w^{1/2} + C$.

Properties of the integration operation. These properties parallel those of the derivative operation. First, note that the derivative of x is 1, so that

$$\int 1 \, dx = x + C,$$

which is correct because

$$\frac{d}{dx}(x + C) = 1.$$

Conventionally, the factor 1 is not written, as is the case for example when we write x rather than one times x. That is,

$$\int dx = \int 1 \, dx = x + C.$$

Similarly, we know that

$$\frac{d}{dx}(3x) = 3,$$

so that

$$\int 3 \, dx = 3x + C$$

and, in general, for any constant k,

$$\int k \, dx = kx + C.$$

Exercise. Find the following: a) $\int(-2) \, dx$. b) $\int dy/2$. c) $\int dz$.
Answer: a) $-2x + C$. b) $(\frac{1}{2})y + C$. c) $z + C$.

As was the case in taking derivatives, a constant factor may be placed inside or outside the operation symbol. For example,

$$\int 3x \, dx = 3 \int x \, dx = 3 \cdot \frac{x^2}{2} + C.$$

We could have written

$$\int 3x \, dx = 3 \int x \, dx = 3\left(\frac{x^2}{2} + K\right) = \frac{3x^2}{2} + 3K$$

but, inasmuch as K is an arbitrary constant, so is $3K$ an arbitrary constant, and only one symbol is required for such a constant. We shall follow convention and write the constant of integration as a single letter, which is usually C.

Again as in the case of taking derivatives, integration may be performed on an expression term by term. Thus,

$$\int(3z^3 + 2z + 5 + m)dz = \int 3 z^3 \, dz + \int 2 z \, dz + \int 5 \, dz + \int m \, dz$$

$$= 3 \int z^3 \, dz + 2 \int z \, dz + 5 \int dz + m \int dz$$

$$= 3\left(\frac{z^4}{4}\right) + 2\left(\frac{z^2}{2}\right) + 5z + mz + C$$

$$= \frac{3z^4}{4} + z^2 + 5z + mz + C.$$

In this example, note that m is to be considered as a constant because the symbol dz specifies the variable is z.

We summarize the last two properties as follows:

$$\int kf(x)dx = k \int f(x)dx$$
$$\int [f(x) \pm g(x)]dx = \int f(x)dx \pm \int g(x)dx.$$

Exercise.   a) Write the symbols for integrating
$$6y - 10y^4 + b - 1$$
with respect to y.   b) Write the integral.
Answer: a) $\int (6y - 10y^4 + b - 1)dy$.   b) $3y^2 - 2y^5 + by - y + C$.

We shall have occasion from time to time to question whether an integral is correct. The answer, of course, is

An indefinite integral is correct if the derivative of the integral is the integrand.

Example. Is the following correct?

$$\int \underbrace{(7x + 5)^2 \, dx}_{\text{integrand}} \overset{?}{=} \underbrace{\frac{(7x + 5)^3}{3} + K.}_{\text{integral}} \tag{1}$$

To check, we find the derivative of the integral,

$$\frac{d}{dx}\left[\frac{(7x + 5)^3}{3} + K \right] = \frac{d}{dx}\left[\frac{(7x + 5)^3}{3} \right] + \frac{d}{dx}(K)$$
$$= \frac{3(7x + 5)^2(7)}{3}$$
$$= (7x + 5)^2(7).$$

The integral is *incorrect* because its derivative contains the factor 7, which does not appear in the integrand. However, this tells us that we can obtain the correct result by dividing the integral in (1) by 7. That is, the correct integral is

$$\int (7x + 5)^2 \, dx = \frac{(7x + 5)^3}{3(7)} + C$$

where, again, we have chosen to use the symbol C rather than $K/7$, which would arise in dividing (1) by 7.

> **Exercise.** Is the following correct? Why or why not?
>
> $$\int (2x + 9)^{-1/2}\, dx \overset{?}{=} (2x + 9)^{1/2} + C.$$
>
> Answer: It is correct because the derivative of $[(2x + 9)^{1/2} + C]$, by application of the function power derivative rule, is the integrand, $(2x + 9)^{-1/2}$.

Integration rule for powers of a linear function. Returning to the correct integral in the preceding example,

$$\int (7x + 5)^2\, dx = \frac{(7x + 5)^3}{3(7)} + C,$$

the integrand is a *linear* function, $(7x + 5)$, to a constant power. The integral can be obtained by proceeding first as we do for a simple power, that is, adding one to the power and dividing by the new power, to give

$$\frac{(7x + 5)^3}{3}$$

provided that we also divide by the coefficient of x, which is 7, and write

$$\frac{(7x + 5)^3}{3(7)} + C.$$

Observe that the constant 5 in the linear expression $(7x + 5)$ has no effect on the result.

In this problem, we are treating $(7x + 5)$ as a single entity, just as we did in performing the chain rule. A standard technique used to handle integration problems like this is usually referred to as "u-substitution." The basic idea is that $(7x + 5)$ is replaced by the letter u since it is treated as a single entity, and the problem is converted to a presumably simpler problem in the new variable u. Continued practice with the technique of u-substitution will help in simplifying complex problems. Let's illustrate the u-substitution technique by resolving our original problem

$$\int (7x + 5)^2 dx.$$

Step 1. Let $u = 7x + 5$.

Step 2. Take the derivative of u with respect to x:

$$\frac{du}{dx} = 7.$$

Step 3. Solve Step 2 for dx:

$$dx = \frac{du}{7}.$$

Step 4. Substitute the appropriate u-expression for every term containing x in the original integral:

$$\int (7x + 5)^2 dx = \int (u^2)\left(\frac{du}{7}\right) = \frac{1}{7}\int u^2 du.$$

Step 5. Integrate the new problem with respect to u:

$$\frac{1}{7}\int u^2 du = \frac{1}{7}\left(\frac{u^3}{3} + C\right) = \frac{u^3}{3 \cdot 7} + C.$$

Step 6. Reverse the substitution process to obtain an answer in terms of the original variable x:

$$\frac{u^3}{3 \cdot 7} + C = \frac{(7x + 5)^3}{3 \cdot 7} + C,$$

so

$$\int (7x + 5)^2 dx = \frac{(7x + 5)^3}{3(7)} + C,$$

which is precisely the same result as before.

At first, this technique may appear to be a tremendous amount of effort for a simple problem. However, not only is it easier than memorizing formulas, but it even allows us to derive the rules themselves. Indeed if the linear function is expressed in general form as

$$mx + b,$$

we may write the following general rule:

Power Rule for Linear Functions

$$\int (mx + b)^n dx = \frac{(mx + b)^{n+1}}{m(n + 1)} + C, \quad n \neq -1.$$

Note that the power rule adds one to the power, divides the result by this new power, and also by the coefficient of x.

Exercise.   a) What would u be substituted for in the power rule above? b) What is du?   Answer: a) $mx + b$. b) $m \cdot dx$.

We wish to emphasize that we could memorize formulas such as the power rule, but this can become cumbersome and is error prone. The u-

substitution technique, on the other hand, works effectively in many situations, as we will see throughout this chapter.

Example. Integrate the following

$$\int \frac{dx}{(5x - 6)^3}.$$

We begin by choosing

$$u = 5x - 6$$

so that

$$\frac{du}{dx} = 5$$

and

$$dx = \frac{du}{5}.$$

Therefore,

$$\int \frac{dx}{(5x - 6)^3} = \int \frac{1}{u^3} \cdot \frac{du}{5} = \frac{1}{5} \int u^{-3} du$$

$$= \frac{1}{5} \left(\frac{u^{-2}}{-2} + C \right) = -\frac{1}{10} \cdot \frac{1}{u^2} + C.$$

Resubstituting, we obtain

$$\int \frac{dx}{(5x - 6)^3} = -\frac{1}{10} \cdot \frac{1}{(5x - 6)^2} + C.$$

Exercise. Find $\int (5 - 2x)^{-3/2} dx$ and write the answer with positive exponents. Answer: $1/(5 - 2x)^{1/2} + C.$

Before turning to a practice problem set, it is worth noting that the product, quotient, and chain rules that applied in taking derivatives do not have general counterparts in integration. As a consequence, it is necessary to pay careful attention to the *form* of the expression to be integrated and be sure that it matches the form of the integration rule being applied. At the moment, we have only the two forms specified in

$$\int x^n dx = \frac{x^{n+1}}{n + 1} + C; \quad n \neq -1$$

$$\int (mx + b)^n dx = \frac{(mx + b)^{n+1}}{m(n + 1)} + C; \quad n \neq -1.$$

13.3 PROBLEM SET 13–1

Write the expression for the indefinite integral. Simplify results where possible. Express answers with positive exponents.

1. $\int dx$.

2. $\int dz$.

3. $\int 5 dy$.

4. $\int (-7) dw$.

5. $\int (1 + x) dx$.

6. $\int (3 - y) dy$.

7. $\int (2x^2 - 3x + 4) dx$.

8. $\int (3y^3 + 4y - 1) dy$.

9. $\int p \, dq$.

10. $\int q \, dp$.

11. $\int (pq) dp$.

12. $\int (pq) dq$.

13. $\int (x^3 + x^4 - 1) dx$.

14. $\int (y^2 + y^5 - 1) dy$.

15. $\int (3y^2 + 5y^4 + 1) dy$.

16. $\int (4x^3 - 6x^5 + 1) dx$.

17. $\int x^{-2} dx$.

18. $\int 7^{-3} dy$.

19. $\int \dfrac{dy}{y^3}$.

20. $\int \dfrac{dx}{x^4}$.

21. $\int (5 - 2y^{-3}) dy$.

22. $\int (7 - 3x^{-4}) dx$.

23. $\int \left(2x - \dfrac{1}{x^2} + 1 \right) dx$.

24. $\int \left(y + \dfrac{2}{y^3} + 1 \right) dy$.

25. $\int p^{1/2} \, dp$.

26. $\int q^{1/3} \, dq$.

27. $\int 3x^{-4/3} \, dx$.

28. $\int 5y^{-3/2} \, dy$.

29. $\int \left(2 - \dfrac{1}{x^2} - \dfrac{2}{3x^{5/3}} \right) dx$.

30. $\int \left(2x - \dfrac{2}{x^3} - \dfrac{1}{4x^{4/3}} \right) dx$.

31. $\int 12(x^2 + x^3) \, dx$.

32. $\int 3(x^2 + 2x) \, dx$.

33. $\int 16(2x - 9)^3 \, dx$.

34. $\int 30(3x + 5)^5 \, dx$.

35. $\int (3x - 9)^{-2} \, dx$.

36. $\int (2x + 3)^{-4} \, dx$.

37. $\int \dfrac{dx}{(5 - 3x)^{1/2}}$.

38. $\int \dfrac{dw}{(7 - 2w)^3}$.

39. $\int \dfrac{8dx}{(2x + 5)^{1/3}}$.

40. $\int \dfrac{12dx}{(3x - 7)^{1/2}}$.

13.4 AREA AND THE DEFINITE INTEGRAL

In differential calculus, we learned that, in geometric terms, the derivative of a function evaluated at a point is the slope of the line tangent to the curve at that point. In this section, we shall show that a form of the integral, in geometric terms, represents an *area* having the integrand function as one of its boundaries. For example, what if we wish to compute the area below the graph of $f(x) = x^2$, above the x-axis, and bounded on the sides by $x = 1$ and $x = 3$, as shown in Figure 13–1?

FIGURE 13–1

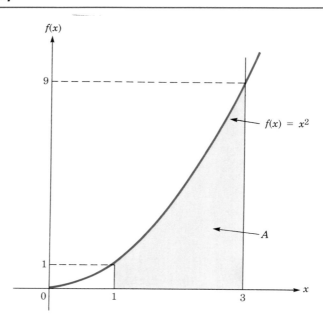

This area is far too irregular to be computed using the area formulas for standard geometric figures. However, we can use a standard geometric figure, such as the rectangle, to approximate this area, as shown on the next page in Figure 13–2. Thus, using ≈ to mean equals approximately,

$$A \approx 1 + 4 = 5 \text{ square units.}$$

We can use 5 as an approximation to the area in question, but clearly this is not a very good approximation because the nonshaded areas under the curve have been omitted. To improve this situation, we can refine the original approximation of Figure 13–2 to a new, better, approximation, such as that shown in Figure 13–3. Now if we add up the areas of all the approximating rectangles, we obtain an approximate area of

$$A \approx \frac{1}{2} + \frac{9}{8} + 2 + \frac{25}{8} = 6\frac{3}{4} \text{ square units.}$$

We can continue to refine each successive approximation by halving the base of each approximating rectangle and forming two new rectangles on the base of the old rectangle.

FIGURE 13–2

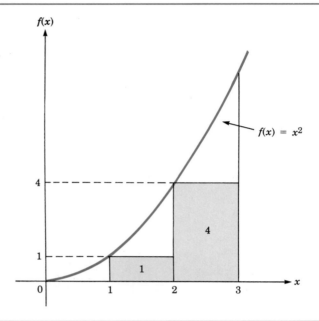

FIGURE 13–3

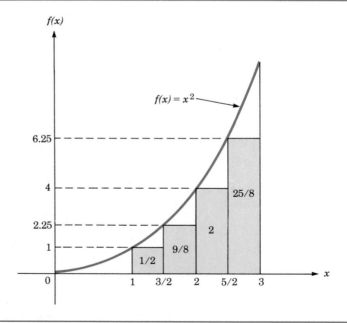

The next approximation would be as shown in Figure 13–4, where

$$A \approx (1)^2 \cdot \frac{1}{4} + \left(\frac{5}{4}\right)^2 \cdot \frac{1}{4} + \left(\frac{3}{2}\right)^2 \cdot \frac{1}{4} + \left(\frac{7}{4}\right)^2 \cdot \frac{1}{4} + (2)^2 \cdot \frac{1}{4} +$$

$$\left(\frac{9}{4}\right)^2 \cdot \frac{1}{4} + \left(\frac{5}{2}\right)^2 \cdot \frac{1}{4} + \left(\frac{11}{4}\right)^2 \cdot \frac{1}{4}$$

$$= \frac{1}{4} + \frac{25}{64} + \frac{9}{16} + \frac{49}{64} + 1 + \frac{81}{64} + \frac{25}{16} + \frac{121}{64} = 7\frac{11}{16}.$$

Note that the width, w, of each rectangle is the same, $w = \frac{1}{4}$, but the height is different for each and equals the square of the left-hand endpoint since this is the value of $f(x) = x^2$ at that point.

FIGURE 13–4

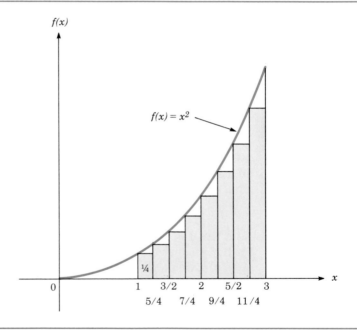

If we put this idea into more general terms, we obtain the picture shown in Figure 13–5. Now the area A will be approximated by

$$A \approx x_0^2 \cdot \Delta x + x_1^2 \cdot \Delta x + x_2^2 \cdot \Delta x + \ldots + x_i^2 \cdot \Delta x + \ldots + x_{n-1}^2 \cdot \Delta x,$$

where $w = \Delta x$ in each rectangle and x_i^2 is the height of the $(i + 1)$st approximating rectangle since $f(x_i) = x_i^2$. This same technique can be

FIGURE 13–5

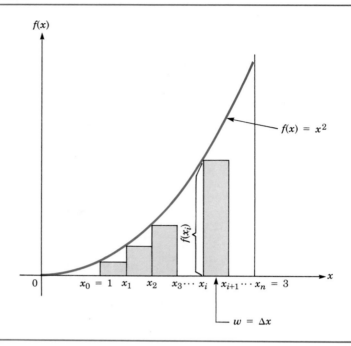

used to compute the area under any curve $f(x)$ and between any two points x_0 and x_n, so in general we have the following approximation formula for the area shown in Figure 13–6:

$$A \approx f(x_1) \cdot \Delta x + f(x_2) \cdot \Delta x + \ldots + f(x_i) \cdot \Delta x + \ldots + f(x_n) \cdot \Delta x.$$

Note that the height of each rectangle in the general case is determined by the smaller of the two possible rectangle heights. Hence for the $(i + 1)$st rectangle, the height is given by min $[f(x_i), f(x_{i+1})]$. Using the sigma notation, we have

$$A \approx \sum_{i=0}^{n-1} \min \, [f(x_i), f(x_{i+1})] \cdot \Delta x.$$

It should be clear from Figure 13–6 that the area is

$$A = \lim_{\Delta x \to 0} \sum_{i=0}^{n-1} \min \, [f(x_i), f(x_{i+1})] \cdot \Delta x.$$

Note that as Δx approaches 0, the number of rectangles, n, approaches

FIGURE 13–6

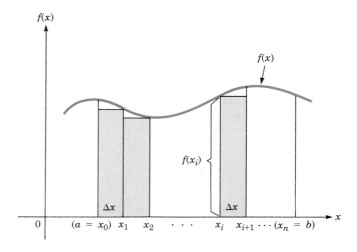

∞. When we take this limit, we symbolize the greek letter Σ in the limit as an elongated S or $\int$ and we replace Δx by dx. Thus,

$$\lim_{\Delta x \to 0} \sum_{i=0}^{n-1} \min \left[f(x_i), f(x_{i+1}) \right] \cdot \Delta x = \int_{(x_0 = a)}^{(x_n = b)} f(x) dx.$$

The term

$$\int_a^b f(x) dx$$

is called the *definite integral* of $f(x)$ from a to b.

From the literature of mathematics a landmark theorem emerges which enables us to compute this definite integral in a very simple way. The importance of this theorem is indicated by its name.

The Fundamental Theorem of Calculus

Let $f(x)$ be continuous on the interval $[a, b]$. If $F(x)$ is an anti-derivative for $f(x)$ on $[a, b]$, then

$$\int_a^b f(x) dx = F(b) - F(a).$$

Thus the area under the curve $f(x)$ from a to b is given by

$$A = \int_a^b f(x)dx = F(b) - F(a) = F(x)\Big|_a^b$$

where the vertical bar means to evaluate the function $F(x)$ at the upper limit b, $F(b)$, and subtract from this the value of the function $F(x)$ at the lower limit a, $F(a)$.

Example. Find the area under the curve $f(x) = x$ from $x = 0$ to $x = 4$, as shown in Figure 13–7.

FIGURE 13–7

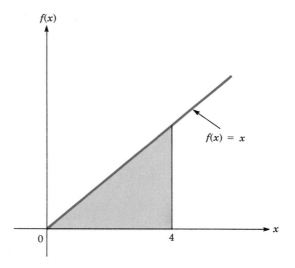

$$A = \int_0^4 xdx = \left(\frac{x^2}{2} + C\right)\Big|_0^4 = \left(\frac{4^2}{2} + C\right) - \left(\frac{0^2}{2} + C\right) = 8 \text{ square units.}$$

Notice the notation $(x^2/2 + C)\ \Big|_0^4$. This means to evaluate the function $(x^2/2 + C)$ at $x = 4$ and subtract from that the value of $(x^2/2 + C)$ at $x = 0$. The function $x^2/2 + C$ is in parentheses since it is the antiderivative of $f(x) = x$.

We could have found this area by using the area formula for a triangle:

$$A = \frac{1}{2} \cdot b \cdot h = \frac{1}{2}(4)(4) = 8 \text{ square units.}$$

Example. Find the area under the curve $f(x) = x^2$ from $x = 1$ to $x = 3$, as shown in Figure 13–8.

$$A = \int_1^3 x^2 dx = \left(\frac{x^3}{3} + C\right)\Big|_1^3 = \left(\frac{27}{3} + C\right) - \left(\frac{1}{3} + C\right)$$

$$= 8\tfrac{2}{3} \text{ square units.}$$

FIGURE 13–8

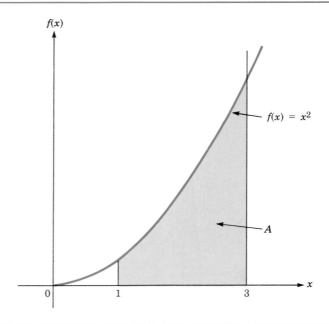

In each of the last two examples notice that the constant C always disappears. Why? Since this is always the case we will no longer use C in our antiderivative form when applying the fundamental theorem of calculus.

Example. Find the area under $f(x) = x^{1/3} + 5$ over the interval $x = 1$ to $x = 8$.

The area sought is shown in Figure 13–9 and is computed as follows:

$$\int_1^8 (x^{1/3} + 5)\, dx = \left(\frac{3}{4}x^{4/3} + 5x\right)\Big|_1^8$$

$$= \left[\frac{3}{4}(8)^{4/3} + 5(8)\right] - \left[\frac{3}{4}(1)^{4/3} + 5(1)\right]$$

$$= \left[\frac{3}{4}(16) + 40\right] - \left[\frac{3}{4} + 5\right]$$

$$= 12 + 40 - \frac{3}{4} - 5$$

$$= 46.25.$$

FIGURE 13–9 (not to scale)

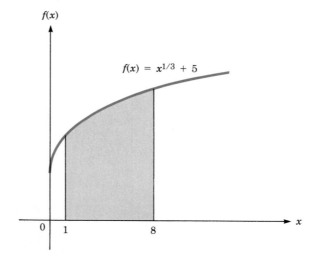

Exercise.   Compute the area under $f(x) = 3x^{1/2} - 2$ over the interval $x = 4$ to $x = 16$.   Answer: 88.

Example. Sketch the function $f(x) = 10x - x^2$, then find the area bounded by the function and the x-axis.

From our work in Chapter 10, we know

$$f(x) = 10x - x^2$$

is a vertical parabola opening downward. The vertex is the local maximum that occurs where $f'(x) = 0$. Hence,

$$f'(x) = 10 - 2x, \quad \text{and} \quad f'(x) \text{ is zero when } x = 5, \quad f(5) = 25,$$

so $(5, 25)$ is the vertex, as shown in Figure 13–10. The curve opens downward from the vertex and so must intersect the x-axis at two points. These points occur where $f(x) = 0$, and we find

$$f(x) = 0 \quad \text{when} \quad \begin{aligned} 10x - x^2 &= 0 \\ x(10 - x) &= 0 \\ x &= 0, 10 \end{aligned}$$

so the intercepts are $(0, 0)$ and $(10, 0)$, as shown in Figure 13–10. The area sought is computed as follows:

$$\int_0^{10} (10x - x^2)dx = \left(5x^2 - \frac{x^3}{3} \right)\Bigg|_0^{10}$$

$$= \left(500 - \frac{1000}{3} \right) - (0 - 0)$$

$$= \frac{500}{3}.$$

FIGURE 13–10 (not to scale)

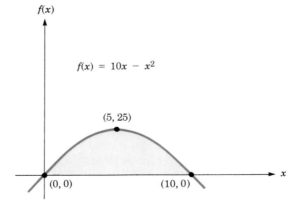

$f(x)$

$f(x) = 10x - x^2$

$(5, 25)$

$(0, 0)$

$(10, 0)$

x

When the endpoints of the interval over which an area is to be computed are given, the computation involves only integrating and evaluating the integral. But, as the last example shows, the problem specification may require that the interval endpoints be found and, in this case, a sketch of the function may be helpful.

Exercise. Sketch the function $f(x) = 16 - x^2$ and compute the area bounded by the curve and the x-axis. Answer: The curve is a parabola with vertex at $(0, 16)$, opening downward, with intercepts $(-4, 0)$ and $(4, 0)$. The area is $256/3$.

Until now, we have only considered areas of the type shown in Figure 13–11 with

$$A_1 = \int_a^b f(x)\,dx.$$

FIGURE 13–11

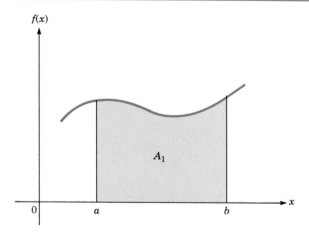

What about areas of the type shown in Figure 13–12? Here

$$A_2 = -\int_a^b f(x)\,dx$$

since all the functional values will give negative heights and all area mea-

FIGURE 13–12

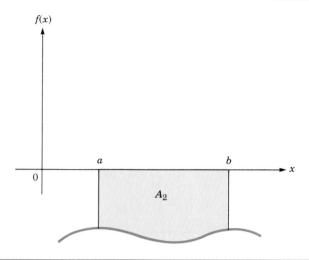

surements must be positive. In general, if we have an area such as shown in Figure 13–13, then the total area between $f(x)$ and the x-axis is given by

$$A = A_1 + A_2 = \int_a^b f(x)\,dx - \int_b^c f(x)\,dx.$$

FIGURE 13–13

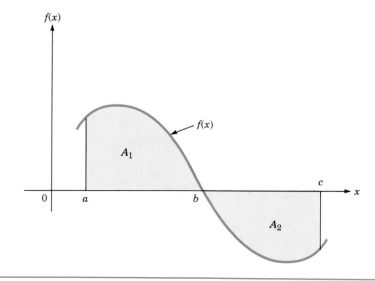

Example. Find the area bounded by the curve $f(x) = x^3 - 3x^2 + 2x$ and the x-axis.

First, we draw a sketch, as shown in Figure 13–14. From this figure, we see that

$$A = A_1 + A_2 = \int_0^1 (x^3 - 3x^2 + 2x)dx - \int_1^2 (x^3 - 3x^2 + 2x)dx$$

$$= \left(\frac{x^4}{4} - x^3 + x^2 \right) \Big|_0^1 - \left(\frac{x^4}{4} - x^3 + x^2 \right) \Big|_1^2$$

$$= \left(\frac{1}{4} - 1 + 1 \right) - (0) - \left(\frac{16}{4} - 8 + 4 \right) + \left(\frac{1}{4} - 1 + 1 \right)$$

$$= \frac{1}{4} - 0 - 0 + \frac{1}{4} = \frac{1}{2} \text{ square unit.}$$

Note that $A_1 = A_2 = \frac{1}{4}$ square unit.

FIGURE 13–14

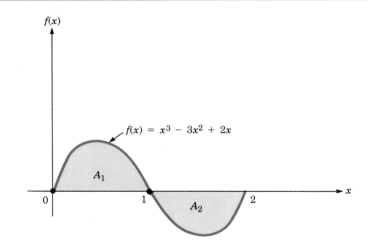

13.5 PROBLEM SET 13–2

Evaluate the following definite integrals:

1. $\int_2^5 2\, dx.$

2. $\int_1^3 3\, dx.$

3. $\int_{-1}^4 2x\, dx.$

4. $\int_{-3}^9 3x\, dx.$

5. $\int_2^6 (x + 1)\, dx.$

6. $\int_{-1}^3 (2x - 1)\, dx.$

7. $\int_0^8 x^{2/3}\, dx.$

8. $\int_0^9 x^{1/2}\, dx.$

9. $\int_1^2 (x^2 - 3x + 5)\, dx.$

13.5 PROBLEM SET 13–2 *(continued)*

10. $\int_0^3 (x^2 + 5x - 2)\, dx.$ **11.** $\int_1^9 (5 + y^{-\frac{1}{2}})\, dy.$ **12.** $\int_1^8 (1 + 2y^{-\frac{1}{3}})\, dy.$

13. $\int_2^6 (2x - 3)^{\frac{1}{2}}\, dx.$ **14.** $\int_1^8 (5x - 4)^{-\frac{1}{2}}\, dx.$ **15.** $\int_1^6 \frac{60\, dx}{(3x + 2)^2}.$

16. $\int_0^6 \frac{20}{(4x + 1)^{\frac{3}{2}}}\, dx.$ **17.** $\int_a^b 3x^2\, dx.$ **18.** $\int_c^d 4x^3\, dx.$

19. $\int_1^n (x + 1)\, dx.$ **20.** $\int_n^1 (2x - 1)\, dx.$

Find the area under the curve of the following functions over the given x-intervals:

21. $f(x) = 2x; x = 1$ to $x = 2.$

22. $f(x) = 3x; x = 1$ to $x = 5.$

23. $f(x) = 3x + 2; x = 1$ to $x = 2.$

24. $f(x) = 2x + 3; x = -1$ to $x = 1.$

25. $f(x) = \frac{6}{x^2}; x = 1$ to $x = 3.$

26. $f(x) = \frac{4}{x^3}; x = 1$ to $x = 2.$

27. $f(x) = \frac{40}{(2x + 1)^2}; x = 0$ to $x = 2.$

28. $f(x) = \frac{50}{x^{\frac{3}{2}}}; x = 1$ to $x = 25.$

Find the areas described in each of the following problems. (Sketches will be helpful.)

29. Find the area bounded by the axes and

$$f(x) = 10 - 0.5x.$$

30. Find the area bounded by the axes and

$$f(x) = 5 + x.$$

31. Find the area bounded by the x-axis and

$$f(x) = 30x - 3x^2.$$

32. Find the area bounded by the x-axis and

$$f(x) = 4x - x^2 + 21.$$

33. Find the area bounded by the x-axis and

$$f(x) = x^3 - 3x^2 - x + 3.$$

34. Find the area bounded by the x-axis and

$$f(x) = x^4 - 5x^2 + 4.$$

---

35. The BASIC program, shown in Program 13–1, approximates the area under the curve $f(x) = x^2$ from $x = a$ to $x = b$ by n rectangles. Underneath the program is a computer run with $a = 1$, $b = 3$, and $n = 10$.

Program 13–1

```
10 REM APPROXIMATION OF AREA UNDER X^2 BY RECTANGLES
20 INPUT "Enter limits a and b, and number of subdivisions n";A,B,N
30 PRINT
40 PRINT " L"," R"," Y","   SUM"
50 W=(B-A)/N
60 FOR I=0 TO N-1
```

13.5 PROBLEM SET 13–2 (*continued*)

```
70 L=A+I*W
80 R=A+(I+1)*W
90 IF (L^2)<(R^2)THEN Y=L^2 ELSE Y=R^2
100 S=S+W*Y
110 PRINT L,R,Y,S
120 NEXT I
130 PRINT "THE AREA IS ";S
140 END

RUN

Enter limits a and b, and number of subdivisions n? 1,3,10
```

L	R	Y	SUM
1	1.2	1	.2
1.2	1.4	1.44	.488
1.4	1.6	1.96	.88
1.6	1.8	2.56	1.392
1.8	2	3.24	2.04
2	2.2	4	2.84
2.2	2.4	4.84	3.808
2.4	2.6	5.76	4.96
2.6	2.8	6.76	6.312
2.8	3	7.84	7.88

```
THE AREA IS  7.88
```

a) Describe what the program is doing line-by-line.

b) Run the program with $n = 10$ for Problems 1 through 28 and 31 through 34.

36. The BASIC program, shown in Program 13–2, approximates the area under the curve $f(x) = x^2$ from $x = a$ to $x = b$ using 100, 200, 300, . . . , 1,000 rectangles. Underneath the program is a computer run with $a = 1$ and $b = 3$.

Program 13–2

```
10 REM APPROXIMATION OF AREA UNDER X^2 USING 100 - 1000 RECTANGLES
20 INPUT "Enter lower limit a and upper limit b";A,B
30 FOR N=100 TO 1000 STEP 100
40 W=(B-A)/N
50 S=0
60 FOR I=0 TO N-1
70 L=A+I*W
80 R=A+(I+1)*W
90 IF (L^2)<(R^2)THEN Y=L^2 ELSE Y=R^2
100 S=S+W*Y
110 NEXT I
120 PRINT "With ";N;" subdivisions, the area is ";S
```

13.5 PROBLEM SET 13–2 (*concluded*)

```
130 NEXT N
140 END

RUN

Enter lower limit a and upper limit b? 1,3
With  100  subdivisions, the area is  8.5868
With  200  subdivisions, the area is  8.6267
With  300  subdivisions, the area is  8.64002
With  400  subdivisions, the area is  8.64667
With  500  subdivisions, the area is  8.65068
With  600  subdivisions, the area is  8.65334
With  700  subdivisions, the area is  8.65524
With  800  subdivisions, the area is  8.65667
With  900  subdivisions, the area is  8.65778
With  1000  subdivisions, the area is  8.65867
```

a) Describe what the program is doing line-
   by-line.
b) Run the program for Problems 1 through
   28 and 31 through 34.

13.6 THE AREA BETWEEN TWO CURVES

In the last section, we discussed areas bounded by a function $f(x)$ and the x-axis. In this section we look at areas determined by two functions $f(x)$ and $g(x)$. We begin with an example.

Example. Find the area bounded by the functions

$$f(x) = 15 - 2x - x^2$$

and

$$g(x) = 9 - x.$$

Here, $f(x)$ is again a parabola opening downward. Its vertex is found in the usual manner to be $(-1, 16)$, as follows:

$$f'(x) = 0: \quad -2 - 2x = 0$$
$$x = -1$$
$$f(-1) = 15 - 2(-1) - (-1)^2 = 16.$$

As shown next, the horizontal intercepts are at $x = -5$ and $x = 3$.

$$f(x) = 0: \quad 15 - 2x - x^2 \quad = 0$$
$$(-x + 3)(x + 5) = 0$$
$$x = 3; \quad x = -5.$$

A sketch of $f(x)$ is shown on Figure 13–15. The function

$$g(x) = 9 - x$$

FIGURE 13–15 (not to scale)

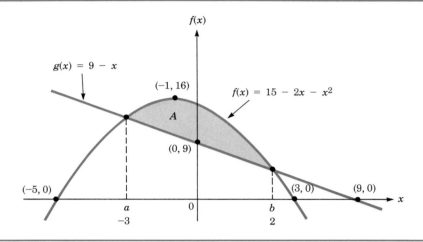

is a straight line that can be plotted from two points. Frequently, the intercepts are the simplest points to find:

$$\text{Horizontal } (x) \text{ intercept:} \quad g(x) = 0$$
$$0 = 9 - x$$
$$x = 9$$
$$\text{Point is } (9, 0).$$
$$\text{Vertical intercept } (x = 0): \quad g(x) = 9 - 0$$
$$g(x) = 9$$
$$\text{Point is } (0, 9).$$

After drawing $g(x)$ on Figure 13–15, we see the specified (shaded) area extends over the interval $x = a$ to $x = b$, where dashed vertical lines have been drawn. We can find this area by taking the area under $f(x)$ over the interval from a to b, which would include also the area under the line $g(x)$, and subtracting from this the area under the line $g(x)$. Thus,

$$A = \int_a^b f(x)dx - \int_a^b g(x)dx,$$

which is the same as

$$A = \int_a^b [f(x) - g(x)]\, dx.$$

The values of a and b are the x-coordinates of the points of intersection of $f(x)$ and $g(x)$. At these points, $g(x) = f(x)$.

$$g(x) = f(x)$$
$$9 - x = 15 - 2x - x^2$$
$$x^2 + x - 6 = 0.$$
$$(x + 3)(x - 2) = 0$$
$$x = -3; \quad x = 2.$$

Hence, $a = -3$ and $b = 2$, so the area is

$$A = \int_{-3}^{2} [f(x) - g(x)] \, dx$$

$$= \int_{-3}^{2} [(15 - 2x - x^2) - (9 - x)] \, dx$$

$$= \int_{-3}^{2} (6 - x - x^2) \, dx$$

$$= \left(6x - \frac{x^2}{2} - \frac{x^3}{3} \right) \Bigg|_{-3}^{2}$$

$$= \left[6(2) - \frac{(2)^2}{2} - \frac{(2)^3}{3} \right] - \left[6(-3) - \frac{(-3)^2}{2} - \frac{(-3)^3}{3} \right]$$

$$= \left[12 - 2 - \frac{8}{3} \right] - \left[-18 - \frac{9}{2} + 9 \right]$$

$$= 19 - \frac{8}{3} + \frac{9}{2} = \frac{114 - 16 + 27}{6} = \frac{125}{6}.$$

It is important to note that

$$A = \int_{a}^{b} [f(x) - g(x)] \, dx$$

and that

$$A \neq \int_{a}^{b} [g(x) - f(x)] \, dx.$$

Why? Because

$$\int_{a}^{b} [g(x) - f(x)] \, dx = -A.$$

We always subtract the smaller function from the larger function or else we would obtain a negative area. Treat a negative answer as a red flag indicating that you made an error and should go back and check your work carefully. Whenever possible, make a sketch before computing the area.

Example. Find the area between the curves

$$f(x) = 3x^3 - 3x$$

and

$$g(x) = x.$$

First we sketch $g(x) = x$, as shown in Figure 13–16. Since $f(x) = 3x^3 - 3x = 3(x)(x - 1)(x + 1)$, $f(x) = 0$ when $x = -1, 0$, and 1. With our knowledge of curve sketching, then, we can generate a rough sketch of $f(x)$, as shown in Figure 13–16.

To find the points of intersection of $f(x)$ and $g(x)$, we let $f(x) = g(x)$

or

$$3x^3 - 3x = x$$
$$3x^3 - 4x = 0$$
$$x(3x^2 - 4) = 0$$
$$x = 0, \pm \frac{2}{\sqrt{3}}.$$

FIGURE 13–16

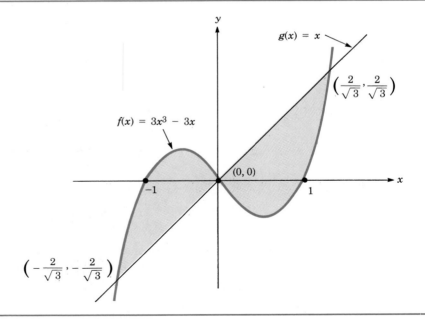

So,

$$A = \int_{-2/\sqrt{3}}^{0} [f(x) - g(x)]dx + \int_{0}^{2/\sqrt{3}} [g(x) - f(x)]dx$$

$$= \int_{-2/\sqrt{3}}^{0} [(3x^3 - 3x) - x]\, dx + \int_{0}^{2/\sqrt{3}} [x - (3x^3 - 3x)]\, dx$$

$$= \int_{-2/\sqrt{3}}^{0} (3x^3 - 4x)\, dx + \int_{0}^{2/\sqrt{3}} (4x - 3x^3)\, dx$$

$$= \left(\frac{3x^4}{4} - 2x^2\right)\Bigg|_{-2/\sqrt{3}}^{0} + \left(2x^2 - \frac{3x^4}{4}\right)\Bigg|_{0}^{2/\sqrt{3}}$$

$$= (0) - \left(\frac{3}{4} \cdot \frac{16}{9} - 2 \cdot \frac{4}{3}\right) + \left(2 \cdot \frac{4}{3} - \frac{3}{4} \cdot \frac{16}{9}\right) - (0)$$

$$= -\frac{4}{3} + \frac{8}{3} + \frac{8}{3} - \frac{4}{3} = \frac{8}{3} \text{ square units.}$$

Take note that we had to break this problem into two parts since from $-2\sqrt{3}$ to 0 the larger function was $f(x)$, but the functions crossed at $x = 0$, and the larger function from 0 to $2\sqrt{3}$ was $g(x)$. An alternative method, without even sketching the graphs, is to find the points of intersection and then determine which is the larger function by testing each function at a point in between. For example, -1 lies between $-2\sqrt{3}$ and $0; f(-1) = 0$ while $g(-1) = -1$, so $f(x)$ is the larger function.

Exercise. a) What is a good test point between 0 and $2\sqrt{3}$? b) Which is the larger function? Answer: a) 1. b) $f(1) = 0$ and $g(1) = 1$, so $g(x)$ is the larger function.

Exercise. a) Sketch $h(x) = 8 - 2x$ and $g(x) = 16 - x^2$. b) Find the points where $g(x)$ and $h(x)$ intersect. c) Compute the area bounded by the functions. Answer: a) $h(x)$ is a straight line passing through $(0, 8)$ and $(4, 0)$; $g(x)$ is a downward opening parabola with vertex at $(0, 16)$ and intercepts $(-4, 0)$; $(4, 0)$. b) $(-2, 12)$ and $(4, 0)$. c) 36.

It will be useful to highlight a few important formulas before we move on to some problems.

$$1. \int_a^b [f(x) \pm g(x)]dx = \int_a^b f(x)dx \pm \int_a^b g(x)dx.$$

$$2. \int_a^b f(x)dx + \int_b^c f(x)dx = \int_a^c f(x)dx.$$

$$3. \int_a^b f(x)dx = -\int_b^a f(x)dx.$$

The first formula follows directly from our discussion of indefinite integrals.

Exercise. Draw a graph to illustrate the second formula.

The third formula follows from the fact that

$$\int_a^b f(x)dx = F(b) - F(a)$$

and

$$-\int_b^a f(x)dx = - [F(a) - F(b)] = F(b) - F(a).$$

13.7 PROBLEM SET 13–3

1. For the functions

   $f(x) = 1 + x$ and $g(x) = 10 - 2x,$

   a) Find the first-quadrant area bounded by the functions and the *y*-axis.
   b) Find the first-quadrant area bounded by the functions and the axes.

2. Find the first-quadrant area bounded by the axes and the functions

   $f(x) = 0.5x + 2; \quad g(x) = 2x - 4.$

3. Find the area bounded by the functions

   $f(x) = x^2 + 1$ and $g(x) = 10.$

4. Find the area bounded by the functions

   $f(x) = 34 - x^2$ and $g(x) = 9.$

5. Find the area bounded by the functions

   $f(x) = x^2 - 8x + 20$ and $g(x) = 14 - x.$

6. Find the area bounded by the functions

   $f(x) = 20 - 2x$ and $g(x) = 12x - 2x^2.$

7. [Note: $f(x)$ is the upper half of a *horizontal* parabola that opens to the right and has the origin as its vertex.] Find the area bounded by

   $f(x) = 8x^{1/2}$ and $g(x) = x^2.$

8. (See Note, Problem 7.) Find the area bounded by

   $f(x) = 6x^{1/2}$ and $g(x) = 0.4x.$

13.7 PROBLEM SET 13–3 (*concluded*)

9. Find the area bounded by the functions

$$f(x) = x^3 \quad \text{and} \quad g(x) = x.$$

10. Find the area bounded by the functions

$$f(x) = x^4 - 5x^2 + 4 \quad \text{and} \quad g(x) = 4.$$

11. a) Modify Program 13–1 of Section 13.5 to find the area between two functions.
   b) Run the program in (a) for Problems 3 through 10.

12. a) Modify Program 13–2 of Section 13.5 to find the area between two functions.
   b) Run the program in (a) for Problems 3 through 10.

13.8 INTERPRETIVE APPLICATIONS OF AREA

The area of the rectangle shown in Figure 13–17 is

$$30(40) = 1200.$$

If asked what this area represents, our reply depends upon what the 30 and 40 represent. Thus, if the rectangle is a piece of level land with dimensions 30 feet by 40 feet, then

$$(30 \text{ feet})(40 \text{ feet}) = 1{,}200 \text{ (feet)}^2,$$

or 1,200 square feet. Here, the *unit of measure* is feet for both numbers, so the product of the numbers is square feet. However, if 30 means 30 gallons of gasoline and 40 means 40 miles per gallon of gasoline, then the first unit is *gallon* and the second is *miles per (divided by) gallon*, and we have

$$(30 \text{ gallons})\left(40 \ \frac{\text{miles}}{\text{gallon}}\right) = 1{,}200 \text{ miles},$$

so the gallon unit cancels and the area of the rectangle represents the 1,200 miles traveled by a car that consumes 30 gallons of gasoline and travels 40 miles per gallon consumed. Once again, if a person rents a motel room for 30 days (unit is *day*) and pays $40 per day (unit is *dollars/day*), we find

$$(30 \text{ days})\left(40 \ \frac{\text{dollars}}{\text{day}}\right) = 1{,}200 \text{ dollars},$$

and the area represents the $1,200 the person pays for the 30-day rental at $40 per day.

In the preceding, observe that miles per gallon and dollars per day are *rates*. The *derivative* of a function also can be interpreted as a rate. Thus, the *total* rent function in the last example is

$$r(t) = (t \text{ days})\left(40 \ \frac{\text{dollars}}{\text{day}}\right)$$
$$r(t) = 40t$$

FIGURE 13–17   **FIGURE 13–18**

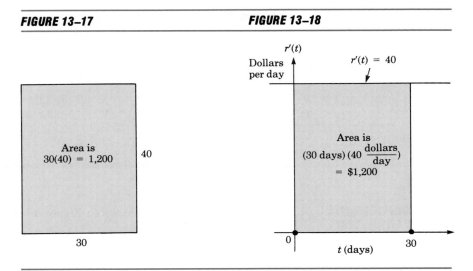

and

$$r'(t) = 40$$

is the rate at which rent changes per additional day's rental. We picture this as in Figure 13–18, with the constant rate function plotted on the vertical axis. Then we can compute the area as

$$\int_0^{30} r'(t)\ dt.$$

Observe that the integrand, $r'(t)$, has the unit (dollars/day), whereas dt, which refers to the horizontal axis, has the unit (days). Hence,

$$r'(t)\ dt$$

or

$$\left(\frac{\text{dollars}}{\text{day}}\right)(\text{days}) = \text{dollars}$$

and

$$\int_0^{30} r'(t)\ dt = \int_0^{30} 40\ dt = 40t\Big|_0^{30} = 1{,}200\ \text{dollars.}$$

The point we wish to emphasize is that for

$$\int_a^b f(x)\ dx$$

an area interpretation is in terms of the product of the unit on the vertical, f(x), axis times the unit of dx, which is the unit on the hori-

zontal axis. This point is important because it arises in numerous applications of integrals.

Example 1. The total amount of coal a country will consume in a period of years depends upon the rate of consumption, and this rate increases as time, t years, increases. Suppose it is estimated that the consumption rate, $r'(t)$, t years from now, will be

$$r'(t) = (20 + 1.2t) \text{ million tons per year.}$$

Compute the total amount of coal the country will consume in the next ten years.

Figure 13–19 shows the rate function, $r'(t)$, as a rising straight line. The shaded area, marked A, is

$$\int_0^{10} (20 + 1.2t)\, dt = (20t + 0.6t^2)\Big|_0^{10}$$
$$= (200 + 60) - (0)$$
$$= 260.$$

The vertical axis has the unit (tons/year) and the horizontal axis has the unit (years). Hence, the number 260 has the unit

$$\left(\frac{\text{tons}}{\text{year}}\right)(\text{years}) = \text{tons}$$

and the area 260 represents 260 million tons consumed in 10 years.

FIGURE 13–19 (not to scale)

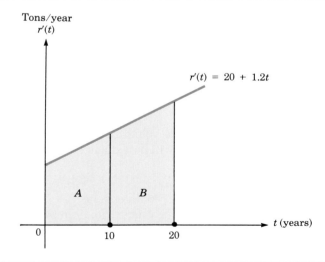

Example 2. (See Example 1.) How much coal will be consumed in the following ten years, that is, during the second decade from now?

The answer here is the area marked as B on Figure 13–19. It is

$$\int_{10}^{20} (20 + 1.2t)\, dt = (20t + 0.6t^2)\Big|_{10}^{20}$$
$$= (400 + 240) - (200 + 60)$$
$$= 380 \text{ million tons.}$$

Example 3. (See Example 1.) If the total supply of coal available to the country now and in the future is 2,500 million tons, how long will it be until the total supply is exhausted?

Here, the total supply will be exhausted when the amount consumed, which is the integral, equals 2500. We write

$$\int_{0}^{T} (20 + 1.2t)\, dt = 2500$$

where T represents the amount of time the coal will last. So we obtain

$$(20t + 0.6t^2)\Big|_{0}^{T} = 2500$$
$$(20T + 0.6T^2) - (0 + 0) = 2500$$
$$0.6T^2 + 20T - 2500 = 0.$$

To solve the quadratic equation just written, we rewrite it as

$$6T^2 + 200T - 25{,}000 = 0$$

or

$$3T^2 + 100T - 12{,}500 = 0$$

Factoring, then, we have

$$(3T + 250)(T - 50) = 0$$

so

$$T = -\frac{250}{3} \quad \text{or} \quad T = 50.$$

The negative value for T is not in the permissible range, so $T = 50$, and the supply will be exhausted in 50 years.

Exercise.   Maintenance cost on a new machine is at the rate of $100t$ dollars per year at time t years. a) Compute total maintenance cost for the first four years. b) How many years will it take for total maintenance cost to amount to $5,000? Answer: a) $800. b) 10 years.

Accounting for a fixed component. In the last exercise, it was assumed, reasonably, that maintenance cost at time $t = 0$ was zero and therefore it was not necessary to take this zero cost into account. Suppose, however, that a company spends \$2,000 to have an advertising campaign prepared and then plans to run the campaign at a cost rate of $C'(t) = 900$ dollars per week at time t weeks. If we compute the total cost of running the campaign for 10 weeks as

$$\int_0^{10} C'(t)\, dt = \int_0^{10} 900\, dt = 900t \Big|_0^{10} = \$9,000,$$

the \$9,000 does not include the fixed preparation cost of \$2,000. The total cost would be

$$\text{Total cost} = \text{Fixed cost} + \int_0^{10} 900\, dt$$
$$= \$2,000 + \$9,000$$
$$= \$11,000.$$

Where does each of the terms on the right-hand side come from? Recall from the fundamental theorem of calculus that

$$\int_0^{10} C'(t)\, dt = C(10) - C(0)$$

since $C(t)$ is an antiderivative of $C'(t)$. Hence

$$C(10) = C(0) + \int_0^{10} C'(t)\, dt.$$

Now $C(10)$ represents the total cost of the advertising campaign after 10 weeks. Since $C(0)$ represents the fixed cost, then

$$\int_0^{10} C'(t)\, dt$$

must represent the variable cost so that, as usual,

$$\text{Total cost} = \text{Fixed cost} + \text{Variable cost.}$$

It is important to realize, as we have just seen, that if a total is obtained by integrating a rate, and a fixed element is present, this element must be added to the value of the definite integral to obtain the correct final value.

Example. The fixed cost incurred when g gallons of paint are produced is \$2,500 and marginal cost at g gallons of output is

$$C'(g) = 0.00045g^2 - 0.18g + 20.$$

Find the total cost of producing 100 gallons.

Here we must recall that marginal cost at output level g gallons is the *rate* at which total cost is changing per additional gallon made. That is, marginal cost has the unit (dollars/gallon) and dg has the unit (gallons). Hence,

$$\int C'(g)\, dg$$

has the unit

$$\left(\frac{\text{dollars}}{\text{gallon}}\right)(\text{gallons}) = \text{dollars}.$$

The total cost of making 100 gallons, fixed cost included, is

$$
\begin{aligned}
C(100) &= \int_0^{100} C'(g)\, dg + C(0) \\
&= \int_0^{100} (0.00045g^2 - 0.18g + 20)\, dg + 2500 \\
&= (0.00015g^3 - 0.09g^2 + 20g)\Big|_0^{100} + 2500 \\
&= [0.00015(100)^3 - (0.09)(100)^2 + 20(100)] - [0] + 2500 \\
&= 1250 + 2500 \\
&= \$3{,}750.
\end{aligned}
$$

Exercise.   Marginal cost at output level p pounds of nails is

$$1 + (p + 1)^{-1/2}$$

and fixed cost is \$400. Find the total cost of making 399 pounds of the product.   Answer: \$837.

13.9 INTERPRETING THE AREA BOUNDED BY TWO FUNCTIONS

Suppose that an operation provided a company income at the rate of $I'(t)$ dollars per day at time t days, where

$$I'(t) = 110 + 4t^{1/2}.$$

The operation was started at an initial fixed expense of \$2,000. Variable expense at the rate of $E'(t)$ per day is incurred at time t days, where

$$E'(t) = 20 + 7t^{1/2}.$$

The income and expense rate functions are shown in Figure 13–20. From a profit maximization viewpoint, the operation should be continued as long as income per day exceeds expense per day; that is, as long as $I'(t)$ is above $E'(t)$ in Figure 13–20. This situation exists up until the intersection point, b, which we find by equating $E'(t)$ and $I'(t)$, thus

FIGURE 13–20 (not to scale)

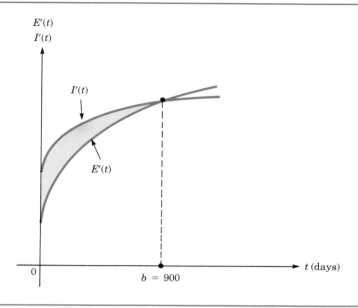

$$20 + 7t^{1/2} = 110 + 4t^{1/2}$$
$$3t^{1/2} = 90$$
$$t^{1/2} = 30$$
$$t = (30)^2$$
$$t = 900 \text{ days,}$$

which is the value shown shown for b in Figure 13–20. If we write

$$\text{Net profit} = \left[\int_0^{900} I'(t)\, dt + I(0) \right] - \left[\int_0^{900} E'(t)\, dt + E(0) \right]$$

then

$$\text{Net profit} = \int_0^{900} I'(t)\, dt - \int_0^{900} E'(t)\, dt - 2000$$

since $I(0) = 0$ and $E(0) = 2000$. Now, on the right, the first term is total income in 900 days, the middle term is total *variable* expense, and the difference in these two is the shaded area in Figure 13–20 and represents profit before the fixed expense of \$2,000. The three terms therefore represent the net profit obtained, and this is the maximum profit, possible only if the operation is terminated at $t = 900$ days. We have

$$\text{Net profit} = \int_0^{900} I'(t)\, dt - \int_0^{900} E'(t)\, dt - 2000$$

$$= \int_0^{900} [I'(t) - E'(t)]\, dt - 2000$$

$$= \int_0^{900} [(110) + 4t^{1/2}) - (20 + 7t^{1/2})]\, dt - 2000$$

$$= \int_0^{900} (90 - 3t^{1/2})\, dt - 2000$$

$$= (90t - 2t^{3/2}) \Big|_0^{900} - 2000$$

$$= [90(900) - 2(900)^{3/2}] - [0] - 2000$$
$$= 81{,}000 - 2(30)^3 - 2000$$
$$= \$25{,}000.$$

Exercise. Income from an operation at time t months from its initiation is at the rate of $(10 + 0.2t)$ thousand dollars per month and variable expense is at the rate of $(5 + 0.3t)$ thousand dollars per month. If fixed start-up cost was \$5,000, find a) The optimum time to terminate the operation. b) The maximum net profit that can be achieved.   Answer: a) 50 months. b) \$120,000.

13.10 CONSUMERS' AND PRODUCERS' SURPLUS

In the economic model of pure competition it is assumed that all consumers (buyers) of a product pay the *same* price per unit for a product. This price comes about by the interplay of competitive market forces and is the price per unit at which the quantity of product consumers are willing and able to buy (called consumer *demand*) is matched by the quantity producers (sellers) are willing and able to supply. The purpose of this section is to illustrate that this competitive situation benefits both consumer and supplier, and to develop a measure of these benefits.

Looking first at the consumer (buyer) side of the situation, it is a matter of observation that even though a product, say gasoline, sells competitively at 99 cents per gallon, there are buyers who would be willing to pay \$3 or more per gallon and, clearly, the lower price established by competition benefits these buyers. Economists use downward sloping curves, called *demand* curves, to represent the observed relationship between the number of units, q, demanded by consumers and $p_d(q)$, the selling price per unit. The subscript d on $p_d(q)$ signifies that this is a demand function to distinguish it from the supply function, which will be introduced later and named $p_s(q)$. Figure 13–21 shows an illustrative demand curve. As the figure shows, low price is accompanied by high demand, and high price is accompanied by low demand. The point $E(q_m, p_m)$ is the *equilibrium* point; that is, the market price that matches

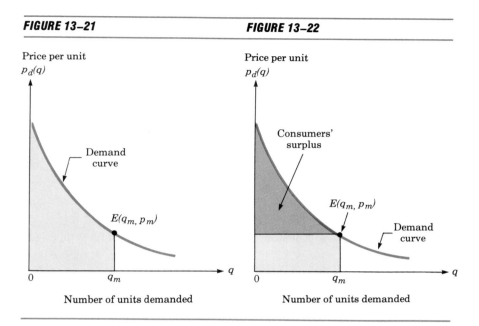

FIGURE 13–21

Price per unit
$p_d(q)$

Demand
curve

$E(q_m, p_m)$

0   q_m

q

Number of units demanded

FIGURE 13–22

Price per unit
$p_d(q)$

Consumers'
surplus

$E(q_m, p_m)$

Demand
curve

0   q_m

q

Number of units demanded

the quantity consumers demand with the quantity producers will supply. The area under the curve,

$$\int_0^{q_m} p_d(q)\, dq,$$

represents dollars because it is the product of price per unit times number of units. This area may be taken as a measure of what consumers might have had to pay for the q_m units if competition did not lead to the constant price, p_m, for all units; that is, if various consumers paid the higher prices on the demand curve to the left of (q_m, p_m). However, at equilibrium, consumers pay p_m dollars per unit for each of the q_m units demanded, so the total paid is $p_m q_m$ dollars, which is the area of the rectangle shown in Figure 13–22. The amount paid, the rectangular area, is less than the whole area under the curve over the interval 0 to q_m, and the *difference* may be taken as a measure of the benefit to consumers of competitive forces that lead to the same unit price for all units sold. Hence, it is called *consumers' surplus* and, as shown by the shaded area on Figure 13–22, it is the total area under the curve over the interval 0 to q_m, minus the area of the rectangle:

$$\textbf{Consumers' Surplus} = \int_0^{q_m} p_d(q)\, dq - p_m q_m.$$

Example. At market equilibrium, consumers demand 625,000 gallons of kerosene, which has the demand function

$$p_d(q) = 25 - 0.6q^{1/2},$$

where q is in thousands of gallons and $p_d(q)$ is in dollars per gallon. Compute consumers' surplus.

First we compute p_m as

$$p_m = p_d(625) = 25 - 0.6(625)^{1/2}$$
$$= 25 - 0.6(25)$$
$$= \$10 \text{ per gallon.}$$

Then,

$$\text{Consumers' surplus} = \int_0^{625} (25 - 0.6q^{1/2}) \, dq - (10)(625)$$

$$= (25q - 0.4q^{3/2}) \Big|_0^{625} - 6250$$

$$= [25(625) - 0.4(625)^{3/2}] - [25(0) - 0.4(0)^{3/2}] - 6250$$
$$= [15{,}625 - 6{,}250] - [0] - 6250$$
$$= \$3{,}125 \text{ thousand.}$$

Exercise.   At market equilibrium, consumers demand 100,000 tons of SAE 90 lubricating oil, which has the demand function $p_d(q) = 110 - 0.5q$, where q is in thousands of tons and $p_d(q)$ is in dollars per ton. Compute consumers' surplus.   Answer: \$2,500 thousand.

Producers' surplus. The relationship between the market price and the quantities producers are willing to supply is expressed as a supply function, $p_s(q)$. The supply curve slopes upward to the right as illustrated in Figure 13–23 because producers are willing to supply more at higher prices than at lower prices. Again, the equilibrium point $E(q_m, p_m)$ is at the price that matches the amount consumers demand with the amount producers are willing to supply. However, producers receive the same unit price, p_m, for all q_m units they produce and sell, so the total received by producers is the product

$$p_m q_m,$$

and this is the area of the rectangle shown in Figure 13–23. But, the supply curve implies that producers would have supplied some units of the product at prices lower than p_m, and the area under the supply curve may be taken as a measure of what producers might have received in the absence of an equilibrium price, that is, if various producers sold some

FIGURE 13–23

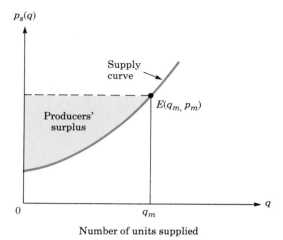

Number of units supplied

units of the product at prices to the left (below) the equilibrium price on the curve. The *difference* between the area of the rectangle and the area under the curve then is a measure of the benefit to producers of market competition that leads to the equilibrium price, p_m, and is called *producers' surplus*. This is the shaded area in Figure 13–23, which is

$$\textbf{Producers' Surplus} = p_m q_m - \int_0^{q_m} p_s(q)\, dq.$$

Example. At market equilibrium, consumers demand 625,000 gallons of kerosene, whose supply function is

$$p_s(q) = 2.5 + 0.3q^{1/2},$$

where q is in thousands of gallons and $p_s(q)$ is in dollars per gallon. Compute producers' surplus.

First we compute the equilibrium price,

$$p_s(625) = 2.5 + 0.3(625)^{1/2}$$
$$= 2.5 + 0.3(25)$$
$$= \$10 \text{ per gallon.}$$

Then, producers' surplus is

$$(10)(625) - \int_0^{625} (2.5 + 0.3q^{1/2})\, dq$$

$$= 6250 - (2.5q + 0.2q^{3/2})\Big|_0^{625}$$
$$= 6250 - [(2.5)(625) + 0.2(625)^{3/2} - (0 + 0)]$$
$$= 6250 - [1562.5 + 0.2(25)^3]$$
$$= 6250 - [1562.5 + 3125]$$
$$= \$1,562.5 \text{ thousand.}$$

Exercise. At market equilibrium, consumers demand 100,000 tons of SAE 90 lubricating oil, whose supply function is

$$p_s(q) = 10 + 0.5q,$$

where q is in thousands of tons and $p_s(q)$ is in dollars per ton. Compute producers' surplus. Answer: \$2,500 thousand.

Now that we have discussed both the demand function and the supply function for a product, we can see that the equilibrium point $E(q_m, p_m)$ occurs at a price where the quantity consumers demand equals the amount producers are willing to supply. That is, $E(q_m, p_m)$ is the intersection point of the supply and demand functions for the product. Thus, in our previous two examples, the product kerosene had supply and demand functions

$$p_s(q) = 2.5 + 0.3q^{1/2}$$
$$p_d(q) = 25 - 0.6q^{1/2}.$$

The equilibrium point occurs where $p_s(q) = p_d(q)$; that is, where

$$2.5 + 0.3q^{1/2} = 25 - 0.6q^{1/2}$$
$$0.9q^{1/2} = 22.5$$
$$q^{1/2} = \frac{22.5}{0.9}$$
$$q^{1/2} = 25$$
$$(q^{1/2})^2 = (25)^2$$
$$q_m = 625.$$

Then, with $q_m = 625$

$$p_s(q) = 2.5 + 0.3(625)^{1/2}$$
$$= 2.5 + 0.3(25)$$
$$p_m = 10.$$

Thus, in the previous two examples, the equilibrium point at demand $q_m = 625,000$ gallons and price $p_m = \$10$ per gallon were the same because they applied to the supply and demand functions for the same product, kerosene. It follows that if we have the supply and demand functions for a product, both producers' and consumers' surplus can be computed by first determining the equilibrium intersection point, then applying the formulas for producers' and consumers' surplus.

Exercise. The supply and demand functions for SAE 90 lubricating oil are

$$p_s(q) = 10 + 0.5q$$
$$p_d(q) = 110 - 0.5q,$$

where q is in thousands of tons and price is in dollars per ton. By review of the previous two exercises, or by starting anew, find: a) The equilibrium point, $E(q_m, p_m)$. b) Producers' surplus. c) Consumers' surplus. Answer: a) (100, 60). b) $2,500 thousand. c) $2,500 thousand.

13.11 PROBLEM SET 13–4

1. Maintenance of newly purchased equipment is expected to cost $(2 + 0.1t)$ thousand dollars per year at time t years.
   a) Compute total maintenance cost during the first six years.
   b) Make a sketch showing what has been computed in (a).
   c) Compute maintenance cost during the second six years.
   d) At what time, t, will the total spent on maintenance reach $60 thousand?

2. A currently new product is expected to be sold at the rate of $(20 - 0.4t)$ thousand dollars per year at time t years, $t < 50$.
   a) Compute total sales during the first 10 years.
   b) Make a sketch showing what has been computed in (a).
   c) Compute total sales during the second 10 years.
   d) At what time, t, will total sales reach $375 thousand?

3. An industry consumes fuel at a rate of $(2 + 0.6t^{1/2})$ million barrels per year at time t years. How much fuel will the industry consume in 25 years?

4. An oil rig pumps oil from a well at the rate of $(360 - 72t^{1/2})$ barrels per year at time t years. How much oil will be pumped in the next nine years?

5. At time t years, an industry consumes fuel at the rate of $(2t + 9)^{1/2}$ million barrels per year. If the total supply of fuel available to the industry now and in the future is 63 million barrels, how many years will the supply last?

6. At time t years, sales of a currently new product are expected to be

$$\frac{10}{(0.5t + 16)^{1/2}}$$

million dollars per year. How many years will it take for total sales to amount to $40 million?

7. The population of a trading area is currently 100 thousand. At time t years from now population will be growing at the rate of

$$\frac{20}{(0.5t + 9)^{1/2}}$$

thousand per year. What will total population be 14 years from now?

13.11 PROBLEM SET 13-4 (*concluded*)

8. A fixed cost of $2 thousand has been incurred in setting up an advertising campaign. Variable cost is expected to be at the rate of $(3 + 0.06t^{1/2})$ thousand dollars per month at time t months. Estimate total cost if the campaign runs 25 months.

9. When t tons of steel are produced, marginal cost in dollars per ton is

$$0.006t^2 - 1.2t + 50.$$

If fixed cost is $1,600, find the total cost of producing 100 tons.

10. When b barrels of whiskey are produced, marginal cost in dollars per barrel is

$$0.0045b^2 - 1.8b + 200.$$

If fixed cost is $4,000, find the total cost of producing 200 barrels.

11. A fixed cost of $50 thousand was incurred in setting up an operation. At time t months thereafter, the operation yields income at the rate of $(20 - 0.3t)$ and incurs expense at the rate of $(10 - 0.1t)$, where both rates are in thousands of dollars per month.
a) What is the optimal time to terminate the operation?
b) What will total profit be at the optimal time of termination?

12. A fixed cost of $4,100 was incurred in setting up an operation. At time t months thereafter, the operation yields income at the rate of $(2000 - 100t^{1/2})$ and incurs expense at the rate of $(200 + 200t^{1/2})$ where both rates are in dollars per month.
a) What is the optimal time to terminate the operation?
b) What will total profit be at the optimal time of termination?

13. The demand function for a product is

$$p_d(q) = 75 - 0.6q,$$

where q is in millions of barrels and $p_d(q)$ is in dollars per barrel. Market equilibrium occurs at a demand of 100 million barrels.
a) Compute consumers' surplus.

b) Make a sketch showing what was computed in (a).

14. The supply function for a product is

$$p_s(q) = 5 + 0.2q,$$

where q is in millions of tons and $p_s(q)$ is in dollars per ton. Market equilibrium occurs at a demand of 50 million tons.
a) Compute producers' surplus.
b) Make a sketch showing what was computed in (a).

15. The supply function for a product is

$$p_s(q) = (4 + 0.2q)^{3/2}$$

where q is in thousands of truckloads and $p_s(q)$ is in dollars per truckload. Market equilibrium occurs at a demand of 60,000 truckloads. Compute producers' surplus.

16. The demand function for a product is

$$p_d(q) = \frac{80}{(0.1q + 0.2)^2}$$

where q is in millions of tons and $p_d(q)$ is in dollars per ton. Market equilibrium occurs at a demand for 18 million tons. Compute consumers' surplus.

17. The supply and demand functions for a product are

$$p_s(q) = 10 + 0.1q \quad \text{and}$$
$$p_d(q) = 100 - 0.2q,$$

where q is in thousands of tons and price is in dollars per ton.
a) Compute consumers' surplus.
b) Compute producers' surplus.

18. The supply and demand functions for a product are

$$p_s(q) = 1 + 0.02q \quad \text{and}$$
$$p_d(q) = 6 - 0.08q,$$

where q is in millions of pounds and price is in dollars per pound.
a) Compute consumers' surplus.
b) Compute producers' surplus.

13.12 THE INTEGRAL OF $(mx + b)^{-1}$

We first consider the special case of

$$\int (mx + b)^{-1}\, dx = \int \frac{1}{mx + b}\, dx = \int \frac{dx}{mx + b}$$

where $m = 1$ and $b = 0$; that is,

$$\int \frac{dx}{x} = \int \frac{1}{x}\, dx.$$

We know that

$$\frac{d}{dx}(\ln x) = \frac{1}{x},$$

and $1/x$ is the integrand of the integral. Hence,

$$\int \frac{1}{x}\, dx = \ln x + C. \qquad (1)$$

Turning next to the general form,

$$\int \frac{1}{mx + b}\, dx,$$

we use the substitution

$$u = mx + b$$

so

$$du = m\, dx$$

and

$$dx = \frac{du}{m}.$$

Then,

$$\int \frac{1}{mx + b}\, dx = \int \frac{1}{u} \cdot \frac{du}{m} = \frac{1}{m} \int \frac{du}{u}.$$

Using (1) to evaluate the latter integral, we have

$$\int \frac{dx}{mx + b} = \frac{1}{m}(\ln u + C)$$

or

$$\int \frac{dx}{mx + b} = \frac{1}{m}\ln(mx + b) + C. \qquad (2)$$

In words, the integral of one over a linear function to the first power is the natural logarithm of the function divided by the coefficient of the variable.

Example. Evaluate $\int_{-1}^{3} \dfrac{4\,dx}{2x + 3}$.

If we have memorized (2), then we write the solution immediately, as follows:

$$4\left[\frac{\ln(2x + 3)}{2}\right]\Bigg|_{-1}^{3}$$

$$= 2[\ln(2x + 3)]\Bigg|_{-1}^{3}$$

$$= 2(\ln 9 - \ln 1)$$

$$= 2(2.19722 - 0)$$

$$= 4.39444.$$

If on the other hand, we do not have (2) at our fingertips, we can then use u-substitution to solve the problem. Let

$$u = 2x + 3$$

so that

$$du = 2dx$$

and

$$dx = \frac{du}{2}.$$

Then

$$\int_{-1}^{3} \frac{4dx}{2x + 3} = \int_{1}^{9} \frac{4}{u} \cdot \frac{du}{2}.$$

Notice that the limits on the integral have changed. When we change the variable of integration from an x to a u, we must simultaneously change the limits of the integral. To find the new limits, we use the substitution equation

$$u = 2x + 3.$$

So, when $x = -1$, $u = 2(-1) + 3 = 1$; and when $x = 3$, $u = 2(3) + 3 = 9$. Therefore,

$$\int_{-1}^{3} \frac{4dx}{2x + 3} = \int_{1}^{9} \frac{2du}{u}.$$

Now from (1)

$$\int_1^9 \frac{2\,du}{u} = 2(\ln u)\Big|_1^9$$
$$= 2(\ln 9 - \ln 1)$$
$$= 2(2.19722 - 0)$$
$$= 4.39444,$$

which is precisely the same result as before.

Exercise. Evaluate $\int_1^3 \frac{6\,dx}{3x - 2}$. Answer: 3.89182.

13.13 PROBLEM SET 13–5

Carry out the following; simplify results where possible.

1. $\int x^{-1}\,dx$.

2. $\int \frac{dx}{x}$.

3. $\int \frac{2\,dx}{x}$.

4. $\int 3x^{-1}\,dx$.

5. $\int x^{-2}\,dx$.

6. $\int \frac{dx}{x^2}$.

7. $\int \frac{dx}{5x + 4}$.

8. $\int \left(\frac{1}{3 - x}\right) dx$.

9. $\int \left(\frac{1}{3 - 0.2x}\right) dx$.

10. $\int 2(0.5x + 1)^{-1}\,dx$.

11. $\int \frac{dx}{(2x - 1)^2}$.

12. $\int \frac{10\,dx}{(5x + 3)^2}$.

13. $\int_1^{10} \frac{dx}{x}$.

14. $\int_1^e x^{-1}\,dx$.

15. $\int_0^2 \frac{dx}{0.5x + 4}$.

16. $\int_5^{10} \left(\frac{1}{0.6x + 1}\right) dx$.

17. If new reserves of a fuel are discovered at the rate of

$$\frac{100}{0.2t + 1}$$

million barrels per year at time t years, find the total amount of fuel that will be discovered in the next 25 years.

18. The demand function for a product is

$$p_d(q) = \frac{50}{0.5q + 1}$$

where q is millions of pounds and $p_d(q)$ is dollars per pound. Compute consumers' surplus if market equilibrium occurs at a demand of 18 million pounds.

13.14 INTEGRALS OF EXPONENTIAL FUNCTIONS

Inasmuch as the derivative of e^x is e^x, it follows that

$$\int e^x \, dx = e^x + C. \tag{1}$$

If the exponent is the linear function $(mx + b)$, then, as in the case in the last section, the integral has m as a divisor. Thus,

---

Exponential Rule, Base e

$$\int e^{mx+b} \, dx = \frac{e^{mx+b}}{m} + C. \tag{2}$$

Example. Evaluate $\displaystyle\int_0^{10} 30e^{0.06x} \, dx$.

If we have memorized (2), then we can notice that the exponent has $m = 0.06$ and $b = 0$. Hence,

$$\int_0^{10} 30e^{0.06x} \, dx = 30\left(\frac{e^{0.06x}}{0.06}\right)\Bigg|_0^{10}$$
$$= 500(e^{0.6} - e^0)$$
$$= 500(1.8221 - 1)$$
$$= 411.$$

If we do not have (2) close at hand, we can again use the u-substitution technique to solve this problem. Let

$$u = 0.06x$$

so that

$$du = 0.06dx$$

and

$$dx = \frac{du}{0.06}.$$

Then

$$\int_0^{10} 30e^{0.06x} \, dx = \int_0^{0.6} 30e^u \, \frac{du}{0.06}.$$

Notice again that the limits have changed. As in the last section, when we change the variable from x to u, we must change the limiting values in the definite integral from limiting values of x to limiting values of u. Since

$$u = 0.06x,$$

then when $x = 0$, $u = (0.06)(0) = 0$; and when $x = 10$, $u = (0.06)(10) = 0.6$. Thus, from (1),

$$\int_0^{0.6} 30e^u \frac{du}{0.06} = \frac{30}{0.06} (e^u) \Big|_0^{0.6}$$

$$= 500(e^{0.6} - e^0)$$

$$= 500(1.8221 - 1)$$

$$= 411.$$

Exercise. Evaluate $\int_1^2 e^{2x-1} \, dx$. Note that b is not zero.

Answer: $0.5(e^3 - e^1) = 8.684$.

Recall that the derivative of an exponential that has a base other than e requires a factor that is the natural logarithm of the base. That is,

$$\frac{d}{dx} a^x = a^x \ln a.$$

It follows that in the inverse process we must divide by $\ln a$. That is,

$$\int a^x \, dx = \frac{a^x}{\ln a} + C.$$

Again, if the exponent is the linear function $(mx + b)$ we can derive a more general formula using u-substitution. In this instance, we obtain

---

Exponential Rule, Base a

$$\int a^{mx+b} \, dx = \frac{a^{mx+b}}{m \ln a} + C. \tag{3}$$

Example. Evaluate $\int_1^2 (0.9)^{2x-1} \, dx$.

Let

$$u = 2x - 1$$

so that

$$du = 2dx$$

and

$$dx = \frac{du}{2}.$$

Then

$$\int_1^2 (0.9)^{2x-1}\, dx = \int_1^3 (0.9)^u \cdot \frac{du}{2}$$

since at $x = 1$, $u = 2 \cdot 1 - 1 = 1$; and at $x = 2$, $u = 2 \cdot 2 - 1 = 3$. Thus,

$$\int_1^2 (0.9)^{2x-1}\, dx = \frac{1}{2} \int_1^3 (0.9)^u\, du$$

$$= \frac{1}{2} \left[\frac{(0.9)^u}{\ln 0.9} \right] \Big|_1^3$$

$$= \frac{(0.9)^3 - (0.9)^1}{2(\ln 0.9)}$$

$$= \frac{0.729 - 0.9}{2(-0.10536)}$$

$$= 0.8115.$$

Exercise.   Evaluate $\int_2^4 (6)^{0.5x}\, dx$.   Answer: 33.49.

Exponentials often arise in applied problems dealing with rates, as illustrated in the following:

Example. A company projects its cost of providing medical care to workers to be at the rate of

$$15e^{0.03t}$$

thousand dollars per year at time t years. a) Compute total medical care cost for the next 10 years. b) How long will it be until total cost amounts to $250 thousand?

The key word in this problem is the word *rate*. The total medical care cost for the next 10 years will be the area under the cost rate curve over the next 10 years. If the cost rate were a constant, say $15 thousand per year, then the total cost over the next 10 years would be simply $(10)(15 \text{ thousand}) = \$150$ thousand. In this problem, however, the cost rate is not a constant, so we need to use the integral to compute the total cost.

Since this example makes no reference to fixed cost, we shall assume there is none, in which case the total cost sought in (a) is, by (2),

$$\int_0^{10} 15e^{0.03t}\, dt = 15\left(\frac{e^{0.03t}}{0.03}\right)\Bigg|_0^{10}$$

$$= 500e^{0.03t}\Bigg|_0^{10}$$

$$= 500(1.3499 - 1)$$

$$= \$175 \text{ thousand.}$$

Part (b) of the example asks us to find the time, T years from now, such that

$$\int_0^T 15e^{0.03t}\, dt = 250.$$

By (2), we find as before

$$500e^{0.03t}\Bigg|_0^T = 250$$

$$500(e^{0.03T} - e^0) = 250$$

$$e^{0.03T} - 1 = \frac{250}{500}$$

$$e^{0.03T} = \frac{250}{500} + 1$$

$$e^{0.03T} = 1.5.$$

We solve for T by first taking the natural logarithm of both sides of the last expression. Thus,

$$\ln e^{0.03T} = \ln 1.5$$

$$0.03T \ln e = \ln 1.5$$

$$0.03T(1) = \ln 1.5$$

$$T = \frac{\ln 1.5}{0.03}$$

$$= \frac{0.40547}{0.03}$$

$$= 13.5 \text{ years.}$$

To better understand the significance of the preceding example, note the cost rate

$$15e^{0.03t}$$

at $t = 0$ is

$$15e^0 = 15,$$

or \$15 thousand per year. If this rate were *constant* over time, then total cost would accumulate to $250 thousand in $250\!/\!15 = 16.7$ years. However, the exponential factor in

$$15e^{0.03t}$$

indicates that the cost rate per year is increasing and this accounts for the fact that cost will accumulate to $250 thousand in 13.5 years rather than 16.7 years.

13.15 PROBLEM SET 13–6

Carry out the following. Simplify results where possible.

1. $\int e^x \, dx$.

2. $\int 2^x \, dx$.

3. $\int 3^{-x} \, dx$.

4. $\int e^{-x} \, dx$.

5. $\int e^{0.5x} \, dx$.

6. $\int 5^{0.2x} \, dx$.

7. $\int (0.5)^{1-0.4x} \, dx$.

8. $\int e^{2-0.5x} \, dx$.

9. $\int 2e^{3-0.1x} \, dx$.

10. $\int 4e^{5-0.2x} \, dx$.

11. $\int \dfrac{dx}{(0.8)^x}$.

12. $\int \dfrac{1}{e^{0.5x}} \, dx$.

Evaluate the following:

13. $\displaystyle\int_0^5 2e^{1-0.2x} \, dx$.

14. $\displaystyle\int_1^2 4e^{2-0.5x} \, dx$.

15. $\displaystyle\int_1^2 10(0.5)^x \, dx$.

16. $\displaystyle\int_0^2 5(0.9)^x \, dx$.

---

17. The total supply of a fuel available now and in the future is 1,000 million barrels. At time t years from now, fuel will be consumed at the rate of

$$10e^{0.05t}$$

million barrels per year.
a) How much fuel will be consumed in the next 20 years?
b) How long will the supply of fuel last?

18. At time t years, the cost of maintaining a facility is at the rate of $12e^{0.08t}$ thousands of dollars per year. Assuming there is no fixed cost involved,
a) Find total maintenance cost for the next 10 years.
b) How long will it take for total maintenance cost to reach $300 thousand?

19. At time t years, interest on a bank account is at the rate of $600e^{0.06t}$ dollars per year.
a) What will be total interest accumulation in 12 years?
b) How long will it take for total interest accumulation to reach $5,000?

20. Sales of a product are projected to be at the rate of $15e^{-0.2t}$ million pounds per year at time t years.
a) Find total sales in the next five years.
b) How long will it take for total sales to reach 60 million pounds?

21. Sales of wheat at time t years are projected to be at the rate of $5 + 15e^{-0.2t}$ million pounds per year. Find total sales in the next five years.

22. Sales of milk at time t years are projected to be at the rate of $10 + 20e^{-0.4t}$ million gal-

13.15 PROBLEM SET 13–6 (*concluded*)

lons per year. Find total sales in the next five years.

23. The supply function for a product is

$$p_s(q) = 5 + e^{0.02q},$$

where q is in thousands of pounds and $p_s(q)$ is in dollars per pound. Market equilibrium occurs at a demand of 40 thousand pounds. Compute producers' surplus.

24. The supply function for a product is

$$p_s(q) = 10 + 2e^{0.05q},$$

where q is in thousands of gallons and $p_s(q)$ is in dollars per gallon. Market equilibrium occurs at a demand of 20 thousand gallons. Compute producers' surplus.

13.16 TABLES OF INTEGRALS

We saw in each of the last two sections that having an integration formula close at hand can simplify the evaluation of definite integrals. Certain integrals should be fixed in your mind and require no reference. These include

$$\int x^n \, dx = \frac{x^{n+1}}{n+1} + C$$

$$\int \frac{1}{x} \, dx = \ln x + C$$

$$\int e^x \, dx = e^x + C$$

$$\int a^x \, dx = \frac{a^x}{\ln a} + C.$$

Most of the problems in this text can be solved using these forms and the technique of u-substitution. Other forms that one might need to evaluate an integral are included in Table 13–1, which is part of the more extensive Table XII–B at the end of the book.

An even more extensive list of rules can be found by consulting a recent edition of *Standard Mathematical Tables*, published by the CRC Press, Boca Raton, Florida. Before illustrating the use of a table of integrals, we should point out that the very general rules for taking derivatives (the chain, product, and quotient rules) do not have counterparts in integration. Consequently, rules presented in tables of integrals were developed by specialized procedures, some quite advanced. Even so, we would look in vain in a table to find a rule for

$$\int e^{x^2} \, dx.$$

There is no rule for this integral and, moreover, there are no integration rules for numerous functions that arise in practice. As a consequence, procedures for approximating values of definite integrals are important in solving applied problems. We shall introduce approximation procedures later under the heading *numerical integration*.

TABLE 13–1

1. $\int (mx + b)^n dx = \dfrac{(mx + b)^{n+1}}{m(n + 1)} + C;\ n \neq -1.$

2. $\int (mx + b)^{-1} dx = \int \dfrac{dx}{mx + b} = \dfrac{\ln (mx + b)}{m} + C.$

3. $\int \dfrac{x\,dx}{mx + b} = \dfrac{x}{m} - \dfrac{b}{m^2} \ln (mx + b) + C.$

4. $\int \dfrac{x\,dx}{(mx + b)^2} = \dfrac{b}{m^2(mx + b)} + \dfrac{\ln (mx + b)}{m^2} + C.$

5. $\int \dfrac{dx}{x(mx + b)} = \dfrac{1}{b} \ln \left(\dfrac{x}{mx + b} \right) + C.$

6. $\int e^{mx+b} dx = \dfrac{e^{mx+b}}{m} + C.$

7. $\int a^{mx+b} dx = \dfrac{a^{mx+b}}{m(\ln a)} + C.$

8. $\int x e^{mx+b} dx = \dfrac{e^{mx+b}(mx - 1)}{m^2} + C.$

9. $\int x a^{mx+b} dx = \dfrac{x a^{mx+b}}{m(\ln a)} - \dfrac{a^{mx+b}}{(m \ln a)^2} + C.$

10. $\int x e^{ax^2+b} dx = \dfrac{e^{ax^2+b}}{2a} + C.$

11. $\int \dfrac{dx}{a + be^{mx}} = \dfrac{mx - \ln(a + be^{mx})}{am} + C.$

12. $\int \ln x\,dx = x(\ln x - 1) + C.$

13. $\int \log x\,dx = x \left(\log x - \dfrac{1}{\ln 10} \right) + C.$

14. $\int \ln (mx + b)\,dx = \dfrac{(mx + b)[\ln(mx + b) - 1]}{m} + C.$

15. $\int \log (mx + b)\,dx = \left(\dfrac{mx + b}{m} \right) \left[\log (mx + b) - \dfrac{1}{\ln 10} \right] + C.$

16. $\int \dfrac{1}{x^2 - a^2} dx = \dfrac{1}{2a} \ln \left| \dfrac{x - a}{x + a} \right| + C,\quad x^2 > a^2.$

17. $\int \dfrac{1}{a^2 - x^2} dx = \dfrac{1}{2a} \ln \dfrac{a + x}{a - x} + C,\quad x^2 < a^2.$

18. $\int \dfrac{1}{x\sqrt{a^2 - x^2}} dx = \dfrac{1}{a} \ln \left| \dfrac{a + \sqrt{a^2 - x^2}}{x} \right| + C,\quad 0 < x < a.$

Note: a, b, k, m, n and C are constants.

To use a table of integral rules, it is necessary to study the *form* of the function to be integrated and, having determined this, the table is searched for the corresponding form. Then constants are matched and the integration is carried out, as illustrated next.

Example. Find

$$\int xe^{0.1\,x}dx.$$

Here the integrand has the form x *times e to a linear function of* x. Running through Table 13–1, we find the corresponding form in Rule 8, which states

$$\int xe^{mx+b}\,dx = \frac{e^{mx+b}(mx-1)}{m^2} + C.$$

To match

$$xe^{0.1\,x} \quad \text{with} \quad xe^{mx+b},$$

it is necessary that

$$m = 0.1 \quad \text{and} \quad b = 0.$$

Therefore, with these values for m and b, we have

$$\int xe^{0.1x}\,dx = \frac{e^{0.1x}(0.1x - 1)}{(0.1)^2} + C$$

$$= \frac{e^{0.1x}(0.1x - 1)}{0.01} + C$$

$$= 100e^{0.1x}(0.1x - 1) + C.$$

Example. Find

$$\int \frac{8x\,dx}{(2x - 3)^2}.$$

Here, the factor 8 remains in the integral and is not considered when determining the form of the function. This form

$$\frac{x}{(2x - 3)^2}$$

is x over the square of a linear function of x, and Rule 4 of Table 13–1 states that

$$\int \frac{x\,dx}{(mx + b)^2} = \frac{b}{m^2(mx + b)} + \frac{1}{m^2}\ln(mx + b) + C.$$

Matching constants in

$$\frac{x}{(2x-3)^2} \quad \text{and} \quad \frac{x}{(mx+b)^2}$$

we see that

$$m = 2 \quad \text{and} \quad b = -3.$$

Consequently,

$$\int \frac{8x\,dx}{(2x-3)^2} = 8\left[\frac{-3}{(2)^2(2x-3)} + \frac{1}{(2)^2}\ln(2x-3)\right] + C$$

$$= \frac{-6}{2x-3} + 2\ln(2x-3) + C.$$

13.17 PROBLEM SET 13–7

Carry out the following using Table XII–B at the end of the book. Simplify where possible.

1. $\int x(2^x)\,dx$.

2. $\int \frac{6x}{2x+1}\,dx$.

3. $\int \frac{2x}{(0.5x+1)^2}\,dx$.

4. $\int xe^x\,dx$.

5. $\int xe^{2-0.5x}\,dx$.

6. $\int \frac{9x\,dx}{(3x+4)^2}$.

7. $\int \frac{2\,dx}{x(0.5x+1)}$.

8. $\int 2xe^{0.4x-1}\,dx$.

9. $\int \frac{2x\,dx}{5x-3}$.

10. $\int \frac{6\,dx}{x(3x+2)}$.

11. $\int xe^{0.1x^2-2}\,dx$.

12. $\int \frac{dx}{1+e^{0.2x}}$.

13. $\int \frac{dx}{1+2e^{0.5x}}$.

14. $\int 2xe^{2-0.5x^2}\,dx$.

15. $\int \frac{2}{x^2-9}\,dx$.

16. $\int \frac{-10}{x^2-16}\,dx$.

17. $\int \frac{3}{x\sqrt{1-9x^2}}\,dx, \quad 0 < x < \frac{1}{3}$.

18. $\int \frac{dx}{x\sqrt{1-16x^2}}, \quad 0 < x < \frac{1}{4}$.

13.18 ASYMPTOTIC AREAS: IMPROPER INTEGRALS

If we write

$$\int_0^5 \frac{1}{x}\,dx,$$

the integrand is *undefined* at $x = 0$. This is one type of *improper* integral, and in this case the definite integral is undefined. The expression

$$\int_1^\infty \frac{1}{x^2} \, dx \qquad (1)$$

is also an improper integral because its upper limit, denoted by the infinity symbol, ∞, is not a number. We shall define (1) to mean the *limit* of

$$\int_1^a \frac{1}{x^2} \, dx$$

as the upper limit a approaches ∞; or

$$\int_1^\infty \frac{1}{x^2} \, dx = \lim_{a \to \infty} \int_1^a \frac{1}{x^2} \, dx.$$

With this definition, the improper integral may or may not have a value (be defined). In the case at hand, if we write

$$\lim_{a \to \infty} \int_1^a \frac{1}{x^2} \, dx = \lim_{a \to \infty} \left(-\frac{1}{x} \right) \Big|_1^a$$

$$= \lim_{a \to \infty} \left[-\frac{1}{a} - \left(-\frac{1}{1} \right) \right], \qquad (2)$$

then we see that as a becomes larger and larger ($a \to \infty$), $1/a$ becomes smaller and smaller, approaching zero as a limit. Thus

$$\lim_{a \to \infty} \left(-\frac{1}{a} \right) = 0,$$

and (2) becomes

$$[0 - (-1)] = 1$$

so

$$\int_1^\infty \frac{1}{x^2} \, dx = 1.$$

Hence, this improper integral is defined and has the value of 1. On the other hand,

$$\int_1^\infty \frac{1}{x} \, dx = \lim_{a \to \infty} (\ln x) \Big|_1^a$$

$$= \lim_{a \to \infty} (\ln a - \ln 1)$$

$$= \lim_{a \to \infty} (\ln a)$$

since ln 1 is 0. Here, as a becomes larger and larger, ln a also becomes larger and larger and does not approach a finite limit. Thus

$$\int_1^\infty \frac{1}{x}\,dx$$

does not exist.

To see the area implication of the integral

$$\int_1^\infty \frac{1}{x^2}\,dx,$$

we sketch the graph of the integrand,

$$f(x) = \frac{1}{x^2}.$$

The important facts to note are, first, that when x is close to zero, $f(x)$ has a large value. For example, with $x = 0.01$ (close to zero)

$$f(0.01) = \frac{1}{(0.01)^2} = \frac{1}{0.0001} = 10{,}000,$$

and the closer x is to zero the larger $f(x)$ becomes, *but x cannot equal zero*. Second, if x becomes very large, $f(x)$ becomes very small. For example, at $x = 100$,

$$f(100) = \frac{1}{(100)^2} = \frac{1}{10{,}000} = 0.0001,$$

and the larger x is, the closer $f(x)$ gets to zero, *but $f(x)$ can never equal zero* no matter how large a number x is. Now refer to Figure 13–24, and note the right branch of the curve. As we move off to the right $(x \to \infty)$, $f(x)$ approaches zero (the x-axis), but does not touch it, and we describe this behavior by saying $f(x)$ approaches the x-axis *asymptotically*, or that the x-axis is an *asymptote* of $f(x)$. Similarly, as we move to the left in the first quadrant, $f(x)$ rises higher and higher as x approaches zero, but x can never be zero, so the curve does not touch the vertical axis, but approaches it asymptotically as x approaches zero. The behavior exhibited by the left branch of Figure 13–24 follows from the fact that

$$f(x) = \frac{1}{x^2}$$

has the same value when x is a given number, whether the number be positive or negative.

As a consequence of the above, when we find

$$\int_1^\infty \left(\frac{1}{x^2}\right) dx = 1$$

we call this result, 1, the area under $f(x)$ over the interval 1 to ∞, even though the area is not completely enclosed by a finite boundary at the

FIGURE 13–24

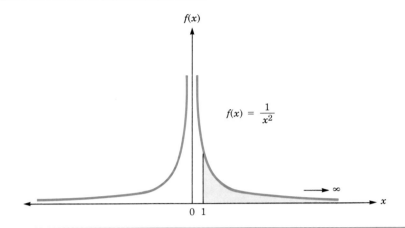

right. This idea of an *asymptotic area* is more than an exercise in apply-ing the limit concept because there are numerous important applications of functions having areas in the asymptotic sense. Indeed, the *normal curve* in the study of probability and statistics as shown in Figure 13–25, has the property under discussion.

Example. Find the value, if one exists, of

$$\int_0^\infty \frac{30\ dx}{(2x + 3)^2}.$$

We write

$$\int_0^\infty \frac{30\ dx}{(2x + 3)^2} = \lim_{a \to \infty} \int_0^a \frac{30\ dx}{(2x + 3)^2}$$

FIGURE 13–25

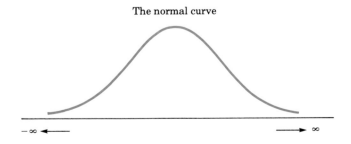

The normal curve

$$= \lim_{a \to \infty} 30 \int_0^a (2x + 3)^{-2} \, dx$$

$$= \lim_{a \to \infty} 30 \left[\frac{(2x + 3)^{-1}}{2(-1)} \right] \Big|_0^a$$

$$= \lim_{a \to \infty} 30 \left[-\frac{1}{2} \left(\frac{1}{2a + 3} - \frac{1}{3} \right) \right].$$

Now as $a \to \infty$, $\dfrac{1}{2a + 3} \to 0$ so we have

$$= 30 \left[-\frac{1}{2} \left(0 - \frac{1}{3} \right) \right]$$

$$= 30 \left(\frac{1}{6} \right) = 5.$$

Exercise. Find the value of the following, if a value exists.

$$\int_6^\infty \frac{3 \, dx}{(2x - 10)^2}.$$

Answer: ¾.

13.19 PROBLEM SET 13–8

Find the value of each of the following, if a value exists.

1. $\displaystyle\int_1^\infty 4x^{-3/2} \, dx.$

2. $\displaystyle\int_2^\infty \frac{6 \, dx}{x^2}.$

3. $\displaystyle\int_{-3}^\infty \frac{dx}{(0.5x + 2.5)^2}.$

4. $\displaystyle\int_3^\infty 3(0.5x + 2.5)^{-3/2} \, dx.$

5. $\displaystyle\int_1^\infty x^{-1/2} \, dx.$

6. $\displaystyle\int_1^\infty x^{-2/3} \, dx.$

7. $\displaystyle\int_0^\infty 5e^{-0.2x} \, dx.$

8. $\displaystyle\int_0^\infty e^{-0.5x} \, dx.$

9. $\displaystyle\int_{25}^\infty \frac{-2}{\sqrt{x}} \, dx.$

10. $\displaystyle\int_{-\infty}^{-4} \frac{1}{x^4} \, dx.$

11. $\displaystyle\int_{-\infty}^{-1} x^2 \, dx.$

12. $\displaystyle\int_1^\infty \frac{1}{x^{1.01}} \, dx$

13. $\displaystyle\int_1^\infty \frac{1}{x^{99}} \, dx.$

14. $\displaystyle\int_{-\infty}^0 e^{4x} \, dx.$

13.19 PROBLEM SET 13–8 (*concluded*)

Use Table 13–1 as necessary for the following:

15. $\displaystyle\int_0^\infty xe^{2x}\,dx.$

16. $\displaystyle\int_{-\infty}^0 xe^{3x}\,dx.$

17. $\displaystyle\int_1^\infty \frac{4}{9x(x+1)}\,dx.$

18. $\displaystyle\int_2^\infty \frac{2}{x(5x+1)}\,dx.$

13.20 NUMERICAL INTEGRATION

Although extensive lists of integration rules are available in published tables, it frequently happens that a table does not have the counterpart of a form that arises in an applied problem. Sometimes it is possible to derive the integration rule for the form at hand either by applying a formal procedure such as the one discussed in the next section, or by some ingenious technique, but there are cases where formal procedures and ingenuity are to no avail. Thus, we note that while

$$\int e^x\,dx = e^x + C$$

is perhaps the simplest of all integration rules, no rule can be found if we write

$$\int e^{x^2}\,dx.$$

Lack of an integration rule poses no particular problem in applications where the value of a definite integral is sought because such values can be approximated quickly and with high accuracy on a computer that has been programmed to carry out numerical (approximate) integration. After the computer has been supplied with the program for numerical integration, we need only supply it with a statement specifying the function to be integrated and the values of the upper and lower limits of integration. The computer will then determine the desired value in less time than we spent supplying it with the problem. Lacking access to a computer, we can also approximate definite integrals easily on calculators. The procedure we shall develop for this purpose is called the *trapezoidal rule.* There are many other techniques that have been developed to approximate the value of definite integrals, but with the high internal speed of the modern computer more efficient procedures save only a negligible amount of actual run time.

The trapezoidal rule approximates the definite integral (which is the area under a curve) by computing the areas of n trapezoids as illustrated in Figure 13–26. To obtain the trapezoids, the interval from a to b, which are the integration limits, is divided into n equal parts, each of width w. That is,

$$w = \frac{b-a}{n}.$$

FIGURE 13–26

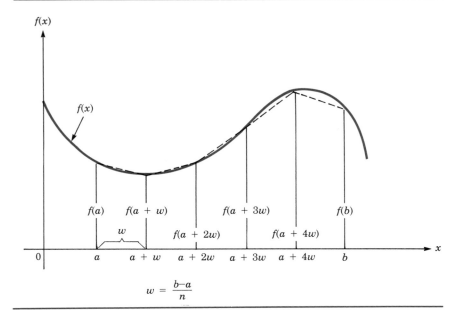

$$w = \frac{b-a}{n}$$

For illustration, Figure 13–26 uses $n = 5$ parts, leading to five trapezoids. The base of the first trapezoid extends from a to $a + w$ and is of width w; the base of the second trapezoid extends from $a + w$ to $a + 2w$ and is of width w, and so on. The x-values of the points delineating the bases are

$$a, \quad a + w, \quad a + 2w, \quad a + 3w, \quad a + 4w, \quad b.$$

Note for later reference that for $n = 5$, the next to the last point in the sequence is $(a + 4w)$, which in general will become $(a + (n - 1)w)$.

The (parallel) sides of the trapezoids are the function values for the points on the x-axis; that is,

$$f(a), \quad f(a + w), \quad f(a + 2w), \quad f(a + 3w), \quad f(a + 4w), \quad f(b),$$

where, again, the next to the last function value will in general be $f(a + (n - 1)w)$.

The area of a trapezoid is computed as one-half the base times the sum of the (parallel) sides. Thus, the area of the first trapezoid is

$$\frac{w}{2}[f(a) + f(a + w)].$$

Exercise.   What is the expression for the area of the second trapezoid?   Answer: $(w/2)[f(a + w) + f(a + 2w)]$.

From the preceding, we see that the sum of the areas of the five trapezoids of Figure 13–26 is:

$$\frac{w}{2}[f(a) + f(a + w)]$$

$$+ \frac{w}{2}[f(a + w) + f(a + 2w)]$$

$$+ \frac{w}{2}[f(a + 2w) + f(a + 3w)]$$

$$+ \frac{w}{2}[f(a + 3w) + f(a + 4w)]$$

$$+ \frac{w}{2}[f(a + 4w) + f(b)].$$

Observe next that if we add up the last expressions, each term in the brackets *except* the first and last, $f(a)$ and $f(b)$, occurs twice, so the sum is

$$\frac{w}{2}[f(a) + 2f(a + w) + 2f(a + 2w) + 2f(a + 3w) + 2f(a + 4w) + f(b)]$$

$$= w\left[\frac{f(a)}{2} + f(a + w) + f(a + 2w) + f(a + 3w) + f(a + 4w) + \frac{f(b)}{2}\right],$$

by bringing the divisor 2 into the bracket. Now, remembering that $a + 4w$ in the next to the last term arose because we had $n = 5$ divisions, it follows that in general, for n divisions, the *next to the last term will be*

$$f(a + (n - 1)w).$$

Using $\approx$ to mean equals approximately, we have the

Trapezoidal Rule

$$\int_a^b f(x)\,dx \approx w\left[\frac{f(a)}{2} + f(a + w) + f(a + 2w)\right.$$

$$\left. + \cdots + f(a + (n - 1)w) + \frac{f(b)}{2}\right],$$

$$\text{where } w = \frac{b - a}{n}.$$

This rule may be stated more compactly by using the summation symbol form as

$$\int_a^b f(x)\,dx \approx w\left\{\frac{f(a)}{2} + \left[\sum_{i=1}^{n-1} f(a + iw)\right] + \frac{f(b)}{2}\right\}.$$

To apply the rule, we first decide the number of subdivisions we wish to use, n, then compute

$$w = \frac{b - a}{n}.$$

With this value of w, we then write the values of

$$a, \quad a + w, \quad a + 2w, \quad \cdots, \quad a + (n - 1)w, \quad b.$$

Next we compute half the function value at a, all of the following function values prior to b, half the function value at b, and sum the results. This sum, multiplied by w, is the approximate value of the definite integral. The greater the number of divisions (the larger n is) the more accurate will be the approximation. The following illustration shows the procedure in a simple case where we can check the outcome.

Example. Approximate the following integral by the trapezoidal rule, using five subdivisions.

$$\int_1^3 x^2 \, dx.$$

Since $n = 5$, the interval width is

$$w = \frac{b - a}{5} = \frac{3 - 1}{5} = \frac{2}{5} = 0.4.$$

The points at which the function x^2 is to be evaluated are $a = 1$, $a + w = 1.4$, and so on as shown in organized fashion in Table 13–2.

TABLE 13–2

Point, x	Function Value, x^2		Numbers to Be Summed
a $= 1$	1	(times ½)	0.50
$a + w$ $= 1.4$	1.96		1.96
$a + 2w = 1.8$	3.24		3.24
$a + 3w = 2.2$	4.84		4.84
$a + 4w = 2.6$	6.76		6.76
b $= 3$	9	(times ½)	4.50
			Sum = 21.80

Answer: $w(\text{Sum}) = 0.4(21.80) = 8.72.$

Hence, from Table 13–2,

$$\int_1^3 x^2 \, dx \approx 8.72.$$

The exact value of this integral is

$$\int_1^3 x^2\, dx = \frac{x^3}{3}\Big|_1^3 = \frac{27}{3} - \frac{1}{3} = \frac{26}{3},$$

which, to two decimals, is 8.67, so our approximation is in error by 8.72 − 8.67 or about 0.05 when $n = 5$ trapezoids are used. Calculations (not shown) provide 8.68 as the approximation when $n = 10$ trapezoids are used, and the error is 8.68 − 8.67, or 0.01 and, of course, larger values of n can be used to reduce the error as much as we wish.

Example. Approximate the following by the area of 10 trapezoids:

$$\int_0^1 e^{x^2}\, dx.$$

In this case, no rule can be applied to determine the correct value of the integral. The approximation with $n = 10$ leads to a subdivision width of

$$w = \frac{b - a}{n} = \frac{1 - 0}{10} = 0.1.$$

The calculations for the approximation are organized in Table 13–3, where the exponential values were taken from a calculator. The answer just obtained,

$$\int_0^1 e^{x^2}\, dx \approx 1.46717,$$

almost certainly contains some meaningless digits at the right, but we cannot say how many. To shed light on this, we carried out the approximation on a computer with $n = 10$ as shown in the BASIC and PASCAL programs of Table 13–4. Note that the resultant area of 1.46717 is precisely the same as that in Table 13–3. Next we carried out approxima-

TABLE 13–3

x	x^2	$f(x) = e^{x^2}$	Numbers to Be Summed	
0.0	0.00	1.0000	(times ½) =	0.5000
0.1	0.01	1.0101		1.0101
0.2	0.04	1.0408		1.0408
0.3	0.09	1.0942		1.0942
0.4	0.16	1.1735		1.1735
0.5	0.25	1.2840		1.2840
0.6	0.36	1.4333		1.4333
0.7	0.49	1.6323		1.6323
0.8	0.64	1.8965		1.8965
0.9	0.81	2.2479		2.2479
1.0	1.00	2.7183	(times ½) =	1.3591
			Sum =	14.6717

Answer: $w(\text{sum}) = 0.1(14.6717) = 1.46717$.

tions with $n = 10, 20, 30, \ldots, 100$ as shown in the BASIC and PASCAL programs of Table 13–5. From this table, it appears that

$$\int_0^1 e^{x^2}\, dx \approx 1.4627$$

accurate to four decimal places.

Exercise.   a) Modify Program 13–3 of Table 13–4 to approximate

$$\int_1^2 \ln x\, dx$$

with $n = 10$. b) Modify Program 13–4 of Table 13–5 to approximate the integral to four decimal places.   Answer: a) 0.385878. b) 0.3863.

TABLE 13–4

Program 13–3 (BASIC)

```
10   REM APPROXIMATION OF AREA UNDER E^(X^2) BY TRAPEZOIDS
20   INPUT "Enter limits a and b, and number of subdivisions n";A,B,N
30   PRINT
40   PRINT " X"," X^2","E^(X^2)","   SUM"
50   W=(B-A)/N
60   FOR I=0 TO N
70   X=A+I*W
80   P=EXP(X^2)
90   IF X=A OR X=B THEN S=S+.5*P
100  IF X>A AND X<B THEN S=S+P
110  PRINT X,X^2,P,S
120  NEXT I
130  PRINT "THE AREA IS ";W*S
140  END

RUN

Enter limits a and b, and number of subdivisions n? 0,1,10
```

X	X^2	E^(X^2)	SUM
0	0	1	.5
.1	.01	1.01005	1.51005
.2	.04	1.04081	2.55086
.3	.09	1.09417	3.64504
.4	.16	1.17351	4.81855
.5	.25	1.28403	6.10257
.6	.36	1.43333	7.5359
.7	.49	1.63232	9.16822
.8	.64	1.89648	11.0647
.9	.81	2.24791	13.3126
1	1	2.71828	14.6717

```
THE AREA IS  1.46717
```

TABLE 13–4 (concluded)

Program 13–3 (PASCAL)

```
program trapezoids(input,output);

  VAR
    x,p,w,a,b,s:real;
    i,n:integer;

  BEGIN
    (* approximation of area under e^(x^2) by trapezoids *)
    writeln('Enter limits a and b, and the number of subdivisions n?');
    writeln;
    readln(a,b,n);
    writeln('x':10,'x^2':10,'e^(x^2)':10,'sum':10);
    writeln;
    w:=(b-a)/n;
    s:=0;
    for i:=0 to n do
      BEGIN
        x:=a+i*w;
        p:=exp(x*x);
        if (x=a) or (x=b) then s:=s+p/2;
        if (x>a) and (x<b) then s:=s+p;
        writeln(x:10:1,x*x:10:2,p:10:5,s:10:5)
      END;
    writeln('The area is ',w*s:8:5)
  END.
$ run

Enter limits a and b, and the number of subdivisions n?

0 1 10

           x        x^2    e^(x^2)        sum

          0.0       0.00   1.00000    0.50000
          0.1       0.01   1.01005    1.51005
          0.2       0.04   1.04081    2.55086
          0.3       0.09   1.09417    3.64504
          0.4       0.16   1.17351    4.81855
          0.5       0.25   1.28403    6.10257
          0.6       0.36   1.43333    7.53590
          0.7       0.49   1.63232    9.16822
          0.8       0.64   1.89648   11.06470
          0.9       0.81   2.24791   13.31261
          1.0       1.00   2.71828   14.67175
The area is  1.46717
```

TABLE 13–5

Program 13–4 (BASIC)

```
10  REM APPROXIMATION OF AREA UNDER E^(X^2) USING 10 - 100 TRAPEZOIDS
20  INPUT "Enter lower limit a and upper limit b";A,B
30  FOR N=10 TO 100 STEP 10
40  W=(B-A)/N
50  S=0
60  FOR I=0 TO N
70  X=A+I*W
80  P=EXP(X^2)
90  IF X=A OR X=B THEN S=S+.5*P
100 IF X>A AND X<B THEN S=S+P
120 NEXT I
130 PRINT "With ";N;" trapezoids, the area is ";W*S
140 NEXT N
150 END

Ready

RUN

Enter lower limit a and upper limit b? 0,1
With  10  trapezoids, the area is  1.46717
With  20  trapezoids, the area is  1.46378
With  30  trapezoids, the area is  1.46316
With  40  trapezoids, the area is  1.46293
With  50  trapezoids, the area is  1.46283
With  60  trapezoids, the area is  1.46278
With  70  trapezoids, the area is  1.46274
With  80  trapezoids, the area is  1.46272
With  90  trapezoids, the area is  1.46271
With  100 trapezoids, the area is  1.4627
```

Program 13–4 (PASCAL)

```
program trapezoids(input,output);

  VAR
    x,p,w,a,b,s:real;
    i,n,m:integer;

  BEGIN
    (* approximation of area under e^(x^2) using 10-100 trapezoids *)
    writeln('Enter lower limit a and upper limit b');
    writeln;
    readln(a,b);
    for n:= 1 to 10 do
      BEGIN
        m:=10*n;
        w:=(b-a)/m;
        s:=0;
        for i:=0 to m do
          BEGIN
            x:=a+i*w;
            p:=exp(x*x);
            if (x=a) or (x=b) then s:=s+p/2;
```

TABLE 13–5 (concluded)

```
            if (x>a) and (x<b) then s:=s+p;
         END;
         writeln('With ',m:4,' trapezoids,the area is ',w*s:10:5)
      END;
   END.
 $ run
 Enter lower limit a and upper limit b

 0 1
 With    10 trapezoids,the area is    1.46717
 With    20 trapezoids,the area is    1.46378
 With    30 trapezoids,the area is    1.46316
 With    40 trapezoids,the area is    1.46293
 With    50 trapezoids,the area is    1.46283
 With    60 trapezoids,the area is    1.46278
 With    70 trapezoids,the area is    1.46274
 With    80 trapezoids,the area is    1.46272
 With    90 trapezoids,the area is    1.46271
 With   100 trapezoids,the area is    1.46270
```

13.21 PROBLEM SET 13–9
Approximate the following by the sum of the areas of n trapezoids. (Trapezoidal rule.)

1. $\int_1^4 \ln x \, dx; n = 6.$

2. $\int_1^4 e^{-x} \, dx; n = 6.$

3. $\int_0^{0.4} e^{-x^2} \, dx; n = 4.$

4. $\int_0^{0.8} e^{x^2} \, dx; n = 4.$

5. $\int_1^2 \frac{x-1}{x+1} \, dx; n = 5.$

6. $\int_2^3 \frac{x+1}{x-1} \, dx; n = 5.$

7. $\int_1^3 \frac{\ln x}{x} \, dx; n = 5.$

8. $\int_0^{0.5} xe^{-x^2} \, dx; n = 5.$

9. $\int_1^3 \frac{x}{e^x} \, dx; n = 4.$

10. $\int_1^2 x \ln x \, dx; n = 5.$

The *normal curve* or, more precisely, the standard normal probability density function, is without question the most important function in probability and statistics. It is

$$f(x) = \frac{1}{\sqrt{2\pi}} e^{-\frac{z^2}{2}} \approx 0.398942e^{-\frac{z^2}{2}}; \quad -\infty < z < \infty.$$

There is no rule for integrating this function to obtain areas, which, in applications, are probabilities. Consequently, to assist the millions of people who use normal probabilities (which includes nearly every student of management and economics), values have been computed and tabulated. Table XI at the end of this book is a typical pre-

13.21 PROBLEM SET 13–9 (*concluded*)

sentation. The entry next to $z = 1$ in Table XI is 0.3413. This means that

$$\frac{1}{\sqrt{2\pi}} \int_0^1 e^{-\frac{z^2}{2}}\, dz = 0.3413$$

to four decimal places. Inasmuch as very few of the millions of users of tables such as XI have any understanding of the source of the numbers, a reader who does problem 11 or 12 can properly claim to be "one in a million."

11. (See the preceding introduction.) Approximate the following integral by the sum of 10 trapezoids.

$$0.398942 \int_0^1 e^{-\frac{z^2}{2}}\, dz.$$

12. Do Problem 11 using 20 trapezoids.

13. a) Modify Program 13–3 to solve Problems 1 through 11.
  b) Modify Program 13–4 to solve Problems 1 through 11.
  c) Using the results of (a) and (b), approximate the integrals in Problems 1 through 11 to four decimal places.

13.22 INTEGRATION BY PARTS

The purpose of this section is to illustrate one formal procedure called "integration by parts" that can be applied to integrate some functions whose integrals are not immediately obvious. There are other formal procedures that the reader can find in more extensive treatments of calculus under the headings of *trigonometric substitution, partial fractions,* and *reduction formulas.* But, it should be remembered that these procedures work only for functions of particular forms.

The method of integration by parts is based on the product formula for derivatives. If $f(x)$ and $g(x)$ are differentiable functions, then we know that

$$\frac{d}{dx}[f(x) \cdot g(x)] = f'(x) \cdot g(x) + f(x) \cdot g'(x). \tag{1}$$

Now let

$$u = f(x) \quad \text{and} \quad v = g(x)$$

so that

$$\frac{du}{dx} = f'(x) \quad \text{and} \quad \frac{dv}{dx} = g'(x).$$

Then (1) becomes

$$\frac{d}{dx}(uv) = v\frac{du}{dx} + u\frac{dv}{dx},$$

or rearranging the terms,

$$u\frac{dv}{dx} = \frac{d}{dx}(uv) - v\frac{du}{dx}. \tag{2}$$

Integrating both sides of (2) with respect to x, we have

$$\int\left[u\frac{dv}{dx}\right]dx = \int\left[\frac{d}{dx}(uv)\right]dx - \int\left[v\frac{du}{dx}\right]dx,$$

which can be restated as

Rule for Integration by Parts

$$\int u\,dv = uv - \int v\,du. \tag{3}$$

Equation (3), the formula for integration by parts, is applied as illustrated by the following examples:

Example. Find $\int \ln x\, dx$.

We first write down the integration-by-parts formula

$$\int u\,dv = uv - \int v\,du$$

and then try to make an appropriate choice for u and dv. Since the left-hand side of the formula must coincide with our problem statement, we choose

$$u = \ln x \quad \text{and} \quad dv = dx.$$

Then

$$du = \frac{1}{x}\,dx \quad \text{and} \quad v = \int dx = x.$$

Any constant may be added to v at this point, so for convenience we choose zero. Now, by (3),

$$\int \ln x\, dx = (\ln x)(x) - \int x\frac{1}{x}\,dx$$
$$= x(\ln x) - x + C$$
$$= x(\ln x - 1) + C.$$

Note that the constant of integration is not necessary until the final step in the integration. Note also that the result is precisely Rule 12 in Table 13–1 of Section 13.16.

Even when integration by parts works, it may take trial and error to get started correctly. The trick is to make the proper selection of the parts.

Example. Integrate the following by parts.

$$\int (e^x) x \, dx.$$

Suppose we try taking $u = e^x$, so that

$$\frac{du}{dx} = \frac{d(e^x)}{dx} = e^x$$

and $du = e^x \, dx.$

The remaining part is $dv = x \, dx$, and

$$\int dv = \int x \, dx$$

$$v = \frac{x^2}{2}.$$

We now have

$$u = e^x; \qquad v = \frac{x^2}{2}$$

$$du = e^x \, dx; \quad dv = x \, dx.$$

Then, applying the rule,

$$\int u \, dv = \int (e^x) x \, dx$$

$$= uv - \int v \, du$$

$$= e^x \left(\frac{x^2}{2}\right) - \int \frac{x^2}{2} e^x dx,$$

and the integral on the right is more difficult than the original problem. Consequently we should start again and choose the parts the other way around. That is, let $u = x$ and $dv = e^x dx$. This leads to

$$u = x; \qquad v = \int e^x \, dx = e^x$$

$$du = dx; \quad dv = e^x \, dx.$$

Hence,

$$\int u \, dv = uv - \int v \, du$$

$$= xe^x - \int e^x dx$$

$$= xe^x - e^x + C$$

$$= e^x(x - 1) + C,$$

which is Rule 8 in Table 13–1 of Section 13.16, with $m = 1$ and $b = 0$.

> **Exercise.**   Integrate by parts $\int x^2 \ln x \, dx$.
> Answer: $\dfrac{x^3}{3} \ln x - \dfrac{x^3}{9} + C$.

13.23 PROBLEM SET 13–10

Carry out the following. Simplify where possible.

1. $\int 3 \ln x \, dx$.

2. $\int 2 \ln x \, dx$.

3. $\int (\ln 2x) \, dx$.

4. $\int (\ln 3x) \, dx$.

5. $\int \ln(2x + 1) \, dx$.

6. $\int \ln(3x + 5) \, dx$.

7. $\int 6 \ln(3x - 2) \, dx$.

8. $\int 4 \ln(2x - 1) \, dx$.

---

9. At time t years, the cost of electric power used by a plant is projected to be at the rate of $4\ln(2t + 6)$ thousand dollars per year. Find total electric power cost for the next seven years.

10. At time t years, production of a food is projected to be at the rate of $9\ln(3t + 5)$ million bushels per year. Find total production in the next five years.

Apply integration by parts and carry out the following:

11. $\int x \ln x \, dx$.

12. $\int x^3 \ln x \, dx$.

13. $\int \dfrac{\ln x}{x^2} \, dx$.

14. $\int \dfrac{x + \ln x}{x^2} \, dx$.

15. $\int x(x + 1)^5 \, dx$.

16. $\int \dfrac{4x}{\sqrt{8 - x}} \, dx$.

17. $\int x\sqrt{1 - x} \, dx$.

18. $\int \dfrac{x}{\sqrt{x - 1}} \, dx$.

19. $\int (x^2 + 8)e^x \, dx$.

20. $\int_0^1 xe^{2x} \, dx$.

21. $\int_1^e x \ln x \, dx$.

22. $\int_0^1 \dfrac{(e^x + 2x)^2}{2} \, dx$.

13.24 DIFFERENTIAL EQUATIONS

Numerous problems earlier in this chapter start with given information about a *rate* and proceed to determine a desired quantity by integrating the rate. The methodology of differential equations, which we introduce in this section, is widely applied in solving such rate problems and, we should remark, such problems occur very frequently in practice.

A differential equation is one that contains a differential or a derivative. As examples, we write

$$y \, dy - x \, dx = 0$$

$$\frac{dy}{dx} = 2x + 1$$

$$\frac{d^2y}{dx^2} + 3\frac{dy}{dx} + x - 1 = 0.$$

The equation last written contains a second derivative and serves to illustrate the fact that differential equations may involve second and higher order derivatives and differentials. However, in this introduction we shall deal only with first-order equations. Before proceeding, we call attention to the use of differentials such as dy and dx as symbols having individual meanings. When these were introduced in differential calculus, it was emphasized that if

$$y = f(x)$$

then

$$\frac{dy}{dx} = f'(x)$$

and dy/dx was not a fraction with dy as numerator and dx as denominator, but a single symbol meaning the same as $f'(x)$. However, when we write

$$\int f'(x)dx,$$

dx appears alone. To achieve consistency, we define dy to be $f'(x)dx$. That is, if

$$\frac{dy}{dx} = f'(x),$$

then

$$dy = f'(x)dx.$$

In terms of symbol manipulation, the last can be thought of as being obtained by multiplying both sides of the preceding equation by dx, and this is how we shall describe the procedure. Thus, for example, if

$$\frac{dy}{dx} = 2x$$

then

$$dy = 2x \, dx$$

is a differential equation that is solved by integrating the left with respect to y and the right with respect to x. That is,

$$\int dy = \int 2x \, dx$$
$$y + C_1 = x^2 + C_2$$
$$y = x^2 + C_2 - C_1.$$

Inasmuch as C_2 and C_1 are arbitrary constants, $C_2 - C_1$ is another arbitrary constant, which we may call C. *We shall follow the practice of writing only one constant for one integration step*, so the solution is

$$y = x^2 + C.$$

A solution such as this, which contains the constant of integration, is called the *general* solution of the differential equation, and each value for C yields a *particular* solution of the differential equation. Thus,

$$y = x^2 + 10$$

is one particular solution, and there are infinitely many particular solutions.

Initial conditions. If we are presented with a differential equation and with a pair of values that must satisfy the solution, the given values are called *initial conditions* or boundary values.

Example. Solve the differential equation

$$dy = x^{1/2} \, dx$$

subject to the initial condition that $y = 10$ when $x = 9$.

We write

$$\int dy = \int x^{1/2} \, dx$$
$$y = \frac{2}{3} x^{3/2} + C.$$

The point $x = 9$, $y = 10$ must satisfy the last equation. Hence,

$$10 = \frac{2}{3}(9)^{3/2} + C$$
$$10 = \frac{2}{3}(3)^3 + C$$
$$10 = 18 + C$$
$$-8 = C,$$

so C must be -8, and the *particular* solution required is

$$y = \frac{2}{3} x^{3/2} - 8.$$

Exercise. Solve the differential equation

$$dy = 2x \, dx$$

subject to the initial condition that $y = 12$ when $x = 3$.
Answer: $y = x^2 + 3$.

13.25 SEPARABLE DIFFERENTIAL EQUATIONS

A differential equation that can be arranged in the form

$$g(y) \, dy = f(x) \, dx,$$

where one side is dy times a function of y and the other side is dx times a function of x, is called a separable differential equation. For example,

$$x \frac{dy}{dx} - 1 = 0,$$

after multiplying both sides by dx, becomes

$$x \, dy - dx = 0$$

or

$$x \, dy = dx$$
$$dy = \frac{dx}{x} \cdot$$

The general solution of the last separated form is

$$\int dy = \int \frac{dx}{x}$$
$$y = \ln x + C.$$

Exercise. Write the general solution of $\dfrac{dy}{dx} - 2x = 1$.
Answer: $y = x^2 + x + C$.

13.26 FORMS OF THE CONSTANT

The definition and rules of logarithms are applied frequently to obtain *explicit* solutions of differential equations. For reference, these are:

1. Definition: If $\ln a = b$, then $a = e^b$.
2. Product: $\ln (ab) = \ln a + \ln b$.
3. Quotient: $\ln (a/b) = \ln a - \ln b$.
4. Power: $\ln (a^b) = b \ln a$.

Example. Find the general solution of the following differential equation in *explicit* form.

$$\frac{dy}{dx} = \frac{y}{x}; \quad x \neq 0.$$

First, multiplying by dx gives

$$dy = \frac{y}{x}\,dx.$$

Then dividing by y provides the separated form

$$\frac{dy}{y} = \frac{dx}{x}.$$

Integrating, we have

$$\int \frac{dy}{y} = \int \frac{dx}{x}$$
$$\ln y = \ln x + C.$$

This solves the equation in terms of $\ln y$, but not explicitly in terms of y. Proceeding, we write

$$\ln y - \ln x = C$$

or

$$\ln \frac{y}{x} = C.$$

We next apply the definition of the natural logarithm and write

$$\frac{y}{x} = e^C.$$

Inasmuch as e is a constant and C is a constant, e^C is a constant, which may be denoted K. That is, there is no need for two constants in the solution. Hence, we have

$$\frac{y}{x} = K$$
$$y = Kx$$

as the *explicit* general solution. This surprisingly simple result is a straight line of slope K that passes through the origin, and a line through the origin is the only function whose slope can be found by dividing the y-coordinate of any one of its points by the x-coordinate; that is,

$$\text{Slope} = \frac{dy}{dx} = \frac{y}{x},$$

which is the initial differential equation. Observe, however, that x cannot equal zero, so the differential equation, and therefore the general solution, is not defined for $x = 0$. As a matter of convenience, we shall assume it to be understood that solutions we write exclude values of the independent variable where the differential equation and/or its solution are not defined.

Exercise. a) Write the following equation in separated form. b) Find the explicit general solution.

$$x \frac{dy}{dx} + y = 0.$$

Answer: a) $dy/y = -dx/x$. b) $y = K/x$.

As another example, consider the equation

$$x \, dy = 2y \, dx.$$

Dividing both sides by xy, we have

$$\frac{x \, dy}{xy} = \frac{2y \, dx}{xy}$$
$$\frac{dy}{y} = \frac{2dx}{x}.$$

Integrating leads to

$$\int \frac{dy}{y} = 2 \int \frac{dx}{x}$$
$$\ln y = 2 \ln x + C.$$

Now, applying logarithm rules,

$$\ln y = \ln x^2 + C$$
$$\ln y - \ln x^2 = C$$
$$\ln \left(\frac{y}{x^2} \right) = C$$
$$\frac{y}{x^2} = e^C = K$$

and we have

$$y = Kx^2$$

as the explicit general solution.

Finally, we remind the reader that the rule of exponents that says

$$e^x \cdot e^C = e^{x+C}$$

can be applied in reverse if an expression similar to the one on the right is encountered. That is

$$e^{x+C} = e^x(e^C) = Ke^x,$$

because if C is an arbitrary constant, so also is e^C an arbitrary constant.

Example. Find the explicit general solution of

$$2x(0.5y + 1)\, dx + dy = 0.$$

First we write

$$dy = -2x(0.5y + 1)\, dx.$$

Division by $(0.5y + 1)$ separates the variables, giving

$$\frac{dy}{0.5y + 1} = -2x\, dx,$$

$$\int \frac{dy}{0.5y + 1} = -2 \int x\, dx.$$

On the left we see a linear form whose integral we recall, or look up in Table 13–1 of Section 13.16, and have

$$\frac{\ln(0.5y + 1)}{0.5} = -2\left(\frac{x^2}{2}\right) + C_1$$

$$\ln(0.5y + 1) = 0.5(-2)\left(\frac{x^2}{2}\right) + 0.5C_1$$

$$= -0.5x^2 + C,$$

where, in the last statement, $0.5C_1$ has been written as another arbitrary constant, C. Application of the logarithm definition leads to

$$0.5y + 1 = e^{-0.5x^2 + C}$$

$$= (e^{-0.5x^2})(e^C)$$

$$= (e^{-0.5x^2})K_1,$$

where e^C has been replaced by another arbitrary constant, K_1. Continuing,

$$0.5y = (e^{-0.5x^2})K_1 - 1$$

$$y = \frac{K_1 e^{-0.5x^2} - 1}{0.5}$$

$$= \frac{K_1}{0.5} e^{-0.5x^2} - \frac{1}{0.5},$$

but $K_1/0.5$ is an arbitrary constant which we shall call K, and then write the explicit general solution,

$$y = Ke^{-0.5x^2} - 2$$

where -2 is *not* an arbitrary constant.

Exercise.   Find the explicit general solution of

$$dy - (2y + 6)\, dx = 0.$$

Answer: $y = Ke^{2x} - 3$.

13.27 PROBLEM SET 13–11

Find the explicit general solution of each of the following:

1. $dy - dx = 0$.

2. $dy - 3x^2\, dx = 0$.

3. $x\, dy = dx$.

4. $dy = y\, dx$.

5. $\dfrac{dy}{dx} = \dfrac{y}{x}$.

6. $\dfrac{dy}{dx} = \dfrac{y}{x^2}$.

7. $2\, dy - \dfrac{y\, dx}{x^{1/2}} = 0$.

8. $x\, dy + y\, dx = 0$.

9. $(0.2x + 3)\, dy = dx$.

10. $(0.5x + 2)\, dy = 2\, dx$.

11. $dy - (0.5y + 2)\, dx = 0$.

12. $dy = (0.2y + 3)\, dx$.

Find the explicit particular solution, using the stated initial conditions:

13. $dy - (x + 1)\, dx$; $y = 26$ when $x = 6$.

14. $\dfrac{dy}{dx} = 2x$; $y = 9$ when $x = 3$.

15. $\dfrac{dy}{dx} = y$; $y = 1.0874$ when $x = 1$.

16. $x\, dy + y\, dx = 0$; $y = 2$ when $x = 3$.

17. $dy = (0.2y + 3)\, dx$; $y = 4$ when $x = 0$.

18. $dy - (0.5y + 2)\, dx = 0$; $y = 1$ when $x = 0$.

19. $x\, dy - y\, dx - dx = 0$; $y = 2$ when $x = 1$.

20. $x\, dy + y\, dx + dx = 0$; $y = 3$ when $x = 2$.

**13.28
APPLICATIONS OF
DIFFERENTIAL
EQUATIONS**

In many applications, including the examples in this section, differential equations arise because the information available consists of an expression for a rate of change, together with initial conditions. When a rate expression is given, it will be helpful in setting up the associated differential equation to keep in mind the *units* associated with the differential and the rate.

Example. Smith owes Brown $100 now, at time $t = 0$, and the amount owed, y, is increasing at the rate of $10 per year at time t years. How much will Smith owe at time $t = 3$ years?

The answer is, of course, $100 + 3(10) = \$130$ because the rate of change is constant. However, we wish to use the example to illustrate the mode of thinking involved in setting up differential equations. To this end, we note that the rate of increase, $10 per year, has (dollars/year) as its unit of measurement. If this rate continued for dt years, where dt therefore has (years) as its unit of measurement, then

$$10\left(\frac{\text{dollars}}{\text{year}}\right) \cdot dt(\text{years}) = 10\ dt\ \text{dollars},$$

so $10dt$ dollars represents the change in the amount owed in time dt years. Calling this change in amount owed dy, we write the differential equation

$$dy = 10\ dt$$

and its general solution is

$$\int dy = \int 10\ dt$$
$$y = 10t + C$$
$$y(t) = 10t + C.$$

From the initial conditions, $y = 100$ at $t = 0$, we have

$$y(0) = 100 = 10(0) + C$$
$$100 = C$$

and the particular solution is

$$y(t) = 10t + 100.$$

Hence, at time $t = 3$ years, Smith will owe

$$y(3) = 10(3) + 100 = \$130.$$

Although the mode of thinking just illustrated is precise only when the rate function is linear, it will, nevertheless, lead to correct statements of differential equations, and we shall apply it in coming illustrations.

Example. A bank account contains $5,000 now, at time $t = 0$, and yields interest at the rate of 6% (0.06) per year, compounded *continuously*. How much will the account contain at $t = 5$ years?

The consequence of continuous compounding is that at any point t in time, the amount in the account at that time $A(t)$ or A is increasing at the rate of 6 percent of that amount, or $0.06A$.

At a rate of

$$0.06A$$

per year, the change in the amount in the account, in dt years, is $0.06A\ dt$, and this change in A is dA. Thus,

$$dA = 0.06A\ dt.$$

We proceed to separate the variables and integrate.

$$\frac{dA}{A} = 0.06 \, dt$$

$$\int \frac{dA}{A} = 0.06 \int dt$$

$$\ln A = 0.06t + C$$

$$A = e^{0.06t+C}$$

$$A = e^{0.06t}(e^{C})$$

$$A = Ke^{0.06t}.$$

The general solution of the differential equation is

$$A(t) = Ke^{0.06t}.$$

To evaluate K, we apply the initial condition $A(0) = \$5,000$.

$$A(0) = 5000 = Ke^{0.06(0)}$$
$$5000 = Ke^{0}$$
$$5000 = K.$$

The particular solution is

$$A(t) = 5000e^{0.06t},$$

so at $t = 5$, we have

$$A(5) = 5000e^{0.06(5)}$$
$$= 5000(e^{0.3})$$
$$= 5000(1.349859)$$
$$= \$6,749.29.$$

Exercise. If the account in the preceding started with P dollars rather than \$5,000, and interest rate i instead of 0.06, what would be the expression for the particular solution?   Answer: $A(t) = Pe^{it}$.

It should be noted that in Chapter 8 this formula was derived by much more laborious means.

Example. An oil company and a farmer upon whose land a well has been drilled agree that the farmer shall receive a royalty of \$2 per barrel of oil produced. The company wishes to pay for a year's output in a lump sum at the year's end. However, the farmer argues that a year's production does not occur all at once at the end of the year, but is spread out uniformly during the year. Consequently, asserts the farmer, his royalty income is generated *continuously* throughout the year but held by the company until the end of the year, and that he should receive interest. Because the flow is continuous, the company agrees to pay interest at the rate of 6 percent per year, compounded continuously, and consider the flow of royalty as being continuous. If the well produces 10,000 barrels in a year, what should the farmer's royalty be?

At the outset, we state that this example contains an idea that may be hard to grasp, and that is the idea of a continuous flow of royalties being compounded continuously. To sort the pieces out, we recall from the last example that whatever the amount A or $A(t)$ is in the account at time t years, that amount will grow at the rate of $0.06A$ dollars per year and in dt years will increase by $0.06A\,dt$ dollars. Next we note that 10,000 barrels per year at \$2 royalty per barrel is a royalty inflow at the rate of \$20,000 per year, which is $20,000\,dt$ dollars in dt years. Hence, there are two components of increase; $0.06A\,dt$ and $20,000\,dt$. The change in the royalty account in dt years is, therefore,

$$dA = 0.06A\ dt + 20{,}000\ dt.$$

We proceed to solve the last differential equation:

$$dA = (0.06A + 20{,}000)\ dt$$

$$\frac{dA}{0.06A + 20{,}000} = dt$$

$$\int \frac{dA}{0.06A + 20{,}000} = \int dt$$

$$\frac{\ln(0.06A + 20{,}000)}{0.06} = t + C_1$$

$$\ln(0.06A + 20{,}000) = 0.06t + 0.06C_1$$

$$= 0.06t + C$$

$$0.06A + 20{,}000 = e^{0.06t + C}$$

$$= (e^{0.06t})(e^C)$$

$$= Ke^{0.06t}$$

$$0.06A = Ke^{0.06t} - 20{,}000$$

$$A = \frac{Ke^{0.06t} - 20{,}000}{0.06}$$

which is an explicit general solution. As to initial conditions, we recall that royalties accumulate from zero at the start of the year, $t = 0$, to the amount at the end of the year. Hence, $A = 0$ at $t = 0$, so

$$A(0) = 0 = \frac{Ke^0 - 20{,}000}{0.06}$$

$$0 = K(1) - 20{,}000$$

$$20{,}000 = K.$$

The particular solution is

$$A = A(t) = \frac{20{,}000e^{0.06t} - 20{,}000}{0.06}$$

$$= \frac{20{,}000(e^{0.06t} - 1)}{0.06}.$$

Consequently, at the end of the year, $t = 1$, the farmer should receive

$$A(1) = \frac{20{,}000(e^{0.06} - 1)}{0.06}$$

$$= \frac{20{,}000(1.0618365 - 1)}{0.06}$$

$$= \$20{,}612.18,$$

which is about $612 more than a lump sum end-of-the-year payment of $20,000.

If, in the last example, money flowed in at the rate of R dollars per year rather than $20,000, and the interest rate was i rather than 0.06, the expression

$$A(t) = \frac{20{,}000(e^{0.06t} - 1)}{0.06}$$

would turn out to be

$$A(t) = \frac{R(e^{it} - 1)}{i},$$

which is the *formula for a continuous flow compounded continuously.*

Example. Suppose that a country has $200 million worth of its old one-dollar bills in circulation and that an average of $2 million worth of one-dollar bills flow through the country's banks each banking day. Starting today, $t = 0$ days, old bills appearing at banks are destroyed and replaced by new one-dollar bills. a) Find the expression for the amount of new currency in circulation at time t banking days. b) How much new currency will be in circulation after 50 banking days?

The key point to note in solving this problem is that even though two million one-dollar bills appear at banks each day, on the average, at any point in time except $t = 0$, not all of these bills will be old bills. For example, at the time when half the old bills have been replaced, only one million of the two million bills appearing will be old bills. Thus, the rate at which old bills appears is a function of t, and is a fraction of $2 million per day. To construct this fraction, we let $N(t)$, or N, be the number (in millions) of *new* bills, in circulation at time t. Then, since we started with 200 million old bills, the number of old bills in circulation is $200 - $ (number of new bills),

$$\text{Number of old bills in circulation} = 200 - N.$$

The total number in circulation remains at 200 million. Hence,

$$\text{Proportion of old bills in circulation} = \frac{200 - N}{200}.$$

Taking this proportion of the total 2 million per day appearing at banks, we have for the rate of increase in the number of new bills, per day:

$$\frac{200 - N}{200} (2) \text{ million per day}$$

$$= \frac{200 - N}{100} \text{ million per day.}$$

Consequently, the change dN in new bills in dt days will be

$$dN = \frac{200 - N}{100} dt.$$

We now solve the last differential equation, as follows:

$$\frac{dN}{200 - N} = \frac{dt}{100} = 0.01 \, dt$$

$$\int \frac{dN}{200 - N} = \int 0.01 \, dt$$

$$-\ln (200 - N) = 0.01t + C$$

$$\ln (200 - N) = -0.01t - C$$

$$200 - N = e^{-0.01t - C}$$

$$= (e^{-C})(e^{-0.01})$$

$$200 - N = Ke^{-0.01t}$$

$$-N = Ke^{-0.01t} - 200$$

$$N = 200 - Ke^{-0.01t}$$

or

$$N(t) = 200 - Ke^{-0.01t}$$

becomes the explicit general solution. At time $t = 0$, no new bills are in circulation, so the initial condition is $N(0) = 0$. Thus,

$$N(0) = 0 = 200 - Ke^0$$

$$0 = 200 - K$$

$$K = 200.$$

Hence,

$$N(t) = 200 - 200e^{-0.01t}$$

$$N(t) = 200(1 - e^{-0.01t})$$

is the explicit particular solution. To find the number of new bills in circulation at time $t = 50$ banking days, we compute

$$N(50) = 200[1 - e^{-0.01(50)}]$$
$$= 200(1 - e^{-0.5})$$
$$= 200(1 - 0.60653)$$
$$= \$78.69 \text{ million.}$$

All of the examples in this section have involved *time* rates of change, and while time rates are very common in practice and the coming problems will all involve time rates, we should not leave the impression that applications of differential equations are restricted to such rates. Thus, all of the marginals in economics (marginal cost, marginal propensity to consume, and so on) are rates not involving time and we could, if we wished to expand our examples, pose problems in terms of these marginals.

13.29 PROBLEM SET 13–12

1. Chris has just opened a sandwich shop and at time t days from opening expects to sell hamburgers at the rate of $150 + 6t$ per day.
   a) Represent total sales after t days by S or $S(t)$ and set up the relevant differential equation.
   b) What are the initial conditions?
   c) Find the particular solution of the differential equation.
   d) How many hamburgers will Chris sell in the first 50 days?
   e) How long will it take for Chris to sell 45,000 hamburgers?

2. (See Problem 1.) At time t days, Chris expects to sell hot dogs at the rate of $100 + 2t$ per day.
   a) Set up the relevant differential equation.
   b) What are the initial conditions?
   c) Find the particular solution of the differential equation.
   d) How many hot dogs will Chris sell in the first 50 days?
   e) How long will it take for Chris to sell 60,000 hot dogs?

3. Population of a town now, at $t = 0$ years, is 100,000. At any time t years, population grows at a per-year rate which is 10 percent of the population at that time.

   a) Set up the relevant differential equation, using $P(t)$ or P as population at time t years.
   b) Find the particular solution of the differential equation.
   c) Compute population 10 years from now.

4. Now, at time $t = 0$, \$2,000 is deposited in a bank account that yields interest at 5 percent per year. Interest is compounded continuously, so that at any point t years in time, the amount in the account grows at an annual rate that is 5 percent of the amount in the account at that time. Let $S(t)$, or S, be the amount in the account at time t years.
   a) Set up the relevant differential equation.
   b) Find the particular solution of the equation.
   c) Compute the amount in the account 20 years from now.

5. A bank account now, at $t = 0$ years, contains \$2,000. Interest, at an annual rate of 8 percent per year, is compounded continuously so that at any time t, the account will increase at the annual rate of 8 percent of the amount in the account at that time. Moreover, money is to be added to the account at a rate of \$500 per year. The addition is to be thought of as a continuous flow

13.29 PROBLEM SET 13–12 (*concluded*)

so that $500 per year is $500 dt in dt years.
a) Let A or A(t) be the amount in the account at time t years and set up the relevant differential equation.
b) Find the particular solution of the differential equation.
c) How much will the account contain 10 years from now?
d) How long will it take for the account balance to grow to $18,500?

6. (See Problem 5.) A bank account now, at t = 0 years, contains $5,000. Interest, at an annual rate of 8 percent, is compounded continuously. However, money is to be withdrawn from the account continuously at the rate of $500 per year.
a) Set up the relevant differential equation.
b) Find the particular solution of the equation.
c) How much will the account contain 10 years from now?

d) How many years will it take to reduce the account balance to zero?

7. The total supply of a fuel available now and in the future is 200 million barrels. At the present moment, t = 0, none of this total supply has been consumed. At time t years, the fuel is being consumed at the rate of

$$5e^{0.01t}$$

billion barrels per year. Let C, or C(t), be the amount consumed at time t years.
a) Set up the relevant differential equation.
b) Find the particular solution of the equation.
c) Compute the total amount of fuel which will be consumed in the next 10 years.
d) How long will the fuel supply last?

8. Solve Problem 7 if annual consumption of the fuel at time t is at the rate of $5e^{0.02t}$ million barrels per year.

13.30 REVIEW PROBLEMS

Write the expression for the indefinite integral. Simplify results where possible. Express answers with positive exponents.

1. $\int dq$.

2. $\int dp$.

3. $\int k\, dx$.

4. $\int 5\, dz$.

5. $\int (1 + y^2)\, dy$.

6. $\int (2 + 3p^2)\, dp$.

7. $\int (a + bx)\, dx$.

8. $\int (1 + cx)\, dx$.

9. $\int 12(2x^2 - x^3 + 3x + 2)\, dx$.

10. $\int 6(10x^4 - 8x^3 + 6x^2 + 4x + 3)\, dx$.

11. $\int (x^{2/3} + 2x^{-3/2})\, dx$.

12. $\int \left(x^2 - \dfrac{1}{x^2} \right) dx$.

13. $\int \left(1 + \dfrac{2}{x^3} + \dfrac{4}{x^{1/2}} \right) dx$.

14. $\int \left(1 - \dfrac{2}{x^{2/3}} \right) dx$.

15. $\int 30(3x - 5)^4\, dx$.

16. $\int \dfrac{15\, dx}{(7 - 5x)^2}$.

17. $\int \dfrac{6\, dx}{(8 - 3x)^{4/3}}$.

18. $\int 12(4x - 9)^{2/3}\, dx$.

13.30 REVIEW PROBLEMS (*continued*)

Evaluate the following definite integrals:

19. $\int_1^5 dx.$

20. $\int_2^5 (1 + x)\, dx.$

21. $\int_1^{16} x^{3/4}\, dx.$

22. $\int_1^2 \left(3 + 4x + \dfrac{10}{x^2}\right) dx.$

23. $\int_2^3 \dfrac{12\, dx}{(3x - 5)^3}.$

24. $\int_0^6 \dfrac{dx}{(0.5x + 1)^2}.$

Express the definite integral in terms of its limits, simplifying where possible.

25. $\int_a^{2a} \left(\dfrac{x}{a} + \dfrac{a}{x^2}\right) dx.$

26. $\int_0^b \dfrac{ab}{(ax + b)^2}\, dx.$

Find the area under the curve of the following functions over the given x-intervals:

27. $f(x) = (8x + 4)^{1/2}, \quad x = 0$ to $x = 4.$

28. $f(x) = \dfrac{20}{(0.5x + 4)^2}, \quad x = 2$ to $x = 12.$

Find the areas described in each of the following problems. (Sketches will be helpful.)

29. Find area bounded by the axes and
$$f(x) = 10 - 0.2x.$$

30. Find the area bounded by an axis and
$$f(x) = 60x - 12x^2 - 48.$$

31. Find the area bounded by the x-axis and
$$f(x) = 3x - x^2 + 18.$$

32. Find the area bounded by
$$f(x) = 19 - x \quad \text{and} \quad g(x) = 25 - x^2.$$

33. Find the first-quadrant area bounded by an axis and
$$f(x) = x^2 \quad \text{and} \quad g(x) = \dfrac{x^2}{2} + 2.$$

---

34. Maintenance cost on newly purchased equipment is expected to be at the rate of $(1 + 0.2t)$ thousand dollars per year at time t years.
a) Compute total maintenance cost during the first five years.
b) Make a sketch showing what was computed in (a).
c) Compute maintenance cost during the second five years.
d) At what time, t, will the total spent on maintenance reach $20 thousand?

35. At time t years, an industry consumes fuel at the rate of $(1 + 0.3t)$ million barrels per year. How much fuel will the industry consume in the next 9 years?

36. At time t years, sales of a currently new product are expected to be at the rate of
$$\dfrac{5}{(0.4t + 1)^{1/2}}$$
million dollars per year. How many years will it take for total sales to amount to $20 million?

37. Selling expense has a fixed component of $5,000 per year, *each year,* and a variable component estimated to be at the rate of $(10 + 0.1t)$ thousand dollars per year at time t years. Estimate total selling expense for the next four years.

38. Sales of a product are projected to be at the rate of $(81 - 3t)^{1/2}$ thousand tons per year at

13.30 REVIEW PROBLEMS (*continued*)

time t years. Find total sales during the next 24 years.

39. Sales of a product are projected to take place at the rate of $(0.9t + 9)^{1/2}$ thousand tons per year at time t years. Find total sales during the next 30 years.

40. The population of a trading area is currently 100 thousand. At time t years from now, population will be growing at the rate of

$$\frac{20}{(0.5t + 9)^{1/2}}$$

thousand per year. How long will it take for population to reach 260 thousand?

41. When t tons of steel are produced, marginal cost in dollars per ton is

$$0.003t^2 - 0.4t + 25.$$

If fixed cost is $1,000, find the total cost of producing 200 tons.

42. A fixed cost of $20,000 was incurred in setting up an operation. At time t months thereafter, income and expense are at the rates, respectively, of $(4100 - 100t^{1/2})$ and $(500 + 260t^{1/2})$ dollars per month.

a) What is the optimal time to terminate the operation?
b) What will total profit be at the optimal time of termination?

43. The demand function for a product is

$$p_d(q) = \frac{100}{(0.2q + 1)^2},$$

where q is in millions of gallons and $p_d(q)$ is in dollars per gallon. Market equilibrium occurs at a demand of 20 million gallons. Compute consumers' surplus.

44. The supply and demand functions for a product are

$$p_s(q) = 2 + 0.06q \quad \text{and}$$
$$p_d(q) = 10 - 0.02q.$$

a) Find the equilibrium market price.
b) Compute producers' surplus.
c) Compute consumers' surplus.
d) Sketch a graph containing both the supply and demand functions. Show by two different shadings which area represents producers' surplus and which represents consumers' surplus.

Carry out the following, simplifying where possible:

45. $\int \dfrac{3}{x}\, dx.$

46. $\int \dfrac{dx}{2x + 3}.$

47. $\int 2(5x + 4)^{-1}\, dx.$

48. $\int \left(\dfrac{1}{0.5x + 10}\right) dx.$

49. $\int_0^{10} 6(2x + 3)^{-1}\, dx.$

50. $\int_5^{50} \dfrac{dx}{0.2x + 1}.$

---

51. If new fuel reserves are discovered at the rate of

$$\frac{40}{0.25t + 1}$$

million tons per year at time t years, find the amount of fuel that will be discovered in the next 20 years.

52. The demand function for a product is

$$p_d(q) = \frac{40}{0.2q + 3},$$

where q is in millions of gallons and $p_d(q)$ is in dollars per gallon. Market equilibrium occurs at a demand of 10 million gallons. Compute consumers' surplus.

13.30 REVIEW PROBLEMS (*continued*)

Carry out the following, simplifying where possible:

53. $\int 6e^{2x+5} \, dx$.

54. $\int e^{-0.5x+1} \, dx$.

55. $\int 2^x \, dx$.

56. $\int 3^{0.5x} \, dx$.

57. $\int_{5}^{10} e^{0.2x-1} \, dx$.

58. $\int \dfrac{2 \, dx}{e^{0.5x-1}}$.

59. $\int 10(0.5)^x \, dx$.

60. $\int_{1}^{2} 10^x (\ln 10) \, dx$.

---

61. The total supply of a fuel available now and in the future is 200 billion barrels. At time t years from now, fuel will be consumed at the rate of
$$2e^{0.08t}$$
billion barrels per year.
a) How much fuel will be consumed in the next 10 years?
b) How long will the fuel supply last?

62. At time t years, interest on a bank account is accumulating at the rate of
$$800e^{0.08t}$$

dollars per year.
a) What will total interest accumulation be in five years?
b) How long will it take for interest accumulation to reach $10,000?

63. The supply function for a product is
$$p_s(q) = 2 + e^{0.01q}$$
where q is in millions of pounds and $p_s(q)$ is in dollars per pound. Market equilibrium occurs at a demand of 100 million pounds. Compute producers' surplus.

Carry out the following, simplifying where possible:

64. $\int 5 \ln x \, dx$.

65. $\int \ln (5x) \, dx$.

66. $\int \ln (0.3x + 5) \, dx$.

67. $\int \ln (10x + 3) \, dx$.

68. $\int_{1}^{5} 10 \ln x \, dx$.

69. $\int_{0}^{4} \ln (5x + 7) \, dx$.

---

70. At a rate t years from now, production of a food is projected to occur at a rate of

$8 \ln (0.5t + 4)$ million bushels per year. Find total production during the next 12 years.

Carry out the following, simplifying results where possible:

71. $\int 4xe^{1-0.25x^2} \, dx$.

72. $\int \dfrac{6 \, dx}{3 + 5e^{2x}}$.

73. $\int \dfrac{4 \, dx}{x(0.4x + 3)}$.

74. $\int \dfrac{2x \, dx}{0.5x + 9}$.

75. $\int 3xe^{5-0.1x} \, dx$.

76. $\int 3x(5^x) \, dx$.

77. $\int \dfrac{9x \, dx}{(3x + 2)^2}$.

78. $\int 5xe^{-0.4x} \, dx$.

79. $\int_{0}^{\infty} 10e^{-0.5x} \, dx$.

80. $\int_{1}^{\infty} 20x^{-5/4} \, dx$.

81. $\int_{0}^{\infty} \dfrac{2 \, dx}{(0.2x + 1)^2}$.

82. $\int_{1}^{\infty} \dfrac{30 \, dx}{x^3}$.

13.30 REVIEW PROBLEMS (*continued*)

Approximate the following by the sum of the areas of *n* trapezoids. (Trapezoidal rule.)

83. $\int_0^3 \ln (x^2 + 1)\, dx;\, n = 6.$

85. $\int_0^2 \dfrac{dx}{\sqrt{4 + x^3}};\, n = 4.$

84. $\int_0^2 e^{0.5x^2 - 0.3}\, dx;\, n = 5.$

Apply integration by parts and carry out the following:

86. $\int xe^x\, dx.$

88. $\int \dfrac{xe^x\, dx}{(1 + x)^2}.$

87. $\int x^2 e^x\, dx.$ (Use answer to Problem 86.)

Find the explicit general solution of each of the following differential equations:

89. $dy + dx = 0.$

93. $x\, dy + 2\, dx = 0.$

90. $3y^2\, dy - 2x\, dx = 0.$

94. $(2x + 3)\, dy = dx.$

91. $x^2\, dy - dx = 0.$

92. $x^2\, dy - y^2\, dx = 0.$

95. $dy - 0.4x(5y + 4)\, dx = 0.$

Find the explicit particular solution for the following, using the stated initial conditions:

96. $dy - 2x\, dx = 0;\, y = 25$ when $x = 5.$

99. $dy - (0.4y + 3)\, dx = 0;$
$y = 2.5$ when $x = 0.$

97. $x^2\, dy - y^2\, dx;\, y = 1.8$ when $x = 18.$

98. $dy - y\, dx = 0;\, y = 10$ when $x = 0.$

---

100. Chris has just opened a pizza shop and at time *t* days from opening expects to sell pizzas at the rate of $50 + 2t$ per day.
  a) Represent total sales after *t* days by *S* or $S(t)$ and set up the relevant differential equation for $dS(t)$.
  b) What are the initial conditions?
  c) Find the particular solution of the differential equation.
  d) How many pizzas will Chris sell in the first 20 days?
  e) How long will it take for Chris to sell 3,600 pizzas?

101. A bank account now, at $t = 0$ years, contains $1,000. Interest accrues at the annual rate of 6 percent per year, but is compounded continuously so that at any time *t*, the account will increase at the annual rate of 6 percent of the amount in the account at that time. Moreover, money is to be added to the account at the rate of $300 per year. The addition is to be thought of as a continuous flow, so that $300 per year is ($300dt) in dt years.
  a) Let *A* or $A(t)$ be the amount in the account at time *t* years and set up the relevant differential equation.
  b) Find the particular solution of the differential equation.
  c) How much will be in the account 10 years from now?

13.30 REVIEW PROBLEMS (*concluded*)

102. A trading area has 20,000 potential customers for a new product and an advertising promotion is planned to sell the product. $R(t)$ is the total number of potential customers who will have responded to the promotion at time t days. At time t days, responses occur at the daily rate of 2 percent of those who have *not* responded.

a) Write the relevant differential equation for $dR(t)$.
b) What are the initial conditions?
c) Find the explicit particular solution of the differential equation.
d) How many of the potential customers will have responded at $t = 10$ days?
e) How many days will it take before 10,000 have responded?

Probability in the Continuous Case

14.1 INTRODUCTION

The binomial rule, discussed in Chapter 9, assigned probabilities to the *number of occurrences* of an event in a certain number of trials. As such, the events were counting numbers, 0, 1, 2, 3, and so on, with no event between a successive pair of these numbers. The set, 0, 1, 2, 3, . . . , is called a *discrete* set because its members are separated. If we were to represent 0, 1, 2, 3, . . . graphically, it would consist of a set of separated points. In this chapter we introduce probability calculations for the *continuous* (as contrasted to discrete) case, and here graphical representation of the set of events consists of a continuous line or line segment. We shall first present the basic ideas in the continuous case by means of relatively simple functions, and then discuss the normal probability model and show some applications of this widely used model.

14.2 THE UNIFORM PROBABILITY DENSITY FUNCTION

Fran, an executive in a company, is expecting a friend to arrive by ship one afternoon. Upon inquiry, Fran learns from a dock official that the ship will certainly arrive between 1 and 6 o'clock, but just when is a matter of chance. Fran decides to assign one (certainty) as the probability of arrival from 1 to 6 o'clock and assume that arrival is equally likely at any time in this interval. Fran has a business appointment that will prevent her from being at the dock from 2 to 3:30 o'clock and calculates the chance that she will not be there when her friend arrives is 0.30 because she will not be present for 1.5 hours in the 5-hour interval from 1 to 6 o'clock; that is, $^{1.5}\!/_5 = 0.3$.

We shall use the preceding to introduce the method of measuring probabilities by areas. Figure 14–1 shows a horizontal interval from 1 to

---

FIGURE 14–1 (not to scale)

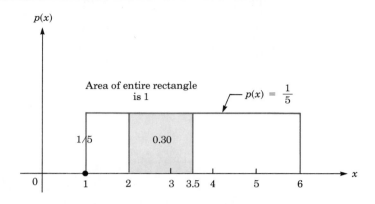

6 representing the time of arrival of Fran's friend. Because time is a *continuous* variable, the interval is a continuous line segment rather than a discrete (separated) set of points. A rectangle of height ⅕ has been drawn over the horizontal base, and its upper boundary is the constant function

$$p(x) = \frac{1}{5}; \quad 1 \le x \le 6.$$

The area of this entire rectangle is

$$A = 5\left(\frac{1}{5}\right) = 1,$$

and the 1 means it is *certain* (probability of 1) that the ship will arrive in this time interval. The shaded area over the horizontal interval from 2 to 3.5 (3:30), which is

$$(3.5 - 2)\left(\frac{1}{5}\right) = 1.5\left(\frac{1}{5}\right) = 0.30,$$

represents the probability that the ship will arrive during this time period. The function $p(x) = ⅕$ is called a *probability density function* or, more briefly, a *density function*. Note carefully that the density function does not provide probabilities. Rather, *areas under a density function over a horizontal interval are probabilities assigned to the horizontal interval*. Density functions are also called *probability distributions*, and we shall use the terms density function and probability distribution interchangeably.

The density function of Figure 14–1 is called the *uniform* density function, or uniform distribution, because it is a constant function representing Fran's assumption that arrival of the ship is *equally likely* to occur anywhere in the interval. Inasmuch as probabilities are areas under a density function, the probability assigned to a horizontal interval is the definite integral of the density function between limits which are the interval endpoints. Thus, in Fran's case, the probability of arrival between 2 and 3.5 is

$$\int_2^{3.5} p(x)\,dx = \int_2^{3.5} \frac{1}{5}\,dx = \frac{1}{5}x\Big|_2^{3.5} = \frac{1}{5}(3.5 - 2) = \frac{1}{5}(1.5) = 0.3,$$

which is precisely the same result as before.

> **Exercise.** By integration find the probability that the ship will arrive between 3 and 3:30 o'clock if $p(x) = \frac{1}{5}$. Answer: 0.10.

One consequence of area assignment of probabilities should be noted; namely, the probability associated with a point is zero. Thus, in Fran's case, the probability that the ship will arrive at *exactly* 2 o'clock is zero, where exactly means an instant (duration zero). This consequence arises because a point (instant) has zero width and the area (probability) over a point necessarily is zero. In applications, of course, we shall be concerned with intervals, so the zero point probability causes no difficulty. However, if we use the symbol

$$P(2 \le x \le 3.5) = 0.3$$

to represent Fran's probability assignment, we should realize that

$$P(2 \le x \le 3.5) = P(2 < x < 3.5)$$

because the probabilities for exactly 2 and exactly 3.5 are zero.

14.3 CONVERTING f(x) TO A DENSITY FUNCTION OVER AN INTERVAL

If we have a function $f(x)$ that is nonnegative over an interval, we can convert $f(x)$ to a density function by dividing $f(x)$ by the total area under $f(x)$ over the interval so that the entire area is adjusted to be 1.

Example. Convert $f(x) = 4x - x^2 - 3$, $1 \le x \le 3$, to a density function.

First we find the total area under $f(x)$ as

$$\int_1^3 (4x - x^2 - 3)\, dx$$

$$= \left(2x^2 - \frac{x^3}{3} - 3x \right)\Big|_1^3$$

$$= \left[2(9) - \frac{27}{3} - 9 \right] - \left[2(1) - \frac{1}{3} - 3 \right]$$

$$= 18 - 9 - 9 - 2 + \frac{1}{3} + 3$$

$$= \frac{4}{3}.$$

Then

$$p(x) = \frac{f(x)}{4/3} = \frac{3}{4} f(x)$$

$$p(x) = \frac{3}{4}(4x - x^2 - 3); \quad 1 \le x \le 3.$$

This function, $p(x)$, is a vertical parabola opening downward, with x-intercepts at $x = 1$ and $x = 3$, as shown in Figure 14–2. The conversion procedure simply changes $f(x)$, which has an area of $4/3$ over the interval, to the density function, $p(x)$, which has an area of 1, as required. Once assured that we have a density function, probabilities for intervals are computed as definite integrals.

Example. For the density function of Figure 14–2, find the probability that a randomly selected value of x will lie in the interval $2 \le x \le 2.5$.

***

FIGURE 14–2

***

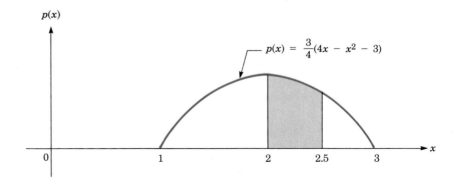

$$p(x) = \frac{3}{4}(4x - x^2 - 3)$$

The desired probability is the shaded area in Figure 14–2. We compute it as

$$\int_2^{2.5} p(x)\,dx = \int_2^{2.5} \frac{3}{4}(4x - x^2 - 3)\,dx$$

$$= \frac{3}{4}\left(2x^2 - \frac{x^3}{3} - 3x\right)\Big|_2^{2.5}$$

$$= \frac{3}{4}\left[\left(-\frac{0.625}{3}\right) - \left(-\frac{2}{3}\right)\right]$$

$$= \frac{3}{4}\left(\frac{1.375}{3}\right) = \frac{1.375}{4} = 0.34375.$$

14.4 PROBLEM SET 14–1

1. a) Convert $f(x) = 20$, $0 \le x \le 10$, to a density function.
  b) Compute the probability that a randomly selected x will lie in the interval $4 \le x \le 7$.

2. a) Convert $f(x) = x$, $0 \le x \le 10$, to a density function.
  b) Compute the probability that a randomly selected x will lie in the interval $4 \le x \le 5$.

3. a) Convert $f(x) = x^{1/2}$, $0 \le x \le 9$, to a density function.
  b) Compute the probability that a ran-

domly selected x will lie in the interval $1 \le x \le 4$.

4. a) Convert $f(x) = 2 - x^{-2}$, $1 \le x \le 20$, to a density function.
  b) Compute the probability that a randomly selected x will lie in the interval $1 < x < 10$.

5. a) Convert $f(x) = 12x - 3x^2$, $0 \le x \le 4$, to a density function.
  b) Compute the probability that a randomly selected x will lie in the interval $0 < x < 2$.

14.5 EXPECTED VALUE

We shall use the opening illustration of the chapter to show the meaning of *expected value*. Recall that Fran assumed a ship was equally likely to arrive at any time during the interval from 1 to 6 o'clock. Now suppose the unlikely circumstance that Fran has repeated occasions to be faced with the same situation and that on each occasion she records the time at which the ship arrives and then computes the average of these times. Because times on the interval 1 to 6 are equally likely to occur, we would expect that, on repeated trials, the average time would be the midpoint of this interval, which is at 3.5, or 3:30 o'clock, and this is called the *expected* time of arrival. Thus, expected value is an average value. What we wish to show first is that Fran's expected value for the time of arrival can be computed as

$$\int_1^6 xp(x)\,dx;$$

that is, the definite integral over the entire range of x's of x times the density function. For Fran's density function, $p(x) = \frac{1}{5}$, we compute the expected value of x, symbolized by $E(x)$, as

$$E(x) = \int_1^6 x\left(\frac{1}{5}\right)dx$$

$$= \frac{1}{5}\left(\frac{x^2}{2}\right)\Big|_1^6$$

$$= \frac{36 - 1}{10} = \frac{35}{10} = 3.5,$$

which is the value anticipated earlier.

Definition. *Expected value of x = E(x) =* $\displaystyle\int_{\text{all }x} xp(x)\,dx.$

In this definition, the "all x" on the integral sign means that the limits on the integral are the endpoints of the entire interval of permissible values of x.

The expected value of x, $E(x)$, is also referred to as the mean (or average) of the x values and is designated by μ (the Greek letter mu). Thus,

$$E(x) = \mu.$$

The mean, μ, has another interpretation that aids understanding; namely, μ is the x-coordinate of the *center of gravity* of a graphical representation of the density function. To see what is meant here, suppose Figure 14–1 was drawn on a piece of cardboard, then the rectangle was cut out with scissors and placed vertically across a knife edge, ($\wedge$), as shown in Figure 14–3. The rectangle would just balance, not tipping down at one side, if the knife edge is at the center of gravity, $\mu = 3.5$.

By way of contrast, consider

$$p(x) = \frac{10 - x}{50}, \quad 0 \leq x \leq 10,$$

which is shown in Figure 14–4. If we cut this triangle out, it will not balance at the midpoint of the base, which is at $x = 5$, but at a point, μ, which is to the left of the midpoint. To see where μ is, we compute

FIGURE 14–3 (not to scale)   **FIGURE 14–4 (not to scale)**

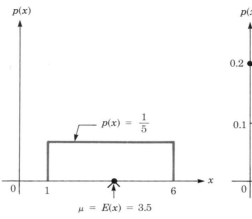

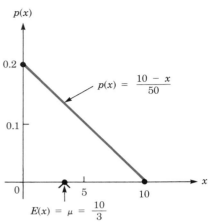

$$\mu = E(x) = \int_0^{10} xp(x)\, dx$$

$$= \int_0^{10} x\left(\frac{10-x}{50}\right) dx$$

$$= \int_0^{10} \frac{10x - x^2}{50}\, dx$$

$$= \frac{1}{50}\left(5x^2 - \frac{x^3}{3}\right)\Big|_0^{10}$$

$$= \frac{1}{50}\left[\left(500 - \frac{1000}{3}\right) - 0\right]$$

$$= 10 - \frac{20}{3} = \frac{10}{3}.$$

Thus, $\mu = {}^{10}\!/\!3$, as shown in Figure 14–4.

Exercise. Find the expected value of x, $E(x) = \mu$, if $p(x) = x/18$, $0 \le x \le 6$. Answer: $\mu = 4$.

Example. Jon sells oil in amounts up to 20 gallons, and uses

$$p(x) = 0.004x + 0.01, \quad 0 \le x \le 20$$

as the density function for amounts purchased by customers. a) Find the average (expected value) of the amounts purchased by customers. b) Estimate the amount that will be purchased by 30 customers.

a) We compute the expected value as

$$\mu = \int_0^{20} xp(x)\,dx = \int_0^{20} x(0.004x + 0.01)\,dx$$

$$= \int_0^{20} (0.004x^2 + 0.01x)\,dx$$

$$= \left(\frac{0.004x^3}{3} + \frac{0.01x^2}{2}\right)\Bigg|_0^{20}$$

$$= \frac{0.004(20)^3}{3} + \frac{0.01(20)^2}{2} - 0$$

$$= \frac{32}{3} + 2$$

$$= \frac{38}{3} \text{ gallons per customer.}$$

b) With an average purchase of 38⁄3 gallons per customer, total purchases by 30 customers would be estimated at

(number of customers)(average purchased per customer)

$$= 30\left(\frac{38}{3}\right) = 380 \text{ gallons.}$$

Exercise.   In the last example, estimate total sales to 90 customers. Answer: 1,140 gallons.

14.6 VARIANCE AND STANDARD DEVIATION

The standard deviation is denoted by the small Greek letter σ (sigma) and its square, σ^2, is called the variance.

Definition. Variance of $x = V(x) = \sigma^2 = \int\limits_{\text{all } x} (x - \mu)^2\, p(x)\,dx.$

The term *variance* has been chosen to emphasize that σ^2 is a measure of variability of x about its mean, μ, and this is captured in the definition by the factor

$$(x - \mu)^2$$

because $x - \mu$ represents a deviation or variation of x from its mean. In the beginning, variance has little, if any, intuitive appeal, but as we proceed through the chapter, the significance of this measure will become clear. For the present, we shall consider only computations of the variance.

Example. Compute the variance and standard deviation of x if its density function is $p(x) = x/288,\ 0 \le x \le 24$.

We must compute μ first. This is

$$\mu = \int_0^{24} x\left(\frac{x}{288}\right) dx = \frac{1}{288} \int_0^{24} x^2\, dx = \frac{1}{288}\left(\frac{x^3}{3}\right)\Big|_0^{24} = \frac{1}{288}\left(\frac{13{,}824}{3}\right) = 16.$$

Next we find

$$V(x) = \sigma^2 = \int_0^{24} (x - \mu)^2\, p(x)\, dx$$

$$= \int_0^{24} (x - 16)^2 \left(\frac{x}{288}\right) dx$$

$$= \frac{1}{288} \int_0^{24} (x^2 - 32x + 256)(x)\, dx$$

$$= \frac{1}{288} \int_0^{24} (x^3 - 32x^2 + 256x)\, dx$$

$$= \frac{1}{288} \left(\frac{x^4}{4} - 32\frac{x^3}{3} + 256\frac{x^2}{2}\right)\Big|_0^{24}$$

$$= \frac{1}{288}(82{,}944 - 147{,}456 + 73{,}728)$$

$$= \frac{9216}{288}$$

$$\sigma^2 = 32$$

$$\sigma = \sqrt{32} = 5.66.$$

Thus, the variance is $\sigma^2 = 32$, and the standard deviation is the square root of the variance, which is approximately $\sigma = 5.66$.

Exercise. Find the mean, variance, and standard deviation of x if the density function is $p(x) = x/72,\ 0 \le x \le 12$. Answer: $\mu = 8$; $V(x) = \sigma^2 = 8$; $\sigma = 2.83$.

Figures 14–5 and 14–6 show the density functions of the last example and exercise. Note that the density function of Figure 14–5 spreads out

FIGURE 14–5 (not to scale)	**FIGURE 14–6 (not to scale)**
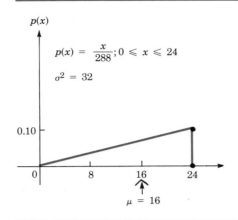	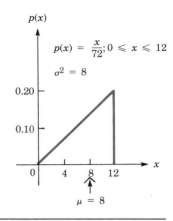

over a wider interval than is the case in Figure 14–6, and it is the spread or variability that is measured by the variance or its square root, the standard deviation. We shall see the importance of σ in more understandable form a little later in the chapter when we introduce the *normal* probability density function.

14.7 PROBLEM SET 14–2

1. Given $p(x) = 0.05$, $0 \le x \le 20$,
   a) Find μ.   b) Find σ^2.   c) Find σ.

2. Given $p(x) = 0.01$, $0 \le x \le 100$,
   a) Find μ.   b) Find σ^2.   c) Find σ.

3. Given $p(x) = \dfrac{x}{18}$, $0 \le x \le 6$,
   a) Find the expected value of x.
   b) Find the variance of x.
   c) Find the standard deviation of x.

4. Given $p(x) = 2x/9$, $0 \le x \le 3$,
   a) Find the expected value of x.
   b) Find the variance of x.
   c) Find the standard deviation of x.

5. Fran sells oil to customers in amounts of x hundred gallons, x going from 0 to 5, with the density function

$$p(x) = 0.04x + 0.1, 0 \le x \le 5.$$

   a) Find average (expected) sales per customer.
   b) Estimate total sales to 72 customers.

6. Sam sells oil to customers in amounts of x thousand gallons, x going from 0 to 2 with the density function

$$p(x) = 0.2x + 0.3, 0 \le x \le 2.$$

   a) Find the average (expected) sales per customer.
   b) Estimate total sales to 90 customers.

7. The density function

$$p(x) = \frac{3(1 - x^2)}{4}, -1 \le x \le 1$$

   is a vertical parabola opening downward, with vertex at (0, 3/4) and intercepts at $(-1, 0)$ and $(1, 0)$.

14.7 PROBLEM SET 14–2 (concluded)

a) Sketch the density function.
b) Why must μ equal zero?
c) Verify that $\mu = 0$.
d) Find the standard deviation of x.

8. The density function

$$p(x) = \frac{3}{32}(4 - x^2), \quad -2 \le x \le 2$$

is a vertical parabola opening downward, with vertex at (0, 3/8) and intercepts at $(-2, 0)$ and $(2, 0)$.

a) Sketch the density function.
b) Why must μ equal zero?
c) Verify that $\mu = 0$.
d) Find the standard deviation of x.

14.8 THE EXPONENTIAL DISTRIBUTION

A commonly occurring applied problem arises in situations where arrival times have to be considered. For example, in a bank where tellers wait upon customers, satisfactory (timely) service depends not only on the number of tellers but the times of arrival of customers. A number of tellers that would be adequate to provide good service to all customers if arrival times were uniformly spaced would not be able to maintain timely service to all if arrivals bunch up from time to time. One model of arrival times that has been useful in some applications is based upon an exponential function of the form

$$p(x) = be^{-bx}, \qquad 0 \le x < \infty. \tag{1}$$

This is a proper density function because it is nonnegative and has the required area of one, as shown next:

$$\int_0^\infty be^{-bx}\,dx = \lim_{a\to\infty}\left(\frac{be^{-bx}}{-b}\right)\Big|_0^a = \lim_{a\to\infty}\left(-e^{-bx}\right)\Big|_0^a$$

$$= -\lim_{a\to\infty}\left(\frac{1}{e^{bx}}\right)\Big|_0^a = -\left(\lim_{a\to\infty}\frac{1}{e^{ba}} - \frac{1}{e^0}\right)$$

$$= -(0 - 1)$$

$$= 1.$$

The expected value of x is

$$\mu = E(x) = \int_0^\infty x(be^{-bx})\,dx$$

$$= b\int_0^\infty xe^{-bx}\,dx.$$

Rule 17 from Table XII–B at the back of the book shows the desired integral is

$$\mu = \lim_{a\to\infty} b\left[\frac{e^{-ba}(-ba - 1)}{b^2}\right]\Big|_0^a = -\frac{1}{b}\lim_{a\to\infty}\left(\frac{ba + 1}{e^{ba}}\right)\Big|_0^a. \tag{2}$$

Thus, the evaluation of (2) requires that we find

$$\lim_{a \to \infty} \left(\frac{ba + 1}{e^{ba}} \right) \qquad (3)$$

and an evaluation of this particular type has not been encountered at a previous point in the text. The problem is that both the numerator, $ba + 1$, and the denominator, e^{ba}, grow without limit (approach ∞) as a goes toward ∞. To those who have developed an understanding of the growth in functions, it will be sufficient to state that the exponential function in the denominator increases much more rapidly than the linear function in the numerator and, as a consequence, the expression in (3) becomes smaller and smaller, approaching zero as a limit as a becomes very large ($a \to \infty$). To *prove* that the limit of (3) is zero, we have to call upon the following application of a procedure known as *L'Hôspital's Rule:*

If $f(x)$ and $g(x)$ approach ∞ as $x \to \infty$, then

$$\lim_{x \to \infty} \frac{f(x)}{g(x)} = \lim_{x \to \infty} \frac{f'(x)}{g'(x)},$$

provided $f'(x)$, $g'(x)$, and the limit of their quotient exist.

To apply the rule to (3), we find the derivative of the numerator and denominator to be:

$$\text{Numerator:} \quad \frac{d}{dx}(bx + 1) = b$$

$$\text{Denominator:} \quad \frac{d}{dx}(e^{bx}) = be^{bx}.$$

Then, by the rule,

$$\lim_{a \to \infty} \left(\frac{ba + 1}{e^{ba}} \right) = \lim_{a \to \infty} \left(\frac{b}{be^{ba}} \right) = \lim_{a \to \infty} \left(\frac{1}{e^{ba}} \right) = 0.$$

Hence, returning to (2),

$$\mu = -\frac{1}{b} \lim_{a \to \infty} \left(\frac{ba + 1}{e^{ba}} \right) \Bigg|_0^a$$

$$= -\frac{1}{b} \left[\lim_{a \to \infty} \left(\frac{ba + 1}{e^{ba}} \right) - \frac{b(0) + 1}{e^0} \right]$$

$$= -\frac{1}{b}(0 - 1)$$

$$= \frac{1}{b}.$$

Consequently,

$$\mu = \frac{1}{b} \quad \text{or} \quad b = \frac{1}{\mu}$$

so that the density function, (1), $p(x) = be^{-bx}$, becomes

Exponential Density Function

$$p(x) = \frac{1}{\mu}(e^{-x/\mu}) = \frac{e^{-x/\mu}}{\mu}.$$

The cumulative exponential density function. Figure 14–7 shows the shape of exponential density functions. The probability that randomly occurring x will be in the interval 0 to a is the shaded area in the figure, which is calculated to be

$$\int_0^a p(x)\,dx = \int_0^a \frac{e^{-x/\mu}}{\mu}\,dx$$

$$= \frac{1}{\mu}\int_0^a e^{-x/\mu}\,dx$$

FIGURE 14–7 (not to scale)

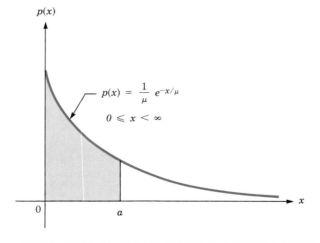

$$= \frac{1}{\mu} \frac{(e^{-x/\mu})}{-1/\mu} \Big|_0^a$$

$$= \frac{1}{\mu} (e^{-x/\mu})(-\mu) \Big|_0^a$$

$$= -(e^{-x/\mu}) \Big|_0^a$$

$$= -(e^{-a/\mu} - e^0)$$

$$= -e^{-a/\mu} + 1$$

$$= 1 - e^{-a/\mu}.$$

The last expression provides the probability over the interval 0 to a specific value of x, namely $x = a$. In general, for any value of x, we may use $P(0 \text{ to } x)$ to represent the probability assigned to the interval from 0 to x and write:

Cumulative Exponential Density Function

$$P(0 \text{ to } x) = 1 - e^{-x/\mu}.$$

Note carefully that a *cumulative* density function is a formula for direct computation of probabilities, but a density function must be integrated to obtain a probability.

Example. If a variable has the exponential distribution with a mean of 10, find the probability that a randomly selected value of the variable lies in the following intervals:

a) 0 to 5.   b) 1 to 4.   c) More than 3.

a) Figure 14–8 shows the desired probability as a shaded area over the interval 0 to 5. The area is

$$P(0 \text{ to } 5) = 1 - e^{-5/10} = 1 - e^{-0.5} = 1 - 0.6065 = 0.3935.$$

b) Figure 14–9 shows the desired probability as a shaded area over the interval 1 to 4. This area is computed as the area over 0 to 4 minus the area over 0 to 1. Thus,

$$P(1 \text{ to } 4) = P(0 \text{ to } 4) - P(0 \text{ to } 1) = 1 - e^{-4/10} - (1 - e^{-1/10})$$
$$= 1 - e^{-0.4} - 1 + e^{-0.1}$$
$$= e^{-0.1} - e^{-0.4}$$
$$= 0.9048 - 0.6703$$
$$= 0.2345.$$

FIGURE 14–8 (*not to scale*)

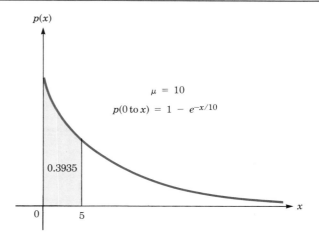

FIGURE 14–9 (*not to scale*)

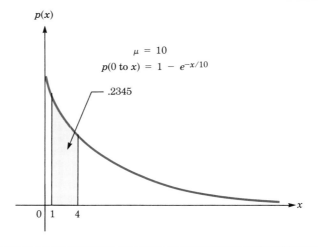

FIGURE 14–10 (not to scale)

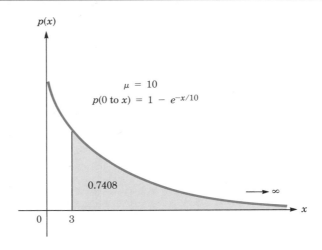

c) Figure 14–10 shows the desired probability for "more than 3" as the *tail* area extending over the interval from 3 to ∞. Because the total area over 0 to ∞ is 1, the shaded area is

$$P(3 \text{ to } \infty) = 1 - P(0 \text{ to } 3) = 1 - (1 - e^{-3/10}) = e^{-0.3} = 0.7408.$$

Exercise. If x has the exponential density function with mean 5, find the probability that a randomly occurring value of x will lie in the interval a) 0 to 5. b) 2 to 3. c) 4 or more. Answer: a) 0.6321. b) 0.1215. c) 0.4493.

The expected value, μ, in the exponential case is the *average interval between occurrences*. This could be the average *time* interval between calls received at a telephone switchboard or the average *distance* traveled between accidents when driving a truck. In neither case, however, is there any compelling reason that the exponential function is appropriate for determining the probability of an occurrence in a given interval. The question, as always, is whether the exponential model adequately describes a real-world situation. In considering the use of the model it should be kept in mind that an interval starts here and now, and a current probability calculation is not influenced by what has already occurred. For example, if the exponential model is used to compute the probability that the next call at a switchboard will come within the next five minutes, the interval starts now, extends five minutes, and the probability is not influenced by occurrence of previous calls. This characteristic sometimes is described by saying the exponential is *memoryless*.

The same term applies in the binomial model; that is, for example, a coin does not have a memory and what happens on the next toss is not influenced by the previous tossing history of the coin.

Example. On the average, 30 customers per hour arrive at a bank. Assuming exponential density, what is the probability that the next customer arrives within the next three minutes?

Here the average of 30 is given *per hour*, but the question has to do with *minutes*. Consequently, the proper value for μ is the average number of minutes between arrivals. We have

$$30 \text{ arrivals in one hour} = 30 \text{ arrivals in 60 minutes}$$

$$\mu = \frac{60 \text{ minutes}}{30 \text{ arrivals}}$$

$$\mu = 2 \text{ minutes between arrivals.}$$

Then,

$$P(0 \text{ to } 3 \text{ minutes}) = 1 - e^{-3/2} = 1 - e^{-1.5} = 1 - 0.2231 = 0.7769.$$

This example shows the exponential density function in applied context and also calls attention to the need for caution in selecting the proper value for μ.

14.9 PROBLEM SET 14–3

Use the cumulative exponential density function for Problems 1 through 6.

1. If $\mu = 2$, find the probabilities for the following intervals.
a) 0 to 3.   b) 2 to 4.   c) More than 5.

2. If $\mu = 4$, find the probabilities for the following intervals.
a) 0 to 2.   b) 3 to 5.   c) More than 4.

3. The average interval between customer arrivals at a gasoline station is four minutes. Find the probability that
a) The next customer arrives in the next three minutes.
b) No customer will arrive during the next two minutes.

4. The average time between breakdowns of a computer is 10 days. Find the probability that
a) The next breakdown will occur in the next five days.

b) There will be no breakdown in the next eight days.

5. On the average, a stockbroker receives 40 calls per eight-hour day from clients.
a) Find the probability that the next call will come during the next hour.
b) If the broker takes a half-hour off, what is the probability that no calls will come while the broker is away?

6. For new television sets of a certain model, the time until first failure of the picture tube averages five years.
a) What is the probability of tube failure in the first nine months?
b) If the manufacturer guarantees to replace the tube if it fails within three months, what is the probability that the manufacturer will *not* have to replace the tube on a newly-purchased set?

14.9 PROBLEM SET 14–3 (concluded)

7. If the function $f(x) = ke^{-4x}$ is to be a density function over $0 \leq x < \infty$, the value of k must be such that the integral over 0 to ∞ equals 1.
   a) Integrate $f(x)$ over the interval 0 to ∞ and write the expression for the definite integral treating k as an unknown constant.
   b) Set the expression in (a) equal to 1, solve for k, and write the density function, $p(x)$.
   c) Find μ, the expected value of x, by integration.

8. If the function $f(x) = k/x^3$ is to be a density function over $1 \leq x < \infty$, the value of k must be such that the integral over 1 to ∞ equals 1.
   a) Integrate $f(x)$ over the interval 1 to ∞ and write the expression for the definite integral, treating k as an unknown constant.
   b) Set the expression in (a) equal to 1, solve for k, and write the density function, $p(x)$.
   c) Find μ, the expected value of x, by integration.

14.10 THE NORMAL DENSITY FUNCTION

The widely-used normal density function (normal distribution) has the bell shape shown in Figure 14–11. The function that is the source of the normal distribution is

$$f(x) = e^{-\frac{1}{2}\left(\frac{x-\mu}{\sigma}\right)^2}, \quad -\infty < x < \infty.$$

To qualify as a density function it is necessary to determine k so that

$$k\int_{-\infty}^{+\infty} f(x)\, dx = 1.$$

By advanced methods, it can be proved that

$$k = \frac{1}{\sigma\sqrt{2\pi}}.$$

Hence the equation of the normal probability density function is

---

Normal Probability Density Function

$$p(x) = \frac{1}{\sigma\sqrt{2\pi}}\, e^{-\frac{1}{2}\left(\frac{x-\mu}{\sigma}\right)^2}.$$

The parameters in $p(x)$ are μ, the mean or expected value, and σ, the standard deviation. As shown in Figure 14–11, a normal distribution has symmetry with respect to a vertical line at μ; that is, in Figure 14–11, the curve has the same height at a point a units to the left or right of μ. The standard deviation measures the variability of x around the mean so that a distribution with a small value of σ concentrates a major proportion of the probability (area) over a small interval around μ. If σ is large, the

FIGURE 14–11

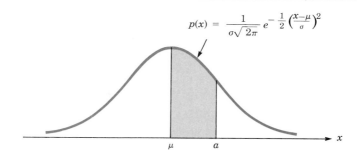

major central proportion of the probability is spread over a wide interval around μ. Often, we specify a normal distribution by $N(\mu, \sigma)$, meaning "normal, with mean mu and standard deviation sigma." For example, $N(100, 5)$ specifies a normal distribution with mean 100, standard deviation 5 (variance 25). This specific distribution function is

$$p(x) = \frac{1}{5\sqrt{2\pi}}\, e^{-\frac{1}{2}\left(\frac{x-100}{5}\right)^2}.$$

Normal curves may be described as being bell-shaped, symmetrical about the mean, and approaching the x-axis asymptotically in both directions.

Exercise. Write the equation of the normal distribution $N(40, 8)$. Geometrically, how would this distribution compare with $N(30, 2)$? Answer:

$$p(x) = \left[\frac{1}{8}\sqrt{2\pi}\right]\left[e^{-\frac{1}{2}\left(\frac{x-40}{8}\right)^2}\right].$$

This distribution would have its mean to the right of $N(30, 2)$ and would spread out more than $N(30, 2)$.

14.11 NORMAL PROBABILITY TABLE

Starting from first principles to find the probability that a randomly selected x will lie in a specified interval, we would try to integrate the normal density function between the interval limits. As it happens, this function cannot be integrated exactly, but it is possible to make approximations using numerical integration. It seems natural to suggest that the approximations for various sets of limits be made and the outcomes tabulated, but this raises a problem. There is not just one normal distribution. There is a normal distribution for each of the limitless combinations of mu and sigma. Fortunately, this latter problem can be handled by changing every normal distribution to a *standard* form. To see how this is done, consider the problem of evaluating

$$\frac{1}{\sigma\sqrt{2\pi}}\int_{\mu}^{a}e^{-\frac{1}{2}\left(\frac{x-\mu}{\sigma}\right)^2}dx.$$

(See Figure 14–11.) We introduce a new variable, z, called the standardized normal deviate, where

$$z = \frac{x-\mu}{\sigma}.$$

We must now make the following conversions:
  If

$$z = \frac{x-\mu}{\sigma}$$

then

$$\frac{dz}{dx} = \frac{d}{dx}\left(\frac{x-\mu}{\sigma}\right) = \frac{1}{\sigma}$$

$$\sigma\, dz = dx.$$

This says we must replace dx in the integral by $\sigma\, dz$. Attention turns next to the limits on the integral. The limit $x = \mu$ becomes

$$z = \frac{x-\mu}{\sigma} = \frac{\mu-\mu}{\sigma} = 0.$$

Similarly, the limit $x = a$ becomes

$$z = \frac{a-\mu}{\sigma}.$$

Substituting, we now have the expression

$$\frac{1}{\sqrt{2\pi}}\int_{0}^{\frac{a-\mu}{\sigma}}e^{-\frac{z^2}{2}}dz$$

in place of the original integral. See Figure 14–12.

To see what has been accomplished, consider the two normal distributions $N(50, 5)$ and $N(78, 2)$. Asked to integrate $N(50, 5)$ between the limits 50, which is μ, and 55, which is a, we find

FIGURE 14-12

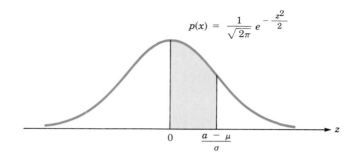

$$z = \frac{55 - 50}{5} = 1$$

for the z corresponding to 55. The z corresponding to μ is, of course, always zero. Our problem here is to integrate the standardized normal distribution from $z = 0$ to $z = 1$.

Suppose, next, we are asked to integrate the second distribution, $N(78, 2)$, between the x limits 78, which is μ, and 80, which is a. We find again that the z limits are 0 and 1. Both problems lead to the evaluation of

$$\frac{1}{\sqrt{2\pi}} \int_0^1 e^{-\frac{z^2}{2}}\, dz.$$

Clearly, the same evaluation arises if the transformation to z yields the interval from $z = 0$ to $z = 1$, no matter what normal distribution is at hand.

Exercise. Given $N(20, 3)$, what z-values correspond to $x = 26$ and $x = 18.5$? Answer: 2, $-\frac{1}{2}$.

Values of the definite integral

$$\frac{1}{\sqrt{2\pi}} \int_0^z e^{-\frac{z^2}{2}}\, dz$$

are given in Table XI at the end of the book for various values of z. We find, for example, when $z = 1$, the tabulated probability is 0.3413.

14.12 USING THE NORMAL PROBABILITY TABLE

The particular manner in which the normal probabilities are given in Table XI must be kept in mind so that the problem at hand will be matched properly with the table. Frequently, a sketch will serve to lessen the chance of improper use of the table.

Example. Given a normal distribution with mean 50 and standard deviation 10, what is the probability that a randomly selected number will lie in the interval from 50 to 65?

The desired probability is shown in Figure 14–13 as the shaded area over the interval from 50 to 65. At the point 65:

$$z = \frac{65 - 50}{10} = 1.5.$$

From Table XI, with $z = 1.5$, we find the desired probability to be 0.4332.

FIGURE 14–13

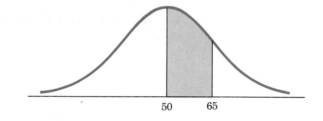

50   65

Example. Given $N(50, 10)$, as in the last example, what is the probability that x will fall in the interval 42 to 50?

As Figure 14–14 shows, 42 lies to the left of the mean. However, the curve is symmetrical. The probability is the same for a given value of z, whether it be positive or negative. Here

$$z = \frac{42 - 50}{10} = -0.8.$$

The desired probability is found by entering Table XI with z equal 0.8. It is 0.2881.

FIGURE 14–14

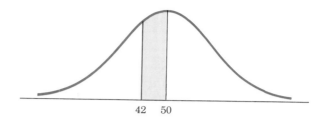

42 50

Exercise. Given $N(50, 10)$ as in the last example, what is the probability that x will be in the interval a) 50 to 62? b) 45 to 50? Answer: a) 0.3849. b) 0.1915.

Example. Given $N(100, 20)$ what is the probability that x will be greater than 145?

The pertinent area is shown in Figure 14–15. It is a *right tail* area. Table XI provides areas only for intervals that start at the mean (that is, at $z = 0$). We can find the desired area by applying the table, then subtracting from 0.5, inasmuch as the entire area to the right of the mean is 0.5.

$$z = \frac{145 - 100}{20} = 2.25.$$

The tabulated entry for $z = 2.25$ is 0.4878. Hence the desired area is

$$0.5000 - 0.4878 = 0.0122.$$

FIGURE 14–15

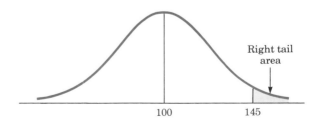

100   145

Right tail
area

Example. Given $N(2, 0.1)$, what is the probability that x will lie in the interval 1.95 to 2.1?

Figure 14–16 shows that we must add two tabulated entries.

FIGURE 14–16

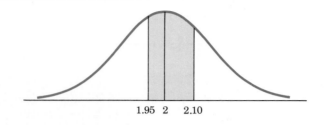

1.95 2   2.10

At 1.95, z is -0.5, and the area is 0.1915.
At 2.1, z is 1, and the area is 0.3413.

Adding, we find the desired probability as

$$0.1915 + 0.3413 = 0.5328.$$

Example. Given $N(15, 2)$, find the probability that x will lie in the interval from 16 to 17.

Analysis of Figure 14–17 shows that the tabulated areas at $z = 1$ and $z = 0.5$ must be subtracted. Hence:

$$0.3413 - 0.1915 = 0.1498.$$

FIGURE 14–17

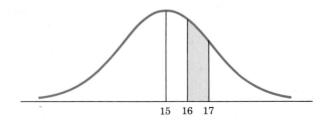

15 16 17

14.13 PROBLEM SET 14–4

1. Given a normal distribution with mean 150 and standard deviation 20, find the area over each of the following intervals:
   a) 150 to 160, inclusive.
   b) 150 up to but not including 160.
   c) Beyond 170.
   d) 160 to 170.
   e) Below 135.
   f) 145 to 165.
   g) 142 to 150.
   h) 138 to 146.

2. Given $N(50, 5)$ find the probability that a randomly selected x will lie in each of the following intervals:
   a) 45 to 65.
   b) 40 to 60.
   c) 35 to 65.
   d) Outside the interval from 40 to 60.
   e) Above 46.
   f) 44 to 48.
   g) Below 55.
   h) Above 56.

3. Given $N(10, 2)$, find the probability that a randomly selected x will lie in each of the following intervals:
   a) Above 6.
   b) 11 to 15.
   c) Below 9.
   d) 8 to 10.
   e) 8 to 9, excluding the end points.
   f) 8 to 12.
   g) Above 11.5.
   h) 9 to 13.
   i) Above 16.

14.14 ESTIMATING THE MEAN AND THE STANDARD DEVIATION

The normal probability density function as a mathematical model can be related approximately to numerous real-world situations. Suppose, for example, that an automatic machine is adjusted to produce shafts that have a diameter of two inches. As shaft after shaft comes off the machine, it is not expected that each shaft will have a diameter of precisely two inches. Shaft diameters will vary somewhat, the amount of variability being dependent upon the precision of the machine. Quality control engineers often assume that the probability of various departures from the nominal figure, two inches, can be estimated by application of the normal distribution.

If we are to apply a normal distribution to a real-world problem, we must have numbers for the mean and standard deviation of the distribution. In the mathematical model, of course, these quantities represent the central point and the degree of spread of an infinite set of values of the variate x. In the real world, we work with a finite set of numbers and think of them as a *sample* of x's drawn at random from the infinite set. The numbers in the sample reflect the central tendency and variability of the infinite set. We estimate the mean and the standard deviation for the infinite set from the numbers in the sample. In the remainder of this section, we shall show how the estimates are made.

Suppose that we select a sample of 10 shafts from the output of a machine and measure the diameter of each shaft, obtaining the numbers in the next table:

Diameters of 10 Shafts, in Inches				
2.00	2.01	1.97	2.02	1.97
1.99	2.03	1.99	2.01	2.01

Because we plan to use the sample to *estimate* μ and σ, we would prefer to have a sample of many more than 10 units. However, our purpose is only to show how the estimates are made, and a small sample will suffice. The mean, μ, for the model, is estimated by computing the mean (the ordinary average) of the sample. The procedure followed in estimating σ starts by estimating the variance, σ^2. Recalling that variance involves the squares of the amounts by which values differ from the mean, we proceed as follows:

1. Find the average of the sample data.
2. Subtract the average from a sample number, and square the difference.
3. Repeat Step 2 for each number in the sample, and then sum all the squares.
4. Divide the sum of squares in Step 3 by $n - 1$, where n is the number of values in the sample. The result of this step is the desired estimate of the variance.[1]

The steps are illustrated in Table 14–1. The difference between each value of x and the sample average, 2, is shown in the second column whose heading is $x - 2$; that is, sample value minus sample average. Note that this column sums to 0. This should always be the case; use this as a check on your arithmetic. The squares of the differences are shown in the third column, whose heading is descriptive of the method for obtaining its entries. The sum of squares is 0.0036; dividing this sum of squares by one less than the number of values in the sample, that is, by $n - 1$ where n is 10, we obtain the variance estimate, 0.0004. The square root of the variance estimate, 0.02, is the estimated standard deviation.

$$\text{Average} = \frac{20}{10} = 2; \quad n = 10.$$

$$\text{Variance estimate} = \frac{0.0036}{9} = 0.0004.$$

$$\text{Standard deviation estimate} = \sqrt{0.0004} = 0.02.$$

---

[1] Statisticians have determined that, for samples, it is more accurate to divide by $n - 1$ rather than n.

TABLE 14-1

Sample Value x	x − 2	(x − 2)²
2.00	0.00	0.0000
1.99	−0.01	0.0001
2.01	0.01	0.0001
2.03	0.03	0.0009
1.97	−0.03	0.0009
1.99	−0.01	0.0001
2.02	0.02	0.0004
2.01	0.01	0.0001
1.97	−0.03	0.0009
2.01	0.01	0.0001
20.00	0.00	0.0036

The summation symbol, Σ, can be put to good use in summarizing instructions for computing estimates of mean and standard deviation. Conventionally, if the variate at hand is x and we wish to indicate the average of a sample of x's, we write the variate with a bar over it, thus: $\bar{x}$. If we now let Σx represent the sum of a set of values of x, and n represent the number of values in the set, the average of the set is

$$\bar{x} = \frac{\Sigma x}{n}.$$

Returning to Table 14-1, n is 10, Σx is 20; hence:

$$\bar{x} = \frac{20}{10} = 2.$$

Turning to the second column of Table 14-1, we express the operation of subtracting the average from each value of x by the instruction $x - \bar{x}$. In the third column, we square each difference, an operation denoted by $(x - \bar{x})^2$. The sum of the third column is expressed as $\Sigma(x - \bar{x})^2$. Finally, dividing the last expression by $n - 1$ provides the variance estimate, which we now label as s^2

$$s^2 = \frac{\Sigma(x - \bar{x})^2}{n - 1}.$$

The standard deviation estimate, s, is

Standard Deviation Estimate

$$s = \sqrt{\frac{\Sigma(x - \bar{x})^2}{n - 1}}.$$

Example. Compute $\bar{x}$ and s for the values of x given in the first column of Table 14–2.

TABLE 14–2

x	x − x̄	(x − x̄)²
5	−2.2	4.84
8	0.8	0.64
8	0.8	0.64
9	1.8	3.24
6	−1.2	1.44
36		10.80

$$\bar{x} = \frac{\Sigma x}{n} = \frac{36}{5} = 7.2$$

$$s^2 = \frac{\Sigma(x - \bar{x})^2}{n - 1} = \frac{10.80}{4} = 2.7$$

$$s = \sqrt{\frac{\Sigma(x - \bar{x})^2}{n - 1}} = \sqrt{\frac{10.80}{4}} = \sqrt{2.7} = 1.64.$$

14.15 PROBLEM SET 14–5

Compute $\bar{x}$ and s for each given set of x's:

1. 8, 8, 9, 6, 4.

2. 17, 15, 14, 20, 18, 16, 10, 12, 15, 13.

3. 8, 13, 12, 13, 10.

4. 2, 2, 6, 5, 1, 5.

5. 0.64, 0.58, 0.57, 0.57, 0.52, 0.58, 0.60, 0.58.

14.16 $N(\mu, \sigma)$ IN ACTUAL USE

In applications the areas for the normal distribution are interpreted as percentages and proportions as well as probability, as we shall see in the examples that follow. In each example the mean and the standard deviation are presumed to have been estimated from sample data by the methods of the previous section.

Example. An automatic filling machine can be set to pour a certain number of ounces of fluid into containers. Data collected from runs of the machine show that the *average* amount of fill per container is, for practical purposes, equal to the machine setting. However, the amount of fill per can varies, and the standard deviation of amount of fill per can has been estimated from sample data to be 0.4 ounces.

a) If the machine is set to pour 32 ounces, what is the probability that a container will receive less than 31.5 ounces?

FIGURE 14–18

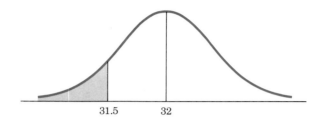

31.5   32

We interpret this problem as one of finding the probability that x will be less than 31.5 in a normal distribution whose mean is 32 and whose standard deviation is 0.4. Figure 14–18 illustrates the probability sought.

$$\text{At } 31.5, \quad z = \frac{31.5 - 32}{0.4} = -1.25.$$

From Table XI, with $z = 1.25$, the tabulated area is 0.3944. The shaded area in the sketch is

$$0.5000 - 0.3944 = 0.1056.$$

We estimate the probability that a can will receive less than 31.5 ounces to be 0.1056.

b) Given the circumstances in (a), what percent of the containers will receive less than 31.5 ounces?

The probability, 0.1056, here is interpreted as the percent equivalent, 10.56 percent; that is, over the long run, about 10.56 percent of the containers will receive less than 31.5 ounces.

c) Given the circumstances in (a), if 1,000 containers are filled, approximately how many will contain less than 31.5 ounces?

Following the interpretation of (b), we find 10.56 percent of 1000. This is

$$0.1056(1000) = 105.6$$

or about 106 containers.

Example. Given the same machine as in the last example, suppose that we wish to set the machine so that not more than 5 percent of the containers will receive less than 32 ounces. What should be the setting?

The nature of this problem is seen in Figure 14–19. We wish to find the mean (the setting) so that the probability below 32 is 0.05 (that is,

FIGURE 14–19

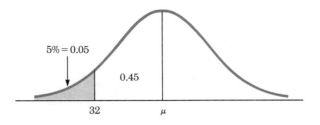

the given 5 percent). This means, by subtraction, that the area over the interval from 32 to μ must be

$$0.5 - 0.05 = 0.45.$$

We can find, by *inverse* use of Table XI, what value of z corresponds to the area 0.45.

Turning to Table XI, we see in the field that 0.4500 is between the tabulated values 0.4495 and 0.4505. The corresponding marginal values, z, are 1.64 and 1.65, respectively. By interpolation, $z = 1.645$.

Now, it is important to understand that in terms of the units of the original problem, *a value of z means z times the standard deviation.* In the present case, $z = 1.645$ means

$$1.645(0.4 \text{ ounces}) = 0.658 \text{ ounces.}$$

Hence, the interval from 32 up to μ is 0.658 ounces, which tells us the machine should be set at

$$\mu = 32 + 0.658 = 32.658 \text{ ounces}$$

if not more than 5 percent of the containers are to receive less than 32 ounces.

The italicized words above refer to the definition

$$z = \frac{x - \mu}{\sigma}$$

from which it follows that

$$z\sigma = x - \mu.$$

The interval $x - \mu$ is the distance from x to the mean. It equals z (for the x in question) times the standard deviation. In passing, we note that the question whether to add $z\sigma$ to x or to subtract $z\sigma$ from x to locate the mean depends upon which side of the mean our sketch shows x to be. In the present case the mean is to the right of 32, so we added $z\sigma$.

FIGURE 14–20

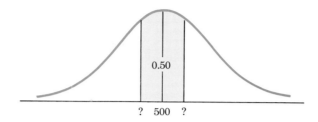

Example. If light bulbs of a certain type have an average burning life of 500 hours and a standard deviation of 40 hours, as estimated from experience, within what limits symmetrically located above and below 500 will the burning lives of half of such bulbs lie?

The desired limits are shown by question marks in Figure 14–20. If we want half (50 percent) of the numbers to fall between these limits, which are symmetrically located with respect to the mean, then 25 percent will be in each of the intervals 500 to ?. Entering Table XI, we find that the z corresponding to an area of 0.25 is 0.675. Hence the length of the interval from 500 to ? is 0.675 times the standard deviation:

$$0.675(40) = 27.$$

The desired limits are

$$500 \pm 27 \quad \text{or} \quad 473 \text{ to } 527 \text{ hours.}$$

Example. A testing service reports the average score on a test as 130 points, and the standard deviation of test scores as 20 points. Jones takes the test and scores 118 points. What is Jones's percentile standing? See Figure 14–21.

FIGURE 14–21

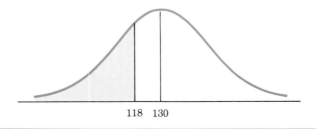

We interpret percentile standing as the percent scoring less than Jones, and estimate it as being the percent below 118 in $N(130, 20)$:

$$z = \frac{130 - 118}{20} = 0.6.$$

From Table XI, with $z = 0.6$, we obtain the area 0.2257. Figure 14–21 shows that the area *below* Jones's 118 points is found by the subtraction

$$0.5000 - 0.2257 = 0.2743 = 27.43\%.$$

Hence, we estimate Jones's score as being at the 27th percentile.

Example. Study of records of the number of units of item K3 in inventory day by day shows average inventory to be 50 units, and the standard deviation of the day-by-day numbers to be 10 units. Suppose that, during a day, 25 units are requested. What is the probability that there will not be enough units in inventory to meet this day's requests?

We interpret this problem as one of finding the probability that x is less than 25 in $N(50, 10)$.

$$z = \frac{25 - 50}{10} = -2.5.$$

From Table XI, with $z = 2.5$, we obtain the area 0.4938. According to Figure 14–22, the desired area is

$$0.5000 - 0.4938 = 0.0062.$$

The probability of not being able to meet the requests is the small figure 0.0062; that is, the chances are only six in a thousand that such requests could not be satisfied.

FIGURE 14–22

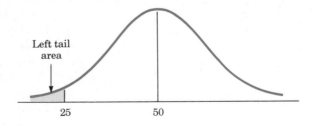

Left tail
area

25   50

14.17 PROBLEM SET 14–6

All problems in this set are to be solved under the assumption that the normal distribution is applicable.

1. Given $N(50, 5)$:
   a) The probability is 0.17 that x will lie in the interval from 50 up to what number?
   b) The probability is 0.10 that x will exceed what number?
   c) The probability is 0.05 that x will be less than what number?
   d) The probability is 0.50 that x will lie in what interval symmetrically located above and below 50?
   e) The probability is 0.95 that x will be less than what number?

2. Assuming that a machine will turn out parts whose average diameter is the figure at which the machine is set, and that the standard deviation has been estimated from sample data to be 0.001 inches:
   a) If the machine is set at 2.00 inches, what percentage of parts made will have diameters exceeding 2.001 inches?
   b) If the machine is set at 0.100 inch, what percentage of parts made will have diameters exceeding 0.098 inches?
   c) If the machine is set at 1.500 inches, and 1,000 parts are made, approximately how many parts will have diameters less than 1.498 inches?
   d) Specifications state that parts are to have 2.000-inch diameter, tolerance plus or minus 0.002; that is, parts whose diameters differ by more than 0.002 from 2.000 are to be classified as defectives. What percent of the parts will be defective?
   e) Within what limits symmetrically located about a setting of 1.575 inches will the diameters of 95 percent of the parts lie?
   f) If the machine is set at 2.250 inches, 5 percent of the parts will have diameters less than what number of inches?
   g) A loss of 40 cents is incurred for every part that is scrapped because its diameter is too *small*. Specifications state that the part is to have diameter 1.500 inches, tolerance ± 0.0015 inches. The machine is set at 1.500 inches. If 2,000 parts are made, what will be the cost of the scrapped undersized parts?

3. The amounts poured by an automatic can-filling machine average out at the machine setting. Collected data indicate that the standard deviation of amounts of fill per can is 0.2 ounce.
   a) If the machine is set to pour 32 ounces, what is the probability that a can will contain less than 31.9 ounces?
   b) If the machine is set to pour 32 ounces, what percent of the cans will contain at least 31.9 ounces?
   c) If the machine is set to pour 32 ounces and 2,000 cans are filled, approximately how many cans will contain less than 31.7 ounces?
   d) If the can label states the contents to be 32 ounces and the machine is set to pour 32.25 ounces, what percent of the cans will be underfilled?
   e) If the can labels state contents to be 16 ounces, at what level should the machine be set if 99 percent of the cans are to contain at least 16 ounces?

4. The average breaking strength of certain connectors is 2,000 pounds, $s = 80$ pounds.
   a) Within what limits symmetrically located about 2000 will the breaking strength of 75 percent of the connectors lie?
   b) What percent of the connectors will have a breaking strength of more than 2,100 pounds?
   c) The breaking strength of 95 percent of the connectors will exceed what number of pounds?

14.17 PROBLEM SET 14–6 (concluded)

d) If a connector with breaking strength less than 1,800 pounds is classified as defective, what percent of connectors will be defective?

5. A testing service reports the average score on a certain test to be 200 points. $s = 25$ points.
   a) What percent of those taking the test score more than 275?
   b) What percent of those taking the test score less than 160?
   c) Half of those taking the test make scores in what interval symmetrically located above and below 200?
   d) Ninety-five percent of those taking the test score above what number of points?
   e) What would be the percentile standing of a person who scored 260 points on the test?

14.18 REVIEW PROBLEMS

1. a) Convert $f(x) = x + 1, 0 \le x \le 10$, to a probability density function.
   b) What is the probability that a randomly selected x will lie in the interval 0 to 1? The interval 5 to 6?

2. a) Convert $f(x) = x^{1/3} - 1, 1 \le x \le 8$, to a probability density function.
   b) Find the probability that a randomly selected x will lie in the interval 1 to 27/8.

3. a) Convert $f(x) = 50, 20 \le x < 45$, to a probability density function.
   b) Find the probability that a randomly selected x will lie in the interval 30 to 40.

4. Convert $f(x) = 10(x + 2)^{-3}, 0 \le x < \infty$, to a probability density function.

5. Given that

$$p(x) = \frac{12x - 3x^2}{32}$$

is a probability density function over the interval $x = 0$ to $x = 4$, find the probability that x will lie in the intervals 0 to 1; 0 to 2; 2 to 3.

6. If $p(x) = kx^{3/2}$ is a probability density function over the interval 0 to 100, what must be the value for k?

7. Given the probability density function $p(x) = 0.02, 0 \le x \le 50$:

   a) Find the expected value, μ.
   b) Find the variance, σ^2.
   c) Find the standard deviation, σ.

8. Given the probability density function $p(x) = 0.012x + 0.04, 0 \le x \le 10$:
   a) Find the expected value, μ.
   b) Find the variance, σ^2.
   c) Find the standard deviation, σ.

9. Find μ, the expected value of x, for the probability density function

$$p(x) = \frac{3}{x^4}, 1 \le x < \infty.$$

10. The quantity of fish brought to port varies from day to day and has the probability density function

$$p(x) = 0.003(x^2 - 20x + 100), 0 \le x \le 10,$$

   where x is in thousands of pounds per day.
   a) Find μ, the expected value of x.
   b) Estimate the total quantity of fish that will be brought to port in a 30-day period.

11. If x has the exponential density function with $\mu = 10$, find the probability that a randomly selected x will be in the interval
    a) 0 to 4.   b) 1 to 5.   c) More than 8.

12. The average interval between arrivals of customers at a bank is two minutes. Assum-

14.18 REVIEW PROBLEMS (*continued*)

ing the exponential density function applies, what is the probability that
a) The next customer will arrive within the next five minutes?
b) No customer will arrive during the next three minutes?

13. On the average, a bank teller provides service to 15 customers per hour. Assuming the exponential density function applies
a) What is the probability that it will take less than five minutes to service the next customer?
b) If customer B comes into the bank at the moment the teller starts servicing A, the only other customer present, what is the probability that B will have to wait more than three minutes for service?

14. Given a normal distribution with mean 30 and standard deviation 6, find the area over each of the following intervals:
a) 30 to 33.
b) 36 to 42.
c) Less than 27.
d) More than 48.
e) 24 to 33.
f) More than 21.

15. Given $N(100, 5)$, find the probability that a randomly selected x will lie in each of the following intervals:
a) 90 to 105.
b) 105 to 115.
c) 92 to 96.
d) Less than 103.
e) More than 88.
f) 112 to 115.

16. Compute the mean, $\bar{x}$, and the standard deviation, s, for each of the following:
a) 3, 7, 7, 9, 14.
b) 3, 5, 7, 7, 8.
c) 15, 15, 15.
d) 1.2, 0.7, 1.2, 1.3.

17. Given $N(20, 4)$:
a) The probability is 0.20 that x will lie in the interval from 20 up to what number?
b) The probability is 0.16 that x will exceed what number?

c) The probability is 0.025 that x will be less than what number?
d) The probability is 0.50 that x will lie in what interval symmetrically located above and below 20?
e) The probability is 0.95 that x will be less than what number?

18. Assuming that a machine will turn out parts whose average diameter is the figure at which the machine is set, and that the standard deviation has been estimated from sample data to be 0.002 inches:
a) If the machine is set at 2.500 inches, what percentage of parts made will have diameters exceeding 2.503 inches?
b) If the machine is set at 2.000 inches, what percentage of parts made will have diameters exceeding 1.999 inches?
c) If the machine is set at 2.250 inches, and 1,000 parts are made, approximately how many parts will have diameters less than 2.245 inches?
d) Specifications state that parts are to have 2.500-inch diameter, plus or minus 0.003; that is, parts whose diameters differ by more than 0.003 from 2.500 are to be classified as defectives. If the machine is set at 2.500 inches, what percent of parts will be defective?
e) Within what limits symmetrically located about a setting of 3.000 inches will the diameters of 95 percent of the parts lie?
f) If the machine is set at 2.500 inches, 10 percent of the parts will have diameters less than what number of inches?
g) A loss of 50 cents is incurred for every part that is scrapped because its diameter is too small. Specifications state that the part is to have diameter 2.000 inches, tolerance ±0.004 inches. If the machine is set at 2.000 inches and 5,000 parts are made, what will be the cost of the scrapped undersized parts?

19. If 100 coins are tossed and the number of heads recorded, the number of heads, x, will be *approximately* normally distributed

14.18 REVIEW PROBLEMS (*concluded*)

with mean 50 and standard deviation 5. Assuming $N(50, 5)$,
a) What percent of the time would more than 65 heads appear in tossing 100 coins?
b) What is the probability that the number of heads will differ by more than 15, one way or the other, from 50?
c) What percent of the time would the number of heads be between 40 and 60?

20. If light bulbs of a certain type have an average burning life of 1,000 hours with a standard deviation of 100 hours,
a) Within what limits symmetrically located above and below 1000 will burning lives of 50 percent of the bulbs fall?
b) If a large number of these bulbs burn continuously, how long will it be before 40 percent have burned out?
c) How many bulbs out of 2000 will have burning lives exceeding 1,250 hours?

21. The amounts poured by an automatic can-filling machine average out at the machine setting. Collected data indicate that the standard deviation of the amounts of fill per can is 1 percent of the machine setting; that is, for example, if the machine is set at 50 ounces, the standard deviation is 1 percent of 50 = 0.50 ounces.
a) If the machine is set to pour 20 ounces, what is the probability that a can will contain less than 19.7 ounces?
b) If the machine is set to pour 50 ounces, how many cans out of 1000 will contain between 49 and 51 ounces?

c) If can labels state contents to be 48 ounces and the machine is set to pour 49 ounces, what percent of the cans will be underfilled?
d) If specifications call for cans to contain at least 100 ounces, and the machine is set to pour 101 ounces, what percent of cans will meet specifications?
e) In (d), if cans cannot hold any more than 102.3 ounces, what percent of cans will overflow?
f) If the maximum amount cans hold is 50.8 ounces and the machine is set at 50 ounces, some cans will overflow. Overflows are defectives and are removed from the batch under production. How many cans will have to be filled if the number left after removing defectives is to be 5000?

22. A testing service reports the average score on a test to be 500 points with a standard deviation of 100 points.
a) What percent of those taking the test score above 600? Above 700?
b) Seventy-five percent of those taking the test make scores in what interval symmetrically located about the average?

23. Inventory on hand for item X is brought up to 150 at the end of each day. Demand for X averages 100 units a day, with a standard deviation of 20 units. On a particular day, what is the probability that demand will exceed inventory on hand?

APPENDIX ONE

Sets

It is not necessary to cover all of this appendix systematically before starting the text. The material contained here is referred to at various points in the text, and it will be sufficient to review the relevant sections when the referral is made.

Some simple notions about groups or collections or *sets* are core ideas in mathematics. We use braces to indicate a set, and specify the *members* or *elements* of the set within the braces. Thus,

$$\{Boston, Wellesley, Newton\}$$

is a set whose members (elements) are the cities Boston, Wellesley, and Newton. Again,

$$\{3, 4, 7, 8\}$$

is a set of numbers whose elements (members) are 3, 4, 7, and 8. The symbols ϵ and $\notin$ are membership symbols, the first being read as "is a member of," the second as "is not a member of." For example,

$$3 \in \{3, 4, 7, 8\}$$
$$5 \notin \{3, 4, 7, 8\}$$

say that 3 is a member (or element) of the set $\{3, 4, 7, 8\}$ but 5 is not an element of this set.

Each element of a set must be unique. For example, in set terminology, the numbers 1, 3, 4, 4 would be a set whose elements are 1, 3, and

813

4. A set may have no elements, a finite number of elements, or an unlimited number of elements. The set with no elements is called the *empty* (or *null*) set and is symbolized by ϕ, without braces. A set with an unlimited number of elements is said to be an *infinite* set. Two sets are *equal* if, and only if, they contain exactly the same elements. The expression

$$\{\text{Integers between 5 and 6}\} = \phi$$

says the set of integers between 5 and 6 has no elements; it is the empty set.

> **Exercise.**   Read the following aloud:
>
> $$\{\text{Red spades in a bridge deck}\} = \phi.$$
>
> Answer: The set of red spades in a bridge deck has no elements.

The expression

$$\{\text{Integers between 5 and 7}\} = \{6\}$$

says that the set of integers between 5 and 7 is the set with the single element, 6. The next expression states that the set of integers between 5 and 10 is the set whose elements are 6, 7, 8, 9

$$\{\text{Integers between 5 and 10}\} = \{6, 7, 8, 9\}.$$

> **Exercise.**   Express in set symbols that the numbers whose square is 25 are 5 and -5. Answer: $\{\text{Numbers whose square is 25}\} = \{5, -5\}$.

The set specified by

$$\{\text{Integers}\}$$

is an infinite set, so we cannot completely list all its members.

> **Exercise.**   Using braces and the symbols for set membership, express the facts that $\frac{1}{2}$ is not an integer and 13 is an integer. Answer: $\frac{1}{2} \notin \{\text{Integers}\}$; $13 \in \{\text{Integers}\}$.

It is conventional to use a capital letter, without braces, when an entire set is to be named by one symbol. For example, we might let E represent the (infinite) set of even integers; thus

$$E = \{\text{Even integers}\}.$$

We may then refer to E by statements such as

$$3 \notin E \quad \text{and} \quad 4 \in E,$$

which say 3 is not a member of E and 4 is a member of E.

Set terminology is not limited to collections of numbers. We may talk, for example, about the set of residents of New York, classifying residents as being members of the set and nonresidents as not being members of the set.

Exercise.   In set symbols, write the relationship of \$ to L, and Q to L, if L = {Capital English letters}.   Answer: $\$ \notin L$. $Q \in L$.

A set is specified by identifying its elements. The *roster* method of specification *lists* each member of the set. The *descriptive* method states the rule or condition that distinguishes members of the set from non-members. Thus,

$$S = \{1, 3, 5, 7, 9\}$$

specifies a set by the roster method. The same set could be specified by the condition that its members be odd numbers between 0 and 10; a descriptive specification therefore would be

$$S = \{\text{Odd numbers between 0 and 10}\}.$$

In either specification it is clear whether an object is or is not a member of the set, for example,

$$3 \in S \quad \text{and} \quad 4 \notin S.$$

Exercise.   Specify W = {Days in the week} by the roster method. Answer: W = {Sunday, Monday, Tuesday, Wednesday, Thursday, Friday, Saturday}.

The set of positive integers, like any infinite set, cannot be listed completely. We may specify the set by the descriptive method as P = {Positive integers} or by

$$P = \{1, 2, 3, \ldots\}$$

where the three dots are read "and so on." We shall classify this last expression as being a roster specification, although in fact it is a roster-like descriptive specification.

> **Exercise.** Specify the set of positive odd integers by the "three dot" convention. Answer: $O = \{1, 3, 5, \ldots\}$.

A1.4 SOLUTION SETS FOR EQUATIONS

The statement, "two plus three equals five," is a *sentence* that can be written as

$$2 + 3 = 5.$$

Similarly, the sentence, "y plus three equals five," can be expressed as

$$y + 3 = 5.$$

Sentences that use the equality symbol $=$ are called equations. If we replace the symbol y by a number that makes the equation become a *true* sentence, the replacement number is a member of the *solution set* of the equation. In the case at hand, the solution set has only one element, 2. We may write

$$\{y : y + 3 = 5\} = \{2\}$$

where the colon is read as *such that*, and the whole statement says *the set of y's such that y + 3 = 5 is the set with the element 2.*

> **Exercise.** a) Write the set symbols for $y + 1 = 6$. b) Translate the symbols $\{y : y - 2 = 10\} = \{12\}$. Answer: a) $\{y : y + 1 = 6\} = \{5\}$. b) The set of y's such that y minus two is ten is the set with the element 12.

A1.5 RELATIONS AND FUNCTIONS

Another core concept in mathematics is the relationship, or correspondence, between the elements of two sets. A kind of correspondence known as a *function* is of particular interest, and to bring out the special nature of a functional relationship, think of one set of elements as the set of mothers and the other set as the set of children. The set of mothers and the set of children are related, obviously, but there is a difference between the relationship of children to mothers and that of mothers to children. To see this difference, let children be the *starting* set and mothers be the *ending* set. If we now take a child from the starting set there is one, *and only one*, corresponding mother in the ending set. This one-to-one correspondence is an example of a *functional* correspondence. If, however, mothers are the starting set and we take a mother from this set, there can be one *or more* corresponding children in the ending set, so we have a relationship that is not one-to-one, and this is not a functional relationship.

One way to specify a function is to write pairs of elements in *order*; that is, the first element is the element from the starting set and the second is the corresponding element from the ending set. Thus, for example, the set of *ordered* pairs

$$\{(\text{child, mother})\}$$

is a function, but

$$\{(\text{mother, child})\}$$

is a relationship, not a function. Similarly, if we let x be any number whatsoever and $2x$ be twice whatever the number x is, the set of ordered pairs

$$\{(x, 2x)\}$$

is a function because for every first number, x, there is one, and only one, second number, $2x$. Clearly, this set of ordered pairs is infinite. Some ordered pairs in the set are

$$(0, 0); \quad (1, 2); \quad (5/2, 5).$$

Usually, we choose to represent functional correspondence by an equation, if it is possible to do so. For example, the function

$$\{(x, 2x)\}$$

can be represented by the equation

$$y = 2x.$$

When it is necessary to specify which element is the starting element, this element is specified in parentheses and is called the *independent* variable. For example, the last equation with functional specification would be

$$y(x) = 2x,$$

meaning x is the starting value *chosen independently* (arbitrarily). For example, taking x as 2, arbitrarily, we find the second element of the ordered pair, symbolized by $y(2)$, to be

$$y(2) = 2 \cdot 2 = 4$$

and the ordered pair

$$(2, 4)$$

is in the *solution set.* The complete (infinite) solution set is *the set of ordered pairs, (x, y), such that y = 2x* and we symbolize this by

$$\{(x, y)\colon y = 2x\}.$$

In the work we shall encounter in this book, it will be helpful to view a function as a *rule* stating how the member of the ending set is obtained for an arbitrarily selected member of the starting set. For example, if we have

$$f(x) = 5x + 1,$$

where $f(x)$ is read as "the f function of x," or "f of x," the rule is

multiply 5 by x, then add 1.

Thus, selecting x arbitrarily to be 20, we find

5 times 20, plus 1 $= 100$ plus 1 $= 101$.

The last is simple substitution. However, we shall have to work with expressions such as

$$f(a + 3),$$

and in such a case it is important to remember that the rule tells us that $f(a + 3)$ means

multiply 5 by $a + 3$, then add 1.

Exercise.   Given $g(z) = 2z + 3$, a) How is $g(z)$ read? b) What is $g(4)$? c) State (write) the function rule. d) How would $g(a + b)$ be obtained? Answer: a) "The g function of z" or "g of z." b) 11. c) Multiply 2 by the value of z, then add 3. d) Multiply 2 by $(a + b)$, then add 3.

FIGURE A1–1   **FIGURE A1–2**

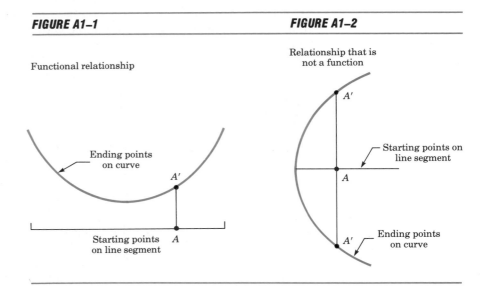

Functional relationship

Relationship that is not a function

Ending points on curve

Starting points on line segment

A'

A

Starting points A on line segment

Ending points on curve

A'

We shall have frequent occasions to represent functions graphically, taking points on a horizontal line as being members of the starting set and a point on the graph *vertically* above or below the starting point as the corresponding member of the ending set. For example, Figure A1–1 represents a functional correspondence because for each point, such as A, in the starting set, there is one and only one point, A', in the ending set. However, the relationship in Figure A1–2 is not a functional correspondence because a vertical line through a member of the starting set intersects the graph (the ending set) in two points.

A1.6 PROBLEM SET A1–1

1. Read the following aloud: for example, $A = \{5, 10, 15, \ldots , 100\}$ is read, "A is the set whose elements are 5, 10, 15, and so on, through 100."
a) $B = \{2, 4, 6\}$.
b) $C = \{0\}$.
c) $Q = \{1, 3, 5, \ldots , 29\}$.
d) $F = \{a, e, i, o, u\}$.
e) $L = \{$George, Charles$\}$.
f) $K = \{2, 4, 6, \ldots\}$.

2. Specify each of the following sets by the descriptive method:
a) $F = \{a, e, i, o, u\}$.
b) $S = \{3, 6, 9, \ldots\}$.
c) $P = \{1, 2, 3, 4, 5\}$.
d) $G = \{A, B, C, D, E\}$.
e) $R = \{100, 101, 102, \ldots\}$.
f) $J = \{-1, -3, -5, \ldots , -101\}$.

3. Specify each of the following by roster:
a) {Odd numbers less than 9}.
b) {First four months of the year}.
c) {Positive even multiples of 7}.
d) $\left\{ \begin{array}{l} \text{Positive numbers, less than 1000,} \\ \text{that are exactly divisible by 5} \end{array} \right\}$.
e) $\left\{ \begin{array}{l} \text{Numbers representing the ratios} \\ \text{formed by dividing integers by 0} \end{array} \right\}$.
f) {Squares of the integers from 1 through 10}.

4. Why is {0} not equal to ϕ?

5. Using set membership symbols and the roster specification of the sets, write the following:

a) 1/2 is not a positive integer.
b) 64 is a multiple of 4.
c) a is a lower case vowel.
d) 4 is not a positive odd number.
e) \$ is not a letter in the lower case English alphabet.
f) This problem does not have a part g.

6. Given $A = \{1, 3, 4, 7\}$; $B = \{3, 7, 12\}$; $C = \{1, 5, 8\}$, write the following sets:
a) The set containing all elements that are members of A, or members of B, or members of both A and B.
b) The set of elements that are members of both A and B.
c) The set of elements that are members of both B and C.
d) The set of elements that are members of A but not members of B.
e) The set of elements that are members of both A and C.
f) The set of elements that are members of all three sets.

7. a) Write the set symbols for $y + 2 = 10$.
b) Translate the symbols $\{y : y + 5 = 8\} = \{3\}$.

8. a) Write the set symbols for $m - 6 = 4$ and its solution set.
b) Translate the symbols $\{q : 2q = 6\} = \{3\}$.

9. What is the solution set for $\{z : 2z + 5 = 2z + 7\}$?

10. What is the solution set for $\{y : 4y + 1 = 12\}$?

A1.6 PROBLEM SET A1–1 (*concluded*)

In Problems 11 through 14, the first mentioned set is the starting set.

11. Each of the United States has two senators.
   a) Is the relationship between the set of states and the set of senators a functional correspondence? Why?
   b) Is the relationship between the set of senators and the set of states a functional correspondence? Why?

12. a) Is the relationship between the set of individual apples in an orchard and the set of individual apple trees in an orchard a functional correspondence? Why?
   b) Is the relationship between the set of apple trees and the set of apples a functional correspondence? Why?

13. Draw a horizontal line and a slant line intersecting the horizontal line, then draw vertical lines intersecting the first two lines. Does the set of points at the intersection of such verticals and the horizontal line have a functional correspondence with the respective set of points at the intersection of verticals and the slant line? Why?

14. Draw a circle and a horizontal line that is a diameter of the circle. If vertical lines are drawn, does the set of points at the intersection of the vertical and the diameter have a functional correspondence with the respective set of points at the intersection of the vertical and the circle? Why?

---

15. If $h(z) = 4z + 7$
   a) How is $h(z)$ read?
   b) What is $h(2)$?
   c) State the function rule.
   d) How would $h(x + 2)$ be obtained?

16. If $f(x) = 3x + 10$
   a) How is $f(x)$ read?
   b) What is $f(5)$?
   c) State the function rule.
   d) How would $f(x + 1)$ be obtained?

17. If $y = 2x + 7$, write the symbolic expression for the solution set.

18. If $y = 5x$, write the symbolic expression for the solution set.

19. Does $y = 10x + 25$ represent a functional correspondence? Why?

20. If the starting set is zero or any whole number and the elements of the ending set are obtained by dividing five by the starting element, is there a functional relationship between the sets? Why?

A1.7 SUBSETS, UNIONS, AND INTERSECTIONS

If every element of a set B is also an element of a set A, then B is called a *subset* of A. For example, if

$$A = \{1, 3, 6, 9\} \quad \text{and} \quad B = \{3, 6\},$$

then B is a subset of A. Moreover, in this example, B is a *proper* subset of A because it does not contain all the elements of A. If

$$C = \{8, 9, 10\} \quad \text{and} \quad D = \{8, 9, 10\},$$

then D is an *improper* subset of C, and vice versa, because all the elements of one are elements of the other. It follows that if two sets are equal, they are improper subsets of each other. The empty set, ϕ, is by definition a proper subset of every set except itself. If $S = \{a, b, c\}$, then the proper subsets of S are

$$\phi, \quad \{a\}, \quad \{b\}, \quad \{c\}, \quad \{a, b\}, \quad \{a, c\}, \quad \text{and} \quad \{b, c\}.$$

Exercise. List all eight subsets of $K = \{2, 4, 6\}$.[1] Answer: ϕ, $\{2\}$, $\{4\}$, $\{6\}$, $\{2, 4\}$, $\{2, 6\}$, $\{4, 6\}$, K.

The *intersection* of two sets A and B is a set whose elements are elements of *both* A and B. The intersection symbol is like an inverted U. Thus

$$A \cap B$$

is read as "A intersection B," or "the intersection of A and B." If we have

$$A = \{4, 8, 9, 11\} \quad \text{and} \quad B = \{8, 11, 14\} \quad \text{and} \quad C = \{3, 5\}$$

then

$$A \cap B = \{8, 11\} \quad \text{and} \quad A \cap C = \phi.$$

The last expression says that the intersection of A and C is the empty set because the two sets have no common members. Sets with no common members also are said to be *disjoint* sets.

Exercise. Given $A = \{a, b, c, d, e\}$ and $B = \{e, f, g, \ldots, z\}$, write $A \cap B$. Answer: $\{e\}$.

The union of sets A and B is a set containing those elements that are members of A or members of B, or members of both A and B. A U-like symbol represents the union; thus,

$$A \cup B$$

is read "A union B" or "the union of A and B." If

$$A = \{a, b, c, d, e\} \quad \text{and} \quad B = \{c, e, f, k\}$$

then

$$A \cup B = \{a, b, c, d, e, f, k\}.$$

Exercise. Find $A \cup B$ if $A = \{2, 7, 8, 9, 13\}$ and $B = \{1, 8, 13, 22\}$. Answer: $\{1, 2, 7, 8, 9, 13, 22\}$.

---

[1] If a set has n elements, then the set will have 2^n subsets, counting the null set and the improper subset.

FIGURE A1–3

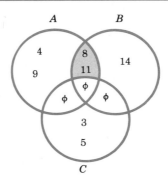

It is helpful to illustrate the ideas of intersection and union diagrammatically as in Figure A1–3. Returning to the earlier example with

$$A = \{4, 8, 9, 11\}, \quad B = \{8, 11, 14\}, \quad \text{and} \quad C = \{3, 5\},$$

if we think of A as a set containing all the points in circle A, and similarly for B and C, then $A \cap B = \{8, 11\}$ is the set of points indicated by the shaded area. In addition, $A \cup B$ is the set of points containing all the points in both circles A and B; $A \cup C$ contains all the points in circles A and C; and $A \cap C = \phi$ because A and C have no points in common, so are disjoint. Note we have adapted the convention of placing the empty set symbol ϕ in an area that has no elements.

A1.8 PROBLEM SET A1–2

1. Figure A shows set R with points $a, b, c, d,$ and e and similarly for sets S and T. Write the following sets by the roster method:

FIGURE A

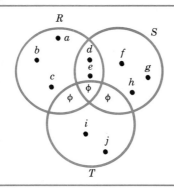

a) $R \cup S$.
b) $R \cup T$.
c) $R \cap S$.
d) $R \cap T$.
e) $S \cup T$.
f) $S \cap T$.

2. If $A = \{1, 3, 5, \ldots\}$, $B = \{0, 2, 4, 6, \ldots\}$, and $C = \{5, 7, 9\}$ write the following sets by the roster method:

a) $A \cup B$.
b) $A \cap B$.
c) $A \cap C$.
d) $B \cap C$.
e) $A \cup C$.

3. If A is the set of face cards in a standard 52-card deck and B is the set of queens, what will be the elements of $A \cup B$ and $A \cap B$?

4. If A is the set of face cards in a standard 52-card deck, B is the set of red cards, and C is the set of nines, what will be the elements in $A \cup B$, $A \cap B$, $A \cap C$, $B \cap C$?

A1.8 PROBLEM SET A1–2 (concluded)

5. If *M* represents the set of all points on one line in a plane, and *N* the points on a different line in the plane, what is $M \cap N$?
   a) If the lines are parallel?
   b) If the lines are not parallel?

6. If *R* means rain tomorrow and *W* means warmer tomorrow, what do the following mean?
   a) $R \cup W$.   b) $R \cap W$.

A1.9 REVIEW PROBLEMS

1. Read the following aloud: for example, $A = \{5, 10, 15, \ldots, 100\}$ is read, "*A* is the set whose elements are 5, 10, 15, and so on, through 100."
   a) $\{5, 6, 7, 9\}$.
   b) $B = \{$Amherst, Babson, Colgate, Dartmouth$\}$.
   c) $C = \{1, 3, 5, 7, \ldots\}$.
   d) $D = \{A, B, C, \ldots, Z\}$.
   e) $E = \left\{1, \dfrac{1}{2}, \dfrac{1}{4}, \dfrac{1}{8}, \ldots\right\}$.
   f) $F = \{$Tim, Dick, Harry$\}$.

2. Specify each of the following sets by the descriptive method:
   a) $A = \{1, 3, 5, 7, 9, \ldots\}$.
   b) $B = \{5, 10, 15, \ldots\}$.
   c) $C = \{101, 102, 103, \ldots, 999\}$.
   d) $D = \{M, A, R, Y\}$.

3. Specify each of the following by the roster method:
   a) $A = \{$Letters in the word HARVARD$\}$.
   b) $B = \{$First nine positive prime numbers$\}$.
   c) $C = \{$Positive odd multiples of 4$\}$.
   d) $D = \{$The first five positive even multiples of 3$\}$.

4. Using set membership symbols and the roster method of specification of the sets, write the following:
   a) The letter *S* is among the letters in the word BABSON.
   b) 7 is not a positive integral multiple of 3.
   c) 3 is not a positive integral power of 2.
   d) 5 is not a lower case English letter.

5. a) Write the set symbols for $t + 1 = 20$ and its solution set.
   b) Translate the symbols $\{y : 3y + 5 = 11\} = \{2\}$.

6. Given the relation $y = x$:
   a) Is the relation a function? Explain.
   b) What is the function rule?
   c) What is meant by the "solution set" for the equation?
   d) How many elements are there in the solution set?
   e) What are the elements in the solution set corresponding to $x = 1, 2, 3, 4$?

7. What is the solution set for $\{t : t = t + 1\}$?

8. Suppose *x* is any positive whole number and *y* is any positive whole number that is an exact divisor of *x*. Is the relation between *y* and *x* a function? Explain.

9. Given $A = \{5, 10, 12, 13, 15\}$; $B = \{2, 10, 13, 14\}$; $C = \{12, 16, 17\}$; write the following sets:
   a) The set containing all elements that are members of *A* or members of *B*, or members of both *A* and *B*.
   b) The set of elements that are members of both *A* and *B*.
   c) The set of elements that are members of both *B* and *C*.
   d) The set of elements that are members of *A* but not members of *B*.
   e) The set of elements that are members of both *A* and *C*.
   f) The set of elements that are members of all three sets.

10. Figure B shows set *R* with points *p, q, r, s,* and *t*, and similarly for sets *S* and *T*. Write the following sets by the roster method:

A1.9 REVIEW PROBLEMS (*concluded*)

a) $R \cup S$.   d) $R \cap T$.
b) $R \cup T$.   e) $S \cup T$.
c) $R \cap S$.   f) $S \cap T$.

FIGURE B

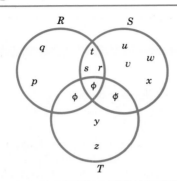

T

---

11. If $A = \{5, 10, 12, 15, 19\}$, $B = \{3, 10, 15\}$, and $C = \{7, 12\}$, write the following sets by the roster method:
a) $A \cup B$.   d) $B \cap C$.
b) $A \cap B$.   e) $A \cup C$.
c) $A \cap C$.   f) $B \cup C$.

12. Make a diagram showing sets R, S, and T (like the diagram in Problem 10) corresponding to the following requirements:
a) $R \cap T = \{x\}$.   d) $R \cup S = \{v, x, y, z\}$.
b) $R \cap S = \{z\}$.   e) $R \cup T = \{w, x, y, z\}$.
c) $T \cap S = \phi$.

13. If sets M and N are, respectively, the sets of points on the perimeters of two concentric circles, what is $M \cap N$?

14. If P is the set of all cars with air conditioners, Q is the set with automatic shifting, and R is the set with manual (or stick) shifting, what are the following?
a) $P \cup Q$.   c) $Q \cap R$.
b) $P \cap Q$.   d) $P \cap R$.

15. a) Write the set symbols for $y + 5 = 15$ and its solution set.
b) Translate the symbols $\{x : x - 2 = 10\} = \{12\}$.

16. What is the solution set for $\{z : z + 7 = 30\}$?

17. Is 5 in the solution set of $\{x : x < 10\}$? Why?

18. If x is a number in the starting set, and the corresponding number in the ending set is any number less than x, do the sets have a functional correspondence?

19. Each secretary in a company works for three executives, and always the same three.
a) Does the starting set of secretaries have a functional correspondence to the set of executives? Why?
b) Does the starting set of executives have a functional correspondence to the set of secretaries?

20. If $f(x) = 20x + 50$
a) How is $f(x)$ read?
b) What is $f(10)$?
c) State the function rule.
d) How would $f(x + 1)$ be obtained?

21. Write the symbolic expression for the solution set of $y = 12x + 6$.

22. Does $z = 3x + 5$ represent a functional correspondence? Why?

23. How many ordered pairs are there in the solution set for $y = x + 3$?

APPENDIX TWO

Elements of Algebra

A2.1 INTRODUCTION

This appendix presents the basic definitions, conventions, and rules of algebra, together with discussions and illustrations of the fundamental properties of numbers. Each topic is accompanied by examples that will meet the needs of those who use isolated parts of the appendix for reference purposes. However, topics are presented in logical order so that the needs of those seeking a substantial review of elements will be met by starting at the beginning and moving in an orderly fashion through the material.

A2.2 THE REAL NUMBERS

The positive and negative whole numbers, with zero, form the set of *integers*. Combining the integers with the fractions, we have the set of *rational* numbers. Thus, a rational number (ratio number) is a number that can be expressed in the form of a fraction that has integers as numerator and denominator. For reasons to be discussed soon, fractions with denominator zero are excluded from our number system.

> **Exercise.** How would the number 1.15 be classified? Answer: This is a rational number because it can be expressed as 115/100, which is the ratio of the two integers 115 and 100.

Numbers such as the square root of 2, the cube root of 6, and π cannot be expressed as a ratio of two integers, and serve as examples of *irrational* numbers. The set of all rational and irrational numbers is called the set of *real* numbers. Only real numbers will be used in this book. Numbers with an imaginary component (that is, a component involving the square root of -1) are not in the set of reals and play no role in our discussions.

A2.3 RULES OF SIGN

The numbers $+2$ and -2 are opposites in the sense that each is the negative of the other. The statement that -2 is the negative of $+2$ is true by definition; the statement that the negative of -2 is $+2$ is a rule that can be derived from definitions and axioms. Thus,

$$-(+2) = -2$$

and

$$-(-2) = +2.$$

Another derived rule justifies the statement

$$+(-2) = -(+2).$$

That is, the positive of the negative of a number is the same as the negative of the positive of the number. As a consequence of this rule, the sign of a number is the same no matter what the *order* is of the signs immediately preceding the number. For example,

$$+[-(-5)] = -[+(-5)] = -[-(+5)].$$

The ultimate sign is shown by working with the last expression to be

$$-[-(+5)] = -[-5] = +5.$$

Exercise.   Write $-[-(-5)]$ with one sign.   Answer: -5.

Any sequence of signs immediately preceding a number can be converted to a single ultimate sign, the ultimate sign being *minus* if the sequence has an *odd* number of *minus* signs, and being *plus* if the sequence has an *even* number of minus signs. For example,

$$-[+(-3)] = +3$$

and

$$-\{-[+(-3)]\} = -3.$$

A2.4 ADDITION AND SUBTRACTION OF SIGNED NUMBERS

If two numbers have the same sign, their sum is found by adding the two numbers and affixing the common sign. Thus,

$$(+4) + (+3) = +7$$

and

$$(-3) + (-4) = -7.$$

> **Exercise.** Add $(-10) + (-4)$. Answer: -14.

The sum of a positive and a negative number is found by taking the difference between the two numbers, disregarding sign, and affixing the sign of the larger to the difference. For example,

$$(+7) + (-3) = +4$$

and

$$(-7) + (+3) = -4.$$

> **Exercise.** Add: $(+5) + (-3)$. Answer: $+2$.

In terms of fundamentals, subtraction is developed from addition. Subtraction can be converted to addition by following the rule that states that subtracting a number is the same as adding its negative. This rule, together with a rule already stated, permits us to write

$$+3 - (+4) = +3 + (-4) = -1.$$

As another example,

$$-3 - (-4) = -3 + (+4) = +1.$$

> **Exercise.** Write as an addition problem, and find the sum: $+5 - (+11)$. Answer: $+5 + (-11) = -6$.

Observe that the minus symbol is used both to designate negative and to indicate the operation of subtraction. Again, the plus symbol designates both positive and the operation of addition. For example, we write $-(+2)$ to designate the *negative* of $+2$, but in the expression $+3 - (+2)$, the same symbol, $-(+2)$, means to *subtract* $+2$. Now, let us adopt two conventions. First, we shall assume that an unsigned number is positive; second, we shall indicate the subtraction of a number by a minus sign, rather than by addition of its negative. Thus, instead of $+3 - (+2)$ we shall write the condensed statement, $3 - 2$. The conventions just stated, taken together with the rule for sign sequence, contribute to simplicity of expression, as illustrated next:

$$+1 + (+2) - (+3) + (-4) - (-5) - [+(-4)]$$

becomes

$$1 + 2 - 3 - 4 + 5 + 4 = 12 - 7 = 5.$$

Exercise. Simplify and evaluate $+(-1) + (-3) - (+2) + (+4) + [-(-6)]$. Answer: 4.

We usually seek to reduce additions and subtractions of signed numbers to simplified form, as just shown. However, in the interest of keeping track of fundamentals, we should be able to convert from the simplified form to an expression in terms of addition of signed numbers. Thus,

$$4 - 3 + 2$$

means

$$+4 + (-3) + (+2).$$

Exercise. What does $2 + 5 - 8$ mean in terms of addition of signed numbers? Answer: $+2 + (+5) + (-8)$.

The negative of the sum of two numbers is the sum of the negatives of the numbers. Thus:

$$-(7 + 5) = (-7) + (-5) = -7 - 5 = -12.$$

It will be observed that as we go from $-(7 + 5)$ to $-7 - 5$, the effect is to remove the parentheses and change the signs of the numbers inside the parentheses. The methodology applies generally; that is, parentheses preceded by a minus sign alone can be removed by changing the sign of each term inside the parentheses. As examples,

$$-(4 - 6) = -4 + 6$$

and

$$-(4 + 8) = -4 - 8.$$

Parentheses preceded by a plus sign alone (or no sign) serve no necessary purpose and may be omitted. Thus,

$$+(8 - 6) = 8 - 6$$

and

$$(2 - 4 + 3) = 2 - 4 + 3.$$

Exercise. Remove grouping symbols: $(2 + 3 - 5) - (5 - 2 + 4)$. Answer: $2 + 3 - 5 - 5 + 2 - 4$.

A2.5
MULTIPLICATION
AND DIVISION OF
SIGNED NUMBERS

Multiplication is a fundamental operation with numbers, and division is defined in terms of multiplication. One rule of sign suffices for both operations—namely, if two numbers have the same sign, their product (or quotient) is positive; if two numbers are of opposite sign, their product (or quotient) is negative. In multiplication, for example,

$$(-4)(-2) = 8$$

and

$$2(-4) = -8.$$

Observe the use of parentheses in the last written expression. In the first, the absence of a symbol between the two sets of parentheses means that the numbers inside the parentheses are to be multiplied. We could have written $-4(-2)$ instead of $(-4)(-2)$ without ambiguity, but multiplication would not be in order if the expression read $(-4) - 2$. The last written number is a difference, not a product.

The division symbol, $\div$, is not used often in algebraic statements. The fractional form of expression is preferred. Thus, 8 divided by 4 is written as $\frac{8}{4}$. Moreover, the general practice in mathematics is to speak of the last number as "8 over 4," not "4 into 8."

According to the rule for division of signed numbers,

$$\frac{8}{-4} = -2, \quad \frac{-8}{4} = -2, \quad \text{and} \quad \frac{-8}{-4} = 2.$$

Exercise. Evaluate: $-2(4)$; $3(6)$; $-(-3)(-5)$; $-4/-2$; $6/-3$; $-(6/-3)$; $-(-6/3)$; $-(-6/-3)$. Answer: -8; 18; -15; 2; -2; 2; 2; -2.

The sign of a term that involves only multiplications and divisions of numbers can be determined by counting the number of minus signs; if the count is odd, the ultimate sign of the term is minus; if the count is even, the ultimate sign of the term is positive. For example,

$$\frac{-4(2)(-3)}{-2(-1)(4)} = 3$$

and

$$\frac{-(-4)(-5)}{2(-1)(-10)} = -1.$$

Exercise. Write as a single signed number: $\dfrac{-2(3)(6)(-10)}{12(-5)}$. Answer: -6.

A2.6 PROBLEM SET A2–1

Reduce to a single signed number, or zero:

1. $-2 + (-3) - [-(-4)] + (-5)$.

2. $-(-8) + 8 - (+3)$.

3. $-(+4) + (-4) - [-(-4)]$.

4. $6 - (+3) + (+5) - (-7) + (-2) - (+10)$.

5. $3.15 - (+1.08) - (-3.27)$.

6. $-4 - (3)(-2) + (-5)(-4)(-1) - (3)(2)$.

7. $-4(3) + (-1)(2)(-6)(-1) -$
    $(-1)(-1)(-1)$.

8. $-(-4 + 3) + [-1(-2)]$.

9. $14(-2) - (-13) + (-3)(-2) - (-5)$.

10. $(3 - 4) - (5 - 2)$.

11. $3 - (-2) - (7 - 5)$.

12. $-5 + (7 - 3) - (2 - 4)$.

13. $+(3 - 6) - (-5 + 4)$.

14. $-(-5 - 7) + (3 - 2)$.

15. $12 - (-3) + (-2) - (+2)$.

16. $-25 - (30 - 10)$.

17. $\dfrac{-3(20)}{-4}$.

18. $\dfrac{5(-2)(3)}{-4(-2.5)}$.

19. $\dfrac{-(-7)}{-2}$.

20. $\dfrac{6(-2)(-1)(-3)}{-(-12)(-2)}$.

21. $\dfrac{-(-26)(16)}{-[-(-13)]}$.

22. $\dfrac{4(-1)(-2)(3)(-7)}{(-5)(-3)(2)}$.

23. $\dfrac{-3 - (5 - 20)}{5 - (-2)}$.

24. $\dfrac{6 - (-7 + 3)}{-[-(-2 + 7)]}$.

25. $\dfrac{-(8 - 3)}{-2 + 3(-1)}$.

26. $\dfrac{40 - 2(-5)}{2 - (15 - 3)}$.

Rewrite as the sum of signed numbers:

27. $3 - 4 + 5 - 2 + 6$.

28. $3 - 2 + 4 - 5$.

29. $-1.5 - 3 - 2.5$.

30. $-3 + 7 - 4 + 2$.

31. $-10 + 7 - 4 + 3$.

32. $12 - 6 + 5 - 7$.

Reduce to a single signed number:

33. $-3(2) + (3 - 7) - (2 + 4)$.

34. $-[-2 + (-3)] - 2(-3) + (-3)(-4)$.

35. $-(3 - 5) + (2 - 6)$.

36. $-[+(-3) + (-5)] + [-2 + (-3)]$.

37. $-[+(-5)] + [-(-3)] + (8 - 4) -$
    $(2 - 6)$.

38. $-(-3) + (-7) + (8) - (-6)$.

A2.7 REPRESENTING NUMBERS BY LETTERS

Mathematics beyond arithmetic is characterized by its use of letter representation of numbers. The sum, difference, and quotient of two numbers in literal form, such as a and b, are written in the usual manner as, respectively, $a + b$, $a - b$, and a/b. The product conventionally is written as ab, the multiplication symbol being omitted. This convention is, of course, in conflict with the place system of decimal notation. For example, 34 means thirty-four, not 3 times 4. We would interpret $34a$ as thirty-four times a, not 3 times 4 times a. It follows that care must be exercised when writing numbers that have literal and numerical factors. Sometimes a dot is employed to indicate multiplication, as in $3 \cdot 4ab$. We shall generally follow the more common practice, already introduced, and use parentheses; thus, $3(4)ab$ or $(3)(4)ab$. The first of the last two expressions is the simpler. The second is equivalent to the first, but uses two sets of parentheses where only one is required.

The first advantage of literal representation of numbers is their utility in stating generalizations. For example, we may illustrate the point that the sum of any two real numbers is a real number by mentioning that the sum of 3 and 4 is 7, and 7 is a real number. To generalize the point and state it as a property of all real numbers, we need a statement that is not restricted to a particular pair of numbers. The statement desired is: *"If a and b are any real numbers, then $a + b$ is a real number."* In this statement the word *any* means that the property applies to *all* real numbers. If someone asks if the statement applies to x and y, we inquire whether x and y are real numbers; if they are, the statement applies, and $x + y$ is a real number. The student will find it helpful to keep in mind the *all* implication of the word *any* in mathematical statements.

The fundamental properties we list for real numbers are formal statements of observations of arithmetic. The very fact that they seem obvious

Property	Addition	Multiplication
1. Closure	If a and b are real, then $a + b$ is real.	If a and b are real, then $a \cdot b$ is real.
2. Identity	There exists a real number 0 such that $$a + 0 = 0 + a = a.$$	There exists a real number 1 such that $a \cdot 1 = 1 \cdot a = a.$
3. Commutative	If a and b are real, then $$a + b = b + a.$$	If a and b are real, then $$a \cdot b = b \cdot a.$$
4. Associative	If a, b, and c are real, then $$(a + b) + c = a + (b + c).$$	If a, b, and c are real, then $$(ab)c = a(bc).$$
5. Distributive	If a, b, and c are real, then $$a(b + c) = a \cdot b + a \cdot c.$$	

is a primary reason for stating them as fundamental properties. The fact that they seem obvious is not, however, justification for thinking time spent on them is wasted. Many questions that perplex beginning students arise simply because of failure to have in mind the fundamental properties of numbers.

We list four fundamental properties for addition and multiplication in the table on the previous page, together with a fifth property which combines both addition and multiplication.

A2.8 IMPORTANCE OF FUNDAMENTAL PROPERTIES

The closure, identity, commutative, associative, and distributive properties of the real numbers are important because they are the fundamental justifications for many of the steps taken in algebraic procedures. Asked if $(a + b)c$ is the same as $c(a + b)$, we answer yes, and cite the commutative law for multiplication as justification. Now,

$$c(a + b) = ca + cb$$

by the distributive property, and the commutative property assures us that the right side can be altered to obtain

$$c(a + b) = ac + bc.$$

From what has been said, it follows that

$$(a + b)c = ac + bc.$$

The point here is that the distributive law does not tell us directly how to expand an expression such as $(2 + a)b$, but we can easily justify by fundamentals that the expansion may be written as

$$(2 + a)b = 2b + ab.$$

Exercise. In $(2)(a)(3) = (2a)(3) = 2(3)(a) = 6a$, what justifies each of the three expressions following the equals sign? Answer: Associative law for multiplication; commutative law for multiplication; associative law for multiplication.

Carrying on one step further, let us learn how to expand

$$(a + b)(c + d).$$

We know by closure that $(a + b)$ is a real number, and the distributive law justifies writing

$$(a + b)(c + d) = (a + b)c + (a + b)d.$$

The right-hand side of the last expression can be expanded, leading to

$$(a + b)(c + d) = (a + b)c + (a + b)d = ac + bc + ad + bd.$$

The distributive law works both ways. Writing it in reverse, we have

$$ab + ac = a(b + c).$$

Converting in this manner from the sum of ab and ac to the product of a by $(b + c)$ is referred to as *factoring*. Hence the distributive property is the fundamental property underlying factoring. When applied to obtain

$$2a + 3a = (2 + 3)a = 5a$$

the procedure is called *combining like terms*. As other examples:

$$2ab - 3ab + 5ab - 6 = 4ab - 6$$
$$4a - 2a + 5b - 2b = 2a + 3b.$$

In the last two examples the associative law for addition justifies the separate combinations of like terms. We may say in general that terms having the same literal factor can be added (subtracted) by adding (subtracting) their numerical coefficients. Thus, in

$$3ab + 4ab - 2ab$$

each term has the same literal factor, ab. Combining the numerical coefficients, we have

$$(3 + 4 - 2)ab = 5ab.$$

Exercise. Remove symbols of grouping and combine like terms: $a(2 - b) - 3(a - 2b)$. Answer: $a(2) - ab - 3a + 6b = 6b - ab - a$.

The following example shows how the fundamental properties come into play. Starting with the expression at the top left, we change to the expression on the next line, indicating on that next line, at the right, the justification for the step:

$$-2a(3b) + ab$$
$$= -2(3b)a + ab \qquad \text{Commutative law, multiplication}$$
$$= -6ba \quad + ab \qquad \text{Associative law, multiplication}$$
$$= -6ab \quad + ab \qquad \text{Commutative law, multiplication}$$
$$= -5ab. \qquad \text{Distributive law (combining like terms, or factoring)}$$

A similar example follows:

$$2 + ba + 3$$
$$= 2 + \quad 3 + ba \qquad \text{Commutative law, addition}$$
$$= \qquad 5 + ba \qquad \text{Associative law, addition}$$
$$= \qquad 5 + ab. \qquad \text{Commutative law, multiplication}$$

We do not mean to suggest by these examples that the fundamental reason for every algebraic step should be cited. We do mean to suggest, and strongly, that continued practice with these fundamentals will help to avoid questions such as:

"Is $(2 + 3b)(-c)$ the same as $-c(2 + 3b)$?"

Exercise. What fundamental law specifies that the two last written expressions are equal? Answer: The commutative law for multiplication.

A2.9 PROBLEM SET A2–2

1. When we write ab or cxy, in what way does algebraic convention differ from the usual decimal notation?

2. What would abc mean in decimal notation?

3. What is the connotation of the word *any* in mathematical statements?

4. If we add the odd number 3 to the odd number 5, the sum is an even number, 8. State this odd-even relationship in a manner that shows it is a fundamental property of integers.

5. Explain the property of closure by using addition of clock numbers as an example.

6. Why does $3a + c$ not mean three times the sum of a and c?

7. How many specific numerical illustrations of the distributive property do you think you could devise?

8. Explain what is meant by the statement that the distributive property equates a product involving a sum to a sum of products.

What fundamental property or convention justifies each of the following?

9. $a(2) = 2a$.

10. $2 - a = -a + 2$.

11. $a(2 + 3) = a2 + a3$.

12. $a + 2 + b = a + b + 2$.

13. $+a = a$.

14. $a(b + c) = (b + c)a$.

15. $a + (-3) = a - 3$.

16. $a2 + a3 = 2a + 3a$.

17. $2 + 3 + b = 5 + b$.

18. $3a2 = 3(2)a$.

19. $3(2)a = 6a$.

20. $+b + (-a) = b - a$.

21. $5 - 4 + b = 1 + b$.

22. $2a + 2b = 2(a + b)$.

23. $a + 2 + b = a + b + 2$.

24. $a + (b + c) = (b + c) + a$.

25. $a(2)(4) = a(8)$.

Combine like terms:

26. $2b + (-3b)$.

27. $2a - 3b + 5a - 2b$.

28. $3abc - 2d - (-2abc)$.

29. $5 - (-3x) + 2 - (+2x)$.

30. $2abc - (-3abc) + 3abc$.

31. $3 + 2a - 3b + 5 - (-2b)$.

A2.9 PROBLEM SET A2–2 (*concluded*)

Name the fundamental property justifying each step:

32. $-b + a$
    $= \quad a - b.$

33. $2b(3a)$
    $= 2b3(a)$
    $= 2(3)ba$
    $= 6ba$
    $= 6ab.$

34. $3 + xy + \ 5 + 3(2ab)$
    $= 3 + 5 \ + xy + 3(2ab)$
    $= \qquad 8 \ + xy + 3(2ab)$
    $= \qquad 8 \ + xy + 6ab.$

35. $3 + a + 2$
    $= 3 + 2 + a$
    $= \qquad 5 + a.$

36. $a + 3 + c + 2$
    $= a + c + 3 + 2$
    $= a + c + 5.$

37. $acdb$
    $= adcb$
    $= adbc.$

Write in algebraic form:

38. The sum of a and b.

39. To a, add the sum of b and c.

40. To the sum of a and b, add twice the product of c and d.

41. From twice the sum of a and b, subtract three times the sum of c and $2d$.

42. Multiply the sum of a, b, and c by the product of 2 and d.

A2.10 REMOVING GROUPING SYMBOLS

Instructions to remove grouping symbols are carried out by systematic application of the distributive property. Thus:

$$a[b - c(d + 2)] = a[b - cd - 2c] = ab - acd - 2ac.$$

Observe that the innermost grouping symbols, the parentheses, were removed first. This order of attack lessens the chance of errors of omission. As another example,

$$a - \{-2 - 3[-4 + (5 - a)]\} = a - \{-2 - 3[-4 + 5 - a]\}$$
$$= a - \{-2 + 12 - 15 + 3a\}$$
$$= a + 2 - 12 + 15 - 3a$$
$$= -2a + 5.$$

> **Exercise.** Remove symbols of grouping and combine like terms: $3x - 2[y - 4(x - 3y)]$. Answer: $11x - 26y$.

Care must be exercised in the interpretation of grouping symbols. Thus,

$$5 - 3(b + c) = 5 - 3b - 3c.$$

If we had wished to indicate that the difference of 5 and 3 was to be multiplied by the sum of b and c, the expression would have been

$$(5 - 3)(b + c) = 2b + 2c.$$

Extension of the distributive property justifies the expansions

$$(3 - a)(2b + 5) = 6b + 15 - 2ab - 5a$$

and

$$(a - b + 2)(c + d) = ac - bc + 2c + ad - bd + 2d.$$

A2.11 DEFINITIONS: EXPRESSION, TERM, FACTOR

Any statement involving mathematical symbols may be referred to as a mathematical *expression*. When an expression consists of parts separated by plus or minus signs, or by an equal sign, the parts, together with their signs, are called *terms* of the expression. Thus, in the expression

$$a + 2b - 3ac + 4$$

the terms are $+a$, $+2b$, $-3ac$, and $+4$.

Each term in an expression consists of one or more *factors*, a factor being one of the separate multipliers in a *product*. Thus, in the expression $2a - 3bc$, the term $+2a$ consists of the two factors, 2 and a; the term $-3bc$ consists of the three factors, -3, b, and c.

The words we have just defined make possible clear descriptions of mathematical statements. We shall provide illustrations for practice purposes. Consider the expression

$$(2a + b)(x + 2y).$$

As written, the expression is a single term consisting of the factors $(2a + b)$ and $(x + 2y)$. We may go on to say that the first factor is an expression containing the two terms, $+2a$ and $+b$; the second factor is also an expression of two terms, $+x$ and $+2y$.

> **Exercise.**   a) The expression $3ab + 4a - 3$ has how many terms? b) What is the composition of the first term? c) Do all the terms have a common factor other than 1? Answer: a) The expression has three terms. b) The first term is composed of the factors 3, a, and b. c) The terms do not have a common factor other than 1.

The distributive property assures us that

$$3(a - 2b + c) = 3a - 6b + 3c.$$

If we think of this last statement as multiplying the parenthetical expression by 3, we come to the general statement that to multiply an expression by a number, we must multiply *each term* of the expression by the number. On the other hand, if we think of

$$3(2a) = 6a$$

as multiplying the term $2a$ by 3, we come to the general statement that to multiply a term by a number, we multiply *one factor* of the term by that number.

According to a rule of sign,

$$-(a - b + 2c) = -a + b - 2c.$$

If we think of this as changing the sign of the parenthetical expression, we see that to change the sign of an expression, we change the sign of every term of the expression. On the other hand, the sign of a term is changed by changing the sign of one of its factors. For instance, thinking of $-[a(-b)(c)(-2)]$ as changing the sign of the bracketed expression, the outcome of the sign change can be written as $-a(-b)(c)(-2)$ or $a(b)(c)(-2)$ or $a(-b)(-c)(-2)$ or $a(-b)(c)(2)$.

Finally, we may state that the sign of a term is unchanged if the signs of an even number of its factors are changed. For example,

$$-ab(-c) = a(-b)(-c) = abc$$

and

$$-3(4 - a) = 3(a - 4).$$

A2.12 ELEMENTARY FACTORING

We are assured by the distributive property that

$$ab + ac = a(b + c).$$

Thinking of this expression as changing from the form on the left to that on the right, we see that the sum of two terms has been converted to the product of two factors. Conversion from the sums and differences of terms to a single term with two or more factors is called *factoring*. Observe that an expression in completely factored form has but one term.

When terms have a factor in common, factoring is carried out by writing the product of the common factor times an expression (in grouping symbols) whose terms are the remaining factors of each of the original terms, as shown in the following examples:

$$2xy + axy = xy(2 + a)$$
$$ax - bx = x(a - b)$$
$$6x + 2y - 4a + 8b = 2(3x + y - 2a + 4b).$$

It is conventional to omit the coefficient one when writing a term, and this convention must be kept in mind when factoring. Thus,

$$ab + b = b(a + 1)$$
$$abc - ab + abd = ab(c - 1 + d).$$

> **Exercise.**   Factor $xy + ax + x$.   Answer: $x(y + a + 1)$.

As another example, we note that each of the terms of

$$2aby - 6abyz - 12xaby$$

has $2aby$ as factors, so we write the factored form as

$$2aby(1 - 3z - 6x).$$

> **Exercise.**   Factor $60xyz - 20axy + 5bxy$.
> Answer: $5xy(12z - 4a + b)$.

Thus far, we have illustrated *monomial* factoring, that is, cases where the common factor has a single term. On rare occasions in this book the need for *binomial* factoring arises. As examples,

$$a(b + 2) - 3(b + 2) = (b + 2)(a - 3)$$
$$(1 + i) + i(1 + i) = (1 + i)(1 + i).$$

> **Exercise.**   Factor $bx + by - x - y$.   Answer: $(x + y)(b - 1)$.

Finally, consider the expression

$$(3x + 4)(2x - 1)$$
$$= 3x(2x - 1) + 4(2x - 1)$$
$$= 6xx - 3x + 8x - 4$$
$$= 6x^2 + 5x - 4$$

where, in the last line, xx is written as x^2 (read as x *squared*). In a number of places in the text, we must do problems like the last one, but in reverse; that is, start with a trinomial that contains a term in x^2, a term in x, and a constant, such as

$$6x^2 + 5x - 4$$

and obtain the equivalent pair of binomial factors,

$$(3x + 4)(2x - 1).$$

We may do this by trial and error. As an example, let us factor

$$12x^2 + 7x - 10. \tag{1}$$

First we write

$$(\quad)(\quad),$$

where each set of parentheses contains two terms, a *first* term and a *second* term. The product of the first terms must be $12x^2$, so the first terms could be x and $12x$, $2x$ and $6x$, $3x$ and $4x$, $6x$ and $2x$, $12x$ and x, or any of the last pairs with signs changed. The product of the second terms must be -10, so the second terms could be 1 and -10, 2 and -5, 5 and -2, 10 and -1, or any of the last four pairs with the sign of both numbers changed. Let us try x and $12x$ as first terms, 1 and -10 as second terms. We fill in the parentheses as follows:

$$(x + 1)(12x - 10).$$

The product of the first terms is $12x^2$, and the product of the second terms is -10, as required. The *test* of our trial is the product of the inner terms $1(12x)$ plus the product of the outer terms $x(-10)$, which is

$$12x - 10x = 2x.$$

Hence,

$$(x + 1)(12x - 10) = 12x^2 + 2x - 10$$

and this does not have the same middle term as the original expression, (1),

$$12x^2 + 7x - 10,$$

so we try another set of first and second terms from our list. For example,

$$(3x + 2)(4x - 5).$$

All we need do at each trial is apply the test mentioned several lines back, and determine if the middle term in the expansion of the trial is the required $7x$. The test here yields

$$2(4x) + (3x)(-5) = 8x - 15x = -7x$$

which is the negative of the desired $7x$ so we need only change the signs of the second (or first) terms. Thus, instead of $(3x + 2)(4x - 5)$ we write $(3x - 2)(4x + 5)$. The test term is now

$$-2(4x) + (3x)5 = -8x + 15x = 7x,$$

so we have the desired factors of the original expression,

$$12x^2 + 7x - 10 = (3x - 2)(4x + 5).$$

With a little practice, the proper pairs of terms usually can be found quite rapidly if we take hints from the original expression and the results of a trial. Thus, in

$$2x^2 - 13x + 20,$$

the second terms have the *positive* product 20, so both must be positive or both must be negative. Inasmuch as the middle term is negative, it follows that both second terms are negative. As a trial, we write

$$(2x - 4)(x - 5)$$

and the test term is $-14x$, which is not the desired $-13x$ in the original. However, we will get the desired middle term if we interchange the second terms of the first trial. Thus,

$$2x^2 - 13x + 20 = (2x - 5)(x - 4).$$

Exercise. Factor $10x^2 + 26x + 12$. Answer: $(5x + 3)(2x + 4)$.

The expression

$$x^2 - 9$$

has a square term and a constant, but no middle term. The first term is the square of x and the second term is the square of 3 (that is, 3 times 3 $= 3^2 = 9$), so the expression is called the *difference of two squares*. By trial and error we find

$$x^2 - 9 = (x + 3)(x - 3).$$

Thus, the difference of the squares of two numbers is the product of the sum of the numbers times the difference of the numbers. As another example, noting that $4a^2 = (2a)(2a)$ and $16b^2 = (4b)(4b)$, we have

$$4a^2 - 16b^2 = (2a + 4b)(2a - 4b).$$

Exercise. Factor: a) $y^2 - 25$. b) $y^2 - 25x^2$.
Answer: a) $(y + 5)(y - 5)$. b) $(y - 5x)(y + 5x)$.

A2.13 PROBLEM SET A2–3

Remove grouping symbols and combine like terms, if any:

1. $2ab(c - 2)$.
2. $(a - 2)(b + 1)$.
3. $2 - 3[1 - (+4)]$.
4. $(c + 2)(a - b + 3)$.

5. $-(-2) + 3[a - (1 - b)]$.
6. $10 - 3[4 - 5(-4 + a)]$.
7. $a - 2\{-3 - 2[5a - 2(a - 6)]\}$.
8. $(3x - 2)[a - 2(b + 3)]$.

A2.13 PROBLEM SET A2-3 (*continued*)

9. $-(a - x - 2b)$.
10. $(2x + 3y)$.
11. $(a - 2b) - b$.
12. $a + (3x + 2)$.
13. $b - 2b(a - 3)$.

14. $ab[c - 2(x - 5)]$.
15. $ax - 2b(a - 1)$.
16. $(a - bx)(3 - c)$.
17. $(a + b + 1)(x + y)$.
18. $(a - 1)(b + 1)$.

Reduce to a single signed number:

19. $-3(2) - 2(1 - 3)$.
20. $\dfrac{(-3)(2) - (-2)(4)}{-3(5) - 2.5(-4)}$
21. $\dfrac{0.017(5 - 1.08) + 2.3[0.5 - 6.2(3.1)]}{-4(0.0025)}$.

22. $\dfrac{12 - (6 - 2)(3 - 1)}{(8 - 3)(-1 - 2) + 6}$.
23. $\dfrac{1.7 - [3 - 17(15.4 - 1.6)]}{-0.8(0.245 - 0.37)}$.

---

24. Define *expression, term,* and *factor,* giving an illustration in each instance.

Factor:

25. $ab - 2b$.
26. $3a + 5a$.
27. $4abc - 2ab + 6a$.
28. $ax - bx + x$.
29. $3ad - 5ac + a$.
30. $4uv - 2xv + 2$.
31. $abx + aby - ab$.
32. $2ax - 6ay + 4az$.
33. $2x + ax + bx$.
34. $-ab - 3ac - a$.
35. $a(x + 1) + b(x + 1)$.

36. $x + 1 + y(x + 1)$.
37. $2(x + y) - a(x + y)$.
38. $ax + bx + ay + by$.
39. $x^2 - x - 2$.
40. $2x^2 - 9x - 5$.
41. $12x^2 - 25x + 12$.
42. $10x^2 + 13x - 3$.
43. $x^2 - x - 6$.
44. $x^2 - 9$.
45. $x^2 - y^2$.
46. $4x^2 - 9y^2$.

Mark (T) for true or (F) for false:

47. ( ) The expression ab has only one factor.
48. ( ) The expression $a + 2b - c$ has three terms.
49. ( ) The expression $a(b - c)$, as written, is a single term.
50. ( ) Referring to $a(b - c)$, it would be proper to say that the expression has two factors.

51. ( ) If ab is to be doubled, both a and b must be doubled.
52. ( ) $(a - b)(-c) = c(b - a)$.
53. ( ) It is correct to state that "to multiply an expression by a number, every factor of each term in the expression must be multiplied by the number."
54. ( ) $-a(-b - c)(-d) = ad(b + c)$.

A2.13 PROBLEM SET A2–3 (*concluded*)

55. ( ) The sign of a term is changed if the sign of any one of its factors is changed.

56. ( ) The parentheses in $a + (b + c)$ are unnecessary.

57. ( ) $3 + 2(a + b) = 5(a + b)$.

58. ( ) $-a - b = +(-b) + (-a)$.

59. ( ) $(a + b) - c = -ac - bc$.

60. ( ) To change the sign of a term, it is sufficient to change the sign of one factor of the term.

A2.14 PROPERTIES OF THE NUMBERS ZERO AND ONE

The number *zero* is unique in several respects. First, for any number a

$$0(a) = 0;$$

that is, zero times any number is zero. Second,

$$a + (-a) = 0;$$

that is, the sum of any number and its negative is zero, and this property defines what we mean by the negative of any number. We also say that in addition, a number and its negative *cancel*, meaning their sum is zero. Third,

$$a + 0 = a - 0 = a;$$

that is, a number is not affected by adding zero to it, or subtracting zero from it. Finally,

$$\frac{a}{0} \text{ is not defined.}$$

We shall find the last statement to be of basic importance in our development of calculus. To understand why $\%$ is not defined, we consider cases such as $\%$ where $a \neq 0$, and $\%$ where a is zero. First recall that $\%$ means to find a number that when multiplied by 3 yields 6. This is the *definition* of division in terms of multiplication, and we prove $\%$ is 2 by stating $6 = (3)(2)$. Applying the definition to

$$\frac{6}{0},$$

we would seek a number which when multiplied by 0 yields 6. There is no such number, because 0 times any number is zero. Hence, expressions such as $\%$, $-\%$, and so on are not defined.

Next consider

$$\frac{0}{0}.$$

The temptation to say that this expression is 1 because $0(1) = 0$, which satisfies the definition of division. However, we could say also the expression is 2, or 3.17, 0, or any number because

$$0(\text{any number}) = 0.$$

It follows that if % were permitted, the results of mathematical operations could be ambiguous or contradictory. To demonstrate the last statement, suppose that a and b both equal 1. Then,

$$a = b,$$

and it is also true if $a = b = 1$ that

$$a^2 = ab$$

and the equality remains if we subtract $b^2 = 1$ from a^2 and from ab, respectively, obtaining

$$a^2 - b^2 = ab - b^2.$$

Factoring shows that

$$(a + b)(a - b) = b(a - b).$$

In general, *except for a division of 0*, if two numbers are equal and we divide them by the same number, the results are equal. If we here neglect the exception of division by zero and divide both numbers in the last equality by $a - b$ (which is zero), we have

$$\frac{(a + b)(a - b)}{(a - b)} = \frac{b(a - b)}{(a - b)}.$$

If we again forget the exception and cancel the $(a - b)$'s, that is, let % = 1, we then have

$$a + b = b.$$

Now recall that at the beginning we had $a = b = 1$. The last statement then would be

$$1 + 1 = 1 \quad \text{or} \quad 2 = 1,$$

which is the contradictory result we sought to demonstrate.

Remember: Expressions such as 5/0, 0/0, or any number divided by zero are not defined. We shall say alternatively that division by zero is impossible, or that it is not permitted.

Summarizing the properties, we state that *for any real number, a:*

$$(0)a = 0$$
$$a + 0 = a - 0 = a$$
$$a + (-a) = 0$$
$$a/0 \text{ is not defined.}$$

The *unique properties of one* exist in reference to multiplication and its inverse, division. Thus a number is unchanged if it is multiplied or divided by one. We have

$$a = (1)a = \frac{a}{1}.$$

The equivalence of a and $1a$ is assumed conventionally in the writing of various algebraic expressions. Any term may be assumed to have a factor of one. Recall the factoring of

$$ab - a = a(b - 1)$$

as an illustration of the point of the last two sentences.

Exercise. A rational number is the quotient of two integers, yet the single number, 4, is rational. Explain. Answer: 4 is the rational number 4/1.

Any number, zero excepted, divided by itself yields a quotient of one. This fact is employed often, as when we write

$$\frac{6}{6} = 1, \quad \text{or} \quad \frac{ab}{ab} = 1, \quad \text{or} \quad \frac{x - y}{x - y} = 1.$$

Circumstances arise also where we may wish to multiply an expression by

$$\frac{6}{6} \quad \text{or} \quad \frac{ab}{ab}$$

and this can be done without changing the expression because it is equivalent to multiplication by one.

The words *cancel* and *cancellation* are used with reference to zero and one. In addition, a number and its negative cancel each other, meaning their sum is zero. In multiplication, a number and its reciprocal cancel, meaning their product is one. Thus:

$$a\left(\frac{1}{a}\right) = 1$$

where $1/a$ is called the reciprocal of a. Often, the latter type of cancellation is thought of in terms of division rather than multiplication of reciprocals. Thus, in ab/a, we think of a over a as being one, so that

$$\frac{ab}{a} = 1(b) = b$$

and we say that the a's cancel. An important rule to keep in mind when working with fractions is that cancellation (replacement by one) can be performed *only for factors common to numerator and denominator.* We cannot cancel the a's in

$$\frac{a + 2}{a}$$

because a is not a factor of the numerator. On the other hand, the numerator of

$$\frac{ax + 2x}{x(b - 1)}$$

can be factored to permit cancellation; thus,

$$\frac{x(a + 2)}{x(b - 1)} = \frac{a + 2}{b - 1},$$

provided $x \neq 0$.

Exercise. x is a factor of what parts of the expression

$$\frac{ax + 2}{x(b - c)}?$$

Answer: x is a factor of the denominator, and of the single term ax in the numerator; x is not a factor of the numerator.

A2.15 PRODUCT OF FRACTIONS

The product of two fractions is the product of their numerators over (divided by) the product of their denominators. For example:

$$\left(\frac{2}{5}\right)\left(\frac{3}{7}\right) = \frac{6}{35}$$

$$\left(\frac{a}{2}\right)\left(\frac{3}{b}\right) = \frac{a(3)}{2b} = \frac{3a}{2b}$$

$$\left[\frac{a(b + 2)}{3}\right]\left(\frac{2}{b}\right) = \frac{a(b + 2)(2)}{3b} = \frac{2a(b + 2)}{3b}.$$

Exercise.   Express as a single fraction without grouping symbols:

$$\left(\frac{3}{x + y}\right)\left(\frac{x - y}{2}\right).$$

Answer: $\dfrac{3x - 3y}{2x + 2y}.$

Generally, cancellation should be performed where it is possible to do so. For example:

$$\left(\frac{6ab}{5c}\right)\left(\frac{c}{3a}\right) = \frac{2b}{5}$$

$$\frac{a(b+2)}{3}\left(\frac{2}{a}\right) = \frac{2(b+2)}{3}$$

$$\left(\frac{2a-2}{b}\right)\left(\frac{1}{2}\right) = \frac{2(a-1)}{b}\left(\frac{1}{2}\right) = \frac{a-1}{b}.$$

As another example, we start with

$$(x+y)\left[3 + \frac{a}{x+y}\right].$$

Any number can be expressed equivalently as the number divided by 1. Thus, the last expression is the same as

$$\frac{(x+y)}{1}\left[\frac{3}{1} + \frac{a}{x+y}\right] = \frac{(x+y)}{1}\left(\frac{3}{1}\right) + \frac{(x+y)}{1}\left(\frac{a}{x+y}\right)$$

$$= \frac{(x+y)(3)}{1} + \frac{a}{1}$$

$$= 3(x+y) + a.$$

Similarly,

$$3\left(\frac{a}{b}\right) = \left(\frac{3}{1}\right)\left(\frac{a}{b}\right) = \frac{3a}{b}$$

$$2\frac{(a-3)}{b} = \left(\frac{2}{1}\right)\frac{(a-3)}{b} = \frac{2(a-3)}{b}.$$

Exercise. Carry out the multiplication, leaving the result as the sum of two fractions:

$$2\frac{a}{b}\left[3 + \frac{x+2}{ax}\right].$$

Answer: $\frac{6a}{b} + \frac{2x+4}{bx}$.

An equivalent expression is obtained if a given expression is multiplied or divided by -1 an even number of times because the net effect is multiplication or division by $+1$. For example, in

$$\frac{b - a}{-2}$$

we may change the sign of numerator and denominator to give

$$\frac{-(b - a)}{-(-2)} = \frac{-b + a}{2} = \frac{a - b}{2}.$$

Keeping in mind that three signs are associated with a fraction (the signs of the numerator and denominator and the sign of the fraction itself), it is helpful to remember that an equivalent fraction results if any *two* of these signs are changed. Thus, the fraction

$$\frac{b - a}{-2}$$

has the three signs shown in parentheses below:

$$(+)\frac{(+)(b - a)}{(-)2},$$

and we changed the signs of the numerator and denominator to yield

$$(+)\frac{(-)(b - a)}{+2} = +\frac{-b + a}{2} = \frac{a - b}{2}.$$

Similarly, in

$$-\frac{2y - x}{3} = (-)\frac{(+)(2y - x)}{(+)3}$$

we may change the sign in front of the fraction and the sign of the numerator to give

$$+\frac{(-)(2y - x)}{+3} = +\frac{-2y + x}{+3} = \frac{x - 2y}{3}.$$

It is important to remember that numerator and denominator are *expressions*, and to change the sign of an expression it is necessary to change the sign of every *term* in the expression, where the change of a term's sign is accomplished by changing the sign of *one* (or an odd number) of the term's *factors*. For example,

$$\frac{(-b - 2)}{3(2a - 5xy)} = (+)\frac{(+)(-b - 2)}{(+)3(2a - 5xy)},$$

where the expression at the right has the three fraction signs indicated in parentheses. Changing the sign of numerator and denominator gives

$$+\frac{(-)(-b - 2)}{(-)3(2a - 5xy)} = +\frac{b + 2}{-6a + 15xy} = \frac{b + 2}{15xy - 6a}.$$

After some practice, you will be able to use sign changes to simplify expressions or to reduce the number of negative signs that appear in expressions. While the latter use may seem inconsequential, it does occur frequently. To show how sign change can lead to simplification, note that

$$3x - \frac{b - a}{a - b} = 3x - \frac{(+)(b - a)}{+(a - b)}$$

$$= 3x + \frac{(-)(b - a)}{+(a - b)}$$

$$= 3x + \frac{-b + a}{a - b}$$

$$= 3x + \frac{a - b}{a - b}$$

$$= 3x + 1.$$

However, in

$$2x - \frac{a - y}{b} = 2x - \frac{+(a - y)}{b}$$

$$= 2x + \frac{-a + y}{b}$$

$$= 2x + \frac{y - a}{b},$$

the sign changes served only to reduce the original two negative signs in the beginning expression to one in the ending expression.

Exercise.   a) Simplify by sign changes $y + \dfrac{2x - z}{z - 2x}$.

b) In $2x - \dfrac{a + 2}{10 - a} = 2x + \dfrac{a + 2}{a - 10}$, what sign changes were made?

Answer: a) $y - 1$. b) The sign of the fraction and the sign of its denominator were changed.

A final point worthy of note in the multiplication of fractions is the use of the word *of* to designate multiplication. Thus, two thirds *of* one half means

$$\left(\frac{2}{3}\right)\left(\frac{1}{2}\right) = \frac{1}{3}.$$

Addition and subtraction of fractions is accomplished by changing each fraction to the same (common) denominator and then placing the sums (differences) of the resultant numerators over the common denominator. A common denominator can always be found by forming the term that has each of the separate denominators as a factor. On the other hand, if all the factors of each denominator are set down and a term is constructed that contains each factor the maximum number of times it appears in any one denominator, this term is called the *lowest common denominator.* Consider

$$\frac{3}{5} + \frac{4}{15} - \frac{2}{3} + \frac{5}{18}.$$

Factors of 5 are 5, 1.
Factors of 15 are 5, 3, 1.
Factors of 3 are 3, 1.
Factors of 18 are 3, 3, 2, 1.
Lowest common denominator is $(5)(3)(3)(2) = 90$.

The mechanical procedure for changing each fraction to the common denominator is illustrated by reference to the fraction ³⁄₅. We divide the lowest common denominator by 5 to obtain the conversion factor ⁹⁰⁄₅, which is 18, and then multiply the numerator, 3, by the conversion factor to obtain 54. By this procedure, ³⁄₅ is changed to ⁵⁴⁄₉₀. We have

$$\frac{3}{5} + \frac{4}{15} - \frac{2}{3} + \frac{5}{18} = \frac{54}{90} + \frac{24}{90} - \frac{60}{90} + \frac{25}{90} = \frac{43}{90}.$$

The mechanical procedure is efficient, but in the interest of emphasizing fundamentals, it should be made clear that the process derives from a fundamental property of the number one; that is, a number is unchanged if it is multiplied by one. For example, when converting ³⁄₅ to a denominator of 90, we observe that 5 must be multiplied by 18 to yield 90, so we multiply ³⁄₅ by ¹⁸⁄₁₈; that is, in this instance the unit multiplier is ¹⁸⁄₁₈. In the case of ⁴⁄₁₅ the unit multiplier is ⁶⁄₆. It follows that the mechanical procedure is a consequence of the more lengthy, but also more fundamental, process shown next:

$$\frac{3}{5} + \frac{4}{15} - \frac{2}{3} + \frac{5}{18} = \frac{3(18)}{5(18)} + \frac{4(6)}{15(6)} - \frac{2(30)}{3(30)} + \frac{5(5)}{18(5)} = \frac{43}{90}.$$

As another example, follow the conversion of each fraction in the next expression to the lowest common denominator, $a(2)(3)$:

$$\frac{2}{a} + \frac{b}{2} + \frac{2c}{3} + \frac{1}{6} = \frac{2}{a}\left(\frac{6}{6}\right) + \frac{b}{2}\left(\frac{3a}{3a}\right) + \frac{2c}{3}\left(\frac{2a}{2a}\right) + \frac{1}{6}\left(\frac{a}{a}\right)$$

$$= \frac{12 + 3ab + 4ac + a}{6a}.$$

Exercise.   Add $5 + \dfrac{2}{y} + \dfrac{3}{4} + \dfrac{1}{2x}$.

Answer: $\dfrac{23xy + 8x + 2y}{4xy}$.

As a final example, consider

$$\frac{5}{3} + \frac{c}{2a} - \frac{c}{a(b + 2)}.$$

The factors of the denominator are, in turn:

$$3, 1$$
$$2, a, 1$$
$$a, (b + 2), 1.$$

The lowest common denominator is $3(2)a(b + 2)$. Hence:

$$\frac{5}{3}\frac{(2a)(b + 2)}{(2a)(b + 2)} + \frac{c}{2a}\frac{(3)(b + 2)}{(3)(b + 2)} - \frac{c}{a(b + 2)}\frac{(3)(2)}{(3)(2)}$$

is equivalent to the original set of fractions. By the associative and commutative properties, all of the denominators may be written as $6a(b + 2)$, so placing all the numerators over the common denominator we have

$$\frac{5(2a)(b + 2) + c(3)(b + 2) - c(3)(2)}{6a(b + 2)}$$

$$= \frac{10a(b + 2) + 3c(b + 2) - 6c}{6a(b + 2)}$$

$$= \frac{10ab + 20a + 3bc + 6c - 6c}{6a(b + 2)}$$

$$= \frac{10ab + 20a + 3bc}{6a(b + 2)}.$$

Exercise.   Add: $\dfrac{1}{x} + \dfrac{2}{y + 1} - \dfrac{2}{3}$.

Answer: $\dfrac{4x + 3y - 2xy + 3}{3x(y + 1)}$.

The division of the fraction a/b by the fraction c/d can be written in the form of a third fraction:

$$\frac{\dfrac{a}{b}}{\dfrac{c}{d}}.$$

This can be simplified if it is multiplied by a suitably chosen one. The objective is to convert from the *complex* fraction (that is, a fraction whose numerator or denominator contains a fraction) to a *simple* fraction (which does not have a fraction in its numerator or denominator). Clearly, we can cancel the c/d of the denominator if we multiply it by d/c. We must then also multiply the numerator by d/c, so that the net effect is multiplication by one. Thus:

$$\frac{\dfrac{a}{b}}{\dfrac{c}{d}} = \frac{\dfrac{a}{b}\left(\dfrac{d}{c}\right)}{\dfrac{c}{d}\left(\dfrac{d}{c}\right)} = \frac{ad}{bc}.$$

The process often is described as "inverting the denominator and multiplying"; that is, invert c/d to give d/c, then multiply the numerator by d/c. This description is adequate when numerator and denominator are in completely factored form, but multiplication by a suitably chosen one not only is a more fundamental description, but also is somewhat more direct when numerator and denominator are not in factored form. Consider the problem of reducing the following to a simple fraction:

$$\frac{\dfrac{a}{2} + \dfrac{1}{3}}{\dfrac{1}{2} + b}.$$

We observe that the lowest common denominator of the terms in the numerator and denominator is 6, so we multiply the fraction by $6/6$. Thus:

$$\frac{6\left(\dfrac{a}{2} + \dfrac{1}{3}\right)}{6\left(\dfrac{1}{2} + b\right)} = \frac{3a + 2}{3 + 6b}.$$

Exercise. Convert to a simple fraction by multiplying numerator and denominator by 12:

$$\frac{\dfrac{1}{2} + \dfrac{1}{3}}{\dfrac{3}{4} + \dfrac{1}{3}}.$$

Answer: $^{10}/_{13}$.

In the next example the lowest common denominator of all terms in numerator and denominator is $3ab$. Hence, we choose our one to be $3ab/3ab$:

$$\frac{\dfrac{2}{a} + \dfrac{1}{b}}{\dfrac{1}{3} + \dfrac{2}{b}} = \frac{\left(\dfrac{2}{a} + \dfrac{1}{b}\right)(3ab)}{\left(\dfrac{1}{3} + \dfrac{2}{b}\right)(3ab)} = \frac{6b + 3a}{ab + 6a}.$$

A2.18 PROBLEM SET A2–4

Mark (T) for true or (F) for false:

1. ( ) 0/0 equals one.
2. ( ) 0/0 equals zero.
3. ( ) No matter what number a is, $a/0$ is meaningless.
4. ( ) If a is not zero, then $0/a$ equals zero.
5. ( ) The product of any number and zero is zero.
6. ( ) The reciprocal of 4 equals 0.25.
7. ( ) The reciprocal of 3 equals 0.3.

8. ( ) In addition, it is said that a number and its reciprocal cancel.
9. ( ) In division, cancellation is the equivalent of substituting the factor one in place of the product of a number and its reciprocal.
10. ( ) Multiplying a number by its reciprocal gives the same result as dividing the number by itself.
11. ( ) "Inverting and multiplying" is equivalent to multiplying by a reciprocal.

12. What does it mean to say a number and its reciprocal cancel?

Simplify by cancellation where possible:

13. $\dfrac{-3a(-6)}{12c}.$

14. $\dfrac{2a - 3}{3}.$

15. $\dfrac{2a - 3a}{-a}.$

16. $\dfrac{2a + 6}{2}.$

A2.18 PROBLEM SET A2–4 (*continued*)

17. $\dfrac{24acd}{4ad}$.

19. $\dfrac{2xy + 6ax + x}{4xy}$.

18. $\dfrac{x + y}{y}$.

20. $4(a + 2)\left(\dfrac{2x}{a + 2}\right)$.

---

21. State the rule for multiplication of fractions.

Multiply, leaving no grouping symbols in the answer:

22. $\dfrac{ab}{2}\left(\dfrac{3}{4}\right)$.

26. $(2)\left(-\dfrac{1}{3}\right)\left(\dfrac{1}{a + b}\right)$.

23. $\dfrac{a + b}{3}\left(\dfrac{2}{5}\right)$.

27. $3(a + 2)\left(\dfrac{1}{3} + \dfrac{2b}{a + 2}\right)$.

24. $\dfrac{-2}{3}\left(\dfrac{9a}{8}\right)$.

28. $6ab\left(\dfrac{2}{3b} - \dfrac{1}{a}\right)$.

25. $(-2)\left(\dfrac{a}{3}\right)\left(\dfrac{b + 2}{-7}\right)$.

Express with a single minus sign:

29. $\dfrac{-b(c - d)}{-2}$.

32. $-\dfrac{-2 + (b - c) - a}{2x(a + b)}$.

30. $-\dfrac{b - 2}{-3 - a}$.

33. $-\dfrac{x + y}{x - y}$.

31. $\dfrac{-2 + (b - c)}{-2a}$.

Reduce to one simple fraction:

34. $\dfrac{2}{3} - \dfrac{1}{2} + \dfrac{1}{6}$.

39. $\dfrac{x}{a - 2} + \dfrac{1}{b} - 2$.

35. $\dfrac{a}{2} - \dfrac{3}{5}$.

40. $\dfrac{x}{2a} - b + \dfrac{3}{a}$.

36. $\dfrac{3}{2a} - \dfrac{1}{6} + \dfrac{2}{5b}$.

41. $3x - \dfrac{1}{2} + \dfrac{2}{12ab}$.

37. $\dfrac{2}{5} - \dfrac{2(a - 10)}{5a} + \dfrac{1}{6}$.

42. $\dfrac{2a}{3(b - 1)} - \dfrac{a - 1}{4} + \dfrac{1}{6}$.

38. $3\frac{1}{2} - 2\frac{1}{3}$.

43. $\dfrac{7}{2(x + 3)} - 3 + \dfrac{5}{4(x + 3)}$.

---

44. Multiply $2\frac{1}{3}$ by $3\frac{1}{4}$, stating the product as a simple fraction.

45. Divide $1\frac{1}{8}$ by $7\frac{1}{3}$, stating the quotient as a simple fraction.

A2.18 PROBLEM SET A2–4 (*concluded*)

Reduce the following complex fractions to simple fractions by multiplying by a suitably chosen one:

46. $\dfrac{\dfrac{1}{2} + \dfrac{1}{3} - \dfrac{1}{4}}{\dfrac{2}{3} - \dfrac{1}{6}}.$

49. $\dfrac{\dfrac{2a}{3b} - \dfrac{1}{c} + 2}{\dfrac{1}{6} - \dfrac{2}{bc}}.$

47. $\dfrac{\dfrac{6}{a} + 2}{-\dfrac{3}{b} + \dfrac{5}{a}}.$

50. $\dfrac{\dfrac{a}{2} + \dfrac{b}{3} - \dfrac{c}{6}}{b - \dfrac{a}{4}}.$

48. $\dfrac{\dfrac{ab}{2} - \dfrac{b-3}{c}}{\dfrac{b}{3} - 1}.$

A2.19 EXPONENTS

The product $(a)(a)(a)(a)(a)$ is denoted by writing a with a superscript of 5; thus, a^5. It is called the fifth power of a. The number a is the *base*, and 5 is the *exponent* of the power. More generally, if n is a positive integer, a^n is read as "a to the nth" and means the term that has a as a factor n times. By convention, we interpret absence of an exponent to mean the exponent is one. We have

$$(a)(a) = a^2$$
$$(a)(a)(a) = a^3$$
$$a = a^1.$$

It is clear that

$$(a^2)(a^3) = (a)(a)[(a)(a)(a)] = a^5.$$

We see that

$$(a^2)(a^3) = a^{2+3} = a^5$$

and it follows that if two powers have the same base, their product is found by writing the common base with the sum of the exponents as its power. For example,

$$x^5(x)x^2 = x^{5+1+2} = x^8$$
$$3a^2(2a^3) = 6a^5$$
$$3^2(3) = 3^3 = 27$$
$$(-2)^3(-2) = (-2)^4 = 16$$
$$(-3)(-3)^2 = (-3)^3 = -27.$$

Exercise. Write $2x^2(3x^5)$ with a single exponent. Answer: $6x^7$.

Turning to division, we have, for example:

$$\frac{a^5}{a^2} = \frac{(a)(a)(a)(a)(a)}{(a)(a)} = (a)(a)(a) = a^3$$

by cancellation. Alternatively, the final exponent, 3, could have been obtained by the subtraction, $5 - 2$, that is, the numerator exponent minus the denominator exponent. In general, if two powers have the same base, their quotient is the common base with an exponent found by the subtraction procedure just mentioned. As examples,

$$\frac{a^4}{a^2} = a^{4-2} = a^2$$

$$\frac{a^2b^3}{ab} = ab^2$$

$$\frac{(a + b)^3}{a + b} = (a + b)^2$$

$$\frac{5^{12}}{5^{10}} = 5^2 = 25$$

$$\frac{3^4(2a^6)}{3a^4} = 54a^2$$

$$\frac{(-2)^5}{(-2)^2} = (-2)^3 = -8$$

$$\frac{(-3)^4(2x^5)}{-3x^2} = (-3)^3(2x^3) = -54x^3.$$

Exercise. Write $(5x^5)/3x^2$ with a single exponent. Answer: $5x^3/3$.

A2.20 ZERO EXPONENT

Following the procedure of the last discussion, we see that for any number a, not zero:

$$\frac{a}{a} = a^{1-1} = a^0.$$

Inasmuch as the beginning expression, a/a, equals one, we conclude that any nonzero number to the zero power equals one. Thus:

$$1^0 = 1, \qquad (ab^3c^2)^0 = 1, \qquad (14.6)^0 = 1, \qquad (-x)^0 = 1.$$

Exercise.   Evaluate $3^0 + (x + 2y)^0$.   Answer: 2

A2.21 NEGATIVE EXPONENTS

When exponents are subtracted, the difference may be negative. For example,

$$\frac{2^3}{2^6} = 2^{3-6} = 2^{-3}.$$

Alternatively, we may evaluate the expression as:

$$\frac{2^3}{2^6} = \frac{(2)(2)(2)}{(2)(2)(2)(2)(2)(2)} = \frac{1}{(2)(2)(2)} = \frac{1}{2^3}.$$

We see that

$$2^{-3} = \frac{1}{2^3}.$$

The general definition applying to a negative exponent is

$$a^{-n} = \frac{1}{a^n}.$$

As illustrations of the definition, we see that

$$2^{-1} = \frac{1}{2^1} = \frac{1}{2}$$

$$3^{-2} = \frac{1}{3^2} = \frac{1}{9}$$

$$ax^{-2} = \frac{a}{1}\left(\frac{1}{x^2}\right) = \frac{a}{x^2}$$

$$\left(\frac{2}{3}\right)^{-1} = \frac{1}{\left(\frac{2}{3}\right)} = \frac{1}{\frac{2}{3}} = 1\left(\frac{3}{2}\right) = \frac{3}{2}$$

$$\left(\frac{1}{3}\right)^{-2} = \frac{1}{\left(\frac{1}{3}\right)^2} = \frac{1}{\frac{1}{9}} = 1\left(\frac{9}{1}\right) = 9.$$

Exercise.   Evaluate $(\tfrac{1}{2})^{-2} + 5(2^{-3})$.   Answer: 37/8.

The following examples are self-explanatory and show how in some expressions we may avoid negative exponents by choice of procedure.

$$\frac{x^3}{x^5} = \frac{1}{x^{5-3}} = \frac{1}{x^2}$$

$$\frac{2x}{x^7} = \frac{2x^1}{x^7} = \frac{2}{x^{7-1}} = \frac{2}{x^6}$$

$$\frac{a^2b^3}{a^4b} = \frac{b^{3-1}}{a^{4-2}} = \frac{b^2}{a^2}.$$

Exercise. Apply the laws of exponents to simplify the following expression and write the result with positive exponents.

$$\frac{3x(x^{-2})y^5}{4x^4y^2}.$$

Answer: $\dfrac{3y^3}{4x^5}.$

Finally, we note that the expression

$$\frac{1 + x^{-n}}{2 + a}$$

is, in effect, a complex fraction because of the fractional nature of x^{-n}. Remembering that

$$x^{-n}(x^n) = x^0 = 1,$$

we may obtain a simple fraction by multiplying by x^n/x^n, as follows:

$$\frac{1 + x^{-n}}{2 + a} = \frac{(1 + x^{-n})x^n}{(2 + a)x^n} = \frac{x^n + 1}{(2 + a)x^n}.$$

As another example of the same procedure:

$$\frac{2 + 3^{-2}}{1 + 3^{-1}} = \left(\frac{2 + 3^{-2}}{1 + 3^{-1}}\right)\left(\frac{3^2}{3^2}\right) = \frac{18 + 1}{9 + 3} = \frac{19}{12}.$$

Exercise. Remove negative exponents by multiplying numerator and denominator by x^n: $\dfrac{1 + x^{-n}}{x^{-n} + 2}.$ Answer: $\dfrac{x^n + 1}{1 + 2x^n}.$

A2.22 POWER TO A POWER

The expression $(a^2)^3$ is an example of a power raised to a power; that is, the second power of a is indicated as being raised to the third power. According to definition:

$$(a^2)^3 = (a^2)(a^2)(a^2)$$

which is a^6 or $a^{(2)(3)}$. The procedure is generalized by stating that in raising a power to a power, exponents are multiplied. As other examples,

$$(2^2)^4 = 2^{(2)(4)} = 2^8 = 256$$
$$(x^3)^2 = x^{(3)(2)} = x^6$$
$$(x^{-1})^4 = x^{(-1)(4)} = x^{-4} = \frac{1}{x^4}$$
$$(5^{-2})^{-1} = 5^{(-2)(-1)} = 5^2 = 25.$$

Exercise.   Evaluate $(2^{-2})^{-3}$.   Answer: 64.

A2.23 FRACTIONAL EXPONENTS

The number

$$8^{1/3}$$

may be read as *eight to the one-third power*. If we apply the rules discussed earlier for integral exponents to this rational fractional exponent, it follows that

$$(8^{1/3})(8^{1/3})(8^{1/3}) = 8^1 = 8,$$

so that the number symbolized as $(8^{1/3})$ must be 2. That is,

$$8^{1/3} = 2.$$

Moreover,

$$8^{2/3} = (8^{1/3})(8^{1/3}) = (2)(2) = 4.$$

Exercise.   Express $8^{4/3}$ as an integer.   Answer: 16.

The number $8^{1/3}$ is also called the *cube root* of 8 and expressed by the *radical* symbol,

$$\sqrt[3]{8}.$$

The number appearing in the opening of the radical symbol is called the *index* of the root, and the number under the symbol, here 8, is called the *radicand*. We note that the index of the root is the denominator of the fractional exponent. In similar fashion,

$$16^{1/2} = \sqrt[2]{16} = \sqrt{16}$$

is called the square root of 16 and, conventionally, the index 2 is not written. That is, if no index number appears on the radical, the index is assumed to be 2.

Both 4 and -4 are square roots of 16 because

$$(4)(4) = (-4)(-4) = 16.$$

Thus,

$$16^{1/2} = \pm 4.$$

Exercise. What are the fourth roots of 16?   Answer: ± 2.

We point out in passing that if we write

$$y(x) = x^{1/2}$$

as a function, then (see Appendix A1) we restrict the square root to its *nonnegative* value because if y is a function of x, there must be one and only one value of y for each value of x.

Even roots of positive numbers have both a positive and a negative value. However, *we shall generally follow the practice of indicating only the positive value for even roots of positive numbers, and using the radical symbol to indicate the principal or positive root.* Even roots of negative numbers are not real numbers. For example, in

$$(-4)^{1/2}(-4)^{1/2} = (-4)^1 = -4,$$

there is no real number for $(-4)^{1/2}$ that will make the statement true. Clearly, $(0)(0) \neq -4$ and, moreover, the product of numbers of like sign cannot be negative, which would be required if $(-4)^{1/2}$ was a real number as required by the statement.

On the other hand, odd roots of negative numbers can be found, as in

$$(-8)^{1/3} = -2.$$

In general, however, if we use a fractional power of a number, x, it will be assumed that x is not negative.

If we write radical expressions at random, the desired root often is irrational and must be approximated. For example,

$$\sqrt{2} = 2^{1/2} = 1.4142$$

to four decimal places. In this appendix, we consider only examples where roots are rational and can be determined by inspection. For example, inspecting

$$4^{3/2}$$

we first write the equivalent numbers

$$4^{3/2} = 4^{(1/2)(3)} = (4^{1/2})^3 = 2^3 = 8.$$

When expressions with fractional exponents are to be evaluated, we strongly urge that the fraction be written first. Thus, in evaluating

$$64^{2/3}$$

we write

$$(64)^{2/3} = (64^{1/3})^2 = 4^2 = 16$$

rather than

$$64^{2/3} = (64^2)^{1/3} = (4096)^{1/3} = 16.$$

The point is simply that the latter procedure, although correct, leads to $(4096)^{1/3}$ and it is not easy to tell at a glance what this cube root is.

Exercise. Evaluate $(27)^{2/3}$. Answer: 9.

Previous rules apply when exponents are fractional or negative, as shown by the following examples:

$$(3^{-2})(3^{-3}) = 3^{-2+(-3)} = 3^{-5} = \frac{1}{3^5} = \frac{1}{243}$$

$$\frac{5^{-6}}{5^{-8}} = 5^{-6-(-8)} = 5^{-6+8} = 5^2 = 25$$

$$(2^{1/3})(2^{1/2}) = 2^{1/3+1/2} = 2^{2/6+3/6} = 2^{5/6}$$

$$\frac{a^{2/3}b^2}{ab} = \frac{a^{2/3}b^2}{a^1 b^1} = \frac{b^{2-1}}{a^{1-2/3}} = \frac{b}{a^{1/3}}$$

$$(a^{1/3})^2 = a^{(1/3)(2)} = a^{2/3}.$$

Fractional powers can be written with radical signs. Thus,

$$16^{3/4} = \left(\sqrt[4]{16}\right)^3 = 2^3 = 8.$$

In general, it is preferable to use fractional exponents rather than radical signs.

A2.24 SUMMARY OF EXPONENT RULES

All the rules for exponents may now be stated in brief form:

If $a \neq 0$, then

$$a^m a^n = a^{m+n}$$

$$\frac{a^m}{a^n} = a^{m-n} = \frac{1}{a^{n-m}}$$

$$(a^m)^n = a^{mn}$$

$$a^0 = 1.$$

The rules of exponents are not restricted to terms having a single factor. We may raise a term to a power by raising each factor of the term to the power. Thus,

$$(2a)^3 = 8a^3$$

$$\left(\frac{a}{2}\right)^2 = \frac{a^2}{4}$$

$$(3x^2y^{1/2})^3 = 27x^6y^{3/2}.$$

Exercise. Express $(4y^4x^3)^{1/2}$ without parentheses. Answer: $2y^2x^{3/2}$.

Observe, however, that in $3a^2$ the absence of parentheses means the exponent applies only to a, not to 3. Again,

$$3(2a^2)^3 = 3(8a^6) = 24a^6.$$

Exponents cannot be applied separately to terms of an expression. In the case of, say, $(a - b)^2$, we cannot simply raise each term to the second power. By definition:

$$(a - b)^2 = (a - b)(a - b).$$

According to the distributive property,

$$(a - b)(a - b) = a^2 - ab - ba + b^2 = a^2 - 2ab + b^2.$$

By way of numerical illustration,

$$(1 - 0.2)^2 = (0.8)^2 = 0.64$$

could be evaluated as

$$(1 - 0.2)(1 - 0.2) = 1^2 - 1(0.2) - 0.2(1) + 0.2^2 = 0.64.$$

This type of exercise is referred to as squaring a binomial, that is, raising the sum of two terms to the second power. We see in general that

$$(a + b)^2 = a^2 + 2ab + b^2$$

and describe the outcome as the "square of the first, plus twice the product of the two, plus the square of the second." Verify that the cube of a binomial is given by

$$(a + b)^3 = a^3 + 3a^2b + 3ab^2 + b^3.$$

Before working the problem set, it will be helpful to practice by verifying the answer stated in each part of the following practice problem set.

A2.25 PRACTICE PROBLEM SET

Look at the following and justify each step by reference to the appropriate rule.

1. $a^{-3}a^5 = a^{-3+5} = a^2$.

2. $(4^{-1})(4^3) = 4^{-1+3} = 4^2 = 16$.

3. $(2^{-3})(2^{-2}) = 2^{-3+(-2)} = 2^{-5} = \dfrac{1}{2^5} = \dfrac{1}{32}$.

4. $\dfrac{5^2}{5^{-3}} = 5^{2-(-3)} = 5^{2+3} = 5^5 = 3125$.

5. $125^{4/3} = (125^{1/3})^4 = 5^4 = 625$.

6. $16^{7/4} = (16^{1/4})^7 = 2^7 = 128$.

7. $27^{-1/3} = \dfrac{1}{27^{1/3}} = \dfrac{1}{3}$.

8. $125^{-2/3} = \dfrac{1}{125^{2/3}} = \dfrac{1}{(125^{1/3})^2} = \dfrac{1}{5^2} = \dfrac{1}{25}$
$= 0.04$.

9. $27^{2/3} = (27^{1/3})^2 = 3^2 = 9$.

10. $9^{-3/2} = \dfrac{1}{9^{3/2}} = \dfrac{1}{3^3} = \dfrac{1}{27}$.

11. $8^{4/3} = 16$.

12. $\sqrt{-4}$ is not a real number.

13. $(2^{-2})(3^{-2}) = \dfrac{1}{4}\left(\dfrac{1}{9}\right) = \dfrac{1}{36}$.

14. $(2^{1/3})(2^{1/2})(2^{1/6}) = 2^{1/3 + 1/2 + 1/6} = 2$.

15. $(1 + 0.01)^2 = (1.01)^2 = 1.0201$.

16. $2^{-2} + 3^{-1} = \dfrac{1}{4} + \dfrac{1}{3} = \dfrac{7}{12}$.

17. $2^3(1 + 2^{-3}) = 2^3 + 2^0 = 8 + 1 = 9$.

18. $(15)^{12}(15)^{-10} = 15^2 = 225$.

19. $\dfrac{10^{-4}}{10^{-2}} = \dfrac{1}{10^{-2+4}} = \dfrac{1}{100}$.

20. $\dfrac{1}{3}(4^{-3/2}) = \dfrac{1}{3}\left(\dfrac{1}{4^{3/2}}\right) = \left(\dfrac{1}{3}\right)\left(\dfrac{1}{8}\right) = \dfrac{1}{24}$.

21. $\dfrac{5 + 2^{-2}}{3} = \dfrac{(5 + 2^{-2})2^2}{(3)(2^2)} = \dfrac{(5)2^2 + 2^0}{3(2^2)} =$
$\dfrac{21}{12} = \dfrac{7}{4}$.

Combine exponents where possible, and simplify. If possible, do not leave grouping symbols, radical signs, or negative exponents in the result:

22. $a^2xa^3x^2 = a^5x^3$.

23. $2x^0 + (2x)^0 = 2 + 1 = 3$.

24. $(a^2b)(a^{-1})b^3(ab)^{-1} = a^{2-1-1}b^{1+3-1} = b^3$.

25. $\dfrac{4x^2b}{(2b)^2} = \dfrac{4x^2b}{4b^2} = \dfrac{x^2}{b}$.

26. $\dfrac{a^3}{(a^x)^2} = \dfrac{a^3}{a^{2x}} = a^{3-2x}$ or $\dfrac{1}{a^{2x-3}}$.

27. $\dfrac{(2^3)(2^x)}{2^{1+x}} = 2^{3+x-(1+x)} = 2^2 = 4$.

28. $\dfrac{(x^{1/3})(y^{2/3})^2}{2(xy)^{1/2}} = \dfrac{x^{1/3}\,y^{4/3}}{2x^{1/2}\,y^{1/2}} = \dfrac{y^{5/6}}{2x^{1/6}}$.

29. $\dfrac{x^{1/3}\sqrt{b}}{b\sqrt{x}} = \dfrac{x^{1/3}b^{1/2}}{bx^{1/2}} = \dfrac{1}{b^{1/2}x^{1/6}}$.

30. $(a - 2b)^2 = a^2 - 4ab + 4b^2$.

31. $\dfrac{1}{3}(3x)^{-2/3} = \dfrac{1}{3(3)^{2/3}(x)^{2/3}} = \dfrac{1}{3^{5/3}x^{2/3}}$.

32. $\dfrac{1 + (1 + x)^{-n}}{x} = \dfrac{[1 + (1 + x)^{-n}](1 + x)^n}{x(1 + x)^n}$
$= \dfrac{(1 + x)^n + 1}{x(1 + x)^n}$.

A2.26 PROBLEM SET A2–5
Evaluate:

1. 2^4.

2. $7(2)^0$.

3. $(1 - 0.02)^{-2}$ to three decimal places.

4. $\left(\dfrac{3}{4}\right)^{-1}$.

5. $(-3)^{-2}(2)^{-3}$.

6. $\dfrac{(10^{-3})(10^5)}{(10^3)(10^{-4})}$.

7. $\sqrt{-16}$.

8. $3^{-1} + \left(\dfrac{2}{3}\right)^{-2}$.

9. 3^{-2}.

10. $(x - 3)^0$.

11. $16^{3/4}$.

12. $\left(\dfrac{1}{8}\right)^{1/3}$.

13. $\dfrac{10^{-4}}{10^{-5}}$.

14. $\dfrac{2}{3}(16)^{-3/4}$.

15. $\sqrt{\dfrac{25}{16}}$.

16. $5x^0 + (ax)^0$.

17. $(25)^4(25)^{-3}$.

18. $(1 + 0.05)^2$.

19. $(32)^{-3/5}$.

20. $\left(\dfrac{2}{3}\right)^{-1} + 2^{-3}$.

21. $\sqrt[3]{125}$.

22. $\left(\dfrac{8}{27}\right)^{-2/3}$.

23. $\dfrac{1 + 3^{-2}}{5}$.

24. $\dfrac{2^{-3} + 2^{-1}}{2^{-1}}$.

25. $3^{-2}(1 + 3^{-1})$.

Combine exponents where possible, and simplify. If possible, do not leave grouping symbols, radical signs, or negative exponents in the result:

26. a^2a.

27. $(ab)(ac)(bc)$.

28. $a^2b^3(ab^4)$.

29. $(abc^2)(a^2cb)$.

30. $(x^2a)(x^2b)$.

31. $\dfrac{a^2b^3}{ab}$.

32. $\dfrac{a^4b^2c}{a^2b^3c^2}$.

33. $\dfrac{xy^3b^3}{x^3yb}$.

34. $\dfrac{a^3(bxy)}{abx^2y}$.

35. $\dfrac{x^3y^2}{x^2y^3}$.

36. $\dfrac{a(bc)^3}{ab^2}$.

37. $\dfrac{(ab)^2(ab)}{a}$.

38. $\dfrac{a(bc)^3}{b(ac)^4}$.

39. $\dfrac{(-3b)^3(2c)^2}{12b^2c}$.

40. $\dfrac{-2b^2(-3c)^2}{-(-bc)^3}$.

41. $(xy^2)(ay^{-2})$.

A2.26 PROBLEM SET A2–5 (*concluded*)

42. $(ab^2c^{-1})(a^2b^{-1}c^2)$.

43. $a(ax)^{-2}$.

44. $\dfrac{2x^{-1}a^3}{(-ax)^2}$.

45. $\dfrac{x^{-2}}{ax}$.

46. $3a^{1/3}b^{1/2}a^2b$.

47. $\dfrac{\sqrt{x}\sqrt[3]{y}}{x^{-1}y^{1/2}}$.

48. $\dfrac{a^{2/3}(b^3)^{1/2}}{\sqrt{a}\sqrt[3]{b}}$.

49. $\dfrac{2}{3}(3x)^{-1/2}$.

50. $\dfrac{2x^{-1/2}\sqrt{y^3}}{3y^{-1/3}\sqrt{x^3}}$.

51. $\dfrac{2 + x^{-2}}{x + 3}$.

52. $\dfrac{(1 - x)^{-1} + 1}{x}$.

53. $\dfrac{x^{-1} + x^{-2}}{3}$.

54. $\dfrac{(ax)^2}{(a^x)^2}$.

55. $\dfrac{x^5 + 4}{x^2 + 2}$.

56. $a(a + b)$.

57. $(a - 3b)^2$.

58. $a(a - b)^2$.

59. $(x - y)(x + y)$.

60. $a(a^{-1} + 1)$.

61. $(a^{1/2} - 1)^2$.

62. $\dfrac{a^{-1} + 2}{a}$.

63. $\dfrac{(3^2)(3^a)}{3^{a-1}}$.

Mark (T) for true or (F) for false:

64. ( ) $(2^3)(3^2) = 6^5$.

65. ( ) $ab^2 = a^2b^2$.

66. ( ) $(2ab)^2 = 4a^2 b^2$.

67. ( ) $\dfrac{a^2}{b^2} = \left(\dfrac{a}{b}\right)^2$.

68. ( ) $(a - b)^2 = a^2 - b^2$.

69. ( ) $(a + 1)^{1/2} = \sqrt{a} + 1$.

70. ( ) $\dfrac{\sqrt[3]{a}}{\sqrt[3]{b}} = \sqrt[3]{\dfrac{a}{b}}$.

71. ( ) $(1 + 0.1)^{-2} = \dfrac{1}{1.21}$.

72. ( ) An expression is raised to a power by raising each of its terms to the power.

73. ( ) The sum of the squares of two numbers is the same as the square of the sum of the two numbers.

74. ( ) $a^{-1} + b^{-1}$ is equivalent to the sum of the reciprocals of a and b.

75. ( ) $0^0 = 1$.

76. ( ) $5x^0 = 1$.

77. ( ) $(1 - 0.02)^{-5} = \dfrac{1}{(0.98)^5}$.

78. ( ) $2x^{-1/2} = \dfrac{2}{x^2}$.

79. ( ) $a^{2/3}$ is the cube root of a^2.

80. ( ) $\sqrt{x^2 + y^2 + z^2} = x + y + z$.

81. ( ) $\sqrt{2x} = 2^{1/2}x^{1/2}$.

82. ( ) $\sqrt{-12}$ is not a real number.

83. ( ) $\dfrac{2a^{1/6}}{b^{1/6}} = 2\left(\dfrac{a}{b}\right)^{1/6}$.

84. ( ) $a^{1/2}$ is called the square of a.

85. ( ) $(a - 2b)^2 = a^2 - 4ab + 4b^2$.

A2.27 REVIEW PROBLEMS
Reduce to a single signed number, or zero:

1. $-4 + (-2) - [+(-3)]$.
2. $-(-8) + (-4) - (+4) + 2$.
3. $-2(3) + (-3)(-4) - (1)(-5)$.
4. $-(-3) + 2\{-[-3(2)]\} - (+10)$.
5. $-5(-2)(-3) + (3)(-2)(-5)$.
6. $\dfrac{-3(-2)(-4)}{8(-5)}$.

7. $\dfrac{-(5)(3)(-4)}{2(-6)}$.
8. $\dfrac{-(-5)(20)}{-\{-[-4]\}}$.
9. $\dfrac{3(2)(5)(-6)}{(-10)(-18)}$.
10. $\dfrac{(-1)(-2)(-3)(-4)}{(-5)(6)}$.

---

11. Rewrite as the sum of signed numbers:
    a) $3 - 4$.
    b) $-1 + 2 - 3$.
    c) $-1 - 2 - 4 + 5$.
    d) $2 + 3$.

12. Reduce to a single signed number:
    a) $-(2 - 5) + 3(-4) - (2 + 1)$.
    b) $-[-2 - (+3)] + (-1)(1 - 3)$.
    c) $-[-(a - b) + (-b + a)]$.

13. What fundamental property or convention justifies each of the following?
    a) $x2y = 2xy$.
    b) $4(3z) = 12z$.
    c) $+2 + (-a) = 2 - a$.
    d) $3x + 6y = 3(x + 2y)$.
    e) $3a + 2 + y = 3a + y + 2$.
    f) $(a + 2) + b = a + (2 + b)$.
    g) $1 + 2 + x = 3 + x$.
    h) $x2 + y3 = 2x + 3y$.
    i) $3 + (-x) = 3 - x$.
    j) $1a = a$.
    k) $2(a + b) = 2a + 2b$.
    l) $5 - xy = -xy + 5$.
    m) $3(x + y) = 3x + 3y$.
    n) $5a + 5b = 5(a + b)$.

14. Combine like terms:
    a) $2 + 5x - 4b + 7 - (-3b)$.
    b) $ab - a(2 - b) + 3a + 5$.
    c) $x(ay - 3) + 2x + 4axy - 7$.
    d) $xy - 2(2 - xy) + 5xy$.

15. Starting with $3x(2y) + 3 + x + 3x$, name the fundamental property that justifies each step:
    a) $3x(2y) + 3 + x + 3x = 3x(2y) + 3 + 4x$.
    b) $\qquad\qquad = 3(2)xy + 3 + 4x$.
    c) $\qquad\qquad = 6xy + 3 + 4x$.
    d) $\qquad\qquad = 6xy + 4x + 3$.
    e) $\qquad\qquad = (6xy + 4x) + 3$.
    f) $\qquad\qquad = 2x(3y + 2) + 3$.

16. Starting with $zy + 5 + 2(3 + 4y)$, name the fundamental property that justifies each step:
    a) $zy + 5 + 2(3 + 4y) = zy + 5 + 2(3) + 2(4y)$.
    b) $\qquad\qquad = zy + 5 + 6 + 2(4y)$.
    c) $\qquad\qquad = zy + 5 + 6 + 8y$.
    d) $\qquad\qquad = zy + 11 + 8y$.
    e) $\qquad\qquad = zy + 8y + 11$.
    f) $\qquad\qquad = yz + y8 + 11$.
    g) $\qquad\qquad = (yz + y8) + 11$.
    h) $\qquad\qquad = y(z + 8) + 11$.

17. Remove grouping symbols and combine like terms:
    a) $x - a\{3 - 2(1 - x)\}$.
    b) $5 - 3[2 - 4(-3 + z)]$.
    c) $3 - 2[a - x + 3(2x - a)]$.
    d) $(3 - a)(x - b + 2)$.
    e) $ax - a\{-2x + 3(2x - 1)\}$.

18. Reduce to a single signed number:

$$-\frac{-3 + 2[-5 - (2 - 7)]}{5 + [2 - 3(2 - 3)]}$$

A2.27 REVIEW PROBLEMS (*concluded*)

19. Factor the following:
   a) $2x + ax$.   g) $a + b + ax + bx$.
   b) $xy + 3xy + axy$.   h) $x^2 + x - 2$.
   c) $2 + 4a + 6b$.   i) $10x^2 + 3x - 1$.
   d) $5xy + 4x$.   j) $6x^2 + 7x - 20$.
   e) $3ax + 6ay + 9a$.   k) $8x^2 + 16x + 6$.
   f) $2(x - 1) + a(x - 1)$.

20. Simplify by cancellation where possible:
   a) $\dfrac{3(3 - a) + x}{2x}$.   c) $\dfrac{x - 2xy}{3x}$.

   b) $\dfrac{3xy}{2x}$.   d) $\dfrac{3}{x - y}[2(x + y)]$.

21. Multiply, leaving no grouping symbols in the answer:
   a) $\left(\dfrac{2x}{3}\right)\left(\dfrac{6a}{b}\right)$.   c) $2(x - y)\left(\dfrac{3a}{x - y} - \dfrac{1}{2}\right)$.

   b) $-2\left(\dfrac{x - 3}{a}\right)$.   d) $10xy\left(\dfrac{1}{5y} - \dfrac{a}{2xy}\right)$.

22. Express with a single minus sign:
   a) $\dfrac{-3x - 2y}{5 - a}$.   c) $-\dfrac{a - b}{-5 - x}$.

   b) $-\dfrac{2a - b}{x + b}$.   d) $\dfrac{a + b}{-5 - x}$.

23. Reduce to one simple fraction:
   a) $\dfrac{1}{3} - \dfrac{1}{6} + \dfrac{3}{4}$.   f) $\dfrac{1}{2x - 3} + \dfrac{b}{3}$.

   b) $\dfrac{a}{b} + 1$.   g) $\dfrac{a}{x + y} - \dfrac{b}{z} + 5$.

   c) $\dfrac{3}{2x} - \dfrac{2}{x} + \dfrac{5}{4x}$.   h) $\dfrac{3}{a} - \dfrac{b}{2} + \dfrac{c}{x + y} - d$.

   d) $\dfrac{y}{x} - 1 + \dfrac{y}{2a}$.   i) Three fourths of $2\frac{1}{2}$.
                      j) $5\frac{1}{4} - 2\frac{1}{3}$.
   e) $\dfrac{1}{12xy} + \dfrac{2}{3} - \dfrac{5}{x}$.   k) $1\frac{7}{8}$ divided by $2\frac{1}{2}$.

24. Reduce the following complex fractions to simple fractions by multiplication by a suitably chosen 1:
   a) $\dfrac{\frac{2}{3} - \frac{1}{4}}{\frac{1}{6} + 1}$.   c) $\dfrac{x - \frac{y - 4}{a}}{\frac{b}{2} + \frac{3}{a}}$.

   b) $\dfrac{\frac{x}{y} - 1}{\frac{2}{3} + \frac{3}{y}}$.   d) $\dfrac{\frac{x}{x + y} - 1}{\frac{2}{x + y}}$.

25. Evaluate:
   a) 3^3.
   b) $2x^0$.
   c) $(2x)^0$.
   d) $(1 - 0.1)^{-2}$ to three decimals.
   e) $\left(\dfrac{2}{3}\right)^{-2}$.
   f) $(2)^{-2}(-2)^2$.
   g) $(75)^{100}(75)^{-98}$.
   h) $3^0 - (2x + 1)^0$.
   i) $\left(\dfrac{1}{16}\right)^{1/4}$.
   j) $\left(\dfrac{1}{16}\right)^{-1/4}$.
   k) $\dfrac{2}{5}(32)^{1/5}$.
   l) $(27)^{2/3}$.
   m) $(125)^{4/3}$.
   n) $(8)^{-2/3}$.

   o) $\left(\dfrac{2}{3}\right)^{-1}$.
   p) $\dfrac{(10)^{-5}(10)^2}{(10)^3(10)^{-8}}$.
   q) $2^{-3}(2^2 + 2^{-1})$.
   r) $\dfrac{3^{-1} - 3^{-2}}{3^{-3}}$.
   s) $\sqrt[3]{64}$.
   t) $(1 + 0.03)^3$.
   u) $\sqrt{-1}$.
   v) $\left(\dfrac{2}{3}\right)^{-2}\left(\dfrac{3}{2}\right)$.
   w) $\sqrt{\dfrac{4}{25}}$.
   x) $(\sqrt[3]{27})^2$.
   y) $\sqrt{16^3}$.
   z) $\sqrt{9^{-3}}$.

26. Combine exponents, where possible, and simplify. If possible, do not leave grouping symbols, radical signs, or negative exponents in the final result:
   a) $a(a^2)(a^3)$.
   b) $xyz(x^2y)$.
   c) $xz(3xy)(2xz)$.
   d) $(abc)^2(ab)$.
   e) $\dfrac{a^2b^3}{abc}$.
   f) $\dfrac{a^2yz^3}{ayz^2}$.
   g) $\dfrac{(3ab)^2(2c)^3}{12ac^2}$.
   h) $\dfrac{(-2x)^3y^2}{4xy}$.
   i) $\dfrac{(ab^{-1}c^2)^3}{2b^2c^2}$.
   j) $\dfrac{(3x^{-2}y)^2}{2x^3y^{-3}}$.
   k) $\dfrac{(-xy^2)^{-3}(2z^2)}{(-2yz)^4}$.
   l) $[(x\sqrt{y})^{3/2}]^2$.
   m) $\dfrac{ax^{1/3}y^{-1/2}}{bx^{1/2}y^{5/3}}$.

   n) $(y^{1/2})^{-3/2}$.
   o) $\dfrac{3}{4}(4y)^{-3/2}$.
   p) $\dfrac{\sqrt[3]{ab}\sqrt{xy}}{9(ab)^{-1}(xy)^{3/2}}$.
   q) $\dfrac{(2a^{1/2}b^{1/3}c)^3}{4abc}$.
   r) $\dfrac{1 + a^{-1}}{1 - a^{-1}}$.
   s) $\dfrac{(a - b)^{-1} - 1}{b^2}$.
   t) $\dfrac{2a^{x-3}a^5}{a^2}$.
   u) $\dfrac{x^{2a}}{x^a}$.
   v) $a^2b^3(ab)^{-5}$.
   w) $x(2 - x)^2$.
   x) $a^2(a^{-2} + a^{-3})$.
   y) $a(a - b)(a + 2b)$.
   z) $(5^{x+1})(5a)^{-3}(5a^3)$.

APPENDIX THREE

Formulas, Equations, Inequalities, and Graphs

A3.1 INTRODUCTION

The distributive property asserts that

$$a(b + c) = ab + ac.$$

Inasmuch as the assertion applies for any numbers, a, b, and c, it is called an identity. On the other hand, the statement

$$x + 5 = 7$$

is true only under the condition that x is 2, and for this reason is called a conditional equality.

A three-lined symbol, $\equiv$, can be used to denote an identity. In this book, however, the two-lined symbol, $=$, is used to denote both identities and conditional equalities because the context makes clear which interpretation of the symbol is relevant. Thus, in Appendix 2 the symbol $=$ means identically equal, whereas in most of the remainder of the book the symbol denotes conditional equality. We shall refer to conditional equalities briefly as equations.

In the equation $x + 5 = 7$, the letter x can be called the unknown, and the value of the unknown that makes the statement true, the number 2, can be called the root of the equation. We may also say that a number that makes the statement of equality true satisfies the equation.

The statement $y = x + 2$ is true for various pairs of values for x and y, and we shall call the letters x and y variables. A particular set of numbers, such as

$$x = -1, \quad y = 1,$$

which satisfy the equation, is a solution of the equation. In this book, we use the *variable, solution* terminology (rather than unknown, root terminology) in the discussion of equations. Thus,

$$y = x + 2$$

will be called an equation in two variables. It has an unlimited number of solutions. The equation

$$x + 5 = 7$$

is an equation in one variable. It has the unique solution $x = 2$.

To solve an equation for a variable means to perform whatever operations are necessary to put the equation in a form in which the stated variable appears by itself (with coefficient one and exponent one) on one side of the equality sign, and the expression on the other side of the equality sign does not contain the stated variable. For example,

$$x - y = 3$$

is not solved for either x or y, but

$$x = y + 3$$

is solved for x, and the equation

$$y = x - 3$$

is solved for y.

Exercise.   Fill in the blanks: The <u>Equation</u> $x + 10 = 4$ has a single <u>Variable</u>, x. The <u>Solution</u> of the <u>Equation</u> is $x = -6$. On the other hand, the <u>Equation</u> $y - x = 7$ has two <u>Variables</u> and has an <u>Unlimited</u> number of solutions: if we write $y - x = 7$ in the alternate form $y = x + 7$, it is said to be <u>Solved</u> for <u>y</u>. Answer: Equation, variable, solution, equation. Equation, variables, unlimited, solved, y.

We now turn to some elementary procedures employed when solving an equation for a variable.

A3.2 SOME AXIOMS

Axioms are statements we assume to be true. For example, we assume that if equals are added to equals, the sums will be equal. Inasmuch as an equation is a statement of equality of the numbers on either side of the equal sign, the axiom says that if we add the same number to both sides of an equation, we shall obtain another equation. For example, if we have the statement

$$x - 3 = 7$$

and we add 3 to each side, we obtain

$$x - 3 + 3 = 7 + 3$$

from which we find $x = 10$, and we have solved the equation for x.

In similar fashion, we assume that if equals are subtracted from equals, the differences are equal; if equals are multiplied by equals, the products are equal; and if equals are divided by equals (division by zero excluded), the quotients are equal. In the context of equations, we say that the solutions of an equation are not altered if the same number is added to both sides, or if the same number is subtracted from both sides, or if both sides are multiplied or divided by the same number.

Examples.

$$x - 2 = 3 \qquad \text{Add 2 to both sides:}$$
$$x - 2 + 2 = 3 + 2$$
$$x = 5.$$

$$x + 2 = 3 \qquad \text{Subtract 2 from both sides:}$$
$$x + 2 - 2 = 3 - 2$$
$$x = 1.$$

$$\frac{x}{3} = 2 \qquad \text{Multiply both sides by 3:}$$
$$3\left(\frac{x}{3}\right) = (3)(2)$$
$$x = 6.$$

$$2x = 7 \qquad \text{Divide both sides by 2:}$$
$$\frac{2x}{2} = \frac{7}{2}$$
$$x = \frac{7}{2}.$$

Exercise. The solution $x = 4$ is obtained by applying which operation to each of the following: $6x = 24$; $x/2 = 2$; $x - 4 = 0$; $x + 2 = 6$? Answer: Divide both sides by 6; multiply both sides by 2; add 4 to both sides; subtract 2 from both sides.

A3.3 SOLUTIONS BY ADDITION AND MULTIPLICATION, WITH INVERSES

The objective in solving an equation for a certain variable is to derive an expression that has that variable alone (coefficient one and exponent one) on one side of the equal sign, and an expression not involving this variable on the other side of the equal sign. Axioms are applied to accomplish this objective. If we are asked to solve

$$ax + b = c$$

for x, we may proceed by subtracting b from both sides to obtain

$$ax = c - b.$$

Next, we divide both sides by a to obtain the desired solution:

$$x = \frac{c - b}{a}.$$

The steps are justified by the axioms. However, it is helpful to understand what steps are required, and this understanding is enhanced if we keep in mind the notion of *inverse* operation. Thus, in solving

$$ax + b = c$$

for x, we wish to remove b from the left side. Inasmuch as b is *added* on the left, we apply the inverse operation and *subtract b* from both sides to obtain

$$ax = c - b.$$

We now observe that x is *multiplied* by a, so we apply the inverse operation and *divide* both sides by a to obtain

$$x = \frac{c - b}{a}.$$

Inverse operations are the tools we need to manipulate equations into desired form.

Be prepared to justify each step taken in the solution of an equation. For brevity, the phrase "both sides of the equation" may be omitted when citing justification for an operation. Thus, for example, "add 3" will be assumed to mean to add 3 to both sides of the equation. For uniformity, it is to be understood that the outcome of each operation performed is shown on the line following the description of the operation. For example,

$$x - 3 = 5 \qquad \text{Add 3:}$$
$$x = 8.$$

Example. Solve for x, citing operations performed:

$$4x - 2 = 2x + 5 \qquad \text{Subtract } 2x:$$
$$2x - 2 = 5 \qquad \text{Add 2:}$$
$$2x = 7 \qquad \text{Divide by 2:}$$
$$x = \frac{7}{2}.$$

Exercise. Solve for x, citing operations performed:
$$3 - 2x = -5x + 7.$$

Answer:

$$3 - 2x = -5x + 7 \qquad \text{Add } 5x\text{:}$$
$$3 + 3x = 7 \qquad \text{Subtract 3:}$$
$$3x = 4 \qquad \text{Divide by 3:}$$
$$x = \frac{4}{3}.$$

Generally, equations containing fractions can be handled most efficiently by finding the lowest common denominator of all the fractions in the equation, and then multiplying both sides by the l.c.d. (lowest common denominator).

Example. Solve for x, citing operations performed:

$$2x - \frac{1}{3} = \frac{x}{2} \qquad \text{Multiply by 6 (the l.c.d.):}$$
$$6(2x) - 6\left(\frac{1}{3}\right) = 6\left(\frac{x}{2}\right) \qquad \text{Carry out multiplications:}$$
$$12x - 2 = 3x \qquad \text{Add 2:}$$
$$12x = 3x + 2 \qquad \text{Subtract } 3x\text{:}$$
$$9x = 2 \qquad \text{Divide by 9:}$$
$$x = \frac{2}{9}.$$

Careful attention should be paid to the fact that each side of an equation is an expression; and to multiply an expression by a number, we must multiply every *term* of the expression by that number.

It is instructive to follow through the tactics of the last example. We observe fractions in the equation, and we know that the denominator of a fraction is canceled (replaced by one, which need not be written) if the fraction is multiplied by a term having the fraction's denominator as a factor. Rather than treat each fraction separately, we make up a term (lowest) that has the denominators of all the fractions as factors. Then, when both sides are multiplied by this term, all denominators are canceled, and we are led to the statement

$$12x - 2 = 3x.$$

We decide to gather terms involving x on the left, other terms on the right. The term -2 is removed from the left by the inverse operation of adding 2. Similarly, the term $+3x$ on the right is removed by the inverse operation of subtracting $3x$ from both sides. We now have $9x = 2$. The 9 must be removed to obtain the desired solution. Inasmuch as 9 is multiplied by x, we apply the inverse operation and divide both sides by 9 to obtain

$$x = \frac{2}{9}.$$

Exercise. Solve for x, citing operations performed:

$$\frac{3x}{4} - 5 = \frac{x}{3}.$$

Answer:

$$\frac{3x}{4} - 5 = \frac{x}{3} \qquad \text{Multiply by 12:}$$
$$9x - 60 = 4x \qquad \text{Subtract } 4x:$$
$$5x - 60 = 0 \qquad \text{Add 60:}$$
$$5x = 60 \qquad \text{Divide by 5:}$$
$$x = 12.$$

If the variable to be solved for is inside a grouping symbol, we remove the grouping symbol, citing the distributive property as justification, and then proceed with the solution. For example,

$$3x - \frac{1}{4} = 2 - \frac{1}{6}[x - (2 - x)] \qquad \text{Multiply by 12:}$$
$$36x - 3 = 24 - 2[x - (2 - x)] \qquad \text{Distributive property:}$$
$$36x - 3 = 24 - 2[x - 2 + x] \qquad \text{Distributive property:}$$
$$36x - 3 = 24 - 2x + 4 - 2x \qquad \text{Add } 4x:$$
$$40x - 3 = 24 + 4 \qquad \text{Add 3:}$$
$$40x = 31 \qquad \text{Divide by 40:}$$
$$x = \frac{31}{40}.$$

In the next example, grouping symbols are introduced to emphasize proper procedure, and then are removed in due course.

$$\frac{2}{3(x - 1)} - \frac{1}{2} = \frac{1}{4} \qquad \text{Multiply by l.c.d. } 3(4)(x - 1):$$

$$3(4)(x - 1)\left[\frac{2}{3(x - 1)}\right] - 3(4)(x - 1)\left(\frac{1}{2}\right) = 3(4)(x - 1)\left(\frac{1}{4}\right).$$

The last equation simplifies to:

$$8 - 6(x - 1) = 3(x - 1) \qquad \text{Distributive property:}$$
$$8 - 6x + 6 = 3x - 3 \qquad \text{Add } 6x; \text{ add 3:}$$
$$17 = 9x \qquad \text{Divide by 9:}$$
$$\frac{17}{9} = x.$$

The same procedures are followed when numbers are in literal form, but the next to the last step often requires factoring. Factoring derives from the distributive property, but we shall follow convention here and cite factoring rather than the distributive property when the need for justification arises.

Example. Solve for x, citing operations performed:

$$\frac{x}{a} - b = 2a(x - b)$$ Multiply by a:

$$x - ab = 2a^2(x - b)$$ Distributive property:

$$x - ab = 2a^2x - 2a^2b$$ Subtract $2a^2x$; add ab:

$$x - 2a^2x = ab - 2a^2b$$ Factor:

$$x(1 - 2a^2) = ab - 2a^2b$$ Divide by $(1 - 2a^2)$:

$$x = \frac{ab - 2a^2b}{1 - 2a^2}.$$

Exercise. Solve for x, citing operations performed:

$$\frac{2x}{a} + \frac{3}{b} = x + 4.$$

Answer:

$$\frac{2x}{a} + \frac{3}{b} = x + 4$$ Multiply by ab:

$$2xb + 3a = abx + 4ab$$ Subtract abx:

$$2xb - abx + 3a = 4ab$$ Subtract $3a$:

$$2xb - abx = 4ab - 3a$$ Factor:

$$x(2b - ab) = 4ab - 3a$$ Divide by $(2b - ab)$:

$$x = \frac{4ab - 3a}{2b - ab}.$$

Example. Solve for x, citing operations performed:

$$a = \frac{x}{1 - nx}$$ Multiply by $(1 - nx)$:

$$a(1 - nx) = x$$ Distributive property:

$$a - anx = x$$ Add anx:

$$a = x + anx$$ Factor:

$$a = x(1 + an)$$ Divide by $(1 + an)$:

$$\frac{a}{1 + an} = x.$$

Example. Solve for y, citing operations performed:

$$\frac{a}{y} - \frac{1}{b} = 2 \qquad \text{Multiply by } yb:$$

$$ab - y = 2by \qquad \text{Add } y:$$

$$ab = 2by + y \qquad \text{Factor:}$$

$$ab = y(2b + 1) \qquad \text{Divide by } (2b + 1):$$

$$\frac{ab}{2b + 1} = y.$$

A3.4 PROBLEM SET A3–1

Solve each of the following for x, citing operations performed:

1. $2x - 3 = x + 4.$

2. $4x + 5 = 2x + 12.$

3. $3x - 7 = 2x + 4.$

4. $5 - 2x = 6.$

5. $7x - 5 = 3 - 4x.$

6. $3 - 2x = x - 4.$

7. $\dfrac{x}{3} + \dfrac{1}{2} = 3x.$

8. $\dfrac{x}{4} + \dfrac{x}{2} = 2 - \dfrac{5x}{8}.$

9. $\dfrac{2x}{5} - \dfrac{3x}{2} = 4.$

10. $1 - \dfrac{x}{3} + \dfrac{x}{2} = x - 4.$

11. $\dfrac{1}{7} - \dfrac{x}{3} = x.$

12. $1 - \dfrac{3x}{7} = 0.$

13. $\dfrac{x + 3}{2} = x - \dfrac{1}{4}.$

14. $\dfrac{5 - 2x}{3} + \dfrac{x}{2} = 1.$

15. $\dfrac{2x - 1}{3} - \dfrac{1 - x}{5} = 0.$

16. $\dfrac{x + 1}{2} - \dfrac{x - 1}{3} = 5.$

17. $bx + 2 = c.$

18. $ax + 2 - x = 0.$

19. $ax + b = cx.$

20. $ax + b = x - b.$

21. $a(x - a) = 2x.$

22. $\dfrac{x}{a} - \dfrac{1}{2} = 2x.$

23. $\dfrac{2}{a - x} + \dfrac{1}{3} = 4.$

24. $y = \dfrac{x}{b - cx}.$

25. $\dfrac{3}{4} - \dfrac{2x}{3} = 2x(a - 1).$

26. $3(x - 2) = 2 - a(x + 2).$

27. $\dfrac{2}{3(x - 2)} + \dfrac{3}{a} - \dfrac{1}{2} = 0.$

28. $ax - \dfrac{b}{2} = c + \dfrac{5[a - 2(b - x)]}{6}.$

29. $\dfrac{b}{a} - x = 2a(b - x).$

30. $x - a(b - x) = 2x - 3.$

31. $3(b - x) = 2 + b[x - (3 - x)].$

32. $b(a + x) = a(b + x),$ where $a \neq b.$

Problem Set A3–1 has afforded practice in citing fundamentals as justification for steps followed in the solutions of equations. From now on, we shall lessen the writing burden by omitting step-by-step justification. The burden can be lightened further by applying the rule of *transposition*, which states that a *term* may be moved from one side of an equation to the other by changing its sign. For example,

$$x - 2a = b$$

becomes

$$x = b + 2a$$

by changing the sign of $-2a$ to $+2a$ and placing $+2a$ on the other side. Similarly,

$$x + 7 = y$$

becomes

$$x = y - 7.$$

The transposition rule is a consequence of the axiom that states that the same number may be added to (subtracted from) both sides of an equation. That is, the change from

$$x + 7 = y$$

to

$$x = y - 7$$

is, in effect, subtracting 7 from both sides of the first equation. Transposition is a handy procedure, but we must keep in mind that it applies to *terms*. It would not be correct to say that any quantity can be moved to the other side by transposition. For example, the 2 in $2x = 6$ is not subject to the rule for transposition because 2 is not a term of the left member of the equation.

> **Exercise.** The change from $ax = b$ to $x = b/a$ is not accomplished by transposition. How is it accomplished? Answer: By dividing both sides of the equation by a.

A3.6 FORMULAS

Computational procedures are described efficiently by formulas employing the symbolism of algebra. Thus, if x is the length and y the width of a rectangle, the area, A, of the rectangle is expressed by the formula $A = xy$. On the one hand, if we are told a rectangle has a length of eight inches and a width of five inches, we compute the area

$$A = (8)(5) = 40 \text{ square inches.}$$

On the other hand, if we are asked how wide a rectangle of 12 inches length should be if its area is to be 84 square inches, we substitute into the equation, obtaining $84 = 12y$. Solving this equation, we find y, the desired width, is seven inches. The point here is that we may wish to use a formula to evaluate a variable other than the one for which the formula is solved, and to do so, we call upon the usual operations for solving equations. Actually, the formula $A = xy$ leads easily to two other formulas:

$$x = \frac{A}{y} \quad \text{and} \quad y = \frac{A}{x}.$$

If we have the formula $A = xy$ and are given values for A and x, we can compute y by substituting the given values directly into the equation and solving for y, or we can solve the literal equation, obtaining

$$y = \frac{A}{x}$$

and then evaluate y by substituting the given values into this equation. Generally, it is more efficient to substitute the given numbers directly into the formula if a single evaluation is to be made. If, however, several evaluations are to be made, the formula should be solved for the desired variable before substituting numbers. For example, suppose that we are given

$$y = 5 \quad \text{and} \quad a = 2$$

and are asked to evaluate x from the formula

$$y = 2(ax - 3).$$

Substituting the given numbers directly into the formula:

$$5 = 2(2x - 3)$$
$$5 = 4x - 6$$
$$11 = 4x$$
$$\frac{11}{4} = x.$$

On the other hand, if we are asked to carry out a whole series of evaluations of x for various values of y and a, it would be more efficient to solve the formula for x to obtain

$$x = \frac{y + 6}{2a}.$$

This formula permits rapid evaluation of x for given values of y and a.

> **Exercise.** If $y = (1 + n)/2$, what would be an efficient way to compute n for many different values of y? Answer: Substitute the values for y into the equation $n = 2y - 1$.

A3.7 EXACT EVALUATIONS

Evaluation by formulas often leads to approximations. Unless care is exercised, these approximations may not be accurate enough for the purpose at hand. Suppose, for example, that we wish to compute $3\frac{1}{3}$ percent of \$1 million. If we change the stated percent to 3.33 percent, and then to the decimal 0.0333, the computation is

$$0.0333(1,000,000) = 33,300.$$

For most purposes the answer obtained would not be satisfactory. We can express the answer to any desired degree of accuracy by changing the stated percent to its exact equivalent, as follows:

$$3\tfrac{1}{3}\% = \frac{3\frac{1}{3}}{100} = \frac{10/3}{100} = \frac{10}{300} = \frac{1}{30}.$$

The computation with exact numbers would be

$$\left(\frac{1}{30}\right)(1,000,000) = 33,333.333 \ldots$$

The point of this example is that if fractions are used up to the last step, the final answer can be carried accurately to as many places as desired.

> **Exercise.** Compute x exactly from $3x + 2 = 1/b$ if b is $2\frac{1}{7}$. Answer: $-\frac{23}{45}$.

As another example, let us evaluate y, given

$$y = \frac{a + b}{1 - r}, \quad a = \frac{1}{3}, \quad b = \frac{1}{2}, \quad \text{and} \quad r = 1\tfrac{1}{3}\%.$$

To express all numbers in the same form, r is changed to its exact fractional equivalent, $\frac{1}{75}$. Substituting this value of r, we obtain

$$y = \frac{1/3 + 1/2}{1 - 1/75}.$$

This is an exact expression for y. If numerator and denominator are each multiplied by 150, we obtain

$$y = \frac{50 + 75}{150 - 2} = \frac{125}{148},$$

which again is an exact expression for y. This result could now be converted to an approximate decimal accurate to as many places as desired.

A3.8 PROBLEM SET A3–2

Given that $k = 12$, $m = 5$, $n = 4$, compute y from the following formulas:

1. $y = \dfrac{km}{n}.$

2. $y = \dfrac{k^2m - n^3}{n^2}.$

3. $y = \dfrac{m}{n/k^2}.$

4. $y = \sqrt[3]{mn} - k.$

5. $y = (n - m)[n - k(m + n)].$

6. $y = \dfrac{8m}{n^2/k}.$

7. $y = \left(\dfrac{kn}{3}\right)^{3/2}.$

8. $y = \left(\dfrac{4}{9k}\right)^{-2/3}.$

9. $y = \left(m^2 - \dfrac{3k}{4}\right)^{5/4}.$

10. $y = m^2n + 3[4k - n(m^3 - k^2)].$

In the following, find the exact value of y in the form of a fraction in lowest terms, given that

$$a = \frac{5}{3}, \quad b = \frac{1}{7}, \quad c = \frac{2}{9}, \quad d = \frac{5}{12}, \quad x = \frac{3}{8}, \quad z = \frac{1}{5}.$$

11. $y = \dfrac{x}{a}.$

12. $y = \dfrac{ab}{2}.$

13. $y = \dfrac{a(b + c)}{3}.$

14. $y = d - \dfrac{1}{a}.$

15. $y = ax + bz.$

16. $y = ax^2 - \dfrac{2a}{b}.$

17. $y = \left(1 - \dfrac{a}{d}\right)^3.$

18. $y = \sqrt[3]{\dfrac{c}{2x}}.$

19. $y = \dfrac{a}{2} - b\sqrt{\dfrac{3d}{5}}.$

20. $y = \dfrac{a + 2c - d}{x - 4a}.$

---

21. Compute y to the nearest cent:

$$y = at + b(t - c)$$
$$a = 16\tfrac{2}{3}\%, \quad b = 15\%, \quad c = \$75{,}000, \text{ and}$$
$$t = \$140{,}000.$$

22. Given that $a = 0.52$, $x = 4$, compute y to two decimal places:

$$y = \dfrac{a}{1 + x/100}.$$

23. The equation relating the cost, C, of an item to its retail price, R, is $C + pR = R$, where p

percent is markup on the retail price.
  a) What markup percent on retail is achieved if an item costs $5 and sells at a retail price of $8?
  b) How much can a merchant pay for an item if he wishes to sell it for $7.50 and achieve a markup which is 20 percent of the retail price?
  c) If a merchant seeks to achieve a markup of 40 percent on retail, at what price should he sell an item which cost him $2.69?

24. The amount of interest, I, earned on P dol-

A3.8 PROBLEM SET A3–2 (concluded)

lars at simple interest of r percent per year for t years is $I = Prt$. Assuming a year to have 360 days:
a) How long will it take for $500 to earn interest in the amount of $20 if the interest rate per year is $4\frac{1}{2}$ percent?
b) How many dollars must be invested at $3\frac{1}{3}$ percent per year if interest in the amount of $75 is to be earned in 50 days?

25. Temperature in degrees Celsius, C, is related to temperature in degrees Fahrenheit, F, by the formula

$$C = \frac{5}{9}(F - 32).$$

Find the Fahrenheit temperature corresponding to the following Celsius readings:
a) 100.   b) 0.   c) -10.6
d) 28.   e) -10.   f) 50.

26. A salesman's earnings, E, amount to 20 percent of his total sales, T, plus a bonus of $12\frac{1}{2}$ percent of any amount he sells in excess of $50,000.
a) Write the equation relating earnings to sales if sales exceed $50,000.
b) What must the man's sales be if he is to earn $10,000? $15,000? $20,000?
c) How much must he sell if his earnings are to be 25 percent of total sales?

27. An executive is to receive compensation, B, amounting to x percent of his company's net profit after taxes. Taxes amount to y percent of net profits after deduction of the executive's compensation.
a) Letting P represent net profits before taxes, complete the following formula:

$$B = x[P - ?(? - ?)].$$

b) If the executive receives 25 percent of net profits after taxes, and taxes amount to 52 percent of net profits after deduction of the executive's compensation, how much must net profits before taxes be if the executive is to receive $50,000?

28. A customer buys an article on the install-

ment plan. The price of the article (or the amount he still owes after making a down payment) is B dollars. The seller adds a carrying charge of C dollars and requires that the debt be paid off by n equal payments. Letting y be the number of payments which would be made in a year (that is, if payments are weekly, y is 52; and if payments are monthly, y is 12), and letting r be the equivalent simple interest rate being paid by the customer, a formula states

$$r = \frac{2yC}{B(n + 1)}.$$

a) An article priced at $500 is purchased. The customer pays $100 down (so B is $400). The seller adds $42 as a carrying charge and requires that the debt be repaid in ten equal monthly installments of $44.20 each. What rate of interest is the customer paying? (Find r, and convert it to percent form.)
b) If the simple interest equivalent of the installment rate is 15 percent, what should be the carrying charge on an article priced at $100 (no down payment) if the debt is to be repaid in 20 equal weekly installments?

29. For each dollar of increase in sales, selling expense increases by $\$p$ where, it is hoped, p is less than 1. The sales level B at which the company will break even if its fixed expenses are $\$F$ is:

$$B = \frac{F}{1 - p}.$$

a) Find B if $F = \$12,000$ and $p = 0.4$.
b) Fixed expenses are $10,000 and management wishes to control p so that breakeven will occur at $12,500. Find p.
c) Repeat (b) if fixed expenses are $20,000 and breakeven is to occur at $32,000.

30. The average cost per unit is $\$A$ when x units are made, and

$$A = \frac{100}{x} + 0.01.$$

A3.8 PROBLEM SET A3–2 (*continued*)

Find the average cost per unit if:
a) 10 units are made.
b) 20 units are made.

How many units should be made if average cost per unit is to be
c) $1.01?   d) $0.41?   e) $0.21?

A3.9 COORDINATE AXES

An axiom of mathematics states that a correspondence exists between the real numbers and the points on a straight line; that is, for each real number, there is one and only one corresponding point on a line, and each point on a line corresponds to one and only one real number. Hence, if we draw a straight line and mark upon it an arbitrary point, zero, all negative real numbers can be represented by points to the left of zero, all positive numbers by points to the right of zero. According to the axiom, each number corresponds to a unique point on the line, and the totality of real numbers corresponds to the line itself.

A pair of rectangular coordinate axes is obtained by drawing two intersecting perpendicular lines, one horizontal, the other vertical. The intersection of the horizontal and vertical axes so obtained is taken as the zero point on each line and is called the *origin*. On the vertical, points above the origin are used to represent positive numbers, points below to represent negative numbers. On the horizontal axis, positive numbers are to the right of the origin, negative numbers to the left.

Any point in the plane of the axes can be located by means of a number pair called the *coordinates* of the point. Conventionally, coordinates are written in the form (a, b), where the first number in the parentheses is the horizontal coordinate, or *abscissa*, and the second number is the vertical coordinate, or *ordinate*. Thus, the point $(2, 3)$ is located by moving two units to the right of the origin, and then three units vertically upward. The procedure is analogous to the method of directing a person from a particular spot (origin) in a city by telling him the point he wishes to reach can be found by going two blocks east, and then three blocks north.

Exercise.   What are the abscissa and the ordinate of a point? Answer: The abscissa is the horizontal coordinate and the ordinate is the vertical coordinate of the point.

Figure A3–1 shows the point $(2, 3)$ just mentioned, together with other aspects of the coordinate system. The axes divide the plane into *quadrants*, which we number counterclockwise I, II, III, and IV as shown in Figure A3–1. In quadrant I, both abscissa and ordinate are positive. In II the abscissa is negative, the ordinate positive. In III both coordinates are negative. In IV the abscissa is positive, the ordinate negative.

FIGURE A3-1

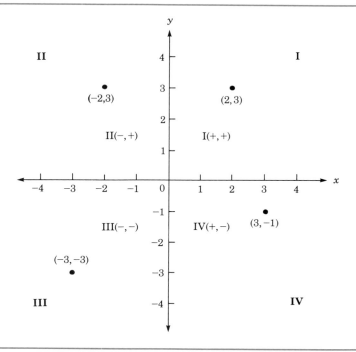

Exercise. In what quadrants are the points $(-2, 3)$, $(3, 5)$, $(2, -3)$, $(-5, -4)$? Answer: II, I, IV, III.

A3.10 PLOTTING OBSERVATIONAL DATA

By observational data we mean numbers collected in real situations—numbers such as costs, sales, units produced, prices, and so on. Frequently, we wish to display such data in a graphical manner, which helps to show relationships that may exist between two variables. Consider the data in Table A3-1.

TABLE A3-1
Production cost per unit of product

Lot number	Number of units in lot (x)	Cost per unit (y)
1	8	$11
2	20	4
3	5	13
4	10	9
5	15	8
6	25	5

FIGURE A3–2

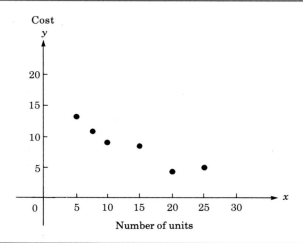

Figure A3–2 is a graphic representation (or, more simply, a graph) of the data of Table A3–1. The numbers of units produced have been assigned the general designation x, the costs per unit the general designation y. Following convention, the numbers x are assigned to the horizontal axis, the numbers y to the vertical. By definition, the vertical variable is called the *dependent* variable, and the horizontal variable is called the *independent* variable. In the present illustration, it is natural to think of production cost as depending on number of units produced, so that cost would be the dependent variable and units produced the independent variable. In many circumstances, however, reference to the vertical axis as the axis of the dependent variable is purely a matter of convention.

The interpretation of Figure A3–2 is simply that unit cost *tends* to decrease as the number of units made increases. It is a graphical illustration of the economies of mass production. We refer to this set of isolated points as a *discrete* set. If we wish to illustrate the relationship by means of a smooth curve, we may sketch in freehand a curve that comes close to the points, although it does not pass through all of the points. The points on the curve are not, of course, records of observations, because actual observations are limited in number, whereas a segment of a smooth curve has an unlimited number of points. However, we might wish to use the smooth curve to estimate costs per unit for numbers of units other than those observed.

Given the equation

$$y = x + 2,$$

we know that for every x, there is a number y such that the number pair (x, y) satisfies the equation. The entire solution set is an infinite set of ordered pairs. We can generate some members (obviously not all) of the solution set by arbitrarily assigning a value for x, then computing the corresponding value for y. For example,

$$\text{if } x = 1, \quad \text{then} \quad y = 1 + 2 = 3$$

and $(1, 3)$ is a member of the solution set. Similarly, if $x = 2$, then $y = 4$, and $(2, 4)$ is another member of the solution set.

> **Exercise.** Find the points in the solution set corresponding to $x = 0$ and $x = 5$. Answer: $(0, 2)$; $(5, 7)$.

We *plot the graph* of an equation by finding and plotting points that satisfy the equation, then sketching in a smooth curve as suggested by the plotted points. In the case at hand, we may tabulate some of the points as in Table A3–2 where the x values are chosen arbitrarily.

The points of Table A3–2 are shown in Figure A3–3 on the next page, where it is clear that all fall on the same straight line. We would also obtain a straight line if we made the graph of

$$y = 3x + 5 \quad \text{or} \quad y = -2x + 7.$$

In general, an equation that can be made into the form

$$y = mx + b,$$

where m and b are constant numbers, has a straight line as its graph and is called a *linear equation*. The graph of such an equation is easily sketched because *two points* suffice to fix a straight line.

TABLE A3–2

	$y = x + 2$	
	x	**y**
	0	2
	1	3
	2	4
	3	5
	4	6
	5	7

FIGURE A3–3

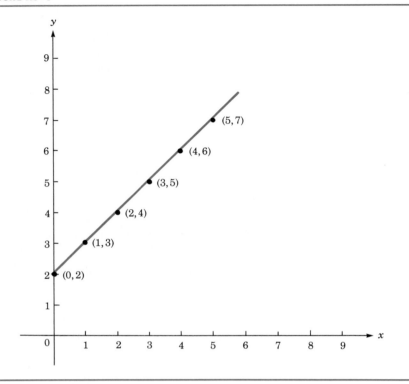

Exercise.   How would you plot the graph of $y = 2x - 3$? Answer: Pick two arbitrary values of x and find the corresponding values of y to obtain two points. Plot the points and use a straightedge to draw a line through them.

A3.12 VERTICAL PARABOLAS

In the equation

$$y = x^2 - 5$$

if we let

$$x = 0, 1, 2, 3, 4, 5$$

in succession, we find the corresponding values of y to be -5, -4, -1, 4, 11, and 20. In this equation the succession of negatives

$$x = -1, -2, -3, -4, -5$$

leads to the same last five values in the preceding sequence of y's. In tabular form, we have the points shown in Table A3–3.

TABLE A3–3

$y = x^2 - 5$	
x	**y**
−5	20
−4	11
−3	4
−2	−1
−1	−4
0	−5
1	−4
2	−1
3	4
4	11
5	20

The general shape of the curve is shown in Figure A3–4. It is clear that the curve will continue to rise at both ends because if we substitute x values of 6, 7, and so on (or -6, -7, and so on), the term x^2 in

$$y = x^2 - 5$$

will overpower the number -5 and make y become larger.

FIGURE A3–4

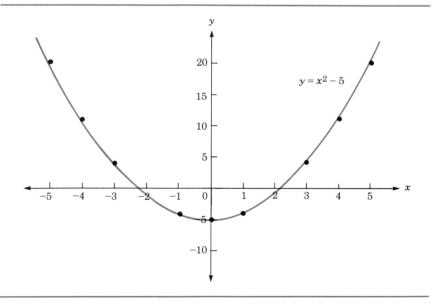

Exercise. Find the coordinates of the points on $y = x^2 - 5$ where $x = 2.5$ and $x = -2.5$. Check the graph in Figure A3–4 by plotting these points. Answer: The points are $(2.5, 1.25)$ and $(-2.5, 1.25)$.

The graph shown in Figure A3–4 is known as a *vertical parabola*. If we plotted points for

$$y = -2x^2 + 5x - 6 \quad \text{or} \quad y = 3x^2 + 5x - 4,$$

we would again obtain vertical parabolas. In general, any equation that can be made into the form

$$y = ax^2 + bx + c,$$

where a, b, c are constant numbers and $a \neq 0$, is a vertical parabola. The "nose" of the parabola is called the *vertex*. If $a > 0$, the parabola opens up; if $a < 0$, the parabola opens down. In the case of Figure A3–4, the vertex lies on the vertical axis. This is always the case if $b = 0$ in $y = ax^2 + bx + c$, as in the plotted equation

$$y = x^2 - 5.$$

Proper positioning of the vertex of a parabola is of key importance in drawing an accurate sketch. This can be done by use of the formula[1] that states that the x-coordinate of the vertex of a vertical parabola occurs at

$$x = -\frac{b}{2a}.$$

Thus, comparing the parabola $y = x^2 - 5$ with $y = ax^2 + bx + c$, we have $a = 1, b = 0, c = -5$, so

$$x = -\frac{0}{2} = 0$$

is the x-coordinate of the vertex. The corresponding y is -5. The vertex is at $(0, -5)$, as shown in Figure A3–4.

As another example, in

$$y = -2x^2 + 12x - 10$$

we have $a = -2, b = 12$. We find

$$x = -\frac{12}{-4} = 3$$

---

[1] Because a vertical parabola is symmetrical with respect to a vertical line through its vertex at $x = v$ (where v stands for vertex) it follows that the y value is the same at $x + v$ and $x - v$. That is, $a(x + v)^2 + b(x + v) + c = a(x - v)^2 + b(x - v) + c$. If we square, collect terms, factor, and solve, we find $x = -b/2a$.

and

$$y = -2(9) + 12(3) - 10 = 8,$$

so $(3, 8)$ is the vertex in this case.

Exercise. Find the coordinates of the vertex of $y = 3x^2 - 12x + 5$. Answer: $(2, -7)$.

In general, peaks and valleys in curves are points of critical importance in sketching accurate graphs. We shall learn more about methods of determining such points and about important interpretations attached to them in Chapter 11. We shall now sketch the graph of the equation of the last exercise

$$y = 3x^2 - 12x + 5.$$

We found the vertex to be $(2, -7)$, and we may compute some other points as shown in Table A3–4. The desired graph is shown in Figure A3–5 on the next page.

TABLE A3–4

$y = 3x^2 - 12x + 5$	
x	**y**
-1	20
0	5
1	-4
2	-7
3	-4
4	5
5	20

Exercise. Plot $y = x^2 - 8x + 15$ in Figure A3–5. Answer: This parabola rises on either side of the vertex at $(4, -1)$, cutting the x-axis at 3 and 5. Other points are $(2, 3)$, $(6, 3)$, $(0, 15)$, and $(8, 15)$.

As another example, the parabola $y = -4x^2 + 7x - 3$ is found to have its vertex at $(\frac{7}{8}, \frac{1}{16})$ and to fall on either side of the vertex. Again, $y = x^2$ is a parabola with vertex at the origin which rises on either side of the vertex.

FIGURE A3–5

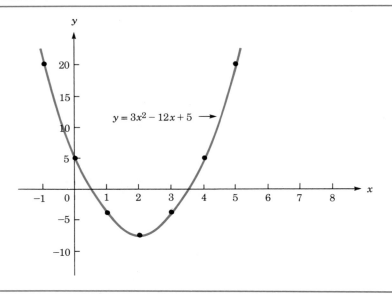

$y = 3x^2 - 12x + 5$

**A3.13 QUADRATIC
EQUATIONS**

A quadratic equation is of the form

$$ax^2 + bx + c = 0,$$

where a, b, and c are constants, with $a \neq 0$. Thus,

$$3x^2 - 12x + 5 = 0 \tag{1}$$

is a quadratic equation with $a = 3$, $b = -12$, and $c = 5$. The solution set consists of the values for x which make the equation a true statement. If we relate this equation to

$$y = 3x^2 - 12x + 5, \tag{2}$$

we see that the solution set of (1) consists of the values of x that make y, in (2), equal to zero. By reference to the graph in Figure A3–5, we see that the graph intersects the x-axis at about $x = 0.5$ and $x = 3.5$, and at these points y, or $3x^2 - 12x + 5$, is zero. An exact determination of the solution set can be found by the *quadratic formula*, which states

$$x = \frac{-b \pm \sqrt{b^2 - 4ac}}{2a}.$$

In the present case,

$$x = \frac{-(-12) \pm \sqrt{144 - 4(3)(5)}}{2(3)} = \frac{12 \pm \sqrt{84}}{6}.$$

Now $\sqrt{84}$ is about 9.17, so

$$x = \frac{12 \pm 9.17}{6}$$

$$= \frac{21.17}{6} \quad \text{or} \quad \frac{2.83}{6}$$

$$= 3.53 \quad \text{or} \quad 0.47,$$

and the solution set may be written as $x_1 = 0.47, x_2 = 3.53$, or $\{0.47, 3.53\}$.

Three cases can arise in the solution of a quadratic. The graphical nature of these cases can be understood by reference to Figure A3–5. In its present state, the graph shows *two different real solutions*. If now we hold the axes fixed and move the curve upward until the vertex is tangent to the x-axis (touches it at a single point), we have the case of *two equal real* solutions. Finally, if we again move the parabola upward, it will not intersect the x-axis, and we have the case of *no real solutions*. Algebraically, these cases relate to the quantity $b^2 - 4ac$ in the quadratic formula,

$$x = \frac{-b \pm \sqrt{b^2 - 4ac}}{2a}.$$

If $b^2 - 4ac$ is *positive* (greater than zero), we have a positive and a negative value for the square root, and there are *two different real* solutions. If $b^2 - 4ac$ is *zero*, we have only one value for x and there are *two equal real* solutions. Finally, if $b^2 - 4ac$ is *negative*, its square root is not a real number, and we have *no real solutions*.

Exercise. Apply the quadratic formula to find the solutions for $x^2 - 9 = 0$. Answer: With $a = 1$, $b = 0$, $c = -9$, we find the two different roots, $x = 3$, and $x = -3$. The same result can be obtained by writing $x^2 = 9$ and noting that the square of $+3$ or -3 equals 9.

If we apply the formula to

$$3x^2 - 5x + 10 = 0,$$

we have,

$$x = \frac{5 \pm \sqrt{25 - 120}}{6} = \frac{5 \pm \sqrt{-95}}{6}$$

and find that this equation has no real solutions.

Exercise. Solve $x^2 - 4x + 4 = 0$ by the quadratic formula. Answer: $x_1 = x_2 = 2$. We have two real equal solutions.

Solution by factoring. The equation

$$(x - 3)(x + 2) = 0$$

is true if either the factor $x - 3 = 0$ or the factor $x + 2 = 0$ because 0 times any number equals zero. Hence, the solutions are $x_1 = 3, x_2 = -2$. Consequently, we can easily find the solutions if the quadratic is factorable. For example,

$$2x^2 + 7x - 15 = 0$$

can be factored to yield

$$(2x - 3)(x + 5) = 0.$$

Setting $2x - 3 = 0$ and $x + 5 = 0$, we have the solutions

$$x_1 = \frac{3}{2}, \quad x_2 = -5.$$

Exercise.   Solve $6x^2 + x - 2 = 0$ by factoring. Answer: $x_1 = \frac{1}{2}$, $x_2 = -\frac{2}{3}$.

Finally, note that the factoring is elementary if the quadratic has no constant term. Thus,

$$2x^2 - 5x = 0$$

factors to

$$x(2x - 5) = 0,$$

so the solutions are $x_1 = 0$ and $x_2 = \frac{5}{2}$.

A3.14 PROBLEM SET A3-3

Graph each of the following:

1. $y = 3x - 1$.

2. $y = x$.

3. $y = -5x + 6$.

4. $2y - 3x = 6$.

5. $y = \frac{x}{2} + 3$.

6. $y = 3x^2$.

7. $y = x^2 - 7$.

8. $y = -2x^2 + 10$.

9. $y = 2x^2 - x$.

10. $y = x^2 + 2x - 6$.

A3.14 PROBLEM SET A3–3 (*concluded*)

Solve by the quadratic formula:

11. $x^2 - 10x + 3 = 0$.

12. $2x^2 + 5x - 2 = 0$.

13. $4x^2 - 12x + 9 = 0$.

14. $3x^2 + 2x + 5 = 0$.

15. $x^2 - 2x = 0$.

Solve by factoring:

16. $x^2 - 3x + 2 = 0$.

17. $3x^2 - 6x = 0$.

18. $6x^2 + 7x - 20 = 0$.

19. $x^2 - 25 = 0$.

20. $2x^2 + 5x - 7 = 0$.

A3.15 DEFINITIONS AND FUNDAMENTAL PROPERTIES OF INEQUALITIES

The symbols of inequality are $<$ and $>$. The first, $<$, means *is less than*; the second, $>$, means *is greater than*. Thus $3 > 2$ is the true statement that 3 is greater than 2, and $5 < 9$ is the true statement that 5 is less than 9. It may be of use to note that the symbols $>$ and $<$ point toward the smaller quantity. The statement $a < b$ is read "a is less than b." If we wish to state that "a is less than or equal to b," we combine the inequality sign with the equality sign and write $a \leq b$. Further practice with the symbols is afforded next:

$a \geq b$ means a is greater than or equal to b.

$a \leq 3$ means a is less than or equal to 3.

$b > 0$ means b is greater than zero; that is, b is positive.

$c < 0$ means c is negative.

$a \geq 0$ means a is not negative.

One of the fundamental properties of the real number system is the property of *order*. We say that the real numbers are ordered in the sense that either any two numbers are equal, or one is greater than the other. Thus, given any two numbers, a and b, one and only one of the following must be true

$$a < b$$
$$a = b$$
$$a > b.$$

To say that a first number is greater than a second implies that a positive number must be added to the second number to make the sum equal the first number. For example, $5 > 2$ implies that a positive number must be added to 2 to make a sum equal to 5. In general,

$a > b$ implies that $a = b + c$, where $c > 0$.
$a < b$ implies that $a + c = b$, where $c > 0$.

The last statement that "a is less than b" implies that a positive number ($c > 0$) must be added to a to make the sum equal b.

It is a consequence of the order property of the real numbers that $-5 < -2$ and $0 > -1$. That is, inasmuch as the positive number 3 must be added to -5 to make the sum equal -2, -5 is less than -2. Again, inasmuch as the positive number 1 must be added to -1 to make the sum 0, 0 is greater than -1.

Exercise.   What argument leads to the conclusion that -10 is greater than -20? (See the immediately preceding paragraph.)

The ordering of numbers can be remembered easily by reference to Figure A3–6. If the number a is to the left of the number b, then $a < b$. If the number a is to the right of the number b, then $a > b$. We see that $-1 < 0, 0 < 1, -2 > -3, 2 > -1$.

FIGURE A3–6

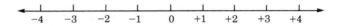

The direction in which an inequality symbol points is referred to as its *sense*, the particular use of the word being in phrases that describe inequalities as being of the *same sense* or of *opposite sense*. Thus, $x < 3$ and $x < -1$ are of the same sense, and $x \leq 5$ and $x \geq 8$ are of opposite sense.

A3.16 FUNDAMENTAL OPERATIONS ON INEQUALITIES

As in the case with equalities, the same number may be added to or subtracted from both sides of an inequality, and both sides may be multiplied by, or divided by, the same *positive* (nonzero) number. However,

Multiplying or dividing both sides of an inequality by the same negative number changes the sense of the inequality.

For example,

$$i_1: \quad -3 > -6$$
$$i_2: \quad 12 < 24 \qquad i_2 \text{ is } -4(i_1).$$

Thus, i_1 is the true statement that -3 is greater than -6. If we multiply both sides of i_1 by -4, we change the sense to get the true statement, i_2, that 12 is less than 24. It will be helpful to check the following sequence of operations.

$$
\begin{array}{lll}
i_1: & 2 > 1 & \\
i_2: & 5 > 4 & \text{Add 3 to both sides of } i_1. \\
i_3: & -30 < -24 & \text{Multiply } i_2 \text{ by } -6. \\
i_4: & 10 > 8 & \text{Divide } i_3 \text{ by } -3. \\
i_5: & -2 > -4 & \text{Subtract 12 from both sides of } i_4. \\
i_6: & -4 < -2 & \text{Read } i_5 \text{ from } right \text{ to } left. \\
i_7: & 2 > 1 & \text{Divide } i_6 \text{ by } -2.
\end{array}
$$

Ordinarily, we read inequalities in the usual manner, from left to right. However, as shown in i_6 of the above, we may, if we wish, read from right to left. For example, just as we can write

$$6 = x \qquad \text{or} \qquad x = 6,$$

so also we may write

$$6 < x \qquad \text{or} \qquad x > 6.$$

It may be helpful in the beginning to note that $>$ resembles an arrowhead and we read "greater than" if we read in the direction the arrow is pointing, and "less than" if we read into the arrowpoint.

A3.17 SOLVING SINGLE INEQUALITIES

Keeping the fundamental operations in mind, we solve a single inequality as shown next.

Example. Solve the following for x:

$$i_1: \quad 3 - 2x \le 7.$$

We proceed to get x alone on one side of the inequality.

$$
\begin{array}{lll}
i_2: & -2x \le 4 & \text{Subtract 3 from both sides of } i_1 \\
i_3: & x \ge -2 & \text{Divide } i_2 \text{ by } -2.
\end{array}
$$

Exercise. Solve $7 - x \ge 3$ for x. Answer: $x \le 4$.

A single equation in two-space has a straight line as its geometric representation. A single *inequality*, on the other hand, is represented by all points on one side of a line, the line itself being included if the equality and inequality signs appear together. If we think of a straight line as dividing a plane in half, we may say that the solutions of an inequality in two-space consist of all points in a *half space*. Consider the inequality

$$2x + 3y \le 6.$$

Our first step in representing the inequality is to draw the line specified by the *equality*

$$2x + 3y = 6.$$

The intercepts are:

$$x = 0; \quad y = 2; \quad \text{point is } (0, 2)$$
$$y = 0; \quad x = 3; \quad \text{point is } (3, 0).$$

The line is shown in Figure A3–7. Notice that the *origin* (0, 0), satisfies the inequality statement

$$2x + 3y \leq 6$$
$$2(0) + 3(0) \leq 6$$
$$0 \leq 6.$$

Thus the origin, which is *below* the line, is in the solution space and *if one point below a line is in the solution space, then all points below the line are in the solution space*. Hence, the solution space consists of all points on the line, or below the line, as indicated by the direction of the arrows on the line. Obviously, the solution space contains an unlimited number of points.

To solve the inequality algebraically, we change the form of the inequality as follows:

$$2x + 3y \leq 6$$
$$3y \leq -2x + 6$$
$$y \leq -\frac{2}{3}x + 2.$$

FIGURE A3–7

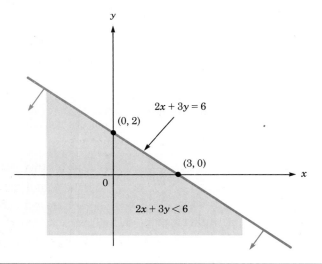

Here, the equality part of

$$y \le$$

means that points *on* the line are included in the solution space and the *less-than* part means points below the line are included. The algebraic solution then is

$$x \text{ arbitrary}$$

$$y \le -\frac{2}{3}x + 2.$$

Thus, if x is assigned any arbitrary value, the last expression states the permissible values for y. For example, if $x = -12$

$$y \le -\frac{2}{3}(-12) + 2$$
$$y \le 8 + 2$$
$$y \le 10$$

and we have $(x = -12, y \le 10)$ as a specific (unlimited) set of solutions.

Example. a) Find the algebraic solution of the inequality

$$3x - 2y < -8.$$

b) On which side of the line (above or below) does the solution space lie? c) Write the specific solution set if $x = 6$.

a) We first solve the inequality, isolating y on the left side, as follows:

$$-2y < -3x - 8$$
$$y > \frac{3}{2}x + 4$$
$$y > 1.5x + 4.$$

The general solution is, therefore,

$$x \text{ arbitrary}$$
$$y > 1.5x + 4.$$

b) The *greater-than* sign, $>$, in the last statement means the solution space is *above* the line. The line itself is *not* included because the statement specifies $y >$, not $y \ge$.

c) If $x = 6$, we have from the general solution

$$y > 1.5(6) + 4$$
$$y > 9 + 4$$
$$y > 13,$$

so the specific solution set is $(x = 6, y > 13)$. Note that $y = 13$ is not in this solution set.

Exercise. Given $x - 3y \leq 12$. a) Write the general algebraic solution. b) On which side of the line does the solution space lie? c) Write the specific solution set if $x = 9$. Answer: a) $y \geq (\frac{1}{3})x - 4$. b) Above the line. c) ($x = 9, y \geq -1$).

To graph solution spaces, the line can be drawn from its intercepts or any two of its points and the side of the line on which the solution space lies indicated by arrows, as in Figure A3–7.

To determine the side of the line on which the solution space lies,

Either: a) Solve for y. Then $y >$ means above the line and $y <$ means below the line.

Or: b) Substitute the origin (0, 0) into the inequality. If the result is a true statement, the half-space is on the same side of the plotted line as the origin. If the result is a false statement, the half-space is on the side of the plotted line which does not contain the origin. Use a point other than (0, 0) if the inequality has no constant term other than zero.

The last sentence says that if we have

$$3y + 2x \geq 0,$$

the line

$$3y + 2x = 0$$

goes through the origin, (0, 0), because

$$3(0) + 2(0) = 0,$$

and every line whose equation has zero as its only constant term passes through the origin. Both intercepts are at the origin, so to get a second point on

$$3y + 2x = 0$$

we give x an arbitrary value, say 3, and compute

$$3y + 2(3) = 0$$
$$3y = -6$$
$$y = -2.$$

The point just determined (3, −2), along with (0, 0), determine the line shown on Figure A3–8. Substituting (0, 0) into $3y + 2x \geq 0$ gives

$$0 + 0 \geq 0,$$

FIGURE A3–8

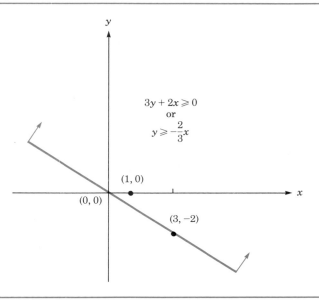

which is true, but it does not tell us on which side of the line the solution space lies because the origin is on the line. However, if we take the point $(1, 0)$ and substitute this into the inequality we find

$$3(0) + 2(1) \geq 0$$
$$2 \geq 0,$$

which is true. From Figure A3–8, we see that $(1, 0)$ is above the line so all points in the solution space are above (or on) the line, as shown by the arrows on Figure A3–8.

The graph of

$$x = 6$$

is a *vertical* line, so the terms above and below have no meaning here. However, if we have

$$x < 6,$$

the *less than* sign, $<$, means the solution space is to the *left* of the vertical line $x = 6$. Similarly, $x > -2$ means the solution space is to the right of the vertical line $x = -2$. Of course,

$$y < 20$$

means the solution space is below the horizontal line $y = 20$, and

$$y > -12$$

means the solution space is above the horizontal line $y = -12$.

A3.18 PROBLEM SET A3–4

Mark (T) for true or (F) for false.

1. ( ) $-3 > -2$.

2. ( ) $a > b$ means a is greater than b.

3. ( ) If $4 < c$, then c could not equal 5.

4. ( ) $a \leq 0$ means a must be positive.

5. ( ) $a \geq 0$ means a must be positive.

6. ( ) If $a < b$, then $a = b + c$ for some positive number c.

7. ( ) If $a > b$, then b is less than a.

8. ( ) If $-a < 2$, then $a < -2$.

9. ( ) If $a - 2 > -5$, then $a > -3$.

10. ( ) If $x \leq y$, then $2x \leq 2y$.

11. ( ) The solution of $2 - 2x > -6$ is $x < 4$.

12. ( ) The origin is in the solution space of $2x + y \leq 8$.

Solve for x:

13. $3x - 2 \leq 4$.

14. $5x + 7 \geq 22$.

15. $5 - 2x > 11$.

16. $4 - 3x < 10$.

17. $4 \leq 3 + 2x$.

18. $5 \geq 6 + 4x$.

In the following: a) Write the general algebraic solution by solving for y. b) On which side of the line does the solution space lie? c) Write the specific solution space for the stated value of x.

19. $3x + 2y \leq 12$; $x = 2$.

20. $2x + 5y \geq 35$; $x = 5$.

21. $7x - 5y \geq 45$; $x = 20$.

22. $3x - 2y \leq 18$; $x = 10$.

State whether or not the origin is in the solution space of each of the following:

23. $3x - 7y \leq 6$.

24. $2y - 3x \geq 4$.

25. $y - 2x \geq -1$.

26. $3x + 2y \leq -5$.

Graph the following in two-space. Indicate by arrows the side of the line on which the solution space lies.

27. $3y - 2x \leq 36$.

28. $2x - 10y \leq 20$.

29. $5x + 2y \geq 40$.

30. $2x + 3y \leq 60$.

31. $y \geq 5$.

32. $x \leq 10$.

33. $x \geq 0$.

34. $y \geq 0$.

35. $y - 3x \leq 0$.

36. $2x + 3y \leq 0$.

A3.19 REVIEW PROBLEMS

Solve for x, citing the operations performed:

1. $3x - 2 = 2x + 5$.

2. $\dfrac{2x}{3} - 1 = 5x$.

3. $\dfrac{3 + 2x}{4} - 2 = x$.

4. $\dfrac{2(a - x)}{b} + 3x = c$.

5. $2a = \dfrac{x}{3 - cx}$.

6. $\dfrac{3}{a(x - 1)} + \dfrac{1}{2} - b = 0$.

7. $5(x - b) = a + b[3 - 2(x + 1)]$.

8. $\dfrac{2}{3} - \dfrac{3x}{4} = 4x(2 - b)$.

9. $x - \dfrac{c}{d} = a - \dfrac{3[2 - b(x - 1)]}{4}$.

10. $\dfrac{1}{1 - x} + 1 = b$.

In the following compute x, given that $a = 6$, $b = 2$, and $c = 10$:

11. $x = \dfrac{ab - c}{b}$.

12. $x = \dfrac{a^2b - b}{c}$.

13. $x = \dfrac{c^2/b}{a}$.

14. $x = \sqrt{c^2 - a^2}$.

15. $x = \left(3c - \dfrac{a}{2}\right)^{1/3}$.

16. $x = (3ab)^{-3/2}$.

17. $x = (c - a - b)[2b - a(c - 5b)]$.

18. $x = \dfrac{a^2/b - c}{b^2}$.

In the following, compute the exact value of y in the form of a fraction in the lowest terms, given that:

$$a = \frac{2}{7}; \quad b = \frac{1}{3}; \quad c = \frac{4}{9}; \quad d = \frac{5}{12}; \quad x = \frac{1}{8}; \quad z = \frac{1}{5}.$$

19. $y = \dfrac{x}{a}$.

20. $y = \dfrac{ab}{2}$.

21. $y = d - \dfrac{1}{a}$.

22. $y = ax + bz$.

23. $y = \left(1 - \dfrac{b}{d}\right)^3$.

24. $y = (1 + 19x)^{1/3}$.

25. $y = \sqrt{c - b}$.

26. $y = \dfrac{b/2 + 3x}{1 + a}$.

---

27. Compute y to the nearest cent:

$$y = at + b(t - c)$$
$$a = 4\tfrac{1}{7}; \quad b = 22\%; \quad c = \$18,000;$$
$$t = \$28,000.$$

28. The equation relating the cost, C, of an item to its retail price, R, is $C + pR = R$, where p

is the percent markup on the retail price.

a) What markup percent on retail is achieved if an item costs \$10 and sells at a retail price of \$15?

b) How much can a merchant pay for an item if he wishes to sell it for \$20 and

A3.19 REVIEW PROBLEMS (*continued*)

achieve a markup that is 30 percent of the retail price?

c) If the merchant seeks to achieve a markup that is 35 percent of the retail price, at what price should he sell an item that cost him $13?

29. Compute y accurate to three decimals if $x = 0.05$:

$$y = \frac{(1 + x)^{-3} + 1}{x}.$$

30. The amount of interest, I, earned on P dollars at simple interest of r percent per year for t years is $I = Prt$. Assuming a year to have 360 days,

a) How many days will it take for $2,000 to earn $50 interest at 4 percent?

b) How many dollars must be invested at $5\frac{1}{3}$ percent if interest in the amount of $100 is to be earned in 90 days?

31. Temperature in degrees Fahrenheit, F, is related to temperature in degrees Celsius, C, by the formula

$$F = \frac{9}{5}C + 32.$$

Find the Celsius temperatures corresponding to the following Fahrenheit readings:

a) 0.   b) 100.   c) 51.   d) -32.

32. When an asset is bought, its initial book value is A. The book value will decline over the N years of the asset's life to the salvage value, S. The ratio of salvage value to initial book value is $s = S/A$. In the straightline method of computing book value from year to year, the appropriate formula is

$$B = A\left[1 - \frac{t}{N}(1 - s)\right],$$

where B is the book value after t years.

a) An asset with an initial book value of $1,000 and a salvage value of $100 after 10 years of life will have what book value after three years?

b) Solve the formula for s.

c) If an asset with an initial book value of

$1,000 and a life of 10 years is quoted as having a book value of $650 after 5 years, find the ratio of the salvage value to the initial value, and find the salvage value.

d) What will the depreciation formula for book value be if the asset has no salvage value?

33. A customer buys an article on the installment plan. The price of the article (or the amount he still owes after making a down payment) is B dollars. The seller adds a carrying charge of C dollars and requires that the debt be paid off by n equal payments. Letting y be the number of payments that would be made in a year (that is, if payments are weekly, y is 52; and if payments are monthly, y is 12), and letting r be the equivalent simple interest rate being paid by the customer, a formula states

$$r = \frac{2yC}{B(n + 1)}.$$

a) An article priced at $200 is purchased. The customer pays $50 down. The seller adds a carrying charge of $28.50 and requires the debt to be repaid in 18 equal monthly installments. What is the amount of the installment and what is the interest rate being charged?

b) If the simple interest equivalent of the installment rate is to be 30 percent, what should be the carrying charge on an article priced at $300 if the debt is to be paid off in 12 monthly installments and no down payment is made?

34. If D (demand) is the number of units of an item that can be sold when the item is priced at p cents per unit, and if

$$D = \frac{20}{p - 1} - 1$$

for values of p greater than 1 but less than 21, at what price will the demand be:

a) 19 units?   b) 9 units?   c) 3 units?

d) 1 unit?

A3.19 REVIEW PROBLEM (*concluded*)

35. Graph the following equations:
a) $y = 2x + 1$.
b) $5y + 4x - 20 = 0$.
c) $y = \dfrac{x}{3}$.
d) $x - y = 1$.
e) $y = 8 - x^2$.
f) $y = x^2 - 10x + 15$.

36. Solve by the quadratic formula:
a) $x^2 - 2x - 2 = 0$.
b) $4x^2 - 4x + 1 = 0$.
c) $x^2 + 2x + 5 = 0$.

37. Solve by factoring:
a) $6x^2 - 5x + 1 = 0$.
b) $16x^2 - 40x + 25 = 0$.
c) $3x^2 - 48x = 0$.
d) $x^2 - 100 = 0$.

In Problems 38–43: a) Solve for y and write the general algebraic solution. b) On which side of the line does the solution space lie? c) Write the specific solution space for the stated value of x.

38. $x - y < 5$; $x = 10$.
39. $x + y > 3$; $x = 1$.
40. $2x - 3y < -5$; $x = 2$.

41. $-2x + 5y > 2$; $x = 4$.
42. $4x - 3y > -5$; $x = 7$.
43. $x - y \le 0$; $x = 5$.

Solve for x:

44. $2 - 3x \le 6$.
45. $2x + 7 \ge 4$.
46. $7 - 4x \le 0$.

47. $3 \ge 5 - 2x$.
48. $0 \le 2x + 3$.
49. $x - 4 \ge 0$.

Answers to Problem Sets

CHAPTER 1

Problem Set 1–1

1. See Figure A. $AB = 6$, $AC = 3$, $DB = 4$.

FIGURE A

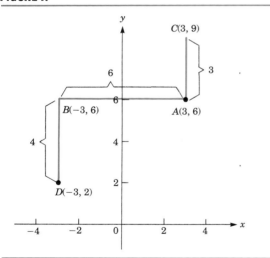

2. $AB = 2$, $AC = 24$, $AD = 17$, $BD = 15$.
3. AB is vertical, CD is horizontal.
4. $y_2 = y_1$, $x_3 = x_1$.   **5.** $y_2 = y_1$, $y_4 = y_3$.
6. a) 40 miles.   b) 70 miles.
7. a) \$16.   b) \$12.   c) See Figure B.
8. Subscript notation preserves the letters x and y to mean abscissa and ordinate for *all* points.
9. 12 blocks.

FIGURE B

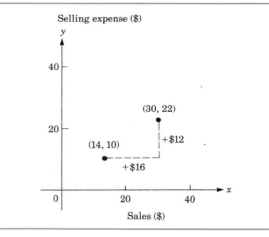

Problem Set 1–2

1. a) (3, 8), (7, 5), 5.
   b) (-1, 6), (5, -2), 10.
   c) (-1, -14), (-10, -2), 15.
2. a) 10.   b) 15.   c) 5.1.
   d) 10.   e) 3.   f) 2.
3. $AB + BC + CA = 140 + 150 + 130 = 420$ miles.
4. a) See Figure C.   b) 25 miles.
5. a) (50, 25).   b) 55.9 feet.   c) 50 feet.

Problem Set 1–2 (*concluded*)

FIGURE C

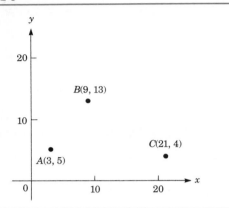

FIGURE D

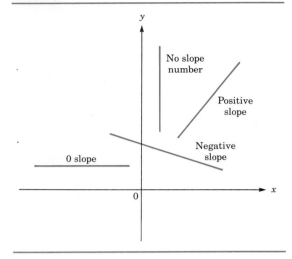

Problem Set 1–3

1. a) The difference of the second (y) coordinates, $y_2 - y_1$.
   b) The difference of the first (x) coordinates, $x_2 - x_1$.
2. a) The steepest line is vertical.
   b) As we go from one point to another on the line, the run is zero, so the slope ratio has a denominator of zero. A ratio with a denominator of zero is not a number.
3. 2/3.
4. Vertical. The plane evidently crashed.
5. 1.   6. a) 8.   b) $8.
7. The slope is 0.96, and $1 - 0.96 = 0.04$. The first is the marginal propensity to consume and the second is the marginal propensity to save. The numbers 0.96 and 0.04 indicate that for an extra $1 of income, consumers spend $0.96 and save $0.04.
8. 1.   9. -1.   10. $-1/8$.
11. Undefined. 12. 0.   13. 0.
14. Undefined. 15. 1.   16. 21/32.
17. -1.   18. $-11/9$. 19. Undefined.
20. 1.   21. $-1/13$. 22. See text.
23. $\dfrac{b-2}{a-3}, \dfrac{2-b}{3-a}$.   24. See Figure D.

25. If a is not zero, there is no number x such that $a/0 = x$; if a is 0, x is ambiguous because it could have any value.
26. F.   27. T.   28. T.   29. T.   30. T.
31. T.   32. T.   33. F.   34. T.

Problem Set 1–4

1. $y = 3x - 5$.   2. $y = -x + 1$.
3. $y = -\dfrac{2}{3}x + \dfrac{14}{3}$.   4. $y = \dfrac{1}{2}x - \dfrac{9}{2}$.
5. $y = -8$.   6. $y = -\dfrac{1}{6}x + \dfrac{22}{3}$.
7. $y = 13x + 57$.   8. $y = 0$.
9. $x = 5$.   10. $x = 0$.   11. $y = 4$.
12. $y = 5x - 23$.   13. $y = -\dfrac{1}{7}x + \dfrac{46}{7}$.
14. $y = \dfrac{6}{7}x + \dfrac{51}{7}$.   15. $y = x$.
16. $y = 9x + 14$.   17. $y = \dfrac{3}{2}x$.
18. $y = 4$.   19. $y = -\dfrac{3}{2}x$.   20. $x = -7$.
21. $y = \dfrac{1}{2}x + \dfrac{7}{2}$.   22. $y = 5$.   23. $y = 0$.
24. $y = -\dfrac{5}{7}x - \dfrac{29}{7}$.   25. $y = 0$.   26. $x = 0$.

Problem Set 1–4 (*continued*)

27. $-24/7$.   **28.** -2.   **29.** $x = -6$.
30. a) $y = 3$.
    b) The tangent is the horizontal line $y = 500$
    and shows the maximum (highest) profit
    is 500.
31. a) $y = 5$.   b) $x = -10$.
32. $y = 0.25x + 50$.   **33.** $y = 3x + 50$.
34. $y = 3x + 10$.   **35.** a) $y = 0.8m + 0.5$.
    b) $E = 0.1V + 50$. The slope is the rate of
    commission.
36. F.   **37.** T.   **38.** T.   **39.** F.   **40.** T.   **41.** T.
42. See Figure E.

FIGURE E

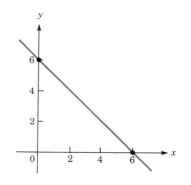

43. See Figure F.

FIGURE F

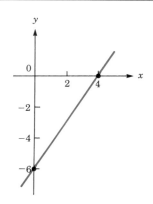

44. See Figure G.

FIGURE G

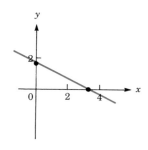

45. See Figure H.

FIGURE H

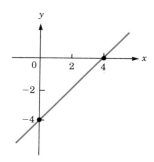

46. See Figure I.

FIGURE I

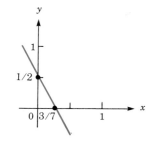

Problem Set 1–4 (*concluded*)

47. 3/2.   **48.** −1.   **49.** 1/3.   **50.** 1.
51. a) $8x + 12y = 96$.
　　b) 1.5 pounds of A per pound of B.
　　c) 2/3 pounds of B per pound of A.
52. $y = 2x − 6$.
53. If the equation is solved for y, the coefficient of x, which is the slope, turns out to be $−a/b$.
54. y/x is cost per unit; $y/x = 3$ or $y = 3x$ is the equation; slope is 3, and intercepts zero (line passes through the origin).
55. a) $y = \frac{3}{2}x + 4$.   b) $y = −3x − 12$.

56. $2,200.   **57.** $y = 2x$.   **58.** $y = 0.8x$.

59. a) D is a right angle; hence, angle 1 is $90° −$ angle BDC. DBC is a right triangle; hence, angle 2 is $90° −$ angle BDC. Therefore, angle 1 = angle 2, and triangles ABD and DBC are similar because they have equal angles. It follows that corresponding sides are in proportion, so that $DB/AB = BC/DB = 1/(DB/BC)$, where DB/AB is the slope of l_2 and DB/BC is the slope of l_1.
　　b) A horizontal and a vertical line do not have reciprocal slopes because 1/0 is not a number.
60. a) 1.25 miles to the right of the origin.
　　b) Because the shortest distance from a point to a line is on a perpendicular to the line.
61. The coordinates of the origin (0, 0), satisfy any equation of the form $ax + by = 0$.
62. F.   **63.** T.   **64.** T.   **65.** T.   **66.** T.
67. T.   **68.** T.   **69.** T.   **70.** T.   **71.** T.

Problem Set 1–5

1. T.   **2.** T.   **3.** F.   **4.** T.   **5.** F.
6. T.   **7.** T.   **8.** T.   **9.** T.   **10.** T.
11. a) 150. b) 170. c) 3. d) 3.40. e) 3.
12. a) $10,000.   b) $10,500.
　　c) $10.   d) $10.
13. a) $y = 5x + 2500$.   b) $10,000.
　　c) $2,500. d) $5. e) $6.25. f) $5.
14. a), b), c) See Figure J.

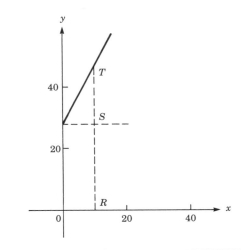

　　d) $RS = 25 =$ fixed cost; $ST = 20 =$ variable cost for 10 units; $RT = 45 =$ total cost for 10 units.
15. a) AB.   b) AD.   c) BD.
　　d) BD/OA.   e) AD/OA.   f) AB/OA.
　　g) EB.   h) BD/OA.
16. a) Setup cost, or fixed cost.
　　b) Variable cost if OM units are made.
　　c) Variable cost per unit.
　　d) Average cost per unit if OM units are made.

Problem Set 1–6

1. T.   **2.** F.   **3.** T.   **4.** T.
5. F.   **6.** T.   **7.** T.   **8.** F.
9. T.   **10.** F.   **11.** F.   **12.** T.
13. a) $R = 5q$. $C = 2q + 60,000$.
　　b) $15,000.   c) Loss of $30,000.
　　d) 20,000 units.   e) $100,000.
　　f) See Figure K.
14. a) $R = 50q$. $C = 20q + 120,000$.
　　b) $180,000.   c) Loss of $90,000.
　　d) 4,000 units.   e) $200,000.
　　f) See Figure L.

Problem Set 1–6 (*continued*)

FIGURE K

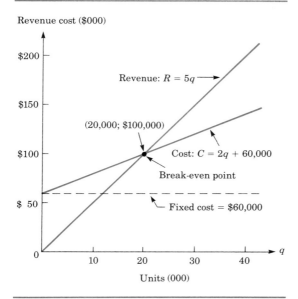

FIGURE L

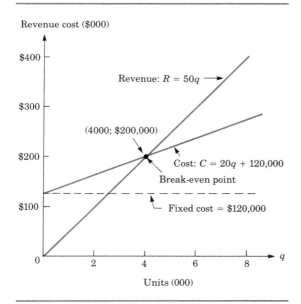

---

15. 2,500 units.   **16.** $5,500,000.
17. a) $200,000.
   b) The company should not shut down, because if it does the loss will be $200,000
   but if it produces and sells 1,000 units
   the loss will be $120,000, which is a
   smaller loss than $200,000.
18. a) $500,000.
   b) The company should not shut down, because if it does the loss will be $500,000
   but if it produces and sells 100,000 units
   the loss will be $450,000, which is a
   smaller loss than $500,000.
19. T.   **20.** T.   **21.** T.   **22.** T.   **23.** T.
24. T.   **25.** F.   **26.** F.   **27.** F.   **28.** T.
29. a) $60,000.   b) $y = 0.62x + 22,800$.
   c) $5,700.   d) See Figure M.

FIGURE M

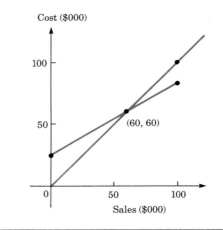

---

30. a) $80,000.   b) $y = 0.55x + 36,000$.
   c) −$2,250.   d) See Figure N.
31. a) $0.47.   b) $29,786.   c) $63,626.
   d) $56,200.   e) $12,614.
32. a) $12,800.   b) $23,800.
   c) $35,000.   d) $3,400 loss.
33. $1,000.
34. a), b) See Figures O and P.

Problem Set 1–6 (*concluded*)

FIGURE N

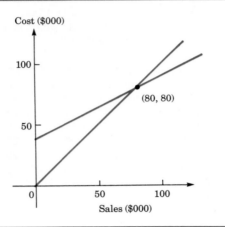

FIGURE O

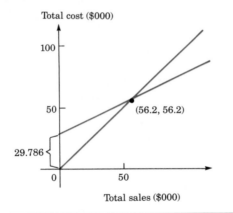

FIGURE P

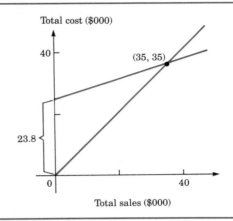

35. The shift is 50 to the left horizontally, so demand is 50 units less at every price level. The shift is 5 downward vertically, so price is $5 per unit less at every level of demand.

36. The shift is 200 to the right horizontally, so demand is 200 units greater at every price level. The shift is 10 upward vertically, so price is $10 per unit higher at every level of demand.

37. a) Demand is a constant number of units at every level of price per unit.
   b) Price per unit is constant at every level of demand.

38. Demand is the constant function $q = 100$ tons per week, a vertical line.

39. The demand function is a horizontal line, $p = $ a constant.

CHAPTER 2

Problem Set 2–1

1. (2, 3). 2. (−1, 4). 3. (1, 1).
4. (3/2, 2). 5. (1/2, 2/3). 6. (1/2, 3/2).
7. 375 liters of regular and 625 liters of un-leaded.
8. Invest $20,000 in Acme and $30,000 in Star.
9. Make 15 double-edged and 10 single-edged.
10. Make 5 captain's and 50 regular.

Problem Set 2–2

1. a) See Figure A. b) $E(70, 15)$.
   c) See Figure A. d) $E'(40, 12)$.
   e) The decrease in demand was accompanied by a lower demand and a lower price per unit at equilibrium.

FIGURE A

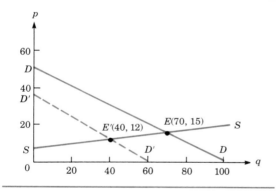

2. a) See Figure B. b) $E(100, 30)$.
   c) See Figure B. d) $E'(80, 38)$.
   e) The decrease in supply was accompanied by a lower supply but a higher price per unit at equilibrium.
3. $E'(125, 35)$. The increase in demand was accompanied by a higher demand and a higher price at equilibrium.
4. $E'(80, 10)$. The increase in supply was accompanied by a higher supply but a lower price at equilibrium.

FIGURE B

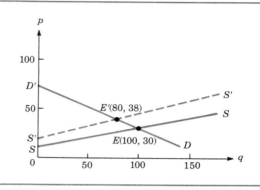

5. The demand function shifted to the right. At the new equilibrium, both demand and price are higher.
6. The supply function shifted to the left. At the new equilibrium, supply is lower but price is higher.
7. The supply function shifted to the right. At the new equilibrium, supply is higher but price is lower.
8. The demand function shifted to the left. At the new equilibrium, both demand and price are lower.
9. The supply function shifted to the right because a right shift of a supply function leads to a new equilibrium in which supply is *higher* but price is *lower*.
10. The demand function shifted to the left because with a left shift in demand *both* demand and price are lower at the new equilibrium.

Problem Set 2–3

1. No solutions. 2. No solutions.
3. No solutions. 4. No solutions.
5. Unlimited number of solutions.
6. Unlimited number of solutions.
7. Unlimited number of solutions.
8. Unlimited number of solutions.

Problem Set 2–4

1. a) A system in which the number of equations is m and the number of variables is n.

   b) A system in which the number of equations is the same as the number of variables.

   c) A system of three equations in two variables.

   d) The total number of variables appearing in the equations of the system.

   e) A linear combination of two equations is an equation formed by taking the sum of p times one equation plus q times the other, where p and q are any numbers.

2. a) x arbitrary, $y = \dfrac{3 - 3x}{4}$.

   b) y and z arbitrary, $x = 15 - 2y + 4z$.

3. a) A false statement, such as $0 = 4$.

   b) An identity, such as $0 = 0$.

4. See text.

5. a) $(3, -2)$. See Figure C.

FIGURE C

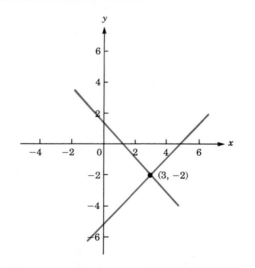

   b) $(3, -2)$. See Figure D.

   c) $(32/17, 3/17)$. See Figure E.

FIGURE D

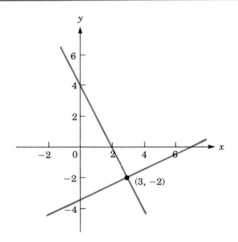

$(3, -2)$

FIGURE E

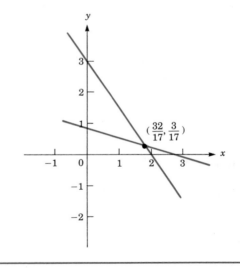

$\left(\dfrac{32}{17}, \dfrac{3}{17} \right)$

6. a) Parallel lines, no solutions.

   b) Lines have same graph.

7. $(1/2, 1, 3/2)$.

8. x arbitrary, $y = x - 2$, $z = 5 - x$.

9. x arbitrary, $y = 3 - 2x$, $z = 5 - 3x$.

10. $(2/5, -3, 3/5)$.

11. No solutions.   **12.** No solutions.

Problem Set 2–4 (*concluded*)

13. x arbitrary, $y = 17 - 17x$, $z = 22 - 9x$.
14. $(1, 2, 3)$.   **15.** No solutions.
16. $(-2, -1, 6)$.

Problem Set 2–5

1. $x = 10$, $y = 15$, $z = 20$.
2. $x = 10$, $y = 15$, $z = 20$.
3. The solution is y arbitrary, $x = 2 + y$,
   $z = 10 - 3y$; however, y must be between 0
   and 3, inclusive.
4. $x = 2$, $y = 0$, $z = 10$.
5. The solution requires that $y = -2$, which is
   not permissible. The problem has no solution.
6. a) z units of C, arbitrary from 5 through 8;
      x units of A, where $x = 80 - 10z$; y units
      of B, where $y = z - 5$.
   b) Maximum is $800, making 30 units of A,
      no B, and 5 units of C.
7. a) z units of C, arbitrary from 0 through 4;
      y units of B, where $y = z$; x units of A,
      where $x = 40 - 10z$.
   b) Maximum is $800, making 40 units of A
      and no B or C.
8. a) $p_1 = \$415$, $q_1 = 65$ units;
      $p_2 = \$445$, $q_2 = 65$ units.
   b) $p_1 = \$474$, $q_1 = 96$ units;
      $p_2 = \$472$, $q_2 = 64$ units.
9. a) $p_1 = \$800$, $q_1 = 100$ units;
      $p_2 = \$400$, $q_2 = 100$ units.
   b) $p_1 = \$740$, $q_1 = 60$ units;
      $p_2 = \$420$, $q_2 = 160$ units.

Problem Set 2–6

1. See Figure F.
2. See Figure G.
3. See Figure H.
4. See Figure I.
5. See Figure J.
6. If $2 \le x \le 30/7$, $0 \le y \le (x - 2)/2$;
   if $30/7 \le x \le 6$, $0 \le y \le (12 - 2x)/3$.
7. $0 \le x \le 52/19$, $(8 - x)/5 \le y \le 12 - 4x$.
8. If $52/19 \le x \le 3$, $12 - 4x \le y \le (8 - x)/5$;
   if $3 \le x \le 8$, $0 \le y \le (8 - x)/5$.

FIGURE F

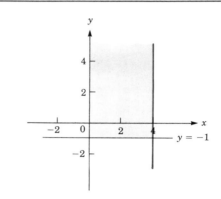

FIGURE G

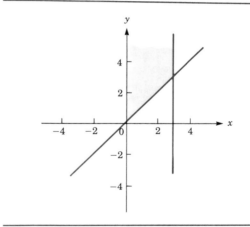

9. If $0 \le x \le 52/19$, $y \ge 12 - 4x$;
   if $52/19 \le x \le 8$, $y \ge (8 - x)/5$;
   if $x \ge 8$, $y \ge 0$.
10. a) $h \le (76 - L)/2$; $0 < L < 76$.
   b) $x \le (108 - L)/4$; $0 < L < 108$.
11. $0 \le x \le 10$, $8 - 0.5x \le y \le (45 - 3x)/5$.
12. $x = 0$, $y = 8$.
13. If $0 \le x \le 320$, $0 \le y \le (2400 - 3x)/8$;
   if $320 \le x \le 500$, $0 \le y \le 500 - x$.

Problem Set 2–6 (*concluded*)

FIGURE H

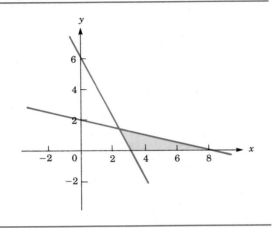

FIGURE I

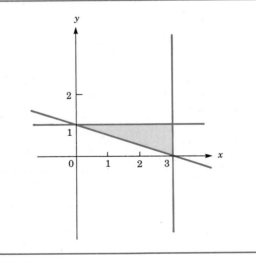

FIGURE J

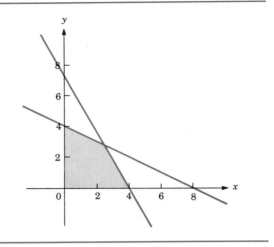

14. a) $0 \le x \le 2, 0 \le y \le 5 - x$;
$2 \le x \le 7/2, 0 \le y \le 7 - 2x$.
b)

x	y
0	0, 1, 2, 3, 4, 5
1	0, 1, 2, 3, 4
2	0, 1, 2, 3
3	0, 1

15. Letting x be the number of single-edged razor blades and y the number of double-edged razor blades,
$0 \le x \le 9/2, 0 \le y \le 2x$;
$9/2 \le x \le 18, 0 \le y \le (36 - 2x)/3$.

16. $0 \le x \le 13, x/4 \le y \le 4x$;
$13 \le x \le 88, x/4 \le y \le (286 - 2x)/5$.

17. $0 \le x \le 20, 0 \le y \le (40 - x)/2$;
$20 \le x \le 27, 0 \le y \le (190 - 6x)/7$;
$27 \le x \le 30, 0 \le y \le (120 - 4x)/3$.

18. $20 \le x \le 24$,
$(190 - 6x)/7 \le y \le (40 - x)/2$;
$24 \le x \le 27$,
$(190 - 6x)/7 \le y \le (120 - 4x)/3$.

CHAPTER 3

Problem Set 3–1

1. a) 7 at (3, 4).   b) 16.5 at (0, 5.5).
   c) 18 at (6, 0).
   d) 12 on line segment joining (6, 0) and (3, 4).
2. a) 58 at (7, 3).   b) 28 at (14, 0).
   c) 44 at (0, 22/5).
   d) 21 on line segment joining (14, 0) and (7, 3).
3. a) 6 at (6, 0).   b) 29 at (3, 2).
   c) 17 at (0, 17).
   d) 17 on line segment joining (0, 17) and (3, 2).
4. a) 15 at (15/2, 0).   b) 19 at (0, 19/2).
   c) 14 at (5, 2).
   d) 60 on line segment joining (5, 2) and (15/2, 0).
5. a) 2.3 at (1, 4).   b) 7 at (2, 3).
   c) 15 at (3, 0).
   d) 15 on line segment joining (1, 4) and (2, 3).
6. a) 92 at (4, 9).   b) 16 at (4, 0).
   c) 77 at (0, 11).
   d) 110 on line segment joining (0, 11) and (4, 9).
7. a) 64/5 at (8/5, 48/5).
   b) 72/5 at (24/5, 24/5).
   c) 32 on line segment joining (8/5, 48/5) and (0, 16).
   d) 48 on line segment joining (24/5, 24/5) and (8/5, 48/5).
8. a) 14 at (4, 10).   b) 46 at (4, 10).
   c) 36 at (0, 18).
   d) 104 on line segment joining (4, 10) and (12, 4).
9. $106 at (9, 2).   10. $32,400 at (12, 6).
11. $61 at (5, 2).   12. $44 at (7, 3).
13. $145 at (13, 4). Machine B is not fully utilized.
14. $22 at (8, 4).   15. $22 at (8, 4).
16. a) $15,600 at (4, 10). No grades are over-produced.
   b) $36,000 on line segment joining (4, 10) and (24, 0). At (4, 10), no grades are overproduced. At all other points, AA and A are both overproduced.

Problem Set 3–2

1. a) 12 at (4,0).   b) 136/7 at (10/7, 36/7).
2. 20.5 at (80, 30).
3. a) 60 at (0, 12) and 45 at (0, 9).
   b) 48 at (6, 6) and 18 at (0, 9).
   c) 36 on line segment joining (0, 12) and (6, 6), and 27 at (0, 9).
4. a) 60 at (0, 12) and 45 at (0, 9).
   b) 40 at (4, 8) and 18 at (0, 9).
   c) 36 on line segment joining (0, 12) and (4, 8), and 27 at (0, 9).
5. See the answers to Problem 3.
6. The feasible solution set is empty, so there is no maximum or minimum.
7. a) 44 at (8, 2) and 42 at (6, 6).
   b) 48 at (6, 6) and 22 at (8, 2).
   c) Maximum and minimum are both 36 on line segment joining (6, 6) and (8, 2).
8. a) Maximum and minimum are both 43 at (7, 4).
   b) Maximum and minimum are both 35 at (7, 4).
   c) Maximum and minimum are both 36 at (7, 4).
9. The feasible solution set is empty so there is no maximum or minimum.
10. a) 33 at (6, 4) and −7 at (0, 0).
    b) 43 at (3, 6) and −2 at (4, 0).
    c) 25 at (0, 0) and 4 at (3, 6).
    d) 50 on line segment joining (4, 0) and (6, 4), and 2 at (0, 4).
11. a) $15,600 at (4, 10). No grades are over-produced.
    b) $36,000 on line segment joining (4, 10) and (10, 7). At (4, 10), no grades are overproduced. At all other points, AA and A are overproduced.
12. $7 at (1, 3).   13. $7.25 at (1.25, 2.25).
14. $0.90 at (3, 1).   15. $0.75 at (1.5, 1.5).

Problem Set 3–3

1. 580 at (520, 320, 0).
2. 228 at (120, 0, 360).
3. 9.5 at (11/3, 0, 2).

Problem Set 3–3 (*concluded*)

4. 30.5 at (1/2, 57/4, 0).
5. $2,000 at (0, 0, 1000).
6. $0.39 at (4/3, 7/3, 7/3).
7. $190 at (0, 40, 75).   **8.** $106 at (2, 3, 6).
9. $26 at (8, 4, 2).   **10.** $46 at (3, 5, 4).

Problem Set 3–4

1. 1,122,750 at (75, 15).
2. a) $165,000 at (1600, 400).
   b) $385,000 at (1000, 3000).
3. a) 23,250 at (50, 50, 20).   b) $9,500.
   c) $5,700 at (30, 30, 60).
4. $26,000 at (4, 10).
5. Maximize
$$2x + y + 4z$$
subject to
$$
\begin{aligned}
x &\leq 50 \quad \text{(redundant)} \\
y &\leq 50 \\
z &\leq 10 \\
x + y + z &\geq 40 \\
x + y + z &\leq 60 \\
z &\geq 5 \\
-x + y &\geq 1 \\
-x + y - 2z &\geq 10 \\
x, y, z &\geq 0. \quad \text{(only } x \geq 0 \text{ needed)}
\end{aligned}
$$
56 corners.

6. Minimize
$$5.75x + 4.75y + 3.75z$$
subject to
$$
\begin{aligned}
x + y + z &\leq 10{,}000 \\
x + y + z &\geq 6{,}000 \\
z &\leq 2{,}000 \\
x, y, z &\geq 1{,}000 \\
x + y - 3z &\geq 0 \\
x, y, z &\geq 0. \quad \text{(redundant)}
\end{aligned}
$$
35 corners.

7. Maximize
$$18x + 23y + 15z$$
subject to
$$
\begin{aligned}
4x + 5y + 3z &\leq 425 \\
x + 2y + z &\leq 140 \\
3x + 4y + 3z &\leq 350 \\
8x + 10y + 9z &\geq 500 \\
7x + 8y + 4z &\geq 400 \\
6x + 6y + 7z &\geq 300 \\
x, y, z &\geq 0.
\end{aligned}
$$
84 corners.

Problem Set 3–4 (*continued*)

8. Maximize

$$0.08S_1 + 0.09S_2 + 0.07S_3 + 0.1B_1 + 0.11B_2 + 0.06N$$

subject to

$$
\begin{aligned}
S_1 + S_2 + S_3 - 0.4B_1 - 0.4B_2 &\leq 0 \\
N &\geq 2{,}500{,}000 \\
S_1 + S_2 + S_3 &\leq 3{,}500{,}000 \\
S_1, S_2, S_3, B_1, B_2 &\leq 3{,}000{,}000 \\
S_1 + S_2 + S_3 + B_1 + B_2 + N &= 10{,}000{,}000 \\
\text{All variables} &\geq 0.
\end{aligned}
$$

9. Maximize

$$30x_{1A} + 60x_{1F} + 100x_{1S} + 75x_{1T} + 5x_{2A} + 80x_{2F} + 65x_{2S} + 110x_{2T}$$

subject to

$$
\begin{aligned}
x_{1A} + x_{2A} &\leq 5{,}000 \\
x_{1F} + x_{2F} &\leq 3{,}000 \\
x_{1S} + x_{2S} &\leq 2{,}000 \\
x_{1T} + x_{2T} &\leq 1{,}000 \\
4x_{1A} + 4x_{1F} + 3x_{1S} &\leq 2{,}100 \\
8x_{1A} + 10x_{1F} + 6x_{1S} + 7x_{1T} &\leq 14{,}000 \\
x_{2A} + 5x_{2S} + 5x_{2T} &\leq 1{,}500 \\
3x_{2A} + 8x_{2F} + 6x_{2T} &\leq 2{,}400 \\
x_{2A} + x_{2F} + 11x_{2S} + 20x_{2T} &\leq 2{,}500 \\
\text{All variables} &\geq 0.
\end{aligned}
$$

10. a) Minimize

$$250x_{JR} + 350x_{JS} + 300x_{AR} + 375x_{AS} + 25x_I$$

subject to

$$
\begin{aligned}
x_{JR} + x_{JS} &\geq 600 \\
x_{AR} + x_{AS} + x_I &\geq 500 \\
x_{JR} &\leq 650 \\
x_{JS} &\leq 200 \\
x_{AR} &\leq 450 \\
x_{AS} &\leq 150 \\
x_{JR} + x_{JS} - x_I &= 600 \\
\text{All variables} &\geq 0.
\end{aligned}
$$

b) Minimize

$$275x_{JRJ} + 275x_{JRA} + 375x_{JSJ} + 375x_{JSA} + 300x_{AR} + 375x_{AS} - 15{,}000$$

subject to

$$
\begin{aligned}
x_{JRJ} + x_{JSJ} &\geq 600 \\
x_{JRA} + x_{JSA} + x_{AR} + x_{AS} &\geq 500 \\
x_{JRJ} + x_{JRA} &\leq 650 \\
x_{JSJ} + x_{JSA} &\leq 200 \\
x_{AR} &\leq 450 \\
x_{AS} &\leq 150 \\
\text{All variables} &\geq 0.
\end{aligned}
$$

If the first constraint is changed to an "$=$", then the objective function is changed to

$$250x_{JRJ} + 275x_{JRA} + 350x_{JSJ} + 375x_{JSA} + 300x_{AR} + 375x_{AS}.$$

11. Minimize

$$x_1 + x_2 + x_3 + x_4 + x_5 + x_6$$

subject to

$$
\begin{aligned}
x_1 + x_6 &\geq 12 \\
x_1 + x_2 &\geq 14 \\
x_2 + x_3 &\geq 16 \\
x_3 + x_4 &\geq 10 \\
x_4 + x_5 &\geq 6 \\
x_5 + x_6 &\geq 9 \\
\text{All } x_i &\geq 0.
\end{aligned}
$$

Problem Set 3–4 (*concluded*)

12. a) (6, 0, 0), 0; (4, 1, 0), 4; (3, 0, 1), 7;
(2, 2, 0), 8; (2, 1, 1), 1; (1, 3, 0), 2;
(1, 0, 7), 4; (0, 2, 1), 5.

b) Minimize
$$4x_2 + 7x_3 + 8x_4 + x_5 + 2x_6 + 4x_7 + 5x_8$$
subject to
$$6x_1 + 4x_2 + 3x_3 + 2x_4 + 2x_5 + x_6 + x_7 \geq 50$$
$$x_2 + 2x_4 + x_5 + 3x_6 + x_8 \geq 75$$
$$x_3 + x_5 + 2x_7 + x_8 \geq 85$$
$$\text{All } x_i \geq 0.$$

c) Minimize
$$60(x_1 + x_2 + x_3 + x_4 + x_5 + x_6) - 3{,}655$$
subject to the constraints in (b).

CHAPTER 4

Problem Set 4–1

1. (3 1 7).

2. $\begin{pmatrix} -2 \\ 2 \end{pmatrix}$.

3. $\begin{pmatrix} 10 \\ 13 \end{pmatrix}$.

4. (8 0 4).

5. $\begin{pmatrix} 21 \\ 6 \end{pmatrix}$.

6. (−10 18 −6).

7. 41.

8. 5.

9. $\begin{pmatrix} 4 & -4 & 0 \\ -2 & 6 & 5 \end{pmatrix}$.

10. $\begin{pmatrix} 3 & 9 \\ 2 & -7 \end{pmatrix}$.

11. $\begin{pmatrix} -2 & -27 & 17 \\ 17 & -2 & -9 \end{pmatrix}$.

12. $\begin{pmatrix} 5 & -4 & 5 \\ 14 & -10 & 15 \end{pmatrix}$.

13. (26 35).

14. $\begin{pmatrix} 3 & 18 \\ 3 & -30 \end{pmatrix}$.

15. $\begin{pmatrix} 13 & 16 \\ 8 & 7 \\ -5 & -9 \end{pmatrix}$.

16. $\begin{pmatrix} 7 & -1 & 5 & 6 \\ 11 & 3 & 8 & 13 \end{pmatrix}$.

17. $\begin{pmatrix} 1 & 4 \\ 2 & 5 \\ 3 & 6 \end{pmatrix}$.

18. $\begin{pmatrix} 1 & 2 & 3 \\ 3 & 2 & 1 \end{pmatrix}$.

19. (0.06 0.07 0.08) $\begin{pmatrix} 3000 \\ 2000 \\ 4000 \end{pmatrix}$ = $640.

20. a) (10 20) $\begin{pmatrix} 8 & 2 & 5 \\ 4 & 8 & 3 \end{pmatrix}$ = (160 180 110).

The first component of the right vector, 160, is 10 batches of Superior times 8 pounds of beef per batch, plus 20 batches of Regular times 4 pounds of beef per batch, for a total of 160 pounds of beef to make the required number of batches. Similarly, we see that 180 pounds of pork and 110 pounds of lamb will be required.

b) $\begin{pmatrix} 8 & 2 & 5 \\ 4 & 8 & 3 \end{pmatrix} \begin{pmatrix} 2.50 \\ 2.00 \\ 3.00 \end{pmatrix} = \begin{pmatrix} 39 \\ 35 \end{pmatrix}$.

The component in the answer, 39, is 8 pounds of beef times $2.50 per pound, plus 2 pounds of pork at $2 per pound, plus 5 pounds of lamb at $3 per pound, so the total cost of a batch of Superior is $39. Similarly, the total cost of a batch of Regular is $35.

Problem Set 4–2

1. $\begin{pmatrix} 2 & 3 \\ 1 & 2 \end{pmatrix} \begin{pmatrix} x_1 \\ x_2 \end{pmatrix} = \begin{pmatrix} 5 \\ 3 \end{pmatrix}$.

2. $\begin{pmatrix} 1 & 2 \\ 2 & 3 \end{pmatrix} \begin{pmatrix} x_1 \\ x_2 \end{pmatrix} + \begin{pmatrix} y_1 \\ y_2 \end{pmatrix} = \begin{pmatrix} 10 \\ 12 \end{pmatrix}$.

3. $\begin{pmatrix} 3 & 0 & 1 & -1 \\ 2 & 1 & 0 & -5 \\ 0 & 1 & 3 & 1 \end{pmatrix} \begin{pmatrix} x_1 \\ x_2 \\ x_3 \\ x_4 \end{pmatrix} \leq \begin{pmatrix} 5 \\ 10 \\ 8 \end{pmatrix}$.

Problem Set 4–2 (*concluded*)

4. $3x_1 + x_2 + 2x_3 = 5$
 $x_1 + 4x_2 + x_3 = 4.$

5. $2x_1 + 3x_2 = 5$
 $4x_1 + 6x_2 = 10$
 $x_1 + 7x_2 = 6.$

6. $3x_1 + x_2 = 2$
 $5x_1 + 4x_2 = 6.$

7. $p_{11}x_1 + p_{12}x_2 + p_{13}x_3 + p_{14}x_4 = q_1$
 $p_{21}x_1 + p_{22}x_2 + p_{23}x_3 + p_{24}x_4 = q_2$
 $p_{31}x_1 + p_{32}x_2 + p_{33}x_3 + p_{34}x_4 = q_3.$

8. $2x_1 + x_2 + 5x_3 + y_1 = 10$
 $4x_1 + 6x_2 + 2x_3 + y_2 = 5.$

9. a) $\boldsymbol{y}$ must be q by 1, and $\boldsymbol{g}$ must be p by 1.
 b) $\boldsymbol{Ay} = \boldsymbol{g}.$

Problem Set 4–3

1. a) 60 percent of customers who last purchased Technics will purchase Technics
 again, and 40 percent will switch to
 Soneton.
 b) (0.55   0.45) and (0.555   0.445).
 c) (5/9 Technics   4/9 Soneton).

2. a) (0.29 spender   0.71 saver).
 b) (1/8 spender   7/8 saver).

3. a) (0.01099 users   0.98901 nonusers).
 b) This is an absorbing chain. The steady
 state is 100 percent users or the state
 vector (1   0).

4. a) (0.20798 owners   0.79202 nonowners).
 b) (0.9901 owners   0.0099 nonowners).

5. a) (0.8519 owners   0.1481 nonowners).
 b) (0.99992 owners   0.00008 nonowners).

6. The new state vector is the original (a b)
 because the ones in the transition matrix
 mean that all in state #1 remain in #1 and
 all in state #2 remain in #2.

7. (0.3   0.1   0.6); (0.1   0.6   0.3);
 (0.6   0.3   0.1).

Problem Set 4–4

1. $\begin{pmatrix} 1 & -3 \\ -2 & 7 \end{pmatrix}.$ **2.** $\begin{pmatrix} 1 & -4 \\ -2 & 9 \end{pmatrix}.$

3. $\begin{pmatrix} 5/4 & -1/2 \\ -3/4 & 1/2 \end{pmatrix}.$ **4.** $\begin{pmatrix} 2 & 1 \\ 1 & 1 \end{pmatrix}.$

5. Inverse does not exist.

6. Inverse does not exist.

7. $\begin{pmatrix} 0 & 1/2 \\ 1/3 & -1/6 \end{pmatrix}.$ **8.** $\begin{pmatrix} -4/7 & 5/7 \\ 3/7 & -2/7 \end{pmatrix}.$

9. $\begin{pmatrix} -3/2 & 1/2 \\ 1 & 0 \end{pmatrix}.$ **10.** $\begin{pmatrix} -5/6 & 3/6 \\ 2/6 & 0 \end{pmatrix}.$

11. $\begin{pmatrix} 1 & 2 & 1 \\ 4 & 5 & -3 \\ 3 & 4 & -2 \end{pmatrix}.$ **12.** $\begin{pmatrix} 3/2 & -3 & -1/2 \\ 2 & -3 & -1 \\ -2 & 4 & 1 \end{pmatrix}.$

13. Inverse does not exist.

14. $\begin{pmatrix} 2 & 2 & 3 \\ 0 & 1 & 1 \\ 1 & 1 & 1 \end{pmatrix}.$ **15.** $\begin{pmatrix} -4/9 & 5/9 & 2/9 \\ -7/9 & 2/9 & 8/9 \\ 2/3 & -1/3 & -1/3 \end{pmatrix}.$

16. Inverse does not exist.

17. a) $\begin{pmatrix} 1 & 0 & 0 \\ 0 & 1 & 0 \\ 0 & 0 & 1 \end{pmatrix}.$ b) $\begin{pmatrix} 1 & 1 & 1 \\ 1 & 1 & 1 \\ 1 & 1 & 1 \end{pmatrix}.$

Problem Set 4–5

1. a) $\boldsymbol{A} = \begin{pmatrix} 8 & 5 \\ 3 & 2 \end{pmatrix}; \boldsymbol{x} = \begin{pmatrix} x_1 \\ x_2 \end{pmatrix}; \boldsymbol{b} = \begin{pmatrix} 2 \\ 1 \end{pmatrix}.$

 b) $(-1 \quad 2).$ c) $\boldsymbol{A}^{-1} = \begin{pmatrix} 2 & -5 \\ -3 & 8 \end{pmatrix}.$

 d) $\begin{pmatrix} x_1 \\ x_2 \end{pmatrix} = \begin{pmatrix} 2 & -5 \\ -3 & 8 \end{pmatrix} \begin{pmatrix} 2 \\ 1 \end{pmatrix}.$

 e) $(-1 \quad 2).$
 f) (1) $(2 \quad -3).$ (2) $(-5 \quad 8).$
  (3) $(-3 \quad 5).$ (4) $(-14 \quad 23).$
  (5) $(-11 \quad 17).$

2. a) $\boldsymbol{A} = \begin{pmatrix} 4 & 3 \\ 9 & 7 \end{pmatrix}; \boldsymbol{x} = \begin{pmatrix} x_1 \\ x_2 \end{pmatrix}; \boldsymbol{b} = \begin{pmatrix} 2 \\ 3 \end{pmatrix}.$

 b) $(5 \quad -6).$ c) $\boldsymbol{A}^{-1} = \begin{pmatrix} 7 & -3 \\ -9 & 4 \end{pmatrix}.$

 d) $\begin{pmatrix} x_1 \\ x_2 \end{pmatrix} = \begin{pmatrix} 7 & -3 \\ -9 & 4 \end{pmatrix} \begin{pmatrix} 2 \\ 3 \end{pmatrix}.$

 e) $(5 \quad -6).$
 f) (1) $(7 \quad -9).$ (2) $(-3 \quad 4).$
  (3) $(4 \quad -5).$ (4) $(11 \quad -14).$
  (5) $(-13 \quad 17).$

3. a) $\boldsymbol{A} = \begin{pmatrix} 6 & 8 \\ 2 & 3 \end{pmatrix}; \boldsymbol{x} = \begin{pmatrix} x_1 \\ x_2 \end{pmatrix}; \boldsymbol{b} = \begin{pmatrix} 3 \\ 1 \end{pmatrix}.$

 b) $(1/2 \quad 0).$ c) $\boldsymbol{A}^{-1} = \begin{pmatrix} 3/2 & -4 \\ -1 & 3 \end{pmatrix}.$

Problem Set 4–5 (concluded)

d) $\begin{pmatrix} x_1 \\ x_2 \end{pmatrix} = \begin{pmatrix} 3/2 & -4 \\ -1 & 3 \end{pmatrix} \begin{pmatrix} 3 \\ 1 \end{pmatrix}$.

e) $(1/2 \quad 0)$.

f) (1) $(-5/2 \quad 2)$. (2) $(-4 \quad 3)$.
(3) $(3/2 \quad -1)$. (4) $(-9 \quad 7)$.
(5) $(-11/2 \quad 4)$.

4. $\begin{pmatrix} 1 & 7/5 \\ 1 & 8/5 \end{pmatrix}$.

5. a) $\mathbf{A} = \begin{pmatrix} 3 & 0 & 5 \\ 2 & 2 & 5 \\ 0 & 1 & 1 \end{pmatrix}; \mathbf{x} = \begin{pmatrix} x_1 \\ x_2 \\ x_3 \end{pmatrix}; \mathbf{b} = \begin{pmatrix} 3 \\ 7 \\ 2 \end{pmatrix}$.

b) $(6 \quad 5 \quad -3)$.

c) $\mathbf{A}^{-1} = \begin{pmatrix} -3 & 5 & -10 \\ -2 & 3 & -5 \\ 2 & -3 & 6 \end{pmatrix}$.

d) $\begin{pmatrix} x_1 \\ x_2 \\ x_3 \end{pmatrix} = \begin{pmatrix} -3 & 5 & -10 \\ -2 & 3 & -5 \\ 2 & -3 & 6 \end{pmatrix} \begin{pmatrix} 3 \\ 7 \\ 2 \end{pmatrix}$.

e) $(6 \quad 5 \quad -3)$.

f) (1) $(-3 \quad -1 \quad 2)$. (2) $(-31 \quad -15 \quad 19)$.
(3) $(7 \quad 3 \quad -4)$. (4) $(7 \quad 6 \quad -4)$.
(5) $(34 \quad 21 \quad -20)$.

6. a) $\mathbf{A} = \begin{pmatrix} 7 & 3 & 0 \\ 0 & 3 & 5 \\ 1 & 1 & 1 \end{pmatrix}; \mathbf{x} = \begin{pmatrix} x_1 \\ x_2 \\ x_3 \end{pmatrix}; \mathbf{b} = \begin{pmatrix} 1 \\ 2 \\ 3 \end{pmatrix}$.

b) $(37 \quad -86 \quad 52)$.

c) $\mathbf{A}^{-1} = \begin{pmatrix} -2 & -3 & 15 \\ 5 & 7 & -35 \\ -3 & -4 & 21 \end{pmatrix}$.

d) $\begin{pmatrix} x_1 \\ x_2 \\ x_3 \end{pmatrix} = \begin{pmatrix} -2 & -3 & 15 \\ 5 & 7 & -35 \\ -3 & -4 & 21 \end{pmatrix} \begin{pmatrix} 1 \\ 2 \\ 3 \end{pmatrix}$.

e) $(37 \quad -86 \quad 52)$.

f) (1) $(16 \quad -37 \quad 22)$.
(2) $(-13 \quad 31 \quad -18)$.
(3) $(-34 \quad 79 \quad -47)$.
(4) $(-2 \quad 8 \quad -5)$. (5) $(3 \quad -7 \quad 4)$.

7. $\begin{pmatrix} 3/2 & -3 & -1/2 \\ 2 & -3 & -1 \\ -2 & 4 & 1 \end{pmatrix}$.

8. b) (1) $(-3 \quad 0 \quad 6)$. (2) $(0 \quad 3 \quad 0)$.
9. b) (1) $(1 \quad 0 \quad 0 \quad 0)$. (2) $(2 \quad -2 \quad 2 \quad -1)$.

10. a) $x_1 + \qquad 2x_3 = H_1$
$\qquad x_2 + 3x_3 = H_2$
$\quad x_1 + 2x_2 \qquad = H_3$.

b) $\mathbf{A} = \begin{pmatrix} 1 & 0 & 2 \\ 0 & 1 & 3 \\ 1 & 2 & 0 \end{pmatrix}$.

$\mathbf{A}^{-1} = \frac{1}{8} \begin{pmatrix} 6 & -4 & 2 \\ -3 & 2 & 3 \\ 1 & 2 & -1 \end{pmatrix}$.

c) $(130 \quad 35 \quad 15)$. d) $(200 \quad 100 \quad 100)$.
e) $(208 \quad 24 \quad 56)$.

11. No solutions. **12.** No solutions.
13. No solutions. **14.** No solutions.
15. Unlimited number of solutions.
16. Unlimited number of solutions.
17. Unlimited number of solutions.
18. Unlimited number of solutions.

Problem Set 4–6

1. $(9, \quad 4)$. **2.** $(-3, \quad -5)$.
3. No solutions.
4. Unlimited number of solutions.
5. $(3, \quad 5, \quad 4)$ **6.** $(-2, \quad -1, \quad 6)$.
7. No solutions.
8. Unlimited number of solutions.
9. $(7, \quad 5, \quad -3)$. **10.** $(8, \quad 9, \quad 2)$.
11. No solutions.
12. Unlimited number of solutions.
13. No solutions.
14. Unlimited number of solutions.
15. No solutions.
16. Unlimited number of solutions.
17. 3 dozens of Luscious Candy and 7 dozens of Delicious Candy.
18. 8 pounds of food X and 4 pounds of food Y.
19. Unlimited number of solutions given by

$$x_1 = \frac{1}{7}x_3 + \frac{17}{7}$$

$$x_2 = -\frac{5}{7}x_3 + \frac{55}{7}.$$

The only solutions with integral coordinates are (3, 5, 4) and (4, 0, 11).

20. Unlimited number of solutions given by

$$x_1 = -2x_4 + 10$$
$$x_2 = \quad 9x_4 - \quad 5$$
$$x_3 = -6x_4 + \quad 8.$$

Problem Set 4–6 (*concluded*)

The only solution with integral coordinates is (8, 4, 2, 1).

Problem Set 4–7

1. 22.   **2.** 15.   **3.** 230.   **4.** 45.

5. 36.   **6.** $\sum_{j=1}^{q} j$.   **7.** $\sum_{j=1}^{n} j^2$.   **8.** $\sum_{j=1}^{4} j^3$.

9. $\sum_{i=1}^{4} (i + 2)$.   **10.** $\sum_{i=1}^{5} (3i)$.

Problem Set 4–8

1. $y_1 + y_2 + y_3 + y_4 + y_5$.
2. $c_1 x_1 + c_2 x_2 + c_3 x_3$.
3. $b_1 y_1 + b_2 y_2 + \cdots + b_n y_n$.
4. $p_1 x_1 + p_2 x_2 + p_3 x_3 + p_4 x_4 + p_5 x_5 = 10$.
5. $a_1 x_1 + a_2 x_2 + \cdots + a_n x_n = c$.

6. $\sum_{i=1}^{4} x_i$.   **7.** $\sum_{i=1}^{6} a_i x_i = b$.

8. $\sum_{i=1}^{9} c_i x_i$.   **9.** $\sum_{i=1}^{q} a_i x_i$.

10. $n = 4$, $a_1 = 1$, $a_2 = 0$, $a_3 = 2$, $a_4 = 5$, $b = 7$.

Problem Set 4–9

1. $a_{11}x_1 + a_{12}x_2 + a_{13}x_3 + a_{14}x_4 = b_1$
  $a_{21}x_1 + a_{22}x_2 + a_{23}x_3 + a_{24}x_4 = b_2$.
2. Maximize
  $c_1 x_1 + c_2 x_2 + c_3 x_3$
  subject to
  $a_{11}x_1 + a_{12}x_2 + a_{13}x_3 \leq b_1$
  $a_{21}x_1 + a_{22}x_2 + a_{23}x_3 \leq b_2$
  $a_{31}x_1 + a_{32}x_2 + a_{33}x_3 \leq b_3$
  $a_{41}x_1 + a_{42}x_2 + a_{43}x_3 \leq b_4$
  $x_1 \geq 0$
  $x_2 \geq 0$
  $x_3 \geq 0$.
3. a) $a_{11}x_1 + a_{12}x_2 + \cdots + a_{1q}x_q = b_1$
  $a_{21}x_1 + a_{22}x_2 + \cdots + a_{2q}x_q = b_2$
  $\vdots \qquad \vdots \qquad\qquad \vdots \qquad \vdots$
  $a_{p1}x_1 + a_{p2}x_2 + \cdots + a_{pq}x_q = b_p$.

b) $\sum_{j=1}^{q} a_{ij}x_j = b_i; i = 1, 2, \cdots, p$.

4. a) Maximize
  $c_1 x_1 + c_2 x_2 + \cdots + c_q x_q$
  subject to
  $a_{11}x_1 + a_{12}x_2 + \cdots + a_{1q}x_q \leq b_1$
  $a_{21}x_1 + a_{22}x_2 + \cdots + a_{2q}x_q \leq b_2$
  $\vdots \qquad \vdots \qquad\qquad \vdots \qquad \vdots$
  $a_{p1}x_1 + a_{p2}x_2 + \cdots + a_{pq}x_q \leq b_p$
  $x_1 \geq 0$
  $x_2 \geq 0$
  $\vdots \qquad \vdots$
  $x_q \geq 0$.

b) Maximize
  $$\sum_{j=1}^{q} c_j x_j$$
  subject to
  $$\sum_{j=1}^{q} a_{ij}x_j \leq b_i; \quad i = 1, 2, \cdots, p$$
  and $x_j \geq 0$ for all j.

5. $\sum_{j=1}^{8} a_{ij}x_j = b_i; \quad i = 1, 2, \cdots, 6$.

6. a) m equations, n variables; $m = 3$, $n = 4$.
  b) $a_{11} = 2$, $a_{12} = 3$, $a_{24} = 8$, $a_{23} = 9$,
   $a_{33} = 7$, $a_{34} = 6$.
  c) $a_{13} = 0$, $b_1 = 20$, $a_{31} = 5$, $a_{22} = 0$,
   $a_{32} = 0$.

7. a) $C = x_1 d_1 + x_2 d_2 + \cdots + x_{10} d_{10}$.
  b) $C = \sum_{i=1}^{10} x_i d_i$.

8. a) $C = x_1 d_1 + x_2 d_2 + \cdots + x_p d_p$.
  b) $C = \sum_{i=1}^{p} x_i d_i$.

Problem Set 4–10

1. 12.   **2.** 21.
3. $x_1 + x_2 + x_3 + x_4 + x_5 - 5a$.
4. $x_1^2 + x_2^2 + x_3^2 + x_4^2 -$
  $2a(x_1 + x_2 + x_3 + x_4) + 4a^2$.
5. 85.   **6.** 0.   **7.** 97.
8. 182.   **9.** 94.5.   **10.** 362.5.

CHAPTER 5

Problem Set 5–1

1.
Preliminary tableau

Basic Variables	θ	Coefficient of				Current Values
		x_1	x_2	s_1	s_2	
s_1	0	4	3	1	0	24
s_2	0	1	2	0	1	11
(max) θ	1	−3	−1	0	0	0

→

↑

Second tableau

Basic Variables	θ	Coefficient of				Current Values
		x_1	x_2	s_1	s_2	
x_1	0	1	3/4	1/4	0	6
s_2	0	0	5/4	−1/4	1	5
(max) θ	1	0	5/4	3/4	0	18

$$x_1 = 6 - \frac{3}{4}x_2 - \frac{1}{4}s_1$$
$$s_2 = 5 - \frac{5}{4}x_2 + \frac{1}{4}s_1.$$

2.
Preliminary tableau

Basic Variables	θ	Coefficient of				Current Values
		x_1	x_2	s_1	s_2	
s_1	0	3	7	1	0	42
s_2	0	1	5	0	1	22
(max) θ	1	−4	−10	0	0	0

→

↑

Second tableau

Basic Variables	θ	Coefficient of				Current Values
		x_1	x_2	s_1	s_2	
s_1	0	8/5	0	1	−7/5	56/5
x_2	0	1/5	1	0	1/5	22/5
(max) θ	1	−2	0	0	2	44

$$s_1 = \frac{56}{5} - \frac{8}{5}x_1 + \frac{7}{5}s_2 \qquad x_2 = \frac{22}{5} - \frac{1}{5}x_1 - \frac{1}{5}s_2.$$

3.
Preliminary tableau

Basic Variables	θ	Coefficient of						Current Values
		x_1	x_2	s_1	s_2	s_3	s_4	
s_1	0	3	1	1	0	0	0	9
s_2	0	1	1	0	1	0	0	5
s_3	0	1	0	0	0	1	0	4
s_4	0	0	1	0	0	0	1	4
(max) θ	1	−0.3	−0.5	0	0	0	0	0

→

↑

Second tableau

Basic Variables	θ	Coefficient of						Current Values
		x_1	x_2	s_1	s_2	s_3	s_4	
s_1	0	3	0	1	0	0	−1	5
s_2	0	1	0	0	1	0	−1	1
s_3	0	1	0	0	0	1	0	4
x_2	0	0	1	0	0	0	1	4
(max) θ	1	−0.3	0	0	0	0	0.5	2

$$s_1 = 5 - 3x_1 + s_4 \qquad s_3 = 4 - x_1$$
$$s_2 = 1 - x_1 + s_4 \qquad x_2 = 4 \qquad - s_4.$$

Problem Set 5–1 (*continued*)

4.
Preliminary tableau

Basic Variables	θ	Coefficient of						Current Values
		x_1	x_2	s_1	s_2	s_3	s_4	
s_1	0	1	1	1	0	0	0	13
s_2	0	1	2	0	1	0	0	22
s_3	0	2	1	0	0	1	0	20
s_4	0	1	0	0	0	0	1	4	→
(max) θ	1	−4	1	0	0	0	0	0

↑

Second tableau

Basic Variables	θ	Coefficient of						Current Values
		x_1	x_2	s_1	s_2	s_3	s_4	
s_1	0	0	1	1	0	0	−1	9
s_2	0	0	2	0	1	0	−1	18
s_3	0	0	1	0	0	1	−2	12
x_1	0	1	0	0	0	0	1	4
(max) θ	1	0	1	0	0	0	4	16

$$s_1 = 9 - x_2 + s_4$$
$$s_2 = 18 - 2x_2 + s_4$$
$$s_3 = 12 - x_2 + 2s_4$$
$$x_1 = 4 \qquad\quad - s_4.$$

5.
Preliminary tableau

Basic Variables	θ	Coefficient of					Current Values
		x_1	x_2	x_3	s_1	s_2	
s_1	0	1	4	3	1	0	1800	→
s_2	0	2	3	1	0	1	2000
(max) θ	1	−0.5	−1	−0.2	0	0	0

↑

Second tableau

Basic Variables	θ	Coefficient of					Current Values
		x_1	x_2	x_3	s_1	s_2	
x_2	0	1/4	1	3/4	1/4	0	450
s_2	0	5/4	0	−5/4	−3/4	1	650
(max) θ	1	−1/4	0	11/20	1/4	0	450

$$x_2 = 450 - \frac{1}{4}x_1 - \frac{3}{4}x_3 - \frac{1}{4}s_1$$
$$s_2 = 650 - \frac{5}{4}x_1 + \frac{5}{4}x_3 + \frac{3}{4}s_1.$$

6.
Preliminary tableau

Basic Variables	θ	Coefficient of						Current Values
		x_1	x_2	x_3	s_1	s_2	s_3	
s_1	0	1	5	0	1	0	0	4	→
s_2	0	0	1	5/2	0	1	0	5
s_3	0	3/2	1	1	0	0	1	15/2
(max) θ	1	−3/2	−5/2	2	0	0	0	0

↑

Second tableau

Basic Variables	θ	Coefficient of						Current Values
		x_1	x_2	x_3	s_1	s_2	s_3	
x_2	0	1/5	1	0	1/5	0	0	4/5
s_2	0	−1/5	0	5/2	−1/5	1	0	21/5
s_3	0	13/10	0	1	−1/5	0	1	67/10
(max) θ	1	−1	0	2	1/2	0	0	2

$$x_2 = \frac{4}{5} - \frac{1}{5}x_1 \qquad\qquad - \frac{1}{5}s_1$$
$$s_2 = \frac{21}{5} + \frac{1}{5}x_1 - \frac{5}{2}x_3 + \frac{1}{5}s_1$$
$$s_3 = \frac{67}{10} - \frac{13}{10}x_1 - x_3 + \frac{1}{5}s_1.$$

Problem Set 5–1 (concluded)

7.
Preliminary tableau

Basic Variables	θ	\multicolumn{3}{c	}{Coefficient of}			Current Values
		x_1	x_2	x_3	s_1 s_2 s_3		
s_1	0	2	2	5	1 0 0		40 →
s_2	0	1	4	2	0 1 0		26
s_3	0	3	1	3	0 0 1		27
(max) θ	1	−8	−6	−12	0 0 0		0

↑

Second tableau

Basic Variables	θ	x_1	x_2	x_3	s_1	s_2 s_3	Current Values
x_3	0	2/5	2/5	1	1/5	0 0	8
s_2	0	1/5	16/5	0	−2/5	1 0	10
s_3	0	9/5	−1/5	0	−3/5	0 1	3
(max) θ	1	−16/5	−6/5	0	12/5	0 0	96

$$x_3 = 8 - \frac{2}{5}x_1 - \frac{2}{5}x_2 - \frac{1}{5}s_1$$
$$s_2 = 10 - \frac{1}{5}x_1 - \frac{16}{5}x_2 + \frac{2}{5}s_1$$
$$s_3 = 3 - \frac{9}{5}x_1 + \frac{1}{5}x_2 + \frac{3}{5}s_1.$$

8.
Preliminary tableau

Basic Variables	θ	x_1	x_2	x_3	s_1	s_2 s_3 s_4 s_5	Current Values
s_1	0	3	2	3	1	0 0 0 0	23 →
s_2	0	1	3	2	0	1 0 0 0	26
s_3	0	2	1	2	0	0 1 0 0	19
s_4	0	4	5	3	0	0 0 1 0	49
s_5	0	3	4	4	0	0 0 0 1	45
(max) θ	1	−5	−3	−4	0	0 0 0 0	0

↑

Second tableau

Basic Variables	θ	x_1	x_2	x_3	s_1	s_2 s_3 s_4 s_5	Current Values
x_1	0	1	2/3	1	1/3	0 0 0 0	23/3
s_2	0	0	7/3	1	−1/3	1 0 0 0	55/3
s_3	0	0	−1/3	0	−2/3	0 1 0 0	11/3
s_4	0	0	7/3	−1	−4/3	0 0 1 0	55/3
s_5	0	0	2	1	−1	0 0 0 1	22
(max) θ	1	0	−1/3	1	5/3	0 0 0 0	115/3

$$x_1 = \frac{23}{3} - \frac{2}{3}x_2 - x_3 - \frac{1}{3}s_1$$
$$s_2 = \frac{55}{3} - \frac{7}{3}x_2 - x_3 + \frac{1}{3}s_1$$
$$s_3 = \frac{11}{3} + \frac{1}{3}x_2 \qquad + \frac{2}{3}s_1$$
$$s_4 = \frac{55}{3} - \frac{7}{3}x_2 + x_3 + \frac{4}{3}s_1$$
$$s_5 = 22 - 2x_2 - x_3 + s_1.$$

Problem Set 5–2

1. 8 at (0, 4). **2.** 28 at (14, 0).
3. 92 at (4, 9). **4.** 92 at (4, 9).
5. 55 at (35, 0, 5). **6.** 60 at (30, 0, 0).
7. 125/2 at (3/2, 29/2, 1/2).
8. 35 at (0, 40/7, 5/7).
9. 27 at (0, 3, 1).
10. 54/5 at (0, 4, 2/5).
11. 335/12 at (0, 5/6, 95/12).
12. 22 at (2, 6, 0). **13.** 9 at (0, 3, 3).
14. 79/7 at (61/7, 5/7, 13/7).
15. $61 at (5, 2).
16. $89 at (5, 8). Machines B and C are not fully utilized.
17. $2,000 at (0, 0, 1000).
18. $190 at (0, 40, 75).

Problem Set 5–3

1. 4/5 at (0, 22/5). **2.** 5 at (0, 3).
3. 10 at (5, 15). **4.** 54 at (0, 8).
5. 17 at (0, 11). **6.** 26 at (0, 8).
7. 3 at (3, 6). **8.** 4 at (0, 4).
9. $3 at (3, 6). **10.** $10,000 at (5, 15).

Problem Set 5–4

1. 28 at (14, 0).
2. 6 on line segment joining (4, 9) and (7, 6).
3. 38 at (6, 1).   **4.** 3 at (6, 1).
5. 27 at (9, 9).   **6.** 90 at (6, 0, 6).
8. 24 on line segment joining (0, 4) and (3, 2).
9. 21 on line segment joining (14, 0) and (7, 3).
10. 7 on line segment joining (5, 2) and (3, 4).
11. 4 on line segment joining (4, 0) and (5, 1).
12. 108 on triangle joining (0, 12, 6), (0, 0, 9), and (12, 0, 6).

Problem Set 5–5

1. Unbounded solution.
2. Unbounded solution.
3. Unbounded solution.
4. 27/10 at (0, 1/40, 9/40).
5. 22 at (0, 13, −6).
6. 9/10 at (1/20, 0, 3/20).
7. a) \$193 at (13, 3, 4).   b) \$193 at (13, 3, 4).
   c) \$1,050 at (12, 6, 0).
8. a) \$365 at (5, 8).   b) \$374 at (5, 8).
   c) \$406 at (0, 8).

Problem Set 5–6

1. Maximize

$$\theta = 20p_1 + 10p_2$$

subject to

$$4p_1 + 6p_2 \le 5$$
$$2p_1 + p_2 \le 3.$$

Initial tableau

Basic Variables	Coefficient of				Current Values	
	p_1	p_2	x_1	x_2		
x_1	[4]	6	1	0	[5]	5/4→
x_2	[2]	1	0	1	[3]	3/2
(max) θ	−20	−10	0	0	0	

↑

2. Maximize

$$\theta = 10p_1 + 20p_2$$

subject to

$$3p_1 + p_2 \le 4$$
$$2p_1 + 2p_2 \le 2.$$

Initial tableau

Basic Variables	Coefficient of				Current Values	
	p_1	p_2	x_1	x_2		
x_1	3	[1]	1	0	[4]	4
x_2	2	[2]	0	1	[2]	1→
(max) θ	−10	−20	0	0	0	

↑

3. Maximize

$$\theta = 2p_1 + 4p_2 + 6p_3$$

subject to

$$3p_1 + 2p_2 + 4p_3 \le 1$$
$$3p_1 + p_2 + 2p_3 \le 1$$
$$p_1 + 2p_3 \le 1.$$

Initial tableau

Basic Variables	Coefficient of						Current Values	
	p_1	p_2	p_3	x_1	x_2	x_3		
x_1	3	2	[4]	1	0	0	[1]	1/4→
x_2	3	1	[2]	0	1	0	[1]	1/2
x_3	1	0	[2]	0	0	1	[1]	1/2
(max) θ	−2	−4	−6	0	0	0	0	

↑

4. Maximize

$$\theta = 10p_1 + 15p_2 + 20p_3$$

subject to

$$p_1 + 2p_2 + 3p_3 \le 2$$
$$p_1 + 3p_2 + p_3 \le 3$$
$$p_1 + p_2 + 2p_3 \le 1.$$

Problem Set 5–6 *(concluded)*

Initial tableau

Basic Variables	Coefficient of						Current Values	
	p_1	p_2	p_3	x_1	x_2	x_3		
x_1	1	2	3	1	0	0	2	2/3
x_2	1	3	1	0	1	0	3	3
x_3	1	1	2	0	0	1	1	1/2→
(max) θ	−10	−15	−20	0	0	0	0	

↑

5. 16 at (0, 8).
6. 42 at (6, 3).
7. 600 at (0, 600, 0).
8. 36 at (0, 22/19, 6/19).
9. $22 at (8, 4).
10. $15,600 at (4, 10). No grades are over-produced.
11. $26 at (8, 4, 2).
12. $14,000 at (8, 4, 2).

Problem Set 5–7

1. a) 94 at (6, 8).   b) 86 at (6, 7).
   c) 92 at (4, 9).

2. 11 to 14; 19 to 26; 17 with no upper limit.
3. a) 88 at (8, 6).
   b) s_3 would have a current value of −4.
4. a) 14 with no upper limit; 13 to 20; 9 to 12.
   b) 33 at (11, 0).
5. a) 9 to 54; 8 to 48.   b) 110 at (6, 0, 8).
6. $138 at (9, 6).   7. 28 at (8, 2).
8. 28 at (8, 2).
9. a) $1,500 at (100, 0, 80).
   b) $30 per man-hour of grinding time and $50 per man-hour of polishing time.
   c) 38 and 45 for grinding time; 23 and 28 for polishing time.
10. a) $125 thousand at (4,9,0).
    b) 1/5 of $1 thousand, or $200, for land purchase and 1/20 of $1 thousand, or $50, for landscaping.
    c) $95 and $103 thousand for land purchase; $38 and $50 thousand for landscaping.
11. a) $58 at (10, 12, 0).
    b) 1/5 of $1, or 20 cents, for forming time and 2/5 of $1, or 40 cents, for painting time.
    c) 140 and 155 minutes for forming time; 60 and 75 minutes for painting time.

CHAPTER 6

Problem Set 6–1

1. 29 at (3, 2).
2. 58 at (7, 3).
3. 40 at (10, 0).
4. 29 at (3, 2).
5. 58 at (7, 3).
6. 32 at (8, 0).
7. 33 at (6, 4).
8. 0 at (0, 0).
9. 90 at (6, 0, 6).
10. 114 at (0, 12, 6).
11. 98 at (0, 12, 6).
12. 126 at (18, 0, 6).
13. 90 at (6, 0, 6).
14. 85 at (5, 5, 3).
15. 114 at (0, 12, 6).
16. 116 at (4, 6, 8).
17. 128 at (2, 3, 6).
18. $172 at (4, 6, 8).
19. $182,000 at (0, 0, 700, 1000, 0, 300, 200, 0).

6. 57 on line segment joining (36, 0, 0) and (12, 0, 6).
7. 32 at (0, 6, 8).   8. 30 at (0, 18, 6).
9. $14,000 at (3, 5, 4).   10. $26 at (8, 4, 2).
11. 34 at (9, 6, 10, 0, 6, 3).
12. a)

	Combinations							
10-inch	6	4	3	2	2	1	1	0
16-inch	0	1	0	2	1	3	0	2
23-inch	0	0	1	0	1	0	2	1
Waste	0	4	7	8	1	2	4	5

b) 85 at (0, 0, 0, 0, 85, 0, 0, 0).
c) 245 at (0, 0, 0, 0, 15, 0, 20, 30).

Problem Set 6–2

1. 29 at (3, 2).
2. 15 at (15/2, 0).
3. 36 at (0, 18).
4. 50 at (10, 0, 5).
5. 56 at (6, 9, 0).

Problem Set 6–3

1. No feasible solutions.
2. No feasible solutions.
3. No feasible solutions.
4. No feasible solutions.
5. No feasible solutions.
6. No feasible solutions.
7. No feasible solutions. **8.** 19 at (3, 2).
9. 60 on line segment joining (15/2, 0) and (5,2).
10. 60 at (0, 12) and 45 at (0, 9).
11. 60 at (0, 12) and 45 at (0, 9).
12. 60 at (0, 12) and 45 at (0, 9).
13. No maximum; minimum is 36 at (6, 6).
14. 28 at (2, 8) and 20 at (4, 4).
15. 86 at (4, 11) and 62 at (4, 7).
16. 14 at (4, 6) and 12 at (6, 0).
17. 44 at (8, 2) and 42 at (6, 6).
18. 63 at (9, 3) and 54 at (6, 6).
19. 42 at (0, 12). **20.** -48 at (0, 0, 12).

Problem Set 6–4

1. a) No lower limit with an upper limit of 54; 13 with no upper limit; no lower limit with an upper limit of 72.
   b) 40 at (0, 20). c) 36 at (0, 18).
   d) p_3 would have a current value of -12.
2. a) 6 with no upper limit; 0 to 16; -4 to 12.
   b) 52 at (7, 9). c) 36 at (6, 6).
   d) s_1 would have a current value of -22.
3. a) 10 with no upper limit; no lower limit with an upper limit of 12; 2 to 10.
   b) 16 at (4, 2). c) 32 at (16, 0).
   d) 12 at (6, 0).

4. a) 14 to 54; no lower limit with an upper limit of 12; 13 to 48.
   b) 46 at (6, 8). c) 38 at (2, 14).
   d) 44 at (8, 2).
5. a) 3 to 12; no lower limit with an upper limit of 12; 6 to 24.
   b) 72 at (8, 8). c) 54 at (6, 6).
   d) 54 at (6, 6). The column entries in (d) are ½ those in (c) because of the relationship between the two respective slack variables.
6. a) 2 to 4. b) 1.5 to 3.
   c) No lower limit with an upper limit of 1.
   d) No lower limit with an upper limit of 1.
7. a) 202 at (14, 0, 8). b) 2 to 14.
   c) No lower limit with an upper limit of 49/3.
   d) 15/2 to 24.
   e) No lower limit with an upper limit of 8/3.
   f) No lower limit with an upper limit of 11/3.
8. a) 4 with no upper limit.
   b) 0 to 3. c) -2 to 8.
9. a) 777 at (0, 0, 15).
   b) 71/2 with no upper limit.
   c) 117/2 with no upper limit.
   d) No lower limit with an upper limit of 36.
   e) 23/2 with no upper limit.
10. a) $P \geq R_2 + R_3$. b) $4 or more.
    c) 4 units or less. d) None.
11. a) $C \leq 2R_2$. b) $6 or less.
    c) 7 units or more; unlimited; unlimited.
12. a) $3P \geq 8R_i + 11R_2$. b) $27 or more.
    c) 3 units or less. d) 3 units or less.
13. a) $2C \leq 24R_1 + 23R_2$. b) $94 or less.
    c) 3 units or more. d) 1 unit or more.

CHAPTER 7

Problem Set 7–1

1. 256. **2.** 8. **3.** 9. **4.** 4.
5. 25. **6.** 3. **7.** 1/3.
8. $e^6 = 403.4288$.
9. $e^{-6} = 0.0025$. **10.** $e^4 = 54.5982$.
11. See Figure A.

FIGURE A

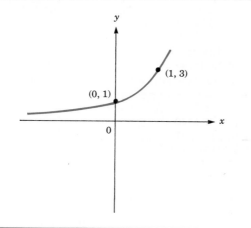

12. See Figure B.

FIGURE B

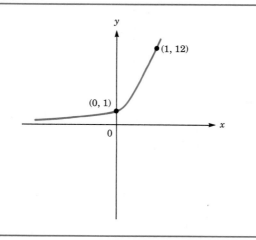

13. See Figure C.

FIGURE C

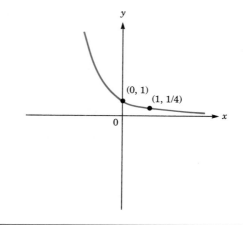

14. See Figure D.

FIGURE D

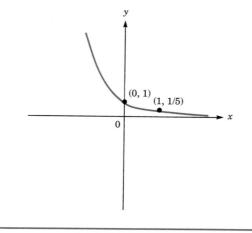

Problem Set 7–1 (*continued*)

15. See Figure E.

17. See Figure G.

FIGURE E

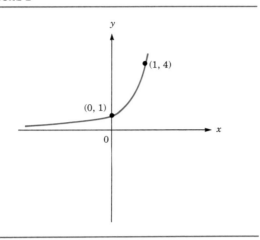

FIGURE G

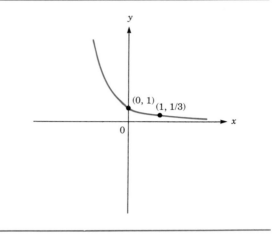

16. See Figure F.

18. See Figure H.

FIGURE F

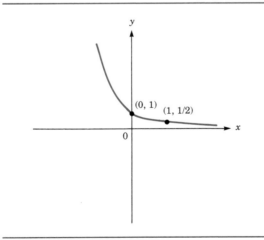

FIGURE H

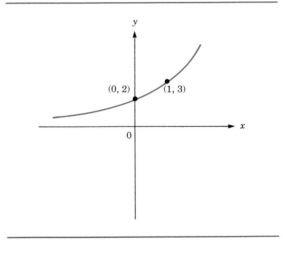

Problem Set 7–1 (concluded)

19. See Figure I.

FIGURE I

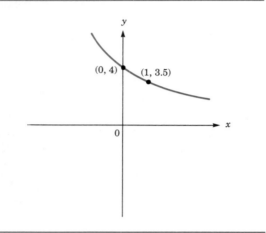

(0, 4)   (1, 3.5)

20. See Figure J.

FIGURE J

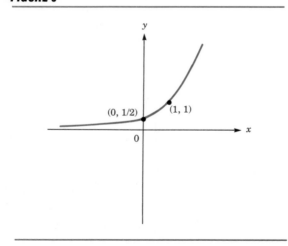

(0, 1/2)   (1, 1)

Problem Set 7–2

1. 1.58496.	**2.** 0.63093.	**3.** 0.69897.
4. 0.77815.	**5.** 0.11103.	**6.** 0.01230.
7. 18.85418.	**8.** 9.00647.	**9.** 0.84510.

10. 0.47712.

11. $\log 125 = \log 5^3 = 3 \log 5 = 3(0.698970)$
$= 2.096910$.

12. $\log 27 = \log 3^3 = 3 \log 3 = 3(0.477121) =$
1.431363.

13. $\log 81 = \log 9^2 = 2 \log 9 = 2(0.954243) =$
1.908486.

14. $\log 625 = \log 5^4 = 4 \log 5 = 4(0.698970)$
$= 2.795880$.

15. 1.53724.	**16.** 4.48289.
17. -3.00000.	**18.** -1.66096.
19. 14.27491.	**20.** 54.44868.

Problem Set 7–3

1. $\log_3 9 = 2$.	**2.** $\log_2 32 = 5$.	**3.** $3^x = N$.
4. $2^y = N$.		**5.** $\log_{1/2} 0.125 = 3$.
6. $\log_{0.2} 0.04 = 2$.		**7.** $16^{1/2} = 4$.
8. $27^{1/3} = 3$.		**9.** $\log_2 0.125 = -3$.
10. $\log_3(1/9) = -2$.		**11.** $5^{-2} = 0.04$.
12. $2^{-4} = 0.0625$.		**13.** $10^2 = 100$.
14. $e^{2.9957} = 20$.		**15.** $e^{2.3026} = 10$.
16. $10^1 = 10$.		**17.** $10^{-0.3010} = 0.5$.
18. $e^{-0.6931} = 0.5$.		**19.** 1. **20.** 1.
21. 2. **22.** 3.		**23.** 1.
24. 1. **25.** 1/2.		**26.** 1/3.

27.
$$\ln(e^{\ln x}) = \ln 2$$
$$\ln x(\ln e) = \ln 2$$
$$\ln x = \ln 2$$
$$\text{antiln } (\ln x) = \text{antiln } (\ln 2)$$
$$x = 2.$$

28.
$$\log(10^{\log x}) = \log 3$$
$$\log x(\log 10) = \log 3$$
$$\log x = \log 3$$
$$\text{antilog}(\log x) = \text{antilog}(\log 3)$$
$$x = 3.$$

29. 5.	**30.** 4.	**31.** 6.	**32.** 5

33. $\ln(x^2 z^3/y^2)$.   **34.** $\log(x^5 y^{1/2}/z^2)$.

35. 4.4.	**36.** -0.6.	**37.** 5.4.
38. 6.8.	**39.** -1.8.	**40.** -2.4.
41. 2.8.	**42.** 1.	**43.** -3.5.
44. -4.66667.	**45.** $\ln x^2 y^3$.	**46.** $\ln(x^3/y^2)$.
47. $\ln x$.	**48.** $2 \ln x$.	**49.** $\ln y^{1/x}$.
50. $\ln x^{1/y}$.	**51.** 1.5220.	**52.** 3.3201.
53. 0.3329.	**54.** 0.9900.	**55.** 0.3499.
56. 0.7183.	**57.** 5.2131.	**58.** 4.7795.
59. 11.23181.	**60.** 6.11626.	**61.** 0.14870.
62. 0.20112.	**63.** 0.09531.	**64.** 0.26246.

CHAPTER 8

Problem Set 8–1

1. a) $35.   b) $535.
2. a) $80.   b) $1,080.
3. a) $45.   b) $1,045.
4. a) $60.   b) $2,060.
5. a) $12.   b) $112.
6. a) $30.   b) $530.
7. a) $36.   b) $236.
8. a) $120.   b) $620.
9. a) $3,600.   b) $8,600.
10. a) $2,400.   b) $6,400.
11. 15 months.   **12.** 18%.   **13.** 8%.
14. $714.29.   **15.** 30 months.
16. 20 months.   **17.** 16%.   **18.** 5%.
19. $400.   **20.** $854.70.   **21.** $904.98.
22. $869.57.   **23.** $1,640.   **24.** $466.25.
25. $2,580.65.   **26.** 12%.   **27.** 14.634%.
28. 9.651%.   **29.** 19.355%.   **30.** 8.802%.
31. 10.427%.   **32.** 13.483%.

Problem Set 8–2

1. $530.66.   **2.** $537.25.   **3.** $8,689.81.
4. $1,379.52.   **5.** $282.68.   **6.** $357.69.
7. $2,880.61.   **8.** $4,801.02.
9. 20.5 years.   **10.** 7.3 years.
11. 3.526%.   **12.** 11.25%.
13. $6,851.14.   **14.** $2,012.99.
15. 8.0 years.   **16.** 17.46%.

Problem Set 8–3

1. $214.55.   **2.** $1,016.70.
3. $3,069.57.   **4.** $2,795.70.
5. $574.37.   **6.** $1,747.31.
7. 78.4 units per man-hour.   **8.** $5,000.
9. $852.16.   **10.** $815.87.

Problem Set 8–4

1. 8.243%.   **2.** 10.25%.   **3.** 12.683%.
4. 16.986%.   **5.** 10.471%.   **6.** 7.186%.
7. 19.562%.   **8.** 9.308%.
9. 9.381%.   **10.** 9.416%.

11. 11%; 11.303%; 11.462%; 11.572%; 11.6%; 11.615%; 11.626%.
12. 14%; 14.49%; 14.752%; 14.934%; 14.981%; 15.006%; 15.024%.

Problem Set 8–5

1. $1,349.86.   **2.** $1,112.77.
3. $7,166.65.   **4.** $5,619.79.
5. $341.93.   **6.** $799.55.   **7.** $913.93.
8. $2,582.12.   **9.** 0.0513.   **10.** 0.0618.
11. 0.0725.   **12.** 0.0833.   **13.** 0.1133.
14. 0.0862.   **15.** 0.0488.   **16.** 0.0953.
17. $19,480.97.   **18.** $4,317.11.
19. $31,267.68.   **20.** $4,782.21.
21. About $1,575,839,260.   **22.** $5,444.39.
23. 0.0822.   **24.** 0.0790.   **25.** 0.0801.

Problem Set 8–6

1. $21,538.44.   **2.** $60,401.98.
3. $81,990.98.   **4.** $396,566.67.
5. $23,787.71.   **6.** $4,307.69.
7. $4,828.51.   **8.** $1,576.44.
9. $6,902.95.   **10.** $687.30.
11. $312,232.31.   **12.** $50,886.21.

Problem Set 8–7

1. $6,540.57.   **2.** $30,107.50.
3. $37,816.56.   **4.** $15,046.30.
5. a) $6,000.00.   b) $5,287.67.
6. a) $53,373.88.   b) $125,000.
7. $47.07.   **8.** $200.61.
9. a) $10,758.49.
   b) $6,000 for interest; $4,758.49 reduction of balance owed.
   c) $5,714.49 for interest; $5,044.00 reduction of balance owed.
10. a) $235.40.
   b) $120 interest; $115.40 reduction of balance owed.
   c) $117.69 interest; $117.71 reduction of balance owed.

Problem Set 8–7 *(concluded)*

11. a) $12,587.95.
 b) $11,250.00 interest; $1,337.95 reduction of balance owed.
12. a) $275.35.
 b) $255.21 interest; $20.14 reduction of balance owed.
13. $86,126.35. **14.** $200,443.11.

Problem Set 8–8

1. $1,146.39. **2.** $232.50.
3. $11,040.20. **4.** $800.80.
5. $2,145.48. **6.** $221,224.81.
7. 38,857. **8.** $178.60. **9.** $6,074.34.
10. $115,573.86. **11.** $3,257.79.

12. $226.11. **13.** $3,888.44.
14. $12,942.29. **15.** $10,119.86.
16. $39,296.11. **17.** $1,414.59.
18. $11,726.87. **19.** $7,357.48.

Problem Set 8–9

1. 6.3%. **2.** 6.9%. **3.** 7.8%.
4. 5.7%. **5.** 10; $54.34. **6.** 29; $16.18.
7. 27; $15,633. **8.** 163; $130,170.
9. $13,497.48. **10.** $205.37.
11. $23,085.36. **12.** $1,185.51.
13. $15,348.58. **14.** $21,225.87.
15. $195.82. **16.** $196.80.
17. $13,467.89. **18.** $109.16
19. $86,697.75. **20.** $217.32.

CHAPTER 9

Problem Set 9–1

1. a) 0.30. b) 0.55. c) 0. d) 0.125.
 e) 0. f) 0.03. g) 0.03. h) 0.15.
 i) 0.20. j) 0.15. k) 0.50.
 l) 0.50. m) 0.775. n) 0.47.
 o) 0.85. p) 0.85. q) 0.70.
 r) 0.50. s) $M \cup S$. t) $B \cup C$.
 u) B or $A' \cap C'$. v) $A' \cap M'$.
 w) $B \cup M$. x) $L \cup C$.
2. a) $P(M|A) = 0.3 = P(M)$.
 b) M and A are independent in the probability sense.
 c) Independent because $P(A|L) = 0.15 = P(A)$, or $P(L|A) = 0.20 = P(L)$.
 d) Not independent, because $P(B|L) = 0.75$ and $P(B) = 0.55$, so $P(B|L) \neq P(B)$.
 e) $P(A \cap B) = 0$. A and B are mutually exclusive.
3. a) 0.42. b) 0.60.
4. a) Yes. $P(WB) = 0$.
 b) No. $P(W|B) = 0$ does not equal $P(W)$, which is 0.20.
 c) No. $P(YW) \neq 0$.
 d) Yes. $P(Y|W) = 78/120 = 0.65$, and $P(Y) = 390/600 = 0.65$.
 e) No. $P(YR) \neq 0$.

 f) No. $P(Y|R) = 270/300 = 0.9$ but $P(Y) = 390/600 = 0.65$, so $P(Y|R) \neq P(Y)$.
5. a) 0.50. b) 0.125. c) 0.275.
 d) 0. e) 0. f) 0. g) 0.25.
 h) 0.625. i) 0.10. j) 0.25. k) 0.40.
 l) 0. m) No. $P(YW) \neq 0$.
 n) No because $P(W|Y) = 10/100 = 0.10$ does not equal $P(W) = 80/400 = 0.20$.
 o) No. $P(WT) \neq 0$.
 p) Yes, $P(W|T) = 50/250 = 0.2$ equals $P(W) = 80/400 = 0.2$.
 q) Yes, $P(RG) = 0$.
 r) No. $P(R|G) = 0$, which does not equal $P(R) = 0.50$.
6. $P(S) = 0.4$, and $P(S|H) = P(S|M) = P(S|L) = 0.4$.
 $P(P) = 0.6$, and $P(H|P) = P(M|P) = P(L|P) = 0.6$.
7.

	H	M	L
Female	20	160	20
Male	10	80	10

Problem Set 9–2

1.

Area	L	M	S	
A	0.03	0.045	0.075	0.15
B	0.15	0.125	0.275	0.55
C	0.02	0.130	0.150	0.30
	0.20	0.30	0.50	1.00

2. a)

	F	F'	
C	0.24	0.36	0.60
C'	0.16	0.24	0.40
	0.40	0.60	1.00

  b) 0.36.   c) 0.76.   d) 0.
  e) 0.40.   f) 0.60.   g) 0.
  h) $P(CF) = 0.24$ and $P(C)P(F) = 0.60(0.40)$
    $= 0.24$. Hence, $P(CF) = P(C)P(F)$, so C
    and F are independent.
  i) F and F' are complementary events.
3. a) 0.79.
  b) As a consequence of these probability
    assignments, $P(A \cup B) = 1.09$, which is
    greater than 1, so the candidate should
    be advised to reassess her subjective
    probabilities.
4. $P(CS) = 0.35$ because $P(CS) = P(C)P(S|C)$
    $= 0.5(0.7) = 0.35$.
5. $P(G|H) = 0.90$, where G means good job
    and H means honors. This follows from the
    rule $P(G|H) = P(GH)/P(H) = 0.09/0.10 =$
    0.90.
6. 0.6.   **7.** 0.9975.   **8.** 0.3.
9. $P(X|Y) = 1/4$; $P(Y|X) = 1/6$.
10. $P(X) = 1/2$; $P(Y) = 2/5$.   **11.** 0.67.
12. a) 1/2.   b) 4/7.   c) 23/70.   d) 47/70.
13. a) 0.35.   b) 0.60.   c) 0.55.   d) 0.45.
14. a) 0.48.   b) 0.16.   **15.** 0.61
16. 0.4015.   **17.** 0.01099.   **18.** 0.07831.
19. a) $P(SC) = 0.5$; $P(S)P(C) = 0.48$;
    $P(SC) \neq P(S)P(C)$.   b) 0.12.
20. a) 1/4000.   b) 3871/4000.
    c) 129/4000.   d) 128/4000.
21. a) 1/12.   b) 7/12.   c) 1/4.   d) 23/36.
22. 0.141.   **23.** 5/6.   **24.** 0.56.
25. 0.9.   **26.** 0.288.   **27.** 0.706.

Problem Set 9–3

1. 0.949.   **2.** 0.678.   **3.** 0.857.
4. a) 0.00336.   b) 0.0198.
5. a) 0.998.   b) 0.664.
6. a) 0.5; 0.5.   b) 0.667; 0.333.
7. 0.308; 0.692.
8. a) 0.13.   b) 0.02.   c) 0.85.
9. 0.4 for John; 0.4 for Anne; 0.2 for Sally.

Problem Set 9–4

1. a) $7/15 = 0.467$.   b) $1/5 = 0.0667$.
  c) $7/15 = 0.467$.
  d) $1 - P(0 \text{ defective}) = 1 - P(GGG) =$
    $1 - (7/10)(6/9)(5/8) = 0.708$.
2. a) 0.9025.   b) 0.0025.
  c) 0.9975.   d) 0.095.
  e) 0.95 because of independence.
3. a) HHH, THH, HTH, HHT, TTH, THT, HTT, TTT.
  b) 0, 1, 2, 3.
  c) Event   HHH   THH   HTH   HHT
    Probability 0.125 0.125 0.125 0.125
                 TTH   THT   HTT   TTT.
                 0.125 0.125 0.125 0.125.
  d) Event   0   1   2   3
    Probability 0.125 0.375 0.375 0.125.
  e) 0.875.   f) 0.50.   g) 0.375.
  h) 0.375.
4. a) Event W_1M W_2M W_1W_2 MW_1 MW_2 W_2W_1.
    Probability 1/6   1/6   1/6   1/6   1/6   1/6.
  b) 1/3.   c) 2/3.   d) 1/3.
5. a) WM.
  b) $P(WM) = P(W)P(M|W) = (2/3)(1/2) = 1/3$.
  c) WW.
  d) $P(WW) = P(W)P(W|W) = (2/3)(1/2) = 1/3$.
6. a) 1/6.   b) 1/2.   c) 1/6.
7. a) $\binom{52}{5} = 2{,}598{,}960$.   b) 2^n.

Problem Set 9–5

1. 3.5; 1.6.   **2.** 3.4; 1.4.   **3.** 2.5; 1.7.
4. 1.2; 1.8.   **5.** 0.3; 1.2.   **6.** -1.7; 1.3.
7. a) No because $\Sigma p(x) > 1$.   b) Yes.
  c) No because -0.25 is not a valid proba-
    bility.
8. a) 35; 215.8; 14.7.   b) See Figure A.
  c) 1; 0.5.

Problem Set 9–5 (concluded)

FIGURE A

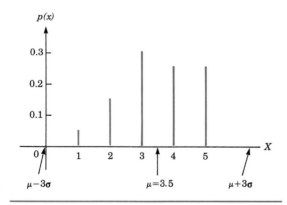

9. a) 3.5; 1.42; 1.2.   b) See Figure B.
   c) 1; 0.55.

FIGURE B

10. $4.

Problem Set 9–6

1. a) 0.441.   b) 0.657.   c) 0.3087.
   d) 0.0513.
2. 0.992.   **3.** 0.913.
4. a) 0.886.   b) 0.655.
5. a) 0.760.   b) 0.0837.   **6.** 5.
7. a) 1/32 = 0.03125.   b) 3/16 = 0.1875.
   c) 5/16, 0.3125.   d) 1/2 = 0.50.
   e) 3/16 = 0.1875.
8. a) 1/1024 = 0.000977.
   b) 1/64 = 0.0156.
   c) 45/512 = 0.0879.
   d) 53/512 = 0.104.
9. a) $\sum_{x=0}^{15} C_x^{100}(0.05)^x(0.95)^{100-x}$.

   b) $\sum_{x=11}^{200} C_x^{200}(0.05)^x(0,95)^{200-x}$.

10. a) 0.993.   b) 0.421.
11. a) 0.642.   b) 0.027.
12. a) 0.983.   b) 0.006.   c) 0.579.
   d) 0.062.   e) 0.377.   f) 0.617.
13. a) 0.115.   b) 0.788.
   c) 1.000 to 3 decimals.   d) 0.032.
   e) 0.210.   f) 0.002.
14. a) 0.349.   b) 0.387.   c) 0.651.
   d) 0.251.
15. a) 0.074.   b) 0.315.   c) 0.012.
   d) 0.389.

Problem Set 9–7

1. 0.   **2.** $0.8.   **3.** Act 2.
4. A_4.   **5.** Make three. EMV = $8.35.
6. a) $42.75.
   b) P(0 loss) = 0.99825 is not stated.
7. Choose A_1 in each case, even though A_2
   presents no chance of loss. At first glance,
   the choice of A_1 may not seem appropriate,
   especially in (c) where there is a 50 percent
   chance of a loss of $1,000. However, $E(A_1)$
   in (c) is $1,000, compared to $E(A_2)$ = $250.

CHAPTER 10

Problem Set 10–1

1. a) 7. b) -8. c) $3a - 2$.
   d) $(3a - 2)^2 = 9a^2 - 12a + 4$.
   e) $3ab - 2$. f) $9y + 10$.
   g) $3x + 1$. h) 3.
2. a) 10. b) 0. c) 1.75.
   d) $(6a + 4)/a^2$. e) $x^2 + 4x + 1.75$.
   f) $a^2 + 5a + 4$. g) $a^2 + a - 2$.
   h) $2x + 2$.
3. a) $a^2y - y^2$. b) $ax^2 - a^2$.
4. a) $2x + 15$. b) $6 + 5y$.
5. a) 0.25. b) 1/3.
   c) $2/a - 3/a^2 = (2a - 3)/a^2$.
   d) $2/(x + 1) - 3/(x + 1)^2$
      $= (2x - 1)/(x + 1)^2$.
6. a) 5. b) 131/16. c) 13.
7. a) Δx means the change in x.
   b) The value of $f(x)$ at the point $x + \Delta x$.
   c) $f(x + \Delta x)$ means the change in $f(x)$ when x changes by Δx.
8. 0.75. **9.** -0.98. **10.** $-3(\Delta x)$.
11. $m(\Delta x)$.
12. a) $2x(\Delta x) + (\Delta x)^2$.
    b) $4x(\Delta x) + 2(\Delta x)^2 - 3(\Delta x)$.
13. a) $4x(\Delta x) + 2(\Delta x)^2$.
    b) $2x(\Delta x) + (\Delta x)^2 + 2(\Delta x)$.
14. a) $0.02 + 2.99$. b) \$3.19. c) \$3.99.
15. a) $0.2g + 0.9$. b) \$2.90. c) \$10.90.

Problem Set 10–2

1. 1. **2.** -13. **3.** ab^2. **4.** a^4. **5.** 0.
6. 1. **7.** Limit does not exist.
8. Limit does not exist. **9.** $(a - 1)^{1/3}$.
10. 5. **11.** $8a$. **12.** $4b$. **13.** 6.
14. 10. **15.** 0. **16.** Limit does not exist.
17. Limit does not exist. **18.** 0.
19. $2x$. **20.** $3x^2$. **21.** $-1/4$. **22.** $-1/25$.
23. 3. **24.** Limit does not exist.
25. 1. **26.** 2. **27.** Limit does not exist.
23. Limit does not exist. **29.** 5/4. **30.** 1.
31. Limit does not exist.
32. c) Limit does not exist.
33. c) -2. **34.** c) 0.

Problem Set 10–3

1. None. **2.** $x = 1$. **3.** None.
4. $x = \pm 2$. **5.** $x = 2$.
6. $x = 2; x = 3$. **7.** $x = 1$.
8. None. **9.** None. **10.** None.
13. Continuous at all $x \geq 0$. See Figure A.

FIGURE A

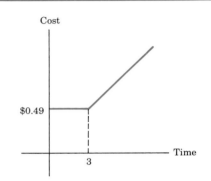

14. Continuous at all $x \geq 0$. See Figure B.

FIGURE B

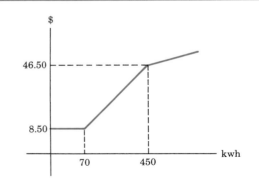

Problem Set 10–4

1. $f'(x) = 3; f'(1) = 3$.
2. $f'(x) = -0.5; f'(1) = -0.5$.

Problem Set 10–4 (*concluded*)

3. $f'(x) = 2x - 2; f'(1) = 0.$
4. $f'(x) = 6x - 12; f'(3) = 6.$
5. $f'(x) = -1/x^2; f'(2) = -1/4.$
6. $f'(x) = -2/x^3; f'(-1) = 2.$
7. $f'(x) = 3x^2 + 2; f'(2) = 14.$
8. $f'(x) = 3x^2 - x + 1; f'(-1) = 5.$
9. $f'(x) = 4x^3; f'(-1) = -4.$
10. $f'(x) = 1/2\sqrt{x}; f'(1) = 1/2.$
11. $f'(x) = \lim\limits_{\Delta x \to 0} \dfrac{(x + \Delta x)^5 - 2(x + \Delta x)^4 - x^5 + 2x^4}{\Delta x}.$
12. $f'(x) = \lim\limits_{\Delta x \to 0} \dfrac{3(x + \Delta x)^6 + 2(x + \Delta x)^3 - 3x^6 - 2x^3}{\Delta x}.$
13. $f'(x) = \lim\limits_{\Delta x \to 0} \dfrac{(x + \Delta x)^{1/3} - x^{1/3}}{\Delta x}.$
14. $f'(x) = \lim\limits_{\Delta x \to 0} \dfrac{(x + \Delta x)^{1/2} - x^{1/2}}{\Delta x}.$

Problem Set 10–5

1. 0.   **2.** 1.   **3.** 1/2.   **4.** 2.   **5.** 1/3.
6. $-3/2.$ **7.** $6x + 2.$ **8.** $x^2 - x + 1.$
9. $0.02x + 2.$ **10.** $1.5x^2 - x.$ **11.** $m.$
12. $2ax + b.$ **13.** $(-2/x^2) + (2/x^3).$
14. $(-1/2x^2) - (3/x^4).$
15. $3x^{1/2} - (2/x^{1/2}) + (2/x^{1/3}) + 2.$
16. $(2/3x^{2/3}) + (4/3)x^{1/3} + 6x^{0.2} + 1.$
17. $(-1/3x^2) - (1/x^{3/2}).$ **18.** $(-1/x^{4/3}) + (3/x^{5/4}).$
19. $6x - 2.$ **20.** $20y.$ **21.** $a.$
22. 0.   **23.** $2kh - (a/3h^{2/3}).$
24. $(-a/m^2) - 6m.$ **25.** 0.   **26.** 0.
27. 2.   **28.** $-4.$ **29.** 1.   **30.** 0.
31. 0.   **32.** $-1.$ **33.** 5/3.   **34.** 1.
35. $x = 1/2.$ **36.** $x = 100.$ **37.** $x = 1/8.$
38. $x = 9/16.$ **39.** $x = 3.$ **40.** $x = 4.$
41. a) \$4 per yard.   b) \$6 per yard.
42. a) \$55 per ton.   b) \$40 per ton.
   c) \$55 per ton.
43. $\dfrac{d}{dx}[f(x) + g(x)] = \lim\limits_{\Delta x \to 0} \left[\dfrac{f(x + \Delta x) + g(x + \Delta x) - f(x) - g(x)}{\Delta x} \right]$

$\qquad\qquad = \lim\limits_{\Delta x \to 0} \left[\dfrac{f(x + \Delta x) - f(x) + g(x + \Delta x) - g(x)}{\Delta x} \right]$

$\qquad\qquad = \lim\limits_{\Delta x \to 0} \left[\dfrac{f(x + \Delta x) - f(x)}{\Delta x} + \dfrac{g(x + \Delta x) - g(x)}{\Delta x} \right]$

$\qquad\qquad = \lim\limits_{\Delta x \to 0} \left[\dfrac{f(x + \Delta x) - f(x)}{\Delta x} \right] + \lim\limits_{\Delta x \to 0} \left[\dfrac{g(x + \Delta x) - g(x)}{\Delta x} \right]$

$\qquad\qquad = \qquad f'(x) + g'(x).$

Problem Set 10–6

1. $30(6x - 5)^4$.   **2.** $10(2x + 6)^4$.
3. $6(2x)^2 = 24x^2$.   **4.** $2/(6x)^{2/3}$.
5. $2/(4x)^{1/2} = 1/x^{1/2}$.   **6.** $12(9x)^{1/3}$.
7. $12(8x - 3)^{1/2}$.   **8.** $20(12x - 9)^{2/3}$.
9. $15(x - 1)(3x^2 - 6x + 2)^{3/2}$.
10. $4(x^2 - 2x + 2)(x^3 - 3x^2 + 6x)^{1/3}$.
11. $1/(2x - 3)^{1/2}$.   **12.** $4x/(3x^2 + 5)^{1/3}$.
13. $-8/(2x - 3)^2$.   **14.** $-18/(3x - 5)^2$.
15. $(-2/x^2)(1/x - 2)$.   **16.** $(6/x^3)(5 - 1/x^2)^2$.
17. $-54/(3x - 5)^3$.
18. $-72/(2x + 10)^4$.
19. $5 - 30/(3x + 2)^2$.
20. $0.1 + 1/(5 - 0.2x)^2$.
21. $3 - 1/(5 + 2x)^{3/2}$.
22. $-2 - 3/2(3x - 7)^{3/2}$.
23. $28/3$.   **24.** $13/2$.

Problem Set 10–7

1. $12x + 11$.   **2.** $19 - 42x$.
3. $9x^2 - 10x + 6$.   **4.** $3(5 - 4x - 5x^2)$.
5. $4x(x - 1)^3 + (x - 1)^4 = (x - 1)^3(5x - 1)$.
6. $3x^2(x + 5)^2 + 2x(x + 5)^3 = 5x(x + 5)^2(x + 2)$.
7. $\dfrac{3x^2(x + 3)^{1/2}}{2} + 2x(x + 3)^{3/2} =$
$x(x + 3)^{1/2}\left(\dfrac{7x}{2} + 6\right)$.

8. $\dfrac{4x^3}{(6x - 1)^{1/3}} + 3x^2(6x - 1)^{2/3} = \dfrac{x^2(22x - 3)}{6x - 1)^{1/3}}$.

9. $\dfrac{4x^2}{(3x^2 + 7)^{2/3}} + 2(3x^2 + 7)^{1/3} = \dfrac{2(5x^2 + 7)}{(3x^2 + 7)^{2/3}}$.

10. $\dfrac{9x^3}{(2x^3 + 5)^{1/2}} + 3(2x^3 + 5)^{1/2} = \dfrac{15(x^3 + 1)}{(2x^3 + 5)^{1/2}}$.

11. $-\dfrac{1}{(x - 1)^2}$.   **12.** $\dfrac{3}{(x + 1)^2}$.

13. $\dfrac{2x(x + 3)}{(2x + 3)^2}$.   **14.** $\dfrac{3x^2(2x + 5)}{(3x + 5)^2}$.

15. $\dfrac{3 - 2x^2}{(3 + 2x^2)^2}$.   **16.** $\dfrac{3(2x^2 + 1)}{(1 - 2x^2)^2}$.

17. $\dfrac{(3x + 2)^{1/2} - \dfrac{3x(3x + 2)^{-1/2}}{2}}{3x + 2} = \dfrac{3x + 4}{2(3x + 2)^{3/2}}$.

18. $\dfrac{2(2x + 3)^{1/2} - 2x(2x + 3)^{-1/2}}{2x + 3} = \dfrac{2(x + 3)}{(2x + 3)^{3/2}}$.

19. $\dfrac{2(x^2 + 5)^{1/3} - \dfrac{2x(2x + 1)(x^2 + 5)^{-2/3}}{3}}{(x^2 + 5)^{2/3}} =$
$\dfrac{2(x^2 - x + 15)}{3(x^2 + 5)^{4/3}}$.

20. $\dfrac{-5(x^3 + 2)^{1/3} - x^2(3 - 5x)(x^3 + 2)^{-2/3}}{(x^3 + 2)^{2/3}} =$
$-\dfrac{3x^2 + 10}{(x^3 + 2)^{4/3}}$.

CHAPTER 11

Problem Set 11–1

1. a) 50 gallons.   b) $5 per gallon.
2. a) $x = 25$ feet.
   c) 25 feet by 25 feet, a square.
   d) 625 square feet.
3. a) $p = 0.50$.
   c) $V(0.5) = 0.025$. $V(0.1) = 0.009$.
4. a) 2000 gallons.
   c) $20,000.

5. (2.5, 6.25) is a local maximum.
6. (3, 2) is a local minimum.
7. (0, 3) is a local maximum.
8. (0, 20) is a local minimum.
9. (5, 85) is a local maximum.
10. (0.5, 0.75) is a local minimum.
11. (0, 12) is a local maximum;
   (8, -244) is a local minimum.

Problem Set 11-1 (*concluded*)

12. (0, 2) is a local maximum;
(2, −2) is a local minimum.
13. $f(x)$ has no local optimum points.
14. $f(x)$ has no local optimum points.
15. (5, −5) is a local maximum;
(2, −32) is a local minimum.
16. (3, 0) is a local maximum;
(1, −4) is a local minimum.
17. (−1, −37) is an endpoint minimum;
(1, 19) is an endpoint maximum.
18. (−2, −98) is an endpoint minimum;
(2, 218) is an endpoint maximum.
19. (2, 52) is a local minimum.
Endpoint maxima at (0, 100) and (3, 85).
20. Endpoint minimum at (0, 0);
endpoint maximum at (2, 200).
21. (1, 5) is a local maximum.
Endpoint minimum at (−1, −3).
22. Endpoint maximum at (0, 30).
23. (4, −8) is a local minimum.
24. (27, 27) is a local maximum.
25. (4, −16) is a local minimum.
26. (125, 25) is a local maximum.
27. (4, 32) is a local minimum;
(−4, −32) is a local maximum.
28. (5, 30) is a local minimum.

Problem Set 11-2

1. $f'(x) = 5x^4 - 8x^3 + 3x^2.$
$f''(x) = 20x^3 - 24x^2 + 6x.$
2. $f'(x) = 3x^2 - 2x - 1.$
$f''(x) = 6x - 2.$
3. $f'(x) = 24x^2 - 4x.$
$f''(x) = 48x - 4.$
4. $f'(x) = 6x^5 - 4x^3 + 6x.$
$f''(x) = 30x^4 - 12x^2 + 6.$
5. $f'(x) = 12x^3 - 15x^2 + 4x.$
$f''(x) = 36x^2 - 30x + 4.$
6. $f'(x) = (5/2)x^{3/2} - 10x + 1.$
$f''(x) = (15/4)x^{1/2} - 10.$
7. $f'(x) = 3(x + 5)^2.$
$f''(x) = 6x + 30.$

8. $f'(x) = x(x^2 + 1).$
$f''(x) = 3x^2 + 1.$
9. $f'(x) = -13/(x - 3)^2.$
$f''(x) = 26/(x - 3)^3.$
10. $f'(x) = -4/(x - 2)^2.$
$f''(x) = 8/(x - 2)^3.$
11. Local minimum at (2, −1).
12. Local minimum at (−5, −34).
13. Local maximum at (1, 5); local minimum at
(3, 1); inflection point at (2, 3).
14. Inflection point at (0, 0).
15. Local maximum at (−2/3, 121/27); local
minimum at (2, −5); inflection point at
(2/3, 7/27).
16. Local maximum at (−3, 24); local minimum
at (1, −8); inflection point at (−1, 8).
17. Local maximum at (−3, 56); local minimum
at (−5, 52); inflection point at (−4, 54).
18. Local minimum at (0, 0).
19. Local minimum at (14, 8).
20. Local minimum at (0, 27); inflection points
at (1, −16) and (3, 0).

Problem Set 11-3

1. a) 50 by 66 feet.   b) $33,000.
2. a) 75 by 99 feet.   b) 7,425 square feet.
3. a) $C(x) = \left(2x + 2\dfrac{A}{x}\right)e + ix.$

b) $x = \sqrt{\dfrac{2Ae}{i + 2e}}.$

4. a) $A(x) = x\left(\dfrac{D - 2ex - ix}{2e}\right).$

b) $x = \dfrac{D}{2(2e + i)}.$

5. a) 90 by 150 feet.   b) $90,000.
6. $210.   **7.** 500 square feet.
8. 18 × 12 inches; area = 216 square inches.
9. 1100 by 660 feet; increase would be 10,000
square feet.
10. a) $A = 2x^2 + 4xL.$
b) $A(x) = 432x - 14x^2.$
c) $x = 108/7;$ $A''(x) = -28$ is always negative, proving we have a maximum.

Problem Set 11–3 (*concluded*)

    d) 108/7 by 108/7 by 3(108/7), or about
    15.4 by 15.4 by 46.3 inches.

11. $x = \dfrac{M}{7}$; $L = \dfrac{3M}{7}$.

12. A cube 4 by 4 by 4 inches; area = 96
    square inches.

13. 10 by 10 by 5 inches; area = 300 square
    inches.

14. 5 by 5 by 10 inches; minimum cost = $300.

15. $2.785.   **16.** One-inch squares.

17. 10/3 by 10/3 inches.

18. $r = 20$ feet; $h = 40$ feet.

19. $r = 24$ feet; $h = 250/9 = 27.8$ feet.

20. Maximum group charge $1,512.50 for 55
    persons or more.

21. a) $80r^2$.   b) $24 - 2r$.
    c) $T(r) = 80r^2(24 - 2r)$.
    d) $r = 8$ miles.   e) $40,960.

22. $175; $24,675.

23. a) $x = (k_1/k_2)^{1/2}$.
    b) 35 miles per hour.

24. a) $x = \left(\dfrac{p + k_1 d}{k_2 d}\right)^{1/2}$.
    b) 74.5 miles per hour.

25. 11,664 cubic inches.

26. 40 miles per hour.

27. 30 miles per hour.

28. $(k_1/k_2)^{1/2}$ miles per hour.

29. $p = 0.10$ yields a maximum because
    $C'(0.1) = 0$ and $C''(0.1)$ is negative.

30. $p = 1/n$.

31. a) $x = 200$ pounds.   b) $1,000.

32. a) $x = 800$ pounds.   b) $8,000.

33. Both sides should be 28.28 inches.

Problem Set 11–4

1. a) $y = 400$ barrels.   b) $164 per barrel.

2. a) $x = 200$ barrels.   b) $150 per barrel.

3. a) $x = 52.5$ thousand gallons.
    b) $14.5 thousand.

4. a) $t = 10$ hours.   b) 2.5 hundred pounds.

5. Q is $Q(0, 125)$.   **6.** Q is $Q(0, 25)$.

7. a) 4 miles.
    b) $24.5 hundred thousand, or $2,450,000.
    c) $160,007.

8. a) 8 miles.
    b) $47.64 hundred thousand, or
    $4,764,000.
    c) $221,639.

9. a) $x = \dfrac{(ab/k)^{1/2} - c}{b}$.

    b) $f''(x) = \dfrac{2ab^2}{(bx + c)^3}$ is positive, so we have
    a local minimum.

10. a) $x = \dfrac{(a/2k)^2 - b}{a} = \dfrac{a}{4k^2} - \dfrac{b}{a}$.

    b) $f''(x) = -\dfrac{a^2}{4(ax + b)^{3/2}}$ is negative, so we
    have a local maximum.

Problem Set 11–5

1. a) N/Q.   b) cN/Q.   c) uQ.
    d) $p(uQ)/2$.
    e) $S(Q) = cN/Q + uN + p(uQ)/2$.
    f) $Q = \sqrt{2cN/pu}$.   g) 240 units.

2. a) $6Kx^2$.   b) W/x^3.

    c) $(W/x^3)(6x^2 d) = \dfrac{6Wd}{x}$.

    d) $C(x) = 6Kx^2 + \dfrac{6Wd}{x}$.

    e) $x = \sqrt[3]{\dfrac{Wd}{2k}}$.   f) $x = 8$ feet.

Problem Set 11–6

1. See Figure A.

FIGURE A

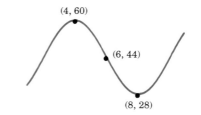

(4, 60)

(6, 44)

(8, 28)

Problem Set 11–6 (*continued*)

2. See Figure B.

FIGURE B

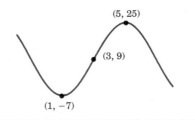

(5, 25)

(3, 9)

(1, −7)

3. See Figure C.

FIGURE C

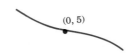

(0, 5)

4. See Figure D.

FIGURE D

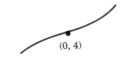

(0, 4)

5. See Figure E.

FIGURE E

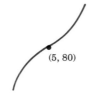

(5, 80)

6. See Figure F.

FIGURE F

(4, 6)

7. See Figure G.

FIGURE G

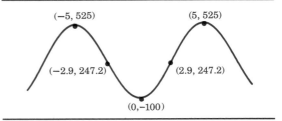

(−5, 525)   (5, 525)

(−2.9, 247.2)   (2.9, 247.2)

(0, −100)

8. See Figure H.

FIGURE H

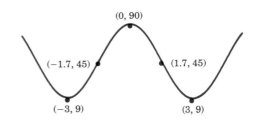

(0, 90)

(−1.7, 45)   (1.7, 45)

(−3, 9)   (3, 9)

9. See Figure I.

FIGURE I

(10, 20)

Problem Set 11–6 (*concluded*)

10. See Figure J.

FIGURE J

$(4, 2)$

11. See Figure K.

FIGURE K

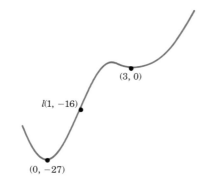

$(3, 0)$

$l(1, -16)$

$(0, -27)$

12. See Figure L.

FIGURE L

$(0, 10)$

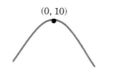

13. b) Inflection point at $(0, 8)$.
c) Local minimum at $(0, 5)$.
d) Local maximum at $(0, 6)$.
e) Inflection point at $(0, 0)$; local minimum at $(9/4, -2187/256)$.
f) Inflection point at $(0, 0)$; local maximum at $(-4/5, 256/3,125)$.

g) Local minimum at $(\sqrt[6]{1/7}, (-6/7)\sqrt[6]{1/7})$.

Problem Set 11–7

1. See Figure M.

FIGURE M

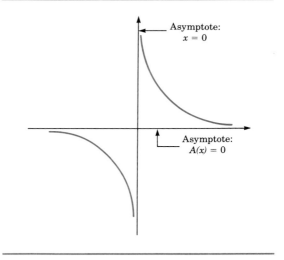

Asymptote:
$x = 0$

Asymptote:
$A(x) = 0$

2. See Figure N.

FIGURE N

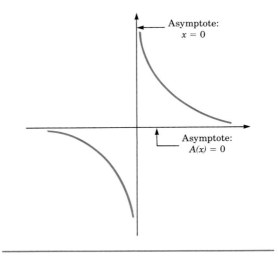

Asymptote:
$x = 0$

Asymptote:
$A(x) = 0$

Problem Set 11–7 (*continued*)

3. See Figure 0.

FIGURE 0

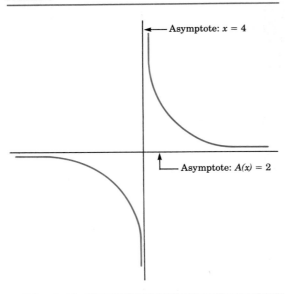

5. See Figure Q.

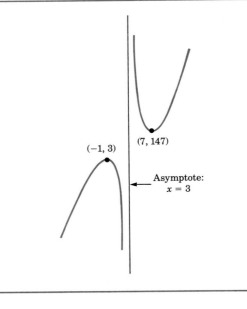

4. See Figure P.

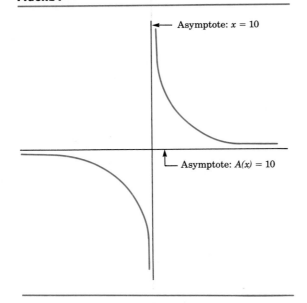

6. See Figure R.

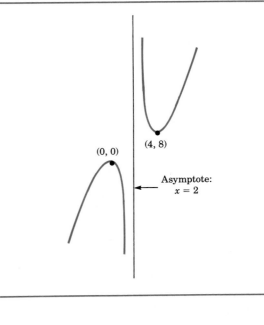

Problem Set 11–7 (concluded)

7. See Figure S.   **8.** See Figure T.

___

FIGURE S
___

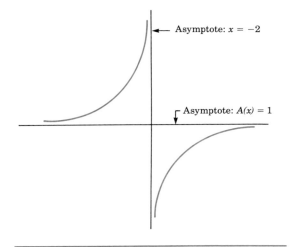

Asymptote: $x = -2$

Asymptote: $A(x) = 1$

___

FIGURE T
___

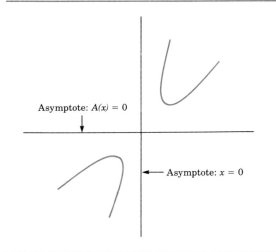

Asymptote: $A(x) = 0$

Asymptote: $x = 0$

___

CHAPTER 12

Problem Set 12–1

1. $f'(x) = 2e^x. \ f''(x) = 2e^x.$
2. $f'(x) = 5^x \ln 5. \ f''(x) = 5^x(\ln 5)^2.$
3. $f'(x) = 7^x \ln 7. \ f''(x) = 7^x(\ln 7)^2.$
4. $f'(x) = 3e^x. \ f''(x) = 3e^x.$
5. $f'(x) = -e^{-0.2x}. \ f''(x) = 0.2e^{-0.2x}.$
6. $f'(x) = -e^{-0.4x}. \ f''(x) = 0.4e^{-0.4x}.$
7. $f'(x) = -2e^{3-0.1x}. \ f''(x) = 0.2e^{3-0.1x}.$
8. $f'(x) = 3e^{0.3x-6}. \ f''(x) = 0.9e^{0.3x-6}.$
9. $f'(x) = 2xe^{x^2}. \ f''(x) = 2e^{x^2}(2x^2 + 1).$
10. $f'(x) = -2xe^{-x^2}. \ f''(x) = 2e^{-x^2}(2x^2 - 1).$
11. $f'(x) = 2.07945(1/2)^{-3x} = 2.07945(2)^{3x}.$
$\quad f''(x) = 4.32411(1/2)^{-3x} = 4.32411(2)^{3x}.$
12. $f'(x) = 0.27489(0.4)^{-0.3x}.$
$\quad f''(x) = 0.07556(0.4)^{-0.3x}.$
13. $f'(x) = 58.27(1.06)^x. \ f''(x) = 3.395(1.06)^x.$

14. $f'(x) = -38.48(1.08)^{-x}.$
$\quad f''(x) = 2.962(1.08)^{-x}.$
15. See Figure A.

___

FIGURE A
___

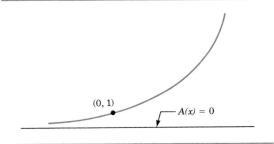

$(0, 1)$

$A(x) = 0$

___

Problem Set 12–1 (*continued*)

16. See Figure B.

FIGURE B

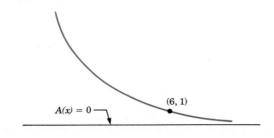

17. See Figure C.

FIGURE C

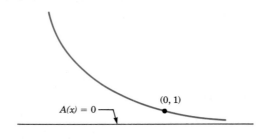

18. See Figure D.

FIGURE D

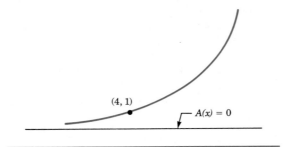

19. See Figure E.

FIGURE E

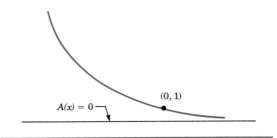

20. See Figure F.

FIGURE F

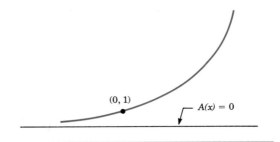

21. See Figure G.

FIGURE G

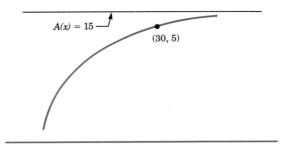

Problem Set 12–1 (*concluded*)

22. See Figure H.

FIGURE H

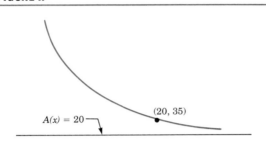

A(x) = 20 ──→   (20, 35)

23. 2.915.
24. a) $t = 252.57286$ days.   b) $882,427.
25. a) $t = 160.94379$ days.   b) $1,024,056.
26. a) $t = 10.058987$ years.   b) $5,163,614.
27. a) $t = 11.453634$ years.   b) $7,381,624.
28. $t = 6.93$ years.   **29.** Maximum is 55.47.
30. Minimum is 1.   **31.** Minimum is 0.52.
32. Maximum is 12.18.
33. Maximum is 145.60.
34. Minimum is 4.85.

Problem Set 12–2

1. $1/x$.   **2.** $3/x$.   **3.** $2/(2x + 3)$.
4. $-1/x$.   **5.** 1.   **6.** $2/3(2x + 5)$.
7. $2(x + 1)/x(x + 2)$.
8. $\dfrac{6x^2 - 6}{2x^3 - 6x} = \dfrac{3(x^2 - 1)}{x(x^2 - 3)}$.
9. $3/2(3x + 2)$.   **10.** Minimum is 16.93.
11. Maximum is 180.26.
12. Minimum is -4.64.
13. Minimum is 2.30.
14. Minimum is 72.78.
15. Minimum is 9.45. (Note that x cannot be negative.)
16. 12 ounces.   **17.** 11.5 ounces.

Problem Set 12–3

1. Cost increases at the (constant) rate of $2.50 per additional book made.
2. At 500 miles, cost is increasing at the rate of

$0.15 per additional mile driven. At 1,000 miles, cost is increasing at the rate of $0.10 per additional mile driven.
3. At $t = 5$ years, the amount in the account is increasing at the rate of $226.16 per additional year. At $t = 10$ years, the amount is increasing at the rate of $332.31 per additional year.
4. At $t = 5$ years, the amount in the account is increasing at the rate of $238.69 per additional year. At $t = 10$ years, the amount is increasing at the rate of $356.09 per additional year.
5. a) $a(x) = \dfrac{16}{x} + 0.2$.   b) $a'(x) = -\dfrac{16}{x^2}$.
At 40 miles, the average cost per mile is decreasing at the rate of $0.01 per additional mile driven.
6. a) $a(x) = 0.01x^2 - 3x + 300 + 10{,}000/x$.
b) $a'(x) = 0.02x - 3 - 10{,}000/x^2$.
c) At 100 tons output, average cost per ton is decreasing at the rate of $2 per additional ton produced. At 500 tons output, average cost per ton is increasing at the rate of $6.96 per additional ton produced.
7. At 100 labor-hours worked, output is increasing at the rate of 0.359 tons per additional labor-hour worked.
8. At $t = 2$ years, sales are increasing at the rate of $17.09 thousand per additional year.
9. At $t = 5$ years, the number of customers in the trading area is increasing at the rate of 39,923 per additional year.
10. At $t = 5$, the function is increasing at the rate of 10 percent per additional unit of x.
11. At $t = 5$ (or any number of) years, customers are increasing at the rate of 10 percent per additional year.
12. At $t = 2$ years, sales are increasing at the rate of 66.7 percent per additional year.
13. At $t = 10$ (or any number of) years, the amount in the account is increasing at the rate of 6.766 percent per additional year.
14. a) 100 units.   b) $\dfrac{N}{i}\left(\dfrac{2NF}{i}\right)^{-1/2} = \dfrac{N}{iL}$.
c) 2 units.
15. a) 200 units.   b) $\dfrac{F}{i}\left(\dfrac{2NF}{i}\right)^{-1/2} = \dfrac{F}{iL}$.
c) Decrease by 10 units.

Problem Set 12–3 (*concluded*)

16. a) $x = 15$.   b) $-50/h^2$.
c) x would decrease by 0.25.
17. a) At $x = 5$, ln x changes at the rate of 0.2 per unit change in x.
b) Increase by 0.0002.   c) 1.60964.
18. a) At $x = 4$, the square root of x changes at the rate of 0.25 per unit change in x.
b) 0.0025.   c) 2.0025.

Problem Set 12–4

1. $\dfrac{df(y)}{dy} \cdot \dfrac{dy}{dx}$.

2. $\dfrac{df(x)}{dx} \cdot \dfrac{dx}{dz}$.

3. $\dfrac{dp(q)}{dq} \cdot \dfrac{dq}{dh}$.

4. $\dfrac{dg(f)}{df} \cdot \dfrac{df}{dw}$.

5. $4y^3 \cdot \dfrac{dy}{dx}$.

6. $3x^2 \cdot \dfrac{dx}{dy}$.

7. $2e^{2w} \cdot \dfrac{dw}{dz}$.

8. $-e^{-0.5p} \cdot \dfrac{dp}{dq}$.

9. $\dfrac{2}{2y + 3} \cdot \dfrac{dy}{dx}$.

10. $\dfrac{2z - 3}{z^2 - 3z} \cdot \dfrac{dz}{dw}$.

11. $x + y \cdot \dfrac{dx}{dy}$.

12. $\left(y - x \cdot \dfrac{dy}{dx} \right) \Big/ y^2$.

13. $2x/3y^2$.

14. $9x^2/5y^4$.

15. $(x^5 + 1)/y(y - 1)$.
16. $2/(20y^4 - 4y + 1)$.
17. $1/(1 - e^{-y}) = e^y/(e^y - 1)$.
18. $1/2(1 - ye^{y^2})$.
19. $-y$ ln y.
20. $1/x$ ln x.
21. $(2x - y^3)/3xy^2$.
22. $2(1 - xy^3)/3x^2y^2$.

23. $\dfrac{1}{1 - \dfrac{dg(y)}{dy}}$.

24. $\dfrac{2z}{2w - \dfrac{df(w)}{dw}}$.

25. a) 0.68.
b) 68 cents of an additional dollar of income is spent.
c) \$3.125.   d) 0.85, or 85 percent.
26. a) 0.63.
b) 63 cents of an additional dollar of income is spent.
c) \$2.70.   d) 0.90, or 90 percent.
27. a) 5.62.   b) 3.51.
28. a) 15.17.   b) 5.26.

Problem Set 12–5

1. a) 3.   b) 0.   c) -2.   d) 0.   e) 0.
2. a) 2.   b) 0.   c) 5.   d) 0.   e) 0.
3. a) $2x + 3$.   b) 2.   c) $2y - 2$.
d) 2.   e) 0.
4. a) $2x - 5$.   b) 2.   c) $-2y + 4$.
d) -2.   e) 0.
5. a) $6x - 2y$.   b) 6.   c) $-2x + 2y$.
d) 2.   e) -2.
6. a) $6x^2 + 3y$.   b) $12x$.   c) $3x + 4$.
d) 0.   e) 3.
7. a) $y^{1/2}/2x^{1/2}$.   b) $-y^{1/2}/4x^{3/2}$.
c) $x^{1/2}/2y^{1/2}$.   d) $-x^{1/2}/4y^{3/2}$.
e) $1/4x^{1/2}y^{1/2}$.
8. a) $2y^{1/3}/3x^{1/3}$.   b) $-2y^{1/3}/9x^{4/3}$.
c) $x^{2/3}/3y^{2/3}$.   d) $-2x^{2/3}/9y^{5/3}$.
e) $2/9x^{1/3}y^{2/3}$.
9. a) $2y^{1/2} - y/x^{2/3}$.   b) $2y/3x^{5/3}$.
c) $(x/y^{1/2}) - 3x^{1/3}$.   d) $-x/2y^{3/2}$.
e) $(1/y^{1/2}) - (1/x^{2/3})$.
10. a) $3x^{1/2}y^2/2$.   b) $3y^2/4x^{1/2}$.   c) $2x^{3/2}y$.
d) $2x^{3/2}$.   e) $3x^{1/2}y$.
11. a) $ye^x(x + 1)$.   b) $ye^x(x + 2)$. c) xe^x.
d) 0.   e) $e^x(x + 1)$.
12. a) y ln y.   b) 0.   c) $x(1 + $ ln $y)$.
d) $x(1 + 1/y)$.   e) $1 + $ ln y.
13. a) $2y/(x + y)^2$.   b) $-4y/(x + y)^3$.
c) $-2x/(x + y)^2$.   d) $4x/(x + y)^3$.
e) $2(x - y)/(x + y)^3$.
14. a) $-2y/(x - y)^2$.   b) $4y/(x - y)^3$.
c) $2x/(x - y)^2$.   d) $4x/(x - y)^3$.
e) $-2(x + y)/(x - y)^3$.
15. a) $3/(3x + 2y)$.   b) $-9/(3x + 2y)^2$.
c) $2/(3x + 2y)$.   d) $-4/(3x + 2y)^2$.
e) $-6/(3x + 2y)^2$.
16. a) $2e^{2x+3y}$.   b) $4e^{2x+3y}$.   c) $3e^{2x+3y}$.
d) $9e^{2x+3y}$.   e) $6e^{2x+3y}$.
17. $6z - 2x$.   **18.** $2w - 3z^2$.   **19.** 2.
20. 6.   **21.** -3.   **22.** 3.
23. a) 7.   b) 3.   c) 0.   d) 2.
e) 0.   f) 0.
24. a) 7.   b) 2.   c) 0.   d) 3.
e) 0.   f) 0.
25. a) 8.   b) 5.   c) 2.   d) -4.
e) -6.   f) 1.
26. a) -14.   b) 2.   c) 4.   d) -11.
e) 2.   f) -5.

Problem Set 12–5 (*concluded*)

27. At the production level of 3 tons of oats and 5 tons of hay, cost is decreasing at the rate of $4 per additional ton of oats and cost is not changing (is stationary) with respect to a change in hay.

28. At the production level of 3 tons of oats and 7 tons of hay, cost is decreasing at the rate of $8 per additional ton of oats and cost is increasing at the rate of $4 per additional ton of hay.

29. At 400 tons of oats and 500 tons of hay:
  a) Profit is increasing at the rate of $10 per additional ton of oats.
  b) Profit is increasing at the rate of $10 per additional ton of hay.
  c) At 600 tons of oats and 500 tons of hay, profit is decreasing at the rate of $10 per additional ton of oats.
  d) At 400 tons of oats and 600 tons of hay, profit is decreasing at the rate of $10 per additional ton of hay.

30. When labor expenditure and capital investment are, respectively, $64 and $27 million:
  a) Output is increasing at the rate of $1.50 per additional $1 of labor expenditure.
  b) Output is increasing at the rate of $7.11 per additional dollar of capital investment.

Problem Set 12–6

1. Minimum is 10.   **2.** Maximum is 23.
3. Maximum is 120.   **4.** Minimum is 50.
5. Minimum is 10.   **6.** Maximum is 52.
7. Saddle point at $f(2, 1) = 0$.
8. Saddle point at $f(0, 0) = 0$.
9. Maximum is 175.

10. Saddle point at $f(6, 5) = 14$.
11. Maximum is 10.   **12.** Minimum is -5.
13. a) 500 gallons of molasses and 550 gallons of maple syrup.
  b) Both P_{xx} and P_{yy} are negative and $D = (0)^2 - (-0.1)(-0.2)$ is negative, so we have a maximum.
  c) $P_{max} = \$42,750$.
14. a) Use machine A for 4 hours and machine B for 6 hours.
  b) Both C_{xx} and C_{yy} are positive and $D = (-2)^2 - 6(2)$ is negative, so we have a minimum.
  c) $C_{min} = \$14$ per unit.
15. $1,400 for 12 salesmen and $40 hundreds of inventory.
16. $94.86 for the first kind and $70.71 for the second kind.
17. a) $L = 400$, $I = 250$.
  b) $C_{min} = \$3,750$.
18. a) $L = 520$, $p = 0.8$.
  b) $C_{LL} = 0.0015$, $C_{pp} = 2600$ and $C_{pL} = 0$. Hence, $D < 0$ and both partials are positive, so we have a minimum.
  c) $C_{min} = \$416,000$.
19. $L = \left[\dfrac{2cd(a + b)}{ab}\right]^{1/2}$.

$I = \dfrac{bL}{a + b} = \left[\dfrac{2bcd}{a(a + b)}\right]^{1/2}$.

Problem Set 12–7

1. $y_t = 1.893 + 0.821x$.
2. $y_t = 9.571 + 0.357x$.
3. $y_t = 9.5 - 1.5x$.
4. $y_t = 11.25 - 2.5x$.
5. $y_t = 26.496 + 0.527x$.
6. $y_t = 32.0029 - 0.0516x$.

CHAPTER 13

Problem Set 13–1

1. $x + C.$ **2.** $z + C.$ **3.** $5y + C.$

4. $-7w + C.$ **5.** $x + \dfrac{x^2}{2} + C.$

6. $3y - \dfrac{y^2}{2} + C.$ **7.** $\dfrac{2x^3}{3} - \dfrac{3x^2}{2} + 4x + C.$

8. $\dfrac{3y^4}{4} + 2y^2 - y + C.$ **9.** $pq + C.$

10. $qp + C.$ **11.** $\dfrac{qp^2}{2} + C.$ **12.** $\dfrac{pq^2}{2} + C.$

13. $\dfrac{x^4}{4} + \dfrac{x^5}{5} - x + C.$ **14.** $\dfrac{y^3}{3} + \dfrac{y^6}{6} - y + C.$

15. $y^3 + y^5 + y + C.$ **16.** $x^4 - x^6 + x + C.$

17. $-\dfrac{1}{x} + C.$ **18.** $\dfrac{y}{343} + C.$

19. $-\dfrac{1}{2y^2} + C.$ **20.** $-\dfrac{1}{3x^3} + C.$

21. $5y + \dfrac{1}{y^2} + C.$ **22.** $7x + \dfrac{1}{x^3} + C.$

23. $x^2 + \dfrac{1}{x} + x + C.$ **24.** $\dfrac{y^2}{2} - \dfrac{1}{y^2} + y + C.$

25. $\dfrac{2p^{3/2}}{3} + C.$ **26.** $\dfrac{3q^{4/3}}{4} + C.$

27. $-\dfrac{9}{x^{1/3}} + C.$ **28.** $-\dfrac{10}{y^{1/2}} + C.$

29. $2x + \dfrac{1}{x} + \dfrac{1}{x^{2/3}} + C.$ **30.** $x^2 + \dfrac{1}{x^2} + \dfrac{3}{4x^{1/3}} + C.$

31. $4x^3 + 3x^4 + C.$ **32.** $x^3 + 3x^2 + C.$

33. $2(2x - 9)^4 + C.$ **34.** $\dfrac{5(3x + 5)^6}{3} + C.$

35. $-\dfrac{1}{3(3x - 9)} + C.$ **36.** $-\dfrac{1}{6(2x + 3)^3} + C.$

37. $-\dfrac{2(5 - 3x)^{1/2}}{3} + C.$ **38.** $\dfrac{1}{4(7 - 2w)^2} + C.$

39. $6(2x + 5)^{2/3} + C.$ **40.** $8(3x - 7)^{1/2} + C.$

Problem Set 13–2

1. 6.   **2.** 6.   **3.** 15.   **4.** 108.   **5.** 20.
6. 4.   **7.** 96/5.   **8.** 18.   **9.** 17/6.
10. 51/2.   **11.** 44.   **12.** 16.   **13.** 26/3.
14. 2.   **15.** 3.   **16.** 8.   **17.** $b^3 - a^3.$

18. $d^4 - c^4.$ **19.** $\dfrac{n^2}{2} + n - \dfrac{3}{2}.$ **20.** $n - n^2.$

21. 3.   **22.** 36.   **23.** 13/2.   **24.** 6.
25. 4.   **26.** 3/2.   **27.** 16.   **28.** 80.
29. 100.   **30.** 25/2.   **31.** 500.
32. 500/3.   **33.** 8.   **34.** 8.

Problem Set 13–3

1. a) 27/2.   b) 23/2.   **2.** 8.   **3.** 36.
4. 500/3.   **5.** 125/6.   **6.** 9.
7. 64/3.   **8.** 3375.   **9.** 1/2.
10. $20\sqrt{5}/3 = 14.9071.$

Problem Set 13–4

1. a) \$13.8 thousand.   b) See Figure A.
c) \$17.4 thousand.   d) 20 years.

FIGURE A

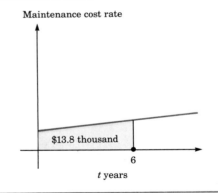

2. a) \$180 thousand.   b) See Figure B.
c) \$140 thousand.   d) 25 years.

Problem Set 13–4 (concluded)

FIGURE B

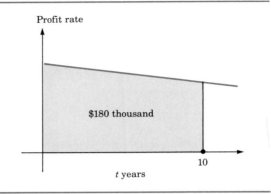

Profit rate

$180 thousand

10

t years

3. 100 million barrels.   **4.** 1,944 barrels.
5. 13.5 years.   **6.** 18 years.
7. $100 + 80 = 180$ thousand.
8. $80 + 2 = \$82$ thousand.
9. $2,600.   **10.** $20,000.
11. a) 50 months.   b) $200 thousand.
12. a) 36 months.   b) $17,500.
13. a) $3,000 million.   b) See Figure C.

FIGURE C

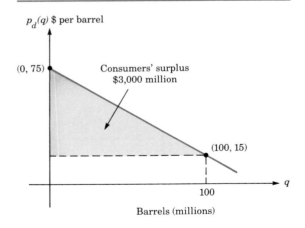

$p_d(q)$ $ per barrel

(0, 75)

Consumers' surplus
$3,000 million

(100, 15)

100

Barrels (millions)

14. a) $250 million.   b) See Figure D.

FIGURE D

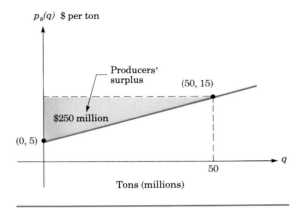

$p_s(q)$ $ per ton

Producers'
surplus

(50, 15)

$250 million

(0, 5)

50

Tons (millions)

15. $1,856 thousand.   **16.** $3,240 million.
17. a) $9,000 thousand.   b) $4,500 thousand.
18. a) $100 million.   b) $25 million.

Problem Set 13–5

1. $\ln x + C.$ **2.** $\ln x + C.$ **3.** $2 \ln x + C.$
4. $3 \ln x + C.$ **5.** $-\dfrac{1}{x} + C.$
6. $-\dfrac{1}{x} + C.$ **7.** $\dfrac{\ln(5x + 4)}{5} + C.$
8. $-\ln(3 - x) + C.$ **9.** $-5 \ln (3 - 0.2x) + C.$
10. $4 \ln(0.5x + 1) + C.$ **11.** $-\dfrac{1}{2(2x - 1)} + C.$
12. $-\dfrac{2}{(5x + 3)} + C.$ **13.** $2.30259.$
14. $1.$ **15.** $0.44629.$ **16.** $0.93269.$
17. 895.9 million barrels.
18. $140.3 million.

Problem Set 13–6

1. $e^x + C.$ **2.** $\dfrac{2^x}{\ln 2} + C.$ **3.** $-\dfrac{3^{-x}}{\ln 3} + C.$
4. $-e^{-x} + C.$ **5.** $2e^{0.5x} + C.$
6. $\dfrac{5(5^{0.2x})}{\ln 5} + C.$ **7.** $\dfrac{-2.5(0.5)^{1-0.4x}}{\ln(0.5)} + C.$
8. $-2e^{2-0.5x} + C.$ **9.** $-20e^{3-0.1x} + C.$
10. $-20e^{5-0.2x} + C.$ **11.** $\dfrac{-1}{(0.8)^x \ln(0.8)} + C.$

Problem Set 13–6 (*concluded*)

12. $-2/e^{0.5x} + C.$ **13.** 17.18.
14. 14.11.   **15.** 3.61.   **16.** 9.02.
17. a) 343.7 million barrels.   b) 35.8 years.
18. a) $183.8 thousand.   b) 13.7 years.
19. a) $10,544.33.   b) 6.76 years.
20. a) 47.41 million pounds.   b) 8.05 years.
21. 72.41 million pounds.
22. 93.23 million gallons.
23. $27.74 thousand.   **24.** $40 thousand.

Problem Set 13–7

1. $\dfrac{x(2^x)}{\ln 2} - \dfrac{2^x}{(\ln 2)^2} + C.$

2. $3x - (3/2)\ln(2x + 1) + C.$

3. $8\left[\dfrac{1}{0.5x + 1} + \ln(0.5x + 1)\right] + C.$

4. $e^x(x - 1) + C.$
5. $-4e^{2 - 0.5x}(0.5x + 1) + C.$

6. $\dfrac{4}{3x + 4} + \ln(3x + 4) + C.$

7. $2\ln\dfrac{x}{0.5x + 1} + C.$

8. $12.5e^{0.4x - 1}(0.4x - 1) + C.$

9. $2\left[\dfrac{x}{5} + \dfrac{3}{25}\ln(5x - 3)\right] + C.$

10. $3\ln\dfrac{x}{3x + 2} + C.$ **11.** $5e^{0.1x^2 - 2} + C.$

12. $5[0.2x - \ln(1 + e^{0.2x})] + C.$
13. $x - 2\ln(1 + 2e^{0.5x}) + C.$

14. $-2e^{2 - 0.5x^2} + C.$ **15.** $(1/3)\ln\left|\dfrac{x - 3}{x + 3}\right| + C.$

16. $(-5/4)\ln\left|\dfrac{x - 4}{x + 4}\right| + C.$

17. $3\ln\left|\dfrac{1 + \sqrt{1 - 9x^2}}{3x}\right| + C.$ **18.** $\ln\left|\dfrac{x + 1}{4x}\right| + C.$

Problem Set 13–8

1. 8.   **2.** 3.   **3.** 2.   **4.** 6.
5. Does not exist.   **6.** Does not exist.
7. 25.   **8.** 2.   **9.** Does not exist.
10. 1/192.   **11.** Does not exist.   **12.** 100.

13. 1/98.   **14.** 1/4.   **15.** Does not exist.
16. $-1/9$.   **17.** $(4/9)\ln 2 = 0.3081$.
18. $2\ln 1.1 = 0.1906$.

Problem Set 13–9

1. 2.53.   **2.** 0.366.   **3.** 0.379.
4. 1.019.   **5.** 0.188.   **6.** 2.391.
7. 0.590.   **8.** 0.110.   **9.** 0.535.
10. 0.639.   **11.** 0.3411.   **12.** 0.3413.

Problem Set 13–10

1. $3x(\ln x - 1) + C.$ **2.** $2x(\ln x - 1) + C.$
3. $x(\ln 2x - 1) + C.$ **4.** $x(\ln 3x - 1) + C.$

5. $\dfrac{(2x + 1)[\ln(2x + 1) - 1]}{2} + C.$

6. $\dfrac{(3x + 5)[\ln(3x + 5) - 1]}{3} + C.$

7. $2(3x - 2)[\ln(3x - 2) - 1] + C.$
8. $2(2x - 1)[\ln(2x - 1) - 1] + C.$
9. $70.33 thousand.
10. 110.6 million bushels.

11. $\dfrac{x^2 \ln x}{2} - \dfrac{x^2}{4} + C.$ **12.** $\dfrac{x^4 \ln x}{4} - \dfrac{x^4}{16} + C.$

13. $-\dfrac{\ln x + 1}{x} + C.$ **14.** $\ln x - \dfrac{\ln x}{x} - \dfrac{1}{x} + C.$

15. $\dfrac{(x + 1)^6 (6x - 1)}{42} + C.$

16. $(-8/3)(8 - x)^{1/2} (5x - 16) + C.$
17. $(-2/15)(1 - x)^{3/2}(7x - 2) + C.$
18. $(-2/3) (x - 1)^{1/2} (x + 2) + C.$
19. $e^x(x^2 - 2x + 10) + C.$

20. $\dfrac{e^2 + 1}{4} = 7.6391.$

21. $\dfrac{e^2 + 1}{4} = 7.6391.$

22. $\dfrac{3e^2 + 29}{12} = 4.2639.$

Problem Set 13–11

1. $y = x + C.$ **2.** $y = x^3 + C.$
3. $y = \ln x + C.$ **4.** $y = Ke^x.$ **5.** $y = Kx.$
6. $y = Ke^{-1/x}.$ **7.** $y = Ke^{x^{1/2}}.$ **8.** $y = K/x.$
9. $y = 5\ln(0.2x + 3) + C.$
10. $y = 4\ln(0.5x + 2) + C.$
11. $y = Ke^{0.5x} - 4.$ **12.** $y = Ke^{0.2x} - 15.$

Problem Set 13–11 (*concluded*)

13. $y = 0.5x^2 + x + 2$. **14.** $y = x^2$.
15. $y = 0.4e^x$. **16.** $y = 6/x$.
17. $y = 19e^{0.2x} - 15$. **18.** $y = 5e^{0.5x} - 4$.
19. $y = 3x - 1$. **20.** $y = 8/x - 1$.

Problem Set 13–12

1. a) $dS = (150 + 6t)\, dt$.
  b) $S = 0$ when $t = 0$.
  c) $S(t) = 150t + 3t^2$. d) 15,000.
  e) 100 days.
2. a) $dS = (100 + 2t)\, dt$.
  b) $S = 0$ when $t = 0$.
  c) $S(t) = 100t + t^2$. d) 7500.
  e) 200 days.

3. a) $dP = 0.1\, Pdt$. b) $P(t) = 100e^{0.1t}$.
  c) \$271.8 thousand.
4. a) $dS = 0.05Sdt$. b) $S(t) = 2000e^{0.05t}$.
  c) \$5,436.56.
5. a) $dS = 0.08Sdt + 500\, dt$.
  b) $S(t) = 8250e^{0.08t} - 6250$.
  c) \$12,110.71. d) 13.7 years.
6. a) $dS = 0.08Sdt - 500\, dt$.
  b) $S(t) = 6250 - 1250e^{0.08t}$.
  c) \$3,468.07. d) 20.1 years.
7. a) $dC = 5e^{0.01t}\, dt$.
  b) $C(t) = 500(e^{0.01t} - 1)$.
  c) 52.6 million barrels. d) 33.6 years.
8. a) $dC = 5e^{0.02t}\, dt$.
  b) $C(t) = 250(e^{0.02t} - 1)$.
  c) 55.4 million barrels. d) 29.4 years.

CHAPTER 14

Problem Set 14–1

1. a) $p(x) = 0.1$. b) 0.3.
2. a) $p(x) = x/50$. b) 0.09.
3. a) $p(x) = x^{1/2}/18$. b) 0.259.
4. a) $p(x) = \dfrac{2 - x^{-2}}{37.05}$. b) 0.462.
5. a) $p(x) = \dfrac{12x - 3x^2}{32}$. b) 0.5.

Problem Set 14–2

1. a) $\mu = 10$. b) $\sigma^2 = 100/3$.
  c) $\sigma = 5.77$.
2. a) $\mu = 50$. b) $\sigma^2 = 2500/3$.
  c) $\sigma = 28.87$.
3. a) $\mu = 4$. b) $\sigma^2 = 2$. c) $\sigma = 1.41$.
4. a) $\mu = 2$. b) $\sigma^2 = 0.5$.
  c) $\sigma = 0.707$.
5. a) 35/12 hundred gallons.
  b) 210 hundred gallons.
6. a) 17/15 thousand gallons.
  b) 102 thousand gallons.
7. a) See Figure A.

FIGURE A

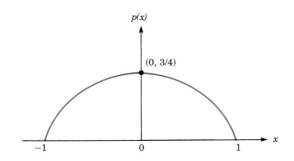

b) The function is symmetrical, so its center
  of gravity is at the midpoint of the x-inter-
  val, which is zero.
c) $\int_{-1}^{1} x \left[\dfrac{3(1 - x^2)}{4} \right] dx = \dfrac{3}{4}\left(\dfrac{x^2}{2} - \dfrac{x^4}{4} \right) \Big|_{-1}^{1} = 0$.
d) $(0.6)^{1/2} = 0.775$.

8. a) See Figure B.
  b) The function is symmetrical, so its center

Problem Set 14–2 (*concluded*)

of gravity is at the midpoint of the *x*-interval, which is zero.

c) $\int_{-2}^{2} x\left[\dfrac{3(4-x^2)}{32}\right] dx = \dfrac{3}{32}\left(2x^2 - \dfrac{x^4}{4}\right)\Big|_{-2}^{2}$
$= 0.$

d) 0.894.

FIGURE B

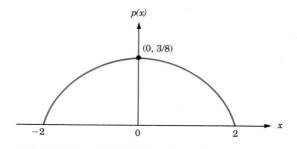

Problem Set 14–3

1. a) 0.7769.   b) 0.2325.   c) 0.0821.
2. a) 0.3935.   b) 0.1859.   c) 0.3679.
3. a) 0.5276.   b) 0.6065.
4. a) 0.3935.   b) 0.4493.
5. a) 0.9933.   b) 0.0821.
6. a) 0.1393.   b) 0.9512.

7. a) $(ke^{-4x}/4)\Big|_{1}^{\infty}$.   b) $k = 4; p(x) = 4e^{-4x}$.

    c) $\mu = 1/4$.

8. a) $(-k/2x^2)\Big|_{1}^{\infty}$.   b) $k = 2$.   c) $\mu = 2$.

Problem Set 14–4

1. a) 0.1915.   b) 0.1915.   c) 0.1587.
    d) 0.1498.   e) 0.2266.   f) 0.3721.
    g) 0.1554.   h) 0.1464.
2. a) 0.8400.   b) 0.9544.   c) 0.9974.
    d) 0.0456.   e) 0.7881.   f) 0.2295.
    g) 0.8413.   h) 0.1151.
3. a) 0.9772.   b) 0.3023.   c) 0.3085.
    d) 0.3413.   e) 0.1498.   f) 0.6826.
    g) 0.2266.   h) 0.6247.   i) 0.0013.

Problem Set 14–5

1. $\bar{x} = 7, s = 2.$ 2. $\bar{x} = 15, s = 2.94.$
3. $\bar{x} = 11.2, s = 2.17.$
4. $\bar{x} = 3.5, s = 2.07.$
5. $\bar{x} = 0.58, s = 0.03.$

Problem Set 14–6

1. a) 52.2.   b) 56.410.   c) 41.775.
    d) 46.6 to 53.4.   e) 58.225.
2. a) 0.1587.   b) 0.9772.   c) 23 parts.
    d) 4.56 percent.   e) 1.5730 to 1.5770.
    f) 2.2484.   g) $53.44.
3. a) 0.3085.   b) 69.15 percent.
    c) 134 cans.   d) 10.56 percent.
    e) 16.465.
4. a) 1908 to 2092.   b) 10.56 percent.
    c) 1868.   d) 0.62 percent.
5. a) 0.13 percent.   b) 5.48 percent.
    c) 183 to 217.   d) 159.
    e) 99th percentile.

APPENDIX 1

Problem Set A1–1

1. a) "*B* is the set whose elements are 2, 4, and 6."
    b) "*C* is the set whose element is 0."
    c) "*Q* is the set whose members are the odd numbers 1 through 29."
    d) "*F* is the set whose elements are the lowercase English vowels."
    e) "*L* is the set whose members are George and Charles."
    f) "*K* is the set of positive even integers starting with 2."
2. a) $F = \{$Lowercase English vowels$\}$.

Problem Set A1–1 (*concluded*)

b) S = {Positive integral multiples of 3}.
c) P = {First five positive integers}.
d) G = {First five uppercase English letters}.
e) R = {Integers greater than 99}.
f) J = {Negative odd integers from -1 through -101}.
    = {Negative odd integers greater than -102}.

3. a) {1, 3, 5, 7}.
b) {January, February, March, April}.
c) {14, 28, 42, . . .}.
d) {5, 10, 15, . . . , 995}.
e) ϕ.   f) {1^2, 2^2, 3^2, . . . , 10^2}.

4. ϕ has no elements, whereas {0} has the element 0.

5. a) $1/2 \notin \{1, 2, 3, . . .\}$.
b) $64 \in \{4, 8, 12, . . .\}$.
c) $a \in \{a, e, i, o, u\}$.
d) $4 \notin \{1, 3, 5, . . .\}$.
e) $\$ \notin \{a, b, c, . . . , z\}$.
f) $g \notin \{a, b, c, d, e, f\}$.

6. a) {1, 3, 4, 7, 12}.   b) {3, 7}.   c) ϕ.
d) {1, 4}.   e) {1}.   f) ϕ.

7. a) {$y : y + 2 = 10$} = {8}.
b) The set of y's such that y plus 5 equals 8 is the set with the single member 3.

8. a) {$m : m - 6 = 4$} = {10}.
b) The set of q's such that two times q is six is the set with the single member 3.

9. ϕ, the empty set.   **10.** {11/4}.

11. a) No, because for each state there are two senators.
b) Yes, because for each senator there is one and only one state.

12. a) Yes, because each apple grows on one and only one tree.
b) No, because one tree may have 0, 1, or more than one apple.

13. Yes, because for each point on the horizontal line there is one and only one point on the slant line.

14. No, because for each point on the diameter there are two points on the circle.

15. a) The h function of z, or h of z.   b) 15.
c) Multiply 4 by the value of z and add 7.
d) Multiply 4 by ($x + 2$) and add 10.

16. a) The f function of x, or f of x.   b) 25.
c) Multiply 3 by the value of x and add 10.
d) Multiply 3 by ($x + 1$) and add 10.

17. {$y : y = 2x + 7$}.   **18.** {$y : y = 5x$}.

19. Yes, because for each value of x there is one and only one value for y.

20. No, because for the starting element 0 there is no ending element; that is, 5/0 is undefined. See Appendix 2, Section 14.

Problem Set A1–2

1. a) {a, b, c, d, e, f, g, h}.
b) {a, b, c, d, e, i, j}.   c) {d, e}.   d) ϕ.
e) {d, e, f, g, h, i, j}.   f) ϕ.

2. a) {0, 1, 2, 3, . . .}   b) ϕ.   c) {5, 7, 9}.
d) ϕ.   e) {1, 3, 5, . . .}.

3. $A \cup B$ = {face cards}; $A \cap B$ = {queens}.

4. Assuming an ace is a face card, and using the notation 3D, $j$$C$ to represent the 3 of diamonds and the jack of clubs, and so on:
$A \cup B$ = {Face card, 2H, 3H, . . . , 10H, 2D, 3D, . . . , 10D}.
$A \cap B$ = {jH, qH, kH, aH, jD, qD, kD, aD}.
$A \cap C$ = ϕ.
$B \cap C$ = {9H, 9D}.

5. a) ϕ.
b) $M \cap N$ is the point at which the lines intersect.

6. a) Rain tomorrow, or warmer tomorrow, or rain and warmer tomorrow.
b) Rain and warmer tomorrow.

APPENDIX 2

Problem Set A2–1

1. -14.	**2.** $+13$.	**3.** -12.	**4.** $+3$.
5. $+5.34$.	**6.** -24.	**7.** -23.	**8.** $+3$.
9. -4.	**10.** -4.	**11.** $+3$.	**12.** $+1$.
13. -2.	**14.** $+13$.	**15.** $+11$.	**16.** -45.
17. $+15$.	**18.** -3.	**19.** $-7/2$.	**20.** $+3/2$.
21. -32.	**22.** $-28/5$.	**23.** $+12/7$.	
24. $+2$.	**25.** $+1$.	**26.** -5.	

27. $+3 + (-4) + (+5) + (-2) + (+6)$.
28. $+3 + (-2) + (+4) + (-5)$.
29. $-1.5 + (-3) + (-2.5)$.
30. $-3 + (+7) + (-4) + (+2)$.
31. $-10 + (+7) + (-4) + (+3)$.
32. $+12 + (-6) + (+5) + (-7)$.

33. -16.	**34.** 23.	**35.** -2.	**36.** 3.
37. 16.	**38.** 10.		

Problem Set A2–2

1. ab means a times b; cxy means c times x times y.

2. $100a + 10b + c$.   **3.** All.

4. If a and b are any odd integers, then $a + b$ is an even integer.

5. Whenever we add two clock numbers (in the time sense), the sum is another clock number.

6. By convention, it is agreed that three times the sum of a and c will be indicated by parentheses; thus, $3(a + c)$.

7. Any (whole) number.

8. In $a(b + c)$, we have the product of the number a by the number $(b + c)$. The distributive property says this product equals the sum of ab and ac.

9. Commutative, multiplication.
10. Commutative, addition.
11. Distributive.   **12.** Commutative, addition.
13. Convention; no sign means assume a plus sign.
14. Commutative, multiplication.
15. Convention; indicate addition of negative by minus sign.
16. Commutative, multiplication.
17. Associative, addition.

18. Commutative, multiplication.
19. Associative, multiplication.
20. Convention; b means $+b$; indicate addition of negative by minus sign.
21. Associative, addition.
22. Distributive property (inverse).
23. Commutative, addition.
24. Commutative, addition.
25. Associative, multiplication.

26. $-b$.	**27.** $7a - 5b$.
28. $5abc - 2d$.	**29.** $7 + x$.
30. $8abc$.	**31.** $8 + 2a - b$.

32. $-b + a$
$\quad = \quad a - b \quad$ Commutative, addition.

33. $\quad 2b(3a)$
$= 2b3(a) \qquad$ Associative, multiplication
$= 2(3)ba \qquad$ Commutative, multiplication
$= 6ba \qquad$ Associative, multiplication
$= 6ab \qquad$ Commutative, multiplication.

34. $\quad 3 + xy + \quad 5 + 3(2ab)$
$= 3 + \quad 5 + xy + 3(2ab) \quad$ Commutative, addition
$= \qquad 8 + xy + 3(2ab) \quad$ Associative, addition
$= \qquad 8 + xy + 6ab \qquad$ Associative, multiplication.

35. $\quad 3 + a + 2$
$= 3 + 2 + a \qquad$ Commutative, addition
$= \quad 5 + a \qquad$ Associative, addition.

36. $\quad a + 3 + c + 2$
$= a + c + 3 + 2 \qquad$ Commutative, addition
$= a + c + 5 \qquad$ Associative, addition.

37. $\quad acdb$
$= adcb \qquad$ Commutative, multiplication
$= adbc \qquad$ Commutative, multiplication.

38. $a + b$.   **39.** $a + (b + c)$.
40. $(a + b) + 2(cd)$.
41. $2(a + b) - 3(c + 2d)$.
42. $2d(a + b + c)$.

Problem Set A2–3

1. $2abc - 4ab$.   **2.** $ab + a - 2b - 2$.
3. 11.   **4.** $ac - bc + 3c + 2a - 2b + 6$.
5. $3a + 3b - 1$.   **6.** $15a - 62$.
7. $13a + 54$.
8. $3ax - 6bx - 18x - 2a + 4b + 12$.
9. $x + 2b - a$.   **10.** $2x + 3y$.
11. $a - 3b$.   **12.** $a + 3x + 2$.

Problem Set A2–3 (concluded)

13. $7b - 2ab$. **14.** $abc - 2abx + 10ab$.
15. $ax - 2ab + 2b$.
16. $3a - ac - 3bc + bcx$.
17. $ax + bx + x + ay + by + y$.
18. $ab + a - b - 1$. **19.** -2. **20.** $-2/5$.
21. $+4298.936$. **22.** $-4/9$. **23.** $+2333$.
24. See text. **25.** $b(a - 2)$.
26. $a(3 + 5) = a(8) = 8a$.
27. $2a(2bc - b + 3)$. **28.** $x(a - b + 1)$.
29. $a(3d - 5c + 1)$. **30.** $2(2uv - xv + 1)$.
31. $ab(x + y - 1)$. **32.** $2a(x - 3y + 2z)$.
33. $x(2 + a + b)$. **34.** $-a(b + 3c + 1)$.
35. $(x + 1)(a + b)$. **36.** $(x + 1)(1 + y)$.
37. $(x + y)(2 - a)$. **38.** $(x + y)(a + b)$.
39. $(x - 2)(x + 1)$. **40.** $(2x + 1)(x - 5)$.
41. $(4x - 3)(3x - 4)$. **42.** $(5x - 1)(2x + 3)$.
43. $(x - 3)(x + 2)$. **44.** $(x + 3)(x - 3)$.
45. $(x - y)(x + y)$. **46.** $(2x + 3y)(2x - 3y)$.
47. F. **48.** T. **49.** T. **50.** T. **51.** F.
52. T. **53.** F. **54.** F. **55.** T. **56.** T.
57. F. **58.** T. **59.** F. **60.** T.

Problem Set A2–4

1. F. **2.** F. **3.** T. **4.** T.
5. T. **6.** T. **7.** F. **8.** F.
9. T. **10.** T. **11.** T.
12. The product of a number and its reciprocal is one.
13. $3a/2c$.
14. Cancellation not possible as the expression stands.
15. 1. **16.** $a + 3$. **17.** $6c$.
18. Cancellation not possible as the expression stands.
19. $(2y + 6a + 1)/4y$. **20.** $8x$.
21. See text. **22.** $3ab/8$.
23. $\dfrac{2a + 2b}{15}$. **24.** $-3a/4$.
25. $\dfrac{2ab + 4a}{21}$. **26.** $\dfrac{-2}{3a + 3b}$.
27. $a + 6b + 2$. **28.** $4a - 6b$.
29. $\dfrac{b(c - d)}{2}$. **30.** $\dfrac{b - 2}{a + 3}$.
31. $\dfrac{2 + (c - b)}{2a}$. **32.** $\dfrac{2 + (c - b) + a}{2x(a + b)}$.

33. $\dfrac{x + y}{y - x}$. **34.** $1/3$. **35.** $\dfrac{5a - 6}{10}$.
36. $\dfrac{45b - 5ab + 12a}{30ab}$. **37.** $\dfrac{a + 24}{6a}$.
38. $7/6$. **39.** $\dfrac{a - 2ab + 4b + bx - 2}{b(a - 2)}$.
40. $\dfrac{x - 2ab + 6}{2a}$. **41.** $\dfrac{18abx - 3ab + 1}{6ab}$.
42. $\dfrac{11a + 5b - 3ab - 5}{12(b - 1)}$.
43. $\dfrac{-(12x + 17)}{4(x + 3)}$. **44.** $91/12$.
45. $27/176$. **46.** $7/6$. **47.** $\dfrac{6b + 2ab}{5b - 3a}$.
48. $\dfrac{3abc - 6b + 18}{2bc - 6c}$.
49. $\dfrac{4ac - 6b + 12bc}{bc - 12}$. **50.** $\dfrac{6a + 4b - 2c}{12b - 3a}$.

Problem Set A2–5

1. 16. **2.** 7. **3.** 1.041. **4.** 4/3.
5. 1/72. **6.** 1000. **7.** Not a real number.
8. 31/12. **9.** 1/9. **10.** 1. **11.** 8.
12. 1/2. **13.** 10. **14.** 1/12. **15.** 5/4.
16. 6. **17.** 25. **18.** 1.1025. **19.** 1/8.
20. 13/8. **21.** 5. **22.** 9/4. **23.** 2/9.
24. 5/4. **25.** 4/27. **26.** a^3. **27.** $a^2b^2c^2$.
28. a^3b^7. **29.** $a^3b^2c^3$. **30.** x^4ab.
31. ab^2. **32.** a^2/bc. **33.** y^2b^2/x^2.
34. a^2/x. **35.** x/y. **36.** bc^3. **37.** a^2b^3.
38. b^2/a^3c. **39.** $-9bc$. **40.** $-18/bc$.
41. ax. **42.** a^3bc. **43.** $1/ax^2$.
44. $2a/x^3$. **45.** $1/ax^3$. **46.** $3a^{7/3}b^{3/2}$.
47. $x^{3/2}/y^{1/6}$. **48.** $a^{1/6}b^{7/6}$. **49.** $2/3^{3/2}x^{1/2}$.
50. $2y^{11/6}/3x^2$. **51.** $\dfrac{2x^2 + 1}{x^3 + 3x^2}$.
52. $\dfrac{2 - x}{x - x^2}$. **53.** $\dfrac{x + 1}{3x^2}$. **54.** $\dfrac{x^2}{a^{2x-2}}$.
55. Exponents in this expression cannot be combined.
56. $a^2 + ab$. **57.** $a^2 - 6ab + 9b^2$.
58. $a^3 - 2a^2b + ab^2$. **59.** $x^2 - y^2$.
60. $1 + a$. **61.** $a - 2a^{1/2} + 1$.
62. $\dfrac{1 + 2a}{a^2}$. **63.** 27. **64.** F. **65.** F.

Problem Set A2–5 (*concluded*)

66. T.   **67.** T.   **68.** F.   **69.** F.   **78.** F.   **79.** T.   **80.** F.   **81.** T.
70. T.   **71.** T.   **72.** F.   **73.** F.   **82.** T.   **83.** T.   **84.** F.   **85.** T.
74. T.   **75.** F.   **76.** F.   **77.** T.

APPENDIX 3

Problem Set A3–1

1. $2x - 3 = x + 4$ Add 3
   $\quad\quad 2x = x + 7$ Subtract x
   $\quad\quad\quad x = 7.$

2. $4x + 5 = 2x + 12$ Subtract 5
   $\quad\quad 4x = 2x + 7$ Subtract $2x$
   $\quad\quad 2x = 7$ Divide by 2
   $\quad\quad\quad x = 7/2.$

3. $3x - 7 = 2x + 4$ Add 7
   $\quad\quad 3x = 2x + 11$ Subtract $2x$
   $\quad\quad\quad x = 11.$

4. $5 - 2x = 6$ Subtract 5
   $\quad -2x = 1$ Divide by -2
   $\quad\quad\quad x = -1/2.$

5. $7x - 5 = 3 - 4x$ Add 5
   $\quad\quad 7x = 8 - 4x$ Add $4x$
   $\quad 11x = 8$ Divide by 11
   $\quad\quad\quad x = 8/11.$

6. $3 - 2x = x - 4$ Subtract 3
   $\quad -2x = x - 7$ Subtract x
   $\quad -3x = -7$ Divide by -3
   $\quad\quad\quad x = 7/3.$

7. $\dfrac{x}{3} + \dfrac{1}{2} = 3x$ Multiply by 6

   $\quad 2x + 3 = 18x$ Subtract 3
   $\quad\quad 2x = 18x - 3$ Subtract $18x$
   $\quad -16x = -3$ Divide by -16
   $\quad\quad\quad x = 3/16.$

8. $\quad\dfrac{x}{4} + \dfrac{x}{2} = 2 - \dfrac{5x}{8}$ Multiply by 8

   $\quad 2x + 4x = 16 - 5x$ Add $5x$
   $2x + 4x + 5x = 16$ Combine like terms
   $\quad\quad 11x = 16$ Divide by 11
   $\quad\quad\quad x = 16/11.$

9. $\dfrac{2x}{5} - \dfrac{3x}{2} = 4$ Multiply by 10

   $\quad 4x - 15x = 40$ Combine like terms

Problem Set A3–1 (*continued*)

$$-11x = 40$$ Divide by -11
$$x = -40/11.$$

10. $\quad 1 - \dfrac{x}{3} + \dfrac{x}{2} = x - 4$ Multiply by 6

$$6 - 2x + 3x = 6x - 24$$ Subtract 6
$$-2x + 3x = 6x - 30$$ Subtract 6x
$$-2x + 3x - 6x = -30$$ Combine like terms
$$-5x = -30$$ Divide by -5
$$x = 6.$$

11. $\quad \dfrac{1}{7} - \dfrac{x}{3} = x$ Multiply by 21

$$3 - 7x = 21x$$ Subtract 3
$$-7x = 21x - 3$$ Subtract 21x
$$-28x = -3$$ Divide by -28
$$x = 3/28.$$

12. $\quad 1 - \dfrac{3x}{7} = 0$ Multiply by 7

$$7 - 3x = 0$$ Subtract 7
$$-3x = -7$$ Divide by -3
$$x = 7/3.$$

13. $\quad \dfrac{x + 3}{2} = x - \dfrac{1}{4}$ Multiply by 4

$$2(x + 3) = 4x - 1$$ Apply distributive property
$$2x + 6 = 4x - 1$$ Subtract 6
$$2x = 4x - 7$$ Subtract 4x
$$-2x = -7$$ Divide by -2
$$x = 7/2.$$

14. $\quad \dfrac{5 - 2x}{3} + \dfrac{x}{2} = 1$ Multiply by 6

$$2(5 - 2x) + 3x = 6$$ Apply distributive property
$$10 - 4x + 3x = 6$$ Subtract 10
$$-4x + 3x = -4$$ Combine like terms
$$-x = -4$$ Divide by -1
$$x = 4.$$

15. $\quad \dfrac{2x - 1}{3} - \dfrac{1 - x}{5} = 0$ Multiply by 15

$$5(2x - 1) - 3(1 - x) = 0$$ Apply distributive property
$$10x - 5 - 3 + 3x = 0$$ Add 8
$$10x + 3x = 8$$ Combine like terms
$$13x = 8$$ Divide by 13
$$x = 8/13.$$

16. $\quad \dfrac{x + 1}{2} - \dfrac{x - 1}{3} = 5$ Multiply by 6

$$3(x + 1) - 2(x - 1) = 30$$ Apply distributive property.
$$3x + 3 - 2x + 2 = 30$$ Subtract 5
$$3x - 2x = 25$$ Combine like terms
$$x = 25.$$

Problem Set A3–1 (*continued*)

17. $bx + 2 = c$ Subtract 2
    $bx = c - 2$ Divide by b
      $x = (c - 2)/b$.

18. $ax + 2 - x = 0$ Subtract 2
    $ax - x = -2$ Factor
    $x(a - 1) = -2$ Divide by $(a - 1)$
        $x = -2/(a - 1)$.

19. $ax + b = cx$ Subtract cx
    $ax - cx + b = 0$ Subtract b
      $ax - cx = -b$ Factor
      $x(a - c) = -b$ Divide by $(a - c)$,
            $x = b/(c - a)$.   change signs

20. $ax + b = x - b$ Subtract b
      $ax = x - 2b$ Subtract x
    $ax - x = -2b$ Factor
    $x(a - 1) = -2b$ Divide by $(a - 1)$
        $x = -2b/(a - 1)$ Change signs of numerator
        $x = 2b/(1 - a)$.   and denominator

21. $a(x - a) = 2x$ Apply distributive property
    $ax - a^2 = 2x$ Add a^2
      $ax = 2x + a^2$ Subtract $2x$
    $ax - 2x = a^2$ Factor
    $x(a - 2) = a^2$ Divide by $(a - 2)$
        $x = a^2/(a - 2)$.

22. $(x/a) - 1/2 = 3x$ Multiply by $2a$.
    $2x - a = 4ax$ Add a
      $2x = 4ax + a$ Subtract $4/ax$
    $2x - 4ax = a$ Factor
    $x(2 - 4a) = a$ Divide by $(2 - 4a)$
        $x = a/(2 - 4a)$.

23. $2/(a - x) + 1/3 = 4$ Multiply by $3(a - x)$
    $6 + a - x = 12(a - x)$ Apply distributive property
    $6 + a - x = 12a - 12x$ Add $12x$
    $6 + a + 11x = 12a$ Subtract $(6 + a)$
        $11x = 11a - 6$ Divide by 11
          $x = (11a - 6)/11$.

24. $y = x/(b - cx)$ Multiply by $(b - cx)$
      $y(b - cx) = x$ Apply distributive property
      $yb - ycx = x$ Add ycx
        $yb = x + ycx$ Factor
        $yb = x(1 + yc)$ Divide by $(1 + yc)$
    $yb/(1 + yc) = x$

    or

            $x = yb/(1 + yc)$.

25. $(3/4) - (2x/3) = 2x(a - 1)$ Multiply by 12
    $9 - 8x = 24x(a - 1)$ Apply distributive property
    $9 - 8x = 24ax - 24x$ Add $8x$
        $9 = 24ax - 16x$ Factor

Problem Set A3–1 (*continued*)

$$9 = x(24a - 16)$$ Divide by $(24a - 16)$
$$9/(24a - 16) = x$$
or
$$x = 9/(24a - 16).$$

26.
$3(x - 2) = 2 - a(x + 2)$	Apply distributive property
$3x - 6 = 2 - ax - 2a$	Add ax
$3x + ax - 6 = 2 - 2a$	Add 6
$3x + ax = 8 - 2a$	Factor
$x(3 + a) = 8 - 2a$	Divide by $(3 + a)$
$x = (8 - 2a)/(3 + a).$	

27.
$2/3(x - 2) + 3/a - 1/2 = 0$	Multiply by $6a(x - 2)$
$4a + 18(x - 2) - 3a(x - 2) = 0$	Apply distributive property
$4a + 18x - 36 - 3ax + 6a = 0$	Subtract $10a$
$18x - 36 - 3ax = -10a$	Add 36
$18x - 3ax = 36 - 10a$	Factor
$x(18 - 3a) = 36 - 10a$	Divide by $(18 - 3a)$
$x = (36 - 10a)/$	
$(18 - 3a).$	

28.
$ax - b/2 = c + 5[a - 2(b - x)]/6$	Multiply by 6
$6ax - 3b = 6c + 5[a - 2(b - x)]$	Apply distributive property
$6ax - 3b = 6c + 5[a - 2b + 2x]$	Apply distributive property
$6ax - 3b = 6c + 5a - 10b + 10x$	Subtract $10x$
$6ax - 10x - 3b = 6c + 5a - 10b$	Add $3b$
$6ax - 10x = 6c + 5a - 7b$	Factor
$x(6a - 10) = 6c + 5a - 7b$	Divide by $(6a - 10)$
$x = (6c + 5a - 7b)/$	
$(6a - 10).$	

29.
$b/a - x = 2a(b - x)$	Multiply by a
$b - ax = 2a^2(b - x)$	Apply distributive property
$b - ax = 2a^2b - 2a^2x$	Add $2a^2x$
$2a^2x + b - ax = 2a^2b$	Subtract b
$2a^2x - ax = 2a^2b - b$	Factor
$x(2a^2 - a) = 2a^2b - b$	Divide by $(2a^2 - a)$
$x = (2a^2b - b)/(2a^2 - a).$	

30.
$x - a(b - x) = 2x - 3$	Apply distributive property
$x - ab + ax = 2x - 3$	Subtract $2x$
$-x - ab + ax = -3$	Add ab
$-x + ax = -3 + ab$	Factor
$x(-1 + a) = -3 + ab$	Divide by $(-1 + a)$
$x = (-3 + ab)/(-1 + a)$	Use commutative property
$x = (ab - 3)/(a - 1).$	

31.
$3(b - x) = 2 + b[x - (3 - x)]$	Apply distributive property
$3b - 3x = 2 + b[x - 3 + x]$	Apply distributive property
$3b - 3x = 2 + bx - 3b + bx$	Subtract $2bx$
$3b - 3x - 2bx = 2 - 3b$	Subtract $3b$
$-3x - 2bx = 2 - 6b$	Factor
$x(-3 - 2b) = 2 - 6b$	Divide by $(-3 - 2b)$

Problem Set A3–1 (*concluded*)

$$x = (2 - 6b)/(-3 - 2b)$$ Change signs of numerator
and denominator

$$x = (6b - 2)/(2b + 3).$$

32. $b(a + x) = a(b + x)$ Apply distributive property
$ba + bx = ab + ax$ Subtract ax
$ba + bx - ax = ab$ Subtract ba
$bx - ax = 0$ Factor
$x(b - a) = 0$ Divide by $(b - a)$
$x = 0.$

Problem Set A3–2

1. 15.   **2.** 41.   **3.** 180.   **4.** 2.
5. 104.   **6.** 30.   **7.** 64.   **8.** 9.
9. 32.   **10.** 472.   **11.** 9/40.   **12.** 5/42.
13. 115/567.   **14.** −11/60.   **15.** 183/280.
16. −4435/192.   **17.** −27.   **18.** 2/3.
19. 16/21.   **20.** −122/453.
21. $33,083.33.   **22.** 0.50.
23. a) 37.5 percent.   b) $6.00.   c) $4.48.
24. a) 320 days.   b) $16,200.
25. a) 212°F.   b) 32°F.   c) 12.92°F.
    d) 82.4°F.   e) 14°F.   f) 122°F.
26. a) $E = 0.2T + 0.125(T - 50,000)$.
    b) $50,000; $65,384.62; $80,769.23.
    c) $83,333.33.
27. a) $B = x[P - y(P - B)]$.   b) $362,500.
28. a) 22.9 percent.   b) $3.03.
29. a) $20,000.   b) 0.2.   c) 0.375.
30. a) $10.01.   b) $5.01.   c) 100.
    d) 250.   e) 500.

Problem Set A3–3

Problems 1 through 10: See Figures A
through J.

FIGURE A

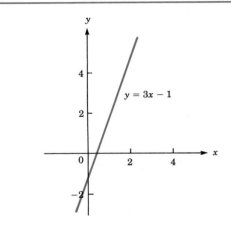

FIGURE B

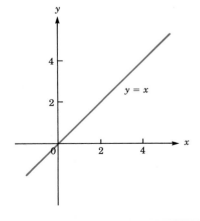

Problem Set A3–3 (*continued*)

FIGURE C

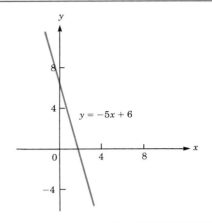

$$y = -5x + 6$$

FIGURE D

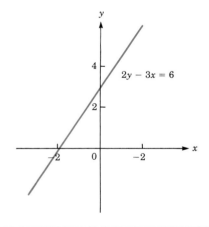

$$2y - 3x = 6$$

FIGURE E

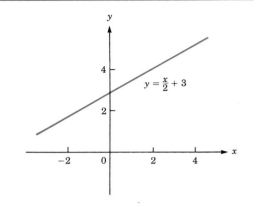

$$y = \frac{x}{2} + 3$$

FIGURE F

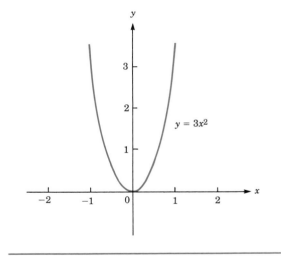

$$y = 3x^2$$

Problem Set A3–3 (*continued*)

FIGURE G

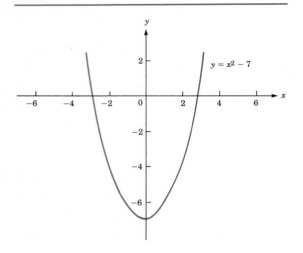

$y = x^2 - 7$

FIGURE H

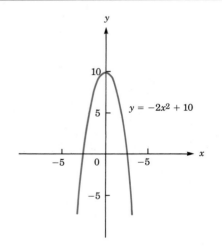

$y = -2x^2 + 10$

FIGURE I

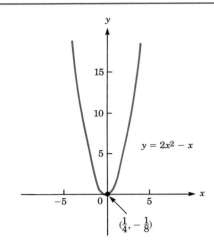

$y = 2x^2 - x$

$(\frac{1}{4}, -\frac{1}{8})$

FIGURE J

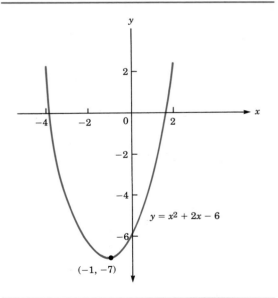

$y = x^2 + 2x - 6$

$(-1, -7)$

Problem Set A3–3 (*concluded*)

11. $x_1 = 9.69; x_2 = 0.31.$
12. $x_1 = 0.35; x_2 = -2.85.$ **13.** $x_1 = x_2 = 3/2.$
14. No real solutions.
15. $x_1 = 0; x_2 = 2.$ **16.** $x_1 = 2; x_2 = 1.$
17. $x_1 = 0; x_2 = 2.$ **18.** $x_1 = -5/2; x_2 = 4/3.$
19. $x_1 = 5; x_2 = -5.$ **20.** $x_1 = -7/2; x_2 = 1.$

Problem Set A3–4

1. F. **2.** T. **3.** F. **4.** F.
5. F. **6.** F. **7.** T. **8.** F.
9. T. **10.** T. **11.** T. **12.** T.
13. $x \le 2.$ **14.** $x \ge 3.$ **15.** $x < -3.$
16. $x > -2.$ **17.** $x \ge 0.5.$ **18.** $x \le -0.25.$
19. a) $y \le 6 - 1.5x.$
  b) On and below the line. c) $y \le 3.$
20. a) $y \ge 7 - 0.4x.$
  b) On and above the line. c) $y \ge 5.$
21. a) $y \le -9 + 1.4x.$
  b) On and below the line. c) $y \le 19.$
22. a) $y \ge -9 + 1.5x.$
  b) On and above the line. c) $y \ge 6.$
23. Yes. **24.** No. **25.** Yes. **26.** No.
27. See Figure K.

FIGURE K

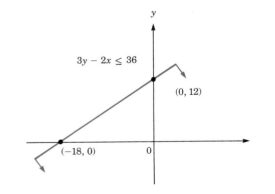

28. See Figure L.

FIGURE L

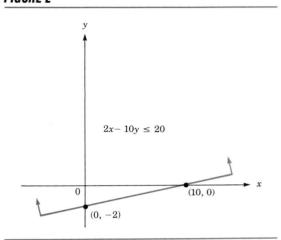

29. See Figure M.

FIGURE M

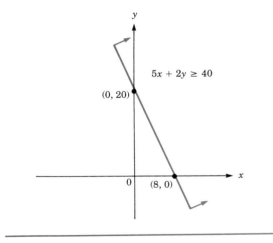

Problem Set A3–4 (*continued*)

30. See Figure N.

FIGURE N

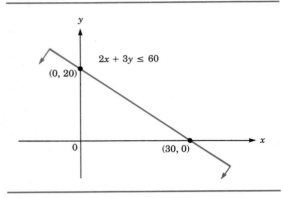

31. See Figure O.

FIGURE O

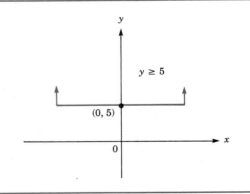

32. See Figure P.

FIGURE P

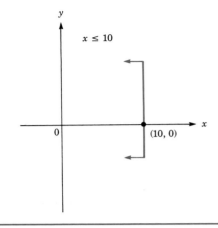

33. See Figure Q.

FIGURE Q

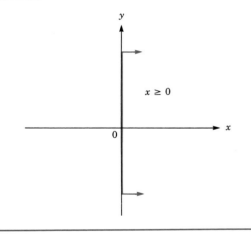

Problem Set A3–4 (*concluded*)

34. See Figure R.

FIGURE R

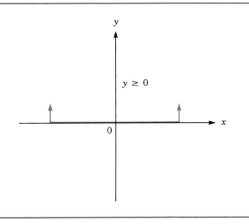

35. See Figure S.

FIGURE S

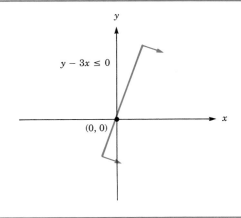

36. See Figure T.

FIGURE T

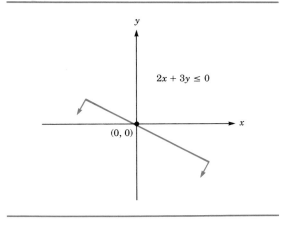

Tables

TABLE I
e^x and e^{-x}

x	e^x	e^{-x}	x	e^x	e^{-x}	x	e^x	e^{-x}	x	e^x	e^{-x}
0.01	1.0101	0.9900	0.31	1.3634	0.7334	0.61	1.8404	0.5434	0.91	2.4843	0.4025
0.02	1.0202	0.9802	0.32	1.3771	0.7261	0.62	1.8589	0.5379	0.92	2.5093	0.3985
0.03	1.0305	0.9704	0.33	1.3910	0.7189	0.63	1.8776	0.5326	0.93	2.5345	0.3946
0.04	1.0408	0.9608	0.34	1.4049	0.7118	0.64	1.8965	0.5273	0.94	2.5600	0.3906
0.05	1.0513	0.9512	0.35	1.4191	0.7047	0.65	1.9155	0.5220	0.95	2.5857	0.3867
0.06	1.0618	0.9418	0.36	1.4333	0.6977	0.66	1.9348	0.5169	0.96	2.6117	0.3829
0.07	1.0725	0.9324	0.37	1.4477	0.6907	0.67	1.9542	0.5117	0.97	2.6379	0.3791
0.08	1.0833	0.9231	0.38	1.4623	0.6839	0.68	1.9739	0.5066	0.98	2.6645	0.3753
0.09	1.0942	0.9139	0.39	1.4770	0.6771	0.69	1.9937	0.5016	0.99	2.6912	0.3716
0.10	1.1052	0.9048	0.40	1.4918	0.6703	0.70	2.0138	0.4966	1.0	2.7183	0.3679
0.11	1.1163	0.8958	0.41	1.5068	0.6637	0.71	2.0340	0.4916	1.1	3.0042	0.3329
0.12	1.1275	0.8869	0.42	1.5220	0.6570	0.72	2.0544	0.4868	1.2	3.3201	0.3012
0.13	1.1388	0.8781	0.43	1.5373	0.6505	0.73	2.0751	0.4819	1.3	3.6693	0.2725
0.14	1.1503	0.8694	0.44	1.5527	0.6440	0.74	2.0959	0.4771	1.4	4.0552	0.2466
0.15	1.1618	0.8607	0.45	1.5683	0.6376	0.75	2.1170	0.4724	1.5	4.4817	0.2231
0.16	1.1735	0.8521	0.46	1.5841	0.6313	0.76	2.1383	0.4677	1.6	4.9530	0.2019
0.17	1.1853	0.8437	0.47	1.6000	0.6250	0.77	2.1598	0.4630	1.7	5.4739	0.1827
0.18	1.1972	0.8353	0.48	1.6161	0.6188	0.78	2.1815	0.4584	1.8	6.0496	0.1653
0.19	1.2092	0.8270	0.49	1.6323	0.6126	0.79	2.2034	0.4538	1.9	6.6859	0.1496
0.20	1.2214	0.8187	0.50	1.6487	0.6065	0.80	2.2255	0.4493	2.0	7.3891	0.1353
0.21	1.2337	0.8106	0.51	1.6653	0.6005	0.81	2.2479	0.4449	2.1	8.1662	0.1225
0.22	1.2461	0.8025	0.52	1.6820	0.5945	0.82	2.2705	0.4404	2.2	9.0250	0.1108
0.23	1.2586	0.7945	0.53	1.6989	0.5886	0.83	2.2933	0.4360	2.3	9.9742	0.1003
0.24	1.2712	0.7866	0.54	1.7160	0.5827	0.84	2.3164	0.4317	2.4	11.0232	0.0907
0.25	1.2840	0.7788	0.55	1.7333	0.5769	0.85	2.3396	0.4274	2.5	12.1825	0.0821
0.26	1.2969	0.7711	0.56	1.7507	0.5712	0.86	2.3632	0.4232	2.6	13.4637	0.0743
0.27	1.3100	0.7634	0.57	1.7683	0.5655	0.87	2.3869	0.4190	2.7	14.8797	0.0672
0.28	1.3231	0.7558	0.58	1.7860	0.5599	0.88	2.4109	0.4148	2.8	16.4446	0.0608
0.29	1.3364	0.7483	0.59	1.8040	0.5543	0.89	2.4351	0.4107	2.9	18.1741	0.0550
0.30	1.3499	0.7408	0.60	1.8221	0.5488	0.90	2.4596	0.4066	3.0	20.0855	0.0498

TABLE II
Natural Logarithms, 0.01 to 4.49. (insert minus sign before shaded numbers)

N	0	1	2	3	4	5	6	7	8	9
0.0		4.60517	3.91202	3.50656	3.21888	2.99573	2.81341	2.65926	2.52573	2.40795
0.1	2.30259	2.20727	2.12026	2.04022	1.96611	1.89712	1.83258	1.77196	1.71480	1.66073
0.2	1.60944	1.56065	1.51413	1.46968	1.42712	1.38629	1.34707	1.30933	1.27297	1.23787
0.3	1.20397	1.17118	1.13943	1.10866	1.07881	1.04982	1.02165	.99425	.96758	.94161
0.4	0.91629	.89160	.86750	.84397	.82098	.79851	.77653	.75502	.73397	.71335

Shaded numbers are negative. Insert minus sign.

N	0	1	2	3	4	5	6	7	8	9
0.5	0.69315	.67334	.65393	.63488	.61619	.59784	.57982	.56212	.54473	.52763
0.6	0.51083	.49430	.47804	.46204	.44629	.43078	.41552	.40048	.38566	.37106
0.7	0.35667	.34249	.32850	.31471	.30111	.28768	.27444	.26136	.24846	.23572
0.8	0.22314	.21072	.19845	.18633	.17435	.16252	.15082	.13926	.12783	.11653
0.9	0.10536	.09431	.08338	.07257	.06188	.05129	.04082	.03046	.02020	.01005

N	0	1	2	3	4	5	6	7	8	9
1.0	0.0 0000	0995	1980	2956	3922	4879	5827	6766	7696	8618
1.1	9531	*0436	*1333	*2222	*3103	*3976	*4842	*5700	*6551	*7395
1.2	0.1 8232	9062	9885	*0701	*1511	*2314	*3111	*3902	*4686	*5464
1.3	0.2 6236	7003	7763	8518	9267	*0010	*0748	*1481	*2208	*2930
1.4	0.3 3647	4359	5066	5767	6464	7156	7844	8526	9204	9878
1.5	0.4 0547	1211	1871	2527	3178	3825	4469	5108	5742	6373
1.6	7000	7623	8243	8858	9470	*0078	*0682	*1282	*1879	*2473
1.7	0.5 3063	3649	4232	4812	5389	5962	6531	7098	7661	8222
1.8	8779	9333	9884	*0432	*0977	*1519	*2058	*2594	*3127	*3658
1.9	0.6 4185	4710	5233	5752	6269	6783	7294	7803	8310	8813
2.0	9315	9813	*0310	*0804	*1295	*1784	*2271	*2755	*3237	*3716
2.1	0.7 4194	4669	5142	5612	6081	6547	7011	7473	7932	8390
2.2	8846	9299	9751	*0200	*0648	*1093	*1536	*1978	*2418	*2855
2.3	0.8 3291	3725	4157	4587	5015	5442	5866	6289	6710	7129
2.4	7547	7963	8377	8789	9200	9609	*0016	*0422	*0826	*1228
2.5	0.9 1629	2028	2426	2822	3216	3609	4001	4391	4779	5166
2.6	5551	5935	6317	6698	7078	7456	7833	8208	8582	8954
2.7	9325	9695	*0063	*0430	*0796	*1160	*1523	*1885	*2245	*2604
2.8	1.0 2962	3318	3674	4028	4380	4732	5082	5431	5779	6126
2.9	6471	6815	7158	7500	7841	8181	8519	8856	9192	9527
3.0	9861	*0194	*0526	*0856	*1186	*1514	*1841	*2168	*2493	*2817
3.1	1.1 3140	3462	3783	4103	4422	4740	5057	5373	5688	6002
3.2	6315	6627	6938	7248	7557	7865	8173	8479	8784	9089
3.3	9392	9695	9996	*0297	*0597	*0896	*1194	*1491	*1788	*2083
3.4	1.2 2378	2671	2964	3256	3547	3837	4127	4415	4703	4990
3.5	5276	5562	5846	6130	6413	6695	6976	7257	7536	7815
3.6	8093	8371	8647	8923	9198	9473	9746	*0019	*0291	*0563
3.7	1.3 0833	1103	1372	1641	1909	2176	2442	2708	2972	3237
3.8	3500	3763	4025	4286	4547	4807	5067	5325	5584	5841
3.9	6098	6354	6609	6864	7118	7372	7624	7877	8128	8379
4.0	8629	8879	9128	9377	9624	9872	*0118	*0364	*0610	*0854
4.1	1.4 1099	1342	1585	1828	2070	2311	2552	2792	3031	3270
4.2	3508	3746	3984	4220	4456	4692	4927	5161	5395	5629
4.3	5862	6094	6326	6557	6787	7018	7247	7476	7705	7933
4.4	8160	8387	8614	8840	9065	9290	9515	9739	9962	*0185

TABLE II (continued)
Natural Logarithms, 4.50 to 8.99

N	0	1	2	3	4	5	6	7	8	9
4.5	1.5 0408	0630	0851	1072	1293	1513	1732	1951	2170	2388
4.6	2606	2823	3039	3256	3471	3687	3902	4116	4330	4543
4.7	4756	4969	5181	5393	5604	5814	6025	6235	6444	6653
4.8	6862	7070	7277	7485	7691	7898	8104	8309	8515	8719
4.9	8924	9127	9331	9534	9737	9939	*0141	*0342	*0543	*0744
5.0	1.6 0944	1144	1343	1542	1741	1939	2137	2334	2531	2728
5.1	2924	3120	3315	3511	3705	3900	4094	4287	4481	4673
5.2	4866	5058	5250	5441	5632	5823	6013	6203	6393	6582
5.3	6771	6959	7147	7335	7523	7710	7896	8083	8269	8455
5.4	8640	8825	9010	9194	9378	9562	9745	9928	*0111	*0293
5.5	1.7 0475	0656	0838	1019	1199	1380	1560	1740	1919	2098
5.6	2277	2455	2633	2811	2988	3166	3342	3519	3695	3871
5.7	4047	4222	4397	4572	4746	4920	5094	5267	5440	5613
5.8	5786	5958	6130	6302	6473	6644	6815	6985	7156	7326
5.9	7495	7665	7834	8002	8171	8339	8507	8675	8842	9009
6.0	9176	9342	9509	9675	9840	*0006	*0171	*0336	*0500	*0665
6.1	1.8 0829	0993	1156	1319	1482	1645	1808	1970	2132	2294
6.2	2455	2616	2777	2938	3098	3258	3418	3578	3737	3896
6.3	4055	4214	4372	4530	4688	4845	5003	5160	5317	5473
6.4	5630	5786	5942	6097	6253	6408	6563	6718	6872	7026
6.5	7180	7334	7487	7641	7794	7947	8099	8251	8403	8555
6.6	8707	8858	9010	9160	9311	9462	9612	9762	9912	*0061
6.7	1.9 0211	0360	0509	0658	0806	0954	1102	1250	1398	1545
6.8	1692	1839	1986	2132	2279	2425	2571	2716	2862	3007
6.9	3152	3297	3442	3586	3730	3874	4018	4162	4305	4448
7.0	4591	4734	4876	5019	5161	5303	5445	5586	5727	5869
7.1	6009	6150	6291	6431	6571	6711	6851	6991	7130	7269
7.2	7408	7547	7685	7824	7962	8100	8238	8376	8513	8650
7.3	8787	8924	9061	9198	9334	9470	9606	9742	9877	*0013
7.4	2.0 0148	0283	0418	0553	0687	0821	0956	1089	1223	1357
7.5	1490	1624	1757	1890	2022	2155	2287	2419	2551	2683
7.6	2815	2946	3078	3209	3340	3471	3601	3732	3862	3992
7.7	4122	4252	4381	4511	4640	4769	4898	5027	5156	5284
7.8	5412	5540	5668	5796	5924	6051	6179	6306	6433	6560
7.9	6686	6813	6939	7065	7191	7317	7443	7568	7694	7819
8.0	7944	8069	8194	8318	8443	8567	8691	8815	8939	9063
8.1	9186	9310	9433	9556	9679	9802	9924	*0047	*0169	*0291
8.2	2.1 0413	0535	0657	0779	0900	1021	1142	1263	1384	1505
8.3	1626	1746	1866	1986	2106	2226	2346	2465	2585	2704
8.4	2823	2942	3061	3180	3298	3417	3535	3653	3771	3889
8.5	4007	4124	4242	4359	4476	4593	4710	4827	4943	5060
8.6	5176	5292	5409	5524	5640	5756	5871	5987	6102	6217
8.7	6332	6447	6562	6677	6791	6905	7020	7134	7248	7361
8.8	7475	7589	7702	7816	7929	8042	8155	8267	8380	8493
8.9	8605	8717	8830	8942	9054	9165	9277	9389	9500	9611

TABLE II (continued)
Natural Logarithms, 9 to 9.99

N	0	1	2	3	4	5	6	7	8	9
9.0	9722	9834	9944	*0055	*0166	*0276	*0387	*0497	*0607	*0717
9.1	2.2 0827	0937	1047	1157	1266	1375	1485	1594	1703	1812
9.2	1920	2029	2138	2246	2354	2462	2570	2678	2786	2894
9.3	3001	3109	3216	3324	3431	3538	3645	3751	3858	3965
9.4	4071	4177	4284	4390	4496	4601	4707	4813	4918	5024
9.5	5129	5234	5339	5444	5549	5654	5759	5863	5968	6072
9.6	6176	6280	6384	6488	6592	6696	6799	6903	7006	7109
9.7	7213	7316	7419	7521	7624	7727	7829	7932	8034	8136
9.8	8238	8340	8442	8544	8646	8747	8849	8950	9051	9152
9.9	9253	9354	9455	9556	9657	9757	9858	9958	*0058	*0158

Natural logarithms, 10 to 99

N	0	1	2	3	4	5	6	7	8	9
1	2.30259	39790	48491	56495	63906	70805	77259	83321	89037	94444
2	99573	*04452	*09104	*13549	*17805	*21888	*25810	*29584	*33220	*36730
3	3.40120	43399	46574	49651	52636	55535	58352	61092	63759	66356
4	68888	71357	73767	76120	78419	80666	82864	85015	87120	89182
5	91202	93183	95124	97029	98898	*00733	*02535	*04305	*06044	*07754
6	4.09434	11087	12713	14313	15888	17439	18965	20469	21951	23411
7	24850	26268	27667	29046	30407	31749	33073	34381	35671	36945
8	38203	39445	40672	41884	43082	44265	45435	46591	47734	48864
9	49981	51086	52179	53260	54329	55388	56435	57471	58497	59512

Natural logarithms, 100 to 349

N	0	1	2	3	4	5	6	7	8	9
10	4.6 0517	1512	2497	3473	4439	5396	6344	7283	8213	9135
11	4.7 0048	0953	1850	2739	3620	4493	5359	6217	7068	7912
12	8749	9579	*0402	*1218	*2028	*2831	*3628	*4419	*5203	*5981
13	4.8 6753	7520	8280	9035	9784	*0527	*1265	*1998	*2725	*3447
14	4.9 4164	4876	5583	6284	6981	7673	8361	9043	9721	*0395
15	5.0 1064	1728	2388	3044	3695	4343	4986	5625	6260	6890
16	7517	8140	8760	9375	9987	*0595	*1199	*1799	*2396	*2990
17	5.1 3580	4166	4749	5329	5906	6479	7048	7615	8178	8739
18	9296	9850	*0401	*0949	*1494	*2036	*2575	*3111	*3644	*4175
19	5.2 4702	5227	5750	6269	6786	7300	7811	8320	8827	9330
20	9832	*0330	*0827	*1321	*1812	*2301	*2788	*3272	*3754	*4233
21	5.3 4711	5186	5659	6129	6598	7064	7528	7990	8450	8907
22	9363	9816	*0268	*0717	*1165	*1610	*2053	*2495	*2935	*3372
23	5.4 3808	4242	4674	5104	5532	5959	6383	6806	7227	7646
24	8064	8480	8894	9306	9717	*0126	*0533	*0939	*1343	*1745
25	5.5 2146	2545	2943	3339	3733	4126	4518	4908	5296	5683
26	6068	6452	6834	7215	7595	7973	8350	8725	9099	9471
27	9842	*0212	*0580	*0947	*1313	*1677	*2040	*2402	*2762	*3121
28	5.6 3479	3835	4191	4545	4897	5249	5599	5948	6296	6643
29	6988	7332	7675	8017	8358	8698	9036	9373	9709	*0044
30	5.7 0378	0711	1043	1373	1703	2031	2359	2685	3010	3334
31	3657	3979	4300	4620	4939	5257	5574	5890	6205	6519
32	6832	7144	7455	7765	8074	8383	8690	8996	9301	9606
33	9909	*0212	*0513	*0814	*1114	*1413	*1711	*2008	*2305	*2600
34	5.8 2895	3188	3481	3773	4064	4354	4644	4932	5220	5507

TABLE II (continued)
Natural Logarithms, 350 to 799

N	0	1	2	3	4	5	6	7	8	9
35	5793	6079	6363	6647	6930	7212	7493	7774	8053	8332
36	8610	8888	9164	9440	9715	9990	*0263	*0536	*0808	*1080
37	5.9 1350	1620	1889	2158	2426	2693	2959	3225	3489	3754
38	4017	4280	4542	4803	5064	5324	5584	5842	6101	6358
39	6615	6871	7126	7381	7635	7889	8141	8394	8645	8896
40	9146	9396	9645	9894	*0141	*0389	*0635	*0881	*1127	*1372
41	6.0 1616	1859	2102	2345	2587	2828	3069	3309	3548	3787
42	4025	4263	4501	4737	4973	5209	5444	5678	5912	6146
43	6379	6611	6843	7074	7304	7535	7764	7993	8222	8450
44	8677	8904	9131	9357	9582	9807	*0032	*0256	*0479	*0702
45	6.1 0925	1147	1368	1589	1810	2030	2249	2468	2687	2905
46	3123	3340	3556	3773	3988	4204	4419	4633	4847	5060
47	5273	5486	5698	5910	6121	6331	6542	6752	6961	7170
48	7379	7587	7794	8002	8208	8415	8621	8826	9032	9236
49	9441	9644	9848	*0051	*0254	*0456	*0658	*0859	*1060	*1261
50	6.2 1461	1661	1860	2059	2258	2456	2654	2851	3048	3245
51	3441	3637	3832	4028	4222	4417	4611	4804	4998	5190
52	5383	5575	5767	5958	6149	6340	6530	6720	6910	7099
53	7288	7476	7664	7852	8040	8227	8413	8600	8786	8972
54	9157	9342	9527	9711	9895	*0079	*0262	*0445	*0628	*0810
55	6.3 0992	1173	1355	1536	1716	1897	2077	2257	2436	2615
56	2794	2972	3150	3328	3505	3683	3859	4036	4212	4388
57	4564	4739	4914	5089	5263	5437	5611	5784	5957	6130
58	6303	6475	6647	6819	6990	7161	7332	7502	7673	7843
59	8012	8182	8351	8519	8688	8856	9024	9192	9359	9526
60	6.3 9693	9859	*0026	*0192	*0357	*0523	*0688	*0853	*1017	*1182
61	6.4 1346	1510	1673	1836	1999	2162	2325	2487	2649	2811
62	2972	3133	3294	3455	3615	3775	3935	4095	4254	4413
63	4572	4731	4889	5047	5205	5362	5520	5677	5834	5990
64	6147	6303	6459	6614	6770	6925	7080	7235	7389	7543
65	7697	7851	8004	8158	8311	8464	8616	8768	8920	9072
66	9224	9375	9527	9677	9828	9979	*0129	*0279	*0429	*0578
67	6.5 0728	0877	1026	1175	1323	1471	1619	1767	1915	2062
68	2209	2356	2503	2649	2796	2942	3088	3233	3379	3524
69	3669	3814	3959	4103	4247	4391	4535	4679	4822	4965
70	5108	5251	5393	5536	5678	5820	5962	6103	6244	6386
71	6526	6667	6808	6948	7088	7228	7368	7508	7647	7786
72	7925	8064	8203	8341	8479	8617	8755	8893	9030	9167
73	9304	9441	9578	9715	9851	9987	*0123	*0259	*0394	*0530
74	6.6 0665	0800	0935	1070	1204	1338	1473	1607	1740	1874
75	2007	2141	2274	2407	2539	2672	2804	2936	3068	3200
76	3332	3463	3595	3726	3857	3988	4118	4249	4379	4509
77	4639	4769	4898	5028	5157	5286	5415	5544	5673	5801
78	5929	6058	6185	6313	6441	6568	6696	6823	6950	7077
79	7203	7330	7456	7582	7708	7834	7960	8085	8211	8336

TABLE II (concluded)
Natural Logarithms, 800 to 1209

N	0	1	2	3	4	5	6	7	8	9
80	8461	8586	8711	8835	8960	9084	9208	9332	9456	9580
81	9703	9827	9950	*0073	*0196	*0319	*0441	*0564	*0686	*0808
82	6.7 0930	1052	1174	1296	1417	1538	1659	1780	1901	2022
83	2143	2263	2383	2503	2623	2743	2863	2982	3102	3221
84	3340	3459	3578	3697	3815	3934	4052	4170	4288	4406
85	4524	4641	4759	4876	4993	5110	5227	5344	5460	5577
86	5693	5809	5926	6041	6157	6273	6388	6504	6619	6734
87	6849	6964	7079	7194	7308	7422	7537	7651	7765	7878
88	7992	8106	8219	8333	8446	8559	8672	8784	8897	9010
89	9122	9234	9347	9459	9571	9682	9794	9906	*0017	*0128
90	6.8 0239	0351	0461	0572	0683	0793	0904	1014	1124	1235
91	1344	1454	1564	1674	1783	1892	2002	2111	2220	2329
92	2437	2546	2655	2763	2871	2979	3087	3195	3303	3411
93	3518	3626	3733	3841	3948	4055	4162	4268	4375	4482
94	4588	4694	4801	4907	5013	5118	5224	5330	5435	5541
95	5646	5751	5857	5961	6066	6171	6276	6380	6485	6589
96	6693	6797	6901	7005	7109	7213	7316	7420	7523	7626
97	7730	7833	7936	8038	8141	8244	8346	8449	8551	8653
98	8755	8857	8959	9061	9163	9264	9366	9467	9568	9669
99	9770	9871	9972	*0073	*0174	*0274	*0375	*0475	*0575	*0675
100	6.9 0776	0875	0975	1075	1175	1274	1374	1473	1572	1672
101	1771	1870	1968	2067	2166	2264	2363	2461	2560	2658
102	2756	2854	2952	3049	3147	3245	3342	3440	3537	3634
103	3731	3828	3925	4022	4119	4216	4312	4409	4505	4601
104	4698	4794	4890	4986	5081	5177	5273	5368	5464	5559
105	5655	5750	5845	5940	6035	6130	6224	6319	6414	6508
106	6602	6697	6791	6885	6979	7073	7167	7261	7354	7448
107	7541	7635	7728	7821	7915	8008	8101	8193	8286	8379
108	8472	8564	8657	8749	8841	8934	9026	9118	9210	9302
109	9393	9485	9577	9668	9760	9851	9942	*0033	*0125	*0216
110	7.0 0307	0397	0488	0579	0670	0760	0851	0941	1031	1121
111	1212	1302	1392	1481	1571	1661	1751	1840	1930	2019
112	2108	2198	2287	2376	2465	2554	2643	2731	2820	2909
113	2997	3086	3174	3262	3351	3439	3527	3615	3703	3791
114	3878	3966	4054	4141	4229	4316	4403	4491	4578	4665
115	4752	4839	4925	5012	5099	5186	5272	5359	5445	5531
116	5618	5704	5790	5876	5962	6048	6133	6219	6305	6390
117	6476	6561	6647	6732	6817	6902	6987	7072	7157	7242
118	7327	7412	7496	7581	7665	7750	7834	7918	8003	8087
119	8171	8255	8339	8423	8506	8590	8674	8757	8841	8924
120	9008	9091	9174	9257	9340	9423	9506	9589	9672	9755

TABLE III
Compound Amount of $1(1 + i)ⁿ

n	1%	2%	3%	4%
1	1.01000	1.02000	1.03000	1.04000
2	1.02010	1.04040	1.06090	1.08160
3	1.03030	1.06121	1.09273	1.12486
4	1.04060	1.08243	1.12551	1.16986
5	1.05101	1.10408	1.15927	1.21665
6	1.06152	1.12616	1.19405	1.26532
7	1.07214	1.14869	1.22987	1.31593
8	1.08286	1.17166	1.26677	1.36857
9	1.09369	1.19509	1.30477	1.42331
10	1.10462	1.21899	1.34392	1.48024
11	1.11567	1.24337	1.38423	1.53945
12	1.12683	1.26824	1.42576	1.60103
13	1.13809	1.29361	1.46853	1.66507
14	1.14947	1.31948	1.51259	1.73168
15	1.16097	1.34587	1.55797	1.80094
16	1.17258	1.37279	1.60471	1.87298
17	1.18430	1.40024	1.65285	1.94790
18	1.19615	1.42825	1.70243	2.02582
19	1.20811	1.45681	1.75351	2.10685
20	1.22019	1.48595	1.80611	2.19112
21	1.23239	1.51567	1.86029	2.27877
22	1.24472	1.54598	1.91610	2.36992
23	1.25716	1.57690	1.97359	2.46472
24	1.26973	1.60844	2.03279	2.56330
25	1.28243	1.64061	2.09378	2.66584
26	1.29526	1.67342	2.15659	2.77247
27	1.30821	1.70689	2.22129	2.88337
28	1.32129	1.74102	2.28793	2.99870
29	1.33450	1.77584	2.35657	3.11865
30	1.34785	1.81136	2.42726	3.24340
31	1.36133	1.84759	2.50008	3.37313
32	1.37494	1.88454	2.57508	3.50806
33	1.38869	1.92223	2.65234	3.64838
34	1.40258	1.96068	2.73191	3.79432
35	1.41660	1.99989	2.81386	3.94609
36	1.43077	2.03989	2.89828	4.10393
37	1.44508	2.08069	2.98523	4.26809
38	1.45953	2.12230	3.07478	4.43881
39	1.47412	2.16474	3.16703	4.61637
40	1.48886	2.20804	3.26204	4.80102

TABLE III (concluded)
Compound Amount of $1(1 + i)^n$

n	5%	6%	7%	8%
1	1.05000	1.06000	1.07000	1.08000
2	1.10250	1.12360	1.14490	1.16640
3	1.15762	1.19102	1.22504	1.25971
4	1.21551	1.26248	1.31080	1.36049
5	1.27628	1.33823	1.40255	1.46933
6	1.34010	1.41852	1.50073	1.58687
7	1.40710	1.50363	1.60578	1.71382
8	1.47746	1.59385	1.71819	1.85093
9	1.55133	1.68975	1.83846	1.99900
10	1.62889	1.79085	1.96715	2.15892
11	1.71034	1.89830	2.10485	2.33164
12	1.79586	2.01220	2.25219	2.51817
13	1.88565	2.13293	2.40985	2.71962
14	1.97993	2.26090	2.57853	2.93719
15	2.07893	2.39656	2.75903	3.17217
16	2.18287	2.54035	2.95216	3.42594
17	2.29202	2.69277	3.15882	3.70002
18	2.40662	2.85434	3.37993	3.99602
19	2.52695	3.02560	3.61653	4.31570
20	2.65330	3.20714	3.86968	4.66096
21	2.78596	3.39956	4.14056	5.03383
22	2.92526	3.60354	4.43040	5.43654
23	3.07152	3.81975	4.74053	5.87146
24	3.22510	4.04893	5.07237	6.34118
25	3.38635	4.29187	5.42743	6.84848
26	3.55567	4.54938	5.80735	7.39635
27	3.73346	4.82235	6.21387	7.98806
28	3.92013	5.11169	6.64884	8.62711
29	4.11614	5.41839	7.11426	9.31727
30	4.32194	5.74349	7.61226	10.06266
31	4.53804	6.08810	8.14511	10.86767
32	4.76494	6.45339	8.71527	11.73708
33	5.00319	6.84059	9.32534	12.67605
34	5.25335	7.25103	9.97811	13.69013
35	5.51602	7.68609	10.67658	14.78534
36	5.79182	8.14725	11.42394	15.96817
37	6.08141	8.63608	12.22362	17.24563
38	6.38548	9.15425	13.07927	18.62528
39	6.70475	9.70351	13.99482	20.11530
40	7.03999	10.28572	14.97446	21.72452

TABLE IV
Present Value of 1(1 + i)$^{-n}$

n	1%	2%	3%	4%
1	0.990099	0.980392	0.970874	0.961538
2	0.980296	0.961169	0.942596	0.924556
3	0.970590	0.942322	0.915142	0.888996
4	0.960980	0.923845	0.888487	0.854804
5	0.951466	0.905731	0.862609	0.821927
6	0.942045	0.887971	0.837484	0.790315
7	0.932718	0.870560	0.831092	0.759918
8	0.923483	0.853490	0.789409	0.730690
9	0.914340	0.836755	0.766417	0.702587
10	0.905287	0.820348	0.744094	0.675564
11	0.896324	0.804263	0.722421	0.649581
12	0.887449	0.788493	0.701380	0.624597
13	0.878663	0.773033	0.680951	0.600574
14	0.869963	0.757875	0.661118	0.577475
15	0.861349	0.743015	0.641862	0.555265
16	0.852821	0.728446	0.623167	0.533908
17	0.844377	0.714163	0.605016	0.513373
18	0.836017	0.700159	0.587395	0.493628
19	0.827740	0.686431	0.570286	0.474642
20	0.819544	0.672971	0.553676	0.456387
21	0.811430	0.659776	0.537549	0.438834
22	0.803396	0.646839	0.521893	0.421955
23	0.795442	0.634156	0.506692	0.405726
24	0.787566	0.621721	0.491934	0.390121
25	0.779768	0.609531	0.477606	0.375117
26	0.772048	0.597579	0.463695	0.360689
27	0.764404	0.585862	0.450189	0.346817
28	0.756836	0.574375	0.437077	0.333477
29	0.749342	0.563112	0.424346	0.320651
30	0.741923	0.552071	0.411987	0.308319
31	0.734577	0.541246	0.399987	0.296460
32	0.727304	0.530633	0.388337	0.285058
33	0.720103	0.520229	0.377026	0.274094
34	0.712973	0.510028	0.366045	0.263552
35	0.705914	0.500028	0.355383	0.253415
36	0.698925	0.490223	0.345032	0.243669
37	0.692005	0.480611	0.334983	0.234297
38	0.685153	0.471187	0.325226	0.225285
39	0.678370	0.461948	0.315754	0.216621
40	0.671653	0.452890	0.306557	0.208289

TABLE IV (concluded)
Present Value of $1 (1 + i)^{-n}

n	5%	6%	7%	8%
1	0.952381	0.943396	0.934579	0.925926
2	0.907029	0.889996	0.873439	0.857339
3	0.863838	0.839619	0.816298	0.793832
4	0.822702	0.792094	0.762895	0.735030
5	0.783526	0.747258	0.712986	0.680583
6	0.746215	0.704961	0.666342	0.630170
7	0.710681	0.665057	0.622750	0.583490
8	0.676839	0.627412	0.582009	0.540269
9	0.644609	0.591898	0.543934	0.500249
10	0.613913	0.558395	0.508349	0.463193
11	0.584679	0.526788	0.475093	0.428883
12	0.556837	0.496969	0.444012	0.397114
13	0.530321	0.468839	0.414964	0.367698
14	0.505068	0.442301	0.387817	0.340461
15	0.481017	0.417265	0.362446	0.315242
16	0.458112	0.393646	0.338735	0.291890
17	0.436297	0.371364	0.316574	0.270269
18	0.415521	0.350344	0.295864	0.250249
19	0.395734	0.330513	0.276508	0.231712
20	0.376889	0.311805	0.258419	0.214548
21	0.358942	0.294155	0.241513	0.198656
22	0.341850	0.277505	0.225713	0.183941
23	0.325571	0.261797	0.210947	0.170315
24	0.310068	0.246979	0.197147	0.157699
25	0.295303	0.232999	0.184249	0.146018
26	0.281241	0.219810	0.172195	0.135202
27	0.267848	0.207368	0.160930	0.125187
28	0.255094	0.195630	0.150402	0.115914
29	0.242946	0.184557	0.140563	0.107328
30	0.231377	0.174110	0.131367	0.099377
31	0.220359	0.164255	0.122773	0.092016
32	0.209866	0.154957	0.114741	0.085200
33	0.199873	0.146186	0.107235	0.078889
34	0.190355	0.137912	0.100219	0.073045
35	0.181290	0.130105	0.093663	0.067635
36	0.172657	0.122741	0.087535	0.062625
37	0.164436	0.115793	0.081809	0.057986
38	0.156605	0.109239	0.076457	0.053690
39	0.149148	0.103056	0.071455	0.049713
40	0.142046	0.097222	0.066780	0.046031

TABLE V

Amount of $1 per Period: $s_{\overline{n}|i} = \dfrac{(1 + i)^n - 1}{i}$

n	1%	2%	3%	4%
1	1.00000	1.00000	1.00000	1.00000
2	2.01000	2.02000	2.03000	2.04000
3	3.03010	3.06040	3.09090	3.12160
4	4.06040	4.12161	4.18363	4.24646
5	5.10101	5.20404	5.30914	5.41632
6	6.15202	6.30812	6.46841	6.63298
7	7.21354	7.43428	7.66246	7.89829
8	8.28567	8.58297	8.89234	9.21423
9	9.36853	9.75463	10.15911	10.58280
10	10.46221	10.94972	11.46388	12.00611
11	11.56683	12.16872	12.80780	13.48635
12	12.68250	13.41209	14.19203	15.02581
13	13.80933	14.68033	15.61779	16.62684
14	14.94742	15.97394	17.08632	18.29191
15	16.09690	17.29342	18.59891	20.02359
16	17.25786	18.63929	20.15688	21.82453
17	18.43044	20.01207	21.76159	23.69751
18	19.61475	21.41231	23.41444	25.64541
19	20.81090	22.84056	25.11687	27.67123
20	22.01900	24.29737	26.87037	29.77808
21	23.23919	25.78332	28.67649	31.96920
22	24.47159	27.29898	30.53678	34.24797
23	25.71630	28.84496	32.45288	36.61789
24	26.97346	30.42186	34.42647	39.08260
25	28.24320	32.03030	36.45926	41.64591
26	29.52563	33.67091	38.55304	44.31174
27	30.82089	35.34432	40.70963	47.08421
28	32.12910	37.05121	42.93092	49.96758
29	33.45039	38.79223	45.21885	52.96629
30	34.78489	40.56808	47.57542	56.08494
31	36.13274	42.37944	50.00268	59.32834
32	37.49407	44.22703	52.50276	62.70147
33	38.86901	46.11157	55.07784	66.20953
34	40.25770	48.03380	57.73018	69.85791
35	41.66028	49.99448	60.46208	73.65222
36	43.07688	51.99437	63.27594	77.59831
37	44.50765	54.03425	66.17422	81.70225
38	45.95272	56.11494	69.15945	85.97034
39	47.41225	58.23724	72.23423	90.40915
40	48.88637	60.40198	75.40126	95.02552

TABLE V (concluded)

Amount of $1 per Period: $s_{\overline{n}|i} = \dfrac{(1+i)^n - 1}{i}$

n	5%	6%	7%	8%
1	1.00000	1.00000	1.00000	1.00000
2	2.05000	2.06000	2.07000	2.08000
3	3.15250	3.18360	3.21490	3.24640
4	4.31012	4.37462	4.43994	4.50611
5	5.52563	5.63709	5.75074	5.86660
6	6.80191	6.97532	7.15329	7.33593
7	8.14201	8.39384	8.65402	8.92280
8	9.54911	9.89747	10.25980	10.63663
9	11.02656	11.49132	11.97799	12.48756
10	12.57789	13.18079	13.81645	14.48656
11	14.20679	14.97164	15.78360	16.64549
12	15.91713	16.86994	17.88845	18.97713
13	17.71298	18.88214	20.14064	21.49530
14	19.59863	21.01507	22.55049	24.21492
15	21.57856	23.27597	25.12902	27.15211
16	23.65749	25.67253	27.88805	30.32428
17	25.84037	28.21288	30.84022	33.75023
18	28.13238	30.90565	33.99903	37.45024
19	30.53900	33.75999	37.37896	41.44626
20	33.06595	36.78559	40.99549	45.76196
21	35.71925	39.99273	44.86518	50.42292
22 . . . . ,	38.50521	43.39229	49.00574	55.45676
23	41.43048	46.99583	53.43614	60.89330
24	44.50200	50.81558	58.17667	66.76476
25	47.72710	54.86451	63.24904	73.10594
26	51.11345	59.15638	68.67647	79.95442
27	54.66913	63.70577	74.48382	87.35077
28	58.40258	68.52811	80.69769	95.33883
29	62.32271	73.63980	87.34653	103.96594
30	66.43885	79.05819	94.46079	113.28321
31	70.76079	84.80168	102.07304	123.34587
32	75.29883	90.88978	110.21815	134.21354
33	80.06377	97.34316	118.93343	145.95062
34	85.06696	104.18375	128.25876	158.62667
35	90.32031	111.43478	138.23688	172.31680
36	95.83632	119.12087	148.91346	187.10215
37	101.62814	127.26812	160.33740	203.07032
38	107.70955	135.90421	172.56102	220.31595
39	114.09502	145.05846	185.64029	238.94122
40	120.79977	154.76197	199.63511	259.05652

TABLE VI

Present Value of \$1 per Period: $a_{\overline{n}|i} = \dfrac{1 - (1 + i)^{-n}}{i}$

n	1%	2%	3%	4%
1	0.99010	0.98039	0.97087	0.96154
2	1.97040	1.94156	1.91347	1.88609
3	2.94099	2.88388	2.82861	2.77509
4	3.90197	3.80773	3.71710	3.62990
5·	4.85343	4.71346	4.57971	4.45182
6	5.79548	5.60143	5.41719	5.24214
7	6.72819	6.47199	6.23028	6.00205
8	7.65168	7.32548	7.01969	6.73274
9	8.56602	8.16224	7.78611	7.43533
10	9.47130	8.98259	8.53020	8.11090
11	10.36763	9.78685	9.25262	8.76048
12	11.25508	10.57534	9.95400	9.38507
13	12.13374	11.34837	10.63496	9.98565
14	13.00370	12.10625	11.29607	10.56312
15	13.86505	12.84926	11.93794	11.11839
16	14.71787	13.57771	12.56110	11.65230
17	15.56225	14.29187	13.16612	12.16567
18	16.39827	14.99203	13.75351	12.65930
19	17.22601	15.67846	14.32380	13.13394
20	18.04555	16.35143	14.87747	13.59033
21	18.85698	17.01121	15.41502	14.02916
22	19.66038	17.65805	15.93692	14.45112
23	20.45582	18.29220	16.44361	14.85684
24	21.24339	18.91393	16.93554	15.24696
25	22.02316	19.52346	17.41315	15.62208
26	22.79520	20.12104	17.87684	15.98277
27	23.55961	20.70690	18.32703	16.32959
28	24.31644	21.28127	18.76411	16.66306
29	25.06579	21.84438	19.18845	16.98371
30	25.80771	22.39646	19.60044	17.29203
31	26.54229	22.93770	20.00043	17.58849
32	27.26959	23.46833	20.38877	17.87355
33	27.98969	23.98856	20.76579	18.14765
34	28.70267	24.49859	21.13184	18.41120
35	29.40858	24.99862	21.48722	18.66461
36	30.10751	25.48884	21.83225	18.90828
37	30.79951	25.96945	22.16724	19.14258
38	31.48466	26.44064	22.49246	19.36786
39	32.16303	26.90259	22.80822	19.58448
40	32.83469	27.35548	23.11477	19.79277

TABLE VI *(concluded)*

Present Value of $1 per Period: $a_{\overline{n}|i} = \dfrac{1 - (1 + i)^{-n}}{i}$

n	5%	6%	7%	8%
1	0.95238	0.94340	0.93458	0.92593
2	1.85941	1.83339	1.80802	1.78326
3	2.72325	2.67301	2.62432	2.57710
4	3.54595	3.46511	3.38721	3.31213
5	4.32948	4.21236	4.10020	3.99271
6	5.07569	4.91732	4.76654	4.62288
7	5.78637	5.58238	5.38929	5.20637
8	6.46321	6.20979	5.97130	5.74664
9	7.10782	6.80169	6.51523	6.24689
10	7.72173	7.36009	7.02358	6.71008
11	8.30641	7.88687	7.49867	7.13896
12	8.86325	7.38384	7.94269	7.53608
13	9.39357	8.85268	8.35765	7.90378
14	9.89864	9.29498	8.74547	8.24424
15	10.37966	9.71225	9.10791	8.55948
16	10.83777	10.10590	9.44665	8.85137
17	11.27407	10.47726	9.76322	9.12164
18	11.68959	10.82760	10.05909	9.37189
19	12.08532	11.15812	10.33560	9.60360
20	12.46221	11.46992	10.59401	9.81815
21	12.82115	11.76408	10.83553	10.01680
22	13.16300	12.04158	11.06124	10.20074
23	13.48857	12.30338	11.27219	10.37106
24	13.79864	12.55036	11.46933	10.52876
25	14.09394	12.78336	11.65358	10.67478
26	14.37519	13.00317	11.82578	10.80998
27	14.64303	13.21053	11.98671	10.93516
28	14.89813	13.40616	12.13711	11.05108
29	15.14107	13.59072	12.27767	11.15841
30	15.37245	13.76483	12.40904	11.25778
31	15.59281	13.92909	12.53181	11.34980
32	15.80268	14.08404	12.64656	11.43500
33	16.00255	14.23023	12.75379	11.51389
34	16.19290	14.36814	12.85401	11.58693
35	16.37419	14.49825	12.94767	11.65457
36	16.54685	14.62099	13.03521	11.71719
37	16.71129	14.73678	13.11702	11.77518
38	16.86789	14.84602	13.19347	11.82887
39	17.01704	14.94907	13.26593	11.87858
40	17.15909	15.04630	13.33171	11.92461

TABLE VII

Per-Period Equivalent of $1 Present Value: $\dfrac{1}{a_{\overline{n}|i}} = \dfrac{i}{1 - (1 + i)^{-n}}$

n	1%	2%	3%	4%
1	1.010000	1.020000	1.030000	1.040000
2	0.507512	0.515050	0.522611	0.530196
3	0.340022	0.346755	0.353530	0.360349
4	0.256281	0.262624	0.269027	0.275490
5	0.206040	0.212158	0.218355	0.224627
6	0.172548	0.178526	0.184598	0.190762
7	0.148628	0.154512	0.160506	0.166610
8	0.130690	0.136510	0.142456	0.148528
9	0.116740	0.122515	0.128434	0.134493
10	0.105582	0.111327	0.117231	0.123291
11	0.096454	0.102178	0.108077	0.114149
12	0.088848	0.094560	0.100462	0.106552
13	0.082415	0.088118	0.094030	0.100144
14	0.076901	0.082602	0.088526	0.094669
15	0.072124	0.077825	0.083767	0.089941
16	0.067945	0.073650	0.079611	0.085820
17	0.064258	0.069970	0.075953	0.082199
18	0.060982	0.066702	0.072709	0.078993
19	0.058052	0.063782	0.069814	0.076139
20	0.055415	0.061157	0.067216	0.073582
21	0.053031	0.058785	0.064872	0.071280
22	0.050864	0.056631	0.062747	0.069199
23	0.048886	0.054668	0.060814	0.067309
24	0.047073	0.052871	0.059047	0.065587
25	0.045407	0.051220	0.057428	0.064012
26	0.043869	0.049699	0.055938	0.062567
27	0.042446	0.048293	0.054564	0.061239
28	0.041124	0.046990	0.053293	0.060013
29	0.039895	0.045778	0.052115	0.058880
30	0.038748	0.044650	0.051019	0.057830
31	0.037676	0.043596	0.049999	0.056855
32	0.036671	0.042611	0.049047	0.055949
33	0.035727	0.041687	0.048156	0.055104
34	0.034840	0.040819	0.047322	0.054315
35	0.034004	0.040002	0.046539	0.053577
36	0.033214	0.039233	0.045804	0.052887
37	0.032468	0.038507	0.045112	0.052240
38	0.031761	0.037821	0.044459	0.051632
39	0.031092	0.037171	0.043844	0.051061
40	0.030456	0.036556	0.043262	0.050523

TABLE VII (concluded)

Per-Period Equivalent of $1 Present Value: $\dfrac{1}{a_{\overline{n}|i}} = \dfrac{i}{1 - (1 + i)^{-n}}$

n	5%	6%	7%	8%
1	1.050000	1.060000	1.070000	1.080000
2	0.537805	0.545437	0.553092	0.560769
3	0.367209	0.374110	0.381052	0.388034
4	0.282012	0.288591	0.295228	0.301921
5	0.230975	0.237396	0.243891	0.250456
6	0.197017	0.203363	0.209796	0.216315
7	0.172820	0.179135	0.185553	0.192072
8	0.154722	0.161036	0.167468	0.174015
9	0.140690	0.147022	0.153486	0.161080
10	0.129505	0.135868	0.142378	0.149029
11	0.120389	0.126793	0.133357	0.140076
12	0.112825	0.119277	0.125902	0.132695
13	0.106456	0.112960	0.119651	0.126522
14	0.101024	0.107585	0.114345	0.121297
15	0.096342	0.102963	0.109795	0.116830
16	0.092270	0.098952	0.105858	0.112977
17	0.088699	0.095445	0.102425	0.109629
18	0.085546	0.092357	0.099412	0.106702
19	0.082745	0.089621	0.096753	0.104128
20	0.080243	0.087185	0.094393	0.101852
21	0.077996	0.085005	0.092289	0.099832
22	0.075971	0.083046	0.090406	0.098032
23	0.074137	0.081278	0.088714	0.096422
24	0.072471	0.079679	0.087189	0.094978
25	0.070952	0.078227	0.085811	0.093679
26	0.069564	0.076904	0.084561	0.092507
27	0.068292	0.075697	0.083426	0.091448
28	0.067123	0.074593	0.082392	0.090489
29	0.066046	0.073580	0.081449	0.089619
30	0.065051	0.072649	0.080586	0.088827
31	0.064132	0.071792	0.079797	0.088107
32	0.063280	0.071002	0.079073	0.087451
33	0.062490	0.070273	0.078408	0.086852
34	0.061755	0.069598	0.077797	0.086304
35	0.061072	0.068974	0.077234	0.085803
36	0.060434	0.068395	0.076715	0.085345
37	0.059840	0.067857	0.076237	0.084924
38	0.059284	0.067358	0.075795	0.084539
39	0.058765	0.066894	0.075387	0.084185
40	0.058278	0.066462	0.075009	0.083860

TABLE VIII

Per-Period Equivalent of $1 Future Value: $\dfrac{1}{s_{\overline{n}|i}} = \dfrac{i}{(1+i)^n - 1} = \dfrac{1}{a_{\overline{n}|i}} - i$

n	1%	2%	3%	4%
1	1.0000000	1.0000000	1.0000000	1.0000000
2	0.4975124	0.4950495	0.4926108	0.4901961
3	0.3300221	0.3267547	0.3235304	0.3203485
4	0.2462811	0.2426238	0.2390270	0.2354900
5	0.1960398	0.1921584	0.1883546	0.1846271
6	0.1625484	0.1585258	0.1545975	0.1507619
7	0.1386283	0.1345120	0.1305064	0.1266096
8	0.1206903	0.1165098	0.1124564	0.1085278
9	0.1067404	0.1025154	0.0984339	0.0944930
10	0.0955821	0.0913265	0.0872305	0.0832909
11	0.0864541	0.0821779	0.0780774	0.0741490
12	0.0788488	0.0745596	0.0704621	0.0665522
13	0.0724148	0.0681184	0.0640295	0.0601437
14	0.0669012	0.0626020	0.0585263	0.0546690
15	0.0621238	0.0578255	0.0537666	0.0499411
16	0.0579446	0.0536501	0.0496108	0.0458200
17	0.0542581	0.0499698	0.0459525	0.0421985
18	0.0509820	0.0467021	0.0427087	0.0389933
19	0.0480518	0.0437818	0.0398139	0.0361386
20	0.0454153	0.0411567	0.0372157	0.0335818
21	0.0430308	0.0387848	0.0348718	0.0312801
22	0.0408637	0.0366314	0.0327474	0.0291988
23	0.0388858	0.0346681	0.0308139	0.0273091
24	0.0370735	0.0328711	0.0290474	0.0255868
25	0.0354068	0.0312204	0.0274279	0.0240120
26	0.0338689	0.0296992	0.0259383	0.0225674
27	0.0324455	0.0282931	0.0245642	0.0212385
28	0.0311244	0.0269897	0.0232932	0.0200130
29	0.0298950	0.0257784	0.0221147	0.0188799
30	0.0287481	0.0246499	0.0210193	0.0178301
31	0.0276757	0.0235963	0.0199989	0.0168554
32	0.0266709	0.0226106	0.0190466	0.0159486
33	0.0257274	0.0216865	0.0181561	0.0151036
34	0.0248400	0.0208187	0.0173220	0.0143148
35	0.0240037	0.0200022	0.0165393	0.0135773
36	0.0232143	0.0192329	0.0158038	0.0128869
37	0.0224680	0.0185068	0.0151116	0.0122396
38	0.0217615	0.0178206	0.0144593	0.0116319
39	0.0210916	0.0171711	0.0138439	0.0110608
40	0.0204556	0.0165557	0.0132624	0.0105235

TABLE VIII (concluded)

Per-Period Equivalent of $1 Future Value: $\dfrac{1}{s_{\overline{n}|i}} = \dfrac{i}{(1+i)^n - 1} = \dfrac{1}{a_{\overline{n}|i}} - i$

n	5%	6%	7%	8%
1	1.0000000	1.0000000	1.0000000	1.0000000
2	0.4878049	0.4854369	0.4830918	0.4807692
3	0.3172086	0.3141098	0.3110517	0.3080335
4	0.2320118	0.2285915	0.2252281	0.2219208
5	0.1809748	0.1773964	0.1738907	0.1704565
6	0.1470175	0.1433626	0.1397958	0.1363154
7	0.1228198	0.1191350	0.1155532	0.1120724
8	0.1047218	0.1010359	0.0974678	0.0940148
9	0.0906901	0.0870222	0.0834865	0.0800797
10	0.0795046	0.0758680	0.0723775	0.0690295
11	0.0703889	0.0667929	0.0633569	0.0600763
12	0.0628254	0.0592770	0.0559020	0.0526950
13	0.0564558	0.0529601	0.0496508	0.0465218
14	0.0510240	0.0475849	0.0443449	0.0412969
15	0.0463423	0.0429628	0.0397946	0.0368295
16	0.0422699	0.0389521	0.0358576	0.0329769
17	0.0386991	0.0354448	0.0324252	0.0296294
18	0.0355462	0.0323565	0.0294126	0.0267021
19	0.0327450	0.0296209	0.0267530	0.0241276
20	0.0302426	0.0271846	0.0243929	0.0218522
21	0.0279961	0.0250045	0.0222890	0.0198323
22	0.0259705	0.0230456	0.0204058	0.0180321
23	0.0241368	0.0212785	0.0187139	0.0164222
24	0.0224709	0.0196790	0.0171890	0.0149780
25	0.0209525	0.0182267	0.0158105	0.0136788
26	0.0195643	0.0169043	0.0145610	0.0125071
27	0.0182919	0.0156972	0.0134257	0.0114481
28	0.0171225	0.0145926	0.0123919	0.0104889
29	0.0160455	0.0135796	0.0114487	0.0096185
30	0.0150514	0.0126489	0.0105864	0.0088274
31	0.0141321	0.0117922	0.0097969	0.0081073
32	0.0132804	0.0110023	0.0090729	0.0074508
33	0.0124900	0.0102729	0.0084081	0.0068516
34	0.0117554	0.0095984	0.0077967	0.0063041
35	0.0110717	0.0089739	0.0072340	0.0058033
36	0.0104345	0.0083948	0.0067153	0.0053447
37	0.0098398	0.0078574	0.0062368	0.0049244
38	0.0092842	0.0073581	0.0057951	0.0045389
39	0.0087646	0.0068938	0.0053868	0.0041851
40	0.0082782	0.0064615	0.0050091	0.0038602

TABLE IX

Monthly Payment for $1 Mortgage: $\dfrac{\dfrac{j}{1200}}{1 - \left(1 + \dfrac{j}{1200}\right)^{-n}}$

Annual Rate j%	Number of Months, n					
	120	180	240	300	360	420
7.00	.0116108479	.0089982827	.0077529894	.0070677920	.0066530250	.0063885636
7.25	.0117401041	.0091286288	.0079037598	.0072280686	.0068217628	.0065646724
7.50	.0118701769	.0092701236	.0080559319	.0073899118	.0069921451	.0067424260
7.75	.0120010631	.0094127575	.0082094856	.0075532876	.0071641225	.0069217594
8.00	.0121327594	.0095565208	.0083644007	.0077181622	.0073376457	.0071026088
8.25	.0122652625	.0097014036	.0085206565	.0078845013	.0075126660	.0072849114
8.50	.0123985689	.0098473956	.0086782324	.0080522708	.0076891348	.0074686057
8.75	.0125326750	.0099944865	.0088371071	.0082214364	.0078670041	.0076536314
9.00	.0126675774	.0101426658	.0089972596	.0083919636	.0080462262	.0078399297
9.25	.0128032722	.0102919229	.0091586683	.0085638184	.0082267543	.0080274432
9.50	.0129397558	.0104422468	.0093213119	.0087369666	.0084085421	.0082161160
9.75	.0130770242	.0105936266	.0094851685	.0089113742	.0085915441	.0084058939
10.00	.0132150737	.0107460512	.0096502165	.0090870075	.0087757157	.0085967243
10.25	.0133539002	.0108995092	.0098164339	.0092638328	.0089610130	.0087885561
10.50	.0134934997	.0110539892	.0099837989	.0094418171	.0091473929	.0089813402
10.75	.0136338680	.0112094798	.0101522895	.0096209272	.0093348136	.0091750290
11.00	.0137750011	.0113659693	.0103218839	.0098011308	.0095232340	.0093695765

TABLE X–A

Cumulative Binomial Distribution for $n = 10$ (Tabulated values are $\sum_{0}^{x} C_x^{10} p^x q^{10-x}$)

Values of x						Values of p							
	0.01	0.05	0.10	0.20	0.30	0.40	0.50	0.60	0.70	0.80	0.90	0.95	0.99
0 ...	.904	.599	.349	.107	.028	.006	.001	.000	.000	.000	.000	.000	.000
1 ...	.996	.914	.736	.376	.149	.046	.011	.002	.000	.000	.000	.000	.000
2 ...	1.000	.988	.930	.678	.383	.167	.055	.012	.002	.000	.000	.000	.000
3 ...	1.000	.999	.987	.879	.650	.382	.172	.055	.011	.001	.000	.000	.000
4 ...	1.000	1.000	.998	.967	.850	.633	.377	.166	.047	.006	.000	.000	.000
5 ...	1.000	1.000	1.000	.994	.953	.834	.623	.367	.150	.033	.002	.000	.000
6 ...	1.000	1.000	1.000	.999	.989	.945	.828	.618	.350	.121	.013	.001	.000
7 ...	1.000	1.000	1.000	1.000	.998	.988	.945	.833	.617	.322	.070	.012	.000
8 ...	1.000	1.000	1.000	1.000	1.000	.998	.989	.954	.851	.624	.264	.086	.004
9 ...	1.000	1.000	1.000	1.000	1.000	1.000	.999	.994	.972	.893	.651	.401	.096
10 ...	1.000	1.000	1.000	1.000	1.000	1.000	1.000	1.000	1.000	1.000	1.000	1.000	1.000

TABLE X–B

Cumulative Binomial Distribution for $n = 25$ (Tabulated values are $\sum_{0}^{x} C_x^{25} p^x q^{25-x}$)

Values of x						Values of p							
	0.01	0.05	0.10	0.20	0.30	0.40	0.50	0.60	0.70	0.80	0.90	0.95	0.99
0	.778	.277	.072	.004	.000	.000	.000	.000	.000	.000	.000	.000	.000
1	.974	.642	.271	.027	.002	.000	.000	.000	.000	.000	.000	.000	.000
2	.998	.873	.537	.098	.009	.000	.000	.000	.000	.000	.000	.000	.000
3	1.000	.966	.764	.234	.033	.002	.000	.000	.000	.000	.000	.000	.000
4	1.000	.993	.902	.421	.090	.009	.000	.000	.000	.000	.000	.000	.000
5	1.000	.999	.967	.617	.193	.029	.002	.000	.000	.000	.000	.000	.000
6	1.000	1.000	.991	.780	.341	.074	.007	.000	.000	.000	.000	.000	.000
7	1.000	1.000	.998	.891	.512	.154	.022	.001	.000	.000	.000	.000	.000
8	1.000	1.000	1.000	.953	.677	.274	.054	.004	.000	.000	.000	.000	.000
9	1.000	1.000	1.000	.983	.811	.425	.115	.013	.000	.000	.000	.000	.000
10	1.000	1.000	1.000	.994	.902	.586	.212	.034	.002	.000	.000	.000	.000
11	1.000	1.000	1.000	.998	.956	.732	.345	.078	.017	.000	.000	.000	.000
12	1.000	1.000	1.000	1.000	.983	.846	.500	.154	.017	.000	.000	.000	.000
13	1.000	1.000	1.000	1.000	.994	.922	.655	.268	.044	.002	.000	.000	.000
14	1.000	1.000	1.000	1.000	.998	.966	.788	.414	.098	.006	.000	.000	.000
15	1.000	1.000	1.000	1.000	1.000	.987	.885	.575	.189	.017	.000	.000	.000
16	1.000	1.000	1.000	1.000	1.000	.996	.946	.726	.323	.047	.000	.000	.000
17	1.000	1.000	1.000	1.000	1.000	.999	.978	.846	.488	.109	.002	.000	.000
18	1.000	1.000	1.000	1.000	1.000	1.000	.993	.926	.659	.220	.009	.000	.000
19	1.000	1.000	1.000	1.000	1.000	1.000	.998	.971	.807	.383	.033	.001	.000
20	1.000	1.000	1.000	1.000	1.000	1.000	1.000	.991	.910	.579	.098	.007	.000
21	1.000	1.000	1.000	1.000	1.000	1.000	1.000	.998	.967	.766	.236	.034	.000
22	1.000	1.000	1.000	1.000	1.000	1.000	1.000	1.000	.991	.902	.463	.127	.002
23	1.000	1.000	1.000	1.000	1.000	1.000	1.000	1.000	.998	.973	.729	.358	.026
24	1.000	1.000	1.000	1.000	1.000	1.000	1.000	1.000	1.000	.996	.928	.723	.222

TABLE XI
Areas under the Normal Curve

Normal Deviate, z	.00	.01	.02	.03	.04	.05	.06	.07	.08	.09
0.0	.0000	.0040	.0080	.0120	.0160	.0199	.0239	.0279	.0319	.0359
0.1	.0398	.0438	.0478	.0517	.0557	.0596	.0636	.0675	.0714	.0753
0.2	.0793	.0832	.0871	.0910	.0948	.0987	.1026	.1064	.1103	.1141
0.3	.1179	.1217	.1255	.1293	.1331	.1368	.1406	.1443	.1480	.1517
0.4	.1554	.1591	.1628	.1664	.1700	.1736	.1772	.1808	.1844	.1879
0.5	.1915	.1950	.1985	.2019	.2054	.2088	.2123	.2157	.2190	.2224
0.6	.2257	.2291	.2324	.2357	.2389	.2422	.2454	.2486	.2517	.2549
0.7	.2580	.2611	.2642	.2673	.2704	.2734	.2764	.2794	.2823	.2852
0.8	.2881	.2910	.2939	.2967	.2995	.3023	.3051	.3078	.3106	.3133
0.9	.3159	.3186	.3212	.3238	.3264	.3289	.3315	.3340	.3365	.3389
1.0	.3413	.3438	.3461	.3485	.3508	.3531	.3554	.3577	.3599	.3621
1.1	.3643	.3665	.3686	.3708	.3729	.3749	.3770	.3790	.3810	.3830
1.2	.3849	.3869	.3888	.3907	.3925	.3944	.3962	.3980	.3997	.4015
1.3	.4032	.4049	.4066	.4082	.4099	.4115	.4131	.4147	.4162	.4177
1.4	.4192	.4207	.4222	.4236	.4251	.4265	.4279	.4292	.4306	.4319
1.5	.4332	.4345	.4357	.4370	.4382	.4394	.4406	.4418	.4429	.4441
1.6	.4452	.4463	.4474	.4484	.4495	.4505	.4515	.4525	.4535	.4545
1.7	.4554	.4564	.4573	.4582	.4591	.4599	.4608	.4616	.4625	.4633
1.8	.4641	.4649	.4656	.4664	.4671	.4678	.4686	.4693	.4699	.4706
1.9	.4713	.4719	.4726	.4732	.4738	.4744	.4750	.4756	.4761	.4767
2.0	.4772	.4778	.4783	.4788	.4793	.4798	.4803	.4808	.4812	.4817
2.1	.4821	.4826	.4830	.4834	.4838	.4842	.4846	.4850	.4854	.4857
2.2	.4861	.4864	.4868	.4871	.4875	.4878	.4881	.4884	.4887	.4890
2.3	.4893	.4896	.4898	.4901	.4904	.4906	.4909	.4911	.4913	.4916
2.4	.4918	.4920	.4922	.4925	.4927	.4929	.4931	.4932	.4934	.4936
2.5	.4938	.4940	.4941	.4943	.4945	.4946	.4948	.4949	.4951	.4952
2.6	.4953	.4955	.4956	.4957	.4959	.4960	.4961	.4962	.4963	.4964
2.7	.4965	.4966	.4967	.4968	.4969	.4970	.4971	.4972	.4973	.4974
2.8	.4974	.4975	.4976	.4977	.4977	.4978	.4979	.4979	.4980	.4981
2.9	.4981	.4982	.4982	.4983	.4984	.4984	.4985	.4985	.4986	.4986
3.0	.4987	.4987	.4987	.4988	.4988	.4989	.4989	.4989	.4990	.4990

Adapted by permission from Ernest Kurnow, Gerald J. Glasser, and Frederick R. Ottman. *Statistics for Business Decisions* (Homewood, Ill.: Richard D. Irwin, 1959), p. 501. © 1959 by Richard D. Irwin, Inc.

TABLE XII–A
Rules for Derivatives

1. $\dfrac{d}{dx}[f(x) + g(x)] = \dfrac{d}{dx}f(x) + \dfrac{d}{dx}g(x).$

2. $\dfrac{d}{dx}[f(x) - g(x)] = \dfrac{d}{dx}f(x) - \dfrac{d}{dx}g(x).$

3. $\dfrac{d}{dx}(a) = 0.$

4. $\dfrac{d}{dx}(x) = 1.$

5. $\dfrac{d}{dx}(ax) = a; \dfrac{d}{dx}af(x) = a\dfrac{d}{dx}f(x).$

6. $\dfrac{d}{dx}(x^n) = nx^{n-1}.$

7. $\dfrac{d}{dx}[f(x)]^n = n[f(x)]^{n-1}f'(x).$

8. $\dfrac{d}{dx}(e^x) = e^x.$

9. $\dfrac{d}{dx}(a^x) = a^x(\ln a).$

10. $\dfrac{d}{dx}[e^{f(x)}] = e^{f(x)}f'(x).$

11. $\dfrac{d}{dx}[a^{f(x)}] = a^{f(x)}[f'(x)](\ln a).$

12. $\dfrac{d}{dx}(\ln x) = \dfrac{1}{x}.$

13. $\dfrac{d}{dx}(\log x) = \dfrac{1}{x(\ln 10)} = \dfrac{0.43429}{x}.$

14. $\dfrac{d}{dx}[\ln f(x)] = \dfrac{1}{f(x)}[f'(x)] = \dfrac{f'(x)}{f(x)}.$

15. $\dfrac{d}{dx}[\log f(x)] = \dfrac{f'(x)}{f(x)(\ln 10)} = \dfrac{(0.43429)f'(x)}{f(x)}.$

16. $\dfrac{d}{dx}f[g(x)] = \dfrac{d}{dg}[f(g)] \cdot \dfrac{d}{dx}g(x).$

17. $\dfrac{d}{dx}[f(x)g(x)] = f(x)g'(x) + g(x)f'(x).$

18. $\dfrac{d}{dx}\left[\dfrac{f(x)}{g(x)}\right] = \dfrac{g(x)f'(x) - f(x)g'(x)}{[g(x)]^2}.$

Note: a and n are constants;
$$\dfrac{d}{dx}f(x) = f'(x); \dfrac{d}{dx}g(x) = g'(x).$$

TABLE XII–B
Rules for Integrals

1. $\int [f(x) + g(x)]dx = \int f(x)dx + \int g(x)dx.$

2. $\int [f(x) - g(x)]dx = \int f(x)dx - \int g(x)dx.$

3. $\int kf(x)dx = k\int f(x)dx.$

4. $\int dx = \int 1dx = x + C.$

5. $\int kdx = kx + C.$

6. $\int x^n dx = \dfrac{x^{n+1}}{n+1} + C; n \neq -1.$

7. $\int x^{-1}dx = \int \dfrac{1}{x}dx = \int \dfrac{dx}{x} = \ln x + C.$

8. $\int (mx + b)^n dx = \dfrac{(mx + b)^{n+1}}{m(n+1)} + C; n \neq -1.$

9. $\int (mx + b)^{-1}dx = \int \dfrac{dx}{mx + b} = \dfrac{\ln (mx + b)}{m} + C.$

10. $\int \dfrac{xdx}{mx + b} = \dfrac{x}{m} - \dfrac{b}{m^2} \ln (mx + b) + C.$

11. $\int \dfrac{xdx}{(mx + b)^2} = \dfrac{b}{m^2(mx + b)} + \dfrac{\ln (mx + b)}{m^2} + C.$

12. $\int \dfrac{dx}{x(mx + b)} = \dfrac{1}{b} \ln \left(\dfrac{x}{mx + b}\right) + C.$

13. $\int e^x dx = e^x + C.$

14. $\int a^x dx = \dfrac{a^x}{\ln a} + C.$

15. $\int e^{mx+b}dx = \dfrac{e^{mx+b}}{m} + C.$

16. $\int a^{mx+b}dx = \dfrac{a^{mx+b}}{m(\ln a)} + C.$

17. $\int xe^{mx+b}dx = \dfrac{e^{mx+b}(mx - 1)}{m^2} + C.$

18. $\int xa^{mx+b}dx = \dfrac{xa^{mx+b}}{m(\ln a)} - \dfrac{a^{mx+b}}{(m \ln a)^2} + C.$

19. $\int xe^{ax^2+b}dx = \dfrac{e^{ax^2+b}}{2a} + C.$

20. $\int \dfrac{dx}{a + be^{mx}} = \dfrac{mx - \ln(a + be^{mx})}{am} + C.$

21. $\int \ln x dx = x(\ln x - 1) + C.$

22. $\int \log x dx = x\left(\log x - \dfrac{1}{\ln 10}\right) + C.$

23. $\int \ln (mx + b)dx = \dfrac{(mx + b)[\ln(mx + b) - 1]}{m} + C.$

24. $\int \log(mx + b)dx = \left(\dfrac{mx + b}{m}\right)\left[\log(mx + b) - \dfrac{1}{\ln 10}\right] + C.$

TABLE XII–B (concluded)

25. $\int \dfrac{1}{x^2 - a^2} dx = \dfrac{1}{2a} \ln \left| \dfrac{x - a}{x + a} \right| + C, \, x^2 > a^2.$

26. $\int \dfrac{1}{a^2 - x^2} dx = \dfrac{1}{2a} \ln \dfrac{a + x}{a - x} + C, \, x^2 < a^2.$

27. $\int \dfrac{1}{x \sqrt{a^2 - x^2}} dx = \dfrac{1}{a} \ln \left| \dfrac{a + \sqrt{a^2 - x^2}}{x} \right| + C, \, 0 < x < a.$

Note: a, b, k, m, n and C are constants.

Index

A

Absolute value, 7
Algebra review, 825–901
Amortization
  defined, 421
  and mortgage payments, 423–24
  schedules, 425–26
  table for, 983
Antiderivatives, 685, 687
Arbitrary variable, 70–72
Asymptote, 612

B

Banker's Rule, 380
Basis, 196–97
Bayes' Rule, 471–73
Big-M method, 286–87
Binomial probability rule, 487, 777
Binomial theorem, 371
Break-even analysis, 39–45

C

Chain rule, 645–51
Charnes, A., 226
Compound discount factor, 399
Computers; *see also by individual*
    program
  and linear relationships, 2
  matrix inversion on, 158
Concave curves, 573
Constraints
  binding, 255
  conversion, 193–95, 206
  degeneracy in, 229
  equal, 112–14, 302–8
  linear, 92
  linearly independent, 120
  mix of, 109–12
  nonnegative, 82

Constraints (*Cont.*)
  in program formulation, 99–100
  redundant, 125, 229
Consumers' surplus, 722–24
Conversion period, 393–94
Cooper, W. W., 226
Corners
  in linear programming, 95, 106
  nonpermissible, 116–17
Cubic, 577
Cumulative binomial distribution
    tables, 984
Current values column, 259–62
Cusps, 564–65

D

Decimal rate, 383
Delta notation, 513–15
Demand function
  horizontal, 47–48
  linear, 45–47, 63–65
  two-product, 77–78
  vertical, 47–48
Derivatives; *see also by function*
  definition of, 536
  first test, 567–69
  function power rule for, 549–52
  partial, 656–59
  product rule for, 553–56
  quotient rule for, 556–58
  rules for, 986
  second test, 573–75
  simple power rule for, 541–43
  with respect to x, 545–47
Difference quotient, 531–34
Differential calculus
  derivatives in, 535–37
  limits in, 516–24
  mutivariate, 622, 656–71
  notation for, 510–13

Differential equations
  defined, 758
  explicit solutions to, 760–63
  general solutions to, 759
  particular solutions to, 759
  separable, 760
  uses for, 757, 764–70
Distance
  formula for, 10–11
  horizontal, 5–7, 12
  vertical, 5–7, 12
Dual problem
  defined, 245, 247
  formation, 246
  solving, 248–49
Dual theorem, 248

E

Elasticity of demand, 48
Endpoints, 566, 569–70
Equilibrium point, 64–65
Events (probabilistic)
  complementary, 454
  defined, 475
  dependent, 449–51
  independent, 449–51, 460
  joint, 447–48
  mutually exclusive, 448, 450–51
  simple, 475
  union of, 453–54
Expected monetary value, 495–98
Expected utility value, 498
Expected value
  defined, 781–82
  in the exponential case, 792–93
Exponents
  defined, 854–55
  fractional, 858–60
  multiplying, 857–58
  negative, 856–57

Exponents (*Cont.*)
  properties of, 349
  rules for, 860–61
  zero, 854–55

F

Functional notation, 510–13
Function power rule, 549–52, 625;
  see also Chain rule
Functions
  area interpretations, 694–706,
    709–17, 720–22
  concave, 573
  consumptive, 651–52
  continuity in, 527–28
  decreasing, 566–69, 574
  defined, 511–12, 816–19
  density, 778–800
    cumulative exponential, 789–90
    exponential, 789
    normal, 794–800
    uniform, 779
  exponential, 623–32
    graphs of, 628–32
    integrals of, 732–34
    properties of, 348–53
    rules for, 625, 628; *see also*
      Chain rule
  increasing, 566–69
  linear, 3–4, 692, 730
  logarithmic, 635–37
  maxima of, 563–66
  minima of, 562–66
  power rules for, 549–52, 625, 692
  rational, 612
  response, 632–33
  value of, 512
Future value
  at compound interest
    BASIC program for, 393
    calculation of, 390–92, 394–95
    PASCAL program for, 393
    table for, 981–82
    time diagram for, 392, 427–30
  of ordinary annuities, 412–15
  at simple interest
    BASIC program for, 382
    calculation of, 381
    PASCAL program for, 382
    time diagram of, 381–83

G–H

Gauss-Jordan inversion
  defined, 153–57

Gauss-Jordan inversion (*Cont.*)
  row operations in, 159
  solving m by n linear systems,
    171–75
  solving n by n linear systems,
    161–65, 167–69
  zeros-first variation of, 157–58
Glasser, Gerald J., 985

Hanna, S., 322
Henderson, A., 226
Hillier, F. S., 267
Histogram, 479

I

Indentity law, 138
Identity matrix, 141–42
Inequalities
  definition of, 891–92
  inconsistent, 80
  linear, 80, 82–83
  redundant, 80, 82
  solving, 892–97
Inflection point, 573
Inner product, 138
Integral calculus
  determining correctness in, 690
  versus differential calculus, 685
  fundamental theorem of, 699
  notation for, 687
  properties of, 688–91
Integrals; *see also* Integration by
    parts
  area interpretations, 694–706,
    709–14
    applications of, 715–17
    with two functions, 720–22
  defined, 687
  definite, 694–99; *see also*
    Numerical integration
  of exponential functions, 732–34
  improper, 740–43
  indefinite, 686–88, 690
  of linear functions, 729–31
  rules for, 987–88
  symbol for, 687
  tables of, 737–39
Integrand, 687, 691
Integration by parts, 754–57
Interest
  compound
    amount on $1 (table), 971–72
    conversion period for, 393–94
    continuous, 405–11, 438

Interest (*Cont.*)
  compound (*cont.*)
    defined, 390
    effective rate of, 402–4
    simple, 378–79
    exact, 380
    ordinary, 380–81
Interest rates
  conversion period, 393–94
  decimal equivalents of, 378
  determination of, 397
  effective, 386–87, 402–3
Intersection symbol, 447, 456
Inventory costs, 602–4
Isocost line, 104–5
Isoprofit line, 106

K–L

Kurnow, Ernest, 985

Least squares
  criterion for, 676
  curve fitting, 675–80
  formulas for, 679
L'Hôspital's Rule, 788
Lieberman, G. J., 267
Limits
  concept of, 516–18
  theorems for, 524–25
  uses for, 518–24
LINDO computer program
  for empty feasible solution set,
    302
  with equal constraints, 311, 319
  minimizing constraints, 317
  sensitivity analysis with, 316–17,
    320, 324
  using, 275, 277–78, 295–96
Linear equations
  in compact summation notation,
    179–80
  defined, 2
  expression of, 20
  graphs of, 2–3, 5–7, 56–58
  matrix representation, 144
  point-slope form, 23
  slope-intercept form, 19
  systems of
    in compact summation
      notation, 181–82
    consistent, 66
    defined, 55
    elimination-substitution
      method, 60–61, 68–69

Linear equations (*Cont.*)
  systems of (*cont.*)
    graphs for, 56–58, 66–67
    inconsistent, 66
    matrix representation, 145
    matrix solution of, 161–65,
      171–75
    m by *n*, 68, 171–75
    optimization in, 73–75
    row operations, 58–59
    solutions for, 56–57
    2 by 2, 55, 162
    3 by 3, 68, 164
  two-point form, 25
Linear inequalities
  nonnegative constraints, 82
  systems of, 80, 82–83
Linear programming
  corners in, 95
  defined, 92–93
  and empty feasible solution, 298–
    302
  and equal constraint, 302–8
  isolines, 104
  maximization in, 93–96
  minimization in, 100
  multivariate, 116–20
  problem formulation, 97–100,
    102–4
  simplex method; *see also* LINDO
      computer program *and* P1P2
      computer program
    alternative optimums, 230–32;
      see also Sensitivity
      analysis
    defined, 192
    disadvantages of, 253
    conversion of constraints, 193–
      95, 206
    feasible solutions in, 195–99,
      207, 209–10
    matrix techniques in, 200–204
    maximizing problems, 214,
      222–29
    minimizing problems, 214, 217–
      21
    and negative ratios, 220, 226,
      233
    with negative variables, 235–39
    outline, 199, 313
    unbound solutions, 233–35
    use of tableaus, 200–204
  solutions in, 106
  summation notation for, 182–83

Linear programming (*Cont.*)
  three-step graphical procedure,
    107
Linear systems; *see* Linear
    equations, systems of
Lines, 12–14, 25–27; *see also* Linear
    equations
Logarithmic function rule, 636; *see
    also* Chain rule
Logarithms
  base 10, 354, 356
  with calculators, 354, 356–57,
    364, 366
  with computers, 369–70
  natural
    computation of, 369–73
    defined, 359, 363
    inverse, 363–64
    tables of, 966–70
  need for, 353
  rules of, 355, 360–61

M

Marginal cost, 543–44
Marginal propensity to consume
  defined, 16, 37–38, 651
  and the multiplier, 652–55
Marginal propensity to save, 16,
    37–38, 651
Markov chains, 150
Mathematical models, 36–37
Matrices; *see also* Gauss-Jordan
    inversion
  adding, 136, 138
  commutable properties of, 140–
    41
  conformable, 139
  defined, 134
  dimension of, 134
  forms of, 144
  identity, 141–42
  inverses of, 153, 165
  multiplying, 135–36, 138–40, 142
  n by *n*, 135
  order of, 134
  row operations on, 151–52
  singular, 159
  square, 135, 141
  subtracting, 136
  symbols for, 143
  transition, 147–49
  zero, 138, 141
Maxima and minima
  global, 564

Maxima and minima (*Cont.*)
  local, 564, 566, 581
  with two independent variables,
    661–65
Mean estimation, 801–3
MINITAB computer program, 483–
    84

N–O

New product analysis, 323–26
Nonnegative constraints, 82
Numerical integration, 745–50

Objective function
  linear, 92
  maximization of, 94–96
  minimization of, 100
  and optimum values, 106
  in problem formulation, 97–100
  sensitivity analysis on, 322–23
  in simplex method, 193–95, 198,
    206, 210, 214, 312
Odds as probabilities, 443–44
Ordinary annuities
  and amortization, 421–26
  with continuous compounding,
    437–38
  future value of, 412–15
  present value of, 419–21
  sinking fund, 415–17
  with unknown interest rates,
    435–36
  with unknown time elements, 436
Ottman, Frederick R., 985

P

Parameters, 675
Payoff tables, 495–97
Phase I-Phase II method; *see also*
    P1P2 computer program
  advantages of, 286
  for empty feasible solution, 298–
    302
  with equal constraints, 302–8
  using, 286–91, 312–14
Pivot column, 207
Pivot row, 208
Point-slope form, 23
Polynomials; *see also* Maxima and
    minima
  degrees of, 576–77
  graphs of, 606–11
P1P2 computer program, 275–77,
    291–95, 308–11

Population (statistical), 444
Present value
  compound interest
    BASIC program for, 401
    calculation of, 399–401
    PASCAL program for, 401–2
  of ordinary annuities, 419–21
  simple interest
    BASIC program for, 385
    formula for, 383–84
    PASCAL program for, 385
    time diagram for, 384
    tables for, 973–74, 977
Primal problem
  defined, 244, 247
  solving, 248–49
Probabilities
  additional rule for, 457
  binomial, 485–93
  conditional, 448–49
  conditional rule for, 459
  cumulative, 491–93
  joint rules for, 459–60
  objective, 445–46
  posterior, 470
  prior, 470
  sources of, 445–46
  subjective, 446
  unconditional, 449
Probability distribution; *see also*
    Functions, density
  area assignment of, 779–80
  binomial, 485–93
    cumulative, 490–93
    defined, 485
    mean of, 488
    standard deviation of, 488
    variance of, 488
  central balance point of, 482
  defined, 480–81, 778–79
  normal, 794–800
  and standard deviation, 482–84,
    801–3
  and variance, 482–484
Proceeds calculation, 384–86
Producers' surplus, 724–27
Product rule, 553–56
Proportion, 29

Q–R

Quadratic equations, 888–90
Quadratics, 577
Quotient rule, 556–58

Random selection, 447
Random variable
  defined, 478
  expected value of, 481
  mean value of, 481; *see also*
    Probability distribution
  properties of, 479–80
  standard deviation of, 482–84
  variance of, 482–484
Rates
  of change, 638–40
  instantaneous, 638, 641
  point, 638
  and sensitivity analysis, 642–43
Reliability (statistical), 444
Row operations
  linear systems, 58–59
  on a matrix, 151–52, 159

S

Saber, J., 322
Saddle points, 664
Sample (statistical), 444
Sample space, 475–77
SAS computer program, 484
Scalar, 135
Schlaifer, Robert, 498
Schrage, L., 275
Sensitivity analysis
  on equal constraints, 319–21
  with LINDO computer program,
    316–17, 320, 324
  on minimizing constraints, 316–
    19
  on objective function, 322–23
  purpose of, 255
  of rates, 642–43
  through vector relationships, 264
Sets
  continuous, 777
  defined, 813
  discrete, 777
  disjoint, 821
  empty, 814
  intersections of, 820–22
  solution, 816
  specification, 815
  subsets of, 820
  terminology for, 813–15
  unions of, 820–22
Shadow price, 255, 262–64, 275
Simplex method; *see* Linear
    programming
Singular matrices, 159

Sinking fund, 415–17
Slope, 12–14, 21
Slope-intercept form, 19–20
SPSS computer program, 484
Square matrix; *see also* Indentity
    matrix
  defined, 135
  Gauss-Jordan computation, 153–
    57
  inverses of, 152–53
  zeros-first computation, 157–58
Standard deviation
  computer programs for, 483–84
  defined, 482–83, 784
  estimating, 801–3
State vector, 148–49
Stationary points, 563-64, 566
Statistical inference, 444
Subscript notation, 7
Substitution rate, 22
Summation symbol
  index of, 178
    for linear equations, 179–80
    for linear programming, 182–83
    for linear systems, 181–82
  use of, 184–86
Supply functions
  linear, 63–65
  two-product, 77–78

T–U

Tableaus, 200–204
Transition matrix, 147
Trapezoidal rule, 745–48
Tree diagrams, 463–64
Two-point form, 25

Union symbol, 453, 456
Unit matrix; *see* Identity matrix
u-substitution technique, 691–92

V–Z

Variables; *see also* Random variable
  artificial, 284, 298
  basic, 196, 214–15, 230
  dependent, 4
  entering, 196, 207–8, 214–15, 222
  independent, 4
  leaving, 197, 208–9, 214–15, 222,
    226
  negative, 235
  nonbasic, 196, 214–15

Variables (*Cont.*)
  slack, 241, 298
  surplus, 246, 250, 298
Variance, 482, 484, 784–85
Vectors
  components of, 134

Vectors (*Cont.*)
  state, 148–49
  symbols for, 143
Vertex, 195–97
Vertical parabolas, 884–88

Wagner, H. M., 267

Yield, 379

Zero matrix, 138, 141

This book has been set Linotron 202, in 10 point
Century, leaded 2 points. Chapter numbers are 20
point Helvetica Bold Condensed and chapter titles
are 30 point Helvetica Bold Condensed. The size of
the type page is 36 picas by 49½ picas.